Annotated Teacher's Edition

MIRRORS & WINDOWS

Connecting with Literature

Level II

EMC
Publishing

ST. PAUL • INDIANAPOLIS

Staff Credits

Senior Editor: Brenda Owens
Editor: Nancy Papsin
Associate Editor: Carley Bomstad
Editorial Assistants: Erin Saladin,
Lindsay Ryan
Permissions Coordinator: Valerie Murphy
Photo Researcher: Brendan Curran
Marketing Managers: Bruce Ayscue,
Laurie Skiba
Cover Designer: Leslie Anderson

Text Designer: Ronan Design
Page Layout Designers: Jack Ross,
Matthias Frasch
Production Editor: Courtney Kost
Production Specialist: Petrina Nyhan
Project Manager: Sara Dovre Wudali,
Buuji, Inc.
Editorial Development and Production:
Nieman Inc.
ATE Composition: Parkwood Composition

Literary Acknowledgments: Literary Acknowledgments appear following the Glossary of Vocabulary Words. We have made every effort to trace the ownership of all copyrighted material and to secure permission from copyright holders. In the event of any question arising as to the use of any material, we will be pleased to make the necessary corrections in future printings. Thanks are due to the authors, publishers, and agents for permission to use the materials indicated.

Art and Photo Credits: Art and Photo Credits appear following the Literary Acknowledgments.

ISBN 978-0-82196-032-5

EMC's *Mirrors & Windows* Is 100% Aligned with the Common Core State Standards

for English Language Arts

Your *Best* Resource for Meeting College and Career Readiness Standards in English Language Arts

Grades 6–12

EMC's *Mirrors & Windows* presents a rigorous and balanced program in reading, writing, speaking and listening, and language. This innovative 6–12 literature program provides extensive and varied preparation opportunities and materials for the Common Core State Standards assessments as well as College and Career Readiness Standards in English Language Arts. The *Mirrors & Windows* program is designed to encourage students to be excellent communicators and lifelong learners.

Mirrors & Windows Scaffolded Reading Support Develops Independent Reading Skills

- The Common Core State Standards establish a "staircase" of increasing complexity in what students must be able to read so that all students are ready for the demands of college- and career-level reading no later than the end of high school.

- *Mirrors & Windows* unique scaffolded reading approach incorporating the **gradual release of responsibility** model promotes the progressive development of reading comprehension so that students advancing through the grades are able to read independently and gain more from whatever they read.

- Each unit in the *Mirrors & Windows* program provides for a **gradual release of responsibility**, moving from

Guided reading — extensive support *before*, *during*, and *after* reading

to

Directed reading — extensive support *before* and *after* reading; less support *during* reading

to

Independent reading — self-monitoring *during* reading; minimal support *before* and *after* reading

Help Your Students Meet Common Core State Standards with Correlated Support Materials

Meeting the Standards Unit Resources

Practice and Apply Strategies and Skills for College and Career Readiness Standards Mastery

- Unit Study Guide with Practice Test correlated to Common Core State Standards in English Language Arts
- Active Reading Model Lessons
- Guided Reading Lessons
- Directed Reading Lessons
- Comparing Literature Lessons
- Independent Reading Lessons
- Writing Workshops

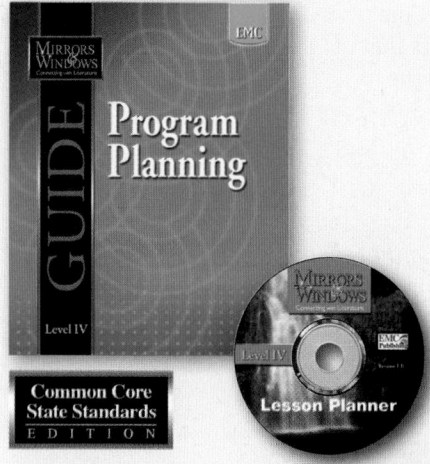

Program Planning Guide and E-Lesson Planner

- Lesson Plans for all the selections in the unit correlated to the Common Core State Standards
- Alternative Teaching Options
- Evaluation Guidelines
- All Common Core State Standards reading text types covered in every grade level

Common Core State Standards
EDITION

Mirrors & Windows Prepares Your Students for Success on Common Core State Standards Assessment Tests

The *Mirrors & Windows* program contains extensive opportunities and support materials to help prepare your students for taking Common Core State Standards assessments.

- Each unit in the textbook offers a fully developed Test Practice Workshop correlated to the English Language Arts Common Core State Standards in reading, writing, and revising and editing. Writing practice includes narrative, expository, and argumentative writing prompts.
- The Language Arts Handbook in the back of each textbook provides an in-depth section on Test-Taking Skills.

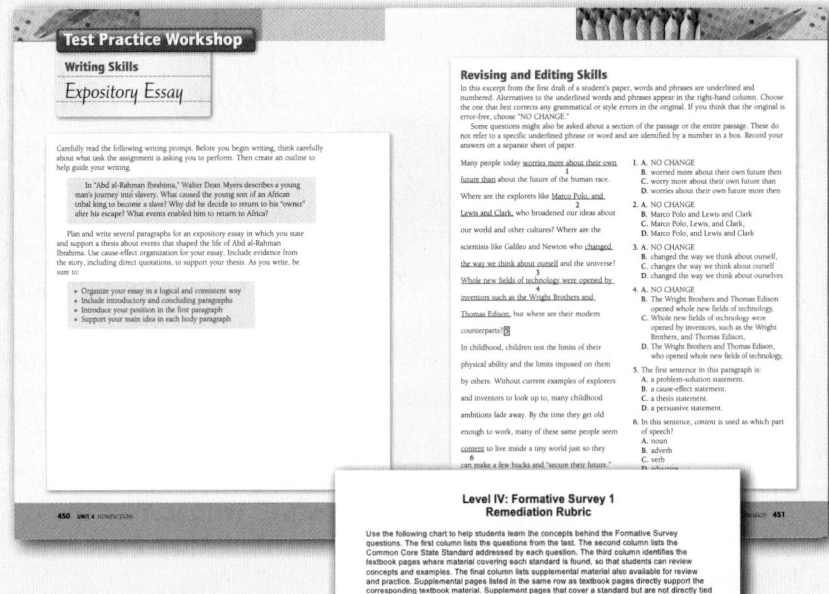

Assessment Guide and ExamView® Assessment Suite

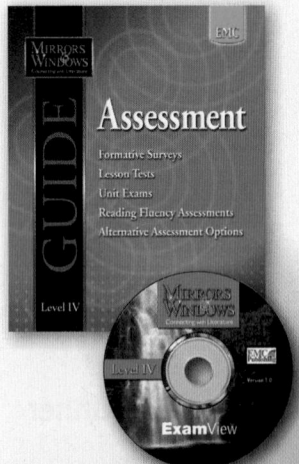

- Selection Test questions in ExamView® are correlated to the English Language Arts Common Core State Standards and labeled by level of difficulty as Easy, Medium, or Difficult.
- Assessment tools include lesson tests and unit exams, oral reading fluency tests, and formative reading surveys correlated to the Common Core State Standards and accompanied by rubrics that prescribe remediation activities provided in the program.

- *Meeting the Standards* unit resource books include a practice test for each unit correlated to the Common Core State Standards.

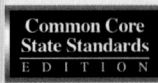

English Language Arts Standards, Grade 7	EMC Pages That Cover the Standards
Reading Standards for Literature	
Key Ideas and Details	
RL.1. Cite several pieces of textual evidence to support analysis of what the text says explicitly as well as inferences drawn from the text.	15, 25, 28, 47, 55, 60, 62, 71, 82, 84, 97, 104, 110, 124, 152, 161, 175, 189, 196, 198, 209, 211, 218, 223, 236, 263, 279, 290, 311, 316, 320, 332, 339, 351, 355, 360, 468, 472, 479, 483, 489, 494, 497, 500, 504, 507, 509, 512, 514, 517, 522, 542, 546, 550, 556, 560, 563, 570, 575, 579, 583, 621, 641, 664, 682, 689, 692, 732, 737, 742, 754, 763, 769, 775, 781, 785, 791, 795
RL.2. Determine a theme or central idea of a text and analyze its development over the course of the text; provide an objective summary of the text.	177, 297, 466, 467, 491, 557, 568, 733, 736
RL.3. Analyze how particular elements of a story or drama interact (e.g., how setting shapes the characters or plot).	11, 14, 18, 23, 25, 30, 35, 36, 40, 47
Craft and Structure	
RL.4. Determine the meaning of words and phrases as they are used in a text, including figurative and connotative meanings; analyze the impact of rhymes and other repetitions of sounds (e.g., alliteration) on a specific verse or stanza of a poem or selection of a story or drama.	73, 154, 160, 199, 257, 259, 312, 340, 415, 475, 476, 479, 481, 482, 483, 485
RL.5. Analyze how a drama's or poem's form or structure (e.g., soliloquy, sonnet) contributes to its meaning.	475, 477, 491, 494, 515, 576
RL.6. Analyze how an author develops and contrasts the points of view of different characters or narrators in a text.	141, 142, 152
Integration of Knowledge and Ideas	
RL.7. Compare and contrast a written story, drama, or poem to its audio, filmed, staged, or multimedia version, analyzing the effects of techniques unique to each medium (e.g., lighting, sound, color, or camera focus and angles in a film).	246–247, 494, 692
RL.8. Delineate and evaluate the argument and specific claims in a text, including the validity of the reasoning as well as the relevance and sufficiency of the evidence.	Not Applicable to Literature per CCSS guidelines
RL.9. Compare and contrast texts in different forms or genres (e.g., stories and poems; historical novels and fantasy stories) in terms of their approaches to similar themes and topics.	27, 62, 104, 174, 198, 210, 289, 311, 339, 350, 386, 387, 405, 414, 421, 499, 514, 565, 643, 686, 692, 744, 756, 785
Range of Reading and Level of Text Complexity	
RL.10. By the end of the year, read and comprehend literature, including stories, dramas, and poems, in the grades 6–8 text complexity band proficiently, with scaffolding as needed at the high end of the range.	105, 111, 125, 220, 224, 237, 352, 356, 361, 518, 520, 523, 584, 586, 588, 591, 593, 694, 709, 796, 803, 805

Reading Standards for Informational Text

Key Ideas and Details	
RI.1. Cite several pieces of textual evidence to support analysis of what the text says explicitly as well as inferences drawn from the text.	279, 295, 385, 393, 402, 406, 411, 414, 420, 422, 442, 446
RI.2. Determine two or more central ideas in a text and analyze their development over the course of the text; provide an objective summary of the text.	27, 291, 294, 396, 821, 835
RI.3. Analyze the interactions between individuals, events, and ideas in a text (e.g., how ideas influence individuals or events, or how individuals influence ideas or events).	272, 295, 309, 311, 316, 332, 402
Craft and Structure	
RI.4. Determine the meaning of words and phrases as they are used in a text, including figurative, connotative, and technical meanings; analyze the impact of specific word choice on meaning and tone.	257, 263, 287, 290, 312, 340, 415
RI.5. Analyze the structure an author uses to organize a text, including how the major sections contribute to the whole and to the development of the ideas.	259, 311, 317, 351, 385, 396, 424
RI.6. Determine an author's point of view or purpose in a text and analyze how the author distinguishes his or her opinion from that of others.	282, 286, 747, 765, 826
Integration of Knowledge and Ideas	
RI.7. Compare and contrast a text to an audio, video, or multimedia version of the text, analyzing each medium's portrayal of the subject (e.g., how the delivery of a speech affects the impact of the words).	316, 414
RI.8. Trace and evaluate the argument and specific claims in a text, assessing whether the reasoning is sound and the evidence is relevant and sufficient to support the claims.	265, 271, 291, 295, 297, 380, 396
RI.9. Analyze how two or more authors writing about the same topic shape their presentations of key information by emphasizing different evidence or advancing different interpretations of texts.	27, 62, 84, 174, 311, 405, 499, 563, 643
Range of Reading and Level of Text Complexity	
RI.10. By the end of the year, read and comprehend literary nonfiction in the grades 6–8 text complexity band proficiently, with scaffolding as needed at the high end of the range.	352, 356, 440, 447, 709

Writing Standards

Text Types and Purposes	

W.1. Write arguments to support claims with clear reasons and relevant evidence.
   a. Introduce claim(s), acknowledge alternate or opposing claims, and organize the reasons and evidence logically.
   b. Support claim(s) with logical reasoning and relevant evidence, using accurate, credible sources and demonstrating an understanding of the topic or text.
   c. Use words, phrases, and clauses to create cohesion and clarify the relationships among claim(s), reasons, and evidence.
   d. Establish and maintain a formal style.
   e. Provide a concluding statement or section that follows from and supports the argument presented.
	316, 509, 575, 710–711, 714, 715, 718, 889–890

W.2. Write informative/explanatory texts to examine a topic and convey ideas, concepts, and information through the selection, organization, and analysis of relevant content.
  a. Introduce a topic clearly, previewing what is to follow; organize ideas, concepts, and information, using strategies such as definition, classification, comparison/contrast, and cause/effect; include formatting (e.g., headings), graphics (e.g., charts, tables), and multimedia when useful to aiding comprehension.
  b. Develop the topic with relevant facts, definitions, concrete details, quotations, or other information and examples.
  c. Use appropriate transitions to create cohesion and clarify the relationships among ideas and concepts.
  d. Use precise language and domain-specific vocabulary to inform about or explain the topic.
  e. Establish and maintain a formal style.
  f. Provide a concluding statement or section that follows from and supports the information or explanation presented.
	126–127, 161, 175, 189, 218, 279, 320, 362–364, 370, 448–449, 504, 524–526, 532, 570, 667, 692, 795, 806–808, 813

W.3. Write narratives to develop real or imagined experiences or events using effective technique, relevant descriptive details, and well-structured event sequences.
  a. Engage and orient the reader by establishing a context and point of view and introducing a narrator and/or characters; organize an event sequence that unfolds naturally and logically.
  b. Use narrative techniques, such as dialogue, pacing, and description, to develop experiences, events, and/or characters.
  c. Use a variety of transition words, phrases, and clauses to convey sequence and signal shifts from one time frame or setting to another.
  d. Use precise words and phrases, relevant descriptive details, and sensory language to capture the action and convey experiences and events.
  e. Provide a conclusion that follows from and reflects on the narrated experiences or events.
	238–240, 242, 245, 483, 594–596, 599, 889–890

Production and Distribution of Writing

W.4. Produce clear and coherent writing in which the development, organization, and style are appropriate to task, purpose, and audience. (Grade-specific expectations for writing types are defined in standards 1–3 above.)	130, 242, 366, 452, 528, 598, 714, 810
W.5. With some guidance and support from peers and adults, develop and strengthen writing as needed by planning, revising, editing, rewriting, or trying a new approach, focusing on how well purpose and audience have been addressed. (Editing for conventions should demonstrate command of Language standards 1–3 up to and including grade 7 on page 52.)	128–130, 239–242, 363–366, 449–452, 525–528, 595–598, 711–714, 807–810
W.6. Use technology, including the Internet, to produce and publish writing and link to and cite sources as well as to interact and collaborate with others, including linking to and citing sources.	62, 130, 175, 339, 366, 452, 528, 598, 714, 769, 810, 896

Research to Build and Present Knowledge

W.7. Conduct short research projects to answer a question, drawing on several sources and generating additional related, focused questions for further research and exploration.	71, 686, 806–810, 816
W.8. Gather relevant information from multiple print and digital sources, using search terms effectively; assess the credibility and accuracy of each source; and quote or paraphrase the data and conclusions of others while avoiding plagiarism and following a standard format for citation.	71, 686, 807, 816

W.9. Draw evidence from literary or informational texts to support analysis, reflection, and research.
  a. Apply *grade 7 Reading standards* to literature (e.g., "Compare and contrast a fictional portrayal of a time, place or character and a historical account of the same period as a means of understanding how authors of fiction use or alter history").
  b. Apply *grade 7 Reading standards* to literary nonfiction (e.g., "Trace and evaluate the argument and specific claims in a text, assessing whether the reasoning is sound and the evidence is relevant and sufficient to support the claims").
	27, 62, 174, 279, 291, 293, 294, 295, 311, 396, 414, 643, 686

Range of Writing	
W.10. Write routinely over extended time frames (time for research, reflection, and revision) and shorter time frames (a single sitting or a day or two) for a range of discipline-specific tasks, purposes, and audiences.	126–131, 161, 189, 238–245, 279, 290, 316, 362–367, 448–453, 524–529, 570, 575, 594–559, 692, 710–715, 785, 795, 806–813

Speaking and Listening

Comprehension and Collaboration

SL.1. Engage effectively in a range of collaborative discussions (one-on-one, in groups, and teacher-led) with diverse partners on *grade 7 topics, texts, and issues,* building on others' ideas and expressing their own clearly. 　a. Come to discussions prepared, having read or researched material under study; explicitly draw on that preparation by referring to evidence on the topic, text, or issue to probe and reflect on ideas under discussion. 　b. Follow rules for collegial discussions, track progress toward specific goals and deadlines, and define individual roles as needed. 　c. Pose questions that elicit elaboration and respond to others' questions and comments with relevant observations and ideas that bring the discussion back on topic as needed. 　d. Acknowledge new information expressed by others, and, when warranted, modify their own views.	47, 211, 316, 468, 479, 483, 494, 737, 785, 802, 914, 915
SL.2. Analyze the main ideas and supporting details presented in diverse media and formats (e.g., visually, quantitatively, orally) and explain how the ideas clarify a topic, text, or issue under study.	279, 376–377, 431, 435, 913
SL.3. Delineate a speaker's argument and specific claims, evaluating the soundness of the reasoning and relevance and sufficiency of the evidence.	279, 376–377, 431, 435, 716–717, 913

Presentation of Knowledge and Ideas

SL.4. Present claims and findings, emphasizing salient points in a focused, coherent manner with pertinent descriptions, facts, details, and examples; use appropriate eye contact, adequate volume, and clear pronunciation.	132–133, 246–247, 368–369, 530–531, 716–717, 814–815, 917
SL.5. Integrate multimedia components and visual displays in presentations to clarify claims and findings and emphasize salient points.	369, 454, 455, 531, 815, 920
SL.6. Adapt speech to a variety of contexts and tasks, demonstrating command of formal English when indicated or appropriate. (See grade 7 Language standards 1 and 3 on page 52 for specific expectations.)	132–133, 246–247, 368–369, 530–531, 600–601, 716–717, 814–815

Language Standards

Conventions of Standard English

L.1. Demonstrate command of the conventions of standard English grammar and usage when writing or speaking. 　a. Explain the function of phrases and clauses in general and their function in specific sentences. 　b. Choose among simple, compound, and compound-complex sentences to signal differing relationships among ideas. 　c. Place phrases and clauses within a sentence, recognizing and correcting misplaced and dangling modifiers.	190, 264, 296, 389, 543, 764, 845, 852–854, 866, 867, 884–887

L.2. Demonstrate command of the conventions of standard English capitalization, punctuation, and spelling when writing.
    a. Use a comma to separate coordinate adjectives (e.g., *It was a fascinating, enjoyable movie* but not *He wore an old[,] green shirt*).
    b. Spell correctly.
	843–850, 851, 871–877

Knowledge of Language	
L.3. Use knowledge of language and its conventions when writing, speaking, reading, or listening. a. Choose language that expresses ideas precisely and concisely, recognizing and eliminating wordiness and redundancy.*	130, 242, 366, 530, 598, 714, 810, 887, 894
Vocabulary Acquisition and Use	

L.4. Determine or clarify the meaning of unknown and multiple-meaning words or phrases based on *grade 7 reading and content*, choosing flexibly from a range of strategies.
    a. Use context (e.g., the overall meaning of a sentence or paragraph; a word's position or function in a sentence) as a clue to the meaning of a word or phrase.
    b. Use common, grade-appropriate Greek or Latin affixes and roots as clues to the meaning of a word (e.g., *belligerent, bellicose, rebel*).
    c. Consult general and specialized reference materials (e.g., dictionaries, glossaries, thesauruses), both print and digital, to find the pronunciation of a word or determine or clarify its precise meaning or its part of speech.
    d. Verify the preliminary determination of the meaning of a word or phrase (e.g., by checking the inferred meaning in context or in a dictionary).
	176, 280, 423, 484, 567, 746, 668, 836, 837–840, 841–842 850

L.5. Demonstrate understanding of figurative language, word relationships, and nuances in word meanings.
    a. Interpret figures of speech (e.g.   literary, biblical, and mythological allusions) in context.
    b. Use the relationship between particular words (e.g., synonym/antonym, analogy) to better understand each of the words.
    c. Distinguish among the connotations (associations) of words with similar denotations (definitions) (e.g., *refined, respectful, polite, diplomatic, condescending*).
	16, 423, 415, 463, 464, 484, 561, 746, 841, 842–843

L.6. Acquire and use accurately grade-appropriate general academic and domain-specific words and phrases; gather vocabulary knowledge when considering a word or phrase important to comprehension or expression.	16, 176, 280, 423, 484, 561, 567, 668, 746, 836–843

Language Progressive Skills

Conventions of Standard English	
L.3.1f. Ensure subject-verb and pronoun-antecedent agreement.	48, 56, 135, 249, 857, 862–864, 868–869
L.3.3a. Choose words and phrases for effect.	180, 240, 452, 598, 897
L.4.1f. Produce complete sentences, recognizing and correcting inappropriate fragments and run-ons.	296, 321, 457, 719, 852, 884
L.4.1g. Correctly use frequently confused words (e.g., to/too/two; there/their).	366, 746, 850
L.4.3b. Choose punctuation for effect.	162, 528, 693, 719, 877, 878–879, 881

L.5.1d. Recognize and correct inappropriate shifts in verb tense.	135, 219, 249, 859–860
L.5.2a. Use punctuation to separate items in a series.	162, 693, 877
L.6.1c. Recognize and correct inappropriate shifts in pronoun number and person.	72, 501, 855, 856–858
L.6.1d. Recognize and correct vague pronouns (i.e., ones with unclear or ambiguous antecedents).	56, 856
L.6.1e. Recognize variations from standard English in their own and others' writing and speaking, and identify and use strategies to improve expression in conventional language.	135, 249, 371, 457, 533, 603, 719, 817
L.6.2a. Use punctuation (commas, parentheses, dashes) to set off nonrestrictive/parenthetical elements.	457, 528, 693, 877, 881
L.6.3a. Vary sentence patterns for meaning, reader/listener interest, and style.	130, 296, 543, 884, 885–887
L.6.3b. Maintain consistency in style and tone.	128, 240, 886–887, 889–890
L.7.1c. Place phrases and clauses within a sentence, recognizing and correcting misplaced and dangling modifiers.	764, 776, 864, 870
L.7.3a. Choose language that expresses ideas precisely and concisely, recognizing and eliminating wordiness and redundancy.	130, 242, 366, 530, 598, 714, 810, 884, 886, 887, 894

Range of Text Types

Literature	
Stories: Includes the subgenres of adventure stories, historical fiction, mysteries, myths, science fiction, realistic fiction, allegories, parodies, satire, and graphic novels	
adventure stories "Rikki-Tikki-Tavi"	86–97
historical fiction "The Inn of Lost Time"	31–46
mysteries "After Twenty Years"	11–14
myths "Persephone and Demeter" "The Secret Name of Ra" "Phaëthon, Son of Apollo" "The Instruction of Indra" "Amaterasu"	728–731 739–742 771–774 778–781 787–790
science fiction "The Foghorn" "The Smallest Dragonboy"	74–82 224–236

Common Core State Standards, Grade 7

realistic fiction "The Portrait" "A Day's Wait" "The War of the Wall" "Uncle Tony's Goat" "Hollywood and the Pits" "The Scholarship Jacket" "Amigo Brothers" "Four Skinny Trees" "The White Umbrella" "Jed's Grandfather"	51–54 58–60 64–70 105–110 142–151 155–160 164–172 178–179 182–188 192–196
allegories Aesop's Fables "Phaëthon, Son of Apollo"	766–768 770–775
parodies from *Ella Enchanted*	815–818
satire "The Rabbits Who Caused All the Trouble"	805–806
graphic novels "The Rabbit and the Tug of War"	807–814
Drama: Includes one-act and multi-act plays, both in written form and on film	
one-act plays "A Defenseless Creature" Film Viewing Activity	612–620
multi-act plays *A Christmas Carol: Scrooge and Marley* *Let Me Hear You Whisper* *The Monsters Are Due on Maple Street* Film Viewing Activity	624–664 670–682 694–708
Poetry: Includes the subgenres of narrative poems, lyrical poems, free verse poems, sonnets, odes, ballads, and epics	
narrative poems "The Village Blacksmith" "Annabelle Lee" "The Highwayman" "The Lost Parrot" "For My Father" "Money Order"	486–488 548–550 551–555 573–574 577–578 581

lyrical poems	
"The Courage That My Mother Had"	197
"in the inner city"	210
"Face It"	289
"Achieving Perspective"	386
"Fire and Ice"	421
"Gold"	467
"Feel Like a Bird"	471
"Blackberry Eating"	482
"Mother to Son"	493
"Under the Apple Tree"	496–497
free verse poems	
"Under the Apple Tree"	496–497
"Unfolding Bud"	507
"How to Eat a Poem"	508
"Two People I Want to Be Like"	518
"Miracles"	520
"I'm Nobody"	585
sonnets	
"Once by the Pacific"	544-546
odes	
"Under the Apple Tree"	496-497
ballads	
"The Village Blacksmith"	485-489
epics	
"Song of Hiawatha"	604

Nonfiction: Includes the subgenres of exposition, argument, and functional text in the form of personal essays, speeches, opinion pieces, essays about art or literature, biographies, memoirs, journalism, and historical, scientific, technical, or economic accounts (including digital sources) written for a broad audience

personal essays	
"Names/Nombres"	283–288
"Was Tarzan a Three-Bandage Man?"	313–315
"Fish Cheeks"	318–319
"The Night the Bed Fell"	356–360
"I am a Native of North America"	403–405
speeches	
from Queen Elizabeth's Speech to Her Last Parliament	277
opinion pieces	
"The Eternal Frontier"	292–294
"A Black Athlete Looks at Education"	310–311
essays about art or literature	
from "Lost In Translation"	513–514
biographies	
from *The Greatest: Muhammad Ali*	173–174
"Elizabeth I"	267–276
"A Bittersweet Memoir"	323–332
"Madam C.J. Walker"	341–347

memoirs	
from *An American Childhood*	258–262
from *Barrio Boy*	352–355
from *An Indian Boy's Story*	564–565

journalism	
"Moving West: A Native American perspective"	755

historical, scientific, technical, or economic accounts (including digital sources) written for a broad audience	
"The Size of Things"	379–385
from *The Sibley Guide to Birds*	391–393
"Ships in the Desert"	397–402
"Mute Dancers: How to Watch a Hummingbird"	409–411
"The Face of the Deep Is Frozen"	416–420
"Dust Changes America"	436–438
"Death in the Open"	440–442
"Astonishing Animals"	443–445
from "The Botany of Desire"	498–499
from "Going Ape Over Language"	683–685

Texts Illustrating the Complexity, Quality, and Range of Student Reading

NOTE: *Mirrors & Windows* offers high-quality literary works that were carefully chosen to enrich and enhance students' understanding of themselves and their world. Each unit in the program presents a diverse body of rich and relevant selections related to a particular theme or topic. The following texts represent the complexity, quality, and range of those selections.

Literature: Stories, Drama, Poetry	
"Annabel Lee" by Edgar Allan Poe (1849)	547–449
"I'm Nobody" by Emily Dickinson (1890)	584
"Rikki-Tikki-Tavi" by Rudyard Kipling (1894)	85–97
"A Day's Wait" by Ernest Hemingway (1933)	57–60
"The Foghorn" by Ray Bradbury (1951)	476–477
A Defenseless Creature by Neil Simon (1973)	611–621
"Four Skinny Trees" by Sandra Cisneros (1984)	177–180

Informational Texts: Literary Nonfiction	
"Dust Changes America" by Margaret Bourke-White (1933)	436–438
from *Off the Court* by Arthur Ashe (1981)	297–309
"Names/Nombres" by Julia Alvarez (1985)	282–288
from *An American Childhood* by Annie Dillard (1988)	257–263
"Ships in the Desert" by Al Gore (2000)	396–402
"Fish Cheeks" by Amy Tan (2003)	317–320

EMC's *Mirrors & Windows* Common Core State Standards Edition includes the full Range of Text Types for Grades 6–12 in every grade level!

Common Core State Standards Range of Text Types	Grade 6	Grade 7	Grade 8	Grade 9	Grade 10	Grade 11	Grade 12
Literature							
Stories: Includes the subgenres of adventure stories, historical fiction, mysteries, myths, science fiction, realistic fiction, allegories, parodies, satire, and graphic novels							
adventure stories	•	•	•	•	•	•	•
historical fiction	•	•	•	•	•	•	•
mysteries	•	•	•	•	•	•	•
myths	•	•	•	•	•	•	•
science fiction	•	•	•	•	•	•	•
realistic fiction	•	•	•	•	•	•	•
allegories	•	•	•	•	•	•	•
parodies	•	•	•	•	•	•	•
satire	•	•	•	•	•	•	•
graphic novels	•	•	•	•	•	•	•
Drama: Includes one-act and multi-act plays, both in written form and on film							
one-act plays	•	•	•	•	•	•	•
multi-act plays	•	•	•	•	•	•	•
Poetry: Includes the subgenres of narrative poems, lyrical poems, free verse poems, sonnets, odes, ballads, and epics							
narrative poems	•	•	•	•	•	•	•
lyrical poems	•	•	•	•	•	•	•
free verse poems	•	•	•	•	•	•	•
sonnets	•	•	•	•	•	•	•
epics	•	•	•	•	•	•	•
Nonfiction: Includes the subgenres of exposition, argument, and functional text in the form of personal essays, speeches, opinion pieces, essays about art or literature, biographies, memoirs, journalism, and historical, scientific, technical, or economic accounts (including digital sources) written for a broad audience							
personal essays	•	•	•	•	•	•	•
speeches	•	•	•	•	•	•	•
opinion pieces	•	•	•	•	•	•	•
essays about art or literature	•	•	•	•	•	•	•
biographies	•	•	•	•	•	•	•
memoirs	•	•	•	•	•	•	•
journalism	•	•	•	•	•	•	•
historical, scientific, technical, or economic accounts (including digital sources) written for a broad audience	•	•	•	•	•	•	•

–Program Overview–

Grades 6–12

Fiction • Nonfiction • Poetry • Drama • Folk Literature • Independent Reading

Great Expectations! Great Results!

Engage students to reflect on and connect personally with literature.

Motivate students to maximize their potential through the **gradual release of responsibility** reading model.

Challenge students to become independent readers, writers, and thinkers.

Try an Innovative Program That's <u>More</u>

Grades 6-8

Grades 9-12

<u>More</u> than great literature.

The student edition is also a resource rich with activities and reading support to motivate students to meet their goals.

- Diverse, interesting, and relevant selections teach the genres and literary elements and engage students in learning.

- Scaffolded instructional approach gradually releases responsibility to the students.

- Independent readings provide students with the opportunity to practice skills and read more on their own.

- Cross-Curricular and Text-to-Text Connections give relevance to literature by linking it to other subjects and students' lives.

(See pages T28–T37, T44–T45.)

<u>More</u> than a Teacher's Edition.

This easy-to-use, flexible management tool will fit your teaching style, and provide daily solutions to your classroom challenges.

- Consistent lesson plans address state standards and provide ongoing assessment opportunities.

- Lesson-planning tools are just a click away to save preparation time.

- Ideas for whole-group and flexible-group instruction provide practical options.

(See pages T38–T43.)

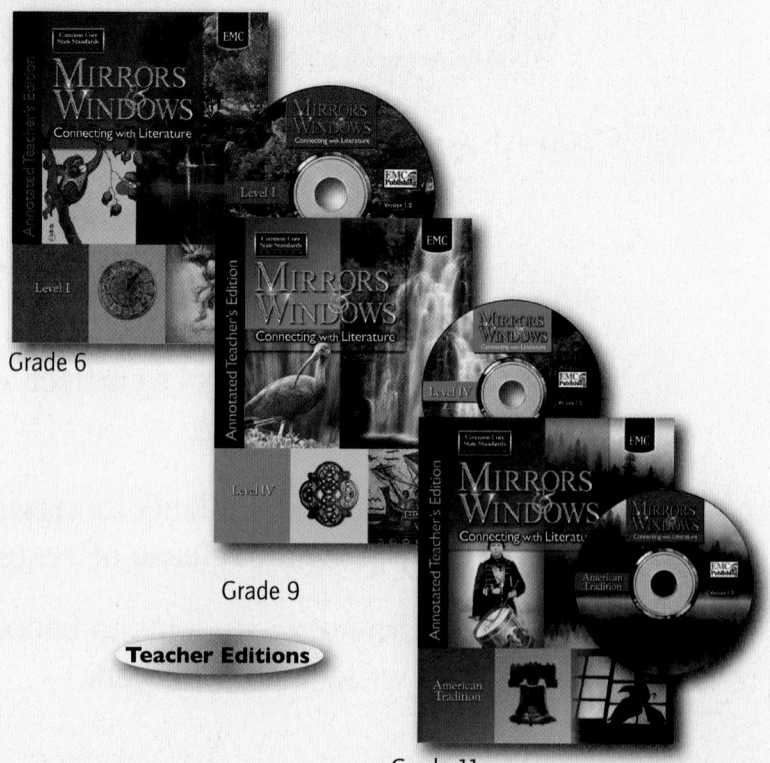

Grade 6

Grade 9

Teacher Editions

Grade 11

Than Just Another Literature Anthology!

More than "stuff" in a box.

This program offers just the right amount of the print and technology resources you need, when you need them, to ensure standards mastery.

- A variety of components provide differentiated materials to meet a range of student abilities and to support English language learners.

- Components are easily stored and available to preview and use.

- State-of-the art technology allows for customization to state standards.

(See pages T22–T27.)

More than scope and sequence.

Concepts, strategies, and activities are taught, practiced, and applied in meaningful contexts for all students.

- The *gradual release of responsibility* reading model provides three levels of reading support to scaffold instruction and develop independent readers.

- Differentiated Instruction focuses on Reading Proficiency, Enrichment, Learning Styles, and English Language Learning.

- Workshops for Vocabulary & Spelling, Grammar & Style, Writing, Speaking & Listening, and Test Practice provide wonderful opportunities for in-depth exploration.

(See pages T18–T19, T30–T37.)

–Program Philosophy and Instructional Design–

"The whole purpose of education is to turn mirrors into windows."

—Sydney J. Harris

Program Overview and Philosophy

Mirrors & Windows: Connecting with Literature, EMC's new literature program for grades 6–12, presents a wide variety of literature to help students reflect on themselves and their world and to connect that understanding to people from other times and places.

Mirrors & Windows responds to the call for increased academic *rigor* that continues to be heard across the nation. Given the lack of rigor in many school programs, today's students are often not engaged in learning and fail to acquire even the most basic skills and knowledge. Using a scaffolded approach, *Mirrors & Windows* provides instruction in essential content and skills and then transfers responsibility for learning to the student.

Program Research and Instructional Design

Scaffolded instruction with the *gradual release of responsibility* model is applied within each unit and across the grades. This approach is based on research that supports the practice of leading students from guided, to directed, to independent reading. Three levels of reading support are provided to gradually transfer responsibility from the teacher and the textbook to the student. The reading support throughout the unit progresses from guided to directed to independent reading.

Guided Reading at the beginning of the unit (Grades 6–10) provides the framework for the teacher to guide students through the reading process. Reading Models walk students through the selections and demonstrate how to analyze literature and apply reading skills and strategies to each genre.

Directed Reading (Grades 6–12), begins the gradual release of responsibility process as the teacher begins to transfer responsibility to the students. Students are directed through explicit pre- and post-reading instruction, but during-reading support is reduced to encourage students to practice reading skills and monitor comprehension on their own.

Independent Reading (Grades 6–12), advances the total release of responsibility from the teacher to the students, who can now apply the skills and knowledge required to read increasingly more difficult selections on their own.

Scaffolding and the Gradual Release of Responsibility

"Since its introduction 25 years ago, the concept of instructional scaffolding has been investigated, elaborated, related to other instructional concepts, and strongly endorsed by virtually every major reading authority. Although different authors define scaffolding slightly differently, three closely related features are essential attributes of effective scaffolding. First, there is the scaffold itself, the temporary and supportive structure that helps a student or group of students accomplish a task they could not accomplish — or could not accomplish as well — without the scaffold. Second, the scaffold must place the learner in what Vygotsky (1978) has termed the zone of proximal development. As explained by Vygotsky, at any particular point in time, children have a circumscribed zone of development or range within which they can learn...Third, over time the teacher must gradually dismantle the scaffold and transfer the responsibility for completing tasks to students..."

Michael F. Graves
Program Reviewer
Professor Emeritus
University of Minnesota

Michael Graves, from *Adolescent Literacy Research and Practice,* ed. Tamara L. Jetton, Janice A. Dole. 2004 Guildford Press.

–Applying Gradual Release of Responsibility–

The *gradual release of responsibility* reading model emphasizes instruction that mentors students into becoming capable thinkers and learners when handling the tasks with which they have not yet developed expertise. Through gradual release, students are:

- exposed to repeated modeling of expert behavior through teacher think-alouds and discussions of effective strategies for learning.

- provided with ongoing guided practice before they are asked to be independent learners.

- encouraged to learn from one another in the context of large group, small group, or independent classroom activities as they experiment with the thinking necessary to succeed in a variety of learning tasks.

Gradual Release of Responsibility Reading Model

Engage ▶	**Guided Reading** ▶ Grades 6–10	**Teacher** guides students through before, during, and after Reading Models.
Motivate ▶	**Directed Reading** ▶ Grades 6–12	**Teacher** directs before and after reading support. **Students** monitor their own comprehension.
Challenge ▶	**Independent Reading** ▶ Grades 6–12	**Students** apply skills and strategies to a variety of texts.

* Adapted from Pearson, P.D., and Gallagher, M.C. (1983)

–Connecting with Literature–

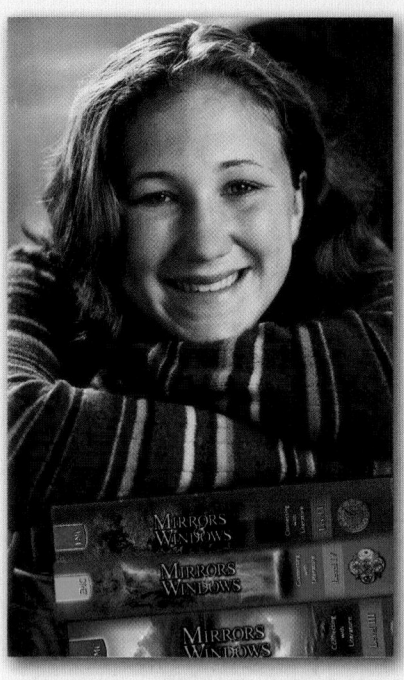

Connecting with the Text

Mirrors & Windows provides multiple opportunities for students to make important connections, including text-to-self, text-to-text, and text-to-world connections.

Text-to-Self Connections Reader's Context questions before reading and *Mirrors & Windows* questions after reading ask essential questions that encourage students to make connections to their own lives and the world around them.

Text-to-Text Connections Connections to a variety of primary sources and informational readings give relevance to literature by helping students to see relationships between literature and other content areas and texts. *(See page T33.)* The three types of text-to-text connections are:

- Informational Text Connections
- Literature Connections
- Primary Source Connections

The Comparing Literature feature pairs two selections that are connected by common literary elements to develop analytical comparison skills. *(See page T32.)*

Text-to-World Connections Cross-Curricular Connections are embedded within selections and provide relevant background information on other subject areas. *(See page T34.)*

Engagement and Reader Response

"...literature allows us to leave the world we inhabited to invest ourselves in imaginary worlds, only to return later to the quotidian events of our lives knowing more about our environment and ourselves than we did before departing. It is the recorded repository of the continuity of human emotions and events, the one subject that can speak across time to evoke from each of us comparable feelings and experiences. Therefore, let us select it carefully and put it to good use—to draw us together while simultaneously respecting our differences."

Edmund J. Farrell
Senior Consultant
Professor Emeritus
University of Texas at Austin

Edmund J. Farrell, from "Tracks in the Sand: On Literary Inclusion." *English in Texas*, Fall/Winter Issue (Vol. 32:2).

–Developing Critical Thinking Skills–

The *Mirrors & Windows* post-reading questions are based on Bloom's Taxonomy of Educational Objectives.

In grades 6–8, **Find Meaning** questions assess students' comprehension of the selections. **Make Judgments** questions address higher level reasoning skills. Questions are paired to build from literal questions to interpretation through synthesis.

In grades 9–12, **Refer to Text** questions that ask students to recall facts from the selections are paired with **Reason with Text** questions that ask students to apply higher level thinking skills. These questions are explicitly labeled based on Bloom's taxonomy, using terminology updated by Lorin Anderson for classroom application. (See chart below.)

Bloom's Original Taxonomy	Anderson's Revised Taxonomy
Knowledge	Remembering
Comprehension	Understanding
Application	Applying
Analysis	Analyzing
Synthesis	Evaluating
Evaluation	Creating

–Extending Learning–

The post-reading material for each selection offers extensive opportunities for students to respond to the literature and to extend their learning through writing and extension activities.

Writing Options Two writing prompts are provided that cover the major modes of writing: *creative, expository, narrative, descriptive,* and *persuasive.*

Extension Activities Two extension activities or projects are offered to expand students' skills in the following areas:

- Media Literacy
- Critical Literacy
- Collaborative Learning
- Lifelong Learning

–Extensive Program Components and Technology Tools–

Engage, Motivate, and Challenge Your Students

Student Edition
Meet All Your State Standards within the Student Edition

- Relevant, interesting, and diverse literature selections
- Three levels of reading support from guided to directed to independent
- Mix of easy, moderate, and challenging selections
- Cross-curricular and Text-to-Text Connections
- In-depth workshops for skills mastery
- Thought-provoking questions

Interactive Student Text on CD
In addition to containing everything in the printed text, the Student Text on CD includes highlighting, note-taking, and bookmarking.

Audio Library
Authentic, dramatic recordings with listening activities offer additional support for developing readers and English language learners, and expand listening skills.

Differentiated Instruction
Intensive instruction and activities provide student support; includes separate resource books for:

- English Language Learners
- Developing Readers
- Advanced Students

Differentiated instruction is also available in CD/DVD format.

Meet Your State Standards Every Day

Meeting the Standards Unit Resources
Practice and Apply Strategies and Skills for State Standards Mastery

- Unit Study Guide with Practice Test
- Active Reading Model Lessons
- Guided Reading Lessons
- Directed Reading Lessons
- Comparing Literature Lessons
- Independent Reading Lessons
- Cumulative Vocabulary Lists
- Available in print and CD/DVD formats

Name_____ Class_____ Date_____

Selection Worksheet 1.2

"The Story of Dædalus and Icarus," page 11

DAILY ORAL LANGUAGE

Rewrite the following sentences, fixing any punctuation, grammar, spelling, or usage errors you may find.

Icarus flew to close to the Sun.

Minerva to save Dædalus nefew from falling to his death turned him into an partridge

Graphic Organizer, page 11

Use the cluster chart provided below to list the examples of foreshadowing in "The Story of Dædalus and Icarus."

Foreshadowing

Dædalus kisses Icarus goodbye

Reader's Journal, page 11

Humans fantasized about flying long before airplanes were invented. Write about an improbable adventure you would like to experience.

Name_____ Class_____ Date_____

Guided Reading Questions

PAGE 12

What is Dædalus's plan for leaving Crete? What does he create?

PAGE 13

According to Dædalus, what should Icarus avoid?

Who looks up in amazement as Icarus flies?

PAGE 14

What ends the flight of Icarus? Where does Icarus fall?

Why had Dædalus's sister sent her son to Dædalus? What sort of mind did the boy have?

What did Dædalus do to his nephew? Why?

What becomes of the young boy?

Respond to the Selection, page 15

"Dædalus and Icarus" is one of the most familiar stories in Western literature. Why do you think it has remained so popular over the centuries?

16   UNIT 1 RESOURCE   © EMC

© EMC   UNIT 1 RESOURCE   17

Save Valuable Classroom Planning Time

Annotated Teacher's Edition (ATE)

One location for accessing, previewing, and planning your use of all program resources.

- Visual Unit Planning Guides
- Complete lesson plans for all selections
- Differentiated instruction for all learners
- Ongoing assessment provided
- Teacher Notes add valuable information
- Extensive vocabulary instruction and resources
- Cross-curricular connections
- Broad range of skills activities

EMC Launchpad (Combined Desktop–Web-based technology)

Complete, customizable application for accessing, previewing, planning, posting, and grading all program resources.

- Include your personal resources
- Post personal lessons on class website
- Access the E-Lesson Planner and E-gradebook
- Access Training Modules for improving computer literacy

Visual Teaching Package

Unit-based lectures, games, art collections, writing workshops, and more, in PowerPoint format, E-Lesson Planner and Teacher Resources DVD.

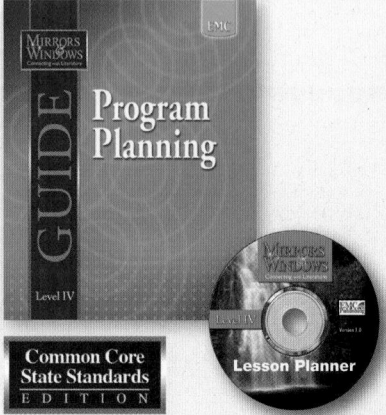

Program Planning Guide and E-Lesson Planner

- Lesson Plans for all the selections in the unit
- Core Standards-Based Selections
- Reading Log and Evaluation Forms
- Lesson plans correlated to state standards in E-Lesson Planner
- Access to all program resources in E-Lesson Planner

Assess Students' Progress and Provide Feedback

 Criterion. Online Writing Evaluation
Publisher's Version

A Web-based tool for students to evaluate their essay writing online before submitting it for teacher review and final evaluation. It saves time in grading the mechanical areas and allows teachers to focus on voice, creativity, and organization.

This service provides these benefits:

- Students are provided with essay topics in key writing modes.
- Students write, submit, and receive annotated diagnostic feedback within 20 seconds.
- Students can revise essays based on feedback or use e-mail to communicate feedback to teachers.

(Grades 9–12)

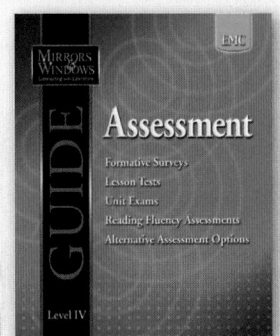

Assessment Guide

The *Assessment Guide* contains the following:

- Formative Surveys
- Lesson Tests
- Unit Exams
- Reading Fluency Assessments
- Alternative Assessment Options
- Remediation Rubrics

EXAMView® Assessment Suite on CD

Easy-to-use and Manage Testing Program

- Leveled multiple choice, short answer, and essay questions
- Ability to select, create, and edit questions to create personalized tests and exams
- Formative Survey test items keyed to state standards with customizable formats

 Go Green!

All print resources available on CD, on DVD, or online.

Enrich Students Beyond the Standards

Exceeding the Standards: Literature & Reading

Extended, unit-based lessons that integrate outside resources, varieties of media, and student creativity to analyze, compare, and fully appreciate literature and culture.

Exceeding the Standards: Test Practice

Timed, unit-based practice tests in formats most commonly found in standard achievement, state-specific, and high-stakes tests and exams. ACT and SAT format practice tests are included at each level.

Exceeding the Standards: Writing

- In-depth lessons to be used as extensions of the Writing Workshops in the student text.
- Developmental, in-depth writing lessons for each of the major writing modes — narrative, descriptive, expository, and persuasive.
- Lessons include models, examples, guidelines, writing checklist, and writing rubric.
- Writing lessons integrate grammar instruction.

Exceeding the Standards: Speaking & Listening

Detailed lessons with explicit instruction expand on the Speaking and Listening Workshops at the end of each unit to further develop speaking and listening skills.

Exceeding the Standards: Vocabulary & Spelling

- Comprehensive developmental Vocabulary and Spelling lessons build word study skills.
- In-depth instruction is modeled using words from the selections in each unit.

Exceeding the Standards: Special Topics

Extended lessons in technology, personal development, and career awareness provide students real-life, practical experience in applied communication skills.

Exceeding the Standards: Grammar & Style

A comprehensive, developmental grammar and style curriculum, taught within the context of selections in each unit.

Exceeding the Standards: Extension Activities

Extended lessons for each of the following catagories:
- Collaborative Learning
- Lifelong Learning
- Media Literacy
- Critical Literacy

Make Your Day Better with Online Resources!

mirrorsandwindows.com
Open Up Your Classroom to a World of Possibilities!

Student and teacher resources, references, technology tools, and state-specific activities to enrich the program.

- Internet links and activities for most literature selections
- Literary links
- Professional development, scholarships, and grant opportunities
- Workshops
- Standardized test-preparation resources
- State-specific information
- Teaching tools
- Online reference materials
- Downloadable Audio Library
- Access to E-Library

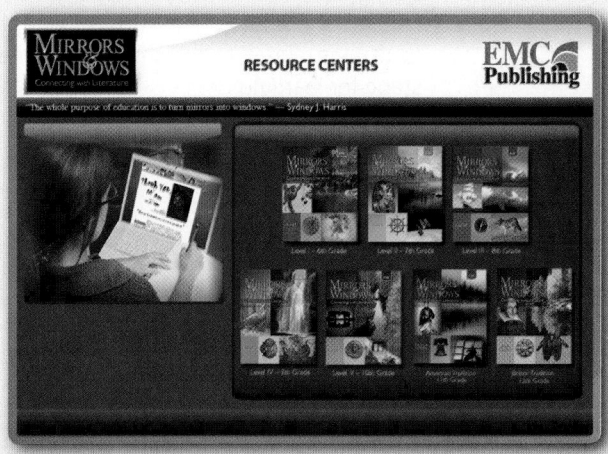

EMC E-Library
Expand Your Classroom Library Instantly

- More than 20,000 pages of literary classics
- 120 long selections, including epic poems, novels, plays, nonfiction, and poetry
- 194 short selections, which include poetry and excerpts
- Ability to view on screen or print out individual selections to plan classes
- Electronic library guide with teaching suggestions, enrichment activities, and reading strategies guidesheets
- Accessed from mirrorsandwindows.com

Audio Library
Authentic, dramatic recordings with listening activities expand students' listening skills and offer additional support for developing readers and English language learners. Accessed from mirrorsandwindows.com

Take a Walk Through
The Student Anthology

Great literature provides mirrors
   that help students reflect on their world
and windows *that lead them into new worlds.*

–Motivate Students to Learn–

Unit Opener

- Introduces the genre and connects students to the literature
- Thought-provoking quote gives insight into literature
- Fine art and photographs connect with the unit theme
- Questions related to the unit theme generate interest and set the stage for learning

Defining Freedom
Nonfiction

"The only education we receive is English education. Surely we must show something for it. But suppose that we had been receiving during the past fifty years education through our vernaculars, what should we have today? We should have today a free India...."
—MOHANDAS GANDHI, "There Is No Salvation for India"

What freedoms do you enjoy that people in other parts of the world do not? This speech was delivered by peace activist Mohandas Gandhi in his struggle to lead India to independence from British rule. As you read this unit, imagine how you would feel if your basic freedoms were challenged.

MOHANDAS GANDHI   AUNG SAN SUU KYI   GARY SOTO   ANNE FRANK   WALTER DEAN MYERS   ZITKALA-ŠA

259

Overview of grades 6–8. Pages shown from grade 6.

Mirrors & Windows

–Prepare Students for Success–

- The genre is introduced and defined before students read the unit selections.
- Detailed and extensive explanations of literary elements are followed by two selections that demonstrate the use of these elements.

Introduction to Nonfiction

Fiction and Nonfiction

Leroy "Satchel" Paige appears in both of the following passages. Though the passages differ in several ways, the main difference is that the first selection is written in first-person point of view and describes an imaginary conversation, and the second is written in third-person point of view and tells facts about Paige and America's baseball leagues. In other words, Gutman's selection is fiction and Littlefield's is nonfiction.

Leroy R. Paige (1906–1982). American baseball player with the Kansas City Monarchs, 1941.

"Ya-hoooo!" shouted Laverne, "If you were white, you would be in the majors for sure."

"Yeah," Satch said, "if."

She meant well, but Laverne's comment seemed to take something out of Satch. I could see his shoulders sag and his head hang a little. I guess he had forgotten about his situation for the moment. Laverne had reminded him that he was the best pitcher in baseball but was banned from playing at the highest level because of the color of his skin.

—DAN GUTMAN, *Satch & Me*

Everywhere these confrontations took place, Satchel Paige would hear the same thing: "If only you were white, you'd be a star in the big leagues." The fault, of course, was not with Satchel. The fault and the shame were with major league baseball, which stubbornly, stupidly clung to the same prejudice that characterized many institutions in the United States besides baseball.

—BILL LITTLEFIELD, "Satchel Paige"

Even though Gutman's fictional novel is about a boy who travels back in time to meet Satchel Paige, many of the novel's events and descriptions are historically accurate. Littlefield's nonfiction selection, on the other hand, is based on research and does not create any imagined situations or details.

In the Introduction to Fiction (page 4), you learned that **fiction** includes any work of prose (writing that is not poetry or drama) that describes an invented or imaginary story. Typical forms of fiction are short stories and novels. **Nonfiction** is writing about real people, places, things, and events. Autobiographies, biographies, journals, essays, histories, and newspaper and magazine articles are all types of nonfiction.

Types of Nonfiction

Among the most common types of nonfiction are autobiography, memoir, biography, and essay.

Autobiography and Memoir

Writing is described as "autobiographical" when the writer presents part or all of his or her own life. There are many types of autobiographical writing, including autobiographies, memoirs, diaries, journals, and letters.

260 UNIT 3 NONFICTION

An **autobiography** is the story of a person's life written by that person. It typically covers the whole of a person's life up to the time of writing. A more focused type of autobiography is the **memoir**, which usually deals with a specific period of a person's life, such as childhood. For example, Gary Soto's "The Jacket" (page 263) is a memoir about a period of Soto's adolescence.

> From my bed, I stared at the jacket. I wanted to cry because it was so ugly and so big that I knew I'd have to wear it a long time. I was a small kid, thin as a young tree, and it would be years before I'd have a new one.
>
> —GARY SOTO, "The Jacket"

Biography

A **biography** is the story of a person's life told by another person. For example, Walter Dean Myers's *Abd al-Rahman Ibrahima* (page 270) is a biography about the son of an African chief who was captured and sold into slavery.

> As the son of a chief Ibrahima was expected to assume a role of political leadership when he came of age. He would also be expected to set a moral example, and to be well versed in his religion. When he reached twelve he was sent to Timbuktu to study.
>
> —WALTER DEAN MYERS, *Abd al-Rahman Ibrahima*

Biographies are often told from the third-person point of view, though biographers may also include autobiographical materials, such as letters, diaries, or journals, so that the reader can gain firsthand knowledge about the subject of the biography.

Essay

An **essay** is a short nonfiction work that makes a point about a single subject. The point that the writer is making is called the **thesis**. For example, in an essay about school uniforms, the thesis might be that uniforms prevent personal expression.

There are many types of essays. A **personal essay** is a short nonfiction work on a single topic related to the life of the writer. The author of a personal essay may tell a story or an anecdote, or reflect on and share feelings about something in his or her life. For example, Carmen Tafolla's "Mi Familia" (page 355) describes her definitions for who makes up a family, and it's not always decided by bloodlines.

> The way I defined family was much like the old funerals I remember. In the front rows were the next of kin, the most greatly affected by the loss, behind them those close, behind them the friends, then the acquaintances and always, somewhere, the people of whom no one knew the exact relationship to the departed…
>
> —CARMEN TAFOLLA, "Mi Familia"

In a **persuasive essay** the writer's goal is to persuade the reader to accept an opinion or point

---

- Each genre begins with a Reading Model, which introduces students to the *Before, During,* and *After* Reading process.
- Following the Reading Model are three Apply the Model selections that provide students with guidance in learning the *Before, During,* and *After* process.

Nonfiction Reading Model

BEFORE READING

Build Background
You need to apply two different types of background to read nonfiction effectively. One is the selection's historical, scientific, or cultural context. Read the **Build Background** and **Meet the Author** to get this kind of information. The other type of background is the personal knowledge you bring to your reading.

Set Purpose
A nonfiction writer writes to inform, describe, persuade, or entertain. Read **Set Purpose** to decide what you want to get out of a selection.

Analyze Literature
A nonfiction writer uses different techniques depending on the type of nonfiction he or she is writing. The **Analyze Literature** feature draws your attention to a key literary element.

Use Reading Skills
The **Use Reading Skills** feature will help you get the most out of your reading. Learn how to apply skills such as determining author's purpose and using context clues. Identify a graphic organizer that will help you apply the skill before and while you read.

DURING READING

Use Reading Strategies
- **Ask questions** about things that seem significant or interesting.
- **Make predictions** about what's going to happen next. As you read, gather more clues to confirm or change your prediction.
- **Visualize** the information. Form pictures in your mind to help you see what the writer is describing.
- **Make inferences**, or educated guesses, about what is not stated directly.
- **Clarify**, or check that you understand, what you read. Reread any difficult parts.

Analyze Literature
What literary elements stand out? Are the descriptions vivid or interesting? As you read, consider how these elements affect your enjoyment and understanding of the selection.

Make Connections
Notice where connections can be made between the selection and your life. What feelings or thoughts do you have while reading?

AFTER READING

Find Meaning
Recall the important details of the selection, such as the sequence of events and setting. Use this information to **interpret**, or explain, the meaning of the selection.

Make Judgments
- **Analyze** the text by examining significant details and determining what they contribute to the meaning.
- **Evaluate** the text by making judgments about how the author creates meaning.

Analyze Literature
Review how the use of literary elements increased your understanding of the selection. For example, did the author use sensory details? How did he or she help shape meaning?

Extend Understanding
Go beyond the text by exploring the selection's ideas through writing or other creative projects.

262 UNIT 3 NONFICTION

–Teach the Gradual Release of Responsibility–

Apply the Model
BEFORE READING
DURING READING
AFTER READING

The Jacket

A Memoir by Gary Soto

GUIDED READING

Build Background

Literary Context Although "The Jacket" reads like a short story, it is actually a memoir, a true story about something that happened to the author when he was in fifth and sixth grade. An autobiographical memoir is a primary, or eyewitness, account of events in the author's life and how he or she felt about them.

Reader's Context How does wearing a favorite item of clothing affect you? How could your clothes influence the way you experience events?

Set Purpose

Preview the memoir's title and first paragraph. As you read, look for ways Soto uses humor to reveal how the events affected him.

Analyze Literature

Memoir A **memoir** is a piece of nonfiction writing that tells a story from the writer's life. Memoirs are about a person's experiences and reactions to historical events. As you read "The Jacket," decide whether Gary Soto is using the memoir to tell about his own experiences or about a historical event that he lived through. Does knowing that the events actually happened to the writer make the story funnier or more interesting to you?

Meet the Author

Gary Soto writes poetry, fiction, and nonfiction. Soto was born in 1952 in Fresno, California, to a Mexican-American family. The family struggled to make ends meet when he was growing up. There were times when Soto had to wear cardboard in his shoes and pick grapes to make money. In college Soto discovered poetry. He began writing his own poems and soon won a national poetry award. Although Soto has written for adults, today he is best known for his writing for young people.

Use Reading Skills

Identify Sequence of Events Using a graphic organizer can help you achieve your purpose in reading. Identifying the sequence of events in a story can help you better understand the plot and allows you to analyze the possible meanings of the events. Create a story strip to record the events in the order in which they happened. Note that not all story events are of equal importance in the plot. Decide which events are significant enough to be recorded.

Soto wants a black leather jacket. → Soto's mother buys him an ugly vinyl jacket.

Preview Vocabulary

vi‑nyl (vī′ nʼl) *adj.*, tough, shiny plastic
swoop (swŭp) *v.*, descend quickly in a sweeping movement
vi‑cious (vĭ′ shas) *adj.*, cruel, fierce
mope (mōp) *v.*, be gloomy or in low spirits

Guided Reading BEFORE

- Build Background, Set Purpose, Analyze Literature
- Meet the Author
- Use Reading Skills
- Preview Vocabulary

vi‑cious (vĭ′ shas) *adj.*, cruel, fierce

mope (mōp) *v.*, be gloomy or in low spirits

But whole pieces still casually flew off my jacket when I played hard, read quietly, or took <u>vicious</u> spelling tests at school. When it became so spotted that my brother began to call me "camouflage,"[6] I flung it over the fence into the alley. Later, however, I swiped the jacket off the ground and went inside to drape it across my lap and <u>mope</u>.

I was called to dinner: steam silvered my mother's glasses as she said grace; my brother and sister with their heads bowed made ugly faces at their glasses of powdered milk. I gagged too, but eagerly ate big rips of buttered tortilla[7] that held scooped-up beans. Finished, I went outside with my jacket across my arm. It was a cold sky. The faces of clouds were piled up, hurting. I climbed the fence, jumping down with a grunt. I started up the alley and soon slipped into my jacket, that green ugly brother who breathed over my shoulder that day and ever since. ✦

DURING READING

Analyze Literature
Memoir How has Soto's tone changed since the beginning of the selection?

6. **camouflage.** Color pattern of green and brown shades designed to blend in with the background, often used in military clothing and equipment
7. **tortilla.** Round, thin, flat bread usually eaten with meat or cheese

MIRRORS
WINDOWS

In this story, Soto says he blames the ugly jacket "for those bad years." Think of a time when you have felt that a situation or experience would have been better if only one thing had been different. Why do you think we allow ourselves to believe that about our pasts?

Guided Reading DURING

- Margin prompts help students analyze literature and develop reading strategies and skills.
- Vocabulary is identified and defined on the page.
- Mirrors & Windows questions encourage students to connect their personal experiences with the selection and the broader world around them.

Apply the Model
BEFORE READING
DURING READING
AFTER READING

Find Meaning

1. (a) What kind of jacket does the narrator want? (b) How does the jacket he receives compare to the jacket he wanted?
2. (a) List some of the unfortunate things that happen to the narrator during the years he wears the jacket. (b) How many of these things does the jacket cause?

Make Judgments

3. (a) Why do you think the narrator teases his dog? (b) Does teasing Brownie help the situation? Explain.
4. Why doesn't the narrator tell his mother that he does not like the jacket?
5. At the end of the memoir, how have the narrator's feelings about the jacket changed?

Analyze Literature

Memoir In autobiographical writing, an author uses tone and word choice to express his or her feelings. How does Soto's use of humor affect the tone of this memoir? Use a cluster chart to record specific details or examples of Soto's word choice that contribute to the tone. Record each detail or example in the outer circles, and write in the center what you think is the overall tone.

detail — "day-old guacamole" — Tone — detail — detail — detail

Extend Understanding

Writing Options

Creative Writing Imagine that you are the narrator in "The Jacket." You have finally outgrown your jacket. Write a **diary entry** explaining how you feel about getting rid of the jacket at last. Add your own sensory details when describing the jacket and your feelings.

Expository Writing "The Jacket" vividly re-creates events in Soto's life and reveals his personal feelings. Write a **literary analysis** of how Soto's tone in this memoir reveals his true feelings about that time in his life. Support your thesis with details from your cluster chart.

Collaborative Learning

Compare Types of Nonfiction Both a memoir and an autobiography are forms of nonfiction written by an author about his or her life. Discuss with a partner the differences between a memoir and an autobiography. Work together to make a chart comparing the features of a memoir to the features of an autobiography. Refer to the Introduction to Nonfiction on page 260 for more information.

Critical Literacy

Read to Interpret In small groups, analyze how the story's meaning would change if the elements of humor were not present in the selection. What does Soto's inclusion of humor indicate about his character and personality?

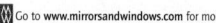 Go to www.mirrorsandwindows.com for more.

THE JACKET **269**

Guided Reading AFTER

- Find Meaning and Make Judgments questions are based on Bloom's taxonomy.
- Analyze Literature explores literary elements.
- Extend Understanding provides two writing options and two extension projects.

T30

–Develop Independent Learners–

DIRECTED READING

from

The Flight of Red Bird:
The Life of Zitkala-Ša

A Memoir re-created from the writings of Zitkala-Ša and the research of Doreen Rappaport

BEFORE READING

Build Background
Cultural Context Until the mid-nineteenth century, the Yankton Sioux hunted buffalo herds across the Great Plains. After the U.S. government forced the Yankton Sioux onto a reservation, they stopped hunting buffalo, but some traditions remained. Zitkala-Ša's mother showed her how to find wild turnips, cherries, and plums that grew on the prairie, and how to preserve meat and fruit. Zitkala-Ša also learned to create beadwork for moccasins, belts, and dresses.

Reader's Context Have you ever imagined what a new place would be like, only to discover it was not what you expected?

Set Purpose
Preview the History Connection (page 317) and predict what Zitkala-Ša's experiences are likely to be at boarding school.

Analyze Literature
Point of View The vantage point from which a story is told is the **point of view.** In first-person point of view, the narrator uses pronouns such as *I* and *we* and is a part of or witness to the action. As you read this memoir, think about how using the first-person point of view helps the reader to understand the experiences presented.

Meet the Author
Zitkala-Ša (1876–1938), whose name means "Red Bird," was born on the Yankton Sioux reservation. In 1884, she attended a boarding school for Native Americans, where she was forced to give up her language, traditional clothing, and customs. She later decided to devote her life to writing and speaking about the unfair treatment of Native Americans in white society.

Use Reading Skills
Draw Conclusions
When you draw conclusions, you gather information from a text to decide what it means. As you read, look for key ideas and supporting points. What conclusions can you draw from this information? Use a chart to track your conclusions.

Key Idea	Zitkala-Ša and friends admire each other's necklaces, moccasins, and belts.
Supporting Points	Zitkala-Ša imagines her friends to be envious of her moccasins.
Overall Conclusion	These items are valued in Zitkala-Ša's culture.

Preview Vocabulary
en • vi • ous (en' vē as) *adj.,* feeling unhappiness or resentment caused by wanting something that someone else has

com • plex (käm' pleks') *adj.,* having many parts that are connected or related in a complicated way

suf • fi • cient • ly (sa fi' shant lē) *adv.,* adequately; with enough to meet all needs

re • buke (ri byük') *n.,* severe criticism

sat • ed (sā' tid) *adj.,* feeling full or satisfied

dis • course (dis' kôrs) *n.,* long talk on a subject

yield (yēld) *v.,* give way to something or someone

THE FLIGHT OF RED BIRD **311**

Directed Reading

- Directed Reading begins the gradual release of responsibility from teacher to students.
- Students continue to be supported with before reading and after reading activities, but the during-reading margin prompts are omitted.
- Students begin to apply the during-reading comprehension skills on their own.

Independent Reading

- Two Independent Readings at the end of each unit provide students with the opportunity to practice skills on their own.

from

The Flight of Red Bird:
The Life of Zitkala-Ša

I heard wonderful stories about the strangers from my friend Judéwin.

A Memoir re-created from the writings of Zitkala-Ša and the research of Doreen Rappaport

from
Woodsong
A Memoir by Gary Paulsen

Whether I lived or died depended on him.

INDEPENDENT READING

Fear comes in many forms but perhaps the worst scare is the one that isn't anticipated; the one that isn't really known about until it's here. A sudden fear. The unexpected.

And again, fire played a role in it.

We have bear trouble. Because we feed processed meat to the dogs there is always the smell of meat around the kennel. In the summer it can be a bit high[1] because the dogs like to "save" their food sometimes for a day or two or four—burying it to dig up later. We live on the edge of wilderness and consequently the meat smell brings any number of visitors from the woods.

Skunks abound, and foxes and coyotes and wolves and weasels—all predators.[2] We once had an eagle live over the kennel for more than a week, scavenging[3] from the dogs, and a crazy group of ravens has pretty much taken over the puppy pen. Ravens are protected by the state and they seem to know it. When I walk toward the puppy pen with the buckets of meat it's a toss-up to see who gets it—the pups or the birds. They have actually pecked the puppies away from the food pans until they have gone through and taken what they want.

Spring, when the bears come, is the worst. They have been in hibernation[4]

1. **a bit high.** Fairly strong
2. **predators.** Animals that live by preying on others
3. **scavenging.** Searching for usable material
4. **hibernation.** State of mental or physical inactivity

Gary Paulsen was born in 1939 in Minnesota. Paulsen learned to be self-sufficient at an early age, working as a trapper, farmer, soldier, truck driver, sailor, construction worker, field engineer, and magazine editor. When he decided to devote himself to writing, he moved to the remote woods of northern Minnesota and lived off the land, supporting himself by hunting and trapping. Paulsen draws on his own experiences to create novels and personal nonfiction that is noted for vivid descriptions of setting, themes of conflict with nature, and the struggle for survival.

351

–Compare Literature and Extend Reading–

Comparing Literature

Satchel Paige
A Biography by Bill Littlefield

THE SHUTOUT
Historical Nonfiction by Patricia C. and Fredrick McKissack Jr.

DIRECTED READING

BEFORE READING

Build Background
Historical Context Patricia C. and Fredrick McKissack Jr.'s "The Shutout" describes the early history of baseball in the Negro leagues. Bill Littlefield's "Satchel Paige" tells the story of a star pitcher of the Negro leagues who became a star in the major leagues, too. African-American players formed the Negro leagues because they were banned from the major leagues until 1947.

Reader's Context Have you ever been excluded from an organization or activity you very much wanted to join? How did you feel? What did you do about it?

Set Purpose
Preview the Historical Context. Read to learn how black players reacted to discrimination by forming their own leagues, hosting their own championships, and developing legendary players.

Meet the Authors

Bill Littlefield has written numerous news articles, reviews, and essays. He currently hosts National Public Radio's "Only a Game," a weekly program about sports. He teaches writing and literature courses at Curry College.

Patricia C. and Fredrick McKissack Jr. are a mother-and-son author team who have written about African-American history. "The Shutout" is from their book *Black Diamond: The Story of the Negro Baseball Leagues.* The book records the relationship between baseball and race and highlights heroes of the Negro leagues.

Compare Literature: Fact vs. Opinion
A **fact** is a statement that can be proven by direct observation or a reliable source. An **opinion** is a statement that expresses an attitude or feeling. As you read, distinguish between fact and opinion in these two selections.

Preview Vocabulary
po·ten·tial (pə ten[t]′ shəl) *adj.,* possible

con·fron·ta·tion (kän′ frən[′] tā′ shən) *n.,* act of meeting face to face, especially in opposition

pre·ju·dice (pre′ jə dəs) *n.,* opinion or judgment formed without sufficient knowledge of a person or group of people

wan·ing (wān′ iŋ) *adj.,* approaching the end

ex·ploit (ek′ sploit′) *n.,* bold deed

an·ec·dote (a′ nik dōt′) *n.,* short, amusing narrative

e·volve (ē vôlv′) *v.,* develop from something else

di·verse (dī vʉrs′) *adj.,* possessing different elements or qualities

in·te·grat·ed (in′ tə grāt′ əd) *adj.,* characterized by equal membership in society

in·fa·mous (in′ fə məs) *adj.,* possessing an extremely bad reputation

(Opposite page) Pitcher Satchel Paige warming up.

332 UNIT 3 NONFICTION

Comparing Literature

- These pairings provide opportunities for students to analyze two selections by comparing and contrasting literary elements.
- At least one Comparing Literature pairing per unit appears in the Directed Reading section, followed by Find Meaning, Make Judgments, and Comparing Literature questions.

For Your Reading List

Independent reading suggestions:
- Appear at the end of each unit.
- Extend the unit theme with relevant, diverse titles.
- Encourage application of reading strategies and skills.

For Your Reading List

The Race to Save the Lord God Bird
by Phillip Hoose

Although once found throughout the southeastern United States, the Ivory-billed Woodpecker has since become a modern endangered species. It was last spotted in 1987 in Cuba. This book details the bird's history through the accounts of people who followed its decline, from artists to scientists to avid bird watchers.

The Land I Lost: Adventures of a Boy in Vietnam
by Huynh Quang Nhuong

This memoir focuses on Nhuong's life as a boy growing up in the Vietnam countryside. Divided into sections that describe individuals as well as animals in the area, the book depicts the importance of animals in Nhuong's lifestyle, such as his water buffalo and the crocodiles that live nearby. The author recalls many interesting encounters between the people of his village and the neighboring animals.

Team Moon: How 400,000 People Landed Apollo 11 on the Moon
by Catherine Thimmesh

When humans first landed on the moon in 1969, it wasn't just the result of the astronauts' hard work. This Sibert Award-winning book tells the story of the moon landing from the perspective of everyone behind the scenes, including workers at Kennedy Space Center, designers who built the spacecraft, and the people responsible for broadcasting the video. The book's photographs and firsthand accounts make the moon landing come to life from a fresh perspective.

Boy
by Roald Dahl

A famous children's author, Roald Dahl has written such classic books as *Matilda, Charlie and the Chocolate Factory,* and *The BFG.* He tells his own story in this memoir. Dahl focuses on his childhood adventures, such as the "Great Mouse Plot." Fans of Dahl's work will be interested to see where he found inspiration for some of his characters, and those less familiar with Dahl's fiction will enjoy his tales of mischief.

Invisible Allies: Microbes That Shape Our Lives
by Jeanette Farrell

In this award-winning book, Farrell describes the tiny microbes that help us survive. After a brief introduction to these microscopic creatures, she describes how microbes help us digest and break down food, and how they play a part in the processes of preserving and producing foods such as bread and cheese.

Good Brother, Bad Brother: The Story of Edwin Booth and John Wilkes Booth
by James Cross Giblin

Edwin and John Wilkes Booth were brothers and aspiring actors until John became famous for assassinating President Abraham Lincoln. The book chronicles the events leading up to Lincoln's assassination through the exciting police efforts to catch Booth, as well as Edwin's later attempts to become a famous actor. The firsthand accounts paint an accurate and engaging picture.

FOR YOUR READING LIST **361**

–Make Text-To-Text Connections–

Text-to-Text Connections add relevance to the literature selections by providing students with background information and context, and by helping them see relationships between literature, informational texts, and primary source materials.

Literature Connection

Primary Source Connection

Informational Text Connection

LITERATURE ▶▶ CONNECTION

In the essay from *All I Really Need to Know I Learned in Kindergarten*, Robert Fulghum uses games as metaphors for the way people interact with each other. Fulghum sees that the world is not always perfect and that people need each other to survive. The following selection is a poem by **Nikki Giovanni** (b. 1943) from her book *My House*. Giovanni grew up in Tennessee and Ohio. Her poetry collections are about civil rights, equality, children, and families. Besides being a poet, Giovanni is an essayist and speaker who teaches writing and literature. As you read, think about the title and theme of the poem and how they connect to Fulghum's main idea.

The World Is Not a Pleasant Place to Be

A Lyric Poem by Nikki Giovanni

the world is not a pleasant place
to be without
someone to hold and be held by

a river would stop
5 its flow if only
a stream were there
to receive it

an ocean would never laugh
if clouds weren't there
10 to kiss her tears

the world is not
a pleasant place to be without
someone

[17 feb 72] ✦

TEXT ←TO→ TEXT CONNECTION Both Robert Fulghum's essay and Nikki Giovanni's poem make a statement about the importance of being with others. If Fulghum uses comparisons to games to support what he believes, what does Giovanni use as evidence? Is Giovanni trying to persuade? Explain.

296 UNIT

PRIMARY SOURCE ▶▶ CONNECTION

Since the 1960s, the National Aeronautics and Space Administration (NASA) has sent astronauts into space. The earliest—and most famous—of the photographs from space were taken by the *Apollo 16* crew, which explored the Moon in the *Lunar Rover*. In 1981, NASA launched the first space shuttle. The photographs in this selection were taken from various satellites and imaging modules orbiting Earth. Study these photographs to imagine the new perspectives astronomers have gained from the space program.

Earth from Space

Photographs from NASA

This true-color image shows North and South America as they would appear from space 35,000 km (22,000 miles) above Earth. The image is a combination of data from two satellites. NASA Goddard Space Flight Center.

386 UNIT 4 NONFICTION

INFORMATIONAL TEXT ▶▶ CONNECTION

Bushmen paintings at Tsodilo Hills, Botswana.

In "There Is No Salvation for India," Gandhi explains why he believes that Indians should be educated in their native languages. The following article is from *Tales from the Times*, a book of stories by the staff of the *New York Times*. This article describes the struggle of the Wayeyi people of Botswana in Africa to keep their native language from dying out. As you read, note why members of the Wayeyi tribe work so hard to preserve their language and customs.

An Old Language Lives

An Article from *Tales from the Times*, by Rachel L. Swarns

In the beginning, there were the rushing rivers, the whispering reeds, the "Kwa! Kwa!" of shrieking herons and the rumble of lions. When the Wayeyi people drifted here some 200 years ago, they thought they had found paradise.

They settled in huts along the green marshes and built canoes to glide through the twisting streams. They fished, harvested water lilies and named the animals, flowers and stars in their language—Shiyeyi.

"First, first people to come here are Wayeyi and Bushmen,"[1] said Baagi Letsapa, as he guided his canoe through the sleepy waterways.

He is a leathery man who still remembers the teachings of his father. He knows that the boiled roots of the sage plant help ease indigestion, that papyrus[2] makes the best sleeping mats and that the ukayi plant produces a poison that kills fish, but not people. This knowledge is disappearing as young people abandon the rivers, the canoes and the old ways. But not without a fight.

Here in the swamps of northern Botswana,[3] the Wayeyi are battling not to disappear. They are just a tiny group in a country dominated by the Tswana people, and for generations tribes like theirs have been discouraged from practicing the traditions that make them different from each other so that there is only one national way. But a few years ago the Wayeyi decided their traditions were too important to fade away. They took the government to court and demanded that their tribe be officially recognized and that their all but forgotten language—a language only the elders of the tribe still speak—be taught in schools.

Critics said they were asking for trouble and that they would pit one tribe against another. Young people are not interested in the old ways, the critics also said. All across southern Africa, young people have left small villages and moved to the cities. Urban

---
1. **Bushmen.** Group of nomadic hunters in southern Africa
2. **papyrus.** Plant that can be made into a material like paper
3. **Botswana.** Country in southern Africa

306 UNIT 3 NONFICTION

–Integrate Cross-Curricular Connections–

Cross-Curricular Connections are embedded within the selections to provide related background information and to connect with other content areas.

SOCIAL STUDIES ▶▶ CONNECTION

Aung San Suu Kyi Aung San Suu Kyi received the Nobel Peace Prize in 1991 for her nonviolent struggle for democracy and human rights in Myanmar. Suu Kyi was not able to attend the awards ceremony in person to receive her prize because she was under house arrest in Myanmar. Although Suu Kyi was released in 1995, the military government severely restricted her words and actions. Suu Kyi continued writing and speaking in support of democracy for Myanmar until she was again placed under house arrest from 2000 to 2002. In May 2003, she was once again arrested, and as of the printing of this book, she remains under house arrest. Many people in Myanmar and in the international community support her struggle and continue to call for her release.

Human rights activists in Manila, Philippines, marched to the Burmese embassy with heart-shaped placards and balloons to symbolize their demand to free Aung San Suu Kyi from house arrest. February, 2007.

there is no way we can win. It has been more than forty years since Burma gained independence.[1] If we ask what progress has been made in these more than forty years, only depressing answers appear. When I visited Myikyina[2] over thirty years ago, there was no problem of electricity—it was always available. Now there is not even enough electricity and we find power in short supply. So we see that in these past thirty years and more there has been not only no progress but actual decline. We must ask ourselves, then: Why has this decline occurred? Most will answer that it is because the BSPP[3] was bad. I won't argue with that, but we must ask again: Why was the BSPP able to last so long, then? I think the answer to this has to do with the people at large. Because we, the citizens, simply stood by and watched, the system was able to last as long as it did. When the time came to take up independence, I think that the BSPP gained control of the government because the citizens failed to carry out the duties of citizenship. If we want a stable democracy in the future, every single one of us must bear this responsibility conscientiously. We must

understand that there is great merit in sacrificing for others and that by so doing we live the full life.

It's not by living to the age of ninety or one hundred that one lives the full life. Some

1. **since Burma gained independence.** Burma won its independence from Great Britain in 1948.
2. **Myikyina.** Capital city of Kachin State in northern Myanmar. Kachin State is one of seven states and seven divisions in Myanmar.
3. **BSPP.** The Burma Socialist Program Party, a political party founded by the military regime that seized power in Burma in 1962 and lasted until 1988
4. **sacrifice.** Give something up for the benefit of something or someone else

de·cline (di klīn´) *n.*, gradual loss of power, health, or prosperity; process of worsening

con·sci·en·tious·ly (kän[t]´ shē en[t]´ shəs lē) *adv.*, guided by a sense of what is right; carefully

mer·it (mer´ ət) *n.*, worthiness, virtue

Social Studies Connection

History Connection

HISTORY ▶▶ CONNECTION

Native American Boarding Schools In the late nineteenth century, many white educators believed that Native Americans' lives would be better if they learned white culture and lived like white people. By 1884, there were forty-nine boarding schools for Native Americans across the country. Here, students were forbidden to speak their native languages or wear native dress. They learned English and trades like carpentry and agriculture. The students were shocked and angered at being forced to give up their traditional culture. Many had a difficult time adjusting to the white system of education. After graduation, many students returned to the reservations, but some found they had forgotten their traditional language and way of life. For others, education at these schools led to successful careers. Most boarding schools were gradually replaced by day schools on the reservations. How did Zitkala-Ša react to losing aspects of her culture at boarding school?

older Indian girls at the table whispered to me, "Wait until you are alone."

"I want my mother and my brother. I want my aunt!" I pleaded in my language, but the ears of the palefaces could not hear me.

We were taken up an incline of wooden boxes, which I later learned to call a stairway. At the top was a quiet, dimly lighted hall. Many narrow beds, with sleeping brown faces peeping out of the coverings, lined the wall. I was tucked into bed with one of the tall girls. She talked to me in my mother tongue, and it soothed me.

I had arrived in the wonderful land of rosy skies, but I was not happy, as I had thought I would be. My long travel and the bewildering sights had exhausted me.

I fell asleep, heaving deep, tired sobs. My tears were left to dry themselves in streaks, because neither my aunt nor my mother was there to wipe them away.

The First Day at School
The first day in the land of red apples was a bitter-cold one. Snow still covered the ground, and the trees were bare. A large bell rang for breakfast, its loud metallic voice crashing through the belfry[17] overhead into our sensitive ears several hours before sunrise. The annoying clatter of shoes gave us no peace. The constant clash of harsh noises, with many voices murmuring an unknown tongue, made a bedlam[18] within which I was securely tied. And though my spirit tore itself in struggling for its lost freedom, all was useless.

A woman with white hair came for us. We were placed in a line with other Indian girls dressed in stiff shoes and closely clinging dresses. The small girls wore sleeved aprons and had shingled (close-cropped and layered) hair.

I felt like sinking to the floor, for my blanket had been stripped from my shoulders. I looked hard at the Indian girls who had been here awhile. They seemed not to care that they were even more immodestly dressed than I in their tight-fitting clothes.

In the dining room I spied the three boys from home, looking as uncomfortable as I felt.

A small bell was tapped and each pupil drew a chair from under the table. I assumed this meant we should sit, so pulled out my chair and slipped into it. But when I turned

17. **belfry.** Tower for a bell
18. **bedlam.** Disturbing scene of confusion and uproar

THE FLIGHT OF RED BIRD **317**

---

homeland in twenty years. The people there were still being captured by slave traders. He would have to send a messenger who knew the countryside, and who knew the Fula. Where would he find such a man?

For a long time Ibrahima did nothing. Finally, some time after the death of Dr. Cox in 1816, Ibrahima wrote the letter that Marschalk suggested. He had little faith in the procedure but felt he had nothing to lose. Marschalk was surprised when Ibrahima appeared with the letter written neatly in Arabic. Since one place in Africa was the same as the next to Marschalk, he sent the letter not to Fouta Djallon but to Morocco.

The government of Morocco did not know Ibrahima but understood from his letter that he was a Moslem. Moroccan officials, in a letter to President James Monroe, pleaded for the release of Ibrahima. The letter reached Henry Clay, the American Secretary of State.

The United States had recently ended a bitter war with Tripoli in north Africa, and welcomed the idea of establishing good relations with Morocco, another north African country. Clay wrote to Foster about Ibrahima.

Foster resented the idea of releasing Ibrahima. The very idea that the government of Morocco had written to Clay and discussed

DURING READING

Analyze Literature
Biography Would Ibrahima's letter be a primary or a secondary source? Why?

GEOGRAPHY ▶▶ CONNECTION

Map of the "Triangular Trade" between Britain, its American colonies, and Africa in the 17th and 18th centuries.

The Triangular Trade West Africa is the area of Africa closest both to Europe and to the Americas. As a result, European trading ships seeking captured Africans often stopped along the coast of West Africa to pick up their human cargo. There were many ports of call along the coast, but Goree Island off the coast of present-day Senegal was the most active port. From there ships sailed west across the Atlantic Ocean. In North America, the enslaved Africans were traded for sugar, rum, and lumber, which were then taken to be sold in Europe. Because this trading route touched on three continents, it was known as the Triangular Trade.

ABD AL-RAHMAN IBRAHIMA **281**

Geography Connection

T34

—Master Language Arts Skills—

Vocabulary & Spelling

Spelling by Syllables

"The charge against us is that we have no initiative."

—MOHANDAS GANDHI, *"There Is No Salvation for India"*

How many syllables does the word *against* have? A **syllable** is a part of a word that contains a single vowel sound. All words have at least one syllable. Understanding how to break words into syllables can help you sound out unfamiliar words and spell them correctly.

There is no single correct way to divide syllables, and sometimes you will see the same word divided two different ways. There are some general guidelines, however, that will help you syllabicate many words. Here are some of them. *V* stands for *vowel* and *C* stands for *consonant*.

Pattern 1: VCV If a word contains a consonant between two vowels, you should usually break the word after the first vowel. Example: **to-ta**l

Pattern 2: VCCV If a word contains two consonants grouped together, you should usually break the word between the two consonants. Example: n**ap-ki**n

Pattern 3: VV If a word contains two vowels, and both vowels are pronounced, divide the word between the two vowels. Example: con-gr**u-e**nt

Pattern 4: Prefixes A prefix always forms a separate syllable. Example: **pre**-pare

Pattern 5: Suffixes A suffix forms a syllable if it contains a vowel. Example: use-**ful**

The suffix *-ed* is only a separate syllable when it follows *d* or *t*. Example: plott-**ed**

The suffix *-y* follows the VCCV rule. Example: hap-**py**

Review the Term

syllable: a part of a word that contains a single vowel sound

Spelling Practice

Write each of the following words, separating syllables with hyphens. Then indicate the pattern (or patterns) the syllable breaks follow. For example: a-gainst VCV

1. native
2. students
3. actual
4. some
5. college
6. fishing
7. Idea
8. downsize
9. uneven
10. accept
11. mislead
12. signal
13. pilot
14. nonsense
15. number
16. hopeful
17. distant
18. nobody
19. fluent
20. doubted
21. amongst
22. applause
23. assured
24. conversation
25. foreigners
26. heritage
27. initiative
28. knowledge
29. vernaculars
30. yourselves

Vocabulary & Spelling

- Concise vocabulary and spelling lessons follow one or two of the literature selections in each unit.
- The lessons incorporate words from the preceding selection.
- Each lesson contains instruction, followed by practice exercises.

Grammar & Style

- As with vocabulary and spelling, concise grammar and style lessons appear several times in each unit.
- These lessons are also paired with the preceding lterature selections.
- Students learn and reinforce their skills in context, as they study literature.

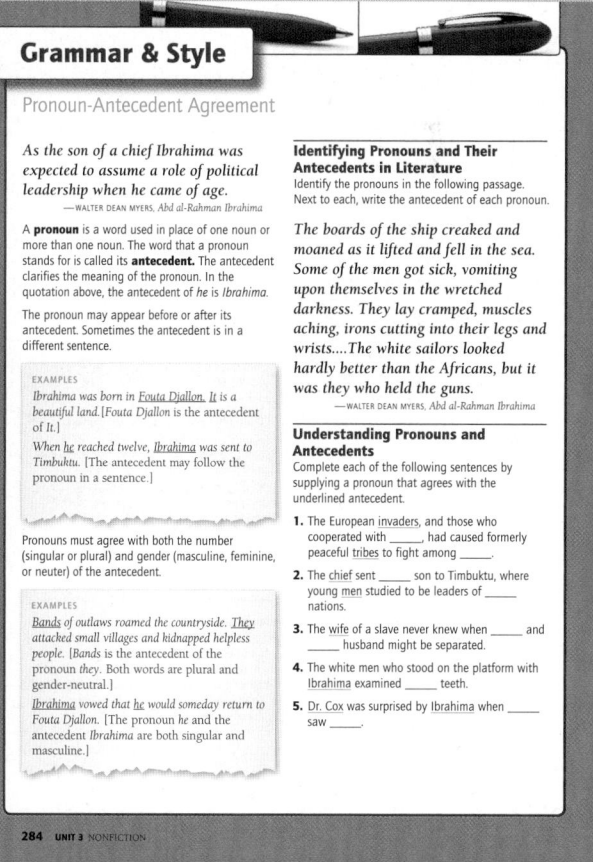

Grammar & Style

Pronoun-Antecedent Agreement

As the son of a chief Ibrahima was expected to assume a role of political leadership when he came of age.

—WALTER DEAN MYERS, *Abd al-Rahman Ibrahima*

A **pronoun** is a word used in place of one noun or more than one noun. The word that a pronoun stands for is called its **antecedent.** The antecedent clarifies the meaning of the pronoun. In the quotation above, the antecedent of *he* is *Ibrahima*.

The pronoun may appear before or after its antecedent. Sometimes the antecedent is in a different sentence.

> **EXAMPLES**
>
> *Ibrahima was born in* Fouta Djallon. It *is a beautiful land.* [*Fouta Djallon* is the antecedent of *It*.]
>
> *When* he *reached twelve,* Ibrahima *was sent to Timbuktu.* [The antecedent may follow the pronoun in a sentence.]

Pronouns must agree with both the number (singular or plural) and gender (masculine, feminine, or neuter) of the antecedent.

> **EXAMPLES**
>
> Bands *of outlaws roamed the countryside.* They *attacked small villages and kidnapped helpless people.* [*Bands* is the antecedent of the pronoun *they*. Both words are plural and gender-neutral.]
>
> Ibrahima *vowed that* he *would someday return to Fouta Djallon.* [The pronoun *he* and the antecedent *Ibrahima* are both singular and masculine.]

Identifying Pronouns and Their Antecedents in Literature

Identify the pronouns in the following passage. Next to each, write the antecedent of each pronoun.

The boards of the ship creaked and moaned as it lifted and fell in the sea. Some of the men got sick, vomiting upon themselves in the wretched darkness. They lay cramped, muscles aching, irons cutting into their legs and wrists....The white sailors looked hardly better than the Africans, but it was they who held the guns.

—WALTER DEAN MYERS, *Abd al-Rahman Ibrahima*

Understanding Pronouns and Antecedents

Complete each of the following sentences by supplying a pronoun that agrees with the underlined antecedent.

1. The European <u>invaders</u>, and those who cooperated with _____, had caused formerly peaceful <u>tribes</u> to fight among _____.

2. The chief sent _____ son to Timbuktu, where young <u>men</u> studied to be leaders of _____ nations.

3. The <u>wife</u> of a slave never knew when _____ and _____ husband might be separated.

4. The white men who stood on the platform with <u>Ibrahima</u> examined _____ teeth.

5. <u>Dr. Cox</u> was surprised by <u>Ibrahima</u> when _____ saw _____.

–Extend Learning with End-of-Unit Workshops–

Writing Workshop

The Writing Workshops provide one extended writing lesson for each unit. All lessons:

- Connect to the unit theme.
- Include a student model.
- Incorporate a fully developed, five-step writing process.
  - Prewrite
  - Draft
  - Revise
  - Edit and Proofread
  - Publish and Present

Writing Workshop

Persuasive Writing

Persuasive Essay

Reading and Writing

In this unit, you read several pieces of persuasive writing. Topics ranged from personal advice, such as letting oneself be "found," to political issues, such as bearing responsibility for life in a democracy. No matter what the topic, writing that presents an opinion or argument is persuasive writing. Standardized tests will often ask you to write persuasively. You will also need persuasive skills in other areas of your life—from getting what you want from a brother or sister to achieving success in the workplace.

In this workshop, you will learn how to write a **persuasive essay.** You will present a clear opinion in a **thesis** or **opinion statement** and back it up with reasons and support. You will also anticipate and address **counterarguments,** which are arguments that oppose your own. The following summary shows a typical persuasive essay assignment. It includes requirements and standards that might not always be stated in an assignment but that you should consider when writing a persuasive essay.

Assignment: Write a persuasive essay in which I present and support a clearly stated opinion.

Goal: Persuade my audience to accept or act on my opinion.

Strategy: Present clear reasons for my opinion, support my reasons, and anticipate and address counterarguments.

Writing Rubric: My persuasive essay should include the following:

- an introduction that clearly states my opinion
- reasons for my opinion
- support for my reasons
- thoughtful answers to counterarguments
- a conclusion with a call to action

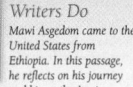

What Great Writers Do
Mawi Asgedom came to the United States from Ethiopia. In this passage, he reflects on his journey and his mother's wise advice. What is his opinion? How does he support and explain it?

My mother's advice in childhood was to pull the covers over my head—that had been the easy part. But her later advice meant, I now realize, that I should know when to pull the covers down and stick my neck out. That's the hard part. Too many of us go through life with the covers over our heads. We want to reach out, but we fear to make ourselves vulnerable. And we are also busy....We race through a world of demands. And then we ask ourselves almost helplessly, "What can we do as individuals?"

—MAWI ASGEDOM, *Of Beetles & Angels*

362 UNIT 3 NONFICTION

Speaking & Listening Workshop

Each unit also includes one complete speaking and listening lesson.

- Students learn and practice oral presentation skills. Topics are related to both school and work.
- Rubrics are provided for evaluation.

Speaking & Listening Workshop

Delivering and Listening to a Persuasive Speech

People are always trying to persuade you to do something. Food companies want you to eat or drink their products. Clothing makers want you to wear their clothes. Now it's your turn. The goal of a **persuasive speech** is to convince others to believe, think, or do something. Actively listening to persuasive speeches helps you make up your own mind based on facts, not emotion.

Planning Your Persuasive Speech
Choose a Topic and Position Think about something you'd like to see changed. Is your weekend curfew too early? Should your teacher give less homework? Select a topic on which people have different opinions. Sum up your position in a strong statement, such as "Students who spend all day in school should have time to socialize with family and friends, earn extra money, or just relax instead of doing hours of homework."

Identify Your Audience Who are you trying to convince? Arguments you use to persuade fellow students might be different from those you use to convince teachers or parents. After identifying your audience, ask yourself, "What kind of arguments will convince these people to agree with me and take action?"

Outline and Research Your Arguments Begin by outlining your arguments. Stating your opinion isn't enough. What facts, statistics, expert opinions, anecdotes, examples, or other details will support your arguments? Consider your own point of view as well as possible arguments that those who disagree might use.

Position: Teachers should give less homework.

Point 1: Describe hours spent getting ready for school, getting to and from school, and at school as a percentage of waking hours.

Point 2: Describe total hours of homework assigned by all teachers. How much time is left in the day?

Point 3: Counterargument: homework is a necessary part of learning—why? Homework only covers school subjects; we learn social skills by associating with others.

Plan Your Opening Grab your audience's interest by telling a short dramatic story related to your point of view; by asking the audience a question, such as "Should people spend all their waking hours working?"; or by using a metaphor (*Feeding your mind only with schoolwork is like feeding your body with only one kind of food*).

368 UNIT 3 NONFICTION

Speaking Rubric

Your presentation will be evaluated on these elements:

Content
- ☐ presentation is clear and well-organized
- ☐ arguments are strong and well-supported
- ☐ opposing arguments are addressed

Delivery and Presentation
- ☐ tone is moderate and reasonable
- ☐ nonverbal communication effectively supports content
- ☐ questions are answered completely and politely

Listening Rubric

As a peer reviewer or audience member, I should do the following:

- ☐ listen quietly and attentively
- ☐ maintain eye contact with speaker
- ☐ ask appropriate questions
- ☐ (as peer reviewer) provide constructive feedback

Mirrors & Windows

Test Practice Workshop

Writing Skills

Persuasive Essay

Read the following excerpt and the writing assignment that follows. Before writing, think about what task the assignment is asking you to perform. Then create an outline to guide your writing.

from "The Fan Club" by Rona Maynard

Rachel crouched on her knees and began very clumsily to gather her scattered treasures. Papers and boxes lay all about, and some of the boxes had broken open, spilling their contents in wild confusion. No one went to help. At last she scrambled to her feet and began fumbling with her notes.

"My—my speech is on shells."

A cold and stony silence had settled upon the room.

"Lots of people collect shells, because they're kind of pretty—sort of, and you just find them on the beach."

"Well, whaddaya know!" It was Steve's voice, softer this time, but all mock amazement. Laura jabbed her notebook with her pencil. Why were they so cruel, so thoughtless? Why did they have to laugh?

Then, suddenly, chairs were shoved aside at the back of the room and there was the sound of many voices whispering. They were standing now, whole rows of them, their faces grinning with delight. Choked giggles, shuffling feet   and then applause   wild, sarcastic, malicious applause. That was when Laura saw that they were all wearing little white cards with a fat, frizzy-haired figure drawn on the front. What did it mean? She looked more closely. "HORTENSKY FAN CLUB," said the bright-red letters.

So that was what the whispering had been all morning. She'd been wrong. They weren't out to get her after all. It was only Rachel.

Diane was nudging her and holding out a card. "Hey, Laura, here's one for you to wear." For a moment Laura stared at the card. She looked from Rachel's red, frightened face to Diane's mocking smile, and she heard the pulsing, frenzied rhythm of the claps and the stamping, faster and faster. Her hands trembled as she picked up the card and pinned it to her sweater. And as she turned, she saw Rachel's stricken look.

"She's a creep, isn't she?" Diane's voice was soft and intimate.

And Laura began to clap.

Assignment: In the passage you just read, Laura encounters peer pressure and makes a choice. Plan and write a **persuasive essay** in which you **state and support a thesis** about the effects of peer pressure on young people and how it should be handled. Include evidence from the passage and your own experience to support your thesis.

Revising and Editing Skills

Each sentence below has one or two blanks. Each blank indicates that a word has been omitted. Choose the word or set of words that, when inserted in the sentence, *best* fits the meaning of the sentence as a whole. Record your answers on a separate sheet of paper.

1. I ___ it my duty to take the ___ in raising funds for the class gift to the teacher.
   A. badgered...privilege
   B. considered...initiative
   C. instilled...potential
   D. destined...techniques
   E. exploited...character

2. The politician's ___ drove him to ___ hundreds of workers for his campaign.
   A. character...instill
   B. privilege...badger
   C. mastery...merit
   D. initiative...swoop
   E. ambition...recruit

3. The coach made his decision based on the ___ that the quarterback's injury would quickly improve.
   A. premise
   B. initiative
   C. tactics
   D. potential
   E. mastery

4. The students were very vocal in their ___ of the professor's ___ lectures.
   A. confirmation...undulating
   B. desegregation...lavish
   C. provision...distorted
   D. condemnation...pedantic
   E. prejudice...sufficient

5. Boats bobbed like corks on the ___ waves.
   A. berserk
   B. undulating
   C. waning
   D. diverse
   E. infamous

6. The author of the biography made it clear that the protagonist's ___ was ___.
   A. conscience...vernacular
   B. anecdote...berserk
   C. tactic...envious
   D. mastery...lavish
   E. character...unimpeachable

7. The actress was ___ for rambling on in the ___ of her Southern roots.
   A. lavish...discourse
   B. distorted...surplus
   C. infamous...vernacular
   D. reasonable...principle
   E. envious...tactics

8. The scientist delivered a ___ lecture about the ___ of space-time.
   A. complex...principle
   B. lavish...democracy
   C. berserk...ambition
   D. vicious...bondage
   E. waning...anecdotes

9. The slave ___ the courage to break free from his ___.
   A. merited...ambition
   B. destined...discourse
   C. badgered...democracy
   D. summoned...bondage
   E. integrated...privilege

10. Because of his ___ attacks on his opponent, support for the candidate was ___.
    A. evolved...sufficient
    B. crucial...vinyl
    C. vicious...waning
    D. conscientious...undulating
    E. diverse...infamous

Test Practice Workshop

- Students practice standardized test formats such as ACT and SAT at the end of each unit.
- The lessons emphasize writing skills, revising and editing skills, and reading skills.
- Topics are related to standard test-prep materials.

Language Arts Handbook

- Complete, easy-to-use student resource at the back of each text to answer questions, provide valuable information, and support the development of students' language arts skills.
- Encourages independent learning.

Language Arts Handbook

Take a Walk Through
The Annotated Teacher's Edition

The Mirrors & Windows Interactive Annotated Teacher's Edition (Desktop or Web-based) provides the instructional tools necessary to enhance the learning experience for all students.

—Choose the Resources You Need—

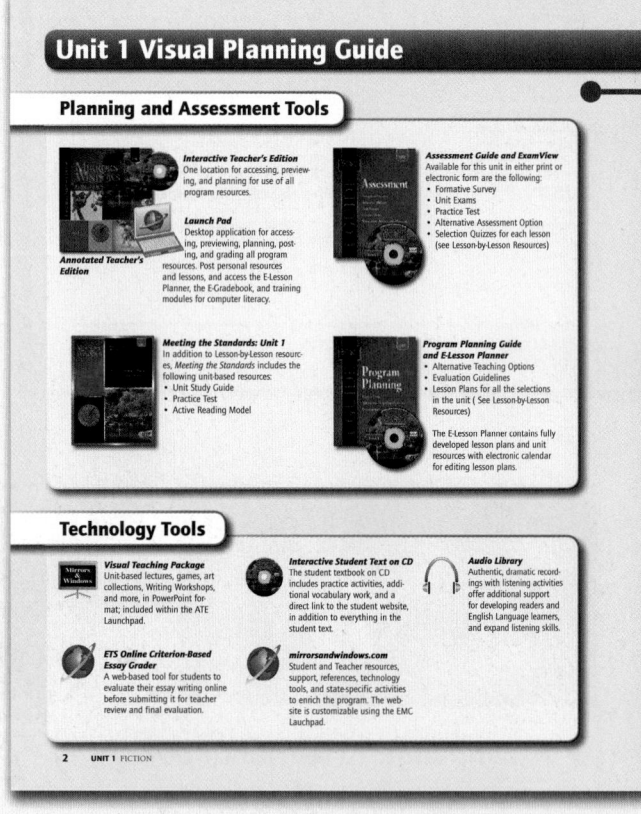

Unit-based Resources

- Unique, at-a-glance teacher planner for efficient decision-making.
- Planning and assessment tools and *Exceeding the Standards* Unit Resources are shown. Technology Tools are displayed for easy reference.

Lesson Resources

- Lesson-by-lesson resource options are pictured.
- Reading level is provided.
- Pacing guidelines are included.

Mirrors & Windows

–Plan Your Day the Easy Way–

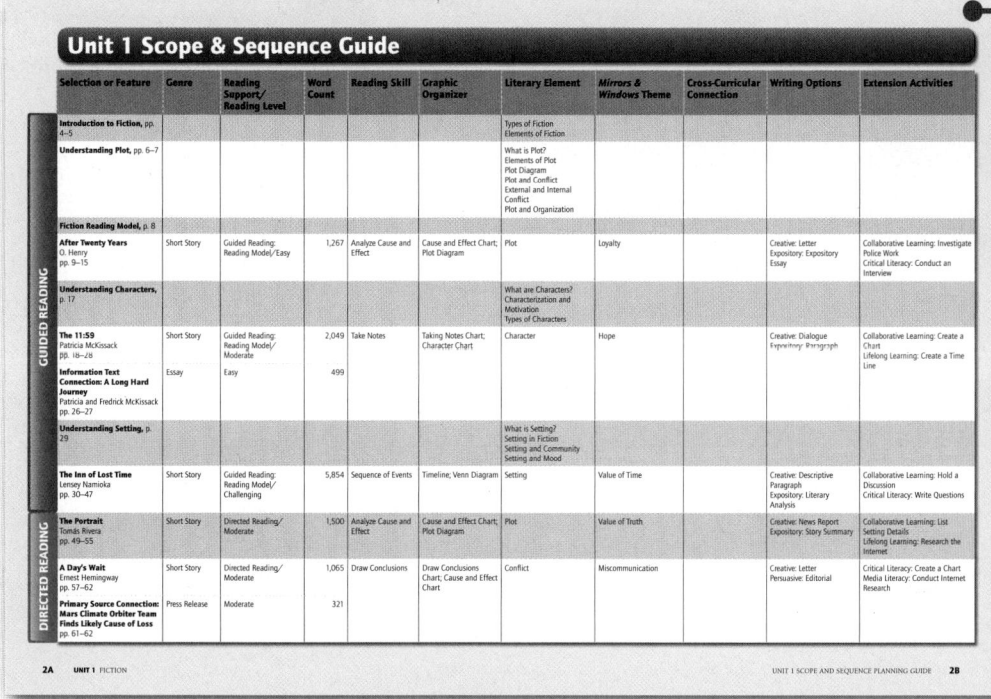

Unit 1 Scope & Sequence Guide

Selection or Feature	Genre	Reading Support/ Reading Level	Word Count	Reading Skill	Graphic Organizer	Literary Element	Mirrors & Windows Theme	Cross-Curricular Connection	Writing Options	Extension Activities
Introduction to Fiction, pp. 4–5						Types of Fiction Elements of Fiction				
Understanding Plot, pp. 6–7						What is Plot? Elements of Plot Plot Diagram Plot and Conflict External and Internal Conflict Plot and Organization				
Fiction Reading Model, p. 8										
After Twenty Years O. Henry pp. 9–15	Short Story	Guided Reading: Reading Model/Easy	1,267	Analyze Cause and Effect	Cause and Effect Chart; Plot Diagram	Plot	Loyalty		Creative: Letter Expository: Expository Essay	Collaborative Learning: Investigate Police Work Critical Literacy: Conduct an Interview
Understanding Characters, p. 17						What are Characters? Characterization and Motivation Types of Characters				
The 11:59 Patricia McKissack pp. 18–28	Short Story	Guided Reading: Reading Model/ Moderate	2,049	Take Notes	Taking Notes Chart; Character Chart	Character	Hope		Creative: Dialogue Expository: Paragraph	Collaborative Learning: Create a Chart Lifelong Learning: Create a Time Line
Information Text Connection: A Long Hard Journey Patricia and Fredrick McKissack pp. 26–27	Essay	Easy	499							
Understanding Setting, p. 29						What is Setting? Setting in Fiction Setting and Community Setting and Mood				
The Inn of Lost Time Lensey Namioka pp. 30–47	Short Story	Guided Reading: Reading Model/ Challenging	5,854	Sequence of Events	Timeline; Venn Diagram	Setting	Value of Time		Creative: Descriptive Paragraph Expository: Literary Analysis	Collaborative Learning: Hold a Discussion Critical Literacy: Write Questions
The Portrait Tomás Rivera pp. 49–55	Short Story	Directed Reading/ Moderate	1,500	Analyze Cause and Effect	Cause and Effect Chart; Plot Diagram	Plot	Value of Truth		Creative: News Report Expository: Story Summary	Collaborative Learning: List Setting Details Lifelong Learning: Research the Internet
A Day's Wait Ernest Hemingway pp. 57–62	Short Story	Directed Reading/ Moderate	1,065	Draw Conclusions	Draw Conclusions Chart; Cause and Effect Chart	Conflict	Miscommunication		Creative: Letter Persuasive: Editorial	Critical Literacy: Create a Chart Media Literacy: Conduct Internet Research
Primary Source Connection: Mars Climate Orbiter Team Finds Likely Cause of Loss pp. 61–62	Press Release	Moderate	321							

GUIDED READING

DIRECTED READING

2A UNIT 1 FICTION

UNIT 1 SCOPE AND SEQUENCE PLANNING GUIDE 2B

Scope & Sequence Guide

- At-a-glance overview of unit selections. For each selection this guide provides information such as genre, reading level, reading skills taught, literary elements taught, themes, and cross-curricular connections.
- Information is organized to make planning easy and efficient.

–Teach Vocabulary Development–

Building Vocabulary

- Overview of all unit vocabulary words and Key Terms.
- Word lists are also referenced at point-of-use with each selection.

Unit 1 Building Vocabulary

The lists below identify the Words in Use and Key Terms within this unit. These words are listed at the bottom of the Teacher's Edition pages at the beginning of each lesson. Vocabulary development activities are provided in the Mastering the Standards Unit book and in Exceeding the Standards: Vocabulary and Spelling.

WORDS IN USE

Preview Vocabulary

Preview Vocabulary are words taken from the sentences within each selection, and are defined in the side margin or at the bottom of the pages on which they appear. The "Preview Vocabulary" section introduces these words in the Before You Read page preceding each selection.

abashed, 87
accost, 60
adornment, 142
afflict, 61
affluence, 169
amenity, 32
analytical, 33
animate, 37
aperture, 66
appertain, 139
assail, 92
avenger, 59
barbarous, 35
barren, 10
career, 111
chagrin, 144
compel, 85
compromise, 16
condone, 34
confer, 95
conscientious, 100
contemplatively, 84
denounce, 88
depreciate, 140
dilapidated, 127

disarming, 30
discreet, 123
distraught, 126
duplication, 142
earnest, 73
eerie, 126
elation, 126
elude, 76
embitter, 16
endeavour, 19
enthralled, 124
evanesce, 117
finesse, 143
formality, 52
frail, 7
futile, 38
gloat, 80
grotesque, 63
heresy, 118
hierarchy, 121
homage, 146
hysterical, 124
iconic, 130
imminent, 113
immoderate, 146

imputation, 139
incessantly, 143
inconsequential, 142
indignantly, 90
inestimable, 144
infallibility, 114
indescent, 113
languor, 19
lasso, 50
latitude, 101
legitimacy, 129
marauder, 17
martyr, 121
meretricious, 141
nocturnal, 147
odious, 149
original, 50
palpable, 21
parsimony, 139
perpetuate, 100
opinion, 17
plight, 17
precipitous, 16
preclude, 59
predominate, 139

premonition, 78
presentable, 9
primacy, 140
prudence, 141
quizzically, 91
reconciliation, 20
reiterate, 115
restraining, 17
retribution, 59
revere, 84
sallow, 103
solace, 127
solicitously, 36
sparse, 102
succession, 65
sullenly, 111
supplements, 143
tangible, 28
tentative, 97
termination, 64
tyranny, 130
usurer, 148
visceral, 129
vortex, 113
wield, 74

marked, 188
misery, 51
mortal, 51
mournful, 112
mystified, 28
naught, 117
nettles, 117
obliterated, 164
obscured, 174
obstinate, 64
oilskin, 52
opaqueness, 29
opposing, 180
palatial, 30
parishioners, 172
remorse, 169
repast, 42
paroxysm, 167

perverse, 187
poised, 163
pompadour, 99
precariously, 115
precipice, 159
privations, 149
prodigy, 177
profound, 121
promoted, 181
pulverizing, 164
quest, 162
rampart, 66
recoiled, 102
relented, 173

repressed, 90
roomers, 7
rowels, 38
ruse, 168
saffron, 171
sanctified, 162
solemnity, 172
sou, 149
spasmodically, 165
spurs, 15
stoop, 10
strictures, 100
succor, 20
surreal, 130
tangy, 155
tattered, 166

turbulent, 99
unfurled, 114
unredressed, 59
vestibule, 139
vexed, 146
vigil, 129
vigilant, 124
virulets, 159
warped, 127
wiles, 22
withered, 96
wont, 17, 60
wrath, 22
wrested, 16
wretchedly, 102

Selection Words

Selection Words are additional words from the reading that may be challenging, but are not central to the selection and are not identified in the prereading section. These words can easily be learned using the story context, and they provide excellent practice for using content clues to find meaning without explicit instruction.

absconded, 61
acquiesced, 16
adorn, 143
antechambers, 144
apparent, 127
ardent, 33
ascetic, 166
balks, 38
beleaguered, 165
benefactor, 173
bow string, 189
brash, 162
brawny, 73
brocades, 102
cascading, 159
cassock, 186

caste, 143
chaplet, 148
chaste, 141
checkmate, 181
chronicle, 142
circumscribing, 64
clattered, 167
consternation, 78
coquettish, 144
cottonwood, 183
cowering, 164
deceitful, 22
descent, 154
discerned, 30
draught, 19

droll, 34
enfolding, 113
entrails, 114
fettered, 64
flagon, 63
follies, 91
foresight, 174
freighted, 129
gallantries, 144
gaunt, 164
gesticulation, 63
gibber, 169
gnarly, 74
gnashing, 74
grunts, 189
humble, 162

imparted, 171
impassioned, 84
imposing, 72
incense, 162
infatuated, 124
ingrained, 130
instigates, 139
lacerated, 29
laments, 77
latching, 10
lilting, 125
linger, 123
loll, 111
lolls, 77
lowly, 181
malodorous, 177

KEY TERMS

Key Terms are commonly referred to as *academic vocabulary*. These terms appear in the instructional material to teach the literary terminology that students need to acquire to understand literature. The repetition of the terms throughout the program ensures student mastery, and provides a solid foundation for the continuing study of literature and language arts.

acquiring, 3
activism, 48
adaptation, 26
adversary, 43
adversity, 136
allegiance, 42
analysis, 192
ancestral, 47
ancestry, 188
aptly, 137
arrogant, 132
aspirations, 108
association, 132
assumption, 44, 58
assembly, 24
authentic, 46
bishop, 189
calculating, 193
château, 106
clarifies, 56
classic, 2
closure, 192
commemorations, 131
complimentary, 45
concrete, 153
connectedness, 135
contempt, 47
context, 3
contradicts, 169
conveyed, 153
critique, 152
crucial, 107
crucial, 12, 107
derive, 106
descent, 70

detest, 68
devoid, 107
dignity, 48
disabilities, 108
dispute, 25
distilled, 135
distinctive, 11, 138
distinguish, 160
documentaries, 129
dominant, 135, 136
eliminate, 198
embellish, 191
empathy, 193
encounters, 12
engaging, 4
enhances, 55
enunciation, 191
envisioned, 164
epidemic, 119
evoke, 132
evolution, 131
executed, 45
extent, 25
factions, 23
fanatic, 133
feverish, 47
flighty, 132
grudge, 192
heritage, 183
heroine, 54
hinder, 25
humility, 152
humorous, 57
immigrant, 82
implacable, 136

implication, 43
implore, 67
impunity, 195
indifferent, 151
industrious, 136
inhabitant, 26
inhumane, 23
insanity, 58
insight, 48
insights, 200
intensity, 12
interment, 82
interpretation, 57
intertwined, 136
intervenes, 12
intonation, 191
intrude, 55
ironic, 164
keen, 25
legacy, 14
legislation, 120
light-hearted, 191
linguistics, 170
lore, 45
lunges, 81
mah-jongg, 170
manipulate, 13
marquisette, 119
martyr, 133
medieval, 58, 180
medium, 135
meticulous, 138
mingle, 151
miseries, 5
murky, 58

mystifying, 70
niche, 46
noble, 195
obsessed, 182
overload, 191
overshadowed, 120
palates, 44
peers, 154
peopled, 138
perceive, 80
plights, 48
plodding, 134
poaching, 25
potluck, 80
premeditated, 66
prim, 119
primitive, 45
principles, 164
prior, 198
proposition, 42
provoke, 132
pseudonym, 138
psychological, 58
quarantine, 105
quest, 152
quest, 23
rank, 106
rebuttal, 43
reflective, 2
reincarnation, 116
remarkable, 133
replicas, 105
resilient, 135
resolves, 3
revelry, 67

2 **UNIT 1** FICTION

UNIT 1 BUILDING VOCABULARY 2

T39

Mirrors & Windows

–Prepare Students *for the* Unit Genre *and* Theme–

Unit Overview

- Important information ensures a successful launch for new and experienced teachers.
- Clear objectives are outlined.
- Launch the Unit strategies for whole class and small groups are provided.

Introduction to Genre

- Launch the Lesson builds on prior knowledge.
- Differentiated Instruction focuses on Reading Proficiency, Enrichment, Learning Styles, and English Language Learners.
- Words in Use and Key Terms are listed for additional vocabulary development.

–Introduce and Preview the Unit Genre Reading Model–

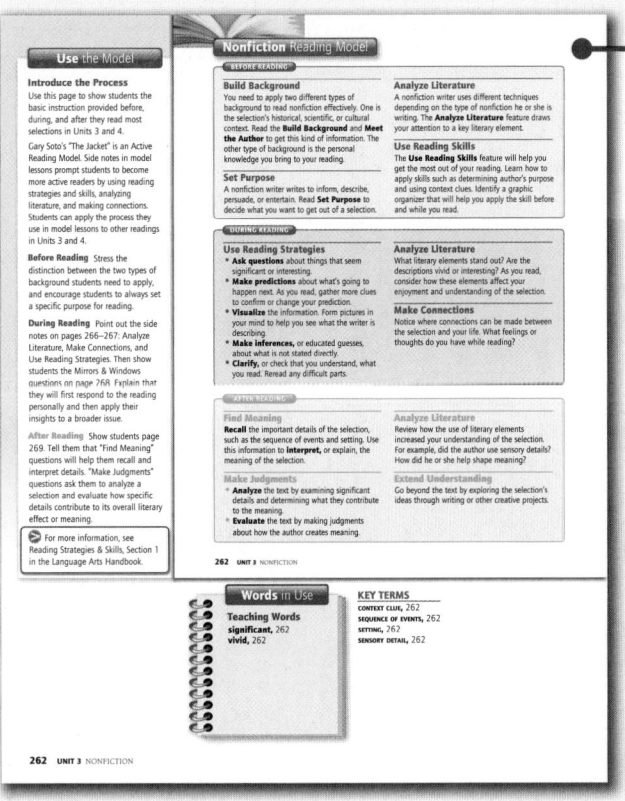

Unit Genre Reading Model

- The Genre Reading Model is taught before the first selection and applied throughout the unit.

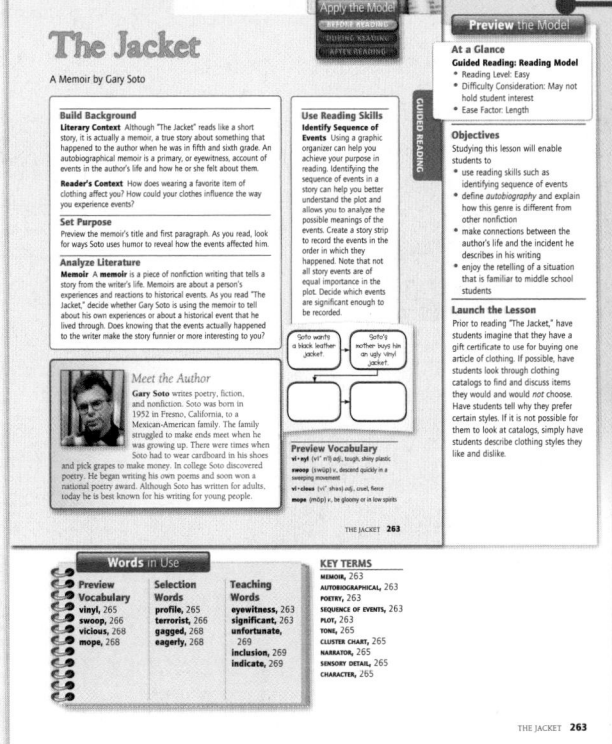

Before Reading

- Guided Reading— teacher guides students (Directed and Independent Reading follow later in the unit).
- At-a Glance provides Reading Level, Difficulty Considerations, and Ease Factors for each selection.
- Lesson objectives are clearly stated.
- Three categories of Words in Use and Key Terms are outlined with page references.

–Teach and Apply the Unit Genre Reading Model–

During Reading

- The *Mirrors & Windows* questions are previewed to prepare students to respond.
- Program Resources are conveniently listed.
- During Reading prompts ask students to Analyze Literature and Use Reading Strategies.

After Reading

- After Reading activities require students to recall and interpret detail, analyze and evaluate, and extend understanding.
- Rubrics for Writing Options are provided.
- Teaching Notes are packed with ideas and activities to stimulate discussion and add new information.

–Practice and Assess Language Arts Skills–

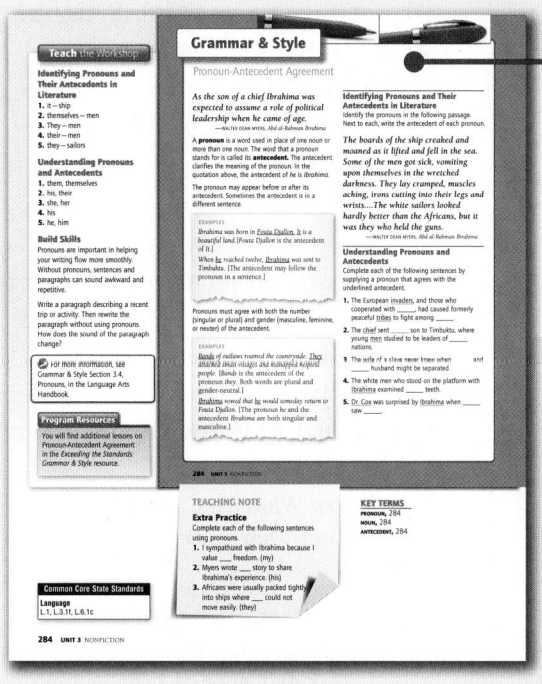

Grammar & Style

- Build Skills activities link grammar and writing instruction.
- Teaching Notes provide Extra Practice.
- Additional instruction is found in the Language Arts Handbook at the end of the text.
- Program Resources are listed.

Test Practice Workshop

- Rubric is provided for the Writing Activity.
- Test-taking tips and standardized test practice activities extend the lesson.

Additional Workshops Not Shown

- Vocabulary & Spelling
- Writing
- Speaking & Listening

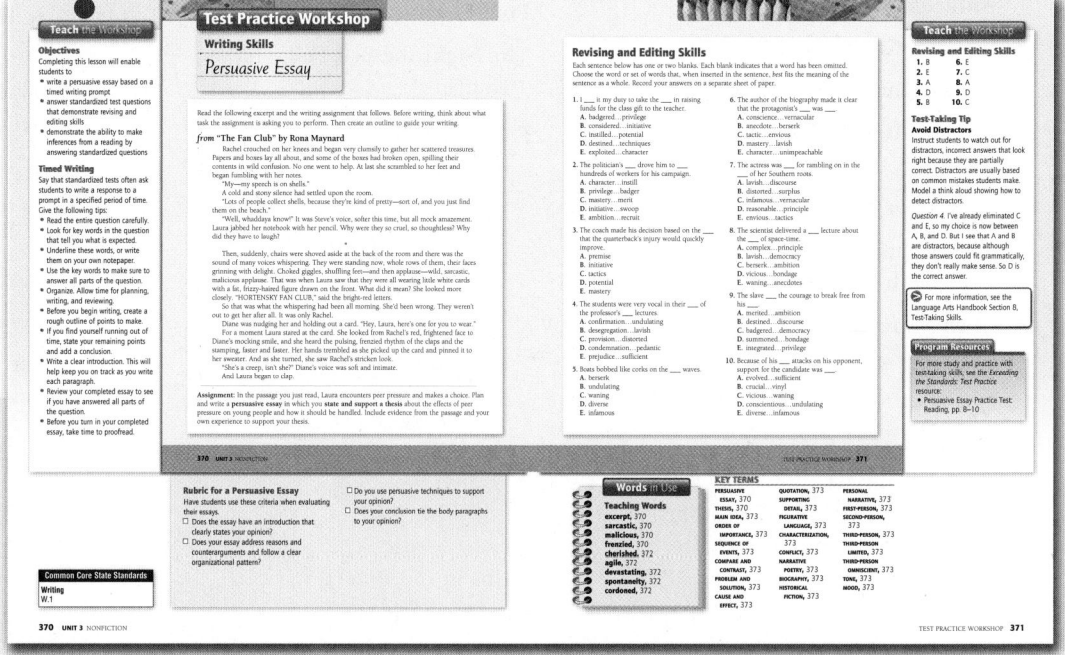

Mirrors & Windows

–Selections by Genre–

–Professional Resources and Research Base–

Teaching Literature

Applebee, A. N. (1993). *Literature in secondary schools: Studies of curriculum and instruction in U.S. schools*. Urbana, IL: National Council of Teachers of English.

Appleman, D. (2000). *Critical encounters in high school English*. Urbana, IL: National Council of Teachers of English.

Raphael, T., and Au, K. H., eds. (1998). *Literature-based instruction: Reshaping the curriculum*. Norwood, MA: Christopher-Gordon.

Rosenblatt, L. (1938, 1996). *Literature as exploration*, 5th ed. New York: MLA.

Teaching Reading Comprehension

Allen, J. (2000). *Yellow brick roads: Shared and guided paths to independent reading 4–12*. Portland, ME: Stenhouse Publishers.

Burke, J. (2000). *Reading reminders: Tools, tips, and techniques*. Portsmouth, NH: Boynton/Cook.

Gallagher, K. (2004). *Deeper reading: Comprehending challenging texts, 4-12*. Portland, ME: Stenhouse Publishers.

Graves, M. F., and Graves, B. B. (1994). *Scaffolding reading experiences: Designs for student success*. Norwood, MA: Christopher-Gordon.

Harvey, S., and Goudvis, A. (2001). *Strategies that work: Teaching comprehension to enhance understanding*. York, ME: Stenhouse Publishers.

Marzano, R. J., Pickering, D. J., and Pollock, J. E. (2001). *Classroom instruction that works: Research-based strategies for increasing student achievement*. Alexandria, VA: Association for Supervision and Curriculum Development.

Pearson, P. D., Roehler, L. R., Dole, J. A., and Duffy, G. G. (1992). Developing expertise in reading comprehension. In J. Samuels and A. Farstrup, eds., *What research has to say about reading instruction*. Newark, DE: International Reading Association.

Rosenblatt, L. (1938, 1996). *Literature as exploration*, 5th ed. New York: MLA.

Tovani, C. (2000). *I read it, but I don't get it: Comprehension strategies for adolescent readers*. Portland, ME: Stenhouse Publishers.

Teaching Vocabulary and Word Study

Anderson, R., and Nagy, W. (1991). Word meanings. In R. Barr, M. Kamil, P. Monsenthal, and P. D. Pearson, eds., *Handbook of reading research*, vol. 2, pp. 690–724. New York: Longman.

Baker, S. K., Simmons, D. C., and Kameenui, E. J. (1995a). *Vocabulary acquisition: Synthesis of the research*. Technical Report No. 13. University of Oregon; National Center to Improve the Tools for Educators

Bos, C. S., and Anders, P. L. (1990). Effects of interactive vocabulary instruction on the vocabulary learning and reading comprehension of junior-high learning-disabled students. *Learning Disability Quarterly*, 13(1), 31–42.

Nagy, W. E. (1988). *Teaching vocabulary to improve reading comprehension*. Urbana, IL: National Council of Teachers of English.

Teaching Grammar and Writing

Behrens, L., and Rosen, L. J. (2002). *Writing and reading across the curriculum*, 8th ed. New York: Addison Wesley.

Fowler, H. W. (1983). *Modern English usage*, 2nd ed. New York: Oxford University Press.

Garner, B. A. (1998). *A dictionary of modern American usage*. New York: Oxford University Press

University of Chicago Pr.ess, The (2003). *The Chicago manual of style: The essential guide for writers, editors, and publishers*, 15th ed. Chicago, IL: University of Chicago Press.

Weaver, C. (1996). *Teaching grammar in context*. Portsmouth, NH: Heinemann

Lesson Planning and Differentiating Instruction

Burke. J. (1999). *The English teacher's companion: A complete guide to classroom, curriculum, and the profession*. Portsmouth, NH: Heinemann.

Daniels, H. (2002). *Literature circles: Voice and choice in the student-centered classroom*, 2nd ed. York, ME: Stenhouse Publishers.

Gallagher, K. (2003). *Reading reasons: Motivational mini-lessons for middle and high school*.

Portland, ME: Stenhouse Publishers.

Gregory, G. H., and Chapman, C. (2002). *Differentiated instructional strategies: One size doesn't fit all*. Thousand Oaks, CA: Corwin Press.

Strickland, D.S. and Alvermann, D. E., eds. (2004). *Bridging the literacy achievement gap grades 4-12*. New York: Teachers College Press.

Vacca, R. T., and Vacca, J. A. (1999). *Content area reading: Literacy and learning across the curriculum*. New York: Longman.

Facilitating Transfer of Learning

Boriarsky, C. (2001). Learning to transfer knowledge from one assignment to the next. Talk delivered at Recreating the Classroom: 91st Annual NCTE Convention, Baltimore, November 16.

Salomen, G. and Perkins, D. N. (1994). Rocky roads to transfer: Rethinking mechanisms of a neglected phenomenon. *Educational Psychologist*, 24(2), 113–142.

Rigor in the Classroom

American Diploma Project, *Ready or Not: Creating a high school diploma thatcounts*. Achieve, Inc., 2004.

Expectations Gap: A 50-state review of high school graduation requirements. Achieve, Inc., 2004.

Jago, C. *With rigor for all*. (2000). Portsmouth, NH: Heinemann.

Assessment

Langer, J. A., ed. (1992). *Literature instruction: A focus on student response*. Urbana, IL: National Council of Teachers of English.

Barr, R., Blachowicz, C. Z., Katz, C., and Kaufman, B. (2001). *Reading diagnosis for teachers: An instructional approach*. New York: Allyn and Bacon.

Gillet, J. W., and Temple, C. (1990). *Understanding reading problems: Assessment and instruction*. New York: HarperCollins.

Johnston, P. (1984). Prior knowledge and reading comprehension test bias. *Reading Research Quarterly*, 19, 219–228.

Sadler, C. R. (2001). *Comprehension strategies for middle grade learners: A handbook for content area teachers*. New York: International Reading Association.

Partial List. Complete list available on request.

MIRRORS & WINDOWS

Connecting with Literature

"The whole purpose of education
is to turn mirrors into windows."

— Sydney J. Harris

MIRRORS & WINDOWS

Connecting with Literature

Level II

EMC
Publishing

ST. PAUL • INDIANAPOLIS

Staff Credits

Senior Editor: Brenda Owens
Editor: Nancy Papsin
Associate Editor: Carley Bomstad
Editorial Assistants: Erin Saladin,
Lindsay Ryan
Permissions Coordinator: Valerie Murphy
Photo Researcher: Brendan Curran
Marketing Managers: Bruce Ayscue,
Laurie Skiba
Cover Designer: Leslie Anderson

Text Designer: Ronan Design
Page Layout Designers: Jack Ross,
Matthias Frasch
Production Editor: Courtney Kost
Production Specialist: Petrina Nyhan
Project Manager: Sara Dovre Wudali,
Buuji, Inc.
Editorial Development and Production:
Nieman Inc.

Literary Acknowledgments: Literary Acknowledgments appear following the Glossary of Vocabulary Words. We have made every effort to trace the ownership of all copyrighted material and to secure permission from copyright holders. In the event of any question arising as to the use of any material, we will be pleased to make the necessary corrections in future printings. Thanks are due to the authors, publishers, and agents for permission to use the materials indicated.

Art and Photo Credits: Art and Photo Credits appear following the Literary Acknowledgments.

ISBN 978-0-82196-031-8

Consultants, Reviewers, and Focus Group Participants

Tracy Pulido
Language Arts Instructor
West Valley High School
Fairbanks, Alaska

Jean Martorana
Reading Specialist/English Teacher
Desert Vista High School
Phoenix, Arizona

Cindy Johnston
English Teacher
Argus High School
Ceres, California

Susan Stoehr
Language Arts Instructor
Aragon High School
San Mateo, California

John Owens
Reading Specialist
St. Vrain Valley Schools
Longmont, Colorado

Fred Smith
Language Arts Instructor
St. Bernard High School
Uncasville, Connecticut

Penny Austin-Richardson
English Department Chair
Seaford Senior High School
Seaford, Delaware

Cecilia Lewis
Language Arts Instructor
Mariner High School
Cape Coral, Florida

Jane Feber
Teacher
Mandarin Middle School
Jacksonville, Florida

Dorothy Fletcher
Language Arts Instructor
Wolfson Senior High School
Jacksonville, Florida

Tamara Doehring
English/Reading Teacher
Melbourne High School
Melbourne, Florida

Patti Magee
English Instructor
Timber Creek High School
Orlando, Florida

Margaret J. Graham
Language Arts/Reading Teacher
Elizabeth Cobb Middle School
Tallahassee, Florida

Elizabeth Steinman
English Instructor
Vero Beach High School
Vero Beach, Florida

Wanda Bagwell
Language Arts Department Chair
Commerce High School
Commerce, Georgia

Betty Deriso
Language Department Chairperson
Crisp County High School
Cordele, Georgia

Dr. Peggy Leland
English Instructor
Chestatee High School
Gainsville, Georgia

Matthew Boedy
Language Arts Instructor
Harlem High School
Harlem, Georgia

Patty Bradshaw
English Department Chair
Harlem High School
Harlem, Georgia

Dawn Faulkner
English Department Chair
Rome High School
Rome, Georgia

Carolyn C. Coleman
AKS Continuous Improvement
    Director
Gwinnett County Public Schools
Suwanee, Georgia

Elisabeth Blumer Thompson
Language Arts Instructor
Swainsboro High School
Swainsboro, Georgia

Toi Walker
English Instructor
Northeast Tifton County High
    School
Tifton, Georgia

Jeanette Rogers
English Instructor
Potlatch Jr.-Sr. High School
Potlatch, Idaho

Gail Taylor
Language Arts Instructor
Rigby High School
Rigby, Idaho

Carey Robin
Language Arts Instructor
St. Francis College Prep
Brookfield, Illinois

Patricia Meyer
English Department Chair
Glenbard East High School
Lombard, Illinois

Liz Rebmann
Language Arts Instructor
Morton High School
Morton, Illinois

Helen Gallagher
English Department Chair
Main East High School
Park Ridge, Illinois

Rosemary Ryan
Dean of Students
Schaumburg High School
Schaumburg, Illinois

Donna Cracraft
English Department Co-Chair/IB
    Coordinator
Pike High School
Indianapolis, Indiana

Consultants, Reviewers, and Focus Group Participants (cont.)

K. C. Salter
Language Arts Instructor
Knightstown High School
Knightstown, Indiana

Lisa Broxterman
Language Arts Instructor
Axtell High School
Axtell, Kansas

Shirley Wells
Language Arts Instructor
Derby High School
Derby, Kansas

Karen Ann Stous
Speech & Drama Teacher
Holton High School
Holton, Kansas

Martha-Jean Rockey
Language Arts Instructor
Troy High School
Troy, Kansas

Shelia Penick
Language Arts Instructor
Yates Center High School
Yates Center, Kansas

John Ermilio
English Teacher
St. Johns High School
Shrewsbury, Massachusetts

James York
English Teacher
Waverly High School
Lansing, Michigan

Mary Spychalla
Gifted Education Coordinator
Valley Middle School
Apple Valley, Minnesota

Shari K. Carlson
Advanced ILA Teacher
Coon Rapids Middle School
Coon Rapids, Minnesota

Rebecca Benz
English Instructor
St. Thomas Academy
Mendota Heights, Minnesota

Michael F. Graves
Professor Emeritus
University of Minnesota
330A Peik Hall
Minneapolis, Minnesota

Kathleen Nelson
English Instructor
New Ulm High School
New Ulm, Minnesota

Adonna Gaspar
Language Arts Teacher
Cooper High School
Robbinsdale, Minnesota

Sara L. Nystuen
English Department Chair; AP
  Instructor
Concordia Academy
Roseville, Minnesota

Tom Backen
English Teacher
Benilde-St. Margaret's School
St. Louis Park, Minnesota

Daniel Sylvester
Jr. High English & American
  Experience Teacher
Benilde-St. Margaret's School
St. Louis Park, Minnesota

Jean Borax
Literacy Coach
Harding High School
St. Paul, Minnesota

Erik Brandt
English Teacher
Harding High School
St. Paul, Minnesota

Kevin Brennan
High School English Teacher
Cretin-Derham Hall
St. Paul, Minnesota

Anna Newcombe
English Instructor
Harding High School
St. Paul, Minnesota

Rosemary Ruffenach
Language Arts Teacher, Consultant,
  and Writer
St. Paul, Minnesota

Nancy Papsin
English Teacher/Educational
  Consultant
White Bear Lake, Minnesota

Shannon Umfleet
Communication Arts Instructor
Northwest High School
Cedar Hill, Missouri

Ken Girard
Language Arts Instructor
Bishop LeBlond High School
St. Joseph, Missouri

Jessica Gall
Language Arts Instructor
Fremont High School
Fremont, Nebraska

Michael Davis
Language Arts Instructor
Millard West High School
Omaha, Nebraska

Lisa Larnerd
English Teacher
Basic High School
Henderson, Nevada

Jo Paulson
Title I Reading Teacher
Camino Real Middle School
Las Cruces, New Mexico

Stacy Biss
Language Arts Instructor
Hackensack High School
Hackensack, New Jersey

J. M. Winchock
Reading Specialist, Adult Literacy
  Instructor
Hillsborough High School
Hillsborough, New Jersey

Consultants, Reviewers, and Focus Group Participants (cont.)

Matthew Cahn
Department of English & Related Arts Supervisor
River Dell High School
Oradell, New Jersey

Jean Mullooly
Language Arts Instructor
Holy Angels High School
Trenton, New Jersey

Fenice Boyd
Assistant Professor, Learning and Instruction
State University of New York at Buffalo
Buffalo, New York

Michael Fedorchuk
Assistant Principal
Auburn High School
Auburn, New York

Robert Balch
English Instructor
Beacon High School
Beacon, New York

Rene A. Roberge
Secondary English/AP English Instructor
Hudson Falls High School
Hudson Falls, New York

Melissa Hedt
Literacy Coach
Asheville Middle School
Asheville, North Carolina

Jane Shoaf
Educational Consultant
Durham, North Carolina

Kimberly Tufts
Department Chair for ELA
Cranberry Middle School
Elk Park, North Carolina

Cheryl Gackle
English Instructor
Kulm High School
Kulm, North Dakota

Barbara Stroh
English Department Chair
Aurora High School
Aurora, Ohio

Mary Jo Bish
Language Arts Instructor
Lake Middle School
Millbury, Ohio

Judy Ellsesser-Painter
Language Arts Instructor
South Webster High School
South Webster, Ohio

Adele Dahlin
English Department Chair
Central Catholic High School
Toledo, Ohio

Joshua Singer
English Instructor
Central Catholic High School
Toledo, Ohio

Debbie Orendorf
Language Arts Instructor
Berlin Brothers Valley High School
Berlin, Pennsylvania

Dona Italiano
English Teacher/Language Arts Coordinator
Souderton Area High School
Souderton, Pennsylvania

Tina Parlier
Secondary English Instructor
Elizabethton High School
Elizabethton, Tennessee

Wayne Luellen
English Instructor
Houston High School
Germantown, Tennessee

Ed Farrell
Senior Consultant
Emeritus Professor of English Education
University of Texas at Austin
Austin, Texas

Terry Ross
Secondary Language Arts Supervisor
Austin Independent School District
Austin, Texas

Angelia Greiner
English Department Chair
Big Sandy High School
Big Sandy, Texas

Sharon Kremer
Educational Consultant
Denton, Texas

E. J. Brletich
Supervisor of English/Language Arts
Spotsylvania City School
Fredericksburg, Virginia

Jeffrey Golub
Educational Consultant
Bothell, Washington

Clifford Aziz
Language Arts Instructor
Washington High School
Tacoma, Washington

Becky Palmer
Reading Teacher
Madison Middle School
Appleton, Wisconsin

Mary Hoppe
English Teacher
Bonduel High School
Bonduel, Wisconsin

Lou Wappel
English, Humanities & Guidance Instructor
St. Lawrence Seminary High School
Mount Calvary, Wisconsin

Gregory R. Kier
Language Arts Instructor
East Elementary School
New Richmond, Wisconsin

CONTENTS IN BRIEF

INDEPENDENT READING

INDEPENDENT READING

LANGUAGE ARTS RESOURCES

Applied English

Speaking & Listening

Test-Taking Skills

LANGUAGE ARTS WORKSHOPS

Writing

Viewing

Test Practice

INDEPENDENT READINGS

> "The whole purpose of education
> is to turn mirrors into windows."
>
> — Sydney J. Harris

Think about when you were young and about to start school for the first time. When you stood in front of the mirror, your view was focused on your own reflection and limited by your own experience. Then the windows of learning began to open your mind to new ideas and new experiences, broadening both your awareness and your curiosity.

As you discovered reading, you learned to connect with what you read and to examine your own ideas and experiences. And the more you read, the more you learned to connect with the ideas and experiences of other people from other times and other places. Great literature provides *mirrors* that help you reflect on your own world and *windows* that lead you into new worlds. This metaphor for the reading experience expresses the power of words to engage and transform you.

EMC's literature program, *Mirrors and Windows: Connecting with Literature,* provides opportunities for you to explore new worlds full of people, cultures, and perspectives different from your own. This book contains stories, essays, plays, and poems by outstanding authors from around the globe. Reading these selections will expand your appreciation of literature and your world view. Studying them will help you examine universal themes such as honesty, integrity, and justice and common emotions such as fear, pride, and belonging. You may already have thought about some of these ideas and feelings yourself.

As you read the selections in this book, try to see yourself in the characters, stories, and themes. Also try to see yourself as a citizen of the world—a world from which you have much to learn and to which you have much to offer.

Unit 1 Visual Planning Guide

Planning and Assessment Tools

Annotated Teacher's Edition
One location for accessing, previewing, and planning for use of all program resources.

Annotated Teacher's Edition

EMC Launchpad
Desktop application for accessing, previewing, planning, posting, and grading all program resources. Post personal resources and lessons, and access the E-Lesson Planner, the E-Gradebook, and training modules for computer literacy.

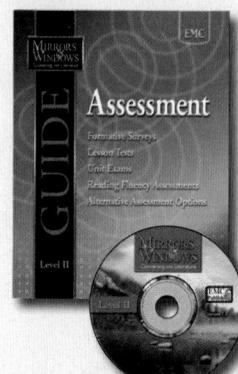

Assessment Guide and ExamView
A variety of assessments are available for this unit in print and electronic forms, including:
• Formative Survey
• Lesson Tests
• Unit Exams
• Alternative Assessment Options
• Reading Fluency Assessments

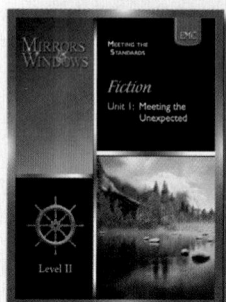

Meeting the Standards: Unit 1
In addition to lesson-by-lesson resources, *Meeting the Standards* includes the following unit-based resources:
• Unit Study Guide
• Practice Test
• Active Reading Model
• Selection Quizzes

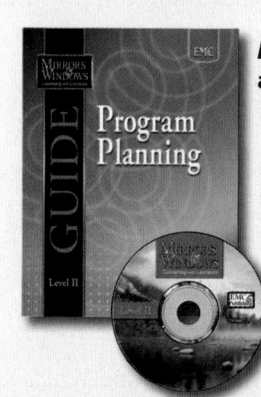

Program Planning Guide and E-Lesson Planner
• Lesson Plans for all the selections in the unit
• Core Standards-Based Selections
• Reading Log and Evaluation Forms

The E-Lesson Planner contains fully developed lesson plans and unit resources with an electronic calendar for editing lesson plans.

Technology Tools

Visual Teaching Package
This package contains unit-based lectures, games, art collections, and Writing Workshops in PowerPoint format; included within the EMC Launchpad.

Interactive Student Text on CD
The student textbook on CD includes highlighting, note-taking, bookmarking, and a direct link to the student website, in addition to everything in the student text.

Audio Library
Authentic, dramatic recordings with listening activities expand listening skills and offer additional support for developing readers and English Language Learners.

ETS Online Criterion-Based Essay Grader (Grades 9–12)
Students can use this ETS web-based tool to evaluate their essays online before submitting them for teacher review and final evaluation.

mirrorsandwindows.com
Student and teacher resources, support, references, technology tools, and state-specific standards are available at **mirrorsandwindows.com.** The website is customizable using the EMC Launchpad.

Unit-Based Resources

Exceeding the Standards Unit Resources

Each of the *Exceeding the Standards* resources provides fully developed lessons to help you extend the textbook lessons and to expand upon the themes and skills covered in the unit. You can also download these lessons from **mirrorsandwindows.com**.

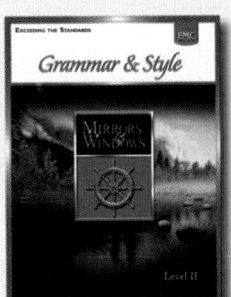

Grammar & Style
This resource contains:
- Five lessons on the Sentence and Parts of Speech, pp. 1–19

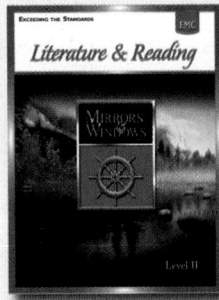

Literature & Reading
This resource contains:
- Summarize Fiction, pp. 1–2

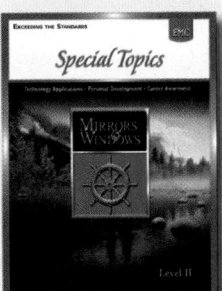

Special Topics
This resource contains:
- Lifelong Learning: The Deifintion of Character: Part 1, pp. 1–2
- Media Literacy: Internet Research, pp. 3–5

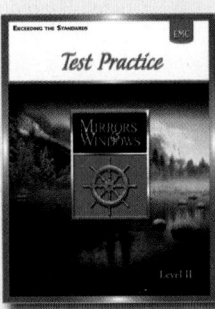

Test Practice
This resource contains:
- Literary Response Practice Test: Reading, pp. 5–6

Writing
This resource contains:
- Narrative Writing: Tell About a Person in Action, pp. 1–6

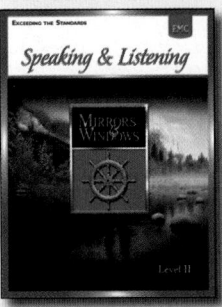

Speaking & Listening
This resource contains the following lesson to expand on the Speaking & Listening Workshop:
- Giving and Actively Listening to Oral Summaries, pp. 1–3.

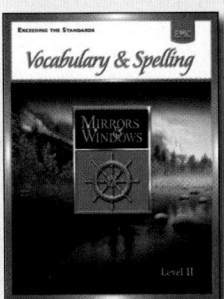

Vocabulary & Spelling
This resource contains:
- Three lessons on Word Study Skills and two lessons on Word Parts, pp. 1–12

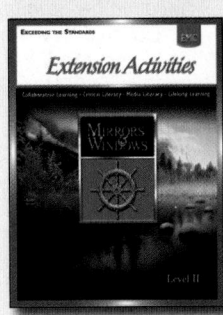

Extension Activities
This resource contains:
- Collaborative Learning: Investigative Police Work, pp. 1–2
- Lifelong Learning: Research the Internet, pp. 3–4

Unit 1 Visual Planning Guide

Reading Level: Easy
Pacing: 3 days

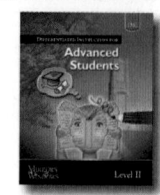 *Meeting the Standards,* Reading Model, pp. 19–28

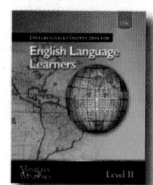 *Advanced Students,* Author/Genre Study, pp. 1–3

English Language Learners, Cause and Effect, pp. 1–9

10

Reading Level: Moderate
Pacing: 4 days

 *Meeting the Standards,* Guided Reading, pp. 29–35

Developing Readers, Make Predictions, pp. 1–3

19

Reading Level: Challenging
Pacing: 3 days

Meeting the Standards, Guided Reading, pp. 36–44

31

Reading Level: Moderate
Pacing: 2 days

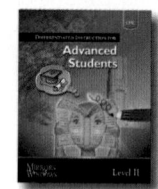 *Meeting the Standards,* Directed Reading, pp. 45–53

Advanced Students, Cultural Connection Project, p. 4

THE PORTRAIT
A Short Story by Tomás Rivera

50

A Day's Wait
A Short Story by Ernest Hemingway

Reading Level: Moderate
Pacing: 2 days

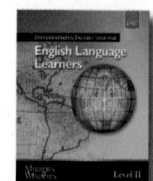 *Meeting the Standards,* Directed Reading, pp. 54–59

English Language Learners, Draw Conclusions, pp. 10–18

58

 Interactive Student Text on CD-ROM

 Selection Lesson Plan

 Web-based Resources

Lesson-by-Lesson Resources

64

Reading Level: Moderate
Pacing: 2 days

Meeting the Standards,
Directed Reading,
pp. 60–66

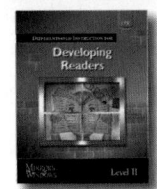
Developing Readers,
Make Connections,
pp. 4–6

Advanced Students,
Historical Context
Project, pp. 5–6

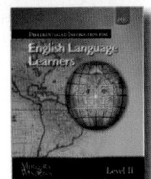
*English Language
Learners,* Cause and
Effect, pp. 19–31

74

Reading Level: Moderate
Pacing: 3 days

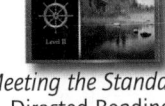
Meeting the Standards,
Directed Reading,
pp. 67–72

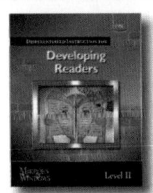
Developing Readers,
Visualize/Text
Organization, pp. 7–12

86

Reading Level: Moderate
Pacing: 4 days

Meeting the Standards,
Comparing Literature,
pp. 73–80

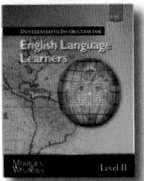
*English Language
Learners,* Personification/
Plot, pp. 32–63

105

Reading Level: Easy
Pacing: 1 day

Meeting the Standards,
Independent Reading,
pp. 81–87

Advanced Students,
Independent Reading
Project, pp. 7–8

111

Reading Level: Challenging
Pacing: 2 days

Meeting the Standards,
Independent Reading,
pp. 88–93

 Lesson Test

 Audio Library

Unit 1 Scope & Sequence Guide

	Selection or Feature	Genre	Reading Support/ Reading Level	Word Count	Reading Skill	Graphic Organizer	
GUIDED READING	**Introduction to Fiction** pp. 4–5						
	Understanding Plot, pp. 6–7						
	Fiction Reading Model, p. 8						
	After Twenty Years O. Henry pp. 9–15	Short Story	Guided Reading: Reading Model/ Moderate	1,267	Analyze Cause and Effect	Cause and Effect Chart; Plot Diagram	
	Understanding Characters p. 17						
	The 11:59 Patricia McKissack pp. 18–28	Short Story	Guided Reading: Reading Model/ Moderate	2,049	Take Notes	Taking Notes Chart; Character Chart	
	Information Text Connection: A Long Hard Journey Patricia and Fredrick McKissack pp. 26–27	Essay	Easy	499			
	Understanding Setting p. 29						
	The Inn of Lost Time Lensey Namioka pp. 30–47	Short Story	Guided Reading: Reading Model/ Challenging	5,854	Sequence of Events	Timeline; Venn Diagram	
DIRECTED READING	**The Portrait** Tomás Rivera pp. 49–55	Short Story	Directed Reading/ Moderate	1,500	Analyze Cause and Effect	Cause and Effect Chart; Plot Diagram	
	A Day's Wait Ernest Hemingway pp. 57–62	Short Story	Directed Reading/ Moderate	1,065	Draw Conclusions	Draw Conclusions Chart; Cause and Effect Chart	
	Informational Text Connection: Mars Climate Orbiter Team Finds Likely Cause of Loss pp. 61–62	Press Release	Moderate	321			

Literary Element	*Mirrors & Windows* Theme	Cross-Curricular Connection	Writing Options	Extension Activities
Types of Fiction Elements of Fiction				
What is Plot? Elements of Plot Plot Diagram Plot and Conflict External and Internal Conflict Plot and Organization				

Plot	Loyalty		Creative: Letter
			Expository: Essay
				Collaborative Learning: Investigate
				  Police Work
				Critical Literacy: Conduct an
				  Interview

What are Characters? Characterization and Motivation Types of Characters				

Character	Hope		Creative: Dialogue
			Expository: Paragraph
				Collaborative Learning: Create a
				  Chart
				Lifelong Learning: Create a Time
				  Line

What is Setting? Setting in Fiction Setting and Community Setting and Mood				

Setting	Value of Time		Creative: Descriptive
			  Paragraph
			Expository: Literary
			  Analysis
				Collaborative Learning: Hold a
				  Discussion
				Critical Literacy: Write Questions

Plot	Value of Truth		Creative: News Report
			Expository: Story Summary
				Collaborative Learning: List
				  Setting Details
				Lifelong Learning: Research the
				  Korean War

Conflict	Miscommunication		Creative: Letter Persuasive: Editorial	Critical Literacy: Create a Chart Media Literacy: Conduct Internet Research

Unit 1 Scope & Sequence Guide

	Selection or Feature	Genre	Reading Support/ Reading Level	Word Count	Reading Skill	Graphic Organizer	
DIRECTED READING	**The War of the Wall** Toni Cade Bambara pp. 63–71	Short Story	Directed Reading/ Moderate	2,709	Analyze Cause and Effect	Cause and Effect Chart; Dialect Chart	
	The Foghorn Ray Bradbury pp. 73–84	Short Story	Directed Reading/ Moderate	3,033	Use Context Clues	Cluster Chart	
	Informational Text Connection: The Aqualung David Macaulay p. 83	Visual Media	Moderate	155			
	Comparing Literature: Rikki-Tikki-Tavi Rudyard Kipling pp. 85–104	Short Story	Directed Reading/ Moderate	5,910		Personification Chart	
	The Green Mamba Roald Dahl pp. 85–104	Autobiography	Directed Reading/ Moderate	2,749			
INDEPENDENT READING	**Uncle Tony's Goat** Leslie Marmon Silko pp. 105–110	Short Story	Independent Reading/ Easy	2,499	Analyze Cause and Effect		
	The Serial Garden Joan Aiken 111–124	Short Story	Independent Reading/ Challenging	6,116	Multiple Levels of Meaning		

Unit 1 Language Arts Workshops

Grammar & Style	Vocabulary & Spelling	Writing	Speaking & Listening	Test Practice
Subject Verb Agreement, p. 48 Pronoun-Antecedent Agreement, p. 56 Nominative and Objective Pronouns, p. 72	Denotation and Connotation, p. 16	Expository Writing: Responding to a Short Story, pp. 126–131	Giving and Actively Listening to Oral Summaries, pp. 132–133	Writing Skills: Literary Response, from *The Snow Goose,* by Paul Gallico, pp. 134 Revising and Editing Skills, p. 135 Reading Skills: "The Dinner Party" by Mona Gardner pp. 136–137

Literary Element	*Mirrors & Windows* Theme	Cross-Curricular Connection	Writing Options	Extension Activities
Dialect	Judging Others	History Connection: *Civil Rights*	Creative: Dialogue Expository: Research Essay	Lifelong Learning: Write a Biography Media Literacy: Analyze Urban Murals
Mood	Patience	Science Connection: *Sea Creatures*	Creative: Job Description Persuasive: Paragraph	Collaborative Learning: Re-create a Scene Media Literacy: Research Underwater Creatures
Compare Literature: Personification	Bravery		Creative: Letter Expository: Compare-and-Contrast Essay	Collaborative Learning: Hold a Panel Discussion Media Literacy: Conduct Internet Research
Plot	Relating to Animals		Creative: Diary Entries	Collaborative Learning: Discuss the Outcome
Setting	Fantasy Worlds		Expository: Essay	Collaborative Learning: Create an Advertising Jingle

Unit 1 Building Vocabulary

The lists below identify the Words in Use and Key Terms within this unit. These words are listed at the bottom of the Teacher's Edition pages at the beginning of each lesson. Vocabulary development activities are provided in the *Meeting the Standards* unit book and in *Exceeding the Standards: Vocabulary & Spelling*.

WORDS IN USE

Preview Vocabulary
Preview Vocabulary are words taken from the sentences within each selection. These words are defined in the side margin or at the bottom of the pages on which they appear. The "Preview Vocabulary" section introduces these words in the Before Reading page preceding each selection.

cower, 88	forlorn, 100	mesmerize, 20	specter, 24
cultivated, 88	habitual, 11	poignant, 33	staunchest, 12
desolate, 33	influenza, 58	primeval, 77	swagger, 11
egotism, 14	intricate, 11	providence, 90	verify, 76
epidemic, 58	manipulate, 103	rapt, 32	worrisome, 21
flush, 59	meager, 19	ravenous, 35	

Selection Words
Selection Words are additional words from the reading that may be challenging but are not central to the selection and are not identified in the prereading section. These words can easily be learned using the story context, and they provide excellent practice for using content clues to find meaning without explicit instruction.

absurdity, 13	deafening, 25	genteel, 26	raveling, 77
accommodations, 26	delicate, 53	implement, 100	rueful, 44
accursed, 41	diaphragm, 83	incalculable, 121	stalwart, 11
apparatus, 77	doggedly, 116	keen, 119	statuettes, 32
ascended, 76	draggled, 87	kindling, 107	swindled, 53
astir, 13	dumbfounded, 98	lacquered, 37	synonymous, 26
beastly, 112	fastened, 24	liberation, 70	thoroughfare, 11
besought, 122	finery, 21	masterpiece, 66	trance, 66
convalescing, 116	flailing, 103	negotiate, 27	trough, 107
covey, 59	fledglings, 89	prophesying, 119	unrivaled, 26
cylinder, 83	gait, 90	purgative, 58	varnished, 59
daintily, 108	gaudy, 113	qualm, 46	

Teaching Words
Teaching Words consist of vocabulary that is used in the directions about the lessons. Teaching words explain to students what to focus on within the selection, help establish the story context, clarify the meaning of literary terms, and define the goals or instructional purpose.

ancestry, 105	colonial, 136	duplicate, 28	imply, 60
anecdote, 28	commotion, 136	eerily, 134	inconsistency, 44
anxiety, 7, 62	complexity, 17	egotism, 16	inevitable, 25
apparition, 134	contemporary, 63	enriches, 110	infer, 33
appealing, 124	convey, 28, 128	evokes, 73	inhabits, 29
associations, 124	coveted, 9	excerpt, 126	instinct, 97
attaché, 136	dangle, 7	exclusively, 18	intensity, 55
bamboo, 29	descriptive, 29	expository, 15	interact, 30
beacon, 73	desolate, 16	Fahrenheit, 6	interfering, 134
burden, 134	dialect, 63	feudal, 30	ironic, 9
capsizing, 79	dialogue, 8	gilded, 29	keen, 16
Celsius, 6	distinctively, 57	graphic organizer, 8	kindling, 29
cephalopod, 79	distinguished, 17	imagery, 35	krait, 85
classify, 17	domains, 30	imaginative, 4	lagged, 57

legible, 130
literary, 4
miserly, 16
motto, 97
narrative, 4
overdependence, 73
plausible, 124

poised, 134
prose, 4
pseudonym, 9
restrictive, 69
scan, 9
sequence, 8
significance, 18

skim, 9, 30, 49
social activist, 63
spare, 57
straddling, 49
terse, 57
thatched, 29
unique, 126

urban, 63
valor, 57
vantage point, 5
vivid, 8
widespread, 124

KEY TERMS

Key Terms are commonly referred to as *academic vocabulary*. These terms appear in the instructional material to teach the terminology that students need to acquire to understand literature. The repetition of the terms throughout the program ensures student mastery and provides a solid foundation for the continuing study of literature and language arts.

antagonist, 5, 17
antecedent, 56
audience, 128, 132
autobiography, 85
body, 128
cause, 62
cause and effect, 9, 49
central conflict, 137
character development, 57
character, 5, 17, 18, 126, 132
character traits, 47
characterization, 17
chronological order, 7
climax, 6, 9, 49, 137
cluster chart, 84, 127
compare, 104
complex sentences, 130
compound, 72
conclusion, 128
conflict, 7, 9, 49, 57
conjunctions, 130
connotations, 16
context clues, 73
contraction, 130
contrast, 104

denotation, 16
dialogue, 28, 57
dynamic character, 17
effect, 62
exposition, 6, 137
external conflict, 7, 57, 137
falling action, 6, 137
fiction, 4
first person point of view, 62
first-person, 5
flashbacks, 7, 47
flat character, 17, 20
foreshadowing, 7, 22
frame story, 47
gender, 56
illustrations, 85
infer, 73
internal conflict, 7, 57, 137
introduction, 128
linking verbs, 72
literary fiction, 4
main character, 18
main idea, 124
major characters, 5, 17
minor characters, 5, 17

mood, 5, 73, 134
motivation, 17, 23
motto, 97
narrator, 104, 110
near synonyms, 16
nominative pronouns, 72
noun, 48
novel, 4
number, 56
objective pronouns, 72
omniscient, 5
oral summary, 132
order of importance, 128
organizational pattern, 128
peer review, 129
personification, 85
plot, 5, 6, 9, 49, 126, 132, 134
plural, 48
point of view, 5
popular fiction, 4
possessive form, 130
predicate nominative, 72
prepositional phrase, 48
pronoun, 56, 72
protagonist, 5, 17, 18, 137

reliable narrator, 84
resolution, 6, 9, 49, 84, 137
rising action, 6
round character, 17, 20
sensory details, 133
sequence, 30
setting, 5, 30, 126, 132, 134
short story, 4, 9, 18, 49, 57, 73, 85, 105, 111
singular, 48
static character, 17
subject, 48, 72
summary, 55, 62, 126
synonyms, 16
theme, 5, 18
thesis, 47, 124, 127
third-person, 5
third-person limited, 5
tone, 128
topic sentence, 128
transitions, 130
unreliable narrator, 84
Venn diagram, 47
verb, 48, 72

Objectives

Studying this unit will help students meet the following objectives:

- Connect the themes expressed in the selections to their own lives and to the world around them
- Identify common forms of fiction, including the short story, as well as the nonfiction genres of essay, visual media, autobiography, and press release
- Identify common elements of fiction, including plot, character, setting, and mood
- Understand variations of literary forms and authors' use of language to develop forms

Reading Strategies

Ask Questions
Clarify
Make Inferences
Make Predictions
Visualize

Reading Skills

Analyze Cause and Effect
Context Clues
Draw Conclusions
Identify Sequence of Events
Take Notes

Literary Elements

Character and Characterization
Conflict
Dialect
Mood
Personification
Plot
Setting

Meeting the Unexpected
Fiction

PATRICIA McKISSACK

RAY BRADBURY

LENSEY NAMIOKA

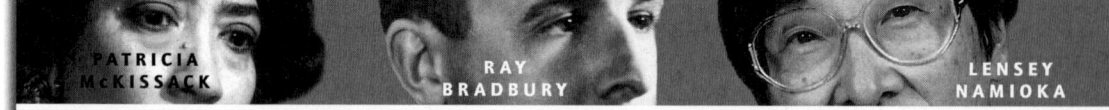

Launch the Unit

Look at the introductory text on page 3. Have students work in small groups to create other questions relating to the unit theme. Model a possible question: "Are surprises always good or always bad?" Have students write down the questions they come up with and keep the list. When the class has completed work on the unit, have students take another look at these questions and tell which selections provide insights that could help answer them.

"You been here now for three months, Johnny, so I better prepare you. About this time of year," he said, studying the murk and fog, "something comes to visit the lighthouse."

—RAY BRADBURY, "The Foghorn"

When have you encountered something you didn't expect? What did you learn from the experience? In his short story "The Foghorn," writer Ray Bradbury describes how two lighthouse keepers encounter a strange sea creature that is lured by the sound of their foghorn. As you read the short stories in the unit, imagine how you might feel if confronted with the unusual, unexplainable, or surprising events that they describe.

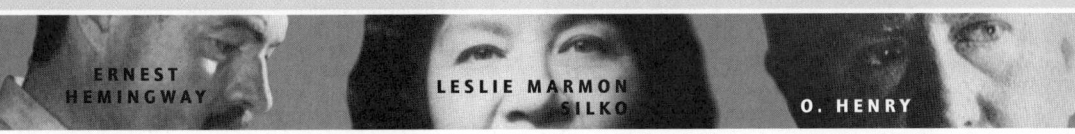

ERNEST HEMINGWAY   LESLIE MARMON SILKO   O. HENRY

3

Writing Options

Creative Writing

Descriptive Paragraph	Job Description
Dialogue	News Report
Diary Entries	Personal Letter

Expository Writing

Analytical Essay	Literary Analysis
Compare-and-Contrast Essay	Position Paragraph
Descriptive Paragraph	Research Essay
Expository Essay	Story Summary

Persuasive Writing

Editorial
Persuasive Paragraph

Language Arts Workshops

Grammar & Style
Subject-Verb Agreement
Pronouns-Antecedent Agreement
Nominative and Objective Pronouns

Vocabulary & Spelling
Denotation and Connotation

Writing Workshop
Response to a Short Story

Speaking & Listening Workshop
Oral Summary of a Short Story

Test Practice Workshop
Literary Response
Revising and Editing Skills
Reading Skills

Program Resources

For a visual reminder of the unit-based resources available for Unit 1, Fiction, see pages 2A and 2B. As you introduce the unit, you may want to provide students with the Unit Study Guide, which is contained in the *Meeting the Standards* resource.

Introduction to Fiction
You may use these "Introduction to Fiction" pages at any point in the unit, as students explore the elements of fiction in the Before Reading and After Reading sections of each selection.

Instead of reading through all the text at once, you may want to begin by having students read the explanations of popular and literary fiction. Then, ask students which general type they would prefer to read in each of the following situations:
- on a two-week vacation
- to discuss with a friend
- in a dentist's waiting room
- for writing a book report
- as the basis for an essay question on a standardized test

Launch the Lesson
Ask students to work in small groups to make a list of really great stories. Go beyond titles, and encourage students to cite actual story lines from short stories, novels, fairy tales, comics, fan fiction, TV shows and movies, science fiction and fantasy, and other popular fiction. Point out that fiction is available via the Internet and in theaters as well as in books.

After everyone has had a chance to suggest a great story, ask students what elements make a story especially good. Help them generalize to identify the main elements of plot, character, and setting.

Introduction to Fiction

"Fear quickened his step. Reaching his small apartment, he hurried up the steps. His heart pounded in his ear, and his left arm tingled. He had an idea, and there wasn't a moment to waste."

—PATRICIA McKISSACK, "The 11:59"

How does this passage make you feel? Does it make you eager to know what will happen next? By creating feelings of expectation, fictional stories can hook readers, making them want to learn more about the characters and what happens to them. A story also provides readers with a window into the fictional lives, thoughts, and experiences of its characters. The very broad category of literature known as **fiction** includes any work of prose (writing other than poetry and drama) that tells an invented or imaginary story.

Types of Fiction

Short Stories and Novels
The two main forms of fiction are the short story and the novel. The **short story** is a brief prose narrative, or story, that usually presents only a single plot, one or two main characters, and one important setting. A **novel** is a long work of prose fiction. Novels often have several plots, many major and minor characters, and numerous settings.

Popular Fiction and Literary Fiction
Another way of dividing fiction is into popular fiction and literary fiction. **Popular fiction** includes subgenres such as mystery, suspense and thriller, horror, science fiction, fantasy, romance, and Western. The works of writers in this book such as Ray Bradbury (famous for his science fiction and fantasy fiction) and Roald Dahl (famous for his fantasy stories) are examples of popular fiction.

Literary fiction does not fit into one of these categories. Writers in this book such as Ernest Hemingway, O. Henry, Sandra Cisneros, and Toni Cade Bambara are considered writers of literary fiction. The dividing line between popular and literary fiction is not clear-cut. For example, some writers of literary fiction, such as Rudyard Kipling, are also well known for their works of popular or imaginative fiction.

Types of Popular Fiction
Here are some of the most widely read types of popular fiction and their common formulas or elements.

- **Mystery:** The main character usually takes on a detective role and tries to uncover clues to a crime or some baffling event.
- **Horror:** Ghosts, monsters, or other dangerous characters may lurk within these stories, whose purpose is to provide a good fright.
- **Science Fiction:** Often the setting is outer space, but it doesn't need to be, as long as advanced technology is a strong element in the story.
- **Fantasy:** Often confused with science fiction, fantasy relies on magic and magical beings instead of technology. Fantasy is often set in another age or world.
- **Westerns:** The setting is important here—the West. The main character is usually a cowboy, often fighting for survival against the wilderness or evildoers.

4 **UNIT 1** FICTION

Words in Use
Teaching Words
prose, 4
narrative, 4
literary, 4
imaginative, 4
vantage point, 5

KEY TERMS
FICTION, 4
SHORT STORY, 4
NOVEL, 4
POPULAR FICTION, 4
LITERARY FICTION, 4
PLOT, 5
CHARACTER, 5
PROTAGONIST, 5
ANTAGONIST, 5
MAJOR CHARACTER, 5

MINOR CHARACTER, 5
SETTING, 5
MOOD, 5
POINT OF VIEW, 5
FIRST-PERSON, 5
THIRD-PERSON, 5
OMNISCIENT, 5
THIRD-PERSON LIMITED, 5
THEME, 5

Elements of Fiction

A piece of fiction is made up of various elements that make it work. Some of these elements include plot, characters, setting, point of view, and theme.

Plot

The plot of a work of fiction is the series of events related to a central conflict, or struggle. The plot typically introduces a conflict, develops it, and eventually resolves it.

Characters

The **characters** are the individuals who take part in the action of a story. The **protagonist** is the most important character in the story. This character is sometimes opposed by an **antagonist,** who is in conflict with the protagonist. In Tomás Rivera's "The Portrait" (page 49), Don Mateo is the protagonist and the portrait salesman is his antagonist.

Major characters play significant roles in the action, and **minor characters** play lesser roles. In Patricia McKissack's "The 11:59" (page 18), Lester Simmons is a major character because the story concentrates on him almost completely. His friends at the shoeshine stand are minor characters because they are only briefly introduced.

Setting

The **setting** of a story is the time, place, and environment in which the events take place. The setting can include the following elements:

- geographic location
- specific sites (such as a building or room)
- time period
- cultural, social, or economic conditions

Setting is important in helping to establish mood, or the emotion created in the reader by part, or all, of the story. The setting of Lensey Namioka's "The Inn of Lost Time" (page 30) includes both the geographic location of Japan and the eighteenth century—the time period in which the story takes place.

Point of View

Point of view is the vantage point from which the story is told—in other words, who is telling the story.

- In *first-person* point of view, the story is told by someone who participates in or witnesses the action; this person, called the *narrator*, uses words such as *I* and *we*.
- In *third-person* point of view, the narrator usually stands outside the action and observes. The narrator uses words such as *he, she, it,* and *they.*
- In a *third-person omniscient* point of view, the thoughts of all the characters are revealed. Piri Thomas's "Amigo Brothers" (page 163) is told from a third-person omniscient point of view.
- In a *third-person limited* point of view, the thoughts of only the narrator or a single character are revealed. Gary Soto's "Seventh Grade" (page 212) is told from a third-person limited point of view.

Theme

The **theme** is the central idea about life that is revealed through a literary work. A *stated theme* is presented directly, but an *implied theme* must be inferred by the reader. Many works of fiction do not have a stated theme but rather have one or more implied themes. A story may also have a stated theme and an implied theme. A stated theme of "The Scholarship Jacket" (page 154) is that earning something is different from buying something. An implied theme is that it is important to stand up for what you believe.

Teach the Genre

Elements of Fiction

For more in-depth information, see the element introductions:
Understanding Plot, pages 6–7
Understanding Characters, page 17
Understanding Setting, page 29
Understanding Point of View, page 140
Understanding Theme, page 153

Differentiated Instruction

English Language Learning

Invite students who recently emigrated from other countries to describe examples of popular fiction they enjoyed there and to name the writers who were their favorites.

Also explain if necessary what it means to *resolve* a conflict (page 5). Tell students this means that the disagreement or problem comes to an end. Usually, actions of the characters resolve the conflict.

Teach the Element

Understanding Plot

Reading skills and strategies that can help students understand plot include analyzing cause and effect, making predictions, and summarizing.

Use Reading Skills

Analyze Cause and Effect Tell students that a story develops from events and motivations. In any plot, one thing leads to another. Mention a current television show or news story with which your students will probably be familiar, and have students identify the causes and effects.

Use Reading Strategies

Make Predictions Have student pairs confer to make a prediction about something that will happen in English class this year. Model a possible response: "I predict that I will end up liking poetry better than I thought I would." Tell students they may also make predictions to appreciate a story's plot. They can anticipate events based on what they learn about people and previous events in their lives. Encourage students to make—and to revise—predictions as they read the selections in this unit.

Literary Element

Understanding Plot

What Is Plot?

When you describe the events that take place in a story, you are describing the plot. The **plot** is a series of related events that drive a short story or novel. The most exciting element of fiction for many readers is the plot, which can keep them guessing what will happen next. What do you think will happen next to Ichabod Crane in the passage on this page from "The Legend of Sleepy Hollow"?

The Elements of Plot

The typical plot contains the following elements: **exposition, rising action, climax, falling action,** and **resolution.** The diagram below shows how these elements shape the development of the plot of Ernest Hemingway's "A Day's Wait" (page 57).

Plot Diagram

Exposition
One morning, the narrator's son Schatz wakes with a headache and looks ill.

Rising Action
The narrator calls a doctor, who takes Schatz's temperature and prescribes flu medicine.

Climax
The narrator comes home to find Schatz causing a commotion. He refuses to let anyone into his room and asks his father how long he has to live.

Falling Action
It is revealed that Schatz doesn't understand the difference between Celsius and Fahrenheit. He thought his fever was much higher than it actually was.

Resolution
Schatz is relieved to learn that he is not going to die and is able to relax after a day of stress.

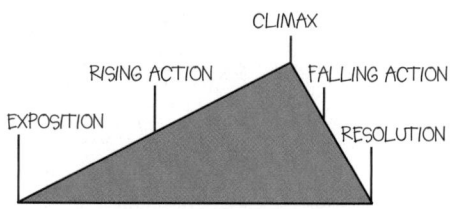

All of the stories of ghosts and goblins that he had heard in the afternoon, now came crowding upon his recollection. The night grew darker and darker....

—WASHINGTON IRVING,
"The Legend of Sleepy Hollow"

CLIMAX

RISING ACTION   FALLING ACTION

EXPOSITION   RESOLUTION

6   UNIT 1 FICTION

Words in Use

Teaching Words
Celsius, 6
Fahrenheit, 6
anxiety, 7
dangle, 7

KEY TERMS

PLOT, 6	EXTERNAL CONFLICT, 7
EXPOSITION, 6	INTERNAL CONFLICT, 7
RISING ACTION, 6	ANTAGONIST, 7
CLIMAX, 6	CHRONOLOGICAL ORDER, 7
FALLING ACTION, 6	FLASHBACKS, 7
RESOLUTION, 6	FORESHADOWING, 7
CONFLICT, 7	

Common Core State Standards

Reading Literature
RL.3

Plot and Conflict

A plot revolves around some type of **conflict,** or struggle. Usually, throughout the course of a story, a central conflict is introduced, developed, and resolved. In units 1 and 2, you will read stories in which characters encounter different kinds of conflict.

External and Internal Conflicts

There are two basic types of conflict, external and internal. An *external conflict* is a struggle that takes place between a character and some outside force. These outside forces are of three principal types:

- another character, or **antagonist** (see Understanding Characters, page 17)
- nature
- society

Conflict with Another Character In Tomás Rivera's "The Portrait" (page 49), the main character, Don Mateo, speaks of confronting the portrait salesman who has taken advantage of him.

> I just grabbed him right then and there. Poor guy couldn't even talk. He was all scared. And I told him that I wanted that portrait of my son....

Conflict with Nature In Ray Bradbury's "The Foghorn" (page 73), the struggle is between the main characters and a force of nature, a strange sea creature attracted by the sound of the foghorn.

Conflict with Society One of the main characters in Borden Deal's "Antaeus" (page 199) is a boy who has his plans to make a roof garden shattered by the building's owner.

> We had grown up aware of adult authority, of policemen and night watchmen and teachers, and this man sounded like all the others. But it was a new thing to T. J.

The other principal type of conflict is *internal conflict,* a struggle that goes on within the main character. In Gish Jen's "The White Umbrella" (page 181), the main character struggles with her own anxiety about fitting in and feeling accepted.

> I stared at the umbrella. I wanted to open it, twirl it around by its slender silver handle; I wanted to dangle it from my wrist on the way to school the way the other girls did.

Plot and Organization

A story has to have a beginning and an end. A story's plot, therefore, is often organized by time. Some stories may present a single day in a character's life, or even an hour, whereas others may span many years. O. Henry's "After Twenty Years" (page 9) takes place in one evening. The events recalled in Cherylene Lee's "Hollywood and the Pits" (page 141) occupy a decade.

Many stories are told in **chronological order,** that is, the events are presented in the order in which they occur in time. Sometimes writers play with time. They use **flashbacks** to tell about something that happened in the past. In Lensey Namioka's "The Inn of Lost Time" (page 30), the narrator begins in the present and then goes back into the past.

> It happened about seven years ago, when I was a green, inexperienced youngster not quite eighteen years old.

Writers use flashbacks to help develop relationships between characters, advance the plot, or add an element of mystery or expectation to a developing narrative.

Another way in which writers play with time is through the use of **foreshadowing,** giving hints or clues about what is going to happen in the future. In Joseph Bruchac's "Jed's Grandfather" (page 191), the main character's dreams suggest coming difficulties.

> He was in the boat, dark water widening between them. The old man stood there on The Island, unaware of the great dark wave coming at him from behind. His eyes were on Jed, but Jed couldn't call out. He couldn't move his arms.

Use Reading Skills

Summarize After covering this material in class, have students work in three small groups to summarize what they have learned. Assign a segment of the essay to each group: Have one group summarize what the class has discussed about each element of the plot, one group summarize the types of conflict, and one group summarize how plot relates to organization. Ask each group to select a spokesperson to share the group's summary with the class.

Analyze Literature

Protagonist and Antagonist This essay identifies an antagonist as a character with whom someone has a conflict. You might want to introduce the term *protagonist* (main character) as well. Tell students they will learn more about protagonists and antagonists later in the unit when they study character in greater detail.

Differentiated Instruction

Reading Proficiency

Have struggling readers read Hemingway's "A Day's Wait" (pages 58–60) before teaching this element. Then, use the marked plot diagram on page 6 to help them grasp the five key elements of the plot.

English Language Learning

English language learners will benefit from internalizing new basic language as well as new academic language. Review the academic terms presented on these pages and point out basic words that might be unfamiliar to ELL students (such as *foghorn*, *watchmen*, and *anxiety*). Have students brainstorm where they would encounter these words in everyday life and then have students define them in their own words.

Use the Model

Introduce the Process

Use this page to show students the basic instruction provided for them before, during, and after reading most fiction selections in Units 1 and 2.

"After Twenty Years" is an Active Reading Model. Side notes in these lessons prompt students to become more active readers by using reading strategies and skills, analyzing literature, and making connections. Students can apply the process they use to read "After Twenty Years" to other stories in Units 1 and 2.

For more information, see Reading Strategies and Skills, Section 1 in the Language Arts Handbook.

Before Reading Stress the distinction between the two types of background students need to apply, and encourage students to always set a specific purpose for reading.

During Reading Point out the side notes in "After Twenty Years": Analyze Literature, Use Reading Strategies, and Use Reading Skills. Then show students the Mirrors & Windows questions on page 14. Explain that they will first respond to the story personally, and then apply their insights to a broader issue.

After Reading Show students page 15. Tell them that "Find Meaning" questions will help them recall and interpret details. "Make Judgments" questions ask them to analyze a selection and evaluate how specific details contribute to its overall literary effect or meaning.

Fiction Reading Model

BEFORE READING

Build Background
You need to apply two types of background to read fiction effectively. One type is the story's literary and historical context. Read the **Build Background** and **Meet the Author** features to get this information. The other type of background is the personal knowledge and experience you bring to your reading.

Set Purpose
A fiction writer presents characters and actions to say something about life. Read **Set Purpose** to decide what you want to get out of the story.

Analyze Literature
A fiction writer uses literary techniques, such as plot and setting, to create meaning. The **Analyze Literature** feature draws your attention to a key literary element in the story.

Use Reading Skills
The **Use Reading Skills** feature will show you skills to help you get the most out of your reading. Learn how to apply skills such as determining author's purpose and using context clues. Identify a graphic organizer that will help you apply the skill before and while you read.

DURING READING

Use Reading Strategies
- **Ask questions** about things that seem significant or interesting.
- **Make predictions** about what's going to happen next. As you read, gather more clues to confirm or change your prediction.
- **Visualize** the story. Form pictures in your mind to help you see the characters, actions, and settings.
- **Make inferences,** or educated guesses, about what is not stated directly.
- **Clarify,** or check that you understand, what you read. Reread any difficult parts.

Analyze Literature
What literary elements stand out? Are the characters vivid and interesting? Is there a strong central conflict? As you read, consider how these elements affect your enjoyment and understanding of the story.

Make Connections
Notice where connections can be made between the story and your life or the world outside the story. What feelings or thoughts do you have while reading the story?

AFTER READING

Find Meaning
Recall the important details of the story, such as the sequence of events and characters' names. Use this information to **interpret,** or explain, the meaning of the story.

Make Judgments
- **Analyze** the text by examining details and deciding what they contribute to the meaning.
- **Evaluate** the text by making judgments about how the author creates meaning.

Analyze Literature
Review how the use of literary elements increases your understanding of the story. For example, if the author uses dialogue, how does it help to shape the story's meaning?

Extend Understanding
Go beyond the text by exploring the story's ideas through writing or other creative projects.

Words in Use

Teaching Words
graphic organizer, 8
vivid, 8
sequence, 8
dialogue, 8

After Twenty Years

A Short Story by O. Henry

Apply the Model
BEFORE READING
DURING READING
AFTER READING

GUIDED READING

Preview the Model

At a Glance
Guided Reading: Reading Model
- Reading Level: Moderate
- Difficulty Considerations: Vocabulary and irony
- Ease Factor: Plot twist

Build Background
Literary Context O. Henry is best known for his use of the ironic, or surprise, ending. His work has been translated into many languages and has been adapted for movies and television. Since 1919 when it was first given, the O. Henry Award has been one of the most coveted prizes for short story writing.

Reader's Context Can you predict what your friends will be like twenty years from now?

Set Purpose
Skim and scan the story for unfamiliar terms. Also, pay attention to words that are defined in footnotes. Based on these words, try to predict what the story will be about.

Analyze Literature
Plot A **plot** is a series of events related to a central **conflict,** or struggle. A plot usually involves the introduction of the conflict, the events that lead to the **climax**—the point of highest tension in the story—and the **resolution,** the point at which the central conflict is resolved. As you read "After Twenty Years," identify the conflict and make predictions about how the conflict will be resolved.

Meet the Author
O. Henry (1862–1910) is the pseudonym of William Sydney Porter, an American short story writer. After working for several years as a bank teller, Porter was convicted of embezzlement. Although it was likely an accounting error, Porter served three years. In prison he began writing short stories using the pen name O. Henry. Upon his release, he moved to New York City.

Use Reading Skills
Analyze Cause and Effect A *cause* is an action or event that results in another event. An *effect* is what happens as the result of an event or action. Analyzing cause-and-effect relationships can help you understand how the events in a story are related. As you read "After Twenty Years," use a chart to keep track of causes and effects.

Cause	Effect
The weather is chilly, rainy, and windy.	The streets are nearly empty.

Preview Vocabulary
ha·bit·u·al (hʉ´ bi ch [ə] wel) *adj.,* behaving in a certain manner by habit

in·tri·cate (in´ tri kət) *adj.,* elaborate

swag·ger (swa´ gər) *n.,* walk with an insolent air; strut

staunch·est (stônch´ est) *adj.,* most loyal or committed

e·go·tism (ē´ gə' ti zəm) *n.,* large sense of self-importance; conceit

Objectives
Studying this lesson will enable students to
- use reading skills such as analyzing cause and effect
- define plot and analyze how characters deal with conflict
- describe the literary accomplishments of O. Henry
- appreciate a story that has an unexpected twist

Launch the Lesson
Tell students that in this story by O. Henry, two friends meet after twenty years. Draw a twenty-year time line on the board, with "now" at one end, and ask students what changes might occur in their lives in five, ten, fifteen, and twenty years. Model examples for students: "In five years, I will be graduating from high school." "In ten years, I will have a well-paying job." After students offer their ideas, ask whether they think their friends will still recognize them in twenty years.

Words in Use

Preview Vocabulary
habitual, 11
intricate, 11
swagger, 11
staunchest, 12
egotism, 14

Selection Words
nigh, 11
thoroughfare, 11
stalwart, 11
astir, 13
absurdity, 13

Teaching Words
ironic, 9
coveted, 9
pseudonym, 9
expository, 15

KEY TERMS
SHORT STORY, 9
SKIM, 9
SCAN, 9
PLOT, 9
CONFLICT, 9
CLIMAX, 9
RESOLUTION, 9
CAUSE AND EFFECT, 9
ESSAY, 15

Common Core State Standards
Reading Literature
RL.1, RL.3

Teach the Model

Summary

A well-dressed man waiting in a doorway tells a New York City policeman—Patrolman Wells—that he has an appointment to meet his old friend Jimmy from twenty years ago. The policeman leaves and soon a police detective approaches and arrests the waiting man, "Silky Bob," because he is wanted by the Chicago police department. A note from Patrolman Wells explains that when he arrived at the appointed time to meet his old friend, he realized that he had seen Bob's picture on a Wanted poster. Instead of confronting Bob, Patrolman Wells left and asked a detective to go back and make the arrest.

 The Mirrors & Windows questions at the end of the story focus on the theme of loyalty. Before students begin reading, ask: How long should you be loyal to a good friend?

Critical Viewing

Have students describe the feeling this painting evokes. Then have them read the first three paragraphs of the story. Ask: "How well does the painting fit the opening scene?" Urge students to explain their answers.

A Short Story by O. Henry

After Twenty Years

10

Program Resources

Planning and Assessment
Program Planning Guide, Selection Lesson Plan
E-Lesson Planner
Assessment Guide, Lesson Test
ExamView

Technology Tools
Interactive Student Text on CD
Visual Teaching Package
Audio Library
mirrorsandwindows.com

Meeting the Standards
Fiction: Unit 1, Active Reading Model, pp. 19–28

Differentiating Instruction
Advanced Students, Author/Genre Study, pp. 1–3
English Language Learners, Cause and Effect, pp. 1–9

"I'm just waiting for a friend. It's an appointment made twenty years ago."

The policeman on the beat[1] moved up the avenue impressively. The impressiveness was <u>habitual</u> and not for show, for spectators were few. The time was barely ten o'clock at night, but chilly gusts of wind with a taste of rain in them had well nigh depeopled the streets.

Trying doors as he went, twirling his club with many <u>intricate</u> and artful movements, turning now and then to cast his watchful eye down the pacific thoroughfare, the officer, with his stalwart form and slight <u>swagger</u>, made a fine picture of a guardian of the peace. The vicinity was one that kept early hours. Now and then you might see the lights of a cigar store or of an all-night lunch counter, but the majority of the doors belonged to business places that had long since been closed.

When about midway of a certain block, the policeman suddenly slowed his walk. In the doorway of a darkened hardware store a man leaned with an unlighted cigar in his mouth. As the policeman walked up to him, the man spoke up quickly.

"It's all right, officer," he said reassuringly. "I'm just waiting for a friend. It's an appointment made twenty years ago. Sounds a little funny to you, doesn't it? Well, I'll explain if you'd like to make certain it's all straight. About that long ago there used to be a restaurant where this store stands—'Big Joe' Brady's restaurant."

"Until five years ago," said the policeman. "It was torn down then."

The man in the doorway struck a match and lit his cigar. The light showed a pale, square-jawed face with keen eyes and a little white scar near his right eyebrow. His scarf pin was a large diamond, oddly set.

"Twenty years ago tonight," said the man, "I dined here at 'Big Joe' Brady's with Jimmy Wells, my best chum and the finest chap in the world. He and I were raised here in New York, just like two

ha·bit·u·al (hə´ bi ch [ə] wel) *adj.*, behaving in a certain manner by habit

in·tri·cate (in´ tri kət) *adj.*, elaborate

swag·ger (swa´ gər) *n.*, walk with an insolent air; strut

DURING READING

Analyze Literature
Plot What do the setting details suggest about possible conflicts in the story? **B**

DURING READING

Use Reading Strategies
Make Inferences What do these details suggest to you about the man in the doorway? **C**

---

1. **beat.** Area regularly patrolled by a policeman

(Opposite page) *Small Town at Night After Snowstorm*, c. 1930. Charles Ephraim Burchfield.

AFTER TWENTY YEARS **11**

Use Reading Skills

Analyze Cause and Effect Point out to students that the man is describing a cause-and-effect relationship to the policeman. The effect is that the man is standing here waiting to meet a friend. The cause is a promise made twenty years ago. **Ⓐ**

Use Reading Skills

Analyze Cause and Effect *Answer:* Twenty years ago he pledged to meet a friend here on this date and at this time. **Ⓑ**

Use Reading Skills

Analyze Cause and Effect *Answer:* The man who went West became too busy with his affairs to maintain the correspondence. **Ⓒ**

Use Reading Strategies

Make Predictions *Answer:* Students will probably think that the partner will show up but that it will somehow be disappointing. Perhaps the partner will be even more successful than the waiting man. **Ⓓ**

> **DURING READING**   **Ⓐ**
> **Use Reading Skills**
> **Analyze Cause and Effect** Why is the man waiting in the doorway? **Ⓑ**

> **DURING READING**
> **Use Reading Skills**
> **Analyze Cause and Effect** Why did the two friends lose contact? **Ⓒ**

staunch·est (stônch´ est)
adj., most loyal or committed

> **DURING READING**
> **Use Reading Strategies**
> **Make Predictions** Will the man's old partner show up? If so, will the man really think it was worth the effort? **Ⓓ**

---

brothers, together. I was eighteen and Jimmy was twenty. The next morning I was to start for the West to make my fortune. You couldn't have dragged Jimmy out of New York; he thought it was the only place on earth. Well, we agreed that night that we would meet here again exactly twenty years from that date and time, no matter what our conditions might be or from what distance we might have to come. We figured that in twenty years each of us ought to have our destiny worked out and our fortunes made, whatever they were going to be."

"It sounds pretty interesting," said the policeman. "Rather a long time between meets, though, it seems to me. Haven't you heard from your friend since you left?"

"Well, yes, for a time we corresponded,"[2] said the other. "But after a year or two we lost track of each other. You see, the West is a pretty big proposition, and I kept hustling around over it pretty lively. But I know Jimmy will meet me here if he's alive, for he always was the truest, staunchest old chap in the world. He'll never forget. I came a thousand miles to stand in this door tonight, and it's worth it if my old partner turns up."

> "A man gets in a groove in New York. It takes the West to put a razor edge on him."

The waiting man pulled out a handsome watch, the lids of it set with small diamonds.

"Three minutes to ten," he announced. "It was exactly ten o'clock when we parted here at the restaurant door."

"Did pretty well out West, didn't you?" asked the policeman.

"You bet! I hope Jimmy has done half as well. He was a kind of plodder,[3] though, good fellow as he was. I've had to compete with

---

2. **corresponded.** Communicated by letter
3. **plodder.** One who works slowly and monotonously; a drudge

---

Differentiated Instruction

English Language Learning

Students may need help with these terms in order to understand the characters' actions and motivations.

on the beat—patrolling the street

trying doors—making sure doors are locked, 11

it's all straight—I'm telling the truth, 11

my pile—my fortune, 13

gets in a groove—gets too comfortable staying in one place, 13

Reading Proficiency

As students read, have them jot down questions, using sticky notes to put the questions on related parts of the selection. Then, as a class, determine which parts of the selection generated the most questions. Reread those parts and, if possible, answer the questions.

some of the sharpest wits going to get my pile. A man gets in a groove in New York. It takes the West to put a razor edge on him." **E**

The policeman twirled his club and took a step or two.

"I'll be on my way. Hope your friend comes around all right. Going to call time on him sharp?"[4]

"I should say not!" said the other. "I'll give him half an hour at least. If Jimmy is alive on earth, he'll be here by that time. So long, officer."

"You've changed lots, Jimmy."

"Good night sir," said the policeman, passing on along his beat, trying doors as he went.

There was now a fine, cold drizzle falling, and the wind had risen from its uncertain puffs into a steady blow. The few foot passengers astir in that quarter hurried dismally and silently along with coat collars turned high and pocketed hands. And in the door of the hardware store the man who had come a thousand miles to fill an appointment, uncertain almost to absurdity, with the friend of his youth, smoked his cigar and waited. **F**

About twenty minutes he waited, and then a tall man in a long overcoat, with collar turned up to his ears, hurried across from the opposite side of the street. He went directly to the waiting man.

"Is that you, Bob?" he asked, doubtfully.

"Is that you, Jimmy Wells?" cried the man in the door.

"Bless my heart!" exclaimed the new arrival, grasping both the other's hands with his own. "It's Bob, sure as fate. I was certain I'd find you here if you were still in existence. Well, well, well!—twenty years is a long time. The old restaurant's gone, Bob; I wish it had lasted, so we could have had another dinner there. How has the West treated you, old man?"

"Bully; it has given me everything I asked it for. You've changed lots, Jimmy. I never thought you were so tall by two or three inches."

---

4. **call time on him sharp.** Leave if he doesn't arrive exactly on time

Teach the Model

> **More About the Author**
The West of the late 1800s and New York City of the early 1900s are settings that were familiar to O. Henry. In the 1880s, he went to the West, where he worked at a variety of jobs, including ranch hand, pharmacist, journalist, and bank teller. He moved to New York City in 1902. **E**

Analyze Literature
Plot and Suspense Ask students how O. Henry creates suspense for the reader. Model a response. "The man has insisted that if Jimmy is alive, he will be there. Now the lonely setting and the use of the word *absurdity* seem to be hinting that Jimmy will not show up. This increases my curiosity." **F**

Reading Skills

Draw Conclusions
Remind students that making a generalization involves making a broad statement about several things based on inferences from text clues and from personal knowledge. Point out that a generalization should include a signal word or phrase such as *most, few, generally, many, some, usually, overall, typically,* or *in general.*

Have students reread the Literary Context paragraph and Meet the Author on page 9 and encourage them to recall any other information they have learned about O. Henry. Then ask students to make a generalization about O. Henry's work. Model a possibility: "O. Henry wrote a lot about con men." Have students identify the textual information and prior knowledge on which they base their generalizations.

Use Reading Strategies
Make Predictions *Answer:* Students may predict that the man from the West will learn something surprising about his old friend. **A**

Analyze Literature
Plot O. Henry's stories are noted for their surprising plot twists. Ask students to describe the plot twist that occurs at the climax of this story. Model a possible response: "Bob was expecting to brag to his old friend about his success; instead, he has been arrested." **B**

Analyze Literature
Plot *Answer:* The dark, cold setting makes the resolution possible, by masking the identity of Jimmy Wells and, later, of the plainclothes policeman. **C**

You may want to ask students to write a journal entry or quick write, or divide students into discussion groups or lead a whole-class discussion about this question. *Answer:* Personal responses will vary. Students may say that loyalty should not be extended to those who break the law, who do not share one's values, or who threaten one's own existence or livelihood.

> **DURING READING**
> **Use Reading Strategies**
> **Make Predictions** Now that the two men have met, what do you think will happen next? **A**

e·go·tism (ē′ gə′ ti zəm)
n., large sense of self-importance; conceit

"Oh, I grew a bit after I was twenty."

"Doing well in New York, Jimmy?"

"Moderately. I have a position in one of the city departments. Come on, Bob; we'll go around to a place I know of and have a good long talk about old times."

The two men started up the street, arm in arm. The man from the West, his <u>egotism</u> enlarged by success, was beginning to outline the history of his career. The other, submerged in his overcoat, listened with interest.

At the corner stood a drugstore, brilliant with electric lights. When they came into this glare, each of them turned simultaneously[5] to gaze upon the other's face.

The man from the West stopped suddenly and released his arm.

"You're not Jimmy Wells," he snapped. "Twenty years is a long time, but not long enough to change a man's nose from a Roman to a pug."[6]

B "It sometimes changes a good man into a bad one," said the tall man. "You've been under arrest for ten minutes, 'Silky' Bob. Chicago thinks you may have dropped over our way and wires[7] us she wants to have a chat with you. Going quietly, are you? That's sensible. Now, before we go to the station, here's a note I was asked to hand to you. You may read it here at the window. It's from Patrolman Wells."

The man from the West unfolded the little piece of paper handed him. His hand was steady when he began to read, but it trembled a little by the time he had finished. The note was rather short.

Bob: I was at the appointed place on time. When you struck the match to light your cigar, I saw it was the face of the man wanted in Chicago. Somehow I couldn't do it myself, so I went around and got a plainclothes man to do the job.

Jimmy   ✥

> **DURING READING**
> **Analyze Literature**
> **Plot** In what way did the setting affect the resolution? **C**

5. **simultaneously.** At the same time
6. **Roman to a pug.** Two distinctly shaped noses
7. **wires.** Communicates by telegram

What circumstances might cause you to do what Jimmy Wells did? What are the limits of loyalty?

Differentiated Instruction

Enrichment
Encourage students to find out more about the time period in which the story is set. Pose the following questions:

- What was the economic and social situation of the West in the late 1800s? What might Silky Bob have done to make his "pile"?
- What long-distance communication systems did people use? How did the telegraph work?

- What are some interesting facts about the early history of the New York City police force?

Allow students to research topics in small groups. Then have them present brief oral reports on their findings. Suggest that they use props or visual aids to enhance their presentations. English language learners should use these visual supports to enhance and confirm their understanding of complex spoken language.

Find Meaning

1. (a) How does the narrator describe the policeman? (b) What does this description suggest about this character?

2. Why does the man in the doorway feel it is necessary to explain his presence to the policeman?

3. (a) What are the most important details of the setting? (b) Why are these details important?

Analyze Literature

Plot Did you predict the climax and the resolution of the story? Use a plot diagram to identify the exposition, climax, and resolution of "After Twenty Years."

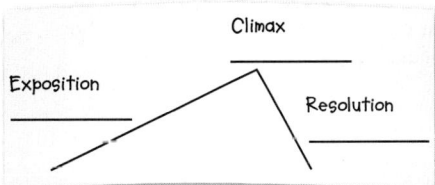

Make Judgments

4. What does the waiting man's description of Jimmy Wells as a "plodder" suggest about his attitude toward his friend?

5. Is it surprising that the waiting man traveled a thousand miles for the meeting? Explain.

6. What overall message, or theme, do you think O. Henry wanted to convey in "After Twenty Years"?

Find Meaning

1. (a) The policeman has a "swagger," is impressive, and has a "watchful eye." (b) He is tough, thorough, competent, responsible, and self-assured.

2. He probably realizes that he looks suspicious and wants to assure the policeman that he has no bad intentions.

3. (a) The dark, cold, windy night is important. (b) The characters are forced to bundle up to protect themselves from the weather. This helps mask their identities.

Make Judgments

4. He seems to feel superior and his attitude is condescending.

5. Students may say it is not, because the man wants to brag to his old partner about his success.

6. Material success, especially when gained illegally, is superficial and fleeting, and cannot buy true friendship or respect.

Analyze Literature

Plot The exposition occurs in the first four paragraphs. The climax is the arrest, and the resolution is the explanation in the note from Jimmy Wells.

Extend Understanding

Writing Options

Creative Writing Imagine that you are Jimmy Wells writing to your former friend after Bob has been sent to jail. Write a **letter** explaining how you feel about what you had to do. Offer to support Bob in turning his life around.

Expository Writing The plainclothes policeman tells Bob that twenty years is long enough to change "a good man into a bad one." Using your cause-and-effect chart, write a short **essay** in which you analyze the causes and effects that brought Bob to justice in "After Twenty Years."

Collaborative Learning

Investigate Police Work With a partner, research how detective work has evolved over the past century. Pay particular attention to how communication, scientific advances, and computers have affected the way detectives work. Prepare a chart or a poster that lists the five most important changes you find.

Critical Literacy

Conduct an Interview Work with a partner to role-play a reporter interviewing the character "Silky" Bob. Find out why he entered a life of crime. Before you begin, work together to prepare a basic time line of Bob's life. Then create a list of questions for the reporter to ask. Take turns playing the reporter's role. Afterward, compare the notes taken by each reporter.

 Go to **www.mirrorsandwindows.com** for more.

Rubrics for Writing Options

You can adapt this as a checklist for students to use as they write.

Creative Writing

☐ Does the writer adopt the persona of Jimmy Wells?

☐ Does the letter clearly describe the decision Jimmy made?

☐ Does the letter offer Jimmy's support in helping Bob turn his life around?

Expository Writing

☐ Does the essay indicate a grasp of the meaning of the plainclothes officer's observation?

☐ Does the essay accurately identify and analyze causes and effects?

☐ Does the essay offer evidence for the writer's opinion based on "After Twenty Years"?

For further instruction, refer students to the following extension activity: Collaborative Learning: Investigate Police Work, *Exceeding the Standards: Extension Activities*, pp. 1–2.

To help students explore literature on a deeper level, assign the following activity: Summarize Fiction, *Exceeding the Standards: Literature & Reading*, pp. 1–2.

Teach the Workshop

Vocabulary Practice

The following are possible answers. Student answers may vary.

1. curious, inquisitive
2. plain, ordinary
3. extraordinary, exceptional
4. selective, exacting
5. relaxed, unhurried, carefree
6. habitual: behaving in a certain manner by habit (neutral)
7. intricate: elaborate (neutral)
8. swagger: walk with an insolent air; strut (negative)
9. egotism: large sense of self-importance; conceit (negative)
10. beat: an area regularly patrolled by a policeman (neutral)

> For more information, see Vocabulary & Spelling Section 2.6, Understanding Denotation and Connotation, in the Language Arts Handbook. Refer to Section 2.7, Spelling, for additional instruction on spelling rules.

Program Resources

You will find additional lessons on Denotation and Connotation in the *Exceeding the Standards: Vocabulary & Spelling* resource.

KEY TERMS

DENOTATION, 16
CONNOTATION, 16
SYNONYM, 16
NEAR SYNONYM, 16

Common Core State Standards

Language
L.5, L.6

Denotation and Connotation

The light showed a pale, square-jawed face with keen eyes and a little white scar near his right eyebrow.

—O. HENRY, "After Twenty Years"

In the passage above, O. Henry describes a man standing in a doorway. In addition to their dictionary meanings, some of the words he uses also have emotional associations.

Every word has a **denotation,** or dictionary definition. In the passage above, *keen* denotes being "extremely sensitive in perception." *Keen* also has **connotations,** or emotional associations, suggesting sharpness and accuracy.

EXAMPLE
unhappy
blue
depressed
desolate

In this example, each word denotes sadness, but each connotes a different level of sadness. You might think of these words as **synonyms,** or words that have basically the same meaning. However, these are **near synonyms,** words that have slightly different meanings.

EXAMPLES
cheap / inexpensive
miserly / frugal
wasteful / generous

In these examples, each pair of words denotes the same meaning. However, one word has positive connotations, and the other negative connotations. *Inexpensive, frugal,* and *generous* are positive, while *cheap, miserly,* and *wasteful* are negative.

Vocabulary Practice

For each of the following words, choose a word with a more positive connotation.

1. nosy
2. bland
3. strange
4. picky
5. lazy

Identify the denotation of each of the following words from "After Twenty Years." Then note whether each word has a positive, neutral, or negative connotation.

6. habitual
7. intricate
8. swagger
9. egotism
10. beat

Spelling Practice
Words with Double Letters

Words with double letters can pose a spelling challenge because you may hear only one occurrence of the letter's sound. To prevent spelling mistakes for these words, you will need to memorize how the words look. For some words, the doubling is caused by a prefix or suffix being added, such as in the word "misspell." Try to figure out which words have doubling caused by affixes (prefixes and suffixes). This list of words from "After Twenty Years" gives examples of words with double letters.

announced	correspond	opposite
appointment	dismally	passengers
beginning	hurried	reassuringly
brilliant	impressive	success
collar	officer	suddenly

TEACHING NOTE
Extra Practice

The three words in each set below are near synonyms. Write each set, scrambled, on the board, and then have students put the words in each set in the order shown, from negative connotation, to neutral connotation, to positive connotation.

1. conspicuous, noticeable, attractive
2. stark, simple, clean
3. bewitch, attract, charm
4. hoard, collect, build up

Words in Use

Teaching Words
keen, 16
desolate, 16
miserly, 16
egotism, 16

Understanding Characters

What Are Characters?
What does this photograph tell you about its subjects? It presents each person visually, but it also suggests something about their personalities. Consider these two people's poses, their facial expressions, and how they are sitting in relation to each other. In this portrait, the photographer has created characters. Writers also create characters. A **character** is an imaginary person or animal who takes part in the action of a literary work.

Characterization and Motivation
In the passage to the right, how is the character of Lester Simmons created? **Characterization** is the act of creating or describing a character. Writers create characters using three major techniques:

- Showing what characters say, do, or think
- Showing what other characters (and the narrator) say or think about them
- Describing what physical features, dress, and personality the characters display

In real life, people do not act for no reason at all. Something—a need, a desire, a feeling, or some other force—causes them to act. Characters respond in the same way. A **motivation** is a force that moves a character to think, feel, or behave in a certain way. Motivation can be either *internal* (from within a character) or *external* (from an outside source).

Types of Characters
The main character in a literary work is called the **protagonist.** A character who struggles against the main character is called an **antagonist.** Characters can also be classified as major characters or minor characters. **Major characters** are ones who play important roles in a work. **Minor characters** are ones who play less important roles.

Another way to classify characters is by how fully they are developed by the writer. A *flat character* is one-dimensional, exhibiting only a single quality or trait. A *round character* is three-dimensional and seems to have all the complexities of an actual human being.

Finally, characters can be distinguished by whether they develop in the course of a literary work or remain the same. A *static character* does not change in the course of a work. A *dynamic character* changes as a result of the story's events.

> *Lester Simmons was a thirty-year retired Pullman car porter—had his gold watch to prove it. "Keeps perfect train time," he often bragged. "Good to the second."*
>
> —PATRICIA McKISSACK,
> "The 11:59"

Understanding Characters
Reading skills and strategies that can help students understand character include distinguishing between major and minor details and making inferences.

Use Reading Skills
Distinguish Between Major and Minor Details Tell students that every detail about a character deserves attention, but that some have more meaning in the story than others. To help students understand the difference between major and minor details, have them name qualities of a familiar, popular character such as Harry Potter. Make a two-column chart on the board, and have the class help you classify the qualities as Major or Minor. After several minutes, reach a consensus on what major qualities define the character's role in the plot, and what minor details help round out the character. Leave the list on the board.

Use Reading Strategies
Make Inferences Remind students that making inferences involves combining clues in the story with their own experiences. Tell them that they will often have to infer a character's motivations. Return to the list of qualities on the board, and ask students to discuss what some of the items suggest about the character.

KEY TERMS
CHARACTER, 17
CHARACTERIZATION, 17
MOTIVATION, 17
PROTAGONIST, 17
ANTAGONIST, 17
MAJOR CHARACTER, 17
MINOR CHARACTER, 17
FLAT CHARACTER, 17
ROUND CHARACTER, 17
STATIC CHARACTER, 17
DYNAMIC CHARACTER, 17

Common Core State Standards

Reading Literature
RL.3

GUIDED READING

The 11:59

A Short Story by Patricia McKissack

Preview the Model

At a Glance
Guided Reading: Reading Model
- Reading Level: Moderate
- Difficulty Consideration: Foreshadowing
- Ease Factors: Short sentences and paragraphs

Objectives
Studying this lesson will enable students to
- use reading skills such as note taking
- analyze character development
- explore the work of Patricia and Frederick McKissack
- synthesize content from different texts to appreciate a story about a dedicated worker

Launch the Lesson
Prior to reading "The 11:59," ask students if they have heard the phrase "self-fulfilling prophecy." Then ask for examples of times when something seemed to come true because they believed in it strongly.

Build Background
Historical Context The Pullman sleeping car was introduced in 1865 to provide train passengers with comfortable sleeping quarters for overnight trips. Pullman porters tended to the sleeping quarters, carried luggage, and assisted passengers. For nearly a century, these porters were almost exclusively African American.

Reader's Context What if you had only a few more hours to live? What would you do or think about in those last few hours?

Set Purpose
Preview the title of the story. Then read to determine what significance the title has for the story's main character.

Analyze Literature
Character Writers make careful choices about how they describe a story's **main character,** or **protagonist.** The changes that a character undergoes during a story can help to reveal the writer's message, or theme, to the reader. As you read "The 11:59," pay attention to how the writer presents the main character and think about what you learn from his behavior and feelings.

Use Reading Skills
Take Notes When you read a short story, it can be helpful to take notes. Writing down the names of the main characters and their traits, details of the story's setting and conflict, and the outcome of the events described can all help you better understand what you have read. As you read "The 11:59," take notes in a chart like the one below.

Characters	Setting	Conflict
Lester Simmons		

Preview Vocabulary
mea·ger (mē′ gər) *adj.*, lacking in quantity or quality

chide (chīd) *v.*, express mild disapproval

mes·mer·ize (mez′ mə rīz′) *v.*, fascinate, spellbind

wor·ri·some (wʉr′ ē səm) *adj.*, causing worry

spec·ter (spek′ tər) *n.*, spirit or ghost

Meet the Author
Patricia McKissack (b. 1944) is an award-winning writer of fiction and nonfiction for young readers. She grew up in Nashville, Tennessee, in the 1940s and 1950s and attended Tennessee State University. After graduation, she married a longtime friend, Fredrick McKissack; started a family; and continued her education, earning a master's degree in 1975. In the 1980s, she and her husband began to write books for children and young adults.

18 UNIT 1 FICTION

Words in Use

Preview Vocabulary
meager, 19
chide, 20
mesmerize, 20
worrisome, 21
specter, 24

Selection Words
finery, 21
fastened, 24
deafening, 25

Teaching Words
exclusively, 18
significance, 18
inevitable, 25
convey, 28
duplicate, 28

KEY TERMS

Common Core State Standards
Reading Literature
RL.1, RL.3

1341

Apply the Model

BEFORE READING

DURING READING

AFTER READING

The 11:59

A Short Story by Patricia McKissack

Ticktock, ticktock.

Lester Simmons was a thirty-year retired Pullman car porter—had his gold watch to prove it. "Keeps perfect train time," he often bragged. "Good to the second."

Daily he went down to the St. Louis Union Station and shined shoes to help supplement[1] his <u>meager</u> twenty-four-dollar-a-month Pullman retirement check. He ate his evening meal at the porter house on Compton Avenue and hung around until late at night talking union, playing bid whist,[2] and spinning yarns with those who were still "travelin' men." In this way Lester stayed in touch with the only family he'd known since 1920.

---

1. **supplement.** Add to
2. **bid whist.** Card game played with partners

> **DURING READING**
>
> **Use Reading Skills**
> **Take Notes** What trait do you notice about Lester right away? **A**

mea·ger (mē´ gər) *adj.*, lacking in quantity or quality

> **DURING READING**
>
> **Analyze Literature**
> **Character** What can you tell about Lester based on how he spends his time? **B**

19

Teach the Model

Summary

Lester Simmons, retired Pullman porter, enjoys telling the chilling tale of the porters' Death Train. According to this tale, a porter hears the whistle of the 11:59 just twenty-four hours before the Death Train arrives to take him on his last ride. When Lester hears the fateful whistle, he spends a suspenseful day trying to stay safe from accidents. But as the time nears, the specter of an old friend appears to remind him that no one can escape the 11:59. Lester chuckles with his friend, the image of the train appears, and Lester's heart gives out.

> **MIRRORS & WINDOWS**
>
> The Mirrors & Windows questions at the end of the story focus on the theme of clinging to hope. Before students begin reading, ask: What makes hope such a powerful emotion?

Use Reading Skills

Take Notes *Answer:* He values punctuality. **A**

Analyze Literature

Character *Answer:* Lester is a hard worker, reliable and self-sufficient. He spends his evenings at the porter house, which shows that he enjoys company. **B**

Program Resources

Planning and Assessment
Program Planning Guide, Selection Lesson Plan
E-Lesson Planner
Assessment Guide, Lesson Test
ExamView

Technology Tools
Interactive Student Text on CD
Visual Teaching Package
Audio Library
mirrorsandwindows.com

Meeting the Standards
Fiction: Unit 1, Guided Reading, pp. 29–35

Differentiating Instruction
Developing Readers, Make Predictions, pp. 1–3

Use Reading Strategies

Make Inferences Model for students how to use information from the story and their own knowledge to make inferences about Lester's character: "Lester has retired, but he works every day, shining shoes. This tells me that he is a hard worker who is probably proud of being self-sufficient."

Analyze Literature

Character *Answer:* Lester wants the younger porters to appreciate and respect the efforts of the porters who came before them; the dialogue suggests that Lester is warm, and values traditions and people. **A**

Analyze Literature

Character *Answer:* Daddy Joe is a flat character; he is described only in terms of a single trait—his superhuman strength. **B**

There was nothing the young porters liked more than listening to Lester tell true stories about the old days, during the founding of the Brotherhood of Sleeping Car Porters, the first black union in the United States. He knew the president, A. Philip Randolph, personally, and proudly boasted that it was Randolph who'd signed him up as a union man back in 1926. He passed his original card around for inspection. "I knew all the founding brothers. Take Brother E. J. Bradley. We hunted many a day together, not for the sport of it but for something to eat. Those were hard times, starting up the union. But we hung in there so you youngsters might have the benefits you enjoy now."

The rookie porters always liked hearing about the thirteen-year struggle between the Brotherhood and the powerful Pullman Company, and how, against all odds, the fledgling[3] union had won recognition and better working conditions.

Everybody enjoyed it too when Lester told tall tales about Daddy Joe, the porters' larger-than-life hero. "Now y'all know the first thing a good Pullman man is expected to do is make up the top and lower berths[4] for the passengers each night."

"Come on, Lester," one of his listeners <u>chided</u>. "You don't need to describe our jobs for us."

"Some of you, maybe not. But some of you, well—" he said, looking over the top of his glasses and raising an eyebrow at a few of the younger porters. "I was just setting the stage." He smiled good-naturedly and went on with his story. "They tell me Daddy Joe could walk flatfooted down the center of the coach and let down berths on both sides of the aisle."

Hearty laughter filled the room, because everyone knew that to accomplish such a feat, Daddy Joe would have to have been superhuman. But that was it: To the men who worked the sleeping cars, Daddy Joe was no less a hero than Paul Bunyan was to the lumberjacks of the Northwestern forests.

"And when the 11:59 pulled up to his door, as big and strong as Daddy Joe was..." Lester continued solemnly. "Well, in the end even he couldn't escape the 11:59." The old storyteller eyed one of the rookie porters he knew had never heard the frightening tale about the porters' Death Train. Lester took joy in <u>mesmerizing</u> his young listeners with all the details.

chide (chīd) *v.*, express mild disapproval

DURING READING

Analyze Literature
Character What does the dialogue between Lester and the younger porters suggest about Lester's character? **A**

DURING READING

Analyze Literature
Character Is Daddy Joe a flat, one-dimensional character or a round, fully developed character? **B**

mes·mer·ize (mez′ mə rīz′) *v.*, fascinate, spellbind

---

3. **fledgling.** Inexperienced
4. **berths.** Places for sleeping

Differentiated Instruction

English Language Learning
Students learning English may need help with the following words and expressions:
hung around—stayed there for a while, 19
spinning yarns—telling stories, 19
union man—member of an association of workers that promotes and protects workers' rights, 20
rookie—inexperienced, 20
berth—built-in bed or bunk, as on a train, 20
dig—slang for "understand," "approve", 25

Enrichment
Students might enjoy visually representing Pullman cars. They can depict the interior of the cars by creating models, dioramas, sketches, diagrams, drawings, or paintings. Have students showcase their work in a Pullman car display.

"Any porter who hears the whistle of the 11:59 has got exactly twenty-four hours to clear up earthly matters. He better be ready when the train comes the next night..." In his creakiest voice, Lester drove home the point. "All us porters got to board that train one day. Ain't no way to escape the final ride on the 11:59."

Silence.

"Lester," a young porter asked, "you know anybody who ever heard the whistle of the 11:59 and lived to tell—"

"Not a living soul!"

Laughter.

"Well," began one of the men, "wonder will we have to make up berths on *that* train?"

"If it's an overnight trip to heaven, you can best be believing there's bound to be a few of us making up the berths," another answered.

"Shucks," a card player stopped to put in. "They say even up in heaven *we* the ones gon' be keeping all that gold and silver polished."

"Speaking of gold and silver," Lester said, remembering. "That reminds me of how I gave Tip Sampson his nickname. Y'all know Tip?"

There were plenty of nods and smiles.

The memory made Lester chuckle. He shifted in his seat to find a more comfortable spot. Then he began. "A woman got on board the *Silver Arrow* in Chicago going to Los Angeles. She was dripping in finery—had on all kinds of gold and diamond jewelry, carried twelve bags. Sampson knocked me down getting to wait on her, figuring she was sure for a big tip. That lady was <u>worrisome</u>! Ooowee! 'Come do this. Go do that. Bring me this.'

"Ain't no way to escape the final ride on the 11:59."

---DURING READING---

Analyze Character
Character What do you think Lester's co-workers thought of him during his career?

---DURING READING---

Use Reading Skills
Context Clues What is *finery*? Use context clues in the surrounding text to determine the meaning of the word. What clues help you determine the words meaning?

wor·ri·some (wʉr´ē səm) *adj.*, causing worry

Teach the Model

Use Reading Strategies
Make Inferences Ask students what they might infer from the silence that falls after Lester's comment. Model a response. "The silence shows that the men take the tale about the 11:59 seriously. Each one is thinking about the day the Death Train will come for him." **C**

Analyze Literature
Character Ask students to consider how Lester's interactions with other characters help reveal his character. Model a possible response: "It seems that Lester and the porters enjoy teasing each other. This shows that Lester is friendly and has a sense of humor."

Use Reading Skills
Context Clues *Answer:* Students may note that the meaning of the word *finery* is given using an example clue. The woman was wearing "all kinds of gold and diamond jewelry." One might conclude that *finery* means "accessories" or "expensive materials."

Vocabulary Skills

Dialect
Explain that dialect is a version of a language spoken by people of a particular place, time, or group. Point out examples: "Keeps perfect train time," "Ain't no way to escape," "Y'all know Tip?" and "And I didn't make it no better."

Note that words at the beginning of sentences may be understood rather than stated. Suggest that reading dialect aloud can help clarify its meaning. Model this: "'Keeps perfect train time' doesn't have a subject, so I'll insert *It* at the beginning of the sentence. This makes sense, since Lester is talking about his gold watch."

Ask students to identify other examples of dialect, read them aloud, and paraphrase or restate them in standard English.

Analyze Literature

Character *Answer:* Lester's story about Tip reveals that he is a keen observer of human nature, he treasures fond memories of his friend, and he has a good sense of humor. **Ⓐ**

Use Reading Strategies

Make Predictions *Answer:* Students may say that the news of Tip, along with the fact that Lester and Willie Beavers are the only two old-timers left, foreshadows that the 11:59 will soon be making another stop, possibly for Lester. **Ⓑ**

History Connection

A. Philip Randolph Asa Philip Randolph (1889–1979) was born in Florida and moved to New York City in 1911, where he attended City College. Seeing the need for black workers to organize, he founded the Brotherhood of Sleeping Car Porters in 1925, serving as president of the union and securing a contract with the Pullman Company in 1937. Randolph worked all of his life to ban segregation; he was one of the leaders of the 1963 Civil Rights March on Washington. He served as president of the Brotherhood of Sleeping Car Porters until his retirement in 1968.

Sampson was running over himself trying to keep that lady happy. When we reached L.A., my passengers all tipped me two or three dollars, as was customary back then.

"When Sampson's Big Money lady got off, she reached into her purse and placed a dime in his outstretched hand. A *dime!* Can you imagine? Ow! You should have seen his face. And I didn't make it no better. Never did let him forget it. I teased him so—went to calling him Tip, and the nickname stuck."

Laughter.

"I haven't heard from ol' Tip in a while. Anybody know anything?"

"You haven't got word, Lester? Tip boarded the 11:59 over in Kansas City about a month ago."

"Sorry to hear that. That just leaves me and Willie Beavers, the last of the old, old-timers here in St. Louis."

Lester looked at his watch—it was a little before midnight. The talkfest had lasted later than usual. He said his good-byes and left, taking his usual route across the Eighteenth Street bridge behind the station.

In the darkness, Lester looked over the yard, picking out familiar shapes—the *Hummingbird,* the *Zephyr.* He'd worked on them both. Train travel wasn't anything like it used to be in the old days—not since people had begun to ride airplanes. "Progress," he scoffed. "Those contraptions will never take the place of a train. No sir!"

Suddenly he felt a sharp pain in his chest. At exactly the same moment he heard the mournful sound of a train whistle, which the wind seemed to carry from some faraway place. Ignoring his pain, Lester looked at the old station. He knew nothing was scheduled to come in or out till early morning. Nervously he lit a match to check the time. 11:59!

"No," he said into the darkness. "I'm not ready. I've got plenty of living yet."

Fear quickened his step. Reaching his small apartment, he hurried up the steps. His heart pounded in his ear, and his left arm tingled. He had an idea, and there wasn't a moment to waste. But his own words haunted him. *Ain't no way to escape the final ride on the 11:59.*

"But I'm gon' try!" Lester spent the rest of the night plotting his escape from fate.

"I won't eat or drink anything all day," he talked himself through his plan. "That way I can't choke, die of food poisoning, or cause a cooking fire."

DURING READING

Analyze Literature
Character What character traits does Lester reveal about himself in telling how he gave Tip his nickname? Explain. **Ⓐ**

DURING READING

Use Reading Strategies
Make Predictions What might this reference to Tip foreshadow? **Ⓑ**

Differentiated Instruction

Kinesthetic Learning

Students can retell Lester's story about Tip. Have them reread the passage several times, committing the events to memory. When they are ready, have them retell the story in their own words, adding their own embellishments. Encourage students to use gestures, movement, and facial expression for emphasis.

Visual Learning

Have students draw a portrait of Lester. It should include details—such as the gold watch—that represent his personality, values, and character. Some students might prefer to make a collage of images related to Lester's life.

Lester shut off the space heater to avoid an explosion, nailed shut all doors and windows to keep out intruders, and unplugged every electrical appliance. Good weather was predicted, but just in case a freak storm came and blew out a window, shooting deadly glass shards in his direction, he moved a straight-backed chair into a far corner, making sure nothing was overhead to fall on him.

"I'll survive," he said, smiling at the prospect of beating Death. "Won't that be a wonderful story to tell at the porter house?" He rubbed his left arm. It felt numb again.

Lester sat silently in his chair all day, too afraid to move. At noon someone knocked on his door. He couldn't answer it. Footsteps... another knock. He didn't answer.

A parade of minutes passed by, equally measured, one behind the other, ticking...ticking...away...The dull pain in his chest returned. He nervously checked his watch every few minutes.

Ticktock, ticktock.

Time had always been on his side. Now it was his enemy. Where had the years gone? Lester reviewed the thirty years he'd spent riding the rails. How different would his life have been if he'd married Louise Henderson and had a gallon of children? What if he'd taken that job at the mill down in Opelika? What if he'd followed his brother to Philly? How different?

Ticktock, ticktock.

So much living had passed so quickly. Lester decided if he had to do it all over again, he'd stand by his choices. His had been a good life. No regrets. No major changes for him.

Ticktock, ticktock.

The times he'd had—both good and bad—what memories. His first and only love had been traveling, and she was a jealous companion. Wonder whatever happened to that girl up in Minneapolis? Thinking about her made him smile. Then he laughed. That *girl* must be close to seventy years old by now.

Ticktock, ticktock.

Daylight was fading quickly. Lester drifted off to sleep, then woke from a nightmare in which, like Jonah, he'd been swallowed by an enormous beast.[5] Even awake he could still hear its heart beating...*ticktock, ticktock*...But then he realized he was hearing his own heartbeat.

Lester couldn't see his watch, but he guessed no more than half an hour had passed. Sleep had overtaken him with such little

---

5. Jonah...beast. Refers to the biblical story of Jonah and the whale

---

DURING READING

Use Reading Skills
Take Notes What is this story's conflict? What do you think the outcome will be? **C**

DURING READING

Analyze Literature
Character What is Lester's motivation for refusing to answer the door? **D**

E

DURING READING

Make Connections
How does Lester's judgment about his life affect your feelings about what is happening to him? **F**

G

Teach the Model

Use Reading Skills
Take Notes *Answer:* The conflict is between Lester and Death. The evidence is that no one escapes the 11:59, so it is unlikely that Lester will prevail. **C**

Analyze Literature
Character *Answer:* Lester is determined to do everything he can to stay alive, so he is trying to maintain tight control over everything around him. Opening the door would introduce an unknown, possibly uncontrollable, factor into the situation. **D**

Analyze Literature
Suspense Ask students how the author builds suspense in this passage. Model a response: "Lester keeps trying to reassure himself that he'll survive, but he nervously checks his watch, and is afraid to answer the door. His arm goes numb, and the *ticktock* sound adds to the tension." **E**

Make Connections
Answer: Students may say this makes it easier for them to accept his impending death. It is comforting to know that he has no regrets about the choices he has made. **F**

Literary Connection
Jonah In the Bible, Jonah tries to escape an assignment from God. Lester is trying to evade Death. **G**

Grammar Skills

Capitalization

Remind students that a proper noun names a specific person, place, or thing and a proper adjective is either formed from a proper noun or a proper noun used as an adjective. Have small groups list proper nouns and proper adjectives from the story. Then ask the groups to sort the names into categories such as "Names of People," "Names of Places," and "Names of Organizations."

Based on their categorized lists, have the groups formulate capitalization rules. Model an example: "The following kinds of proper nouns/adjectives should be capitalized: names of places, names of people . . ." Have groups share their results.

Use Reading Strategies

Make Predictions Invite students to review the predictions they made about whether Lester's plan will work. Model how to weigh new evidence and adjust predictions: "In spite of all of Lester's precautions, he has been having chest pain and numbness in his arm. I'm going to change my prediction. I think that Lester will board the 11:59 tonight."

> ### ▶ More by This Author
>
> Students who like "The 11:59" might enjoy other stories by Patricia McKissack from *The Dark Thirty: Southern Tales of the Supernatural.*

TEACHING NOTE

Self-Generated Questioning

Divide the class into small groups. Have the members of each group brainstorm and jot down questions they would like to ask Lester. Model a possible question: "Why did you retire?" Instruct each group to pass its questions to another group. Then each group should use what they know about Lester to answer the questions it receives. Have groups share some of their questions and answers with the rest of the class.

"I'm too smart for that, Death..."

spec•ter (spek´ tər) *n.,* spirit or ghost

resistance. Would Death, that shapeless shadow, slip in that easily? Where was he lurking? *Yea, though I walk through the valley of the shadow of death, I will fear no evil...*The Twenty-third Psalm was the only prayer Lester knew, and he repeated it over and over, hoping it would comfort him.

Lester rubbed his tingling arm. He could hear the blood rushing past his ear and up the side of his head. He longed to know what time it was, but that meant he had to light a match—too risky. What if there was a gas leak? The match would set off an explosion. "I'm too smart for that, Death," he said.

Ticktock, ticktock.

It was late. He could feel it. Stiffness seized his legs and made them tremble. How much longer? he wondered. Was he close to winning?

Then in the fearful silence he heard a train whistle. His ears strained to identify the sound, making sure it *was* a whistle. No mistake. It came again, the same as the night before. Lester answered it with a groan.

Ticktock, ticktock.

He could hear Time ticking away in his head. Gas leak or not, he had to see his watch. Striking a match, Lester quickly checked the time. 11:57.

Although there was no gas explosion, a tiny explosion erupted in his heart.

Ticktock, ticktock.

Just a little more time. The whistle sounded again. Closer than before. Lester struggled to move, but he felt fastened to the chair. Now he could hear the engine puffing, pulling a heavy load. It was hard for him to breathe, too, and the pain in his chest weighed heavier and heavier.

Ticktock, ticktock.

Time had run out! Lester's mind reached for an explanation that made sense. But reason failed when a glowing phantom dressed in the porters' blue uniform stepped out of the grayness of Lester's confusion.

"It's *your* time, good brother." The <u>specter</u> spoke in a thousand familiar voices.

Freed of any restraint now, Lester stood, bathed in a peaceful calm that had its own glow. "Is that you, Tip?" he asked, squinting to focus on his old friend standing in the strange light.

24 UNIT 1 FICTION

Vocabulary Skills

Context Clues

Write this sentence on the board: "You can often figure out the meaning of a word by looking for clues in the context, or the surrounding words and sentences." Point out that in this sentence, the comma and the word *or* signals that *context* is "the surrounding words and sentences." Tell students that to find context clues they can look for commas, dashes, and such signal words or phrases as *such as, that is, or,* and *in other words.*

Have students identify the context clues for the underlined words in this sentence:

Sam knew he would still be hungry after he ate his <u>meager</u> breakfast.

"It's me, ol' partner. Come to remind you that none of us can escape the last ride on the 11:59."

"I know. I know," Lester said, chuckling. "But man, I had to try."

Tip smiled. "I can dig it. So did I."

"That'll just leave Willie, won't it?"

"Not for long."

"I'm ready."

Lester saw the great beam of the single headlight and heard the deafening whistle blast one last time before the engine tore through the front of the apartment, shattering glass and splintering wood, collapsing everything in its path, including Lester's heart.

When Lester didn't show up at the shoeshine stand two days running, friends went over to his place and found him on the floor. His eyes were fixed on something quite amazing—his gold watch, stopped at exactly 11:59. ❖

DURING READING

Analyze Literature
Character Based on what you know about Lester, is his acceptance of his fate surprising? Explain. **A**

Lester tells Tip he "had to try" to fight off Death. Have you ever clung to something you knew you would lose? How can clinging to hope help us come to terms with the inevitable?

Find Meaning

1. (a) How does Lester spend his evenings after he retires from his job as a Pullman porter? (b) Why does he spend his evenings in this way?

2. (a) What physical symptoms does Lester feel during his last day alive? (b) What do you think is happening to Lester?

3. (a) What time is on Lester's watch when his friends find him two days later? (b) Why does his watch read that time?

Make Judgments

4. (a) What does the reader learn about the lives of porters and their relationships with one another from this story? (b) What things did the porters share that reinforced their bonds with one another?

5. (a) How does Lester's mood change when he first hears the 11:59? (b) What does this mood change tell you about Lester's personality?

6. (a) How does Lester feel when he sees who the porter on the 11:59 is? (b) What does the manner in which they talk tell you about Lester's mood or attitude?

Analyze Literature

Character *Answer:* It is not surprising, because talking to his old friend Tip helps him realize that although he will leave some relationships behind, other relationships will continue. **A**

 Answer: Responses will vary. Clinging to hope may give a person strength and determination.

Find Meaning

1. (a) He spends his evenings with the porters, playing cards and telling stories. (b) He enjoys their company.

2. (a) He feels a sharp pain in his chest, numbness and tingling in his left arm, and stiffness in his legs. Later, he feels an "explosion" in his heart, has trouble breathing, and feels as if there is a great weight on his chest. (b) He is having a heart attack.

3. (a) The watch says 11:59. (b) That is when Lester died.

Make Judgments

4. (a) The story gives a good general picture of the lives of the porters. (b) They share stories.

5. (a) Lester goes from feeling jovial to feeling terrified, then determined to fight for his life. (b) Lester enjoys life and doesn't want to leave his friends; he is determined and resourceful.

6. (a) He feels calmer. (b) Lester now accepts what is happening.

Speaking & Listening Skills

Evaluate and Interpret Literary Texts

Have students analyze what makes Lester a good storyteller. Suggest that pairs concentrate on Lester's character and work together to make a list of the storytelling techniques he uses. Then have students practice telling Lester's story. Students who complete the Creative Writing activity on page 28 may choose, instead, to present their dialogues about how Lester outsmarts Death.

Encourage students to use the storytelling techniques from the lists they have made to add drama and suspense to their tale. Suggest that they tell the story to the class.

In "The 11:59," Patricia McKissack tells a fictional story about a Pullman porter, weaving in details about the porters' struggle to build a union. The following excerpt is from *A Long Hard Journey: The Story of the Pullman Porter*, by **Patricia** and **Fredrick McKissack.** Their book focuses on the Pullman porters' fight to build a union. The McKissacks have written many histories, biographies, and fictional works about African Americans.

from A Long Hard Journey: The Story of the Pullman Porter

An Essay by Patricia and Fredrick McKissack

Railroading has an unusual number of "firsts," making it difficult to target a single invention, event, or date as the *beginning* of American railroads. The earliest mention of an American-built, steam-propelled carriage was in 1804, developed by a Philadelphian, Oliver Evans. The Mohawk & Hudson Line boasted that in 1826, theirs was the first chartered American railroad. However, in 1825 Colonel John Stevens's steam-powered, rack-rail engine with wooden cogged wheels was the first machine to carry passengers on wooden cogged tracks in the United States. John B. Javis's first use of the steam locomotive in the Western Hemisphere made passenger travel faster and more comfortable and opened the way for the Baltimore & Ohio, the first American chartered passenger line.

As eastern railroads expanded westward toward the Mississippi River, the demand for better overnight accommodations increased. On September 1, 1859, a new chapter in railroad history began when George Mortimer Pullman's first sleeping car made its debut[1] run between Bloomington, Illinois, and Chicago.

The original Pullman car was described as a "primitive thing," but shortly after the Civil War, George Pullman developed a sleeping car that was unrivaled in design and service. Giving each traveler pampered treatment—making him feel special—was the Pullman hallmark. But George Pullman didn't give the personalized service for which his name became synonymous. Thousands of porters helped make the legendary Pullman service a reality.

Beginning in 1867, Pullman staffed his earliest cars with the former genteel servants of the Plantation South. His decisions to hire ex-slaves set a business precedent and for nearly a century *all* Pullman porters were black. These emancipated[2] slaves repaid Pullman with loyalty and dedicated service. Grateful for the opportunity to stand proudly beside other working people, the early porters worked willingly and joyfully, graciously receiving passengers, carrying their

1. **debut.** First
2. **emancipated.** Freed

luggage, making up the berths, serving beverages and food, keeping the guests happy—and all with a smile. These men did their jobs so well they became known as the "Ambassadors of Hospitality."

Seventy years later, the gratitude had worn thin. The new generation of free-born, more informed porters was not satisfied with the Pullman Company's long hours, low wages, and unfair company policies. Their smiles changed to pleas in the beginning, then shouts of protest. Unable to get the powerful Pullman Company to negotiate in good faith, the porters united under the leadership of A. Philip Randolph, and in 1925, against all odds, they formed the first black-controlled union: the Brotherhood of Sleeping Car Porters.

The Brotherhood was the largest representative of black workers in America. It was also the first union admitted to the American Federation of Labor (AFL)[3] as a full member, and the first black union to negotiate a contract with a major corporation.

The porters' struggle for recognition and fair treatment is a classic David-and-Goliath story. A handful of black workers squared off against one of American history's corporate mega-giants and won. ✤

3. **American Federation of Labor (AFL).** Federation of labor unions founded in 1886

TEXT ⟷ TEXT CONNECTION	Both Patricia McKissack's story and the excerpt from Patricia and Fredrick McKissack's book give information about the Pullman porters. Compare and contrast the kinds of information each selection presents. What do the details about Lester's life and death reveal about the Pullman porters? Summarize the texts in ways that maintain meaning and logical order. **A**

Review the Model

Analyze Literature

Character The author describes Lester as a hard worker who is proud of his contributions to his profession. He enjoys the company of his fellow porters and is respected and well liked. By the end of the story, the reader likes and respects Lester and understands why, although he loved his life, he willingly boards the 11:59.

Analyze Literature

Character Writers use a variety of techniques to create characters to whom readers can relate and who can convey lessons about life. Use a chart to analyze how the author creates the character of Lester in "The 11:59." Then analyze, in one or two sentences, how the reader is made to feel about Lester at the end of the story.

Lester's Character	
Habits/Behaviors	Relationships with Others
hard worker	friendly

Extend Understanding

Writing Options

Creative Writing Imagine that Lester beat the 11:59. Write a brief **dialogue** in which Lester tells the other porters about how he outsmarted Death. Review Lester's story about Tip and the wealthy lady and try to duplicate Lester's storytelling style. With a partner, read aloud your dialogue for the class.

Narrative Writing When friends gather at a funeral, they often take turns telling stories and sharing memories of the departed. Write a **paragraph** about Lester's life and personality that you might share at Lester's funeral with his friends from the porter house. Include an example or an anecdote to illustrate a memorable character trait. Share your work with the class.

Collaborative Learning

Create a Chart With a partner, skim and scan "The 11:59" to find as many examples of foreshadowing as you can. List each example in the left column of a two-column chart. In the right column, explain what the example foreshadows. When you finish, compare your chart with your classmates' charts and identify similarities and differences.

Lifelong Learning

Create a Time Line Imagine that you have been asked to direct a video documentary. Use the library or the Internet to research the history of the Pullman porters. Take careful notes and be sure to write down dates of events. Then use your notes to create an illustrated time line of the most important events in the history of the Pullman porters. Present your time line to the class and explain how your video will treat each event.

Go to **www.mirrorsandwindows.com** for more.

Rubrics for Writing Options

You can adapt this as a checklist for students to use as they write.

Creative Writing
- ☐ Does the dialogue adopt Lester's storytelling style?
- ☐ Does Lester clearly describe outsmarting Death?
- ☐ Are the porters' responses to Lester's story believable?

Narrative Writing
- ☐ Does the paragraph contain an example or anecdote?
- ☐ Does the paragraph clearly describe Lester's life and personality?
- ☐ Is the paragraph tailored to appeal to the audience of porters?

Literary Element

Understanding Setting

What Is Setting?

Where was this photograph taken? What details in the photograph help you answer this question? These details relate to the setting of the picture. In the same way, writers use the details of setting to tell a reader when and where the events of a story are taking place. The **setting** of a literary work is the time and place in which it happens.

Setting in Fiction

Writers create setting in many different ways. Setting can be revealed through imagery in descriptive passages, but it can also be developed through action and dialogue. In fiction, setting is often revealed by descriptions of the following:

- seasons and weather
- landscapes, cities, and towns
- buildings and vehicles
- furniture and clothing

Setting and Community

Setting can also be revealed by how characters talk and behave. For example, in the following passage from "Uncle Tony's Goat" (page 105), how does the author use details of setting to tell the reader about the community that inhabits that setting?

My sister helped out around the house mostly, and I was supposed to carry water from the hydrant and bring in kindling. I helped my father look after the horses and pigs, and Uncle Tony milked the goats and fed them.

Setting and Mood

Setting is an important element in the creation of **mood,** the feeling or emotion created by a literary work. How would you describe the mood generated by the details of setting in the passage from "The Inn of Lost Time"?

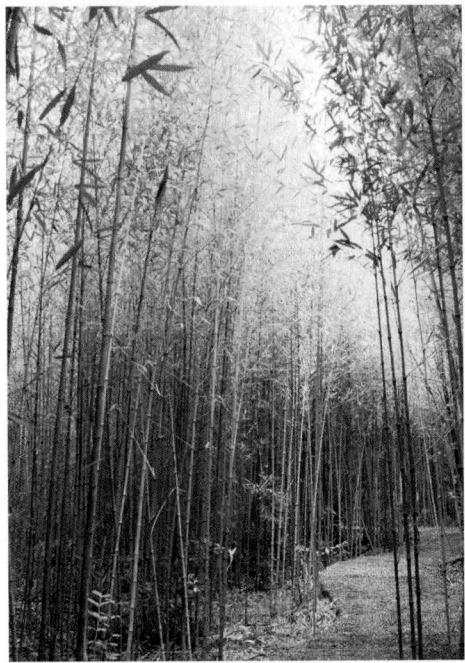

The sun was just beginning to set. We passed a bamboo grove, and in the low evening light the thin leaves turned into little golden knives. I saw a gilded clump of bamboo shoots. The sight made me think of the delicious dish they would make when boiled in soy sauce.

We hurried forward. To our delight we soon came to a clearing with a thatched house standing in the middle. The fragrant smell of rice was now so strong that we were certain a meal was being prepared inside.

—LENSEY NAMIOKA, "The Inn of Lost Time"

LITERARY ELEMENT **29**

Teach the Element

Understanding Setting

Reading strategies and skills that can help students understand setting include visualizing and activating prior knowledge.

Use Reading Strategies

Visualize Remind students that the physical appearance of a place is just one part of a setting. Then encourage them to review what they know about the setting of a story they have already read (such as "After Twenty Years" or "The 11:59"). Have them briefly work in small groups to sketch the setting, using their visualizing skills. Encourage them to try to convey a mood with each sketch.

Use Reading Skills

Activate Prior Knowledge Mention a story you have already read as a class. Ask students what they knew about the story's time or place *before* they read it. Write their remarks on the board. Then, ask how much their prior knowledge influenced their assumptions about the setting of that story. Elicit the observation that readers regularly use their prior knowledge to develop a sense of the setting—place, time, and even mood—of a work of fiction.

Words in Use

Teaching Words
- descriptive, 29
- inhabits, 29
- kindling, 29
- bamboo, 29
- gilded, 29
- thatched, 29

KEY TERMS

SETTING, 29
IMAGERY, 29
DIALOGUE, 29
MOOD, 29

Common Core State Standards

Reading Literature
RL.3

LITERARY ELEMENT **29**

Preview the Model

At a Glance
Guided Reading: Reading Model
- Reading Level: Challenging
- Difficulty Considerations: Length, frame story, and vocabulary
- Ease Factor: Interesting plot

The Inn of Lost Time

A Short Story by Lensey Namioka

Objectives
Studying this lesson will enable students to
- use reading skills such as analyzing sequence of events
- explain how setting affects plot
- sample the historical fiction of Lensey Namioka
- appreciate a story with an interplay of mystery, confusion, and truth

Launch the Lesson
Tell students that "The Inn of Lost Time" is a mysterious story with a surprise ending. Ask them to recall ghost stories or strange, scary stories that they have learned at sleepovers, on camping trips, or at other gatherings. Encourage students to sit in a circle and share some of the mysterious stories that are part of their own oral tradition.

GUIDED READING

Build Background
Historical Context In feudal Japan (1100s to 1800s), the country was broken up into many domains, each held by a lord, or land baron. The feudal lord's land was protected by samurai, members of the warrior class, who were the only people allowed to carry weapons. This story takes place during the 1700s, a period of famine and civil wars. Many landowners could no longer afford to keep their samurai, and these master-less samurai, or ronin, wandered the countryside looking for work.

Reader's Context Do you ever say things like "I can't wait until I'm older"? What if you could skip years of your life?

Set Purpose
Skim the text and predict what effect the setting of the story will have on the plot. Read to find out if your prediction is accurate.

Analyze Literature
Setting In addition to physical descriptions of time and place, **setting** also includes the broader cultural, social, and historical background in which a story's characters live and interact. As you read "The Inn of Lost Time," record the setting details that the writer presents and consider the effect that the setting has on the characters and the plot.

Use Reading Skills
Sequence of Events As you read "The Inn of Lost Time," use a time line to track the sequence of events. Begin by recording the first events mentioned in the story. Complete the time line by adding the events that occur before and after these events. Look for signal words such as *before*, *after*, *then*, *while*, and *later*.

Before ————————— After

farmer tells story to children

Preview Vocabulary
rapt (rapt) *adj.*, mentally engrossed or absorbed

des•o•late (deˊ sə lət) *adj.*, lonely, sad

poi•gnant (poiˊ nyənt) *adj.*, deeply affecting or touching; somber

rav•en•ous (raˊ və nəs) *adj.*, very eager for food

com•pen•sate (kämˊ pən sāt') *v.*, balance, offset, repay

Meet the Author
Lensey Namioka was born in 1929 in Beijing, China. Her family moved to the United States when she was nine. Namioka taught mathematics before her interest in the history of her husband's family led her to write about feudal Japan. Zenta and Matsuzo, the ronin in "The Inn of Lost Time," appear in several of her historical mystery novels.

Words in Use

Preview Vocabulary	Selection Words	Teaching Words
rapt, 32	**statuettes,** 32	**feudal,** 30
desolate, 33	**lacquered,** 37	**domains,** 30
poignant, 33	**accursed,** 41	**interact,** 30
ravenous, 35	**rueful,** 44	**infer,** 33
compensate, 36	**qualm,** 46	**inconsistency,** 44

KEY TERMS
SKIM, 30
SETTING, 30
SEQUENCE, 30
IMAGERY, 35
VENN DIAGRAM, 47
CHARACTER TRAIT, 47
FRAME STORY, 47
FLASHBACK, 47
SUSPENSE, 47
THESIS, 47

Common Core State Standards
Reading Literature
RL.1, RL.3

Speaking and Listening
SL.1

The INN of Lost Time

A Short Story by Lensey Namioka

"He had lost the most precious thing of all: time."

31

Summary

This is a story within a story. In the frame of the story, two samurai visit an inn owned by a farmer and his wife. One of the samurai, Zenta, tells a story about something that happened to him in the past, when he stayed at an inn where time was lost. The action then shifts back to the present—the frame—and Zenta reveals something surprising about the inn in which they are staying.

 MIRRORS & WINDOWS The Mirrors & Windows questions at the end of the story focus on the theme of the monetary value of time. Before students begin reading, ask: How much would you pay for the chance to relive an event that you missed?

Program Resources

Planning and Assessment
Program Planning Guide, Selection Lesson Plan
E-Lesson Planner
Assessment Guide, Lesson Test
ExamView

Technology Tools
Interactive Student Text on CD
Visual Teaching Package
Audio Library
mirrorsandwindows.com

Meeting the Standards
Fiction: Unit 1, Guided Reading, pp. 36–44

Literary Connection
Urashima Taro The tale of Urashima Taro is a well-known Japanese fairy tale that has inspired several Japanese movies, a short story by Ursula K. Le Guin ("Another Story" in *A Fisherman of the Inland Sea*), the video games *Okami* and *Onimusha*, and a ballet by choreographer Erika Akoh. Playwright Coleman A. Jennings has adapted the story as *The Honorable Urashima Taro*, a play widely performed in colleges and schools. **A**

Analyze Literature
Setting *Answer:* The ronin are in the home of a farmer and wife, in the main room. The room is lit only by the charcoal fire. The references to troubled times, civil wars, and samurai indicate that the scene takes place in Japan, several centuries ago. **B**

Make Connections
Invite students to think of stories they asked to hear over and over again when they were young. Have students compile a short list of favorite stories and allow them to share and compare the stories. **C**

"Will you promise to sleep if I tell you a story?" said the father. He pretended to put on a stern expression.

"Yes! Yes!" the three little boys chanted in unison. It sounded like a nightly routine.

The two guests smiled as they listened to the exchange. They were wandering ronin, or unemployed samurai, and they enjoyed watching this cozy family scene.

The father gave the guests a helpless look. "What can I do? I have to tell them a story, or these little rascals will give us no peace." **A** Clearing his throat, he turned to the boys. "All right. The story tonight is about Urashima Taro."

Instantly the three boys became still. Sitting with their legs tucked under them, the three little boys, aged five, four, and three, looked like a descending row of stone statuettes. Matsuzo, the younger of the two ronin, was reminded of the wayside half-body statues of Jizo, the God of Travelers and Protector of Children.

Behind the boys the farmer's wife took up a pair of iron chopsticks and stirred the ashes of the fire in the charcoal brazier.[1] A momentary glow brightened the room. The lean faces of the two ronin, lit by the fire, suddenly looked fierce and hungry.

The farmer knew that the two ronin were supposed to use their arms in defense of the weak. But in these troubled times, with the country torn apart by civil wars, the samurai didn't always live up to their honorable code.

Then the fire died down again and the subdued red light softened the features of the two ronin. The farmer relaxed and began his story.

The tale of Urashima Taro is familiar to every Japanese. No doubt **C** the three little boys had heard their father tell it before—and more than once. But they listened with <u>rapt</u> attention.

Urashima Taro, a fisherman, rescued a turtle from some boys who were battering it with stones. The grateful turtle rewarded Taro by carrying him on his back to the bottom of the sea, where he lived happily with the Princess of the Underseas. But Taro soon became homesick for his native village and asked to go back on land. The princess gave him a box to take with him but warned him not to peek inside.

When Taro went back to his village, he found the place quite changed. In his home he found his parents gone and living there was

DURING READING

Analyze Literature
Setting What do the details tell you about where the ronin are and when this scene takes place? **B**

rapt (rapt) *adj.*, mentally engrossed or absorbed

---

1. **brazier.** Pan for holding burning coals

Differentiated Instruction

Reading Proficiency
Because sharing stories through the oral tradition is a theme in this story, you might ask a storyteller, or perhaps an older student with an interest in acting, to read the Urashima Taro story aloud as expressively as possible. Students can then read "The Inn of Lost Time" on their own, paying close attention to the During Reading questions and writing out their answers.

English Language Learning
Help students define the following words and expressions:

statuettes—small statues, 32
bizarre—strange or unusual, 34
basin—bowl, 36
vandalize—damage intentionally, 40
depressions—hollows or holes, 44

another old couple. He was stunned to learn that the aged husband was his own son whom he had last seen as a baby. Taro thought he had spent only a pleasant week or two undersea with the princess. On land, seventy-two years had passed! His parents and most of his old friends had long since died.

Underline: Desolate, Taro decided to open the box given him by the princess. As soon as he looked inside he changed in an instant from a young man to a decrepit[2] old man of more than ninety.

des·o·late (dĕ´ sə lət)
adj., lonely, sad

At the end of the story the boys were close to tears. Even Matsuzo found himself deeply touched. He wondered why the farmer had told his sons such a poignant bedtime story. Wouldn't they worry all evening instead of going to sleep?

But the boys recovered quickly. They were soon laughing and jostling each other, and they made no objections when their mother shooed them toward bed. Standing in order of age, they bowed politely to the guests, and then lay down on the mattresses spread out for them on the floor. Within minutes the sound of their regular breathing told the guests that they were asleep.

poi·gnant (poi´ nyənt)
adj., deeply affecting or touching; somber

> **DURING READING**
> **Analyze Literature** **D**
> **Setting** Based on the details in this passage, what can you infer about the farmer's house?

Zenta, the older of the two ronin, sighed as he glanced at the peaceful young faces. "I wish I could fall asleep so quickly. The story of Urashima Taro is one of the saddest that I know among our folk tales."

The farmer looked proudly at his sleeping sons. "They're stout lads. Nothing bothers them much."

The farmer's wife poured tea for the guests and apologized. "I'm sorry this is only poor tea made from coarse leaves."

Zenta hastened to reassure her. "It's warm and heartening on a chilly autumn evening."

"You know what I think is the saddest part of the Urashima Taro story?" said Matsuzo, picking up his cup and sipping the tea. "It's that Taro lost not only his family

Urashima Taro (manuscript illustration), 1688–1704. Unknown artist.

---

2. decrepit. Broken down; weak

Analyze Literature
Setting *Answer:* The boys' mattresses are spread on the floor of the same room in which the adults are gathered. This may be the only room in the house, indicating that the family is poor. **D**

Reading Skills

Monitor Comprehension
Explain that the setting of this story is key to unraveling its mystery. Students can use a chart to record information as they read. Recording and comparing the setting details from each part of the story will help them understand the plot twist at the end.

Remind students to distinguish between the frame story and the inner story. They could have a chart with two main columns: Frame Story and Inner Story. Under Frame Story, they can list details of the present-day farmer's cottage. Under Inner Story, they can list two sets of details, one set about the Inn seven years ago, and the other about the Inn after time is lost.

Analyze Literature

Characterization Ask students to describe Zenta's and Matsuzo's character traits. How does the author convey these character traits to the reader? Model a possible response: "They both behave politely to the farmer and his family. Zenta's reassurance of the farmer's wife shows that he is kind, and Matsuzo is touched by the bedtime story, which shows that he is thoughtful."

Analyze Literature

Suspense Ask students how Zenta makes Matsuzo eager to hear his story. Model a possible response: "Zenta's cryptic remark about the 'strange affair' he isn't proud of makes Matsuzo curious, particularly since Zenta has never before spoken of this experience." **A**

Use Reading Skills

Sequence of Events *Answer:* The story recounts events that took place seven years ago, when Zenta was nearly eighteen years old. **B**

Analyze Literature

Setting *Answer:* The new wealth of the merchant class is creating some upheaval in Japanese society. As power shifts from one class to another, some groups, such as landowners and samurai, must find new ways of supporting themselves. **C**

and friends, but a big piece of his life as well. He had lost the most precious thing of all: time."

The farmer nodded agreement. "I wouldn't sell even one year of my life for money. As for losing seventy-two years, no amount of gold will make up for that!"

Zenta put his cup down on the floor and looked curiously at the farmer. "It's interesting that you should say that. I had an opportunity once to observe exactly how much gold a person was willing to pay for some lost years of his life." He smiled grimly. "In this case the man went as far as one gold piece for each year he lost."

"That's bizarre!" said Matsuzo. "You never told me about it."

A "It happened long before I met you," said Zenta. He drank some tea and smiled ruefully.[3] "Besides, I'm not particularly proud of the part I played in that strange affair."

"Let's hear the story!" urged Matsuzo. "You've made us all curious."

The farmer waited expectantly. His wife sat down quietly behind her husband and folded her hands. Her eyes looked intently at Zenta.

"Very well, then," said Zenta. "Actually, my story bears some resemblance to that of Urashima Taro..."

> **DURING READING**
>
> **Use Reading Skills**
> **Sequence of Events** When did the events of Zenta's story take place? **B**

It happened about seven years ago, when I was a green, inexperienced youngster not quite eighteen years old. But I had had a good training in arms, and I was able to get a job as a bodyguard for a wealthy merchant from Sakai.

As you know, wealthy merchants are relatively new in our country. Traditionally the rich have been noblemen, landowners, and warlords with thousands of followers. Merchants, considered as parasites[4] in our society, are a despised class. But our civil wars have made people unusually mobile and stimulated trade between various parts of the country. The merchants have taken advantage of this to conduct businesses on a scale our fathers could not imagine. Some of them have become more wealthy than a warlord with thousands of samurai under his command.

> **DURING READING**
>
> **Analyze Literature**
> **Setting** What do these details reveal about the Japanese society that serves as a background for the story? **C**

The man I was escorting,[5] Tokubei, was one of this new breed of wealthy merchants. He was trading not only with outlying provinces

---

3. **ruefully.** In a regretful way
4. **parasites.** People who make a habit of taking advantage of others
5. **escorting.** Accompanying; guiding

Differentiated Instruction

Enrichment

Tell students that the tale of Urashima Taro has been performed in Japanese theater. Have small groups research a traditional form of Japanese theater, such as Noh, Kabuki, or puppet theater. Each student should be responsible for researching a specific aspect of the theater, such as the design of the stage or of the theater, the costumes or masks actors wear, types of puppets used, music,

the types of plays performed, when the type of theater was popular, and so on.

Each group should then present its findings to the class. Ask students which form of theater they think would be best for performing Urashimo Taro's story.

but even with the Portuguese from across the sea. On this particular] **D**
journey he was not carrying much gold with him. If he had, I'm sure
he would have hired an older and more experienced bodyguard. But
if the need should arise, he could always write a message to his
clerks at home and have money forwarded to him. It's important to] **E**
remember this.

The second day of our journey was a particularly grueling one,
with several steep hills to climb. As the day was drawing to its close,
we began to consider where we should spend the night. I knew that
within an hour's walking was a hot-spring resort known to have
several attractive inns.

But Tokubei, my employer, said he was already very tired and
wanted to stop. He had heard of the resort, and knew the inns there
were expensive. Wealthy as he was, he did not want to spend more
money than he had to.

While we stood talking, a smell reached our noses, a wonderful
smell of freshly cooked rice. Suddenly I felt <u>ravenous</u>. From the way
Tokubei swallowed, I knew he was feeling just as hungry.

We looked around eagerly, but the area was forested and we
could not see very far in any direction. The tantalizing smell seemed
to grow and I could feel the saliva filling my mouth.

"There's an inn around here, somewhere," muttered Tokubei.
"I'm sure of it."

We followed our noses. We had to leave the well-traveled
highway and take a narrow, winding footpath. But the mouth-
watering smell of the rice and the vision of fluffy, freshly aired cotton
quilts drew us on.

The sun was just beginning to set. We passed a bamboo grove,
and in the low evening light the thin leaves turned into little golden
knives. I saw a gilded clump of bamboo shoots. The sight made me
think of the delicious dish they would make when boiled in soy
sauce.

We hurried forward. To our delight we soon came to a clearing
with a thatched house standing in the middle. The fragrant smell of
rice was now so strong that we were certain a meal was being
prepared inside.

Standing in front of the house was a pretty girl beaming at us
with a welcoming smile. "Please honor us with your presence," she
said, beckoning.

There was something a little unusual about one of her hands,
but, being hungry and eager to enter the house, I did not stop to
observe closely.

rav•en•ous (raˊ və nəs)
adj., very eager for food

DURING READING

Analyze Literature
Setting How does the
imagery in this passage
explain why Tokubei and
Zenta leave the highway to
search for an unknown inn? **F**

THE INN OF LOST TIME **35**

History Connection

Seclusion Policy The comment
about trading with the Portuguese is
significant. In the 1630s, in order to
control trade and prevent rebellions,
Japan's military regime had instituted
a policy of national seclusion, closing
the country to trade with outside
merchants. A special edict in 1639
banned Portuguese ships from visiting
Japan. Trade was allowed only with
licensed Korean, Dutch, and Chinese
merchants. The policy of seclusion,
known as *sakoku* ("closed country"),
lasted for 200 years. **D**

Use Reading Strategies

Clarify Call attention to the fact
that Zenta advises his listeners to
remember a particular point. Model
how to clarify information: "I want to
be sure I know what Zenta means by
this, so I'll reread the preceding
sentence. That sentence says Tokubei
can have his clerks send money. I'll
keep this in mind as I read on." **E**

Analyze Literature

Setting *Answer:* The tantalizing smell
of freshly cooked rice makes them
realize that they are very hungry, and
the "vision of freshly aired cotton
quilts" appeals to their desire for a
comfortable place to rest. They assume
that only an inn would offer these
comforts, so they search for it. **F**

Writing Skills

Sensory Details

Tell students to imagine that they and their families
have just spent the night in an expensive hotel that
had run-down, seedy rooms and poor service. Have
them write a letter of complaint to the hotel's
management describing the bad experience and
requesting a refund. Remind students to use sensory
details to make the description vivid and realistic.

Point out that in "The Inn of Lost Time," Lensey
Namioka uses pleasant sensory details to describe
the comforts Zenta and Tokubei imagine as they
approach the inn. To make their letters of complaint
convincing, students will need to use unpleasant
sensory details. Invite students to read their letters
aloud to the class.

Analyze Literature

Setting *Answer:* It is odd that the inn is hidden away from the highway, but Zenta is too hungry to be suspicious. **Ⓐ**

Analyze Literature

Foreshadowing Ask students what might be foreshadowed by Zenta's comment that he should have wondered why the inn was "hidden away from the highway." Model a response: "Zenta's use of the word *danger* seems to hint that there is something sinister about the inn's location. The travelers are about to encounter a problem." **Ⓑ**

Use Reading Skills

Monitor Comprehension Make sure students understand that Zenta is reflecting on an event in the past. Ask: "What has Zenta learned since he first saw the inn in the forest?" (He should have been suspicious.) **Ⓒ**

DURING READING

Analyze Literature
Setting What is odd about the location of the inn? Why isn't Zenta suspicious? **Ⓐ**

Ⓑ You will say, of course, that it was my duty as a bodyguard to be suspicious and to look out for danger. Youth and inexperience should not have prevented me from wondering why an inn should be found hidden away from the highway. As it was, my stomach growled, and I didn't even hesitate but followed Tokubei to the house.

Before stepping up to enter, we were given basins of water to wash our feet. As the girl handed us towels for drying, I saw what was unusual about her left hand: she had six fingers.

Tokubei had noticed it as well. When the girl turned away to empty the basins, he nudged me. "Did you see her left hand? She had—" He broke off in confusion as the girl turned around, but she didn't seem to have heard.

Ⓒ The inn was peaceful and quiet, and we soon discovered the reason why. We were the only guests. Again, I should have been suspicious. I told you that I'm not proud of the part I played.

Tokubei turned to me and grinned. "It seems that there are no other guests. We should be able to get extra service for the same amount of money."

The girl led us to a spacious room which was like the principal chamber of a private residence. Cushions were set out for us on the floor and we began to shed our traveling gear to make ourselves comfortable.

The door opened and a grizzled-haired man entered. Despite his vigorous-looking[6] face his back was a little bent and I guessed his age to be about fifty. After bowing and greeting us he apologized in advance for the service. "We have not always been innkeepers here," he said, "and you may find the accommodations lacking. Our good intentions must make up for our inexperience. However, to <u>compensate</u> for our inadequacies,[7] we will charge a lower fee than that of an inn with an established reputation."

com•pen•sate (käm´ pən sāt´) *v.*, balance, offset, repay

Tokubei nodded graciously, highly pleased by the words of our host, and the evening began well. It continued well when the girl came back with some flasks of wine, cups, and dishes of salty snacks.

While the girl served the wine, the host looked with interest at my swords. From the few remarks he made, I gathered that he was a former samurai, forced by circumstances to turn his house into an inn.

---

6. **vigorous.** Lively; energetic
7. **inadequacies.** Shortcomings

Differentiated Instruction

Visual Learning

Zenta and Tokubei's approach to the inn through the bamboo grove functions in the plot of the story. Work with students to list and analyze the sensory details and figurative language used to describe their walk along the narrow footpath and their first sight of the inn.

Have students individually use the list of details to create a drawing of the travelers' approach to the inn, including as many details from the story as possible. Encourage students to share and compare their completed drawings and ask them to point out details that correspond to the text.

Having become a bodyguard to a tight-fisted merchant, I was in no position to feel superior to a ronin turned innkeeper. Socially, therefore, we were more or less equal.

We exchanged polite remarks with our host while we drank and tasted the salty snacks. I looked around at the pleasant room. It showed excellent taste, and I especially admired a vase standing in the alcove.

My host caught my eyes on it. "We still have a few good things that we didn't have to sell," he said. His voice held a trace of bitterness. "Please look at the panels of these doors. They were painted by a fine artist."

Tokubei and I looked at the pair of sliding doors. Each panel contained a landscape painting, the right panel depicting a winter scene and the left one the same scene in late summer. Our host's words were no idle[8] boast. The pictures were indeed beautiful.

Tokubei rose and approached the screens for a closer look. When he sat down again, his eyes were calculating. No doubt he was trying to estimate what price the paintings would fetch.

After my third drink I began to feel very tired. Perhaps it was the result of drinking on an empty stomach. I was glad when the girl brought in two dinner trays and a lacquered container of rice. Uncovering the rice container, she began filling our bowls.

Again I noticed her strange left hand with its six fingers. Any other girl would have tried to keep that hand hidden, but this girl made no effort to do so. If anything, she seemed to use that hand more than her other one when she served us. The extra little finger always stuck out from the hand, as if inviting comment.

The hand fascinated me so much that I kept my eyes on it, and soon forgot to eat. After a while the hand looked blurry. And then everything else began to look blurry. The last thing I remembered was the sight of Tokubei shaking his head, as if trying to clear it.

When I opened my eyes again, I knew that time had passed, but not how much time. My next thought was that it was cold. It was not only extremely cold but damp.

I rolled over and sat up. I reached immediately for my swords and found them safe on the ground beside me. On the ground? What was I doing on the ground? My last memory was of staying at an inn with a merchant called Tokubei.

---

8. **idle.** Without worth or basis in fact

> When I opened my eyes again, I knew that time had passed, but not how much time.

Use Reading Skills

Sequence of Events *Answer:* Zenta stares so long at the six fingers on the girl's left hand that he forgets to eat. Things begin to look blurry and he notices Tokubei shaking his head. Then he opens his eyes, feeling that some time has passed, and realizes that he is outside on the ground, with his swords beside him. **Ⓐ**

Make Connections

Answer: Students may say that they would assume they had been drugged, robbed, and placed outside by the thieves. **Ⓑ**

Analyze Literature

Suspense Ask students how these new developments help create suspense for the reader. Model a response: "I'm very puzzled, now. If robbery wasn't the motive, then what was? I want to keep reading to find out." **Ⓒ**

DURING READING

Use Reading Skills
Sequence of Events Zenta has three drinks and the girl serves the rice. What happens after that? **Ⓐ**

DURING READING

Make Connections
What assumption would you make if you found yourself in this situation? **Ⓑ**

The thought of Tokubei put me into a panic. I was his bodyguard, and instead of watching over him, I had fallen asleep and had awakened in a strange place.

I looked around frantically and saw that he was lying on the ground not far from where I was. Had he been killed?

I got up shakily, and when I stood up my head was swimming. But my sense of urgency gave some strength to my legs. I stumbled over to my employer and to my great relief found him breathing—breathing heavily, in fact.

When I shook his shoulder, he grunted and finally opened his eyes. "Where am I?" he asked thickly.

It was a reasonable question. I looked around and saw that we had been lying in a bamboo grove. By the light I guessed that it was early morning, and the reason I felt cold and damp was because my clothes were wet with dew.

"It's cold!" said Tokubei, shivering and climbing unsteadily to his feet. He looked around slowly, and his eyes became wide with disbelief. "What happened? I thought we were staying at an inn!"

His words came as a relief. One of the possibilities I had considered was that I had gone mad and that the whole episode with the inn was something I had imagined. Now I knew that Tokubei had the same memory of the inn. I had not imagined it.

But why were we out here on the cold ground, instead of on comfortable mattresses in the inn?

"They must have drugged us and robbed us," said Tokubei. He turned and looked at me furiously. "A fine bodyguard you are!"

There was nothing I could say to that. But at least we were both alive and unharmed. "Did they take all your money?" I asked.

Tokubei had already taken his wallet out of his sash and was peering inside. "That's funny! My money is still here!"

This was certainly unexpected. What did the innkeeper and his strange daughter intend to do by drugging us and moving us outside? **Ⓒ**

At least things were not as bad as we had feared. We had not lost anything except a comfortable night's sleep, although from the heaviness in my head I had certainly slept deeply enough—and long enough too. Exactly how much time had elapsed[9] since we drank wine with our host?

All we had to do now was find the highway again and continue

---

9. **elapsed.** Passed

Differentiated Instruction

Enrichment

Point out that the setting details in this story accurately represent feudal Japan. Inform students that to write this story, Lensey Namioka had to research social, political, and economic conditions in feudal Japan. Note that creative writers often have to do research to make their writing seem believable and accurate, especially when their writing is set in another place or time. Encourage students to write a brief work of fiction (a poem, a description, or a very short story) set in another place and time in which they are interested. Students should research this place and time before they write their fictional piece. Ask students to share their work with the class.

our journey. Tokubei suddenly chuckled. "I didn't even have to pay for our night's lodging!"

As we walked from the bamboo grove, I saw the familiar clump of bamboo shoots, and we found ourselves standing in the same clearing again. Before our eyes was the thatched house. Only it was somehow different. Perhaps things looked different in the daylight than at dusk.

But the difference was more than a change of light. As we approached the house slowly, like sleepwalkers, we saw that the thatching was much darker. On the previous evening the thatching had looked fresh and new. Now it was dark with age. Daylight should make things appear brighter, not darker. The plastering of the walls also looked more dingy.[10]

Tokubei and I stopped to look at each other before we went closer. He was pale, and I knew that I looked no less frightened. Something was terribly wrong. I loosened my sword in its scabbard.

We finally gathered the courage to go up to the house. Since Tokubei seemed unable to find his voice, I spoke out. "Is anyone there?"

After a moment we heard shuffling footsteps and the front door slid open. The face of an old woman appeared. "Yes?" she inquired. Her voice was creaky with age.

What set my heart pounding with panic, however, was not her voice. It was the sight of her left hand holding on to the frame of the door. The hand was wrinkled and crooked with the arthritis of old age—and it had six fingers.

I heard a gasp beside me and knew that Tokubei had noticed the hand as well.

The door opened wider and a man appeared beside the old woman. At first I thought it was our host of the previous night. But this man was much younger, although the resemblance was strong. He carried himself straighter and his hair was black, while the innkeeper had been grizzled and slightly bent with age.

"Please excuse my mother," said the man. "Her hearing is not good. Can we help you in some way?"

Tokubei finally found his voice. "Isn't this the inn where we stayed last night?"

The man stared. "Inn? We are not innkeepers here!"

"Yes, you are!" insisted Tokubei. "Your daughter invited us in

> **DURING READING**
>
> **Analyze Literature**
> **Setting** What is different about the outside of the house? **D**

10. **dingy.** Dirty or discolored; showing signs of wear or neglect

Cultural Connection

Samurai Philosophy Respect for one's elders is an aspect of Neo-Confucianism, a guiding philosophy Japan absorbed from China in the twelfth century. As a samurai, Zenta probably adhered to the Confucian ideals of respect for the social order, obedience to superiors, and proper rules of conduct. Point out to students that this cultural precept plays a role in the story. **A**

Analyze Literature

Setting *Answer:* One of the painted screens on the door has been torn and carefully mended, and Tokubei is sure no one would vandalize a valuable painting just to play a joke. **B**

Analyze Literature

Suspense Encourage students to consider how suspense builds during the conversation that Zenta and Tokubei have with the young man and the old woman. What new questions does the encounter raise in their minds? Guide students to cite the growing "evidence" that Zenta and Tokubei have slept for fifty years, such as seeing that the paintings are faded and torn, learning that the old woman's grandfather ran an inn about fifty years ago, learning other guests have disappeared—and then the old woman's sudden recognition of Zenta and Tokubei. Model how this evidence provokes questions: "I wonder, now, if the two men have slipped into the future or slept for fifty years without aging."

Urashima on the Turtle, 1882. Yoshitoshi.

"I've lost fifty years! Fifty years of my life went by while I slept at this accursed inn!"

DURING READING

Analyze Literature
Setting What detail in the house convinces Tokubei that the host is not just playing a joke? Explain. **B**

---

and served us with wine. You must have put something in the wine!"

The man frowned. "You are serious? Are you sure you didn't drink too much at your inn and wander off?"

"No, I didn't drink too much!" said Tokubei, almost shouting. "I hardly drank at all! Your daughter, the one with six fingers in her hand, started to pour me a second cup of wine..." His voice trailed off, and he stared again at the left hand of the old woman.

"I don't have a daughter," said the man slowly. "My mother here is the one who has six fingers in her left hand, although I hardly think it polite of you to mention it."

"I'm getting dizzy," muttered Tokubei and began to totter.

"I think you'd better come in and rest a bit," the man said to him gruffly. He glanced at me. "Perhaps you wish to join your friend. You don't share his delusion[11] about the inn, I hope?"

"I wouldn't presume to contradict my elders," I said carefully. Since both Tokubei and the owner of the house were my elders, I wasn't committing myself. In truth I didn't know what to believe, but I did want a look at the inside of the house. **A**

The inside was almost the same as it was before but the differences were there when I looked closely. We entered the same room with the alcove and the pair of painted doors. The vase I had admired was no longer there, but the doors showed the same landscapes painted by a master. I peered closely at the pictures and saw that the colors looked faded. What was more, the left panel, the one depicting a winter scene, had a long tear in one corner. It had been painstakingly mended, but the damage was impossible to hide completely.

Tokubei saw what I was staring at and he became even paler. At this stage we had both considered the possibility that a hoax of some sort had been played on us. The torn screen convinced Tokubei that our host had not played a joke: the owner of a valuable painting would never vandalize it for a trivial reason.

As for me, I was far more disturbed by the sight of the sixth finger on the old woman's hand. Could the young girl have disguised

---

11. delusion. Incorrect perception of reality

Differentiated Instruction

Visual Learning

Suggest that students use a comparison chart or other graphic organizer to list visual details about

- the man and woman who were at the inn when Zenta and Tokubei first arrived and
- the man and woman who were at the inn after Zenta and Tokubei slept outdoors.

Allow students to sketch their impressions if they prefer. Then have them discuss the similarities and differences they find.

herself as an old crone? She could put rice powder in her hair to whiten it, but she could not transform her pretty straight fingers into old fingers twisted with arthritis. The woman here with us now was genuinely old, at least fifty years older than the girl.

It was this same old woman who finally gave us our greatest shock. "It's interesting that you should mention an inn, gentlemen," she croaked. "My father used to operate an inn. After he died, my husband and I turned this back into a private residence. We didn't need the income, you see."

"Your...your...f-father?" stammered Tokubei.

"Yes," replied the old woman. "He was a ronin, forced to go into innkeeping when he lost his position. But he never liked the work. Besides, our inn had begun to acquire an unfortunate reputation. Some of our guests disappeared, you see."

Even before she finished speaking, a horrible suspicion had begun to dawn on me. Her father had been an innkeeper, she said, her father who used to be a ronin. The man who had been our host was a ronin turned innkeeper. Could this mean that this old woman was actually the same person as the young girl we had seen?

I sat stunned while I tried to absorb the implications. What had happened to us? Was it possible that Tokubei and I had slept while this young girl grew into a mature woman, got married, and bore a son, a son who was now an adult? If that was the case, then we had slept for fifty years!

The old woman's next words confirmed my fears. "I recognize you now! You are two of the lost guests from our inn! The other lost ones I don't remember so well, but I remember you because your disappearance made me so sad. Such a handsome youth, I thought, what a pity that he should have gone the way of the others!"

A high wail came from Tokubei, who began to keen[12] and rock himself back and forth. "I've lost fifty years! Fifty years of my life went by while I slept at this accursed inn!"

The inn was indeed accursed. Was the fate of the other guests similar to ours? "Did anyone else return as we did, fifty years later?" I asked.

The old woman looked uncertain and turned to her son. He frowned thoughtfully. "From time to time wild-looking people have come to us with stories similar to yours. Some of them went mad with the shock."

---

12. **keen.** Lament or complain loudly

DURING READING

Use Reading Skills
Sequence of Events What sequence of events is suggested to Zenta by the old woman's words? **C**

Use Reading Skills

Analyze Cause and Effect Ask students what causes Tokubei to believe that he's lost his business and his wife. Model a response: "If he has been asleep for fifty years, then his wife may be dead, she may have remarried, or she may be very old, and his business has probably been sold or has gone bankrupt." **A**

Analyze Literature

Setting *Answer:* The people believe that it is possible for an evil spirit to inhabit a place; they think such a spirit has the power and ability to "steal time" from people's lives. **B**

Analyze Literature

Fantasy Ask students what elements of fantasy are evident in this passage. Have them explain whether they think the story will or will not turn out to be a fantasy. Model a response: "The passage contains unreal elements such as the evil spirit and the spell. These are typical elements of fantasy, but most of the story is realistic, so I need to read more before I decide." **C**

TEACHING NOTE

Self-Generated Questioning

Tell students to create two or more questions about the situation that Zenta and Tokubei have found themselves in, along with notes on how to answer the questions. Model a possible question: "What is the scariest aspect of this for Tokubei?" Have some of the students share their questions with the class.

"They would wake up twenty, thirty, or even fifty years later."

A Tokubei wailed again. "I've lost my business! I've lost my wife, my young and beautiful wife! We had been married only a couple of months!"

A gruesome chuckle came from the old woman. "You may not have lost your wife. It's just that she's become an old hag like me!"

That did not console Tokubei, whose keening became louder. Although my relationship with my employer had not been characterized by much respect on either side, I did begin to feel very sorry for him. He was right: he had lost his world.

As for me, the loss was less traumatic.[13] I had left home under extremely painful circumstances, and had spent the next three years wandering. I had no friends and no one I could call a relation. The only thing I had was my duty to my employer. Somehow, some way, I had to help him.

"Did no one find an explanation for these disappearances?" I asked. "Perhaps if we knew the reason why, we might find some way to reverse the process."

The old woman began to nod eagerly. "The priestess! Tell them about the shrine priestess!"

"Well," said the man, "I'm not sure if it would work in your case...."

"What? What would work?" demanded Tokubei. His eyes were feverish.

C "There was a case of one returning guest who consulted the priestess at our local shrine," said the man. "She went into a trance and revealed that there was an evil spirit dwelling in the bamboo grove here. This spirit would put unwary[14] travelers into a long, unnatural sleep. They would wake up twenty, thirty, or even fifty years later."

"Yes, but you said something worked in his case," said Tokubei.

The man seemed reluctant to go on. "I don't like to see you cheated, so I'm not sure I should be telling you this."

"Tell me! Tell me!" demanded Tokubei. The host's reluctance only made him more impatient.

"The priestess promised to make a spell that would undo the work of the evil spirit," said the man. "But she demanded a large sum of money, for she said that she had to burn some very rare and costly incense before she could begin the spell."

> **DURING READING**
>
> **Analyze Literature**
> **Setting** What do the details about the evil spirit reveal about people's beliefs in this time and place? **B**

13. **traumatic.** Shocking
14. **unwary.** Easily fooled

Vocabulary Skills

Irregular Verbs

Remind students that irregular verbs are those that do not follow the regular pattern of adding *-d* or *-ed* to the present form in order to form the past and the past participle. Many irregular verbs have the same spelling in the past and past participle forms *(sleep/slept/has, have slept)*. Others have different forms *(begin/began/has, have begun)*.

Have students complete each sentence with the correct form of the verb in parenthesis.

1. Zenta (see) something unusual about the girl's left hand.

2. The girl (lead) them to a large room.

3. They (drink) wine and (eat) snacks before dinner.

At the mention of money Tokubei sat back. The hectic flush died down on his face and his eyes narrowed. "How much money?" he asked.

The host shook his head. "In my opinion the priestess is a fraud[15] and makes outrageous claims about her powers. We try to have as little to do with her as possible."

"Yes, but did her spell work?" asked Tokubei. "If it worked, she's no fraud!"

"At least the stranger disappeared again," cackled the old woman. "Maybe he went back to his own time. Maybe he walked into a river."

Tokubei's eyes narrowed further. "How much money did the priestess demand?" he asked again.

"I think it was one gold piece for every year lost," said the host. He hurriedly added, "Mind you, I still wouldn't trust the priestess."

"Then it would cost me fifty gold pieces to get back to my own time," muttered Tokubei. He looked up. "I don't carry that much money with me."

"No, you don't," agreed the host.

Something alerted me about the way he said that. It was as if the host knew already that Tokubei did not carry much money on him. **D**

Meanwhile Tokubei sighed. He had come to a decision. "I do have the means to obtain more money, however. I can send a message to my chief clerk and he will remit[16] the money when he sees my seal."

"Your chief clerk may be dead by now," I reminded him.

"You're right!" moaned Tokubei. "My business will be under a new management and nobody will even remember my name!"

"And your wife will have remarried," said the old woman, with one of her chuckles. I found it hard to believe that the gentle young girl who had served us wine could turn into this dreadful harridan.[17]

"Sending the message may be a waste of time," agreed the host.

"What waste of time!" cried Tokubei. "Why shouldn't I waste time? I've wasted fifty years already! Anyway, I've made up my mind. I'm sending that message."

"I still think you shouldn't trust the priestess," said the host. **E**

That only made Tokubei all the more determined to send for the money. However, he was not quite resigned to the amount. "Fifty

---

DURING READING

Use Reading Strategies
Clarify The Latin phrase *carpe diem* applies to this story. Identify the meaning of this foreign phrase and explain how it fits with this section of the story. **F**

---

15. **fraud.** One who cheats or deceives
16. **remit.** Send (money)
17. **harridan.** Ill-tempered woman

Analyze Literature
Foreshadowing Ask students what Zenta's comment about "something" that alerted him might foreshadow. Model a response: "Zenta's comment hints that he is suspicious and that he will continue to question the idea that they lost fifty years." **D**

Use Reading Skills
Analyze Cause and Effect Point out that the host keeps advising Tokubei not to trust the priestess. Ask students to explain the effect these warnings have on Tokubei. Is this the effect the host is hoping for? Model a possible response: "The warnings only make Tokubei more determined to believe in the powers of the priestess. If the host is setting up a hoax, he may be using reverse psychology. By appearing to discredit the priestess, he is attempting to convince Tokubei that he has no interest in the money." **E**

Use Reading Strategies
Clarify The Latin phrase *carpe diem* means literally "pluck the day" and is oftened translated to "seize the day." Tokubei has decided that after fifty years of wandering around lost in time, this is the day he is going to send a message asking for money that he hopes will help him get back to his own time. **F**

Vocabulary Skills

Prefixes and Suffixes
Remind students that prefixes and suffixes are word parts that add or change the meaning of the base words to which they are added. Ask students to record the meanings of the following prefixes and suffixes. Allow them to use a dictionary.

prefixes: *con-, dis-, pre-, re-, un-*
suffixes: *-ance, -ish, -ly, -ship*

Challenge students to find as many examples of these prefixes and suffixes as they can on pages 42 and 43 of the story. Ask them to define the words they find, using what they know about the prefixes and suffixes.

Use Reading Skills

Sequence of Events *Answer:* He notices that the clump of bamboo shoots is in the same place as when he last saw it, and that it looks almost exactly the same as it did then, except that each shoot had grown about an inch taller, which is a reasonable amount for bamboo to grow overnight. **Ⓐ**

gold pieces is a large sum. Surely the priestess can buy incense for less than that amount?"

"Why don't you try giving her thirty gold pieces?" cackled the old woman. "Then the priestess will send you back thirty years, and your wife will only be middle-aged."

While Tokubei was still arguing with himself about the exact sum to send for, I decided to have a look at the bamboo grove. "I'm going for a walk," I announced, rising and picking up my sword from the floor beside me.

The host turned sharply to look at me. For an instant a faint, rueful smile appeared on his lips. Then he looked away.

Outside, I went straight to the clump of shoots in the bamboo grove. On the previous night—or what I perceived as the previous night—I had noticed that clump of bamboo shoots particularly, because I had been so hungry that I pictured them being cut up and boiled.

The clump of bamboo shoots was still in the same place. That in itself proved nothing, since bamboo could spring up anywhere, including the place where a clump had existed fifty years earlier. But what settled the matter in my mind was that the clump looked almost exactly the way it did when I had seen it before, except that every shoot was about an inch taller. That was a reasonable amount for bamboo shoots to grow overnight.

Overnight. Tokubei and I had slept on the ground here overnight. We had not slept here for a period of fifty years.

Once I knew that, I was able to see another inconsistency: the door panels with the painted landscapes. The painting with the winter scene had been on the right last night and it was on the left this morning. It wasn't simply a case of the panels changing places, because the depressions in the panel for the handholds had been reversed. In other words, what I saw just now was not a pair of paintings faded and torn by age. They were an entirely different pair of paintings.

But how did the pretty young girl change into an old woman? The answer was that if the screens could be different ones, so could the women. I had seen one woman, a young girl, last night. This morning I saw a different woman, an old hag.

The darkening of the thatched roof? Simply blow ashes over the roof. The grizzled-haired host of last night could be the same man who claimed to be his grandson today. It would be a simple matter for a young man to put gray in his hair and assume a stoop.

> **DURING READING**
>
> **Use Reading Skills**
> **Sequence of Events** What inconsistency does Zenta discover in the old woman's story of lost time? **Ⓐ**

Differentiated Instruction

Enrichment

Tell students that *carpe diem* is a Latin phrase meaning "seize the day." The *carpe diem* theme in literature advises people to enjoy themselves while they have a chance, because life is short and time passes quickly. Share the following quotation from Robert Herrick (1591–1674) with students and ask them how its theme relates to that of "The Inn of Lost Time."

"Gather ye rosebuds while ye may
Old Time is still a-flying
And this same flower that
      smiles to-day
To-morrow will be dying."

Invite students to brainstorm or research other quotations that express this theme.

And the purpose of the hoax? To make Tokubei send for fifty pieces of gold, of course. It was clever of the man to accuse the shrine priestess of fraud and pretend reluctance to let Tokubei send his message.

I couldn't even feel angry toward the man and his daughter—or mother, sister, wife, whatever. He could have killed me and taken my swords, which he clearly admired. Perhaps he was really a ronin and felt sympathetic toward another one.

When I returned to the house, Tokubei was looking resigned. "I've decided to send for the whole fifty gold pieces." He sighed.

"Don't bother," I said. "In fact we should be leaving as soon as possible. We shouldn't even stop here for a drink, especially not of wine."

Tokubei stared. "What do you mean? If I go back home, I'll find everything changed!"

"Nothing will be changed," I told him. "Your wife will be as young and beautiful as ever."

"I don't understand," he said. "Fifty years…"

"It's a joke," I said. "The people here have a peculiar sense of humor, and they've played a joke on us."

Tokubei's mouth hung open. Finally he closed it with a snap. He stared at the host, and his face became first red and then purple. "You—you were trying to swindle me!" He turned furiously to me. "And you let them do this!"

"I'm not letting them," I pointed out. "That's why we're leaving right now."

"Are you going to let them get away with this?" demanded Tokubei. "They might try to swindle someone else!"

"They only went to this much trouble when they heard of the arrival of a fine fat fish like you," I said. I looked deliberately at the host. "I'm sure they won't be tempted to try the same trick again."

"And that's the end of your story?" asked Matsuzo. "You and Tokubei just went away? How did you know the so-called innkeeper wouldn't try the trick on some other luckless traveler?"

Zenta shook his head. "I didn't know. I merely guessed that once the trick was exposed, they wouldn't take the chance of trying it again. Of course I thought about revisiting the place to check if the people there were leading an honest life."

"Why didn't you?" asked Matsuzo. "Maybe we could go together. You've made me curious about that family now."

"Then you can satisfy your curiosity," said Zenta, smiling. He

DURING READING

Use Reading Skills
Sequence of Events How does this paragraph signal a shift from the flashback to the "frame" story? **C**

Teach the Model

Analyze Literature
Make Inferences Ask students why Zenta doesn't feel angry about the hoax. Model a response: "He seems to admire the cleverness of the ruse, and he also feels a connection with the man because as a ronin himself, he knows that he could easily find himself in desperate need of money." **B**

Use Reading Skills
Sequence of Events *Answer:* Matsuzo, a character who appears only in the "frame" story, asks if this is "the end" of Zenta's story. Also, there is a shift from first-person narrator to third-person narrator, which helps signal the time change. **C**

Grammar Skills

Commas with Introductory Phrases
Ask a volunteer to read aloud this sentence from the story: "As you know, wealthy merchants are relatively new in our country." Note that a comma indicates the natural pause that a speaker makes after using an introductory phrase. Read aloud the sentence without the pause. This will demonstrate that the pause keeps the reader from running together words and phrases that should be kept apart for clarity.

Have students decide where to place the comma in the following sentences.
1. Yes I'd like to hear that story.
2. In fact it happened more than seven years ago.
3. By the way the tea was delicious.

Analyze Literature

Plot Ask students how this simple action of the farmer's wife advances the plot. Model a response: "This is the turning point, or climax, of the story, because the farmer's wife is revealing that she was involved in the hoax Zenta has just described." **A**

Analyze Literature

Setting *Answer:* They are at the house Zenta visited several years ago when he thought he had lost fifty years. **B**

Use Reading Skills

Sequence of Events *Answer:* Five years after their visit, their host found work with a warlord, but just a month after that he was killed in battle. **C**

Analyze Literature

Humor Ask students why everyone laughs when Matsuzo refused a cup of tea. What does this reveal about the characters? Model a response: "They remember that the woman drugged Zenta seven years earlier. The humor shows that the characters trust each other." **D**

Answer: Some students might be willing to trade ten years for money; others wouldn't want to miss relationships or experiences for any price.

---

held his cup out for more tea, and the farmer's wife came forward to pour.

A Only now she used both hands to hold the pot, and for the first time Matsuzo saw her left hand. He gasped. The hand had six fingers.

"Who was the old woman?" Zenta asked the farmer's wife.

"She was my grandmother," she replied. "Having six fingers is something that runs in my family."

At last Matsuzo found his voice. "You mean this is the very house you visited? This is the inn where time was lost?"

"Where we thought we lost fifty years," said Zenta. "Perhaps I should have warned you first. But I was almost certain that we'd be safe this time. And I see that I was right."

He turned to the woman again. "You and your husband are farmers now, aren't you? What happened to the man who was the host?"

C "He's dead," she said quietly. "He was my brother, and he was telling you the truth when he said that he was a ronin. Two years ago he found work with another warlord, but he was killed in battle only a month later."

Matsuzo was peering at the pair of sliding doors, which he hadn't noticed before. "I see that you've put up the faded set of paintings. The winter scene is on the left side."

The woman nodded. "We sold the newer pair of doors. My husband said that we're farmers now and that people in our position don't need valuable paintings. We used the money to buy some new farm implements."

She took up the teapot again. "Would you like another cup of tea?" she asked Matsuzo.

Staring at her left hand, Matsuzo had a sudden qualm. "I—I don't think I want any more."

D Everybody laughed. ✤

DURING READING

Analyze Literature
Setting Where are Zenta and Matsuzo staying now? **B**

DURING READING

Use Reading Skills
Sequence of Events What happened to their host after Zenta and Tokubei's visit to the inn? **C**

MIRRORS & WINDOWS

What if you could sell ten years of your life? What amount, if any, would make it worthwhile to lose the possibilities those years might hold for you? What do you think time is worth?

TEACHING NOTE

Self-Generated Questioning

Divide the class into two groups, Description and Dialogue. Have each group generate three or four questions about Namioka's writing techniques in its area. Model some sample questions:

• "How does Namioka use verbs to enhance descriptions?"

• "How does Namioka use punctuation in writing dialogue?"

When groups finish, have them exchange lists and try to answer the other group's questions.

Find Meaning

1. (a) What do Zenta and Tokubei notice that is unusual about the girl at the inn? (b) Why do you suppose the girl, and later the old woman, makes no effort to hide her left hand?

2. (a) While Tokubei and the host are arguing about whether Tokubei should send for money, what does Zenta decide to do, and how does the host respond? (b) Why does a rueful smile appear on the host's lips?

Analyze Literature

Setting Setting often has an effect on plot. Use a Venn diagram to list the details that describe the inn when Zenta and Tokubei arrive and "after fifty years," when they awaken from their drugged sleep. What details are the same? What details are different? How do these details influence the plot?

Make Judgments

3. (a) What words, behaviors, and gestures demonstrate Tokubei's attitude about money? (b) How do these attitudes affect his response when he learns about the hoax?

4. (a) Why do you think the innkeeper decides to try to swindle the two travelers? (b) Do you think he feels guilty? Explain.

5. Why do you think Zenta is more forgiving of the innkeeper and his family than Tokubei is?

Extend Understanding

Writing Options

Creative Writing Imagine that you are Tokubei and that you have decided to make a police report. Write a **descriptive paragraph** to help the police make an identification of the innkeepers. Include character traits as well as physical descriptions. Support your statements with evidence from the story.

Expository Writing Consider how Zenta's story would be different if the "frame" story featuring Zenta, Matsuzo, and the farmer's family were removed. Write a short **literary analysis** of "The Inn of Lost Time" in which you examine how the author's use of flashback helps increase suspense. Include a thesis and support.

Collaborative Learning

Hold a Discussion With a partner, discuss how you might react if you realized that a great deal of time had passed while you slept or had been unconscious as a result of an accident or illness. Would you be upset? frightened? confused? Write a few sentences to summarize your feelings.

Critical Literacy

Write Questions Prepare a set of questions that you would ask Tokubei to prompt him to tell his version of the story. Read aloud your questions to the class and invite volunteers to supply Tokubei's answers.

MW Go to **www.mirrorsandwindows.com** for more.

Find Meaning

1. (a) She has six fingers on her left hand. (b) It will help convince the guests that a long time has elapsed.

2. (a) He decides to go outside for a walk. The host turns sharply to look at him. (b) The host may be thinking that when Zenta looks outside, he will figure out what really happened.

Make Judgments

3. (a) Tokubei tries to avoid expensive inns, tries to get his "lost" time back for a reduced fee, and sighs when he decides to send for gold. (b) He thinks those responsible for the hoax should be punished.

4. (a) The innkeeper's poverty and Tokubei's obvious wealth are motivations. (b) He may not feel guilty, because he despises merchants, but he may feel guilty about tricking a fellow samurai.

5. Zenta may feel kinship with the innkeeper because he was once a samurai and because Zenta, too, despises what Tokubei stands for.

Analyze Literature

Setting *Answers:*

Inn on Arrival: new thatching; smell of rice; cushions on floor; vase in alcove; beautiful paintings; girl with six fingers on left hand

Same: thatched house in bamboo grove; spacious main room; alcove; sliding doors

Inn After Fifty Years: dingy thatching; no vase; faded, torn paintings; old woman with six fingers on left hand; *very similar to the farmer's house*

Rubrics for Writing Options

You can adapt this as a checklist for students to use as they write.

Creative Writing

☐ Does the description include adjectives that accurately describe the character?

☐ Does the description include personality traits?

☐ Does the description include evidence or examples from the story?

Expository Writing

☐ Does the analysis indicate an understanding of flashback?

☐ Does the analysis clearly explain how the connection between the flashback and the frame story creates suspense?

☐ Does the analysis include a thesis statement and offer supporting evidence from the story?

Teach the Workshop

Sentence Improvement

1. merchants
2. tale
3. Zenta
4. innkeepers
5. Tokubei
6. screens
7. is
8. pass
9. are
10. guests

Build Skills

Some students may think that the *s* in third-person singular verbs creates a "plural verb." Tell students that a verb with an *s* almost always goes with a singular subject. Run through several examples of first-person, second-person, and third-person singular and plural regular verbs. Have students listen for the *s*. For instance:

- I sing, you sing, he sings; we sing, you sing, they sing
- I eat, you eat, she eats; we eat, you eat, they eat

> For more information, see Grammar & Style Section 3.7, Agreement, in the Language Arts Handbook.

Program Resources

You will find additional lessons on Subject-Verb Agreement in the *Exceeding the Standards: Grammar & Style* resource.

Subject-Verb Agreement

Identifying Subject-Verb Agreement

The sun was just beginning to set.

—LENSEY NAMIOKA, "The Inn of Lost Time"

In the sentence above, the subject *sun* is singular. A verb must agree with the subject in number. Number refers to whether the subject is singular or plural. If the subject is plural, the verb must also be plural. If the subject is singular, the verb must also be singular. Then the singular subject *sun* needs the singular verb *was*.

> **EXAMPLE**
> *The <u>inn</u> in the woods <u>was</u> dark in the evening.*

In this example, the subject and verb are separated by a prepositional phrase. The prepositional phrase *in the woods* modifies the subject, *inn*. The subject is singular, so the verb, *was*, is also singular. If you are not sure of the subject-verb agreement in a sentence with a prepositional phrase, try rewriting the sentence without the phrase.

Fixing Subject-Verb Agreement

> **INCORRECT**
> *One of the innkeepers give the ronin a dinner of rice and vegetables.*

In the sentence above, the verb *give* agrees with *innkeepers*, the noun it follows. However, *innkeepers* is not the subject. *Innkeepers* is part of the prepositional phrase *of the innkeepers*. The subject is *one*, which is singular. The verb *give* is plural. To fix the sentence, change the verb to *gives*, the singular form. Note that the singular form of many verbs ends in an *-s*.

> **INCORRECT**
> *Tokubei want to discover what happened as he slept.*

In this example, the subject *Tokubei* is singular, but the verb *want* is plural. To fix the sentence, change the verb to *wants*, the singular form.

Sentence Improvement

For each of the following sentences, select the word that best completes the sentence. Then rewrite the sentences on a separate sheet of paper.

1. Wealthy (merchant / merchants) usually complain more than others.
2. The farmer's (tale / tales) about Urashima Taro is famous.
3. (Zenta / The two ronin) waits for the end of the story.
4. The (innkeeper / innkeepers) were not telling the truth.
5. (Tokubei / The innkeepers) is suspicious of the situation.
6. The painted (screen / screens) seem different from the night before.
7. That inn by the two pine trees (are / is) very old.
8. The travelers in the bamboo grove (pass / passes) the inn.
9. Inside of the inn, the guests (are / is) sleeping.
10. The (guest / guests) on the path were very hungry.

KEY TERMS

SUBJECT, 48
SINGULAR, 48
VERB, 48
PLURAL, 48
PREPOSITIONAL PHRASE, 48
NOUN, 48

Differentiated Instruction

English Language Learning

Ask students to give oral presentations that utilize correct subject-verb agreement. First ask the students to write their presentation, then ask them to present it to the class. Writing and speaking activities such as these will help English language learners use a variety of grammatical structures with increasing accuracy and ease.

Common Core State Standards

Language
L.3.1f

THE PORTRAIT

A Short Story by Tomás Rivera

At a Glance
Directed Reading
- Reading Level: Moderate
- Difficulty Considerations: Abrupt shifts and lack of speaker tags
- Ease Factor: Suspense

BEFORE READING

Build Background
Literary Context Mexican-American literature is sometimes referred to as Chicano literature. A main subject of Chicano literature is the experiences of newcomers to the United States. Mexican-American writers, such as Tomás Rivera, often describe the many challenges and pleasures associated with straddling two different cultures.

Reader's Context Imagine that you have a treasured photograph of a well-loved pet, friend, or relative whom you will never see again. What might cause you to trust that photograph with a stranger?

Set Purpose
Preview the title and skim the first page of text. Make a prediction about the story's conflict and its resolution. Then read to determine if your prediction is accurate. You may change your prediction as you gain new information from the story.

Analyze Literature
Plot A **plot** is a series of events related to a central problem, or **conflict.** A typical plot begins with the introduction of the conflict, followed by events that lead to the **climax,** which is the point of highest tension or excitement in the story. The **resolution** is the point at which the central conflict is resolved. As you read "The Portrait," identify the central conflict, climax, and resolution.

Use Reading Skills
Analyze Cause and Effect When you analyze cause and effect, you look for a logical relationship between a cause or several causes and one or more effects. Sometimes signal words such as *because*, *since*, and *therefore* signal cause-and-effect relationships. Keeping track of what happens in a story can help you better understand the story events. As you read "The Portrait," use a chart to keep track of causes and effects.

Cause:	Effect:
Portrait salesman shows samples	Wife wants portrait of son

Objectives
Studying this lesson will enable students to
- use reading skills such as analyzing cause and effect
- define *plot* and recognize the elements of plot in the selection
- describe literary accomplishments of Tomás Rivera and explain the influence of Mexican-American culture on his writing
- appreciate a story of loss and remembrance

Launch the Lesson
Prior to reading "The Portrait," ask students how they would respond if someone tricked them out of a lot of money. How would they feel about that person? How would they feel about themselves? What would they do?

Meet the Author
Tomás Rivera (1935–1984) was the son of migrant farm workers, but he went on to earn a Ph.D. in Romance Languages and Literature. Rivera's published work includes novels, short stories, poetry, and essays, written in English and Spanish. His fiction is known for its realistic portrayal of the enduring spirit and strong family and community ties of Mexican-American migrant workers.

Selection Words
delicate, 53
swindled, 53

Teaching Words
straddling, 49
intensity, 55

KEY TERMS
SHORT STORY, 49
SKIM, 49
PLOT, 49
CONFLICT, 49
CLIMAX, 49
RESOLUTION, 49
CAUSE AND EFFECT, 49
SUMMARY, 55

Common Core State Standards
Reading Literature
RL.1

Summary

A salesman convinces migrant worker Don Mateo and his wife to purchase an expensive three-dimensional portrait of their only son, Chuy, who was killed in the Korean War. They hand over their only photograph of Chuy, pay cash, as the salesman insists, and await delivery of the finished portrait. Many weeks later, a sack of wet, worm-eaten photographs is found near the dump, and Chuy's ruined photograph is among them. Don Mateo goes to San Antonio, finds the salesman, and insists that he provide the portrait of Chuy. Since the photograph has been ruined, the man must create the portrait from memory. He finally delivers the portrait to Don Mateo, who is pleased, and perhaps a little surprised, when people point out that Chuy had a remarkable resemblance to Don Mateo.

 The Mirrors & Windows questions at the end of the story focus on the theme of the value of truth. Before students begin reading, ask: When, if ever, is it all right to ignore the truth?

Private First Class Eugene A. Obregon was awarded the Medal of Honor in Korea for giving his life to save a fellow soldier.

THE PORTRAIT

A Short Story by Tomás Rivera

50

Program Resources

Planning and Assessment
Program Planning Guide, Selection Lesson Plan
E-Lesson Planner
Assessment Guide, Lesson Test
ExamView

Technology Tools
Interactive Student Text on CD
Visual Teaching Package
Audio Library
mirrorsandwindows.com

Meeting the Standards
Fiction: Unit 1, Directed Reading, pp. 45–53

Differentiating Instruction
Advanced Students, Cultural Connection
   Project, p. 4

As soon as the people returned from up north the portrait salesmen began arriving from San Antonio. They would come to rake in.[1] They knew that the workers had money and that was why, as Dad used to say, they would flock in. They carried suitcases packed with samples and always wore white shirts and ties; that way they looked more important and the people believed everything they would tell them and invite them into their homes without giving it much thought. I think that down deep they even longed for their children to one day be like them. In any event, they would arrive and make their way down the dusty streets, going house to house carrying suitcases full of samples.

I remember once I was at the house of one of my father's friends when one of these salesmen arrived. I also remember that that particular one seemed a little frightened and timid. Don Mateo asked him to come in because he wanted to do business.

"Good afternoon, traveler. I would like to tell you about something new that we're offering this year."

"Well, let's see, let's see..."

"Well, sir, see, you give us a picture, any picture you may have, and we will not only enlarge it for you but we'll also set it in a wooden frame like this one and we'll shape the image a little, like this—three dimensional, as they say."

"And what for?"

"So that it will look real. That way...look, let me show you...see? Doesn't he look real, like he's alive?"

"Man, he sure does. Look, vieja.[2] This looks great. Well, you know, we wanted to send some pictures to be enlarged...but now,

this must cost a lot, right?"

"No, I'll tell you, it costs about the same. Of course, it takes more time."

"Well, tell me, how much?"

"For as little as thirty dollars we'll deliver it to you done with inlays[3] just like this, one this size."

"Boy, that's expensive! Didn't you say it didn't cost a lot more? Do you take installments?"

"Well, I'll tell you, we have a new manager and he wants everything in cash. It's very fine work. We'll make it look like real. Shaped like that, with inlays...take a look. What do you think? Some fine work, wouldn't you say? We can have it all finished for you in a month. You just tell us what color you want the clothes to be and we'll come by with it all finished one day when you least expect, framed and all. Yes, sir, a month at the longest. But like I say, this man, who's the new manager, he wants the full payment in cash. He's very demanding, even with us."

"Yes, but it's much too expensive."

"Well, yes. But the thing is, this is very fine work. You can't say you've ever seen portraits done like this, with wood inlays."

"No, well, that's true. What do you think, vieja?"

"Well, I like it a lot. Why don't we order one? And if it turns out good...my Chuy...may he rest in peace. It's the only picture we have of him. We took it right before he left for Korea. Poor m'ijo,[4] we never saw him again. See...this is his picture. Do

> **It's the only picture we have of him.**

---

1. **rake in.** Make lots of money
2. **vieja.** Old woman; wife (Spanish)
3. **inlays.** Material set into a surface in pieces to form a design
4. **m'ijo.** My son (Spanish; a contraction of *mi hijo*)

THE PORTRAIT **51**

Teach the Selection

Use Reading Strategies
Ask Questions Remind students that good readers ask questions as they read a story. Model some questions that the story's first paragraphs might prompt a reader to ask: "Who are the 'people' who returned from up north? What did they do there? What are the salesmen selling? What does Don Mateo want to buy?"

History Connection
U.S. Migrant Workers Use of migratory farm workers in the United States dates back to the late nineteenth century, when big businesses began taking over agriculture. In the 1920s there were as many as two million migrant farm workers in the United States. Today, that figure may be between 800,000 and 900,000. Migrant workers travel from farm to farm, harvesting fruit and vegetables. Without the migrant workers, U.S. farmers would not be able to harvest their crops.

Analyze Literature
Character Ask students what the dialogue reveals about the salesman. Point out that he blames the requirement of full payment in cash on his new manager. Ask students if they think the salesman is honest. Have them support their opinions with evidence from the text. **A**

Differentiated Instruction

Reading Proficiency
Students may need help understanding the setting. Have them read page 49 carefully before they begin the story, and explain that the story is set in a community of migrant workers not far from San Antonio, Texas. People go north to do seasonal farm work, sometimes for months at a time. When the work runs out, they come back home with their pay.

Auditory Learning
The dialogue in the story does not include speaker tags. To clarify which characters are speaking, assign the parts of the narrator, the salesman, Don Mateo, and Don Mateo's wife to fluent readers and have them read the story aloud while the class reads along silently.

History Connection

The Korean War In 1950, the Democratic People's Republic of Korea (North Korea) invaded the Republic of Korea (South Korea). The United Nations sent troops from the United States and several other nations to help with the defense of South Korea. Millions of soldiers and civilians died in the war, which lasted until a cease-fire agreement was signed in 1953. The country remains divided.

52 UNIT 1 FICTION

Differentiated Instruction

English Language Learning

Volunteers who are fluent in Spanish might enjoy explaining the Spanish words in the story. Students learning English may need help with the meanings of these words and expressions:

three-dimensional — appearing to have depth, 51
installments — payments made at intervals, 51
caught on — understood, 53
swindled — cheated, 53

Enrichment

Encourage interested students to learn more about migratory farm workers in the United States. Suggest they might focus on housing and working conditions, health and safety, family life, schooling for children of migrant workers, or historical changes in the cultural identity of migrant workers.

you think you can make it like that, make it look like he's alive?"

"Sure, we can. You know, we've done a lot of them in soldier's uniforms and shaped it, like you see in this sample, with inlays. Why, it's more than just a portrait. Sure. You just tell me what size you want and whether you want a round or square frame. What do you say? How should I write it down?"

"What do you say, vieja, should we have it done like this one?"

"Well, I've already told you what I think. I would like to have m'ijo's picture fixed up like that and in color."

"All right, go ahead and write it down. But you take good care of that picture for us because it's the only one we have of our son grown up. He was going to send us one all dressed up in uniform with the American and Mexican flags crossed over his head, but he no sooner got there when a letter arrived telling us that he was lost in action.[5] So you take good care of it."

"Don't you worry. We're responsible people. And we understand the sacrifices that you people make. Don't worry. And you just wait and see, when we bring it, you'll see how pretty it's gonna look. What do you say, should we make the uniform navy blue?"

"But he's not wearing a uniform in that picture."

"No, but that's just a matter of fixing it up with some wood fiber overlays. Look at these. This one, he didn't have a uniform on but we put one on him. So what do you say? Should we make it navy blue?"

A

And two more weeks had passed by the time they made the discovery.

"All right."

"Don't you worry about the picture."

And that was how they spent the entire day, going house to house, street by street, their suitcases stuffed with pictures. As it turned out, a whole lot of people had ordered enlargements of that kind.

"They should be delivering those portraits soon, don't you think?"

"I think so, it's delicate work and takes more time. That's some fine work those people do. Did you see how real those pictures looked?"

"Yeah, sure. They do some fine work. You can't deny that. But it's already been over a month since they passed by here."

B

"Yes, but from here they went on through all the towns picking up pictures...all the way to San Antonio for sure. So it'll probably take a little longer."

"That's true, that's true."

And two more weeks had passed by the time they made the discovery. Some very heavy rains had come and some children, who were playing in one of the tunnels leading to the dump, found a sack full of pictures, all worm-eaten and soaking wet. The only reason that they could tell that these were pictures was because there were a lot of them and most of them the same size and with faces that could just barely be made out. Everybody caught on right away. Don Mateo was so angry that he took off to San Antonio to find the so and so who had swindled them.

---

5. **lost in action.** Killed in battle

A

Teach the Selection

Use Reading Strategies
Make Predictions Have students make a prediction about the portrait that Don Mateo has ordered. Model how to base a prediction on details in the text by pointing out how many times the salesman repeats "Don't you worry" in this passage. **A**

Use Reading Skills
Analyze Cause and Effect Ask students what Don Mateo and his wife think are the reasons they have not yet received Chuy's portrait. (The intricate work is taking more time than expected; many people ordered portraits.) Then have students read the next paragraph to find out the real reason. **B**

Grammar Skills

Sentence Fragments
"We'll make it look like real. Shaped like that, with inlays . . . take a look. What do you think? Some fine work, wouldn't you say?"

Ask students to identify the sentence fragments — groups of words that don't express a complete thought — in this passage. Remind them that to express a complete thought, a sentence needs a subject and a predicate. Note that authors may deliberately use sentence fragments to create natural-sounding dialogue, but formal writing, such as for school assignments, should not contain fragments. Ask students to correct this fragment:

"Shaped like that, with inlays . . ."

Analyze Literature

Setting Remind students that a story's setting includes cultural, social, and economic conditions as well as time and place. Ask students how important the cultural details are to the setting and to the resolution of this story's conflict. Model a response by naming some cultural details, such as those relating to the closeness of the Mexican-American community and Don Mateo's certainty that he would find the salesman.

Analyze Literature

Plot Ask students to explain the resolution of the conflict in their own words. Model how to begin: "Don Mateo's problem was that he did not get the portrait he paid for, and Chuy's picture was destroyed. The problem was solved when . . ." **A**

Answer: Some students may say that it is always better to know the truth; others may say that it depends on the circumstances. Students' opinions about the relative value of truth or happiness will vary.

More by This Author

Students who like "The Portrait" might enjoy Tomás Rivera's short story collection, *The Harvest.*

"Well, you know, I stayed in Esteban's house. And every day I went with him to the market to sell produce. I helped him with everything. I had faith that I would run into that son of a gun some day soon. Then, after I'd been there for a few days, I started going out to the different barrios[6] and I found out a lot that way. It wasn't so much the money that upset me. It was my poor vieja, crying and all because we'd lost the only picture we had of Chuy. We found it in the sack with all the other pictures but it was already ruined, you know."

"I see, but tell me, how did you find him?"

"Well, you see, to make a long story short, he came by the stand at the market one day. He stood right in front of us and bought some vegetables. It was like he was trying to remember who I was. Of course, I recognized him right off. Because when you're angry enough, you don't forget a face. I just grabbed him right then and there. Poor guy couldn't even talk. He was all scared. And I told him that I wanted that portrait of my son and that I wanted it three

"**W**ell, to be honest, I don't remember too well how Chuy looked."

dimensional and that he'd best get it for me or I'd let him have it. And I went with him to where he lived. And I put him to work right then and there. The poor guy didn't know where to begin. He had to do it all from memory."

"And how did he do it?"

"I don't know. I suppose if you're scared enough, you're capable of doing anything. Three days later he brought me the portrait all finished, just like you see it there on that table by the Virgin. Now tell me, how do you like the way my boy looks?"

"Well, to be honest, I don't remember too well how Chuy looked. But he was beginning to look more and more like you, isn't that so?" **A**

"Yes, I would say so. That's what everybody tells me now. That Chuy's a chip off the old block and that he was already looking like me. There's the portrait. Like they say, one and the same." ✤

---

6. *barrios.* Neighborhoods (Spanish)

MIRRORS & WINDOWS

How satisfying did you find the ending of the story? If knowing the truth about something would make you unhappy, would you want to know the truth, or would you rather not know but remain happy? What do you think is more important: truth or happiness?

Differentiated Instruction

Reading Proficiency

Tell students that summarizing is a skill that can help them read fiction. Remind them that when you summarize, you retell the main events in a selection (or a part of a long selection) using your own words. Ask them to summarize "The Portrait."

Enrichment

Have interested students use the Internet to find out about historical three-dimensional portraiture or contemporary, computerized three-dimensional portraiture. Topics can range from old-fashioned cameo carvings to holograms. Ask students to narrow the topic, research basic methods for creating the portraits, and identify possible sources of examples they could show the class.

Find Meaning

1. Why do the portrait salesmen dress the way they do?
2. (a) Who is Chuy? (b) Why is Chuy's photograph so important to Don Mateo and his wife?
3. (a) Why does Don Mateo travel to San Antonio? (b) What does he do there?

Analyze Literature

Plot In a plot, once the conflict is identified, the events build in intensity until the action reaches the climax, the moment at which the outcome of the conflict is decided. Then the resolution concludes the story. On a plot diagram, indicate the climax and the resolution of "The Portrait." Explain at what points you verified or changed your predictions about the outcome of the story.

Make Judgments

4. What is your opinion of what the salesman says about his manager? Why might he say this?
5. After Don Mateo gives the photograph of his son to the salesman, what clues help you to predict what will happen next?
6. (a) How does the portrait salesman manage to create the new portrait? (b) Do you think the salesman should have simply refunded the money? Explain.

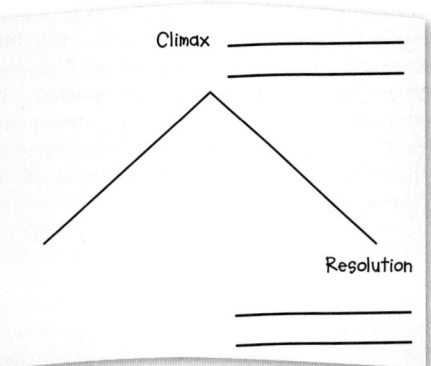

Extend Understanding

Writing Options

Creative Writing Write a **news report** for a local radio station about the incidents described in the story. Remember that a good news report begins with an attention-grabbing first line. Be sure to answer the questions of *who, what, where, when, why,* and *how.* Present your news report to the class.

Expository Writing In a brief **story summary,** describe the problem faced by Don Mateo in the story and the steps he takes to solve the problem. Also consider the problem that the portrait salesman has when Don Mateo wants him to create the portrait of Chuy from memory. How does he solve the problem? Does the story end happily for Don Mateo? Explain.

Collaborative Learning

List Setting Details In small groups, discuss the setting of "The Portrait." Create a list of details from the story that helped you determine the time period and the locations. Use this list to analyze how both time and place influence the theme or message of the selection. Present your conclusions to the class.

Lifelong Learning

Research the Internet Use the Internet to gather information about Hispanic Americans who served in the Korean War (1950–1953). Find out about Hispanic-American recipients of the Medal of Honor, and create a "Wall of Honor" for them in the classroom.

 Go to **www.mirrorsandwindows.com** for more.

THE PORTRAIT **55**

Find Meaning

1. The salesmen want to look responsible and trustworthy.
2. (a) Chuy is Don Mateo's son, who was killed in the Korean War. (b) It is the only picture his parents have of him as a young man.
3. (a) He goes to find the salesman who cheated him. (b) He helps a friend at the market and visits different barrios.

Make Judgments

4. The salesman probably made it up so that he could blame the prices and terms on someone else. He wants his customers to think he's on their side.
5. The salesman makes too many promises; perhaps the portrait will not be delivered as promised.
6. (a) He uses Don Mateo as the model. (b) He may have done the right thing, because what Don Mateo really wanted was not money, but a memento.

Analyze Literature

Plot Don Mateo confronting the salesman at the vegetable stand is the climax, and the portrait on display in Don Mateo's home represents the resolution. Students' explanations about their predictions will vary.

Program Resources

For further instruction, refer students to the following extension activity: Lifelong Learning: Research the Internet, *Exceeding the Standards: Extension Activities,* pp. 3–4.

Rubrics for Writing Options

You can adapt this as a checklist for students to use as they write.

Creative Writing

☐ Does the news report begin with an attention-grabbing first line?
☐ Does the report contain accurate facts and details?
☐ Does the report answer the questions *who, what, where, when, why,* and *how*?

Expository Writing

☐ Does the story summary describe the central problem and its solution?
☐ Does the summary describe the salesman's problem and how he solved it?
☐ Does the summary evaluate the outcome?

Teach the Workshop

Sentence Improvement

1. D
2. A
3. A

Build Skills

Some writers may choose a pronoun that leaves the antecedent vague or unclear, rather than being incorrect in gender or number. Often, students say *This* or *That,* referring to the preceding sentence. For example:

> I went to the garden and studied the summer sunlight on the grass. That was a beautiful thing.

Tell students they can often make an antecedent clearer by adding a noun after the pronoun *This* or *That.* In the example here, the writer could say:

> I went to the garden and studied the summer sunlight on the grass. That sunlight was a beautiful thing.

> ⊃ For more information, see Grammar & Style Section 3.7, Agreement, in the Language Arts Handbook.

Program Resources

You will find additional lessons on Pronoun-Antecedent Agreement in the *Exceeding the Standards: Grammar & Style* resource.

KEY TERMS

PRONOUN, 56
GENDER, 56
NUMBER, 56
ANTECEDENT, 56

Pronoun-Antecedent Agreement

Gender Agreement

Don Mateo was so angry that he took off to San Antonio....

—TOMÁS RIVERA, "The Portrait"

Pronouns must agree with their antecedents. That means pronouns must have the same number and gender as the word or words they refer to. **Gender** is the form a pronoun takes to show whether it is masculine, feminine, or gender neutral. **Number** refers to the singular or plural. In the sentence above, the antecedent *Don Mateo* is masculine, so the pronoun used is *he. Don Mateo* is singular, so the pronoun is also singular.

> **EXAMPLE**
> *Don Mateo went to the market. It was crowded with people.*

In this example, the pronoun *it* is gender neutral. Use *it* when the antecedent is not a person.

Unclear Antecedents

Make sure that the antecedent of each pronoun is clear and does not seem to refer to more than one pronoun. Also, avoid the pronouns *that, this, it,* and *which* when the antecedent is unclear.

> **EXAMPLE**
> *Many families were confused and angry. This was understandable.*

Clarify by restating the antecedent.

> **EXAMPLE**
> *Many families were confused and angry. Their feelings were understandable.*

A pronoun may sometimes seem to refer to multiple antecedents. In the following example, the antecedent of the pronoun *he* is unclear.

> **EXAMPLE**
> *After Don Mateo visited Esteban, he was pleased.*

Reword the sentence or remove the pronoun to correct this problem.

> **EXAMPLE**
> *Don Mateo was pleased after visiting Esteban.*

Sentence Improvement

For each of the following sentences, select the best revision of the underlined portion.

1. <u>Vieja was unhappy. She cried all day.</u>
  A. Vieja was unhappy. It cried all day.
  B. Vieja was unhappy. They cried all day.
  C. Vieja was unhappy. We cried all day.
  D. NO CHANGE

2. The townspeople found the rotting bag beneath a bridge. <u>They were sitting in a puddle of water.</u>
  A. It was sitting in a puddle of water.
  B. He was sitting in a puddle of water.
  C. She was sitting in a puddle of water.
  D. NO CHANGE

3. Don Mateo and Esteban were angry with the salesman. <u>He couldn't understand why the portrait would cost so much.</u>
  A. Esteban couldn't understand why the portrait would cost so much.
  B. She couldn't understand why the portrait would cost so much.
  C. It couldn't understand why the portrait would cost so much.
  D. NO CHANGE

TEACHING NOTE

Extra Practice

Have students identify the antecedent for the underlined pronoun in each sentence. If the antecedent is unclear, have students tell you how you might correct the writing to make the antecedent clear.

1. Eleanor and Lenore often turned in <u>their</u> work at the same time. (Eleanor and Lenore)
2. The horse tossed <u>its</u> sparkling head. (horse)
3. All of the children yelled at the clowns and threw their candy at <u>them</u>. (clowns)
4. After ordering her lunch, Jenna and Jake moved to the back of the line and waited for <u>it</u>. (lunch; some students may say *line.* If so, have them correct the sentence to clarify the antecedent.)

Common Core State Standards

Language
L.3.1f, L.6.1d

A Day's Wait

A Short Story by Ernest Hemingway

BEFORE READING

Build Background

Cultural Context The metric system was introduced in France in the 1790s in order to standardize units of measurement, which varied widely from country to country and even from town to town. In 1875, many countries, including the United States, signed the *Treaty of the Meter*, establishing the International Bureau of Weights and Measures. English-speaking countries have lagged in adopting the metric system. The United Kingdom did not begin to use metric units until 1965.

Reader's Context When has misinformation or lack of information caused you to be frightened of something?

Set Purpose

One way writers develop their characters is through dialogue. As you read "A Day's Wait," examine how the dialogue influences character development.

Analyze Literature

Conflict The plot of a story centers on a **conflict,** or struggle, that the main character has with internal or external forces. An *internal conflict* involves the character's struggle with emotions such as fear or love. An *external conflict* involves a struggle with outside forces such as nature, another character, or society. As you read "A Day's Wait," examine the conflict and try to determine if it is internal or external. Record your answers.

Meet the Author

Ernest Hemingway (1899–1961) is considered one of the greatest fiction writers of the twentieth century. His stories and novels, written in a distinctively spare and terse prose style, often reflect his lifelong love of hunting, fishing, and outdoor adventure. During World War I, an eye problem prevented him from joining the U.S. Army, so he served with an ambulance unit. He was wounded in the war and was awarded the Italian Silver Medal for Valor. Hemingway received a Pulitzer Prize in 1953 and the Nobel Prize for Literature in 1954.

Use Reading Skills

Draw Conclusions

When you draw conclusions, you use evidence from the text to support your ideas about characters, conflicts, and other literary elements. As you read "A Day's Wait," use a two-column chart to record details from this story. List details about the characters in the left-hand column and your conclusions about them in the right.

Details: Schatz keeps repeating that he is "all right."	Details:

Conclusions:

Preview Vocabulary

in·flu·en·za (in′ flu[′] en´ zə) *n.*, viral disease characterized by fever, muscular aches, and respiratory distress

ep·i·dem·ic (e′ pə de´ mik) *n.*, outbreak of contagious disease that spreads rapidly

flush (flʊsh) *adj.*, having a red color to the skin

Preview the Selection

At a Glance

Directed Reading

- Reading Level: Moderate
- Difficulty Consideration: Dialogue
- Ease Factor: Length

Objectives

Studying this lesson will enable students to

- use reading skills such as drawing conclusions
- analyze how characters deal with conflict
- describe the writing style of Ernest Hemingway and explain how his work influenced other writers
- appreciate a story about courage

Launch the Lesson

Before reading "A Day's Wait," ask students what it is like to have to stay in bed with an illness or an injury. What experience have they had like this? How did it feel? Did they worry, or were they bored? How did they pass the time?

 MIRRORS & WINDOWS The Mirrors & Windows questions at the end of the story focus on the theme of miscommunication. Before students begin reading, ask: Has an adult ever assumed you understood something when, in fact, you did not?

Words in Use

Preview Vocabulary
influenza, 58
epidemic, 58
flush, 59

Selection Words
purgative, 58
varnished, 59
covey, 59

Teaching Words
lagged, 57
distinctively, 57
spare, 57
terse, 57
valor, 57
imply, 60
anxiety, 62

KEY TERMS

SHORT STORY, 57
DIALOGUE, 57
CHARACTER DEVELOPMENT, 57
CONFLICT, 57
INTERNAL CONFLICT, 57
EXTERNAL CONFLICT, 57
CAUSE , 62
EFFECT, 62
FIRST PERSON
  POINT OF VIEW, 62
SUMMARY, 62

Common Core State Standards

Reading Literature
RL.1

Summary
Nine-year-old Schatz is feverish. The doctor says his temperature is one hundred and two. The doctor diagnoses a mild case of influenza and recommends bed rest and medication. The boy's father reads to him for a while, but Schatz says he need not stay if it "bothers" him, so the father goes out for a while. When he returns, Schatz, who is now extremely tense, asks how long it will be before he dies. After some discussion, the father learns that Schatz thought the doctor had taken his temperature with a Celsius thermometer. Knowing that a normal temperature in that system is thirty-seven degrees, Schatz had been waiting all day to die.

Analyze Literature
Characterization Ask students what the dialogue and the characters' actions reveal about them. Model a response: "The narrator's questions and instructions to Schatz show that he is caring and concerned. Calling the doctor immediately shows responsibility. The boy's responses indicate that he is determined and resigned." **A**

A Day's Wait

A Short Story by Ernest Hemingway

He came into the room to shut the windows while we were still in bed and I saw he looked ill. He was shivering, his face was white, and he walked slowly as though it ached to move.

"What's the matter, Schatz?"

"I've got a headache."

"You better go back to bed."

"No. I'm all right."

"You go to bed. I'll see you when I'm dressed."

A

But when I came downstairs he was dressed, sitting by the fire, looking a very sick and miserable boy of nine years. When I put my hand on his forehead I knew he had a fever.

"You go up to bed," I said, "you're sick."

"I'm all right," he said.

When the doctor came he took the boy's temperature.

"What is it?" I asked him.

"One hundred and two."

Downstairs, the doctor left three different medicines in different colored capsules with instructions for giving them. One was to bring down the fever, another a purgative, the third to overcome an acid condition. The germs of <u>influenza</u> can only exist in an acid condition, he explained. He seemed to know all about influenza and said there was nothing to worry about if the fever did not go above one hundred and four degrees. This was a light <u>epidemic</u> of flu and there was no danger if you avoided pneumonia.[1]

Back in the room I wrote the boy's temperature down and made a note of the time to give the various capsules.

"Do you want me to read to you?"

---

1. **pneumonia.** Disease marked by inflammation of the lungs

in·flu·en·za (in′ flu[′] en′ zə) *n.*, viral disease characterized by fever, muscular aches, and respiratory distress

ep·i·dem·ic (e′ pə de′ mik) *n.*, outbreak of contagious disease that spreads rapidly

58

Program Resources

Planning and Assessment
Program Planning Guide, Selection Lesson Plan
E-Lesson Planner
Assessment Guide, Lesson Test
ExamView

Technology Tools
Interactive Student Text on CD
Visual Teaching Package
Audio Library
mirrorsandwindows.com

Meeting the Standards
Fiction: Unit 1, Directed Reading, pp. 54–59

Differentiating Instruction
English Language Learners, Draw Conclusions, pp. 10–18

"All right. If you want to," said the boy. His face was very white and there were dark areas under his eyes. He lay still in the bed and seemed very detached from what was going on.

I thought perhaps he was a little lightheaded...

I read aloud from Howard Pyle's *Book of Pirates*; but I could see he was not following what I was reading.

"How do you feel, Schatz?" I asked him.

"Just the same, so far," he said.

I sat at the foot of the bed and read to myself while I waited for it to be time to give another capsule. It would have been natural for him to go to sleep, but when I looked up he was looking at the foot of the bed, looking very strangely.

"Why don't you try to go to sleep? I'll wake you up for the medicine."

"I'd rather stay awake."

After a while he said to me, "You don't have to stay in here with me, Papa, if it bothers you."

"It doesn't bother me."

"No, I mean you don't have to stay if it's going to bother you."

I thought perhaps he was a little lightheaded and after giving him the prescribed capsules at eleven o'clock I went out for a while. It was a bright, cold day, the ground covered with a sleet that had frozen so that it seemed as if all the bare trees, the bushes, the cut brush and all the grass and the bare ground had been varnished with ice. I took the young Irish setter for a little walk up the road and along a frozen creek, but it was difficult to stand or walk on the glassy surface and the red dog slipped and slithered and I fell twice, hard, once dropping my gun

B

and having it slide away over the ice.

We flushed[2] a covey of quail under a high clay bank with overhanging brush and I killed two as they went out of sight over the top of the bank. Some of the covey lit[3] in trees but most of them scattered into brush piles and it was necessary to jump on the ice-coated mounds of brush several times before they would flush. Coming out while you were poised unsteadily on the icy, springy brush they made difficult shooting, and I killed two, missed five and started back pleased to have found a covey close to the house and happy there were so many left to find on another day.

At the house they said the boy had refused to let anyone come into the room.

"You can't come in," he said. "You mustn't get what I have."

"Something like a hundred," I said.

I went up to him and found him in exactly the position I had left him, white-faced, but with the tops of his cheeks flushed by the fever, staring still as he had stared at the foot of the bed.

I took his temperature.

"What is it?"

"Something like a hundred," I said. It was one hundred and two and four tenths.

"It was a hundred and two," he said.

"Who said so?"

---

2. **flushed.** Frightened a game bird from cover
3. **covey lit.** Flock of birds came to rest

flush (flush) *adj.,* having a red color to the skin

Analyze Literature

Conflict Point out that while his father thought Schatz was fighting influenza, the boy was actually engaged in an internal conflict with his fear of death. **Ⓐ**

Answer. Students may say they would feel emotionally wrung out. They might suggest that, in the future, father and son should try harder to explain their thoughts and emotions.

Find Meaning

1. (a) There are both internal and external conflicts. (b) The internal conflict is central, because its resolution reveals the most about the main character.

2. (a) He knows the boy isn't seriously ill. (b) The boy may have felt let down about being left, as he thought, to die alone.

3. (a) He doesn't realize that there are different temperature scales, and he assumes his temperature is life-threatening. (b) His reaction may be reasonable for someone who is determined to be very strong.

Make Judgments

4. (a) Schatz doesn't want to worry his father. (b) He is self-sufficient and reserved.

5. The two have a somewhat distant, formal relationship.

"The doctor."

"Your temperature is all right," I said. "It's nothing to worry about."

"I don't worry," he said. "but I can't keep from thinking."

"Don't think," I said. "Just take it easy."

"I'm taking it easy," he said and looked straight ahead. He was evidently holding tight on to himself about something.

"Take this with water."

"Do you think it will do any good?"

"Of course it will."

I sat down and opened the *Pirate* book and commenced[4] to read, but I could see he was not following, so I stopped.

"About what time do you think I'm going to die?" he asked.

"What?"

"About how long will it be before I die?"

"You aren't going to die. What's the matter with you?"

"Oh, yes, I am. I heard him say a hundred and two."

"People don't die with a fever of one hundred and two. That's a silly way to talk."

"I know they do. At school in France the boys told me you can't live with forty-four degrees. I've got a hundred and two."

Ⓐ He had been waiting to die all day, ever since nine o'clock in the morning.

"You poor Schatz," I said. "Poor old Schatz. It's like miles and kilometers. You aren't going to die. That's a different thermometer. On that thermometer thirty-seven is normal. On this kind it's ninety-eight."

"Are you sure?"

"Absolutely," I said. "It's like miles and kilometers. You know, like how many kilometers we make when we drive seventy miles in the car?"

"Oh," he said.

But his gaze at the foot of the bed relaxed slowly. The hold over himself relaxed too, finally, and the next day it was very slack and he cried very easily at little things that were of no importance. ✤

---

4. commenced. Began

How would you feel at the end of the story if you were Schatz? What advice would you give him or his father to help them avoid future misunderstandings? How does communication play a vital role in solving and preventing problems?

Find Meaning

1. (a) What kind(s) of conflict can be found in this story? (b) What is the most important conflict in the story? Why?

2. (a) Why does the father go hunting instead of staying by his son's bedside? (b) How do you think the boy felt when his father went out?

3. (a) What causes the boy to think he is going to die? (b) Does his reaction seem reasonable? Why or why not?

Make Judgments

4. (a) At the beginning of the story, why does Schatz keep insisting that he's "all right"? (b) What does this behavior suggest about his character?

5. The narrator often refers to his son as "the boy." What does this imply about their relationship?

Differentiated Instruction

Enrichment

Some students might be interested in reporting on the 1918 influenza pandemic. Suggest that they find information on the number of fatalities worldwide, the spread of the disease, its effect on communities, flu treatments, and preventive measures. Other students could research the development and use of influenza vaccine.

Have students prepare oral reports to share their research with the class. Encourage them to use visual aids such as maps, charts, graphs, photographs, and drawings. Students should use these visual supports to enhance and confirm their understanding of complex spoken language.

In "A Day's Wait," a young boy's misunderstanding about a thermometer reading causes him to believe that he is about to die, and he spends an entire day in extreme, but needless, anxiety. The following selection is a press release from the National Aeronautics and Space Administration (NASA) that describes how a misunderstanding about units of measure affected a Mars space mission.

Mars Climate Orbiter Team Finds Likely Cause of Loss

A Press Release by NASA

A failure to recognize and correct an error in a transfer of information between the Mars Climate Orbiter spacecraft team in Colorado and the mission navigation team in California led to the loss of the spacecraft last week, preliminary findings by NASA's Jet Propulsion Laboratory internal peer review[1] indicate.

"People sometimes make errors," said Dr. Edward Weiler, NASA's Associate Administrator for Space Science. "The problem here was not the error, it was the failure of NASA's systems engineering,[2] and the checks and balances in our processes to detect the error. That's why we lost the spacecraft."

The peer review preliminary findings indicate that one team used English units (e.g., inches, feet and pounds) while the other used metric units for a key spacecraft operation. This information was critical to the maneuvers[3] required to place the spacecraft in the proper Mars orbit.

"Our inability to recognize and correct this simple error has had major implications," said Dr. Edward Stone, director of the Jet Propulsion Laboratory. "We have underway a thorough investigation to understand this issue."

Two separate review committees have already been formed to investigate the loss of Mars Climate Orbiter: an internal JPL peer group and a special review board of JPL and outside experts. An independent NASA failure review board will be formed shortly.

"Our clear short-term goal is to maximize the likelihood of a successful landing of the Mars Polar Lander on December 3," said Weiler. "The lessons from these reviews will be applied across the board in the future."

Mars Climate Orbiter was one of a series of missions in a long-term program of Mars

---

1. **peer review.** Process of subjecting work to the scrutiny of experts
2. **systems engineering.** Overall planning, design, and specifications for a project
3. **maneuvers.** Controlled movements

MARS CLIMATE ORBITER **61**

Teach the Connection

Media Connection
Press Releases Tell students that a press release is a written or recorded statement that an organization provides to the news media. Its purpose is to announce something that has news value. A press release may be mailed, faxed, or e-mailed to newspapers, magazines, radio stations, and television stations. Unlike a news article, which contains facts gathered by a reporter, a press release usually provides only information that is favorable to the organization that issues it.

Alert students may notice that the press release lacks the final comma in a series. Tell them that press releases usually are written in "Associated Press style," which does not require the final comma.

Use Reading Skills
Read Aloud Have students read aloud the press release as a televised news report. The "reporter" can read the body of the release, and two other students can read the quotations of Dr. Edward Weiler and Dr. Edward Stone. Encourage students to discuss what background visuals they would use for the "news story."

Research Skills

Compare Sources
Tell students that when gathering information for a research paper, they should compare the information from at least two reliable sources. If there are any discrepancies, they will need to find additional sources. Tell students that websites with .edu, .org, or .gov in the address generally provide reliable information.

Ask students to locate a website that provides a tool or chart for quickly converting between the U.S. and metric systems of measurement. Work with students to come up with keywords they can enter in a search engine to find the information they need (for example, *metric conversion*).

Common Core State Standards
Reading Literature
RL.1, RL.9
Reading Informational
RI.9
Writing
W.9

Science Connection

Costs of Mistakes You may wish to tell students that the lost spacecraft cost at least $125 million. Adding the costs of launching and monitoring the craft puts the total loss at nearly $300 million.

Text-to-Text Connection

Answer: Students should identify Schatz's confusion in Hemingway's short story and NASA's failure to complete its Mars Polar Landing Mission as similarities. They are very similar mistakes. The outcomes of the mistakes differ—NASA's failure cost more money than Schatz's fearful afternoon, but Schatz's experience could have serious emotional consequences. In both cases, people are likely to be more careful in the future.

Analyze Literature

Conflict Students could identify Schatz's misunderstanding of his temperature as a cause and his worry-filled afternoon as the effect, summarizing this as "Schatz spends a miserable day waiting to die because he misunderstands his temperature reading."

 More by This Author
Students who like "A Day's Wait" might enjoy Hemingway's novella *The Old Man and the Sea.*

---

exploration managed by the Jet Propulsion Laboratory for NASA's Office of Space Science, Washington, DC. JPL's industrial partner is Lockheed Martin Astronautics, Denver, CO. JPL is a division of the California Institute of Technology, Pasadena, CA. ❖

 TEXT TO **TEXT** CONNECTION   Both Hemingway's story and NASA's press release focus on mistakes related to units of measurement. In each selection, how do different measurement systems create problems? What is similar about the mistakes that are made? What is different?

AFTER READING

Analyze Literature

Conflict Identifying cause-and-effect relationships in a story helps you understand what happened and why. A *cause* is an event or action that brings about an *effect,* or outcome. Use a chart to analyze the cause and the effect of the conflict in "A Day's Wait." Then summarize the cause-and-effect relationship in a brief statement.

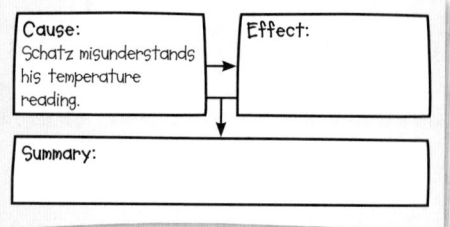

Extend Understanding

Writing Options

Creative Writing Write a **letter** to a friend in which you give a real or fictional account of a misunderstanding that caused you to experience anxiety. Use the first-person point of view, and include a summary of how the experience changed you.

Persuasive Writing Write an **editorial** for your local newspaper stating why all schools and industries in the United States should use metric measurements instead of the measurement system currently used in the United States. State your position in the topic sentence. Then argue for your position, including at least three reasons for your position. Organize your reasons by order of importance, and provide examples or supporting facts. Conclude your editorial by restating your position.

Critical Literacy

Create a Chart Create a chart for Schatz that shows the Fahrenheit equivalents for Celsius temperatures from 36 to 44 degrees. You can use library resources to research Fahrenheit and Celsius conversion formulas, or you can find a converter on the Internet, such as the one provided by the National Weather Service.

Media Literacy

Conduct Internet Research Perform key word searches with a search engine or an electronic library database to locate information about a problem or confusing situation caused by unit conversion. Summarize the information in one or two paragraphs, and present it to the class.

 Go to **www.mirrorsandwindows.com** for more.

Rubrics for Writing Options

You can adapt this as a checklist for students to use as they write.

Creative Writing
☐ Does the letter use first-person point of view?
☐ Does the account describe an internal conflict?
☐ Does the letter describe how the experience changed the writer?

Persuasive Writing
☐ Does the editorial include a topic sentence that clearly states the writer's opinion?
☐ Are at least three reasons included, organized by order of importance?
☐ Does the editorial include supporting examples or facts?
☐ Does the conclusion restate the writer's position?

The War of the Wall

A Short Story by Toni Cade Bambara

BEFORE READING

Build Background
Cultural Context Outdoor urban murals, or paintings on walls, emerged as a form of public art in the United States during the 1960s and 1970s. Urban murals have the potential to bring together communities through the expression of common interests and values. The themes often relate to the community in which the mural is located. The images often include cultural and religious symbols, historical events, contemporary events, and historical and contemporary leaders and personalities.

Reader's Context Where do you and your friends or family like to gather to relax and have fun? How would you feel if a stranger started to make a major change in that place?

Set Purpose
Paying attention to what the characters say, do, and think can help you understand why they feel or behave a certain way. Read to determine how the characters' needs, desires, or feelings affect their motivations.

Analyze Literature
Dialect A **dialect** is a version of a language spoken by people of a particular place, time, or group. Writers use dialect to develop characters, to establish setting, and to create a mood. As you read "The War of the Wall," think about what the characters' dialect tells you about them and what it adds to the atmosphere, or mood, of the story.

Meet the Author
Toni Cade Bambara (1939–1995) was deeply influenced by the Harlem, New York community where she spent the first years of her life. She published her first short story shortly after college. As a college professor, writer, social activist, and filmmaker, Bambara worked throughout her life to fight oppression and injustice. The themes of family and community are woven throughout Bambara's work.

Use Reading Skills
Analyze Cause and Effect In fiction, sometimes one event explains *why* another event takes place. The event that explains why is a *cause;* the event that results is an *effect.* Understanding cause-and-effect relationships can help you grasp the meaning of a story. Sometimes a single cause has several effects, and an effect can have several causes. As you read "The War of the Wall," use a chart to keep track of causes and effects.

Cause:	Effect:
A stranger is painting the wall that is the neighborhood's gathering place.	The narrator is angry.

Preview Vocabulary
mas·ter·piece (mas´ tər pēs') *n.,* artist's greatest work

trance (tran[t]s) *n.,* state of detachment from one's physical surroundings

lib·er·a·tion (lĭ' bə rā´ shən) *n.,* state of being free or of achieving civil rights

Preview the Selection

At a Glance
Directed Reading
- Reading Level: Moderate
- Difficulty Consideration: Historical references
- Ease Factor: Interesting plot

Objectives
Studying this lesson will enable students to
- use reading skills such as analyzing cause and effect
- define dialect and recognize its effect in the selection
- describe literary accomplishments of Toni Cade Bambara and explain how the Harlem community influenced her writing
- appreciate a story of creativity and discovery

Launch the Lesson
Before reading "The War of the Wall," ask students to share their ideas about a place they have—or would like to have—in their community where people can gather casually to enjoy outdoor activities and each other's company.

THE WAR OF THE WALL • **63**

Words in Use

Preview Vocabulary	Selection Words	Teaching Words
masterpiece, 66	courtesies, 65	urban, 63
trance, 66	aromas, 65	contemporary, 63
liberation, 70	scheme, 68	dialect, 63
		social activist, 63
		restrictive, 69

KEY TERMS
DIALECT, 63
MOOD, 63
CAUSE, 63
EFFECT, 63
SETTING, 71
DIALOGUE, 71
TONE, 71

Common Core State Standards
Reading Literature
RL.1
Writing
W.7, W.8

Teach the Selection

Summary

The narrator and Lou are outraged because a woman is beginning to paint a mural on "their" wall, a favorite gathering place in the neighborhood and a place where they have written an inscription to memorialize Jimmy Lyons, who was killed in Vietnam. Unsuccessful at stopping the artist, the two children decide to deface the mural with spray paint. Before they can carry out their plan, though, they find the entire neighborhood gathered around the completed mural, exclaiming over its depictions of African-American heroes and members of the community. A special inscription dedicates the wall to Jimmy Lyons and reveals that the artist is his cousin.

 The Mirrors & Windows questions at the end of the story focus on the theme of judging other people. Before students begin reading, ask: How does your neighborhood treat newcomers?

The War of the Wall

A Short Story by Toni Cade Bambara

64

Program Resources

Planning and Assessment
Program Planning Guide, Selection Lesson Plan
E-Lesson Planner
Assessment Guide, Lesson Test
ExamView

Technology Tools
Interactive Student Text on CD
Visual Teaching Package
Audio Library
mirrorsandwindows.com

Meeting the Standards
Fiction: Unit 1, Directed Reading, pp. 60–66

Differentiating Instruction
Developing Readers, Make Connections, pp. 4–6
Advanced Students, Historical Context Project, pp. 5–6
English Language Learners, Cause and Effect, pp. 19–31

M e and Lou had no time for courtesies. We were late for school. So we just flat out told the painter lady to quit messing with the wall. It was our wall, and she had no right coming into our neighborhood painting on it. Stirring in the paint bucket and not even looking at us, she mumbled something about Mr. Eubanks, the barber, giving her permission. That had nothing to do with it as far as we were concerned. We've been pitching pennies against that wall since we were little kids. Old folks have been dragging their chairs out to sit in the shade of the wall for years. Big kids have been playing handball against the wall since so-called integration[1] when the crazies 'cross town poured cement in our pool so we couldn't use it. I'd sprained my neck one time boosting my cousin Lou up to chisel Jimmy Lyons's name into the wall when we found out he was never coming home from the war in Vietnam to take us fishing.

"If you lean close," Lou said, leaning hipshot against her beat-up car, "you'll get a whiff of bubble gum and kids' sweat. And that'll tell you something—that this wall belongs to the kids of Taliaferro Street." **A** I thought Lou sounded very convincing. But the painter lady paid us no mind. She just snapped the brim of her straw hat down and hauled her bucket up the ladder.

"You're not even from around here," I hollered up after her. The license plates on her old piece of car said "New York." Lou dragged me away because I was about to grab hold of that ladder and shake it. And then we'd really be late for school.

When we came from school, the wall was slick with white. The painter lady was running string across the wall and taping it here and there. Me and Lou leaned against the gumball machine outside the pool hall and watched. She had strings up and down and back and forth. Then she began chalking them with a hunk of blue chalk.

So we just flat out told the painter lady to quit messing with the wall.

The Morris twins crossed the street, hanging back at the curb next to the beat-up car. The twin with the red ribbons was hugging a jug of cloudy lemonade. The one with yellow ribbons was holding a plate of dinner away from her dress. The painter lady began snapping the strings. The blue chalk dust measured off halves and quarters up and down and sideways too. Lou was about to say how hip it all was, but I dropped my book satchel on his toes to remind him we were at war.

B Some good aromas were drifting our way from the plate leaking pot likker[2] onto the Morris girl's white socks. I could tell from where I stood that under the tinfoil was baked ham, collard greens, and candied yams. And knowing Mrs. Morris, who sometimes bakes for my mama's restaurant, a slab of buttered cornbread was probably up

---

1. **integration.** Ending of segregation, or the separation of races
2. **pot likker.** Cooking juices

Teach the Selection

Analyze Literature
Characterization Ask students what the details in the first paragraph tell them about the narrator. Model a response based on one detail: "The narrator's use of the term 'so-called' to describe integration indicates that the narrator is African-American and has strong opinions."

Analyze Literature
Setting Point out the sensory images the author uses to describe the wall, such as "a whiff of bubble gum and kids' sweat." Suggest that students use a chart as they read to keep track of setting details and changes in the wall. **A**

Analyze Literature
Plot Ask students to make a prediction about the conflict in the story. Model a response: "The conflict will be between the narrator and the painter. I think that the narrator will try to stop the painter from working on the wall." **B**

Differentiated Instruction

Enrichment
Invite students to research outdoor urban murals in your own community or in cities around the United States. Students can use library or Internet sources to locate photographs of the murals. Have students display the murals and explain their subjects and themes. Ask students to find out who painted each mural and when it was painted. Suggest that they also try to find out how the neighborhood felt about the mural while it was being planned and painted, and how the neighborhood felt about it after it was completed. Then have the class vote on the urban mural they like best. Ask students to explain the reasons for their choice.

Cultural Connection

African American Cuisine The meal that the Morris twins offer to the painter is typical of African-American cuisine, sometimes called "soul food." It includes traditional foods from Africa, such as yams, grains, legumes, okra, and onions. It also includes foods that enslaved Africans on American plantations received either as rations or as discards from the plantation kitchen. They made creative use of ingredients such as turnip and beet tops, pokeweed, collards, dandelion greens, cornmeal, and molasses. For meat, they relied mostly on parts of the pig not used in the plantation kitchen—pig's feet, pig's ears, ham hocks, and tripe. The meat and greens were cooked in big pots with onions, garlic, and spices.

Use Reading Strategies

Make Inferences Ask students to consider what the scene with the Morris girls implies about the character of the neighborhood. Model a possible response: "This seems to be a neighborhood where people know each other and are friendly and hospitable." **Ⓐ**

---

under there too, sopping up some of the pot likker. Me and Lou rolled our eyes, wishing somebody would send us some dinner. But the painter lady didn't even turn around. She was pulling the strings down and prying bits of tape loose.

Side Pocket came strolling out of the pool hall to see what Lou and me were studying so hard. He gave the painter lady the once-over, checking out her paint-spattered jeans, her chalky T-shirt, her floppy-brimmed straw hat. He hitched up his pants and glided over toward the painter lady, who kept right on with what she was doing.

"Watcha got there, sweetheart?" he asked the twin with the plate.

"Suppah," she said all soft and countrylike.

"For her," the one with the jug added, jerking her chin toward the painter lady's back.

Still she didn't turn around. She was rearing back on her heels, her hands jammed into her back pockets, her face squinched up like the <u>masterpiece</u> she had in mind was taking shape on the wall by magic. We could have been gophers crawled up into a rotten hollow for all she cared. She didn't even say hello to anybody. Lou was muttering something about how great her concentration was. I butt him with my hip, and his elbow slid off the gum machine.

"Good evening," Side Pocket said in his best ain't-I-fine voice. But the painter lady was moving from the milk crate to the step stool to the ladder, moving up and down fast, scribbling all over the wall like a crazy person. We looked at Side Pocket. He looked at the twins. The twins looked at us. The painter lady was giving a show. It was like those old-timey music movies where the dancer taps on the tabletop and then starts jumping all over the furniture, kicking chairs

over and not skipping a beat. She didn't even look where she was stepping. And for a minute there, hanging on the ladder to reach a far spot, she looked like she was going to tip right over.

"Ahh," Side Pocket cleared his throat and moved fast to catch the ladder. "These young ladies here have brought you some supper."

"Ma'am?" The twins stepped forward. Finally the painter turned around, her eyes "full of sky," as my grandmama would say.

We could have been gophers crawled up into a rotten hollow for all she cared.

Then she stepped down like she was in a <u>trance</u>. She wiped her hands on her jeans as the Morris twins offered up the plate and the jug. She rolled back the tinfoil, then wagged her head as though something terrible was on the plate.

"Thank your mother very much," she said, sounding like her mouth was full of sky too. "I've brought my own dinner along." And then, without even excusing herself, she went back up the ladder, drawing on the wall in a wild way. Side Pocket whistled one of **Ⓐ**

---

mas·ter·piece (mas′ tər pēs′) *n.*, artist's greatest work
trance (tran[t]s) *n.*, state of detachment from one's physical surroundings

---

Reading Skills

Skim and Scan

Tell students that previewing a selection can help them focus their attention and connect with their prior knowledge. Previewing involves reading, scanning, and skimming. To preview, they should:
1. Read the title.
2. Scan the illustrations.
3. Skim the first paragraph.

Students can use what they learn to make predictions about the characters, plot, and setting, and they can list any questions they have about unfamiliar words or concepts. Previewing can also help them decide how to read the selection. If it looks complicated, they can read it slowly or read it several times. Have students preview "The War of the Wall" and share their predictions and questions.

those oh-brother breathy whistles and went back into the pool hall. The Morris twins shifted their weight from one foot to the other, then crossed the street and went home. Lou had to drag me away, I was so mad. We couldn't wait to get to the firehouse to tell my daddy all about this rude woman who'd stolen our wall.

All the way back to the block to help my mama out at the restaurant, me and Lou kept asking my daddy for ways to run the painter lady out of town. But my daddy was busy talking about the trip to the country and telling Lou he could come too because Grandmama can always use an extra pair of hands on the farm.

Later that night, while me and Lou were in the back doing our chores, we found out that the painter lady was a liar. She came into the restaurant and leaned against the glass of the steam table, talking about how starved she was. I was scrubbing pots and Lou was chopping onions, but we could hear her through the service window. She was asking Mama was that a ham hock in the greens, and was that a neck bone in the pole beans, and were there any vegetables cooked without meat, especially pork.

"I don't care who your spiritual leader is," Mama said in that way of hers. "If you eat in the community, sistuh, you gonna eat pig by-and-by, one way or t'other." **C**

Me and Lou were cracking up in the kitchen, and several customers at the counter were clearing their throats, waiting for Mama to really fix her wagon for not speaking to the elders when she came in. The painter lady took a stool at the counter and went right on with her questions. Was there cheese in the baked macaroni, she wanted to know? Were there eggs in the salad? Was it honey or sugar in the iced tea? Mama was fixing Pop Johnson's plate. And every time the painter lady asked a fool question, Mama would dump another spoonful of rice on the pile. She was tapping her foot and heating up in a dangerous way. But Pop Johnson was happy as he could be. Me and Lou peeked through the service window, wondering what planet the painter lady came from. Who ever heard of baked macaroni without cheese, or potato salad without eggs? **D**

"Do you have any bread made with unbleached flour?" the painter lady asked Mama. There was a long pause, as though everybody in the restaurant was holding their breath, wondering if Mama would dump the next spoonful on the painter lady's head. She didn't. But when she set Pop Johnson's plate down, it came down with a bang. When Mama finally took her order, the starving lady all of a sudden couldn't make up her mind whether she wanted a vegetable plate or fish and a salad. She finally settled on the broiled trout and a tossed salad. But just when Mama reached for a plate to serve her, the painter lady leaned over the counter with her finger all up in the air.

"Excuse me," she said. "One more thing." Mama was holding the plate like a Frisbee,

THE WAR OF THE WALL **67**

Vocabulary Skills

Idioms

Remind students that an idiom is an informal expression whose meaning cannot be understood from the meaning of the individual words in the expression. One way to understand an idiom is to form a mental image of it. For example, *to open fire on* someone does not mean to literally shoot the person, but the image these words create conveys strong hostility, leading to the understanding that *to open fire on* means "to express anger verbally." Ask students what mental images they form when they think about the following idioms.

1. run out of town
2. cracking up
3. fix her wagon

Analyze Literature

Plot Point out that the conflict between Mama and the painter lady over the dinner fuels the narrator's dislike of the woman, and prompts the narrator to try to gain Mama's support in stopping the artist's work. Ask students to describe Mama's attitude toward the conflict. (Mama regrets her annoyance with the painter; she doesn't share the narrator's concern about the wall.) **A**

Cultural Connection

Graffiti Explain that the word *graffiti* is the plural of the Italian word *graffito* and is related to *sgraffito*, which is a way of scratching a design into a surface; this technique was often used to decorate ceramics. In ancient times, *graffiti* referred to inscriptions or decorations scratched on walls. In modern times, the word has become associated with vandalism, usually by spray-painting exterior walls or sidewalks with intricate designs and symbols. **B**

Use Reading Strategies

Clarify Students may not understand why the painter turned down the dinner the Morris twins offered, or why she asks so many questions at the restaurant about the ingredients of each dish. Point out that the painter is most likely a vegetarian, and asks questions to determine which dishes contain no meat. Explain that when Mama says, "I don't care who your spiritual leader is," she is referring to the fact that some religions advocate a vegetarian diet.

tapping that foot, one hand on her hip. "Can I get raw beets in that tossed salad?"

"You will get," Mama said, leaning her face close to the painter lady's, "whatever Lou back there tossed. Now sit down." And the painter lady sat back down on her stool and shut right up.

A All the way to the country, me and Lou tried to get Mama to open fire on the painter lady. But Mama said that seeing as how she was from the North, you couldn't expect her to have any manners. Then Mama said she was sorry she'd been so impatient with the woman because she seemed like a decent person and was simply trying to stick to a very strict diet. Me and Lou didn't want to hear that. Who did that lady think she was, coming into our neighborhood and taking over our wall?

"Welllllll," Mama drawled, pulling into the filling station so Daddy could take the wheel, "it's hard on an artist, ya know. They can't always get people to look at their work. So she's just doing her work in the open, that's all."

Me and Lou definitely did not want to hear that. Why couldn't she set up an easel downtown or draw on the sidewalk in her own neighborhood? Mama told us to quit fussing so much; she was tired and wanted to rest. She climbed into the back seat and dropped down into the warm hollow Daddy had made in the pillow.

All weekend long, me and Lou tried to scheme up ways to recapture our wall. Daddy and Mama said they were sick of hearing about it. Grandmama turned up the TV to drown us out. On the late news was a story about the New York subways. When a train came roaring into the station all covered from top to bottom, windows too, with

All weekend long, me and Lou tried to scheme up ways to recapture our wall.

writings and drawings done with spray paint, me and Lou slapped five. Mama said it was too bad kids in New York had nothing better to do than spray paint all over the trains. **B** Daddy said that in the cities, even grown-ups wrote all over the trains and buildings too. Daddy called it "graffiti." Grandmama called it a shame.

We couldn't wait to get out of school on Monday. We couldn't find any black spray paint anywhere. But in a junky hardware

---

Differentiated Instruction

Reading Proficiency

Students may stumble over the dialect in the story. To help them read it more fluently, have them read along while you and a confident student read some of the dialogue (with dialect) aloud.

Kinesthetic Learning

Students may benefit from acting out the restaurant scene in which the painter's questions cause Mama to start "tapping her foot and heating up in a dangerous way." After they act it out, ask students to explain how this scene contributes to the plot, characters, and setting.

store downtown we found a can of white epoxy paint, the kind you touch up old refrigerators with when they get splotchy and peely. We spent our whole allowance on it. And because it was too late to use our bus passes, we had to walk all the way home lugging our book satchels and gym shoes, and the bag with the epoxy. When we reached the corner of Taliaferro and Fifth, it looked like a block party or something. Half the neighborhood was gathered on the sidewalk in front of the wall. I looked at Lou, he looked at me. We both looked at the bag with the epoxy and wondered how we were going to work our scheme. The painter lady's car was nowhere in sight. But there were too many people standing around to do anything. Side Pocket and his buddies were leaning on their cue sticks, hunching each other. Daddy was there with a lineman he catches a ride with on Mondays. Mrs. Morris had her arms flung around the shoulders of the twins on either side of her. Mama was talking with some of her customers, many of them with napkins still at the throat. Mr. Eubanks came out of the barbershop, followed by a man in a striped poncho, half his face shaved, the other half full of foam.

"She really did it, didn't she?" Mr. Eubanks huffed out his chest. Lots of folks answered right quick that she surely did when they saw the straight razor in his hand.

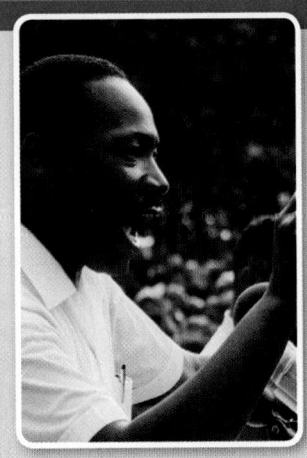

(C) Mama beckoned us over. And then we saw it. The wall. Reds, greens, figures outlined in black. Swirls of purple and orange. Storms of blues and yellows. It was something. I recognized some of the faces right off. There was Martin Luther King, Jr. And there was a man with glasses on and his mouth open like he was laying down a heavy rap. Daddy came up alongside and reminded us that was Minister Malcolm X. The serious

HISTORY ▶▶ CONNECTION

Civil Rights Throughout the first half of the twentieth century, African Americans struggled against restrictive segregation laws. In spite of the 1954 Supreme Court ruling against segregation in public schools, segregation and discrimination persisted. The Civil Rights era of the 1960s was inspired by leaders such as Martin Luther King, Jr., who encouraged blacks and whites to engage in demonstrations, sit-ins, and "freedom rides" in order to achieve integration and voting rights for African Americans. Why might it be important to remember these historical events? **(E)**

woman with a rifle I knew was Harriet Tubman because my grandmama has pictures of her all over the house. And I knew Mrs. Fannie Lou Hamer 'cause a signed photograph of her hangs in the restaurant next to the calendar.

Then I let my eyes follow what looked like a vine. It trailed past a man with a horn, a woman with a big white flower in her hair, a handsome dude in a tuxedo seated at a

Use Reading Strategies

Ask Questions Prompt students to ask questions about the actions of the narrator and Lou on Monday. ("Why do they want to buy black spray paint? Do they plan to cover up the mural with it? Will the white epoxy paint cover up the mural? What will happen if they get caught defacing the mural?") **(C)**

Analyze Literature

Setting Ask students what details in the description of the scene help convey the mood of excitement. (One man is half-shaved, diners are still wearing their napkins—people have stopped what they were doing to rush out and look at the wall.) **(D)**

History Connection

Civil Rights *Answer:* Answers will vary. Many students will say that it is good to honor cultural heroes and that the lessons of the past have relevance for the present. **(E)**

Grammar Skills

Punctuate Dialogue

"Good evening," the young man said.

Display this sentence and explain that the young man's exact words are enclosed in quotation marks. A comma separates his words from the rest of the sentence.

"I'm hungry," she said. "What is today's special?"

Point out that all punctuation marks that go with the direct quotation itself, such as the question mark here, fall inside the quotation marks. Note that a direct quotation should begin with a capital letter. Have students punctuate the following quotations.

1. This meal said the woman is delicious
2. Come here he said look at this wall

History Connection

Colonialism in Africa By the early 1900s, European powers had colonized almost all of Africa, exploiting natural resources and restricting the population's freedom. African resistance to colonialism grew throughout the twentieth century and peaked after World War II. Ghana achieved independence in 1957. Tanzania was one of fourteen African countries to become independent in the 1960s. Guinea-Bissau, Angola, and Mozambique won independence in the 1970s. **Ⓐ**

Make Connections

Ask students how the inscription changes their feelings about the painter lady. (What they perceived as rudeness may have been caused by her grief for her cousin.) **Ⓑ**

Answer: Students may say that most snap judgments are negative because they result from something that triggers a negative emotional response. Factors that may lead people to make snap judgments include jealousy, fear, unwillingness to accept change, territoriality, and distrust of "outsiders."

---

piano, and a man with a goatee[3] holding a book. When I looked more closely, I realized that what had looked like flowers were really faces. One face with yellow petals looked just like Frieda Morris. One with red petals looked just like Hattie Morris. I could hardly believe my eyes.

...as though he'd been waiting all his life to give this lesson.

"Notice," Side Pocket said, stepping close to the wall with his cue stick like a classroom pointer. "These are the flags of <u>liberation</u>," he said in a voice I'd never heard him use before. We all stepped closer while he pointed and spoke. "Red, black and green," he said, his pointer falling on the leaflike flags of the vine. "Our liberation flag. And **Ⓐ** here, Ghana, there Tanzania. Guinea-Bissau, Angola, Mozambique."[4] Side Pocket sounded very tall, as though he'd been waiting all his life to give this lesson.

Mama tapped us on the shoulder and pointed to a high section of the wall. There was a fierce-looking man with his arms crossed against his chest guarding a bunch of children. His muscles bulged, and he looked a lot like my daddy. One kid was looking at

a row of books. Lou hunched me 'cause the kid looked like me. The one that looked like Lou was spinning a globe on the tip of his finger like a basketball. There were other kids there with microscopes and compasses. And the more I looked, the more it looked like the fierce man was not so much guarding the kids as defending their right to do what they were doing.

Then Lou gasped and dropped the paint bag and ran forward, running his hands over a rainbow. He had to tiptoe and stretch to do it, it was so high. I couldn't breathe either. The painter lady had found the chisel marks and had painted Jimmy Lyons's name in a rainbow.

"Read the inscription,[5] honey," Mrs. Morris said, urging little Frieda forward. She didn't have to urge much. Frieda marched right up, bent down, and in a loud voice that made everybody quit oohing and ahhing and listen, she read,

Ⓑ *To the People of Taliaferro Street*
I Dedicate This Wall of Respect
Painted in Memory of My Cousin
Jimmy Lyons ❖

---

3. **goatee.** Small beard on the chin, sometimes trimmed into a point
4. **Ghana, Tanzania, Guinea-Bissau, Angola, Mozambique.** African countries that were once under European domination
5. **inscription.** Message written or carved on a surface

lib·er·a·tion (lǐ' bə rā´ shən) *n.*, state of being free or of achieving civil rights

Have you ever made a snap judgment about someone and later regretted it? Are snap judgments more often positive or negative? What are some of the factors that lead people to make snap judgments about others?

Differentiated Instruction

Visual Learning

Invite students to sketch their ideas of what the completed mural looks like. Ask them to add a caption for each person portrayed in the mural. Captions should include the person's name and a fact about the person's life. When they are done, ask students to explain what the wall now means to the neighborhood.

English Language Learning

Students may be confused by the nonstandard English of the characters' dialect. Pair English language learners with English-proficient readers and ask the proficient students to clarify any confusing dialogue by rephrasing it as standard English.

Find Meaning

1. (a) What is the setting of the story? (b) What details provide clues about the time and place?

2. (a) How do the children of Taliaferro Street feel about the wall? Explain. (b) Why are they angry with the painter?

3. (a) What do the narrator and Lou decide to do in order to "recapture" their wall? (b) What causes them to change their plan?

Analyze Literature

Dialect Writers use dialect to create a realistic mood, or atmosphere, in a story. In "The War of the Wall," the narrator uses dialect in telling the story as well as in the dialogue. Scan the story for examples of dialect. Use a chart to record examples of dialect and to describe the mood or feeling the dialect creates. Discuss how the use of dialect heightens the conflict with the painter.

Dialect Examples	Effect on Mood
"If you eat in the community, sistuh, you gonna eat pig by-and-by, one way or t'other."	

Make Judgments

4. (a) What words would you use to describe the painter's behavior? (b) Why do you think the author portrayed the painter in this way?

5. (a) Are the adults as angry with the painter as the children are? Explain. (b) What might explain their attitude?

6. (a) How does the narrator's attitude toward the painter change? (b) What lesson might be learned from the narrator's experience?

Extend Understanding

Writing Options

Creative Writing Tone is a speaker's emotional attitude toward the subject. Use the narrator's dialect to write the **dialogue** that the narrator and Lou might have had as they planned the wall's "recapture." Remember that they "slapped five" after they saw the spray-painted subway trains. Try to capture that attitude, or tone, in your dialogue. With a partner, read aloud your dialogue for the class.

Expository Writing Write a brief **research essay** that explains, for teenagers from another country, the Civil Rights era that is reflected in this story. Connect the historical and cultural setting to examples from the story. Be sure to cite the sources from which you draw your information.

Lifelong Learning

Write a Biography Research the life of one of the people depicted in the mural, using both primary sources (firsthand accounts such as letters and diaries) and secondary sources (descriptions or explanations of primary sources such as encyclopedias and textbooks). Write a brief biography to be placed in a classroom resource center.

Media Literacy

Analyze Urban Murals Use the Internet to locate at least three images of urban murals like the one in the story. With these images, prepare an actual or virtual slide show for your classmates in which you evaluate and analyze the images, describe the artists' purposes, and state your own opinion.

 Go to **www.mirrorsandwindows.com** for more.

THE WAR OF THE WALL **71**

Find Meaning

1. (a) It is the 1970s, in the U.S. South. (b) Clues include the Vietnam war, the dialect, the "soul food" dinner, the neighborhood pool hall and restaurant, and busses.

2. (a) The wall belongs to the community, because people play and gather there, and it has a memorial to Jimmy Lyons. (b) No stranger has a right to change "their" wall.

3. (a) They decide to cover the art with spray paint, and they buy paint. (b) They see that the painting honors their history and community.

Make Judgments

4. (a) Words might include *rude, distant, abrupt, superior, show-off, creative, finicky,* and *reserved.* (b) The painter's behavior and the reaction to it help build suspense.

5. (a) The adults are not as angry. After taking the dinner order, Mama adopts a tolerant attitude. (b) The adults may know who the painter is and her plans for the wall.

6. (a) At the beginning, the narrator is angry; at the end, the narrator is respectful. (b) Don't make snap judgments.

Analyze Literature

Dialect Many examples are possible. One would be: "If you eat in the community, sistuh, you gonna eat pig by-and-by, one way or t'other," which creates a hostile mood. The community's dialect contrasts with the painter's speech, emphasizing her status as an outsider.

Rubrics for Writing Options

You can adapt this as a checklist for students to use as they write.

Creative Writing

☐ Does the student's dialogue capture the narrator's tone of defiance and determination?

☐ Does the dialogue make use of dialect?

☐ Does the dialogue set forth a plan that logically connects to the spray-painted subway trains?

Expository Writing

☐ Does the research essay provide relevant information about the Civil Rights era?

☐ Does the essay include examples from the story and show how they reflect the historical and cultural setting?

☐ Does the essay cite reference sources?

Sentence Improvement

1. she
2. We, her
3. she
4. him
5. me
6. I

Build Skills

It can be challenging to choose the correct pronoun when faced with either a compound object of a preposition or a predicate pronoun.

A compound object of a preposition calls for an objective pronoun, but sometimes the position of the prepositional phrase suggests that nominative would be correct. Give this example:

• For Bill and her (not for Bill and she), it was a big surprise.

A predicate pronoun completes a sentence with a form of the verb *to be*. Work with a volunteer to model answering the telephone. Have the volunteer ask "Is [your name] there?" Answer "This is he/she." Offer some other examples. They may sound awkward, but assure students that they are correct. Let them reverse the sentences to hear it.

• The smartest students are we (not *us;* we are the smartest students).
• The villain is probably she (not *her;* she is probably the villain).

> For more information, see Grammar & Style Section 3.4, Pronouns, in the Language Arts Handbook.

Grammar & Style

Nominative and Objective Pronouns

Nominative Pronouns

I recognized some of the faces right off.
—TONI CADE BAMBARA, "The War of the Wall"

In the sentence above, the pronoun *I* is the subject of the verb *recognized*. When a pronoun is the subject of a verb, you use the **nominative** case of the pronoun. The nominative case includes *I, you, he, she, it, we,* and *they.*

Sometimes the subject of a verb is compound. This can be confusing. If you are not sure which pronoun to use, try each part of the sentence separately.

> **EXAMPLE**
> *Lou and (me / I) bought white paint to cover the mural.*

Look closely at the sentence to choose the correct pronoun. The nominative pronoun will still be correct without the word *Lou. Me bought white paint* is incorrect, so the pronoun must be *I.*

When a pronoun or noun appears after a linking verb and refers back to the subject of the sentence, it is called a **predicate nominative.**

> **EXAMPLE**
> *The painter lady is she.*

In the above example, the predicate nominative is *she,* and the subject of the sentence is *painter lady.* Remember to use nominative pronouns after linking verbs.

Objective Pronouns

Lou had to drag me away...
—TONI CADE BAMBARA, "The War of the Wall"

In this sentence, the pronoun *me* is the object of the verb *drag.* What was dragged away? *Me.* When the verb acts upon an object, you use the **objective** case of the pronoun. The objective case includes *me, you, him, her, it, us,* and *them.*

> **EXAMPLE**
> *Mama told Lou and (me / I) to stop fussing so much.*

As above, if you are not sure which pronoun to use, try each part of the sentence separately.

The objective pronoun will still be correct if you remove the word *Lou. Mama told I to stop fussing so much* is incorrect. The correct pronoun must be *me.*

Like the subject of a sentence, the object can sometimes be compound. If you are not sure which pronoun to use, try each part of the sentence separately.

Sentence Improvement

For each of the following sentences, choose the correct pronoun in parentheses.

1. The children couldn't believe that (her / she) refused Mrs. Morris's hospitality.
2. (We / us) told (her / she) about the painter lady's rudeness.
3. The artist is probably (her / she).
4. We wanted (he / him) to help run the painter lady out of town, but Daddy refused.
5. The mural included paintings of Daddy and (I / me).
6. Mama and (me / I) were amazed by all the pictures on the wall.

KEY TERMS

PRONOUN, 72
SUBJECT, 72
VERB, 72
NOMINATIVE PRONOUN, 72
COMPOUND, 72
PREDICATE NOMINATIVE, 72
LINKING VERB, 72
OBJECTIVE PRONOUN, 72

Program Resources

You will find additional lessons on Nominative and Objective Pronouns in the *Exceeding the Standards: Grammar & Style* resource.

Common Core State Standards

Language
L.6.1c

The Foghorn

A Short Story by Ray Bradbury

BEFORE READING

Build Background

Historical Context Lighthouses date back to ancient Egypt, where beacon fires were kept lit to guide ships. The first lighthouse in the United States was built in 1716. Early lighthouses used candles, fires, and oil lamps to create light. In the late 1800s, electricity was first used. Early audio warnings included bells, whistles, cannons, and rockets. Steam-powered foghorns began to be widely used in the 1860s. With the increased use of electricity and radar in the twentieth century, the need for lighthouses declined.

Reader's Context If you feared that you might be the last person in the world, what would you do to try to find another human being?

Set Purpose

Preview the title of the story and think about what you can infer about the setting. Where are foghorns most commonly used? Read to determine what role the foghorn plays in the story.

Analyze Literature

Mood The **mood** of a story is the emotional response that it evokes in the reader. Writers use a variety of techniques to create mood, including word choice and setting details. As you read "The Foghorn," make a list of words and details that create feelings and emotions for you.

Meet the Author

Ray Bradbury (b. 1920) has won countless awards for his science fiction and fantasy. In 1934, Bradbury's family moved from Illinois to Los Angeles, California, where, as a high school student, he first became interested in writing. His short stories and novels are poetic and fanciful, but they address serious themes such as the value of individuality and modern society's overdependence on technology.

Use Reading Skills
Use Context Clues
Preview the vocabulary words from this story as they are used in the sentences below. Try to unlock the meaning of each word using the context clues provided.

1. Before you turn in your research paper, <u>verify</u> the facts to make sure they are accurate.
2. The archaeologists are searching for clues about the ancient <u>primeval</u> world of the dinosaurs.
3. Don't worry—if you fail this test, it's nothing to <u>brood</u> about.

Preview Vocabulary

ver·i·fy (ver´ ə fī´) v., test or check for correctness

pri·me·val (prī mē´ vəl) adj., from the earliest ages

brood (brüd) v., dwell on a gloomy subject; worry

Preview the Selection

At a Glance
Directed Reading
- Reading Level: Moderate
- Difficulty Consideration: Vocabulary
- Ease Factor: Style

Objectives

Studying this lesson will enable students to
- use reading skills such as context clues
- analyze mood
- experience Ray Bradbury's style of storytelling
- synthesize content from different texts

Launch the Lesson

Before reading "The Foghorn," discuss with students whether people are necessarily lonely when they are alone. Ask them to consider the following questions: "How is it possible to feel lonely in a crowd? Why might the feeling of loneliness be more painful than the feeling of being alone? When you feel lonely, what can you do about your situation?"

THE FOGHORN **73**

Words in Use

Preview Vocabulary	Selection Words	Teaching Words
verify, 76	ascended, 76	beacon, 73
primeval, 77	apparatus, 77	evokes, 73
brood, 80	raveling, 77	overdependence, 73
		capsizing, 79
		cephalopod, 79

Common Core State Standards

Reading Literature
RL.1, RL.4

Teach the Selection

Summary

McDunn is keeper of the Lonesome Bay lighthouse, which is perched on a rock two miles out in the ocean. On a foggy November night, a gigantic, long-necked dinosaur-like creature comes swimming toward the lighthouse, answering the foghorn's call with its own. It comes every year at this time, McDunn tells the narrator, probably because the lonely ancient creature thinks the foghorn is one of its own kind. As an experiment, McDunn turns off the foghorn, and the creature, in frustration and despair, destroys the lighthouse and swims away. When rescuers come the next day, McDunn, who knows that the creature won't return, tells them that the waves caused the lighthouse to crumble.

 MIRRORS & WINDOWS The Mirrors & Windows questions at the end of the story focus on the theme of patience. Before students begin reading, ask: How long should a person wait for happiness?

The Foghorn

A Short Story by Ray Bradbury

74

Program Resources

Planning and Assessment
Program Planning Guide, Selection Lesson Plan
E-Lesson Planner
Assessment Guide, Lesson Test
ExamView

Technology Tools
Interactive Student Text on CD
Visual Teaching Package
Audio Library
mirrorsandwindows.com

Meeting the Standards
Fiction: Unit 1, Directed Reading, pp. 67–72

Differentiating Instruction
Developing Readers, Visualize/Text
  organization, pp. 7–12

> ## "One night, years ago,
> ## I was here alone, when all of the fish of the sea
> ## surfaced out there."

Out there in the cold water, far from land, we waited every night for the coming of the fog, and it came, and we oiled the brass machinery and lit the fog light up in the stone tower. Feeling like two birds in the gray sky, McDunn and I sent the light touching out, red, then white, then red again, to eye the lonely ships. If they did not see our light, then there was always our Voice, the great deep cry of our Fog Horn. It shuddered through the rags of mist to startle the gulls away like decks of scattered cards and make the waves turn high and foam.

"It's a lonely life, but you're used to it now, aren't you?" asked McDunn.

"Yes," I said. "You're a good talker, thank the Lord."

"Well, it's your turn on land tomorrow," he said, smiling, "to dance with the ladies."

"What do you think, McDunn, when I leave you out here alone?"

"On the mysteries of the sea." McDunn lit his pipe. It was a quarter past seven on a cold November evening, the heat on, the light switching its tail in two hundred directions, the Fog Horn bumbling in the high throat of the tower. There wasn't a town for a hundred miles down the coast, just a road, which came lonely through dead country to the sea, with few cars on it, a stretch of two miles of cold water out to our rock, and rare few ships.

"The mysteries of the sea," said McDunn thoughtfully. "You know, the ocean's the biggest snowflake ever? It rolls and swells a thousand shapes and colors, no two alike. Strange. One night, years ago, I was here alone, when all of the fish of the sea surfaced out there. Something made them swim in and lie in the bay, sort of trembling. They stared up at the tower light going red, white, red, white across them so I could see their funny eyes. I turned cold. They were like a big peacock's tail, moving out there until midnight. Then, without so much as a sound, they slipped away. The million of them was gone. I kind of think maybe, in some sort of way, they came all those miles to worship. Strange. But think how the tower must look to them, standing seventy feet above the water, the God-light flashing out from it, and the tower declaring itself with a monster voice. They never came back, those fish, but don't you think for a while they thought they were in the Presence?"

(A) I shivered. I looked out at the long gray lawn of the sea stretching away into nothing and nowhere.

"Oh, the sea's full." McDunn puffed his pipe nervously, blinking. He had been nervous all day and hadn't said why. "For all our engines and so-called submarines, it'll be ten thousand centuries before we set foot on the real bottom of the sunken lands, in the

Differentiated Instruction

English Language Learning
Define the following words and expressions for students:

beard of a comet—long tail of melting dust and gas that trails off an icy rock that orbits the sun, 76
duffel—large waterproof bag, 76
reek—stench or smell, 81

Use Reading Strategies

Make Inferences Based on McDunn's story about the gathering of the fish and on what he says about the undersea world, ask students how he feels about sea creatures. (He feels awestruck by how ancient they are; he feels sympathetic toward them; he thinks they have feelings.)

Analyze Literature

Setting Point out that the lighthouse is compared to an animal again, with its "eye" of light and the Fog Horn that sounds "like an animal." Tell students to keep in mind that the Fog Horn blows steadily throughout the story. Suggest that they consider the effects of such personification as they read. **A**

Use Reading Strategies

Make Predictions Ask students what they think will visit the lighthouse. Tell them to check and change their predictions as they continue to read. **B**

fairy kingdoms there, and know real terror. Think of it. It's still the year 300,000 Before Christ down under there. While we've paraded around with trumpets, lopping off each other's countries and heads, they have been living beneath the sea twelve miles deep and cold in a time as old as the beard of a comet." **B**

"Yes, it's an old world."

"Come on. I got something special I been saving up to tell you."

We ascended the eighty steps, talking and taking our time. At the top, McDunn switched off the room lights so there'd be no reflection in the plate glass. The great eye of the light was humming, turning easily in its oiled socket. The Fog Horn was blowing steadily, once every fifteen seconds.

daft.[1] But tonight's the latest I can put it off, for if my calendar's marked right from last year, tonight's the night it comes. I won't go into detail; you'll have to see it yourself. Just sit down there. If you want, tomorrow you can pack your duffel and take the motorboat into land and get your car parked there at the dinghy pier[2] on the cape and drive on back to some little inland town and keep your lights burning nights. I won't question or blame you. It's happened three years now, and this is the only time anyone's been here with me to <u>verify</u> it. You wait and watch."

Half an hour passed with only a few whispers between us. When we grew tired waiting, McDunn began describing some of his ideas to me. He had some theories about the Fog Horn itself.

"About this time of year," he said, studying the murk and fog, "something comes to visit the lighthouse."

A "Sounds like an animal, don't it?" McDunn nodded to himself. "A big lonely animal crying in the night. Sitting here on the edge of ten billion years calling out to the Deeps, I'm here, I'm here, I'm here. And the Deeps do answer, yes, they do. You been here now for three months, Johnny, so I better prepare you. About this time of year," he said, studying the murk and fog, "something comes to visit the lighthouse."

"The swarms of fish like you said?"

"No, this is something else. I've put off telling you because you might think I'm

"One day many years ago a man walked along and stood in the sound of the ocean on a cold sunless shore and said, 'We need a voice to call across the water, to warn ships. I'll make one. I'll make a voice like all of time and all of the fog that ever was; I'll make a voice that is like an empty bed beside you all night long, and like an empty house when you open the door, and like trees in autumn with no leaves. A sound like the birds flying

---

1. daft. Insane; crazy
2. dinghy pier. Docking place for small boats

ver•i•fy (ver´ ə fī') v., test or check for correctness

Differentiated Instruction

Reading Proficiency
Have small groups create time lines for the story. As they read, they should add such events as when McDunn first came to the lighthouse, when Johnny started working there, and when the fish gathered in the sea. Tell students they may use their completed time lines to review the story and as guides for retelling the story.

Enrichment
Some students might wish to debate the possibility of the continued existence of dinosaur-like creatures. As a class, create a large pro-and-con chart on the board, listing reasons for and against the likelihood of such a creature's existence.

> *The head rose a full forty feet above the water on a slender and beautiful dark neck.*

south, crying, and a sound like November wind and the sea on the hard, cold shore. I'll make a sound that's so alone that no one can miss it, that whoever hears it will weep in their souls, and hearths will seem warmer, and being inside will seem better to all who hear it in the distant towns. I'll make me a sound and an apparatus and they'll call it a Fog Horn and whoever hears it will know the sadness of eternity and the briefness of life.'"

The Fog Horn blew.

"I made up that story," said McDunn quietly, "to try to explain why this thing keeps coming back to the lighthouse every year. The Fog Horn calls it, I think, and it comes...."

"But—" I said.

"Sssst!" said McDunn. "There!"
He nodded out to the Deeps.

Something was swimming toward the lighthouse tower.

It was a cold night, as I have said; the high tower was cold, the light was coming and going, and the Fog Horn, calling and calling through the raveling mist. You couldn't see far and you couldn't see plain, but there was the deep sea moving on its way about the night earth, flat and quiet, the color of gray mud, and here were the two of us alone in the high tower, and there, far out at first, was a ripple, followed by a wave, a rising, a bubble, a bit of froth. And then, from the surface of the cold sea came a head, a large head, dark-colored, with immense

eyes, and then a neck. And then—not a body—but more neck and more! The head rose a full forty feet above the water on a slender and beautiful dark neck. Only then did the body, like a slender little island of black coral and shells and crayfish, drip up from the subterranean. There was a flicker of tail. In all, from head to tip of tail, I estimated the monster at ninety or a hundred feet. **C**

I don't know what I said. I said something.

"Steady, boy, steady," whispered McDunn.

"It's impossible!" I said.

"No, Johnny, *we're* impossible. *It's* like it always was ten million years ago. *It* hasn't changed. It's *us* and the land that've changed, become impossible. Us!"

It swam slowly and with a great dark majesty out in the icy waters, far away. The fog came and went about it, momentarily erasing its shape. One of the monster eyes caught and held and flashed back our immense light, red, white, red, white, like a disk held high and sending a message in <u>primeval</u> code. It was as silent as the fog through which it swam.

"It's a dinosaur of some sort!" I crouched down holding to the stair rail.

"Yes, one of the tribe."

"But they died out!"

---

pri·me·val (prī mē´ vəl) *adj.*, from the earliest ages

THE FOGHORN **77**

Cultural Connection
Sea Monsters Many seafaring cultures have legends and tales of sea monsters. The "monsters" of these legends might actually be animals such as giant squid, octopuses, or giant sharks. Various lakes around the world, such as Loch Ness in Scotland, are also said to be inhabited by "monsters." Stories about "Nessie" may have their roots in Scottish folklore about kelpies. A kelpie is an evil water spirit that comes onto shore in the form of a horse; it lures children into the water and devours them. Tales such as this were commonly told to keep children away from the lake's edge. Most sightings of the Loch Ness monster have twentieth-century origins, and several hoaxes have been uncovered related to claimed sightings, photographs, and even footprints (which were made using a stuffed hippopotamus foot). However, sonar explorations of the lake in the 1980s and 1990s produced some mysterious indications of large, moving underwater objects that could be alive. **C**

Vocabulary Skills

Concrete and Abstract Nouns

terror	ideas	eternity
sea	man	life
animal	voice	year

Display this list of nouns and ask students to identify the persons, places, and things that they can see, hear, touch, taste, or smell. Explain that these are concrete nouns: They represent things a person can experience with the senses. The remaining words are abstract nouns: They represent ideas, concepts, and emotions. Have students list as many concrete and abstract nouns as they can find on a page from "The Foghorn." Then invite them to share and compare their lists.

Science Connection

Living Fossils Science does not support the idea that sea or lake monsters may be dinosaurs that have been staying alive in "the Deeps." The ancient reptile most like the sea monster in "The Foghorn" is the plesiosaur, which is also similar to descriptions of the Loch Ness Monster. It was a long-necked aquatic reptile that lived in the Mesozoic age. Plesiosaurs were cold blooded and could not have survived in the cold temperatures of "the Deeps." Also, because they breathed air, they would have to surface several times a day. **A**

Use Reading Strategies

Visualize Read this paragraph aloud with dramatic expression to demonstrate how Bradbury's short sentences, repetition, and visual and auditory images convey what Johnny sees and hears as the monster approaches. Then ask students to describe the scene in their own words. **B**

Literary Connection

Science Fiction The "Golden Age" of science fiction lasted from about 1937 through the 1950s. During this time, readership increased and writers such as Robert Heinlein, Isaac Asimov, and Theodore Sturgeon flourished. This Bradbury story was first published in June of 1951, with the title "The Beast from 20,000 Fathoms."

A "No, only hid away in the Deeps. Deep, deep down in the deepest Deeps. Isn't *that* a word now, Johnny, a real word, it says so much: the Deeps. There's all the coldness and darkness and deepness in a word like that."

"What'll we do?"

"Do? We got our job, we can't leave. Besides, we're safer here than in any boat trying to get to land. That thing's as big as a destroyer and almost as swift."

"But here, why does it come *here*?"

The next moment I had my answer.

The Fog Horn blew.

And the monster answered.

A cry came across a million years of water and mist. A cry so anguished[3] and alone that it shuddered in my head and my body. The monster cried out at the tower. The Fog Horn blew. The monster roared again. **B** The Fog Horn blew. The monster opened its great toothed mouth and the sound that came from it was the sound of the Fog Horn itself. Lonely and vast and far away. The sound of isolation, a viewless sea, a cold night, apartness. That was the sound.

"Now," whispered McDunn, "do you know why it comes here?"

---

3. **anguished.** Feeling great suffering or pain

78   UNIT 1 FICTION

Differentiated Instruction

Enrichment

Have students reread the passage in which McDunn tells his fanciful story about the invention of the Fog Horn. Ask students to list and discuss the similes he uses to describe Fog Horn's sound: "a voice like all of time and all of the fog that ever was"; "like an empty bed beside you"; "like an empty house"; "like trees in autumn with no leaves"; "like the birds flying south, crying"; "like November wind and the sea on the hard cold, shore." Ask students to think of other sounds that convey a similar lonely, mournful feeling. Possible answers might include train whistles, bagpipes, or other musical instruments. Then challenge students to write similes that describe these sounds.

I nodded.

"All year long, poor monster there thousand miles at sea, and twenty miles deep maybe, biding its time, perhaps it's a million years old, this one creature. Think of it, waiting a million years. Could *you* wait that long? Maybe it's the last of its kind. I sort of think that's true. Anyway, here come men on land and build this lighthouse, five years ago. And set up their Fog Horn and sound it and sound it out toward the place where you bury yourself in sleep and sea memories of a world where there were thousands like yourself, but now you're alone, all alone in a world not made for you, a world where you have to hide.

"But the sound of the Fog Horn comes and goes, comes and goes, and you stir from the muddy bottom of the Deeps, and your eyes open like the lenses of two-foot cameras and you move, slow, slow, for you have the ocean sea on your shoulders, heavy. But that Fog Horn comes through a thousand miles of water, faint and familiar, and the furnace in your belly stokes up, and you begin to rise, slow, slow. You feed yourself on great slakes of cod and minnow, on rivers of jellyfish, and you rise slow through the autumn

months, through September when the fogs started, through October with more fog and the horn still calling you on, and then, late in November, after pressurizing yourself day by day, a few feet higher every hour, you are near the surface and still alive. You've got to go slow; if you surfaced all at once you'd explode. So it takes you all of three months to surface, and then a number of days to swim through the cold waters to the lighthouse. And there you are, out there, in the night, Johnny, the biggest monster in creation. And here's the lighthouse calling to you, with a long neck like your neck sticking way up out of the water, and a body like your body, and, most important of all, a

SCIENCE ▶▶ CONNECTION

Sea Creatures Many ancient tales and legends describe gigantic sea creatures that rise up from the deep, capsizing ships and terrifying mariners. In September 2004, Japanese scientists snapped rare photographic images of a real-life gigantic deep-sea creature—the giant squid. This cephalopod, with a beaked head and long tentacles, is one of the world's largest animals, growing to forty-six feet long. Live giant squid have rarely been sighted in the wild. Knowing that sperm whales are predators of giant squid, researchers from the Ogasawara Whale Watching Association in Japan tracked sperm whales in the North Pacific Ocean and used a baited fishing line to attract the squid. As the squid's tentacles wrapped around the bait and became snagged on the hook, the scientists took more than five hundred photographs. When the squid escaped, it left behind a tentacle that measured eighteen feet long. How likely is it that other strange creatures may be living at the bottom of the sea, undiscovered by humans? **C**

(Opposite page) *The Loch Ness Monster,* c. 1935. Gino d'Achille. Private collection.

THE FOGHORN **79**

Teach the Selection

Science Connection
Sea Creatures *Answer:* Answers will vary. Some students may claim that because the ocean is so vast, not everything has been discovered. **C**

Use Reading Skills
Use Context Clues Ask students to use context clues to determine the meaning of the word *pressurizing.* Model a response: "In previous sentences, McDunn has said 'you move slow, slow, for you have the ocean sea on your shoulders, heavy.' Then, a few sentences later, he says 'if you surfaced all at once, you'd explode,' so I think that *pressurizing* is coming slowly to the surface, like scuba divers do, to keep air in the lungs from expanding too rapidly." **D**

▷ More by This Author
Students who like "The Foghorn" might enjoy reading "A Sound of Thunder" by Ray Bradbury.

TEACHING NOTE
Self-Generated Questioning
Divide the class into small groups and have the groups brainstorm and jot down questions they would like to ask about the sea monster in the story. Model a possible question: "What does the sea monster normally eat?" Instruct each group to pass its questions to another group. Then members of each group should use what they know about the monster to answer the questions the group receives. Have the groups share some of their questions and answers as a class.

Research Skills

Multimedia Sources
Have students use research skills to locate audio and multimedia sources of whale sounds. Divide the class into two groups. Have one group use the Internet to locate recordings and have the second group use a library. Challenge each group to listen to at least five recordings, and then provide a full citation of the best recording. They may use these criteria to judge the best:

- clarity of sound—there is no static or other interference
- consistent volume—soft and loud sounds are audible at the same volume setting
- ease of use—the medium (CD, website, etc.) is easy to locate and navigate

Science Connection

Life in the Deep Scientists have discovered hydrothermal vents on the seafloor. These geysers shoot super-heated water—as hot as 750 °F—up through cracks in Earth's crust. Scientists did not expect to find life in the crushing pressures, darkness, and extreme temperatures of the vents, but they found a variety of unusual creatures living near them, including bacteria, tubeworms, and vent crabs.

Analyze Literature

Setting Ask students why the author periodically repeats the line "The Fog Horn blew." What effect does this create? (It heightens tension by seeming almost like an alarm bell as the monster approaches, crying out in response.) **A**

Use Reading Strategies

Make Inferences Ask students what inferences they might make about McDunn's past, based on these comments. (He seems to be speaking from bitter experience. He identifies with the monster's loneliness and anger because someone he loved left him and hurt him.) **B**

---

voice like your voice. Do you understand now, Johnny, do you understand?"

The Fog Horn blew.

The monster answered.

I saw it all, I knew it all—the million years of waiting alone, for someone to come back who never came back. The million years of isolation at the bottom of the sea, the insanity of time there, while the skies cleared of reptile-birds, the swamps dried on the continental lands, the sloths and saber-tooths[4] had their day and sank in tar pits, and men ran like white ants upon the hills.

A The Fog Horn blew.

"Last year," said McDunn, "that creature swam round and round, round and round, all night. Not coming too near, puzzled,

I'd say. Afraid, maybe. And a bit angry after coming all this way. But the next day, unexpectedly, the fog lifted, the sun came out fresh, the sky was as blue as a painting. And the monster swam off away from the heat and the silence and didn't come back. I suppose it's been <u>brooding</u> on it **C** for a year now, thinking it over from every which way."

The monster was only a hundred yards off now, it and the Fog Horn crying at each other. As the lights hit them, the monster's eyes were fire and ice, fire and ice.

B "That's life for you," said McDunn. "Someone always waiting for someone who never comes home. Always someone loving some thing more than that thing loves

them. And after a while you want to destroy whatever that thing is, so it can't hurt you no more."

The monster was rushing at the lighthouse.

The Fog Horn blew.

"Let's see what happens," said McDunn. He switched the Fog Horn off.

The ensuing minute of silence was so intense that we could hear our hearts pounding in the glassed area of the tower, could hear the slow greased turn of the light.

The monster stopped and froze. Its great lantern eyes blinked. Its mouth gaped. It gave a sort of rumble, like a volcano. It twitched its head this way and that, as if to seek the

As the lights hit them, the monster's eyes were fire and ice, fire and ice.

sounds now dwindled off into the fog. It peered at the lighthouse. It rumbled again. Then its eyes caught fire. It reared up, threshed the water, and rushed at the tower, its eyes filled with angry torment.

"McDunn!" I cried. "Switch on the horn!"

McDunn fumbled with the switch. But even as he flicked it on, the monster was rearing up. I had a glimpse of its gigantic paws, fishskin glittering in webs between the finger-like projections, clawing at the tower. The huge eyes on the right side of its anguished head glittered before me like a

---

4. **saber-tooths.** Prehistoric tigers with large teeth

brood (brüd) *v.*, dwell on a gloomy subject; worry

Differentiated Instruction

Reading Proficiency

Have students add events to their time lines (see page 76), rereading passages as necessary to clarify information. Point out that McDunn says the fogs start in September, so that is when the Fog Horn begins to sound its warnings for ships. Note that McDunn thinks it takes the creature from September to late November to rise up out of the Deeps.

Visual Learning

Invite students to create a drawing, painting, or other visual that helps to explain McDunn's ideas about the sea monster. They can include details related to the lighthouse and the Deeps, as well as to the sea monster. When they are done, ask students to tell you how the ideas contribute to Bradbury's characterization of McDunn.

The monster gasped and cried. The tower was gone.

cauldron into which I might drop, screaming. The tower shook. The Fog Horn cried, the monster cried. It seized the tower and gnashed[5] at the glass, which shattered in upon us.

McDunn seized my arm. "Downstairs!"

The tower rocked, trembled, and started to give. The Fog Horn and the monster roared. We stumbled and half fell down the stairs. "Quick!"

We reached the bottom as the tower buckled down toward us. We ducked under the stairs into the small stone cellar. There were a thousand concussions as the rocks rained down. The Fog Horn stopped abruptly. The monster crashed upon the tower. The tower fell. We knelt together, McDunn and I, holding tight, while our world exploded.

Then it was over, and there was nothing but darkness and the wash of the sea on the raw stones.

That and the other sound.

"Listen," said McDunn quietly. "Listen."

We waited a moment. And then I began to hear it. First a great vacuumed sucking of air, and then the lament,[6] the bewilderment, the loneliness of the great monster, folded over and upon us, above us, so that the sickening reek of its body filled the air, a stone's thickness away from our cellar. The monster gasped and cried. The tower was gone. The light was gone. The thing that had called to it across a million years was gone. And the monster was opening its mouth and **(D)**

sending out great sounds. The sounds of a Fog Horn, again and again. And ships far at sea, not finding the light, not seeing anything, but passing and hearing late that night, must've thought: There it is, the lonely sound, the Lonesome Bay horn. All's well. We've rounded the cape.

And so it went for the rest of that night. The sun was hot and yellow the next afternoon when the rescuers came out to dig us from our stoned-under cellar.

"It fell apart, is all," said Mr. McDunn gravely. "We had a few bad knocks from the waves and it just crumbled." He pinched my arm. **(E)**

There was nothing to see. The ocean was calm, the sky blue. The only thing was a great algaic[7] stink from the green matter that covered the fallen tower stones and the shore rocks. Flies buzzed about. The ocean washed empty on the shore.

The next year they built a new lighthouse, but by that time I had a job in the little town and a wife and a good small warm house that glowed yellow on autumn nights, the doors locked, the chimney puffing smoke. As for McDunn, he was master of the new lighthouse, built to his own specifications, out of steel-reinforced concrete. "Just in case," he said.

The new lighthouse was ready in November. I drove down alone one evening late and parked my car and looked across the

---

5. **gnashed.** Struck with the teeth
6. **lament.** Loud mourning; wailing
7. **algaic.** Made up of algae, or simple water organisms

Answer: Some would wait as long as it takes; some would give up when it becomes obvious that reaching a goal is impossible. Others would adapt to changing circumstances.

Find Meaning

1. (a) They work at a lighthouse in the ocean. (b) McDunn's stories help lighten the atmosphere of the place.
2. (a) He says, "No, Johnny, *we're* impossible." (b) He means that human society is harder to believe or explain than the sea creature.
3. (a) It destroys them. (b) The creature realizes how truly alone it is and lashes out in despair.

Make Judgments

4. (a) He is thoughtful, intelligent, imaginative, and a good storyteller. (b) It foreshadows the creature's appearance and relates to the theme.
5. (a) McDunn feels sympathy for it. He calls it "that poor monster" and describes how lonely it feels. (b) He may have had to come to terms with loneliness, so he can imagine how the creature feels.
6. (a) and (b) "The Fog Horn blew" repeats, more frequently as the sea creature approaches, building suspense. The words *lonely* and *alone* repeat, emphasizing the mood and theme. McDunn repeats the words *voice* and *sound* in his story about the invention of the foghorn.

---

gray waters and listened to the new horn sounding, once, twice, three, four times a minute far out there, by itself.

The monster?

It never came back.

"It's gone away," said McDunn. "It's gone back to the Deeps. It's learned you can't love anything too much in this world. It's gone into the deepest Deeps to wait another million years. Ah, the poor thing! Waiting out there, and waiting out there, while man comes and goes on this pitiful little planet. Waiting and waiting."

I sat in my car, listening. I couldn't see the lighthouse or the light standing out in Lonesome Bay. I could only hear the Horn, the Horn, the Horn. It sounded like the monster calling.

I sat there wishing there was something I could say. ❖

The sea creature in "The Foghorn" waited thousands of years in hopes of seeing others of its kind. How long would you be willing to wait for something you really wanted? When might it be best to abandon a goal?

Find Meaning

1. (a) Where do the narrator and McDunn work? (b) Why do you think the narrator says he is thankful that McDunn is so talkative?
2. (a) As the creature comes into view, how does McDunn answer Johnny's exclamation, "It's impossible"? (b) What does McDunn mean by his response?
3. (a) What does the sea creature do to the foghorn and the lighthouse? (b) What do you think causes the sea creature to react in this way?

Make Judgments

4. (a) What words would you use to describe the character of McDunn? (b) Why do you think the author chose to have McDunn tell the story about the night that all the fish of the sea surfaced?
5. (a) What attitude does McDunn have toward the sea creature? (b) What might explain this attitude?
6. (a) What are some examples of the author's use of repetition in the story? (b) What effect does each example create?

Reading Skills

Compare and Contrast

To help students tell the difference between fantasy and science fiction, point out the following elements of each genre.

Fantasy

- plot—relies on magic and magical beings
- setting—often another age or world with imaginary elements

Science Fiction

- plot—relies on scientific principles
- setting—often outer space; may also be the future, the distant past, other planets, or worlds beneath the ground or the sea

Have students categorize titles of fantasy and science fiction stories they have read.

In "The Foghorn," an ancient sea creature has existed for centuries in the ocean, unknown to the humans who now populate the earth and try to penetrate the ocean's mysteries. The aqualung, which is described in the following selection from **David Macaulay's** book, *The New Way Things Work,* was developed as a tool to help scientists explore the underwater world and learn about the creatures that live there. Before you read "The Aqualung," preview the title and the diagram. What do you expect to learn from reading this selection?

THE AQUALUNG

With the aid of an aqualung or scuba (Self-Contained Underwater Breathing Apparatus), a diver can stay underwater for long periods. This device does away with the need for a diving suit by supplying air at changing pressures during a dive.

The diver's body is under pressure from the surrounding water, which becomes greater the deeper one dives. The air inside the diver's lungs is at about the same pressure as the water. The air in the cylinder is at high pressure. The aqualung's regulator has two stages that reduce the pressure of the air coming from the cylinder to the same pressure as the water so that the diver can breathe in. The first-stage valve, worked by a spring, opens to admit air at a set pressure always greater than water pressure. The second-stage valve, worked by a lever, opens by suction to admit air at water pressure.

AIR CYLINDER
SPRING
FIRST-STAGE VALVE
SECOND-STAGE VALVE
REGULATOR
LEVER

BREATHING IN
As the diver inhales, the air pressure in the air tubes falls. The diaphragm is sucked in, pushed by the greater pressure of water on the outside of the diaphragm. The lever opens the second-stage valve, admitting more air to the diver.

BREATHING OUT
As the diver breathes out, the air pressure in the air tubes rises, pushing the diaphragm down to shut off the incoming air. The one-way valve opens to expel the exhaled air to the sea.

DIAPHRAGM
AIR TUBE
MOUTHPIECE

KEY
- AIR FROM CYLINDER
- AIR AT SET PRESSURE
- AIR JUST ABOVE WATER PRESSURE
- AIR JUST BELOW WATER PRESSURE

ONE-WAY VALVE
AIR TUBE

THE AQUALUNG **83**

Teach the Connection

Use Reading Skills

Text Structure Remind students that a key is a guide that aids in interpreting and identifying significant marks on maps, graphs, charts, diagrams, and tables. Captions explain a visual item or graphic in writing. Labels are simple headers or titles within a graphic that give names to different parts; they also help readers understand the graphic and develop vocabulary.

Ask students what they learn from the key in "The Aqualung" diagram. What do they learn from the captions in the diagram? the labels? (The key shows what the different colors in the diagram indicate. The captions explain in detail what happens as the diver breathes in and breathes out. The labels identify different parts of the aqualung.)

TEACHING NOTE

Brainstorm Topics

Have pairs or small groups work together to brainstorm topics for a science fiction or fantasy story that they will write. Suggest that they use a cluster diagram. In the center circle, they can write Science Fiction or Fantasy. Around that they can add and connect related words or ideas. Have students work on their clusters for three or four minutes. Then invite them to individually freewrite about one of the ideas.

Words in Use

"The Aqualung"
Selection Words
cylinder, 83
diaphragm, 83

Common Core State Standards

Reading Literature
RL.1

Reading Informational
RI.9

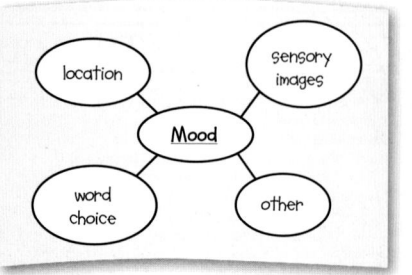

TEXT ← TO → TEXT
CONNECTION

In "The Foghorn," McDunn imagines what life must be like at the bottom of the ocean. He says, "For all our engines and so-called submarines, it'll be ten thousand centuries before we set foot on the real bottom of the sunken lands...." After reading "The Aqualung," do you agree with McDunn? Why or why not?

AFTER READING

Analyze Literature
Mood Use a cluster chart to organize the words and details that created emotional responses for you as you read the story. Think about the various emotions that the story evokes and in one or two sentences, describe the overall mood of the story.

Extend Understanding

Writing Options

Creative Writing Since Johnny has found a job in the town, McDunn needs a new assistant lighthouse keeper. Write a **job description** for the position. Remember that you want to attract applicants who will get along with McDunn and who will not mind the lonely location.

Persuasive Writing How reliable is Johnny's version of what happened? In one column of a two-column chart, list details from the story showing that Johnny is a reliable narrator; in the other column, list details showing that he is unreliable. Take a position and write a short **paragraph** in which you explain to a group of researchers why they should or should not try to find the sea creature.

Collaborative Learning

Re-create a Scene In small groups, review "The Foghorn" and discuss the descriptions in the story. As a group, choose one of the author's scenes to re-create in a drawing, a painting, a stage scene, or an audio recording. Think about the sights, sounds, and sensations that make the author's descriptions effective.

Media Literacy

Research Underwater Creatures A number of legendary creatures, such as the Loch Ness Monster, are reportedly living in lakes, rivers, and seas around the world. Use the Internet to research these creatures. Keep a log with information about each creature and the websites you visit. Which creature do you find the most believable? Why? Finally, assess whether the websites you viewed used the correct level of formality and tone on their pages and explain how they might improve.

⋈ Go to **www.mirrorsandwindows.com** for more.

Rikki-Tikki-Tavi

A Short Story by Rudyard Kipling

The Green Mamba

An Autobiography by Roald Dahl

At a Glance

Directed Reading

"Rikki-Tikki-Tavi"
- Reading Level: Moderate
- Difficulty Considerations: Many characters, selection length
- Ease Factor: Vocabulary

"The Green Mamba"
- Reading Level: Moderate
- Difficulty Considerations: Unfamiliar setting, long sentences
- Ease Factor: Exciting events

DIRECTED READING

BEFORE READING

Build Background

Scientific Context Both Rudyard Kipling's "Rikki-tikki-tavi" and Roald Dahl's "The Green Mamba" present encounters with dangerous snakes. Of the more than 2,700 species of snakes on Earth, about 375 are poisonous, including the green mamba, the cobra, and the krait.

Reader's Context Who is the most courageous person you've ever met? What do you think made that person so brave?

Set Purpose

Look at the illustrations on page 93 and page 103. What different feelings do you get from each image? As you read the story and autobiography, note how each work deals with the different feelings aroused by the presence of danger.

Meet the Authors

Rudyard Kipling (1865–1936) was born in India and cared for by a native nurse, who told him Indian legends. "Rikki-tikki-tavi" is a story in one of his most popular works, *The Jungle Book*.

Roald Dahl (1916–1990) lived a life of adventure before becoming a writer. His first job involved traveling across what was then the British colony of Tanganyika and is today the independent country of Tanzania. During World War II, he was a fighter pilot with the Royal Air Force until injuries forced him to take a desk job.

Compare Literature: Personification

Personification is a figure of speech in which something not human, such as an animal, object, or idea, is described as if it were human. To understand the technique of personification, use a chart to record the different characteristics given to the snakes in each work.

"Rikki-tikki-tavi"	"The Green Mamba"
Nag—wicked, cold-hearted, able to speak	

Preview Vocabulary

cul·ti·vat·ed (kʉl´ tə vāt´ əd) *adj.*, prepared for growing plants

cow·er (kaù´ [ə]r) *v.*, shrink and tremble as from anger, threats, or blows

prov·i·dence (präv´ ə dəns) *n.*, valuable gift; godsend

for·lorn (fər lôrn´) *adj.*, sad; lonely; hopeless

ma·nip·u·late (mə nip´ yə lāt) *v.*, treat or operate with the hands in a skillful manner

Objectives

Studying this lesson will enable students to
- compare literary selections of different genres
- use reading skills such as previewing texts
- describe personification
- name literary accomplishments of Rudyard Kipling and Roald Dahl
- observe skills that help people and animals handle the unexpected

Launch the Lesson

Tell students "Rikki-tikki-tavi" is a story about a mongoose that protects a family from snakes. Ask students to recall stories they know about animals that have saved people's lives.

Ask students what they would do if they saw a dangerous animal entering their house like the narrator in "The Green Mamba" does. How would they communicate with people inside? How would they "neutralize the threat" that the animal poses?

RIKKI-TIKKI-TAVI / THE GREEN MAMBA **85**

Words in Use

"Rikki-Tikki-Tavi"

Preview Vocabulary
cultivated, 88
cower, 88
providence, 90

Selection Words
draggled, 87
fledglings, 89
gait, 90

Teaching Words
krait, 85
instinct, 97
motto, 97

KEY TERMS

SHORT STORY, 85
AUTOBIOGRAPHY, 85
ILLUSTRATION, 85
PERSONIFICATION, 85
MOTTO, 97
NARRATOR, 104
COMPARE, 104
CONTRAST, 104

Common Core State Standards

Reading Literature
RL.1

Teach the Selection

Summary
Teddy, the child of an English family in India, finds a young mongoose called Rikki-tikki-tavi. The mongoose first fights off a dangerous pair of cobras, Nag and Nagaina, that live in the family's garden. Next, Rikki-tikki-tavi protects Teddy by killing a deadly snake named Karait. Determined to drive away the mongoose, Nag enters the family's home at night to kill them. Rikki-tikki-tavi battles Nag until Teddy's father arrives and kills the cobra with a gun. Nagaina tries to avenge Nag by killing Teddy, but the mongoose drives her off and pursues the cobra into her burrow, where he kills her.

The Mirrors & Windows questions at the end of the story focus on the theme of bravery. Before students begin reading, ask: Where does bravery come from?

Rikki-Tikki-Tavi, 1937. Andre Collot. Bibliotheque Nationale, Paris.

Rikki-Tikki-Tavi

A Short Story by Rudyard Kipling

This is the story of the great war that Rikki-tikki-tavi fought single-handed, through the bathrooms of the big bungalow in Segowlee cantonment.[1] Darzee, the tailorbird, helped him, and Chuchundra, the muskrat, who never comes out into the middle of the floor but always creeps round by the wall, gave him advice; but Rikki-tikki did the real fighting.

He was a mongoose, rather like a little cat in his fur and his tail but quite like a weasel in his head and his habits. His eyes and the end of his restless nose were pink; he could

---

1. **Segowlee cantonment.** Living quarters for British troops in the town of Segowlee in India

86

Program Resources

Planning and Assessment
Program Planning Guide, Selection Lesson Plan
E-Lesson Planner
Assessment Guide, Lesson Test
ExamView

Technology Tools
Interactive Student Text on CD
Visual Teaching Package
Audio Library
mirrorsandwindows.com

Meeting the Standards
Fiction: Unit 1, Comparing Literature, pp. 73–80

Differentiating Instruction
English Language Learners, Personification/ Plot, pp. 32–63

scratch himself anywhere he pleased with any leg, front or back, that he chose to use; he could fluff up his tail till it looked like a bottlebrush, and his war cry as he scuttled through the long grass was *Rikk-tikk-tikki-tikki-tchk!*

One day, a high summer flood washed him out of the burrow where he lived with his father and mother and carried him, kicking and clucking, down a roadside ditch. He found a little wisp of grass floating there and clung to it till he lost his senses. When he revived, he was lying in the hot sun in the middle of a garden path, very draggled indeed, and a small boy was saying: "Here's a dead mongoose. Let's have a funeral."

"No," said his mother; "let's take him in and dry him. Perhaps he isn't really dead."

They took him into the house, and a big man picked him up between his finger and thumb and said he was not dead but half choked; so they wrapped him in cotton wool and warmed him over a little fire, and he opened his eyes and sneezed.

"Now," said the big man (he was an Englishman who had just moved into the bungalow), "don't frighten him, and we'll see what he'll do."

It is the hardest thing in the world to frighten a mongoose, because he is eaten up from nose to tail with curiosity. The motto of all the mongoose family is "Run and find out," and Rikki-tikki was a true mongoose. He looked at the cotton wool, decided that it was not good to eat, ran all round the table, sat up and put his fur in order, scratched himself, and jumped on the small boy's shoulder.

"Don't be frightened, Teddy," said his father. "That's his way of making friends."

"Ouch! He's tickling under my chin," said Teddy.

Rikki-tikki looked down between the boy's collar and neck, snuffed at his ear, and climbed down to the floor, where he sat rubbing his nose.

"Good gracious," said Teddy's mother, "and that's a wild creature! I suppose he's so tame because we've been kind to him."

"All mongooses are like that," said her husband. "If Teddy doesn't pick him up by the tail or try to put him in a cage, he'll run in and out of the house all day long. Let's give him something to eat."

They gave him a little piece of raw meat. Rikki-tikki liked it immensely, and when it was finished, he went out into the veranda and sat in the sunshine and fluffed up his fur to make it dry to the roots. Then he felt better.

"There are more things to find out about in this house," he said to himself, "than all my family could find out in all their lives. I shall certainly stay and find out."

He spent all that day roaming over the house. He nearly drowned himself in the bathtubs, put his nose into the ink on a writing table, and burnt it on the end of the big man's cigar, for he climbed up in the big man's lap to see how writing was done. At nightfall he ran into Teddy's nursery to watch how kerosene lamps were lighted, and when Teddy went to bed, Rikki-tikki climbed up too; but he was a restless companion, because he had to get up and attend to every noise all through the night and find out what made it. Teddy's mother and father came in,

It is the hardest thing in the world to frighten a mongoose....

Analyze Literature

Personification Tell students that personification is a figure of speech in which something nonhuman is described as if it were human. In this story, it is clear that Rikki-tikki-tavi is a mongoose, not a person. However, Kipling gives Rikki-tikki-tavi many human qualities. Ask students to list some of the human qualities Rikki-tikki-tavi has so far. Model one possible quality, such as "making friends" or "curiosity."

Literary Connection

Beast Fables The stories in Kipling's *Jungle Books,* including "Rikki-tikki-tavi," are beast fables. Tell students that in beast fables, animals have human qualities. Like all fables, beast fables operate on two levels: They have a literal level, and they teach a lesson. India is the source of many beast fables. Kipling heard many animal stories as a child.

Reading Proficiency

To help students keep track of the many characters in "Rikki-tikki-tavi," ask them to write the name of each character they encounter, and then to list two descriptive phrases for each character as they read. Model this strategy by offering possible phrases for one character; for example, "Karait—tiny brown snake; deadly."

Visual Learning

Students may practice their understanding of plot and sequence by making a plot diagram or a story strip for "Rikki-tikki-tavi." Encourage visual learners to create one of the organizers and fill it in as they read the story.

Make Connections

Ask students why they think the family feels safe with Rikki-tikki-tavi. Then ask students if they have animals around their homes that make them feel safe. Have volunteers describe why the animal they name makes them feel safe. **A**

the last thing, to look at their boy, and Rikki-tikki was awake on the pillow. "I don't like that," said Teddy's mother; "he may bite the child." "He'll do no such thing," said the father. "Teddy's safer with that little beast than if he had a bloodhound to watch him. If a snake came into the nursery now—"

But Teddy's mother wouldn't think of anything so awful.

Early in the morning, Rikki-tikki came to early breakfast in the veranda riding on Teddy's shoulder, and they gave him banana and some boiled egg; and he sat on all their laps one after the other, because every well-brought-up mongoose always hopes to be a house mongoose someday and have rooms to run about in; and Rikki-tikki's mother (she used to live in the General's house at Segowlee) had carefully told Rikki what to do if ever he came across white men.

Then Rikki-tikki went out into the garden to see what was to be seen. It was a large garden, only half <u>cultivated</u>, with bushes, as big as summer houses, of Marshal Niel roses; lime and orange trees; clumps of bamboos; and thickets of high grass. Rikki-tikki licked his lips. "This is a splendid hunting ground," he said, and his tail grew bottlebrushy at the thought of it, and he scuttled up and down the garden, snuffing here and there till he heard very sorrowful voices in a thorn bush.

It was Darzee, the tailorbird, and his wife. They had made a beautiful nest by pulling two big leaves together and stitching them up the edges with fibers and had filled the hollow with cotton and downy fluff. The nest swayed to and fro as they sat on the rim and cried.

"What is the matter?" asked Rikki-tikki.

"We are very miserable," said Darzee.

"One of our babies fell out of the nest yesterday and Nag ate him."

"H'm!" said Rikki-tikki, "that is very sad—but I am a stranger here. Who is Nag?"

Darzee and his wife only <u>cowered</u> down in the nest without answering, for from the thick grass at the foot of the bush there came a low hiss—a horrid, cold sound that made Rikki-tikki jump back two clear feet. Then inch by inch out of the grass rose up the head and spread hood of Nag, the big black cobra, and he was five feet long from tongue to tail. When he had lifted one third of himself clear of the ground, he stayed balancing to and fro exactly as a dandelion tuft balances in the wind, and he looked at Rikki-tikki with the wicked snake's eyes that never change their expression, whatever the snake may be thinking of.

"Who is Nag?" said he. "I am Nag. The great God Brahm[2] put his mark upon all our people, when the first cobra spread his hood to keep the sun off Brahm as he slept. Look, and be afraid!"

He spread out his hood more than ever, and Rikki-tikki saw the spectacle mark on the back of it that looks exactly like the eye part of a hook-and-eye fastening. He was afraid for the minute; but it is impossible for a mongoose to stay frightened for any length of time, and though Rikki-tikki had never met a live cobra before, his mother had fed him on dead ones, and he knew that all a grown mongoose's business in life was to fight and eat snakes. Nag knew that too, and

"Be careful. I am Death!"

2. **Brahm.** Short for *Brahma*, the creator of the universe according to Hindu religion

cul·ti·vat·ed (kʉl′ tə vāt′ id) *adj.*, prepared for growing plants

cow·er (kaủ′ [ə]r) *v.*, shrink and tremble as from anger, threats, or blows

Differentiated Instruction

English Language Learning

Use this part of the story to help English language learners recognize contractions. Have students work in pairs to identify such contractions as *he's, here's, that's, let's, don't, doesn't, we'll, he'll,* and *we've.* Have students spell out the words from which the contractions are made. You might also help them distinguish contractions from possessives.

Auditory Learning

Have students practice saying Rikki-tikki-tavi's name and making the sounds he makes, as written in the text. Ask students to offer other examples of alliteration (repeating initial consonants) or onomatopoeia (words that sound like what they mean) that convey animal sounds.

at the bottom of his cold heart, he was afraid.

"Well," said Rikki-tikki, and his tail began to fluff up again, "marks or no marks, do you think it is right for you to eat fledglings out of a nest?"

Nag was thinking to himself and watching the least little movement in the grass behind Rikki-tikki. He knew that mongooses in the garden meant death sooner or later for him and his family, but he wanted to get Rikki-tikki off his guard. So he dropped his head a little and put it on one side.

"Let us talk," he said. "You eat eggs. Why should not I eat birds?"

"Behind you! Look behind you!" sang Darzee.

Rikki-tikki knew better than to waste time in staring. He jumped up in the air as high as he could go, and just under him whizzed by the head of Nagaina, Nag's wicked wife. She had crept up behind him as he was talking, to make an end of him; and he heard her savage hiss as the stroke missed. He came down almost across her back, and if he had been an old mongoose, he would have known that then was the time to break her back with one bite; but he was afraid of the terrible lashing return stroke of the cobra. He bit, indeed, but did not bite long enough, and he jumped clear of the whisking tail, leaving Nagaina torn and angry.

"Wicked, wicked Darzee!" said Nag, lashing up as high as he could reach toward the nest in the thorn bush; but Darzee had built it out of reach of snakes, and it only swayed to and fro.

Rikki-tikki felt his eyes growing red and hot (when a mongoose's eyes grow red, he is angry), and he sat back on his tail and hind legs like a little kangaroo, and looked all round him, and chattered with rage. But

Nag and Nagaina had disappeared into the grass. When a snake misses its stroke, it never says anything or gives any sign of what it means to do next. Rikki-tikki did not care to follow them, for he did not feel sure that he could manage two snakes at once. So he trotted off to the gravel path near the house and sat down to think. It was a serious matter for him. If you read the old books of natural history, you will find they say that when the mongoose fights the snake and happens to get bitten, he runs off and eats some herb that cures him. That is not true. The victory is only a matter of quickness of eye and quickness of foot—snake's blow against the mongoose's jump—and as no eye can follow the motion of a snake's head when it strikes, this makes things much more wonderful than any magic herb. Rikki-tikki knew he was a young mongoose, and it made him all the more pleased to think that he had managed to escape a blow from behind. It gave him confidence in himself, and when Teddy came running down the path, Rikki-tikki was ready to be petted. But just as Teddy was stooping, something wriggled a little in the dust and a tiny voice said: "Be careful. I am Death!" It was Karait, the dusty brown snakeling that lies for choice on the dusty earth; and

◄ ►

Teach the Selection

Use Reading Strategies
Make Predictions Tell students that most of the characters in the story have now been introduced. Ask them to predict what the main conflict in the story will be, based on what they know of the characters so far. Model a response: "The main conflict will involve the cobras attacking Rikki-tikki-tavi." **B**

Use Reading Strategies
Visualize Point out that personification, like characterization, can involve using precise physical descriptions. Have them review what they have read so far and pick out one or two strong visual details about Rikki-tikki-tavi. Ask volunteers to describe the *human* qualities that each detail evokes. Model a possible answer, such as "When Rikki-tikki-tavi sat up and put his fur in order, it reminded me of how a man who just woke up from a nap straightens out his wrinkly sweater."

Writing Skills

Figurative Language
Remind students that onomatopoeia is the use of words or phrases that sound like what they mean. Give them some examples from the story, such as *snuffling*, *fluff*, and *whizzed by*.

Ask students to work in pairs to create a character sketch of an animal. Tell them to draft, revise, and finalize a sketch of one to three paragraphs. At least once in each paragraph—but as often as they want—have them use onomatopoeia as they describe their animal. When students have finished, have each pair read the sketch aloud to the class.

Analyze Literature

Suspense Tell students that suspense is a feeling of being anxious or curious. To create suspense, writers raise questions in a reader's mind and evoke strong emotions. Ask students how Kipling creates suspense in this story. (Dangerous snakes have been defeated, but the two most dangerous have not been killed. Rikki-tikki-tavi is young and inexperienced, so we wonder whether he will survive more snake attacks.) **Ⓐ**

History Connection

England in India From 1600 to the 1850s, the British East India Company established trading outposts and gained property and power in India. After the Company suppressed a bloody revolt in 1858, the British government dissolved the Company and began ruling India. This was the period known as the Raj. Britain's Queen Victoria became Empress of India in 1877. The Raj lasted until 1947, when India achieved independence.

TEACHING NOTE

Media Literacy

Encourage interested students to find a video or DVD of "Rikki-tikki-tavi." (They will most likely find a 1975 animated version.) Set aside time for the students to watch the video and prepare a brief review for the rest of the class. Students should say how closely the video follows Kipling's original plot, characters, and use of language.

---

his bite is as dangerous as the cobra's. But he is so small that nobody thinks of him, and so he does the more harm to people.

Rikki-tikki's eyes grew red again, and he danced up to Karait with the peculiar rocking, swaying motion that he had inherited from his family. It looks very funny, but it is so perfectly balanced a gait that you can fly off from it at any angle you please; and in dealing with snakes this is an advantage. If Rikki-tikki had only known, he was doing a much more dangerous thing than fighting Nag, for Karait is so small and can turn so quickly that unless Rikki bit him close to the back of the head, he would get **Ⓐ** the return stroke in his eye or his lip. But Rikki did not know; his eyes were all red, and he rocked back and forth, looking for a good place to hold. Karait struck out, Rikki jumped sideways and tried to run in, but the wicked little dusty gray head lashed within a fraction of his shoulder, and he had to jump over the body, and the head followed his heels close.

Teddy shouted to the house: "Oh, look here! Our mongoose is killing a snake," and Rikki-tikki heard a scream from Teddy's mother. His father ran out with a stick, but by the time he came up, Karait had lunged out once too far, and Rikki-tikki had sprung, jumped on the snake's back, dropped his head far between his forelegs, bitten as high up the back as he could get hold, and rolled away. That bite paralyzed Karait, and Rikki-tikki was just going to eat him up from the tail, after the custom of his family at dinner, when he remembered that a full meal makes a slow mongoose, and if he wanted all his strength and quickness ready, he must keep himself thin. He went away for a dust bath under the castor-oil bushes, while Teddy's father beat the dead Karait. "What is the use of that?" thought Rikki-tikki; "I have settled it all"; and then Teddy's mother picked him up

from the dust and hugged him, crying that he had saved Teddy from death, and Teddy's father said that he was a <u>providence</u>, and Teddy looked on with big, scared eyes. Rikki-tikki was rather amused at all the fuss, which, of course, he did not understand. Teddy's mother might just as well have petted Teddy for playing in the dust. Rikki was thoroughly enjoying himself.

That night at dinner, walking to and fro among the wineglasses on the table, he might have stuffed himself three times over with nice things; but he remembered Nag and Nagaina, and though it was very pleasant to be patted and petted by Teddy's mother and to sit on Teddy's shoulder, his eyes would get red from time to time, and he would go off into his long war cry of *Rikk-tikk-tikki-tikki-tchk!*

Teddy carried him off to bed and insisted on Rikki-tikki's sleeping under his chin. Rikki-tikki was too well bred to bite or scratch, but as soon as Teddy was asleep, he went off for his nightly walk round the house, and in the dark he ran up against Chuchundra, the muskrat, creeping round by the wall. Chuchundra is a brokenhearted little beast. He whimpers and cheeps all night, trying to make up his mind to run into the middle of the room; but he never gets there.

"Don't kill me," said Chuchundra, almost weeping. "Rikki-tikki, don't kill me!"

"Do you think a snake killer kills muskrats?" said Rikki-tikki scornfully.

"Those who kill snakes get killed by snakes," said Chuchundra, more sorrowfully than ever. "And how am I to be sure that Nag won't mistake me for you some dark night?"

"There's not the least danger," said Rikki-tikki, "but Nag is in the garden, and I know you don't go there."

---

prov·i·dence (präv´ ə dəns) *n.*, valuable gift; godsend

Differentiated Instruction

Kinesthetic Learning

Have volunteers enact one of the conversations in the story so far. The performers should choose a conversation, and then everyone in the class should reread it to review the words, gestures, emotions, and expressions involved. Discuss as a class whether the enactment incorporated the main verbal and nonverbal components of the story. Use this discussion to review characterization.

Have less-able readers read the story along with an audio recording. Several recordings of "Rikki-tikki-tavi" are available. Encourage English language learners to ask for information about unknown words or expressions they encounter in the selection.

"My cousin Chua, the rat, told me—" said Chuchundra, and then he stopped.

"Told you what?"

"H'sh! Nag is everywhere, Rikki-tikki. You should have talked to Chua in the garden."

"I didn't—so you must tell me. Quick, Chuchundra, or I'll bite you!"

Chuchundra sat down and cried till the tears rolled off his whiskers. "I am a very poor man," he sobbed. "I never had spirit enough to run out into the middle of the room. H'sh! I mustn't tell you anything. Can't you *hear*, Rikki-tikki?"

Rikki-tikki listened. The house was as still as still, but he thought he could just catch the faintest *scratch-scratch* in the world—a noise as faint as that of a wasp walking on a windowpane—the dry scratch of a snake's scales on brickwork.

"That's Nag or Nagaina," he said to himself, "and he is crawling into the bathroom sluice.³ You're right, Chuchundra; I should have talked to Chua."

He stole off to Teddy's bathroom, but there was nothing there, and then to Teddy's mother's bathroom. At the bottom of the smooth plaster wall there was a brick pulled out to make a sluice for the bathwater, and as Rikki-tikki stole in by the masonry curb where the bath is put, he heard Nag and Nagaina whispering together outside in the moonlight.

"When the house is emptied of people," said Nagaina to her husband, "*he* will have to go away, and then the garden will be our own again. Go in quietly, and remember that the big man who killed Karait is the first one to bite. Then come out and tell me, and we will hunt for Rikki-tikki together."

"But are you sure that there is anything to be gained by killing the people?" said Nag.

"Everything. When there were no people in the bungalow, did we have any mongoose in the garden? So long as the bungalow is empty, we are king and queen of the garden; and remember that as soon as our eggs in the melon bed hatch (as they may tomorrow), our children will need room and quiet."

"I had not thought of that," said Nag. "I will go, but there is no need that we should hunt for Rikki-tikki afterward. I will kill the big man and his wife, and the child if I can, and come away quietly. Then the bungalow will be empty, and Rikki-tikki will go."

Rikki-tikki tingled all over with rage and hatred at this, and then Nag's head came through the sluice, and his five feet of cold body followed it. Angry as he was, Rikki-tikki was very frightened as he saw the size of the big cobra. Nag coiled himself up, raised his head, and looked into the bathroom in the dark, and Rikki could see his eyes glitter.

"Now, if I kill him here, Nagaina will know; and if I fight him on the open floor, the odds are in his favor. What am I to do?" said Rikki-tikki-tavi.

Nag waved to and fro, and then Rikki-tikki heard him drinking from the biggest water jar that was used to fill the bath. "That is good," said the snake. "Now, when Karait was killed, the big man had a stick. He may have that stick still, but when he comes in to bathe in the morning, he will not have a stick. I shall wait here till he comes. Nagaina—do you hear me?—I shall wait here in the cool till daytime."

> "Those who kill snakes get killed by snakes...."

---

3. sluice. Valve through which water is run

Use Reading Strategies
Ask Questions Have pairs of students briefly pause in their reading and ask each other questions to determine whether or not the main events of the plot have yet taken place. Model one possible question, such as "Is the rising action over?" or "Has the climax occurred yet?"

Science Connection
Mongoose Misuse The mongoose is so good at what it does, people imported the animal to islands in the West Indies in 1872, and to Fiji and Hawaii in 1883, in a plan to rid the islands' sugar cane fields of rats. The plan backfired, however, because the mongooses ate birds as well as small mammals (such as rodents) and reptiles (including turtles and snakes). Furthermore, mongooses carry rabies and other diseases that threaten livestock. Mongooses have literally driven many island species into extinction.

There was no answer from outside, so Rikki-tikki knew Nagaina had gone away. Nag coiled himself down, coil by coil, round the bulge at the bottom of the water jar, and Rikki-tikki stayed still as death. After an hour he began to move, muscle by muscle, toward the jar. Nag was asleep, and Rikki-tikki looked at his big back, wondering which would be the best place for a good hold. "If I don't break his back at the first jump," said Rikki, "he can still fight; and if he fights—O Rikki!" He looked at the thickness of the neck below the hood, but that was too much for him; and a bite near the tail would only make Nag savage.

"It must be the head," he said at last, "the head above the hood; and when I am once there, I must not let go."

Then he jumped. The head was lying a little clear of the water jar, under the curve of it; and as his teeth met, Rikki braced his back against the bulge of the red earthenware to hold down the head. This gave him just one second's purchase,[4] and he made the most of it. Then he was battered to and fro as a rat is shaken by a dog—to and fro on the floor, up and down, and round in great circles, but his eyes were red and he held on as the body cartwhipped over the floor, upsetting the tin dipper and the soap dish and the flesh brush, and banged against the tin side of the bath. As he held, he closed his jaws tighter and tighter, for he made sure he would be banged to death, and for the honor of his family, he preferred to be found with his teeth locked. He was dizzy, aching, and felt shaken to pieces, when something went off like a thunderclap just behind him; a hot wind knocked him senseless and red fire singed his

...a hot wind knocked him senseless and red fire singed his fur.

fur. The big man had been wakened by the noise and had fired both barrels of a shotgun into Nag just behind the hood.

Rikki-tikki held on with his eyes shut, for now he was quite sure he was dead; but the head did not move, and the big man picked him up and said: "It's the mongoose again, Alice; the little chap has saved *our* lives now." Then Teddy's mother came in with a very white face and saw what was left of Nag, and Rikki-tikki dragged himself to Teddy's bedroom and spent half the rest of the night shaking himself tenderly to find out whether he really was broken into forty pieces, as he fancied.

When morning came, he was very stiff but well pleased with his doings. "Now I have Nagaina to settle with, and she will be worse than five Nags, and there's no knowing when the eggs she spoke of will hatch. Goodness! I must go and see Darzee," he said.

Without waiting for breakfast, Rikki-tikki ran to the thorn bush, where Darzee was singing a song of triumph at the top of his voice. The news of Nag's death was all over the garden, for the sweeper had thrown the body on the rubbish heap.

"Oh, you stupid tuft of feathers!" said Rikki-tikki angrily. "Is this the time to sing?"

"Nag is dead—is dead—is dead!" sang Darzee. "The valiant Rikki-tikki caught him by the head and held fast. The big man brought the bang-stick, and Nag fell in two pieces! He will never eat my babies again."

"All that's true enough, but where's

---

4. purchase. Firm hold

(Opposite page) *Rikki-Tikki-Tavi* (illustration), 1937. Louis Joseph Soulas. Bibliotheque Nationale, Paris.

Differentiated Instruction

English Language Learning
Point out to students that the dialogue between Nag and Nagaina outside the house, which Rikki-tikki-tavi overhears, is formal English. The snakes do not speak with contractions. Some students may recognize the subjunctive mood; you may wish to draw students' attention to it.

Enrichment
Encourage interested students to use library or Internet resources to find pictures of mongooses and king cobras. Tell them to try to locate pictures they can use to demonstrate the relative sizes of the two animals. Have them research other animals mongooses attack and find similar pictures. (There is often a great size disparity.) Let them share their discoveries with the class.

Make Connections

Have students stop reading for a moment and discuss whether Rikki-tikki-tavi is brave or reckless. If he were a human being instead of a mongoose, what would they say?

Critical Viewing

Looking at a Painting Tell students that they can "read" a painting by studying details of the subject, composition (arrangement of parts), color, and style. Write those words on the board and use the questions below as starting points for analysis.

Subject

- What is pictured in this painting?
- How are the animals pictured relating to one another?

Composition

- How has the artist made the mongoose the center of the composition?
- How does the composition contribute to the overall effect of the painting?

Color

- What colors predominate in this painting?
- What mood do these colors create?

Style

- Would you describe this painter's style as realistic or abstract? Why?
- What comment does this painting make about the story?

Identify Multiple Levels of Meaning

Remind students that the animals in this story have both literal roles in the plot and symbolic or moral roles. Encourage students to keep track of these dual roles. Sketch a chart on the board with the column headings Character, Literal Role, and Symbolic/Moral Role. Encourage students to fill in the columns for each character — Rikki-tikki-tavi, Darzee, Darzee's wife, Nag, Nagaina, and Chuchundra — based on what they have already read. They can change or add to the chart as they continue reading.

Use Reading Strategies

Make Inferences Remind students that making an inference involves combining new information with what they already know. Ask students what they can infer from Rikki-tikki-tavi's questions to Darzee and Darzee's wife (such as "Is this the time to sing?" "Where's Nagaina?" and "Have you ever heard where she keeps her eggs?"). Specifically, what can they infer from Rikki-tikki's interest in Nagaina's nest? (He wants to get rid of all the cobras.) **A**

Analyze Literature

Character Have students review the discussion of static and dynamic characters on page 17. Ask whether they think Darzee and his wife are static or dynamic in their appearances so far. Students will probably say they are static. Then, point out that static characters can play prominent roles in a story, even if they do not change over the course of the plot.

Nagaina?" said Rikki-tikki, looking carefully round him.

"Nagaina came to the bathroom sluice and called for Nag," Darzee went on; "and Nag came out on the end of a stick—the sweeper picked him up on the end of a stick and threw him upon the rubbish heap. Let us sing about the great, the red-eyed Rikki-tikki!" and Darzee filled his throat and sang.

A "If I could get up to your nest, I'd roll your babies out!" said Rikki-tikki. "You don't know when to do the right thing at the right time. You're safe enough in your nest there, but it's war for me down here. Stop singing a minute, Darzee."

"For the great, beautiful Rikki-tikki's sake I will stop," said Darzee. "What is it, O Killer of the terrible Nag?"

"Where is Nagaina, for the third time?"

"On the rubbish heap by the stables, mourning for Nag. Great is Rikki-tikki with the white teeth."

"Bother my white teeth! Have you ever heard where she keeps her eggs?"

"In the melon bed, on the end nearest the wall, where the sun strikes nearly all day. She hid them there weeks ago."

"And you never thought it worthwhile to tell me? The end nearest the wall, you said?"

"Rikki-tikki, you are not going to eat her eggs?"

"Not eat exactly; no. Darzee, if you have a grain of sense, you will fly off to the stables and pretend that your wing is broken and let Nagaina chase you away to the bush. I must get to the melon bed, and if I went there now, she'd see me."

Darzee was a featherbrained little fellow who could never hold more than one idea at a time in his head, and just because he knew that Nagaina's children were born in eggs like his own, he didn't think at first that it was fair to kill them. But his wife was a sensible

bird, and she knew that cobra's eggs meant young cobras later on; so she flew off from the nest and left Darzee to keep the babies warm and continue his song about the death of Nag. Darzee was very like a man in some ways.

She fluttered in front of Nagaina by the rubbish heap and cried out, "Oh, my wing is broken! The boy in the house threw a stone at me and broke it." Then she fluttered more desperately than ever.

Nagaina lifted up her head and hissed, "You warned Rikki-tikki when I would have killed him. Indeed and truly, you've chosen a bad place to be lame in." And she moved toward Darzee's wife, slipping along over the dust.

"The boy broke it with a stone!" shrieked Darzee's wife.

"Well! It may be some consolation to you when you're dead to know that I shall settle accounts with the boy. My husband lies on the rubbish heap this morning, but before night the boy in the house will lie very still. What is the use of running away? I am sure to catch you. Little fool, look at me!"

Darzee's wife knew better than to do *that*, for a bird who looks at a snake's eyes gets so frightened that she cannot move. Darzee's wife fluttered on, piping sorrowfully and never leaving the ground, and Nagaina quickened her pace.

Rikki-tikki heard them going up the path from the stables, and he raced for the end of the melon patch near the wall. There, in the warm litter above the melons, very cunningly hidden, he found twenty-five eggs about the size of a bantam's eggs but with whitish skins instead of shells.

"I was not a day too soon," he said, for he could see the baby cobras curled up inside the skin, and he knew that the minute they were hatched, they could each kill a man or a mongoose. He bit off the tops of the eggs as

---

Differentiated Instruction

English Language Learning

Review with students the paragraph that characterizes Darzee and his wife, beginning with "Darzee was a featherbrained little fellow." Explain that *featherbrained* means "empty-headed." Ask students for examples of terms from their own languages that mean the same thing. Also, make sure students see the humor in the last sentence of the paragraph.

Auditory Learning

Have two volunteers present an oral interpretation of the conversation between Darzee's wife and Nagaina. Encourage them to express the appropriate emotions in the dialogue. When they are done, ask students to tell you what this exchange contributes to the plot.

fast as he could, taking care to crush the young cobras, and turned over the litter from time to time to see whether he had missed any. At last there were only three eggs left, and Rikki-tikki began to chuckle to himself, when he heard Darzee's wife screaming:

"Rikki-tikki, I led Nagaina toward the house, and she has gone into the veranda, and—oh, come quickly—she means killing!"

Rikki-tikki smashed two eggs, and tumbled backward down the melon bed with the third egg in his mouth, and scuttled to the veranda as hard as he could put foot to the ground. Teddy and his mother and father were there at early breakfast, but Rikki-tikki saw that they were not eating anything. They sat stone still, and their faces were white. Nagaina was coiled up on the matting by Teddy's chair, within easy striking distance of Teddy's bare leg, and she was swaying to and fro, singing a song of triumph.

"Son of the big man that killed Nag," she hissed, "stay still. I am not ready yet. Wait a little. Keep very still, all you three! If you move, I strike, and if you do not move, I strike. Oh, foolish people, who killed my Nag!"

Teddy's eyes were fixed on his father, and all his father could do was to whisper, "Sit still, Teddy. You mustn't move. Teddy, keep still."

Then Rikki-tikki came up and cried: "Turn round, Nagaina; turn and fight!"

"All in good time," said she, without moving her eyes. "I will settle my account with *you* presently. Look at your friends,

Rikki-tikki. They are still and white. They are afraid. They dare not move, and if you come a step nearer, I strike."

"Look at your eggs," said Rikki-tikki, "in the melon bed near the wall. Go and look, Nagaina!"

The big snake turned half round and saw the egg on the veranda. "Ah-h! Give it to me," she said.

Rikki-tikki put his paws one on each side of the egg, and his eyes were blood-red. "What price for a snake's egg? For a young cobra? For a young king cobra? For the last—the very last of the brood? The ants are eating all the others down by the melon bed."

Nagaina spun clear round, forgetting everything for the sake of the one egg; and Rikki-tikki saw Teddy's father shoot out a big hand, catch Teddy by the shoulder, and drag him across the little table with the teacups, safe and out of reach of Nagaina.

"Tricked! Tricked! Tricked! *Rikk-tck-tck!*" chuckled Rikki-tikki. "The boy is safe, and it was I—I—I that caught Nag by the hood last night in the bathroom." Then he began to jump up and down, all four feet together, his head close to the floor. "He threw me to and fro, but he could not shake me off. He was dead before the big man blew him in two. I did it! *Rikki-tikki-tck-tck!* Come then, Nagaina. Come and fight with me. You shall not be a widow long."

Nagaina saw that she had lost her chance of killing Teddy, and the egg lay between Rikki-tikki's paws. "Give me the egg, Rikki-tikki. Give me the last of my eggs,

> "If you move, I strike, and if you do not move, I strike."

Use Reading Skills

Identify Sequence of Events Ask students to identify the change in plot development that occurs while Rikki-tikki-tavi is destroying the cobra eggs. (In leading Nagaina toward the house, Darzee's wife unintentionally endangers the family.) Ask how they would show this type of simultaneous action on a time line or story strip. (One could show it with two labels or frames stacked vertically.)

Science Connection

Snake Facts Ask students to tell you a few general things they know about snakes. After receiving several responses, remind them that snakes do not generate their own body heat, so they are cold when their environment is cold, as Nag is cold in the bathroom. Also tell students that snake eggs do not have hard shells like bird eggs. You might also tell students that most adult snakes can control the amount of venom in a bite. Some bites are "dry," meaning they have no venom at all.

Reading Skills

Summarize

As students finish reading "Rikki-tikki-tavi," ask them to summarize the story in three paragraphs, as follows:

1. **Setting:** Describe the setting of the main action in the story. Include details about the inside and outside of the family bungalow.

2. **Characters**: Describe each main character. If students believe there are minor characters, have students list them in a single sentence at the end of the paragraph.

3. **Plot:** Use one sentence apiece to articulate the exposition, the rising action, the climax, the falling action, and the resolution of the plot.

Analyze Literature

Motivation Remind students that a character's motivation is what forces or leads the character to act in a specific way. Ask each student to pick one character in this story and describe its motivation. Model a response: "Darzee's motivation is to stay safe so he can make up songs."

Analyze Literature

Plot Ask students to review "Understanding Plot" on pages 6–7. Then raise the question of where the climax occurs in "Rikki-tikki-tavi." Ask whether there is just one climax, or if there are several. (The plot seems to climax with the killing of Nag, but then Nagaina becomes angry, so there is another climax when Rikki-tikki-tavi kills Nagaina.) Consider revisiting previous discussions of conflict. Based on students' opinions of the main conflict, whether it is external or internal, and who participates in the conflict, ask them to name a single incident, or climax, that seems to lead to resolution of this conflict.

and I will go away and never come back," she said, lowering her hood.

"Yes, you will go away, and you will never come back; for you will go to the rubbish heap with Nag. Fight, widow! The big man has gone for his gun! Fight!"

Rikki-tikki was bounding all round Nagaina, keeping just out of reach of her stroke, his little eyes like hot coals. Nagaina gathered herself together and flung out at him. Rikki-tikki jumped up and backwards. Again and again and again she struck, and each time her head came with a whack on the matting of the veranda and she gathered herself together like a watch spring. Then Rikki-tikki danced in a circle to get behind her, and Nagaina spun round to keep her head to his head, so that the rustle of her tail on the matting sounded like dry leaves blown along by the wind.

He had forgotten the egg. It still lay on the veranda, and Nagaina came nearer and nearer to it, till at last, while Rikki-tikki was drawing breath, she caught it in her mouth, turned to the veranda steps, and flew like an arrow down the path, with Rikki-tikki behind her. When the cobra runs for her life, she goes like a whiplash flicked across a horse's neck. Rikki-tikki knew that he must catch her or all the trouble would begin again. She headed straight for the long grass by the thorn bush, and as he was running, Rikki-tikki heard Darzee still singing his foolish little song of triumph. But Darzee's wife was wiser. She flew off her nest as Nagaina came along and flapped her wings about Nagaina's head. If Darzee had helped, they might have turned her, but Nagaina only lowered her hood and went on. Still, the instant's delay brought Rikki-tikki up to her, and as she plunged into the rat hole where she and Nag used to live, his little white teeth were clenched on her tail and he went down with her—and very few mongooses, however

wise and old they may be, care to follow a cobra into its hole. It was dark in the hole, and Rikki-tikki never knew when it might open out and give Nagaina room to turn and strike at him. He held on savagely and stuck out his feet to act as brakes on the dark slope of the hot, moist earth. Then the grass by the mouth of the hole stopped waving, and Darzee said: "It is all over with Rikki-tikki! We must sing his death song. Valiant Rikki-tikki is dead! For Nagaina will surely kill him underground."

So he sang a very mournful song that he made up on the spur of the minute, and just as he got to the most touching part, the grass quivered again, and Rikki-tikki, covered with dirt, dragged himself out of the hole leg by leg, licking his whiskers. Darzee stopped with a little shout. Rikki-tikki shook some of the dust out of his fur and sneezed. "It is all over," he said. "The widow will never come out again." And the red ants that live between the grass stems heard him and began to troop down one after another to see if he had spoken the truth.

Rikki-tikki curled himself up in the grass and slept where he was—slept and slept till it was late in the afternoon, for he had done a hard day's work.

"Now," he said, when he awoke, "I will go back to the house. Tell the Coppersmith, Darzee, and he will tell the garden that Nagaina is dead."

The Coppersmith is a bird who makes a noise exactly like the beating of a little hammer on a copper pot, and the reason he is always making it is because he is the town crier to every Indian garden and tells all the news to everybody who cares to listen. As Rikki-tikki went up the path, he heard his "attention" notes like a tiny dinner gong and then the steady "*Ding-dong-tock! Nag is dead—dong! Nagaina is dead! Ding-dong-*

Vocabulary Skills

Foreign Words in English

Read aloud the first sentence of "Rikki-tikki-tavi." Ask students if they know what a bungalow is. Explain that in the United States, a bungalow is a small house. The word comes from India, where a bungalow is a one-story house with a wide veranda.

Have students find the foreign origins of these other words from "Rikki-tikki-tavi" and "The Green Mamba."

1. mongoose (India)
2. veranda (India, Iran, or Portugal)
3. cigar (Spain or Central America)
4. bantam (Indonesia)
5. mosquito (Spain and Portugal)
6. sofa (Turkey)

tock!" That set all the birds in the garden singing and the frogs croaking, for Nag and Nagaina used to eat frogs as well as little birds.

When Rikki got to the house, Teddy and Teddy's mother (she looked very white still, for she had been fainting) and Teddy's father came out and almost cried over him; and that night he ate all that was given him till he could eat no more and went to bed on Teddy's shoulder, where Teddy's mother saw him when she came to look late at night.

"Just think, he saved all our lives."

"He saved our lives and Teddy's life," she said to her husband. "Just think, he saved all our lives."

Rikki-tikki woke up with a jump, for the mongooses are light sleepers.

"Oh, it's you," he said. "What are you bothering for? All the cobras are dead; and if they weren't, I'm here."

Rikki-tikki had a right to be proud of himself, but he did not grow too proud, and he kept that garden as a mongoose should keep it, with tooth and jump and spring and bite, till never a cobra dared show its head inside the walls. ❖

Is Rikki-tikki-tavi "brave" in killing the snakes, or is he just doing what a mongoose does? Is courage more like an instinct we are born with or like a habit we can learn?

Find Meaning
1. (a) In "Rikki-tikki-tavi," what is the motto of the mongoose family? (b) What does this motto tell you about Rikki-tikki?
2. (a) What is the plan Nag and Nagaina come up with to regain the garden as their territory? (b) Why would the plan get rid of Rikki-tikki?

Make Judgments
3. (a) What different battles does Rikki-tikki fight? (b) In your opinion, in which of these battles does the mongoose show the greatest courage? Explain your answer.
4. (a) How do animals and people respond to Rikki-tikki? (b) How do these responses help shape the character of the mongoose?

Teach the Selection

MIRRORS & WINDOWS

Answer: Because Rikki-tikki-tavi is personified, he seems capable of human qualities such as courage. His bravery is also consistent with his character as a mongoose. Students will differ on whether courage can be learned or results from an individual's nature.

Find Meaning
1. (a) The motto is "run and find out." (b) It says Rikki-tikki is curious and daring.
2. (a) The cobras plan to kill the family in the house. (b) They hope that without people in the house, Rikki-tikki will leave the garden.

Make Judgments
3. (a) Rikki-tikki fights Nag and Nagaina together, fights Karait, fights Nag in the house, and fights Nagaina in her den. (b) Most students will choose the fights with Nag in the house and with Nagaina in her den; the mongoose fights his opponents under very difficult circumstances.
4. (a) The animals, other than the snakes, and the people greatly admire him. (b) These responses help portray him as a heroic warrior.

Writing Skills

Develop a Personified Character
Briefly review the main techniques of characterization (see page 17) and discuss how Kipling uses them in "Rikki-tikki-tavi." Then challenge students to develop their own personified characters, using these instructions.
1. Select a non-human, living or nonliving thing to be the personified character.
2. Briefly describe the character's appearance and personality.
3. Write something that the character says, does, or thinks. Have students note the setting and plot in which the character exists.
4. Write a sentence or two about how other characters would react to this character.

The Green Mamba

An Autobiography by Roald Dahl

Oh, those snakes! How I hated them! They were the only fearful thing about Tanganyika, and a newcomer very quickly learned to identify most of them and to know which were deadly and which were simply poisonous. The killers, apart from the black mambas, were the green mambas, the cobras and the tiny little puff adders that looked very much like small sticks lying motionless in the middle of a dusty path, and so easy to step on.

One Sunday evening I was invited to go and have a sundowner[1] at the house of an Englishman called Fuller who worked in the **A** Customs office[2] in Dar es Salaam. He lived with his wife and two small children in a plain white wooden house that stood alone some way back from the road in a rough grassy piece of ground with coconut trees scattered about. I was walking across the grass toward the house and was about twenty yards away when I saw a large green snake go gliding straight up the veranda[3] steps of Fuller's house and in through the open front door. The brilliant yellowy-green skin and its great size made me certain it was a green mamba, a creature almost as deadly as the black mamba, and for a few seconds I was so startled and dumbfounded and horrified that I froze to the spot. Then I pulled myself together and ran round to the back of the house shouting, "Mr. Fuller! Mr. Fuller!"

> "There's a green mamba in your living room!"

1. **sundowner.** Evening refreshment
2. **Customs office.** Government agency that controls taxes on imports and exports
3. **veranda.** Open-air porch, usually with a roof

98

Mrs. Fuller popped her head out of an upstairs window. "What on earth's the matter?" she said.

"You've got a large green mamba in your front room!" I shouted. "I saw it go up the veranda steps and right in through the door!"

"Fred!" Mrs. Fuller shouted, turning round. "Fred! Come here!"

Freddy Fuller's round red face appeared at the window beside his wife. "What's up?" he asked.

"There's a green mamba in your living room!" I shouted.

Without hesitation and without wasting time with more questions, he said to me, "Stay there. I'm going to lower the children down to you one at a time." He was completely cool and unruffled.[4] He didn't even raise his voice.

A small girl was lowered down to me by her wrists and I was able to catch her easily by the legs. Then came a small boy. Then Freddy Fuller lowered his wife and I caught her by the waist and put her on the ground. Then came Fuller himself. He hung by his hands from the windowsill and when he let go he landed neatly on his two feet.

We stood in a little group on the grass at the back of the house and I told Fuller exactly what I had seen.

The mother was holding the two children by the hand, one on each side of her. They didn't seem to be particularly alarmed.

"What happens now?" I asked.

"Go down to the road, all of you," Fuller said. "I'm off to fetch the snake-man." He trotted away and got into his small ancient black car and drove off. Mrs. Fuller and the two small children and I went down to the road and sat in the shade of a large mango tree.

"Who is this snake-man?" I asked Mrs. Fuller.

"He is an old Englishman who has been out here for years," Mrs. Fuller said. "He actually *likes* snakes. He understands them and never kills them. He catches them and sells them to zoos and laboratories all over the world. Every native for miles around knows about him and whenever one of them sees a snake, he marks its hiding place and runs, often for great distances, to tell the snake-man. Then the snake-man comes along and captures it. The snake-man's strict rule is that he will never buy a captured snake from the natives."

"Why not?" I asked.

"To discourage them from trying to catch snakes themselves," Mrs. Fuller said. "In his early days he used to buy caught snakes, but so many natives got bitten trying to catch them, and so many died, that he decided to put a stop to it. Now any native who brings in a caught snake, no matter how rare, gets turned away."

"That's good," I said.

"What is the snake-man's name?" I asked.

"Donald Macfarlane," she said. "I believe he's Scottish."

"Is the snake in the house, Mummy?" the small girl asked.

"Yes, darling. But the snake-man is going to get it out."

"He'll bite Jack," the girl said.

"Oh, my God!" Mrs. Fuller cried, jumping to her feet. "I forgot about Jack!" She began calling out, "Jack! Come here, Jack! Jack!... Jack!...Jack!"

The children jumped up as well and all of them started calling to the dog. But no dog came out of the open front door.

---

4. **unruffled.** Poised; calm

Teach the Selection

Analyze Literature
Autobiography Tell students that autobiography is a form of nonfiction in which a person tells his or her own life story. The only difference between the setting, plot, and characters in short stories, such as "Rikki-tikki-tavi," and in autobiographies is that in the autobiography, they are real rather than made up.

Analyze Literature
Setting Review with students "Understanding Setting" on page 29. Then ask students to read the first two paragraphs of "The Green Mamba." Have students describe to you the physical setting (house, road, trees, yard) and the time (Sunday evening). Ask them also to describe how the setting "feels" based on the people in it.

▶ More About the Author
"The Green Mamba" comes from Roald Dahl's book, *Going Solo*. The book is a collection of autobiographical essays about his experiences while serving as a fighter pilot in Africa during World War II (1939–1945).

Writing Skills

Use Similes
Remind students that a simile is a comparison that contains the word *like* or *as*. Memorable similes usually compare two things that are not alike—for example, Dahl compares a snake's movement to the quick open-and-shut of a camera shutter.

Tell students that the snake-man in "The Green Mamba" "moved like a leopard, with soft slow catlike strides." Ask a volunteer to demonstrate this kind of movement, or demonstrate it yourself. Then, ask students to pick a person in their lives who moves in a distinctive way. Have each student write a description of this movement using one or more similes.

Science Connection

Snake Danger Poison and venom can both be deadly; the difference is that poison is absorbed or eaten, while venom is injected. Snakes are the only venomous animals that use their venom for offense as well as self-defense. It is hard to identify the world's most dangerous snakes, because the most venomous snake may be so rare that it never attacks a human being, while a less-venomous snake can kill many people because it attacks more often. The mamba is an aggressive snake, which makes it especially dangerous.

History Connection

Shell Oil In the late 1930s, Dahl was a salesman for Shell Oil in Tanganyika, which was then governed by the British. Europeans had long been attracted to the African continent for its mineral wealth. Shell was British and, at the time, the world's largest oil company. **A**

"He's bitten Jack!" the small girl cried out. "He must have bitten him!" She began to cry and so did her brother, who was a year or so younger than she was. Mrs. Fuller looked grim.

"Jack's probably hiding upstairs," she said. "You know how clever he is."

Mrs. Fuller and I seated ourselves again on the grass, but the children remained standing. In between their tears they went on calling to the dog.

"Would you like me to take you down to the Maddens' house?" their mother asked.

"No!" they cried. "No, no, no! We want Jack!"

"Here's Daddy!" Mrs. Fuller cried, pointing at the tiny black car coming up the road in a swirl of dust. I noticed a long wooden pole sticking out through one of the car windows.

The children ran to meet the car. "Jack's inside the house and he's been bitten by the snake!" they wailed. "We know he's been bitten! He doesn't come when we call him!"

Mr. Fuller and the snake-man got out of the car. The snake-man was small and very old, probably over seventy. He wore leather boots made of thick cowhide and he had long gauntlet-type gloves[5] on his hands made of the same stuff. The gloves reached above his elbows. In his right hand he carried an extraordinary implement, an eight-foot-long wooden pole with a forked end. The two prongs of the fork were made, so it seemed, of black rubber, about an inch thick and quite flexible, and it was clear that if the fork was pressed against the ground the two

It lay there like a long, beautiful, deadly shaft of green glass, quite motionless, perhaps asleep.

prongs would bend outward, allowing the neck of the fork to go down as close to the ground as necessary. In his left hand he carried an ordinary brown sack.

Donald Macfarlane, the snake-man, may have been old and small but he was an impressive-looking character. His eyes were pale blue, deep-set in a face round and dark and wrinkled as a walnut. Above the blue eyes, the eyebrows were thick and startlingly white, but the hair on his head was almost black. In spite of the thick leather boots, he moved like a leopard, with soft slow catlike strides, and he came straight up to me and said, "Who are you?"

A "He's with Shell,"[6] Fuller said. "He hasn't been here long."

"You want to watch?" the snake-man said to me.

"Watch?" I said, wavering. "Watch? How do you mean watch? I mean where from? Not in the house?"

"You can stand out on the veranda and look through the window," the snake-man said.

"Come on," Fuller said. "We'll both watch."

"Now don't do anything silly," Mrs. Fuller said.

The two children stood there <u>forlorn</u> and miserable, with tears all over their cheeks.

The snake-man and Fuller and I walked over the grass toward the house, and as we approached the veranda steps the snake-man

---

5. gauntlet-type gloves. Protective gloves
6. Shell. Shell Oil, the company Dahl flew for

for•lorn (fər lôrn´) *adj.*, sad; lonely; hopeless

English Language Learning

Tell students that in English, writers often make adjectives by connecting several words with hyphens. Help them find these examples in the text, and ask questions to be sure students grasp their meaning.

- gauntlet-type [gloves], 100
- eight-foot-long [wooden pole], 100
- impressive-looking [character], 100
- deep-set [eyes], 100
- backward-curving [position], 102

You might also note that the hyphenated word *snake-man* is a noun.

whispered, "Tread softly on the wooden boards or he'll pick up the vibration. Wait until I've gone in, then walk up quietly and stand by the window."

The snake-man went up the steps first and he made absolutely no sound at all with his feet. He moved soft and catlike onto the veranda and straight through the front door and then he quickly but very quietly closed the door behind him.

I felt better with the door closed. What I mean is I felt better for myself. I certainly didn't feel better for the snake-man. I figured he was committing suicide. I followed Fuller onto the veranda and we both crept over to the window. The window was open, but it had a fine mesh mosquito netting all over it. That made me feel better still. We peered through the netting.

The living room was simple and ordinary, coconut matting on the floor, a red sofa, a coffee table and a couple of armchairs. The dog was sprawled on the matting under the coffee table, a large Airedale with curly brown and black hair. He was stone dead.

The snake-man was standing absolutely still just inside the door of the living room. The brown sack was now slung over his left shoulder and he was grasping the long pole with both hands, holding it out in front of him, parallel to the ground. I couldn't see the snake. I didn't think the snake-man had seen it yet either.

A minute went by...two minutes...three... four...five. Nobody moved. There was death in that room. The air was heavy with death and the snake-man stood as motionless as a pillar of stone, with the long rod held out in front of him.

And still he waited. Another minute...and another...and another.

And now I saw the snake-man beginning to bend his knees. Very slowly he bent his knees until he was almost squatting on the floor, and from that position he tried to peer under the sofa and the armchairs.

And still it didn't look as though he was seeing anything.

Slowly he straightened his legs again, and then his head began to swivel around the room. Over to the right, in the far corner, a staircase led up to the floor above. The snake-man looked at the stairs, and I knew very well what was going through his head. Quite abruptly, he took one step forward and stopped.

Nothing happened.

A moment later I caught sight of the snake. It was lying full-length along the skirting[7] of the right-hand wall, but hidden from the snake-man's view by the back of the sofa. It lay there like a long, beautiful, deadly shaft of green glass, quite motionless, perhaps asleep. It was facing away from us who were at the window, with its small triangular head resting on the matting near the foot of the stairs.

I nudged Fuller and whispered, "It's over there against the wall." I pointed and Fuller saw the snake. At once, he started waving both hands, palms outward, back and forth across the window, hoping to get the snake-man's attention. The snake-man didn't see him. Very softly, Fuller said, "Pssst!" and the snake-man looked up sharply. Fuller

B

7. **skirting.** Baseboard

RIKKI-TIKKI-TAVI / THE GREEN MAMBA **101**

◄ ►

Teach the Selection

Use Reading Strategies
Make Inferences Remind students that when they infer, they combine what they already know with new information. Ask them to reread the paragraph that begins "I felt better with the door closed." Then ask what they can infer about the speaker's feelings from the paragraph they just read. (The speaker is afraid, even though people have assured him that the snake-man knows what he is doing.) **B**

Make Connections
Tell students to compare, in their minds, the family's response to the mamba in "The Green Mamba" and the family's response to the cobra in "Rikki-tikki-tavi." Ask: "Which family's response is more realistic? How can the families' circumstances explain their responses?"

Grammar Skills

Ellipses
Tell students that three dots in a row make up a type of punctuation called ellipses points. Ellipses points indicate where material has been left out — for example, where part of a quoted passage has been omitted. Ellipses points can show that an idea trails off. Some writers, like Dahl in "The Green Mamba," use ellipses points to show silence or inactivity.

Write this sentence on the board. Have students tell you where to add ellipses points:

"Keep still, my lovely," the snake-man whispered. "Don't move now. Keep still. No one's going to hurt you."

Analyze Literature

Characterization Remind students that characterization involves three main techniques:

1. Showing what characters say, do, or think

2. Showing what other characters (and the narrator) say or think about them

3. Describing what physical features, dress, and personality the characters display

Ask students, based on what they have read so far, which technique Dahl uses the most to characterize the snake-man. (He describes the man's physical appearance and personality.)

Use Reading Strategies

Make Predictions Ask students to predict how the snake-man will get the snake out of the house. Have them visualize the snake-man's pole and the grip he first has on the snake, and then speculate about how he can maneuver the pole to control the animal. As they finish reading the selection, ask students how close their predictions were to the truth. **Ⓐ**

---

pointed. The snake-man understood and gave a nod.

Now the snake-man began working his way very very slowly to the back wall of the room so as to get a view of the snake behind the sofa. He never walked on his toes as you or I would have done. His feet remained flat on the ground all the time. The cowhide boots were like moccasins, with neither soles nor heels. Gradually, he worked his way over to the back wall, and from there he was able to see at least the head and two or three feet of the snake itself.

But the snake also saw him. With a movement so fast it was invisible, the snake's head came up about two feet off the floor and the front of the body arched backwards, ready to strike. Almost simultaneously, it bunched its whole body into a series of curves, ready to flash forward.

The snake-man was just a bit too far away from the snake to reach it with the end of his pole. He waited, staring at the snake, and the snake stared back at him with two small malevolent[8] black eyes.

Then the snake-man started speaking to the snake. "Come along, my pretty," he whispered in a soft wheedling[9] voice. "There's a good boy. Nobody's going to hurt you. Nobody's going to harm you, my pretty little thing. Just lie still and relax..." He took a step forward toward the snake, holding the pole out in front of him. **Ⓐ**

What the snake did next was so fast that the whole movement couldn't have taken more than a hundredth of a second, like the flick of a camera shutter. There was a green flash as the snake darted forward at least ten feet and struck at the snake-man's leg.

The sack started jumping about as though there were fifty angry rats inside it....

Nobody could have got out of the way of that one. I heard the snake's head strike against the thick cowhide boot with a sharp little crack, and then at once the head was back in that same deadly backward-curving position, ready to strike again.

"There's a good boy," the snake-man said softly. "There's a clever boy. There's a lovely fellow. You mustn't get excited. Keep calm and everything's going to be all right." As he was speaking, he was slowly lowering the end of the pole until the forked prongs were about twelve inches above the middle of the snake's body. "There's a lovely fellow," he whispered. "There's a good kind little chap. Keep still now, my beauty. Keep still, my pretty. Keep quite still. Daddy's not going to hurt you."

I could see a thin dark trickle of venom running down the snake-man's right boot where the snake had struck.

The snake, head raised and arcing[10] backwards, was as tense as a tight-wound spring and ready to strike again. "Keep still, my lovely," the snake-man whispered. "Don't move now. Keep still. No one's going to hurt you."

Then *wham*, the rubber prongs came down right across the snake's body, about midway along its length, and pinned it to the floor. All I could see was a green blur as the snake thrashed around furiously in an effort to free itself. But the snake-man kept up the

---

8. malevolent. Having or showing hatred
9. wheedling. Coaxing; flattering
10. arcing. Following a curved course

Differentiated Instruction

English Language Learning

Define *simile* for English learners. Have students read the next-to-last paragraph of "The Green Mamba," pausing to ask how the snake makes the sack seem "as though there were fifty angry rats inside it" (the snake twists and turns inside the sack). Then ask how the snake-man is able to hold that sack "as if it contained no more than a few pounds of potatoes." Make sure students understand the difference between how agitated the snake is and how calm the snake-man is.

pressure on the prongs and the snake was trapped.

What happens next? I wondered. There was no way he could catch hold of that madly twisting flailing length of green muscle with his hands, and even if he could have done so, the head would surely have flashed around and bitten him in the face.

Holding the very end of the eight-foot pole, the snake-man began to work his way round the room until he was at the tail end of the snake. Then, in spite of the flailing and the thrashing, he started pushing the prongs forward along the snake's body toward the head. Very very slowly he did it, pushing the

rubber prongs forward over the snake's flailing body, keeping the snake pinned down all the time and pushing, pushing, pushing the long wooden rod forward millimeter by millimeter. It was a fascinating and frightening thing to watch, the little man with white eyebrows and black hair carefully <u>manipulating</u> his long implement and sliding the fork ever so slowly along the length of the twisting snake toward the head. The snake's body was thumping against the coconut matting with such a noise that if you had been upstairs you might have thought two big men were wrestling on the floor.

Then at last the prongs were right behind the head itself, pinning it down, and at that point the snake-man reached forward with one gloved hand and grasped the snake very firmly by the neck. He threw away the pole. He took the sack off his shoulder with his free hand. He lifted the great, still twisting length of the deadly green snake and pushed the head into the sack. Then he let go the head and bundled the rest of the creature in and closed the sack. The sack started jumping about as though there were fifty angry rats inside it, but the snake-man was now totally relaxed and he held the sack casually in one hand as if it contained no more than a few pounds of potatoes. He stooped and picked up his pole from the floor, then he turned and looked toward the window where we were peering in.

"Pity about the dog," he said. "You'd better get it out of the way before the children see it." ❖

ma·nip·u·late (mə nip´ yə lāt) *v.*, treat or operate with the hands in a skillful manner

![Mirrors & Windows] Who do you think shows more courage—the snake-man or Rikki-tikki-tavi? How is their behavior in the presence of danger similar? How is it different?

Analyze Literature

Personification Remind students that in "Rikki-tikki-tavi," all the animal characters had personalities. Ask if they think the snake in "The Green Mamba" is personified. (The snake has "malevolent black eyes," implying that it wants to hurt someone. More than personifying the snake, however, Dahl portrays the snake-man talking to the snake as if it were human—for example, "You mustn't get excited. Keep calm and everything's going to be all right.")

Use Reading Strategies

Clarify Have students review the description of how the snake-man gets the snake into the bag. Tell them to make sure they understand exactly how the process works. If they are unable to follow a part of the description, have them write a question to ask other students so they can clarify what they have read. **B**

![Mirrors & Windows] *Answer:* Most students will feel Rikki-tikki shows much more courage than the snake-man. Both characters face danger without showing fear. Rikki-tikki's courage comes from being a mongoose, while the snake-man's results from his experience.

Speaking & Listening Skills

Prepare an Informal Debate

Ask students: "Is it right for people to live where there are dangerous animals?"

Randomly separate the class into two groups. Assign one group the affirmative side: People should live anywhere they want, and should drive out dangerous animals. Give the other group the negative side: People should avoid living where there are dangerous animals.

Give each group five minutes to prepare a brief statement of its position and choose a person to deliver it. Then have the groups make their opening statements. Follow up by having students informally debate the issue, and reach a class consensus on the better position.

Review the Selections

Find Meaning

1. (a) He is cool and unruffled. (b) He feels confident that he can control the situation.

2. (a) All three worry about the dog and call frantically for him. (b) The dog serves as a focus for the family's fears and as evidence of how dangerous the snake is.

3. He regards it as a dangerous, beautiful animal worthy of respect.

Make Judgments

4. (a) The narrator describes the snake "gliding," having "brilliant yellow-green skin," being "like a long, beautiful, deadly shaft of green glass," and striking like "a green flash." (b) He creates the effect of strength, beauty, and danger.

5. (a) He was "old and small but . . . an impressive looking character" who "moved like a leopard," and "whispered in a soft wheedling voice." (b) The man is a fearless snake enthusiast who is both gentle and skillful in capturing the animals.

Compare Literature

Personification

1. He gives them names, intelligence, and emotions such as hatred and fear.

2. No; none of the snake's traits (strength, swiftness, beauty) are exclusively human.

3. Some students may think the personified snakes in "Rikki-tikki-tavi," are more frightening; others may feel that the deadliness of the green mamba is more frightening.

Comparing Literature

AFTER READING

Find Meaning

1. (a) How does Mr. Fuller respond to the news that the snake has entered his living room? (b) Based on his actions, how do you think Mr. Fuller feels about the snake?

2. (a) How do the children and Mrs. Fuller respond when they realize the dog is still in the house? (b) What role does the dog play in the story?

3. What is the snake-man's attitude toward the snake? Explain.

Compare Literature

Personification When a writer uses personification, he or she gives human intelligence, emotions, abilities, and other traits to non-human characters. Review the characteristics of the snakes in "Rikki-tikki-tavi" and "The Green Mamba" that you recorded in your chart to answer the following questions.

Make Judgments

4. (a) What words and phrases does the narrator use to describe the green mamba and its actions? (b) What effect does he create with his descriptions of the snake?

5. (a) What words and phrases does the narrator use to describe the snake-man and his actions? (b) What is the effect of his characterization of the snake-man?

1. How does the author personify Karait, Nag, and Nagaina in "Rikki-tikki-tavi"?

2. Does the author personify the snake in "The Green Mamba"? Explain your answer.

3. Which snakes—those in "Rikki-tikki-tavi" or the green mamba—do you find more frightening? Why do you feel this way?

Extend Understanding

Writing Options

Creative Writing Imagine that the snake-man was writing a **letter** to a friend who also studies snakes describing the events in "Rikki-tikki-tavi." Keep in mind the attitude toward snakes he shows in "The Green Mamba" in creating his version of the story of Rikki-tikki's battles with Karait, Nag, and Nagaina.

Expository Writing Write a brief **compare-and-contrast essay** examining the similarities and differences between the settings, characters, and themes of "Rikki-tikki-tavi" and "The Green Mamba." You may organize your essay either by examining all three elements first in one work and then in the other or by discussing each literary element in turn. Share your work with the class.

Collaborative Learning

Hold a Panel Discussion Use "Rikki-tikki-tavi" and "The Green Mamba" as jumping-off points in a discussion about what personal characteristics enable individuals to perform well in a crisis. Keep a list of such traits as you discuss them, and at the conclusion, vote to determine which are the three most important characteristics.

Media Literacy

Conduct Internet Research Use the Internet to research information for a comparison study of the western green mamba *(Dendroaspis viridis)* and the king cobra *(Ophiophagus hannah)*. Find out facts about their size, appearance, habitat, range, and habits. Determine which of the two snakes represents a greater danger to human beings.

 Go to **www.mirrorsandwindows.com** for more.

Rubrics for Writing Options

You can adapt this as a checklist for students to use as they write.

Creative Writing

☐ Does the letter clearly identify the writer as the snake-man?

☐ Does the letter accurately describe the events in "Rikki-tikki-tavi"?

☐ Does the letter describe the events in a manner consistent with the character of the snake-man?

Expository Writing

☐ Does the essay accurately describe the settings, characters, and themes in each story?

☐ Does the essay maintain a consistent and logical organization?

☐ Does the essay effectively compare and contrast literary elements from each story?

UNCLE TONY'S GOAT

A Short Story
by Leslie Marmon Silko

"Something will get hurt. Maybe even one of you."

We had a hard time finding the right kind of string to use. We knew we needed gut to string our bows the way the men did, but we were little kids and we didn't know how to get any. So Kenny went to his house and brought back a ball of white cotton string that his mother used to string red chili with. It was thick and soft and it didn't make very good bowstring. As soon as we got the bows made we sat down again on the sand bank above the stream and started skinning willow twigs for arrows. It was past noon, and the tall willows behind us made cool shade. There were lots of little minnows that day, flashing in the shallow water, swimming back and forth wildly like they weren't sure if they really wanted to go up or down the stream; it was a day for minnows that we were always hoping for—we could have filled our rusty coffee cans and old pickle jars full. But this was the first time for making bows and arrows, and the minnows weren't much different from the sand or the rocks now. The secret is the arrows. The ones we made were crooked, and when we shot them they didn't go straight—they flew around in arcs and curves; so we crawled through the leaves and branches, deep into the willow groves, looking for the best, the straightest willow branches. But even after we skinned the sticky wet bark from them and whittled the knobs off, they still weren't

Although she is of mixed ancestry—Laguna Pueblo, Mexican, and European—**Leslie Marmon Silko** has always identified most closely with the Native American part of her background. Born in 1948, she was raised on the Laguna Pueblo reservation where she grew up hearing traditional stories. She draws on her Native American heritage in her writing, which includes poetry, novels, short stories, essays, articles, and film scripts. Her story "Uncle Tony's Goat" grew out of a late-night telephone conversation with an old friend and fellow Pueblo Indian, the poet Simon Ortiz, who told her a story about a mean billy goat.

105

Preview the Selection

At a Glance
Independent Reading
- Reading Level: Easy
- Difficulty Considerations: None
- Ease Factor: Simple plot

Objectives
Reading this selection will enable students to do the following:
- read with developing fluency
- read silently with comprehension for a sustained period of time

Launch the Lesson
Prior to reading "Uncle Tony's Goat," ask students to recall memorable encounters they have had with animals. Then ask: "Do animals have long memories or hold grudges?"

The Mirrors & Windows questions at the end of the story focus on the theme of relating to animals. Before students begin reading, ask: Where would you draw the line between tame animals and wild animals?

TEACHING NOTE
Although this selection is presented in the student edition as an independent reading, teaching support has been provided should you choose to cover it in class.

Program Resources

Planning and Assessment
Program Planning Guide, Selection Lesson Plan
E-Lesson Planner
Assessment Guide, Lesson Test
ExamView

Technology Tools
Interactive Student Text on CD
Visual Teaching Package
Audio Library
mirrorsandwindows.com

Meeting the Standards
Fiction: Unit 1, Independent Reading, pp. 81–87

Differentiating Instruction
Advanced Students, Independent Reading Project, pp. 7–8

Common Core State Standards
Reading Literature
RL.1, RL.10

Summary

Uncle Tony has a special attachment to his billy goat. One day the seven-year-old narrator and his friends practice shooting their homemade arrows at the nanny goats and kids. The goats are unharmed, but the narrator feels the billy goat staring at him. Soon afterward, the billy goat knocks the narrator down. The boy suffers only a small cut, but Uncle Tony sadly locks the billy goat in the pen. All day at school the boy worries that Uncle Tony will kill the goat. He arrives home to find that the goat has escaped and Uncle Tony is going after it on horseback. Three days later, Uncle Tony returns without the goat. Uncle Tony isn't upset, though; he smiles when he speaks of the stubborn goat.

Analyze Literature

Setting Ask students what the details in the first three paragraphs of the story tell them about the setting. (It is a rural community in a warm climate. The children play near a stream under willow trees; people grow chili peppers; there is a church nearby; and goats graze in a hillside field.)

straight. Finally we went ahead and made notches at the end of each arrow to hook in the bowstring, and we started practicing, thinking maybe we could learn to shoot the crooked arrows straight.

We left the river each of us with a handful of damp, yellow arrows and our fresh-skinned willow bows. We walked slowly and shot arrows at bushes, big rocks, and the juniper tree that grows by Pino's sheep pen. They were working better just like we had figured; they still didn't fly straight, but now we could compensate[1] for that by the way we aimed them. We were going up to the church to shoot at the cats old Sister Julian kept outside the cloister.[2] We didn't want to hurt anything, just to have new kinds of things to shoot at.

But before we got to the church we went past the grassy hill where my uncle Tony's goats were grazing. A few of them were lying down chewing their cud[3] peacefully, and they didn't seem to notice us. The billy goat was lying down, but he was watching us closely like he already knew about little kids. His yellow goat eyes didn't blink, and he stared with a wide, hostile[4] look. The grazing goats made good deer for our bows. We shot all our arrows at the nanny goats and their kids; they skipped away from the careening[5] arrows and never lost the rhythm of their greedy chewing as they continued to nibble the weeds and grass on the hillside. The billy goat was lying there watching us and taking us into his memory. As we ran down the road toward the church and Sister Julian's cats, I looked back, and my uncle Tony's billy goat was still watching me.

> The billy goat never forgot the bows and arrows....

My uncle and my father were sitting on the bench outside the house when we walked by. It was September now, and the farming was almost over, except for bringing home the melons and a few pumpkins. They were mending ropes and bridles and feeling the afternoon sun. We held our bows and arrows out in front of us so they could see them. My father smiled and kept braiding the strips of leather in his hand, but my uncle Tony put down the bridle and pieces of scrap leather he was working on and looked at each of us kids slowly. He was old, getting some white hair—he was my mother's oldest brother, the one that scolded us when we told lies or broke things.

"You'd better not be shooting at things," he said, "only at rocks or trees. Something will get hurt. Maybe even one of you."

We all nodded in agreement and tried to hold the bows and arrows less conspicuously[6] down at our sides; when he turned back to his work we hurried away before he took the bows away from us like he did the time we made the slingshot. He caught us shooting rocks at an old wrecked car; its windows were all busted out anyway, but he took the slingshot away. I always wondered what he did with it and with the knives we made ourselves out of tin cans. When I was much older I asked my mother, "What did he ever do with those knives and slingshots he took

---

1. **compensate.** Offset or counterbalance an effect
2. **cloister.** Convent, or residence of nuns
3. **cud.** Partially digested food chewed a second time by cows, goats, and other grazing animals
4. **hostile.** Unfriendly
5. **careening.** Moving wildly; uncontrolled
6. **conspicuously.** In a very noticeable way

Words in Use

Selection Words	Teaching Words
kindling, 107	**ancestry,** 105
trough, 107	**enriches,** 110
daintily, 108	

away from us?" She was kneading[7] bread on the kitchen table at the time and was probably busy thinking about the fire in the oven outside. "I don't know," she said; "you ought to ask him yourself." But I never did. I thought about it lots of times, but I never did. It would have been like getting caught all over again.

A

The goats were valuable. We got milk and meat from them. My uncle was careful to see that all the goats were treated properly; the worst scolding my older sister ever got was when my mother caught her and some of her friends chasing the newborn kids. My mother kept saying over and over again, "It's a good thing I saw you; what if your uncle had seen you?" and even though we kids were very young then, we understood very well what she meant.

The billy goat never forgot the bows and arrows, even after the bows had cracked and split and the crooked, whittled arrows were all lost. This goat was big and black and important to my uncle Tony because he'd paid a lot to get him and because he wasn't an ordinary goat. Uncle Tony had bought him from a white man, and then he'd hauled him in the back of the pickup all the way from Quemado.[8] And my uncle was the only person who could touch this goat. If a stranger or one of us kids got too near him, the mane[9] on the billy goat's neck would stand on end and the goat would rear up on his hind legs and dance forward trying to reach the person with his long, spiral horns. This billy goat smelled bad, and none of us cared if we couldn't pet him. But my uncle took good care of this goat. The goat would let Uncle Tony brush him with

"Get up, big goat!"

the horse brush and scratch him around the base of his horns. Uncle Tony talked to the billy goat—in the morning when he unpenned the goats and in the evening when he gave them their hay and closed the gate for the night. I never paid too much attention to what he said to the billy goat; usually it was something like "Get up, big goat! You've slept long enough," or "Move over, big goat, and let the others have something to eat." I think Uncle Tony was proud of that billy goat.

We all had chores to do around home. My sister helped out around the house mostly, and I was supposed to carry water from the hydrant[10] and bring in kindling. I helped my father look after the horses and pigs, and Uncle Tony milked the goats and fed them. One morning near the end of September I was out feeding the pigs their table scraps and pig mash;[11] I'd given the pigs their food, and I was watching them squeal and snap at each other as they crowded into the feed trough. Behind me I could hear the milk squirting into the eight-pound lard pail that Uncle Tony used for milking.

When he finished milking he noticed me standing there; he motioned toward the goats still inside the pen. "Run the rest of them out," he said as he untied the two milk goats and carried the milk to the house.

B I was seven years old, and I understood that everyone, including my uncle, expected me to handle more chores; so I hurried over to the goat pen and swung the tall wire gate

---

7. **kneading.** Pressing or squeezing with the hands
8. **Quemado.** Town in west central New Mexico
9. **mane.** Hair growing about the neck of some animals
10. **hydrant.** Pipe that discharges water
11. **mash.** Animal feed

Use Reading Skills
Analyze Cause and Effect Ask students why, even as a grown man, the narrator doesn't want to ask Uncle Tony about the knives and slingshots. (Uncle Tony still has a strong influence on the narrator, and the narrator still feels like a naughty child risking Uncle Tony's disapproval.) **A**

Analyze Literature
Sensory Details Point out that the author uses sensory details to describe the billy goat and how it reacts to different people. Ask students to identify these sensory details. (With strangers, visual and tactile details include the goat's mane standing on end, his rearing up and dancing forward, his threatening with his long, spiral horns, and his unpleasant odor; with Uncle Tony, visual and tactile images include Uncle Tony brushing the goat and scratching him about the horns affectionately.) **B**

> **More by This Author**
> Students who like "Uncle Tony's Goat" might enjoy the stories, poems, photographs, and personal accounts in Silko's collection *Storyteller.*

Differentiated Instruction

English Language Learning
Have students read the story in pairs. Remind them to use the footnotes to find definitions of difficult or unusual words used in the story. If an unknown word is not defined in the footnotes, tell students to continue reading to see if the context will help them clarify the meaning. If necessary, they can pause in their reading to look up words in a dictionary. Students can also jot down unknown words as they read and look up their definitions after they finish reading the story. Encourage students to record each word with its definition, pronunciation, and a drawing or a context sentence on an index card. They can use these word cards as study aids.

Use Reading Strategies

Make Predictions Point out to students that the narrator thinks the billy goat has never forgotten the incident with the bows and arrows. Ask them to predict what will happen next. **Ⓐ**

History Connection

Laguna Pueblo For the setting of this story the author may have drawn from her own knowledge of the Laguna Pueblo, which is located 45 miles west of Albuquerque, New Mexico. Evidence shows that Native Americans have lived here for thousands of years. *Laguna* is the name the Spanish gave to the community in 1699. The people who live there call it Ka-waikah or Kawaik, which means "Lake People." Farming and raising livestock were the traditional occupations in the six villages that make up the pueblo. A more recent occupation is uranium mining, which has added to the prosperity of the pueblo. Today, the Laguna Pueblo has a population of nearly 8,000 people.

Analyze Literature

Plot Ask students what they think is the climax of the story. Remind them that the climax is the point of highest tension or the turning point. (The billy goat's charge combines tension and dramatic action.) **Ⓑ**

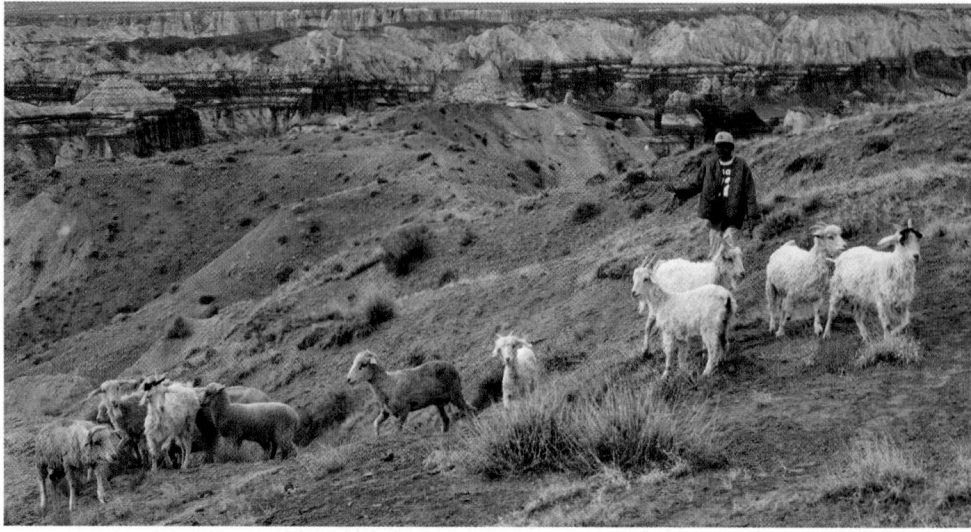

open. The does and kids came prancing out. They trotted daintily past the pigpen and scattered out, intent on finding leaves and grass to eat. It wasn't until then I noticed that the billy goat hadn't come out of the little wooden shed inside the goat pen. I stood outside the pen and tried to look inside the wooden shelter, but it was still early and the morning sun left the inside of the shelter in deep shadow. I stood there for a while, hoping that he would come out by himself, **Ⓐ** but I realized that he'd recognized me and that he wouldn't come out. I understood right away what was happening and my fear of him was in my bowels and down my neck; I was shaking.

Finally my uncle came out of the house; it was time for breakfast. "What's wrong?" he called out from the door.

"The billy goat won't come out," I yelled back, hoping he would look disgusted and come do it himself.

"Get in there and get him out," he said as he went back into the house.

I looked around quickly for a stick or broom handle, or even a big rock, but I couldn't find anything. I walked into the pen slowly, concentrating on the darkness beyond the shed door; I circled to the back of the shed and kicked at the boards, hoping to make the billy goat run out. I put my eye up to a crack between the boards, and I could see he was standing up now and that his yellow eyes were on mine.

My mother was yelling at me to hurry up, and Uncle Tony was watching. I stepped around into the low doorway, and the goat **Ⓑ** charged toward me, feet first. I had dirt in my mouth and up my nose and there was blood running past my eye; my head ached. Uncle Tony carried me to the house; his face was stiff with anger, and I remembered what he'd always told us about animals; they won't bother you unless you bother them first. I didn't start to cry until my mother hugged me close and wiped my face with a damp

Progressive Verb Forms

Display the following examples:

The boys <u>are walking</u> to the church.

Uncle Tony <u>was sitting</u> on the bench.

He <u>will be feeding</u> the goats soon.

Say that these sentences contain progressive verb forms, which use a helping verb (*are, was, will be*) plus a verb ending in *-ing*. The present progressive indicates that an action is ongoing. Past progressive indicates an action that happened while another action occurred. Future progressive indicates an action that will take place in the future. Ask students to rewrite each of these sentences using the form of the verb indicated.

1. Present progressive: The boys (make) bows and arrows.
2. Past progressive: Uncle Tony (eat) lunch.
3. Future progressive: He (milk) the goats later.

wash rag. It was only a little cut above my eyebrow, and she sent me to school anyway with a Band-Aid on my forehead.

Uncle Tony locked the billy goat in the pen. He didn't say what he was going to do with the goat, but when he left with my father to haul firewood, he made sure the gate to the pen was wired tightly shut. He looked at the goat quietly and with sadness; he said something to the goat, but the yellow eyes stared past him.

"What's he going to do with the goat?" I asked my mother before I went to catch the school bus.

"He ought to get rid of it," she said. "We can't have that goat knocking people down for no good reason."

I didn't feel good at school. The teacher sent me to the nurse's office and the nurse made me lie down. Whenever I closed my eyes I could see the goat and my uncle, and I felt a stiffness in my throat and chest. I got off the school bus slowly, so the other kids would go ahead without me. I walked slowly and wished I could be away from home for a while. I could go over to Grandma's house, but she would ask me if my mother knew where I was and I would have to say no, and she would make me go home first to ask. So I walked very slowly, because I didn't want to see the black goat's hide hanging over the corral fence.

When I got to the house I didn't see a goat hide or the goat, but Uncle Tony was on his horse and my mother was standing beside the horse holding a canteen and a flour sack bundle tied with brown string. I was

---

12. **roan gelding.** Reddish brown male horse that has been neutered
13. **piñon.** Small evergreen

---

frightened at what this meant. My uncle looked down at me from the saddle.

"The goat ran away," he said. "Jumped out of the pen somehow. I saw him just as he went over the hill beyond the river. He stopped at the top of the hill and he looked back this way."

Uncle Tony nodded at my mother and me and then he left; we watched his old roan gelding[12] splash across the stream and labor up the steep path beyond the river. Then they were over the top of the hill and gone.

Uncle Tony was gone for three days. He came home early on the morning of the fourth day, before we had eaten breakfast or fed the animals. He was glad to be home, he said, because he was getting too old for such long rides. He called me over and looked closely at the cut above my eye. It had scabbed over good, and I wasn't wearing a Band-Aid any more; he examined it very carefully before he let me go. He stirred some sugar into his coffee.

"That miserable goat," he said. "I followed him for three days. He was headed south, going straight to Quemado. I never could catch up to him." My uncle shook his head. "The first time I saw him he was already in the piñon[13] forest, halfway into the mountains already. I could see him most of the time, off in the distance a mile or two. He

---

Teach the Selection

Use Reading Strategies
Make Inferences Point out that after the goat charged him, the narrator remembered Uncle Tony had said animals "won't bother you unless you bother them first" (page 108). Ask students why the boy feels upset when he thinks of the goat and his uncle. (He knows his uncle likes the goat; his mother wants the uncle to "get rid of" the goat; and he thinks the bow and arrow incident provoked the goat into knocking him down, so he feels responsible for causing his uncle the pain of losing his goat.) **C**

Science Connection
Goats Spanish explorers brought goats to North America in the 1500s. Goats supply people with meat, milk, cheese, wool, and leather. Goats are grazers, but they can survive on less grass than cows or sheep require. Male goats are known for their rank odor. Wild goats generally live in herds. Uncle Tony's goat may have gone back to his former home, or he may have become "feral," surviving in the wild.

Reading Skills

Use Graphic Organizers
Point out to students that paying attention to sensory details as they read will help them visualize, or imagine, story events. Ask students to identify images or words and phrases in the encounter between the narrator and the goat that contain sensory details. Suggest that they use a chart to identify these details.

Sight	"the darkness beyond the shed door" and "his yellow eyes were on mine"
Sound	"mother was yelling"
Touch	"blood running" "head ached"
Taste	"dirt in my mouth"
Smell	

Answer: Responses may depend on students' familiarity with animals. Those who have pets or care for livestock may have a positive attitude; students with little experience of animals may find them frightening. Students may say the experience of living with animals helps people express affection and exercise responsibility.

Analyze and Extend

1. (a) He regards animals—such as Sister Julian's cats or Uncle Tony's goats—as things to shoot at. They are only objects. (b) By frightening and then hurting the narrator, the billy goat forces him to recognize that an animal can have feelings.

2. (a) Uncle Tony paid a lot for the goat, and he was the only person who could touch the goat. (b) He is proud that the animal eluded him.

3. Animals are not simply toys or pets. The narrator has also come to understand his Uncle Tony better.

Rubric for Creative Writing

You can adapt this as a checklist for students to use as they write.

☐ Does the diary entry clearly present the events of the story?

☐ Is the entry written in the narrator's voice?

---

would stop sometimes and look back." Uncle Tony paused and drank some more coffee. "I stopped at night. I had to. He stopped too, and in the morning we would start out again. The trail just gets higher and steeper. Yesterday morning there was frost on top of the blanket when I woke up and we were in the big pines and red oak leaves. I couldn't see him any more because the forest is too thick. So I turned around." Tony finished the cup of coffee. "He's probably in Quemado by now."

I looked at him again, standing there by the door, ready to go milk the nanny goats.

"There wasn't ever a goat like that one," he said, "but if that's the way he's going to act, O.K. then. That stubborn goat was just too mean anyway."

He smiled at me and his voice was strong and happy when he said this.

 What do you find most appealing about animals? What do you find most frightening? How do you think the experience of living with animals enriches people's lives?

Analyze and Extend

1. (a) How does the narrator respond to animals at the beginning of the story? (b) How does this reaction change?

2. (a) What does Uncle Tony value about the goat? (b) How does he view the animal at the end of the story?

3. What lesson do you think this experience teaches the narrator?

Creative Writing Imagine that the narrator of "Uncle Tony's Goat" keeps a diary. Re-create the major events of the story as **diary entries.** Adopt an appropriate style in your entries.

(Remember that the narrator is seven years old.) You might want to add illustrations to your entries, showing how the narrator sees Uncle Tony, the goat, and other characters in the story.

Collaborative Learning Work with a small group of fellow students to discuss the outcome of the story. Consider the following questions: Why do you think the story ended the way it did? If you had been writing the story, how would you have ended it? How would you describe the ending of the story?

Go to **www.mirrorsandwindows.com** for more.

Differentiated Instruction

Enrichment

Encourage students to cooperatively create a guide to Laguna Pueblo writers and artists. In their guide they should include a bibliography of works by Leslie Marmon Silko, Simon Ortiz, and Paula Gunn Allen, and brief descriptions of the works of artist DeHaven Solimon Chaffins, potter Michael Kanteena, and photographer Lee Marmon. Students can include brief reviews and illustrations in their guides.

Visual Learning

Students may enjoy drawing their impressions of the billy goat. Suggest that they include as many details as they can from the description in the story. They might also want to include Uncle Tony in the drawing to convey something about his attitude toward the animal.

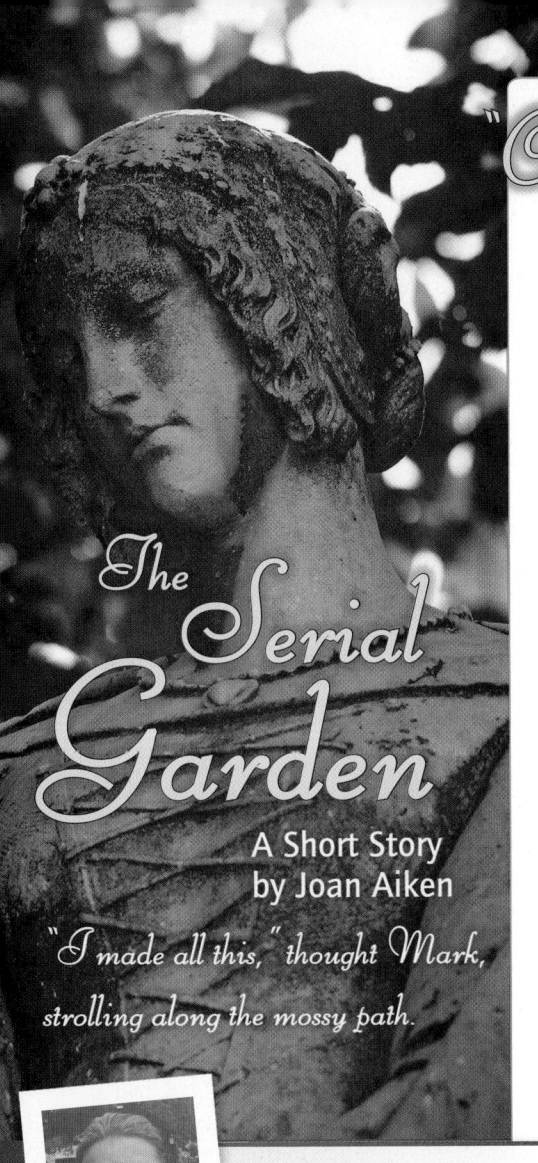

The Serial Garden

A Short Story by Joan Aiken

"I made all this," thought Mark, strolling along the mossy path.

Joan Aiken grew up telling stories. Born in Sussex, England, in 1924, she exchanged tales with her brother about imaginary lands. She was fascinated by mysterious happenings and loved to read stories by Charles Dickens, Rudyard Kipling, Edgar Allan Poe, and Jane Austen. In "The Serial Garden," she presents a new approach to a familiar theme of fantasy literature, the alternative world. Instead of falling down a rabbit hole into Wonderland like Alice, young Mark Armitage gains entry to his fantasy world by assembling the cutouts on the back of a box of breakfast cereal.

"C old rice pudding for breakfast?" said Mark, looking at it with disfavor.

"Don't be fussy," said his mother. "You're the only one who's complaining." This was unfair, for she and Mark were the only members of the family at table, Harriet having developed measles while staying with a school friend, while Mr. Armitage had somehow managed to lock himself in the larder.[1] Mrs. Armitage never had anything but toast and marmalade for breakfast anyway.

Mark went on scowling at the chilly-looking pudding. It had come straight out of the fridge, which was not in the larder.

"If you don't like it," said Mrs. Armitage, "unless you want Daddy to pass your corn flakes through the larder ventilator,[2] flake by flake, you'd better run down to Miss Pride and get a small packet of cereal. She opens at eight; Hickmans doesn't open till nine. It's no use waiting till the blacksmith comes to let your father out; I'm sure he won't be here for hours yet."

There came a gloomy banging from the direction of the larder, just to remind them that Mr. Armitage was alive and suffering in there.

"*You're* all right," shouted Mark heartlessly as he passed the larder door.

---

1. **larder.** Pantry
2. **ventilator.** Device used to bring in fresh air and drive out foul air; fan

Program Resources

Planning and Assessment
Program Planning Guide, Selection Lesson Plan
E-Lesson Planner
Assessment Guide, Lesson Test
ExamView

Technology Tools
Interactive Student Text on CD
Visual Teaching Package
Audio Library
mirrorsandwindows.com

Meeting the Standards
Fiction: Unit 1, Independent Reading, pp. 88–93

Preview the Selection

At a Glance
Independent Reading
- Reading Level: Challenging
- Difficulty Considerations: Length and vocabulary
- Ease Factor: Opening lines

Objectives
Reading this selection will enable students to do the following:
- read with developing fluency
- read silently with comprehension for a sustained period of time

Launch the Lesson
Tell students that in "The Serial Garden," an advertising jingle functions as a magic spell. Ask them for some of their favorite jingles. Write several on the board and ask what makes them effective.

TEACHING NOTE
Although this selection is presented in the student edition as an independent reading, teaching support has been provided should you choose to cover it in class.

Common Core State Standards
Reading Literature
RL.1, RL.10

111

Summary

Mark Armitage assembles a cardboard garden he cuts from the back of cereal boxes. He discovers that by singing a tune he can transport himself into this garden, which is enchanted. On one visit, he meets a princess. She tells Mark she was in love with the court music teacher, whom her father the king would not permit her to marry. So she created the garden by magic and fled into it to await her sweetheart. Fifty years later, she is still waiting. Mark discovers that the princess is waiting for his own music teacher, but his attempt to reunite the two fails when his mother destroys the cardboard garden.

MIRRORS & WINDOWS The Mirrors & Windows questions at the end of the story focus on the theme of fantasy worlds. Before students begin reading, ask: If you could create your own alternative world, what would it be like?

Use Reading Skills
Identify Multiple Levels of Meaning

Ask students to define the homophones *cereal* and *serial*. If necessary, point out that Aiken uses this play on words in the story's title. She develops the idea of serial cereal boxes as part of the plot. Tell students to be alert for other plays on words in the story.

"There's nothing to stop *you* having cornflakes. Oh, I forgot, the milk's in the fridge. Well, have cheese and pickles then. Or treacle tart."[3]

Even through the zinc grating[4] on the door, he could hear his father shudder at the thought of treacle tart and pickles for breakfast. Mr. Armitage's imprisonment was his own fault, though; he had sworn that he was going to find out where the mouse got into the larder if it took him all night, watching and waiting. He had shut himself in, so that no member of the family should come bursting in and disturb his vigil.[5] The larder door had a spring catch that sometimes jammed; it was bad luck that this turned out to be one of the times.

Mark ran across the fields to Miss Pride's shop at Sticks Corner and asked if she had any corn flakes.

"Oh, I don't think I have any left, dear," Miss Pride said woefully. "I'll have a look....I think I sold the last packet a week ago Tuesday."

"What about the one in the window?"

"That's a dummy, dear."

Ⓐ Miss Pride's shop window was full of nasty, dingy old cardboard cartons with nothing inside them, and several empty display stands that had fallen down and never been propped up again. Inside the shop were a few small, tired-looking tins and jars, which had a worn and scratched appearance as if mice had tried them and given up. Miss Pride herself was small and wan,[6] with yellowish gray hair; she rooted rather hopelessly in a pile of empty boxes. Mark's mother never bought any groceries from Miss Pride's if she could help it, since the day when she had found a label inside the foil wrapping of a cream cheese saying,

"This cheese should be eaten before May 11, 1899."

"No corn flakes I'm afraid, dear."

"Any wheat crispies? Puffed corn? Rice nuts?"

"No, dear. Nothing left, only Brekkfast Brikks."

"Never heard of *them*," said Mark doubtfully.

"Or I've a jar of Ovo here. You spread it on bread. That's nice for breakfast," said Miss Pride, with a sudden burst of salesmanship. Mark thought the Ovo looked beastly, like yellow paint, so he took the packet of Brekkfast Brikks. At least it wasn't very big.... On the front of the box was a picture of a fat, repulsive, fair-haired boy, rather like the chubby Augustus, banging on his plate with his spoon.

"They look like tiny doormats," said Mrs. Armitage, as Mark shoveled some Brikks into the bowl.

"They taste like them, too. Gosh," said Mark, "I must hurry or I'll be late for school. There's rather a nice cutout garden on the back of the packet, though; don't throw it away when it's empty, Mother. Goodby, Daddy," he shouted through the larder door; "hope Mr. Ellis comes soon to let you out." And he dashed off to catch the school bus.

At breakfast next morning Mark had a huge helping of Brekkfast Brikks and persuaded his father to try them.

"They taste just like esparto grass,"[7] said Mr. Armitage fretfully.[8]

---

3. **treacle tart.** Pastry with a sweet molasses filling
4. **zinc grating.** Metal framework on a door
5. **vigil.** Watchful wakefulness during the usual hours of sleep
6. **wan.** Pale; sickly
7. **esparto grass.** Coarse grass used to make rope
8. **fretfully.** Irritably

Words in Use

Selection Words
beastly, 112
gaudy, 113
doggedly, 116
convalescing, 116
prophesying, 119
keen, 119
incalculable, 121
besought, 122

Teaching Words
widespread, 124
plausible, 124
associations, 124
appealing, 124

KEY TERMS
SHORT STORY, 111
MAIN IDEA, 124
THESIS, 124

"Yes, I know, but do take some more, Daddy. I want to cut out the model garden; it's so lovely."

"Rather pleasant, I must say. It looks like an eighteenth-century German engraving," his father agreed. "It certainly was a stroke of genius putting it on the packet. No one would ever buy these things to eat for pleasure. Pass me the sugar, please. And the cream. And the strawberries."

It was the half-term holiday, so after breakfast Mark was able to take the empty packet away to the playroom and get on with the job of cutting out the stone walls, the row of little trees, the fountain, the yew arch,[9] the two green lawns, and the tiny clumps of brilliant flowers. He knew better than to "stick tabs in slots and secure with paste," as the directions suggested; he had made models from packets before and knew they always fell to pieces unless they were firmly bound together with transparent sticky tape.

It was a long, fiddling, pleasurable job.

Nobody interrupted him. Mrs. Armitage cleaned the playroom only once every six months or so, when she made a ferocious descent on it and tidied up the tape recorders, roller skates, meteorological sets, and dismantled railway engines, and threw away countless old magazines, stringless tennis rackets, abandoned paintings, and unsuccessful models. There were always bitter complaints from Mark and Harriet;

then they forgot and things piled up again till next time.

As Mark worked, his eye was caught by a verse on the outside of the packet:

"Brekkfast Brikks to start the day
Make you fit in every way.
Children bang their plates with glee
At Brekkfast Brikks for lunch and tea!
Brekkfast Brikks for supper too
Give peaceful sleep the whole night through."

"Blimey," thought Mark, sticking a cedar tree into the middle of the lawn and then bending a stone wall round at dotted lines A, B, C, and D. "I wouldn't want anything for breakfast, lunch, tea, and supper, not even Christmas pudding. Certainly not Brekkfast Brikks."

He propped a clump of gaudy scarlet flowers against the wall and stuck them in place.

The words of the rhyme kept coming into his head as he worked, and presently he found that they went rather well to a tune that was running through his mind, and he began to hum, and then to sing. Mark often did this when he was alone and busy.

"Brekkfast Brikks to sta-art the day,
Ma-ake you fi-it in every way—

"Blow, where did I put that little bit of sticky tape? Oh, there it is.

"Children bang their pla-ates with glee
At Brekkfast Brikks for lunch and tea

"Slit gate with razor blade, it says; but it'll have to be a penknife.

---

9. **yew arch.** Gateway in a garden made out of yew branches. A yew is an evergreen bush.

THE SERIAL GARDEN **113**

Teach the Selection

Use Reading Strategies
Visualize Point out to students that in "The Serial Garden," the author provides many sensory details to help readers visualize such settings as Miss Pride's shop and the Armitage children's playroom. Ask them to identify some details that will help them visualize each of these settings. Possible responses:

- Miss Pride's shop—dingy old cardboard cartons, empty display stands, tired-looking tins and jars **A**
- playroom—old magazines, stringless tennis rackets, abandoned paintings **B**

Differentiated Instruction

Reading Proficiency
Struggling readers and students learning English may need definitions of some unfamiliar words in the story.
repulsive—disgusting, offensive, 112
ferocious—extreme, intense, 113
gaudy—bright, showy, but in bad taste, 113
booty—any gain, prize, or gift, 116
tantalizing—tempting, 117

Enrichment
Encourage students to find images of famous gardens. Students should use the Internet or the school or local library to find books on gardens to share with the class. Urge them to find examples of several different types of gardens, such as European formal gardens, English landscape gardens, and Japanese gardens.

Analyze Literature

Plot Tell students that in a fantasy such as "The Serial Garden," plot development often depends on magic. Ask them to identify the point at which magic is introduced into the plot of "The Serial Garden." (Magic is introduced when Mark sings the jingle and is suddenly in the model garden.) **Ⓐ**

Make Connections

Ask students how they responded to Mark's reaction to the garden's usefulness as a hiding place. Would this have been their first reaction to a discovery of a magical place such as the garden? What would their first reaction have been? **Ⓑ**

Analyze Literature

Character Have students look back at the Understanding Characters feature (page 17) and review the different types of characters. Ask them to consider how Mark fits into these categories. Model a response for determining whether Mark is a flat or round character: "Mark is not one-dimensional, so he is a round character."

"Brekkfast Brikks for supper toohoo
Give peaceful sleep the whole night throughoo...."

"Hullo. That's funny," said Mark.

Ⓐ It was funny. The openwork iron gate he had just stuck in position now suddenly towered above him. On either side, to right and left, ran the high stone wall, stretching away into foggy distance. Over the top of the wall he could see tall trees, yews and cypresses and others he didn't know.

"Well, that's the neatest trick I ever saw," said Mark. "I wonder if the gate will open."

He chuckled as he tried it, thinking of the larder door. The gate did open, and he went through into the garden.

One of the things that had already struck him as he cut them out was that the flowers were not at all in the right proportions. But they were all the nicer for that. There were huge, velvety violets and pansies the size of saucers; the hollyhocks were as big as dinner plates and the turf was sprinkled with enormous daisies. The roses, on the other hand, were miniature, no bigger than cuffbuttons. There were real fish in the fountain, bright pink.

"I made all this," thought Mark, strolling along the mossy path to the yew arch. "Won't Harriet be surprised when she sees it. I wish she could see it now. I wonder what made it come alive like that."

He passed through the yew arch as he said this, and discovered that on the other side there was nothing but gray, foggy blackness. This, of course, was where his cardboard garden had ended. He turned through the archway and gazed with pride at a border of huge, scarlet tropical flowers that were perhaps supposed to be geraniums but

certainly hadn't turned out that way.

"I know! Of course, it was the rhyme, the rhyme on the packet."

He recited it. Nothing happened. "Perhaps you have to sing it," he thought and (feeling a little foolish) he sang it through to the tune that fitted so well. At once, faster than blowing out a match, the garden drew itself together and shrank into its cardboard again, leaving Mark outside.

Ⓑ "What a marvelous hiding place it'll make when I don't want people to come bothering," he thought. He sang the spell once more, just to make sure that it worked, and there was the mossy wall, the stately iron gate, and the treetops. He stepped in and looked back. No playroom to be seen, only gray blankness.

Reading Skills

Take Notes

Tell students that using a graphic organizer is a good way to take notes on literary works they read. Have them create a graphic organizer to keep notes about the two settings in "The Serial Garden"—Mark's home and the princess's garden. They might use a table like this.

Mark's Home	
Princess's Garden	

At that moment he was startled by a tremendous clanging, the sort of sound the Trump of Doom[10] would make if it was a dinner bell. "Blow," he thought. "I suppose that's lunch." He sang the spell for the fourth time; immediately he was in the playroom, and the garden was on the floor beside him, and Agnes was still ringing the dinner bell outside the door.

"All right, I heard," he shouted. "Just coming."

He glanced hurriedly over the remains of the packet to see if it bore any mention of the fact that the cutout garden had magic properties. It did not. He did, however, learn that this was Section Three of the Beautiful Brekkfast Brikk Garden Series, and that Sections One, Two, Four, Five, and Six would be found on other packets. In case of difficulty in obtaining supplies, please write to Fruhstucksgeschirrziegelsteinindustrie (Great Britain), Lily Road, Shepherds Bush.

"Elevenpence a packet," Mark murmured to himself, going to lunch with unwashed hands. "Five elevens are thirty-five. Thirty-five pennies are—no, that's wrong. Fifty-five pence are four-and-sevenpence. Father, if I mow the lawn and carry coal every day for a month, can I have four shillings[11] and sevenpence?"

"You don't want to buy another space gun, do you?" said Mr. Armitage looking at him suspiciously. "Because one is quite enough in this family."

"No, it's not for a space gun, I swear."

"Oh, very well."

"And can I have the four-and-seven now?"

Mr. Armitage gave it reluctantly. "But that lawn has to be like velvet, mind," he said.

"And if there's any falling off in the coal supply, I shall demand my money back."

"No, no, there won't be," Mark promised in reply. As soon as lunch was over, he dashed down to Miss Pride's. Was there a chance that she would have sections One, Two, Four, Five, and Six? He felt certain that no other shop had even heard of Brekkfast Brikks, so she was his only hope, apart from the address in Shepherds Bush.

"Oh, I don't know, I'm sure," Miss Pride said, sounding very doubtful— and more than a little surprised. "There might just be a couple on the bottom shelf— yes, here we are."

They were sections Four and Five, bent and dusty, but intact, Mark saw with relief. "Don't you suppose you have any more anywhere?" he pleaded.

"I'll look in the cellar but I can't promise. I haven't had deliveries of any of these for a long time. Made by some foreign firm they were; people didn't seem very keen on them," Miss Pride said aggrievedly.[12] She opened a door revealing a flight of damp stone stairs. Mark followed her down them like a bloodhound on the trail.

The cellar was a fearful confusion of mildewed, tattered, and toppling cartons, some full, some empty. Mark was nearly knocked cold by a shower of pilchards[13] in tins, which he dislodged onto himself from the top of a heap of boxes. At last Miss Pride, with a cry of triumph, unearthed a little cache[14] of Brekkfast Brikks, three packets

---

10. **Trump of Doom.** Trumpet blast believed to announce the end of the world
11. **shillings.** Former British coins, each worth twelve pennies (or pence)
12. **aggrievedly.** In an annoyed way
13. **pilchards.** Small fish of the herring family
14. **cache.** Secret, hidden supply

Teach the Selection

Cultural Connection

Romanticism You may wish to tell students that in the late 1700s and early 1800s, a cultural movement known as Romanticism changed European literature and the visual arts. Romanticism also changed the way Europeans designed gardens. Previously, formal gardens with elaborate plantings in geometric patterns had been the fashion. Under the influence of Romanticism, landscape gardens that imitated wild nature became popular.

Writing Skills

Precise Language

Show students that to create vivid pictures in the reader's mind, writers use verbs that have strong connotations. For example, "Mark *galloped* home with his booty and met his father on the porch." Ask students to make a list as they read of the verbs Aiken uses to make her writing more dramatic (for example, "Mark stood *hugging* himself with satisfaction"; "tears, which slowly began to *trickle* down his thin cheeks"; "*scribbling* crotchets and minims"; "Furniture was being *shoved* about"). Instruct students to use their lists as inspiration in creating their own descriptive paragraphs. Students should use a variety of grade-appropriate sentence lengths as well as a variety of sentence types. Refer students to page 130 for more information on sentence variety and length.

Alternative-World Fantasy *"The Serial Garden"* belongs to the alternative-world type of fantasy, which includes many familiar works of fiction, such as Lewis Carroll's *Alice in Wonderland* and *Through the Looking Glass,* L. Frank Baum's Oz series, C. S. Lewis's Narnia series, and Norton Juster's *The Phantom Tollbooth.*

"There, isn't that a piece of luck now!"

which turned out to be the remaining sections, Six, One, and Two.

"There, isn't that a piece of luck now!" she said, looking quite faint with all the excitement. It was indeed rare for Miss Pride to sell as many as five packets of the same thing at one time.

Mark galloped home with his booty and met his father on the porch. Mr. Armitage let out a groan of dismay.

"I'd almost rather you'd bought a space gun," he said. Mark chanted in reply:

> "Brekkfast Brikks for supper too
> Give peaceful sleep the whole night
>   through."

"I don't want peaceful sleep," Mr. Armitage said. "I intend to spend tonight mousewatching again. I'm tired of finding footprints in the Stilton."[15]

During the next few days, Mark's parents watched anxiously to see, Mr. Armitage said, whether Mark would start to sprout esparto grass instead of hair. For he doggedly ate Brekkfast Brikks for lunch, with soup, or sprinkled over his pudding; for tea, with jam; and for supper, lightly fried in dripping, not to mention, of course, the immense helpings he had for breakfast, with sugar and milk.

---

15. **Stilton.** Strongly flavored British cheese
16. *paté de foie gras.* Puréed goose livers (French)
17. **espaliers.** Trees trained to grow on a trellis, or framework
18. **flagged.** Paved with flagstones

Mr. Armitage, for his part, soon gave out; he said he wouldn't taste another Brekkfast Brikk even if it were wrapped in an inch-thick layer of *paté de foie gras.*[16] Mark regretted that Harriet, who was a handy and uncritical eater, was still away, convalescing from her measles with an aunt.

In two days, the second packet was finished (sundial, paved garden, and espaliers).[17] Mark cut it out, fastened it together, and joined it onto Section Three with trembling hands. "Would the spell work for this section, too?" He sang the rhyme in rather a quavering voice, but luckily the plywood door was shut, and there was no one to hear him. Yes! The gate grew again above him, and when he opened it and ran across the lawn through the yew arch, he found himself in a flagged[18] garden full of flowers like huge blue cabbages.

Mark stood hugging himself with satisfaction and then began to wander about smelling the flowers, which had a spicy perfume most unlike any flower he could think of. Suddenly he pricked up his ears. Had he caught a sound? There! It was like somebody crying and seemed to come from the other side of the hedge. He ran to the next opening and looked through. Nothing; only gray mist and emptiness. But, unless he had imagined it, just before he got there, he thought his eye had caught the flash of white-and-gold draperies swishing past the gateway.

Differentiated Instruction

English Language Learning
Students learning English may have difficulty with Aiken's use of adjectives, particularly those used as intensifiers, such as "ferocious descent," "fearful confusion" and "fiddling task." Suggest that students identify adjectives that give them trouble, and then have them work in pairs to find their meanings.

"Do you think Mark's all right?" Mrs. Armitage said to her husband next day. "He seems to be in such a dream all the time."

"Boy's gone clean off his rocker, if you ask me," grumbled Mr. Armitage. "It's all these doormats he's eating. Can't be good to stuff your insides with moldy jute.[19] Still, I'm bound to say he's cut the lawn very decently and seems to be remembering the coal. I'd better take a day off from the office and drive you over to the shore for a picnic; sea air will do him good."

Mrs. Armitage suggested to Mark that he should slack off on the Brekkfast Brikks, but he was so horrified that she had to abandon the idea. But, she said, he was to run four times round the garden every morning before breakfast. Mark almost said, "Which garden?" but stopped just in time. He had cut out and completed another large lawn, with a lake and weeping willows; and on the far side of the lake he had a tantalizing glimpse of a figure dressed in white and gold who moved away and was lost before he could get there.

After munching his way through the fourth packet, he was able to add on a broad grass walk bordered by curiously clipped trees. At the end of the walk, he could see the white-and-gold person, but when he ran to the spot, no one was there—the walk ended in the usual gray mist.

When he had finished and had cut out the fifth packet (an orchard), a terrible thing happened to him. For two days he could not remember the tune that worked the spell. He tried other tunes, but they were no use. He sat in the playroom singing till he was hoarse or silent with despair. Suppose he never remembered it again?

---

19. jute. Strong rope made from plant fibers
20. plantains. Banana-like fruit

His mother shook her head at him that evening and said he looked as if he needed a dose. "It's lucky we're going to Shinglemud Bay for the day tomorrow," she said. "That ought to do you good."

"Oh, *blow*. I'd forgotten about that," Mark said. "Need I go?"

His mother stared at him in utter astonishment. 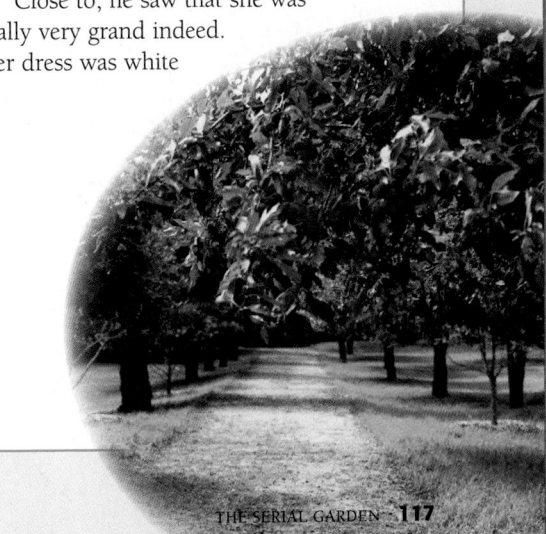 **A**

But in the middle of the night he remembered the right tune, leaped out of bed in a tremendous hurry, and ran down to the playroom without even waiting to put on his dressing gown and slippers.

The orchard was most wonderful, for instead of mere apples, its trees bore oranges, lemons, limes and all sorts of tropical fruits whose names he did not know, and there were melons and pineapples growing, and plantains[20] and avocados. Better still, he saw the lady in her white and gold waiting at the end of an alley and was able to draw near enough to speak to her.

"Who are you?" she asked. She seemed very much astonished at the sight of him.

"My name's Mark Armitage," he said politely. "Is this your garden?"

Close to, he saw that she was really very grand indeed. Her dress was white

Use Reading Strategies

Ask Questions Why does Mark's mother stare at him in "utter astonishment" when he asks if he needs to go to Shinglemud Bay? (She is very surprised that he doesn't want to spend a day at the beach.) **A**

Vocabulary Skills

Words from Mythology

Point out that the word *tantalizing* (paragraph 3) comes from the Greek myth of Tantalus, who was punished with eternal hunger and thirst in the Underworld for offending the gods. The gods forced Tantalus to stand in a pool of water under a fruit tree with low branches. If he reached for some fruit, the branches lifted it beyond his grasp. If he bent down for a drink, the water level sank so he could not reach it. Ask students to use a dictionary to research the myths behind the following English words:

1. odyssey
2. titanic
3. labyrinth
4. echo
5. atlas

Cultural Connection

German Nouns Aiken may be poking some gentle fun at the German language. Nouns in German often consist of many words strung together. For example, the name of the fictional cereal maker, Fruhstucksgeschirrziegelsteinindustrie, consists of four words that literally mean "breakfast tableware clay brick maker." The princess's home of Saxe-Hoffenpoffen-und-Hamster is more nonsensical. Although the German word *hoffen* means "to hope," and *und* means "and," this name sounds more like "huff and puff and hamster." (In German, *hamster* means "hamster.") **A**

Analyze Literature

Character Have students review the techniques of characterization in "Understanding Characters" on page 17. Ask them to identify which techniques the writer uses to develop the character of the princess. Model one technique: "The writer develops this character by describing her appearance and dress." Ask what these details suggest about her. Then ask students for other techniques and interpretations.

118 UNIT 1 FICTION

satin embroidered with pearls, and swept the ground; she had a gold scarf and her hair, dressed high and powdered, was confined in a small, gold-and-pearl tiara. Her face was rather plain, pink with a long nose, but she had a kind expression and beautiful gray eyes.

"Indeed it is," she announced with hauteur.[21] "I am Princess Sophia Maria Louisa of Saxe-Hoffenpoffen-und-Hamster. What are you doing here, pray?"

A "Well," Mark explained cautiously, "it seemed to come about through singing a tune."

"Indeed. That is most interesting. Did the tune, perhaps, go like this?"

The princess hummed a few bars.

"That's it! How did you know?"

"Why, you foolish boy, it was I who put the spell on the garden, to make it come alive when the tune is played or sung."

"I say!" Mark was full of admiration. "Can you do spells as well as being a princess?"

She drew herself up. "Naturally! At the court of Saxe-Hoffenpoffen, where I was educated, all princesses were taught a little magic, not so much as to be vulgar, just enough to get out of social difficulties."

"Jolly useful," Mark said. "How did you work the spell for the garden, then?"

"Why, you see," (the princess was obviously delighted to have somebody to talk to; she sat on a stone seat and patted it, inviting Mark to do likewise) "I had the misfortune to fall in love with Herr Rudolf, the court Kapellmeister,[22] who taught me music. Oh, he was so kind and handsome! And he was most talented, but my father, of

---

21. **hauteur.** Disdainful pride; snobbery
22. **Kapellmeister.** Conductor of a choir or an orchestra in Germany

Differentiated Instruction

Kinesthetic Learning

Mark finds assembling the model garden "a long, fiddling, pleasurable job." Encourage students to bring in an example of a similar type of project that they enjoy doing. For example, students might bring in model kits, sewing projects, beadwork, and jewelry. Students can describe how long these projects take, what skills, tools, and materials they require, and what is satisfying about the pastimes. After students share their work, ask how their experiences help them understand the character of Mark.

❧ ✳ ❧

*"Can you do spells as well
as being a princess?"*

❧ ✳ ❧

course, would not hear of my marrying him because he was only a common person."

"So what did you do?"

"I arranged to vanish, of course. Rudi had given me a beautiful book with many pictures of gardens. My father kept strict watch to see I did not run away, so I used to slip between the pages of the book when I wanted to be alone. Then, when we decided to marry, I asked my maid to take the book to Rudi. And I sent him a note telling him to play the tune when he received the book. But I believe that spiteful Gertrud must have played me false and never taken the book, for more than fifty years have now passed and I have been here all alone, waiting in the garden, and Rudi has never come. Oh, Rudi, Rudi," she exclaimed, wringing her hands and crying a little, "where can you be? It is so long—so long!"

"Fifty years," Mark said kindly, reckoning that must make her nearly seventy. "I must say you don't look it."

"Of course I do not, dumbhead. For me, I make it that time does not touch me. But tell me, how did you know the tune that works the spell? It was taught me by dear Rudi."

"I'm not sure where I picked it up," Mark confessed. "For all I know it may be one of the Top Ten. I'll ask my music teacher; he's sure to know. Perhaps he'll have heard of your Rudolf too."

B

Privately Mark feared that Rudolf might very well have died by now, but he did not like to depress Princess Sophia Maria by such a suggestion, so he bade her a polite good night, promising to come back as soon as he could with another section of the garden and any news he could pick up.

He planned to go and see Mr. Johansen, his music teacher, next morning, but he had forgotten the family trip to the beach. There was just time to scribble a hasty post card to the British office of Fruhstucksgeschirrziegelsteinindustrie, asking them if they could inform him from what source they had obtained the pictures used on the packets of Brekkfast Brikks. Then Mr. Armitage drove his wife and son to Shinglemud Bay, gloomily prophesying wet weather.

In fact, the weather turned out fine, and Mark found it quite restful to swim and play beach cricket and eat ham sandwiches and lie in the sun. For he had been struck by a horrid thought: suppose he should forget the tune again when he was inside the garden— would he be stuck there, like Father in the larder? It was a lovely place to go and wander at will, but somehow he didn't fancy spending the next fifty years there with Princess Sophia Maria. Would she oblige him by singing the spell if he forgot it, or would she be too keen on company to let him go? He was not inclined to take any chances.

It was late when they arrived home, too late, Mark thought, to disturb Mr. Johansen, who was elderly and kept early hours. Mark ate a huge helping of sardines on Brekkfast Brikks for supper—he was dying to finish Section Six—but did not visit the garden that night.

Teach the Selection

Use Reading Strategies
Make Predictions When the princess asks Mark where he heard the tune that evokes the garden, saying "It was taught me by my dear Rudi," Mark says, "I'll ask my music teacher; he's sure to know." Ask students to predict what will happen when Mark asks Mr. Johansen, his music teacher, about the tune and about Rudolf. (Mr. Johansen will turn out to be the princess's Rudi.) **B**

Vocabulary Skills

Context Clues: Appositives
Tell students that some context clues are appositives, words or phrases that means the same thing as an unfamiliar word. For example, in "The fairy godmother sang an incantation, a magic spell that transformed the pumpkin into a coach," the appositive phrase "magic spell" gives a context clue to the meaning of *incantation*. Ask students to

identify the appositive clue to the italicized word in each of these sentences.
1. It was time for the *showdown*, a competition between the two best players on the opposing teams.
2. Afterward they retired to the *cantina*, a favorite little restaurant of her father's.
3. He ordered the rice and fish dish, a spicy *paella*.

Use Reading Strategies

Ask Questions Ask students why the author might have included the detail about the mouse chewing a hole in the packet of Brekkfast Brikks. (This detail shows the relationship between the cardboard garden created from the cut-outs and the "real" garden inhabited by the princess.) **A**

Analyze Literature

Setting Have students look back at "Understanding Setting"on page 29 and review the different types of details writers use to develop setting in fiction. Ask students which details in this story develop the setting of the garden. (Setting details include the different kinds of trees and plants, the various structures, and the costume worn by the princess.)

Next morning's breakfast (Brikks with hot milk for a change) finished the last packet—and just as well, for the larder mouse, which Mr. Armitage still had not caught, was discovered to have nibbled the bottom left-hand corner of the packet, slightly damaging an ornamental grotto[23] in a grove of lime trees. Rather worried about this, Mark decided to make up the last section straightaway, in case the magic had been affected. By now he was becoming very skillful at the tiny, fiddling task of cutting out the little tabs and slipping them into the little slots; the job did not take long to finish. Mark attached Section Six to Section Five and then, drawing a deep breath, sang the incantation[24] once more. With immense relief, he watched the mossy wall and rusty gate grow out of the playroom floor; all was well.

He raced across the lawn, round the lake, along the avenue, through the orchard, and into the lime grove. The scent of the lime flowers was sweeter than a cake baking.

Princess Sophia Maria came towards him from the grotto, looking slightly put out.

"Good morning!" she greeted Mark. "Do you bring me any news?"

"I haven't been to see my music teacher yet," Mark confessed. "I was a bit anxious because there was a hole—"

A "Ach, yes, a hole in the grotto! I have just been looking. Some wild beast must have made its way in, and I am afraid it may come again. See, it has made tracks like those of a big bear." She showed him some enormous footprints in the soft sand of the grotto floor. Mark stopped up the hole with prickly branches and promised to bring a dog when he next came, though he felt fairly sure the mouse would not return.

"I can borrow a dog from my teacher—he has plenty. I'll be back in an hour or so—see you then," he said.

"*Auf Wiedersehen,*[25] my dear young friend."

Mark ran along the village street to Mr. Johansen's house, Houndshaven Cottage. He knew better than to knock at the door because Mr. Johansen would be either practicing his violin or out in the barn at the back, and in any case the sound of barking was generally loud enough to drown any noise short of gunfire.

Besides giving music lessons at Mark's school, Mr. Johansen kept a guest house for dogs whose owners were abroad or on holiday. He was extremely kind to the guests and did his best to make them feel at home in every way, finding out from their owners what were their favorite foods, and letting them sleep on his own bed, turn about. He spent all his spare time with them, talking to them and playing either his violin or long-playing records of domestic sounds likely to appeal to the canine fancy—such as knives being sharpened, cars starting up, and children playing ball games.

Mark could hear Mr. Johansen playing Brahms's lullaby in the barn, so he went out there; the music was making some of the more susceptible inmates feel homesick: howls, sympathetic moans, and long, shuddering sighs came from the numerous comfortably carpeted cubicles all the way down the barn.

Mr. Johansen reached the end of the piece as Mark entered. He put down his fiddle and smiled welcomingly.

---

23. grotto. Cavelike house or shrine
24. incantation. Magic spell
25. *Auf Wiedersehen.* Goodbye (German)

Differentiated Instruction

Auditory and Kinesthetic Learning
Have small groups of students prepare oral interpretations of different scenes from "The Serial Garden." Have them practice reading with emotion, pausing, varying volume and pace, emphasizing certain words and phrases, and using gestures and facial expressions. After their presentations, have them explain what preparing their oral interpretations taught them about the story.

ʒ✻ʒ

"...if I whistle a tune to you, can
you write it down for me?"

ʒ✻ʒ

"*Ach, how gut!* It is the young Mark."

"Hullo, sir."

"You know," confided Mr. Johansen, "I play to many audiences in my life all over the world, but never anywhere do I get such a response as from zese dear doggies—it is really remarkable. But come in, come into ze house and have some coffee cake."

Mr. Johansen was a gentle, white-haired, elderly man; he walked slowly with a slight stoop and had a kindly, sad face with large, dark eyes. He looked rather like some sort of dog himself, Mark always thought, perhaps a collie or a long-haired dachshund.

"Sir," Mark said, "if I whistle a tune to you, can you write it down for me?"

"Why, yes, I shall be most happy," Mr. Johansen said, pouring coffee for both of them.

So Mark whistled his tune once more; as he came to the end, he was surprised to see the music master's eyes fill with tears, which slowly began to trickle down his thin cheeks.

"It recalls my youth, zat piece," he explained, wiping the tears away and rapidly scribbling crotchets and minims[26] on a piece of music paper. "Many times I am whistling it myself—it is wissout doubt from me you learn it—but always it is reminding me of how happy I was long ago when I wrote it."

"You *wrote* that tune?" Mark said, much excited.

"Why yes. What is so strange in zat? Many, many tunes haf I written."

"Well—" Mark said, "I won't tell you just yet in case I'm mistaken—I'll have to see somebody else first. Do you mind if I dash off right away? Oh, and might I borrow a dog—preferably a good ratter?"

"In zat case, better have my dear Lotta—alzough she is so old she is ze best of zem all," Mr. Johansen said proudly. Lotta was his own dog, an enormous, shaggy, lumbering animal, with a tail like a palm tree and feet the size of electric polishers; she was reputed to be of incalculable age; Mr. Johansen called her his strudel-hound. She knew Mark well and came along with him quite biddably,[27] though it was rather like leading a mammoth.

Luckily, his mother, refreshed by her day at the sea, was heavily engaged with Agnes the maid in spring cleaning. Furniture was being shoved about, and everyone was too busy to notice Mark and Lotta slip into the playroom.

A letter addressed to Mark lay among the clutter on the table; he opened and read it while Lotta foraged happily among the piles of magazines and tennis nets and cricket bats and rusting electronic equipment, managing to upset several things and increase the general state of huggermugger in the room.

Dear Sir, (the letter said—it was from Messrs. Digit, Digit, & Rule, a firm of chartered accountants)—We are in receipt of your inquiry as to the source of pictures on packets of Brekkfast Brikks. We are pleased to inform you that these were reproduced from the illustrations of a little-known 18th-century German work, *Steinbergen's Gartenbuch.* Unfortunately, the only known remaining copy of this book

---

26. crotchets and minims. Musical notation
27. biddably. Obediently

Teach the Selection

Use Reading Strategies
Make Inferences Ask students what they can infer from the facts of the "incalculable age" of Mr. Johansen's dog Lotta and her continued puppy-like friskiness. (The dog must be subject to the same suspension of time as the princess.) **B**

Grammar Skills

Verbs with Indefinite Pronouns

The indefinite pronouns *all, any, most, none,* and *some* can take either singular or plural verbs. The pronoun takes a singular verb when it refers to a portion of something or to a single person, place, or thing. It takes a plural verb when it refers to a number of individual persons, places, or things. For example, <u>Some</u> of the lawn <u>was</u> lit by the sun (singular); <u>Some</u> of the children <u>were</u> present (plural).

Ask students to identify the correct form of the verb in the following sentences.
1. Most of the dogs (barks / <u>bark</u>) loudly.
2. All of that cereal (<u>tastes</u> / taste) like cardboard.

Analyze Literature

Character Ask students to identify the major character or characters in "The Serial Garden." (Most students will identify Mark as the major character. Some may also include the princess as a major character because she is central to the plot of the story. All the other characters, including Mark's parents, Miss Pride, and Mr. Johansen, are minor characters.)

You might also ask if Mark is a static or a dynamic character. Model a possible response: "He doesn't really develop in the course of the story, so he is a static character."

TEACHING NOTE

Self-Generated Questioning

Have students work in pairs. Have each pair of students create a question about the selection. Model a possible question: "What would have happened if Rudi and the princess reunited?" Ask students to then draw a picture, a chart, or another type of graphic that answers the question.

---

was burnt in the disastrous fire that destroyed the factory and premises of Mssrs. Fruhstucksgeschirrziegelsteinindustrie two months ago. The firm has now gone into liquidation and we are winding up their effects.

Yours faithfully,

P. J. Zero, Gen. Sec.

"*Steinbergen's Gartenbuch,*" Mark thought. "That must have been the book that Princess Sophia Maria used for the spell—probably the same copy. Oh, well, since it's burned, it's lucky the pictures were reproduced on the Brekkfast Brikks packets. Come on, Lotta, let's go and find a nice princess then. Good girl! Rats! Chase 'em!"

He sang the spell, and Lotta, all enthusiasm, followed him into the garden.

They did not have to go far before they saw the princess—she was sitting sunning herself on the rim of the fountain. But what happened then was unexpected. Lotta let out the most extraordinary cry—whine, bark, and howl all in one—and hurled herself towards the princess like a rocket.

"Hey! Look out! Lotta! *Heel!*" Mark shouted in alarm. But Lotta, with her great paws on the princess's shoulders, had about a yard of salmon-pink tongue out, and was washing the princess's face all over with frantic affection.

The princess was just as excited. "Lotta, Lotta! She knows me; it's dear Lotta; it must be! Where did you get her?" she cried to Mark, hugging the enormous dog, whose tail was going round

faster than a turbo prop.

"Why, she belongs to my music master, Mr. Johansen, and it's he who made up the tune," Mark said.

The princess turned quite white and had to sit down on the fountain's rim again.

"*Johansen?* Rudolf Johansen? My Rudi! At last! After all these years! Oh, run, run, and fetch him immediately, please! Immediately!"

Mark hesitated a moment.

"Please make haste!" she besought him. "Why do you wait?"

"It's only—well, you won't be surprised if he's quite *old*, will you? Remember he hasn't been in a garden keeping young like you."

"All that will change," the princess said confidently. "He has only to eat the fruit of the garden. Why, look at Lotta—when she was a puppy, for a joke I gave her a fig from this tree, and you can see she is a puppy still, though she must be older than any other dog in the world! Oh, please hurry to bring Rudi here."

"Why don't you come with me to his house?"

"That would not be correct etiquette," she said with dignity. "After all, I *am* royal."

"Okay," said Mark. "I'll fetch him. Hope he doesn't think I'm crackers."

"Give him this." The princess took off a locket on a gold chain. It had a miniature of a romantically handsome young man with dark, curling hair. "My Rudi," she explained fondly. Mark could just trace a faint resemblance to Mr. Johansen.

Grammar Skills

Commonly Confused Words

Point out that words may be confused for other words if they sound alike (*here/hear*) or if their spelling is very similar (*proposition/preposition*). Remind students that to determine the correct meaning, they should pay attention to how a word is used. Have them select the correct word in each of the following sentences.

1. He said he would meet me (*hear, here*) at ten o'clock.
2. The policeman left (*then, than*) to finish walking his beat.
3. The salesman posed an interesting (*proposition, preposition*) to the shoppers.
4. "I like (*you're, your*) watch," he said.

He took the locket and hurried away. At the gate, something made him look back: the princess and Lotta were sitting at the edge of the fountain, side by side. The princess had an arm round Lotta's neck; with the other hand she waved to him, just a little.

"Hurry!" she called again.

Mark made his way out of the house, through the spring-cleaning chaos, and flew down the village to Houndshaven Cottage. Mr. Johansen was in the house this time, boiling up a noisome[28] mass of meat and bones for the dogs' dinner. Mark said nothing at all, just handed him the locket. He took one look at it and staggered, putting his hand to his heart; anxiously, Mark led him to a chair.

"Are you all right, sir?"

"Yes, yes! It was only ze shock. Where did you get ziss, my boy?"

So Mark told him.

Surprisingly, Mr. Johansen did not find anything odd about the story; he nodded his head several times as Mark related the various points.

"Yes, yes, her letter, I have it still—" he pulled out a worn little scrap of paper, "but ze *Gartenbuch* it reached me never. Zat wicked Gertrud must haf sold it to some bookseller who sold it to Fruhstucksgeschirrziegelsteinindustrie. And so she has been waiting all zis time! My poor little Sophie!"

"Are you strong enough to come to her now?" Mark asked.

"*Natürlich!* But first we must give ze dogs zeir dinner; zey must not go hungry."

So they fed the dogs, which was a long job, as there were at least sixty and each had a different diet, including some very odd preferences like Swiss roll spread with

✣ ❋ ✣

*"Yes, yes, her letter,
I have it still—"*

✣ ❋ ✣

Marmite and yeast pills wrapped in slices of caramel. Privately, Mark thought the dogs were a bit spoiled, but Mr. Johansen was very careful to see that each visitor had just what it fancied.

"After all, zey are not mine! Must I not take good care of zem?"

At least two hours had gone by before the last willow-pattern plate was licked clean and they were free to go. Mark made rings round Mr. Johansen all the way up the village; the music master limped quietly along, smiling a little; from time to time he said, "Gently, my friend. We do not run a race. Remember, I am an old man."

That was just what Mark did remember. He longed to see Mr. Johansen young and happy once more.

The chaos in the Armitage house had changed its location: the front hall was now clean, tidy, and damp; the rumpus of vacuuming had shifted to the playroom. With a black hollow of apprehension in his middle, Mark ran through the open door and stopped, aghast. All the toys, tools, weapons, boxes, magazines, and bits of machinery had been rammed into the cupboards; the floor where his garden had been laid out was bare. Mrs. Armitage was in the playroom taking down the curtains.

"Mother! Where's my Brekkfast Brikks garden?"

---

28. **noisome.** Offensive to the sense of smell

Teach the Selection

History Connection
The Advertising Business

Advertising in the modern sense really began in the 1800s in Europe and the United States. An enormous expansion in manufacturing and business and improvements in printing technology prompted its development. The first advertising agencies began by selling advertising space in newspapers. The twentieth century saw a huge growth of the advertising industry, as advertising media expanded to include radio and television, and agencies began creating entire campaigns for their clients.

Grammar Skills

Commas in a Series

Remind students that commas separate words in a series. Three or more items make a series.

Have students rewrite the following sentences to correctly punctuate them with commas.

1. Miss Pride's shop contained cartons tins and jars.
2. There were violets, pansies and hollyhocks in the garden.
3. Mark asked Miss Pride if she had sections One, Two, Three, Four Five and Six.
4. Mrs. Armitage had cleaned up all the toys tools and magazines from the playroom.

Answer: Students should be able to give reasons to support their choices. They may mention love of adventure or desire to escape ordinary life.

Analyze and Extend

1. His immediate willingness to accept the garden's reality suggests he is fairly imaginative; his pleased anticipation of using the garden as a good place to hide indicates a sense of humor and a desire for privacy.

2. The everyday settings help make the alternative world of the garden more believable and more fantastic.

3. Some students may feel the ending would have been stronger and more satisfying with the princess and Rudi reunited; others may find the ending unexpected and refreshing.

"Oh, darling, you didn't want it, did you? It was all dusty; I thought you'd finished with it. I'm afraid I've burned it in the furnace. Really you *must* try not to let this room get into such a clutter; it's perfectly disgraceful. Why, hullo, Mr. Johansen," she added in embarrassment. "I didn't see you. I'm afraid you've called at the worst possible moment. But I'm sure you'll understand how it is at spring-cleaning time."

She rolled up her bundle of curtains, glancing worriedly at Mr. Johansen; he looked rather odd, she thought. But he gave her his tired, gentle smile and said, "Why, yes, Mrs. Armitage, I understand, I understand very well. Come, Mark. We have no business here, you can see."

Speechlessly, Mark followed him. What was there to say?

"Never mind," Mrs. Armitage called after Mark. "The Rice Nuts pack has a helicopter on it."

Every week in The Times newspaper you will see this advertisement:

BREKKFAST BRIKKS PACKETS.
£100 offered for any in good condition, whether empty or full.

So, if you have any, you know where to send them.

But Mark is growing anxious; none have come in yet, and every day Mr. Johansen seems a little thinner and more elderly. Besides, what will the princess be thinking? ✤

What is your favorite alternative world in literature or films? What qualities of this world make it particularly appealing to you? Why do you think literature that depicts fantasy worlds—from Homer's *Odyssey* to J. K. Rowling's Harry Potter series—has such a widespread appeal?

Analyze and Extend

1. What does Mark's reaction to his discovery of the garden suggest about his personality?

2. How do the everyday settings of the story affect your perception of the garden?

3. This story could have ended with Rudolf and the princess living happily ever after. Is the actual ending stronger or weaker than a typical "fairy tale" ending? Explain.

Expository Writing One definition of fantasy is "the plausible impossible," that is, it makes things that actually couldn't happen seem possible and real. Write a brief **essay** analyzing how Joan Aiken makes her alternative world seem real. State your main idea in your thesis, focusing on one or two literary elements that made this fantasy world believable. Support your thesis with examples from the story.

Collaborative Learning Working with other students, create an advertising jingle like the Brekkfast Brikks song. The jingle should promote a food or product that is generally not considered tasty or exciting. What descriptive words or associations would you use to make the product more appealing to consumers?

Go to **www.mirrorsandwindows.com** for more.

Differentiated Instruction

Enrichment

Interested students might research the development of advertising slogans or the creation of advertising characters (such as Mr. Peanut, the Jolly Green Giant, and Elsie the Cow). Ask several students to collaborate and do a visual presentation for the class.

Rubric for Expository Writing

You can adapt this as a checklist for students to use as they write.

☐ Does the essay's introduction clearly express a thesis?

☐ Does the body offer examples from the story?

☐ Does the essay focus on one or two literary elements?

For Your Reading List

A Wrinkle in Time
by Madeleine L'Engle

In this Newbery Award–winning classic, high school student Meg Murry is worried about her father, who has been missing for a year. One stormy night, the mysterious Mrs. Whatsit arrives at the Murrys' door with important news. Mrs. Whatsit tells the family that they must journey through a tesseract, a kind of wrinkle in time, to save Mr. Murry.

Tuck Everlasting
by Natalie Babbitt

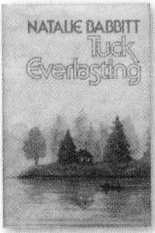

Ten-year-old Winnie Foster hates her strict and smothering life. One day she sets off into the woods to get away from everything. Instead of solitude, Winnie finds the Tuck family living there. Winnie wonders why anyone would choose to be so isolated, so the family lets her in on their secret. The deep woods are not safe, though, and soon Winnie must rescue her friends from the law.

The Devil's Arithmetic
by Jane Yolen

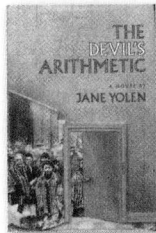

During the Jewish holiday of Passover, twelve-year-old Hannah Stern is chosen to open the door during the Seder, to symbolically welcome the prophet Elijah to the family meal. When she opens the door, Hannah suddenly finds herself in Poland in 1942, where everyone thinks she is Chaya Abramowicz.

Bradbury Stories: 100 of His Most Celebrated Tales
by Ray Bradbury

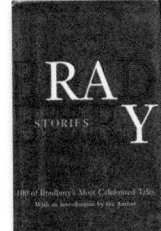

Ray Bradbury has written a wide variety of stories, from horror and fantasy to realistic fiction and humorous anecdotes. What characterizes all of Bradbury's fiction is a natural-born storyteller's delight in the creation of wonder. Selected by the writer, this recent collection includes many of Bradbury's best-known fiction, including "The Flying Machine" and excerpts from *The Martian Chronicles*.

Eragon
by Christopher Paolini

Eragon, a farm boy living in a world much like medieval Europe, finds a magical blue stone that turns out to be a dragon's egg. When the egg hatches, an evil king comes looking for the baby dragon, burning down Eragon's farm and killing his uncle. Thus begins a series of adventures that involve immortal elves, mining dwarves, a wizard, and a magical red sword.

Zazoo
by Richard Mosher

Swimming in her quiet canal, Zazoo spies Marius, a bird-watching boy on a bike. When he asks for information about her quiet French village, she grows curious and begins asking her own questions. Zazoo slowly uncovers the story of her adoptive grandfather's early life. She learns of the "Awful Time" during World War II. But as the story is revealed, old pains are healed and new romance sparked.

Independent Reading Activity

Help students link their reading to the unit theme, Meeting the Unexpected. Ask how fiction can help readers better cope with surprises. You might try this as an in-class activity: Have students read silently a fiction work of their choosing for at least twenty minutes. Then have students identify what ideas this short story or novel can give a reader about dealing with the unexpected.

▶ EMC E-Library

The EMC E-Library contains more than twenty thousand pages of literary classics that students may read independently. An Electronic Library Guide provides teaching suggestions, enrichment activities, and reading strategy guidesheets.

TEACHING NOTE

Start a Book Club

Tell students that one pleasure of independent reading is sharing the experience with other readers. Suggest that they form classroom book clubs, small groups that meet to exchange insights, interpretations, and questions about books. Have groups select one of the books suggested here (or another book) by consensus. Urge book clubs to create participation guidelines.

Program Resources

EMC Access Editions

For additional independent reading, you may wish to refer students to one of EMC's Access Edition titles such as Madeleine L'Engle's *A Wrinkle in Time*. Each Access Edition contains a thorough study apparatus, including background information, literal comprehension questions, footnotes, vocabulary definitions, critical thinking questions, and related projects and activities. An Assessment Manual offering worksheets is available for each Access Edition.

Common Core State Standards

Reading Literature
RL.10

Teach the Workshop

Objectives

This lesson will help students write a literary response essay that has

- an effective introduction
- a clear thesis statement
- a clear organizational pattern
- a conclusion restating the thesis

Launch the Lesson

Have students suggest several feelings someone could have in response to a reading, such as curiosity, excitement, nervousness, and pleasure. Point out that even negative feelings, such as being bored or annoyed while reading, are legitimate responses to literature. Encourage students to remember their strongest responses as they choose a story on which to base their literary response essays.

Cultural Connection

Buck Rogers Ray Bradbury refers to Buck Rogers comics, which may be unfamiliar to students. Explain that Buck Rogers is a fictional outer space adventurer in the 25th century. The comic strip was an example of science fiction. It developed with the development of space exploration in the real world.

Program Resources

Additional writing workshops are available in the *Exceeding the Standards: Writing* resource.

Writing Workshop

Expository Writing

Responding to a Short Story

Reading and Writing

In this unit, you read short stories about the unexpected, including a criminal who runs out of time, time catching up to a Pullman porter, and lost time at a mysterious inn. How did you respond to each of these stories?

As you read a story, you react to it, forming opinions about the characters, setting, plot, and the story as a whole. Perhaps you liked a story in the unit because you could relate to a character or could visualize the setting described. In this workshop, you will learn how to write a **response to a piece of literature.** In a response to literature, you not only tell how you reacted to a selection, you explain your reaction with specific details and examples from the text. The following summary includes a description of your assignment, your goals, strategies, and a writing rubric, that is, a set of standards by which you can judge how well you completed your assignment. You will use this rubric in drafting and revising your response.

Assignment: Write a response to a short story I have read.

Goal: Present a clear and engaging response to a story or an aspect of a story.

Strategy: Organize my main points and support them with evidence from the story.

Writing Rubric: My response to literature should include the following:

- a compelling introduction that clearly states my response
- a clear organizational pattern
- textual evidence that supports my main ideas
- varied sentences to engage the reader
- a conclusion that sums up my response

What Great Writers Do

Ray Bradbury is the author of many novels and short stories. In the following excerpt, Bradbury discusses how he came to embrace his unique literary tastes. When writing a response essay, why is it important to express your own opinions?

In October 1929 I looked at that one comic strip, with its view of the future, and I thought, "That's where I belong." I started to collect Buck Rogers comic strips. And everybody in the fifth grade made fun of me. I continued to collect them for about a month, and then I listened to the critics. And I tore up my comic strips. That's the worst thing I ever did. Two or three days later, I broke down. I was crying, and I said to myself, "Why am I crying? Whose funeral am I going to? Who died?" And the answer was, "Me." I'd torn up the future.

Words in Use

Teaching Words
excerpt, 126
unique, 126
convey, 128
legible, 130

KEY TERMS

CHARACTER, 126	TOPIC SENTENCE, 128
SETTING, 126	CONCLUSION, 128
PLOT, 126	AUDIENCE, 128
SUMMARY, 126	TONE, 128
CLUSTER CHART, 127	PEER REVIEW, 129
THESIS, 127	COMPLEX SENTENCE, 130
ORGANIZATIONAL PATTERN, 128	CONJUNCTION, 130
ORDER OF IMPORTANCE, 128	TRANSITION, 130
INTRODUCTION, 128	CONTRACTION, 130
BODY, 128	POSSESSIVE FORM, 130

Common Core State Standards

Reading Literature
RL.10

1. PREWRITE

Narrowing Your Topic

Think of the stories from the unit that stand out in your mind. Which stories surprised you? Which were the most interesting or changed your perspective on something? Perhaps there was a particular character or other aspect of the story that influenced your reaction. As you consider stories to write about, make sure the one you choose will give you enough to discuss.

Gathering Details

Once you have chosen a story to write about, gather specific details from the story that caused you to react the way you did. As you draft, you will use these details to support your ideas. One way to gather and organize details about a character or main idea is by using a cluster chart.

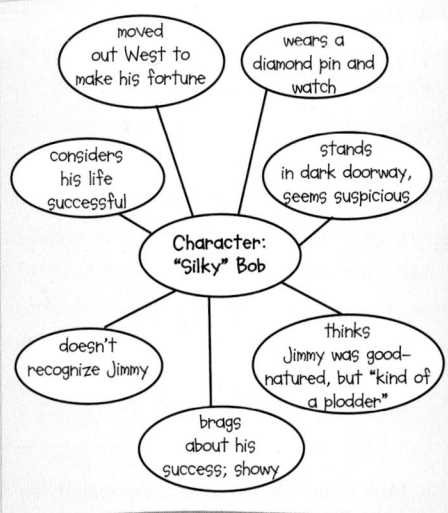

Deciding on Your Purpose

Now that you have gathered details, ask yourself questions to help you decide on your thesis, or the point you want to make about the story. Ask questions about the parts of the story that most affected your reaction to it.

> 1. What is my opinion of the main characters?
> 2. What do the characters learn?
> 3. Is the setting important? Why?
> 4. Which events were most interesting or surprising?
> 5. What was the message, or theme, of the story?

In your thesis, give your response to the story and tell which parts of the story created this effect. In the sample below, the writer felt the story was suspenseful and surprising due to the realistic descriptions.

> The realistic descriptions made this story suspenseful and surprising to me because they reveal who each character really is, despite how the characters see themselves.

Prewrite

Choosing a Story Encourage students to choose the story to which they had the strongest reaction. If nothing particularly affected a student, ask him or her to pick the story he or she can write the most about. Tell students they will need to write at least three paragraphs, and preferably five or six, about whatever they select.

Gathering and Organizing Details Remind students to review any notes they took or graphic organizers they constructed as they read the story. Suggest that they include at least three quotations from the literature in their organizers — quotes they think they can use in their essays.

What Great Writers Do

Many writers say that strong feelings are good sources for writing. Here is one example.

I always tell would-be writers to search their own memories for a time when they experienced a strong emotion: fear, anger, joy, sorrow, guilt. How, as a result of the experience that created that emotion, did they change? There is where the story lies.

— LOIS LOWRY, AUTHOR OF *Number the Stars*

Differentiated Instruction

Reading Proficiency

To help students understand the lesson, tell them what the assignment will be and show them the student model. Point out that the lesson is organized into five steps. Then have students read and summarize the instructions for each step before they begin the assignment.

English Language Learning

Students learning English may want to take some extra time with the Ray Bradbury quote. Make sure they understand that Bradbury is saying he should not have doubted — or should have trusted — his own fascination with science fiction, no matter what the other fifth graders said.

Teach the Workshop

Draft

Choosing an Organization Remind students that they can choose from a variety of organizational strategies; order of importance is just one. Other options include chronological organization, compare-and-contrast organization, and cause-and-effect organization. Model some examples:

Cause and effect—"I hated this story (effect) because the characters were stereotyped and the plot was predictable (causes)."

Chronological—"When I began this story, I could not have predicted the end. It starts . . ."

Compare and contrast—"This story is the best example of historical fiction in the collection. It is more realistic than . . ."

Putting Your Thoughts on Paper Remind students to devise a topic sentence for each paragraph in their plan. Even if they replace these sentences later, the sentences will provide a useful road map for the draft.

Audience and Tone Have students imagine delivering their essays aloud to a group of people. Encourage them to visualize the people and detect the attitudes their speaking conveys. Then ask each student to make a note of his or her ideal audience and tone.

2. DRAFT

Organizing Ideas

Once you have created a thesis and have gathered enough ideas to write about, decide how to organize your ideas. Choose an **organizational pattern** that will help you convey your ideas clearly and effectively. To emphasize your strongest points, organize them by **order of importance.** That is, place your most important point either first or last for the most impact.

Order of Importance

Least Important Point
↓
More Important Point
↓
Most Important Point

Putting Your Thoughts on Paper

Your essay should have three main parts: an introduction, body paragraphs, and a conclusion. In your introduction, summarize the basic plot of the story and include your thesis. In your body paragraphs, organize your main points by order of importance. Remember that each paragraph should focus on one main idea about the story that in turn supports your thesis. These main ideas will be stated in each paragraph's **topic sentence.** Support each main idea with specific details, examples, and quotations from the story. Then explain how these details support your main ideas. The last paragraph, or **conclusion,** should sum up your main points and restate your thesis. Before drafting, create a plan to identify the main parts of your response.

Use your plan as a guide. You may want to write from beginning to end to create your first draft, and reread and revise only after you have finished the first draft. Or you may want to write each paragraph, then reread to revise it point by point.

Intro
- Identify the story "After Twenty Years" by O. Henry.
- Summarize the important parts of the story.
- Include my thesis statement.

Body
- State my least important point and support it.
- State my more important point and support it.
- State my most important point and support it.

Conclusion
- Sum up my main points.
- Restate my thesis.

Audience and Tone

As you write, keep in mind who will read your response. This is your **audience.** Your audience could be your teacher or your classmates, for example. Make sure you give enough background information so your audience can understand your response. If your audience has also read the story, only summarize the main parts. Use your introduction to "hook," or engage, your audience.

Your **tone** is your attitude toward the subject you are writing about. Your tone tells the reader how you feel about the story, characters, or other subjects you discuss. The tone you take can be formal or informal, and it can show attitudes such as sympathy, humor, disgust, and admiration. Your response should sound natural, but not too casual.

Differentiated Instruction

English Language Learning

English learners may use words without fully understanding their connotations. When they have completed rough drafts, pair them with native English speakers as mentors. Have the mentors read the drafts, explain missed connotations, and suggest replacement words.

Enrichment

Let good writers imagine writing a hook for several different audiences. Give them three diverse audience options, such as teenagers eating on a cruise ship, rodeo riders waiting for their competitions to start, and sunbathers at a country club pool. For each audience, have students identify what their hooks would be, and then ask them to describe any differences in tone among the hooks.

3. REVISE

Evaluating Your Draft

Now that your draft is complete, look over your own paper for strengths and weaknesses. To get the best evaluation of your writing, however, conduct a **peer review.** Exchange papers with a classmate and discuss ways you can improve your paper.

Below is part of a draft of a response to literature. The annotations to the right indicate the reasons for the changes marked in the draft.

Revising Checklist

- ☐ Does the introduction state the thesis?
- ☐ Is the response clearly organized?
- ☐ Are the main ideas supported with specific details and examples?
- ☐ Does the conclusion sum up the thesis and main points?

Friends who meet again after several years are often shocked at how different their lives are. In "After Twenty Years" by O. Henry, ~~is a story about~~ two friends. ~~They~~ meet again after twenty years~~.~~*, under surprising circumstances. The friends, Bob and Jimmy, are scheduled to meet at a restaurant where they had dinner* twenty years ago. *The realistic descriptions made this story suspenseful and surprising to me because they reveal who each character really is, despite how the characters see themselves.*

The dark, shadowy setting of the story suggests that appearances may not be what they seem. When the police officer sees Bob, he is in a dark doorway. Neither man seems to recognize the other in the darkness.

The suspense and unexpected twist in "After Twenty Years" make this an engaging story. ~~Also, the story reminds me of the "Inn of Lost Time."~~ The realistic descriptions gradually reveal the true qualities of each character, whether the characters see that truth or not.

> *Add a hook and interesting details to engage your reader.*

> *In your thesis, specify what parts of the story made you respond the way you did.*

> *Make sure each body paragraph has a topic sentence.*

> *Delete any details that are off topic.*

Revise

Point out that the revising stage is an effective time for students to review their organizational patterns and make sure they follow a pattern consistently. Also, encourage students to choose peer reviewers who have not written about the same story. Remind students to review essays as objectively as possible so they can offer the most detailed and constructive feedback.

What Great Writers Do

To encourage students to develop strong hooks for their essays, read them this quotation from twentieth-century American writer Dorothy Parker.

This is not a novel to be tossed aside lightly. It should be thrown with great force.

Writing Skills

Topic Sentences

Remind students that they may state a paragraph's main idea with a topic sentence. (The main idea may also be unstated, conveyed instead by an accumulation of information in the sentences.) After reading the following group of sentences aloud, ask students what a good topic sentence would be.

Marjorie held her head in her hands. Everyone stared at her. Many were thinking "it could have been me" but they weren't saying a word. (Possible answer: Marjorie was incredibly embarrassed.)

Edit and Proofread

Sentence Variety If students enjoyed the process of peer review, have them exchange papers with new "peers." Instruct them to identify and circle repetitive sentence styles.

Commonly Confused Words Hold a brief brainstorming session on commonly confused words. Let students identify things they think other people often confuse. If necessary, prompt students to think of words they always have to check twice, or ask what errors they saw when they were conducting peer reviews.

Proofreading Suggest to students that they may want to make several proofreading passes—one for spelling, one for punctuation, and one for capitalization.

▶ Edit and Proofread

Students may want to use proofreader's marks when correcting their work. Refer them to the Language Arts Handbook, Writing Section 4.1, Proofreader's Symbols.

▶ Publish and Present

Before students begin their final version, they might benefit from reading in the Language Arts Handbook, Writing Section 4.1, Writing Follow-up.

4. EDIT AND PROOFREAD

Focus: Sentence Variety

Including a variety of sentences in your response will make your writing more interesting. As you revise your draft, check that the length and type of your sentences vary. If you have several short, choppy sentences in a row, combine some of them with conjunctions to create complex sentences. Use transitions to connect ideas.

> Yet, Jimmy sees through Bob's bragging. Jimmy feels loyalty toward his old friend. He cannot arrest him himself.

> Yet, *though* Jimmy sees through Bob's bragging, Jimmy feels loyalty toward his old friend, *and* he cannot arrest him himself.

If many of your sentences start or end the same way, revise them to add variety. Add introductory phrases, or change the order of the clauses.

Focus: Commonly Confused Words

Some words can be confusing when you are writing. Review words such as *were* and *we're*, *its* and *it's*, and *affect* and *effect* as you revise. If you are confused as to which word to use, look up the word in a dictionary.

> In the story, it's "barely 10 o'clock at night," and the street is "depeopled."

If you substitute the words *it is* for the contraction *it's,* you will notice that the correct word was used. The word *its* is the possessive form of the word *it.*

Proofreading

Proofreading for Errors When you proofread, you look for mistakes in the mechanics of your writing. Now is the time to correct mistakes in spelling, punctuation, and capitalization. Use proofreader's marks to highlight any errors you find. (See the Language Arts Handbook, section 4.1, for a list of proofreader's marks.)

5. PUBLISH AND PRESENT

Final Draft

Clean Copy Now that you have revised, edited, and proofread your paper, make a clean copy for presentation. Handwritten papers should be neat and legible. If you are working with a word processing program, double-space the lines of text and use a readable typeface. Follow your teacher's presentation guidelines before submitting your work.

Differentiated Instruction

Reading Proficiency

Work with struggling readers as they proofread their own material. Help individuals focus on problem areas you have already identified. If two or more students have the same chronic problems with grammar and usage, you might use this stage of the writing process to help them correct the problems together.

English Language Learning

Encourage students to increase their accuracy and ease in both speaking and writing English by having them read their expository essay aloud to the class or to a partner. Essays should include a variety of sentence types and connecting words to vary sentence length. In turn, students should listen to the presentations and provide constructive feedback.

Student Model

After Twenty Years
by Sonia Mendoza

Friends who meet again after several years are often shocked at how different their lives are. In "After Twenty Years" by O. Henry, two friends meet again after twenty years, under surprising circumstances. The friends, Bob and Jimmy, are scheduled to meet at a restaurant where they had dinner twenty years ago. A man calls Bob's name and Bob believes the man is Jimmy. When they reach better light, however, Bob realizes his perceptions have been wrong. The realistic descriptions made this story suspenseful and surprising to me because they reveal who each character really is, despite how the characters see themselves.

The dark, shadowy setting of the story suggests that appearances may not be what they seem. In the story, it's "barely 10 o'clock at night," and the street is "depeopled." When the police officer sees Bob, he is in a dark doorway. Neither man seems to recognize the other in the darkness. The few people out are unrecognizable with their "coat collars turned high." When the man claiming to be Jimmy arrives, he has his "collar turned up to his ears," suggesting he, too, may not be who he seems.

The descriptions of Jimmy reveal he is impressive and observant, despite what others might think. He sees Bob immediately, even though Bob is standing in a dark doorway, and Bob doesn't recognize him. When Bob talks about Jimmy, he says he was "a kind of plodder, though good-natured fellow." The detail suggests that Bob is not impressed by Jimmy's humble traits. As Bob brags about life out West, Jimmy doesn't seem interested in such showy success. Yet, though Jimmy sees through Bob's bragging, Jimmy feels loyalty toward his old friend, and he cannot arrest him himself.

The descriptions of Bob add suspense to the story, and they reveal that he cannot see himself or others for who they really are. "Silky" Bob is sure his life has turned out better than Jimmy's. After growing up in New York, he moved out West to make his fortune. There, Bob says, "I've had to compete with some of the sharpest wits to get my pile." His pile, it seems, included a life of crime. Yet, though Bob has "keen eyes," he is never able to see himself and his success for what it really is until he is arrested as a criminal.

The suspense and unexpected twist in "After Twenty Years" make this an engaging story. The realistic descriptions gradually reveal the true qualities of each character, whether the characters see that truth or not.

Names the story and its author

Summarizes the important points of the story

Presents a clear thesis statement that responds to one aspect of the story

Is organized in a clear, logical way

Includes clear topic sentences for body paragraphs

Supports the thesis by providing clear explanations

Supports main ideas with specific details and quoted evidence from the story

Sums up the main points without repeating the thesis exactly

Teach the Workshop

Student Model
Direct students' attention to the model. Point out the side notes that identify the major parts of the essay, the introduction, the body, and the conclusion.

What Great Writers Do
Most writers find inspiration in what they have read. Share with students the following observation by an author in this unit.

My favorite stories came from fairytales, myths and legends also, but my favorite story of all times was The Ugly Duckling. *And I loved that story so much, because it parallels my life and my culture; you know, I was cast aside and told that, 'You're not as beautiful as' and 'You're not' and 'You don't have anything to offer.'*

— PATRICIA MCKISSACK,
AUTHOR OF "The 11:59"

Writing Skills

Outlines
Students may benefit from outlining the model. This will help them see the framework on which the writer built her literary response. Begin by having students identify the introduction, body paragraphs, and conclusion. Have them jot down the main idea of each paragraph.

Then, divide the class into two groups. Have one group prepare a rough outline. This should have main ideas, with supporting details listed under each. Ask the second group to prepare a formal outline. This outline will have headings and subheadings with numbers and letters. When groups have finished, compare the outlines. Ask students to explain any major differences.

Teach the Workshop

Objectives
Participating in this lesson will help students deliver an oral summary of a short story that
- clearly presents the main details of the plot
- conveys the setting and characters using sensory details

Launch the Lesson
Ask students to describe the qualities of a good storyteller. Model a possible response: "My grandfather tells great stories. He makes the characters seem really bizarre." Ask them what kinds of skills they would like to work on to become effective storytellers. Point out that they can experiment with these skills by summarizing stories they have read.

Literary Connection
Storytelling Remind students that most cultures have long traditions of oral storytelling. The Greek poet Homer, for example, inherited a storytelling tradition stretching back centuries, to the time of the Trojan War. Tell students they can locate some roots of a culture's oral tradition by finding stories about how the culture came to be.

> For more information, see the Language Arts Handbook Section 7, Speaking & Listening.

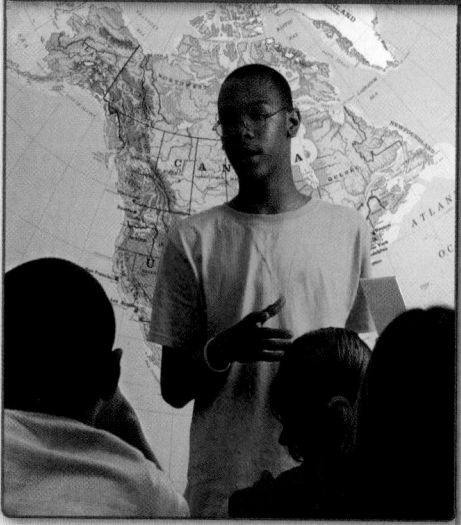

Giving and Actively Listening to Oral Summaries

Imagine a friend has asked you to describe a movie you have just seen or a story you have read recently. What information would you give your friend? Would you talk just about the plot? Or would you describe the setting and the characters? An effective oral summary should discuss all of these elements. An **oral summary** is a presentation that conveys the plot, setting, characters, and other elements of a literary work through spoken words rather than writing.

In this workshop you will learn how to plan and deliver an oral summary of a short story. You will also learn how to listen effectively to someone else's presentation. This workshop includes a rubric, a set of standards to use in evaluating either your own presentation or someone else's.

Planning an Oral Summary
Choose a Story Many short stories would make good subjects for an oral summary. Here are a few points to keep in mind when choosing a story for an oral summary.

- Pick a story that you feel strongly about, since you will communicate your own enthusiasm—or lack of it—to your audience.
- Don't pick a story that is so long and complicated that your presentation becomes bogged down in too many plot details and you lose your audience's attention.
- Don't pick a story that is so brief that your presentation will seem skimpy.

Identify Your Audience How you develop your oral summary will depend on who your audience is. Is the audience familiar with the short story? Will you need to provide any background information? Be prepared to answer questions from your audience.

Summarize the Plot Once you have selected the story for your oral presentation, make sure that you know the plot thoroughly. The best way to do this is to create a plot summary. In preparing your summary, include all the main events of the narrative, but avoid unimportant details. Use brief key words and phrases to remind yourself of key plot elements. If you had decided to base your presentation on "The Serial Garden," for example, your key word plot summary might look like this:

- Mark assembles model garden on cereal box
- transports himself into enchanted garden
- meets princess who created garden
- she loved court music teacher
- vanished into garden to await him
- plan failed; still waiting
- he is Mark's music teacher
- Mark tries to reunite the two; plan fails
- mother destroys cardboard model

Differentiated Instruction

English Language Learning
Pair English language learners with advanced students. Ask the English learners to tell a story about the country they came from. Encourage advanced students to listen closely, to prompt storytellers with English words where necessary, and to use gestures and facial expressions to draw the story out. Afterward, identify as a class the listening and speaking skills students found most useful.

KEY TERMS
ORAL SUMMARY, 132
PLOT, 132
SETTING, 132
CHARACTER, 132
AUDIENCE, 132
SENSORY DETAIL, 133

Common Core State Standards
Speaking and Listening
SL.4, SL.6

Use Sensory Details In addition to presenting the plot of the short story you have chosen, your oral summary should help your audience *imagine* it. To do this, use sensory details, or descriptive words that appeal to the five senses. Sensory details will help your audience imagine the setting and characters and can be created through word choice. For example, if you wanted to convey the setting of the enchanted garden in "The Serial Garden," you might use words that suggest rich, glowing color, such as *golden* or *emerald*. To help your audience see the princess, you might use phrases such as "dressed in white satin," "covered with jewels," "pink-faced," or "long-nosed." As with the plot summary, use key words and phrases to remind you of sensory details.

Rehearse Your Summary Once you have prepared the materials for your oral summary, try practicing your presentation in front of a mirror, or use a video recorder to monitor your communication and delivery. Make sure to self-correct any errors in pronunciation or delivery. Remember that if you have practiced and are prepared, your presentation will go smoothly.

Evaluating Your Presentation

Before you deliver your oral summary to an audience, work with a partner to evaluate it. As with the revision of a piece of writing, a peer reviewer can help you improve your presentation. Respond to your reviewer's feedback on what you did well and on what could be improved. If you are asked to be a peer reviewer, remember to listen attentively and provide constructive feedback, which means that you should be respectful and polite whether you give criticism or praise. Whether you work alone or with a peer reviewer, use the rubric on this page to evaluate your oral summary.

Delivering Your Oral Summary

Nonverbal communication is an important part of listening and speaking. As you deliver your oral summary, remember to make eye contact with the audience. Try to stand still and avoid any movements that can distract your listeners. Adjust the pacing of your delivery, and vary the tone and volume of your voice to keep your audience focused and interested.

Listening Actively Just as it is important to be an effective speaker, it is also necessary to be an effective listener. To listen effectively, maintain eye contact with the speaker. Remain silent during the presentation, and ask questions when appropriate.

Speaking Rubric

Your oral summary will be evaluated on the following elements:

Content
- ☐ clear presentation of main details of the plot
- ☐ sensory details that convey setting and characters

Delivery and Presentation
- ☐ appropriate volume
- ☐ appropriate pacing
- ☐ effective nonverbal expression

Listening Rubric

As a peer reviewer or audience member, you should do the following:

- ☐ listen quietly and attentively
- ☐ maintain eye contact with speaker
- ☐ ask appropriate questions
- ☐ (as peer reviewer) provide constructive feedback

Evaluating an Oral Summary
Have partners use the rubric to create a feedback checklist for preparing and evaluating their oral summaries. Encourage them to incorporate into the checklist any additional criteria you have provided.

Delivering an Oral Summary
Demonstrate to students that a normal conversational voice may not be loud enough when they give their oral summaries. Explain that, like teachers and actors, they need to project their voices. This means they need to practice effectively focusing their voices. Students can establish an appropriate volume by delivering a portion of their summary to a partner standing at the back of the room.

Listening Skills
Encourage students to listen attentively. Consider inviting listeners to break into several groups based on the rubric, such as groups to listen for the plot, for sensory details related to setting, and for volume and pacing. You can also assign a small group to evaluate the nonverbal aspects of the presentation. Suggest that students write down questions only after the summary has been delivered. This way, listening will command their full attention.

Program Resources

To expand upon this workshop lesson, Giving and Listening to Oral Summaries, see the *Exceeding the Standards: Speaking & Listening* resource.

Speaking & Listening Skills

Using Inflection

Tell students that they will have to speak with expression. This means introducing inflection, or variety, into their voices. Inflection can come through changes in pitch (high and low), volume (loudness), pacing, and emphasis. Have students practice inflection by reading aloud these sentences, emphasizing the italicized word in each.

- *Latin* is the language of our ancestors.
- Latin *is* the language of our ancestors.
- Latin is *the* language of our ancestors.
- Latin is the *language* of our ancestors.
- Latin is the language of *our* ancestors.

Objectives

Completing this lesson will enable students to

- write a response to literature based on a timed writing prompt
- answer standardized test questions that demonstrate revising and editing skills
- demonstrate the ability to make inferences from a reading by answering standardized questions

Timed Writing

Say that standardized tests often ask students to write a response to a prompt in a specified period of time. Give the following tips:

- Read the entire question carefully.
- Look for key words in the question that tell you what is expected.
- Underline these words or write them on your own notepaper.
- Use the key words to make sure you answer all parts of the question.
- Organize. Allow time for planning, writing, and reviewing.
- Before you begin writing, create a rough outline of points to make.
- Write a clear introduction. This will help keep you on track as you write each paragraph.
- If you find yourself running out of time, state your remaining points and add a conclusion.
- Review your completed essay to see if you have answered all parts of the question.
- Before you turn in your completed essay, take time to proofread.

Test Practice Workshop

Writing Skills

Literary Response

Read the following short excerpt and the writing assignment that follows. Before you begin writing, think carefully about what task the assignment is asking you to perform. Then create an outline to help guide your writing.

from *The Snow Goose* by Paul Gallico

One November afternoon, three years after Rhayader had come to the Great Marsh, a child approached the lighthouse studio by means of the sea wall. In her arms she carried a burden.

She was no more than twelve, slender, dirty, nervous and timid as a bird, but beneath the grime as eerily beautiful as a marsh faery. She was pure Saxon, large-boned, fair, and a head to which her body was yet to grow, and deep-set, violet-colored eyes.

She was desperately frightened of the ugly man she had come to see, for legend had already begun to gather about Rhayader, and the native wild-fowlers hated him for interfering with their sport.

But greater than her fear was the need of that which she bore. For locked in her child's heart was the knowledge, picked up somewhere in the swampland, that this ogre who lived in the lighthouse had magic that could heal injured things.

She had never seen Rhayader before and was close to fleeing in panic at the dark apparition that appeared at the studio door, drawn by her footsteps—the black head and beard, the sinister hump, and the crooked claw.

She stood there staring, poised like a disturbed marsh bird for instant flight.

But his voice was deep and kind when he spoke to her.

"What is it, child?"

She stood her ground and then edged timidly forward. The thing she carried in her arms was a large white bird, and it was quite still. There were stains of blood on its whiteness and on her kirtle where she had held it to her.

The girl placed it in his arms. "I found it, sir. It's hurted. Is it still alive?"

Assignment: What methods of **characterization** does the author use to develop the two characters in this passage? Plan and write several paragraphs in which you explain how the use of characterization helps the reader to understand the girl's motivation for approaching the man in the lighthouse. What about the old man assists her in overcoming her own fears? Include evidence from this passage in your response.

Rubric for a Response to Literature

Have students use these criteria for evaluating their literary responses.

- ☐ Does the response to literature have a compelling introduction that clearly states a response?
- ☐ Does the response follow a clear organizational pattern?
- ☐ Does textual evidence support the main ideas?
- ☐ Does the essay have a conclusion that sums up the response?

Common Core State Standards

Language
L.3.1f, L.5.1d, L.6.1e

Revising and Editing Skills

For each of the following questions, choose the *best* revision of the underlined portion of the sentence. If you feel that the underlined portion should not be changed, choose option (A), which repeats the phrasing of the original. Record your answers on a separate sheet of paper.

1. Because we studied so hard, <u>were much happier than</u> the rest of the class.
   A. were much happier than
   B. were much happier, than
   C. were much happier; than
   D. we're much happier than
   E. your much happier than

2. <u>John and he went to visit their</u> grandparents in Arkansas over winter break.
   A. John and he went to visit their
   B. John and him went to visit their
   C. Him and John went to visit their
   D. John and he went to visit they're
   E. Him and John went to visit they are

3. The <u>senator, along with his supporters, were</u> unhappy with the outcome of the election.
   A. senator, along with his supporters, were
   B. senator, along with his supporters, was
   C. senator, along with him supporters, were
   D. senator, along with his supporters, are
   E. senator along with his supporters were

4. Thanks to Johnny, <u>were nearly done with</u> the project.
   A. were nearly done with
   B. were done nearly with
   C. we is nearly done with
   D. we was nearly done with
   E. we're nearly done with

5. Sarah and Haifa <u>were not going to bring their clubs</u> to the course.
   A. were not going to bring their clubs
   B. isn't going to bring their clubs
   C. we're not going to bring their clubs
   D. is not going to bring their clubs
   E. have not bring their clubs

6. <u>The principal is him.</u>
   A. The principal is him.
   B. The principal was him.
   C. The principal were him.
   D. The principal is he.
   E. The principal were he.

7. Monica <u>was unsympathetic to Marie and I.</u>
   A. was unsympathetic to Marie and I.
   B. is unsympathetic to Marie and I.
   C. was unsympathetic to Marie and me.
   D. unsympathetically was to Marie and I.
   E. were unsympathetic to Marie and me.

8. Juan and Tony could not avoid their homework, <u>no matter how hard he tried.</u>
   A. no matter how hard he tried.
   B. no matter how hard we tried.
   C. No matter how hard he tried.
   D. no matter how hard us tried.
   E. no matter how hard they tried.

9. Allen, as well as Allen's three sisters, <u>are going to attend</u> the afternoon's events.
   A. are going to attend
   B. were going to attend
   C. we're going to attend
   D. is going to attend
   E. have attended

10. <u>Were not supposed to use water</u> during the drought.
   A. Were not supposed to use water
   B. We're not supposed to use water
   C. Were is supposed to use water
   D. Were not supposing to use water
   E. Not supposed to use water

Teach the Workshop

Revising and Editing Skills
1. D
2. A
3. B
4. E
5. A
6. D
7. C
8. E
9. D
10. B

Test-Taking Tip
Avoid Distractors

Instruct students to watch out for distractors, incorrect answers that look right because they are partially correct. Distractors are usually based on common mistakes students make. Model a think-aloud showing how to detect distractors.

Question 7. I've already eliminated A, B, and D, so my choice is now between C and E. But I see that E is a distractor, because although it's otherwise correct, the subject and verb don't match. So C is the correct answer.

> For more information, see the Language Arts Handbook Section 8, Test-Taking Skills.

Program Resources

For more study and practice with test-taking skills, see the *Exceeding the Standards: Test Practice* resource:
- Literary Response Practice Test: Reading, pp. 5–6

Words in Use

Teaching Words
burden, 134
eerily, 134
interfering, 134
apparition, 134
poised, 134
colonial, 136
attaché, 136
commotion, 136

KEY TERMS

SETTING, 134
PLOT, 134
MOOD, 134
EXPOSITION, 137
CLIMAX, 137
FALLING ACTION, 137
RESOLUTION, 137
PROTAGONIST, 137
CENTRAL CONFLICT, 137
INTERNAL CONFLICT, 137
EXTERNAL CONFLICT, 137

Reading Comprehension Tests

Tell students that reading comprehension tests give a short piece of writing and then ask several questions about it. The questions may ask students to figure out something based on information in the passage. Urge students to keep the following tips in mind:

- Read all the questions quickly.
- Read the passage with the questions in mind.
- Reread the first question carefully.
- Scan the passage, looking for key words. When you find a key word, slow down and read carefully.
- Answer the first question.
- Repeat this process to answer all the rest of the questions.

Reading Skills

Carefully read the following passage. Then, on a separate piece of paper, answer each question.

"The Dinner Party" by Mona Gardner

The country is India. A colonial official and his wife are giving a large dinner party. They are seated with their guests—army officers and government attachés and their wives, and a visiting American naturalist—in their spacious dining room, which has a bare marble floor, open rafters and wide glass doors opening onto a
5   veranda.

A spirited discussion springs up between a young girl who insists that women have outgrown the jumping-on-a-chair-at-the-sight-of-a-mouse era and a colonel who says that they haven't.

"A woman's unfailing reaction in any crisis," the colonel says, "is to scream.
10 And while a man may feel like it, he has that ounce more of nerve control than a woman has. And that last ounce is what counts." The American does not join in the argument but watches the other guests. As he looks, he sees a strange expression come over the face of the hostess. She is staring straight ahead, her muscles contracting slightly. With a slight gesture she summons the native boy
15 standing behind her chair and whispers to him. The boy's eyes widen: he quickly leaves the room.

Of the guests, none except the American notices this or sees the boy place a bowl of milk on the veranda just outside the open doors.

The American comes to with a start. In India, milk in a bowl means only one
20 thing—bait for a snake. He realizes there must be a cobra in the room. He looks up at the rafters—the likeliest place—but they are bare. Three corners of the room are empty, and in the fourth the servants are waiting to serve the next course. There is only one place left—under the table.

His first impulse is to jump back and warn the others, but he knows the
25 commotion would frighten the cobra into striking. He speaks quickly, the tone of his voice so arresting that it sobers everyone.

"I want to know just what control everyone at this table has. I will count to three hundred—that's five minutes—and not one of you is to move a muscle. Those who move will forfeit fifty rupees. Ready!" The twenty people sit like stone
30 images while he counts. He is saying, "...two hundred and eighty..." when, out of the corner of his eye, he sees the cobra emerge and make for the bowl of milk. Screams ring out as he jumps to slam the veranda doors safely shut.

"You were right, Colonel!" the host exclaims. "A man has just shown us an example of perfect control."
35 "Just a minute," the American says, turning to his hostess. "Mrs. Wynnes, how did you know that cobra was in the room?" A faint smile lights up the woman's face as she replies: "Because it was crawling across my foot."

Differentiated Instruction

English Language Learning

Students learning English will need help with the academic vocabulary used in standardized tests. Explain the following terms used in this workshop:
outline—short summary or description, usually arranged as a series of key points, 134
evidence—facts that support an argument, 134
definition—meaning of a word, 137

In order to help students internalize these new terms, ask them to rewrite the definitions using their own words and then use the terms in a paragraph or journal entry. Verify that they understand the academic terms based on these activities.

1. Based on the context, which of the following is the *best* definition of the word *spacious* in line 3?
   A. big and open
   B. uncomfortable
   C. quiet
   D. very small
   E. crooked

2. Lines 1 through 16 can *best* be described as the
   A. exposition.
   B. climax.
   C. climax and falling action.
   D. falling action.
   E. resolution.

3. Based on the context, which of the following is the *best* definition of the word *forfeit* in line 29?
   A. to bet
   B. to take
   C. to consider
   D. to taper off
   E. to lose

4. What motivates the naturalist to ask the dinner guests to enter into a contest?
   A. He wants to alert the guests to the presence of a snake.
   B. He wants to closely watch the hostess.
   C. He wants to test the colonel's theory.
   D. He wants to win fifty rupees.
   E. He wants to keep everyone completely still.

5. The protagonist of this passage is
   A. the naturalist.
   B. the colonel.
   C. the colonial official.
   D. the boy.
   E. the snake.

6. Which of the following *best* describes the central conflict of this passage?
   A. Members of a dinner party are arguing over a colonel's claim that women are less courageous than men.
   B. People at a dinner party use a snake to solve a dispute.
   C. People at a dinner party are engaged in a contest to see who can hold still the longest.
   D. A cobra has crawled into a dinner party, but those who have noticed cannot alert the rest of the party safely.
   E. A servant at a dinner party attempts to murder the guests as they eat.

7. The conflict in this passage is primarily
   A. internal.
   B. external.
   C. indirect.
   D. resolution.
   E. falling action.

8. The setting of this passage is best described as a
   A. small house.
   B. veranda.
   C. living room.
   D. dining room.
   E. garden.

Reading Skills
1. A
2. A
3. E
4. E
5. A
6. D
7. B
8. D

Test-Taking Skills

Eliminate Incorrect Responses

Point out that a key skill in working with multiple-choice questions is eliminating incorrect responses. Demonstrate this skill by modeling a think-aloud for one question in the Reading Skills section.

Question 1. The word *spacious* sounds like *space.* That seems to eliminate B, C, and E. Line 1 calls the setting a "large dinner," and lines 2 and 3 say a lot of people are in this room, so A is probably correct.

Select another question and have the class work as a group to eliminate the incorrect responses.

Unit 2 Visual Planning Guide

Planning and Assessment Tools

Annotated Teacher's Edition

Annotated Teacher's Edition
One location for accessing, previewing, and planning for use of all program resources.

EMC Launchpad
Desktop application for accessing, previewing, planning, posting, and grading all program resources. Post personal resources and lessons, and access the E-Lesson Planner, the E-Gradebook, and training modules for computer literacy.

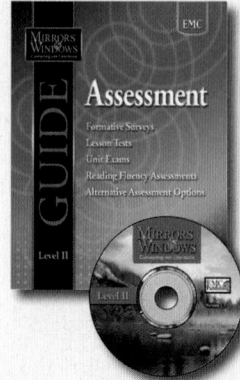

Assessment Guide and ExamView
A variety of assessments are available for this unit in print and electronic forms, including:
- Formative Survey
- Lesson Tests
- Unit Exams
- Alternative Assessment Options
- Reading Fluency Assessments

Meeting the Standards: Unit 2
In addition to lesson-by-lesson resources, *Meeting the Standards* includes the following unit-based resources:
- Unit Study Guide
- Practice Test
- Active Reading Model
- Selection Quizzes

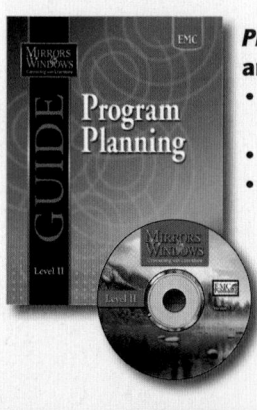

Program Planning Guide and *E-Lesson Planner*
- Lesson Plans for all the selections in the unit
- Core Standards-Based Selections
- Reading Log and Evaluation Forms

The E-Lesson Planner contains fully developed lesson plans and unit resources with an electronic calendar for editing lesson plans.

Technology Tools

Visual Teaching Package
This package contains unit-based lectures, games, art collections, and Writing Workshops in PowerPoint format; included within the EMC Launchpad.

Interactive Student Text on CD
The student textbook on CD includes highlighting, note-taking, bookmarking, and a direct link to the student website, in addition to everything in the student text.

Audio Library
Authentic, dramatic recordings with listening activities expand listening skills and offer additional support for developing readers and English Language Learners.

ETS Online Criterion-Based Essay Grader (Grades 9–12)
Students can use this ETS web-based tool to evaluate their essays online before submitting them for teacher review and final evaluation.

mirrorsandwindows.com
Student and teacher resources, support, references, technology tools, and state-specific standards are available at **mirrorsandwindows.com.** The website is customizable using the EMC Launchpad.

Unit-Based Resources

Exceeding the Standards Unit Resources

Each of the *Exceeding the Standards* resources provides fully developed lessons to help you extend the textbook lessons and to expand upon the themes and skills covered in the unit. You can also download these lessons from **mirrorsandwindows.com**.

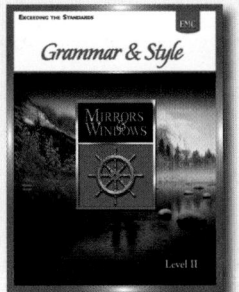
Grammar & Style
This resource contains:
- Four lessons on Nouns, pp. 20–32
- Five lessons on Pronouns, pp. 33–48

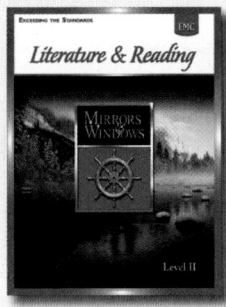
Literature & Reading
This resource contains:
- Read Fiction Aloud, pp. 3-5

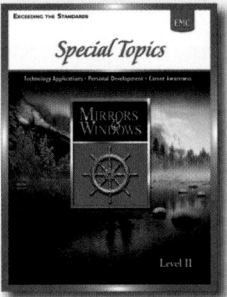
Special Topics
This resource contains:
- Lifelong Learning: The Definition of Character: Part 2, pp. 6–7
- Media Literacy: Using Microsoft Word, pp. 8–9

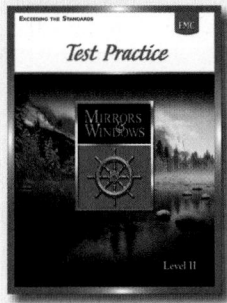
Test Practice
This resource contains:
- Literary Response Practice Test: Timed Writing, p. 7

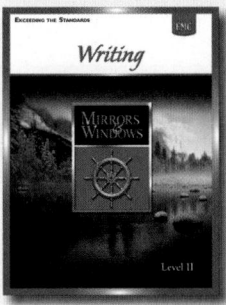
Writing
This resource contains:
- Descriptive Writing: Describe a Dreamlike Atmosphere, pp. 7–13

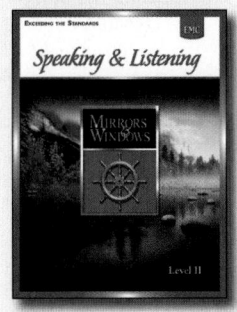
Speaking & Listening
This resource contains the following lesson to expand on the Speaking & Listening Workshop:
- Giving and Actively Listening to Literary Presentations, pp. 4–6

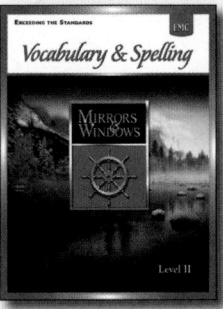
Vocabulary & Spelling
This resource contains:
- Four lessons on Studying Syllables, pp. 13–20.

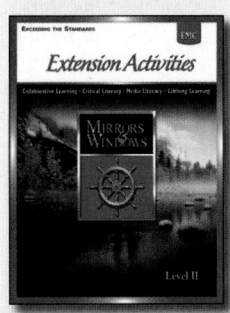
Extension Activities
This resource contains:
- Media Literacy: Dig for Details, pp. 5–6
- Critical Literacy: Explore an Allusion, p. 7

Unit 2 Visual Planning Guide

(142)

Reading Level: Moderate
Pacing: 3 days

Meeting the Standards,
Reading Model,
pp. 19–24

Developing Readers,
Take Notes, pp. 13–15

---

(155)

Reading Level: Easy
Pacing: 3 days

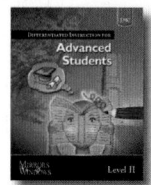

Meeting the Standards,
Guided Reading,
pp. 25–31

Advanced Students,
Theme Study, p. 9

---

(164)

Reading Level: Moderate
Pacing: 3 days

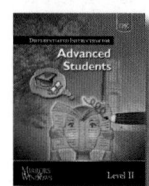

Meeting the Standards,
Directed Reading,
pp. 32–42

Advanced Students,
Author Study,
pp. 10–11

Reading Level: Easy
Pacing: 1 day

Meeting the Standards,
Directed Reading,
pp. 43–46

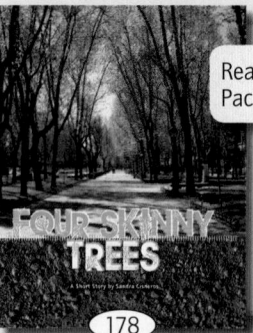
(178)

Reading Level: Easy
Pacing: 2 days

Meeting the Standards,
Directed Reading,
pp. 47–53

---

(182)

 Interactive Student
Text on CD-ROM

 Selection
Lesson Plan

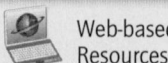 Web-based
Resources

Lesson-by-Lesson Resources

Reading Level: Directed
Reading Pacing: 3 days

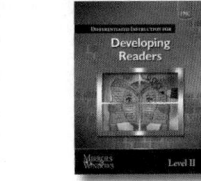

Meeting the Standards, Compare Literature, pp. 54–61

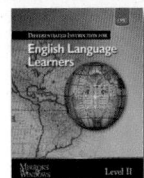

Developing Readers, Make Predictions, pp. 16–18

English Language Learners, Media Ideas, pp. 64–69

192

Reading Level: Moderate
Pacing: 3 days

Meeting the Standards, Directed Reading, pp. 62–65

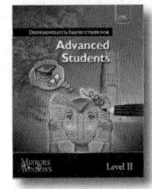

Advanced Students, Comparing Genres, p. 12

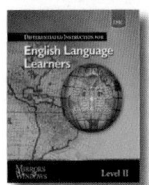

English Language Learners, Use Context Clues, pp. 70–85

200

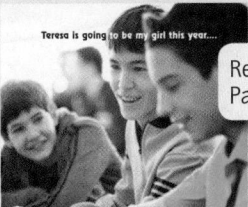

Reading Level: Easy
Pacing: 2 days

Meeting the Standards, Directed Reading, pp. 69–73

213

Reading Level: Easy
Pacing: 1 day

Meeting the Standards, Independent Reading, pp. 74–80

220

Reading Level: Challenging
Pacing: 2 days

Meeting the Standards, Independent Reading, pp. 81–87

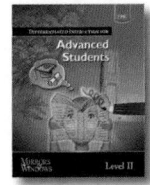

Advanced Students, Symbolism Analysis, p. 13

224

 Lesson Test   Audio Library

Unit 2 Scope & Sequence Guide

Selection or Feature	Genre	Reading Support/ Reading Level	Word Count	Reading Skill	Graphic Organizer	
Understanding Point of View, p. 140						
Hollywood and the Pits Cherylene Lee pp. 141–152	Short Story	Guided Reading: Reading Model/ Moderate	3,624	Analyze Cause and Effect	Cause-Effect Chart; POV Chart	
Understanding Theme p. 153						
The Scholarship Jacket Marta Salinas pp. 154–161	Short Story	Guided Reading: Reading Model/Easy	1,968	Context Clues	Theme Map	
Amigo Brothers Piri Thomas pp. 163–175	Short Story	Directed Reading/ Moderate	3,470	Draw Conclusions	Drawing Conclusions Log; POV Chart	
Informational Text Connection: from **The Greatest: Muhammad Ali** Walter Dean Myers pp. 173–174	Biography	Easy	599			
Four Skinny Trees Sandra Cisneros pp. 177–180	Short Story	Directed Reading/Easy	209	Identify Main Idea	Main Idea Map; Description Chart	
The White Umbrella Gish Jen pp. 181–189	Short Story	Directed Reading/Easy	2,844	Compare and Contrast	Compare and Contrast Chart; Mood Map	
Jed's Grandfather Joseph Bruchac pp. 191–198	Short Story	Directed Reading/ Moderate	1,988		Compare Tone Chart	
The Courage that My Mother Had Edna St. Vincent Millay pp. 191–198	Lyric Poem	Directed Reading/Easy	99			
Antaeus Borden Deal pp. 199–211	Short Story	Directed Reading/ Moderate	4,111	Context Clues	Cause-and-Effect Chart	
Literature Connection: in the inner city Lucille Clifton p. 210	Lyric Poem	Moderate	64			
Seventh Grade Gary Soto pp. 212–218	Short Story	Directed Reading/Easy	1,909	Sequence of Events	Timeline; Character Chart	

GUIDED READING

DIRECTED READING

Literary Element	*Mirrors & Windows* Theme	Cross-Curricular Connection	Writing Options	Extension Activities
What is Point of View? Point of View in Fiction				
Point of View	Perception	Science Connection: *Geologic Time*	Creative: Journal Entry Expository: Literary Response	Collaborative Learning: Infer the Author's Purpose Media Literacy: Dig for Details
What is Theme? Themes and Topics Stated and Implied Themes				
Theme	Guardians		Creative: Acceptance Speech Expository: Epository Paragraph	Lifelong Learning: Find Famous Awards Collaborative Learning: Communicate by Computer
Point of View	Competition		Creative: Dialogue Expository: Expository Essay	Collaborative Learning: Write a Script Media Literacy: Conduct Internet Research
Description	Symbolism		Creative: Descriptive Essay Expository: Literary Response	Collaborative Learning: Give Complex Instructions Lifelong Learning: Describe a Tree
Mood	Conflicting Emotions		Creative: Diary Entry Expository: Expository Paragraph	Collaborative Learning: Relate Mood to Point of View Lifelong Learning: Explore a Symbol
Compare Literature: Tone	Inheritance		Creative: Poem Expository: Compare-and-Contrast Essay	Collaborative Learning: Study Native Languages Lifelong Learning: Dream Research
Conflict	Accomplishment	History Connection: Victory Gardens	Creative: Business Letter Expository: Literary Response	Collaborative Learning: Discuss Motivation Critical Literacy: Explore an Allusion
Character	Image		Creative: Short Story Expository: Expository Essay	Lifelong Learning: Get Romantic Critical Literacy: Ask the Author

Unit 2 Scope & Sequence Guide

	Selection or Feature	Genre	Reading Support/ Reading Level	Word Count	Reading Skill	Graphic Organizer	
INDEPENDENT READING	**Papa's Parrot** Cynthia Rylant pp. 220–223	Short Story	Independent Reading/ Easy	1,027	Identify Sequence of Events		
	The Smallest Dragonboy Anne McCaffrey pp. 224–236	Short Story	Independent Reading/ Challenging	5,230	Analyze Cause and Effect		

Unit 2 Language Arts Workshops

Grammar & Style	Vocabulary & Spelling	Writing	Speaking & Listening	Test Practice
Comma Use, p. 162 Independent and Dependent Clauses, p. 190 Consistent Verb Tense, p. 219	Prefixes, Roots, and Suffixes, p. 176	Narrative Writing: Writing a Short Story, pp. 238–245	Giving and Actively Listening to Literary Presentations, pp. 246–247	Writing Skills: Literary Response, p. 249 Revising and Editing Skills, p. 249 Reading Skills: from "The Ground is Always Damp" by Luci Tapahonso, pp. 250–251

Literary Element	*Mirrors & Windows* Theme	Cross-Curricular Connection	Writing Options	Extension Activities
Theme	Staying in Touch		Creative: Journal Entry	Lifelong Learning: Research Mimicry
Character	Apprehension		Persuasive: Book Review	Collaborative Learning: Research Conventions of Epic Tales

Unit 2 Building Vocabulary

The lists below identify the Words in Use and Key Terms within this unit. These words are listed at the bottom of the Teacher's Edition pages at the beginning of each lesson. Vocabulary development activities are provided in the *Meeting the Standards* unit book and in *Exceeding the Standards: Vocabulary & Spelling*.

WORDS IN USE

Preview Vocabulary
Preview Vocabulary are words taken from the sentences within each selection. These words are defined in the side margin or at the bottom of the pages on which they appear. The "Preview Vocabulary" section introduces these words in the Before Reading page preceding each selection.

absentmindedly, 156	dispel, 170	laborious, 205	surge, 172
barrage, 143	domain, 203	obsessed, 142	tether, 194
coincidence, 157	dub, 143	predator, 149	trough, 192
conviction, 214	ferocity, 214	revelation, 187	trudge, 215
credibility, 183	flail, 171	scavenger, 149	wary, 168
desecrate, 206	flourish, 207	scepter, 184	withdrawn, 159
devastating, 165	inert, 205	scowl, 214	
dismay, 157	kindling, 193	stupendous, 183	

Selection Words
Selection Words are additional words from the reading that may be challenging but are not central to the selection and are not identified in the prereading section. These words can easily be learned using the story context, and they provide excellent practice for using content clues to find meaning without explicit instruction.

agile, 156	enamel, 193	merely, 220	raucous, 196
archaeological, 142	enviable, 225	mottled, 224	resolute, 202
barrage, 165	evasion, 228	obscure, 202	roused, 231
blubbery, 221	falsify, 157	pang, 183	shrewd, 204
chauffeured, 144	ferocious, 179	percale, 194	skewing, 147
claret, 172	groveling, 150	perturbed, 227	spectrum, 174
consternation, 235	imminent, 226	perversion, 149	toilsome, 205
deposition, 151	immobilized, 144	piteous, 235	torrent, 168
desolation, 231	inevitable, 173	populace, 216	vile, 160
dignitaries, 169	levied, 207	quivering, 184	welterweight, 166
eke, 184	lilt, 183	raggedy, 179	

Teaching Words
Teaching Words consist of vocabulary that is used in the directions about the lessons. Teaching words explain to students what to focus on within the selection, help establish the story context, clarify the meaning of literary terms, and define the goals or instructional purpose.

academically, 248	epochs, 148	motivations, 161	provoking, 238
activist, 154	era, 148	multiethnic, 181	regretted, 223
ammunition, 199	fend, 160	multigenerational, 181	represent, 179
asphalt, 141	foundation, 198	narrative, 219	resemble, 180
authoritative, 198	genuinely, 223	nostalgic, 251	rubric, 238
canned, 203	habitual, 219	pacing, 247	subject, 190
clause, 190	impoverished, 220	pesticide, 154	symbolize, 179
collage, 238	influence, 141	petroleum, 141	tension, 181, 240
consensus, 211	insight, 210	physique, 172	traditional, 181
consistent, 191, 219	inspiration, 198	portrayal, 174	universally, 219
constructive, 247	isolated, 220	predicate, 190	vivid, 180, 238
context, 154	linguistic, 198	profiles, 175	
convey, 247	mimicry, 223	prose, 177	

KEY TERMS

Key Terms are commonly referred to as *academic vocabulary*. These terms appear in the instructional material to teach the terminology that students need to acquire to understand literature. The repetition of the terms throughout the program ensures student mastery and provides a solid foundation for the continuing study of literature and language arts.

adjective clause, 190
adverb clause, 190
allusion, 211
audience, 246
autobiographical, 212
cause, 141, 211
central conflict, 181
character, 177, 212, 238
characterization, 251
chronological order, 212, 240
climax, 181, 238
cluster chart, 189, 239
compare, 181, 198
complete sentence, 190
conclusion, 218
conflict, 199, 238, 251
connotations, 191
context clues, 154, 199
contrast, 181, 198
dependent clause, 190
description, 177, 251
dialect, 251

dialogue, 175, 241, 246, 251
dictionary, 218
dynamic character, 212, 223, 251
effect, 141, 211
encyclopedia, 218
external conflict, 199, 251
figurative language, 177
first-person point of view, 141, 251
folklore, 236
imagery, 177
independent clause, 190
indirect conflict, 251
internal conflict, 199, 251
limited, 163
limited point of view, 251
limited third-person narrator, 163
literary presentation, 246
lyric poem, 191
main character, 199, 212
main idea, 161, 177, 236, 248

minor character, 212
mood, 141, 180, 181, 251
motivation, 163, 189, 211
narrator, 141, 161, 163, 181, 211
nouns, 190
omniscient, 163
paraphrase, 236
past tense, 219
peer review, 241
personification, 177
plot, 141, 163, 181, 199, 238
point of view, 141, 163, 239, 246
precise language, 177
predicate, 190
present tense, 219
pronouns, 190
protagonist, 251
punctuation, 246
resolution, 175, 181, 240, 251
second-person point of view, 141
sensory details, 177, 181, 247, 251

sequence, 212
setting, 181, 191, 238
short story, 141, 154, 163, 177, 181, 191, 199, 212, 220, 224, 238
static character, 212, 223, 251
story map, 239
summarize, 189, 218, 223
summary, 236
symbol, 189, 198, 236
theme, 154, 199, 251
thesis statement, 175, 218
third-person limited, 239
third-person omniscient, 239
third-person point of view, 141, 163, 251
time line, 212
tone, 189, 191, 240, 251
unreliable character, 251
verb, 190, 218, 219, 242

UNIT 2 OVERVIEW Fiction

Objectives
Studying this unit will help students meet the following objectives:
- Connect the themes expressed in the selections to their own lives and to the world around them
- Identify common forms of fiction, including the short story, as well as examples of other genres such as biography and poetry
- Understand different elements of fiction, such as point of view and theme
- Understand variations of literary forms and authors' use of language to develop forms

Reading Strategies
Ask Questions
Clarify
Make Inferences
Make Predictions
Visualize

Reading Skills
Analyze Cause and Effect
Compare and Contrast
Context Clues
Draw Conclusions
Identify Main Idea
Identify Sequence of Events

Literary Elements
Character
Conflict
Description
Mood
Point of View
Theme
Tone

Learning Values
Fiction

Unit 2

SANDRA CISNEROS   GARY SOTO   CHERYLENE LEE

Launch the Unit

Have students work in small groups to define the word *values*. Encourage groups to brainstorm definitions for one minute, then to concur on a single working definition. When this is done, have each group create three questions they could ask about how people learn values. Each group should pass its definition and its questions to another group, and then attempt to answer the questions it receives.

> "But T. J. kept the vision bright within us, his words shrewd and calculated toward the fulfillment of his dream; and he worked harder than any of us. He seemed driven toward a goal that we couldn't see...."

—BORDEN DEAL, "Antaeus"

How do you respond when faced with a challenge? In "Antaeus," T. J. is a newcomer to the city. Though he struggles at first, he is able to excite his friends with his dream of creating a roof garden. As you read the unit, consider how you approach difficult situations. Do you always stay true to your values?

EDNA ST. VINCENT MILLAY   PIRI THOMAS   GISH JEN

139

Program Resources

For a visual reminder of the unit-based resources available for Unit 2, Fiction, see pages 138A and 138B. As you introduce the unit, you may want to provide students with the Unit Study Guide, which is contained in the *Meeting the Standards* resource.

Understanding Point of View

Reading skills and strategies that can help students understand point of view include skimming, scanning, and clarifying.

Use Reading Skills

Skim and Scan Tell students that by identifying whether a writer uses first-person or third-person pronouns, it is fairly easy to determine the narrator's point of view. Caution them to be careful, however, when they skim or scan a story to look for pronouns. A third-person narrator can report conversations in which people use first-person pronouns, and a first-person narrator naturally will use third-person pronouns when describing other people.

Use Reading Strategies

Clarify Suggest to students that in order to ensure they understand a story's point of view, they should clarify who the narrator is. Rather than rely on pronouns alone, they can ask themselves what the narrator knows and does not know, how the narrator fits into the story, and whether the narrator is objective or subjective in relaying events that occur as the plot develops.

KEY TERMS

POINT OF VIEW, 140
FIRST-PERSON POINT OF VIEW, 140
THIRD-PERSON POINT OF VIEW, 140
THIRD-PERSON OMNISCIENT, 140
NARRATOR, 140
THIRD-PERSON LIMITED POINT OF VIEW, 140

Literary Element

Understanding Point of View

What Is Point of View?

Each of these photographs shows the same subject—a man motorcycling down a rural road. What is different about them? The main difference is the point of view. One photograph shows the motorcyclist from the point of view of another person; the other shows the scene from the point of view of the motorcyclist himself. Point of view is an important element in fiction as well as photography.

Point of View in Fiction

Each of the passages to the right gives an account of a story's main character observing something. Who is the narrator in each? In other words, who is telling the story? How do you know? The vantage point from which a writer presents the events and characters of a story is called the **point of view.**

First-Person Point of View In "Hollywood and the Pits," the story is told from a *first-person point of view.* In other words, the narrator is a character in the story and describes the events. You can tell that a story is told from a first-person point of view because the narrator uses such pronouns as *I* and *we.* In a story told from the first-person point of view, the information must be limited to what the character experiences or knows. A story told in first person often has a heightened intensity, however, because the narrator is experiencing the events that he or she describes.

Third-Person Point of View In the passage from "Jed's Grandfather," the story is told from a *third-person point of view.* In this case, the narrator is usually not a character. The third-person point of view is indicated by the narrator's use of such pronouns as *he, she, it,* and *they.* If a story is told from a *third-person omniscient* ("all-knowing") point of view, the narrator is able to relate everything about all the characters—their experiences, thoughts, and feelings. In a *third-person limited* point of view, the narrator chiefly presents the perspective of only one character.

> I breathed, ate, slept, dreamed about the La Brea Tar Pits. I spent summer days working the archaeological dig, and in dreams saw the bones glistening....
>
> —CHERYLENE LEE, "Hollywood and the Pits"

> Gulls began swooping down in front of them. They were grey and white. From their yellow beaks came those raucous squawks which seemed to Jed to be the one thing which linked them to the rock they flew up from.
>
> —JOSEPH BRUCHAC, "Jed's Grandfather"

Differentiated Instruction

Enrichment

Invite students who read widely to find examples of stories written in each point of view—first-person, third-person omniscient, and third-person limited. Have them bring to class one-paragraph examples to share.

Visual Learning

Use the photographs on this page to prompt visual learners to offer other visual examples of point of view, or vantage point. Ask them to find samples of distant, close-up, interior, and exterior points of view. When students have found such visual examples, invite the class to associate each one with a literary point of view.

Common Core State Standards

Reading Literature
RL.3

HOLLYWOOD and the Pits

A Short Story by Cherylene Lee

GUIDED READING

Preview the Model

At a Glance
Guided Reading: Reading Model
- Reading Level: Moderate
- Difficulty Consideration: Two narrative voices
- Ease Factor: Familiar themes

Objectives
Studying this lesson will enable students to
- use reading skills such as analyzing cause and effect
- define point of view and recognize its effect in the selection
- describe how Cherylene Lee establishes mood and tone
- appreciate a story based on the author's personal experiences

Launch the Lesson
Before reading "Hollywood and the Pits," ask students what they think it would be like to be a child star. What would be the advantages and disadvantages? Would getting older be an advantage or a disadvantage? List advantages and disadvantages on the board. Then, ask students to decide whether or not the advantages outweigh the disadvantages.

Build Background
Scientific Context The La Brea Tar Pits are a major tourist attraction in Los Angeles, California. They began to form nearly 40,000 years ago, when the area was home to such animals as saber-toothed cats, ground sloths, and mammoths. The "tar" is really asphalt, which seeps out of petroleum deposits. Animals entered a watering hole and were trapped by tar under the water. The remains of the animals churn in the tar.

Reader's Context How is becoming a teenager like falling into tar? Do parents really remember what growing up is like?

Set Purpose
Before you begin reading, skim the story for unfamiliar terms. Make a list of terms you need to look up.

Analyze Literature
Point of View A story's **point of view** reflects the vantage point of the narrator. With the *first-person point of view*, the narrator is part of the action, but with the *third-person point of view*, the narrator observes the action. "Hollywood and the Pits" uses both points of view. As you read, think about how the alternating points of view influence the mood, the plot, and your understanding of the main character.

Use Reading Skills
Analyze Cause and Effect You can keep track of causes and effects in this story by creating a cause-effect chart. As you read, create a cause-effect chart like the one below.

Cause: Narrator begins to grow up. → Effect:

Preview Vocabulary
ob•sessed (əb sest´) *adj.*, preoccupied

dub (dub) *v.*, give a nickname

bar•rage (bə räzh´) *n.*, outpouring of many things at once

pred•a•tor (pred´ ə tər) *n.*, animal that gets food by capturing and eating other animals

scav•en•ger (scav´ ən jər) *n.*, animal that gets food by eating the dead bodies of other animals

Meet the Author
Cherylene Lee (b. 1954) grew up in Los Angeles, California, and appeared in television shows, movies, and stage plays when she was a child. In college, she studied paleontology—fossils and prehistoric life—and geology—Earth's structure. Today she writes stories, poems, and plays. She is best known for her plays, including one set at the La Brea Tar Pits called *Mixed Messages*.

HOLLYWOOD AND THE PITS **141**

Words in Use

Common Core State Standards
Reading Literature
RL.1, RL.6

Summary

The narrator became a Hollywood actor when she was three. At fifteen, she has grown too old for the roles she once got easily. While her mother laments the decline in her daughter's acting career, the narrator becomes obsessed by a totally different Hollywood scene—the La Brea Tar Pits. As a volunteer, she digs for fossils of animals that got trapped in the black, gooey sand eons ago. In the process, she realizes that she doesn't have to be young and adorable to be of value.

MIRRORS & WINDOWS The Mirrors & Windows questions at the end of the story focus on the theme of perception. Before students begin reading, ask: What does it feel like when people say how grown-up you are?

Analyze Literature

Plot Ask students to explain the conflict the narrator seems to be having with her mother. (Her mother doesn't understand her obsession with the tar pits.) Ⓐ

Analyze Literature

Point of View *Answer:* The narrator is part of the action and was a child actor in Hollywood. Ⓑ

Apply the Model

- BEFORE READING
- DURING READING
- AFTER READING

HOLLYWOOD and the Pits

A Short Story by Cherylene Lee

> I lost myself there and found something else.

ob·sessed (əb sest´) *adj.,* preoccupied

DURING READING

Analyze Literature
Point of View Is the narrator part of the action? What else can you tell about the narrator so far? Ⓑ

1968, when I was fifteen, the pit opened its secret to me. I breathed, ate, slept, dreamed about the La Brea Tar Pits. I spent summer days working the archaeological dig, and in dreams saw the bones glistening, the broken pelvises, the skulls, the vertebrae[1] looped like a woman's pearls hanging on an invisible cord. I welcomed those dreams. I wanted to know where the next skeleton was, identify it, record its position, discover whether it was whole or not. I wanted to know where to dig in the coarse, black, gooey sand. I lost myself there and found something else.

Ⓐ My mother thought something was wrong with me. Was it good for a teenager to be fascinated by death? Especially animal death in the Pleistocene?[2] Was it normal to be so <u>obsessed</u> by a sticky brown hole in the ground in the center of Los Angeles? I don't know if it was normal or not, but it seemed perfectly logical to me. After all, I grew up in Hollywood, a place where dreams and nightmares can often take the same shape. What else would a child actor do?

"Thank you very much, dear. We'll be letting you know."

---

1. **the broken pelvises, the skulls, the vertebrae.** Bones from the hip, head, and spine (backbone)
2. **Pleistocene.** Geologic epoch that spans 10,000 to 1.6 million years ago

142

Program Resources

Planning and Assessment
Program Planning Guide, Selection Lesson Plan
E-Lesson Planner
Assessment Guide, Lesson Test
ExamView

Technology Tools
Interactive Student Text on CD
Visual Teaching Package
Audio Library
mirrorsandwindows.com

Meeting the Standards
Fiction: Unit 2, Reading Model, pp. 19–24

Differentiating Instruction
Developing Readers, Take Notes, pp. 13–15

I knew what that meant. It meant I would never hear from them again. I didn't get the job. I heard that phrase a lot that year.

I walked out of the plush office, leaving behind the casting director, producer, director, writer, and whoever else came to listen to my reading for a semiregular role on a family sitcom. The carpet made no sound when I opened and shut the door.

I passed the other girls waiting in the reception room, each poring over her script. The mothers were waiting in a separate room, chattering about their daughters' latest commercials, interviews, callbacks, jobs. It sounded like every Oriental[3] kid in Hollywood was working except me.

My mother used to have a lot to say in those waiting rooms. Ever since I was three, when I started at the Meglin Kiddie Dance Studio, I was <u>dubbed</u> "The Chinese Shirley Temple"—always the one to be picked at auditions and interviews, always the one to get the speaking lines, always called "the one-shot kid," because I could do my scenes in one take—even tight close-ups.[4] My mother would only talk about me behind my back because she didn't want me to hear her brag, but I knew that she was proud. In a way I was proud too, though I never dared admit it. I didn't want to be called a showoff. But I didn't exactly know what I did to be proud of either. I only knew that at fifteen I was now being passed over at all these interviews when before I would be chosen.

My mother looked at my face hopefully when I came into the room. I gave her a quick shake of the head. She looked bewildered.[5] I felt bad for my mother then. How could I explain it to her? I didn't understand it myself. We left, saying polite good-byes to all the other mothers.

We didn't say anything until the studio parking lot, where we had to search for our old blue Chevy among rows and rows of parked cars baking in the Hollywood heat.

"How did it go? Did you read clearly? Did you tell them you're available?"

"I don't think they care if I'm available or not, Ma."

"Didn't you read well? Did you remember to look up so they could see your eyes? Did they ask you if you could play the piano? Did you tell them you could learn?"

The <u>barrage</u> of questions stopped when we finally spotted our

---

C **dub** (dŭb) *v.,* give a nickname

bar·rage (bə räzh´) *n.,* outpouring of many things at once

---

3. **Oriental.** Old term for Asian
4. **tight close-ups.** Film shots in which a performer's face fills the camera lens
5. **bewildered.** Puzzled

Point of View Ask students to identify the point of view in the italicized text. Ask: "How is its tone different from that of the regular text?" (It is in third-person point of view. The tone is impersonal and informative.) **A**

Science Connection
Tar Millions of years ago, time and pressure changed organic deposits in an ocean basin near today's La Brea Tar Pits into oil. For the last 40,000 years, the oil has been making its way to the surface and seeping onto the ground. When it reaches the ground, kerosene and other lighter elements evaporate, leaving behind asphalt, the lowest grade of crude oil. This thick, heavy, sticky substance is commonly called "tar."

Use Reading Skills
Analyze Cause and Effect *Answer:* Her sister recommended her for a role. **B**

Use Reading Strategies
Make Inferences Ask students what they can infer about the narrator's parents. How involved were they with the girls' careers? What did the girls' careers mean to them? Model a response: "They both support the girls' careers, the mother with time and the father with money. However, it seems that the mother has made their careers *her* career." **C**

To me the applause sometimes sounded like static, sometimes like distant waves.

DURING READING

Use Reading Skills
Analyze Cause and Effect What launched the narrator's Hollywood career? **B**

---

car. I didn't answer her. My mother asked about the piano because I lost out in an audition once to a Chinese girl who already knew how to play.

My mother took off the towel that shielded the steering wheel from the heat. "You're getting to be such a big girl," she said, starting the car in neutral. "But don't worry, there's always next time. You have what it takes. That's special." She put the car into forward and we drove through a parking lot that had an endless number of identical cars all facing the same direction. We drove back home in silence.

A *In the La Brea Tar Pits many of the excavated bones belong to juvenile[6] mammals. Thousands of years ago thirsty young animals in the area were drawn to watering holes, not knowing they were traps. Those inviting pools had false bottoms made of sticky tar, which immobilized its victims and preserved their bones when they died. Innocence trapped by ignorance. The tar pits record that well.*

I suppose a lot of my getting into show business in the first place was a matter of luck—being in the right place at the right time. My sister, seven years older than me, was a member of the Meglin Kiddie Dance Studio long before I started lessons. Once during the annual recital held at the Shrine Auditorium, she was spotted by a Hollywood agent who handled only Oriental performers. The agent sent my sister out for a role in the CBS *Playhouse 90* television show *The Family Nobody Wanted*. The producer said she was too tall for the part. But true to my mother's training of always having a positive reply, my sister said to the producer, "But I have a younger sister…" which started my show-biz career at the tender age of three.

C My sister and I were lucky. We enjoyed singing and dancing, we were natural hams, and our parents never discouraged us. In fact they were our biggest fans. My mother chauffeured us to all our dance lessons, lessons we begged to take. She drove us to interviews, took us to studios, went on location with us, drilled us on our lines, made sure we kept up our schoolwork and didn't sass back the tutors hired by studios to teach us for three hours a day. She never complained about being a stage mother. She said that we made her proud.

My father must have felt pride too, because he paid for a choreographer to put together our sister act: "The World Famous

6. **juvenile.** Young

Differentiated Instruction

English Language Learning
Students learning English may need help with the following words and expressions in order to understand the main character and the plot.
archaeological—having to do with the scientific study of the life and culture of the past, 142
sass—talk rudely to, 144
corny—unsophisticated, old-fashioned, 145

shrimp or *small fry*—informal terms for a small person or a child, 146
Tootsie Pop—type of lollipop or round candy on a stick, 147
cascading—falling, like a waterfall, 148
herbivores—plant-eating animals, 149
City of Angels—another name for Los Angeles, 149

Lee Sisters," fifteen minutes of song and dance, real vaudeville[7] stuff. We joked about that a lot, "Yeah, the Lee Sisters—Ug-Lee and Home-Lee," but we definitely had a good time. So did our parents. Our father especially liked our getting booked into Las Vegas at the New Frontier Hotel on the Strip. He liked to gamble there, though he said the craps tables in that hotel were "cold," not like the casinos in downtown Las Vegas, where all the "hot" action took place.

In Las Vegas our sister act was part of a show called "Oriental Holiday." The show was about a Hollywood producer going to the Far East, finding undiscovered talent, and bringing it back to the U.S. We did two shows a night in the main showroom, one at eight and one at twelve, and on weekends a third show at two in the morning. It ran the entire summer, often to standing-room-only audiences—a thousand people a show.

Our sister act worked because of the age and height difference. My sister then was fourteen and nearly five foot two; I was seven and very small for my age—people thought we were cute. We had song-and-dance routines to old tunes like "Ma, He's Making Eyes at Me," "Together," and "I'm Following You," and my father hired a writer to adapt the lyrics to "I Enjoy Being a Girl," which came out "We Enjoy Being Chinese." We also told corny jokes, but the Las Vegas audience seemed to enjoy it. Here we were, two kids, staying up late and jumping around, and getting paid besides. To me the applause sometimes sounded like static, sometimes like distant waves. It always amazed me when people applauded. The owner of the hotel liked us so much, he invited us back to perform in shows for three summers in a row. That was before I grew too tall and the sister act didn't seem so cute anymore.

Many of the skeletons in the tar pits are found incomplete— particularly the skeletons of the young, which have only soft cartilage connecting the bones. In life the soft tissue allows for growth, but in death it dissolves quickly. Thus the skeletons of young animals are more apt to be scattered, especially the vertebrae protecting the spinal cord. In the tar pits, the central ends of many vertebrae are found unconnected to any skeleton. Such bone fragments are shaped like valentines, disks that are slightly lobed—heart-shaped shields that have lost their connection to what they were meant to protect.

Cherylene Lee (left) and her sister performing on television in 1959.

DURING READING

Make Connections
What does the tone of this writing remind you of? Explain. F

---
7. vaudeville. Theatrical variety show

Use Reading Skills
Analyze Cause and Effect Ask students why the narrator believes their sister act worked so well. (The difference in their heights and ages made them cute and appealing.) **D**

Analyze Literature
Point of View Have students describe how the narrator's tone changes when she makes the comment about growing too tall. (The tone switches from nostalgic and lighthearted to matter-of-fact and slightly sarcastic.) **E**

Use Reading Skills
Monitor Comprehension Tell students that if they have trouble understanding the concepts in the italicized text they can try reading the text more slowly, and can go back and reread if necessary.

Make Connections
Answer: The passage will probably remind students of a textbook or a brochure. **F**

Reading Skills

Monitor Comprehension
Some students may be interested in reading more about fossils, the Pleistocene age, and/or the fossil discoveries at the La Brea Tar Pits. When reading science texts, students should apply the following strategies to get the most from their reading experience.

- Skim the text to get a general idea of what it is about.
- Read slowly to understand main ideas.
- Take notes about facts and details.
- Ask questions about words or ideas that are unclear.
- Stop occasionally to check comprehension by summarizing what you have read so far.

Use Reading Skills

Determine Sequence of Events Ask students to point out words and phrases that show the sequence of changes in the narrator's acting opportunities and in her mother's attitude toward her (such as "When I was younger," "When I turned fifteen," and "Before that summer"). **A**

Make Connections

Have students share anecdotes about changes that came unexpectedly as they got older and bigger. How do their own experiences affect their feelings for the narrator? (Most will sympathize with her.) **B**

TEACHING NOTE

Ask the Author

Divide the class into small groups, and have the groups brainstorm and jot down questions they would like to ask Cherylene Lee. Model a question: "Do you still volunteer at the Tar Pits?" Instruct each group to pass its questions to another group, and then pretend it is Lee and try to answer the questions it receives. Have the groups share some of their questions and answers as a class.

I never felt my mother pushed me to do something I didn't want to do. But I always knew if something I did pleased her. She was generous with her praise, and I was sensitive when she withheld it. I didn't like to disappoint her.

I took to performing easily, and since I had started out so young, making movies or doing shows didn't feel like anything special. It was part of my childhood—like going to the dentist one morning or going to school the next. I didn't wonder if I wanted a particular role or wanted to be in a show or how I would feel if I didn't get in. Until I was fifteen, it never occurred to me that one day I wouldn't get parts or that I might not "have what it takes."

A When I was younger, I got a lot of roles because I was so small for my age. When I was nine years old, I could pass for five or six. I was really short. I was always teased about it when I was in elementary school, but I didn't mind because my height got me movie jobs. I could read and memorize lines that actual five-year-olds couldn't. My mother told people she made me sleep in a drawer so I wouldn't grow any bigger.

But when I turned fifteen, it was as if my body, which hadn't grown for so many years, suddenly made up for lost time. I grew five inches in seven months. My mother was amazed. Even I couldn't get used to it. I kept knocking into things, my clothes didn't fit right, **B** I felt awkward and clumsy when I moved. Dumb things that I had gotten away with, like paying children's prices at the movies instead of junior admission, I couldn't do anymore. I wasn't a shrimp or a small fry any longer. I was suddenly normal.

Before that summer my mother had always claimed she wanted me to be normal. She didn't want me to become spoiled by the attention I received when I was working at the studios. I still had chores to do at home, went to public school when I wasn't working, was punished severely when I behaved badly. She didn't want me to feel I was different just because I was in the movies. When I was eight, I was interviewed by a reporter who wanted to know if I thought I had a big head.

"Sure," I said.

"No you don't," my mother interrupted, which was really unusual, because she generally never said anything. She wanted me to speak for myself.

I didn't understand the question. My sister had always made fun of my head. She said my body was too tiny for the weight—I looked

---

Differentiated Instruction

English Language Learning

Students learning English may need help understanding the meaning of the following idioms used in the text.

have what it takes—possess the necessary skills and temperament to succeed, 146

pass for [five or six]—appear to be younger than one is, 146

made up for lost time—happened quickly, 146

speak for myself—say what I really think, 146

Visual Learning

Visual learners may benefit from visualizing the process of how animals became trapped in the tar pits. Ask students to gather in groups of three or four to review the italicized passages. Then have students work together to draw a series of sketches that illustrates the animal entrapment. Students can share their drawings with the class.

like a walking Tootsie Pop. I thought the reporter was making the same observation.

"She better not get that way," my mother said fiercely. "She's not any different from anyone else. She's just lucky and small for her age."

The reporter turned to my mother, "Some parents push their children to act. The kids feel like they're used."

"I don't do that—I'm not that way," my mother told the reporter.

But when she was sitting silently in all those waiting rooms while I was being turned down for one job after another, I could almost feel her wanting to shout, "Use her. Use her. What is wrong with her? Doesn't she have it anymore?" I didn't know what I had had that I didn't seem to have anymore. My mother had told the reporter that I was like everyone else. But when my life was like everyone else's, why was she disappointed?

The churning action of the La Brea Tar Pits makes interpreting the record of past events extremely difficult. The usual order of deposition[8]—the oldest on the bottom, the youngest on the top— loses all meaning when some of the oldest fossils can be brought to the surface by the movement of natural gas. One must look for an undisturbed spot, a place untouched by the action of underground springs or natural gas or human interference. Complete skeletons become important, because they indicate areas of least disturbance. But such spots of calm are rare. Whole blocks of the tar pit can become displaced,[9] making false sequences of the past, skewing the interpretation for what is the true order of nature.

That year before my sixteenth birthday, my mother seemed to spend a lot of time looking through my old scrapbooks, staring at all the eight-by-ten glossies of the shows that I had done. In the summer we visited with my grandmother often, since I wasn't working and had lots of free time. I would go out to the garden to read or sunbathe, but I could hear my mother and grandmother talking.

"She was so cute back then. She worked with Gene Kelly when she was five years old. She was so smart for her age. I don't know what's wrong with her."

"She's fifteen."

---

8. **order of deposition.** Sequence in which layers of sediment are left behind when water flows over an area and then recedes
9. **Whole blocks of the tar pit can become displaced.** Tar is warm enough to flow very slowly, and whole sections can move from one place to another.

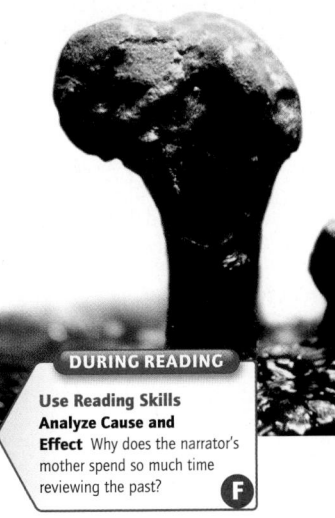

DURING READING

Make Connections
What feeling do you think the author wants to convey by this comparison to a Tootsie Pop? **C**

DURING READING

Make Connections
Why might most parents have mixed feelings about whether a child should be "normal"? **D**

DURING READING

Use Reading Skills
Analyze Cause and Effect Why does the narrator's mother spend so much time reviewing the past? **F**

Teach the Model

Make Connections
Answer: Most students will say the author wants readers to find this funny. Some may think the author wants them to feel sympathy for the narrator. **C**

Make Connections
Answer: Most students will say parents want their children to be special, but also to be accepted. **D**

Use Reading Skills
Analyze Cause and Effect Ask students why the discovery of whole skeletons matters, and what effect this has on scientific interpretations. (Whole skeletons show that those places have not been disturbed, so the scientists' conclusions are apt to be accurate.) **E**

Use Reading Skills
Analyze Cause and Effect *Answer:* She is trying to make sense of what has changed. **F**

Analyze Literature
Character Ask students what the conversation between the narrator's mother and grandmother reveals about their attitudes toward the narrator. Model a possible response: "The narrator's grandmother seems to realize that the narrator has grown up and is ready to move in a new direction, away from movies and performing. The narrator's mother doesn't want to let go of the past." **G**

Grammar Skills

Passive Voice and Active Voice
Remind students that active-voice verbs express ideas more directly than passive-voice verbs. Give them this example:
Passive voice: The fossil <u>was examined</u> by scientists.
Active voice: Scientists <u>examined</u> the fossil.

Have students identify the passive verb in these sentences, and then revise each sentence so the verb is active.

1. Hundreds of fossil bones were collected by volunteers.
2. The story of these ancient animals is revealed through a museum exhibit.
3. The saber-tooth cat has been named California's state fossil.

Science Connection

Geologic Time *Answer:* It is recent in terms of geologic time. **A**

Use Reading Skills

Analyze Cause and Effect Ask students why the narrator's hair won't stay in knots. What effect does this have on the narrator? (Her hair is too springy and young to stay in knots. It increases the narrator's frustrations with all the changes that are taking place in her life.) **B**

"She's too young to be an ingénue[10] and too old to be cute. The studios forget so quickly. By the time she's old enough to play an ingénue, they won't remember her."

"Does she have to work in the movies? Hand me the scissors."

My grandmother was making false eyelashes using the hair from her hairbrush. When she was young she had incredible hair. I saw an old photograph of her when it flowed beyond her waist like a cascading black waterfall. At seventy, her hair was still black as night, which made her few strands of silver look like shooting stars. But her hair had thinned greatly with age. It sometimes fell out in clumps. She wore it brushed back in a bun with a hairpiece for added fullness. My grandmother had always been proud of her hair, but once she started making false eyelashes from it, she wasn't proud of the way it looked anymore. She said she was proud of it now because it made her useful.

It was painstaking work—tying knots into strands of hair, then tying them together to form feathery little crescents. Her glamorous false eyelashes were much sought after. Theatrical makeup artists waited months for her work. But my grandmother said what she liked was that she was doing something, making a contribution, and besides it didn't cost her anything. No overhead. "Till I go bald," she often joked.

She tried to teach me her art that summer, but for some reason strands of my hair wouldn't stay tied in knots.

B "Too springy," my grandmother said. "Your hair is still too young." And because I was frustrated then, frustrated with everything about my life, she added, "You have to wait until your hair falls out, like mine. Something to look forward to, eh?" She had laughed and patted my hand.

SCIENCE ▶▶ CONNECTION

Geologic Time Evidence in rocks indicates that Earth is more than four billion years old. Scientists use big categories to measure this much time. The largest category of geologic time is the *era*. We are in the Cenozoic Era, which began sixty-five million years ago, after dinosaurs became extinct. An era is divided into *periods*, and periods are split into *epochs*. We live in the Quaternary Period, which started less than two million years ago. The La Brea Tar Pits formed during the last part of the Pleistocene Epoch of the Quaternary Period, approximately forty-thousand years ago. In terms of geologic time, would you say this is recently, or very long ago? **A**

---

10. **ingénue.** Inexperienced young woman

Vocabulary Skills

Jargon

Jargon is the special vocabulary used by a specific group or profession. Although writers use jargon to add authenticity to their work, for readers it can interfere with comprehension.

"Hollywood and the Pits" contains jargon from the entertainment industry. To figure out the meaning of unfamiliar terms or familiar words used in new ways, students can use context clues. For example, by using context, they can figure out that *take* in the story means "an uninterrupted filming session."

Tell students that if context doesn't help them understand a word, they can write it down. Later, they can find its meaning in a dictionary.

My mother was going on and on about my lack of work, what might be wrong, that something she couldn't quite put her finger on. I heard my grandmother reply, but I didn't catch it all: "Movies are just make-believe, not real life. Like what I make with my hair that falls out—false. False eyelashes. Not meant to last." **C**

The remains in the La Brea Tar Pits are mostly of carnivorous animals. Very few herbivores are found—the ratio is five to one, a perversion of the natural food chain.[11] The ratio is easy to explain. Thousands of years ago a thirsty animal sought a drink from the pools of water only to find itself trapped by the bottom, gooey with subterranean oil. A shriek of agony from the trapped victim drew flesh-eating <u>predators</u>, which were then trapped themselves by the very same ooze which provided the bait. The cycle repeated itself countless times. The number of victims grew, lured by the image of easy food, the deception of an easy kill. The animals piled on top of one another. For over ten thousand years the promise of the place drew animals of all sorts, mostly predators and <u>scavengers</u>—dire wolves,[12] panthers, coyotes, vultures—all hungry for their chance. Most were sucked down against their will in those watering holes destined to be called the La Brea Tar Pits in a place to be named the City of Angels, home of Hollywood movie stars.

I spent a lot of time by myself that summer, wondering what it was that I didn't have anymore. Could I get it back? How could I if I didn't know what it was?

That's when I discovered the La Brea Tar Pits. Hidden behind the County Art Museum on trendy Wilshire Boulevard, I found a job that didn't require me to be small or cute for my age. I didn't have to audition. No one said, "Thank you very much, we'll call you." Or if they did, they meant it. I volunteered my time one afternoon, and my fascination stuck—like tar on the bones of a saber-toothed tiger. **E**

My mother didn't understand what had changed me. I didn't understand it myself. But I liked going to the La Brea Tar Pits. It meant I could get really messy and I was doing it with a purpose. I didn't feel awkward there. I could wear old stained pants. I could wear T-shirts with holes in them. I could wear disgustingly filthy sneakers and it was all perfectly justified. It wasn't a costume for a

pred·a·tor (pred´ ə tər)
n., animal that gets food by capturing and eating other animals

scav·en·ger (scav´ ən jər)
n., animal that gets food by eating the dead bodies of other animals

DURING READING

**Use Reading Skills
Analyze Cause and Effect** Why are there so many predator and scavenger remains in the tar pits? **D**

---

11. **perversion of the natural food chain.** Plant-eaters (herbivores) usually greatly outnumber meat-eaters (carnivores); a perversion reverses this relationship.
12. **dire wolves.** Members of an extinct species of California wolf *(Canis dirus)*

Teach the Model

Analyze Literature
Mood Ask students what they think the author wants readers to feel about the narrator's life as a movie actor. (The author probably wants readers to recognize that it is hollow and lacks real meaning.) **C**

Use Reading Skills
Analyze Cause and Effect *Answer:* Predators got stuck in tar when they pursued prey, and after they died, scavengers came to eat their bodies and also got stuck in the tar. **D**

Analyze Literature
Mood Ask students to describe the mood the author creates when she links the tar pits to Hollywood. (The mood is dark and depressing.)

Cultural Connection
Tar Pits Tourism The La Brea Tar Pits are located in the historic and culturally rich district of Los Angeles known as the Miracle Mile. Other attractions in the immediate area, which is sometimes called Museum Row, include the Petersen Automotive Museum, The Los Angeles County Museum of Art, and the Museum of Miniatures. Upscale shops and restaurants, as well as entertainment-industry companies, also occupy the densely populated, affluent area. **E**

Research Skills

Primary and Secondary Sources

Tell students that they can use both primary and secondary sources. A primary source is a firsthand account of an event. A journal an archaeologist keeps on a dig would be a primary source. A secondary source is something written by someone who has not directly experienced an event. A magazine article about fossil discoveries could be a secondary source.

Have students identify the following materials as primary or secondary sources of information about fossils.

1. A mystery novel in which an archaeologist is the main character
2. An autobiography by an archaeologist
3. An essay by a student who attended an archaeology camp
4. An encyclopedia article about fossils

Cultural Connection

Tar Pit Exhibit You may wish to tell students that the mammoth in the photograph is a reconstruction, part of an outdoor exhibit at the La Brea Tar Pits. The animal is in the process of being trapped; its mate and child stand on the bank of the pit, unable to save it.

Use Reading Strategies

Make Inferences *Answer:* The narrator is not trying as hard to please her mother as before, and she has stopped trying to alleviate her mother's uncertainty. The narrator no longer expresses interest in show business, even though her mother does. **A**

Analyze Literature

Plot Ask students how they think the narrator's conflict has changed—if at all—by this point in the story.

Analyze Literature

Point of View Ask students what else the narrator may be telling the reader when she says that she wondered a lot about how the animals fell into the trap. (She may be saying that it will take time for her to figure out how she, and other entertainers, fell into the Hollywood trap.) **B**

Independent Reading

Students who like "Hollywood and the Pits" might enjoy other stories in *American Dragons: Twenty-Five Asian American Voices.*

role in a film or a part in a TV sitcom. My mother didn't mind my dressing like that when she knew I was off to the pits. That was okay so long as I didn't track tar back into the house. I started going to the pits every day, and my mother wondered why. She couldn't believe I would rather be groveling in tar than going on auditions or interviews.

While my mother wasn't proud of the La Brea Tar Pits (she didn't know or care what a fossil was), she didn't discourage me either. She drove me there, the same way she used to drive me to the studios.

"Wouldn't you rather be doing a show in Las Vegas than scrambling around in a pit?" she asked.

"I'm not in a show in Las Vegas, Ma. The Lee Sisters are retired." My older sister had married and was starting a family of her own.

"But if you could choose between…"

"There isn't a choice."

"You really like this tar-pit stuff, or are you just waiting until you can get real work in the movies?"

I didn't answer.

My mother sighed. "You could do it if you wanted, if you really wanted. You still have what it takes."

I didn't know about that. But then, I couldn't explain what drew me to the tar pits either. Maybe it was the bones, finding out what they were, which animal they belonged to, imagining how they got **B** [there, how they fell into the trap. I wondered about that a lot.

> **DURING READING**
>
> **Use Reading Strategies**
> **Make Inferences** How has the narrator's relationship with her mother changed by this point in the plot? **A**

Differentiated Instruction

Enrichment

Some students may be interested in taking a trip to a local museum to see the fossils that archaeologists, like the ones who work in the La Brea Tar Pits, uncover. You may want to talk to the students' science teacher to see if you can coordinate a joint trip.

Suggest that students prepare for their museum visit by creating a list of questions that they would like answered. Offer these examples:

- What animal is the fossil from?
- Where was the fossil found?
- What does the fossil reveal about the creature that once lived?
- What does the discovery reveal about the times in which the creature lived?

At the La Brea Tar Pits, everything dug out of the pit is saved—including the sticky sand that covered the bones through the ages. Each bucket of sand is washed, sieved, and examined for pollen grains, insect remains, any evidence of past life. Even the grain size is recorded—the percentage of silt to sand to gravel that reveals the history of deposition, erosion, and disturbance. No single fossil, no one observation, is significant enough to tell the entire story. All the evidence must be weighed before a semblance of truth emerges.

The tar pits had its lessons. I was learning I had to work slowly, become observant, to concentrate. I learned about time in a way that I would never experience—not in hours, days, and months, but in thousands and thousands of years. I imagined what the past must have been like, envisioned Los Angeles as a sweeping basin, perhaps slightly colder and more humid, a time before people and studios arrived. The tar pits recorded a warming trend; the kinds of animals found there reflected the changing climate. The ones unadapted disappeared. No trace of their kind was found in the area. The ones adapted to warmer weather left a record of bones in the pit. Amid that collection of ancient skeletons, surrounded by evidence of death, I was finding a secret preserved over thousands and thousands of years. There was something cruel about natural selection[13] and the survival of the fittest. Even those successful individuals that "had what it took" for adaptation still wound up in the pits.

I never found out if I had what it took, not the way my mother meant. But I did adapt to the truth: I wasn't a Chinese Shirley Temple any longer, cute and short for my age. I had grown up. Maybe not on a Hollywood movie set, but in the La Brea Tar Pits. ❖

---

13. **natural selection.** Process in which individuals and groups best adjusted to the environment survive and reproduce

> **DURING READING**
>
> **Use Reading Skills**
> **Analyze Cause and Effect** Why does the narrator prefer the tar pits to a career in show business? **C**

> **DURING READING**
>
> **Use Reading Skills**
> **Analyze Cause and Effect** How have the La Brea Tar Pits helped the narrator gain perspective on her life? **D**

 At one point, the narrator says, "I didn't know what I had had that I didn't seem to have anymore." Do you ever feel like you've changed, but people close to you don't seem to notice? Why might this be a common feeling?

Use Reading Skills
Analyze Cause and Effect *Answer:* She can be messy with a purpose; she doesn't feel awkward there; she is fascinated by the pits; and she likes the process of learning about the past. **C**

Use Reading Skills
Analyze Cause and Effect *Answer:* Studying the tar pits has taught her to adapt to change. **D**

 You may want to ask students to write a journal entry or quick write, or divide students into discussion groups or lead a whole-class discussion about this question. *Answer:* Most students will have felt some confusion or ambivalence about getting older.

Writing Skills

Cause-and-Effect Order

Point out that writers use cause-and-effect order to help readers understand how events are connected. Often, a single cause will have more than one effect, and a single effect will have more than one cause. Writers use transitions such as *because, and so, as a result,* and *therefore* to signal cause-and-effect order.

Have students work in pairs to develop a cause-and-effect paragraph about the changes in the relationship between the narrator and her mother. Students can use a chart similar to the one on page 141 to keep track of causes and effects as they plan and draft their paragraphs. Remind them to use transitions.

Review the Model

Find Meaning

1. (a) She no longer gets parts.
(b) She does not understand it very well at first, but her understanding grows over the course of the story.
2. The narrator's mother shows support, pride, expectations, disappointment, and nostalgia.

Make Judgments

3. (a) Students may say the narrator volunteered because she had free time, since she was not getting acting roles. They may also say the narrator liked the pits because the job did not depend on her being young or cute.
(b) Many students will note that the narrator does not feel awkward at the tar pits, as she does now at auditions. This gives her a more mature and positive outlook.
4. (a) Young, thirsty animals came to the pits, as did predators and scavengers. (b) Students may say that people are drawn to show business in the same way—and that some could be at risk of getting stuck in something dangerous.
5. Many students will say the narrator enjoys her tar-pit time more because she is comfortable there.

Analyze Literature

Point of View Students may say the changes between first and third person help move the action along, or that the third-person segments offer insight into the narrator of the first-person segments. The mood shifts with the point of view. If you wish, ask students to provide text support, such as examples, for their responses.

Find Meaning

1. (a) How did the narrator's experiences at auditions change? (b) How well does the narrator understand why her experiences are different?
2. How does the narrator's mother act toward the narrator?

Analyze Literature

Point of View Summarize how Cherylene Lee's use of both first-person and third-person points of view affects the mood and plot of "Hollywood and the Pits." Make a graphic organizer like this one so you can record your key impressions.

Make Judgments

3. (a) What inspired the narrator to volunteer at the La Brea Tar Pits? (b) How did volunteering there change her outlook on life?
4. (a) What kinds of animals were drawn to the tar pits? (b) How might they resemble people?
5. Which part of her life do you think the narrator has enjoyed the most? Why?

	First-Person Narrator (Hollywood)	Third-Person Narrator (The Pits)
How this influences the plot	Presents an internal conflict	Presents an external conflict
How this influences the mood		

Extend Understanding

Writing Options

Creative Writing Imagine that you are creating a time capsule in your backyard. What objects would you include? Write a **journal entry** in which you describe these things and your reasons for including them. When you are finished, share your entry with the class.

Expository Writing How would you describe this story to a friend? Write a three-paragraph **literary response** that describes the conflicts the narrator and her mother experience. Identify each conflict as internal or external and use examples from the story. In your final sentences, tell how the plot resolves each of the conflicts. Make certain you summarize the story in a way that maintains logical order.

Collaborative Learning

Infer the Author's Purpose In a small group, discuss why the story includes the scientific information on the tar pits. What might the tar pits represent? Take notes on your discussion, and then summarize the group's thoughts in one or two paragraphs.

Media Literacy

Dig for Details Use the Internet to find information on an archaeological site in or near your state. Then write a letter to the site director with two or three questions about the site. For example, ask about the fossils scientists have discovered there.

Go to **www.mirrorsandwindows.com** for more.

Program Resources

For further instruction, refer students to the following extension activity: Media Literacy: Dig for Details, *Exceeding the Standards: Extension Activities*, pp. 5–6.

Rubrics for Writing Options

You can adapt this as a checklist for students to use as they write.

Creative Writing

☐ Does the entry start with a list of items from a time capsule?
☐ Does the entry give reasons for students' choices?

Expository Writing

☐ Does the literary response cover both the narrator and her mother?
☐ Does the literary response identify conflicts as either internal or external, and use examples from the story?
☐ Do the last sentences tell how the plot resolves each conflict?
☐ Does the summary maintain logical order?

Understanding Theme

What Is Theme?

What is the main point being made in the passage below from *Peter Pan*, J. M. Barrie's most famous work? In answering this question, you are identifying the theme. A **theme** is the central idea of a literary work.

Themes and Topics

The theme is not the same as the topic. A topic is the subject of a literary work, that is, what it is about. For example, the topic of this novel is Peter Pan's adventures in Neverland. The theme is a general observation based on that topic. Literary works can share the same topic but have different themes. For example, you might have two stories that are both on the topic of sports. One story's theme might be stated: "Sports are a wonderful way to get some exercise and make friends." The other story's theme might be stated: "Sports are overrated; I prefer a good book." The topic is the same, but the themes are very different.

Stated and Implied Themes

Sometimes the central idea of a literary work is presented directly. This is called a *stated theme.* More often, however, the theme of a literary work is not presented directly and must be inferred by the reader. This is an *implied theme.* For example, the theme in the passage from *Peter Pan* is "growing up is both natural and something to be desired." Some works can have both a stated theme and an implied theme—or even several themes—either stated or implied.

Maude Adams as Peter Pan, c. 20th century. Sigismond de Ivanowski.

> *That was the last time the girl Wendy ever saw him. For a little longer she tried for his sake not to have growing pains; and she felt she was untrue to him when she got a prize for general knowledge. But the years came and went without bringing the careless boy; and when they met again Wendy was a married woman, and Peter was no more to her than a little dust in the box in which she had kept her toys. Wendy was grown up. You need not be sorry for her.*
>
> —J. M. BARRIE, *Peter Pan*

At a Glance
Guided Reading: Reading Model
- Reading Level: Easy
- Difficulty Considerations: None
- Ease Factor: Familiar themes

Objectives
Studying this lesson will enable students to
- use reading skills such as context clues
- identify a theme by examining characterization, dialogue, and plot
- infer Marta Salinas's purpose and explore how she achieves it
- appreciate a story about justice

Launch the Lesson
Prior to reading "The Scholarship Jacket," ask students to recall special awards they have received. Ask what they did to earn these awards. Then ask how they would have felt if, through no fault of their own, one of these awards had been given to someone less worthy. You might have students create a list of words associated with these feelings.

GUIDED READING

Apply the Model
BEFORE READING
DURING READING
AFTER READING

THE SCHOLARSHIP JACKET

A Short Story by Marta Salinas

Build Background
Cultural Context The term *valedictorian* comes from the Latin *vale dicere*, which means, literally, "to say farewell." The *valedictorian* makes the valedictory speech, which in turn means "a speech of farewell." A valedictorian is not necessarily the top academic achiever. Many people argue that schools should choose a top student for more than academic achievement—for well-rounded combinations of schoolwork, athletic ability, social skills, and creative talents instead.

Reader's Context When have you felt passed over for recognition that you deserved?

Set Purpose
Based on the title and information in Build Background, predict what this story will be about. Then read to find out how well you predicted the story's theme.

Analyze Literature
Theme The **theme** of a story is the main message the author wants to express. To determine the theme, read the story and then think about it for a while. Ask yourself questions such as: Of all the ideas in this story, what could I say in one sentence that would sum up the author's main point? Write your answer in your notebook.

Meet the Author
Marta Salinas is best known for being an environmental activist. In and around McFarland, California, a "cancer cluster" developed when Salinas's children were young. She became a community organizer and spoke out about potential pesticide poisoning. As a result, the U.S. Environmental Protection Agency conducted a detailed study of the area. Salinas has written articles for California newspapers and magazines, as well as this story.

Use Reading Skills
Context Clues Preview the vocabulary words from this selection as they are used below. Try to unlock the meaning of each word using context clues in the sentences.

1. I was so nervous for my interview that I <u>absentmindedly</u> got on the wrong train.
2. Our meeting at the music store was unplanned, a complete <u>coincidence.</u>
3. When he saw the broken glass, his eyes opened wide and his jaw dropped in <u>dismay.</u>
4. Arlis was so <u>withdrawn,</u> she had turned to face the wall and did not respond to the nurse.

Preview Vocabulary
ab·sent·mind·ed·ly
(ab' sənt mīn´ dəd lē) *adv.*, lost in thought; unaware

co·in·ci·dence (kō in[t]´ sə dən[t]s) *n.*, chance occurrence

dis·may (dis mā´) *n.*, sudden loss of courage; shock

with·drawn (wi<u>th</u> drôn´) *adj.*, introverted; unresponsive

154 UNIT 2 FICTION

Common Core State Standards

Reading Literature
RL.1, RL.4

Writing
W.2, W.10

Words in Use

THE SCHOLARSHIP JACKET

A Short Story
by Marta Salinas

Apply the Model
BEFORE READING
DURING READING
AFTER READING

Why did they have to change the rules just when it was my turn to win the jacket?

155

Teach the Model

Summary

With a stellar academic record for all eight years of school, Martha (called Marta at home) has earned the right to receive the coveted gold and green scholarship jacket at her eighth grade graduation ceremony. So Martha is shocked when she accidentally learns that the jacket may, instead, go to a less-worthy classmate, the daughter of a wealthy, influential gentleman in the community. Inspired by her grandfather's wisdom and her own sense of justice, Martha finds the courage to stand up for what is fair and is rightly awarded the jacket.

MIRRORS & WINDOWS The Mirrors & Windows questions at the end of the story focus on the theme of guardians. Before students begin reading, ask: What is the best way to deal with unfair adults?

Independent Reading

Students who like "The Scholarship Jacket" might enjoy *Cuentos Chicanos: A Short Story Anthology* and *Growing Up Chicano*.

Program Resources

Planning and Assessment
Program Planning Guide, Selection Lesson Plan
E-Lesson Planner
Assessment Guide, Lesson Test
ExamView

Technology Tools
Interactive Student Text on CD
Visual Teaching Package
Audio Library
mirrorsandwindows.com

Meeting the Standards
Fiction: Unit 2, Guided Reading, pp. 25–31

Differentiating Instruction
Advanced Students, Theme Study, p. 9

Analyze Literature

Theme *Answer:* She could not participate in sports because doing so cost money. **Ⓐ**

Cultural Connection

Academic Recognition Schools have traditionally recognized students for academic excellence. Most schools publish an honor roll or principal's list—the names of students who have achieved a specific grade average for one or more terms. Many schools present academic achievement awards at the end of the school year and at graduation ceremonies. These can include regional and national awards, such as the National Honor Roll, the President's Award for Educational Excellence, and the President's Award for Educational Achievement.

The small Texas school that I attended carried out a tradition every year during the eighth grade graduation; a beautiful gold and green jacket, the school colors, was awarded to the class valedictorian, the student who had maintained the highest grades for eight years. The scholarship jacket had a big gold *S* on the left front side and the winner's name was written in gold letters on the pocket.

My oldest sister Rosie had won the jacket a few years back and I fully expected to win also. I was fourteen and in the eighth grade. I had been a straight A student since the first grade, and the last year I had looked forward to owning that jacket. My father was a farm laborer who couldn't earn enough money to feed eight children, so when I was six I was given to my grandparents to raise. We couldn't participate in sports at school because there were registration fees, uniform costs, and trips out of town; so even though we were quite agile and athletic, there would never be a sports school jacket for us. This one, the scholarship jacket, was our only chance.

In May, close to graduation, spring fever struck, and no one paid any attention in class; instead we stared out the windows and at each other, wanting to speed up the last few weeks of school. I despaired every time I looked in the mirror. Pencil thin, not a curve anywhere, I was called "Beanpole" and "String Bean" and I knew that's what I looked like. A flat chest, no hips, and a brain, that's what I had. That really isn't much for a fourteen-year-old to work with, I thought, as I absentmindedly wandered from my history class to the gym. Another hour of sweating in basketball and displaying my toothpick legs was coming up. Then I remembered my P.E. shorts were still in a bag under my desk where I'd forgotten them. I had to walk all the way back and get them. Coach Thompson was a real bear if anyone wasn't dressed for P.E. She had said I was a good forward and once she even tried to talk Grandma into letting me join the team. Grandma, of course, said no.

I was almost back at my classroom's door when I heard angry voices and arguing. I stopped. I didn't mean to eavesdrop;[1] I just hesitated, not knowing what to do. I needed those shorts and I was going to be late, but I didn't want to interrupt an argument between my teachers. I recognized the voices: Mr. Schmidt, my history teacher, and Mr. Boone, my math teacher. They seemed to be arguing about me. I couldn't believe it. I still remember the shock

> **DURING READING**
>
> **Analyze Literature**
> **Theme** Why won't the narrator get a school jacket for sports? **Ⓐ**

ab · sent · mind · ed · ly
(ab' sənt mīn´ dəd lē)
adv., lost in thought; unaware

---

1. **eavesdrop.** Secretly listen to someone else's private conversation

---

Differentiated Instruction

Reading Proficiency

Have students listen to you read aloud sections of the story, and then have them read aloud with you. Some students may also benefit from reading with a partner, alternating paragraphs or pages, and offering help when needed.

English Language Learning

Explain the following expressions to students learning English.

school colors—specific colors (usually two), used for uniforms and other objects related to the school and school activities, 156

straight A student—a student who receives the grade of A or A+ in all courses, 156

P.E.—abbreviation for physical education, or gym class, 156 that rooted me flat against the wall as if I were trying to blend in with the graffiti written there.

"I refuse to do it! I don't care who her father is, her grades don't even begin to compare to Martha's. I won't lie or falsify records. Martha has a straight A plus average and you know it." That was Mr. Schmidt and he sounded very angry. Mr. Boone's voice sounded calm and quiet.

"Look, Joann's father is not only on the Board, he owns the only store in town; we could say it was a close tie and—"

The pounding in my ears drowned out the rest of the words, only a word here and there filtered through. "...Martha is Mexican.... resign....won't do it...." Mr. Schmidt came rushing out, and luckily for me went down the opposite way toward the auditorium, so he didn't see me. Shaking, I waited a few minutes and then went in and grabbed my bag and fled from the room. Mr. Boone looked up when I came in but didn't say anything. To this day I don't remember if I got in trouble in P.E. for being late or how I made it through the rest of the afternoon. I went home very sad and cried into my pillow that night so grandmother wouldn't hear me. It seemed a cruel <u>coincidence</u> that I had overheard that conversation.

The next day when the principal called me into his office, I knew what it would be about. He looked uncomfortable and unhappy. I decided I wasn't going to make it any easier for him so I looked him straight in the eye. He looked away and fidgeted with the papers on his desk.

"Martha," he said, "there's been a change in policy this year regarding the scholarship jacket. As you know, it has always been free." He cleared his throat and continued. "This year the Board decided to charge fifteen dollars—which still won't cover the complete cost of the jacket."

I stared at him in shock and a small sound of <u>dismay</u> escaped my throat. I hadn't expected this. He still avoided looking in my eyes.

"So if you are unable to pay the fifteen dollars for the jacket, it will be given to the next one in line."

Standing with all the dignity I could muster,[2] I said, "I'll speak to my grandfather about it, sir, and let you know tomorrow." I cried on the walk home from the bus stop. The dirt road was a quarter of a mile from the highway, so by the time I got home, my eyes were red and puffy.

---

2. **muster.** Call forth; collect

DURING READING

Analyze Literature
Theme What does Mr. Schmidt refuse to do? **B**

co·in·ci·dence
(kō ĭn[t]´ sə dən[t]s) *n.*, chance occurrence

DURING READING

Analyze Literature
Theme How does the narrator know what the principal wants? **D**

dis·may (dis mā´) *n.*, sudden loss of courage; shock

Teach the Model

Analyze Literature

Theme *Answer:* He refuses to falsify grades or go along with a plan to give the scholarship jacket to someone other than Martha. **B**

Use Reading Strategies

Ask Questions Tell students that asking questions as they read can help them better understand the characters' feelings and actions. Model questions that this paragraph might prompt a reader to ask: "What does being Mexican have to do with the teachers' argument? Why didn't Mr. Boone say anything? What does Martha mean by 'cruel coincidence'?" **C**

Analyze Literature

Theme *Answer:* She overheard the teachers arguing about giving the jacket to someone else. **D**

Analyze Literature

Theme Point out to students that they can often determine the theme of a story by examining the story's conflict or problem and how the main character deals with it. Ask students what problem Martha faces and how she plans to deal with it. (She needs fifteen dollars to pay for the scholarship jacket. She plans to ask her grandfather for the money.) **E**

Reading Skills

Identify Author's Purpose

Remind students that authors usually have one or more purposes for writing. Give examples of purposes, such as to tell a story and to persuade. Ask students to identify Marta Salinas's main purpose for writing "The Scholarship Jacket." Then, encourage them to answer the following questions as they read to determine what else she may want readers to understand.

1. What kinds of details does the author use to describe the characters, especially Martha?
2. Why did the author choose these specific details? What does she want me to understand about Martha? Grandpa? Martha's teachers?
3. Does the author just want to tell a story, or is she trying to make a point?

Analyze Literature

Theme *Answer:* Students may point out that she really wants the money, and that if she tells the truth, she will convince her grandfather it is for something essential. **Ⓐ**

Analyze Literature

Dialogue In fiction, dialogue helps reveal the personalities of characters and their relationships with one another. Dialogue also helps move the story along. Ask students to pause after they read the dialogue that begins here. Have them tell you what the dialogue reveals about Grandpa and his relationship with Martha. (Grandpa is patient, thoughtful, gentle, and kind. Their relationship is mutually respectful.) **Ⓑ**

Analyze Literature

Character Offer students an opportunity to consider how the names Marta and Martha relate to the main character and the story's theme.

TEACHING NOTE

Self-Generated Questioning

Have students work in pairs, and divide the selection into as many sections as you have pairs. Give each pair a section of the selection to read. Instruct students to write down any questions that they have about characters or events as they read. Model a possible question: "Why doesn't the narrator insist on being called Marta at school?" Have pairs share their questions and develop answers with the class.

"Where's Grandpa?" I asked Grandma, looking down at the floor so she wouldn't ask me why I'd been crying. She was sewing on a quilt and didn't look up.

"I think he's out back working in the bean field."

I went outside and looked out at the fields. There he was. I could see him walking between the rows, his body bent over the little plants, hoe in hand. I walked slowly out to him, trying to think how I could best ask him for the money. There was a cool breeze blowing and a sweet smell of mesquite³ in the air, but I didn't appreciate it. I kicked at a dirt clod. I wanted that jacket so much. It was more than just being a valedictorian and giving a little thank you speech for the jacket on graduation night. It represented eight years of hard work and expectation. I knew I had to be honest with Grandpa; it was my only chance. He saw me and looked up.

He waited for me to speak. I cleared my throat nervously and clasped my hands behind my back so he wouldn't see them shaking. "Grandpa, I have a big favor to ask you," I said in Spanish, the only language he knew. He still waited silently. I tried again. "Grandpa, this year the principal said the scholarship jacket is not going to be

> **DURING READING**
>
> **Analyze Literature**
> **Theme** Why is being honest the narrator's only chance? **Ⓐ**
>
> **Ⓑ**

---

3. **mesquite.** Small tree or shrub with sweet pods and fragrant wood

Grammar Skills

Subordinating Conjunctions

Remind students that a subordinating conjunction (*if, as if, even though, just when, because,* and *after*) joins a dependent or subordinate clause to a main or independent clause in a sentence. Write these pairs of sentences on the board. Ask students to combine ideas into a single sentence, using a subordinating conjunction.

1. (a) Rita has been nominated for class president. (b) Rita is a responsible student with strong leadership qualities.
2. (a) The principal revealed the winner of this year's academic scholarship. (b) Several students were disappointed.

free. It's going to cost fifteen dollars and I have to take the money in tomorrow, otherwise it'll be given to someone else." The last words came out in an eager rush. Grandpa straightened up tiredly and leaned his chin on the hoe handle. He looked out over the field that was filled with the tiny green bean plants. I waited, desperately hoping he'd say I could have the money.

He turned to me and asked quietly, "What does a scholarship jacket mean?"

I answered quickly; maybe there was a chance. "It means you've earned it by having the highest grades for eight years and that's why they're giving it to you." Too late I realized the significance of my words. Grandpa knew that I understood it was not a matter of money. It wasn't that. He went back to hoeing the weeds that sprang up between the delicate little bean plants. It was a time consuming job; sometimes the small shoots were right next to each other. Finally he spoke again.

"Then if you pay for it, Marta,[4] it's not a scholarship jacket, is it? Tell your principal I will not pay the fifteen dollars."

I walked back to the house and locked myself in the bathroom for a long time. I was angry with grandfather even though I knew he was right, and I was angry with the Board, whoever they were. Why did they have to change the rules just when it was my turn to win the jacket?

It was a very sad and withdrawn girl who dragged into the principal's office the next day. This time he did look me in the eyes.

"What did your grandfather say?"

I sat very straight in my chair.

"He said to tell you he won't pay the fifteen dollars."

The principal muttered something I couldn't understand under his breath, and walked over to the window. He stood looking out at something outside. He looked bigger than usual when he stood up; he was a tall gaunt[5] man with gray hair, and I watched the back of his head while I waited for him to speak.

"Why?" he finally asked. "Your grandfather has the money. Doesn't he own a small bean farm?"

I looked at him, forcing my eyes to stay dry. "He said if I had to pay for it, then it wouldn't be a scholarship jacket," I said and stood up to leave. "I guess you'll just have to give it to Joann." I hadn't

---

4. **Marta.** The narrator is called *Martha* at school and *Marta* at home.
5. **gaunt.** Very thin and angular

He turned to me and asked quietly, "What does a scholarship jacket mean?"

with·drawn (with drôn′) *adj.,* introverted; unresponsive

DURING READING

Analyze Literature
Theme What does it mean that the principal meets her eyes today and not yesterday? **E**

Make Connections

Ask students to explain, based on their own experience, what Martha means by this sentence. (Students will identify with verbal slips, and may also describe the feeling of being startled when their words say more than they mean to.) **C**

Cultural Connection

School Boards Every public school district in the United States is governed by a school board. The members of the board are ordinary citizens who reside within the boundaries of the district, and are either elected by the people or appointed by the governor. The primary responsibility of most school boards is to set policies that establish the direction of education within the district. Other responsibilities keep the district operating normally. These include recruiting staff, approving curriculums, and creating a budget. **D**

Analyze Literature

Theme *Answer:* Several similar answers are possible: The principal expects Martha to respond to the fee request, so he is not as ashamed today as he was yesterday; he was lying yesterday, and today he does not have to lie again; he is more prepared for Martha's disappointment today than he was before. **E**

Persuasive Speech

Ask students to imagine what Martha might say in her valedictorian speech if, instead of simply expressing her gratitude for the scholarship jacket (see the Creative Writing prompt on page 161), she expresses her feelings about why the scholarship jacket should continue to be awarded solely for academic excellence.

Give students time to prepare and practice a persuasive speech that Martha might give. Remind them that an effective persuasive speech relies on logical reasoning and avoids emotional or unfair language. Then have them deliver their speeches. Have classmates evaluate the speeches based on their organization, content, delivery, and persuasiveness.

Use Reading Strategies

Make Predictions Ask students what might happen next. (The principal could change his mind, or he could say he's sorry, but he can't change the new policy.) **A**

Use Reading Skills

Context Clues *Answer:* It means something like "nasty." **B**

Analyze Literature

Plot Remind students that in the resolution of a plot, the main character's conflict comes to an end. Ask students to describe the resolution in this story. Then ask if they find it satisfying. **C**

Use Reading Strategies

Make Inferences Ask: "What can you infer from the pat and the smile that Grandpa gives Martha?" (He wants to let her know that she did the right thing and he is proud of her.) **D**

Answer: Students probably have had this experience. They may have been grateful or they may have felt annoyed. Some students may distinguish between times when adults helpfully intervene with other adults on a young person's behalf, and when adults interfere unnecessarily in conflicts between students and their peers.

DURING READING

Use Reading Skills
Context Clues Based on context clues, what does *vile* mean? **B**

A meant to say that; it had just slipped out. I was almost to the door when he stopped me.

"Martha—wait."

I turned and looked at him, waiting. What did he want now? I could feel my heart pounding. Something bitter and vile tasting was coming up in my mouth; I was afraid I was going to be sick. I didn't need any sympathy speeches. He sighed loudly and went back to his big desk. He looked at me, biting his lip, as if thinking.

C "Okay. We'll make an exception in your case. I'll tell the Board, you'll get your jacket."

I could hardly believe it. I spoke in a trembling rush. "Oh, thank you sir!" Suddenly I felt great. I didn't know about adrenalin[6] in those days, but I knew something was pumping through me, making me feel as tall as the sky. I wanted to yell, jump, run the mile, do something. I ran out so I could cry in the hall where there was no one to see me. At the end of the day, Mr. Schmidt winked at me and said, "I hear you're getting a scholarship jacket this year."

His face looked as happy and innocent as a baby's, but I knew better. Without answering I gave him a quick hug and ran to the bus. I cried on the walk home again, but this time because I was so happy. I couldn't wait to tell Grandpa and ran straight to the field. I joined him in the row where he was working and without saying anything I crouched down and started pulling up the weeds with my hands. Grandpa worked alongside me for a few minutes, but he didn't ask what had happened. After I had a little pile of weeds between the rows, I stood up and faced him.

"The principal said he's making an exception for me, Grandpa, and I'm getting the jacket after all. That's after I told him what you said."

D Grandpa didn't say anything, he just gave me a pat on the shoulder and a smile. He pulled out the crumpled red handkerchief that he always carried in his back pocket and wiped the sweat off his forehead.

"Better go see if your grandmother needs any help with supper."

I gave him a big grin. He didn't fool me. I skipped and ran back to the house whistling some silly tune. ✢

6. **adrenalin.** Hormone that gives a person a burst of energy

When has an older person stepped into a situation to stand up for you? Do you think it's always a good thing, or should adults let young people fend for themselves?

Differentiated Instruction

Enrichment

Interested students might research regional and national academic awards and scholarships available to middle school students. Suggest that students begin their research in the school's guidance department. Students can also use the Internet and library resources. Tell students to take notes that explain what the award or scholarship is; who sponsors it; how students can qualify or apply for it; and how and when the award or scholarship is presented. Students can combine the results of their research and publish a compilation in a pamphlet to display in the classroom or library.

Find Meaning

1. (a) What does the scholarship jacket reward? (b) Why would the school give it to someone who does not meet the usual criteria?
2. (a) Why can't the narrator participate in sports? (b) Why does the narrator want the scholarship jacket so much?
3. Which teacher supports the narrator? Why?

Analyze Literature

Theme Review your answers to the During Reading questions on the pages of the "The Scholarship Jacket." Using those responses, make a theme map to determine the story's theme or themes. Draw a large circle labeled "Theme(s)," and then put smaller circles around it. Write details from the story in the smaller circles. Then fill in the center circle.

Make Judgments

4. Compare Mr. Schmidt and Mr. Boone. Who do you think is the better person? Why?
5. Compare the actions of the principal and the narrator's grandfather. Who acts more responsibly? Explain.
6. (a) Why does the narrator finally get the scholarship jacket? (b) What does this suggest the theme of the story could be?

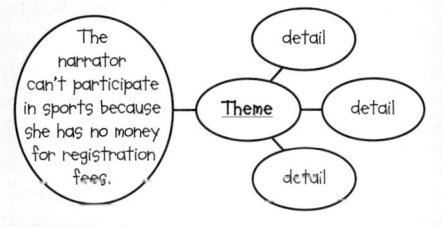

Extend Understanding

Writing Options

Creative Writing Take the role of the narrator in "The Scholarship Jacket" and prepare a one-paragraph **acceptance speech** with a clear main idea. Your speech should cover several key points that support your main idea.

Expository Writing Imagine you have agreed to read this story aloud to a class of fifth graders. Before you start, help them anticipate the story's overall message. Use your theme map to draft an **expository paragraph** in which you explain the story's theme. Support your explanation with evidence from the story.

Lifelong Learning

Find Famous Awards Use the Internet to research the history of a famous award, such as the Nobel Prize for Literature or the Academy Award for directing a movie. Create a list of the criteria used to pick the winners. Prepare a poster of your list.

Collaborative Learning

Communicate by Computer In a small group, discuss what caused Martha, the principal, Mr. Boone, and Mr. Schmidt to make the decisions they made. Consider motivations such as pride, prejudice, and self-respect. Create a list of these reasons, and exchange it electronically with another small group.

Go to www.mirrorsandwindows.com for more.

THE SCHOLARSHIP JACKET **161**

Find Meaning

1. (a) The jacket rewards good grades. (b) Some may say that social pressure has persuaded the Board to award the jacket to the daughter of a prominent man. Some may say the school wants to take advantage of a poor student to favor someone wealthier, or to honor a non-Mexican more than a Mexican.
2. (a) She does not have the money to pay participation fees. (b) The jacket represents the investments she has made to excel academically.
3. Mr. Schmidt supports her out of his ethical and moral convictions. He wants to be fair, and he will not lie.

Make Judgments

4. Students will probably think Schmidt is the better person because he does not give in to pressure.
5. The principal tries to deny Martha the jacket, while her grandfather points out that she has already earned it. Most will say the grandfather acts more honestly and responsibly.
6. (a) Students will probably say it is because she stands up for her right to what she has earned. (b) Many will say the theme is about standing up for your rights.

Analyze Literature

Theme The theme in the center of a student's map should match the theme he or she expressed in response to Question 6. Details may come from responses to During Reading questions. All details should relate directly to the theme.

Rubrics for Writing Options

You can adapt this as a checklist for students to use as they write.

Creative Writing

☐ Does the student write as if giving Martha's acceptance speech?
☐ Is the speech limited to two or three main points?
☐ Does the student connect the main points in complete sentences?
☐ Are the student's ideas confined to a single paragraph?

Expository Writing

☐ Does the expository paragraph clearly state the story's theme?
☐ Does the paragraph include examples from the story?
☐ Is the paragraph geared toward students who have not read or heard the story at all?

Sentence Improvement
1. A
2. B
3. C

Build Skills
Students may ask for guidance about what constitutes a long or a short clause. Emphasize that they should use a comma between clauses when the comma helps them avoid any possible confusion. Consider reading the first Sentence Improvement example aloud, without inflection. Then read the corrected version. Ask students which is clearer to them.

> ▶ For more information, see Grammar & Style Section 3.15, Punctuation, in the Language Arts Handbook.

Program Resources
You will find additional lessons on Comma Use in the *Exceeding the Standards: Grammar & Style* resource.

KEY TERMS
COMPOUND SENTENCE, 162
INDEPENDENT CLAUSE, 162
COORDINATING CONJUNCTION, 162
COMMA, 162

Grammar & Style

Comma Use

Commas and Compound Sentences

I had been a straight A student since the first grade, and the last year I had looked forward to owning that jacket.

—MARTA SALINAS, "The Scholarship Jacket"

In this compound sentence, two independent, or main, clauses are joined by the coordinating conjunction *and*. (Other coordinating conjunctions are *but, or, nor, for,* and *yet*.) Because these clauses are long, you should use a comma before the conjunction. When the two independent clauses are very short, you can sometimes omit the comma.

> EXAMPLE
> *Martha is a good student and she wants to win the jacket.*

Even if a compound sentence is short, include a comma if the sentence would be confusing without it. In the first of the two examples, the sentence sounds odd. Add a comma to make it clear.

> EXAMPLES
> *Martha weeds but her Grandpa works too.*
> *Martha weeds, but her Grandpa works too.*

Commas in a Series
You should always use commas to separate items in a series. Three or more words make a series.

> EXAMPLE
> *Martha says that she has good grades, good attendance, and a good attitude.*

It is not necessary to use commas if the items in the series are linked by conjunctions.

> EXAMPLE
> *Martha says that she has good grades and good attendance and a good attitude.*

Sentence Improvement
For each of the following sentences, select the response that indicates the *best* revision.

1. Martha asks for fifteen dollars but Grandpa refuses to give the money to her.
   A. Martha asks for fifteen dollars, but Grandpa refuses to give the money to her.
   B. Martha asks for fifteen dollars but, Grandpa refuses to give the money to her.
   C. Martha asks for fifteen dollars, but, Grandpa refuses to give the money to her.
   D. NO CHANGE

2. Martha spoke with her teachers her grandpa and her grandma.
   A. Martha spoke with her teachers her grandpa, and her grandma.
   B. Martha spoke with her teachers and her grandpa and her grandma.
   C. Martha spoke with her teachers, her grandpa her grandma.
   D. NO CHANGE

3. Martha's family couldn't afford registration fees uniform costs and trips out of town.
   A. Martha's family couldn't afford registration fees, uniform costs and trips out of town.
   B. Martha's family couldn't afford registration fees uniform costs, and trips out of town.
   C. Martha's family couldn't afford registration fees, uniform costs, and trips out of town.
   D. NO CHANGE

TEACHING NOTE

Extra Practice
Each of the following sentences would benefit from having a comma. Give students the sentences and have them add the comma or commas where appropriate.

1. Gerald[,] Delores[,] Marcus[,] and Lloyd went to the gym[,] but once they got there they used different equipment.

2. My cats act as if they don't know who I am[,] yet they come running when I take the can opener out of the drawer.

3. Eleven new students entered the first[,] second[,] and third grades yesterday.

4. You have to find a place away from city lights[,] or you must go to a planetarium[,] to see stars clearly.

Common Core State Standards
Language
L.4.3b, L.5.2a

Amigo Brothers

A Short Story
by Piri Thomas

Preview the Selection

At a Glance
Directed Reading
- Reading Level: Moderate
- Difficulty Consideration: Vocabulary
- Ease Factor: Vivid description

DIRECTED READING

BEFORE READING

Build Background
Literary Context Writers create characters in three principal ways. They can show what a character says, does, and thinks. They can show what other characters say about a character. Also, they can describe a character's physical traits. Piri Thomas develops the characters in "Amigo Brothers" in these three ways.

Reader's Context Have you ever had to compete against a friend? How did it affect your relationship?

Set Purpose
Preview the story by reading the first three paragraphs. How are the two main characters similar? How are they different? Do you think their relationship will change during the story?

Analyze Literature
Point of View This story is written from the *third-person point of view*, which means the narrator is not part of the action. A third-person narrator can be omniscient or limited. An *omniscient* narrator knows everything about the characters and the plot. A *limited third-person* narrator knows only some things, such as what anyone observing the characters and situation could see. As you read, think about whether the narrator of "Amigo Brothers" is omniscient or limited. Record your thoughts.

Meet the Author
Piri Thomas (b. 1928) grew up in Spanish Harlem, part of New York City. As a youth, he was a gang member and spent time in prison. He wrote an autobiography called *Down These Mean Streets* in which he tries to persuade other gang members to change. Today, Thomas is known for reaching out to youth who are at risk for problems with drugs and crime.

Use Reading Skills
Draw Conclusions The plot of "Amigo Brothers" depends on the characters' competing motivations. Both friends want to win a boxing match, but they don't want to hurt each other. To determine the overall message of the story, keep track of the characters' motivations and actions as well as the key points in the plot. Use a drawing conclusions log like the one below to take notes as you read.

Preview Vocabulary
dev•a•stat•ing (de´ və stā´ tiŋ) *adj.*, overwhelming

war•y (wer´ ē) *adj.*, cautious

dis•pel (di spel´) *v.*, break up; make vanish

flail (flāl) *v.*, swing

surge (sʉrj) *v.*, rise and move forward

Objectives
Studying this lesson will enable students to
- use reading skills such as drawing conclusions
- define point of view and recognize the effect of a third-person omniscient narrator in the selection
- describe the work of Piri Thomas and see how his personal experiences influenced his writing
- appreciate a story about the endurance of true friendship

Launch the Lesson
Before reading "Amigo Brothers," tell students that they are about to read a story in which two friends compete for something that means a lot to both of them. Write the phrase *friendly competition* on the board. Ask students what the phrase means to them, using their own experiences to support their ideas. Ask: "Can a friendly competition ever be about something meaningful to either of the competitors?" After students have answered, have the class compose a sentence that expresses its opinion.

AMIGO BROTHERS **163**

Words in Use

Common Core State Standards

Reading Literature
RL.3

Summary

Having grown up together in the same tough New York City neighborhood, Antonio Cruz and Felix Vargas share a deep friendship and a passion for boxing. When they learn that they are to fight each other in the Golden Gloves Championship Tournament, they vow not to let their friendship influence the competition, and not to let the outcome of the fight affect their friendship. True to their word, the amigos fight without restraint. When the bout is over, their friendship is the victor.

The Mirrors & Windows questions at the end of the story focus on the theme of competition. Before students begin reading, ask: What character traits does it take to win at an individual sport, like swimming, tennis, or boxing?

Art Connection

P. J. Crook is known for painting large crowds. In many of her paintings, people are so packed together that it becomes difficult to focus on their individual characteristics. The crowd watching this fight is typical of her work.

The Big Fight, c. 20th century. P. J. Crook. Private collection.

A Short Story by Piri Thomas

Antonio knew the dynamite that was stored in his amigo brother's fist.

164

Program Resources

Planning and Assessment
Program Planning Guide, Selection Lesson Plan
E-Lesson Planner
Assessment Guide, Lesson Test
ExamView

Technology Tools
Interactive Student Text on CD
Visual Teaching Package
Audio Library
mirrorsandwindows.com

Meeting the Standards
Fiction: Unit 2, Directed Reading, pp. 32–42

Differentiating Instruction
Advanced Students, Author Study, pp. 10–11

Antonio Cruz and Felix Vargas were both seventeen years old. They were so together in friendship that they felt themselves to be brothers. They had known each other since childhood, growing up on the lower east side of Manhattan in the same tenement building[1] on Fifth Street between Avenue A and Avenue B.

Antonio was fair, lean, and lanky, while Felix was dark, short, and husky. Antonio's hair was always falling over his eyes, while Felix wore his black hair in a natural Afro style.

Each youngster had a dream of someday becoming lightweight champion of the world. Every chance they had the boys worked out, sometimes at the Boys Club on 10th Street and Avenue A and sometimes at the pro's gym on 14th Street. Early morning sunrises would find them running along the East River Drive, wrapped in sweat shirts, short towels around their necks, and handkerchiefs Apache style around their foreheads.

While some youngsters were into street negatives, Antonio and Felix slept, ate, rapped, and dreamt positive. Between them, they had a collection of *Fight* magazines second to none, plus a scrapbook filled with torn tickets to every boxing match they had ever attended, and some clippings of their own. If asked a question about any given fighter, they would immediately zip out from their memory banks divisions, weights, records of fights, knock-outs, technical knock-outs,[2] and draws or losses.

Each had fought many bouts[3] representing their community and had won two gold-plated medals plus a silver and bronze medallion. The difference was in their style. Antonio's lean form and long reach made him the better boxer, while Felix's short and muscular frame made him the better slugger. Whenever they had met in the ring for sparring sessions,[4] it had always been hot and heavy.

Now, after a series of elimination bouts,[5] they had been informed that they were to meet each other in the division finals that were scheduled for the seventh of August, two weeks away—the winner to represent the Boys Club in the Golden Gloves Championship Tournament.

The two boys continued to run together along the East River Drive. But even when joking with each other, they both sensed a wall rising between them.

One morning less than a week before their bout, they met as usual for their daily work-out. They fooled around with a few jabs at the air, slapped skin, and then took off, running lightly along the dirty East River's edge.

Antonio glanced at Felix who kept his eyes purposely straight ahead, pausing from time to time to do some fancy leg work while throwing one-twos followed by upper cuts to an imaginary jaw. Antonio then beat the air with a barrage of body blows and short <u>devastating</u> lefts with an overhand jaw-breaking right. After a mile or so, Felix puffed and said, "Let's stop a while, bro. I think we both got something to say to each other." Antonio nodded. It was not natural to be acting as though nothing unusual was happening when two ace-boon buddies were going to be blasting each other within a few short days.

They rested their elbows on the railing separating them from the river. Antonio

---

1. **tenement building.** Large residential rental building in a city
2. **technical knock-outs.** Fights that are stopped when a referee decides one boxer is too badly hurt to continue
3. **bouts.** Athletic matches
4. **sparring sessions.** Informal matches in which boxers practice being on the offense and the defense
5. **elimination bouts.** Series of contests in which only the winner of each contest continues in the competition

dev·a·stat·ing (deˊ və stā′ tiŋ) *adj.*, overwhelming

AMIGO BROTHERS **165**

Analyze Literature

Plot Have students describe the conflict that the upcoming division finals create for Antonio and Felix. Is this conflict internal or external? (The two friends have to fight each other. The conflict is internal because while before they shared a mutual goal, now their goals conflict—each wants to win the fight and represent the Boys Club in the Golden Gloves Championship Tournament. They are also worried about hurting each other. Students may note that an external conflict, the fight, prompts the internal conflict.) **A**

Use Reading Skills

Draw Conclusions Ask students why they think Antonio admires the courage of the tugboat. (Antonio refers to the tugboat's "welterweight size." He probably thinks of himself as the tugboat, powerful beyond its slight appearance.) **B**

---

wiped his face with his short towel. The sunrise was now creating day.

Felix leaned heavily on the river's railing and stared across to the shores of Brooklyn. Finally, he broke the silence.

A "Man, I don't know how to come out with it."

Antonio helped. "It's about our fight, right?"

"Yeah, right." Felix's eyes squinted at the rising orange sun.

"I've been thinking about it too, *panín*.[6] In fact, since we found out it was going to be me and you, I've been awake at night, pulling punches on you, trying not to hurt you."

"Same here. It ain't natural not to think about the fight. I mean, we both are *cheverote*[7] fighters and we both want to win. But only one of us can win. There ain't no draws[8] in the eliminations."

Felix tapped Antonio gently on the shoulder. "I don't mean to sound like I'm bragging, bro. But I wanna win, fair and square."

Antonio nodded quietly. "Yeah. We both know that in the ring the better man wins. Friend or no friend, brother or no..."

Felix finished it for him. "Brother. Tony, let's promise something right here. Okay?"

B "If it's fair, *hermano*,[9] I'm for it." Antonio admired the courage of a tugboat pulling a barge five times its welterweight size.

"It's fair, Tony. When we get into the ring, it's gotta be like we never met. We gotta be like two heavy strangers that want the same thing and only one can have it. You understand, don'tcha?"

"*Sí*, I know." Tony smiled. "No pulling punches. We go all the way."

"Yeah, that's right. Listen, Tony. Don't you think it's a good idea if we don't see each other until the day of the fight? I'm going to stay with my Aunt Lucy in the Bronx.[10] I can use Gleason's Gym for working out. My manager says he got some sparring partners with more or less your style."

---

6. *panín* (pä nēn´). Pal (Spanish)
7. *cheverote* (shev´ ər ōt). Great (Spanish)
8. **draws.** Ties
9. *hermano* (hər män´ ō). Brother (Spanish)
10. **the Bronx.** Part of New York City just north of Manhattan

---

Differentiated Instruction

Reading Proficiency

Students may have trouble following ideas in long sentences, such as the sentence that begins, "Between them, they had a collection of *Fight* magazines . . ." on page 165. Have students reread these sentences to make sure they have understood the details and the overall meaning.

English Language Learning

While the use of English and Spanish slang in the story adds authenticity, students learning English may have difficulty with it. Ask English-speaking and Spanish-speaking students to interpret such slang expressions as "slapped skin" and "ace-boon buddies." Then ask students to provide similar expressions in their first languages. Encourage English language learners to ask about other unknown words or expressions they have encountered.

Tony scratched his nose pensively.[11] "Yeah, it would be better for our heads." He held out his hand, palm upward. "Deal?"

"Deal." Felix lightly slapped open skin.

"Ready for some more running?" Tony asked lamely.

"Naw, bro. Let's cut it here. You go on. I kinda like to get things together in my head."

"You ain't worried, are you?" Tony asked.

"No way, man." Felix laughed out loud. "I got too much smarts for that. I just think it's cooler if we split right here. After the fight, we can get it together again like nothing ever happened."

The amigo brothers were not ashamed to hug each other tightly.

"Guess you're right. Watch yourself, Felix. I hear there's some pretty heavy dudes up in the Bronx. *Suavecito,*[12] okay?"

"Okay. You watch yourself too, *sabe?*"[13]

Tony jogged away. Felix watched his friend disappear from view, throwing rights and lefts. Both fighters had a lot of psyching up to do before the big fight.

The days in training passed much too slowly. Although they kept out of each other's way, they were aware of each other's progress via the ghetto grapevine.

The evening before the big fight, Tony made his way to the roof of his tenement. In the quiet early dark, he peered over the ledge. Six stories below the lights of the city blinked and the sounds of cars mingled with the curses and the laughter of children in the street. He tried not to think of Felix, feeling he had succeeded in psyching his mind. But only in the ring would he really know. To spare Felix hurt, he would have to knock him out, early and quick.

Up in the South Bronx, Felix decided to take in a movie in an effort to keep Antonio's face away from his fists. The flick was *The Champion* with Kirk Douglas, the third time Felix was seeing it.

C

11. **pensively.** Thoughtfully
12. *suavecito* (swäv´ a sē' tō). Smooth; take it easy (Spanish)
13. *Sabe?* (sä bā´). Understand? (Spanish)

AMIGO BROTHERS **167**

AMIGO BROTHERS **167**

Use Reading Strategies

Clarify Ask students why Antonio believes it would be best to knock Felix out early (page 167). How does this compare to what Felix imagines as he watches the movie? (Antonio understands that a quick knockout will be less punishing than a prolonged fight in which he batters Felix. At the movies, Felix imagines himself being beaten mercilessly by Antonio, but then suddenly taking command and winning the fight.) **Ⓐ**

Use Reading Strategies

Ask Questions Encourage students to ask themselves why Felix does all those boxing moves as he walks up the street. Model other questions that these paragraphs might prompt readers to ask: "Is Felix afraid of the other kids? Is Felix disappointed that they don't challenge him to a fight?" **Ⓑ**

Use Reading Skills

Analyze Cause and Effect Ask students what effect the upcoming fight is having on Antonio's thoughts about his friendship with Felix. How does Antonio react to these thoughts? (The upcoming fight is causing Antonio to doubt the strength of their friendship. He pushes the thoughts out of his mind and vows to think of Felix in the ring as his opponent, not as his friend.) **Ⓒ**

The champion was getting hit hard. He was saved only by the sound of the bell.

Felix became the champ and Tony the challenger.

Ⓐ The movie audience was going out of its head. The challenger, confident that he had the championship in the bag, threw a left. The champ countered with a dynamite right.

Felix's right arm felt the shock. Antonio's face, superimposed on the screen, was hit by the awesome blow. Felix saw himself in the ring, blasting Antonio against the ropes. The champ had to be forcibly restrained. The challenger was allowed to crumble slowly to the canvas.

When Felix finally left the theatre, he had figured out how to psyche himself for tomorrow's fight. It was Felix the Champion vs. Antonio the Challenger.

He walked up some dark streets, deserted except for small pockets of <u>wary</u>-looking kids wearing gang colors. Despite the fact that he was Puerto Rican like them, they eyed him as **Ⓑ** a stranger to their turf. Felix did a fast shuffle, bobbing and weaving, while letting loose a torrent of blows that would demolish whatever got in its way. It seemed to impress the brothers, who went about their own business.

Finding no takers, Felix decided to split to his aunt's. Walking the streets had not relaxed him, neither had the fight flick. All it had done was to stir him up. He let himself quietly into his Aunt Lucy's apartment and went straight to bed, falling into a fitful sleep with sounds of the gong for Round One.

Antonio was passing some heavy time on **Ⓒ** his rooftop. How would the fight tomorrow affect his relationship with Felix? After all, fighting was like any other profession. Friendship had nothing to do with it. A gnawing doubt crept in. He cut negative thinking real quick by doing some speedy fancy dance steps, bobbing and weaving like

mercury.[14] The night air was blurred with perpetual motions of left hooks and right crosses. Felix, his *amigo* brother, was not going to be Felix at all in the ring. Just an opponent with another face. Antonio went to sleep, hearing the opening bell for the first round. Like his friend in the South Bronx, he prayed for victory, via a quick clean knockout in the first round.

Large posters plastered all over the walls of local shops announced the fight between Antonio Cruz and Felix Vargas as the main bout.

The fight had created great interest in the neighborhood. Antonio and Felix were well liked and respected. Each had his own loyal following. Antonio's fans counted on his boxing skills. On the other side, Felix's admirers trusted in his dynamite-packed fists.

Felix had returned to his apartment early in the morning of August 7th and stayed there, hoping to avoid seeing Antonio. He turned the radio on to *salsa* music sounds and then tried to read while waiting for word from his manager.

The fight was scheduled to take place in Tompkins Square Park.[15] It had been decided that the gymnasium of the Boys Club was not large enough to hold all the people who were sure to attend. In Tompkins Square Park, everyone who wanted could view the fight, whether from ringside or window fire escapes or tenement rooftops.

The morning of the fight Tompkins Square was a beehive of activity with numerous workers setting up the ring, the seats, and the guest speakers' stand. The scheduled bouts began shortly after noon and the park had begun filling up even earlier.

---

14. **mercury.** Metal that is liquid at room temperature
15. **Tompkins Square Park.** Only large open space on Manhattan's lower east side

war•y (wer´ ē) *adj.,* cautious

Vocabulary Skills

Idioms

Tell students that an idiom is an expression in which a group of words together has a different meaning from the exact meaning of the individual words. For example, to understand the idiom *second to none* on page 165, they have to go beyond the dictionary meaning of the words and consider what the words mean together, which is "better than anything else."

Have students list idioms in this story, such as *memory banks, hot and heavy, took off, come out with it, fair and square,* and *via the [ghetto] grapevine.* Tell them to use context and prior knowledge to write the meaning of each idiom, and to check their meanings in a dictionary.

The local junior high school across from Tompkins Square Park served as the dressing room for all the fighters. Each was given a separate classroom with desk tops, covered with mats, serving as resting tables. Antonio thought he caught a glimpse of Felix waving to him from a room at the far end of the corridor. He waved back just in case it had been him. **D**

The fighters changed from their street clothes into fighting gear. Antonio wore white trunks, black socks, and black shoes. Felix wore sky blue trunks, red socks, and white boxing shoes. Each had dressing gowns to match their fighting trunks with their names neatly stitched on the back.

The loudspeakers blared into the open windows of the school. There were speeches by dignitaries, community leaders, and great boxers of yesteryear. Some were well prepared, some improvised on the spot. They all carried the same message of great pleasure and honor at being part of such a historic event. This great day was in the tradition of champions emerging from the streets of the lower east side.

Interwoven with the speeches were the sounds of the other boxing events. After the sixth bout, Felix was much relieved when his trainer Charlie said, "Time change. Quick knock-out. This is it. We're on."

Waiting time was over. Felix was escorted from the classroom by a dozen fans in white T-shirts with the word FELIX across their fronts.

Antonio was escorted down a different stairwell and guided through a roped-off path.

As the two climbed into the ring, the crowd exploded with a roar. Antonio and Felix both bowed gracefully and then raised their arms in acknowledgment. **E**

Antonio tried to be cool, but even as the roar was in its first birth, he turned slowly to meet Felix's eyes looking directly into his. Felix nodded his head and Antonio responded. And both as one, just as quickly, turned away to face his own corner.

Bong—bong—bong. The roar turned to stillness.

"Ladies and Gentlemen. *Señores y Señoras.*"

The announcer spoke slowly, pleased at his bilingual efforts.

"Now the moment we have all been waiting for—the main event between two fine young Puerto Rican fighters, products of our lower east side. In this corner, weighing 134 pounds, Felix Vargas. And in this corner, weighing 133 pounds, Antonio Cruz. The winner will represent the Boys Club in the tournament of champions, the Golden Gloves. There will be no draw. May the best man win."

AMIGO BROTHERS **169**

Analyze Literature

Point of View Ask students how the narrator helps them visualize what is going on around the fighters. (The narrator provides details about the sounds of the crowd and the actions of the referee and the boys' trainers.) **Ⓐ**

Use Reading Skills

Draw Conclusions Have students use the details that show Antonio and Felix touching gloves, dancing to their corners, and crossing themselves to draw conclusions about the boys' attitudes and spirit before the fight. Remind students to continue to record character motivations and actions in their drawing conclusions log. **Ⓑ**

Analyze Literature

Characterization Ask students to point out details that help them recognize Felix and Antonio as experienced, enthusiastic fighters. (Antonio danced, his left hand pumping jabs. Felix bobbed and weaved. Students may cite details about avoiding blows and stopping at the sound of the bell.) **Ⓒ**

Use Reading Skills

Draw Conclusions Have students pause here and tell you who they think is winning the fight and why they think this. (Students may say that Antonio is winning the fight at this point because he has inflicted some punishing blows to Felix's head, while he has avoided being hit in the head himself.) **Ⓓ**

Boxer Right, c. 20th century. Carol Tatham. Private collection.

Ⓐ The cheering of the crowd shook the window panes of the old buildings surrounding Tompkins Square Park. At the center of the ring, the referee was giving instructions to the youngsters.

"Keep your punches up. No low blows. No punching on the back of the head. Keep your heads up. Understand. Let's have a clean fight. Now shake hands and come out fighting."

Ⓑ Both youngsters touched gloves and nodded. They turned and danced quickly to their corners. Their head towels and dressing gowns were lifted neatly from their shoulders by their trainers' nimble fingers. Antonio crossed himself.[16] Felix did the same.

Ⓒ BONG! BONG! ROUND ONE. Felix and Antonio turned and faced each other squarely in a fighting pose. Felix wasted no time. He came in fast, head low, half hunched toward his right shoulder, and lashed out with a straight left. He missed a right cross as Antonio slipped the punch and countered with one-two-three lefts that snapped Felix's head back, sending a mild shock coursing through him. If Felix had any small doubt about their friendship affecting their fight, it was being neatly <u>dispelled.</u>

Antonio danced, a joy to behold. His left hand was like a piston pumping jabs one right after another with seeming ease. Felix bobbed and weaved and never stopped boring in.[17] He knew that at long range he was at a disadvantage. Antonio had too much reach on him. Only by coming in close could Felix hope to achieve the dreamed-of knockout.

Antonio knew the dynamite that was stored in his *amigo* brother's fist. He ducked a short right and missed a left hook. Felix trapped him against the ropes just long enough to pour some punishing rights and lefts to Antonio's hard midsection. Antonio slipped away from Felix, crashing two lefts to his head, which set Felix's right ear to ringing.

Bong! Both *amigos* froze a punch well on its way, sending up a roar of approval for good sportsmanship.

Ⓓ Felix walked briskly back to his corner. His right ear had not stopped ringing. Antonio gracefully danced his way toward his stool none the worse, except for glowing glove burns, showing angry red against the whiteness of his midribs.

"Watch that right, Tony." His trainer talked into his ear. "Remember Felix always goes to the body. He'll want you to drop your hands for his overhand left or right. Got it?"

---

16. **crossed himself.** Made a gesture to invoke religious protection
17. **boring in.** Making one's way steadily against resistance

---

dis•pel (di spel´) *v.,* break up; make vanish

Differentiated Instruction

Visual Learning

Students can enhance their understanding of the anxiety, restlessness, and excitement that both Felix and Antonio experience leading up to the moment that they climb into the ring. Suggest that they create a cartoon story strip for "Amigo Brothers" with split frames that show Felix on one side of the split and Antonio on the other. Students can use their story strips to summarize the story so far, compare and contrast the two main characters, and make predictions about what might happen next and how the story will end.

Antonio nodded, spraying water out between his teeth. He felt better as his sore midsection was being firmly rubbed.

Felix's corner was also busy.

"You gotta get in there, fella." Felix's trainer poured water over his curly Afro locks. "Get in there or he's gonna chop you up from way back."

Bong! Bong! Round two. Felix was off his stool and rushed Antonio like a bull, sending a hard right to his head. Beads of water exploded from Antonio's long hair.

Antonio, hurt, sent back a blurring barrage of lefts and rights that only meant pain to Felix, who returned with a short left to the head followed by a looping right to the body. Antonio countered with his own flurry, forcing Felix to give ground. But not for long.

Felix bobbed and weaved, bobbed and weaved, occasionally punching his two gloves together.

Antonio waited for the rush that was sure to come. Felix closed in and feinted[18] with his left shoulder and threw his right instead. Lights suddenly exploded inside Felix's head as Antonio slipped the blow and hit him with a pistonlike left catching him flush on the point of his chin.

Bedlam[19] broke loose as Felix's legs momentarily buckled. He fought off a series of rights and lefts and came back with a strong right that taught Antonio respect.

Antonio danced in carefully. He knew Felix had the habit of playing possum[20] when hurt, to sucker[21] an opponent within reach of the powerful bombs he carried in each fist.

A right to the head slowed Antonio's pretty dancing. He answered with his own left at Felix's right eye that began puffing up within three seconds.

Antonio, a bit too eager, moved in too close and Felix had him entangled into a rip-roaring, punching toe-to-toe slugfest that brought the whole Tompkins Square Park screaming to its feet.

Rights to the body. Lefts to the head. Neither fighter was giving an inch. Suddenly a short right caught Antonio squarely on the chin. His long legs turned to jelly and his arms flailed out desperately. Felix, grunting like a bull, threw wild punches from every direction. Antonio, groggy, bobbed and weaved, evading most of the blows. Suddenly his head cleared. His left flashed out hard and straight catching Felix on the bridge of his nose.

Felix lashed back with a haymaker,[22] right off the ghetto streets. At the same instant, his eye caught another left hook from Antonio. Felix swung out trying to clear the pain. Only the frenzied screaming of those along ringside let him know that he had dropped Antonio. Fighting off the growing haze, Antonio struggled to his feet, got up, ducked, and threw a smashing right that dropped Felix flat on his back.

Felix got up as fast as he could in his own corner, groggy but still game.[23] He didn't even hear the count. In a fog, he heard the roaring of the crowd, who seemed to have gone insane. His head cleared to hear the bell sound at the end of the round. He was very glad. His trainer sat him down on the stool.

In his corner, Antonio was doing what all fighters do when they are hurt. They sit and smile at everyone.

The referee signaled the ring doctor to check the fighters out. He did so and then gave his okay. The cold water sponges brought clarity to both *amigo* brothers. They were rubbed until their circulation ran free.

---

18. **feinted.** Pretended to aim at one place and then hit elsewhere
19. **bedlam.** Loud confusion
20. **playing possum.** Pretending to be dead by lying motionless
21. **sucker.** Deceive; lure under false pretenses
22. **haymaker.** Powerful blow
23. **still game.** Still willing to compete

flail (flāl) *v.*, swing

Teach the Selection

▶ More About the Author
Piri Thomas began writing while he was in prison as a way to pass the time and to alleviate some of the loneliness. Even when he had no one else in the world to talk to, he could talk to his paper. For him, writing was a way "to get rid of all this agony. . . It brings clarity," he said. Critics have admired Thomas's honest portrayal of the cold, tough realities of life in the ghetto, and his ability to connect with readers in spite of the fact that the Spanish Harlem dialect and prison slang that his characters use are not familiar to most of his readers.

Make Connections
Ask students if they are surprised at the intensity of the fight. Have them explain their responses. (Most students will probably say they are not surprised because they already knew how much winning meant to both boys.)

Use Reading Strategies
Clarify Students may feel lost by the time they get to the end of the description of the fast-paced action in round two. If students are confused, suggest that they go back and reread this section of the text. Encourage them to ask questions about any words or phrases that they don't understand and discuss ways that they could figure out their meaning.

Speaking & Listening Skills

Dramatic Reading
Have students prepare dramatic readings of the fight scene from "Amigo Brothers." Separate the class into six groups. Break the text into six parts (use the *bong* bell sound as a visual clue), like this: (1) The announcer introduces the fighters. (2) Round one (3) Round two (4) Round three (5) The bell sounds, ending the fight. (6) The announcer is about to announce the winner.

Assign each group a section of the text. Have students practice reading with emotion, varying volume and pace, emphasizing certain words and phrases, and using appropriate gestures and facial expressions. When they are ready, have the groups present their scenes in order.

Answer: Students may say most winners rely on skill and control rather than on brute strength.

Find Meaning

1. They have known each other a long time; they talk, spend almost all their time together, and share a dream and an attitude.
2. (a) Antonio is lanky, fair, and lean; Felix is dark, short, and husky. Antonio has a long reach and is the "better boxer"; Felix comes in close and is the "better slugger." (b) They dress alike, are both committed to winning, know a lot about boxing, and know each other's styles.
3. (a) Each wants to win. (b) They had to stop thinking of each other as friends and stop being afraid to hurt each other.
4. Felix imagines himself as the champion and Antonio as the challenger.

Make Judgments

5. (a) Opinions will vary. (b) Most students will say yes, because neither lets up to protect his friend. Some may say no, because it turned out they did not really care who won.
6. They could be friends forever because the fight tested their friendship, or they may have to go their separate ways as competitors.

Bong! Round three—the final round. Up to now it had been tic-tac-toe, pretty much even. But everyone knew there could be no draw and this round would decide the winner.

This time, to Felix's surprise, it was Antonio who came out fast, charging across the ring. Felix braced himself but couldn't ward off the barrage of punches. Antonio drove Felix hard against the ropes.

The crowd ate it up. Thus far the two had fought with *mucho corazón*.²⁴ Felix tapped his gloves and commenced his attack anew. Antonio, throwing boxer's caution to the winds, jumped in to meet him.

Both pounded away. Neither gave an inch and neither fell to the canvas. Felix's left eye was tightly closed. Claret red blood poured from Antonio's nose. They fought toe-to-toe.

The sounds of their blows were loud in contrast to the silence of a crowd gone completely mute. The referee was stunned by their savagery.

Bong! Bong! Bong! The bell sounded over and over again. Felix and Antonio were past hearing. Their blows continued to pound on each other like hailstones.

Finally the referee and the two trainers pried Felix and Antonio apart. Cold water was poured over them to bring them back to their senses.

They looked around and then rushed toward each other. A cry of alarm <u>surged</u> through Tompkins Square Park. Was this a fight to the death instead of a boxing match?

The fear soon gave way to wave upon wave of cheering as the two *amigos* embraced.

No matter what the decision, they knew they would always be champions to each other.

BONG! BONG! BONG! "Ladies and Gentlemen. *Señores* and *Señoras*. The winner and representative to the Golden Gloves Tournament of Champions is..."

The announcer turned to point to the winner and found himself alone. Arm in arm the champions had already left the ring. ✤

---

24. *mucho corazón* (mü chō′ kôr ō zōn′). Big heart; much courage (Spanish)

surge (sᴜrj) *v.*, rise and move forward

Who do you know who has the courage to "go all out" in a competition? Have you ever seen a winning competitor who seemed out of control? Are winners always people who keep themselves under control?

Find Meaning

1. What makes Antonio and Felix such good friends?
2. (a) How are the *amigo* brothers different in physique and style? (b) How are they similar?
3. (a) What were the friends' goals for the final fight? (b) Based on these goals, what did they have to do to prepare?
4. During training, Felix decides to see a movie called *The Champion*. How does seeing the movie help him prepare for the fight?

Make Judgments

5. (a) Although Felix and Antonio decide to act as if they never met, do you think they really acted that way in the ring? (b) Did the friends meet their goals for the fight? Explain your answer.
6. How long do you think Felix and Antonio can continue being best friends? Why?

Differentiated Instruction

Enrichment

Encourage students who are interested in learning about the art of boxing to visit a gym where young amateur boxers train. Before they go, they should reread "Amigo Brothers" to note boxing terms, techniques, and rules that they would like to learn more about. Have them use their notes to create a list of questions to ask trainers and boxers at the gym. Students can present their findings orally to the class. To enhance their reports, students can display labeled photographs of boxers demonstrating different techniques.

Remind students to make sure that they have adult permission and supervision when they visit the gym, and that they also have permission from the boxers and trainers to take photographs.

In "Amigo Brothers," Piri Thomas presents two boxers in heated competition. The following is an excerpt from *The Greatest: Muhammad Ali*, a biography by **Walter Dean Myers.** Myers was born in 1937 in West Virginia but soon moved to New York City. Myers conducts extensive research for his nonfiction writing. As you read, imagine Antonio and Felix experiencing what Myers describes.

from The Greatest: Muhammad Ali

A Biography by Walter Dean Myers

Each time a fighter steps into the ring he knows there will be a cost. For the glory of the possible win there will be a price measured in units of pain. He will have an idea, if he is honest with himself, of just how much pain he will have to endure on a given night, how much blood he will lose, and just how long it will take for his body to recover from the inevitable battering. Every fight hurts. Every fight damages the body. Some damage the soul.

Fights are often decided in the dressing room as the fighter extends his imagination to the glare of ringside. The image of the impending[1] battle flickers through his mind, and he visualizes himself winning, punishing his opponent more than he is punished. He sees himself using his style, using those tools most comfortable to him, to control the fight. Muhammad Ali could see himself moving quickly, throwing out lightning jabs, leaning back, just out of the reach of the desperate hooks. He saw himself frustrating his opponent, imposing his will on the fight. But even if he was convinced that he could win the fight, convinced beyond the hype and the false bravado[2] he offered to the press, he must still have assessed how much suffering he could bear to carry it off.

When the pain comes, it can be excruciating.[3] A two hundred-pound heavyweight at the top of his form can deliver a devastating blow. A good single blow to the face can break the neck of an ordinary person. Those watching on television or at ringside can scream at a fighter who lies helplessly against the ropes or who has stumbled heavily to the canvas, to get back into the fight. But few fight fans have ever been hit with even a glancing blow from a real fighter. They don't know the courage it takes to continue when the body is screaming to give it up.

Body punches bruise the muscles that help a fighter turn and lift his arms. They push the ribs out of shape; they bruise and tear the internal organs. Hours after the fight

---

1. **impending.** Upcoming
2. **false bravado.** Pretend display of courage
3. **excruciating.** Sharp; nearly intolerable

THE GREATEST **173**

Words in Use

from *The Greatest: Muhammad Ali*
Selection Words
inevitable, 173
spectrum, 174

Teach the Connection

Use Reading Skills

Summarize Point out to students that both "Amigo Brothers" and "The Greatest: Muhammad Ali" contain information about boxers and the sport of boxing. Ask students to list what they've learned from both sources and and then to synthesize their notes into a one-paragraph summary.

Text-to-Text Connection

Answer: Antonio and Felix do use visualization to prepare for their fight, but they try to imagine winning without hurting each other too much. Myers describes, in brutal detail, the effects of a devastating blow to the face, the damage to internal organs, and the pain that fighters live with after a fight. His focus is on how destructive fighting is to the head and body. Thomas also seems to give a realistic picture of the actual match, showing its brutality as well as the calculations each competitor makes in an effort to win, but his focus is on the characters and their resilient spirits.

the torn tissue and bleeding show up as a bloody tint in the urine.

A fighter's head throbs. Cuts are alive with pain as they are slammed again and again or as a glove is scraped across the exposed nerves. Forehead cuts bleed into the eyes and give color to the violence. Fighters hurt. They survive by accepting the agony of fighting as a way of life.

In the top ranks there are trainers and doctors at ringside, and other doctors to examine and care for the boxer. At the lower end of the spectrum there is less medical attention, less time to heal between fights, less money for good treatment.

Whether the medical treatment received before and after a fight is good or bad, the damage to the body is still done. Mostly, the body is forgiving. It will usually heal. The major physical problems that fighters encounter are with the eyes and with the brain. Physicians have long studied the effects of fighting, and especially of taking blows to the head. Some feel that boxing can be made safer. Others disagree: They feel that as long as the aim of professional fighting is to do damage to the head and body, it will be a dangerous sport. Just how destructive is fighting to the human body? Doctors debate, but fighters know. ❖

> **TEXT ← TO → TEXT CONNECTION**
>
> Myers writes that a fighter "visualizes himself winning, punishing his opponent more than he is punished." Compare Myers's description of a fight with the way Thomas describes the fight between Felix and Antonio. Based on what Myers writes, do you think Thomas gives a realistic portrayal of a boxing match? Explain.

174 UNIT 2 FICTION

Differentiated Instruction

Auditory Learning

Point out that the narrator says that during the fight, "Antonio danced, a joy to behold." Encourage students to try to picture the fight as a choreographed dance. Tell them to select an appropriate piece of music to go with the fight.

Invite them to imagine creating an interpretive dance based on the movements described in the fight scene. Provide time for students to locate music, listen to it, and share it with the class. Have students explain how the music captures the tone and/or mood of the fight.

174 UNIT 2 FICTION

Analyze Literature

Point of View In what ways does the third-person narrator in "Amigo Brothers" help advance the story's plot? For example, how does the narrator's omniscient point of view affect your understanding of the characters' motivations, actions, and personalities? Put your ideas in a two-column chart.

Detail of Omniscient Narration	Effect on My Understanding
"Antonio and Felix slept, ate, rapped, and dreamt positive."	Even though Antonio and Felix are surrounded by negative influences, they stay positive.

Extend Understanding

Writing Options

Creative Writing Imagine that your class is creating a short scene about what happens to Antonio and Felix immediately after the fight. Decide in your mind who you would have act the part of each fighter. Then write a five- to ten-line **dialogue** between Antonio and Felix. Refer to the story for examples of how the two friends talk to each other. When you are done, consider sharing dialogues with a friend and reading them aloud.

Expository Writing Using your drawing conclusions log, examine how the characters' motivations and actions lead to the resolution of the plot. Synthesize your work into a four-paragraph **expository essay** that maintains the meaning and logical order of the selection. Create a thesis statement and use two or three examples from the text to form paragraphs supporting your thesis.

Collaborative Learning

Write a Script When radio or television stations broadcast sporting events, they often have a color commentator. This person describes the action and talks during lulls, giving statistics and other background information to keep listeners interested. Have members of your group skim the story. Then work together to write a short color commentary script for a specific part of the fight. Read your script aloud in class.

Media Literacy

Conduct Internet Research Using the Internet, research the history of the Golden Gloves tournament. Investigate the various weight divisions and the age restrictions. Using the official competition website, create a list of some famous winners, including the years they won. Choose two of these people. Then do further Internet research to write a brief summary of their later achievements. Put your information into two profiles that you can display and discuss in class.

Go to www.mirrorsandwindows.com for more.

Analyze Literature

Point of View Student charts may suggest that the omniscient narrator is able to give a better portrait of these two fighters' personalities. This kind of narration helps readers understand the struggles the fighters face and their dedication to the sport.

Rubrics for Writing Options

You can adapt this as a checklist for students to use as they write.

Creative Writing

☐ Is the exchange five to ten lines long?
☐ Does it take place after the story?
☐ Do speech patterns approximate those in the story's exchanges between Felix and Antonio?

Expository Writing

☐ Is the essay four paragraphs long?
☐ Does the essay open with a thesis statement about how well the characters' motivations and actions predicted the resolution?
☐ Does the body include at least two examples from the text?
☐ Is the summary organized in a logical manner?

Vocabulary Practice

Sample answers are given below.

1. root: *psych* from Greek *psychē* meaning "breath, principle of life, life, soul"; **suffix:** *-logy* from French *-logie,* from Latin *-logia,* from Greek, from *logos* meaning "word"; **meaning:** "science of the mind"

2. root: *cryp* from Latin *crypta,* from Greek *kryptē,* from feminine of *kryptos* meaning "hidden," from *kryptein* meaning "to hide"; **suffix:** *-grapher* from Latin *-graphum,* from Greek *-graphon,* from neuter of *-graphos* meaning "written," from *graphein* meaning "to write"; **meaning:** "person who writes hidden words"

3. root: *nym* from Middle English *nimphe,* from Middle French, from Latin *nympha* meaning "bride," *nymph,* from Greek *nymphē*; **prefix:** *ant-* from Middle English, from Latin, *against,* from Greek, from *anti*; **meaning:** "opposite name"

4. root: *impose* from Middle French *imposer,* from Latin *imponere,* meaning literally "to put upon" (perfect indicative *imposui*), from *in-* + *ponere* meaning "to put"; **prefix:** *super-* from Latin, meaning "over, above, in addition, from" *super* meaning "over, above, on top of"; **meaning:** "laid over something else"

> ⏵ For more information, see Vocabulary & Spelling Section 2.2; Breaking Words Into Base Words, Word Roots, Prefixes, and Suffixes, in the Language Arts Handbook. Refer to Section 2.7, Spelling, for additional instruction on spelling rules.

You will find additional lessons on Prefixes, Roots, and Suffixes in the *Exceeding the Standards: Vocabulary & Spelling* resource.

Common Core State Standards

Language
L.4, L.5

Vocabulary & Spelling

Prefixes, Roots, and Suffixes

They were so together in friendship that they felt themselves to be brothers.

—PIRI THOMAS, "Amigo Brothers"

Many words are formed by adding prefixes and suffixes to base words. In the sentence above, the word *friendship* is an example of a word formed by the addition of a suffix. The suffix *-ship,* meaning "state of," added to the root, or base word *friend,* creates *friendship,* meaning "the state of friendship."

A **root** or **base word** is a word to which a prefix or suffix is added. A **prefix** is a letter or group of letters added to the beginning of a base word to change its meaning. A **suffix** is a letter or group of letters added to the end of a base word to change its meaning.

> **EXAMPLES**
>
> *inter + woven = interwoven*
> *mid + section = midsection*
> *light + ly = lightly*
> *power + ful = powerful*

Below are some common word parts and their origins.

Prefix	Meaning	Origin
auto-	"self"	Greek
bi-	"two"	Latin
micro-	"small"	Greek
mid-	"middle"	Anglo-Saxon
super-	"above, over"	Latin
un-	"not"	Anglo-Saxon

Suffix	Meaning	Origin
-able	"capable of being"	Latin
-cracy	"form of government"	Greek
-ic	"like, having the nature of"	Latin & Greek
-ist	"one who"	Latin
-ful	"full of"	Anglo-Saxon
-ness	"state or quality of"	Anglo-Saxon
-ship	"state of"	Anglo-Saxon

Root	Meaning	Origin
aud	"sound"	Anglo-Saxon
cine	"motion"	Latin
graph	"write"	Greek
junct	"join"	Latin
nym	"name"	Greek
psych	"of the mind"	Greek

Vocabulary Practice

Identify the roots, prefixes, and suffixes for each of the following academic terms along with their origin and meaning. Write the meaning of each term in your own words. Use a dictionary if you need help.

1. psychology
2. cryptographer
3. antonym
4. superimpose
5. bilingual
6. topography

Spelling Practice

Words with Prefixes, Roots, or Suffixes

Being able to recognize common prefixes, roots, and suffixes will help to make you a better speller because you will know how to spell the affix (prefix or suffix) or the root when you hear it. Some affixes you will recognize immediately, such as adding *s* or *es* to the end of a noun to make it plural; others are less common. Examine this list of words to determine which affixes and root words have been used. Remember that most word parts come from Latin, Greek, or Anglo-Saxon origins. For more information, refer to the Language Arts Handbook 2.2, Breaking Words Into Base Words, Word Roots, Prefixes, and Suffixes.

approval	desperately	occasionally
audience	dispelled	perpetual
analogy	elimination	succeeded
circulation	geometry	technical
commence	imaginary	
confident	immediately	

PREFIX, 176
ROOT, 176
SUFFIX, 176
ANTONYM, 176
BASE WORD, 176

Extra Practice

Students often have experience with identifying prefixes and suffixes. Roots, or base words, are more difficult to identify. Have students use a dictionary to find the roots of the following words. Once they find the roots, have them give an example of another English word that contains it.

Dictionaries differ in the amount of detail they provide. These are sample answers.

1. confide (*fidere,* trust; fidelity)
2. legend (*legere,* read; legible)
3. territory (*terra,* land; terrestrial)
4. inscription (*scribere,* write; script)

FOUR SKINNY TREES

A Short Story by Sandra Cisneros

At a Glance
Directed Reading
- Reading Level: Easy
- Difficulty Consideration: Imagery
- Ease Factor: Length

DIRECTED READING

BEFORE READING

Build Background
Literary Context "Four Skinny Trees" is from the book *The House on Mango Street,* which was first published in 1984. Cisneros began writing the pieces in the book when she was studying poetry as a graduate student. Poets use language in special ways so that its sound reflects its meaning. Although *The House on Mango Street* is called a novel, the book's structure and voice reflect Cisneros's training as a poet.

Reader's Context How are trees like people? Have you ever imagined that a tree, a flower, or another growing thing had a personality?

Set Purpose
Look at how long this selection is. It has four paragraphs. As a short story, it is very short. Read to find out how a person can tell an entire story in a prose piece of this length.

Analyze Literature
Description Writing that portrays a character, object, or scene is **description**. In this kind of writing, **sensory details** and precise language create vivid mental pictures, or **imagery.** Descriptions often contain **figurative language,** such as **personification.** "Four Skinny Trees" describes trees as if they are human, an example of personification. As you read, take time to let the sensory details and figurative language have an effect on you.

Use Reading Skills
Identify Main Idea To identify the main idea, or theme, of a piece of fiction, examine details such as characters' thoughts and actions, the author's choice of words, the point of view from which the story is told, and the main conflict. To determine the main idea of "Four Skinny Trees," use a main idea map like the one below. List details in the outer ovals and the main idea in the center.

The trees are skinny and pointy like the speaker.

detail

Main Idea or Theme

detail

detail

Objectives
Studying this lesson will enable students to
- use reading strategies such as asking questions
- define description and recognize the literal and figurative meanings of sensory language
- describe the literary accomplishments of Sandra Cisneros, recognize how her Mexican heritage and childhood experiences inspired her work, and appreciate how she applies poetic techniques to prose
- read a story on the themes of alienation, identity, and struggle

Launch the Lesson
Prior to reading "Four Skinny Trees," a short story by Sandra Cisneros, ask students to think about a time when they felt awkward and out of place. Then ask them to suggest words and phrases that describe the thoughts and emotions that accompanied that experience. List ideas on the board. Model a wide range of examples, such as *embarrassed, isolated, angry, aggressive, indifferent,* and *sad.* After students have listed ideas, ask them which thoughts and feelings other people are most likely to sympathize with and understand.

Meet the Author
Sandra Cisneros (b. 1954) grew up in Chicago with six brothers. Her father was Mexican and her mother was Mexican American. After finishing graduate school, she worked as a teacher and poet in schools. *The House on Mango Street* is her most popular book, but she has published another novel as well as short stories, poems, and a bilingual children's book. She lives in San Antonio, Texas, today.

FOUR SKINNY TREES **177**

Words in Use

Selection Words
raggedy, 179
ferocious, 179

Teaching Words
prose, 177
symbolize, 179
represent, 179
resemble, 180
vivid, 180

KEY TERMS
SHORT STORY, 177
DESCRIPTION, 177
CHARACTER, 177
SENSORY DETAIL, 177
PRECISE LANGUAGE, 177
IMAGERY, 177
FIGURATIVE LANGUAGE, 177
PERSONIFICATION, 177
MAIN IDEA, 177
MOOD, 180

Common Core State Standards
Reading Literature
RL.2
Language
L.3.3a

Teach the Selection

Summary

The narrator looks out her window to the sidewalk, where the city has planted four skinny, pitiful trees. In the narrator's mind, she and these scraggly trees share the same secret. While both appear trapped in the hard city landscape, they actually possess a ferocious will to put down roots, reach new heights, and, above all, survive.

 MIRRORS & WINDOWS The Mirrors & Windows questions at the end of the story focus on the theme of symbolism. Before students begin reading, ask: Why do people—not just writers—personify things?

Use Reading Strategies

Ask Questions Point out to students that good readers ask lots of questions before and as they read. Model for students questions that the title and first two sentences of the story might prompt a reader to ask: "Is this story about trees or is it about the narrator? Is the narrator a part of the story? If so, the story is told from a first-person point of view."

▶ More by This Author

Students who enjoy "Four Skinny Trees" might enjoy reading other vignettes in Cisneros's *The House on Mango Street.*

FOUR SKINNY TREES

A Short Story by Sandra Cisneros

178

Program Resources

Planning and Assessment
Program Planning Guide, Selection Lesson Plan
E-Lesson Planner
Assessment Guide, Lesson Test
ExamView

Technology Tools
Interactive Student Text on CD
Visual Teaching Package
Audio Library
mirrorsandwindows.com

Meeting the Standards
Fiction: Unit 2, Directed Reading, pp. 43–46

Four who grew despite concrete.

They are the only ones who understand me. I am the only one who understands them. Four skinny trees with skinny necks and pointy elbows like mine. Four who do not belong here but are here. Four raggedy excuses planted by the city. From our room we can hear them, but Nenny[1] just sleeps and doesn't appreciate these things.

Their strength is secret. They send ferocious roots beneath the ground. They grow up and they grow down and grab the earth between their hairy toes and bite the sky with violent teeth and never quit their anger. This is how they keep.

Let one forget his reason for being, they'd all droop like tulips in a glass, each with their arms around the other. Keep, keep, keep, trees say when I sleep. They teach.

When I am too sad and too skinny to keep keeping, when I am a tiny thing against so many bricks, then it is I look at trees. When there is nothing left to look at on this street. Four who grew despite concrete. Four who reach and do not forget to reach. Four whose only reason is to be and be. ❖

 A

---

1. **Nenny.** Narrator's younger sister, who shares her room

Think about the things you always see when you look out the window at home. What do you feel especially close to? What is one thing you see that could symbolize your life? Can a nonhuman object ever completely represent a human being?

Literary Connection

Prose Poems "Four Skinny Trees" has all the characteristics of a prose poem. It flows like prose without the conventional line breaks of a poem, yet it has a definite rhythm. It has strong imagery (*ferocious roots*), figurative language (*They . . . bite the sky with violent teeth*), internal rhyme (*street, concrete*), assonance (*keep, trees, sleep, teach*), and repetition (*understand, four skinny trees, keep,* and *be*). Encourage student to read the story aloud to appreciate its poetic quality.

Analyze Literature

Description Ask students which descriptive details reveal the narrator's awareness that people live not just for themselves, but for each other (*tulips in a glass, each with their arms around the other*). **A**

M**IRRORS** & **W**INDOWS

Answer: Each student should try to find one object from his or her window view that at least partially reflects his or her personality or physical qualities. Most will note that a non-human object cannot represent all of a human being, but some may point out that a symbol does not have to be completely accurate to represent something effectively.

Differentiated Instruction

Reading Proficiency

Some students may benefit from working in pairs to read and understand the extended metaphor that runs through the story. Pair students of similar reading ability. Have partners take turns reading one sentence, two sentences, or an entire paragraph. Then have partners explain to each other what they think the narrator is saying in those sentences or the paragraph. If students still have trouble interpreting the figurative elements of the story, encourage them to ask for help from you or from their classmates.

Review the Selection

Find Meaning

1. (a) They have "skinny necks and pointy elbows." (b) The trees, like the narrator, are stuck in a place they do not belong, have secret strength, are angry, keep reaching for more, and exist just to exist.

2. The city probably planted the trees to beautify the neighborhood.

3. Nenny does not appreciate what the trees say, which is "keep," or what the trees teach.

4. (a) If one tree forgets its "reason for being," all will droop. (b) All the trees support each other.

Make Judgments

5. Students may cite the trees' ability to understand the narrator, their "necks" and "elbows," and the sounds the narrator hears.

6. (a) Anger allows them to survive. (b) The word may mean "survive," "stay strong," or "remember why you exist."

7. (a) Possible answers include sad, tired, small, empty, and reassured. (b) Their presence may reassure the narrator, or they make her feel less discouraged and lonely.

Analyze Literature

Description Students will choose various descriptions. Their charts should include an image, as well as a paraphrase of the description. Allow students to assign any reasonable meanings. Moods may be angry, powerful, sad, dangerous, and united.

Find Meaning

1. (a) Physically, how do the trees resemble the narrator? (b) How do the trees resemble the narrator emotionally?

2. Who put the trees where they are, and why?

3. What doesn't Nenny appreciate?

4. (a) What would cause all the trees to droop? (b) Why aren't the trees drooping now?

Analyze Literature

Description Sensory details affect a story's mood. Select two descriptions from "Four Skinny Trees" that put a vivid picture in your mind. Read them aloud if you like. Evaluate how the descriptions sound and what they mean. Put your ideas in a chart. Then name a mood that is created by the combination of these images.

Make Judgments

5. Find an example of personification in the first paragraph. What quality does it give to the trees?

6. (a) What does anger do for the trees? (b) What does the narrator mean by the word *keep*?

7. (a) How does the narrator feel in the last paragraph? (b) How do the trees affect the narrator's feelings?

Description	Image	Meaning
Grab the earth between their hairy toes	Animal feet squeezing wet soil	Wild and strong, not tame and gentle

---

Extend Understanding

Writing Options

Creative Writing Close your eyes and picture the view from your favorite window. It can be a window at home, a car window, or any other window with a view. Then imagine that you want to re-create the view for someone else. Write a short **descriptive essay** about the scene you see. Use precise words and sensory details, and use figurative language if possible.

Expository Writing Reread "Four Skinny Trees" to analyze the narrator's emotions. To begin, connect the narrator and her emotions to your own experiences. Write a two-paragraph **literary response.** Using examples from the story, tell how the narrator's emotions impressed you. Try to relate her emotions to her circumstances or the setting.

Collaborative Learning

Give Complex Instructions With a partner, take turns giving oral instructions to perform specific tasks, answer questions, or solve problems. Set at time limit for each speaker and switch when your time is up. Focus your instructions on researching or analyzing the selection or its theme.

Lifelong Learning

Describe a Tree Using the Internet, the library, or a phone call to your local park district, find out which trees grow naturally in your area. Then choose one type of tree and find out more about it. Write a short description of the tree, using sensory details to create a vivid image.

Go to **www.mirrorsandwindows.com** for more.

Rubrics for Writing Options

You can adapt this as a checklist for students to use as they write.

Creative Writing
☐ Did the student choose a specific view?
☐ Does the essay include details that would be meaningful to someone else?
☐ Does the essay contain effective sensory details and figurative language?

Expository Writing
☐ Does the response connect the fictional narrator and her emotions to actual personal experiences?
☐ Does the response relate the narrator's emotions to her setting or circumstances?

The White Umbrella

A Short Story by Gish Jen

Preview the Selection

At a Glance
Directed Reading
- Reading Level: Easy
- Difficulty Considerations: None
- Ease Factor: Familiar themes

BEFORE READING

Build Background
Literary Context In a traditional plot, the central conflict is resolved after the climax of the story. Gish Jen's stories don't always have a resolution. Instead, her characters live with tensions that are part of ongoing relationships. Jen has said, "Opposites don't fight each other, but belong together and can intensify each other, and are simply in the nature of the world."

Reader's Context Imagine a teacher asking you to give a reason for what one of your parents is doing right now. What would you say?

Set Purpose
Read the opening scene of the story, the first eight paragraphs. Based on this exchange, try to predict what the theme—the central idea—of the story is going to be.

Analyze Literature
Mood The **mood** of a work of fiction is the way the author wants you to feel as you read it. The setting, descriptive language, and sensory details all affect a story's mood. As you read "The White Umbrella," try to pay attention to your own feelings about the story and the characters, especially the narrator. When you have finished reading, see if you can summarize the mood of the story in a single word.

Use Reading Skills
Compare and Contrast The main character in this story is the narrator. As you read, pay attention to her personality. Use a character chart like the one below to record your first impressions of her. Then, at the end of the story, think about the narrator's personality again. Write down your impressions. How are they similar to and different from your first impressions?

Narrator	Behavior Toward Other People	Internal State
proud	bossy toward her sister	embarrassed to be poor

Preview Vocabulary
cred·i·bil·i·ty (kreʹ də biʹ lə tē) *n.*, believability; ability to inspire belief

stu·pen·dous (stŭ penʹ dəs) *adj.*, marvelous; awe-inspiring

scep·ter (sepʹ tər) *n.*, tall staff or baton that a ruler carries as a symbol of authority

rev·e·la·tion (reʹ və lāʹ shən) *n.*, act of revealing or showing, usually something astonishing or enlightening

Meet the Author
Gish Jen (b. 1956) grew up in the New York City area. In college she considered being a lawyer or a doctor, and then she went to business school. She left business school and has been writing ever since. Her works explore identity and the American dream. Many of her stories and novels are about multigenerational, multiethnic families whose members must cope with how they feel about their heritage.

Objectives
Studying this lesson will enable students to
- use reading skills such as comparing and contrasting
- define mood and recognize how descriptive language and sensory details contribute to the mood
- describe the literary accomplishments of Gish Jen and how Chinese-American heritage influences her writing
- appreciate a story about the desire to belong and family loyalty

Launch the Lesson
Tell students that in "The White Umbrella," a plain white umbrella becomes an object of deep beauty to the narrator. Ask if they have ever become fascinated with an ordinary object and came to want it more than anything. Ask them to supply words and phrases that describe how they felt then—when they desired the object (such as *riveted, had to have it*)—and now, as they look back on how they acted because of that desire (such as *embarrassed, mystified*).

THE WHITE UMBRELLA **181**

Words in Use

Common Core State Standards
Reading Literature
RL.1
Writing
W.2, W.10

Summary

The narrator of the story is so ashamed that her mother works that she lies about it to her piano teacher, Miss Crosman. When the narrator spots a white umbrella in the piano room, she becomes infatuated with its sleek, perfect beauty, which is everything, she believes, she is not. After her lesson, the narrator insists on waiting for her mother in the rain. She is overcome with joy when Miss Crosman brings her the umbrella and tells her she can keep it. On the way home, the narrator realizes that taking the umbrella represents a betrayal of her mother, so she throws it in a sewer.

MIRRORS & WINDOWS The Mirrors & Windows questions at the end of the story focus on the theme of conflicting emotions. Before students begin reading, ask: How does it feel when two emotions compete for your attention?

The White Umbrella

A Short Story by Gish Jen

"This is the most beautiful umbrella I have ever seen," I said.

182

Program Resources

Planning and Assessment
Program Planning Guide, Selection Lesson Plan
E-Lesson Planner
Assessment Guide, Lesson Test
ExamView

Technology Tools
Interactive Student Text on CD
Visual Teaching Package
mirrorsandwindows.com

Meeting the Standards
Fiction: Unit 2, Directed Reading, pp. 47–53

When I was twelve, my mother went to work without telling me or my little sister.

"Not that we need the second income." The lilt of her accent drifted from the kitchen up to the top of the stairs, where Mona and I were listening.

"No," said my father, in a barely audible voice. "Not like the Lee family." **Ⓐ**

The Lees were the only other Chinese family in town. I remembered how sorry my parents had felt for Mrs. Lee when she started waitressing downtown the year before; and so when my mother began coming home late, I didn't say anything and tried to keep Mona from saying anything either.

"But why shouldn't I?" she argued. "Lots of people's mothers work."

"Those are American people," I said. **Ⓑ**

"So what do you think we are? I can do the pledge of allegiance with my eyes closed."

Nevertheless, she tried to be discreet;[1] and if my mother wasn't home by 5:30, we would start cooking by ourselves, to make sure dinner would be on time. Mona would wash the vegetables and put on the rice; I would chop.

For weeks we wondered what kind of work she was doing. I imagined that she was selling perfume, testing dessert recipes for the local newspaper. Or maybe she was working for the florist. Now that she had learned to drive, she might be delivering boxes of roses to people.

"I don't think so," said Mona as we walked to our piano lesson after school. "She would've hit something by now."

A gust of wind littered the street with leaves.

"Maybe we better hurry up," she went on, looking at the sky. "It's going to pour."

"But we're too early." Her lesson didn't begin until 4:00, mine until 4:30, so we usually tried to walk as slowly as we could.

"And anyway, those aren't the kind of clouds that rain. Those are cumulus clouds."

We arrived out of breath and wet.

"Oh, you poor, poor dears," said old Miss Crosman. "Why don't you call me the next time it's like this out? If your mother won't drive you, I can come pick you up."

"No, that's okay," I answered. Mona wrung her hair out on Miss Crosman's rug. "We just couldn't get the roof of our car to close, is all. We took it to the beach last summer and got sand in the mechanism." I pronounced this last word carefully, as if the credibility of my lie depended on its middle syllable. "It's never been the same." I thought for a second. "It's a convertible." **Ⓒ**

"Well then make yourselves at home." She exchanged looks with Eugenie Roberts, whose lesson we were interrupting. Eugenie smiled good-naturedly. "The towels are in the closet across from the bathroom."

Huddling at the end of Miss Crosman's nine foot leatherette couch, Mona and I watched Eugenie play. She was a grade ahead of me and, according to school rumor, had a boyfriend in high school. I believed it....She had auburn hair, blue eyes, and, I noted with a particular pang, a pure white folding umbrella.

"I can't see," whispered Mona.

"So clean your glasses."

"My glasses *are* clean. You're in the way."

I looked at her. "They look dirty to me."

"That's because *your* glasses are dirty."

Eugenie came bouncing to the end of her piece.

"Oh! Just stupendous!" Miss Crosman hugged her, then looked up as Eugenie's

---

1. discreet. Using good judgment, especially when deciding how much to say

cred•i•bil•i•ty (kre′ də bi′ lə tē) *n.*, believability; ability to inspire belief

stu•pen•dous (stū pen′ dəs) *adj.*, marvelous; awe-inspiring

Analyze Literature

Mood Ask students how they think the author wants them to feel about Eugenie. Model for students how the author's choice of words helps create that feeling: "In this section, I notice the expressions *pure white, radiant, royalty,* and *quivering sun.* These words remind me of a fairy tale. I think the author wants me to feel as if Eugenie is perfection, like a fairy tale princess, and far superior to the narrator." **A**

Analyze Literature

Mood Ask students how the description of the umbrella contributes to the mood of this section. (The umbrella glows like a magic wand, adding to the fairy-tale, dreamlike mood surrounding the description of Eugenie, whom the narrator thinks owns the umbrella.) **B**

Literary Connection

Asian-American Writers Gish Jen is one of several critically acclaimed Asian-American female authors who draw inspiration from their personal knowledge of the Chinese-American immigrant experience. Students might enjoy the works of other Asian-American female writers, including Lensey Namioka (author of "The Inn of Lost Time" on page 30), Amy Tan (author of "Fish Cheeks" on page 317), Uchida Yoshiko, and Lan Samantha Chang.

mother walked in. "Stupendous!" she said again. "Oh! Mrs. Roberts! Your daughter has a gift, a real gift. It's an honor to teach her."

Mrs. Roberts, radiant with pride, swept her daughter out of the room as if she were royalty, born to the piano bench. Watching the way Eugenie carried herself, I sat up and concentrated so hard on sucking in my stomach that I did not realize until the Robertses were gone that Eugenie had left her umbrella. As Mona began to play, I jumped up and ran to the window, meaning to call to them—only to see their brake lights flash then fade at the stop sign at the corner. As if to allow them passage, the rain had let up; a quivering sun lit their way.

The umbrella glowed like a <u>scepter</u> on the blue carpet while Mona, slumping over the keyboard, managed to eke out a fair rendition[2] of a cat fight. At the end of the piece, Miss Crosman asked her to stand up.

"Stay right there," she said, then came back a minute later with a towel to cover the bench. "You must be cold," she continued. "Shall I call your mother and have her bring over some dry clothes?"

"No," answered Mona. "She won't come because she..."

"She's too busy," I broke in from the back of the room.

"I see." Miss Crosman sighed and shook her head a little. "Your glasses are filthy, honey," she said to Mona. "Shall I clean them for you?"

Sisterly embarrassment seized me. Why hadn't Mona wiped her lenses when I told her to? As she resumed abuse of the piano, I stared at the umbrella. I wanted to open it, twirl it around by its slender silver handle; I wanted to dangle it from my wrist on the

---

2. **rendition.** Performance

scep•ter (sep´ tər) *n.,* tall staff or baton that a ruler carries as a symbol of authority

Reading Skills

Ask Questions

Point out to students that using a graphic organizer is a good way to keep track of questions that they have about story characters and plot as they read. Have them create a graphic organizer to write questions about the characters and plot in "The White Umbrella." They can also record any answers they figure out as they continue reading or through discussion with classmates. They might use a chart like this:

Questions I Have	Answers from Text

way to school the way the other girls did. I wondered what Miss Crosman would say if I offered to bring it to Eugenie at school tomorrow. She would be impressed with my consideration for others; Eugenie would be pleased to have it back; and I would have possession of the umbrella for an entire night. I looked at it again, toying with the idea of asking for one for Christmas. I knew, however, how my mother would react.

"Things," she would say. "What's the matter with a raincoat? All you want is things, just like an American."

C I stared at the umbrella. I wanted to open it, twirl it around by its slender silver handle....

Sitting down for my lesson, I was careful to keep the towel under me and sit up straight.

"I'll bet you can't see a thing either," said Miss Crosman, reaching for my glasses. "And you can relax, you poor dear....This isn't a boot camp."[3]

When Miss Crosman finally allowed me to start playing, I played extra well, as well as I possibly could. See, I told her with my fingers. You don't have to feel sorry for me.

"That was wonderful," said Miss Crosman. "Oh! Just wonderful."

An entire constellation rose in my heart.

"And guess what," I announced proudly. "I have a surprise for you."

Then I played a second piece for her, a much more difficult one that she had not assigned.

"Oh! That was stupendous," she said without hugging me. "Stupendous! You are a genius, young lady. If your mother had started you younger, you'd be playing like Eugenie Roberts by now!"

I looked at the keyboard, wishing that I had still a third, even more difficult

piece to play for her. I wanted to tell her that I was the school spelling bee champion, that I wasn't ticklish, that I could do karate.

"My mother is a concert pianist," I said. **D**

She looked at me for a long moment, then finally, without saying anything, hugged me. I didn't say anything about bringing the umbrella to Eugenie at school.

The steps were dry when Mona and I sat down to wait for my mother.

"Do you want to wait inside?" Miss Crosman looked anxiously at the sky.

"No," I said. "Our mother will be here any minute."

"In a while," said Mona.

"Any minute," I said again, even though my mother had been at least twenty minutes late every week since she started working.

According to the church clock across the street we had been waiting twenty-five minutes when Miss Crosman came out again.

"Shall I give you ladies a ride home?"

"No," I said. "Our mother is coming any minute."

"Shall I at least give her a call and remind her you're here? Maybe she forgot about you."

"I don't think she _forgot_," said Mona.

"Shall I give her a call anyway? Just to be safe?"

"I bet she already left," I said. "How could she forget about us?"

Miss Crosman went in to call.

"There's no answer," she said, coming back out.

"See, she's on her way," I said.

"Are you sure you wouldn't like to come in?"

E

---

3. **boot camp.** Camp for military basic training, usually perceived as being surprisingly tough

---

THE WHITE UMBRELLA **185**

Teach the Selection

Use Reading Skills

Infer Author's Perspective Have students explain what the narrator's imaginary conversation with her mother reveals about the author's perspective on growing up in an immigrant family in America. Model a response: "The clash of cultures can make it a struggle for children who want to fit in and be like everyone else." **C**

Use Reading Skills

Compare and Contrast Ask students to think about why the narrator lies to Miss Crosman about her mother's being a concert pianist. Tell them to ask themselves if this suggests a change in the narrator's personality or attitude since the beginning of the story. **D**

Analyze Literature

Setting Ask students to describe the shift in setting from the previous passage and explain how this shift affects the story. (The setting has shifted from inside the house to outside, where the narrator and her sister wait for their mother to pick them up. This provides an opportunity for the teacher to offer the girls a ride home and dinner, and for the narrator to maintain her lie.) **E**

Differentiated Instruction

Reading Proficiency

Use "The White Umbrella" as an example of how students can use figurative language to express ideas in speaking and writing. Provide examples of similes from the selection (such as "The umbrella glowed like a scepter") and discuss the image that the simile brings to mind. Then ask students to choose an object in the classroom, and have them use a simile to describe it. Encourage students to keep a notebook of similes that they encounter as they read, either examples that appeal to them or phrases they create themselves.

Gish Jen believes her characters and their struggles transcend ethnic boundaries, so she sometimes bristles when reviewers classify her as an Asian-American author. Still, Jen does focus on Asian-American characters with problems that arise from their cultural background, and she admits it's impossible for her to separate the creative process from her heritage. According to reviewers, what distinguishes Jen from other Asian-American female authors is her sardonic wit and her ability to make readers ask themselves, "Who am I?"

Use Reading Skills

Compare and Contrast Have students explain how Mona's attitude toward her mother's job shows that she has not changed during the story, and how this contrasts to her sister's attitude. (At the beginning of the story, Mona couldn't understand why she shouldn't say anything about her mother's job, and here she expresses the same attitude. In contrast, her sister will lie to keep it a secret.) **A**

Analyze Literature

Mood Ask students how the mood changes after Miss Crosman offers the narrator a blanket and umbrella. (The mood changes from a feeling of cold despair and loneliness to a sudden feeling of warmth and hopeful expectation.) **B**

"No," said Mona.

"Yes," I said. I pointed at my sister. "She meant yes too. She meant no, she wouldn't like to go in."

Miss Crosman looked at her watch. "It's 5:30 now, ladies. My pot roast will be coming out in fifteen minutes. Maybe you'd like to come in and have some then?"

"My mother's almost here," I said. "She's on her way."

We watched and watched the street. I tried to imagine what my mother was doing; I tried to imagine her writing messages in the sky, even though I knew she was afraid of planes. I watched as the branches of Miss Crosman's big willow tree started to sway; they had all been trimmed to exactly the same height off the ground, so that they looked beautiful, like hair in the wind.

It started to rain.

"Miss Crosman is coming out again," said Mona.

"Don't let her talk you into going inside," I whispered.

"Why not?"

"Because that would mean Mom isn't really coming any minute."

A "But she isn't," said Mona. "She's *working*."

"Shhh! Miss Crosman is going to hear you."

"She's working! She's working! She's working!"

I put my hand over her mouth, but she licked it, and so I was wiping my hand on my wet dress when the front door opened.

"We're getting even *wetter*," said Mona right away. "Wetter and wetter."

"Shall we all go in?" Miss Crosman pulled Mona to her feet. "Before you young ladies catch pneumonia? You've been out here an hour already."

"We're *freezing*." Mona looked up at Miss Crosman. "Do you have any hot chocolate? We're going to catch *pneumonia*."

"I'm not going in," I said. "My mother's coming any minute."

"Come on," said Mona. "Use your *noggin*."[4]

"Any minute."

"Come on, Mona," Miss Crosman opened the door. "Shall we get you inside first?"

"See you in the hospital," said Mona as she went in. "See you in the hospital with *pneumonia*."

I stared out into the empty street. The rain was pricking me all over; I was cold; I wanted to go inside. I wanted to be able to let myself go inside. If Miss Crosman came out again, I decided, I would go in.

B She came out with a blanket and the white umbrella.

I could not believe that I was actually holding the umbrella, opening it. It sprang up by itself as if it were alive, as if that were what it wanted to do—as if it belonged in my hands, above my head. I stared up at the network of silver spokes, then spun the umbrella around and around and around. It was so clean and white that it seemed to glow, to illuminate everything around it. "It's beautiful," I said.

Miss Crosman sat down next to me, on one end of the blanket. I moved the umbrella over so that it covered that too. I could feel the rain on my left shoulder and shivered. She put her arm around me.

"You poor, poor dear."

I knew that I was in store for another bolt of sympathy, and braced myself by staring up into the umbrella.

"You know, I very much wanted to have children when I was younger," she continued.

"You did?"

She stared at me a minute. Her face looked dry and crusty, like day-old frosting.

---

4. **noggin.** Head

Sensory Details

Point out that using sensory details helps writers create vivid pictures in readers' minds, heightening their interest and involvement in the text. Call attention to Jen's use of sensory details in this story, For example, help students recognize why having the narrator say "a quivering sun lit their way" and "An entire constellation rose in my heart" conveys so much more about the narrator's personality and feelings than if she had simply said "It was sunny" and "I was happy."

Ask students to find a passage in their own writing—using their journals or assignments they have saved—that they can improve with sensory details. After they have changed the passage, have them describe the changes to a classmate.

"I did. But then I never got married."

I twirled the umbrella around again.

"This is the most beautiful umbrella I have ever seen," I said. "Ever, in my whole life."

"Do you have an umbrella?"

"No. But my mother's going to get me one just like this for Christmas."

"Is she? I tell you what. You don't have to wait until Christmas. You can have this one."

"But this one belongs to Eugenie Roberts," I protested. "I have to give it back to her tomorrow in school."

"Who told you it belongs to Eugenie? It's not Eugenie's. It's mine. And now I'm giving it to you, so it's yours."

"It is?"

She hugged me tighter. "That's right. It's all yours."

"It's mine?" I didn't know what to say. "Mine?" Suddenly I was jumping up and down in the rain. "It's beautiful! Oh! It's beautiful!" I laughed.

Miss Crosman laughed too, even though she was getting all wet

"Thank you, Miss Crosman. Thank you very much. Thanks a zillion. It's beautiful. It's *stupendous!*"

I could not believe that I was actually holding the umbrella, opening it.

"You're quite welcome," she said.

"Thank you," I said again, but that didn't seem like enough. Suddenly I knew just what she wanted to hear. "I wish you were my mother."

Right away I felt bad.

"You shouldn't say that," she said, but her face was opening into a huge smile as the lights of my mother's car cautiously turned the corner. I quickly collapsed the umbrella and put it up my skirt, holding onto it from the outside, through the material.

"Mona!" I shouted into the house. "Mona! Hurry up! Mom's here! I told you she was coming!"

Then I ran away from Miss Crosman, down to the curb. Mona came tearing up to my side as my mother neared the house. We both backed up a few feet so that in case she went onto the curb, she wouldn't run us over.

"But why didn't you go inside with Mona?" my mother asked on the way home. She had taken off her own coat to put over me and had the heat on high.

"She wasn't using her noggin," said Mona, next to me in the back seat.

"I should call next time," said my mother. "I just don't like to say where I am."

That was when she finally told us that she was working as a check-out clerk in the A&P.[5] She was supposed to be on the day shift, but the other employees were unreliable, and her boss had promised her a promotion if she would stay until the evening shift filled in.

For a moment no one said anything. Even Mona seemed to find the revelation disappointing.

---

5. A&P. Grocery store

---

rev·e·la·tion (re' və lā´ shən) *n.*, act of revealing or showing, usually something astonishing or enlightening

THE WHITE UMBRELLA **187**

Teach the Selection

Cultural Connection

Umbrellas In Chinese custom, umbrellas are never given as gifts; they are signs of bad luck. The Chinese word for *umbrella* sounds like a Chinese word that means "separation" or "break apart," so giving an umbrella is a sign that a relationship will end. On the other hand, in the ancient Chinese culture, the umbrella, or parasol, was associated with royalty and rank. It shaded the person carrying it from the sun, and therefore became a symbol of protection. **C**

Analyze Literature

Characterization Ask students to describe the teacher's personality using details in the story. (She is kind. She offers the girls towels to dry off, praises students' piano playing, and offers to drive the girls home and give them supper. She gives the narrator the umbrella. She doesn't reveal that she suspects the narrator is lying about her mother.)

Analyze Literature

Plot Ask students if the umbrella solves the narrator's problem. Model a response: "The narrator coveted the umbrella, so she is overjoyed when Miss Crosman gives it to her. But instead of saying thank you, she says, 'I wish you were my mother,' which she immediately regrets. When she sees her mother she feels guilty. She hides the umbrella because it now represents a betrayal of her mother." **D**

Differentiated Instruction

Enrichment

Interested students may enjoy working independently or with a partner to write an ode to the white umbrella that so captivated the narrator. Explain that an *ode* is usually a serious poem, written in a lofty style as a tribute to a person or a thing. Provide an example of formal and serious odes, such as "Ode to the West Wind" by Percy

Bysshe Shelley and "Ode on a Grecian Urn" by John Keats, as well as an example of a more light-hearted ode, such as Pablo Neruda's "Ode to My Socks."

Suggest that students skim the story for sensory and concrete details about the umbrella that they can incorporate into their odes.

Use Reading Skills

Compare and Contrast Remind students to record their final impressions of the narrator's personality in their character charts so that they can compare those impressions to their impressions at the beginning of and during the story.

Analyze Literature

Mood Ask students to compare the mood surrounding the umbrella earlier in the story to the mood surrounding it at the end. (The mood changes from dreamy and magical to one of harsh reality.)

Answer: Most students will identify with having mixed feelings. Some may say that they would be unable to act at all in the narrator's situation. Others may say they would act on one or the other emotion, that they would behave unpredictably, or that they would act upset.

"A promotion already!" she said, finally. I listened to the windshield wipers.

"You're so quiet." My mother looked at me in the rear view mirror. "What's the matter?"

"I wish you would quit," I said after a moment.

She sighed. "The Chinese have a saying: one beam cannot hold the roof up."

"But Eugenie Roberts's father supports their family."

She sighed once more. "Eugenie Roberts's father is Eugenie Roberts's father," she said.

As we entered the downtown area, Mona started leaning hard against me every time the car turned right, trying to push me over. Remembering what I had said to Miss Crosman, I tried to maneuver the umbrella under my leg so she wouldn't feel it.

"What's under your skirt?" Mona wanted to know as we came to a traffic light. My mother, watching us in the rear view mirror again, rolled slowly to a stop.

"What's the matter?" she asked.

"There's something under her skirt," said Mona, pulling at me. "Under her skirt."

Meanwhile, a man crossing the street started to yell at us. "Who do you think you are, lady?" he said. "You're blocking the whole crosswalk."

We all froze. Other people walking by stopped to watch.

"Didn't you hear me?" he went on, starting to thump on the hood with his fist.

"Don't you speak English?"

My mother began to back up, but the car behind us honked. Luckily, the light turned green right after that. She sighed in relief.

"What were you saying, Mona?" she asked.

We wouldn't have hit the car behind us that hard if he hadn't been moving too but as it was, our car bucked violently, throwing us all first back and then forward.

"Uh oh," said Mona when we stopped. "Another accident."

I was relieved to have attention diverted from the umbrella. Then I noticed my mother's head, tilted back onto the seat. Her eyes were closed.

"Mom!" I screamed. "Mom! Wake up!"

She opened her eyes. "Please don't yell," she said. "Enough people are going to yell already."

"I thought you were dead," I said, starting to cry. "I thought you were dead."

She turned around, looked at me intently, then put her hand to my forehead.

"Sick," she confirmed. "Some kind of sick is giving you crazy ideas."

As the man from the car behind us started tapping on the window, I moved the umbrella away from my leg. Then Mona and my mother were getting out of the car. I got out after them; and while everyone else was inspecting the damage we'd done, I threw the umbrella down a sewer. ❖

When have you felt two emotions, like shame and anger, at the same time? What kinds of things make people feel conflicting emotions?

Differentiated Instruction

Kinesthetic Learning

Have volunteers dramatize one of the conversations in the story. Provide time for the entire class to review the selected conversation, paying special attention to the words, facial expressions, and gestures that the characters use, and how these contribute to the tone and mood of the conversation. After the dramatization, have students evaluate the performance, using the following criteria:

- Was it entertaining?
- Was it easy to understand and follow?
- Did performers use appropriate facial expressions, gestures, and tones of voice?
- Did performers correctly interpret the mood and tone of the conversation?

Find Meaning

1. (a) Which of the narrator's parents is the focus of the story? (b) Why doesn't the narrator want other people to know about her parents?
2. (a) What are some lies the narrator tells to the piano teacher? (b) Why does she lie?
3. (a) How does the piano teacher show her sympathy for the narrator? (b) How does the narrator respond to the piano teacher?
4. How is the narrator feeling when her mother arrives at the piano teacher's house?

Analyze Literature

Mood Description helps establish the mood of a story. Review the part of the story when both girls are waiting for their mother after the piano lesson, before Mona goes inside. Look for sensory details and pay attention to the narrator's thoughts. Put those things in the outer circles of a cluster chart. Then write one or two words in the center circle that capture the mood.

Make Judgments

5. How does the narrator change over the course of the story? What aspects of her personality stay the same?
6. What does the white umbrella represent to the narrator when she sees it at Miss Crosman's house?
7. Why does the narrator throw away the umbrella?

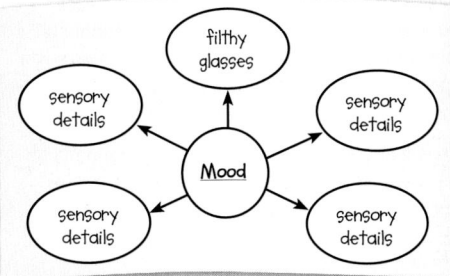

Extend Understanding

Writing Options

Creative Writing Imagine that you are the narrator of "The White Umbrella." Write a **diary entry** about why you threw the umbrella down the sewer. Use the diary to work through your motivations. In other words, try to explain your actions to yourself. At the end of the entry, write one sentence that summarizes why you threw away the umbrella.

Expository Writing Write an **expository paragraph** about the tone of "The White Umbrella." Tone is the writer's attitude toward his or her subject. It can be funny, sad, or serious, for example. Introduce your paragraph with a topic sentence that names the overall tone of the story. Give examples of how the writer creates this tone. Conclude by stating how the tone might affect a reader's response.

Collaborative Learning

Relate Mood to Point of View With a partner, talk about how the first-person point of view affects the mood of "The White Umbrella." Ask each other such questions as: How do the narrator's feelings about her family affect the mood? How do her feelings about herself affect the mood? Write a sentence that relates the mood to the first-person point of view.

Lifelong Learning

Explore a Symbol In Chinese culture, the umbrella has a long history as a cultural symbol and a practical device. Learn more about China's relationship with the umbrella. Use reference books or Internet search engines. Search with terms such as *umbrella*, *China*, and *history*. Use visual aids to present your findings to the class.

Go to **www.mirrorsandwindows.com** for more.

THE WHITE UMBRELLA **189**

Find Meaning

1. (a) The narrator's mother is the focus. (b) She worries that others may judge her family harshly.
2. (a) She says that the family car is a convertible; that her mother is a concert pianist, will "be here any minute," and will get her an umbrella for Christmas; and that she wishes Miss Crosman were her mother. (b) She may be trying to impress the teacher or cover up her insecurities.
3. (a) The teacher does not challenge the narrator's lies or force her to come inside. She brings her a blanket and gives her the umbrella. (b) The narrator ignores some kindnesses and shows gratitude for the umbrella.
4. The narrator is relieved to see her mother, but feels guilty because of what she said to Miss Crosman.

Make Judgments

5. The narrator is bossy and defensive. However, after receiving the umbrella she starts to feel guilty about betraying her mother and realizes that she needs her mother more than the umbrella.
6. It probably represents prosperity.
7. The umbrella now represents the narrator's selfishness and discontent.

Analyze Literature

Mood Details include the dry steps, Miss Crosman looking anxiously at the sky and her watch, the willow branches looking like hair, and the rain. The narrator thinks a lot about time. She imagines her mother writing in the sky. The mood could be tense, unsettling, or anticipatory.

Rubrics for Writing Options

You can adapt this as a checklist for students to use as they write.

Creative Writing

☐ Did the student adopt the persona of the narrator?
☐ Does the student include one or more motivations for throwing away the umbrella?
☐ Does the final sentence summarize the student's reasoning?

Expository Writing

☐ Does the topic sentence name a single, overall tone?
☐ Does the body include examples of how the writer creates the tone through her use of language?
☐ Does the conclusion suggest an effect this tone could have on a reader?

Identifying Clauses

1. As Eugenie and her mother left (dependent) the rain stopped falling (independent)

2. She wanted the white umbrella (independent) that Eugenie had left behind (dependent)

3. Miss Crosman praised Eugenie (independent) because she played so well (dependent)

4. The two girls stood (independent) where the rain was falling (dependent)

5. The narrator played a piano piece (independent) that she had not been assigned (dependent)

6. She held the umbrella (independent) as if it belonged to her (dependent)

7. As the man crossed the street (dependent) he yelled at us (independent)

8. Miss Crosman sat down on the couch (independent) where the narrator was sitting (dependent)

9. The girls' mother arrived (independent) after her shift at the grocery was through (dependent)

10. When their mother was late (dependent) the girls would start dinner (independent)

➤ For more information, see Grammar & Style Section 3.12, Clauses, in the Language Arts Handbook.

Independent and Dependent Clauses

When I was twelve, my mother went to work without telling me or my little sister.

—GISH JEN, "The White Umbrella"

An **independent** (or main) clause has a subject and a predicate and can function as a complete sentence. A **dependent** (or subordinate) clause also has a subject and a predicate but cannot stand alone. In the passage above, *When I was twelve* is a dependent clause. It cannot stand by itself as a complete sentence.

Dependent clauses can function as several parts of speech. Two common types of dependent clauses are adverb and adjective clauses.

Adverb Clauses

An **adverb clause** is a dependent clause that functions as an adverb. Like adverbs, adverb clauses answer such questions as when, where, why, and how an action took place. In the passage above, for example, the dependent clause modifies the verb *went* and tells when this action occurred.

> EXAMPLE
>
> *She ran to the window, so that she could see the street.*

In this example, the dependent clause *so that she could see the street* modifies the verb *ran* and tells why the action took place.

Adjective Clauses

An **adjective clause** is a dependent clause that functions as an adjective. Like adjectives, adjective clauses modify nouns or pronouns.

> EXAMPLE
>
> *The narrator's family lives in a town that has only one other Chinese family.*

In this example, the adjective clause *that has only one other Chinese family* modifies the noun *town*.

> EXAMPLE
>
> *They who arrive first will get the best seats.*

In this example, the adjective clause *who arrive first* modifies the pronoun *they*.

Identifying Clauses

For each of the following sentences, identify the independent and dependent clauses.

1. As Eugenie and her mother left, the rain stopped falling.
2. She wanted the white umbrella that Eugenie had left behind.
3. Miss Crosman praised Eugenie because she played so well.
4. The two girls stood where the rain was falling.
5. The narrator played a piano piece that she had not been assigned.
6. She held the umbrella as if it belonged to her.
7. As the man crossed the street, he yelled at us.
8. Miss Crosman sat down on the couch where the narrator was sitting.
9. The girls' mother arrived after her shift at the grocery store was through.
10. When their mother was late, the girls would start dinner.

KEY TERMS

INDEPENDENT CLAUSE, 190	VERB, 190
PREDICATE, 190	ADJECTIVE CLAUSE, 190
COMPLETE SENTENCE, 190	NOUNS, 190
DEPENDENT CLAUSE, 190	PRONOUNS, 190
ADVERB CLAUSE, 190	

Jed's Grandfather
A Short Story by Joseph Bruchac

The Courage That My Mother Had
A Lyric Poem by Edna St. Vincent Millay

Preview the Selections

At a Glance
Directed Reading
"Jed's Grandfather"
- Reading Level: Moderate
- Difficulty Consideration: Subject matter
- Ease Factor: Length

"The Courage That My Mother Had"
- Reading Level: Easy
- Difficulty Consideration: Metaphors
- Ease Factor: Length

BEFORE READING

Build Background
Literary Context The setting of a literary work—place and time—almost always contributes to its meaning. Bruchac's story has both a real setting and a dream setting, both of which help the reader understand the characters and what happens in the plot. Millay's poem mentions a place, New England, in describing a person.

Reader's Context Think of elderly relatives you have known. What do you admire about them? Have they ever been ill? How did this make you feel?

Set Purpose
Read the first three paragraphs of "Jed's Grandfather," and then read the title of Edna St. Vincent Millay's poem. Try to think of what both writers seem to value about people. Then read both works to find out if these values stay consistent throughout the texts.

Compare Literature:
Tone The writer's or speaker's attitude toward his or her subject is the **tone.** Word choice is a key tool for creating tone: How a writer says things implies how he or she feels. To help you detect tone, consider the words the author uses along with the connotations of those words. Use a three-column chart like this to compare the tone of each piece.

	Bruchac	Millay
Details	pancakes don't taste right	
Tone		

Preview Vocabulary
trough (trôf) *n.*, long, shallow container

kind·ling (kin´ [d] liŋ) *n.*, material used to start a fire, often dry sticks

teth·er (te´ thər) *n.*, rope or chain that allows an animal to move in a limited area

Objectives
Studying this lesson will enable students to
- compare literary selections of different genres
- use reading strategies such as asking questions and clarifying
- define tone and recognize how a writer establishes tone
- compare the effects of tone in two literary works
- enjoy literature about the wisdom and strength of elders

Launch the Lesson
In "Jed's Grandfather," the main character identifies with a sparrow and compares his grandfather to an ash tree. Ask students to write down one thing in nature that they identify with. Have students share and explain their choices.

Before reading "The Courage That My Mother Had," have students complete the following sentence starter: *Courage is _____.* Then ask them to think of someone whose life is an example of that kind of courage.

Meet the Authors

Joseph Bruchac (b. 1942) was raised by his grandparents in the Adirondack Mountains of New York. By heritage he is part Native American (Abenaki), and he draws on that heritage in his writing and storytelling.

Edna St. Vincent Millay (1892–1950) grew up on the coast of Maine. Her parents divorced when she was eight, after which she and her sisters lived with their mother, a nurse. Millay wrote poetry and plays almost all of her life.

JED'S GRANDFATHER / THE COURAGE THAT MY MOTHER HAD **191**

Words in Use

"Jed's Grandfather"

Preview Vocabulary
trough, 192
kindling, 193
tether, 194

Selection Words
enamel, 193
percale, 194
raucous, 196

Teaching Words
consistent, 191
inspiration, 198
foundation, 198
linguistic, 198
authoritative, 198

KEY TERMS
SHORT STORY, 191
LYRIC POEM, 191
SETTING, 191
TONE, 191
CONNOTATION, 191
SYMBOL, 198
COMPARE, 198
CONTRAST, 198

Common Core State Standards
Reading Literature
RL.1

Summary

Jed has a disturbing dream in which he becomes separated from his grandfather and then can only watch as his grandfather is about to be swept away in a wave. The dream reflects the sadness and helplessness Jed feels because his beloved grandfather is dying of cancer. Jed has avoided visiting his grandfather's house, but when his mother asks him to take his grandfather breakfast, Jed cannot refuse. While Jed and his grandfather, who has stopped eating, feed the breakfast to the gulls, Jed becomes aware of his grandfather's quiet acceptance of death and realizes that he must accept it, too.

MIRRORS & WINDOWS

The Mirrors & Windows questions at the end of "Jed's Grandfather," and at the end of "The Courage That My Mother Had" on page 197, focus on the theme of inheritance.

Before students begin reading the story, ask: Why do so many older people seem wise?

Before students begin reading the poem, ask: What is special about things we inherit?

Jed's Grandfather

A Short Story by Joseph Bruchac

Jed slowly worked the handle of the backyard pitcher pump. He watched the water lap from side to side in waves as he tilted the bucket back and forth. The patterns of the dream were still going through his head. They hadn't been washed away with the first splash of water from the <u>trough</u>, water so cold that a paper-thin layer of ice still had to be brushed away these early spring mornings. Washing his face usually cleared whatever cobwebs of sleep still clung to his face and his thoughts, but it hadn't happened this morning. The dream was still with him.

The swallows had flown up now. The red sun was a finger's width above the hill. He looked up and watched the swallows darting, stitching the face of the sky the way his mother's needle covered a piece of cloth. The other birds, shorter-winged, fluttered in groups, as if afraid to fly by themselves the way the swallows did. The swallows were the adventurous ones. He remembered how his grandfather first pointed out to him the way a swallow can dart down to the surface of a lake and scoop up a mouthful of water without landing. They had watched swallows

trough (trôf) *n.*, long, shallow container

192

Program Resources

Planning and Assessment
Program Planning Guide, Selection Lesson Plan
E-Lesson Planner
Assessment Guide, Lesson Test
ExamView

Technology Tools
Interactive Student Text on CD
Visual Teaching Package
Audio Library
mirrorsandwindows.com

Meeting the Standards
Fiction: Unit 2, Comparing Literature, pp. 54–61

Differentiating Instruction
Developing Readers, Make Predictions, pp. 16–18
English Language Learners, Main Ideas, pp. 64–69

doing that, drinking from the pond below the house that day last blueberry season[1] when Grandfather rowed him out to The Island.

Usually the sight of the swallows in the morning sky would drive everything else out of his thoughts. He'd arch his back, lift his chin, hold out his arms, hearing his Grandfather's soft voice guiding him. "You want to be a swallow, Jeddy? You can do it. Just feel the wind under ye. That's it."

That wouldn't work this morning. The dream was too strong. He was in the boat, dark water widening between them. The old man stood there on The Island, unaware of the great dark wave coming at him from behind. His eyes were on Jed, but Jed couldn't call out. He couldn't move his arms. He wanted to turn into a swallow, fly out and rescue him, but he was paralyzed. Then the water between them began to open like a crack in the earth...

"Jed!" It was his mother's voice. Jed looked up. The bucket was filled and overflowing around his feet. A chicken was scurrying around the edge of the spreading water, now and then lifting a foot and shaking it as the water touched it. Jed carried the bucket into the kitchen.

His parents were at the table. Jed bent his arms and arched his back, hefting the bucket up onto the sink shelf.

"You're getting stronger every day, son," his father said, thin hand around a steaming mug. Behind him the wood stove crackled, a sound Jed had always loved. The steam from his father's coffee rose through the cold morning air of the kitchen. Jed could smell the coffee. It was a good smell, just as good

but not quite the same as that smell when he ground the beans in the coffee mill with its blue enamel sides. But even the good smell of the coffee couldn't drive away the dream. It was there, between him and the things which were good and pleasant in his life, there the way a thick fog comes between a boat and the land. He was on the boat. He didn't know which way was home. **A**

Jed's mother smiled at him, wiped her hands on her apron. It was the first time he had really noticed the way his mother always wiped her hands on her apron before she spoke when they were at the table. She used the same care with her words that she did in making their food. All around Jed were familiar things, things known and loved, but he was seeing them for the first time...the small crystal dog in the east window where a bull's-eye pane of glass split the sun like a prism and painted a rainbow on the wall near the stairs...the woodbox with its splintery top which sometimes snagged his left thumb when he went for an armful of <u>kindling</u>...the rocking chair which always caught the last rays of the setting sun, the chair which was empty now... **C**

"He just takes after his..." his mother was saying. She stopped in mid-sentence. Jed finished the sentence in his own mind. *He takes after his grandfather.* Jed's father was a good man, hard-working, but he never had the strength of his wife's people, the Sabaels. That was why he worked as a clerk at the

Washing his face usually cleared whatever cobwebs of sleep still clung to his face and his thoughts, but it hadn't happened this morning.

---

1. **blueberry season.** July and August

kind • ling (kin´ [d] liŋ) *n.,* material used to start a fire, often dry sticks

Differentiated Instruction

Reading Proficiency
Have students use a plot line or a story map to keep track of characters and events in this story. Tell students to fill in the graphic organizer as they read. If they become confused about what is happening at any point in the story, they can look back at the details they have already recorded in their plot lines or story maps to refresh their memories about what has happened so far.

Kinesthetic Learning
Have kinesthetic learners pay attention to how birds and people move in this story. After they read, have them explain how these movements contribute to characterization.

Use Reading Strategies

Clarify Students may not realize that Jed is reliving his dream as he tries to eat his breakfast. For clarification, have students reread the first paragraph of the story and the paragraph on page 193 that describes the dream. **Ⓐ**

Analyze Literature

Tone Ask students how the choice of words that explain the tradition of basket making contributes to the tone of the story. Tell them to record these word choices in their comparison charts (see page 191). **Ⓑ**

Analyze Literature

Symbolism Ask students to interpret the symbolism of the small boat and its tether outside Jed's grandfather's house. Model a response: "I think the boat represents Jed's grandfather and its tether represents his ties to earth. Like the boat, Jed's grandfather may not be exerting a lot of energy to be free, but he is still anxious and ready to leave." **Ⓒ**

---

store in town three miles from the farm. It was Jed's grandfather, straight as an ash,[2] who always did the work around the farm. Jed was only ten, but he was already as strong as his father.

"Jed," his mother said, her hands smoothing her apron, "you aren't eating."

Ⓐ The pancakes were dry in his mouth. He knew they were good. They were the pancakes his mother was famous for at church socials. They were light and smelled of the goodness of a summer wheatfield, but he couldn't taste them. Instead he tasted the moist air within the fog, felt the pressure of the building storm throb around his temples as the great dark wave lifted.

Jed's father was saying something to his mother. What was it? Starving himself? Jed hadn't heard the words for sure over the roaring of the wave.

"Are you sure?" his mother said.

"You're his daughter," Jed's father answered. He spoke in the same quiet voice Jed heard him use when he answered a customer who asked what to buy to get rid of potato bugs or whether the percale was what she really wanted for her money's worth.

Jed's mother rose and walked over to the stove. She took the plate which had been warming there and covered it with a cloth. She put the cloth-covered plate, some silverware and a stoppered bottle into a **Ⓑ** basket. Jed recognized the basket. It was one Grandfather made. He remembered the sounds of the mallet as his grandfather pounded the side of the felled ash tree to break loose the withes[3] he'd trim to size. His grandfather had shown him the steps many times, shown him by doing. He felt as if the way of making a basket was woven into

"Come," the old man called out, making that simple word one of many meanings.

him the way the pattern of a web is woven into a spider's limbs. It was a craft passed down for more generations than the Sabaels could count, passed down before Jed's father's people had stepped from their ships onto these shores. For a moment the thought of Grandfather's sure hands weaving a basket drove away the dream. Then the pounding of the mallet became the pounding of whitecaps against the side of the boat and he saw the old man's figure made small by the lifting darkness.

"Take this down to the Little House, Jed," his mother said. She was holding the basket out to him. Jed looked up into her eyes for a moment and then reached out his hand.

No smoke was rising from the chimney. Had it been rising it would have traced a perfect line up the face of the mountains and sky above Indian Lake. That was the way smoke rose on spring mornings such as this from the small one-roomed house his grandfather had built where the field fell away, green becoming the grey of stone, then the blue of **Ⓒ** water. A small boat was tied to a pole that jutted out of the water. The boat moved with the water the way a horse moves when tied to a rail...not pulling hard enough to break free, hardly even putting a strain on its <u>tether</u>, but showing in its motion how anxious it is to be on its way. The boat was still there. But there was no smoke.

Jed drew in a breath, feeling it catch in his stiff throat. But before he could speak he heard his grandfather's voice.

---

2. **ash.** Tree with thin bark and bendable wood
3. **withes.** Thin, bendable branches or twigs

teth·er (te´ thər) *n.*, rope or chain that allows an animal to move in a limited area

---

Differentiated Instruction

Visual Learning

Some students might find it helpful to illustrate different scenes in the story, such as the ones that describe Jed's dream, breakfast with his parents, and Jed's visit with his grandfather. Students can use their illustrations to discuss Jed's relationship to the characters and to summarize the whole story or parts of the story, which is a good way to check comprehension.

English Language Learning

English language learners will benefit from internalizing new, content-based words, such as *trough*, *kindling*, and *tether*. Ask students to write a paragraph that uses the three words and illustrates that they understand each word's meaning. Consider providing them with new basic words to incorporate into their paragraphs.

"Come," the old man called out, making that simple word one of many meanings. It meant he knew who was there. It meant Jed was welcome. It meant something else, too. It was like the words in the old language his grandfather seldom spoke, the language few people knew he knew. Jed pulled gently at the locust[4] post which held up the small open gate. It creaked as he pulled at it, but the old wood was still firm. A locust post can stay in the ground a hundred years and still bend any nail you're fool enough to try to drive into it. A hundred years.

Jed went in. Joseph Sabael was sitting on the edge of his cot. There was a blanket around his shoulders and he was wearing his woolens,[5] but his feet were bare. There was no rug on the floor, no fire in the stove. It was cold in the Little House, but not as cold as Jed had thought it would be. There was a faint odor in the air, one Jed had not really noticed before. It confused him.

"That's just how the cancer smells, Jeddy," his grandfather said. "Don't pay it no mind. It's just as natural as anything else."

Jed looked at him. Joseph Sabael had always been a tall man, but never one whose frame put on bulk. His shoulders had been broad, but not heavy. His arms had always been long and sinewy[6] like the others in the town who worked the land or the big woods, not the ham-thick sort of arm which turned to softness with age. Like an ash tree's limbs, that was how his grandfather's arms had seemed. But now there was a different look to the old man. His eyes had fallen back into their sockets and one could see the bones beneath the skin in his arms. As he sat hands clasping the blanket about him, it seemed as if his shoulders were folding in around his chest. Jed held out the basket.

---

4. **locust.** Tree with hard, stiff wood
5. **woolens.** Warm underclothing
6. **sinewy.** Tough and stringy

Cultural Connection
Native American Elders In traditional Native American culture, elders (grandparents and great-grandparents) are revered in the family and the entire tribal community. According to custom, elders teach children the Native language and pass on family values, beliefs, and traditions, while simultaneously instilling a sense of pride in their heritage. **D**

Analyze Literature
Setting Have students describe the inside of Joseph Sabael's house in their own words. Ask them how the setting details contribute to tone. (The details describe a cold place with an odd odor. Students may say the tone is stark or bleak.) **E**

Use Reading Skills
Draw Conclusions Ask students what the description of Jed's grandfather suggests. Are they surprised by this? (Most students will conclude that Jed's grandfather is sick and dying. Most won't be surprised, because Jed's dream and sadness in the story have pointed to this.) **F**

Writing Skills

Character Sketch
Tell students that a character sketch is a brief word picture that captures a person's essence. A character sketch often includes a description of a person's physical appearance, personality traits, relationships with other people, interests, and opinions and beliefs about life.

Ask students to write a one-paragraph character sketch of either Jed or his grandfather. Tell them to reread the story, looking for details to include in the sketch. After they have finished their sketches, have students share them with the class. Students may find it interesting to note features that other students chose to include in their sketches.

Answer: Most will say Jed inherits physical strength and feelings for nature, and will recommend taking an interest in older relatives.

Find Meaning

1. (a) He observes swallows, shorter-winged birds, a chicken, and gulls. (b) He would like to be a swallow, to fly alone, to be adventurous, and to rescue his grandfather.

2. (a) Jed smells coffee and his grandfather's cancer. (b) The coffee represents home. The cancer smell represents his grandfather's death.

3. In the dream, the boat is where Jed is paralyzed and disoriented. In real life, Jed's grandfather used the boat to row Jed to The Island.

4. Grandfather may be starving himself.

Make Judgments

5. (a) Jed's grandfather once had physical strength. Students may also cite his knowledge. (b) Jed takes after his grandfather physically. It disturbs Jed that his grandfather is losing strength.

6. It makes Jed less worried and makes him admire his grandfather.

7. (a) It makes Jed feel paralyzed, trapped, powerless, and afraid. (b) Jed visits his grandfather and together they feed the gulls. Jed begins to accept his grandfather's coming death.

"Mama sent you this," he said.

"I be glad she let you come," Grandfather said. He didn't reach out his hands for the basket.

"I wasn't sure I wanted to until now," Jed said. He heard his own voice as if it were the voice of a stranger.

His grandfather nodded. Very slowly, he got up from the bed. It seemed to Jed as if he were watching something happen as strange and wonderful, as magical as a tree uprooting itself and stepping across the woodlot.[7] Joseph Sabael walked very slowly to the back door of the Little House. Jed opened it for him. Together they stepped out into the light from the open water, a light which made Jed's eyes squint against the brightness of it all. His grandfather sat down carefully in the rough wooden chair which faced The Island. Again Jed smelled that strange odor, but now he knew what it was and he was not confused. It was his grandfather's death.

Gulls began swooping down in front of them. They were grey and white. From their yellow beaks came those raucous squawks which seemed to Jed to be the one thing which linked them to the rock they flew up from. Those voices, rough and filled with the earth, were all that kept the gulls from flying up and up forever until they blended with the sky.

His grandfather made a small motion with his hand and Jed opened the basket. He removed the cloth from the plate. The heat rose up to touch the back of his hand. With his fingers he broke the pancakes up into small pieces. Then, piece by piece, he tossed them up into the air. Swooping, diving, squabbling in mid-air, the gulls caught them all. Not one piece touched the waveless lake. ❖

---

7. **woodlot.** Place where people grow trees to use for fuel, building, and paper

---

MIRRORS & WINDOWS

What has Jed inherited from his grandfather? Have you inherited anything similar from one of your grandparents? How can a person be sure to receive knowledge from previous generations?

Find Meaning

1. (a) What kinds of birds does Jed observe in the story? (b) Which kind of bird would Jed like to be, and why?

2. (a) What are two different smells Jed experiences in the story? (b) What do these smells represent?

3. What role does the boat play in Jed's dream and in his real life?

4. Who in the story is starving himself?

Make Judgments

5. (a) What kind or kinds of strength does Jed's grandfather have? (b) How does this strength affect Jed?

6. Near the end of the story, as his grandfather stands, "It seemed to Jed as if he were watching something happen as strange and wonderful, as magical as a tree uprooting itself and stepping across the woodlot." What do you think this image suggests about Jed's thoughts and feelings?

7. (a) How does Jed's lingering dream make him feel? (b) What happens in the story that frees Jed from the feeling of the dream?

Differentiated Instruction

Enrichment

Encourage students to express their own feelings about death and dying in a poem, short story, or personal essay. Students might wish to write about their own experiences with losing a loved one. However, for some students this topic may be too difficult or painful. Suggest, instead, that they write about the repeated cycle of living and dying in nature.

Before students begin writing, encourage them to explore symbols that they could use to represent death and the process of dying in their writing. Suggest that they create a web with the phrase "death and dying" in the center, and possible symbols in the radiating circles. Students can refer to their webs as they write.

The **Courage**
That My Mother Had

A Lyric Poem by
Edna St. Vincent Millay

Teach the Selection

Analyze Literature

Tone Ask students to focus on lines 9 and 10 and think about how the words and punctuation contribute to the overall tone of the poem. Model a response: "The words sound cold to me. The exclamation point and dash make me think the speaker is angry or annoyed with her mother." **A**

MIRRORS
WINDOWS

Answer: Students may say it is wrong to want to inherit something specific, because having a particular desire may lead to disappointment. Others may say it is right to want to inherit something they admire.

The courage that my mother had
Went with her, and is with her still:
Rock from New England quarried;[1]
Now granite in a granite[2] hill.

The golden brooch[3] my mother wore
She left behind for me to wear;
I have no thing I treasure more:
Yet, it is something I could spare.

Oh, if instead she'd left to me
The thing she took into the grave!— **A**
That courage like a rock, which she
Has no more need of, and I have. ❖

---
1. **quarried.** Excavated; dug
2. **granite.** Very hard igneous rock
3. **brooch.** Piece of jewelry worn as a pin near the neck

MIRRORS
WINDOWS

If you had to pick just one thing to inherit from your mother or father, what would it be? Is it right to want to inherit something in particular?

197

Speaking & Listening Skills

Define Group Roles

Tell students that when they are assigned a group research project, each group member should take a specific responsibility. This ensures that the work is evenly distributed, no work is duplicated, and all the goals of the assignment are met. Students can apply the guidelines at right to define group roles for the Collaborative Learning activity on page 198.

- Choose a group leader to conduct meetings and record assignments, schedules, and so on. (This role can be rotated.)
- Choose one or two members to collect and organize research materials.
- Assign each member of the group a different type of resource to use for research, such as the Internet, periodicals, books, and interviews.

Common Core State Standards

Reading Literature
RL.1, RL.9

Review the Selections

Find Meaning

1. Her mother's courage is like "rock from New England quarried" and "granite in a granite hill."
2. (a) The speaker has a golden brooch. (b) The brooch has sentimental value to the speaker, and may have monetary value as well.
3. The speaker wants courage.

Make Judgments

4. (a) Gold is prettier and has more monetary value than rock. (b) The speaker would rather have the rocklike courage of her mother.
5. The speaker "needs" the courage, but the poem does not say why. Since the speaker's mother "has no more need of" it, the speaker may not want it to go to waste.
6. (a) Students will probably say the speaker would ask her mother for courage. (b) Students may imagine that the mother will give the courage willingly, or that she will tell the speaker to develop her own courage.

Compare Literature
Tone
1. Possibilities include *dark water widening, great dark wave, coming . . . from behind, unaware, paralyzed, a crack in the earth,* and *roaring wave.*
2. Rock and granite suggest something hard and permanent. Their use contributes to a tone of longing because the speaker wants stability. The speaker treasures the brooch, but it is decorative, so it may symbolize something superficial and may contribute to a dissatisfied tone.

Comparing Literature

Find Meaning
1. To what does the speaker compare her mother's courage in the first stanza?
2. (a) What does the speaker have that belonged to her mother? (b) How valuable is it?
3. What does the speaker want that she does not have?

Compare Literature
Tone Both of these writers chose their words carefully. The connotations of some of those words influence the tone of each work. Refer to the chart in which you recorded the tone in "Jed's Grandfather" and "The Courage That My Mother Had" to answer the questions on the right.

Make Judgments
4. (a) How does gold compare to rock? (b) Which would the speaker rather have?
5. Why does the speaker want her mother's courage?
6. (a) If the speaker could talk to her mother, what do you think the speaker would say? (b) What would her mother say?

1. What words used to describe Jed's dream most influence the story's tone?
2. How do the words *rock, granite,* and *courage* contribute to the tone and theme of the poem?

Extend Understanding

Writing Options
Creative Writing Write a short **poem** that you could show to your own parents. Use either Bruchac's story or Millay's poem as inspiration. The poem should be about something you would like to inherit from a grandparent, an aunt or uncle, or one of your parents. Try to use at least one symbol in the poem, but no more than three. Draft your poem; then revise it to remove unnecessary words. When you think you are done, give it a title.

Expository Writing Write a paragraph in the form of a **compare-and-contrast essay** in which you compare and contrast the feelings of the speaker in Millay's poem with Jed's feelings for his grandfather. Use what you have determined about the tone of each piece as a foundation for describing these feelings. After you have synthesized these two selections into the essay, summarize the texts in a way that maintains their meaning and logical order.

Collaborative Learning
Study Native Languages Joseph Bruchac has spent much of his life learning about his Abenaki heritage. The Abenaki language is an Algonquian language. These were the languages of the native people who met the first North American colonists. In a small group, find out more about the native people from this linguistic family. Make brief summaries of what you learned and present your findings to the class.

Lifelong Learning
Dream Research Use resources in your school or public library to find out how Native Americans felt and thought about dreams. Find a resource that is authoritative and reliable. You may have to start by researching Native American folklore. When you know something about the role of dreams in Native American traditions, write a short paragraph about it. In a second paragraph, compare what you learned to the way your own culture views dreams today.

Go to www.mirrorsandwindows.com for more.

Rubrics for Writing Options
You can adapt this as a checklist for students to use as they write.

Creative Writing
☐ Is the poem about inheriting something from an older relative, and could the student show the poem to a parent?
☐ Does the poem draw inspiration from "Jed's Grandfather" or "The Courage That My Mother Had"?
☐ Does the poem include symbols?
☐ Does the poem have a title?

Expository Writing
☐ Does the paragraph describe the feelings of both the poem's speaker and Jed?
☐ Does the student compare and contrast tones?
☐ Does the summary maintain meaning and a logical order?

Antaeus

A Short Story by Borden Deal

At a Glance
Directed Reading
- Reading Level: Moderate
- Difficulty Consideration: Vocabulary
- Ease Factor: Interesting plot

DIRECTED READING

BEFORE READING

Build Background
Historical Context During the Great Depression of the 1930s, the farm economy collapsed in much of the South. When the United States entered World War II in 1941, many farm laborers had already moved to the cities to look for work. The war industries, such as steel making and ammunition production, drew even more workers to the cities. "Antaeus" is set in a city during World War II.

Reader's Context What connects you to the place you live? If you moved, could you reproduce that feeling somewhere else?

Set Purpose
Preview "Antaeus" by reading the first paragraph. Use the paragraph to predict the story's plot and theme.

Analyze Literature
Conflict The **plot** in a work of fiction usually develops because of a **conflict,** or struggle. A conflict can be *internal,* within a single character. A conflict can also be *external,* between a character and an outside force. As you read, identify the main character and the type of conflict.

Use Reading Skills
Context Clues Preview the vocabulary words as they appear in the sentences below. Try to unlock the meaning of each word using the context clues in the sentences.

1. From the highest tower, the queen could see all of her land, the full extent of her <u>domain.</u>
2. The cat slept so deeply in the sunlight that its feet did not even twitch; its body was totally <u>inert.</u>
3. The child <u>flourished</u> with good food and loving care, growing five inches in one summer.

Preview Vocabulary
do•main (dō mān´) *n.,* land that a person owns; rightful territory

la•bo•ri•ous (lə bôr´ ē əs) *adj.,* produced by hard work

in•ert (i nɐrt´) *adj.,* still; unmoving

des•e•crate (des´ i krāt´) *v.,* treat with disrespect

flour•ish (flɐr´ ish) *v.,* grow luxuriously

Meet the Author
Borden Deal (1922–1985) grew up in Mississippi as part of a farming family. His family lost its land in the Great Depression, and his father died when he was sixteen. Deal worked as a firefighter, on a showboat, and in the U.S. Navy. He began publishing novels in his mid-thirties, writing about life and culture in the South. Often, his novels and stories focus on the connections people have to the land and how these connections shape their identities.

Objectives
Studying this lesson will enable students to
- use reading skills such as context clues
- define conflict and recognize how causes and effects reveal a story's main conflict
- describe the literary accomplishments of Borden Deal and how his family history influenced his writing
- appreciate a story that contains a literary allusion

Launch the Lesson
Tell students that in "Antaeus," boys work together to build a garden on the top of a factory building. Ask students to think about the problems that building a rooftop garden would present and to offer suggestions for overcoming these problems. List ideas in a two-column Problem-Solution chart on the board. Students can then compare their ideas to what actually happens in the story.

ANTAEUS **199**

Preview Vocabulary
domain, 203
laborious, 205
inert, 205
desecrate, 206
flourish, 207

Selection Words
resolute, 202
obscure, 202
shrewd, 204
toilsome, 205
levied, 207

Teaching Words
ammunition, 199
canned, 203
insight, 210
consensus, 211

Common Core State Standards
Reading Literature
RL.1, RL.4

Antaeus

A Short Story by Borden Deal

Summary

It is wartime, and T. J.'s family has moved from a farm in rural Alabama to an apartment building in a northern city. A boy who lives in T. J.'s building takes T. J. to meet the members of his gang, who hang out on the roof of a nearby factory. T. J., who raised his own crops in Alabama, wants the gang to help him build a garden on the tar-covered roof. At first, the gang thinks he is insane, but soon they're lugging dirt up for their very own roof garden. The factory owner surprises the boys on the roof and vows to have the garden destroyed. An angry T. J. runs away after he and the boys destroy the garden themselves, and disappears for two weeks.

MIRRORS & WINDOWS The Mirrors & Windows questions at the end of the story focus on the theme of accomplishment. Before students begin reading, ask: Why do people get so much satisfaction from gardening and artistic pursuits?

200

Program Resources

Planning and Assessment
Program Planning Guide, Selection Lesson Plan
E-Lesson Planner
Assessment Guide, Lesson Test
ExamView

Technology Tools
Interactive Student Text on CD
Visual Teaching Package
Audio Library
mirrorsandwindows.com

Meeting the Standards
Fiction: Unit 2, Directed Reading, pp. 62–65

Differentiating Instruction
Advanced Students, Comparing Genres, p. 12
English Language Learners, Use Context Clues, pp. 70–85

Tenement Flats (Family Flats), c. 1934. Millard Sheets. Smithsonian American Art Museum, Washington, DC.

> *I remember the first day I took T. J. up there to meet the gang.*

This was during the wartime, when lots of people were coming North for jobs in factories and war industries, when people moved around a lot more than they do now, and sometimes kids were thrown into new groups and new lives that were completely different from anything they had ever known before. I remember this one kid, T. J. his name was, from somewhere down South, whose family moved into our building during that time. They'd come North with everything they owned piled into the back seat of an old-model sedan that you wouldn't expect could make the trip, with T. J. and his three younger sisters riding shakily on top of the load of junk.

Our building was just like all the others there, with families crowded into a few rooms, and I guess there were twenty-five or thirty kids about my age in that one building. Of course, there were a few of us who formed a gang and ran together all the time

after school, and I was the one who brought T. J. in and started the whole thing.

The building right next door to us was a factory where they made walking dolls. It was a low building with a flat, tarred roof that had a parapet[1] all around it about head-high, and we'd found out a long time before that no one, not even the watchman, paid any attention to the roof because it was higher than any of the other buildings around. So my gang used the roof as a headquarters. We could get up there by crossing over to the fire escape from our own roof on a plank and then going on up. It was a secret place for us, where nobody else could go without our permission.

I remember the day I first took T. J. up there to meet the gang. He was a stocky, robust kid with a shock of white hair, **A** nothing sissy about him except his voice; he

---

1. **parapet.** Low wall around the edge of a roof or platform

Teach the Selection

History Connection

Wartime Employment When the United States entered World War II, the country began to recover from the high unemployment rates of the Great Depression. However, most jobs were in factories that produced materials for fighting the war. Urban areas, which had already absorbed rural families during the Depression, grew even more crowded as farm families migrated to the cities in search of these factory jobs.

Analyze Literature

Setting Ask students to identify the setting. Then have them point out details in the first three paragraphs that show the story is set in a poor, crowded, industrial section of a northern city during the war.

Use Reading Skills

Use Context Clues Ask students how they can use context clues to figure out what the narrator means when he describes T. J. as robust. Model a response: "I'm not sure what *robust* means. The narrator says that T. J. was stocky and that there was nothing sissy about him. I know that a stocky person has a broad solid body, and that the word *sissy* often implies weakness. I think that the narrator is trying to say T. J. was strong and healthy looking." **A**

Differentiated Instruction

Reading Proficiency

Guide students through previewing and predicting. Read the Before Reading page and the quotations within the story. Suggest that students also skim the footnotes. Then have them predict what the story will be about. Next, read the first paragraph. Ask: "Would you like to modify your predictions or make new ones?"

Encourage students to keep predicting as they read. Assign specific places for students to stop and predict what will happen next. For example:

- after T. J. says "We could make our own field right here"
- after the three men in suits surprise the boys
- after Blackie tells T. J. "They own the building"

Use Reading Strategies

Make Inferences Point out to students that this is the second time the narrator says that T. J. was not a sissy. Ask students why they think the narrator feels it necessary to emphasize this fact. (The narrator and his friends call themselves a gang, which implies they think of themselves as tough. The narrator may be saying that T. J. qualified to be part of the gang because there was nothing timid or cowardly about him.) **Ⓐ**

Use Reading Skills

Use Context Clues Point to the word *resolute* in the text. Ask students to identify context clues in the surrounding text that could help them figure out that *resolute* means "displaying a firm or determined manner." Students should identify the phrase "knowledge of his rightness." **Ⓑ**

Analyze Literature

Conflict Ask students to describe T. J.'s conflict. Who or what are the opposing forces in this conflict? Model a response: "T. J. is used to living in a place where he can plant and raise crops, but in the city there are no such places. The conflict is between T. J.'s desire to make something grow and the city's cold, hard landscape."

---

talked in this slow, gentle voice like you never heard before. He talked different from any of us and you noticed it right away. But I liked him anyway, so I told him to come on up.

We climbed up over the parapet and dropped down on the roof. The rest of the gang were already there.

"Hi," I said. I jerked my thumb at T. J. "He just moved into the building yesterday."

He just stood there, not scared or anything, just looking, like the first time you see somebody you're not sure you're going to like.

"Hi," Blackie said. "Where are you from?"

"Marion County," T. J. said.

We laughed. "Marion County?" I said. "Where's that?"

He looked at me for a moment like I was a stranger, too. "It's in Alabama," he said, like I ought to know where it was.

"What's your name?" Charley said.

"T. J.," he said, looking back at him. He had pale blue eyes that looked washed-out but he looked directly at Charley, waiting for **Ⓐ** his reaction. He'll be all right, I thought. No sissy in him, except that voice. Who ever talked like that?

"T. J.," Blackie said. "That's just initials. What's your real name? Nobody in the world has just initials."

"I do," he said. "And they're T. J. That's all the name I got."

Ⓑ His voice was resolute with the knowledge of his rightness, and for a moment no one had anything to say. T. J. looked around at the rooftop and down at the black tar under his feet. "Down yonder where I come from," he said, "we played out

in the woods. Don't you-all have no woods around here?"

"Naw," Blackie said. "There's the park a few blocks over, but it's full of kids and cops and old women. You can't do a thing."

T. J. kept looking at the tar under his feet. "You mean you ain't got no fields to raise nothing in?...no watermelons or nothing?"

"Naw," I said scornfully. "What do you want to grow something for? The folks can buy everything they need at the store."

He looked at me again with that strange, unknowing look. "In Marion County," he said, "I had my own acre of cotton and my own acre of corn. It was mine to plant and make ever' year."

He sounded like it was something to be proud of, and in some obscure way it made the rest of us angry. Blackie said, "Who'd want to have their own acre of cotton and corn? That's just work. What can you do with an acre of cotton and corn?"

T. J. looked at him. "Well, you get part of the bale offen your acre,"[2] he said seriously. "And I fed my acre of corn to my calf."

We didn't really know what he was talking about, so we were more puzzled than angry; otherwise, I guess, we'd have chased him off the roof and wouldn't let him be part of our gang. But he was strange and different, and we were all attracted by his stolid[3] sense of rightness and belonging, maybe by the strange softness of his voice

> *He moved his foot against the black tar. "We could make our own field right here," he said softly, thoughtfully.*

2. **you get part of the bale offen your acre.** When T. J. farmed someone else's land, he shared the crop with the owner and was able to keep part of it for himself.
3. **stolid.** Unemotional

English Language Learning

Students learning English may need help understanding T. J.'s southern dialect, which includes expressions such as "down yonder," "you-all," and "ourn," as well as his use of nonstandard English that includes double negatives, "ain't," and sentences such as "Come spring we could raise us what we want to."

Have English learners work with fluent partners to read aloud the dialogue and then put the dialogue into standard English. Remind students to use footnotes. Students should ask for more assistance if they cannot interpret the dialogue on their own.

contrasting our own tones of speech into harshness.

He moved his foot against the black tar. "We could make our own field right here," he said softly, thoughtfully. "Come spring we could raise us what we want to—watermelons and garden truck[4] and no telling what all."

HISTORY ▶▶ CONNECTION

Victory Gardens During World War I and World War II, the U.S. government asked citizens to grow their own fruits and vegetables at home. This allowed the government to send canned and preserved food overseas to feed the troops. City people planted in yards and vacant lots and on rooftops. Neighbors cooperated to maintain community food supplies. During World War II, more than twenty million of these "victory gardens" helped people on the home front feel they were contributing to the war effort. Considering the story's setting, what do you think about T. J. and the gang's roof garden? Explain. **F**

"You'd have to be a good farmer to make these tar roofs grow any watermelons," I said. We all laughed.

But T. J. looked serious. "We could haul us some dirt up here," he said. "And spread it out even and water it, and before you know it, we'd have us a crop in here." He looked at us intently. "Wouldn't that be fun?"

"They wouldn't let us," Blackie said quickly.

"I thought you said this was you-all's roof," T. J. said to me. "That you-all could do anything you wanted to up here."

"They've never bothered us," I said. I felt the idea beginning to catch fire in me. It was **D**

a big idea, and it took a while for it to sink in; but the more I thought about it, the better I liked it. "Say," I said to the gang. "He might have something there. Just make us a regular roof garden, with flowers and grass and trees and everything. And all ours, too," I said. "We wouldn't let anybody up here except the ones we wanted to."

"It'd take a while to grow trees," T. J. said quickly, but we weren't paying any attention to him. They were all talking about it suddenly, all excited with the idea after I'd put it in a way they could catch hold of it. Only rich people had roof gardens, we knew, and the idea of our own private <u>domain</u> excited them.

"We could bring it up in sacks and boxes," Blackie said. "We'd have to do it while the folks weren't paying any attention to us, for we'd have to come up to the roof of our building and then cross over with it."

"Where could we get the dirt?" somebody said worriedly.

"Out of those vacant lots over close to school," Blackie said. "Nobody'd notice if we scraped it up."

C I slapped T. J. on the shoulder. "Man, you had a wonderful idea," I said, and everybody grinned at him, remembering that he had started it. "Our own private roof garden."

He grinned back. "It'll be ourn," he said. "All ourn." Then he looked thoughtful again.

---

4. **garden truck.** Vegetables grown for market

---

do•main (dō mān´) *n.,* land that a person owns; rightful territory

Teach the Selection

Analyze Literature

Suspense Say that authors add suspense by raising questions in the reader's mind about whether something is possible or may happen. Ask students how Deal builds suspense in this section of the story. (He raises such questions as "Is it really possible to grow something on a tar roof? Will T. J. be able to convince the gang? What problems will he encounter?") **C**

Use Reading Skills

Use Context Clues Have students use context clues to explain what the phrase *catch fire* means in the selection. (It means "stir up feelings inside.") **D**

Analyze Literature

Tone Ask students how the dialogue in this scene adds to its tone. (The boys get more and more excited as they discuss the possibility of the roof garden, which helps create an excited, anticipatory tone.) **E**

History Connection

Victory Gardens *Answer:* Most students will say the reprimand was not justified, but some may point out that the gang was not motivated to grow crops by the war effort, and it did not occur to the factory owner that this could be a victory garden. **F**

Grammar Skills

Coordinating Conjunctions

Remind students that a coordinating conjunction is a word, such as *and, but, for,* and *so,* that joins words of equal importance in a sentence.

The boys worked hard, <u>for</u> they were inspired by T. J.'s vision <u>and</u> enthusiasm.

Give students the following passage, and have them find the coordinating conjunctions and the words they join.

T. J. planted an acre of corn and an acre of cotton back home in Alabama. In the city, there were no open fields, but there was the factory rooftop. It was not the best place for planting grass or raising crops, yet it was flat and open.

Use Reading Skills

Analyze Cause and Effect Ask students why T. J. has the boys put all the dirt in one corner of the building. (He knows that if the boys can see results, they will be more likely to keep working hard.) Ⓐ

Analyze Literature

Narrator Point out that the narrator of "Antaeus" is an adult, describing an event that took place when he was a boy. Telling the story from an adult perspective gives the narrator insight into the characters and events that he never would have had as a boy. It allows him to reflect on why things happened as they did. Ⓑ

Use Reading Skills

Use Context Clues Ask students to explain how context helps them understand that here *calculated* is an adjective that means "carefully considered" and not a verb that means "figured out an amount." (The words "shrewd" and "fulfillment of his dream" are clues to meaning here.) Ⓒ

TEACHING NOTE

Self-Generated Questioning

Divide the class into groups and have each group create one or more questions about the story. Model a possible question: "What planting process does the gang follow?" Then ask each group to prepare and act out answers to the questions, using appropriate gestures and sound effects. Have the rest of the class guess the questions being acted out.

"Maybe I can lay my hands on some cotton seed, too. You think we could raise us some cotton?" We'd started big projects before at one time or another, like any gang of kids, but they'd always petered out for lack of organization and direction. But this one didn't; somehow or other T. J. kept it going all through the winter months. He kept talking about the watermelons and the cotton we'd raise, come spring, and when even that wouldn't work, he'd switch around to my idea of flowers and grass and trees, though Ⓑ he was always honest enough to add that it'd take a while to get any trees started. He always had it on his mind, and he'd mention it in school, getting them lined up to carry dirt that afternoon, saying in a casual way that he reckoned a few more weeks ought to see the job through.

Ⓐ Our little area of private earth grew slowly. T. J. was smart enough to start in one corner of the building, heaping up the carried earth two or three feet thick so that we had an immediate result to look at, to contemplate with awe. Some of the evenings T. J. alone was carrying earth up to the building, the rest of the gang distracted by other enterprises or interests, but T. J. kept Ⓒ plugging along on his own, and eventually we'd all come back to him again, and then our own little acre would grow more rapidly.

He was careful about the kind of dirt he'd let us carry up there, and more than once he dumped a sandy load over the parapet into the areaway below because it wasn't good enough. He found out the kinds of earth in all the vacant lots for blocks around. He'd pick it up and feel it and smell it, frozen though it was sometimes, and then he'd say it was good growing soil or it wasn't worth anything, and we'd have to go on somewhere else.

Ⓑ Thinking about it now, I don't see how he kept us at it. It was hard work, lugging paper sacks and boxes of dirt all the way up the stairs of our own building, keeping out of the way of the grown-ups so they wouldn't catch on to what we were doing. They probably wouldn't have cared, for they didn't pay much attention to us, but we wanted to keep it secret anyway. Then we had to go through the trap door to our roof, teeter[5] over a plank to the fire escape, then climb two or three stories to the parapet, and drop them down onto the roof. All that for a small pile of earth that sometimes didn't seem worth the effort. But T. J. kept the vision bright within us, his words shrewd and Ⓒ calculated toward the fulfillment of his dream; and he worked harder than any of us. He seemed driven toward a goal that we couldn't see, a particular point in time that

---

5. teeter. Wobble

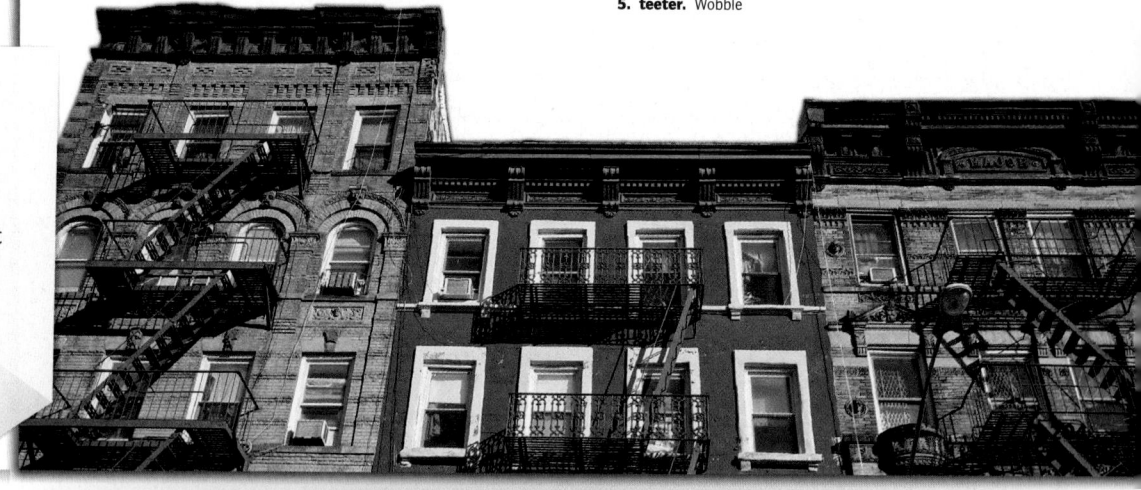

Find Pronunciations

Point out to students that they can use the pronunciation key and phonetic respellings in a dictionary to figure out how to pronounce unfamiliar words in the story.

• The pronunciation key has symbols that show how to say letters and combinations of letters.

• The phonetic respelling shows how to say a word using the pronunciation key.

For practice, ask volunteers to demonstrate how to use the pronunciation key and phonetic respellings in the classroom dictionary by saying the words out loud. Have them give the correct pronunciations for these words from the selection: *resolute, enterprises, laborious, Antaeus,* and *bravado.* Students should attempt to recognize elements of the English sound system such as consonant and vowel sounds by listening to these and other unfamiliar words.

would be definitely marked by signs and wonders that only he could see.

The <u>laborious</u> earth just lay there during the cold months, <u>inert</u> and lifeless, the clods lumpy and cold under our feet when we walked over it. But one day it rained, and afterward there was a softness in the air, and the earth was live and giving again with moisture and warmth.

That evening T. J. smelled the air, his nostrils dilating with the odor of the earth under his feet. "It's spring," he said, and there was a gladness rising in his voice that filled us all with the same feeling. "It's mighty late for it, but it's spring. I'd just about decided it wasn't never gonna get here at all."

We were all sniffing at the air, too, trying to smell it the way that T. J. did, and I can still remember the sweet odor of the earth under our feet. It was the first time in my life that spring and spring earth had meant anything to me. I looked at T. J. then, knowing in a faint way the hunger within him through the toilsome winter months, knowing the dream that lay behind his plan. He was a new Antaeus,[6] preparing his own bed of strength.

D

"Planting time," he said. "We'll have to find us some seed."

"What do we do?" Blackie said. "How do we do it?"

"First we'll have to break up the clods," T. J. said. "That won't be hard to do. Then we plant the seed, and after a while they come up. Then you got you a crop." He frowned. "But you ain't got it raised yet. You got to tend it and hoe it and take care of it, and all the time it's growing and growing, while you're awake and while you're asleep. Then you lay it by when it's growed[7]

"You-all seem mighty set on raising some grass," he said.

and let it ripen, and then you got you a crop."

"There's these wholesale seed houses over on Sixth," I said. "We could probably swipe some grass seed over there."

T. J. looked at the earth. "You-all seem mighty set on raising some grass," he said. "I ain't never put no effort into that. I spent all my life trying not to raise grass."

"But it's pretty," Blackie said. "We could play on it and take sunbaths on it. Like having our own lawn. Lots of people got lawns."

"Well," T. J. said. He looked at the rest of us, hesitant for the first time. He kept on looking at us for a moment. "I did have it in mind to raise some corn and vegetables. But we'll plant grass."

E

He was smart. He knew where to give in. And I don't suppose it made any difference to him, really. He just wanted to grow something, even if it was grass.

"Of course," he said. "I do think we ought to plant a row of watermelons. They'd be mighty nice to eat while we was a-laying on that grass."

We all laughed. "All right," I said. "We'll plant us a row of watermelons."

Things went very quickly then. Perhaps half the roof was covered with the earth, the half that wasn't broken by ventilators,[8] and

---

6. **Antaeus.** Mythological giant who gained strength from touching Earth. Hercules defeated Antaeus by holding him off the ground until he weakened and died.
7. **Then you lay it by when it's growed.** To lay by a crop is to tend to it for the last time before harvesting. After laying by, a farmer leaves the crop to mature on its own.
8. **ventilators.** Mechanisms, such as ducts or fans, for getting rid of old air and bringing fresh air into a building

la·bo·ri·ous (lə bôr´ ē əs) *adj.*, produced by hard work
in·ert (i nʉrt´) *adj.*, still; unmoving

Teach the Selection

Literary Connection

Myth of Antaeus According to myth, King Antaeus of Libya was the son of Poseidon, the Olympian god of the sea, and Gaia, the goddess of earth. When strangers wandered onto Antaeus's land, they were forced to wrestle the powerful giant, who was invincible as long as he remained in contact with earth. If Antaeus was victorious, as he often was, he would then kill his opponent. When the powerful Hercules, son of Zeus, wrestled Antaeus, he was unable to defeat him until he discovered that Antaeus's strength was derived from his contact with earth. Hercules lifted Antaeus and held him off the ground until Antaeus died.

Analyze Literature

Characterization Ask students what the narrator wants readers to understand about T. J. when he compares him to Antaeus. (The narrator believes that T. J. lived for the land, and that his strength and leadership qualities came from his love for the earth and his ability to make things grow.) **D**

Analyze Literature

Conflict Ask students to describe the conflict that arises between T. J. and the gang about what to plant. How is this conflict resolved? (T. J. wants to plant corn and vegetables. The gang wants to plant grass. T. J. gives in because he just wants to grow something.) **E**

Research Skills

Identify a Contemporary Topic

Tell students they can use library resources and an Internet search engine to identify topics for a research report. Library resources include nonfiction books and materials in the reference section, such as magazines, newspapers, CDs, and periodical guides. The Internet has numerous resources that can help students explore a topic. Many search engines offer advanced search features for narrowing a topic.

Ask students to identify a suitable topic for a four-page research report on today's green roofs. Students can then describe the process that they used to identify topics. Interested students can use their research to write a report.

Use Reading Strategies

Visualize Encourage students to use sensory details in the text, plus what they already know, to visualize the boys as they look at the grass. What are the boys' expressions? **Ⓐ**

Use Reading Skills

Use Context Clues Ask students how the look of shame on Blackie's face can help them understand the word *bravado*. Model a response: "Someone who is ashamed is not likely to act with confidence. I think *bravado* has the opposite meaning. Blackie acted with confidence when he first stepped on the grass." **Ⓑ**

Critical Viewing

Reading a Photograph Tell students they can "read" a photograph much like a story. They can examine details and use prior knowledge and imagination to draw conclusions and make inferences about setting, characters, and events. Write those headings on the board. Use the teacher questions on the side of page 207 to help students analyze the picture.

Independent Reading

Students might also enjoy stories in the anthology *Big City Cool: Short Stories About Urban Youth.*

---

we swiped pocketfuls of grass seed from the open bins in the wholesale seed house, mingling among the buyers on Saturdays and during the school lunch hour. T. J. showed us how to prepare the earth, breaking up the clods and smoothing it and sowing the grass seed. It looked rich and black now with moisture, receiving of the seed, and it seemed that the grass sprang up overnight, pale green in the early spring.

Ⓐ We couldn't keep from looking at it, unable to believe that we had created this delicate growth. We looked at T. J. with understanding now, knowing the fulfillment of the plan he had carried alone within his mind. We had worked without full understanding of the task, but he had known all the time.

We found that we couldn't walk or play on the delicate blades, as we had expected to, but we didn't mind. It was enough just to look at it, to realize that it was the work of our own hands, and each evening, the whole gang was there, trying to measure the growth that had been achieved that day.

One time a foot was placed on the plot of ground, one time only, Blackie stepping onto **Ⓑ** it with sudden bravado. Then he looked at the crushed blades and there was shame in his face. He did not do it again. This was his grass, too, and not to be <u>desecrated</u>. No one said anything, for it was not necessary.

T. J. had reserved a small section for watermelons, and he was still trying to find some seed for it. The wholesale house didn't have any watermelon seed, and we didn't know where we could lay our hands on them. T. J. shaped the earth into mounds, ready to receive them, three mounds lying in

We couldn't keep from looking at it, unable to believe that we had created this delicate growth.

a straight line along the edge of the grass plot.

We had just about decided that we'd have to buy the seed if we were to get them. It was a violation of our principles, but we were anxious to get the watermelons started. Somewhere or other, T. J. got his hands on a seed catalog and brought it one evening to our roof garden.

"We can order them now," he said, showing us the catalog. "Look!"

We all crowded around, looking at the fat, green watermelons pictured in full color on the pages. Some of them were split open, showing the red, tempting meat, making our mouths water.

"Now we got to scrape up some seed money," T. J. said, looking at us. "I got a quarter. How much you-all got?"

We made up a couple of dollars among us and T. J. nodded his head. "That'll be more than enough. Now we got to decide what kind to get. I think them Kleckley Sweets. What do you-all think?"

He was going into esoteric[9] matters beyond our reach. We hadn't even known there were different kinds of melons. So we just nodded our heads and agreed that yes, we thought the Kleckley Sweets too.

"I'll order them tonight," T. J. said. "We ought to have them in a few days."

"What are you boys doing up here?" an adult voice said behind us.

It startled us, for no one had ever come up here before, in all the time we had been using the roof of the factory. We jerked around and saw three men standing near the

---

9. esoteric. Understood by only a small group of people

des•e•crate (des´ i krāt´) *v.*, treat with disrespect

Differentiated Instruction

Visual Learning

Although the narrator describes T. J.'s physical appearance and his "slow, gentle voice" to help readers visualize him, the narrator does not describe himself, Blackie, or any other members of the gang. Have visual learners tell you how this difference affects their feelings about the characters.

Kinesthetic Learning

Have students enact the confrontation between the factory owner and T. J. Have them prepare by rereading the dialogue and the narrator's comments about the two characters. Use this activity to discuss external conflict and how a character's personality affects what happens next in a story.

Critical Viewing
Ask students these questions.
Setting What is the setting of this photograph? What details help you understand the setting? How is the setting similar to that of "Antaeus"?

Characters Who are the people in this photograph? What do their expressions and postures suggest about their personalities? Do any of the boys remind you of characters in "Antaeus"? In what way?

Events What do you think the women in the background are talking about? What do you think the boys were doing before this photograph was taken? What might they decide to do next?

trap door at the other end of the roof. They weren't policemen, or night watchmen, but three men in plump business suits, looking at us. They walked toward us.

"What are you boys doing up here?" the one in the middle said again.

We stood still, guilt heavy among us, levied by the tone of voice,[10] and looked at the three strangers.

The men stared at the grass <u>flourishing</u> behind us. "What's this?" the man said. "How did this get up here?"

"Sure is growing good, ain't it?" T. J. said conversationally. "We planted it."

The men kept looking at the grass as if they didn't believe it. It was a thick carpet over the earth now, a patch of deep greenness startling in the sterile industrial surroundings.

"Yes, sir," T. J. said proudly. "We toted that earth up here and planted that grass."

He fluttered the seed catalog. "And we're just fixing to plant us some watermelon."

The man looked at him then, his eyes strange and faraway. "What do you mean, putting this on the roof of my building?" he said. "Do you want to go to jail?"

T. J. looked shaken. The rest of us were silent, frightened by the authority of his voice. We had grown up aware of adult authority, of policemen and night watchmen and teachers, and this man sounded like all the others. But it was a new thing to T. J.

"Well, you wasn't using the roof," T. J. said. He paused a moment and added shrewdly, "So we just thought to pretty it up a little bit."

---

10. **levied by the tone of voice.** Judged by the attitude more than by words

---

flour • ish (flʉr´ ish) v., grow luxuriously

Use Reading Skills
Analyze Cause and Effect Ask students what may have happened to bring the factory owner up to the roof. (The owner may have noticed that the roof was sagging, or someone may have seen the boys.) **C**

Analyze Literature
Characterization Have students compare the reactions of T. J. and the gang when the men arrive on the roof. (While the boys are intimidated, T. J. truly believes he has beautified the roof and that the men will be able to appreciate that.) **D**

Use Reading Skills
Use Context Clues Ask students what *sterile* means here ("barren" or "bare.") **E**

Clarify

Point out to students that short stories often contain references to topics in science, social studies, math, art, and other subjects that they can explore through reading in these areas. For example, as they read in "Antaeus" about how the gang measured the growth of the grass, students may wonder how much grass typically grows in a day and under what conditions. Reading an article about grass in an encyclopedia may answer this question.

Ask students to identify topics from other curriculum areas suggested by characters and events in the story. Encourage students to read more about these topics in textbooks and other reference sources.

Analyze Literature

Conflict Have students explain the conflict expressed in the faces of the gang members and in T. J.'s face. (The gang's faces show that they know they cannot stop the factory owner from destroying the garden. T. J.'s face shows that he won't allow them to destroy it.) **Ⓐ**

Analyze Literature

Conflict Encourage students to visualize T. J. and the gang as they destroy the roof garden. In their opinion, is T. J.'s decision to destroy the roof garden himself a satisfactory resolution to the conflict between him and the factory owner? Why or why not? (Most students will say that by destroying it himself, he did not let the factory owner defeat him.) **Ⓑ**

Independent Reading

Students might also enjoy stories in the anthology *Big City Cool: Short Stories About Urban Youth.*

"And sag it so I'd have to rebuild it," the man said sharply. He started turning away, saying to another man beside him, "See that all that junk is shoveled off by tomorrow."

"Yes, sir," the man said.

T. J. started forward. "You can't do that," he said. "We toted it up here, and it's our earth. We planted it and raised it and toted it up here."

The man stared at him coldly. "But it's my building," he said. "It's to be shoveled off tomorrow."

"It's our earth," T. J. said desperately. "You ain't got no right!"

The men walked on without listening and descended clumsily through the trap door. T. J. stood looking after them, his body tense with anger, until they had disappeared. They wouldn't even argue with him, wouldn't let him defend his earth rights.

He turned to us. "We won't let 'em do it," he said fiercely. "We'll stay up here all day tomorrow and the day after that, and we won't let 'em do it."

We just looked at him. We knew that there was no stopping it.

Ⓐ He saw it in our faces, and his face wavered for a moment before he gripped it into determination. "They ain't got no right," he said. "It's our earth. It's our land. Can't nobody touch a man's own land."

We kept looking at him, listening to the words but knowing that it was no use. The adult world had descended on us even in our richest dream, and we knew there was no calculating the adult world, no fighting it, no winning against it.

We started moving slowly toward the parapet and the fire escape, avoiding a last look at the green beauty of the earth that T. J. had planted for us, had planted deeply in our minds as well as in our experience. We filed slowly over the edge and down the

steps to the plank, T. J. coming last, and all of us could feel the weight of his grief behind us.

"Wait a minute," he said suddenly, his voice harsh with the effort of calling.

We stopped and turned, held by the tone of his voice, and looked up at him standing above us on the fire escape.

"We can't stop them?" he said, looking down at us, his face strange in the dusky light. "There ain't no way to stop 'em?"

"No," Blackie said with finality. "They own the building."

We stood still for a moment, looking up at T. J., caught into inaction by the decision working in his face. He stared back at us, and his face was pale and mean in the poor light, with a bald nakedness in his skin like cripples have sometimes.

Ⓑ "They ain't gonna touch my earth," he said fiercely. "They ain't gonna lay a hand on it! Come on."

He turned around and started up the fire escape again, almost running against the effort of climbing. We followed more slowly, not knowing what he intended to do. By the time we reached him, he had seized a board and thrust it into the soil, scooping it up and flinging it over the parapet into the areaway below. He straightened and looked at us.

"They can't touch it," he said. "I won't let 'em lay a dirty hand on it!"

We saw it then. He stooped to his labor again, and we followed, the gusts of his anger moving in frenzied labor among us as we scattered along the edge of the earth, scooping it and throwing it over the parapet, destroying with anger the growth we had nurtured with such tender care. The soil carried so laboriously upward to the light and the sun cascaded swiftly into the dark areaway, the green blades of grass crumpled and twisted in the falling.

208 UNIT 2 FICTION

Differentiated Instruction

Enrichment

Some students may want to try designing a private rooftop garden for a building in the community. Have students create a working plan that includes

- choosing a building and determining how to get permission to build the garden;

- deciding what kind of garden they want, such as vegetable, flower, grass, or container;
- identifying the USDA growing zone and selecting plants suitable for the zone; and
- drawing a blueprint for the garden.

It took less time than you would think; the task of destruction is infinitely easier than that of creation. We stopped at the end, leaving only a scattering of loose soil, and when it was finally over, a stillness stood among the group and over the factory building. We looked down at the bare sterility of black tar, felt the harsh texture of it under the soles of our shoes, and the anger had gone out of us, leaving only a sore aching in our minds, like overstretched muscles.

T. J. stood for a moment, his breathing slowing from anger and effort, caught into the same contemplation of destruction as all of us. He stooped slowly, finally, and picked up a lonely blade of grass left trampled under our feet and put it between his teeth, tasting it, sucking the greenness out of it into his mouth. Then he started walking toward the fire escape, moving before any of us were ready to move, and disappeared over the edge.

We followed him, but he was already halfway down to the ground, going on past the board where we crossed over, climbing down into the areaway. We saw the last section swing down with his weight, and then he stood on the concrete below us, looking at the small pile of anonymous earth scattered by our throwing. Then he walked across the place where we could see him and disappeared toward the street without glancing back, without looking up to see us watching him.

They did not find him for two weeks.

Then the Nashville police caught him just outside the Nashville freight yards. He was walking along the railroad track, still heading South, still heading home.

As for us, who had no remembered home to call us, none of us ever again climbed the escapeway to the roof. ✤

How does it feel to plant a garden, write a poem, play music, or create a work of art? What is so special about the feeling a person gets from growing plants or making something beautiful?

Find Meaning

1. (a) What brings T. J. and his family to the North? (b) Why does the narrator's gang let T. J. in?
2. Why does T. J. want to grow crops?
3. (a) How does the gang manage to plant the grass? (b) How does T. J.'s project affect the gang?

Make Judgments

4. If no one knew they were using the roof, why does the gang keep their project a secret?
5. (a) Once grass is growing, the narrator says about the gang and T. J., "We had worked without full understanding of the task, but he had known all the time." What does the narrator mean by "full understanding"? (b) Why hadn't the gang understood this before?
6. Why does T. J. destroy the garden himself?

ANTAEUS **209**

Teach the Selection

Make Connections
Ask students how they felt after T. J. and the boys destroyed the garden.

> *Answer:* Students will probably identify with a sense of accomplishment. Most will say that the feeling is special because of investing time and skill and because the result is beautiful.

Find Meaning

1. (a) The family moved North to look for work. (b) T. J. wasn't intimidated by the boys, and his roof garden idea appealed to them.
2. He wanted to grow crops to remind himself of home or because he missed having his own acres.
3. (a) They carried soil up to the roof, broke up the soil, stole grass seed, and planted it. (b) It gave the gang a purpose and a sense of accomplishment.

Make Judgments

4. The boys knew they were trespassing. They may also have habitually kept their activities secret.
5. (a) The narrator is probably referring to the reasons behind some of their tasks. (b) The gang had never done this before.
6. T. J. felt he and the gang owned the garden ("It's our earth. It's our land."), and he didn't want anyone else to desecrate it.

Reading Skills

Clarify
Remind students that when they read a story like "Antaeus," they can draw on prior knowledge (what they've learned and experienced in their lives) to understand unfamiliar words, draw conclusions and make inferences about characters and events, and predict what will happen next. Ask students:

- to use prior knowledge to explain one example of figurative language in the story.
- how their prior knowledge about gangs influenced their opinions of the narrator at the beginning of the story. What did they learn as they read that may have changed that opinion?
- how their prior knowledge helped them predict what the factory owner would do.

Teach the Connection

Use Reading Strategies

Make Inferences Ask students how they think the speaker feels about the inner city and about living there. (By calling the inner city "home" and "no place," the speaker reveals mixed emotions about the city, along with an awareness of its shortcomings. However, the lines "happy to be alive/and in the inner city" suggest that the speaker prefers living there in spite of its shortcomings.)

Text-to-Text Connection

Answer: The poem's speaker implies that uptown residents are like dead men, while people in the inner city are alive. T. J.'s dream of growing crops and the gang's enthusiasm for the project suggest that city people lack opportunities to make gardens or to otherwise create pleasant places for themselves.

"Antaeus" reveals some deep differences between city and country living. In the following poem, the speaker highlights some differences between two parts of a city. **Lucille Clifton** was born in 1936 in a small town near Buffalo, New York. She is a university professor in Maryland and has published many poetry collections, children's books, and a memoir. Her African-American heritage and her own family have inspired many of her works. Read the poem for insight into what "home" means to someone living in a city.

in the inner city

A Lyric Poem by Lucille Clifton

in the inner city
or
like we call it
home
we think a lot about uptown[1]
and the silent nights
and the houses straight as
dead men
and the pastel[2] lights
and we hang on to our no place
happy to be alive
and in the inner city
or
like we call it
home ✤

---

1. **uptown.** Residential part of a city away from the center, usually considered safer and more well off than the inner city
2. **pastel.** Pale, light color

TEXT ←→ TEXT
CONNECTION

"Antaeus" and "in the inner city" both deal with contrasts. The poem's speaker contrasts the inner city "home" with uptown, while the story's narrator contrasts city life with T. J.'s dreams. How does the speaker compare the inner city to uptown? What do T. J.'s dreams tell you about day-to-day life in the city?

210   **UNIT 2** FICTION

Differentiated Instruction

Reading Proficiency

Although the poem appears simple and contains fairly simple vocabulary, students may have trouble reading it because it is not punctuated or divided into sentences. Read the poem aloud for them or have them listen to a recording of the poem so they can hear the natural pauses. Then have them read the poem aloud or softly to themselves.

Analyze Literature

Conflict The conflict in "Antaeus" is between T. J. and an outside force. It is an external conflict. Identify the main conflict using a cause-and-effect chart. List at least three causes and effects from the story. Then, based on your cause-and-effect examples, state what you think is the story's main conflict.

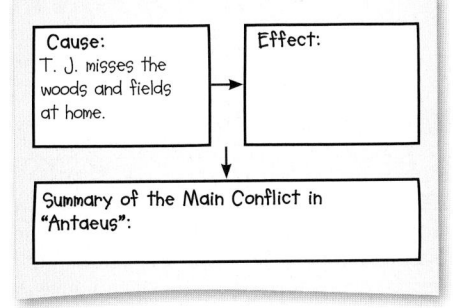

Cause:
T. J. misses the woods and fields at home.

Effect:

Summary of the Main Conflict in "Antaeus":

Extend Understanding

Writing Options

Creative Writing Imagine that you are the narrator of "Antaeus." T. J. has been brought back to the city, and you want to help him plant a garden. You decide to formally request use of the factory roof for a victory garden. Write a **business letter** to the factory owner. Follow the instructions for writing a business letter in Language Arts Handbook 6.3, on pages 909–910 of this textbook. In the body of your letter, use evidence to support arguments in favor of growing a garden in this space.

Expository Writing Write a short **literary response** that evaluates the ending of "Antaeus." Name the main conflict in the story and give an example from the text to illustrate it. Then state how the ending resolves the conflict. Finish by showing how T. J. and the gang would have been better off if they had been able to keep their garden.

Collaborative Learning

Discuss Motivation A motivation is a force that moves a character to think, feel, or behave in a certain way. In a small group, discuss T. J.'s motivation. Why did he want crops? Why did he join the narrator's gang? Why did he agree to plant grass? And why did he destroy the garden and leave the city? When your group has reached a consensus on answers to these questions, have a volunteer write one or two sentences summarizing T. J.'s motivation.

Critical Literacy

Explore an Allusion The title of Deal's story is a literary allusion, an indirect reference to something that explains or enriches the story. Use a library or the Internet to find out about the myth of Antaeus. Compare Antaeus and T. J. Make a poster that explains how they are similar and how they are different.

 Go to **www.mirrorsandwindows.com** for more.

Review the Selection

Analyze Literature

Conflict Students' lists of causes and effects will vary, but should follow the plot. For example, they could give as a cause "The gang hauls dirt to the roof" and as an effect "In spring, the roof is ready for grass seed." They may infer a cause that brings the factory owner to the roof. The main conflict is between the desire T. J. and the gang have to beautify their private spot and the fact that the building owner does not want them on the roof.

Program Resources

For further instruction, refer students to the following extension activity. Critical Literacy: Explore an Allusion, *Exceeding the Standards: Extension Activities,* p. 7.

Rubrics for Writing Options

You can adapt this as a checklist for students to use as they write.

Creative Writing

☐ Does the letter apply the conventions of a formal business letter?

☐ Is the letter addressed to the factory owner?

☐ Does the letter persuasively advocate growing a victory garden on the roof?

Expository Writing

☐ Does the literary response identify the main conflict and give an example from the story?

☐ Does the literary response relate the conflict to the plot resolution at the end of the story?

☐ Does the literary response conclude with a statement about how a garden would benefit T. J. and the gang?

Seventh Grade

A Short Story by Gary Soto

BEFORE READING

Build Background
Literary Context As a young man, Gary Soto was impressed with writers who used everyday language to write about real places and common experiences. In his own writing, Soto draws from his experiences growing up Mexican American in California's Central Valley. From writing poetry in college, he turned to autobiographical essays and finally to fiction for adults and young people.

Reader's Context Think back to your first day of school this year. What hopes and plans did you have for the months ahead?

Set Purpose
Skim the first two paragraphs of the story. Based on the title and those paragraphs, predict how likely it is that Victor will succeed. Read the story to find out if your prediction is correct.

Analyze Literature
Character A story always has a **main character**—in this case, Victor—and usually one or more **minor characters.** Sometimes a character is *static,* meaning that he or she doesn't change over the course of the story. Other times, a character is dynamic. From the beginning of the story to the end, a *dynamic* character has experiences that change his or her personality and behavior. As you read, pay attention to how Victor's character changes.

Meet the Author

Gary Soto was born in 1952 and raised in Fresno, California. He did not do well in school, but he loved the school library. Today he is both a poet and a novelist, and he writes for young people and adults. He travels widely to connect with readers. He is also a Young People's Ambassador for the United Farm Workers of America, a large labor union. During many appearances he introduces students to the union's history and activities.

212 UNIT 2 FICTION

Use Reading Skills
Sequence of Events
Most stories are told in chronological order. This means that the events are told in the order in which they occurred. The events can happen within a character's mind or in the setting of the story. Write down the sequence of events in a story using a time line. As you read, follow Victor through his day from beginning to end and record the key events on your time line.

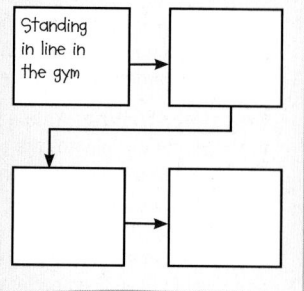

Preview Vocabulary
scowl (skaů[ə]l) *v.,* lower the eyebrows, as if squinting or frowning

fe·roc·i·ty (fə räs´ ət ē) *n.,* fierceness or intensity

con·vic·tion (kən vik´ shən) *n.,* belief; self-confidence; boldness

trudge (trŭj) *v.,* walk heavily; plod

Words in Use

Preview Vocabulary
scowl, 214
ferocity, 214
conviction, 214
trudge, 215

Selection Words
populace, 216

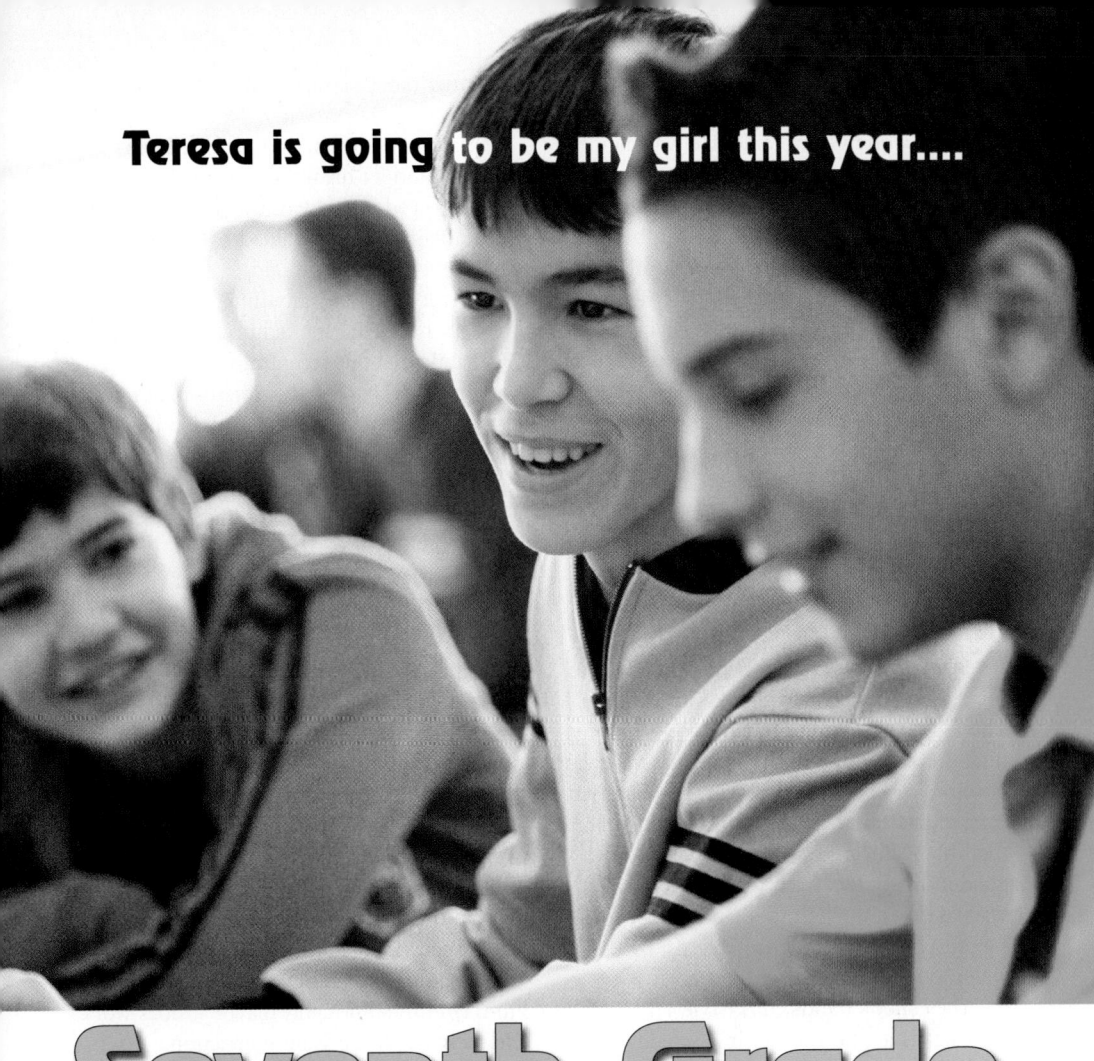

Teresa is going to be my girl this year....

Seventh Grade

A Short Story by Gary Soto

213

Teach the Selection

Summary

It is the first day of seventh grade. While Victor's friend Michael tries scowling to attract girls, Victor has decided to take French to be close to Teresa, the girl he likes. In French class, Victor tries to impress Teresa by pretending to know French. But when Mr. Bueller, his teacher, asks him a question in French, Victor can only respond in garbled syllables. To Victor's surprise and relief, Mr. Bueller doesn't give him away. Teresa is so impressed that after class she asks Victor for help with French. Filled with love for Teresa and gratitude for Mr. Bueller, Victor runs to the library for some French books. He has to learn French as quickly as possible.

 The Mirrors & Windows questions at the end of the story focus on the theme of image. Before students begin reading, ask: How much would you change yourself to impress someone?

▶ More About the Author

Gary Soto bases his characters and their struggles on his own experiences growing up in a Mexican-American neighborhood. The details may reflect Soto's heritage, but because of Soto's perception of human nature and language, his characters and themes have universal appeal.

Program Resources

Planning and Assessment
Program Planning Guide, Selection Lesson Plan
E-Lesson Planner
Assessment Guide, Lesson Test
ExamView

Technology Tools
Interactive Student Text on CD
Visual Teaching Package
Audio Library
mirrorsandwindows.com

Meeting the Standards
Fiction: Unit 2, Directed Reading, pp. 69–73

History Connection

Fresno Fresno, in the center of California's agriculturally rich Central Valley, provides the backdrop for most of Gary Soto's stories. In 1849, during the California Gold Rush, the region was flooded with prospectors and investors hoping to become instantly rich. When the Gold Rush ended, investors realized that the region was ideal for farming. In the 1870s and 1880s, with the construction of irrigation canals and a rail line, the town of Fresno grew and flourished. Fresno officially became a town on October 12, 1885. **A**

Analyze Literature

Character Students have to identify what they know about a dynamic character at the beginning of a story in order to know how the character changes by the end of the story. Ask students what they know about Victor so far. (He's Mexican-American. He is friends with Michael. He thinks Michael's scowling is weird. He likes Teresa. He lives and goes to school in Fresno. He picked grapes to earn money for clothes. He speaks Spanish and English, but not French. He's not good in math.)

O n the first day of school, Victor stood in line half an hour before he came to a wobbly card table. He was handed a packet of papers and a computer card on which he listed his one elective, French. He already spoke Spanish and English, but he thought some day he might travel to France, **A** where it was cool; not like Fresno,[1] where summer days reached 110 degrees in the shade. There were rivers in France and huge churches, and fair-skinned people everywhere, the way there were brown people all around Victor.

Michael thinks making a face makes him handsome.

Besides, Teresa, a girl he had liked since they were in catechism classes[2] at Saint Theresa's, was taking French, too. With any luck they would be in the same class. Teresa is going to be my girl this year, he promised himself as he left the gym full of students in their new fall clothes. She was cute. And good in math, too, Victor thought as he walked down the hall to his homeroom. He ran into his friend, Michael Torres, by the water fountain that never turned off.

They shook hands, *raza*-style,[3] and jerked their heads at one another in a *saludo de vato*.[4] "How come you're making a face?" asked Victor.

"I ain't making a face, *ese*. This is my face." Michael said his face had changed during the summer. He had read a *GQ* magazine[5] that his older brother had borrowed from the Book Mobile and noticed that the male models all had the same look on their faces. They would stand, one arm around a beautiful woman, and scowl. They would sit at a pool, their rippled stomachs dark with shadow, and scowl. They would sit

at dinner tables, cool drinks in their hands, and scowl.

"I think it works," Michael said. He scowled and let his upper lip quiver. His teeth showed along with the ferocity of his soul. "Belinda Reyes walked by a while ago and looked at me," he said.

Victor didn't say anything, though he thought his friend looked pretty strange. They talked about recent movies, baseball, their parents, and the horrors of picking grapes in order to buy their fall clothes. Picking grapes was like living in Siberia,[6] except hot and more boring.

"What classes are you taking?" Michael said, scowling.

"French. How 'bout you?"

"Spanish. I ain't so good at it, even if I'm Mexican."

"I'm not either, but I'm better at it than math, that's for sure."

A tinny, three-beat bell propelled students to their homerooms. The two friends socked each other in the arm and went their ways, Victor thinking, man, that's weird. Michael thinks making a face makes him handsome.

On the way to his homeroom, Victor tried a scowl. He felt foolish, until out of the corner of his eye he saw a girl looking at him. Umm, he thought, maybe it does work. He scowled with greater conviction.

---

1. **Fresno.** Inland city in California's major agricultural region
2. **catechism classes.** Religious instruction
3. **raza-style.** In the style of Mexicans or Mexican Americans
4. **saludo de vato** (sä lüd´ ō də vä tō´). Greeting between friends (Spanish)
5. **GQ magazine.** Fashion and style magazine for men
6. **Siberia.** Vast area of northern Asia with a harsh environment where the Soviet Union used to send prisoners

---

scowl (skaů[ə]l) *v.*, lower the eyebrows, as if squinting or frowning

fe•roc•i•ty (fə räs´ ət ē) *n.*, fierceness or intensity

con•vic•tion (kən vik´ shən) *n.*, belief; self-confidence; boldness

---

Differentiated Instruction

English Language Learning

Students learning English may have difficulty with Soto's choice of vivid verbs, especially those that have multiple meanings or contain word parts with multiple meanings. Examples include *jerked*, *socked*, *herded*, *bustled*, and *beamed*. Suggest that students identify verbs that give them trouble and have them work with fluent partners to identify their meanings in context. Partners can also discuss the meaning of idioms that they encounter as they read, such as "on the sly" and "catch her eye."

In homeroom, roll was taken, emergency cards were passed out, and they were given a bulletin to take home to their parents. The principal, Mr. Belton, spoke over the crackling loudspeaker, welcoming the students to a new year, new experiences, and new friendships. The students squirmed in their chairs and ignored him. They were anxious to go to first period. Victor sat calmly, thinking of Teresa, who sat two rows away, reading a paperback novel. This would be his lucky year. She was in his homeroom, and would probably be in his English and math classes. And, of course, French.

The bell rang for first period, and the students herded noisily through the door. Only Teresa lingered, talking with the homeroom teacher.

"So you think I should talk to Mrs. Gaines?" she asked the teacher. "She would know about ballet?"

"She would be a good bet," the teacher said. Then added, "Or the gym teacher, Mrs. Garza."

Victor lingered, keeping his head down

and staring at his desk. He wanted to leave when she did so he could bump into her and say something clever.

He watched her on the sly. As she turned to leave, he stood up and hurried to the door, where he managed to catch her eye.

> **He wanted to leave when she did so he could bump into her and say something clever.**

She smiled and said, "Hi, Victor."

He smiled back and said, "Yeah, that's me." His brown face blushed. Why hadn't he said, "Hi, Teresa," or "How was your summer?" or something nice? **B**

As Teresa walked down the hall, Victor walked the other way, looking back, admiring how gracefully she walked, one foot in front of the other. So much for being in the same class, he thought. As he <u>trudged</u> to English, he practiced scowling. **C**

In English they reviewed the parts of speech. Mr. Lucas, a portly man, waddled down the aisle, asking, "What is a noun?"

"A person, place, or thing," said the class in unison.

"Yes, now somebody give me an example of a person—give, Victor Rodriguez."

"Teresa," Victor said automatically. Some of the girls giggled. They knew he had a crush on Teresa. He felt himself blushing again. **D**

"Correct," Mr. Lucas said. "Now provide me with a place."

Mr. Lucas called on a freckled kid who answered, "Teresa's house with a kitchen full of big brothers."

---

trudge (trʉj′) v., walk heavily; plod

Make Connections

Ask students why they think Victor blushes when he speaks to Teresa. Then have students suggest things they might say in a similar situation. **B**

Analyze Literature

Humor Point out to students that Soto achieves a humorous tone in this story through broad exaggeration, such as Michael's scowling, and through subtle irony such as Victor's admiration of Teresa's walk, which, in fact, is how everyone walks, by putting one foot in front of the other. **C**

Analyze Literature

Plot Have students describe Victor's problem and tell whether his conflict is mainly internal (within himself) or external (with an outside force). (Victor wants Teresa to be his girlfriend. The conflict is internal. Victor has to overcome shyness and a fear of rejection to get close to her.) **D**

TEACHING NOTE

Self-Generated Questioning

Divide the class into two groups, Character and Dialogue. Have each group write three or four questions about Soto's writing techniques in its area. Model some possible questions:

- "How much time does Soto spend physically describing the characters?"
- "Is all of the dialogue appropriate for the speaker's age?"

Then have groups take turns reading aloud their questions for the other group to try to answer.

Reading Skills

Author's Perspective

Point out to students that they can use what characters say, do, and think in a story to figure out the author's perspective, or viewpoint, on different subjects. Encourage students to use a chart to keep track of details in "Seventh Grade." A good chart will have columns for the four main characters, Victor, Michael, Teresa, and Mr. Bueller. For each character, students can record (1) What he/she says, (2) what he/she does, and (3) what he/she thinks. Students can then use their notes to infer Soto's perspective on subjects such as school, adolescence, friendship, and boy-girl relationships.

Use Reading Skills

Identify Sequence of Events Ask: "What does Victor do after he leaves the cafeteria, before he goes to French, and why?" (He goes outside, onto the school campus, hoping to see Teresa.) **A**

Use Reading Strategies

Make Predictions Tell students to think about what they know about Victor so far. Do they think he'll work up the courage to approach Teresa? What will be the outcome? (He will probably try to talk to Teresa again. She smiles at him so she seems to like him. They will at least be friends.) **B**

Analyze Literature

Setting Ask students where this part of the story takes place and why it's important to the plot. (The setting is French class. It's where Victor hopes to begin his quest to make Teresa his girlfriend.) **C**

Use Reading Strategies

Visualize Have students picture the scene in which Victor pretends to speak French. What effect does it have on their feelings for Victor? (The scene will probably make them feel embarrassment for Victor, but may make them like him even more.) **D**

After English, Victor had math, his weakest subject. He sat in the back by the window, hoping that he would not be called on. Victor understood most of the problems, but some of the stuff looked like the teacher made it up as she went along. It was confusing, like the inside of a watch. **B**

> **Mr. Bueller, wrinkling his face in curiosity, asked him to speak up.**

After math he had a fifteen-minute break, then social studies, and, finally, lunch. He bought a tuna casserole with buttered rolls, some fruit cocktail, and milk. He sat with Michael, who practiced scowling between bites. **C**

Girls walked by and looked at him.

"See what I mean, Vic?" Michael scowled. "They love it."

"Yeah, I guess so."

They ate slowly, Victor scanning the horizon for a glimpse of Teresa. He didn't see her. She must have brought lunch, he thought, and is eating outside. Victor scraped his plate and left Michael, who was busy scowling at a girl two tables away.

The small, triangle-shaped campus bustled with students talking about their new classes. Everyone was in a sunny mood. Victor hurried to the bag lunch area, where he sat down and opened his math book. He moved his lips as if he were reading, but his mind was somewhere else. He raised his eyes slowly and looked around. No Teresa. **A** **D**

He lowered his eyes, pretending to study, then looked slowly to the left. No Teresa. He turned a page in the book and stared at some math problems that scared him because he knew he would have to do them eventually. He looked to the right. Still no sign of her. He stretched out lazily in an attempt to disguise his snooping.

Then he saw her. She was sitting with a girlfriend under a plum tree. Victor moved to a table near her and daydreamed about taking her to a movie. When the bell sounded, Teresa looked up, and their eyes met. She smiled sweetly and gathered her books. Her next class was French, same as Victor's.

They were among the last students to arrive in class, so all the good desks in the back had already been taken. Victor was forced to sit near the front, a few desks away from Teresa, while Mr. Bueller wrote French words on the chalkboard. The bell rang, and Mr. Bueller wiped his hands, turned to the class, and said, *"Bonjour."*[7]

"Bonjour," braved a few students.

"Bonjour," Victor whispered. He wondered if Teresa heard him. Mr. Bueller said that if the students studied hard, at the end of the year they could go to France and be understood by the populace.

One kid raised his hand and asked, "What's 'populace'?"

"The people, the people of France."

Mr. Bueller asked if anyone knew French. Victor raised his hand, wanting to impress Teresa. The teacher beamed and said, *"Très bien. Parlez-vous français?"*[8]

Victor didn't know what to say. The teacher wet his lips and asked something else in French. The room grew silent. Victor felt all eyes staring at him. He tried to bluff his way out by making noises that sounded French.

"La me vave me con le grandma," he said uncertainly.

Mr. Bueller, wrinkling his face in curiosity, asked him to speak up.

Great rosebushes of red bloomed on Victor's cheeks. A river of nervous sweat ran

---

7. Bonjour. Good day (French)
8. Très bien. Parlez-vous français? Very good. Do you speak French? (French)

Grammar Skills

Infinitives

Remind students that in an infinitive, a verb follows the word *to*. In a prepositional phrase, *to* is followed by a noun or pronoun. For example:

Joe began to sweat (infinitive) whenever he spoke to Ana. (prepositional phrase).

Give students these sentences, and have them tell whether the underlined words are infinitives (I) or prepositional phrases (P).

1. The bell rang to start the school day. (I)
2. We couldn't find our way to homeroom. (P)
3. Mr. Knowles asked me to pass out assignment sheets to the class. (I, P)
4. He was trying to act cool, but he tripped. (I)
5. She was too shy to say anything to him. (I, P)

down his palms. He felt awful. Teresa sat a few desks away, no doubt thinking he was a fool. Without looking at Mr. Bueller, Victor mumbled, "Frenchie oh wewe gee in September." **E**

Mr. Bueller asked Victor to repeat what he had said.

"Frenchie oh wewe gee in September," Victor repeated.

Mr. Bueller understood that the boy didn't know French and turned away. He walked to the blackboard and pointed to the words on the board with his steel-edged ruler. **F**

"*Le bateau*," he sang.

"*Le bateau*," the students repeated.

"*Le bateau est sur l'eau*,"[9] he sang.

"*Le bateau est sur l'eau*."

Victor was too weak from failure to join the class. He stared at the board and wished he had taken Spanish, not French. Better yet, he wished he could start his life over. He had never been so embarrassed. He bit his thumb until he tore off a sliver of skin.

The bell sounded for fifth period, and Victor shot out of the room, avoiding the stares of the other kids, but had to return for his math book. He looked sheepishly at the teacher, who was erasing the board, then widened his eyes in terror at Teresa who stood in front of him. "I didn't know you knew French," she said. "That was good."

Mr. Bueller looked at Victor, and Victor looked back. Oh please, don't say anything, Victor pleaded with his eyes. I'll wash your car, mow your lawn, walk your dog—anything! I'll be your best student and I'll clean your erasers after school.

Mr. Bueller shuffled through the papers on his desk. He smiled and hummed as he sat down to work. He remembered his college years when he dated a girlfriend in borrowed cars. She thought he was rich **D**

> **Oh please, don't say anything, Victor pleaded with his eyes.**

because each time he picked her up he had a different car. It was fun until he had spent all his money on her and had to write home to his parents because he was broke.

Victor couldn't stand to look at Teresa. He was sweaty with shame. "Yeah, well, I picked up a few things from movies and books and stuff like that." They left the class together. Teresa asked him if he would help her with her French. **G**

"Sure, anytime," Victor said.

"I won't be bothering you, will I?"

"Oh no, I like being bothered."

"*Bonjour*," Teresa said, leaving him outside her next class. She smiled and pushed wisps of hair from her face.

"Yeah, right, *bonjour*," Victor said. He turned and headed to his class. The rose-bushes of shame on his face became bouquets of love. Teresa is a great girl, he thought. And Mr. Bueller is a good guy.

He raced to metal shop. After metal shop there was biology, and after biology a long sprint to the public library, where he checked out three French textbooks.

He was going to like seventh grade. ❖

---

9. ***Le bateau est sur l'eau.*** The boat is on the water. (French)

Have you ever tried to change your look? How much effort should people expend trying to impress each other?

SEVENTH GRADE **217**

Analyze Literature

Character Ask students how Victor has changed so far in the story. (Before, he was almost too shy to say anything to Teresa. Now he risks embarrassment just to impress her.) **E**

Use Reading Skills

Retell Sequence Ask: "What does Mr. Bueller do after Victor pretends to speak French?" (He continues to teach the class without revealing that Victor was speaking nonsense.) **F**

Use Reading Strategies

Make Inferences Ask students to tell what happens after French class and to infer why Victor is surprised. (Teresa asks Victor for help with French. He was sure she knew he had only pretended to speak the language.) **G**

Answer: Most students will identify with the kind of experimenting Michael Torres and Victor do in the story. Many students will say that personality matters more than appearance, and some may point out that Victor attracts Teresa's attention through his actions, not his looks.

Writing Skills

Personal Anecdotes

Remind students that writers like Gary Soto often draw on their own life experiences to develop ideas for stories. Then challenge students to write a brief anecdote based on one of their own seventh-grade experiences, using these guidelines.

1. Select an interesting or amusing topic. To recall events, look through personal journals or talk with teachers and classmates.

2. List details and events to include in the anecdote, and check that they are in sequence.

3. Write the anecdote using first-person point of view. Use catchy dialogue and descriptive details to make the experience real for readers.

Review the Selection

Find Meaning

1. (a) He scowls for no obvious reason. (b) Victor thinks the scowl is strange, but he doesn't say so, and later tries scowling himself.
2. Victor would like Teresa to be his girlfriend.
3. (a) They bloom on his cheeks in French class. (b) They represent self-consciousness or embarrassment.

Make Judgments

4. (a) Mr. Bueller gives Victor an opportunity to show how much French he knows, but does not say anything when Victor demonstrates that he cannot really speak French. (b) They have both taken a risk to impress a girl.
5. (a) At first, he feels foolish. (b) No; Teresa responds to Victor's interest in her and to his apparent skill in speaking French. Also, Victor makes every effort to be in Teresa's presence, so she can't help paying attention to him.
6. Victor changes the most. He is the only character whose thoughts and feelings we know much about. All we know about Michael and Teresa comes through their brief interactions with Victor.

Analyze Literature

Character The events in charts should match the ones students used in their time lines. Students will probably say that the main change in Victor is an increase in self-confidence.

Find Meaning

1. (a) What does Michael Torres do on the first day of school that surprises Victor? (b) How does Victor respond to Michael?
2. What is Victor's big goal for this school year?
3. (a) When do "great rosebushes of red" bloom on Victor's cheeks? (b) What do the rosebushes represent?

Analyze Literature

Character Analyze Victor to find out how he changes during the story. Use a character chart and the time line you created earlier to track Victor's progress. In the left column, write the events you included on your time line. In the right column, write one or two words that describe how Victor feels during each event. When you are done, use one sentence to summarize the main change in Victor.

Make Judgments

4. (a) How does Mr. Bueller, the French teacher, treat Victor? (b) What do Victor and Mr. Bueller have in common?
5. (a) When Victor first tries scowling, how does he feel? (b) Does Victor's scowling attract Teresa? If not, how does he get her attention?
6. Which character in the story—Victor, Michael, or Teresa—changes the most? Explain.

Event	How Victor Feels
standing in line in the gym	optimistic

Summary Sentence:

Extend Understanding

Writing Options

Creative Writing With a classmate, draft a story about Victor's second day of school. Write a very **short story,** no longer than two paragraphs, to use as a starting point. Think about your own day at school for some ideas. Use the third-person point of view. With your partner, practice reading the story aloud. When you finish, present your story to the class.

Expository Writing Mentally review your own experiences in seventh grade, especially the first day. Then write an **expository essay** to compare your experiences with Victor's. In just one or two paragraphs, draft a thesis statement, a body with examples, and a conclusion. When you are done, trade your essay with a classmate. You and your partner should provide feedback about each other's essays.

Lifelong Learning

Get Romantic French and Spanish are both called "Romance languages." What does this mean? Use a dictionary or encyclopedia to find out. As part of your research, identify at least one other Romance language. Then choose one simple English word, like *school* or *sleep,* and find the word for it in French, Spanish, or another Romance language or languages. Make a chart of the words you have translated.

Critical Literacy

Ask the Author Think over the story of Victor and his first day of school. Then compose a list of questions you would like to ask Gary Soto about how he wrote the story. Start by jotting down any questions that are already in your mind. Then organize your questions and make sure you ask at least one question about the characters and one question about the sequence of events. When you are done, trade the list with a partner and compare your questions.

 Go to **www.mirrorsandwindows.com** for more.

Rubrics for Writing Options

You can adapt this as a checklist for students to use as they write.

Creative Writing

☐ Does the story clearly indicate it is Victor's second day of school?
☐ Does the story have a plot?
☐ Does the story use third-person point of view?

Expository Writing

☐ Does the thesis statement focus on comparing personal experiences with Victor's?
☐ Does the body of the essay include examples?
☐ Does the essay have a conclusion that relates to the thesis statement?

Grammar & Style

Consistent Verb Tense

The bell sounded for fifth period, and Victor shot out of the room, avoiding the stares of the other kids, but had to return for his math book.

—GARY SOTO, "Seventh Grade"

In this passage, each of the verbs—*sounded, shot*, and *had*—is in the past tense. When actions take place at the same time, the verbs that express these actions should be in the same tense. Good writers maintain a consistent verb tense in their writing.

> **INCORRECT**
>
> Last summer I <u>took</u> a long bicycle trip and <u>enjoy</u> the outdoors.

In this example, the first verb, *took*, is in the past tense, and the second verb, *enjoy*, is in the present tense. To correct this, make both verbs the same tense.

> **CORRECT**
>
> Last summer I <u>took</u> a long bicycle trip and <u>enjoyed</u> the outdoors.

When writing a literary analysis or other literary essay, maintain the present tense. Because the author is writing to a present reader in the present moment, you should refer to characters, settings, plots, and the author in the present tense.

> **CORRECT**
>
> Victor <u>is</u> both a believable and interesting character.

When you are writing a narrative essay, be sure to maintain a consistent tense between paragraphs.

> **CORRECT**
>
> I <u>walked</u> to the store to purchase a loaf of bread for my grandmother.
>
> I <u>felt</u> happy that I could help.

Most often, personal narratives and short stories are written in the past tense. When describing something habitual or universally true, however, use the present tense.

> **CORRECT**
>
> Victor <u>studied</u> for the test. He <u>wasn't</u> too worried. Victor usually <u>gets</u> straight As.

Sentence Improvement

For each of the following sentences, select the correct form of the verb in parentheses.

1. Last night I went to the movies and (see / saw) a Japanese samurai film.
2. Washington Irving was the author of many short stories, including "Rip Van Winkle," which he (writes / wrote) about a sleepy New Englander.
3. When Hannibal's troops (had crossed / cross) the Alps, they rested briefly before marching southward into Italy.
4. In Soto's story, Victor is a seventh-grader who (decides / decided) to take French.
5. She (turns / turned) off the television set and went to bed.

Sentence Improvement

1. saw
2. wrote
3. had crossed
4. decides
5. turned

Build Skills

When students have practiced sufficiently with maintaining a verb tense in a sentence, have them move on to paragraphs. Have pairs of students exchange samples of their own writing that are at least one paragraph long. Each student should choose a paragraph, identify the verb tense used in the first sentence, and then see if verb tenses are used correctly in the rest of the paragraph.

Point out that verb tenses can mix in a paragraph as long as the verbs refer to things happening at different times. For example, "Lottie explained that whenever she has rhubarb, she makes a rhubarb pie."

Review students' work and offer opportunities to discuss common problems or good examples of using multiple tenses correctly and consistently.

> ▶ For more information, see Grammar & Style Section 3.5, Verbs, in the Language Arts Handbook.

Words in Use

Teaching Words
consistent, 219
narrative, 219
habitual, 219
universally, 219

KEY TERMS

VERB, 219
PAST TENSE, 219
PRESENT TENSE, 219

Program Resources

You will find additional lessons on Consistent Verb Tense in the *Exceeding the Standards: Grammar & Style* resource.

Common Core State Standards

Language
L.5.1d

Preview the Selection

At a Glance
Independent Reading
- Reading Level: Easy
- Difficulty Considerations: None
- Ease Factor: Straightforward

Objectives
Reading this selection will enable students to do the following:
- read with developing fluency
- read silently with comprehension for a sustained period of time

Launch the Lesson
Tell students that the story they are about to read, "Papa's Parrot," is about a boy whose life is changed by a pet parrot. Write the following statement on the board: *Animals make just as good, if not better, friends and companions than people.* Have students briefly debate this statement, providing reasons and examples to support their opinions.

TEACHING NOTE
Although this selection is presented in the student edition as an independent reading, teaching support has been provided should you choose to cover it in class.

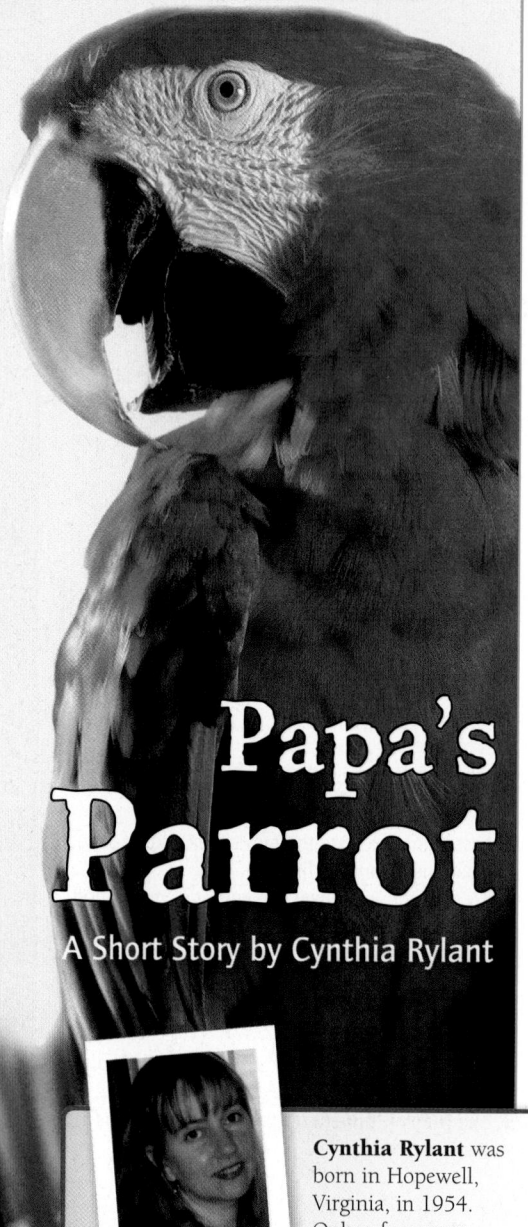

Papa's Parrot
A Short Story by Cynthia Rylant

Cynthia Rylant was born in Hopewell, Virginia, in 1954. Only a few years later, though, Rylant moved to a small town in the Appalachian Mountains. Due to her family's isolated and impoverished circumstances, she did not see a children's book until the age of twenty-three, and was unaware that such books existed. Today, Rylant is widely known for her works aimed at younger readers, including picture books and nonfiction. Rylant's 1992 novel *Missing May* won the Newbery Award.

220

Though his father was fat and merely owned a candy and nut shop, Harry Tillian liked his papa. Harry stopped liking candy and nuts when he was around seven, but, in spite of this, he and Mr. Tillian had remained friends and were still friends the year Harry turned twelve.

For years, after school, Harry had always stopped in to see his father at work. Many of Harry's friends stopped there, too, to spend a few cents choosing penny candy from the giant bins or to sample Mr. Tillian's latest batch of roasted peanuts. Mr. Tillian looked forward to seeing his son and his son's friends every day. He liked the company.

When Harry entered junior high school, though, he didn't come by the candy and nut shop as often. Nor did his friends. They were older and they had more spending money. They went to a burger place. They played video games. They shopped for records. None of them were much interested in candy and nuts anymore.

A new group of children came to Mr. Tillian's shop now. But not Harry Tillian and his friends.

The year Harry turned twelve was also the year Mr. Tillian got a parrot. He went to a pet store one day and bought one for more money than he could really afford. He brought the parrot to his shop, set its cage near the sign for maple clusters, and named it Rocky.

Program Resources

Planning and Assessment
Program Planning Guide, Selection Lesson Plan
E-Lesson Planner
Assessment Guide, Lesson Test
ExamView

Technology Tools
Interactive Student Text on CD
Visual Teaching Package
mirrorsandwindows.com

Meeting the Standards
Fiction: Unit 2, Independent Reading, pp. 74–80

Common Core State Standards

Reading Literature
RL.1, RL.10

Harry thought this was the strangest thing his father had ever done, and he told him so, but Mr. Tillian just ignored him.

Rocky was good company for Mr. Tillian. When business was slow, Mr. Tillian would turn on a small color television he had sitting in a corner, and he and Rocky would watch the soap operas. Rocky liked to scream when the romantic music came on, and Mr. Tillian would yell at him to shut up, but they seemed to enjoy themselves.

The year Harry turned twelve was also the year Mr. Tillian got a parrot.

The more Mr. Tillian grew to like his parrot, and the more he talked to it instead of to people, the more embarrassed Harry became. Harry would stroll past the shop, on his way somewhere else, and he'd take a quick look inside to see what his dad was doing. Mr. Tillian was always talking to the bird. So Harry kept walking.

At home things were different. Harry and his father joked with each other at the dinner table as they always had—Mr. Tillian teasing Harry about his smelly socks; Harry teasing Mr. Tillian about his blubbery stomach. At home things seemed all right.

But one day, Mr. Tillian became ill. He had been at work, unpacking boxes of caramels, when he had grabbed his chest and fallen over on top of the candy. A customer

had found him, and he was taken to the hospital in an ambulance.

Mr. Tillian couldn't leave the hospital. He lay in bed, tubes in his arms, and he worried about his shop. New shipments of candy and nuts would be arriving. Rocky would be hungry. Who would take care of things?

Harry said he would. Harry told his father that he would go to the store every day after school and unpack boxes. He would sort out all the candy and nuts. He would even feed Rocky.

So, the next morning, while Mr. Tillian lay in his hospital bed, Harry took the shop key to school with him. After school he left his friends and walked to the empty shop alone. In all the days of his life, Harry had never seen the shop closed after school. Harry didn't even remember what the CLOSED sign looked like. The key stuck in the lock three times, and inside he had to search all the walls for the light switch.

The shop was as his father had left it. Even the caramels were still spilled on the floor. Harry bent down and picked them up one by one, dropping them back in the boxes. The bird in its cage watched him silently.

Harry opened the new boxes his father hadn't gotten to. Peppermints. Jawbreakers. Toffee creams. Strawberry kisses. Harry traveled from bin to bin, putting the candies where they belonged.

"Hello!"

Harry jumped, spilling a box of jawbreakers.

"Hello, Rocky!"

Harry stared at the parrot. He had

Summary

When Harry Tillian enters junior high, he and his friends suddenly outgrow their habit of stopping by his father's candy store after school each day. Unaware of how much those visits meant to his father, Harry thinks it's strange when Mr. Tillian buys a parrot to keep him company at the store. Then one day, Mr. Tillian is rushed to the hospital. Trying to ease his father's mind, Harry agrees to take care of the store and Rocky, the parrot, after school. Rocky reveals to Harry just how much his father has missed him.

MIRRORS & WINDOWS The Mirrors & Windows questions at the end of the story focus on the theme of staying in touch. Before students begin reading, ask: What makes children grow away from their parents?

Use Reading Strategies

Make Inferences Ask students if they think it's a coincidence that Mr. Tillian buys the parrot the same year that Harry turns twelve, and have them explain their answers. (Mr. Tillian buys the parrot because Harry isn't coming around any more and he's lonely.)

Words in Use

Selection Words
merely, 220
blubbery, 221

Teaching Words
isolated, 220
impoverished, 220
regretted, 223
genuinely, 223
mimicry, 223

KEY TERMS

SHORT STORY, 220
STATIC CHARACTER, 223
DYNAMIC CHARACTER, 223
SUMMARIZE, 223

Use Reading Skills

Identify Sequence of Events Have students tell what happens the day before Harry goes to the candy shop. (First, Harry's father becomes ill and is rushed to the hospital. Then Harry goes to see him and agrees to take care of the shop and the parrot.)

Make Connections

Ask students how Harry's response to the parrot affects their attitude toward him. (Most students will feel sympathy because they realize he is worried about his father. Some may say they don't like him as a result.)

Analyze Literature

Theme Remind students that the theme of a story is the central idea the author wants readers to get. Ask them to state the theme of "Papa's Parrot." (Young people can get so busy with friends and activities that they neglect their own families who love them.)

More by This Author

Students who like "Papa's Parrot" might enjoy other short stories by Cynthia Rylant, such as "Slower Than the Rest," "A Crush," and "Shay."

forgotten it was there. The bird had been so quiet, and Harry had been thinking only of the candy.

"Hello," Harry said.

"Hello, Rocky!" answered the parrot.

Harry walked slowly over to the cage. The parrot's food cup was empty. Its water was dirty. The bottom of the cage was a mess.

Harry carried the cage into the back room.

"Hello, Rocky!"

"Is that all you can say, you dumb bird?" Harry mumbled. The bird said nothing else.

Harry cleaned the bottom of the cage, refilled the food and water cups, and then put the cage back in its place and resumed sorting the candy.

"Where's Harry?"

Harry looked up.

"Where's Harry?"

Harry stared at the parrot.

"Where's Harry?"

Chills ran down Harry's back. What could the bird mean? It was something from "The Twilight Zone."[1]

"Where's Harry?"

Harry swallowed and said, "I'm here. I'm here, you stupid bird."

---

1. **The Twilight Zone.** Long-running science fiction television program that aired in the 1960s

222   UNIT 2 FICTION

Differentiated Instruction

Reading Proficiency

The lack of speaker tags in parts of the conversation between Harry and the parrot may make it difficult for students to follow the conversation and to understand what is happening. Point out that any dialogue in this scene that is _not_ followed by a comma and the speaker's name belongs to Rocky, the parrot.

Enrichment

Interested students might enjoy researching parrots and learning more about their ability to speak. Students should use the Internet or your school or local library to find books and articles on parrots. Encourage them to prepare a brief oral report to share findings with classmates.

"You stupid bird!" said the parrot.

Well, at least he's got one thing straight, thought Harry.

"Miss him! Miss him! Where's Harry? You stupid bird!"

Harry stood with a handful of peppermints.

"What?" he asked.

"Where's Harry?" said the parrot.

"I'm *here*, you stupid bird! I'm here!" Harry yelled. He threw the peppermints at the cage, and the bird screamed and clung to its perch.

Harry sobbed, "I'm here." The tears were coming.

"I'm here. I'm here, you stupid bird."

Harry leaned over the glass counter. "Papa." Harry buried his face in his arms. "Where's Harry?" repeated the bird.

Harry sighed and wiped his face on his sleeve. He watched the parrot. He understood now: someone had been saying, for a long time, "Where's Harry? Miss him."

Harry finished his unpacking and then swept the floor of the shop. He checked the furnace so the bird wouldn't get cold. Then he left to go visit his papa.

Have you ever regretted losing touch with a family member? Have you ever wished you could be more open with your parents or better understand how they saw the world? Why do you think it is important for people to remain in touch with their loved ones?

Analyze and Extend

1. (a) Why did Harry and his friends stop going to Mr. Tillian's candy shop? (b) How do you think this made Mr. Tillian feel?

2. Do you think Mr. Tillian genuinely enjoyed his relationship with the parrot, or was he simply using the parrot as a replacement for his son? Explain.

3. Is Harry a static character, which is a character that remains essentially the same, or a dynamic character, which is a character that changes through the course of the story? Explain your answer.

Creative Writing Imagine that you are Harry. The events described in this story have already taken place and you have gone home after visiting your father. Write a **journal entry** to summarize the events that took place, and explain how they made you feel. Try to capture the style in which Harry would write.

Lifelong Learning Research the ability of parrots to mimic human speech. Then research other mimics in nature. Compare the different kinds of animal mimicry. Use a graphic organizer or an outline to organize your information. Present your findings to the class.

Go to **www.mirrorsandwindows.com** for more.

Answer: Answers will vary. Most will say that they have wanted to better understand their parents. Students might argue that people should stay in touch with loved ones because the future is always uncertain.

Analyze and Extend

1. (a) Harry and his friends stopped going to Mr. Tillian's candy shop because they grew too old. Also, Harry stopped liking candy and nuts. (b) It made Mr. Tillian feel unhappy.

2. Answers will vary. Most students will claim that while Mr. Tillian genuinely enjoyed his relationship with the parrot, he also used it as a replacement for his son.

3. Harry is a dynamic character. During the course of the story Harry grows up, stops visiting his father, and then learns to value his relationship with his father.

Rubric for Creative Writing

You can adapt this as a checklist for students to use as they write.

☐ Does the journal entry describe Harry's feelings?

☐ Does the journal entry summarize the events of the story?

☐ Does the journal entry capture Harry's voice?

Reading Skills

Identify Text Structure

Remind students that the climax of a story is the most exciting point in the plot. Something happens to decide how the central conflict will end. The resolution is when the conflict ends, leading to the conclusion. In stories as short as "Papa's Parrot," the climax, resolution, and ending often come close together.

Help students state the conflict in this story (for example, "Harry doesn't understand his father's attachment to Rocky"). Then have them identify the climax and the resolution. (The climax is when Harry becomes enraged at Rocky. The resolution is when Harry understands why Rocky keeps saying, "Where's Harry? Miss him.")

Preview the Selection

At a Glance
Independent Reading
- Reading Level: Challenging
- Difficulty Considerations: Vocabulary and setting
- Ease Factors: Sympathetic main character and interesting plot

Objectives
Reading this selection will enable students to do the following:
- read with developing fluency
- read silently with comprehension for a sustained period of time

Launch the Lesson
Have students freewrite for five minutes in response to these questions: "What is a dragon? What do dragons look like? Where do dragons live? Are dragons good or evil?" Then work as a class to write a dictionary-style definition of a dragon, based on the freewriting ideas. Students can revise the definition after they read "The Smallest Dragonboy."

TEACHING NOTE
Although this selection is presented in the student edition as an independent reading, teaching support has been provided should you choose to cover it in class.

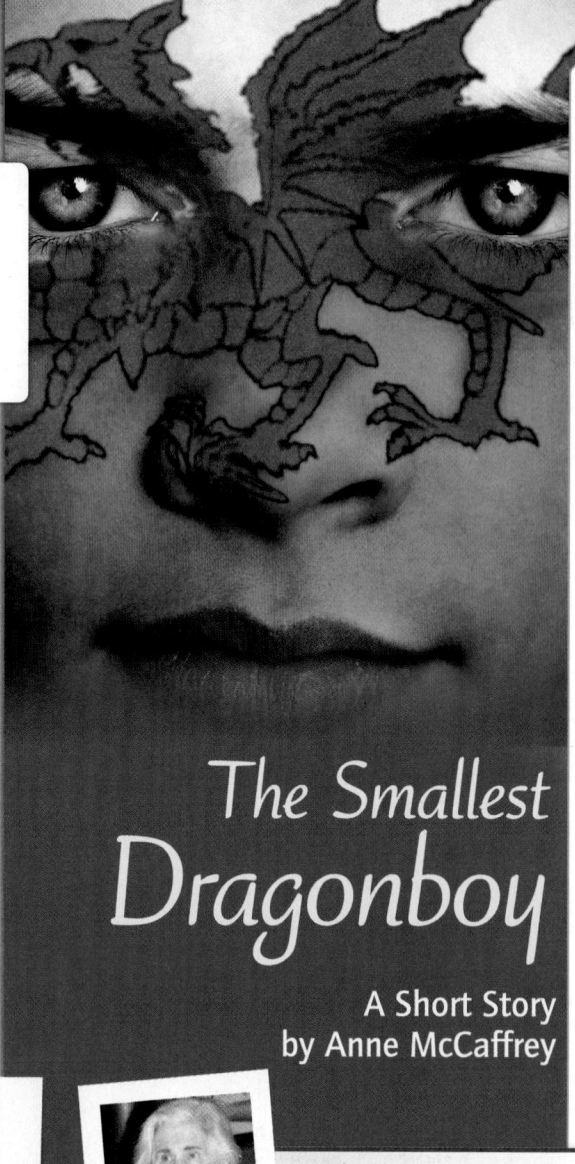

The Smallest Dragonboy

A Short Story
by Anne McCaffrey

Anne McCaffrey (b. 1926) is known for her many works of science fiction and fantasy. However, she is best known for her Dragonriders of Pern series. This series focuses on the planet Pern, which is populated with dragons and magic as well as high technology and other science fiction elements. Her first short story in the Dragonriders series, "Weyr Search," was awarded the prestigious Hugo Award in 1968, making McCaffrey the first female winner of a Hugo Award for fiction. Currently there are about twenty Dragonrider books, including two collections of short stories.

224

Although Keevan lengthened his walking stride as far as his legs would stretch, he couldn't quite keep up with the other candidates. He knew he would be teased again.

Just as he knew many other things that his foster mother told him he ought not to know, Keevan knew that Beterli, the most senior of the boys, set that spanking pace just to embarrass him, the smallest dragonboy. Keevan would arrive, tail fork-end of the group, breathless, chest heaving, and maybe get a stern look from the instructing wingsecond.

Dragonriders, even if they were still only hopeful candidates for the glowing eggs which were hardening on the hot sands of the Hatching Ground cavern, were expected to be punctual and prepared. Sloth[1] was not tolerated by the weyrleader of Benden Weyr. A good record was especially important now. It was very near hatching time, when the baby dragons would crack their mottled shells and stagger forth to choose their lifetime companions. The very thought of that glorious moment made Keevan's breath catch in his throat. To be chosen—to be a dragonrider! To sit astride the neck of the winged beast with the jeweled eyes: to be his friend in telepathic communion[2] with him for

---

1. **sloth.** Laziness
2. **telepathic communion.** Ability to share thoughts with another mind without speaking

---

Program Resources

Planning and Assessment
Program Planning Guide, Selection Lesson Plan
E-Lesson Planner
Assessment Guide, Lesson Test
ExamView

Technology Tools
Interactive Student Text on CD
Visual Teaching Package
mirrorsandwindows.com

Meeting the Standards
Fiction: Unit 2, Independent Reading, pp. 81–87

Differentiating Instruction
Advanced Students, Symbolism Analysis, p. 13

Common Core State Standards
Reading Literature
RL.1, RL.10

life; to be his companion in good times and fighting extremes; to fly effortlessly over the lands of Pern! Or, thrillingly, *between* to any point anywhere on the world! Flying *between* was done on dragonback or not at all, and it was dangerous.

Keevan glanced upward, past the black mouths of the weyr caves in which grown dragons and their chosen riders lived, toward the Star Stones that crowned the ridge of the old volcano that was Benden Weyr. On the height, the blue watch dragon, his rider mounted on his neck, stretched the great transparent pinions[3] that carried him on the winds of Pern to fight the evil Thread[4] that fell at certain times from the sky. The many-faceted rainbow jewels of his eyes glistened momentarily in the greeny sun. He folded his great wings to his back, and the watchpair resumed their statuesque[5] pose of alertness.

Then the enticing[6] view was obscured as Keevan passed into the Hatching Ground cavern. The sands underfoot were hot, even through heavy wher-hide boots. How the bootmaker had protested having to sew so small! Keevan was forced to wonder again why being small was reprehensible.[7] People were always calling him "babe" and shooing him away as being "too small" or "too young" for this or that. Keevan was constantly working, twice as hard as any other boy his age, to prove himself capable. What if his muscles weren't as big as Beterli's? They were just as hard. And if he couldn't overpower anyone in a wrestling match, he could outdistance everyone in a footrace.

"Maybe if you run fast enough," Beterli had jeered on the occasion when Keevan had been goaded to boast of his swiftness, "you could catch a dragon. That's the only way

you'll make a dragonrider!"

"You just wait and see, Beterli, you just wait," Keevan had replied. He would have liked to wipe the contemptuous[8] smile from

"As we well know, there are only forty eggs and seventy-two candidates."

Beterli's face, but the guy didn't fight fair even when the wingsecond was watching. "No one knows what Impresses[9] a dragon!"

"They've got to be able to *find* you first, babe!"

Yes, being the smallest candidate was not an enviable position. It was therefore imperative[10] that Keevan Impress a dragon in his first hatching. That would wipe the smile off every face in the cavern, and accord him the respect due any dragonrider, even the smallest one.

Besides, no one knew exactly what Impressed the baby dragons as they struggled from their shells in search of their lifetime partners.

"I like to believe that dragons see into a

---

3. **pinions.** Outer parts of a bird's wings
4. **Thread.** Spore from outer space that feeds on living things and that the dragonriders fight
5. **statuesque.** Statuelike; unmoving
6. **enticing.** Tempting
7. **reprehensible.** Unacceptable; deserving condemnation
8. **contemptuous.** Showing contempt or scorn
9. **Impresses.** Dragonriders become telepathically connected to their dragons through *Impression.*
10. **imperative.** Very important

Summary
Keevan knows chances of being chosen as a dragonrider at his first hatching are slim. There are seventy-two boys and only forty eggs. In spite of the odds and constant teasing by Beterli and other older candidates, Keevan remains hopeful. Still, after Beterli breaks Keevan's leg, Keevan nearly misses Hatching Day. With determination, Keevan stumbles his way onto the hatching field, where he is chosen by a bronze, the rarest, most prestigious of all dragons.

MIRRORS & WINDOWS The Mirrors & Windows questions at the end of the story focus on the theme of apprehension. Before students begin reading, ask: What are the benefits of worrying?

Use Reading Strategies
Clarify Encourage students to reread the first few paragraphs of the story to make sure they understand the setting, who the main characters are, and the conflict. If they don't understand these elements, have them use questions to clarify points before reading on.

Analyze Literature
Character Ask students what Keevan's reply to Beterli's teasing tells you about Keevan's character. (He believes in himself and is not afraid of Beterli.) Ⓐ

Words in Use

Analyze Literature

Plot Model for students identifying details of the exposition: "This story takes place in Bendyn Weyr, on the planet Pern, where dragons with riders patrol the skies and fight the evil Thread. Keevan is the main character. It is near hatching time and Keevan's goal is to be chosen as a dragonrider. His problem is that he is small, and it's not easy for him to keep up with the other bigger, older candidates. He is also constantly being teased and embarrassed by Beterli." Encourage students to write details in their graphic organizers.

Science Connection

Imprinting Dragons bond with their partners soon after hatching through a process called "Impressing." The author probably got this idea from the scientific concept called imprinting. Imprinting (like the fictional Impressing) is an instinctive process, especially among birds. A newly hatched duck, for example, will follow and imitate the first moving object it sees, choosing that object as its parent. Usually, the first thing a duckling sees is its mother. However, if the first thing the animal sees is a person, it is likely to choose the person as its parent.

---

man's heart," Keevan's foster mother, Mende, told him. "If they find goodness, honesty, a flexible mind, patience, courage—and you've that in quantity, dear Keevan—that's what dragons look for. I've seen many a well-grown lad left standing on the sands, Hatching Day, in favor of someone not so strong or tall or handsome. And if my memory serves me" (which it usually did—Mende knew every word of every Harper's tale worth telling, although Keevan did not interrupt her to say so), "I don't believe that F'lar, our weyrleader, was all that tall when bronze Mnementh chose him. And Mnementh was the only bronze dragon of that hatching."

Dreams of Impressing a bronze were beyond Keevan's boldest reflections, although that goal dominated the thoughts of every other hopeful candidate. Green dragons were small and fast and more numerous. There was more prestige[11] in Impressing a blue or a brown than a green. Being practical, Keevan seldom dreamed as high as a big fighting brown, like Canth, F'nor's fine fellow, the biggest brown on all Pern. But to fly a bronze? Bronzes were almost as big as the queen, and only they took the air when a queen flew at mating time. A bronze rider could aspire to become weyrleader! Well, Keevan would console himself, brown riders could aspire to become wingseconds, and that wasn't bad. He'd even settle for a green dragon: they were small, but so was he. No matter! He simply had to Impress a dragon his first time in the Hatching Ground. Then no one in the weyr would taunt him anymore for being so small.

"Shells," thought Keevan now, "but the sands are hot!"

"Impression time is imminent,

candidates," the wingsecond was saying as everyone crowded respectfully close to him. "See the extent of the striations[12] on this promising egg." The stretch marks *were* larger than yesterday.

Everyone leaned forward and nodded thoughtfully. That particular egg was the one Beterli had marked as his own, and no other candidate dared, on pain of being beaten by Beterli on the first opportunity, to approach it. The egg was marked by a large yellowish splotch in the shape of a dragon backwinging to land, talons outstretched to grasp rock. Everyone knew that bronze eggs bore distinctive markings. And naturally, Beterli, who'd been presented at eight Impressions already and was the biggest of the candidates, had chosen it.

"I'd say that the great opening day is almost upon us," the wingsecond went on, and then his face assumed a grave expression. "As we well know, there are only forty eggs and seventy-two candidates." Some of you may be disappointed on the great day. That doesn't necessarily mean you aren't dragonrider material, just that *the* dragon for you hasn't been shelled. You'll have other hatchings, and it's no disgrace to be left behind an Impression or two. Or more."

Keevan was positive that the wingsecond's eyes rested on Beterli, who'd been stood off at so many Impressions already. Keevan tried to squinch[13] down so the wingsecond wouldn't notice him. Keevan had been reminded too often that he was eligible to be a candidate by one day only. He, of all the hopefuls, was most likely to be

---

11. **prestige.** Honor
12. **striations.** Grooves
13. **squinch.** Crouch down

Reading Skills

Take Notes

Tell students that using a graphic organizer is an efficient, organized way to take notes about setting, characters, and plot as they read a story. They can use a completed graphic organizer to summarize a story, to study for a class test, or to prepare a literary response. Have students create a graphic organizer to keep notes about the plot of "The Smallest Dragonboy." They might use a plot diagram similar to the one on page 6 or a plot chart with the heads Exposition, Rising Action, Climax. Falling Action, and Resolution.

left standing on the great day. One more reason why he simply had to Impress at his first hatching.

"Now move about among the eggs," wingsecond said. "Touch them. We don't know that it does any good, but it certainly doesn't do any harm."

Some of the boys laughed nervously, but everyone immediately began to circulate among the eggs. Beterli stepped up officiously to "his" egg, daring anyone to come near it. Keevan smiled, because he had already touched it...every inspection day ...as the others were leaving the Hatching Ground, when no one could see him crouch and stroke it.

Keevan had an egg he concentrated on too, one drawn slightly to the far side of the others. The shell bore a soft greenish blue tinge with a faint creamy swirl design. The

consensus[14] was that this egg contained a mere green, so Keevan was rarely bothered by rivals. He was somewhat perturbed then to see Beterli wandering over to him.

"I don't know why you're allowed in this Impression, Keevan. There are enough of us without a babe," Beterli said, shaking his head.

"I'm of age." Keevan kept his voice level, telling himself not to be bothered by mere words.

"Yah!" Beterli made a show of standing on his toe tips. "You can't even see over an egg; Hatching Day, you better get in front or the dragons won't see you at all. 'Course, you could get run down that way in the mad scramble. Oh, I forget, you can run fast, can't you?"

"You'd better make sure a dragon sees *you*, this time, Beterli," Keevan replied. "You're almost overage, aren't you?"

Beterli flushed and took a step forward, hand half-raised. Keevan stood his ground, but if Beterli advanced one more step, he would call the wingsecond. No one fought on the Hatching Ground. Surely Beterli knew that much.

Fortunately, at that moment the wingsecond called the boys together and led them from the Hatching Ground to start on evening chores.

There were "glows" to be replenished in the main kitchen caverns and sleeping cubicles, the major hallways, and the queen's apartment. Firestone sacks had to be filled against Thread attack, and black rock brought to the kitchen

---

14. **consensus.** Agreement among a group

Analyze Literature
Motivation Tell students that the more they learn about characters, the easier it will be to understand their motivations. Ask why Beterli is so mean to Keevan. Model a response: "Beterli has gone through many Impressions without being chosen. He is probably feeling insecure. He's a bully, so he takes his anxiety out on someone smaller, like Keevan." Ⓐ

Use Reading Skills
Compare and Contrast Ask students to compare and contrast Keevan and Beterli. (Keevan is small and about to enter his first hatching. He is not very muscular but he is fast, and he follows the rules. Beterli is muscular and strong, but mean and likely to break the rules.)

Use Reading Strategies
Make Predictions Ask students to predict whether a dragon will choose Beterli this time. Do they think Keevan will be chosen? Why or why not? (Students should understand that Beterli probably hasn't been chosen yet because he is a mean-spirited bully, and it's not likely he'll be chosen this time. Keevan, on the other hand, will probably be chosen because of the qualities Mende pointed out earlier.) Ⓑ

Differentiated Instruction

Reading Proficiency
To help students keep track of characters in the story, encourage them to write the name of each character they encounter, and one or two descriptive details that will help them remember the character and why he or she is important to the story. Provide the following example: Keevan—smallest, youngest dragonboy; candidate to be a dragonrider.

Some students may find it helpful to use a two-column chart with the heads Characters and Details to keep track of characters. If students become confused during reading, they can quickly refer to their lists or charts to refresh their memories about a character.

Use Reading Strategies

Ask Questions Encourage students to ask questions to fully understand the responsibilities of dragonriders during a Thread attack, and to understand the ability of dragons to spew fire to sear Thread. **Ⓐ**

Analyze Literature

Plot Ask students to explain how specifics of the dragonriders' conversation intensify the conflict, because the conversation complicates Keevan's problem and threatens to ruin his chances of achieving his goal. (They are discussing the possibility of eliminating the youngest boys from the Impression. If this happens, Keevan, who is the youngest of all, will be eliminated, and he won't be chosen by a dragon.) **Ⓑ**

hearths. The boys fell to their chores, tantalized by the odors of roasting meat. The population of the weyr began to assemble for the evening meal, and the dragonriders came in from the Feeding Ground or their sweep checks.

It was the time of day Keevan liked best: once the chores were done, before dinner was served, a fellow could often get close to the dragonriders and listen to their talk. Tonight Keevan's father, K'last, was at the main dragonrider table. It puzzled Keevan how his father, a brown rider and a tall man, could *be* his father—because he, Keevan, was so small. It obviously never puzzled K'last when he deigned to notice his small son: "In a few more turns, you'll be as tall as I am—or taller!"

K'last was pouring Benden drink all around the table. The dragonriders were relaxing. There'd be no Thread attack for three more days, and they'd be in the mood to tell tall tales, better than Harper yarns, about impossible maneuvers they'd done a-dragonback. When Thread attack was closer, their talk would change to a discussion of tactics of evasion, of going *between,* how long to suspend there until the burning but fragile Thread would freeze and crack and fall harmlessly off dragon and man. They would dispute the exact moment to feed firestone to the dragon so he'd have the best flame ready to sear Thread midair and render it harmless to ground—and man—below. There was such a lot to know and understand about being a dragonrider that sometimes Keevan was overwhelmed. How would he ever be able to remember everything he ought to know at the right moment? He couldn't dare ask such a question; this would only have given

additional weight to the notion that he was too young yet to be a dragonrider.

"Having older candidates makes good sense," L'vel was saying, as Keevan settled down near the table. "Why waste four to five years of a dragon's fighting prime until his rider grows up enough to stand the rigors?" L'vel had Impressed a blue of Ramoth's first clutch.[15] Most of the candidates thought L'vel was marvelous because he spoke up in front of the older riders, who awed them. "That was well enough in the Interval when you didn't need to mount the full weyr complement to fight Thread. But not now. Not with more eligible candidates than ever. Let the babes wait."

"Any boy who is over twelve turns has the right to stand in the Hatching Ground," K'last replied, a slight smile on his face. He never argued or got angry. Keevan wished he were more like his father. And oh, how he wished he were a brown rider! "Only a dragon...each particular dragon...knows what he wants in a rider. We certainly can't tell. Time and again the theorists," and K'last's smile deepened as his eyes swept those at the table, "are surprised by dragon choice. *They* never seem to make mistakes, however."

"Now, K'last, just look at the roster this Impression. Seventy-two boys and only forty eggs. Drop off the twelve youngest, and there's still a good field for the hatchlings to choose from. Shells! There are a couple of weyrlings unable to see over a wher egg much less a dragon! And years before they can ride Thread."

"True enough, but the weyr is scarcely under fighting strength, and if the youngest Impress, they'll be old enough to fight when

---

15. clutch. Group of eggs

Differentiated Instruction

Reading Proficiency

Most students who are unfamiliar with McCaffrey's stories will find it necessary to use context clues to translate the Pern language. However, struggling readers and students learning English may find that the translation process makes it harder to follow the story's action. You might divide the story into

manageable chunks for students to read aloud with a bilingual partner who can offer help when necessary. Emphasize that students should not read on until they are sure they have understood what they have read so far.

the oldest of our current dragons go *between* from senility."

"Half the weyrbred lads have already been through several Impressions," one of the bronze riders said then. "I'd say drop some of

"Only a dragon...
each particular dragon...
knows what he wants
in a rider."

them off this time. Give the untried a chance."

"There's nothing wrong in presenting a clutch with as wide a choice as possible," said the weyrleader, who had joined the table with Lessa, the weyrwoman.

"Has there ever been a case," she said, smiling in her odd way at the riders, "where a hatchling didn't choose?"

Her suggestion was almost heretical[16] and drew astonished gasps from everyone, including the boys.

F'lar laughed. "You say the most outrageous things, Lessa."

"Well, *has* there ever been a case when a dragon didn't choose?"

"Can't say as I recall one," K'last replied.

"Then we continue in this tradition," Lessa said firmly, as if that ended the matter.

But it didn't. The argument ranged from one table to the other all through dinner, with some favoring a weeding out of the candidates to the most likely, lopping off those who were very young or who had multiple opportunities to Impress. All the candidates were in a swivet,[17] though such a

departure from tradition would be to the advantage of many. As the evening progressed, more riders were favoring eliminating the youngest and those who'd passed four or more Impressions unchosen. Keevan felt he could bear such a dictum if only Beterli was also eliminated. But this seemed less likely than that Keevan would be tuffed out, since the weyr's need was for fighting dragons and riders.

By the time the evening meal was over, no decision had been reached, although the weyrleader had promised to give the matter due consideration.

He might have slept on the problem, but few of the candidates did. Tempers were uncertain in the sleeping caverns next morning as the boys were routed out of their beds to carry water and black rock and cover the "glows." Mende had to call Keevan to order twice for clumsiness.

"Whatever is the matter with you, boy?" she demanded in exasperation when he tipped black rock short of the bin and sooted up the hearth.

"They're going to keep me from this Impression."

"What?" Mende stared at him. "Who?"

"You heard them talking at dinner last night. They're going to tuff the babes from the hatching."

Mende regarded him a moment longer before touching his arm gently. "There's lots of talk around a supper table, Keevan. And it cools as soon as the supper. I've heard the same nonsense before every hatching, but nothing is ever changed."

---

16. **heretical.** Something that goes against established thought or tradition
17. **swivet.** State of confusion

Teach the Selection

Literary Connection
Fantasy or Science Fiction? A fantasy is an extremely unrealistic story with imaginary elements that have no or little basis in reality. Science fiction is imaginative literature based on actual scientific principles, discoveries, or laws. While many reviewers classify "The Smallest Dragonboy" and other works by Anne McCaffrey as fantasy, the author herself expresses her thoughts on that subject rather emphatically: "I am a storyteller of science fiction and wish that label attached to my work in that field. I make this point as I am often classified, erroneously, as a fantasy writer." Consider asking students why McCaffrey might feel this way.

Use Reading Strategies
Visualize Have students picture the scene in the caverns after the boys wake up. Ask students what it conveys about the thoughts and feelings of Keevan and the other candidates. (The boys act edgy. Keevan is clumsy and spills black rock, causing soot to rise. Because of what they overheard the night before, he and the other boys are obviously worried about being eliminated from the Impression.) **C**

Reading Skills

Use Context Clues
Remind students that context clues include descriptions and examples. For practice, have students read the description of a dragonrider at the beginning of the story. Then ask them to use that description to determine the meaning of *dragonboy* (a young boy waiting for a newly hatched dragon to choose him as a rider and lifetime companion). Encourage students to use descriptions and examples to figure out the meaning of the following words as they are used in the story: *wingsecond, between, watchpair, Impress/ Impression, backwinging, glows,* and *turns.*

Make Connections

Do students think that, in Keevan's place, they would feel reassured by what Mende says? Why or why not? (Many will say yes, because Keevan is one of her fosterlings and she says that all her fosterlings make dragonriders. Some may have doubts, because Keevan may be left out of the Impression.) **A**

Analyze Literature

Suspense Ask students how this introduction to Keevan's encounter with Beterli adds suspense to the plot. (The narrator says, "if he hadn't been on that chore," suggesting something bad is going to happen. Then Beterli asks Keevan if he's heard the news in a sly, smug way. Has Keevan been eliminated from the Impression?) **B**

Literary Connection

Dragons Dragons are familiar figures in English literature. In the English epic *Beowulf*, the title character battles a fierce fire-breathing dragon until both die. In 1898, Kenneth Grahame published the humorous children's story "The Reluctant Dragon," in which a dragon who doesn't like fighting eventually becomes friends with the other characters. One of the most famous and fearsome dragons in literature is Smaug, a character in J. R. R. Tolkien's *The Hobbit*, published in 1937.

"There's always a first time," Keevan answered, copying one of her own phrases.

"That'll be enough of that, Keevan. Finish your job. If the clutch does hatch today, we'll need full rock bins for the feast, and you **A** won't be around to do the filling. All my fosterlings make dragonriders."

"The first time?" Keevan was bold enough to ask as he scooted off with the rockbarrow.

Perhaps, Keevan thought later, if he hadn't been on that chore just when Beterli was also fetching black rock, things might have turned out differently. But he had dutifully trundled[18] the barrow to the outdoor bunker for another load just as Beterli arrived on a similar errand.

B "Heard the news, babe?" asked Beterli. He was grinning from ear to ear, and he put an

---

18. **trundled.** Moved something slowly

Differentiated Instruction

Auditory Learning

Have volunteers present an oral interpretation of the confrontation between Keevan and Beterli on these pages. Encourage them to capture the personalities and emotions of the characters.

English Language Learning

Ask students learning English to tell the word for *dragon* in their languages. Then ask them to share stories about dragons, and any superstitions or beliefs associated with dragons from their cultures. English-speaking students from different ethnic backgrounds may also enjoy sharing stories and beliefs about dragons passed down in their families.

unnecessary emphasis on the final insulting word.

"The eggs are cracking?" Keevan all but dropped the loaded shovel. Several anxieties flicked through his mind then; he was black with rock dust—would he have time to wash before donning the white tunic of candidacy? And if the eggs were hatching, why hadn't the candidates been recalled by the wingsecond?

"Naw! Guess again!" Beterli was much too pleased with himself.

With a sinking heart Keevan knew what the news must be, and he could only stare with intense desolation at the older boy. **C**

"C'mon! Guess, babe!"

"I've no time for guessing games," Keevan managed to say with indifference. He began to shovel black rock into his barrow as fast as he could.

"I said, 'guess.'" Beterli grabbed the shovel.

"And I said I'd no time for guessing games."

Beterli wrenched the shovel from Keevan's hands. "Guess!"

"I'll have the shovel back, Beterli." Keevan straightened up, but he didn't come up to Beterli's bulky shoulder. From somewhere, other boys appeared, some with barrows, some mysteriously alerted to the prospect of a confrontation among their numbers.

"Babes don't give orders to candidates around here, babe!"

"Hatching?" he cried.

Someone sniggered and Keevan knew, incredibly, that he must've been dropped from the candidacy.

He yanked the shovel from Beterli's loosened grasp. Snarling, the older boy tried to regain possession, but Keevan clung with all his strength to the handle, dragged back and forth as the stronger boy jerked the shovel about.

With a sudden, unexpected movement, Beterli rammed the handle into Keevan's chest, knocking him over the barrow handles. Keevan felt a sharp, painful jab behind his left ear, an unbearable pain in his right shin, and then a painless nothingness.

Mende's angry voice roused him, and startled, he tried to throw back the covers, thinking he'd overslept. But he couldn't move, so firmly was he tucked into his bed. And then the constriction of a bandage on his head and the dull sickishness in his leg brought back recent occurrences.

"Hatching?" he cried.

"No, lovey," said Mende, and her voice was suddenly very kind, her hand cool and gentle on his forehead. "Though there's some

Dragons and other beasts, 1390–1430. Boucicaut Master. Bibliotheque Nationale, Paris.

Visual Literacy

Interpret a Painting Give students time to examine the painting. Ask students how the dragons in this painting compare to their mental images of the dragons in "The Smallest Dragonboy." (Students may point out that the bodies of the dragons in the painting have the characteristics of other animals not traditionally associated with dragons, such as dogs, foxes, and chickens. None of the beasts in the painting looks particularly friendly. The dragons in the story probably fit the more traditional image of large fire-breathing winged beasts, and the dragons in the story are friends and companions of humans.)

Use Reading Skills

Use Context Clues Ask students to use prior knowledge and the surrounding text to explain what *desolation* means. (The narrator says that Keevan "knew what the news must be," which is that he is no longer a dragonboy candidate. Since it's Keevan's dream to be chosen by a dragon on Hatching Day, he must have a look of incredible sadness on his face.) **C**

Research Skills

Bibliographic Entries

Remind students that a bibliography lists sources used to write a research report. The bibliography usually appears at the end of the report. Items in a bibliography are arranged alphabetically by the author's last name, or by the first word in the title if the author's name is repeated or unknown. Have students use the library to compile a bibliography of books in Ann McCaffrey's "Dragonriders of Pern" and "Harper Hall" series. Give them formatting guidelines, or use the following examples.

McCaffrey, Anne. *Dragonflight.* New York: Walker & Co., 1969.

_____. *The White Dragon.* New York: Del Rey, 1978.

Analyze Literature

Dialogue Remind students that authors use dialogue to move a plot along. Have students explain how the dialogue beside Keevan's bed helps move the plot forward. (The dialogue reveals that Keevan's leg is broken, that he is still a candidate, that the hatching hasn't happened yet, and that Beterli has been dropped as a candidate. The dialogue makes readers anticipate what will happen at the hatching.)

Make Connections

Ask: "What do you think of Keevan's reluctance to tattle on Beterli? How do you feel about what has happened to Beterli?" (Most students will agree that Keevan shows strength of character by not tattling, and that Beterli got what he deserved.) **A**

---

as won't be at any hatching again." Her voice took on a stern edge.

Keevan looked beyond her to see the weyrwoman, who was frowning with irritation.

"Keevan, will you tell me what occurred at the black-rock bunker?" Lessa asked, but her voice wasn't angry.

He remembered Beterli now and the quarrel over the shovel and...what had **A** Mende said about some not being at any hatching? Much as he hated Beterli, he couldn't bring himself to tattle on Beterli and force him out of candidacy.

"Come, lad," and a note of impatience crept into the weyrwoman's voice. "I merely want to know what happened from you, too. Mende said she sent you for black-rock. Beterli—and every weyrling in the cavern—seems to have been on the same errand. What happened?"

"Beterli took the shovel. I hadn't finished with it."

"There's more than one shovel. What did he *say* to you?"

"He'd heard the news."

"What news?" The weyrwoman was suddenly amused.

"That...that...there'd been changes."

"Is that what he said?"

"Not exactly."

"What did he say? C'mon, lad. I've heard from everyone else, you know."

"He said for me to guess the news."

"And you fell for that old gag?" The weyrwoman's irritation returned.

"Consider all the talk last night at supper, Lessa," said Mende. "Of course the boy would think he'd been eliminated."

"In effect, he is, with a broken skull and leg." She touched his arm, a rare gesture of sympathy in her. "Be that as it may, Keevan, you'll have other Impressions. Beterli will not. There are certain rules that must be observed by all candidates, and his conduct proves him unacceptable to the weyr."

She smiled at Mende and then left.

"I'm still a candidate?" Keevan asked urgently.

"Well, you are and you aren't, lovey," his foster mother said. "Is the numb weed working?" she asked, and when he nodded, she said, "You just rest. I'll bring you some nice broth."

At any other time in his life, Keevan would have relished such cosseting,[19] but he lay there worrying. Beterli had been dismissed. Would the others think it was his fault? But everyone was there! Beterli provoked the fight. His worry increased, because although he heard excited comings and goings in the passageway, no one tweaked back the curtain across the sleeping alcove he shared with five other boys. Surely one of them would have to come in sometime. No, they were all avoiding him. And something else was wrong. Only he didn't know what.

Mende returned with broth and beachberry bread.

"Why doesn't anyone come see me, Mende? I haven't done anything wrong, have I? I didn't ask to have Beterli tuffed out."

Mende soothed him, saying everyone was busy with noontime chores and no one was mad at him. They were giving him a chance to rest in quiet. The numb weed made him drowsy, and her words were fair enough. He

---

19. **cosseting.** Protecting

Differentiated Instruction

Visual Learning

Some students might like to create a storyboard to keep track of the sequence of events in the story. Tell them to divide a large piece of art paper into six blocks and to illustrate a key scene in each block. Students can add captions to describe what is happening in each scene.

permitted his fears to dissipate. Until he
heard the humming. It started low, too
low to be heard. Rather he felt it in the
broken shin bone and his sore head.
And thought, at first, it was an effect of
the numb weed. Then the hum grew,
augmented[20] by additional sources. Two
things registered suddenly in Keevan's
groggy mind: The only white
candidate's robe still on the pegs in the
chamber was his; and dragons hummed
when a clutch was being laid or being
hatched. Impression! And he was flat
abed.

B

C

Bitter, bitter disappointment
turned the warm broth sour in his
belly. Even the small voice telling him
that he'd have other opportunities failed to
alleviate[21] his crushing depression. *This* was
the Impression that mattered! This was his
chance to show *everyone* from Mende to
K'last to L'vel and even the weyrleaders that
he, Keevan, was worthy of being a
dragonrider.

He twisted in bed, fighting against the
tears that threatened to choke him.
Dragonmen don't cry! Dragonmen learn to
live with pain....

Pain? The leg didn't actually pain him as
he rolled about on his bedding. His head felt
sort of stiff from the tightness of the bandage.
He sat up, an effort in itself since the numb
weed made exertion difficult. He touched the
splinted leg, but the knee was unhampered.
He had no feeling in his bone, really. He
swung himself carefully to the side of his bed
and slowly stood. The room wanted to swim
about him. He closed his eyes, which made
the dizziness worse, and he had to clutch the
bedpost.

Gingerly he took a step. The broken leg

dragged. It hurt in spite of the numb weed,
but what was pain to a dragonman?

No one had said he couldn't go to the
Impression. "You are and you aren't," were
Mende's exact words.

Clinging to the bedpost, he jerked off his
bedshirt. Stretching his arm to the utmost, he
jerked his white candidate's tunic from the
peg. Jamming first one arm and then the
other into the holes, he pulled it over his
head. Too bad about the belt. He couldn't
wait. He hobbled to the door, hung on to the
curtain to steady himself. The weight on his
leg was unwieldy. He'd not get very far
without something to lean on. Down by the
bathing pool was one of the long crooknecked
poles used to retrieve clothes from the hot
washing troughs. But it was down there, and
he was on the level above. And there was no
one nearby to come to his aid: everyone

---

20. **augmented.** Amplified
21. **alleviate.** Relieve

THE SMALLEST DRAGONBOY **233**

Teach the Selection

Science Connection

Bone Healing After a broken leg is
set in a cast, the pain gradually
subsides. However, the healing
process itself can take anywhere from
several weeks to months, depending
on the severity of the break. In some
patients, the healing process takes
unusually long, so scientists are
experimenting with faster ways to
heal broken bones. One method
involves using ultrasound waves,
which are applied directly to the area
of the break to stimulate bone
growth. McCaffrey may have had this
idea in mind when she described the
humming Keevan hears. **B**

Use Reading Skills

Identify Cause and Effect Ask why
Keevan is bothered by the sight of his
robe on the peg and the low hum.
(He realizes the hatching is taking
place and he's missing it.) **C**

Analyze Literature

Symbolism Ask students what they
think Keevan's broken leg symbolizes.
(It may symbolize the obstacles he has
to overcome to become a dragonrider,
or his strength, courage, and faith in
himself, or his transition from
childhood to adulthood.)

Use Reading Strategies

Visualize Read aloud the paragraph
that describes Keevan's efforts to get
to the Hatching Ground. Ask students
to use the details to "see" Keevan's
determination and inner strength.

Reading Skills

Monitor Comprehension

Remind students that they should take time to
check whether they understand what they are
reading. One way to check understanding is to ask
questions about the setting, characters, events, and
the author's purpose as they read and after they
read. For example, they might ask: "What made the
character do this? Does it make sense that this
happened? What does the author want me to think
or know here?" They can also summarize parts or all
of the story, reread a passage carefully to clarify
what they don't understand, and predict what will
happen next and then read on to confirm or change
their predictions. Have students explain how they
used one or more of these strategies as they read
"The Smallest Dragonboy."

Analyze Literature

Onomatopoeia Remind students that *onomatopoeia* means using words or phrases that sound like what they mean. Authors use onomatopoeia in a story to help readers "hear" what is happening and make them feel as if they are part of the action. Ask students what sounds they "hear" coming from the Hatching Ground (for example, *humming*, *thump thud*, *oohs*, *susurrus*, *crooning*, and *squawks*.) Ⓐ

Make Connections

Have students think of times in their lives when they struggled to get something that they wanted very badly, only to be disappointed in the end. Ask students to use their own thoughts and feelings about that experience to imagine what Keevan is thinking and feeling at his first sight of the cracked eggs. Ⓑ

> **More by This Author**
>
> Students who like "The Smallest Dragonboy" might enjoy reading McCaffrey's *The Dragonriders of Pern* and *On Dragonwings*.

would be in the Hatching Ground right now, eagerly waiting for the first egg to crack.

The humming increased in volume and tempo, an urgency to which Keevan responded, knowing that his time was all too limited if he was to join the ranks of the hopeful boys standing about the cracking eggs. But if he hurried down the ramp, he'd fall flat on his face.

He could, of course, go flat on his rear end, the way crawling children did. He sat down, the jar sending a stab of pain through his leg and up to the wound on the back of his head. Gritting his teeth and blinking away the tears, Keevan scrabbled down the ramp. He had to wait a moment at the bottom to catch his breath. He got to one knee, the injured leg straight out in front of him. Somehow, he managed to push himself erect, though the room wanted to tip over his ears. It wasn't far to the crooked stick, but it seemed an age before he had it in his hand.

Then the humming stopped!

Ⓑ Keevan cried out and began to hobble frantically across the cavern, out to the bowl of the weyr. Never had the distance between the living caverns and the Hatching Ground seemed so great. Never had the weyr been silent, breathless. As if the multitude of people and dragons watching the hatching held every breath in suspense. Not even the weyr muttered down the steep sides of the bowl. The only sounds to break the stillness were Keevan's ragged breathing and the thump thud of his stick on the hard-packed ground. Sometimes he had to hop twice on his good leg to maintain his balance. Twice he fell into the sand and had to pull himself up on the stick, his white tunic no longer spotless. Once he jarred himself so badly he couldn't get up immediately.

Ⓐ Then he heard the first exhalation of the crowd, the oohs, the muted cheer, the susurrus[22] of excited whispers. An egg had cracked, and the dragon had chosen his rider. Desperation increased Keevan's hobble. Would he never reach the arching mouth of the Hatching Ground?

> *An egg had cracked, and the dragon had chosen his rider.*

Another cheer and an excited spate of applause spurred Keevan to greater effort. If he didn't get there in moments, there'd be no unpaired hatchling left. Then he was actually staggering into the Hatching Ground, the sands hot on his bare feet.

No one noticed his entrance or his halting progress. And Keevan could see nothing but the backs of the white-robed candidates, seventy of them ringing the area around the eggs. Then one side would surge forward or back and there'd be a cheer. Another dragon had been Impressed. Suddenly a large gap appeared in the white human wall, and Keevan had his first sight of the eggs. There didn't seem to be *any* left uncracked, and he could see the lucky boys standing beside wobble-legged dragons. He could hear the unmistakable plaintive[23] crooning of hatchlings and their squawks of protest as they'd fall awkwardly in the sand.

---

22. susurrus. Whispering sound
23. plaintive. Sounding sad

Differentiated Instruction

Kinesthetic Learning

Have volunteers enact the critical sequence of events at the climax of the story, from when Keevan discovers that the Impression has begun until the ending. Everyone in the class should reread this section of the text to recall the words, gestures, emotions, and expressions involved. Performers should present their enactment for the class, incorporating all the dramatic elements in the scene, including not just Keevan's actions, but the background sounds and behavior of other characters, too. After the presentation, discuss as a class whether the performers captured both the meaning and the emotional quality of the scene.

Suddenly he wished that he hadn't left his bed, that he'd stayed away from the Hatching Ground. Now everyone would see his ignominious[24] failure. He scrambled now as desperately to reach the shadowy walls of the Hatching Ground as he had struggled to cross the bowl. He mustn't be seen.

He didn't notice, therefore, that the shifting group of boys remaining had begun to drift in his direction. The hard pace he had set himself and his cruel disappointment took their double toll of Keevan. He tripped and collapsed sobbing to the warm sands. He didn't see the consternation in the watching weyrfolk above the Hatching Ground, nor did he hear the excited whispers of speculation.[25] He didn't know that the weyrleader and weyrwoman had dropped to the arena and were making their way toward the knot of boys slowly moving in the direction of the archway.

"Never seen anything like it," the weyrleader was saying. "Only thirty-nine riders chosen. And the bronze trying to leave the Hatching Ground without making Impression!"

"A case in point of what I said last night," the weyrwoman replied, "where a hatchling makes no choice because the right boy isn't there."

"There's only Beterli and K'last's young one missing. And there's a full wing of likely boys to choose from...."

"None acceptable, apparently. Where is the creature going? He's not heading for the entrance after all. Oh, what have we there, in the shadows?"

Keevan heard with dismay the sound of voices nearing him. He tried to burrow in to the sand. The mere thought of how he would be teased and taunted now was unbearable.

Don't worry! Please don't worry! The thought was urgent, but not his own.

C Someone kicked sand over Keevan and butted roughly against him.

"Go away. Leave me alone!" he cried.

Why? was the injured-sounding question inserted into his mind. There was no voice, no tone, but the question was there, perfectly clear, in his head.

Incredulous, Keevan lifted his head and stared into the glowing jeweled eyes of a small bronze dragon. His wings were wet; the tips hung drooping to the sand. And he sagged in the middle on his unsteady legs, although he was making a great effort to keep erect.

Keevan dragged himself to his knees, oblivious to the pain of his leg. He wasn't even aware that he was ringed by the boys passed over, while thirty-one pairs of resentful eyes watched him Impress the dragon. The weyrleaders looked on, amused and surprised at the draconic choice, which could not be forced. Could not be questioned. Could not be changed.

D *Why?* asked the dragon again. *Don't you like me?* His eyes whirled with anxiety, and his tone was so piteous that Keevan staggered forward and threw his arms around the dragon's neck, stroking his eye ridges, patting the damp, soft hide, opening the fragile-looking wings to dry them, and assuring the hatchling wordlessly over and over again that he was the most perfect, most beautiful, most beloved dragon in the entire weyr; in all the weyrs of Pern.

"What's his name, K'van?" asked Lessa,

---

24. **ignominious** (ig′ nə mi′ nē əs). Shameful
25. **speculation.** Theory

Use Reading Skills
Identify Sequence of Events Ask students what happens after Keevan realizes he may have missed his chance for an Impression. (He tries to sneak away. Meanwhile the crowd has begun to drift toward him, where he has collapsed onto the sand. Something is happening to make the crowd concerned and excited.) **C**

Use Reading Strategies
Make Predictions Tell students to reread the dialogue between the weyrleader and the weyrwoman, until the moment they notice Keevan in the shadows. Based on the dialogue and what has already happened, what do they think will happen next? (Most will predict that the bronze will go to Keevan and make an Impression with him.) **D**

Analyze Literature
Theme Remind students that the theme of a story is the main message the author wants readers to get. Model how to figure out the theme: "To figure out the theme of 'The Smallest Dragonboy,' I ask questions about the main character and his conflict: What does Keevan want at the beginning of the story? What obstacles must he face and how does he overcome them? What has he learned or how has he changed at the end of the story? Answers to these questions tell me that the theme is believing in yourself."

Grammar Skills

Superlative Adjectives
Keevan uses superlative adjectives when he assures the hatchling that he is "the most perfect, most beautiful, most beloved dragon" in the weyr. Superlative adjectives compare three or more nouns. Explain that to form most superlative adjectives. add *–est* to short adjectives (for instance, *smallest*). Add *most* before longer adjectives with two or more syllables not ending in *y*. For example, Beterli was the *most senior* of the boys.

Ask students to write the superlative form for each adjective below. Then, have them use each adjective in a sentence.
1. bold
2. selfish
3. considerate

Analyze and Extend

1. Beterli was insecure.

2. (a) Keevan left his bed because of his dedication to becoming a dragonrider. (b) Some students might argue that if he had not gone to the Hatching Ground, the bronze dragon would have found his way to Keevan anyway. Others will say Keevan's courageous behavior led to the story's outcome.

3. Students may list dragons, Thread, and the ability to communicate telepathically. These elements shape how characters respond to the world, and help define conflicts in the plot.

Rubric for Persuasive Writing

You can adapt this as a checklist for students to use as they write.

☐ Does the review begin with a summary of the story?

☐ Does the review state an opinion of the selection?

☐ Does the review support the opinion with evidence?

---

smiling warmly at the new dragonrider. K'van stared up at her for a long moment. Lessa would know as soon as he did. Lessa was the only person who could "receive" from all dragons, not only her own Ramoth. Then he gave her a radiant smile, recognizing the traditional shortening of his name that raised him forever to the rank of dragonrider.

My name is Heath, thought the dragon mildly and hiccuped in sudden urgency: *I'm hungry.*

"Dragons are born hungry," said Lessa, laughing. "F'lar, give the boy a hand. He can barely manage his own legs, much less a dragon's."

K'van remembered his stick and drew himself up. "We'll be just fine, thank you."

"You may be the smallest dragonrider ever, young K'van, but you're the bravest," said F'lar.

And Heath agreed! Pride and joy so leaped in both chests that K'van wondered if his heart would burst right out of his body. He looped an arm around Heath's neck and the pair—the smallest dragonboy, and the hatchling who wouldn't choose anybody else—walked out of the Hatching Ground together forever.

When have you felt as if you were not ready for something important, like the first day of school or some other life-changing event? Were your feelings justified? Why might it not be helpful for people, like Keevan in "The Smallest Dragonboy," to worry too much about whether or not they are ready for life-changing experiences?

Analyze and Extend

1. Why do you think Beterli treated Keevan the way he did?

2. (a) What motivated Keevan to leave his bed and go to the Hatching Ground after breaking his leg? (b) What do you think would have happened if he had stayed in bed?

3. List examples of the various elements of fantasy in the story. How do these elements affect the characters? How do they affect the plot?

Persuasive Writing Using your library, locate a recent book review in a local or national newspaper or magazine. Read the review, noting the tone and the reviewer's main idea. Then write your own two-paragraph book review of "The Smallest Dragonboy." Give your opinion and present evidence, including paraphrases and direct quotations, in support of it. At the start of your review, be sure to give a brief summary of "The Smallest Dragonboy." When you are done, present your review using gestures as well as the proper speaking rate, volume, and eye contact.

Collaborative Learning An epic tale is a long story, often told in verse. In the English epic *Beowulf*, the title character battles a fierce fire-breathing dragon. With a partner, research and describe the conventions of epic tales and determine whether "The Smallest Dragonboy" contains any similar elements.

Go to **www.mirrorsandwindows.com** for more.

Differentiated Instruction

Enrichment

Some students might enjoy writing an interview with Heath (the dragon) to learn why he chose Keevan to be his rider and lifetime partner. Tell students to prepare a list of questions to ask Heath to find out, for example, what experiences and feelings he remembers from inside the egg, what he felt when he first hatched, how he located Keevan, and why he chose him. Remind students that since

Heath can only communicate telepathically, they will have to choose a character from the story who can "receive" his thoughts and relay them to the interviewer. After they have written their interviews, students may enlist the help of two other classmates to present the interview as a dramatic reading to the rest of the class.

For Your Reading List

The Outcasts of 19 Schuyler Place
by E. L. Konigsburg

After being ejected from summer camp, Margaret Rose Kane moves in with her two great uncles, Alex and Morris. However, controversy is brewing in the neighborhood over the three massive, colorful, and strange towers her uncles have been building in their backyard. Can Margaret save her uncles' giant works of art?

Holes
by Louis Sachar

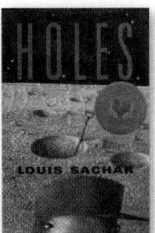

In this Newbery Award winning novel, Stanley Yelnats—whose name reads the same both backward and forward—has been sent to Camp Green Lake to be rehabilitated for a crime he did not commit. In a dried-up Texas lake, the campers of Camp Green Lake are forced every day to dig hole after hole after hole. Stanley soon learns that the camp is not all it at first appears.

Pictures of Hollis Woods
by Patricia Reilly Giff

Hollis Woods wants a loving family but can't seem to stop running away from foster homes. Eventually she finds Josie, a retired teacher, who shares Hollis's love of art. Sadly, Josie seems to be losing her memory, while Hollis still misses the Regans, her last foster family. As the story progresses, the reason for Hollis's departure from the Regan household is slowly revealed.

Al Capone Does My Shirts
by Gennifer Choldenko

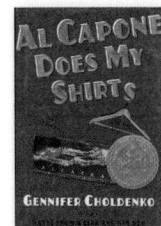

After Moose Flanagan's father takes a job as a prison guard, the Flanagan family is forced to move to Alcatraz Island. Moose must cope with his new environment, help take care of his sister, and deal with the warden's daughter Piper, who always seems to be scheming.

Romiette and Julio
by Sharon Draper

In an Internet chat room, Romiette Cappelle meets Julio Montague. Soon they discover that they attend the same high school and start seeing each other, ignoring both their parents' prejudices and threats from a local gang violently opposed to interracial dating. A retelling of Shakespeare's Romeo and Juliet, the novel brings readers the play's romance and feuding, but with a happier ending.

The Chosen
by Chaim Potok

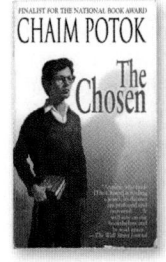

Reuven and Danny, two boys growing up in Brooklyn, New York, meet by accident during a softball game. As they become friends, they must learn to negotiate the differences in their families' religious practices as well as confusion, love, loss, and other trials of adolescence. Eventually, the differences between the characters open each of them to new worlds.

Program Resources

EMC Access Editions
For additional independent reading, you may wish to refer students to one of EMC's Access Edition titles such as Stephen Crane's *Red Badge of Courage* or Virginia Driving Hawk Sneve's *High Elk's Treasure*. Each Access Edition contains a thorough study apparatus, including background information, literal comprehension questions, footnotes, vocabulary definitions, critical thinking questions, and related projects and activities. An Assessment Manual offering worksheets is available for each Access Edition.

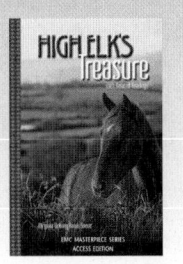

Independent Reading

Independent Reading Activity
Help students link their reading to the unit theme, Learning Values. Ask how fiction can possibly teach human values. Model one response: "Stories show me how people make choices, and the right choices always seem to reflect the value of being fair." You might try an in-class activity: Have students read silently a fiction work of their choosing for at least twenty minutes. Then have students identify what ideas this short story or novel can give a reader about values.

EMC E-Library
The EMC E-Library contains over twenty thousand pages of literary classics that students may read independently. An Electronic Library Guide provides teaching suggestions, enrichment activities, and reading strategy guidesheets.

TEACHING NOTE

Activate Prior Knowledge
Offer students an opportunity to evaluate their own development as readers. Tell students you would like them to recall and think about the reading they have done in the past year. If you wish, prompt them with questions: "How much fiction have you read in the past year? How much nonfiction? What is your favorite kind of reading now, and how does that compare to last year?" Provide several minutes for quiet thinking.

Common Core State Standards

Reading Literature
RL.10

Objectives

Participating in this lesson will help students write a short story that

- develops complex, believable characters
- has a vivid setting
- has a logically organized plot
- maintains one point of view

Launch the Lesson

Ask students if they can agree on the best short story they've read in class so far. Use the ensuing discussion to elicit observations about what makes a character, a setting, and a plot especially appealing. Tell students they can now create the kinds of characters, settings, and plots they like most.

Literary Connection

Muses Walter Dean Myers has his wife create a collage of characters that he cuts out, probably from magazines. The collage acts like a muse. Tell students that a *muse* is a source of inspiration, a person or thing that visits a writer and makes suggestions. In Greek mythology, there were nine Muses, daughters of Zeus and the goddess of memory, Mnemosyne. Ask students to think of muses in their own creative lives.

Writing Workshop

Narrative Writing

Writing a Short Story

Reading and Writing

You have read stories about values in the unit from such writers as Joseph Bruchac, Sandra Cisneros, and Gary Soto. These selections feature the basic elements of short stories: character development, setting, conflict, plot structure, and dialogue. You will from time to time be asked to write a short story on a particular topic or to develop a character and a believable plot.

In this workshop you will learn how to write a **short story.** You may want to begin this assignment by determining the kind of characters you would like to develop and how you might make these characters believable and complex. Decide how important your setting will be to your story. Consider what conflicts your characters might face and how they could resolve those conflicts through a series of events. Keep in mind that a good story is entertaining, thought provoking, and interesting to its readers. Look at the following writing rubric. This set of standards will help you judge whether or not you have achieved your goal of writing a successful short story. You will use this rubric in both drafting and revising your story.

- **Assignment:** Write a short story that develops believable characters, setting, and plot.
- **Goal:** Create a story that is interesting and enjoyable for my audience.
- **Strategy:** Create well-developed characters and a detailed setting. Create a plot in which a conflict rises to a climax and is resolved at the end.
- **Writing Rubric:** My short story should include the following:
  - complex and believable characters
  - a vivid setting
  - a logically organized plot that includes a conflict, exposition, rising action, climax, falling action, and resolution
  - a consistent point of view

What Great Writers Do

Walter Dean Myers is a great lover of writing. Here is what he has to say about his approach to writing and revising fiction.

When I work, what I'll do is outline the story first. That forces me to do the thinking. I cut out pictures of all my characters and my wife puts them into a collage, which goes on the wall above the computer. When I walk into the room I can see the characters, and I just get very close to them. I rush through a first draft, and then I go back and rewrite, because I can usually see what the problems are going to be ahead of me. Rewriting is more fun for me than writing is.

Words in Use

Teaching Words
provoking, 238
rubric, 238
vivid, 238
collage, 238
tension, 240

KEY TERMS

SHORT STORY, 238	STORY MAP, 239
CHARACTER, 238	CLUSTER CHART, 239
CONFLICTS, 238	CHRONOLOGICAL
SETTING, 238	ORDER, 240
PLOT, 238	RESOLUTION, 240
CLIMAX, 238	TONE, 240
POINT OF VIEW, 239	PEER REVIEW, 241
THIRD-PERSON	DIALOGUE, 241
LIMITED, 239	FIRST-PERSON
THIRD-PERSON	POINT OF VIEW, 242
OMNISCIENT, 239	

Common Core State Standards

Writing
W.3, W.4, W.5, W.10
Language
L.3

1. PREWRITE

Choosing Your Topic

Planning the Parts of Your Story The topic of your story is who and what you will write about. You may want to begin developing your story by using the *who, when, where, what,* and *how* method.

Who? Do you have a character in mind? What would this character be like? Consider what beliefs, qualities, or problems this character would have.

When and Where? When and where your story takes place is its setting. Think about how important your setting will be. Is it just background, or does it play a strong role in the conflict and its resolution? For instance, consider a story that takes place in an old castle in the 1900s as opposed to a bustling street in present-day New York. No matter which setting you choose, be sure it fits the characters and events in your story.

What? Once you have a main character in mind, decide what will happen to him or her. What conflict will your character face? Maybe the conflict is one you have personally experienced or imagined. The conflict can be with another character, with a situation or outside force (such as nature or society), or within the character's mind.

How? The plot, or series of events, will grow out of the conflict. After the conflict is introduced, the conflict develops with each event until it reaches a climax or turning point. After the climax, the conflict must be resolved in a satisfactory way.

Gathering Details

Now concentrate on the details of the characters, setting, and plot. Use your imagination, but let these ideas guide you:

1. Develop your characters through descriptive details, action, and dialogue.
2. Describe the setting in vivid detail.
3. Bring the conflict to a climax or turning point, and then resolve it by the story's end.

4. Decide on point of view—first-person, third-person limited, or third-person omniscient—and maintain that point of view throughout the story.

To help you keep track of your characters, setting, and plot, use a story map. Here is how one student approached writing his short story.

Characters
James, age 12
Zack, age 12
Zack's mom

Setting
School gym, after school for intramural game of volleyball (present day)

Conflict
Teams are being formed for intramural volleyball. Zack is small for his age, and he wants badly to play on any team, but especially with the Tigers. James, Zack's best friend, makes the team, but Zack doesn't.

The writer used a cluster chart to further develop each character. Keep track of a character's traits by clustering them into categories including physical traits, personality, feelings, and goals.

Personality
good leader, determined, fair, honest

Goals
have fun, win fairly, have a tough team, win all games

James, team leader of the Tigers

Physical Traits
tall, strong, athletic

Teach the Workshop

Prewrite

Deciding on a Topic Model the process of choosing a topic: "I want to write a romantic story about a boy and girl who pretend not to like each other. I have to make up believable characters that aren't based on anyone I really know, but I can combine things I've experienced with what I can imagine. I'll make the setting a summer camp in Minnesota."

Gathering Details Point out that students can make separate cluster charts for plot, characters, and setting. Suggest that they begin by putting the conflict in the story into words. You can continue modeling: "The central conflict in my story is within one of the characters, who is scared to admit to being in love with the other one." Tell students that once they articulate the conflict, they can probably start imagining what the story's climax will be.

What Great Writers Do

My settings begin with real places, real neighborhoods, but after that the imaginative process takes over and what's real and what's made up blur in often inextricable ways.

NOVELIST DIANE MCKINNEY WHETSTONE

Differentiated Instruction

Reading Proficiency

To help students understand the lesson, tell them what the assignment will be and show them the student model. Point out that the lesson is organized into five steps. Then have students read and summarize the instructions for each step before they begin the assignment.

Enrichment

Have interested students use library and Internet resources to learn about the writing habits of their favorite fiction authors. Ask them to share useful tips with the class.

Draft

Organizing Ideas Point out that chronological order is easy and logical, but students can include foreshadowing and flashbacks in their stories. Model a possible plan for this: "As the characters meet up day after day at camp, each remembers how they have seen each other at neighborhood parties and during various school performances since kindergarten. More than once, each one remembers how fun it was to act in the fifth-grade musical together."

Filling in the Blanks As students follow the recommendations in the text, assure them that they can outline their stories in any order. Beginning with the climax might be easiest for some. Then they can think through the steps that would lead up to it, and make sure the exposition introduces the proper elements.

What Great Writers Do

Writers find their work satisfying, even though it can be difficult. Here, Elie Wiesel describes how characters can motivate a person to write.

Writers write because they cannot allow the characters that inhabit them to suffocate them. These characters want to get out, to breathe fresh air and partake of the wine of friendship; were they to remain locked in, they would forcibly break down the walls. It is they who force the writer to tell their stories.

2. DRAFT

Organizing Ideas

Once you have gathered details about the story, plan how the plot will develop. Often, the most logical and effective way to organize stories is by the order the events occurred, or **chronological order.** Study the main parts of a story and what is introduced or developed in each.

> **Beginning**
> 1. **Exposition:** introduces the main characters, setting, and conflict
>
> **Middle**
> 2. **Rising Action:** develops the conflict through a series of events
> 3. **Climax or Turning Point:** creates the point of highest tension or excitement
>
> **End**
> 4. **Resolution:** resolves the conflict

Putting Your Thoughts on Paper

When writing your first draft, organize your characters, setting, conflict, and plot in a logical plan like that shown here. At this stage, focus mainly on developing the conflict. Try to outline the series of events that will lead to the turning point, and, finally, the resolution of your story. Don't worry if you don't have all the events determined before you begin writing. More ideas will come once you begin drafting, but use your plan as a starting point.

> 1. **Exposition**
> **Characters:** James, Zack, Zack's mom
> **Setting:** present day, during volleyball tryouts
> **Conflict:** James and Zack are great friends, but James is a better athlete.
>
> 2. **Rising Action**
>   1. James makes the team, but Zack does not.
>   2. Zack tries out for a different team.
>   3. Zack makes the team.
>
> 3. **Climax or Turning Point**
>   Zack's first game is against James and the Tigers. Everyone is surprised at how well Zack plays.
>
> 4. **Resolution**
>   Zack's team loses, but not before he receives praise from his good friend, James.

Making Connections

The Right Tone As you draft, pay attention to the tone of your writing. Your **tone,** or attitude toward your subject, should be more natural and informal in a short story than in most other types of writing, such as essays. Make sure your dialogue sounds true to the character and to the way people actually speak. Try reading parts of your story—especially the dialogue—out loud to see if it sounds smooth and natural.

Differentiated Instruction

Visual and Kinesthetic Learning

If students feel stuck, encourage them to use the board to sketch the curve of a plot diagram. Have them draw or name the characters present at the beginning of the story. Urge them to sketch the interactions of the characters at the climax of the story. For the resolution of the story, ask them to draw the face of each character with an appropriate expression.

Reading Proficiency

Have students work in pairs to complete their story plans. Each student should describe the conflict of his or her story to the other. The listener should then ask questions such as "What would make the people do this?" and "How will the characters resolve this situation?" Students may also return to the *who, when, where, what,* and *how* method of questioning.

Evaluating Your Draft

As you reread your draft, look for areas to improve. You may want to exchange papers and do a **peer review.** Evaluate each other's work and discuss ideas for revision. Use the checklist as a guide.

Below is a draft of the first part of the short story, "A Chance to Play." Changes have been made within the body of the text and reasons for the changes are given on the right.

Revising Checklist

☐ Are the characters well-developed and introduced at the beginning?

☐ Is the setting described in detail?

☐ Is the story organized logically?

☐ Is the dialogue natural and effective?

☐ Is there a consistent point of view?

"James McDermott!" I heard the coach call off the next name on the list. James, who was sitting next to me, tightened his laces one last time and stood up. "Good luck," I said as he gave me a thumbs-up and ran over to the coach standing by the volleyball net. *The gym echoed with shouts and the squeak of sneakers against the floor as players practiced serving and setting.*

> *Introduce the setting in the exposition. Use sensory details to make the setting vivid.*

James had always been good at sports, especially volleyball, for as long as I had known him. I never let him know how I secretly wished I could be like him. It seemed like he and everyone else in the seventh grade was growing taller and stronger, but I was still as short and small as I had always been. *I wanted to try out for volleyball, but even James took one look at me and said, "Maybe volleyball just isn't for you." That hurt, coming from my best friend, but he never lied to me before and was always the kindest guy I had ever known.*

> *Introduce the conflict within the first few paragraphs.*

After a few moments James came back with a smile on his face.

"Did you make it?" I asked.

"Yeah, they said no one else could spike the ball like me." James grabbed his stuff and we went out into the parking lot.

Teach the Workshop

Revise

Evaluating Dialogue Remind students that characters and the plot develop together. Suggest that they evaluate each dialogue in the story to see if it advances the plot.

Evaluating a Draft Instruct students to listen for a consistent point of view and a believable tone as they review their own work. When they have done as much as they can in the available time, suggest that they conduct a peer review. Be sure they understand the rubric.

Allow ample time for students to read the story they receive to review. Schedule peer review exchanges when each student will have several minutes to deliver his or her review, and when each writer will have time to thoughtfully absorb the comments and ask questions for clarification.

What Great Writers Do

Point out that in acknowledgments, writers thank people who read their draft manuscript. Here, Joseph Bruchac refers to people who helped him with his novel *Code Talker.*

In 2001 I was fortunate enough to spend some time with two more code talkers, Jesse Samuel Smith and Keith Wilson . . . Mr. Wilson was even kind enough to read my manuscript in first draft. I'd better stop here because I could go on for pages about the people who helped me along the way.

Writing Skills

Mood

Remind students that the mood is the feeling a writer wants the reader to get. As they respond to their own revision notes and their peer reviews, have students consider mood. In particular, have them review the story's setting. Tell them to make sure their settings are detailed enough to create a mood.

Write each of these sentences on the board, and then ask students to improve the mood by adding sensory details.

1. The boathouse was an unpleasant place to meet.

2. He could not see which boat she was in.

3. She paddled a canoe like a pro.

4. He stared at the wall.

Edit and Proofread

Students may want to use proofreader's marks when correcting their work. Refer them to the Language Arts Handbook Writing Section 4.1, Proofreader's Symbols.

What Great Writers Do

You might want to tell students that some people enjoy editing more than writing. Mystery writer Lisa Scottoline says: *"Editing is the treat only after the first draft is finished."*

Publish and Present

Before students begin their final version, they might benefit from reading the Language Arts Handbook, Writing 4.1, Writing Follow-up.

Focus: Maintaining a Consistent Point of View

Point of view is the perspective from which an author presents the action and characters in a story. If the person who experiences the action tells the story, it is being told from the *first-person point of view.* If the narrator is outside of the action, then the story is being told from the *third-person point of view.* If the narrator is all-knowing and can tell the reader about any and every character's thoughts, ideas, feelings, and actions, then the story is being told from the *third-person omniscient point of view.*

Whatever point of view you choose, maintain that point of view throughout the story. Check your writing carefully to be sure your point of view is consistent. If you decide your story would be better told from a different point of view, be sure to go back and make that change throughout.

I was just so sick of thinking about how I could never be as good as James. ~~Zack~~ *I* turned on some music, and for a while ~~he~~ *I* was finally able to stop thinking about volleyball and the other kids until my mom called me down for dinner.

Focus: Punctuating Dialogue

Recall the rules for punctuating dialogue:

1. Enclose direct speech within quotation marks.
2. Place any commas or end punctuation of a direct quotation inside the quotation marks.
3. When a speech tag comes before the speaker's words, use a comma after the speech tag. Begin the words of the speaker with a capital letter.
4. When a speech tag comes after the speaker's words, use a comma after the speaker's words.
5. Start a new paragraph when the speaker changes.

"What's your name?" one of the girls sitting next to me asked.
"Z-Zack," I stuttered.

Embedded Quotations When a speaker quotes what another character said, use embedded quotations. Place the character's direct speech in double quotation marks and the words the character is quoting in single quotation marks.

"He told me, 'Maybe volleyball just isn't for you.' But it's not just volleyball. It always seems like everything goes his way."

Proofreading

Proofreading for Errors Proofread your story for mechanical errors. Use proofreader's marks to correct mistakes. (See the Language Arts Handbook, section 4.1, for a list of proofreader's marks.)

5. PUBLISH AND PRESENT

Final Draft

Presentation Make a clean final version of your story. Handwritten stories should be neat and legible. Typed stories should be double-spaced and in a standard typeface. Check your teacher's guidelines before submitting your paper.

Differentiated Instruction

English Language Learning

Use this opportunity to gauge progress among English learners. Have them show you their editing and proofreading to see how well they have absorbed spelling and grammar lessons you have given. Take time to correct and discuss any consistent problems in these areas before students prepare final drafts.

Student Model

A Chance to Play
by John McCombs

"James McDermott!" I heard the coach call off the next name on the list. James, who was sitting next to me, tightened his laces one last time and stood up. "Good luck," I said as he gave me a thumbs-up and ran over to the coach standing by the volleyball net. The gym echoed with shouts and the squeak of sneakers against the floor as players practiced serving and setting.

James had always been good at sports, especially volleyball, for as long as I had known him. I never let him know how I secretly wished I could be like him. It seemed like he and everyone else in the seventh grade was growing taller and stronger, but I was still as short and small as I had always been. I wanted to try out for volleyball, but even James took one look at me and said, "Maybe volleyball just isn't for you." That hurt, coming from my best friend, but he never lied to me before and was always the kindest guy I had ever known.

After a few moments James came back with a smile on his face.
"Did you make it?" I asked.
"Yeah, they said no one else could spike the ball like me." James grabbed his stuff and we went out into the parking lot. "Coach said practices start next week. This year's team is going to be great," James said as we sat down on a bench.
"Yeah, I just wish I could be a part of it," I said without really thinking about my words.
Suddenly I saw my mom pull up in her red car and I walked over and got in without saying a word.
"So did James make the team?" my mom asked.
"Yeah," I replied. "They said he was the best."
"That's wonderful, I'm sure his parents are proud of him."
I didn't say anything.
"Is something wrong?" my mom asked.
"I just wish that I could be as athletic as James." I fiddled with the radio station. "He told me, 'Maybe volleyball just isn't for you.' But it's not just volleyball. It always seems like everything goes his way."
"That's no way to talk. James just has different gifts than you do."
When we finally got home, I went up to my room and lay down on my bed. I was just so sick of thinking about how I could never be as good as James. I turned on some music, and for a while I was finally able

Introduces the main characters and the conflict

Introduces and describes the setting in vivid detail

Introduces the first event and begins the rising action

Develops the conflict and adds suspense

Teach the Workshop

Student Model
Using the Model Direct students' attention to the model. Point out the side notes that identify the flow of the story—the beginning, middle, and end. Ask them to look for the parts of a plot: exposition, rising action, climax, falling action, and resolution.

Some students might benefit from outlining the model to grasp the writer's strategies. They may also create graphic organizers, such as cluster charts, to investigate the writer's development of character and setting.

Writing Skills

Sensory Details

Remind students that sensory details enhance descriptions. They can use sensory details to make their settings, characters, and the events of the plot vivid and memorable. Introduce them to the idea of a Sensory Detail Chart. Encourage them to make one for each character and for each setting.

A Sensory Detail Chart has one column each for the senses of sight, sound, touch, taste, and smell. Urge students to put something in each column, even if they don't think they will use it in their final stories.

Using Suspense

Tell students that suspense is a feeling of expectation, anxiety, or curiosity. Writers create suspense by raising questions in the reader's mind and by using details that create strong emotions. (Students may recall learning about suspense if they read "The Serial Garden" in Unit 1.)

Ask students to work in pairs to ask and answer questions about how this writer builds suspense. Model some possible questions: "When do you start to wonder how Zack feels about sports, or about James? What sensory details create strong emotions for you?"

Student Model CONTINUED

to stop thinking about volleyball and the other kids until my mom called me down for dinner.

As we ate dinner, my mom slid a piece of paper across the table.

"What's this?" I asked as I skimmed the page.

"It's an after-school program at the community center for boys and girls who want to play volleyball. I thought that since you can't play for the Tigers, maybe you'd want to play for another team."

"When are tryouts?" I asked my mom.

"This weekend, do you want to go?"

Before I could answer, my eyes stopped on one little piece of text.

"What is it?" my mom asked.

"They play in the same league as the Tigers. I'll be playing against my own school!" I couldn't believe it.

"Well, that's great; you'll get to play against your friends."

The idea of playing against the Tigers didn't excite me one bit. They were the best in the city, and I didn't want to look stupid in front of all my friends. Still, I decided to try out since playing on a team was a dream of mine, and I might finally get the chance.

That Saturday, my mom drove me over to the community center. They had the whole gym set up for tryouts. I sat down on a bench with a few other kids and waited for my name to be called.

> *Develops the conflict and adds suspense*

"What's your name?" one of the girls sitting next to me asked.

"Z-Zack," I stuttered. She laughed a little.

"Are you nervous?" she asked.

"Yeah, just a little."

"Don't worry; I'm sure you'll make it. By the way, my name is Chris."

Before I could say anything else, I heard someone yell out, "Zack Atkinson!"

I stood up slowly. My legs were shaking.

"Good luck," Chris said as I walked over to the coach.

The coach threw the ball in the air, and I stuck my hands out as it came down. The ball bounced off the side of my hand. I wanted to disappear.

"Hey, Zack, just relax. Trust me, you'll get it," the coach said as he grabbed another ball.

> *Uses natural, believable dialogue to develop the characters*

This time as he threw the ball in the air I calmed down and was able to return it to him. I felt so good; I couldn't believe I actually returned it. The tryouts went on until I was finally the one serving.

> *Maintains a consistent point of view*

Differentiated Instruction

English Language Learning

After students have read the model, you might invite English learners to plan new stories in their native languages, and then describe them to you verbally. Encourage them to talk through their ideas in English. Particularly encourage them to summarize the plot, so you can judge how well they understand that element of fiction.

"Whenever you're ready," the coach said. I threw the ball over my head and hit it with all my strength. The ball flew over the net and landed in the back corner of the other side of the gym.

"That was a great hit, Zack!"

I smiled and continued serving balls over the net.

When tryouts were finally over, the coach posted a list of the names and positions of the team. I searched eagerly for mine until I finally saw it. I was the starting server! Before I had time to celebrate, one of the coaches blew a whistle, and everybody walked over.

"All right everyone, now that you know your positions, we have an exhibition game tomorrow at 1 PM before the official season starts. I expect you all to be there and ready to go. We're playing the Tigers at Manhattan Middle School." My heart skipped a beat. Tomorrow I would play against my own school and James.

One o'clock sneaked up on me the next day, and before I knew it, we were warming up in Manhattan's gym. I spotted James on the other side of the court, and when he saw me, he looked stunned.

Finally the ref blew a whistle, starting the game. I got in position and grabbed the ball. I threw it in the air and smacked it across the net. The ball landed out of bounds. My cheeks felt flushed. I was mortified.

The Tigers took the ball and served it over perfectly, but Chris jumped above the net and spiked the ball on the Tigers' side.

The game seemed to drag on and on with the score going back and forth until finally it was 20 to 17 and our ball. The Tigers only needed one more point to win. I set up the ball and hit it over. It landed in the back right corner: ace. I set up again and hit it over. This time it landed in the front left corner: ace. With one more point we could tie the game.

"Keep it up, Zack, you can do it!" Chris yelled. I threw the ball over my head and hit it. This time one of the Tigers returned it. One of our setters just barely tipped it back over the net. Suddenly I saw James jump up and spike the ball straight towards the middle. I dove for it, but it bounced off my hands. The game was over. I wanted to just lie there forever, but one of the guys extended his hand and helped me up.

"You did great out there. I've never seen a server play so well," he said, and the rest of the team agreed. After the Tigers were done cheering, James came over and shook my hand.

"I was wrong about you Zack; you really can play."

"Yeah, you did really great too. I couldn't believe that spike."

"I have a feeling this season is going to be the best one yet."

> Maintains a consistent point of view

> Provides details about the characters' thoughts, feelings, and physical characteristics to make them more complex and interesting

> Builds tension toward a climax

> Resolves the conflict and brings the story to a satisfying close

Teach the Workshop

Building Tension

As the second-to-last annotation says, the writer builds tension toward the climax of the plot. Point out this annotation to students, and ask them to reiterate what the main conflict is in this story. (They should recognize that Zack has strong feelings about being compared to James, even if it is only Zack making the comparisons.) Then ask for several volunteers to define the word *tension*. Elicit definitions that go beyond the role of tension in a work of fiction, such as *stress, tightness, discomfort,* and *worry*. Then, ask student to identify events and sensory details that contribute to the building tension. (They will probably focus on the details of the play-by-play.)

Speaking & Listening Skills

Choral Reading

Tell students that the best way to determine if dialogue is believable is to read it out loud. Then have students form two groups to prepare a choral reading of part of the model. Give groups time to conduct one read-through and use group discussion to refine the presentation. Ask each group to present its reading in front of the class.

After the readings, ask the following questions and allow students to respond.

- Is the dialogue natural?
- If there is unnatural dialogue, how did it make you feel about the characters?
- What have you learned from this experience that will help you write dialogue in the future?

Teach the Workshop

Objectives

Participating in this lesson will help students deliver literary presentations that

- appeal to their audience
- contain vivid sensory details and descriptive words
- exhibit appropriate pacing for tone and purpose
- engage listeners with dialogue
- employ effective nonverbal expression

Launch the Lesson

Ask students why they think children like having stories read aloud to them. Beyond the fact that young children usually cannot read on their own, what engages them as listeners? Then ask: "What grabs you as a listener?" Tell students they will learn effective tools for reading aloud by studying this workshop.

> For more information, see the Language Arts Handbook Section 7, Speaking & Listening.

Program Resources

To expand upon this workshop lesson, Giving and Actively Listening to Literary Presentations, see the *Exceeding the Standards: Speaking & Listening* resource.

To help students explore literature on a deeper level, assign the following activity: Read Fiction Aloud, *Exceeding the Standards: Literature & Reading*, pp. 3–5.

Giving and Actively Listening to Literary Presentations

You have just written an exciting story, or maybe you have just read an excellent short story or poem. You want to share the passage with another person. You could let that person read it to him or herself. Or you could present the piece of literature aloud. This is called a **literary presentation.**

In this workshop you will learn how to plan and deliver an effective literary presentation. You will also learn how to effectively listen to someone else's presentation. This workshop includes a rubric, a set of standards to use in evaluating either your own presentation or someone else's.

Planning a Literary Presentation

Choose a Piece of Literature You have read a variety of stories and a couple of poems in this unit. You have also written your own short story. Here are a few points to keep in mind when choosing a story for a literary presentation:

- Which story or poem struck you the most? Choose a story or poem that you would like to hear read.
- Read aloud the first few lines. Does the story or poem sound like one you can effectively deliver to an audience?
- Can you give the story or poem the surprise or dramatic reading that it demands?

Identify Your Audience What literature you choose and how you present it will depend partly on who your audience is. Is the audience familiar with the story or poem? Be prepared to answer questions or even accept criticism from your audience.

Review Your Literature Once you have chosen the selection you will present, read it silently. Use the following tips to evaluate if the story or poem is a good one to be read aloud.

- Identify the point of view. Is it told from the first-person point of view? Decide how you will adjust your voice and body language as you present your story.
- How easy or difficult will it be for you to switch character roles in dialogue or become the narrator when necessary?
- Look at the punctuation. Does it suggest emotions or pauses in speech?
- How much emotion is called for, and how much can you deliver?

Common Core State Standards

Reading Literature
RL.7

Speaking and Listening
SL.4, SL.6

Words in Use

Teaching Words
convey, 247
constructive, 247
pacing, 247

KEY TERMS

LITERARY PRESENTATION, 246
AUDIENCE, 246
POINT OF VIEW, 246
DIALOGUE, 246
PUNCTUATION, 246
SENSORY DETAIL, 247

Word Choice and Sensory Details Sensory details are details that appeal to one of the five senses. If you are reading your own short story, ask yourself: Have I effectively used words to convey emotion or paint a picture of what I want the audience to see in their minds? If you are presenting a story or poem by another writer, consider whether or not you can visualize where and when the story takes place or how a character looks, thinks, or feels. Remember to convey this when you give your presentation to the class.

Evaluating Your Literary Presentation

As with the revision of your writing, a peer reviewer can help improve your presentation. Remember, your reviewer has your best interest in mind when he or she critiques the way you deliver a line or a piece of dialogue. If you are reviewing someone else's presentation, keep in mind that you should give helpful suggestions for improving the presentation. Be respectful in your criticism, and give constructive feedback. Use the rubric on this page to help you evaluate your literary presentation.

Delivering Your Literary Presentation

Nonverbal communication is just as important in giving a literary presentation as speaking is. When you read your story or poem, look at your audience, use facial expressions to convey emotion, and use your body to convey a character's attitude. Remember your pacing, and do not race through a reading, mumble (unless the story calls for it), or read too loudly. Keep your audience interested and focused on the story.

Listen Actively Respect is the key to active listening. Be attentive to the speaker's words, and follow the story's plot. Respond appropriately to funny or surprising parts, and ask questions when appropriate.

Speaking Rubric

Your presentation will be evaluated on these elements:

Content

☐ literature is appropriate for audience

☐ literature contains vivid sensory details

☐ literature uses descriptive words

Delivery and Presentation

☐ engaging presentation of dialogue

☐ appropriate pacing for tone and purpose of literature

☐ effective nonverbal expression

Listening Rubric

As a peer reviewer or audience member, you should do the following:

☐ listen quietly and attentively

☐ maintain eye contact with speaker

☐ ask appropriate questions

☐ (as peer reviewer) provide constructive feedback

Dramatizing

Tell students that making a literary presentation is similar to acting in a play. If they are reading fiction, encourage them to think through what their plot, setting, and characters mean, and to consider ways to bring those literary elements alive. If they are reading poems, have students think about mood and tone and the emotion they want to evoke.

Preparing for Presentations

Give students opportunities to practice their presentations alone and with peer reviewers. Offer these tips:

- If the story is long, consider creating a cutting, which means selecting a portion of the story to read.
- Decide whether the presentation will be clearer with speech tags (such as "she said") or without them.
- Make sure the material will be easy for the presenter to see when reading in front of an audience. This may mean retyping the material or copying it and adding various cues.
- Prepare a short introduction to the work, especially if the audience will be unfamiliar with the writer or type of literature.

Differentiated Instruction

English Language Learning

Invite students from other countries to tell short stories or poems in their native languages. Encourage them to model appropriate pacing, tone, and expression. As a class, identify the nonverbal elements that make strong impressions on listeners.

Enrichment

Tell students that high schools often offer "oral interpretation" in speech classes. Many college communications and theater departments offer oral interpretation courses as well. Some people have careers reading literature aloud. Encourage interested students to find examples of college course descriptions and/or biographies of professional storytellers to share with the class.

Objectives

Completing this lesson will enable students to

- write a literary response based on a timed writing prompt
- answer standardized test questions that demonstrate revising and editing skills
- demonstrate the ability to make inferences from a reading by answering standardized questions

Timed Writing

Say that standardized tests often ask students to write a response to a prompt in a specified period of time. Give the following tips:

- Read the entire question carefully.
- Look for key words in the question that tell you what is expected.
- Underline these words or write them on your own notepaper.
- Use the key words to make sure you answer all parts of the question.
- Organize. Allow time for planning, writing, and reviewing.
- Before you begin writing, create a rough outline of points to make.
- Write a clear introduction. This will help keep you on track as you write each paragraph.
- If you find yourself running out of time, state your remaining points and add a conclusion.
- Review your completed essay to see if you have answered all parts of the question.
- Before you turn in your completed essay, take time to proofread.

Writing Skills

Literary Response

Carefully read the following writing prompt. Before you begin writing, think carefully about what task the assignment is asking you to perform. Then create an outline to help guide your writing.

> In Marta Salinas's short story "The Scholarship Jacket," the main character, Martha, learns that the school principal is going to make her pay money in order to be eligible for the scholarship jacket—an honor awarded to the most academically successful student. When Martha asks her grandfather if he will pay the fifteen-dollar fee, he responds, "Then if you pay for it, Marta, it's not a scholarship jacket, is it? Tell your principal I will not pay the fifteen dollars." Do you believe Martha's grandfather made the right choice?

In your essay, take a position on the grandfather's decision. Use evidence from the story, including direct quotations, in support of your position. As you write, be sure to:

- Organize your essay in a logical and consistent way
- Include introductory and concluding paragraphs
- Introduce your position in the first paragraph
- Support your main idea in each body paragraph

Rubric for a Literary Response

Have students use these criteria for evaluating their literary responses.

- ☐ Does the response have an introductory paragraph that clearly states a position?
- ☐ Is the response organized logically and consistently?
- ☐ Does each body paragraph have material that supports the main idea, including such evidence as direct quotations from the story?
- ☐ Does the essay have a concluding paragraph?

Common Core State Standards

Language
L.3.1f, L.5.1d, L.6.1e

Revising and Editing Skills

In the following excerpt from the first draft of a student's paper, words and phrases are underlined and numbered. Alternatives to the underlined words and phrases appear in the right-hand column. Choose the alternative that best corrects any grammatical or style errors in the original. If you think the original is error-free, choose *NO CHANGE*.

You may also be asked questions about a section of the passage or the entire passage. These questions do not refer to a specific underlined phrase or word and are identified by a number in a box. Record your answers on a separate sheet of paper.

In Gish Jen's story "The White Umbrella"
                                    1
many different things motivate the characters.

The story's narrator wants to be like everybody

else, and her sister Mona wanted to be happy.
                              2
Her parents are just trying to provide what's best
                                              3
for she and her sister. Each character's motivation

play an important role in the development of the
      4
plot and the story's overall mood. 5

The story's narrator is ashamed that their

mother has taken a job working at a grocery

store. She wants her mother to stay at home and

be "normal." The narrator's feelings are partly the

result of how she compares herself to others and

of how her parents talk about other families.

Early in the story she says "I remembered how
                      6
sorry my parents had felt for Mrs. Lee when she

started waitressing downtown the year before."

1. A. NO CHANGE
   B. "The White Umbrella,"
   C. The White Umbrella
   D. "The White Umbrella;"

2. A. NO CHANGE
   B. Mona wants to be happy
   C. Mona wanted happy
   D. wanted to be happy, Mona

3. A. NO CHANGE
   B. what are best for she and her sister
   C. what's best for her and her sister
   D. what's best for she and she sister

4. A. NO CHANGE
   B. playing an important role
   C. have played an important role
   D. plays an important role

5. Which of the following *best* summarizes the thesis, or main idea, of this essay?
   A. The characters' motivations contribute to the plot and mood.
   B. The characters' motivations are in conflict.
   C. The narrator should pay more attention to her parents.
   D. The plot has the greatest influence on the mood.

6. A. NO CHANGE
   B. she says;
   C. she says,
   D. she said

Words in Use

Teaching Words
academically, 248
nostalgic, 251

KEY TERMS

Tell students that reading comprehension tests give a short piece of writing and then ask several questions about it. The questions may ask students to figure out something based on information in the passage. Urge students to keep the following tips in mind:

- Read all the questions quickly.
- Read the passage with the questions in mind.
- Reread the first question carefully.
- Scan the passage, looking for key words. When you find a key word, slow down and read carefully.
- Answer the first question.
- Repeat this process to answer all the rest of the questions.

Reading Skills

Carefully read the following passage. Then, on a separate piece of paper, answer each question.

from "The Ground Is Always Damp" by Luci Tapahonso

One night Leona dreamt that she was sitting outside her parents' home in the bright sunlight. The many trees, the small dusty chickens scratching nearby, and a single cloud above cast sharp dark shadows on the smooth yard. The sudden familiarity of the detailed shadows and clean air startled and awakened her, and
5 later she spoke aloud, addressing her mother who was hundreds of miles away.

"Shimá, my mother, it's cloudy here most of the time. The ground is always damp, and Mom, I don't care to kneel down and sift dirt through my fingers. One day last week, the sun came out for a few hours, and the shadows were soft and furry on the brown grass. That's the way it is here, my mother."

10 Even though Leona hadn't seen her parents in months, she talked to them silently every day. She imagined that they listened, then responded by explaining things or asking long, detailed questions. Leona did this thoughtfully and felt that they did the same in their daily conversations about her and her children. They wondered what the weather was like and what kind of house Leona and her family
15 lived in. She was certain about this. The difference was that they spoke aloud to each other, or to the various brothers and sisters who lived nearby.

In her dreams, she was always there in New Mexico, driving the winding roads to Taos, watching the harvest dances at Laguna, or maybe selling hay and watermelons with her brothers. In her dreams, she laughed, talking and joking
20 easily in Navajo and English. She woke herself up sometimes because she had laughed aloud, or said, "Aye-e-e"—that old familiar teasing expression.

The New Mexico sky is clear and empty. It is a deep blue, almost turquoise, and Leona's family lives surrounded by the Carriso Mountains in the west, the Sleeping Ute Mountains in the north, the La Plata in the east and the Chuska
25 Mountain range to the southwest. They rely on the distance, the thin, clean air, and the mountains to alert them to rain, thunderstorms, dust storms, and intense heat. At various times, her brothers stand looking across the horizon to see what is in store. They can see fifty miles or more in each direction.

In contrast, when Leona looks to the east most mornings, the sky is gray, the
30 air thick with frost, and the wind blows cold dampness.

"My mother, there are no mountains here, and I can't see very far because the air is thick and heavy with a scent I can't recognize. I haven't been able to smell the arrival of snow here, or to distinguish between the different kinds of rain scent. The rain seems all the same here, except in degree, and it is constant."

English Language Learning

Students learning English will need help with the academic vocabulary used in standardized tests. Explain the following terms used in this workshop: *prompt*—cue, something to help one begin, 248. A "writing prompt" is usually a detailed paragraph of instruction.

outline—short summary or description, usually arranged as a series of key points, 248
position—opinion or point to be discussed, 248
evidence—facts that support an argument, 248

Help students internalize these academic terms by asking them to write a short story or expository paragraph that uses these words correctly and effectively. Confirm their understanding of the terms by reviewing their work.

1. The sentence that begins in line 2 can best be
described as
   A. theme.
   B. description.
   C. tone.
   D. characterization.

2. Who is Shimá?
   A. Leona
   B. Leona's grandmother
   C. Leona's sister
   D. Leona's mother

3. Which of the following *best* describes the
paragraph beginning on line 22?
   A. It explains the story's conflict.
   B. It describes the protagonist.
   C. It is filled with sensory details.
   D. It is filled with dialect.

4. Based on the context, what is the meaning of
degree in line 34?
   A. texture
   B. shape
   C. color
   D. amount

5. From the text, you could infer that Leona is
   A. an adult.
   B. a small child.
   C. an old woman.
   D. an only child.

6. Which of the following *best* describes the
tone of the narrator's dialogue?
   A. unsure
   B. humorous
   C. sorrowful
   D. happy

7. The character of the story's narrator can be
described as
   A. dynamic.
   B. static.
   C. unreliable.
   D. implied.

8. The conflict in this passage is primarily
   A. internal.
   B. external.
   C. indirect.
   D. resolution.

9. The mood of this passage can best be
described as
   A. nostalgic.
   B. excited.
   C. suspenseful.
   D. energetic.

10. This story is written from which point of
view?
   A. first-person
   B. second-person
   C. third-person
   D. limited

Teach the Workshop

Reading Skills
   1. B
   2. D
   3. C
   4. D
   5. A
   6. C
   7. B
   8. A
   9. A
   10. C

Test-Taking Skills

Eliminate Incorrect Responses

Tell students that a key skill in answering multiple-
choice questions is eliminating incorrect responses.
Demonstrate this skill by modeling a think-aloud for
one question in the Reading Skills section.

Question 10. The three kinds of point of view we
have learned are first-person, third-person
omniscient, and third-person limited. That eliminates
B and D. I see the pronoun "I" in the second

paragraph and the last paragraph, but it looks like
those are quotes of what a person is saying. Taking
everything into account, the answer must be C,
third-person.

Select another question and have the class work as
a group to eliminate the incorrect responses.

Unit 3 Visual Planning Guide

Planning and Assessment Tools

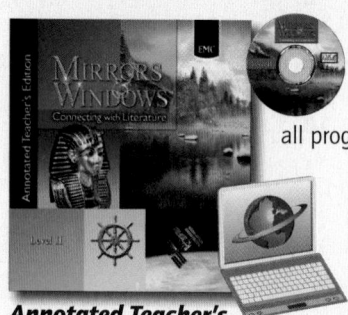

Annotated Teacher's Edition
One location for accessing, previewing, and planning for use of all program resources.

Annotated Teacher's Edition

EMC Launchpad
Desktop application for accessing, previewing, planning, posting, and grading all program resources. Post personal resources and lessons, and access the E-Lesson Planner, the E-Gradebook, and training modules for computer literacy.

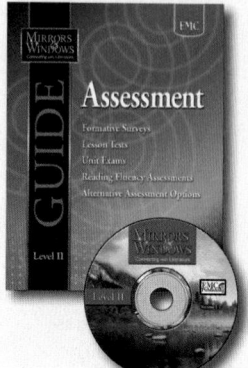

Assessment Guide and ExamView
A variety of assessments are available for this unit in print and electronic forms, including:
- Formative Survey
- Lesson Tests
- Unit Exams
- Alternative Assessment Options
- Reading Fluency Assessments

Meeting the Standards: Unit 3
In addition to lesson-by-lesson resources, *Meeting the Standards* includes the following unit-based resources:
- Unit Study Guide
- Practice Test
- Active Reading Model
- Selection Quizzes

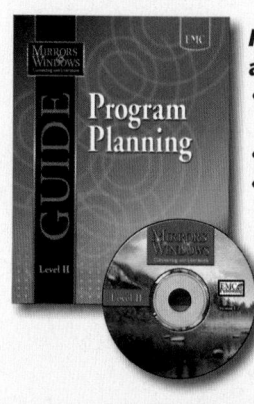

Program Planning Guide and E-Lesson Planner
- Lesson Plans for all the selections in the unit
- Core Standards-Based Selections
- Reading Log and Evaluation Forms

The E-Lesson Planner contains fully developed lesson plans and unit resources with an electronic calendar for editing lesson plans.

Technology Tools

Visual Teaching Package
This package contains unit-based lectures, games, art collections, and Writing Workshops in PowerPoint format; included within the EMC Launchpad.

Interactive Student Text on CD
The student textbook on CD includes highlighting, note-taking, bookmarking, and a direct link to the student website, in addition to everything in the student text.

Audio Library
Authentic, dramatic recordings with listening activities expand listening skills and offer additional support for developing readers and English Language Learners.

ETS Online Criterion-Based Essay Grader (Grades 9–12)
Students can use this ETS web-based tool to evaluate their essays online before submitting them for teacher review and final evaluation.

mirrorsandwindows.com
Student and teacher resources, support, references, technology tools, and state-specific standards are available at **mirrorsandwindows.com.** The website is customizable using the EMC Launchpad.

Unit-Based Resources

Exceeding the Standards Unit Resources

Each of the *Exceeding the Standards* resources provides fully developed lessons to help you extend the textbook lessons and to expand upon the themes and skills covered in the unit. You can also download these lessons from **mirrorsandwindows.com**.

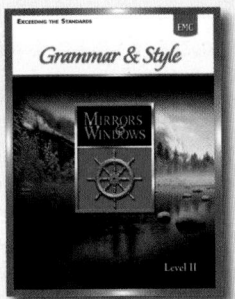

Grammar & Style
This resource contains:
- Seven lessons on Verbs, pp. 49–74
- Two lessons on Subject-Verb Agreement and Usage, pp. 75–81

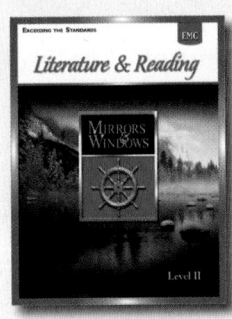

Literature & Reading
This resource contains:
- Distinguish between Fiction and Nonfiction, pp. 6–7

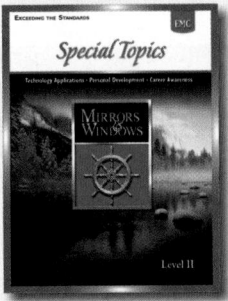

Special Topics
This resource contains:
- Lifelong Learning: Analyzing Yourself: Part 1, pp. 10–11
- Media Literacy: Using PowerPoint, pp. 12–13

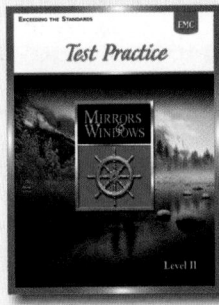

Test Practice
This resource contains:
- Expository Essay Practice Test: Revising and Editing, pp. 8–9

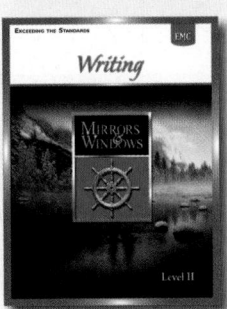

Writing
This resource contains:
- Persuasive Writing: Write a Persuasive Essay, pp. 14–22

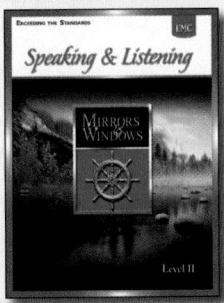

Speaking & Listening
This resource contains the following lesson to expand on the Speaking & Listening Workshop:
- Giving and Actively Listening to Informative Presentations, 7–9

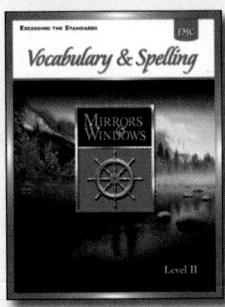

Vocabulary & Spelling
This resource contains:
- Four lessons on Spelling Patterns, pp. 21–34

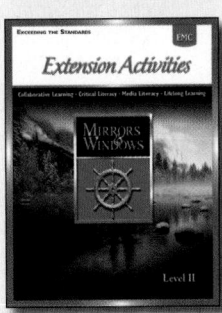

Extension Activities
This resource contains:
- Collaborative Learning: Identifying Facts and Opinions, p. 8
- Media Literacy: Analyze Advertisements, pp. 9–10

Unit 3 Visual Planning Guide

 Reading Level: Challenging
Pacing: 2 days

 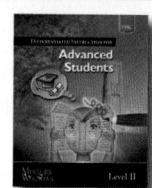

Meeting the Standards, Reading Model, pp. 19–26

Developing Readers, Unlock Word Meaning, pp. 19–21

Advanced Students, Memoir Writing, pp. 14–15

258

  Reading Level: Moderate
Pacing: 4 days

 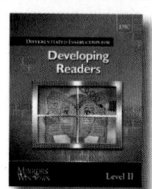

Meeting the Standards, Guided Reading, pp. 27–34

Developing Readers, Use Text Organization, pp. 22–24

266

  Reading Level: Moderate
Pacing: 3 days

  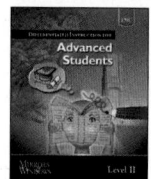

Meeting the Standards, Guided Reading, pp. 34–40

English Language Learners, Author's Purpose, pp. 86–95

Advanced Students, Comparing Literature Activity, p. 16

283

  Reading Level: Moderate
Pacing: 2 days

The Eternal Frontier

Meeting the Standards, Guided Reading, pp. 41–46

292

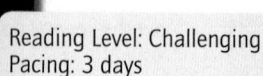 **Reading Level: Challenging**
Pacing: 3 days

Meeting the Standards, Directed Reading, pp. 47–52

Developing Readers, Take Notes, pp. 25–27

298

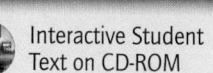 Interactive Student Text on CD-ROM

  Selection Lesson Plan

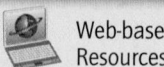 Web-based Resources

Lesson-by-Lesson Resources

Reading Level: Easy
Pacing: 1 day

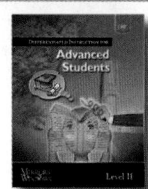

Meeting the Standards,
Directed Reading,
pp. 53–56

Advanced Students,
Biographical Research
Project, pp. 17–18

313

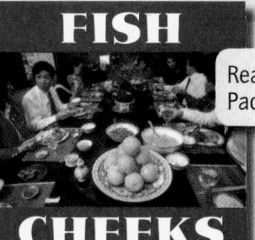

Reading Level: Easy
Pacing: 1 day

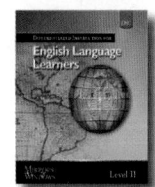

Meeting the Standards,
Directed Reading,
pp. 57–61

*English Language
Learners,* Analyze Text
Structure, pp. 96–102

318

Reading Level: Moderate
Pacing: 3 days

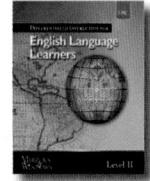

Meeting the Standards,
Directed Reading,
pp. 62–70

English Language Learners,
Characterization,
pp. 103–119

323

Reading Level: Moderate
Pacing: 3 days

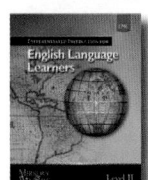

Meeting the Standards,
Directed Reading,
pp. 62–70

English Language Learners,
Characterization,
pp. 103–119

333

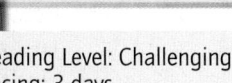

Reading Level: Challenging
Pacing: 3 days

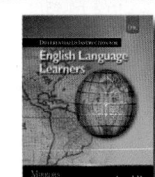

Meeting the Standards,
Directed Reading,
pp. 71–81

*English Language
Learners,* Use Context
Clues, pp. 120–131

341

 Lesson Test   Audio Library

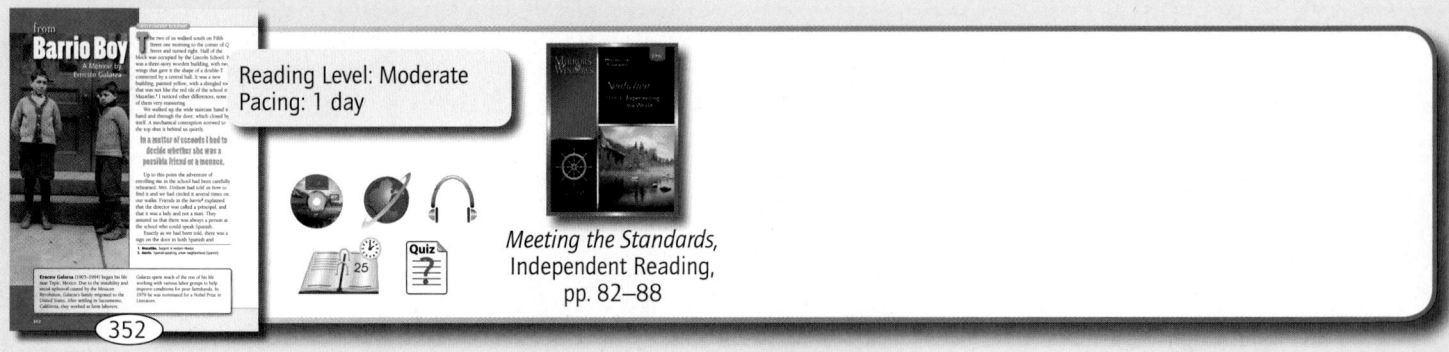

Reading Level: Moderate
Pacing: 1 day

Quiz
?

Meeting the Standards,
Independent Reading,
pp. 82–88

Unit 3 Scope & Sequence Guide

Selection or Feature	Genre	Reading Support/ Reading Level	Word Count	Reading Skill	Graphic Organizer	
Introduction to Nonfiction pp. 254–255						
Nonfiction Reading Model p. 256						
from An American Childhood Annie Dillard pp. 257–263	Memoir	Guided Reading: Reading Model/ Challenging	1,770	Context Clues	Details and Opinions Chart	
Elizabeth I Milton Meltzer pp. 265–279	Biography	Guided Reading/ Moderate	3,273	Distinguish Fact from Opinion	Fact/Opinion Chart; Detail Web	
Primary Source Connection: from **Queen Elizabeth's Speech to Her Last Parliament** Queen Elizabeth I p. 277	Speech	Challenging	181			
Written with a Diamond on Her Window at Woodstock Queen Elizabeth I p. 277	Poem	Moderate	11			
Written in Her French Psalter Queen Elizabeth I p. 277	Poem	Moderate	25			
from Letter to Mary, Queen of Scots, 1586 Queen Elizabeth I p. 277	Letter	Moderate	91			

GUIDED READING

Reading Level: Moderate
Pacing: 1 day

Meeting the Standards,
Independent Reading,
pp. 89–94

Advanced Students,
Independent Author
Study, pp. 19–20

Literary Element	*Mirrors & Windows* Theme	Cross-Curricular Connection	Writing Options	Extension Activities
Fiction and Nonfiction Types of Nonfiction				
Autobiography	Memories		Creative and Expository: Screenplay and Essay Expository: Critical Analysis	Collaborative Learning: Analyze Tone Lifelong Learning: Write a Book Summary
Biography	Leadership	Cultural Connection: *The Renaissance*	Creative: Dialogue Expository: Expository Paragraph	Collaborative Learning: Analyze Speech Critical Literacy: Conduct an Interview

Unit 3 Scope & Sequence Guide

Selection or Feature	Genre	Reading Support/ Reading Level	Word Count	Reading Skill	Graphic Organizer	
Understanding the Essay p. 281						
Names/Nombres Julia Alvarez pp. 282–290	Personal Essay	Guided Reading/ Moderate	1,372	Identify Author's Purpose	Author's Purpose Chart; Details Web	
Literature Connection: Face It Janet S. Wong p.289	Lyric Poem	Easy	46			
The Eternal Frontier Louis L'Amour pp. 291–295	Persuasive Essay	Guided Reading/ Moderate	629	Analyze Main Idea and Supporting Details	Main Idea Map; Logic/ Appeals Chart	
from **Off the Court** Arthur Ashe pp. 297–311	Autobiography	Directed Reading/ Challenging	5,513	Identify Main Idea	Main Idea Map; Sensory Details Chart	
Informational Text Connection: A Black Athlete Looks at Education Arthur Ashe p. 310–311	Editorial	Moderate	477			
Was Tarzan a Three-Bandage Man? Bill Cosby pp. 312–316	Personal Essay	Directed Reading/Easy	507	Context Clues	Purpose Chart	
Fish Cheeks Amy Tan pp. 317–320	Personal Essay	Directed Reading/Easy	516	Analyze Text Structure	Sequence Map; Sensory Details Chart	
Comparing Literature: A Bittersweet Memoir Jerry Izenberg pp. 322–339	Biography	Directed Reading/ Moderate	4,678		Characterization Chart	
Searching for January W.P. Kinsella pp. 322–339	Short Story	Directed Reading/ Moderate	2,081			
Madam C.J. Walker Jim Haskins pp. 340–351	Biography	Directed Reading/ Challenging	2,493	Context Clues		
Literature Connection: The Sunflower Quilting Bee at Arles Faith Ringgold pp. 348–350	Story Quilt	Moderate	784			

Literary Element	*Mirrors & Windows* Theme	Cross-Curricular Connection	Writing Options	Extension Activities
What is an Essay? Elements of an Essay Types of Essays				
Personal Essay	Fitting In	Geography Connection: *The Dominican Republic*	Creative: Invitation Expository: Expository Paragraph	Lifelong Learning: Gather Historical Information Critical Literacy: Conduct a Panel Discussion
Persuasive Essay	Exploration		Creative: Personal Letter Expository: Literary Response	Collaborative Learning: Identify Facts, Opinions, and Commonplace Assertations Media Literacy: Evaluate Media Reports on Space
Description	Overcoming Discrimination		Creative: Autobiographical Essay Expository: Biographical Sketch	Collaborative Learning: Research a Sport Critical Literacy: Question and Answer
Purpose	Imitating Heroes	History Connection: *Jackie Robinson*	Creative: Personal Letter Persuasive: Persuasive Paragraph	Critical Literacy: Analyze Adaptions Media Literacy: Discuss Humorous Writing
Sensory Details	Diversity		Creative: Dialogue Expository: Expository Essay	Collaborative: Hold a Small-Group Discussion Lifelong Learning: Research Holidays of Other Cultures
Compare Literature: Characterization	Fame		Creative: News Article Expository: Compare and Contrast Essay	Collaborative Learning: Create a Dialogue Media Literacy: Conduct Internet Research
	Yearning for the Past			
Introduction and Conclusion	Helping Others		Creative: Jingle Expository: Biography	Critical Literacy: Analyze a Speech Media Literacy: Analyze Advertisements

Unit 3 Scope & Sequence Guide

	Selection or Feature	Genre	Reading Support/ Reading Level	Word Count	Reading Skill	Graphic Organizer	
INDEPENDENT READING	from **Barrio Boy** Ernesto Galarza pp. 352–355	Memoir	Independent Reading/ Moderate	1,605	Identify Author's Purpose		
	The Night the Bed Fell James Thurber pp. 356–360	Personal Essay	Independent Reading/ Moderate	1,759	Compare and Contrast		

Unit 3 Language Arts Workshops

Grammar & Style	Vocabulary & Spelling	Writing	Speaking & Listening	Test Practice
Phrases, p. 264 Sentence Types, p. 296 Fragments and Run-on Sentences, p. 321	Greek, Latin, and Anglo-Saxon Roots, p. 280	Expository Writing: Cause-and-Effect Essay, pp. 362–367	Giving and Actively Listening to Informative Presentations, pp. 368–369	Writing Skills: Expository Essay, p. 370 Revising and Editing, p. 371 Reading Skills: from "Flying" by Reeve Lindbergh, pp. 372–373

Literary Element	*Mirrors & Windows* Theme	Cross-Curricular Connection	Writing Options	Extension Activities
Personal Narrative	Alienation		Persuasive: Newspaper Editorial	Collaborative Learning: Discuss the Importance of a Strong Education
Purpose	Storytelling		Descriptive: Descriptive Essay	Critical Literacy: Create a List of Questions You Would Like to Ask the Author

Unit 3 Building Vocabulary

The lists below identify the Words in Use and Key Terms within this unit. These words are listed at the bottom of the Teacher's Edition pages at the beginning of each lesson. Vocabulary development activities are provided in the *Meeting the Standards* unit book and in *Exceeding the Standards: Vocabulary & Spelling*.

WORDS IN USE

Preview Vocabulary

Preview Vocabulary are words taken from the sentences within each selection. These words are defined in the side margin or at the bottom of the pages on which they appear. The "Preview Vocabulary" section introduces these words in the Before Reading page preceding each selection.

ambition, 346	dominant, 300	noisome, 259	rebuff, 305
antidote, 293	emulate, 314	ominous, 274	recruit, 345
appalling, 319	exasperate, 261	physiologically, 299	repress, 304
astute, 346	forfeit, 274	pluck, 319	rumpled, 319
brace, 325	impasse, 303	preliminary, 293	segregate, 342
conjecture, 326	incorporate, 294	prerogative, 261	subsequent, 259
dejectedly, 315	lavish, 346	prestige, 268	tedium, 262
delineate, 324	lithely, 334	prosperity, 270	
directive, 273	locomotion, 314	provision, 342	

Selection Words

Selection Words are additional words from the reading that may be challenging but are not central to the selection and are not identified in the prereading section. These words can easily be learned using the story context, and they provide excellent practice for using content clues to find meaning without explicit instruction.

ailments, 275	engulf, 338	mobilized, 353	specify, 286
assimilate, 309	enticed, 277	niche, 299	spendthrift, 270
avid, 346	ethnicity, 286	obnoxious, 353	statecraft, 271
bales, 335	exposé, 348	ominous, 357	tormented, 350
bounty, 277	flanked, 353	oppression, 348	torque, 300
cautious, 260	foreign, 355	overseer, 327	tourniquets, 315
chaotic, 287	formidable, 353	perilous, 359	transcontinental, 293
commencement, 288	hearsay, 262	pungent, 359	transistors, 294
commend, 277	hypertension, 346	recitations, 354	transoceanic, 293
commerce, 267	incorporate, 314	reign, 270	tyranny, 277
deity, 301	ingenuity, 338	rejuvenation, 347	uncanny, 359
disposition, 358	innuendoes, 305	reviver, 357	undercurrent, 329
dissuading, 357	malfunction, 338	salve, 344	vaulted, 258
enamel, 259	maneuvered, 353	sharecroppers, 342	

Teaching Words

Teaching Words consist of vocabulary that is used in the directions about the lessons. Teaching words explain to students what to focus on within the selection, help establish the story context, clarify the meaning of literary terms, and define the goals or instructional purpose.

affiliate, 314	camaraderie, 309	ecosystem, 363	flourish, 265
analyze, 256	carrion, 255	effectively, 256	forbade, 284
anecdote, 255	chronologically, 257	emulated, 371	forfeited, 371
anthology, 295	circumstances, 363	enabled, 265	governing, 279
anticipated, 365	conjecture, 371	enunciation, 369	heckled, 314
antidote, 371	contracted, 297	equidistant, 280	heir, 265
armada, 280	contribute, 256, 363	equilateral, 280	humorist, 356
artisan, 280	convoluted, 287	evaluate, 256	immigrants, 355
aviator, 372	coronation, 280	exasperated, 371	impasse, 371
avid, 291	criteria, 263	expedition, 370	improbable, 356
bazaar, 287	delegation, 265	extensive, 254	incoherent, 255
bias, 295	derived, 280	firsthand, 255	indicate, 364

informal, 281
instability, 352
interpret, 256
jeers, 314
jurisdiction, 280
lighthearted, 281
manageable, 363
migrated, 352
monarchy, 265
nonverbal, 369

ominous, 371
omitted, 371
perilous, 372
petitions, 255
photosynthesis, 280
piloted, 291
prerogative, 371
presiding, 265
prestige, 280, 371
rebuffed, 371

recall, 256
redirected, 356
rephrasing, 369
repressed, 371
reverence, 263
revival, 280
specialized, 368
succession, 280
tandem, 372
technical, 368

tedium, 371
tethered, 372
transfusion, 297
treasure trove, 262
undertook, 254
unnecessarily, 366
upheaval, 352
vantage point, 281
vivid, 257
watershed, 362

KEY TERMS

Key Terms are commonly referred to as *academic vocabulary.* These terms appear in the instructional material to teach the terminology that students need to acquire to understand literature. The repetition of the terms throughout the program ensures student mastery and provides a solid foundation for the continuing study of literature and language arts.

analyze, 256
anecdote, 316
Anglo-Saxon root, 280
annotation, 365
audience, 281, 368
author's purpose, 281, 282
autobiography, 255, 257, 297, 373
base word, 280
biographical sketch, 311
biography, 255, 265, 322, 340, 373
body, 281, 364
cause, 370
cause-and-effect essay, 362
cause-and-effect organization, 364
characterization, 322
chart, 369
chronological, 317
clause, 321
comma, 321
conclusion, 281, 316, 340, 364, 369
conflict, 288, 373
conjunction, 321
context clue, 256, 257, 312, 340

description, 297
dialogue, 279, 311, 320, 321, 360
direct characterization, 339
editorial, 310, 355
effect, 370
essay, 255, 281
evaluate, 256
expository essay, 281, 370
fact, 265, 295
feedback, 369
fiction, 254
figurative language, 373
first-person point of view, 282
first-person, 373
foreshadowing, 373
graph, 369
Greek root, 280
independent clause, 321
indirect characterization, 339
informative presentation, 368
interpret, 256
introduction, 281, 340, 364, 369
introductory sentence, 316
Latin root, 280
literary response, 295
main idea, 291, 297, 355, 368

memoir, 255, 257, 322, 352, 373
narrative, 254, 317
narrator, 370
news article, 339
nonfiction, 254, 256, 265, 281, 297, 340
opinion, 265, 295
organizational pattern, 362
outline, 355, 370
parallelism, 255
paraphrase, 355
peer review, 365
personal essay, 281, 282, 312, 317, 356
personification, 373
persuasive essay, 281, 291
phrase, 297, 321
point of view, 281, 360, 373
precise language, 295, 360
predict, 265
pronoun, 281, 282
proofread, 366
protagonist, 373
punctuation, 321, 364
purpose, 312, 360
recall, 256, 277
repetition, 295

review, 263
rhetorical question, 255
run-on sentence, 321
second-person, 373
semicolon, 321
sensory detail, 256, 295, 297, 317, 360
sentence fragments, 321
sequence, 317
sequence of events, 256
setting, 256
short story, 322
skim, 282
summarize, 282, 316
supporting detail, 291
text structure, 317
theme, 290, 373
thesis, 255, 355, 362, 370
thesis statement, 279, 363
third-person limited, 373
third-person omniscient, 373
third-person point of view, 255
third-person, 373
tone, 263, 281, 290, 316, 363, 368, 373

Objectives

Studying this unit will help students meet the following objectives:

- Connect the themes expressed in the selections to their own lives and to the world around them
- Identify common forms of nonfiction
- Understand different elements of nonfiction, including *autobiography, biography, personal essay, persuasive essay, description, purpose, sensory details, characterization,* and *introduction and conclusion*
- Understand variations of literary forms and authors' use of language to develop forms

Reading Strategies

Ask Questions
Clarify
Make Inferences
Make Predictions
Visualize

Reading Skills

Analyze Main Idea and Supporting
  Details
Analyze Text Structure
Context Clues
Distinguish Fact from Opinion
Identify Author's Purpose
Identify Main Idea

Literary Elements

Autobiography	Personal Essay
Biography	Persuasive Essay
Characterization	Purpose
Description	Sensory Details
Introduction and	
Conclusion	

Experiencing the World
Nonfiction

JAMES THURBER   AMY TAN   ARTHUR ASHE

Launch the Unit

Have students work in small groups to create questions that relate to the unit theme. Model this by proposing a question such as: "What does it feel like to experience the world through someone else's eyes?" Have the groups write down their questions and keep the lists. When the class has completed work on the unit, have students revisit the questions and identify selections that help answer them.

"...my mother said to me, 'You want to be the same as American girls on the outside....But inside you must always be Chinese. You must be proud you are different. Your only shame is to have shame.'"

—AMY TAN, "Fish Cheeks"

Sometimes we feel the need to express an idea, to describe our experiences, or to make a statement about something we believe. In Amy Tan's personal essay "Fish Cheeks," she describes an experience in her youth that helped her to understand the importance of self-acceptance. As you read the nonfiction in this unit, consider what each author is trying to say about him- or herself or the world.

JERRY IZENBERG   LOUIS L'AMOUR   BILL COSBY

253

Program Resources

For a visual reminder of the unit-based resources available for Unit 3, Nonfiction, see pages 252A and 252B. As you introduce the unit, you may want to provide students with the Unit Study Guide, which is contained in the *Meeting the Standards* resource.

Introduction to Nonfiction

You may choose to draw students' attention to the Introduction to Nonfiction as they explore types of nonfiction in the unit's selections. In Before Reading and During Reading sections of each selection, they will read about visual media, informational text, and essays, for example. This material can help them fit individual selections into the larger genre of nonfiction.

You may also want to have students discuss reasons they might write nonfiction themselves. Ask what they have written in the past for each of these kinds of assignments or purposes:

- report on a science experiment
- letter to an older relative
- e-mail to a friend
- summary of a summer vacation
- text message
- blog

Launch the Lesson

Ask students to give you examples of nonfiction material they have read in the past few days. Most will refer to newspapers and textbooks. Help students appreciate that much of what they see — street signs, posters, company names, instruction sheets, and advertisements — can be considered nonfiction. Nonfiction is not imaginary, so its topics are real people, places, things, and events.

Introduction to Nonfiction

Both of the following passages deal with baseball great Roberto Clemente. How do they differ?

"I am surprised. More than surprised. You are Roberto Clemente, the baseball player?"

"Of course."

"You were lost at sea?"

"Until now."

"There's something not quite right."

"Like what?" says Clemente.

"Like what year do you think this is?"

"When we took off it was 1972, but New Year's Eve. We crashed in the ocean. It must be January fifth or sixth, maybe even the seventh, 1973."

— W. P. KINSELLA, "Searching for January"

"It was almost midnight," recalls Rudy Hernandez, a former teammate of Roberto's.

"We were having this party in my restaurant, and somebody turned on the radio and the announcer was saying that Roberto's plane was feared missing. And then, because my place is on the beach, we saw these giant floodlights crisscrossing the waves, and we heard the sound of the helicopters and the little search planes."

— JERRY IZENBERG, *A Bittersweet Memoir*

Roberto Clemente, outfielder for the Pittsburgh Pirates, in 1964.

Fiction and Nonfiction

These two passages differ in several ways, including writing style. But one very important difference is that Kinsella's re-creation of Clemente in this passage is imaginary, and Izenberg's is an attempt to describe actual events. To put it another way, Kinsella's short story is fiction, and Izenberg's biography is nonfiction.

Fiction is often highly realistic. Kinsella is known for his extensive knowledge of baseball and its history, and he draws on this when writing his fiction, yet his narrative is still invented. On the other hand, Izenberg undertook extensive research and interviews when writing his biography.

In the Introduction to Fiction (page 4), you learned that **fiction** includes any work of prose (writing that is not poetry or drama) that describes an invented or imaginary story. Typical forms of fiction are short stories and novels. **Nonfiction** is writing about real people, places, things, and events. Autobiographies, biographies, journals, essays, histories, and newspaper and magazine articles are all types of nonfiction.

Common Core State Standards

Reading Informational
RI.3

Words in Use

Teaching Words

extensive, 254
undertook, 254
incoherent, 255
firsthand, 255
anecdote, 255
carrion, 255
petitions, 255

KEY TERMS

NARRATIVE, 254
FICTION, 254
NONFICTION, 254
AUTOBIOGRAPHY, 255
MEMOIR, 255
BIOGRAPHY, 255
THIRD-PERSON POINT OF VIEW, 255
ESSAY, 255
THESIS, 255
PARALLELISM, 255
RHETORICAL QUESTION, 255

Types of Nonfiction

Among the most common types of nonfiction are autobiography and memoir, biography, and essay.

Autobiography and Memoir

Writing is described as "autobiographical" when the writer presents parts or the whole of his or her own life. There are many types of autobiographical writing, including autobiographies, memoirs, diaries, journals, and letters.

An **autobiography** is told from the *first-person point of view* and is the story of a person's life written by that person. It typically covers the whole of a person's life up to the time of writing. A more focused type of autobiography is the **memoir**, which usually deals with a specific period of a person's life. Annie Dillard's *An American Childhood* (page 257) is a memoir about her childhood.

> The suggestions of adults were uncertain and incoherent. They gave you Nancy Drew with one hand and *Little Women* with the other. They mixed good and bad books together because they could not distinguish between them. Any book which contained children, or short adults, or animals, was felt to be a children's book.

Biography

A **biography** is the story of a person's life told by another person. Milton Meltzer's "Elizabeth I" (page 265) is a biography about one of England's greatest rulers.

> Elizabeth I came to the throne of England in 1558 at the age of twenty-five. It was not a happy time for a young woman to take the responsibility for ruling a kingdom.

Biographies are told from the *third-person point of view,* although writers of biography may also include autobiographical materials, such as letters, diaries, or journals, so that the reader may gain some firsthand knowledge about the person whose life story is being told.

Essay

An **essay** is a short nonfiction work that makes a point about a single subject. The point that the writer is making is the **thesis.** For example, in an essay about school uniforms, the thesis might be that uniforms prevent personal expression.

There are many types of essays. A **personal essay** is a short nonfiction work on a single topic related to the life of the writer. The author of a personal essay may tell a story or an anecdote or reflect on and share thoughts and feelings about something in his or her life.

In a **persuasive essay,** the writer's goal is to persuade the reader to accept a point of view. For example, in "The Eternal Frontier" (page 291), Louis L'Amour tries to make his readers understand the importance of space exploration.

> One might ask—why outer space, when so much remains to be done here? If that had been the spirit of man we would still be hunters and food gatherers, growling over the bones of carrion in a cave somewhere.

Newspaper editorials and petitions are common examples of persuasive writing. Writers of persuasive essays use a variety of techniques to make an argument, including appealing to both logic and emotion, using parallel construction to add force to their statements, and asking rhetorical questions. **Parallelism** is the use of the same grammatical constructions to express ideas of equal importance. A **rhetorical question** is a question asked by an author to reinforce an idea.

Teach the Genre

Elements of Nonfiction
For more in-depth information, see the element introduction Understanding the Essay, page 281.

TEACHING NOTE

Most students will have read one or more biographies. Ask for recommendations of good biographies. Then, have students reach a consensus about the qualities that make a biography particularly good. Draw out the observation that good nonfiction includes compelling details, interesting facts and anecdotes, and clear structure.

Differentiated Instruction

Reading Proficiency
Many students can be motivated to read newspapers and popular magazines. Ask students to bring in samples of the newspapers and magazines they routinely see at home or at the homes of friends. Have each student select a favorite article and explain why is it interesting. Discuss with students the literary elements that make this type of nonfiction appealing to readers, such as current topics, short paragraphs, and clear organizational strategies.

Enrichment
For additional materials that students can read on their own, direct them to the For Your Reading List on page 361.

Use the Model

Introduce the Process

Use this page to show students the basic instruction provided before, during, and after they read most selections in Units 3 and 4.

The excerpt from Annie Dillard's *An American Childhood* is an Active Reading Model. Side notes in model lessons prompt students to become more active readers by using reading strategies and skills, analyzing literature, and making connections. Students can apply the process they use in model lessons to other readings in Units 3 and 4.

For more information, see Reading Strategies & Skills, Section 1 in the Language Arts Handbook.

Before Reading Stress the two types of background students need to apply, and encourage students always to set a purpose for reading.

During Reading Point out the side notes on pages 259–260: Analyze Literature, Use Reading Skills, and Make Connections. Then show students the Mirrors & Windows questions on page 262. Explain that they will first respond to the reading personally, and then apply their insights to a broader issue.

After Reading Show students page 263. Tell them that "Find Meaning" questions help them recall and interpret details. "Make Judgments" questions ask them to analyze a selection and evaluate how specific details contribute to its overall meaning.

Nonfiction Reading Model

BEFORE READING

Build Background
You need to apply two types of background to read a piece of nonfiction effectively. One is the selection's historical, scientific, or cultural context. Read the **Build Background** and **Meet the Author** features to get this kind of information. The other type of background is the personal knowledge you bring to your reading.

Set Purpose
A nonfiction writer writes to inform, describe, persuade, or entertain. Read **Set Purpose** to decide what you want to get out of the selection.

Analyze Literature
A nonfiction writer uses different techniques depending on the type of nonfiction he or she is writing. The **Analyze Literature** feature draws your attention to a key literary element.

Use Reading Skills
The **Use Reading Skills** feature will show you skills to help you get the most out of your reading. Learn how to apply skills such as determining author's purpose and using context clues. Identify a graphic organizer that will help you apply the skill before and while you read.

DURING READING

Use Reading Strategies
- **Ask questions** about things that seem significant or interesting.
- **Make predictions** about what's going to happen next. As you read, gather more clues to confirm or change your prediction.
- **Visualize** the information. Form pictures in your mind to help you see what the writer is describing.
- **Make inferences,** or educated guesses, about what is not stated directly.
- **Clarify,** or check that you understand, what you read. Reread any difficult parts.

Analyze Literature
What literary elements stand out? As you read, consider how these elements affect your enjoyment and understanding of the selection.

Make Connections
Notice where connections can be made between the information presented in the selection and your life.

AFTER READING

Find Meaning
Recall the important details of the selection, such as the sequence of events and settings. Use this information to **interpret,** or explain, the meaning of the selection.

Make Judgments
- **Analyze** the text by examining details and deciding what they contribute to the meaning.
- **Evaluate** the text by making judgments about how the author creates meaning.

Analyze Literature
Review how the use of literary elements increased your understanding of the selection. For example, did the author use sensory details? How did they help shape meaning?

Extend
Go beyond the text by exploring the selection's ideas through writing or other creative projects.

256 UNIT 3 NONFICTION

Words in Use

Teaching Words
effectively, 256
recall, 256
interpret, 256
analyze, 256
contribute, 256
evaluate, 256

KEY TERMS
NONFICTION, 256
CONTEXT CLUE, 256
SEQUENCE OF EVENT, 256
SETTING, 256
SENSORY DETAIL, 256

from An American Childhood

A Memoir by Annie Dillard

Build Background

Literary Context Annie Dillard is best known as a nature writer. Her Pulitzer Prize–winning collection of essays, *Pilgrim at Tinker Creek* (1974), follows in the tradition of Henry David Thoreau's *Walden* (1854). In her nature writing, Dillard, like Thoreau, combines vivid descriptions of nature with personal reflections on human nature, philosophy, and spirituality. This memoir describes Dillard's early fascination with nature writing.

Reader's Context What do you remember about your first visit to a library?

Set Purpose

Preview the first paragraph to predict what the author will reveal about her thoughts, feelings, and actions.

Analyze Literature

Autobiography An **autobiography** is a work that describes the life of the author, often chronologically. Autobiographies are written from the first-person point of view, using pronouns such as *I* and *me*. One type of autobiographical writing is the **memoir,** in which a writer recalls experiences of a particular time in his or her life. As you read this selection, notice how Dillard uses details to help the reader share her experiences.

Meet the Author

Annie Dillard (b. 1945) has written many books and essays about her life, about nature, and about her experiences in nature. She has also written poetry and novels. Dillard grew up in Pittsburgh, Pennsylvania, and taught at Wesleyan College in Middletown, Connecticut. Still a passionate reader, Dillard keeps lists of "Books I Have Read." Dillard says, "I just read, read, read, read. That's all I do."

Use Reading Skills

Context Clues Preview the vocabulary words from this selection as they are used in the sentences below. Try to unlock the meaning of each word using the context clues provided in the sentences.

1. The first arrow I shot hit the bull's eye, but my <u>subsequent</u> shots missed.
2. Marta wrinkled her nose at the skunk's <u>noisome</u> odor.
3. It is the <u>prerogative</u> of the coach to decide who plays on the team.
4. John's bad attitude and complaining began to <u>exasperate</u> the others.
5. The <u>tedium</u> of fishing always makes Hank doze off.

Preview Vocabulary

sub·se·quent (sŭb´ si kwənt) *adj.*, following in time, order, or place

noi·some (nôi´ səm) *adj.*, offensive smell; objectionable

pre·rog·a·tive (pri räg´ ət iv) *n.*, special power or privilege

ex·as·per·at·ed (ig zas´ pə rāt' ed) *adj.*, irritated

te·di·um (tē´ dē əm) *n.*, boredom

Preview the Model

At a Glance

Guided Reading: Reading Model
- Reading Level: Challenging
- Difficulty Considerations: Vocabulary and style
- Ease Factor: Sympathetic narrator

Objectives

Studying this lesson will enable students to

- use reading skills such as context clues
- define autobiography and memoir and recognize how this selection is an example of those genres
- describe the influence books and reading had on Annie Dillard
- appreciate how childhood experiences helped shape a writer

Launch the Lesson

Tell students they are about to read a writer's account of how, as a child, she was given access to the grown-up world of books at the library. Invite them to talk about their own experiences growing up: How did they feel when they were first considered responsible enough to participate in something adults do?

Words in Use

Preview Vocabulary	Selection Words	Teaching Words
subsequent, 259	vaulted, 258	vivid, 257
noisome, 259	enamel, 259	chronologically, 257
prerogative, 261	cautious, 260	treasure trove, 262
exasperate, 261	hearsay, 262	criteria, 263
tedium, 262		reverence, 263

KEY TERMS

Common Core State Standards

Reading Literature
RL.1, RL.4

Reading Informational
RI.4, RI.5

Teach the Model

Summary

In this excerpt from her memoir, Annie Dillard recalls how she was given access to the adult section at her local library. There, among the nonfiction books, she discovers a favorite, *The Field Book of Ponds and Streams.* She reads it often and becomes fascinated with the card in the back of the book, which shows that many other people have checked out the book. She wonders who they are and imagines meeting them. Dillard goes on to discuss her troubles choosing fiction books she likes. She finds adults' recommendations unreliable and the number of choices on the shelves overwhelming. She feels many books that start well get less interesting after the protagonists grow up. Dillard describes how reading was a private act for her at that time, one she could not imagine sharing with others.

The Mirrors & Windows questions at the end of the selection focus on the theme of memories. Before students start to read, ask: What is your most precious memento of your childhood?

from An American Childhood

Students with Books, 1966. Jacob Lawrence. Private collection.

A Memoir by Annie Dillard

The people of Homewood... they dreamed of ponds and streams.

The Homewood Library had graven across its enormous stone facade: FREE TO THE PEOPLE. In the evenings, neighborhood people—the men and women of Homewood—browsed in the library, and brought their children. By day, the two vaulted rooms, the adults' and children's sections, were almost empty. The kind Homewood librarians, after a trial period, had given me a card to the adult section. This was an enormous silent room with marble floors. Nonfiction was on the left.

Beside the farthest wall, and under leaded windows set ten feet from the floor, so that no human being could ever see anything from

258

them—next to the wall, and at the farthest remove from the idle librarians at their curved wooden counter, and from the oak bench where my mother waited in her camel's-hair coat chatting with the librarians or reading—stood the last and darkest and most obscure of the tall nonfiction stacks: NEGRO HISTORY and NATURAL HISTORY. It was in Natural History, in the cool darkness of a bottom shelf, that I found *The Field Book of Ponds and Streams*.

The Field Book of Ponds and Streams was a small, blue-bound book printed in fine type on thin paper, like *The Book of Common Prayer*. Its third chapter explained how to make sweep nets, plankton nets, glassbottomed buckets, and killing jars. It specified how to mount slides, how to label insects on their pins, and how to set up a freshwater aquarium.

One was to go into "the field" wearing hip boots and perhaps a head net for mosquitoes. One carried in a "rucksack"[1] half a dozen corked test tubes, a smattering of screw-top baby-food jars, a white enamel tray, assorted pipettes[2] and eyedroppers, an artillery of cheesecloth nets, a notebook, a hand lens, perhaps a map, and *The Field Book of Ponds and Streams*. This field—unlike the fields I had seen, such as the field where Walter Milligan played football—was evidently very well watered, for there one could find, and distinguish among, daphniae, planaria, water pennies, stonefly larvae, dragonfly nymphs, salamander larvae, tadpoles, snakes, and turtles, all of which one could carry home.

That anyone had lived the fine life described in Chapter 3 astonished me. Although the title page indicated quite plainly that one Ann Haven Morgan had written *The Field Book of Ponds and Streams*, I nevertheless imagined, perhaps from the authority and freedom of it, that the author was a man. It would be good to write him and assure him that someone had found his book, in the dark near the marble floor in the Homewood Library. I would, in the same letter or in a <u>subsequent</u> one, ask him a question outside the scope of his book, which was where I personally might find a pond, or a stream. But I did not know how to address such a letter, of course, or how to learn if he was still alive.

I was afraid, too, that my letter would disappoint him by betraying my ignorance, which was just beginning to attract my own notice. What, for example, was this <u>noisome</u> sounding substance called cheesecloth, and what do scientists do with it? What, when

---

1. **rucksack.** Knapsack
2. **pipettes.** Small tubes for holding fluid

DURING READING

Use Reading Skills
Text Organization What kind of organizational pattern does the author use in the first two paragraphs? How effective is this pattern? What do you learn from it? **A**

DURING READING

Analyze Literature
Autobiography What experience is the author sharing with the reader? **B**

DURING READING

Use Reading Skills
Context Clues What are *planaria*? What clues in the text help you determine this? **C**

DURING READING

Use Reading Skills
Context Clues The word *authority* has multiple meanings. Use the surrounding text to identify the meaning of *authority* as it appears in this context. **E**

sub•se•quent
(sŭb´ si kwənt) *adj.*, following in time, order, or place

noi•some (noi´ səm) *adj.*, offensive smell; objectionable

Analyze Literature
Autobiography Ask students to consider the title *An American Childhood*. What does it say about how Dillard wishes to present herself? (It sounds generic, as if she is describing the life of almost anyone in the United States.) Ask: "How does information in the text support the title?"

Use Reading Skills
Text Organization *Answer:* She uses spatial organization. This pattern is effective because it helps readers visualize the setting and connect their own experience with the author's. **A**

Analyze Literature
Autobiography *Answer:* She is sharing a childhood visit to the local library. **B**

Use Reading Skills
Context Clues *Answer:* They are small creatures that live in streams. Other items in the list are small creatures that live in streams. **C**

Use Reading Skills
Context Clues Tell students that when they encounter unfamiliar words as part of a series in a sentence, they should look at the other items in the list and note the ones that are familiar. Unknown words should belong to the same part of speech and have related meanings. Have students examine the names of creatures listed along with planaria. Suggest that Dillard does not expect them to know or look up all these words. Instead, she uses the list to evoke the sense of mystery she felt reading *The Field Book of Ponds and Streams*. **D**

Use Reading Skills
Context Clues Surrounding context shows that the word *authority* describes the book or author's firm tone so "power to influence" or "confidence" would be correct. **E**

Reading Skills

Compare and Contrast
Ask students to name the different kinds—or categories—of texts Dillard talks about (nonfiction, especially natural history, and fiction, including books with children or animals, seagoing adventures, novels by Mark Twain, Charles Dickens, and other authors, old-fashioned love stories, Modern Library classics, and *Mad* magazine).

Have the class compile a recommended reading list made up of their favorite books, plus the ones Annie Dillard recommends, and arrange the titles in appropriate categories. Encourage students to consult the list when they need something to read. Suggest that they to broaden their experience by trying books from unfamiliar categories.

Make Connections

Answer: This may make students feel more sympathetic toward Dillard and help them identify with her. **A**

Make Connections

Note how Dillard's discovery that other people have read *The Field Book* inspires her to feel fellowship and sympathy for them. Ask students if they have ever felt alone for some reason, then discovered that others share the same experience. Invite volunteers to tell their stories. **B**

Analyze Literature

Setting Remind students that setting is the location and time in which a work takes place. Have them look for clues in the selection that identify its setting.

Science Connection

Field Guides A field guide (or field book) is an illustrated manual for identifying animals or plants in nature ("out in the field"). Guides usually focus on a specific category of natural object and a particular geographic region. *The Sibley Guide to Birds* (page 391) is a field guide. Bring examples of other field guides for students to examine, or ask them to investigate field guides at the library. If any students have ever used such a manual, invite them to talk about their experiences.

> **DURING READING**
>
> **Make Connections**
> How does the admission, at the beginning of this paragraph, that she was afraid affect your feelings about Dillard? **A**

you really got down to it, was enamel? If candy could, notoriously, "eat through enamel," why would anyone make trays out of it? Where—short of robbing a museum—might a fifth-grade student at the Ellis School on Fifth Avenue obtain such a legendary item as a wooden bucket?

The Field Book of Ponds and Streams was a shocker from beginning to end. The greatest shock came at the end.

When you checked out a book from the Homewood Library, the librarian wrote your number on the book's card and stamped the date on a sheet glued to the book's last page. When I checked out *The Field Book of Ponds and Streams* for the second time, I noticed the book's card. It was almost full. There were numbers on both sides. My hearty author and I were not alone in the world, after all. With us, and sharing our enthusiasm for dragonfly larvae and single-celled plants were, apparently, many Negro adults. Who were these people? Had they, in Pittsburgh's Homewood section, found ponds? Had they found streams? At home, I read the book again; I studied the drawings; I reread Chapter 3; then I settled in to study the due-date slip. People read this book in every season. Seven or eight people were reading this book every year, even during the war.

Every year, I read again *The Field Book of Ponds and Streams*. Often, when I was in the vicinity, I simply visited it. I sat on the marble floor and studied the book's card. There was my number. There was the number of someone else who had checked it out more than once. Might I contact this person and cheer him up? For I assumed that, like me, he had found pickings pretty slim in Pittsburgh.

The people of Homewood, some of whom live in visible poverty, on crowded streets among burned-out houses—they dreamed of ponds and streams. They were saving to buy microscopes. In their bedrooms they fashioned plankton nets. But their hopes were even more vain than mine, for I was a child, and anything might happen; they were adults, living in Homewood. There was neither pond nor stream on the streetcar routes. The Homewood residents whom I knew had little money and little free time. The marble floor was beginning to chill me. It was not fair.

I had been driven into nonfiction against my wishes. I wanted to read fiction, but I had learned to be cautious about it.

"When you open a book," the sentimental library posters said, "anything can happen." This was so. A book of fiction was a bomb.

Differentiated Instruction

Reading Proficiency

Struggling readers may have difficulty with Dillard's long sentences. Point out that these sentences are often long because they contain lists, or series, of items. Review the use of the comma to separate items in a series. Encourage students to read the selection out loud, pausing at each comma, to improve comprehension.

Visual Learning

The selection is rich with tactile details that evoke the library setting and how Dillard felt there. To help students experience the description more vividly, ask them to fill out a sensory details chart (see page 320) as they read. Ask them to think about their own experiences in libraries, and especially how the libraries looked, sounded, and felt.

It was a land mine you wanted to go off. You wanted it to blow your whole day. Unfortunately, hundreds of thousands of books were duds. They had been rusting out of everyone's way for so long that they no longer worked. There was no way to distinguish the duds from the live mines except to throw yourself at them headlong, one by one.

The suggestions of adults were uncertain and incoherent. They gave you Nancy Drew with one hand and *Little Women* with the other. They mixed good and bad books together because they could not distinguish between them. Any book which contained children, or short adults, or animals, was felt to be a children's book. So also was any book about the sea—as though danger or even fresh air were a child's <u>prerogative</u>—or any book by Charles Dickens or Mark Twain. Virtually all British books, actually, were children's books; no one understood children like the British. Suited to female children were love stories set in any century but this one. Consequently one had read, <u>exasperated</u> often to fury, *Pickwick Papers, Désirée, Wuthering Heights, Lad, a Dog, Gulliver's Travels, Gone With the Wind, Robinson Crusoe,* Nordhoff and Hall's *Bounty* trilogy, *Moby-Dick, The Five Little Peppers, Innocents Abroad, Lord Jim, Old Yeller.*

The fiction stacks at the Homewood Library, their volumes alphabetized by author, baffled me. How could I learn to choose a novel? That I could not easily reach the top two shelves helped limit choices a little. Still, on the lower shelves I saw too many books: Mary Johnson, *Sweet Rocket;* Samuel Johnson, *Rasselas;* James Jones, *From Here to Eternity.* I checked out the last because I had heard of it; it was good. I decided to check out books I had heard of. I had heard of *The Mill on the Floss.* I read it, and it was good. On its binding was printed a figure, a man dancing or running; I had noticed this figure before. Like so many children before and after me, I learned to seek out this logo, the Modern Library colophon.[3]

The going was always rocky. I couldn't count on Modern Library the way I could count on, say, *Mad* magazine, which never failed to slay me. *Native Son* was good, *Walden* was pretty good, *The Interpretation of Dreams* was okay, and *The Education of Henry Adams* was awful. *Ulysses,* a very famous book, was also awful. *Confessions* by Augustine, whose title promised so much, was a bust. *Confessions* by Jean-Jacques Rousseau was much better, though it fell apart halfway through.

---

3. colophon. Publisher's identifying imprint

DURING READING

**Analyze Literature
Autobiography** How does Dillard feel about the books that adults recommended? Why do you think she feels this way? **D**

pre·rog·a·tive
(pri räg´ ət iv) *n.,* special power or privilege

ex·as·per·at·ed
(ig zas´ pə rāt' ed) *adj.,* irritated

> A book of fiction was a bomb. It was a land mine you wanted to go off.

Teach the Model

Analyze Literature

Metaphor Remind students that a metaphor is a figure of speech in which one thing is referred to as if it were another. Explain that sometimes an author uses a metaphor more than once in a piece, or uses other related comparisons. This is known as an "extended metaphor" or "sustained metaphor." The paragraph that contains the metaphorical statement *A book of fiction was a bomb* is an example of this. Have students point out the language used to sustain the comparison (*land mine, go off, blow, duds, rusting, live mines*). **C**

Analyze Literature

Autobiography *Answer:* Dillard is exasperated and annoyed by many of these books. She seems to think that books featuring children are too boring or too silly. **D**

Literary Connection

Nature Writing *An American Childhood* contains much information about how Annie Dillard became a writer who often focused on natural subjects. Explain that "nature writing" is an established literary genre. Other famous nature writers include Henry David Thoreau, Rachel Carson, and Diane Ackerman. Consider having each student seek out an example of nature writing (a book, essay, or poem) and share it with classmates.

Writing Skills

Supporting Details

Remind students that a successful critical analysis includes a thesis that expresses the writer's opinion. The writer must then give supporting details—reasons—in the order most likely to convince readers to agree. Work as a class to identify Dillard's main idea and list her supporting details.

EXAMPLE:

main idea: Finding good fiction is hard.

supporting details:
- The alphabetical organization of library shelves does not showcase good books.
- The Modern Library imprint doesn't reliably identify good books.
- Child protagonists are interesting, but often they grow up and become boring.

Analyze Literature

Autobiography *Answer:* Dillard goes on to give examples of two books that lack excitement in the second half. She suggests that when she is older she may appreciate these parts of the books more. **Ⓐ**

Use Reading Strategies

Make Inferences Remind students that an inference is a conclusion based on the information they are given combined with what they know about life. Ask students to reread the last paragraph of the selection, focusing on Dillard's description of her father. What do they think Dillard might wish them to infer from this description? (The father had indeed read the books he saw her carrying, and he raised his eyebrows either because he doubted she was mature enough for them or because he was amused.) **Ⓑ**

You may want to ask students to write a journal entry or quick write, or divide students into discussion groups or lead a whole-class discussion about this question. *Answer:* Students may cite favorite books, toys, or found objects, or experiences such as a birthday party, learning to ride a bicycle, or holiday celebrations.

DURING READING

Analyze Literature
Autobiography How does Dillard support her claim about "most books"? What realization does she have about her taste in books? **Ⓐ**

te·di·um (tē´ dē əm) *n.,* boredom

In fact, it was a plain truth that most books fell apart halfway through. They fell apart as their protagonists quit, without any apparent reluctance, like idiots diving voluntarily into buckets, the most interesting part of their lives, and entered upon decades of unrelieved <u>tedium</u>. I was forewarned, and would not so bobble my adult life; when things got dull, I would go to sea.

Jude the Obscure was the type case. It starts out so well. Halfway through, its author forgot how to write. After Jude got married, his life was over, but the book went on for hundreds of pages while he stewed in his own juices. The same thing happened in *The Little Shepherd of Kingdom Come,* which Mother brought me from a fair. It was simply a hazard of reading. Only a heartsick loyalty to the protagonists of the early chapters, to the eager children they had been, kept me reading chronological narratives to their bitter ends. Perhaps later, when I had become an architect, I would enjoy the latter halves of books more.

This was the most private and obscure part of life, this Homewood Library; a vaulted marble edifice[4] in a mostly decent Negro neighborhood, the silent stacks of which I pondered in deep concentration for many years. There seemed then, happily, to be an infinitude[5] of books.

Ⓑ I no more expected anyone else on earth to have read a book I had read than I expected someone else to have twirled the same blade of grass. I would never meet those Homewood people who were borrowing *The Field Book of Ponds and Streams;* the people who read my favorite books were invisible or in hiding, underground. Father occasionally raised his big eyebrows at the title of some volume I was hurrying off with, quite as if he knew what it contained—but I thought he must know of it by hearsay, for none of it seemed to make much difference to him. Books swept me away, one after the other, this way and that; I made endless vows according to their lights, for I believed them. ❖

4. **edifice.** Large building
5. **infinitude.** Quality of being infinite or without end

What item or experience from your childhood can unlock a treasure trove of memories for you? What kinds of things can people learn from memories of their childhood?

Differentiated Instruction

English Language Learning

Ask students learning English to write down any questions that come to them as they read the selection. These might include unfamiliar vocabulary (such as *stacks,* in the context of the library) and phrases (such as *The going was always rocky*), or even questions about practices such as checking out a book at a library. Afterward, have students present their questions so that classmates can provide explanations.

Enrichment

The author of *The Field Book of Ponds and Streams* was a pioneer in her own right. Have students investigate Ann Haven Morgan and the publishing history of her book. Ask students to share the results of their research with the class.

Find Meaning

1. (a) What information does *The Field Book of Ponds and Streams* contain? (b) Why do you think Dillard is so fascinated by this book?

2. (a) What does Dillard notice about the book's card? (b) What is her reaction? (c) Why does she react this way?

3. (a) What does Dillard say happens to many books of fiction "halfway through"? (b) What do you think she means by this?

Analyze Literature

Autobiography How does Annie Dillard help the reader share her experiences? Use a chart to list examples of concrete details and feelings or opinions in *An American Childhood*. Then, in one or two brief paragraphs, summarize the effectiveness of these details, feelings, and opinions in conveying her experiences.

Make Judgments

4. (a) What criteria would Dillard use to judge whether or not a book is good? (b) What books would you suggest for Dillard? Explain your answer.

5. (a) What words would you use to describe how Dillard responds to books? (b) Do you think her responses will change as she gets older? Explain.

Concrete Details	Feelings/Opinions
The Field Book of Ponds and Streams was printed on thin paper like a prayer book.	reverence; an important book

Extend Understanding

Writing Options

Creative and Expository Writing Imagine that you are a television screenwriter. Write a screenplay based on the excerpt you just read from Annie Dillard's memoir, *An American Childhood*. After you have finished your screenplay, write an essay describing the structural and substantive differences between the excerpt and your screenplay.

Expository Writing An author's voice expresses his or her personality and attitudes. How would you describe Annie Dillard's voice in this passage? Analyze Dillard's voice, or use of language, tone, and sentence structure, in a brief one-page **critical analysis**. Be sure to include a thesis statement and evidence from the text.

Collaborative Learning

Analyze Tone The tone of a selection reflects how the author feels about his or her subject. Think of how you would instruct someone to identify and analyze the tone of the selection. Meet with a partner and take turns giving oral instructions and following oral instructions. Record your work.

Lifelong Learning

Write a Book Summary Select one of the pieces of fiction that Dillard mentions in the selection and research its plot. Write a brief summary of the book's plot for a teacher interested in recommending books to students.

W Go to **www.mirrorsandwindows.com** for more.

AN AMERICAN CHILDHOOD **263**

Review the Model

Find Meaning

1. (a) It contains information on how to investigate ponds and streams. (b) She has little access to the natural world the book describes, so it seems exotic and sparks her imagination.

2. (a) It is almost full. (b) She is curious about the other people on the card. (c) She knows that they have even less access to ponds and streams than she does, and she wonders why they would spend their time reading the book.

3. (a) They fall apart. (b) She loses interest in the main characters, who tend to fall into decades of tedium.

Make Judgments

4. (a) Responses will vary (for example, in a good book, the protagonist is lively and active from the beginning to the very end). (b) Be sure students explain their recommendations.

5. (a) Students may offer words like *passionately, emotionally, angrily,* and *enthusiastically.* (b) Her responses may change because she will read more and will take a calmer, less intense approach to books; some may say her intense personality and her strong response to books are unlikely to change.

Analyze Literature

Autobiography Students should note that Dillard's concrete details help the reader visualize her surroundings. Her strong words create vivid images.

Rubrics for Writing Options

You can adapt this as a checklist for students to use as they write.

Creative Writing

☐ Does the review summarize the book and name its title and author?

☐ Does the review clearly state an opinion of the book?

☐ Does the review provide examples to back up the opinion?

Expository Writing

☐ Does the analysis indicate a clear understanding of author's voice?

☐ Does the analysis accurately describe Dillard's voice?

☐ Does the analysis show how language, tone, and sentence structure convey the author's voice?

Teach the Workshop

Identifying Phrases

1. In the afternoon (prepositional)
2. gathered in the stacks (participial)
3. Inside *The Field Book of Ponds and Streams* (prepositional)
4. beside the card catalog (prepositional)
5. Kneeling on the library's floor (participial)

> For more information, see Grammar & Style Section 3.11, Phrases, in the Language Arts Handbook.

Program Resources

You will find additional lessons on Phrases in the *Exceeding the Standards: Grammar & Style* resource.

KEY TERMS

CLAUSE, 264
PHRASE, 264
SUBJECT, 264
VERB, 264
PREPOSITIONAL PHRASE, 264
PREPOSITION, 264
MODIFIER, 264
ADJECTIVE, 264
ADVERB, 264
NOUN, 264
PARTICIPLE, 264
PARTICIPIAL PHRASE, 264

Grammar & Style

Phrases

Prepositional Phrases

The kind Homewood librarians, after a trial period, had given me a card....

—ANNIE DILLARD, "An American Childhood"

In this sentence, the independent, or main, clause is broken up by a **phrase.** A phrase is a group of words used as a single part of speech. A phrase lacks a subject, a verb, or both. One of the most common kinds of phrases is the prepositional phrase. A **prepositional phrase** consists of a preposition, its object, and any modifiers of that object. In the above sentence, the word *after* is the preposition; *trial period* is the object.

> EXAMPLE
> *I read in the library's nonfiction section.*

A prepositional phrase adds information to a sentence by modifying another word in that sentence. For example, *in the library's nonfiction section* modifies *read.* Prepositional phrases can function as either adjectives or adverbs. The above is an adverb because it modifies a verb. The following example contains a phrase that acts as an adjective, modifying a noun.

> EXAMPLE
> *The shelves in the library were dusty and cluttered.*

Participial Phrases

A **participle** is a verb form ending in *-ing, -d,* or *-ed* that acts as an adjective, modifying a noun or pronoun. A **participial phrase** is made up of a participle and all of its modifiers, which may include objects, nouns, adjectives, adverbs, and prepositional phrases. The entire phrase acts as an adjective.

> EXAMPLE
> *Walking in the rows, I was able to find my books.*

The participle *walking* and the prepositional phrase *in the rows* make up the participial phrase that modifies *I.*

Be sure to place the participial phrase close to the word it modifies. Otherwise, you may say something you don't mean.

> EXAMPLE
> *I considered the importance of the book standing in the Homewood parking lot.*

In this example, the sentence seems to say that the book is standing in the parking lot.

Identifying Phrases

On a separate piece of paper, identify the phrase in each of the following sentences. Then describe the type of phrase it is: prepositional or participial.

1. In the afternoon I hurried home.
2. The librarians gathered in the stacks.
3. Inside *The Field Book of Ponds and Streams,* there were many interesting facts.
4. There were a dozen books beside the card catalog.
5. Kneeling on the library's floor, I was able to find my card.

TEACHING NOTE

Extra Practice

Write these sentences on the board, and have students identify the participial (single underscore) and/or prepositional (double underscore) phrases in each sentence.

1. Just <u>before we left</u>, I heard hummingbirds <u>fluttering at the back door</u>.
2. <u>Haunted by his memories</u>, he waited fearfully <u>outside the doctor's office</u>.
3. Derek talked <u>in a high-pitched voice</u>, hardly stopping to draw a breath.
4. Marla was tired <u>of the many picky rules instituted by her boss</u>.
5. Everyone <u>gathered on the stage</u> called out <u>to the departing audience members</u>.

Common Core State Standards

Language
L.1

Elizabeth I

A Biography by Milton Meltzer

Preview the Model

At a Glance
Guided Reading: Reading Model
- Reading Level: Moderate
- Difficulty Consideration: Vocabulary
- Ease Factor: Opening paragraph

Build Background

Historical Context Elizabeth I ruled as queen of England from 1558 until her death in 1603. In the long history of the English monarchy, only five women have held the position of sole ruler of England. Each woman came to the throne because the presiding male ruler or heir had died or because there was no male heir at all. Elizabeth inherited the crown from her father, King Henry VIII. She also inherited the conflict he had created between the English monarchy and the Catholic church.

Reader's Context If you were a queen or king, how would you capture the respect and loyalty of your citizens?

Set Purpose

Preview the first paragraph, and predict how Queen Elizabeth succeeded in making England a great nation. Read to find out how accurate your predictions are.

Analyze Literature

Biography A **biography** is the story of a person's life told by another person. Biographies may be book length or only a few pages. Biographers may interview their subjects, or they may find out about their subjects through research. Most biographers try to convey a balanced picture of a person's life. As you read, decide whether Milton Meltzer presents a fair and objective picture of Elizabeth.

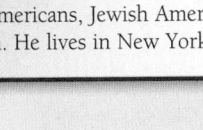

Meet the Author

Milton Meltzer was born in Worcester, Massachusetts, in 1915. He is best known for his nonfiction books for young adult readers and for his books on American history. He has written more than eighty books on such topics as black Americans, Jewish Americans, and the American Revolution. He lives in New York City.

Use Reading Skills

Distinguish Fact from Opinion A *fact* is a statement that can be proven. An *opinion* is a statement that expresses an attitude or desire. Opinions may be supported by facts, but they cannot be proven true or false. Create a chart to record facts and opinions in "Elizabeth I." Put fact statements in the first column. Record opinion statements in the second column.

Fact:
Queen Elizabeth was the daughter of Henry VIII and his second wife, Anne Boleyn.

Opinion:
Queen Elizabeth was one of the most remarkable women who ever lived.

Preview Vocabulary

pres•tige (pre stēzh´) *n.,* status; standing in general opinion

pros•per•i•ty (prä spur´ ə tē) *n.,* condition of being successful or thriving, especially economic well-being

di•rec•tive (də rek´ tiv) *n.,* order or form of guidance

om•i•nous (äm´ ə nəs) *adj.,* foreboding or foreshadowing evil

for•feit (for´ fət) *v.,* lose or fail to win the right to something by some error, offense, or crime

Objectives

Studying this lesson will enable students to
- use reading skills such as distinguishing fact from opinion
- define *biography* and study an example of the form
- explore biographer Milton Meltzer's treatment of a major historical figure in conjunction with some of the subject's own writing
- appreciate the life of a person who played a pivotal role in history

Launch the Lesson

Before students read "Elizabeth I," note that Elizabeth's experiences were in many ways very different from students' own—both because she was born nearly 500 years ago and because she was a queen. Even so, the biography creates a very human portrait. Ask students to notice things that are familiar as they read. Have they felt the same emotions? Can they imagine what it was like to live then? What must it have been like to be in Elizabeth's situation?

ELIZABETH I **265**

Words in Use

Preview Vocabulary	Selection Words	Teaching Words
prestige, 268	commerce, 267	monarchy, 265
prosperity, 270	spendthrift, 270	presiding, 265
directive, 273	reign, 270	heir, 265
ominous, 274	statecraft, 271	enabled, 265
forfeit, 274	ailments, 275	flourish, 265
		delegation, 265
		governing, 279

KEY TERMS

PREDICT, 265
BIOGRAPHY, 265
NONFICTION, 265
FACT, 265
OPINION, 265
RECALL, 277
DIALOGUE, 279
THESIS STATEMENT, 279

Common Core State Standards

Reading Informational
RI.3, RI.8

Summary

Born to King Henry VIII's second wife, young Elizabeth received an extensive education, unusual for a woman of the time, to prepare her in case she inherited the throne. After the deaths of her younger brother and older sister, both of whom were crowned before her, Elizabeth became queen. Meltzer describes Elizabeth's refusal to marry despite continued pressure to do so, her efforts to please her subjects with impressive displays, and the cultural and economic changes that occurred in England during her reign. He explains the threat the Catholic Church posed to Elizabeth's Protestant government, along with the sometimes ruthless actions she took to maintain power. Although her infirmities began to show as she aged, she remained vigorous. She died of a fever at the age of 63.

MIRRORS & WINDOWS The Mirrors & Windows questions at the end of the selection focus on the theme of leadership. Before students start to read, ask: What is the one absolutely necessary quality of a good national leader?

Apply the Model

BEFORE READING
DURING READING
AFTER READING

Elizabeth I

A Biography by Milton Meltzer

266

Program Resources

Planning and Assessment
Program Planning Guide, Selection Lesson Plan
E-Lesson Planner
Assessment Guide, Lesson Test
ExamView

Technology Tools
Interactive Student Text on CD
Visual Teaching Package
Audio Library
mirrorsandwindows.com

Meeting the Standards
Nonfiction: Unit 3, Guided Reading, pp. 27–34

Differentiating Instruction
Developing Readers, Use Text Organization, pp. 22–24

"Good Queen Bess" her people called her. But "good" is a tame word for one of the most remarkable women who ever lived. Elizabeth I came to the throne of England in 1558 at the age of twenty-five. It was not a happy time for a young woman to take the responsibility for ruling a kingdom. Religious conflicts, a huge government debt, and heavy losses in a war with France had brought England low. But by the time of Elizabeth's death forty-five years later, England had experienced one of the greatest periods in its long history. Under Elizabeth's leadership, England had become united as a nation; its industry and commerce, its arts and sciences had flourished; and it was ranked among the great powers of Europe.

Elizabeth was the daughter of King Henry VIII and his second wife, Anne Boleyn. At the age of two she lost her mother when Henry had Anne's head chopped off. Not a good start for a child. But her father placed her in the care of one lord or lady after another, and the lively little girl with the reddish-gold hair, pale skin, and golden-brown eyes won everyone's affection.

Almost from her infancy Elizabeth was trained to stand in for ruling men, in case the need should arise. So she had to master whatever they were expected to know and do. Her tutors found the child to be an eager student. She learned history, geography, mathematics, and the elements of astronomy and architecture. She mastered four modern languages—French, Italian, Spanish, and Flemish[1]—as well as classic Greek and Latin. She wrote in a beautiful script that was like a work of art. The earliest portrait painted of her—when she was thirteen—shows a girl with innocent eyes holding a book in her long and delicate hands, already confident and queenly in her bearing.

She was a strong-willed girl who liked to give orders. She loved to be out on horseback, and rode so fast it frightened the men assigned to protect her. She loved dancing too—she never gave it up. Even in her old age she was seen one moonlit night dancing by herself in the garden.

Elizabeth had a half sister, Mary, born of Henry's first wife, Catherine of Aragon. Many years later came Elizabeth, the child of Anne Boleyn, and four years after, her half brother, Edward, the son of Henry's third wife, Jane Seymour. After Henry died, because

And why should she, the absolute ruler of England, allow a man to sit alongside her as king?

DURING READING
Use Reading Strategies
Make Inferences What does this tell you about Elizabeth's father? **B**

DURING READING
Use Reading Strategies
Make Predictions What does this suggest about Elizabeth's future? **C**

---

1. **Flemish.** Language spoken in Flanders, a small region in parts of northern France, Belgium, and the Netherlands

(Opposite page) *Queen Elizabeth I in Coronation Robes,* c. 1559. National Portrait Gallery, London.

ELIZABETH I **267**

Teach the Model

Use Reading Strategies
Visualize Note that the biographer includes vivid details to help readers imagine what the young Elizabeth looked like. Ask students to pause to study her portrait and to look at the artwork on page 269. What would students say the writer accomplishes by including these visual details? (They help make Elizabeth seem more like a real person.) **A**

Use Reading Strategies
Make Inferences *Answer:* He was cruel and obviously had complete power over his wife's fate without interference from Parliament. **B**

Use Reading Strategies
Make Predictions *Answer:* She seems well equipped to be a queen, who needs to be strong-willed and comfortable giving orders. **C**

Analyze Literature
Denotation and Connotation
Remind students that denotation is the literal meaning of a word, while its connotation includes emotional associations and other ideas that influence how people interpret the word.

Draw students' attention to the beginning of the selection. What is Meltzer saying about the adjective *good* in regard to Queen Elizabeth? (While *good* denotes positive feelings toward her, its connotations are too mild—"tame"—to effectively express how remarkable she was.)

Differentiated Instruction

English Language Learning
Remind students to preview the vocabulary and footnotes. Explain these words and expressions to help them better comprehend the reading. Verify that students understand the meaning of these basic and content-based words and phrases by asking them to write sentences that use these newly acquired words.

spendthrift—a person who wastes money (*thrift,* however, means "careful use of money"), 270

give free rein—let someone do whatever they want (a reference to horseback riding, in which a rider uses "reins" to control the horse), 270

right arm—used metaphorically for a person whose help makes it possible to carry out a job, 275

nip . . . in the bud—stop something in its early stages (reference to preventing a plant's bud from growing into a flower or leaf), 275

boxed their ears—hit on the side of the head, 275

ELIZABETH I **267**

Use Reading Strategies

Make Inferences *Answer:* It suggests that women rarely held positions of power in England at the time. **A**

Analyze Literature

Biography Note that successful biographical writing includes factual information, such as dates and statistics, as well as quotations. (Such writing also includes interpretations of factual information and its effect on the subject of the biography.) Ask students to point out some examples of factual information and quotations in the selection. (Examples include the date Elizabeth was crowned, November 17, 1558; the number of people in her household, 120; and Elizabeth's question, "Am I not a queen because God has chosen me . . . ?")

Analyze Literature

Tone Have students describe the tone of the piece so far and explain their answers. (The tone is friendly and conversational. Students may point to the way the author addresses readers directly, telling them to *remember,* and the way he asks questions.) **B**

Analyze Literature

Biography *Answer:* He is reinforcing his point that marriage would not logically appeal to her. **C**

"Am I not a queen because God has chosen me to be a queen?"

DURING READING

Use Reading Strategies
Make Inferences What does this statement of the people's disbelief suggest about the role of women in their society? **A**

pres•tige (pre stēzh´) *n.,* status; standing in general opinion

DURING READING

Analyze Literature
Biography Why do you think the biographer asks whether or not marriage looked promising to Elizabeth? **C**

---

succession[2] came first through the male, ten-year-old Edward was crowned king. But he lived only another six years. Now Mary took the throne and, soon after, married King Philip II of Spain, a Catholic monarch like herself. He was twenty-seven and she thirty-eight. But they were rarely together, each ruling their own kingdom. Mary died of cancer at the age of forty-two. That made Elizabeth the monarch.

When she came to the throne on November 17, 1558, it was a day to be marked by celebrations, then and long after. As Her Majesty passed down a London street, an astonished housewife exclaimed, "Oh, Lord! The Queen is a woman!" For there were still many who could scarcely believe they were to be ruled by another woman. Elizabeth herself would say with mock modesty that she was "a mere woman." But everyone soon learned she was a very special woman. "Am I not a queen because God has chosen me to be a queen?" she demanded.

As princess and later as queen, Elizabeth lived in various palaces, with much coming and going; each time she moved, she took along her household staff of 120 people. Often the changes were required because there was no sanitation. The smelly palaces had to be emptied so they could be "aired and sweetened."

Even before Elizabeth came of age there was much talk of when she would marry, and whom. Marriages among the nobility and royalty were arranged not for love, but for practical reasons—to add land holdings, to strengthen the prestige and power of families, to cement an alliance of nations against a common enemy.

And remember, from the most ancient times, kings claimed that they as men were born to rule by divine right. That is, God had ordained that the crown should pass through the male line of descent. But when the king's wife had no male child, it meant trouble. Who then would rule? That crisis often led to civil war as various factions battled for the power to name a king. Many disputed Elizabeth's right to the throne, and as long as she had neither husband nor successor, her life was in danger.

Ever since Elizabeth was eight, however, she had said again and again, "I will never marry." Did marriage look promising to a girl whose father had six wives, two of whom, including her own mother, he had beheaded? Yet she liked to hear of people who wanted to marry her.

---

2. **succession.** Order of persons having a right to the throne

---

Differentiated Instruction

Enrichment

Mentions of such daily life issues as girls' education during Elizabeth's day or the poor state of sanitation might inspire students to further investigate those and other aspects of daily life in Elizabethan England. Have students do research at the library or online and report their findings to the class.

Reading Proficiency

Because the selection is rich in details, struggling readers may benefit from making an outline of it as they read. Review the outline format. Remind them that they should write down the topic of each paragraph and then note the main supporting details the author provides.

And there was no shortage of suitors.[3] She continued to insist she wished to live unmarried. No matter how often she said it, men did not believe it. Understandably, since she often made a prince or duke who had come to court her believe she was finally ready to give in—only at the last moment to back out. Once, to a delegation from Parliament come to beg her to marry, she declared, "I am already bound unto a husband, which is the Kingdom of England."

And why should she, the absolute ruler of England, allow a man to sit alongside her as king? The power of husbands over wives in that century—and even now, in many places of this world—was so

DURING READING

Analyze Literature
Biography What does Elizabeth's statement tell you about her commitments?

D

---

3. **suitors.** Men who court or pay loving attention to a woman in order to marry her

PROCESSION OF QUEEN ELIZABETH TO HUNSDON HOUSE

Queen Elizabeth I in Procession with Her Courtiers, 1825. Sarah Countess of Essex. Private collection.

ELIZABETH I   **269**

Analyze Literature

Biography *Answer:* She is firm in her belief that she owes her affection and loyalty to the kingdom. **D**

Art Connection

Ask students to pause and examine this painting. Tell them that they can make inferences and use context clues from the painting, just as they can use these strategies and skills with a reading. Ask: "Based on this painting, what do you think the word *courtiers* means? What can you infer about the court and courtiers?"

Challenge interested students to use library and Internet resources to find out why such a procession might have taken place and how often such processions occurred. Students may delve further into the "world of the painting" by investigating the dress and posture of the courtiers, Elizabeth's appearance and probably age, and other works by the artist.

Reading Skills

Distinguish Fact from Opinion

Remind students that bias is a person's own outlook or belief, which can affect the way he or she thinks about things. The word *bias* is often used as a synonym for *prejudice,* but bias does not have to be negative. Expressions of the author's personality—or bias—can contribute in a positive way to the tone of a piece.

Explain that readers can usually detect bias through the author's choice of words with emotional associations. Ask students to find examples of language in the text that suggests Meltzer's bias and to interpret the statements. For example, on page 270 when Meltzer writes about *the hideous sport of bear-baiting,* the word *hideous* reveals that Meltzer, personally, finds bear-baiting offensive.

Analyze Literature
Biography *Answer:* Most students will say that Meltzer is trying to further demonstrate Elizabeth's commitment to her country and to proper governance. **A**

Analyze Literature
Characterization Ask students to focus on the description of Queen Elizabeth and her finery, as well as the description of the parties she attended. Ask: "What kind of person emerges from these details?" (The descriptions could be of a woman who may have been sensible about money, but who also enjoyed participating in lavish displays and dazzling her subjects.) **B**

> **DURING READING**
> **Analyze Literature**
> **Biography** Why do you think Meltzer includes this information about Elizabeth's spending? **A**

pros·per·i·ty
(prä spər′ ə tē) *n.*, condition of being successful or thriving, especially economic well-being

Above everything else, Elizabeth wanted to have her people think well of her.

great that a husband might snatch the reins of power from her and leave her with the title but not the authority she loved to exercise.

Was it fun to be queen? As monarch, she commanded great wealth, inherited from her father, and people who wanted favors were always enriching her with lavish presents. She was no spendthrift, however. She hated to see money wasted, whether her own or the kingdom's. Early on she began keeping careful household account books, and later she would do the same with the royal accounts. Always she urged her counselors to carry out orders as inexpensively as possible.

Above everything else, Elizabeth wanted to have her people think well of her. Her deepest desire was to assure them of peace and prosperity. And why not make a grand personal impression upon them at the same time? In her mature years she gave free rein to her love of jewels and staged brilliant displays for the court and the people. Her dresses were decorated with large rubies, emeralds, and diamonds, and she wore jeweled necklaces, bracelets, and rings. In her hair, at her ears, and around her neck she wore pearls—the symbol of virginity.

During her reign she made many great processions through London, the people wild with excitement, crowding the streets—for the English, like most people, loved spectacle. In the first of them, her coronation, she wore gold robes as she was crowned. Trumpets sounded, pipes and drums played, the organ pealed, bells rang. Then came the state banquet in Westminster Hall. It began at 3:00 P.M., and went on till 1:00 A.M.

Elizabeth was often entertained at house parties. One of them, given by the Earl of Leicester in Kenilworth Castle, lasted for eighteen days in July. Thirty other distinguished guests were invited. The great number of their servants (together with Leicester's) turned the palace into a small town. When darkness fell, candles glittered everywhere, indoors and out, creating a fairyland. Musicians sang and played, the guests danced in the garden, and such a great display of fireworks exploded that the heavens thundered and the castle shook. Then came a pleasure relished in those days: the hideous sport of bear-baiting. A pack of dogs was let loose in an inner courtyard to scratch and bite and tear at thirteen tormented bears. Still, the happy guests retained their appetite for a "most delicious banquet of 300 dishes."

Differentiated Instruction

Enrichment
Many films have been made about the life of Queen Elizabeth I. Interested students may wish to view one of them and report their impressions of it to the class. In particular, ask them to consider how the portrait of Elizabeth in the film compares to the portrait Milton Meltzer creates.

The tremendous festival at Kenilworth was only one of the highlights of Elizabeth's summer festival. She moved from one great house to another all season long, always at the enormous expense of her hosts. They had little to complain of, however, for their wealth was often the product of the queen's generous bestowal[4] of special privileges. In recognition of his high rank and in return for his support, she granted the Duke of Norfolk a license to import carpets from Turkey free of duty. The Earl of Essex was favored with the profitable right to tax imported sweet wines. Other pets[5] got rich from a monopoly on the importation[6] of or taxation of silks, satins, salt, tobacco, starch.

England was a small nation at that time: less than four million people, about as many as live in Arizona today. But the English were a young people, coming to maturity with new worlds opening up to them, in the mind and across the seas. A rebirth of culture—the Renaissance[7]—had begun in the 1400s. With the revival of interest in the literature of the ancient Greek and Roman worlds came the beginning of a great age of discovery. This period marked the transition from medieval to modern times. The arts and sciences were influenced by changes in economic life. All the nation was swept up in the vast tides of change. Merchants, bankers, the gentry,[8] artisans,[9] seamen, miners—men and women of every class and condition—felt themselves part of the national venture.

At the heart of change in England was the queen. But no king or queen rules alone, no matter how authoritative or arrogant they may be. They usually look to others for advice, advice they may follow or reject. Elizabeth appointed ministers to handle the various departments of government, and made Sir William Cecil, then thirty-eight, her principal adviser. He was a brilliant, hardworking master of statecraft, devoted to her and England's well-being, and as ruthless as she and the nation's interests required. When he died in old age, his son Robert replaced him at her side.

So great was the queen's role, however, that her time became known as the Age of Elizabeth. Not only did many fine musicians

> **DURING READING**
> **Use Reading Strategies**
> **Clarify** How does the author support the idea that kings or queens usually look for advice? **C**

4. **bestowal.** Gift
5. **pets.** Persons treated with unusual kindness; favorites
6. **monopoly on the importation.** Exclusive control over the trade in foreign goods
7. **Renaissance** (re′ nə sän[t]s′). Revival of art and learning in Europe
8. **gentry.** Upper class of people
9. **artisans.** Artists and craftspeople

Use Reading Strategies

Clarify *Answer:* The author writes that Elizabeth appointed ministers for "various departments" and a principal adviser, Sir William Cecil, who was replaced by his son. **C**

Grammar Skills

Interrupters

Remind students that interrupters are words or phrases that break (interrupt) the flow of thought in a sentence to insert new information. Punctuation indicates how dramatic the break should be. Commas set off interrupters that blend fairly smoothly into the sentence. Dashes and parentheses emphasize the new information more. Ask students to find examples of interrupters in the selection.

EXAMPLE:
- Commas: "Then, <u>too,</u> there were the daring explorers . . ."
- Dashes: "The effect of this directive was to turn practicing Catholics<u>—about half of the English, most of them loyal—</u>into potential traitors."
- Parentheses: When Elizabeth's older half sister, Mary <u>(who remained Catholic)</u>, married . . ."

flower, but writers too, such as Christopher Marlowe and John Donne and Ben Jonson and Edmund Spenser. And above all, the incomparable William Shakespeare, whose plays were sometimes performed at court. Astronomers, naturalists, mathematicians, geographers, and architects pioneered in their fields.

CULTURAL ▶▶ CONNECTION

The Renaissance Roughly stretching from the fourteenth to the sixteenth century, the Renaissance was a period of rebirth for the arts and sciences in Europe and marks the transition between the Medieval period and the modern world. The Renaissance was also a time of rediscovery of Classical ideas and art from ancient Greece and Rome. Artists such as Leonardo da Vinci and writers such as Shakespeare and Dante created their masterpieces during this fertile time. In part, tolerance of new ideas enabled the arts and sciences to flourish. How do you think Elizabeth influenced the development of the Renaissance in England? **A**

Then, too, there were the daring explorers who pushed English expansion overseas. One of the queen's favorites, Sir Walter Raleigh, planned the colony of Virginia in America and named it for her, the Virgin Queen. The queen herself put money into several of the great voyages, keeping close watch over the plans and their results. She supported Sir Francis Drake on his three-year voyage around the world, profiting mightily from the immense loot he captured from Spanish ships taken in the Pacific. **B**

> **DURING READING**
>
> **Use Reading Strategies**
> **Make Predictions** How might have her father's actions affected Elizabeth? **C**

For Elizabeth, one of the most urgent problems was the question of religion. Her father had broken with the Catholic church and launched the English Reformation, creating the Church of England, with himself at its head. When Elizabeth's older half sister, Mary (who remained Catholic), married the Catholic king of Spain, Philip II, she reconciled England with the Church of Rome. In Mary's brief reign she persecuted those Protestants who refused to conform, executing some 270 of them. **D**

When Elizabeth became queen upon Mary's death, she said she hoped religion would not prevent her people from living together in peaceful unity. She did not want to pry into people's souls or

272 UNIT 3 NONFICTION

question their faith. But in 1570, Pope Pius V excommunicated[10] her, denied her right to the throne, and declared her subjects owed her no allegiance. A directive from the pope's office decreed that the assassination of Queen Elizabeth would not be regarded as a sin. The effect of this directive was to turn practicing Catholics—about half of the English, most of them loyal—into potential traitors.

Though Elizabeth had wanted to pursue a middle way of toleration, circumstances threatened to overwhelm her. She had to beware of several Catholic monarchs of Europe who wished to see a Protestant England overthrown. Philip II of Spain sent ambassadors to England to urge Catholics to rise against Elizabeth, put her cousin Mary[11] on the throne, and restore Roman Catholicism as the national faith. The line between power, politics, and religion was becoming very thin.

Missionary priests living abroad were sent into England to stir up opposition to the queen. But the English Catholics as a body never rebelled, nor did they ever intend to. Still, missionary priests such as Edmund Campion were convicted of plotting against Elizabeth and executed.

In 1588 a long-threatened invasion of England by Spain was launched by Philip II. He mistakenly believed that the English Catholics were waiting to welcome him. News of his armada[12] of 130 big ships carrying 17,000 soldiers was terrifying. But the queen did not panic. She supervised the high command personally, meanwhile rallying popular support for the defense of the realm and sending troops to protect the coasts while Sir Francis Drake's ships set out to attack the Spanish fleet.

The Spanish Armada was defeated in three battles, its ships dispersed. When the news came of the tremendous victory, the citizens took to the streets, shouting for joy.

The defeat of the Spanish Armada did not end Spain's aggression against England. The Jesuits[13] in England, who were especially identified with Spain, continued to be persecuted. Richard Topcliffe, a notorious hater of Catholics, was given authority to track down suspects. He examined them under torture to force information about people who had sheltered them. The treatment of them was so vicious and cruel that the victims welcomed death as a release from their agony.

---

10. **excommunicated.** Excluded from a church or a religious community
11. **Mary.** Mary Stuart, the Queen of Scotland, not Elizabeth's half sister
12. **armada.** Large fleet of warships
13. **Jesuits.** Members of the Roman Catholic Society of Jesus

di·rec·tive (də rek′ tiv)
n., order or form of guidance

The line between power, politics, and religion was becoming very thin.

> **DURING READING**
> **Use Reading Skills**
> **Distinguish Fact from Opinion** Why is this paragraph's first sentence a statement of fact? **E**

ELIZABETH I **273**

Teach the Model

Use Reading Skills
Distinguish Fact from Opinion
Remind students that facts are concrete details that can be confirmed, while opinions are personal beliefs. Although a biographer's opinions about a subject can help readers formulate their own opinions, students should learn to recognize them as opinions and not mistake them for fact. Have students point out opinions in the selection (such as the description of William Shakespeare as *incomparable*).

Use Reading Skills
Distinguish Fact from Opinion
Answer: The statement can be verified using reliable sources based on English documents. **E**

Grammar Skills

Participles

Tell students that a participle is a verb form that they can use as an adjective or to form complex verb tenses, such as the past participle. Challenge them to provide examples of the ways participles can be used. For example:

- As a part of a verb: The door was creaking.
- As a modifier A creaking door should be oiled.

Have students find examples of participles in the selection and identify them as verbs or modifiers. Have them give the full form of the verbs and tell what nouns are being modified. Possible answers include (Verbs) *had experienced, was crowned, were decorated* and (Modifiers) *ruling men, astonished housewife, jeweled necklaces.*

ELIZABETH I **273**

Cultural Connection

Libel Seditious libel—criticizing the government—was made illegal in Great Britain in 1275. At that time, the crime was limited to what people might say or perhaps write in a letter. After Johannes Gutenberg perfected the printing press in the mid-fifteenth century, people could spread their opinions much more widely by handing out pamphlets, or little booklets. This made negative and critical expressions of opinion seem like an even greater threat. **Ⓐ**

Analyze Literature

Biography *Answer:* Answers will vary. Many students will say they found the violence of these actions surprising and it changed their opinion of Elizabeth. Others will claim that her actions were justified—or that she must genuinely have felt that they were—and that the actions did not change their opinions. **Ⓑ**

---

om•i•nous (äm´ ə nəs) *adj.*, foreboding or foreshadowing evil

for•feit (for´ fət) *v.*, lose or fail to win the right to something by some error, offense, or crime

> **DURING READING**
>
> **Analyze Literature**
> **Biography** How does this information about these punishments affect your understanding of Elizabeth? **Ⓑ**

During Elizabeth's reign several plots to assassinate her were uncovered. Elizabeth managed to give the impression that she was not frightened, but those close to her knew she was. When one of the major plots proved to center around Elizabeth's cousin, Mary Queen of Scots, Elizabeth found it almost intolerable to put to death a crowned queen. Yet she ordered the use of torture on Mary's co-conspirators, and in the end, Mary was beheaded. A song composed by William Byrd at the time suggests how <u>ominous</u> the news of a monarch's execution was:

> The noble famous Queen
> who lost her head of late
> Doth show that kings as well as clowns
> Are bound to fortune's fate,
> And that no earthly Prince
> Can so secure his crown
> But fortune with her whirling wheel
> Hath power to pull them down.

When two earls combined forces against her, Elizabeth's troops overcame them. The queen was so enraged she ordered that 800 of the mostly poor rebels be hanged. But she spared the lives of their wealthy leaders so that they might enrich her, either by buying their pardons or by <u>forfeiting</u> their lands.

Elizabeth came down hard on writers who criticized her actions. John Stubbs, a zealous[14] Puritan, wrote a pamphlet expressing horror at the possibility the queen might marry a French Catholic. The queen had Stubbs and his publisher tried and convicted for seditious libel.[15] How dare Stubbs say publicly she was too old to marry, and that the much younger French suitor could not possibly be in love with her? Elizabeth was merciless as she invoked the penalty for libel. With a butcher's cleaver, the executioner cut the right hands off Stubbs and his publisher. Not an uncommon punishment. **Ⓐ**

How did Elizabeth learn of all these plots and conspiracies? How did she know what plans Philip II of Spain was devising to invade her kingdom? Spies and secret agents—they were her eyes and ears. Crucial to the flow of information was Sir Francis Walsingham. Trained as a lawyer, he lived on the Continent[16] for years, mastering the languages and the ins and outs of European affairs. Upon his return home, he was asked by Sir William Cecil,

---

14. **zealous.** Filled with eagerness in pursuit of something
15. **seditious libel.** Crime of lying to create opposition to authority
16. **Continent.** European continent

Differentiated Instruction

Enrichment

Students interested in learning more about Elizabeth's life may want to read one of many excellent biographies of the queen, such as *Behind the Mask: The Life of Queen Elizabeth* by Jane Resh Thomas. They may also be interested in classic or recent film treatments of her life. Suggest that students conduct library research to create lists of ten possible biographies, fictional treatments of Elizabeth, and film or television treatments of her life. Display their lists in class.

the queen's right arm, to gather information on the doings and plans of foreign governments. Soon he was made chief of England's secret service. He placed over seventy agents and spies in the courts of Europe. And of course he watched closely the activities of people at home suspected of disloyalty. Letters to and from them were secretly opened, to nip plots in the bud.

Monarchs had absolute power. Elizabeth could arrest anyone, including the topmost ranks of the nobility, and imprison them in the Tower of London even if they had not committed any legal offense. The only thing that held her back was her fear of public opinion. It upset her when a crowd gathered at a public execution and was so disgusted by the butchery that they let out roars of disapproval. Still, like all rulers, Elizabeth said she believed that "born a sovereign princess" she enjoyed "the privilege common to all kings" and was "exempt from human jurisdiction[17] and subject only to the judgement of God."

Despite her blazing nervous energy, Elizabeth was often sick. Her ailments were anxiously reported and discussed. For the English believed her survival was their only guarantee of freedom from foreign invasion and civil war. Once, suffering a raging toothache for the first time, the queen feared the pain of having an extraction. She had never had a tooth pulled and was terrified. To reassure her, an old friend, the Bishop of London, had her watch while the dental surgeon pulled out one of the bishop's own good teeth. And then she consented to have her own taken out.

It was commonly believed then that kings and queens had the magical power to cure disease in their subjects. Eager to demonstrate that she too had the sacred power of royalty, Elizabeth prayed intensely before using the royal touch on people with scrofula, a nasty skin disease. Her chaplain said he watched "her exquisite hands, boldly, and without disgust, pressing the sores and ulcers." In one day it was reported that she healed thirty-eight persons. But if she did not feel divinely inspired, she would not try her touch.

Even in the last decade of her life, Elizabeth's energy was astonishing. She was as watchful as always over the affairs of state, though sometimes forgetful. But age made her more irritable; she sometimes shouted at her ladies and even boxed their ears. She was less able to control rival factions out for power, and became so fearful of assassins she rarely left her palaces.

---

17. **jurisdiction.** Authority to apply the law

Elizabeth came down hard on writers who criticized her actions.

DURING READING

Analyze Literature
Biography Why might the author have included this detail about the queen's toothache? **D**

Teach the Model

Make Connections
Meltzer describes several ruthless acts Queen Elizabeth commits. On the board, write this quotation by Lord John Emerich Dalberg Acton: "Power tends to corrupt and absolute power corrupts absolutely." Do students think that Queen Elizabeth might have been corrupted by the power she wielded? Have them explain their responses. **C**

Analyze Literature
Biography *Answer:* Her fear of having a tooth extracted makes her seem more like an ordinary human being, with the same fear of pain that all humans have. The detail fleshes out the queenly portrait. **D**

Grammar Skills

Participles and Gerunds
Tell students that, like participles, gerunds end in -*ing*. However, gerunds are nouns. Challenge them to provide examples of the ways gerunds can be used. For example: Creaking can occur when you forget to oil a door's hinges.

Have students find examples of words ending in -*ing* in the selection and identify them as participles—verbs and modifiers—or as gerunds. See page 273 for examples of participles. Examples of gerunds include *bearing, coming and going,* and *bear-baiting.*

Answer: Impressions and examples will vary. Students may say many world leaders could learn from Elizabeth's dedication and ability.

Find Meaning

1. Henry VIII had her beheaded.

2. (a) Some people disputed her right to the throne. (b) She had many processions (which the people liked), traveled throughout the country, and tried to promote religious harmony.

3. (a) Henry's marriage record and treatment of his wives might have discouraged Elizabeth. (b) She said her husband was England.

Make Judgments

4. Students can infer that people were impressed with Elizabeth's glittering appearance and could boast that they had seen the queen.

5. (a) Henry opposed the Catholic Church and created the Church of England. Catholics in England did not want to renounce their faith. (b) Although she wanted to be tolerant, Elizabeth was fearful and responded vigorously to threats.

6. She was one of the most influential rulers of all time.

A portrait of her done when she was approaching sixty shows her in a great white silk dress studded with aglets[18] of black onyx, coral, and pearl. She wears three ropes of translucent pearls and stands on a map of England, her England. An ambassador reported that at sixty-three she looked old, but her figure was still beautiful, and her conversation was as brilliant and charming as ever.

There was dancing at court every evening, a pastime she still enjoyed. When it came to displays of gallantry by eager young men, she could act a bit vain and foolish, although never letting any hopeful get out of bounds.

In early 1603 Elizabeth developed a bad cold that led to a serious fever, and then she fell into a stupor[19] for four days. As she lay dying, all of London became strangely silent. On March 24, the life of a rare genius ended. The nation went into mourning.

"Old age came upon me as a surprise, like a frost," she once wrote. ❖

DURING READING

Make Connections
Do you agree that Elizabeth was "a rare genius"? **A**

18. **aglets.** Ornamental pins
19. **stupor.** State of shock or greatly dulled sense

MIRRORS & WINDOWS What are your impressions of Elizabeth? Who in the modern world do you think shares some or many of her traits? How does Elizabeth compare with heads of countries today? What could today's leaders learn from her?

Find Meaning

1. What happened to Elizabeth's mother?

2. (a) What were people's attitudes toward having a female ruler? (b) How did Elizabeth deal with these attitudes?

3. (a) The author suggests some reasons for Elizabeth's refusal to marry. What are these reasons? (b) What did Elizabeth herself declare about this matter to a delegation from Parliament?

Make Judgments

4. Why do you think people were impressed with Elizabeth's grand processions through London?

5. (a) What was at the heart of the religious conflict in England? (b) How did Elizabeth deal with this conflict?

6. Why do you think the author chose Elizabeth as the subject of a biography?

Differentiated Instruction

Kinesthetic Learning

To help students further familiarize themselves with the period, have them find a short scene from a work by an Elizabethan playwright (such as William Shakespeare, Christopher Marlowe, Ben Jonson, or Thomas Kyd), rehearse it, and perform it for classmates. Ask each group to begin its presentation by briefly telling the plot of the play and explaining how the scene fits into the action.

In "Elizabeth I," Milton Meltzer tells of the life of a remarkable English queen. The following selection includes part of a speech Elizabeth gave to the English Parliament, two of her poems, and an excerpt from a letter she wrote to Mary Queen of Scots. As you read, recall what you already know about Elizabeth's life.

Writings by Queen Elizabeth I

from **Queen Elizabeth's Speech to Her Last Parliament**

> Mr. Speaker,
>
> And if my Princely bounty have been abused, and my Grants turned to the hurt of my People contrary to my will and meaning, or if any in Authority under me have neglected, or converted what I have committed unto them, I hope God they will not lay their culps[1] to my charge.
>
> To be a King, and wear a Crown, is a thing more glorious to them that see it, than it is pleasant to them that bear it: for my self, I never was so much enticed with the glorious name of a King, or the royal authority of a Queen, as delighted that god hath made me His Instrument to maintain His Truth and Glory, and to defend this Kingdome from dishonor, damage, tyranny, and oppression....
>
> Thus Mr. Speaker, I commend me to your loyal Loves, and yours to my best care and your further Councils, & I pray you Mr. Controller, & Mr. Secretary, and you of my council, that before these Gentlemen depart into their Countries you bring them all to kiss my Hand. ♣

---

1. **culps.** Blame

WRITINGS BY QUEEN ELIZABETH I **277**

Analyze Literature

Setting Note that in speeches and letters, the author may not describe a setting the way fiction writers do. However, such documents still contain clues about setting. Challenge students to identify these. Students should note that sentence structure, word choices, and spellings are characteristic of an archaic form of English, which helps readers identify the setting as Renaissance England.

Use Reading Skills

Analyze Effects of Form on Content Ask students how the forms of the four related readings relate to the content of the pieces. Possible responses:

- Speech: The formal address, closing, and prose are suited to impressing an audience of powerful people.
- Poems: The strict rhyme and meter and limited length are suited to expressing private thoughts and impressions.
- Letter: The more casual prose is similar to a face-to-face conversation.

Writing Skills

Business and Personal Letters
Have students compare Elizabeth's speech to Parliament to her personal letter to Queen Mary. Encourage them to note elements that contribute to formality and tone, such as word choice and sentence structure.

Ask students to write two short letters expressing interest in a job: one to an imaginary employer, and another to a friend. Remind them to pay attention to the formality and tone of each letter.

Common Core State Standards

Reading Literature
RL.1

Reading Informational
RI.1

Writing
W.2, W.9, W.10

Teach the Connection

Science Connection

Diamonds Discuss the fact that Elizabeth was able to scratch words into a window using a diamond. Explain that particles in a diamond are very tightly packed, making it so hard that the only natural material that can scratch a diamond is another diamond. Glass, on the other hand, is made primarily of quartz, which can be scratched by a number of other materials. **A**

Analyze Literature

Meter Tell students that meter, or rhythm, is the pattern of beats in a poem. Model how to divide a line of this poetry into two-syllable units known as "metrical feet," and then mark the strong and weak beats in each foot. (Note that in Elizabethan times, the syllable *-ed* at the end of words was pronounced more often than in modern English. Also note that Elizabeth used a metrical foot called an iamb, which consists of an unstressed syllable followed by a stressed syllable.) For example:

No CROOK / *ed* LEG, / *no* BLEAR / *ed* EYE,

Challenge students to mark the beats in the remaining lines of the poems.

Text-to-Text Connection

Answer: Many students will claim that Elizabeth's poems reveal her innermost thoughts; the poems present a slightly different, more intimate, portrait of her. Others may say that her speech to Parliament reinforces what they already learned.

A Written with a Diamond on Her Window at Woodstock

Much suspected of me,
Nothing proved can be,
Quoth[2] Elizabeth prisoner. ♣

Written in Her French Psalter[3]

No crooked leg, no bleared[4] eye,
No part deformed out of kind,
Nor yet so ugly half can be
As is the inward suspicious mind. ♣

from **Letter to Mary Queen of Scots, 1586**

You have in various ways and manners attempted to take my life and to bring my kingdom to destruction by bloodshed. I have never proceeded so harshly against you, but have, on the contrary, protected and maintained you like myself. These treasons will be proved to you and all made manifest.[5] Yet it is my will, that you answer the nobles and peers of the kingdom as if I were myself present. I therefore require, charge, and command that you make answer for I have been well informed of your arrogance. ♣

2. **quoth.** Said
3. **psalter.** Prayer book
4. **bleared.** Watery
5. **manifest.** Evident; clear

TEXT TO TEXT CONNECTION Both Milton Meltzer's biography and Elizabeth's writings present insights into Elizabeth's life. Compare and contrast what each writer tells. Which selection or selections most reveal Elizabeth's innermost thoughts? Do Elizabeth's writings support the picture of her character as portrayed by Meltzer?

278 UNIT 3 NONFICTION

Differentiated Instruction

Enrichment

Explain to students that when Elizabeth calls herself a prisoner in her poem, it is not a metaphor — she really was a prisoner in the palace at Woodstock. She had even spent time in the much grimmer Tower of London. This was because her half-sister Mary was queen at the time and feared conspirators might be plotting to overthrow her and have Elizabeth crowned instead. Have students find out more about Elizabeth's life during this difficult time and speculate about what her poems might mean when considered in that context.

Analyze Literature

Biography Biographers typically present both facts and opinions about their subjects. Given this selection, what do you think is the biographer's overall opinion of Elizabeth? Do you think he admires her? What evidence from the story supports your answer? Use a web like the one on the right to record words and phrases that indicate whether or not Meltzer admires Elizabeth.

Now review the selection and list any facts that support the biographer's opinion. For example, does Meltzer provide any evidence that Elizabeth was a genius? In a separate list, record any facts that contradict the biographer's opinion. Compare the two lists. Do you think the author's opinion of Elizabeth is fair and accurate? Explain your answer.

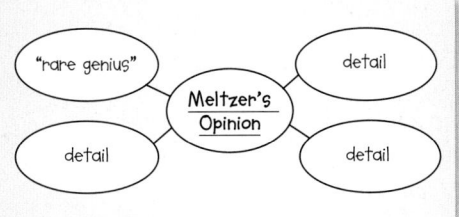

Extend Understanding

Writing Options

Creative Writing Write a one- or two-page **dialogue** between Elizabeth and one of her suitors. Assume that Elizabeth has already said she is not going to marry. Assume also that the suitor is convinced he can change her mind. The suitor should try to persuade Elizabeth by suggesting various logical and emotional advantages to her marriage with him. Elizabeth should respond accordingly. Present your dialogue to the class.

Expository Writing In the excerpt from her last speech to Parliament, Elizabeth says, "To be a King, and wear a Crown, is a thing more glorious to them that see it, than it is pleasant to them that bear it...." In an **expository paragraph,** explain why Elizabeth might have felt this way, given the events of her life. Include a thesis statement and evidence from Meltzer's biography in your paragraph.

Collaborative Learning

Analyze Speech Government leaders are known for giving persuasive speeches. A **policy speech** attempts to persuade listeners to support a change in government policy. These often contain quotations from experts and arguments that address policy issues. In a group, identify and read the text of a contemporary policy speech. Interpret the speaker's purpose by asking questions or making comments about the evidence presented. Finally, analyze the structure of the speech's central argument and identify the different types of evidence used to support the argument. Present your findings to the class.

Critical Literacy

Conduct an Interview Working in pairs, with one person acting as reporter and the other as Elizabeth, conduct an interview. The interview might cover such topics as Elizabeth's views on marriage and government, her leisure activities, and her opinions about religion.

 Go to **www.mirrorsandwindows.com** for more.

Review the Model

Analyze Literature

Biography Most will agree that Meltzer admires Elizabeth. They might point to his use of words like *genius* and phrases like *the most remarkable woman who ever lived.* In deciding whether the biographer's opinion is fair, they should recognize that the author has presented facts that support his opinion, and that other sources may offer facts that support a different opinion.

Rubrics for Writing Options

You can adapt this as a checklist for students to use as they write.

Creative Writing
☐ Does the dialogue include both a suitor and Elizabeth?
☐ Does the dialogue offer logical and emotional appeals in the suitor's arguments in support of marriage?

Expository Writing
☐ Does the paragraph explain why Elizabeth may have felt this way?
☐ Does the paragraph include textual evidence?
☐ Does the paragraph include a thesis statement?

Vocabulary Practice

1. from the Latin *scriptum* meaning "writing, lines, or marks in a book"

2. from the Latin *successionem* or *successio* meaning "a following after, a coming into another's place, result"

3. from the Latin *prosperus* meaning "doing well"

4. from the Latin *coronare* meaning "to crown"

5. from the Latin *revivere* meaning "to live again"

6. from the Latin *jurisdictionem* meaning "administration of justice or the power to administer justice"

7. from the Old English *blæse* meaning "torch"

8. from the Latin *ars* meaning "practicing a trade or handicraft"

9. from the Latin *renasci* meaning "to be born again"

10. from the Latin *armata* meaning "a fleet of warships"

For more information, see Vocabulary & Spelling Section 2.2: Breaking Words into Base Words, Root Words, Prefixes, and Suffixes, in the Language Arts Handbook. Refer to Section 2.7, Spelling, for additional instruction on spelling rules.

Program Resources

You will find additional lessons on Greek, Latin, and Anglo-Saxon Roots in the *Exceeding the Standards: Vocabulary & Spelling* resource.

Vocabulary & Spelling

Greek, Latin, and Anglo-Saxon Roots

She learned history, geography, mathematics, and the elements of astronomy and architecture.

—MILTON MELTZER, "Elizabeth I"

Thousands of common English words are formed from **Latin** and **Greek roots** or base words. In the sentence above, the word *geography* is formed by joining two Greek roots: *geo* meaning "earth" and *graph* meaning "describe." *Architecture* is formed from the Greek roots *arkhi* meaning "chief" and *tekton* meaning "builder."

Anglo-Saxon roots are derived from Old English, which was spoken from the fifth to the twelfth century. The meaning of some modern words is different from the root meaning. For example, *prestige* comes from the Latin word *praestigium*, which meant "deceptive" or "full of tricks." Today, the word means "status," or "standing in general opinion."

Common Roots

Root Word	Meaning	Origin	English Words
alt	"high"	Latin	altitude, altimeter
bio	"life"	Greek	biology, bionic
duc	"lead, bring, take"	Latin	produce, deduce
kno	"skill"	Anglo-Saxon	know, knowledge
nym	"name"	Greek	synonym, antonym
side	"boundary, edge"	Anglo-Saxon	inside, sideline

Root Word	Meaning	Origin	English Words
fare	"go"	Anglo-Saxon	farewell, welfare
spell	"recite"	Anglo-Saxon	spelling, gospel
aster	"star"	Greek	asteroid, asterisk
photo	"light"	Greek	photography, photosynthesis
equi	"equal"	Latin	equilateral, equidistant

Vocabulary Practice

Use a dictionary to find the roots or base words for each of these words from "Elizabeth I." Then write the meaning as it is used in the text.

1. script
2. succession
3. prosperity
4. coronation
5. revival
6. jurisdiction
7. blazing
8. artisans
9. Renaissance
10. armada

Spelling Practice

Words with *ei* or *ie*

A common rule for the vowel combination *ei* or *ie* is the following: "*I* before *e*, except after *c* or when sounded long *a* as in *neighbor* or *weigh*." However, that saying does not cover every instance. Examine this list of words from "Elizabeth I" to see if they follow this rule.

ancient	foreign	priests
believe	forfeiting	reign
chief	friend	reins
eighteen	medieval	sciences
fields	neither	sovereign

KEY TERMS

LATIN ROOT, 280
GREEK ROOT, 280
BASE WORD, 280
ANGLO-SAXON ROOT, 280

Common Core State Standards

Language
L.4, L.6

TEACHING NOTE

Spelling Practice

Verify that students employ English spelling patterns and rules (such as the *ie* and *ei* rule) with increasing accuracy by checking over their written work. Consider asking students to write a paragraph that includes the following words: *believe, field, neighbor, thief, piece,* and *height.* Be sure to read these words aloud so students utilize their own spelling skills.

Words in Use

Teaching Words

derived, 280
prestige, 280
photosynthesis, 280
equilateral, 280
equidistant, 280
succession, 280
coronation, 280

revival, 280
jurisdiction, 280
artisan, 280
armada, 280

Understanding the Essay

What Is an Essay?

An **essay** is a short nonfiction work that expresses a writer's thoughts about a single subject. A well-written essay clearly presents information and usually has an introduction, body, and conclusion.

Elements of an Essay

Essays all share some common elements.

An **author's purpose** is the goal or aim the writer wants to accomplish with his or her essay. For example, an author might write to inform, to explain, to entertain, to tell a story, or to persuade.

The **audience** is the person or group for whom the author is writing. Audiences affect the way an author writes. For example, an essay intended for an audience unfamiliar with the essay's subject would contain little technical vocabulary.

Tone is the writer's attitude toward the subject or the reader. For example, a writer might use a lighthearted, informal tone when writing about something happy or funny.

Voice is the way a writer uses language to reflect his or her unique personality and attitude toward topic, form, and audience. A writer expresses voice through tone, word choice, and sentence structure.

Point of View is the vantage point from which a story is told. Most essays are written in either the first- or third-person point of view. If a story is told from the first-person point of view, the narrator uses the pronouns *I* and *we* and is a part of the action. When a story is told from a third-person point of view, the narrator is outside the action and uses pronouns such as *he, she, it,* and *they*.

Types of Essays

There are three main types of essays.

A **personal essay** is a short nonfiction work on a single topic related to the life of the writer. A personal essay is written from the author's point of view and often uses the pronouns *I* and *me*.

> *I write to find out what I'm thinking. I write to find out who I am. I write to understand things.*
>
> —JULIA ALVAREZ

A **persuasive essay** presents an argument in order to persuade or convince a reader. The writer supports his or her argument with evidence, such as facts and examples.

An **expository essay** is written to communicate facts. Since the main purpose is to inform, the tone is usually formal. The expository essays that you will encounter in this book appear in Unit 4. For example, Robert Jastrow's "The Size of Things" (page 378) communicates information about the size of the universe.

LITERARY ELEMENT **281**

Teach the Element

Understanding the Essay

Reading strategies and skills that can help students understand the essay include clarifying and identifying text structure.

Use Reading Strategies

Clarify Students may want to practice their clarifying strategies with many selections in this unit. For instance, Julia Alvarez and Louis L'Amour have different purposes and write in different genres, yet each appeals to emotions in order to heighten readers' engagement with the text. Students may wish to pause while reading Alvarez's essay to clarify her purpose or her theme. They may wish to pause as they read L'Amour's essay to distinguish between facts and opinions.

Use Reading Skills

Identify Text Structure Writers use various organizational plans in persuasive, personal, and expository essays. Encourage students to practice identifying cause-and-effect, compare-contrast, and problem-solution organization as they read.

TEACHING NOTE

Tell students that as they read essays, they should remember that they can check additional sources of information on a topic. They can combine new information with the information in an essay, and then draw conclusions about how well or completely the essay writer describes a topic.

Teaching Words
lighthearted, 281
informal, 281
vantage point, 281

KEY TERMS

ESSAY, 281
NONFICTION, 281
INTRODUCTION, 281
BODY, 281
CONCLUSION, 281
AUTHOR'S PURPOSE, 281
AUDIENCE, 281
TONE, 281
VOICE, 281

POINT OF VIEW, 281
PRONOUN, 281
PERSONAL ESSAY, 281
PERSUASIVE ESSAY, 281
EXPOSITORY ESSAY, 281

Common Core State Standards

Reading Informational
RI.3

Names/Nombres

A Personal Essay by Julia Alvarez

Preview the Model

At a Glance
Guided Reading: Reading Model
- Reading Level: Moderate
- Difficulty Considerations: Footnotes and vocabulary
- Ease Factor: Length

Objectives
Studying this lesson will enable students to
- use reading skills such as identifying the author's purpose
- define *personal essay* and recognize an example of the genre
- describe the literary accomplishments of Julia Alvarez
- appreciate a story about the experience of coming to the United States from another country

Launch the Lesson
Instigate a class discussion about students' relationships with their own names. Ask such questions as: "What is your full name, and where did it come from? Does any name express a cultural heritage? Do you have nicknames? How do you feel when people mispronounce your name or get it wrong? Would you change your name if you could? If so, why, and what would the new name be?"

▶ More by This Author
Students who like this story might enjoy the novels of Julia Alvarez, especially *How the Garcia Girls Lost Their Accents*.

GUIDED READING

Build Background
Historical Context Julia Alvarez was raised in the Dominican Republic, a Spanish-speaking island country in the Caribbean. At the time of Alvarez's birth, the Dominican Republic was ruled by a dictator, Rafael Trujillo. Alvarez's father joined the underground movement that attempted to overthrow Trujillo, but the attempt failed, and in 1960 her family fled to New York City.

Reader's Context How would you feel if everyone suddenly started addressing you by a new name?

Set Purpose
Skim the text to look for unfamiliar terms. Identify and define these terms ahead of time to read without interruption.

Analyze Literature
Personal Essay A short nonfiction work that is written to express the writer's thoughts about a single subject is called a **personal essay.** Personal essays are written from the first-person point of view, using pronouns such as *I* and *we*. Personal essays frequently reveal something about the life of the essay's author and can be written for a variety of purposes.

Meet the Author

Julia Alvarez (b. 1950) was ten years old when her family moved back to New York City from the Dominican Republic. Julia worked hard to be proficient in English. She says that having to "pay close attention to each word [was] great training for a writer." She has taught at several colleges and universities and is writer-in-residence at Middlebury College in Vermont. Her works of fiction include *How the Garcia Girls Lost Their Accents* and *Yo!* Alvarez has also published several poetry collections.

Use Reading Skills
Identify Author's Purpose Using a graphic organizer can help you determine whether the author's main purpose for writing is to inform, to entertain, or to persuade. Look at the title, skim the selection, and read the footnotes. Then write your observations in the Before Reading section of the chart. Next, read the essay and list the main ideas the author communicates in the During Reading section. Then, in the After Reading section, summarize the author's purpose.

Before Reading	During Reading	After Reading
The author speaks two languages.		

Preview Vocabulary
eth·ni·ci·ty (eth ni´ sə tē) *n.*, belonging to a racial, cultural, or national group

spec·i·fy (spe´ sə fi´) *v.*, state explicitly

cha·ot·ic (kā ät´ ik) *adj.*, in a state of disorder or confusion

com·mence·ment (kəm men[t]s´ mənt) *adj.*, graduation

282 UNIT 3 NONFICTION

Words in Use

Selection Words
ethnicity, 286
specify, 286
chaotic, 287
commencement, 288

Teaching Words
forbade, 284
bazaar, 287
convoluted, 287

KEY TERMS

Common Core State Standards
Reading Informational
RI.4, RI.6

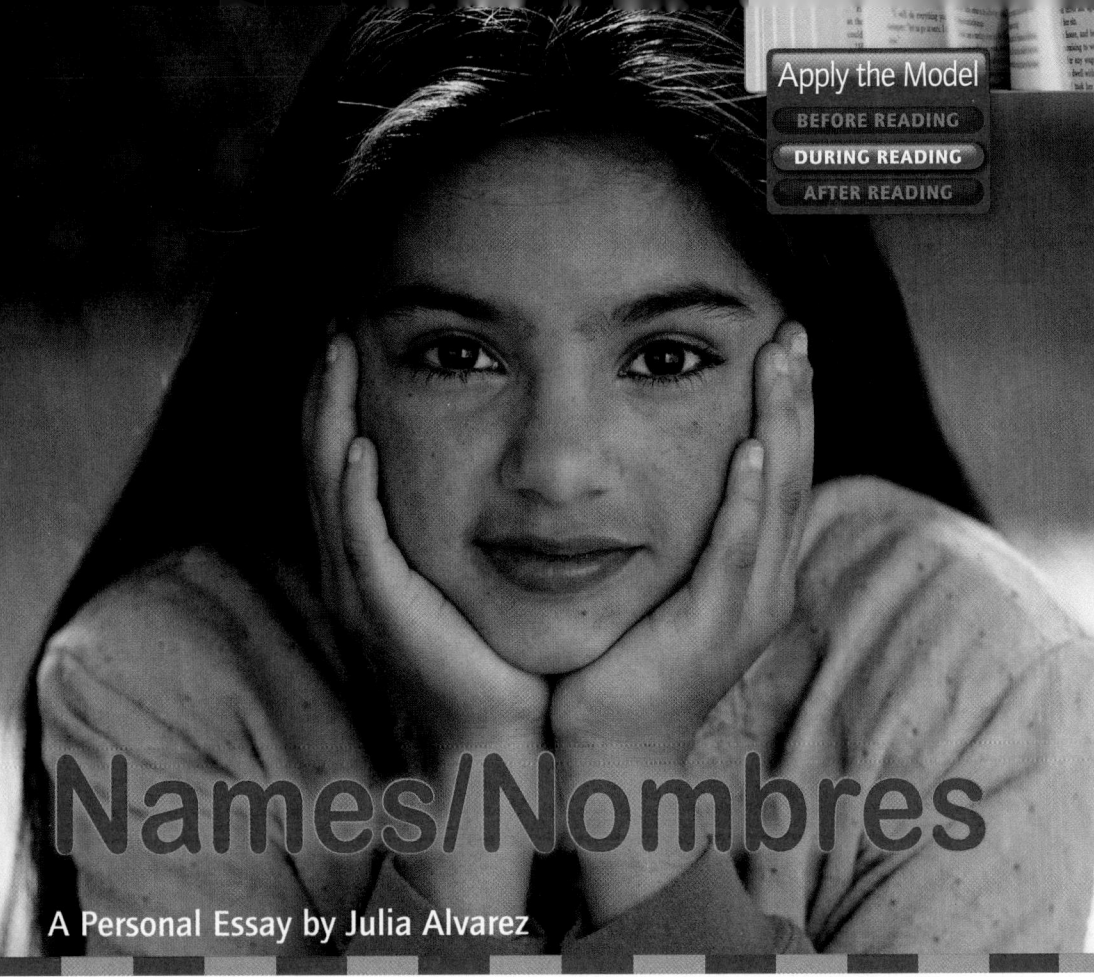

Names/Nombres

A Personal Essay by Julia Alvarez

Teach the Model

Summary

Julia Alvarez, a writer of Dominican heritage, explains how her sense of identity developed by examining the many names by which she was known from her arrival in the United States to the time she left for college. At first, she was upset by the way so many people mispronounced her name and the names of her family members. After a while, as a popular girl at school, she came to like the American versions of her names and the nicknames her friends gave her. By the end of the essay, she has begun to identify with several different names and wonders which one will be most associated with her when she grows up to be a writer.

MIRRORS & WINDOWS The Mirrors & Windows questions at the end of the selection focus on the theme of fitting in. Before students begin reading, ask: What's the biggest advantage of "fitting in" at school?

When we arrived in New York City, our names changed almost immediately. At Immigration, the officer asked my father, *Mister Elbures,* if he had anything to declare. My father shook his head no, and we were waved through.

I was too afraid we wouldn't be let in if I corrected the man's pronunciation, but I said our name to myself, opening my mouth wide for the organ blast of the *a,* trilling my tongue for the drumroll of the *r, All-vah-rrr-es!* How could anyone get *Elbures* out of that orchestra of sound?

At the hotel my mother was *Missus Alburest,* and I was *little girl,* as in, "Hey, little girl, stop riding the elevator up and down. It's *not a toy.*"

When we moved into our apartment building, the super called my father *Mister Alberase,* and the neighbors who became mother's

"Say your name in Spanish, oh, please say it!"

283

Program Resources

Planning and Assessment
Program Planning Guide, Selection Lesson Plan
E-Lesson Planner
Assessment Guide, Lesson Test
ExamView

Technology Tools
Interactive Student Text on CD
Visual Teaching Package
Audio Library
mirrorsandwindows.com

Meeting the Standards
Nonfiction: Unit 3, Guided Reading, pp. 34–40

Differentiating Instruction
Advanced Students, Comparing Literature Activity, p. 16
English Language Learners, Author's Purpose, pp. 86–95

Analyze Literature

Personal Essay Remind students that a personal essay is a short nonfiction work about a specific topic related to the author's life. Note that it is very closely related to memoir (a literary account of a writer's life, usually limited to a specific period). Talk about ways of distinguishing personal essay from memoir. (Students should agree that an essay is narrower in scope and shorter than a memoir.)

Make Connections

Answer: Hoo-lee-tah is the name that her family has used for her since she was a baby, so it makes her feel young and coddled, while *Alcatraz* is the name given to her by her "troublemaking" friends. **A**

Foreign Words

Note that often a foreign term looks or sounds like a word with a similar meaning in English; this can help a person determine its meaning. Students may also be able to use context clues. For example, using both pronunciation and context clues, they can analyze the title, "Names/Nombres," to determine that *nombres* means "names." *Nombres* might sound a little more like the English word *numbers*. However, paired with *names,* its meaning becomes clear. Suggest that students preview foreign terms before reading the selection. Have them say the words out loud, using the pronunciations in the footnotes.

JUDY ALCATRAZ, the name on the "Wanted" poster would read.

> **DURING READING**
>
> **Make Connections**
> Why do you think the name *Judy Alcatraz* is so much more appealing to the author than *"Hoo-lee-tah"*? **A**

friends pronounced her name *Jew-lee-ah* instead of *Hoo-lee-ah.* I, her namesake, was known as *Hoo-lee-tah* at home. But at school I was *Judy* or *Judith,* and once an English teacher mistook me for *Juliet.*

It took a while to get used to my new names. I wondered if I shouldn't correct my teachers and new friends. But my mother argued that it didn't matter. "You know what your friend Shakespeare said, '*A rose by any other name would smell as sweet.*'" My family had gotten into the habit of calling any famous author "my friend" because I had begun to write poems and stories in English class.

By the time I was in high school, I was a popular kid, and it showed in my name. Friends called me *Jules* or *Hey Jude,* and once a group of troublemaking friends my mother forbade me to hang out with called me *Alcatraz.*[1] I was *Hoo-lee-tah* only to Mami and Papi and uncles and aunts who came over to eat *sancocho*[2] on Sunday afternoons—old world folk whom I would just as soon go back to where they came from and leave me to pursue whatever mischief I wanted to in America. JUDY ALCATRAZ, the name on the "Wanted" poster would read. Who would ever trace her to me?

My older sister had the hardest time getting an American name for herself because *Mauricia* did not translate into English. Ironically, although she had the most foreign-sounding name, she and I were the Americans in the family. We had been born in New York City when our parents had first tried immigration and then gone back "home," too homesick to stay. My mother often told the story of how she almost changed my sister's name in the hospital.

After the delivery, Mami and some other new mothers were cooing over their newborn sons and daughters and exchanging names, weights and delivery stories. My mother was embarrassed among the Sallys and Janes, Georges and Johns to reveal the rich, noisy name of *Mauricia,* so when her turn came to brag, she gave her baby's name as *Maureen.*

"Why'd ya give her an Irish name with so many pretty Spanish names to choose from?" one of the women asked.

My mother blushed and admitted her baby's real name to the group. Her mother-in-law had recently died, she apologized, and her husband had insisted that the first daughter be named after his mother, *Mauran.* My mother thought it the ugliest name she had

---

1. **Alcatraz.** From the mid-1930s to the mid-1960s, a maximum-security prison for America's toughest criminals
2. **sancocho** (san kô´ chō). Caribbean meat stew (Spanish)

Differentiated Instruction

Auditory Learning

This selection provides an outstanding opportunity for native Spanish speakers in the class to contribute. If possible, have them read sections of the essay aloud. In addition to giving the readers more practice with English, this is the best way to show how the Spanish words should sound.

Enrichment

Unlike the Alvarez family, some immigrants change their names, maybe to make them easier for English speakers to pronounce, or to try to fit in—or to hide their origins. Students may want to investigate this. For some, a name change might be part of family history. Encourage students to use library and Internet sources, and family input if applicable, and to report their findings.

ever heard, and talked my father into what she believed was an improvement, a combination of *Mauran* and her own mother's name, *Felicia.*

"Her name is *Mao-ree-shee-ah*," my mother said to the group of women.

"Why, that's a beautiful name," the other mothers cried. "*Moor-ee-sha, Moor-ee-sha,*" she cooed into the pink blanket. *Moor-ee-sha* it was when we returned to the States eleven years later. Sometimes, American tongues found that mispronunciation tough to say and called her *Maria* or *Marsha* or *Maudy* from her nickname *Maury*. I pitied her. What an awful name to have to transport across borders!

GEOGRAPHY ▶▶ CONNECTION

The Dominican Republic The Dominican Republic occupies two thirds of the island of Hispaniola, which is part of the Greater Antilles chain in the Caribbean Sea. Haiti occupies the remaining third of the island. The Atlantic Ocean is to the north, and the Caribbean Sea is to the south; the island of Puerto Rico is to the east, and Cuba is to the west. The capital city of the Dominican Republic is Santo Domingo. It is a mountainous country, with many rivers and fertile land. The climate is tropical, with a rainy season from May to November. Christopher Columbus landed on Hispaniola in 1492 and founded the first European settlement in America there. Why might it be difficult for Julia to adapt to her new environment? **C**

NAMES/NOMBRES **285**

Reading Skills

Identify Author's Purpose
Review the difference between theme (a central idea in a literary work) and purpose (the author's aim in writing the piece). Note that theme and purpose are rarely stated in literature. To figure out the theme, students can ask themselves, "What idea is the author exploring in this work?" To figure out the purpose, they can ask, "Why did the author write this?" Discuss possible answers to these questions as they apply to this selection. Ideas include:
- She is exploring the idea that a person's name helps define a person's identity.
- She is exploring the idea that different names can apply to different stages of life.
- She is writing to entertain readers with humor.
- She is writing to share her experience.

NAMES/NOMBRES **285**

Use Reading Skills

Identify Author's Purpose Remind students that an author may have more than one purpose in writing a piece. Usually, students' task is to decide what they consider the primary purpose. Discuss purposes Alvarez might have had in writing "Names/Nombres." These include to entertain, to explain, and to share.

Use Reading Skills

Author's Purpose *Answer:* Both anecdotes describe in a humorous way how non-Spanish-speaking people surprise the Alvarezes by embracing their Spanish names. The purpose of the anecdotes is both to explain and to entertain. **A**

eth·ni·ci·ty
(eth ni´ sə tē) *n.*, belonging to a racial, cultural, or national group

DURING READING

Use Reading Skills
Author's Purpose Compare the anecdotes about the two sisters' names. What point do you think the author is making? **A**

spec·i·fy (spe´ sə fī') *v.*, state explicitly

My little sister, Ana, had the easiest time of all. She was plain *Anne*—that is, only her name was plain, for she turned out to be the pale, blond "American beauty" in the family. The only Hispanic thing about her was the affectionate nicknames her boyfriends sometimes gave her. *Anita*, or, as one goofy guy used to sing to her to the tune of the banana advertisement, *Anita Banana.*

Later, during her college years in the late sixties, there was a push to pronounce Third World[3] names correctly. I remember calling her long distance at her group house and a roommate answering.

"Can I speak to Ana?" I asked, pronouncing her name the American way.

"Ana?" The man's voice hesitated. "Oh! You must mean *Ah-nah!*"

Our first few years in the States, though, ethnicity was not yet "in." Those were the blond, blue-eyed, bobby-sock years of junior high and high school before the sixties ushered in peasant blouses, hoop earrings, *sarapes.*[4] My initial desire to be known by my correct Dominican name faded. I just wanted to be Judy and merge with the Sallys and Janes in my class. But, inevitably, my accent and coloring gave me away. "So where are you from, Judy?"

"New York," I told my classmates. After all, I had been born blocks away at Columbia-Presbyterian Hospital.

"I mean, *originally.*"

"From the Caribbean," I answered vaguely, for if I specified, no one was quite sure on what continent our island was located.

"Really? I've been to Bermuda. We went last April for spring vacation. I got the worst sunburn! So, are you from Portoriko?"[5]

"No," I sighed. "From the Dominican Republic."

"Where's that?"

"South of Bermuda."

They were just being curious, I knew, but I burned with shame whenever they singled me out as a "foreigner," a rare, exotic friend.

"Say your name in Spanish, oh, please say it!" I had made mouths drop one day by rattling off my full name, which, according to Dominican custom, included my middle names, Mother's and Father's surnames for four generations back.

---

3. **Third World.** Developing countries of Latin America, Africa, and Asia
4. **sarapes** (sə rä´ pēs). Woolen shawls or ponchos (Spanish)
5. **Portoriko.** Puerto Rico

Differentiated Instruction

Reading Proficiency

Less-proficient readers may be unsure how to begin using context clues. Review ways to consider context, such as:

• Is the unfamiliar word a thing (noun) or an action (verb), or does it describe something (adjectives, adverbs)? Example: In *trilling my tongue*, trilling must be an action, something the tongue can do.

• Do familiar words around the unfamiliar one provide clues? Example: In *to eat sancocho*, sancocho must be food.

• Does the action around the word contain clues? Example: *Mami and some other mothers were cooing over their newborn sons and daughters.* Have students imagine mothers with their babies—what do they do?

Civil flag of the Dominican Republic.

"Julia Altagracia María Teresa Álvarez Tavares Perello Espaillat Julia Pérez Rochet Gonzálcz." I pronounced it slowly, a name as <u>chaotic</u> with sounds as a Middle Eastern bazaar or market day in a South American village.

My Dominican heritage was never more apparent than when my extended family attended school occasions. For my graduation, they all came, the whole lot of aunts and uncles and the many little cousins who snuck in without tickets. They sat in the first row in order to better understand the Americans' fast-spoken English. But how could they listen when they were constantly speaking among themselves in florid-sounding phrases, rococo[6] consonants, rich, rhyming vowels?

Introducing them to my friends was a further trial to me. These relatives had such complicated names and there were so many of them, and their relationships to myself were so convoluted. There was my Tía[7] Josefina, who was not really an aunt but a much older cousin. And her daughter, Aida Margarita, who was adopted, una hija de crianza.[8] My uncle of affection, Tío José, brought my madrina[9] Tía Amelia and her comadre[10] Tía Pilar. My friends rarely had more than a "Mom and Dad" to introduce.

---

6. **rococo.** Fancy, flamboyant
7. **Tía** (tē´ ä). Aunt (Spanish); Tío (tē´ ō) is uncle.
8. **una hija de crianza** (ú´ nä ē´ hä de krē än´ sä). An adopted daughter (Spanish)
9. **madrina** (mä drē nä). Godmother (Spanish)
10. **comadre** (kō mä´ drā). Close friend (Spanish)

---DURING READING---

Analyze Literature
Personal Essay What does the author want to communicate to the reader about her attitude toward her name? **B**

cha·ot·ic (kā ät´ ik) *adj.*, in a state of disorder or confusion

---DURING READING---

Use Reading Skills
Meaning of Words Knowing the meaning of foreign words, such as *madrina* and *comadre*, can be helpful. Identify the meaning and origin of the following foreign words and phrases: *que sera sera*, *eureka*, and *ad nauseam*. **C**

Teach the Model

Analyze Literature
Personal Essay *Answer:* She is proud of it, yet also is ashamed of how exotic it could make her seem. **B**

Use Reading Skills
Meaning of Words *Possible answers: Que sera sera* is a Spanish phrase that means "whatever will be, will be." The word *eureka* Greek and is an exclamation of excitement meaning "I have found it." The term *ad nauseam* is Latin phrase used to describe an argument that has been continuing "to the point of nausea." It can also mean that something has been addressed extensively and everyone involved is sick and tired of it. **C**

Grammar Skills

Compound and Complex Sentences
Review definitions of compound and complex sentences: A compound sentence contains two or more independent clauses linked by a comma and coordinating conjunction or by a semicolon; a complex sentence contains an independent clause and one or more subordinate clauses.

Ask students to find compound and complex sentences in the reading and identify them by type.

Examples include (independent clauses underlined; subordinate clause in italics):

- ". . . <u>I burned with shame</u> *whenever they singled me out . . .*" (complex)
- <u>These relatives had such complicated names </u>and <u>there were so many of them</u>, and <u>their relationships to myself were so convoluted.</u> (compound)

Analyze Literature

Personal Essay *Answer:* The last two sentences of the essay hark back to the first three paragraphs, and also prompt the reader to notice that the author's name is "Julia Alvarez." **A**

 Answer: Students may say people fear being considered different.

Find Meaning

1. (a) It changes. (b) She does this to reassure herself.

2. (a) It doesn't matter what names people use. (b) Yes; she becomes known as Jules, Jude, and Alcatraz.

3. (a) She thinks it may be better to use a more American-sounding name. (b) It foreshadows her conflict over her desire to have a name like those of her American classmates.

Make Judgments

4. People of other cultures have trouble pronouncing it correctly.

5. It reveals her ambivalence.

6. (a) She wants to be like her classmates, and her family is something of an obstacle. (b) No; she describes her family members with affection and respect and seems to enjoy her graduation party.

7. (a) She uses Julia Alvarez. (b) She has decided to be true to her heritage.

---

com·mence·ment
(kəm men[t]s´ mənt) *adj.*, graduation

After the <u>commencement</u> ceremony, my family waited outside in the parking lot while my friends and I signed yearbooks with nicknames which recalled our high school good times: "Beans" and "Pepperoni" and "Alcatraz." We hugged and cried and promised to keep in touch.

Our goodbyes went on too long. I heard my father's voice calling out across the parking lot, "*Hoo-lee-tah! Vámonos!*"[11]

Back home, my *tíos* and *tías* and *primas*,[12] Mami and Papi, and *mis hermanas*[13] had a party for me with sancocho and a store-bought *pudín*,[14] inscribed with *Happy Graduation, Julie*. There were many gifts—that was a plus to a large family! I got several wallets and a suitcase with my initials and a graduation charm from my godmother and money from my uncles. The biggest gift was a portable typewriter from my parents for writing my stories and poems.

Someday, the family predicted, my name would be well-known throughout the United States. I laughed to myself, wondering which one I would go by. ✤

> **DURING READING**
>
> **Analyze Literature**
> **Personal Essay** How does the conclusion of the essay tie back to the beginning? **A**

11. *Vámonos* (vä´ mä nōs'). Let's go (Spanish)
12. *primas* (prē´ mäs'). Cousins (Spanish)
13. *mis hermanas* (mēs är mä´ näs). My sisters (Spanish)
14. *pudín* (pù dēn´). Pudding (Spanish)

 Julia Alvarez, at one point, was willing to change her name to Judy to be more like her classmates. What would you have done in her place? Why do you think people feel the need to fit in?

Find Meaning

1. (a) According to the author, what happens to her family's name at Immigration? (b) Why do you think she repeats the family's name to herself?

2. (a) What does the author's mother advise about correcting the pronunciation of teachers and new friends? (b) Does she follow her mother's advice? Explain.

3. (a) Why does Mrs. Alvarez almost change her daughter's name at the hospital? (b) What conflict does this anecdote foreshadow in the author's life?

Make Judgments

4. Why does Alvarez say that her older sister's name is "an awful name to have to transport across borders"?

5. Although the author says she dislikes being considered "exotic" by her classmates, she takes pleasure in "rattling off" her full name for them. What does this reveal about her feelings?

6. (a) Why does the author describe how her family differs from the families of her classmates? (b) Are these differences really important to her? Explain.

7. (a) What name does the author use when she becomes a professional writer? (b) What does this say about her attitude toward her name?

Differentiated Instruction

English Language Learning

Use the Alvarez reading to help English learners practice deciphering appositives. Remind them that an appositive is a word or group of words that renames a noun. If the noun is one of a kind, then commas are put around the appositive to show that it's extra information. If there are no commas, the appositive is essential to identifying the object or person being renamed. Have students point out nouns and their appositives in the selection. For example: Tía Josefina's daughter = Aida Margarita = *una hija de crianza* (an adopted daughter).

In her personal essay, "Names/Nombres," Julia Alvarez reflects on immigration, cultural heritage, and identity. The writer of the following poem, **Janet S. Wong,** was born in the United States to parents who had emigrated from China and Korea. Wong's poetry reflects her cultural heritage and her Asian-American identity. As you read "Face It," think about the significance of the poem's title.

Face It

A Lyric Poem by Janet S. Wong

My nose belongs
to Guangdong, China—
short and round, a Jang family nose.

My eyes belong
to Alsace, France—
wide like Grandmother Hemmerling's.

But my mouth, my big-talking mouth,
belongs
to me, alone. ❖

| TEXT ⟷ TO ⟷ TEXT CONNECTION | Both Julia Alvarez's essay and Janet Wong's poem explore ideas about cultural heritage and identity. In what ways are the two selections similar? In what ways do they differ? How important is cultural heritage to Alvarez and to the speaker in the poem? |

FACE IT **289**

Teach the Connection

Geography Connection
Author Background Guangdong is a province in southeastern China. Its capital is the port city of Guangzhou, known in the West as Canton. The Chinese food students are familiar with is likely to be Cantonese. The city is known for its cuisine, and Chinese immigrants introduced it to the United States. Alsace is a region of eastern France, along the borders of Switzerland and Germany. The region was under German rule consistently from about the ninth to the seventeenth centuries and sporadically until after World War II. Because of this, the culture there is a mixture of French and German. Most residents speak a German dialect known as Alsatian.

Use Reading Skills
Read Aloud Tell students that a good way to understand poetry is to read it aloud. Ask several students to read the poem aloud. Note that both repeated readings and hearing different people's interpretations can spark thoughts and ideas.

Text-to-Text Connection
Answer: The cross-cultural backgrounds of the writers and their acceptance of themselves are similarities. The essay's narrator had to struggle to learn self-acceptance, whereas there is no trace of struggle in the poem. The narrator and speaker differ in how much they value cultural heritage.

Reading Skills

Make Inferences
Remind students that inferences are conclusions reached using both clues in a piece of writing and the reader's own knowledge. Note that understanding "Face It" requires a reader to make inferences. Go through the poem, having students talk about the inferences they make and the knowledge they use to make them.

EXAMPLE:
- Stanza 1: The speaker has relatives from China.
- It helps to know the custom of remarking on family resemblances in a person's features.
- Stanza 3: Although he or she may look like other people, the speaker feels unique.
- It helps to know that a "big mouth" is someone who talks a lot.

Common Core State Standards
Reading Literature
RL.1, RL.9
Reading Informational
RI.4
Writing
W.10

Analyze Literature

Personal Essay Students' charts will vary. Some students might identify Alvarez's tone as vibrant. Others will claim that it is humorous. Make sure that students use evidence from the text in their charts.

Analyze Literature

Personal Essay A personal essay is greatly affected by its tone. Tone is the author's attitude toward his or her subject. For example, an author's tone might be humorous, angry, or thoughtful. Use this web to determine the tone of "Names/Nombres." Write details from the essay in the outer ovals. Then write the tone in the center oval.

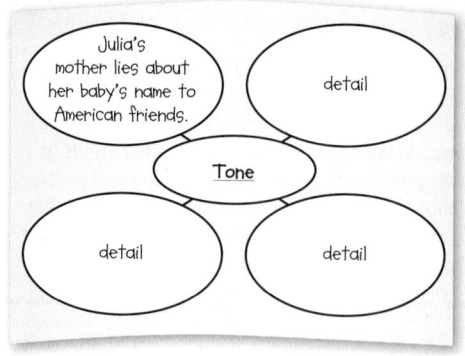

Julia's mother lies about her baby's name to American friends.

detail

Tone

detail

detail

Extend Understanding

Writing Options

Creative Writing Pretend that you are Julia and you want to invite one of your family members to attend your graduation. Write an **invitation** to this family member, stating why you would like the person to come. Note how you feel about the event. Remember to include the date, time, and location of the ceremony.

Expository Writing Is the theme, or central idea, of "Name/Nombres" stated in the essay or is it implied? Write an **expository paragraph** in which you describe the theme. Provide examples from the essay that support your analysis. Share your analysis with the class.

Lifelong Learning

Gather Historical Information Learn more about Alvarez's background by researching the history of the Dominican Republic, where she spent her first ten years. Write a short history of the nation on note cards or in an outline, and then present your findings to the class.

Critical Literacy

Conduct a Panel Discussion What's in a name? Use "Names/Nombres" as a starting point for discussing the importance of names. Do you agree with Shakespeare that "A rose by any other name would smell as sweet"? Can a person's name affect his or her self-image or how others perceive him or her? What do you think parents should consider when they decide on names for their children?

 Go to **www.mirrorsandwindows.com** for more.

Rubrics for Writing Options

You can adapt this as a checklist for students to use as they write.

Creative Writing
☐ Does the invitation have a consistent first-person point of view?
☐ Does the invitation include reference to the writer's personal desire to have the family member attend the event?
☐ Does the invitation name the event and include details of date, time, and location?

Expository Writing
☐ Does the paragraph accurately describe the theme of the essay?
☐ Does the paragraph explain whether the theme is stated or unstated?
☐ Does the paragraph include examples from the essay that support the theme?

The Eternal Frontier

A Persuasive Essay by Louis L'Amour

Build Background
Scientific Context When *Apollo 11* landed on the moon in 1969, extensive space exploration seemed within reach. In the 1970s, satellites were put into orbit, space stations were planned and piloted, and robotic missions were launched. In 1984, the year this essay was written, President Reagan announced plans to build an international space station. This meant that funds were going to be concentrated more on the space station than on sending rockets to explore the solar system.

Reader's Context What do you think is the most important frontier today? The most exciting? The most challenging?

Set Purpose
As you read the essay, pay attention to how the author appeals to both your emotions and logic.

Analyze Literature
Persuasive Essay In a **persuasive essay,** the author expresses a particular viewpoint and attempts to sway the reader to agree with that position. In addition to presenting logical arguments based on reasons and evidence, an author may use persuasive techniques that rely on faulty reasoning or emotional appeals. As you read "The Eternal Frontier," decide what the author's viewpoint is and evaluate the evidence he provides to support that viewpoint.

Use Reading Skills
Analyze Main Idea and Supporting Details To identify the main idea of "The Eternal Frontier," gather details in a main idea map. Then examine the details to determine the author's overall message.

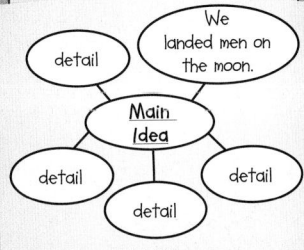

Preview Vocabulary
pre•lim•i•nar•y (pri li´ mə ner' ē) *adj.*, preparing for the main action or event

an•ti•dote (an´ ti dōt') *n.*, remedy

in•cor•po•rate (in kôr´ pə rāt') *v.*, combine into one body

Meet the Author
Louis L'Amour (1908–1988) grew up in North Dakota listening to stories about his grandfather's experiences in the Civil War. L'Amour became an avid reader of history and adventure books. As a young man, L'Amour worked as a lumberjack, a seaman, and a boxer. After serving in World War II, L'Amour began writing Westerns for magazines. By the 1980s, he was a best-selling author. He was the first novelist to be awarded a Congressional gold medal. In 1984, he received the Presidential Medal of Freedom.

THE ETERNAL FRONTIER **291**

Preview the Model

At a Glance
Guided Reading: Reading Model
- Reading Level: Moderate
- Difficulty Consideration: Abstract ideas
- Ease Factor: Length

Objectives
Studying this lesson will enable students to
- use reading skills such as analyzing the main idea and supporting details to assess a persuasive argument
- define *persuasive essay* and study an example
- describe the literary accomplishments of Louis L'Amour
- appreciate an author's assessment of what humankind's future will be

Launch the Lesson
Note that in his essay, "The External Frontier," Louis L'Amour describes space exploration as an adventure, like the pioneers' push westward in this country's early years. Ask students to think about how the two kinds of adventures seem similar and different. Which would they rather do, make their way into an unknown part of our planet, or venture into space? Why?

Words in Use

Preview Vocabulary	Selection Words	Teaching Words
preliminary, 293	transcontinen-tal, 293	piloted, 291
antidote, 293	transoceanic, 293	avid, 291
incorporate, 294	transistors, 294	bias, 295
		anthology, 295

Common Core State Standards
Reading Informational
RI.1, RI.2, RI.3, RI.8
Writing
W.9

Summary

Louis L'Amour says that the present-day equivalent to the Western frontier is outer space. He thinks people should explore and settle it just as they did the Old West. To support his view, he points out how rapidly technological innovation has progressed and mentions humankind's urge to explore the unknown. He reminds readers that people have already made the first exploratory space journeys, and that many conveniences are by-products of the space program. He ends by urging readers not to settle for living in the past and to look toward the future.

The Mirrors & Windows questions at the end of the selection focus on the theme of exploration. Before students begin to read, ask: What percentage of the annual U.S. budget do you think should go toward exploring space?

Use Reading Skills

Summarize A good way of evaluating the success of a writer's persuasive technique is to make a reader's journal entry for it. Have students draw a vertical line down the center of a sheet of paper and label the left column "Argument" and the right column "Reaction." As students read, they should note the author's arguments and then document what they think of them.

The Eternal Frontier

A Persuasive Essay by Louis L'Amour

292

Planning and Assessment
Program Planning Guide, Selection Lesson Plan
E-Lesson Planner
Assessment Guide, Lesson Test
ExamView

Technology Tools
Interactive Student Text on CD
Visual Teaching Package
Audio Library
mirrorsandwindows.com

Meeting the Standards
Nonfiction: Unit 3, Guided Reading, pp. 41–46

The question I am most often asked is, "Where is the frontier now?"

The answer should be obvious. Our frontier lies in outer space. The moon, the asteroids, the planets, these are mere stepping stones, where we will test ourselves, learn needful lessons, and grow in knowledge before we attempt those frontiers beyond our solar system. Outer space is a frontier without end, the eternal frontier, an everlasting challenge to explorers not [only] of other planets and other solar systems but also of the mind of man.

All that has gone before was <u>preliminary</u>. We have been preparing ourselves mentally for what lies ahead. Many problems remain, but if we can avoid a devastating[1] war we shall move with a rapidity scarcely to be believed. In the past seventy years we have developed the automobile, radio, television, transcontinental and transoceanic flight, and the electrification of the country, among a multitude of other such developments. In 1900 there were 144 miles of surfaced road in the United States. Now there are over 3,000,000. Paved roads and the development of the automobile have gone hand in hand, the automobile being civilized man's <u>antidote</u> to overpopulation.

What is needed now is leaders with perspective; we need leadership on a thousand fronts, but they must be men and women who can take the long view and help to shape the outlines of our future. There will always be the nay-sayers,[2] those who cling to our lovely green planet as a baby clings to its mother, but there will be others like those who have taken us this far along the path to a limitless future.

We are a people born to the frontier. It has been a part of our thinking, waking, and sleeping since men first landed on this continent. The frontier is the line that separates the known from the unknown wherever it may be, and we have a driving need to see what lies beyond....

A few years ago we moved into outer space. We landed men on the moon; we sent a vehicle beyond the limits of the solar system, a vehicle still moving farther and farther into that limitless distance.[3]

1. **devastating.** Extremely destructive
2. **nay-sayers.** People who disagree
3. **we sent a vehicle...into that limitless distance.** Reference to *Voyager 1*, an unmanned probe launched in 1977 to explore the far reaches of the universe

pre·lim·i·nar·y
(pri liˊ mə nerˈ ē) *adj.*,
preparing for the main action
or event

an·ti·dote (anˊ ti dōtˈ) *n.*,
remedy

> **DURING READING**
>
> **Analyze Literature
> Persuasive Essay** How
> would you paraphrase the
> argument in this paragraph?

Teach the Model

Use Reading Skills

Analyze Main Idea and Supporting Details In small groups, have students share the main idea maps they made for Use Reading Skills (page 291). Students may find that others noted items they missed, or have a different take on things. Allow students to adjust their maps as they wish, based on the discussion.

Use Reading Skills

Distinguish Fact from Opinion Note that readers may occasionally wish to check a fact cited by an author to make sure it is correct. Challenge students to pick a factual detail from the piece (for example, the number of miles of U.S. road in 1900) and to try to confirm it through online or library research. **A**

Analyze Literature

Persuasive Essay *Answer:*
Paraphrase: "We need strong leaders with vision to guide our future. There will always be people who do not see the big picture, who are scared of the future." **B**

> ### ▷ More About the Author
> L'Amour published ninety novels—three books a year after 1955—as well as short stories, TV and film scripts, articles, and his autobiography. He is most famous for his meticulously researched Westerns.

Differentiated Instruction

Reading Proficiency
Help less-confident readers identify words that project the author's feelings. Model a few examples, such as *obvious* (implies complete certainty) and *nay-sayers* (implies disapproval of their negative attitude). Ask students to look for other words that have emotional resonance and to explain their choices.

Enrichment
Students may wish to study space exploration and colonization by investigating other visions of the future. Have them narrow their topic for research. Some may wish to examine fictional depictions in novels or films. Others might focus on real-world endeavors, such as NASA projects or the work of the SETI (Search for Extraterrestrial Intelligence) Institute.

Use Reading Skills

Analyze Main Idea and Supporting Details *Answer:* Space is limitless, a frontier people could explore forever. **A**

Analyze Literature

Persuasive Essay Remind students that an author's goal in a persuasive essay is to convince readers to agree. Note it can be very effective to acknowledge the existence of dissenting views and then to argue convincingly against them. Ask: "How do you feel L'Amour responds to the view that there is still too much to be done on Earth to begin exploring space?" **B**

Make Connections

Answer: L'Amour's answer is emotional, not logical. Students' explanations will vary. **C**

 MIRRORS & WINDOWS *Answer:* Students may say that L'Amour's viewpoint is valid, and that space exploration is crucial to the sciences and the future of humanity. Others may argue that money spent exploring space could be better used solving problems on our planet. Students may say humanity has often been driven to explore for practical purposes, such as acquiring land or food, and also out of curiosity.

> **DURING READING**
> **Use Reading Skills**
> **Analyze Main Idea and Supporting Details** What is the author's main point in this paragraph? **A**

> **DURING READING**
> **Make Connections**
> Does L'Amour provide a logical answer to his question? Do you agree with what he says? Explain. **C**

in·cor·po·rate (in kôr′ pə rāt′) *v.*, combine into one body

If our world were to die tomorrow, that tiny vehicle would go on and on forever, carrying its mighty message to the stars. Out there, someone, sometime, would know that once we existed, that we had the vision and we made the effort. Mankind is not bound by its atmospheric envelope or by its gravitational field, nor is the mind of man bound by any limits at all.

B One might ask—why outer space, when so much remains to be done here? If that had been the spirit of man we would still be hunters and food gatherers, growling over the bones of carrion[4] in a cave somewhere. It is our destiny to move out, to accept the challenge, to dare the unknown. It is our destiny to achieve.

Yet we must not forget that along the way to outer space whole industries are springing into being that did not exist before. The computer age has arisen in part from the space effort, which gave great impetus[5] to the development of computing devices. Transistors, chips, integrated circuits, Teflon, new medicines, new ways of treating diseases, new ways of performing operations, all these and a multitude of other developments that enable man to live and to live better are linked to the space effort. Most of these developments have been so <u>incorporated</u> into our day-to-day life that they are taken for granted, their origin not considered.

If we are content to live in the past, we have no future. And today is the past. ❖

---
4. **carrion.** Dead and decaying flesh
5. **impetus.** Stimulus; force or energy associated with movement

 MIRRORS & WINDOWS Do you agree with L'Amour's viewpoint? Should humanity be trying to explore space? Why do you think exploration has been such a consistent part of human life for so long?

294

English Language Learning
Explain that when L'Amour began writing, it was traditional to use masculine forms (such as *mankind, mind/spirit of man*) to describe people in general. Today writers try to avoid such "gendered" language. Have students think of "nongendered" equivalents to L'Amour's choices (such as *humankind* or *humanity, human mind/spirit.*)

Kinesthetic Learning
Hold a debate. Divide the class into three groups: one to argue for L'Amour's stance, one to argue against, and one to judge the debate. Have students prepare; students in the judging group should come up with probing questions to ask the debaters. Have each team present its argument; allow the judges to ask questions and deliberate before announcing the winning team.

Find Meaning

1. (a) What does Louis L'Amour think is "today's" frontier? (b) Why does he describe the moon, asteroids, and planets as stepping stones?

2. Why does L'Amour include the comparison between the number of paved roads in the United States in 1900 and the number of paved roads now?

Analyze Literature

Persuasive Essay What is Louis L'Amour's attitude, or bias, about the topic of this essay? Use a chart to list appeals to logic and appeals to emotion that he uses to persuade readers to agree with his viewpoint. Which appeals are most effective? Which are least effective?

Appeals to Logic	Appeals to Emotion
The developments of the past seventy years show how quickly we can make progress.	Nay-sayers are like babies clinging to their mothers.

Make Judgments

3. When L'Amour recounts the achievements of the moon landing, how does his use of words, phrases, and repetition reveal his opinion of these efforts?

4. Why does L'Amour include a list of the space program's accomplishments?

5. L'Amour says, "If we are content to live in the past, we have no future. And today is the past." What does he mean by this statement?

Extend Understanding

Writing Options

Creative Writing Imagine that you are a member of the first colony on Mars. Write a **personal letter** to your family describing your experiences. Include some comparisons between life on Mars and life on Earth. Use sensory details and precise language when describing life on Mars.

Expository Writing Imagine that you are an editor putting together an anthology, or collection, of essays and articles about space exploration. Write a **literary response** to "The Eternal Frontier" in which you evaluate the overall effectiveness of this essay. Explain why you will or will not include the essay in your collection.

Collaborative Learning

Identify Facts, Opinions, and Commonplace

Assertions *Factual claims* are statements that can be proven, *opinions* are statements that express attitudes or desires, and *commonplace assertions* are claims that are generally considered true. In a small group, complete a three-column chart listing facts, opinions, and commonplace assertions from "The Eternal Frontier." Then read a scientific essay, news article, encyclopedia entry, or other informative text about outer space and complete a fact / opinion / commonplace assertion chart for it.

Media Literacy

Evaluate Media Reports on Space Identify several different websites, newspapers, or magazines that make predictions about the future of space travel. Which is the most persuasive? Why?

Go to www.mirrorsandwindows.com for more.

THE ETERNAL FRONTIER **295**

Find Meaning

1. (a) He thinks it is space. (b) He thinks that exploring them is just preparation for exploring the far reaches of the solar system.

2. He is implying that we can make similar rapid progress in space travel.

Make Judgments

3. His words and phrases reveal that his opinion is high.

4. He is claiming that the space program has a positive effect on our economy, health, and way of life.

5. We must constantly plan for the future and think about new ways of doing things; we cannot progress if we cling to the past or to the present.

Analyze Literature

Persuasive Essay *Answers:* Students' opinions about which appeals are most effective will vary. Appeals to logic include: The developments of the past seventy years show how quickly we can make progress; we have already started to explore outer space; space exploration gives rise to new inventions and industries. Appeals to emotion include: Nay-sayers are like babies clinging to their mothers; "Mankind is not bound . . . nor is the mind of man bound by any limits at all"; "It is our destiny to move out, to accept the challenge, to dare the unknown."

Rubrics for Writing Options

You can adapt this as a checklist for students to use as they write.

Creative Writing

☐ Does the student use the correct format for a personal letter?

☐ Does the letter include descriptions of experiences?

☐ Does the letter include comparisons between Mars and Earth?

Expository Writing

☐ Does the response evaluate the overall effectiveness of the essay?

☐ Does the response provide examples to support the evaluations?

☐ Does the response explain why the essay will or will not be included in the anthology?

Program Resources

For further instruction, refer students to the following extension activity: Collaborative Learning: Identify Facts and Opinions, *Exceeding the Standards: Extension Activities*, p. 8.

Teach the Workshop

Identifying Sentence Types

1. Why should we explore space, when Earth is our home? (interrogative)

2. If we do not travel to the frontiers, we will betray ourselves. (declarative)

3. Wouldn't humanity still be trapped in the Dark Ages if it hadn't embraced exploration? (interrogative)

4. Explore new frontiers. (imperative or, with exclamation mark, exclamatory)

5. Space exploration is the only path that is open to humanity. (declarative)

> For more information, see Grammar & Style Section 3.1, The Sentence, in the Language Arts Handbook.

Program Resources

You will find additional lessons on Sentence Types in the *Exceeding the Standards: Grammar & Style* resource.

KEY TERMS

DECLARATIVE SENTENCE, 296
PERIOD, 296
IMPERATIVE SENTENCE, 296
INTERROGATIVE SENTENCE, 296
QUESTION MARK, 296
EXCLAMATORY SENTENCE, 296
EXCLAMATION POINT, 296
PUNCTUATION, 296

Sentence Types

Sentence Variety

"Where is the frontier now?"
The answer should be obvious.

—LOUIS L'AMOUR, "The Eternal Frontier"

Varying your sentences can make your writing more enjoyable to read. You can introduce variety by changing the lengths of your sentences and by using different grammatical constructions. Another method is the use of different sentence types. In the above quotation, the writer asks a question and makes a statement. Questions and statements are two different types of sentences. There are four main types: the declarative, the imperative, the interrogative, and the exclamatory sentence.

Declarative and Imperative Sentences

A **declarative sentence** makes a statement and ends with a period. The declarative is the most common kind of sentence.

> EXAMPLES
>
> *Space travel is important to the future of humanity.*
>
> *There will always be new frontiers.*

An **imperative sentence** gives a command or makes a request. These kinds of sentences frequently appear in dialogue. Often, the understood subject of these sentences is *you*.

> EXAMPLES
>
> *Do not allow yourself to be lulled into a sense of satisfaction.*
>
> *Travel to the moon, to the other planets, and then to the edge of the solar system.*

Interrogative and Exclamatory Sentences

An **interrogative sentence** asks a question. Interrogative sentences always end in question marks.

> EXAMPLES
>
> *What is the future of humanity, if not in space?*
>
> *How can people deny the importance of exploration?*

An **exclamatory sentence** expresses a strong feeling and ends with an exclamation point. Be careful when using exclamatory sentences and the exclamation point; both are frequently overused.

> EXAMPLE
>
> *We must explore space, now!*

Identifying Sentence Types

On a separate sheet of paper, rewrite these sentences with correct end punctuation—a period, question mark, or exclamation point. Next to each sentence, write what kind of sentence it is.

1. Why should we explore space, when Earth is our home

2. If we do not travel to the frontiers, we will betray ourselves

3. Wouldn't humanity still be trapped in the Dark Ages if it hadn't embraced exploration

4. Explore new frontiers

5. Space exploration is the only path that is open to humanity

Differentiated Instruction

English Language Learning

English language learners will benefit from writing and speaking using a variety of sentence types. Students may practice reading the examples of the workshop aloud or they could create a variety of new sentences to read aloud to the class.

Common Core State Standards

Language
L.1, L.4.1f, L.6.3a

TEACHING NOTE

Extra Practice

Write these sentences on the board. Have students tell you how to revise them to create the type of sentence indicated in parentheses.

1. You have to read all those library books. (interrogative; Have you read all those library books?)

2. Let's get going. (exclamatory; Let's go!)

3. Will you please get busy doing your homework? (imperative; Get busy doing your homework.)

4. Javier, come here. (interrogative; Javier, would you come here?)

5. They must have seen us coming! (declarative; They must have seen us coming.)

from OFF THE COURT

An Autobiography by Arthur Ashe

Build Background

Historical Context From its earliest days, tennis was a sport played mostly by Britain's wealthiest people. As tennis took hold in the United States, private country clubs became the exclusive sites of play. Membership rules at these clubs automatically excluded blacks. In the 1940s and 1950s, when Arthur Ashe was a young boy eager to join the sport, African-American tennis players could only play on courts in black sections of town and were kept out of tournaments in which white athletes played.

Reader's Context Have you ever come face to face with discrimination of any type? How did you handle the situation?

Set Purpose

Use Build Background, the story title, and the first paragraph to preview the excerpt from *Off the Court.* Based on your preview, what do you predict the autobiography will focus on?

Analyze Literature

Description Writing that portrays a character, action, object, or scene is called **description.** Many descriptions use **sensory details,** words and phrases that describe how things look, sound, smell, taste, or feel. As you read the excerpt from *Off the Court,* be aware of how Ashe uses sensory details to bring the reader into his story.

Meet the Author

Arthur Ashe was born in 1943 in Richmond, Virginia, and eventually became one of the top junior players in the nation. After college, he won the U.S. Open, and in 1975 he won both the Wimbledon and World Championship Tennis men's singles titles. He died in 1993 of AIDS, contracted from a blood transfusion after open-heart surgery. Arthur Ashe Stadium was dedicated in Flushing Meadows, New York, in 1996, and in 2005, the U.S. Postal Service issued a stamp honoring Ashe.

Use Reading Skills

Identify Main Idea The main idea in a piece of nonfiction is often not stated directly. You can use a main idea map to help you find the main idea. Collect the details from the text, and then use these details to determine the main idea of a selection.

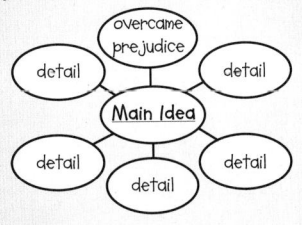

Preview Vocabulary

phys•i•o•log•i•cal•ly (fĭ' zē ə lä' ji k[ə]lē) *adv.*, relating to bodily function

dom•i•nant (dä' mə nənt) *adj.*, having the most control or influence

im•passe (im' pas') *n.*, situation with no escape

re•press (ri pres') *v.*, hold in by self-control

re•buff (ri bəf') *n.*, refusal to meet an advance or offer

At a Glance
Directed Reading
- Reading Level: Challenging
- Difficulty Considerations: Length and vocabulary
- Ease Factor: Style

Objectives
Studying this lesson will enable students to
- use reading skills such as analyzing the author's perspective
- define *description* and understand how sensory detail contributes to description
- define the athletic and literary accomplishments of Arthur Ashe
- gain understanding of the discrimination African Americans often experienced during the 1960s and of the mindset required to succeed in professional sports

Launch the Lesson
Prior to reading the excerpt from Arthur Ashe's autobiography *Off the Court,* ask students to think about their own goals in life. How hard would they fight for them? What if people said they *couldn't* do what they want to? Ask students to consider, as they read, how Ashe's determination to succeed might inspire them in their own endeavors.

Words in Use

Preview Vocabulary
physiologically, 299
dominant, 300
impasse, 303
repress, 304
rebuff, 305

Selection Words
niche, 299
torque, 300
deity, 301
innuendoes, 305
assimilate, 309

Teaching Words
contracted, 297
transfusion, 297
camaraderie, 309

KEY TERMS
AUTOBIOGRAPHY, 297
DESCRIPTION, 297
SENSORY DETAIL, 297
PHRASE, 297
MAIN IDEA, 297
NONFICTION, 297
EDITORIAL, 310
DIALOGUE, 311
BIOGRAPHICAL SKETCH, 311

Common Core State Standards
Reading Literature
RL.2

Reading Informational
RI.3, RI.8

Summary

Ashe opens by explaining why he was physically better suited to tennis than to other sports. He describes how he began taking tennis lessons. As he improves at tennis, Ashe stays interested in other sports, especially baseball, and has several boyhood heroes. At ten, he is discovered by R. W. Johnson, a coach working to train black players to compete at the national level. Ashe describes his progress under Johnson and his first years of tournament play.

At seventeen Ashe moves to St. Louis for his senior year, so he can train through the winter. He makes progress that year as an athlete, a student, and personally—"I came out of my shell." That November, after winning his first title, he is offered a scholarship to UCLA and accepts.

Ashe ends by discussing the discrimination he experienced as he worked to overcome "assumptions of inequality." He notes that he received support from his own community, but not from the white people in his hometown.

The Mirrors & Windows questions at the end of the selection focus on the theme of overcoming discrimination. Before students begin reading, ask: How do individuals learn to stand up for themselves?

from

OFF THE COURT

An Autobiography by Arthur Ashe

Arthur Ashe in 1968 during the Wimbledon Tennis Tournament in London, England.

298

Program Resources

Planning and Assessment
Program Planning Guide, Selection Lesson Plan
E-Lesson Planner
Assessment Guide, Lesson Test
ExamView

Technology Tools
Interactive Student Text on CD
Visual Teaching Package
Audio Library
mirrorsandwindows.com

Meeting the Standards
Nonfiction: Unit 3, Directed Reading, pp. 47–52

Differentiating Instruction
Developing Readers, Take Notes, pp. 25–27

I WAS TOO SMALL FOR ANY SPORT BUT TENNIS.

You can't compare tennis with baseball, basketball, or football. When Jackie Robinson broke the color line in 1947 with the Brooklyn Dodgers, dozens of good baseball players in the Negro leagues were waiting to follow. When Althea Gibson, the first prominent black in tennis, won national grass-court titles at Forest Hills in 1957 and 1958, there was no reservoir of black talent waiting to walk in if the door ever opened. Blacks had no identification with the sport— on or off the court. Tennis is a difficult game to learn. Very difficult. You have to be a generalist. You can't be a specialist and excel in tennis. You have to become adept in about four or five different sets of exercises, none of which are the same. Physiologically, serving a tennis ball is nothing like hitting a forehand; they're two completely different actions. Hitting a volley is not like hitting an overhead;[1] they too are two completely different functions. You must learn how to do all of them.

I was too small for any sport but tennis. I learned to swim when I was very young, but I was always a bit afraid of water, even if there was no way to avoid Brook Pool on my doorstep. My father wouldn't let me play football because of my size, which was a disappointment, so I tried to make up for it by working harder in other activities. When I wasn't sitting on the front porch of our house buried in a book, I played baseball, basketball, and tennis.

The four tennis courts just outside our side door were used fairly regularly by a handful of black people in Richmond. The all-black Richmond Racquet Club used Brook Field as its home base. As I grew increasingly sensitive to matters of race and color, I noticed that most of the black tennis players came from the educated, well-to-do segment of our community—principals, doctors, dentists, and lawyers. As a seven-year-old trying to find his niche in a complex, segregated society, I found that significant.

The students at Virginia Union also made good use of the courts in the spring. Their campus was just beyond Brook Field and they had just two courts of their own. They practiced at the playground and played teams from other colleges. Ron Charity spent more time on the courts than anyone else. For hours and hours, he hit balls against the wall or served to an empty court. Even my untrained eye could see an unusual grace in his swing, an agility that surpassed most of his opponents.

I watched him play against another school one afternoon. He dominated his opponent and won. His name was whispered around the gaggle of girlfriends, relatives, tennis buffs, and curious bystanders who drifted over from the football fields, baseball diamonds, and basketball courts. Ron Charity, they said, was one of the best black players in the country. I was properly impressed.

The next afternoon, he was out on the courts again, working on his serve. I watched for a while. Finally, he noticed me for the first time.

"What's your name?"

"Arthur Ashe, Junior."

"Your dad runs the playground?"

"Yes, sir."

He nodded and went back to his serve. His wooden racquet flashed high above his head in the late afternoon sun and sliced through the silence. White balls rocketed to

---

1. overhead. Stroke made above the height of the head

---

phys·i·o·log·i·cal·ly (fĭ' zē ə lä´ ji k[ə] lē) *adv.*, relating to bodily function

---

Make Connections

Ask students to pay attention to Ashe's assessment of his strengths and weaknesses. Have them think about something that they do well themselves. What are their own strengths and weaknesses in that area? How can they make the best use of their strengths to minimize the effects of their weaknesses?

TEACHING NOTE

Visualize

To help students visualize what Ashe is describing, it may be helpful for them to watch a portion of a tennis match (live or recorded). Ask them to discuss their reactions to the sport. What makes it exciting? What makes it challenging? Does watching the game help to clarify what Ashe is saying about tennis?

the corners of the opposing court. After a while, he stopped and looked at me again.

"You play tennis?"

I shrugged. I had batted some old tennis balls around with the twelve-dollar nylon-strung racquet that had found its way into the wooden equipment box under my bedroom window.

"You want to learn?"

I nodded. At that age, any sport was a challenge I felt I could master. "You got a racquet. Go get it," he said.

Ron Charity was a patient teacher with an understanding of my strengths and limitations. I weighed about fifty pounds. To get a tennis ball across the net and seventy-eight feet down court with a twenty-seven-inch racquet required a firm grip to withstand the torque from off-center hits.

Ron had me use an Eastern forehand grip, like shaking hands with my racquet. This is the best grip for beginners for three reasons: one, the hand is firmly behind the racquet handle at the moment the ball touches the string—a solid support system; two, it allows the best grip for an all-court attack, either down the line, cross-court, or down the middle; three, as I would learn later, it is a good starting point for future experimentation.

Ron stood on the other side of the net and tossed thousands of balls to me in the year that followed. I concentrated on form, my stroke, and getting the ball over the net. When I was alone and couldn't find someone to hit with me, I played against a backboard. Tennis became something I could do by

myself, like reading a book, and I soon found myself absorbed in workouts without worrying about friends.

Pound for pound, I was a good little athlete—not a Lynn Swann or Kurt Thomas[2]—but someone with agility, speed, coordination, and a will to win. If all those elements could produce timing, I was on my way. Timing is the most important element in tennis. It separates players into different levels. John McEnroe, Ilie Nastase, and Evonne Goolagong have it in spades. They were born with it. Some good players have good timing with their hands but not with their feet. John Newcombe had great hands, but his feet were average. Rod Laver's feet were A+, but his hands rated an "A." Billie Jean King had great hands and feet. I would rate my hands and feet at the "B" level.

The eyes also play a vital role in timing. People are right-eyed and left-eyed, just as they are right-handed, and left-handed, right-footed and left-footed. When someone focuses on a tennis ball, one eye—and one eye alone—does the focusing. In turning aside during a backswing, the <u>dominant</u> eye can lose contact with the ball momentarily. At 120 miles an hour, a tennis ball can elude the best eyes. From the beginning, I had no trouble waiting for just the right moment. Because of my lack of size and weight, however, I had to develop a semi-lob off the forehand as a form of survival.

> I grew up aware that I was a Negro, colored, black,...and other less flattering terms.

---

2. Lynn Swann or Kurt Thomas. Famous athletes in football and gymnastics, respectively

dom•i•nant (dä′ mə nənt) *adj.,* having the most control or influence

Differentiated Instruction

Reading Proficiency

Students may have difficulty with the tennis terms in the story. Have them read the Before Reading page and footnotes carefully. Tell them that if they run into a term or concept they don't understand, they should try to figure it out from context. If they are unable to do this, they should jot down their question in a notebook and read on. After students have finished the selection, you might have them ask their questions as part of a class discussion and allow other students to help them discover the answers.

I was aware of the limitations of my height and build and soon accepted the fact that basketball and football were not for me. But baseball was a sport that demanded agility and determination rather than bulk or height. The baseball diamond and tennis court became my homes.

Baseball had special meaning for all colored boys because of Jackie Robinson. Joe Louis was still a big name in boxing, but he was finishing up his career and most of us only heard about his days of glory as heavyweight champion from our parents. As soon as the Brooklyn Dodgers signed Jackie Robinson, every black man, woman, and child in America became a Dodger fan. The New York Yankees had a farm club in Richmond, the Braves, but they were not very popular with blacks because they were so slow to integrate. In 1978, George Steinbrenner, the Yankee owner, offered me a job on his staff. We talked about it over a hamburger at P. J.'s, but I had to turn it down.

One of the highlights of my summers was the baseball school run by Maxie Robinson, the father of the present ABC-TV anchorman.[3] Even in those days, summer camps and schools were big; Mr. Robinson was the football, basketball, and track coach at Armstrong High School, highly respected and a disciplinarian like Daddy. Every day from nine to twelve-thirty, he taught baseball fundamentals. Later in the summer, the school took a trip to Washington to see the Senators[4] play. I could have cared less if they won. I was a Dodger fan.

The trip was fun. It also was a reminder of our segregated world. Contradictions between the slogans of democracy and equality and our reality were sharpened in the District of Columbia. We could not go to certain places. Even where we were not

barred, we were not welcome. I grew up aware that I was a Negro, colored, black,... and other less flattering terms.

Heroes also were few—or so I thought. In the South, black heroes who made waves were discouraged. Booker T. Washington was recognized because he stressed self-help and education, and posed no threat to "the natural order of things." Paul Robeson[5] was moderately popular among blacks. His politics, which we didn't fully understand at the time, made us uneasy. Now, he has been elevated to near deity status. Everybody admired Ralph Bunche,[6] especially after he won the Nobel Peace Prize for his Middle East negotiations. George Washington Carver, who made the peanut fashionable long before Jimmy Carter, was highly regarded. I knew about Maggie Walker, president and founder of Consolidated Bank and Trust, Richmond's first black bank. She was the first woman bank president, black or white, in the country.

Like most black children, I held Abe Lincoln in high esteem because I had been taught that he freed the slaves, though for the wrong reasons. My one contemporary white hero was Gene Autry. I liked him because he was the underdog. Roy Rogers was the so-called "king of the cowboys," but Gene Autry was my man. My father took me to see him when I was six years old and I was impressed by the tricks he did with his horse, Champion. Playing cowboys and Indians as a kid, I insisted on being Gene Autry.

Ⓐ

3. **present ABC-TV anchorman.** Max Robinson, the first black network television anchor, died in 1988.
4. **Senators.** There were two baseball teams by this name in Washington, D.C. The first was moved to Minneapolis-St. Paul in 1961 and renamed the Minnesota Twins. The second team was moved to Arlington in 1971 and renamed the Texas Rangers.
5. **Paul Robeson.** (1898–1976) African-American singer and actor
6. **Ralph Bunche.** (1904–1971) Distinguished African-American diplomat with a long career in the United Nations

Teach the Selection

Analyze Literature
Setting Remind students that setting is the time and place in which a story happens. Talk about how Ashe helps establish setting in this paragraph. (Students should recognize that his discussion of the famous people of the day establishes the era of the story, as well as the fact that it takes place in a black community.)

Cultural Connection
Gene Autry Gene Autry (1907–1998) was known as the "Singing Cowboy." He was popular in radio, film, and television and, true to his wholesome, all-American image, served in World War II. Although he might have had a show business rivalry with Roy Rogers (1911–1998), who challenged his position as the country's most popular musical cowboy, the two men were close friends. In 1961, Autry, a lifelong baseball fan, became owner of the Anaheim, California, team. The title of his autobiography, *Back in the Saddle Again*, came from his theme song. Ⓐ

Writing Skills

Topic Sentences
Review topic sentences with students:
- The topic sentence states what a paragraph will be about.
- It also relates to the main idea of the piece.
- Often it appears at the beginning of the paragraph, although it can be anywhere.
- The rest of the paragraph should support the topic sentence.

Have students pick out topic sentences from paragraphs in the selection. Discuss how the other details in the paragraphs relate to the topic sentence and how the topic sentence supports the main idea of the piece.

Use Reading Skills
Analyze Author's Perspective
Note that all writing reflects its author's perspective, or viewpoint. Taking into account word choice can help students analyze this. Challenge students to point out passages that reflect Ashe's perspective and explain how they do this. Model an example: "In describing how he met Dr. Johnson, Ashe uses the first person, but chooses words that express only how he saw the event as a boy—at the time, he didn't know why Johnson was there. This creates the sense that the adults in Ashe's life made decisions that shaped his future." **Ⓐ**

Analyze Literature
Dialogue Remind students that dialogue is conversation presented in writing. Authors usually use it when they want to convey information in a vivid, lifelike way. Note that in this passage, after Ashe uses speaker tags for the first two lines of speech, he presents five lines of dialogue without tags. As long as it is clear who is speaking (as it is here) this technique helps to move the dialogue along quickly and make it seem like a realistic conversation. **Ⓑ**

In the spring of 1954, Virginia Union hosted the Central Intercollegiate Athletic Association Tennis Tournament. The CIAA was an association of black colleges. I was ten and had been taking lessons from Ron Charity for about three years. During a break in the action, I started hitting some balls on the court that was not in use.

"Somebody wants to meet you," Ron said, approaching the court.

I followed him to a table that was under the tree outside the side door of my house. Seated at the table was the tournament director, recording scores and directing players to the proper courts. Dr. R. W. Johnson was five feet ten inches tall, dark-skinned and handsome, with wavy brown hair and a small scar on his upper lip.

"Dr. Johnson," Ron Charity said, "this is Arthur Ashe, Junior."

He shook my hand and looked me over quizzically. "I understand you're ten years old."

"Yes, sir."

"You've been playing three years."

"Yes, sir."

"You like tennis?"

"Yes, sir."

He nodded, asked a few more questions, and dismissed me. I went back to the empty court, but felt him watching me as I played. When I glanced over, he was talking to Ron. Later that day, he talked to my father for a long time.

After the matches, Daddy spoke to me about this Dr. Johnson. "Arthur Junior," he began. I could tell from the form of address that this was to be a serious conversation. "Dr. Johnson works with young tennis players. He'd like you to come down to his place for a couple of weeks in the summer so you can play against other good players every day. You'll also have a chance to travel to some other tournaments."

If the chance to play against other boys had not been enough, the word "travel" would have done it. Here was a chance to explore the world beyond the pages of my old *National Geographics*. I had been to South Hill in the summer and had traveled to Chicago by train with my grandmother. But Dr. Johnson's offer was almost too good to be true. I had no trouble accepting.

Robert Walter Johnson was born in North Carolina, educated at Lincoln University in Pennsylvania, where he was a black All-American running back. He attended Meharry Medical College in Nashville and was a general practitioner[7] in Lynchburg, Virginia. "Dr. J," as we called him, took up tennis to stay in shape and became a major figure in the American Tennis Association, the black equivalent of the USLTA, until his death in 1971. His obsession was the development of good black junior tennis players.

One year, while driving home from Washington, D.C., he saw a huge sign announcing the "USLTA Inter-Scholastic Championship." He parked his car and watched all those white boys in white tennis uniforms competing against each other. He went to the tournament director and asked if any blacks had ever played. After a long discussion the officials agreed they would accept two black finalists from an all-black qualifying event every year. The first year Dr. Johnson brought players, they lost, 6–0, 6–0, in the first round. He was terribly embarrassed but vowed he would produce a player to win that tournament. I won it in 1961.

Dr. Johnson spent most of his days at his office in the Johnson Medical Building on Fifth Street. He would come home after office hours and play tennis, frequently with some of his cronies. Miss Erdice Creecy, his

---
7. **general practitioner.** Family doctor

Differentiated Instruction

English Language Learning
Point out the following vocabulary words and expressions in the selection.
- *broke the color line*—entered a world previously occupied only by white players, 299
- *well-to-do*—wealthy, well-off, 299
- *racquet*—older spelling of *racket*, 299
- *make waves*—cause trouble, 301
- *quizzically*—in a questioning way, 302

- *social graces*—good manners, 305
- *pet phrase*—favorite thing to say, 305
- *street-wise*—tough, knowledgeable about how to handle tricky situations, 307
- *parochial*—literally, having to do with the community that attends a single church; by extension, narrow-minded, limited to one's immediate surroundings, 309

lifelong secretary and private nurse, supervised his office and three-story house on Pierce Street. The basement of the house was equipped with showers, a recreation room, bar, and a shelf full of books on tennis. I read them all. Dr. Johnson had a tennis court behind his house, a rose garden, and a kennel for his hunting dogs.

> **I** *was suddenly exposed to a world of black tennis whose dimensions I had not imagined.*

Almost all our training and practicing was done in the morning and early afternoon so Dr. Johnson could have the court around five o'clock. I spent only two weeks with him that first summer but immediately ran into problems. Ron Charity had been my first teacher, and I patterned my game after him. He had worked for a long time with me on my backhand; I felt I could do anything with it. The key was a very long and early backswing. The ball had to be hit way out in front to allow for as much racquet momentum as possible. My timing on my backhand was very good. But I used a standard backhand grip, and that became the source of my troubles.

Dr. Johnson's son, Bobby, who did a lot of the teaching, wanted to change my backhand the first day I was in Lynchburg.

"Mr. Charity showed me the other way," I protested. I didn't want to change my grip. I felt I could hit all day and not miss.

"I'm your teacher now and I want to change it," Bobby said firmly. I stood my ground.

"Well, if you want Ron Charity to teach you," Bobby said, "why don't you go home?"

We had reached an <u>impasse</u>. Dr. Johnson called my father. Two hours later, the blue Ford screeched to a stop in the driveway. Daddy listened to the explanations of the problem. He turned to me. "Dr. Johnson is teaching you now, Arthur Junior. You do what they say." Daddy then got in his car and drove back to Richmond. **C**

It was that simple. I always obeyed my father. They had no more trouble with me. But to tell the truth, I didn't really change the grip on my backhand that much.

During those two weeks, Dr. Johnson took me to two tournaments, the Southeastern ATA in Durham, North Carolina, and the Mall Tennis Club tournament in Washington. I was suddenly exposed to a world of black tennis whose dimensions I had not imagined. There was black tennis in virtually every major city along the East Coast and in the South, the Midwest, and California.

Because I was the youngest player at Dr. Johnson's, I had the dirtiest jobs. I cleaned his doghouse and weeded his rose gardens. Yet I had acquired these skills from my father, who often had a dozen dogs around Brook Field. I swept sidewalks, made beds, washed dishes, and rolled the tennis court. I didn't enjoy these things, but I understood this as my way of paying back, so I did those chores as quickly as I could.

I also had to use the court when nobody else wanted it so the backboard became my challenge. Sometimes the neighbors would complain about my pounding the backboard at 7 a.m. But by the time breakfast came around, I had put in a good forty-five minutes on the board. Those sessions were fantasy times. I imagined that I was Pancho

---

im·passe (im´ pas´) *n.*, situation with no escape

Teach the Selection

Analyze Literature
Characterization Have students reread the anecdote about the disagreement Ashe had with Bobby about his backhand. Point out that the story reveals a great deal about Ashe's character, and have students explain why this is so. Students should note that even though Ashe responded obediently to his father, he confides that he did not really change his backhand. The story shows him to be determined, self-confident, and stubborn, as well as respectful to authority figures. **C**

Grammar Skills

Single and Compound Predicates
Remind students that a predicate is the main verb in a sentence. The simplest sentence consists of a single subject and a single predicate: "<u>I</u> | <u>stood</u> my ground." A sentence with a compound predicate has more than one main verb that relates to the same subject: "<u>Daddy</u> | then <u>got</u> in his car and <u>drove</u> back to Richmond."

Have students identify sentences from the selection that have single predicates and sentences that have compound predicates. Ask them to write the sentences on the board, underlining subjects once and predicates twice. Make sure students understand that in a compound predicates, all verbs share one subject.

Segregation The events Ashe describes are happening at a turbulent time in the South. Segregation, the legally mandated separation of the races in many aspects of life, is still in full effect, so Ashe and his peers must learn ways to cope with the system. The next year, 1954, one of the first steps in the long, difficult process of ending segregation will take place. In the case of *Brown v. Board of Education* the Supreme Court will decide that it is unconstitutional for schools to be segregated.

Gonzales[8] or another famous tennis player in a critical situation, at deuce, set point, match point.[9] In practices, Bobby Johnson would make us run patterns. We had to hit so many down the line, so many cross-court, maybe a cross-court then a down-the-line, come to the net and put away the volley. We had daily contests: who could hit the most forehands without an error, the most forehand returns of serve, deep forehand shots, forehand approach shots, forehand passing shots. Then we ran through the whole series for the backhand.

I noticed early that I had more endurance than the older boys. I was smaller, couldn't hit as hard or serve as fast, but I could last longer. So I would try to go as long as I could in the practice sessions and against the backboard without missing. I also began to learn the standard tennis principles: on

approach shots, go down the line, not cross-court; no drop shots from the baseline; when in doubt, hit a semi-lob deep down the middle; get 70 percent of your first serves in.

There were also maxims meant only for little black Southern boys: when in doubt, call your opponent's shot good; if you're serving the game before the change of ends, pick up the balls on your side and hand them to your opponent during the crossover. Dr. Johnson knew we were going into territory that was often hostile and he wanted our behavior to be beyond reproach. It would be years before I understood the emotional toll of repressing anger and natural frustration.

---

8. Pancho Gonzales. (1928–1995) Mexican-American tennis player
9. deuce, set point, match point. Scores in a tennis match

re·press (ri pres´) *v.,* hold in by self-control

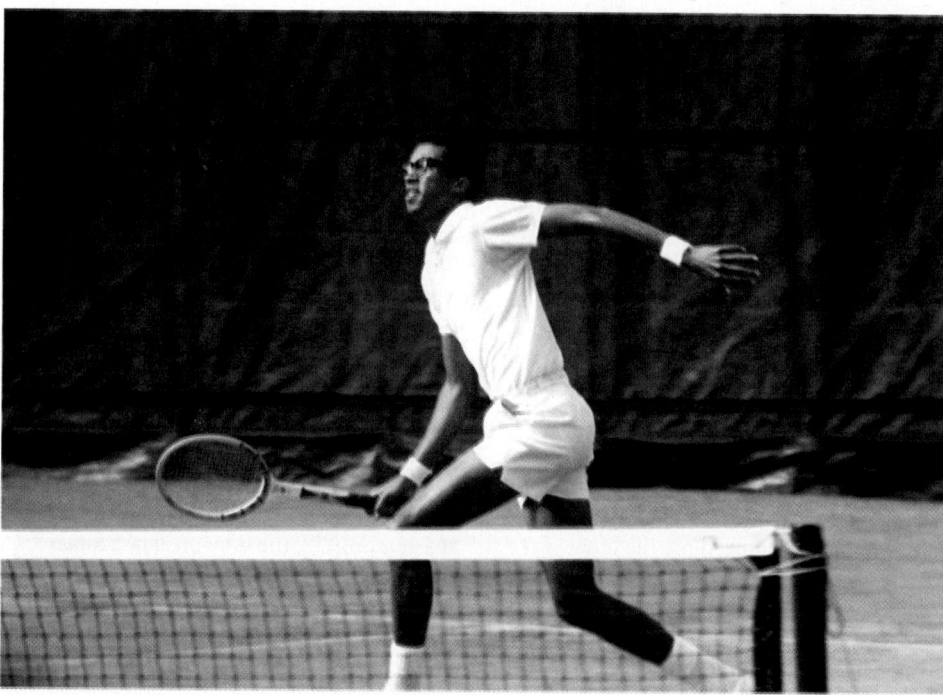

Arthur Ashe playing against Rod Laver of Australia during the 1968 Wimbledon Tennis Tournament.

Enrichment
Students may be curious about the historical figures and other contemporary references throughout Ashe's text. To enrich their understanding of the reading, have students work together to compile a list of the historical figures and topics mentioned. Have each student choose a topic from the list (avoiding duplication) and research it further before presenting findings to the class.

That summer of '53 was symbolic because it marked the first steps on the road from Richmond. In subsequent years, traveling with Ron Charity and others stressed the importance of camaraderie. Blacks could not eat in restaurants, so we brought our fried chicken, potato salad, and rolls in bags and passed the Thermos around the car. Spending weekends as a guest in someone's house taught me more about social graces than I could have ever learned elsewhere.

I also learned on the court. During a tournament at Barraud Park in Norfolk, I had won the first set against another boy my age and was leading in the second when I started feeling sorry for him. It happens all the time among club players, but not on the prize-money tour anymore. I decided to let my opponent win a few games by making a few intentional errors. I lost the second set, was down, 2–0, in the third, and then began to panic. I tried to come back, but the more I pressed, the more mistakes I made. I lost the third set—and the match. My opponent was elated; I was in tears, angry at myself. It was an important lesson. There would be other occasions when I felt sorry for someone, but I never again let such sympathies affect my game...

My first seventeen years set the stage for the way I view the world. I grew up as an underdog, so I rent from Avis instead of Hertz now. As I played more and more against white juniors, I realized I was fighting assumptions about black inferiorities. Dr. Johnson tried to combat our insecurities by making "the white boys" the ultimate opponent.

"You're not going to beat those white boys playing like that," he would say. "Hit that to a white boy and you'll go home early," was another of his pet phrases.

Knowing that I would not be admitted to certain tournaments protected me from direct rebuffs. O. H. Parrish and some others I played against were terrific guys—period. Some others were too well-mannered to express racism crudely. No player ever refused to appear on court with me. No official ever called me a name. But the indirect rebuffs and innuendoes left their scars.

> I noticed early that I had more endurance than the older boys.

(A) The same year that I beat O. H. in the Middle Atlantic Juniors, some kids ransacked the log cabins where we had been housed for the tournament. Officials tried to place the blame on me and phoned Dr. Johnson. **(B)**

"What do you know about this?" he asked, after I had returned to Lynchburg.

"I don't know anything about it," I said, nervous that I was being implicated and that my future tennis travel could be in jeopardy. "Honest—I don't, Dr. Johnson."

"I believe you, Arthur," he said. "They said they're just investigating, but I wanted to be sure."

Not all of my encounters were harsh. During the National Interscholastics in Charlottesville in 1960, Butch Newman, Cliff Buchholz, and Charlie Pasarell asked me to join them at a movie. I turned them down because I knew I wouldn't get in—but the

re·buff (ri bəf´) n., refusal to meet an advance or offer

Use Reading Skills
Identify Cause and Effect Remind students that in a narrative, sometimes the author explains *why* something happens. Note that a cause can have more than one effect. Have students consider Ashe's story of this match. In this sequence of events, what is the cause? (Ashe feels sorry for his opponent.) What are the effects? (He decides to let the boy win a few games; the boy begins to win on his own; Ashe panics and plays worse; Ashe loses; he learns never to give in to sympathy.) **(A)**

Use Reading Skills
Identify Sequence of Events Remind students that for the most part, narratives are presented in chronological order. However, that doesn't mean events are presented day by day or year by year. In telling his story, Ashe sometimes refers to things that happened before or that would follow. To keep readers oriented, he must use verbal cues. This paragraph orients readers by explaining that he's about to describe something that happened "the same year that I beat O. H." A few paragraphs later, he specifies that he is talking about events in 1960. **(B)**

Reading Skills

Take Notes

Point out to students that a time line is a very effective graphic organizer for taking notes on an autobiographical reading. It will help them remember more and keep the sequence of events straight in their minds. To expand on the idea, after students have taken reading notes in time-line format, have them form small groups to create an illustrated time line for display.

Students can use their own notes, the supplemental information in their texts, and additional research about Ashe's life and the state of Civil Rights at that time. Provide poster board or butcher paper so students can present their work large scale, and display the finished time lines in the classroom.

Make Connections

Discuss Ashe's anecdote about the friends who try to go to the movies with him and leave when he is not admitted. How would students characterize the friends' actions? What would they have done in those circumstances? What else would they do to support a friend? **A**

guys wouldn't take no for an answer. When we got to the theater, the reaction was predictable.

A "You can't go in," the woman in the ticket booth said. I wasn't surprised by her statement. But I was slightly elated when Cliff said, "Well, if he can't go in, none of us will go." And all of us left.

> *I won more than my share of matches by out-thinking opponents.*

That summer, Daddy and Dr. Johnson faced their own decision. I had won a number of important regional titles and was ranked among the top junior players in the country. Ever the realist, Daddy knew there were few opportunities for a tennis player to make a living from his sport (this was in the days before open tennis). He knew the obstacles I would face as a black tennis player; yet he felt obliged to give me, as the best young black to come along since Althea Gibson, an opportunity to go as far as I could. My peers, the juniors who had become my friends in many cases, would continue to progress, and the Californians could play all year. To keep up with them, I had to be able to play winter tennis. And there were no such opportunities in Richmond.

The solution was to spend my senior year in high school in St. Louis, Missouri, at the home of Richard Hudlin, a good friend of Dr. Johnson and another tennis buff. The move was practical because each summer I had roamed farther and farther away from home. St. Louis would be the final break with Richmond.

Everybody goes through stages in life when they wish they could change things about themselves or their circumstances. As a sophomore at Maggie Walker, I had made the varsity baseball team and pitched one inning in our first game that spring. The next morning J. Harry Williams, the principal, called me into his office.

"Arthur Junior," he said bluntly. "I'm kicking you off the baseball team."

I was stunned. "Why, Mr. Williams?"

"Arthur, you've got a great future ahead of you as a tennis player. You've gone further than any other black male, and I don't want to risk you getting hurt."

I was deeply disappointed. But the loss was tempered by his acknowledgement that there was something special about my tennis. Spending my senior year in St. Louis gave me the chance not only to change my tennis game but also my personality.

I was always rather shy and studious. I was good in tennis and baseball, but socially I was shy. I came out of my shell in St. Louis, partly because they made such a fuss over me and nobody knew anything about me. I could be a different person, and nobody would ever know the difference. After growing up in a community where everybody knew who I was, either because of my father or because of my tennis, I could be anything I wanted in St. Louis. Because I had a straight-A average and had already taken subjects in Richmond as a junior that were being taught only to seniors at Sumner High School, I was often allowed to study on my own.

It amazed me that I had a higher GPA than anybody else in the school. I would have been valedictorian of my senior class at Sumner, with the highest grade-point average, except that I had been in school only one year and didn't qualify. Still, grades aren't everything.

TEACHING NOTE

Ask the Author

Have students imagine that they are going to have the chance to interview Arthur Ashe. Ask them to review the reading, make a list of the questions they would like to ask him, and then write one or two of the questions that interest them most on a slip of paper. Model a question: "Would you like to be competing against today's pros?" Choose slips of paper and read the questions aloud to the

class. How do students think Ashe would have responded? Why?

To expand on the exercise, before reading the questions show students footage from an interview or documentary featuring Arthur Ashe (such as the 1994 HBO documentary *Arthur Ashe: Citizen of the World*).

St. Louis was north of the Mason-Dixon Line, so I thought Sumner would have white students. The city had an integrated school system, but Sumner was in an all-black **B** neighborhood. It was a different sort of neighborhood from Richmond's North Side. The kids were more street-wise, and you had to be tougher to survive. There were more kids in the school, and you didn't get that feeling of community that you did at Maggie Walker. People helped one another out in Richmond, even though there was an unwritten feeling that blacks in the public schools in the South were inferior.

Separate-but-equal was the house line for defending dual school systems in Virginia then. It was really separate and unequal. Many black teachers in the southern public schools had only bachelor's degrees. The amount of public money spent on the black schools per pupil was obviously less than the amount of money spent on the white schools per pupil. Many job opportunities were just closed to blacks, so the curriculum at black public schools was often geared toward the jobs that a black graduate could expect to find when he or she graduated, which wasn't very much. You could drive a truck, teach, become a doctor, lawyer, or undertaker; the best blue-collar job was considered that of a mailman.

Mr. Hudlin, his wife, and their son welcomed me into their home. Mr. Hudlin was a teacher at Sumner and his wife Jane was a registered nurse. Mr. Hudlin had been the captain of the tennis team at the University of Chicago in 1924 and had a tennis court in the backyard of his home.

His son, Dickie, was a ninth-grader, and we got along fairly well. But I think there was an element of jealousy because of the attention my tennis got from his father. Ironically, Mr. Hudlin wanted nothing more than to have his son become a great player, but Dickie just hated tennis.

My game had evolved considerably from the deep lob that was my main weapon at age seven. Aware that junior tennis depended heavily on consistency, Dr.

Arthur Ashe holds the Wimbledon Gentlemen's Singles Trophy in 1975.

Johnson's plan for my development concentrated on ground strokes. This theory was a serious mistake—but fortunately, one that was correctable.

Dr. J's court at home was clay and few clay-court players, especially juniors, venture **C** to the net. He saw tennis as a game of ground strokes and sound strategy. He believed that a smart player with average strokes could out-think and beat players with better strokes and poor strategy. Up to a point, he was right, and I won more than my share of matches by out-thinking opponents.

OFF THE COURT **307**

Teach the Selection

Analyze Literature

Description Remind students that description portrays a character, object, or scene. Ask students to review this passage, paying attention to how Ashe compares and contrasts St. Louis and Richmond. Have them create a two-column chart, with one column labeled *St. Louis* and the other labeled *Richmond,* and record details about each city. **B**

Science Connection

Tennis Courts Explain that there are three basic types of tennis courts, made of different materials, that affect the game differently.

- hard court—a surface of concrete or other hard, solid material
- grass court—short-mowed grass on packed earth
- clay court—crushed claylike material (originally natural clay, but now often brick, rock, or synthetic)

Clay courts are considered "slower" than other surfaces because balls lose speed when they hit the ground and bounce higher; players have more time to get to them. Hard courts are "faster" because the ball bounces less and keeps moving fast after striking the ground. Grass is the "fastest," because the ball bounces the least and the uneven grass may cause the ball to go in an unexpected direction; players must be very quick to get in position for the return shot. **C**

Research Skills

Key Word Searches

Remind students that the key words they use in computer searches will affect the relevancy of their results. State good practices for key word searches, such as:

- Make sure the spelling is accurate. If a misspelling does return results, the results are not likely to be reliable (since reliable sites should not contain spelling errors).

- Be specific. Searching for *dogs* will return far too many results. Adding more words can help—say, *poodles* and *intelligence.*
- Use "advanced search" for greater precision. Many search engines provide a form of advanced search, which allows users to restrict a search in various ways, for example to a range of dates.

History Connection

African-American Tennis Stars A number of top-ranked tennis players in the United States today are black. They include James Blake (b. 1979), who is consistently ranked among the top ten men's players in the world. Women include the sisters Venus Williams (b. 1980) and Serena Williams (b. 1981), Ahsha Rolle (b. 1985), and Jamea Jackson (b. 1986).

But the appearance of California players, with their upbringing on faster hard courts and the serve-and-volley power game, forced a change in my style. At age sixteen, I had to learn to volley in a hurry and make the jump to the eighteen-and-unders. But once I got to St. Louis, I practiced every day at the St. Louis Armory, on a wooden floor. A wooden floor is fast and slick, balls skid off the floor and accelerate after they bounce. I had to shorten my backswing to play well. With my old round-house backswing, the ball would have been in the back fence before I started moving my racquet forward.

A fast wooden floor also gives a player a false sense of confidence about his serve. Even an average serve seems formidable when it skids off a slick floor. It could have lulled me into accepting the shortcomings on my serve, but Mr. Hudlin and Larry Miller, a white pro, told me to lean forward and put more muscle into my service motion.

I started to return serve differently. Usually, I would stand just behind the baseline and wait for the ball. Now I dropped back a yard and a half or so and charged the ball when my opponent served. I had never been comfortable charging the ball because of my clay-court background, but with my new aggressiveness, I developed new techniques to catch the ball on the rise. In the course of some weight-shifting drills suggested by Larry, I developed a topspin backhand, which worked very well for moving the ball cross-court as I charged forward.

I also changed my grip from the Eastern to the Continental. It is a less secure way of holding the racquet for the forehand, but it allows you to hit everything—forehand, backhand, volley[10] or serve—with the same grip. The disadvantage is that flat forehands are very difficult to hit with this grip. I began to observe my opponents' grips to figure out what they could and could not do.

In November 1960 I won my first USLTA national title, the National Junior Indoors. At Christmas, on the way back to St. Louis from the Orange Bowl Juniors in Miami Beach, I stopped off in Richmond to visit my family. While I was at home, I got a telephone call one afternoon.

"Arthur, this is J. D. Morgan," the voice on the telephone said. There was a pause. "I'm the tennis coach at UCLA. We're preparing to offer you a scholarship to come out and play for us."

You could have knocked me over with a feather. I was thrilled beyond belief. I said yes even before he finished his offer. I had no idea that UCLA had any interest in me. I would get offers from Michigan, Michigan State, Arizona, and Hampton Institute later, but every junior player knew that UCLA and USC were the schools for tennis.

My father understood my elation but did not understand the significance of UCLA. He supported my decision to go to California, although he was clearly upset at having me move still farther away from the family.

Mr. Hudlin also realized the importance of my UCLA scholarship, and Dr. Johnson was as thrilled as I was. My senior year capped my long career as a junior player. After fulfilling Dr. Johnson's dream of producing a winner in the Interscholastics, I reached the semifinals of the National Jaycees and the National Juniors. By graduation, I was the fifth-ranked junior in the country and a member of the Junior Davis Cup team that traveled together that summer.

Of course, there was a great deal of fuss about being the "first black" Junior Davis Cup player, the "first black" to get a tennis scholarship to UCLA, the "first black" to win at Charlottesville, etc. Those comments

---

10. volley. Return of a ball before it touches the ground

Reading Proficiency

Less-confident readers may benefit from discussing Ashe's closing thoughts. To help students explore the implications of his statements, ask them to paraphrase—or express in their own words—the meaning of selected sentences. Model an example: Original: "The fact that this kind of accomplishment by a black player got so much attention was an indication that we still had so far to go."

Paraphrase: "A great performance by a black athlete should have been as normal as a great performance by a white one. The fact that it caused such a fuss showed how much work was still needed to convince people that blacks were equal."

always put me under pressure to justify my accomplishments on racial grounds, as if sports were the cutting edge of our nation's move toward improved race relations. The fact that this kind of accomplishment by a black player got so much attention was an indication that we still had so far to go.

The questions asked in 1960 and 1961 served to remind me of my isolated status in tennis. I played in clubs where the only blacks were waiters, gardeners, and busboys. I knew there was apprehension in some circles about my presence, but I was not about to embarrass myself or anybody else. I was polite, fairly well educated, and I knew which fork to use because I had done some catering with my father.

I was moved into the world of tennis that had little in common with the black experience. The game had a history and tradition I was expected to assimilate, but much of that history and many of those traditions were hostile to me. When I decided to leave Richmond, I left all that Richmond stood for at the time—its segregation, its conservatism, its parochial[11] thinking, its slow progress toward equality, its lack of opportunity for talented black people. I had no intention then of coming back. And I really never would, except to see my family, and for a few tournaments and a Davis Cup match years later.

When I got national recognition as a tennis player in my senior year in high school, it was an important step in my personal campaign to overcome assumptions of inequality. But I also knew that no one in Richmond's white tennis establishment had done anything to help me to get where I was. My memories and experiences about Richmond remain firmly rooted in the 1960s. The support I got—from teachers, relatives, and people like Ron Charity and Dr. Johnson—prepared me for the life I would lead outside the South. ❖

---

11. parochial. Narrow

How would you feel if you were prevented from competing in a sport or going to a public place because of your skin color? What do you think contributed most to Ashe's success? Is success in a given field more a matter of luck or a matter of hard work?

Find Meaning

1. (a) Where did Ashe first learn tennis? (b) How did his physical limitations affect his attraction to tennis?

2. (a) What dispute did Ashe have with Dr. Johnson's son, Bobby? (b) How was the dispute resolved?

3. How did Ashe's personality change in St. Louis?

Make Judgments

4. Ashe says that "traveling with Ron Charity and others stressed the importance of camaraderie," or spirit of friendship. Why was camaraderie important?

5. (a) What social experiences did Ashe have as a result of tennis that he otherwise might not have had? (b) How did these experiences help shape Ashe's view of life and his values?

6. How did Ashe view the discrimination he experienced as a tennis player?

OFF THE COURT **309**

Vocabulary Skills

Use Context Clues

Ashe often discusses technical aspects of tennis, and he may use terms students do not know (for example, *torque* and *semi-lob*). They can tell from the context that such terms are tennis related, even though this may not reveal precise meanings.

Discuss the idea that the technical information is not central to Ashe's purpose for writing—although it would be if he were writing a tennis instruction manual. Tell students not to get distracted by tennis-related words they don't fully understand. If they would like to investigate such terms further, they can keep a list as they read and look up definitions later.

After his competitive tennis days were over, **Arthur Ashe** expanded his career to include coaching, fund-raising, and writing. He wrote this editorial for the *New York Times* in 1977. Because of Ashe's fame, newspapers and other organizations valued his views on athletics and education. As you read, notice the sensory details Ashe uses to support his main idea.

A Black Athlete Looks at Education

An Editorial by Arthur Ashe

(A) Since my sophomore year at UCLA, I have become convinced that we blacks spend too much time on the playing fields and too little time in the libraries. Consider these facts: for the major professional sports of hockey, football, basketball, baseball, golf, tennis and boxing, there are roughly only 3170 major league positions available (attributing 200 positions to golf, 200 to tennis and 100 to boxing). And the annual turnover is small.

There must be some way to assure that those who try but don't make it to pro sports don't wind up on street corners or in unemployment lines. Unfortunately, our most widely recognized role models are athletes and entertainers—"runnin'" and "jumpin'" and "singin'" and "dancin'."

Our greatest heroes of the century have been athletes—Jack Johnson, Joe Louis, and Muhammad Ali.[1] Racial and economic discrimination forced us to channel our energies into athletics and entertainment. These were the ways out of the ghetto, the ways to get that Cadillac, those regular shoes, that cashmere sport coat.

Somehow, parents must instill a desire for learning alongside the desire to be Walt Frazier.[2] Why not start by sending black professional athletes into high schools to explain the facts of life?

I have often addressed high school audiences and my message is always the same: "For every hour you spend on the athletic field, spend two in the library. Even if you make it as a pro athlete, your career will be over by the time you are 35. You will need that diploma."

Have these pro athletes explain what happens if you break a leg, get a sore arm, have one bad year or don't make the cut for five or six tournaments. Explain to them the star system, wherein for every star earning millions there are six or seven others making $15,000 or $20,000 or $30,000. Invite a bench-warmer or a guy who didn't make it. Ask him if he sleeps every night. Ask him whether he was graduated. Ask him what he would do if he became disabled tomorrow. Ask him where his old high school athletic buddies are.

We have been on the same roads—sports and entertainment—too long. We need to

---

1. **Jack Johnson, Joe Louis, and Muhammad Ali.** Twentieth-century African-American boxers
2. **Walt Frazier.** Black basketball player for the New York Knicks (1967–1977) and the Cleveland Cavaliers (1977–1980)

Teach the Connection

Use Reading Skills
Identify the Main Idea Note that in persuasive writing, the task of identifying the main idea is often much simpler than in other kinds of writing. This is because the author must state his or her opinion clearly, usually right at the beginning. Have students identify the earliest words in the selection that express Ashe's main idea. (They should agree that in the first sentence, "we blacks spend too much time on the playing fields and too little time in the libraries" expresses this.) **(A)**

Analyze Literature
Editorial and Autobiography
Remind students that an editorial is a short piece expressing the author's opinion about a topic, which appears in a publication such as a newspaper or magazine. An author's purpose (or goal) in writing an editorial is to persuade. By contrast, autobiography tells the story of the writer's life; the purpose is to explain.

Ask students to notice as they read how Ashe's voice (his expression of his outlook and personality) in the editorial is similar to his voice in the main selection. Do they feel that having read the autobiography deepens their understanding of the editorial? How?

Differentiated Instruction

Auditory Learning
Ask students to prepare a three- to five-minute speech in response to Ashe's editorial. Say that they may
- agree with his point of view,
- disagree with his point of view,
- relate his point of view to groups other than African Americans, or
- explain the situation from the point of view of a young person just starting out in life.

Tell students they must support their positions with effective reasoning and pertinent facts. Have students present their speeches to classmates. Ask listeners to take notes so they can provide feedback after all the presentations have been made.

Common Core State Standards

Reading Literature
RL.1, RL.9

Reading Informational
RI.3, RI.5, RI.9

pull over, fill up at the library and speed away to Congress and the Supreme Court, the unions and the business world.

I'll never forget how proud my grandmother was when I graduated from UCLA. Never mind the Davis Cup. Never mind the Wimbledon title. To this day, she still doesn't know what those names mean. What mattered to her was that of her more than thirty children and grandchildren, I was the first to be graduated from college, and a famous college at that. Somehow, that made up for all those floors she scrubbed all those years. ❧

TEXT ←**TO**→ **TEXT**
CONNECTION

The excerpt from Ashe's autobiography and his editorial both deal with being an African-American athlete. Compare and contrast the purpose and content of each selection. Be sure to describe the structural and substantive differences between the two.

AFTER READING

Analyze Literature

Description A writer's use of sensory details helps to portray a character, object, action, or scene. Use a chart to analyze the effect of specific sensory details in the excerpt from *Off the Court*. Then describe the overall mood of the autobiography using two or three key words.

Sensory Detail	Effect
too small for any sport but tennis	

Extend Understanding

Writing Options

Creative Writing Write an **autobiographical essay** about an event in your past. The event should be something that affected you strongly and that you think will interest your readers. Use dialogue and sensory details to create a realistic effect. Share your essay with the class.

Expository Writing Write a one-paragraph **biographical sketch** of Arthur Ashe. Use information from his autobiography, including quotations and paraphrases, and information you gather from the Internet or library. Write as though your sketch will be published in a reference work about famous athletes.

Collaborative Learning

Research a Sport With a partner, research a sport you would like to know more about. Prepare a basic overview of the sport, and present your overview to the class using drawings, photographs, puppets, or demonstrations as supporting visuals.

Critical Literacy

Question and Answer Many famous minority athletes have broken racial and social barriers. Look for information on one or two male or female minority athletes. First, create a set of questions you would like to ask them. Then, research answers to those questions. Report your findings in a question-and-answer format and post your work on the class bulletin board.

 Go to www.mirrorsandwindows.com for more.

Review the Selection

Text-to-Text Connection
Answer: As a star athlete with a college degree, Ashe is uniquely qualified to discuss this topic and provide an insightful perspective. Many students will agree with Ashe's sentiment. Students descriptions of the structural and substantive differences will vary. Verify that their comparisons discuss purpose, content, and structure.

Analyze Literature

Description Students' descriptions of mood will vary. Be sure the sensory details they choose relate to the mood they state.

Rubrics for Writing Options

You can adapt this as a checklist for students to use as they write.

Creative Writing

- [ ] Does the essay maintain a consistent first-person point of view?
- [ ] Does the essay use dialogue and sensory details?
- [ ] Will the event interest readers?

Expository Writing

- [ ] Does the sketch present an accurate portrait of Ashe?
- [ ] Does the sketch use information from Ashe's autobiography, including quotations and paraphrases?
- [ ] Does the sketch include information gathered from Internet or library research?

Was **Tarzan** a **Three-Bandage** Man?

A Personal Essay by Bill Cosby

At a Glance
Directed Reading
- Reading Level: Easy
- Difficulty Considerations: None
- Ease Factors: Humor and simple language

Objectives
Studying this lesson will enable students to

- use reading skills such as context clues
- define *purpose* and recognize the author's purpose for writing
- define the literary and comedic accomplishments of Bill Cosby
- appreciate humorous anecdotes about growing up

Launch the Lesson
Before reading "Was Tarzan a Three-Bandage Man?" encourage students to talk about their own heroes, either in sports or another field. Have they ever done anything just because a hero did it? What? Ask them also to talk about times they did something silly that they thought was cool. How did their families react? Are they able to laugh about that now?

BEFORE READING

Build Background
Literary Context The title of this personal essay is a humorous reference to a literary character first created in 1912 by author Edgar Rice Burroughs. *Tarzan of the Apes* was the first book in a series featuring Tarzan, who lived in an African jungle and was known for his strength and courage in the face of danger. Also the title character of several movies, Tarzan was played by various actors over the years.

Reader's Context What do you admire in a person? Is it his or her strength, courage, talent, or something else?

Set Purpose
Based on the title of this essay, do you think it will be serious or humorous?

Analyze Literature
Purpose A writer's **purpose** is his or her goal. For example, people might write to inform, to entertain, or to persuade. Sometimes a writer may have more than one purpose. As you read "Was Tarzan a Three-Bandage Man?" try to determine the author's purpose. Think about how well he achieves this purpose.

Use Reading Skills
Context Clues Preview the vocabulary words from this selection as they are used in the sentences below. Try to unlock the meaning of each word using the context clues in the sentences.

1. Walking backward is a difficult means of <u>locomotion</u>.
2. I tried to <u>emulate</u> my mother's good cooking, but my dishes never tasted the same as hers.
3. We knew Phil had failed his math test because we saw him sitting <u>dejectedly</u> with his head in his hands.

Preview Vocabulary
lo‧co‧mo‧tion (lō' kə mō´ shən) *n.*, power or act of moving from one place to another

em‧u‧late (em´ yə lāt') *v.*, imitate

de‧jec‧ted‧ly (di jek´ təd lē) *adv.*, sadly; showing lack of confidence

Meet the Author
Bill Cosby was born in 1937 in Philadelphia. He has been called "one of the most influential performers of the second half of the twentieth century." Most Americans recognize Cosby from two popular television shows: *I Spy* and *The Cosby Show*. He has known success as a comedian, actor, and writer, and his books have sold millions of copies. In recent years in his public appearances, he has urged more parental involvement in the lives of young people.

(Opposite page) Sugar Ray Robinson wrapping his hands before a fight in 1956.

Words in Use

Preview Vocabulary	Selection Words	Teaching Words
locomotion, 314	incorporate, 314	heckled, 314
emulate, 314	tourniquets, 315	affiliate, 314
dejectedly, 315		jeers, 314

KEY TERMS

Common Core State Standards
Reading Literature
RL.1, RL.4

Reading Informational
RI.3, RI.4, RI.7

Was Tarzan a Three-Bandage Man?

A Personal Essay by
Bill Cosby

"My mother says I gotta stop wearin' a bandage. She wants my whole head to show."

313

Teach the Selection

Summary

In this humorous autobiographical essay, Bill Cosby tells how he and his boyhood friends used to imitate their sports heroes' physical characteristics. First he tells how they tried to walk pigeon-toed and bowlegged. Next, he tells how they wore Band-Aids so they would look like their favorite prize fighters. Each time Cosby describes what he did, he also describes his mother's dubious responses to it. Her sarcastic comments reveal how silly he must have looked. Finally, Cosby's mother tells him he is not allowed to wear a Band-Aid. His friends console him by saying one bandage isn't enough anyway—he needs two to look really tough. Cosby finishes by joking that he and his friends should have considered that the truly tough guys were the ones who caused the injuries that led the heroes to require bandages.

The Mirrors & Windows questions at the end of the selection focus on the theme of imitating heroes. Before students begin reading, ask: What makes "national heroes" so attractive to people?

Program Resources

Planning and Assessment
Program Planning Guide, Selection Lesson Plan
E-Lesson Planner
Assessment Guide, Lesson Test
ExamView

Technology Tools
Interactive Student Text on CD
Visual Teaching Package
Audio Library
mirrorsandwindows.com

Meeting the Standards
Nonfiction: Unit 3, Directed Reading,
    pp. 53–56

Differentiating Instruction
Advanced Students, Biographical Research
    Project, pp. 17–18

314 UNIT 3 NONFICTION

Teach the Selection

Analyze Literature

Identify Author's Purpose Cosby's purpose is, at least in part, to entertain. He does this with humor, particularly through sarcasm. Draw students' attention to the dialogue between Cosby and his mother, and note that much of the humor results from the mother's sarcasm. Have students point out examples of sarcasm and explain what the mother means. **Ⓐ**

History Connection

Jackie Robinson *Answer:* Jackie Robinson was both a great athlete and the first African American to play in major league baseball. He was a Civil Rights leader and an athlete, and so a natural role model for Cosby and his friends. **Ⓑ**

Use Reading Skills

Use Context Clues Explain that writers sometimes add context clues to give readers an idea of what something means. Soon after his mother mentions *Swiss Family Robinson*, Cosby includes dialogue that contains a clue: "You'd know who they are if you read more books. . . ." **Ⓒ**

In the days before athletes had learned how to incorporate themselves, they were shining heroes to American kids. In fact, they were such heroes to me and my friends that we even imitated their walks. When Jackie Robinson,[1] a pigeon-toed walker, became famous, we walked pigeon-toed, a painful form of <u>locomotion</u> unless you were Robinson or a pigeon.

"Why you walkin' like that?" said my mother one day.

"This is Jackie *Robinson's* walk," I proudly replied.

Ⓐ "There's somethin' wrong with his shoes?"

"He's the fastest man in baseball."

"He'd be faster if he didn't walk like that. His mother should make him walk right."

A few months later, when football season began, I stopped imitating Robinson and began to walk bowlegged like a player named Buddy Helm.

"Why you always tryin' to change the shape of your legs?" said my mother. "You keep doin' that an' they'll fall off—an' I'm not gettin' you new ones."

Although baseball and football stars inspired us, our real heroes were the famous prize fighters, and the way to <u>emulate</u> a fighter was to walk around with a Band-Aid over one eye. People with acne walked around that way too, but we hoped it was clear that we were worshipping good fists and not bad skin.

The first time my mother saw me being Sugar Ray,[2] not Jackie Robinson, she said, "What's that bandage for?"

"Oh, nuthin'," I replied.

"Now that's a new kinda stupid answer.

That bandage gotta be coverin' somethin'—besides your entire brain."

"Well, it's just for show. I wanna look like Sugar Ray Robinson."

"The fastest man in baseball."

"No, that's a different one."

HISTORY ▶▶ CONNECTION

Jackie Robinson Jackie Robinson excelled in most sports in high school and at the University of California, but as an African American, he was often heckled by players on opposing teams. His professional career began when he joined the Kansas City Monarchs of the Negro American League. There, he was spotted by Branch Rickey, president of the Brooklyn Dodgers. Rickey signed Robinson to play for the Montreal Royals. A year later Rickey pulled him from the minor-league affiliate, and Robinson played the 1947 season with the Brooklyn Dodgers. Despite the jeers and insults of some fans and team members, he was named Major League Rookie of the Year. Robinson was inducted into baseball's Hall of Fame in 1962. Why might Robinson have been a hero to young Cosby and his friends? **Ⓑ**

"You doin' *Swiss Family Robinson*[3] next?"

"*Swiss Family Robinson?* They live in the projects?"

Ⓒ "You'd know who they are if you read more books instead of makin' yourself look like an accident. Why can't you try to imitate someone like Booker T. Washington?"[4]

---

1. **Jackie Robinson.** (1919–1972) First African American in the twentieth century to play in the major leagues
2. **Sugar Ray.** (1921–1989) Ray Robinson, known as "Sugar Ray," was a world champion prize fighter six times.
3. **Swiss Family Robinson.** Story for young people written in 1812 that tells of a family wrecked on a desert island
4. **Booker T. Washington.** (1856–1915) African American born into slavery who became a teacher and founded Tuskegee Institute in Alabama

lo•co•mo•tion (lō′ kə mō′ shən) *n.*, power or act of moving from one place to another

em•u•late (em′ yə lāt′) *v.*, imitate

Differentiated Instruction

Enrichment

Students who enjoy this selection may enjoy researching the evolution of the Fat Albert character (who has a small role) and his friends. Suggest that they investigate the history of the character's appearance, from stand-up comedy routines to the educational cartoon popular in the 1970s to the 2004 movie, and then prepare a multimedia presentation for classmates.

Kinesthetic Learning

Comedy is one of the most difficult genres to write (or perform) successfully. Ask students to examine the selection, asking themselves, "What makes this funny?" Then challenge them to rehearse and present the selection as a comedic skit.

"Who does he play for?"

"Bill, let's put it this way: you take off that bandage right now or I'll have your father move you up to stitches."

The following morning on the street, I <u>dejectedly</u> told the boys, "My mother says I gotta stop wearin' a bandage. She wants my whole head to show."

"What's wrong with that woman?" said Fat Albert. "She won't let you do *nuthin'*."

"It's okay, Cos," said Junior, "cause one bandage ain't enough anyway. My brother says the really tough guys wear two."

"One over each eye?" I asked him.

"Or one eye and one nose," he said.

"Man, I wouldn't want to mess with no two-bandage man," said Eddie.

And perhaps the toughest guys of all wore tourniquets around their necks. We were capable of such attire, for we were never more ridiculous than when we were trying to be tough and cool. Most ridiculous, of course, was that our hero worshipping was backwards: we should have been emulating the men who had *caused* the need for bandages. ♣

> **de•jec•ted•ly** (di jek′ təd lē) *adv.*, sadly; showing lack of confidence

When have you tried to physically emulate one of your heroes? How might a person's attempt to copy a hero be useful? How might it be dangerous?

WAS TARZAN A THREE-BANDAGE MAN? **315**

Grammar Skills

Comparative and Superlative Adjectives

Review comparative and superlative adjectives:

- A comparative adjective describes one thing in comparison to another. It is usually formed by adding *-er* to a one-syllable adjective or using *more* or *less* before a multisyllabic adjective.

- A superlative adjective describes how something stands out from everything else in comparison. It is usually formed by adding *-est* to a one-syllable adjective or using *most* or *least* before a multisyllabic adjective.

Challenge students to find comparative and superlative adjectives in the selection (for example, "He's the fastest man in baseball" and "He'd be faster if he didn't walk like that.")

Review the Selection

Find Meaning

1. They imitate his pigeon-toed walk.
2. They greatly admire prizefighters, who often appear with at least one bandage.

Make Judgments

3. (a) She keeps tabs on what he is doing and wearing, and he tries to explain his actions. (b) The dialogue adds humor to the tone.
4. He sees that it was silly to copy such superficial attributes. He jokes that he was emulating the wrong people; he should have been emulating those who caused the prizefighters to wear bandages.
5. Famous people can have a lot of influence, especially on young people.

Analyze Literature

Purpose Cosby's primary purpose is to entertain. By including his mother's reactions to his efforts to imitate his heroes, he gradually and humorously conveys that his efforts were misguided.

Find Meaning

1. What do Cosby and his friends do to show that Jackie Robinson is their hero?
2. What does wearing a bandage over one eye indicate about Cosby and his friends?

Make Judgments

3. (a) What is the relationship between Cosby and his mother? (b) How is the tone of this essay affected by the dialogue between Cosby and his mother?
4. How does the author later view his attempts to emulate his heroes?
5. What does this essay tell you about the influence famous people have?

Analyze Literature

Purpose A writer uses specific details to help achieve the purpose of an essay. Use a chart to analyze Cosby's purpose.

Before Reading
Identify the author's purpose, the type of writing he or she uses, and the ideas he or she wants to communicate.
During Reading
Gather ideas that the author communicates to readers.
After Reading
Summarize the ideas the author communicates. Explain how these ideas help fulfill the author's purpose.

Extend Understanding

Writing Options

Creative Writing Think about some funny event that has happened to you or to someone in your family. Write your own humorous anecdote in a **personal letter** that you plan on sending to a close friend. Include as many vivid details as you can.

Persuasive Writing Why is it good (or bad) for young people to admire and copy sports figures? In the introductory sentence of a **persuasive paragraph,** state your answer to this question. Try to appeal to both emotion and logic. In the conclusion, sum up your reasons for feeling as you do. Share your work with the class.

Critical Literacy

Analyze Adaptations Works of nonfiction are often changed or adapted into another medium or genre. Find an adaptation of an autobiography or a diary and describe the structural and substantive differences between the two. An example would be the autobiography *Farewell to Manzanar* by Jeanne Wakatsuki Houston and the 1976 television movie.

Media Literacy

Discuss Humorous Writing In small groups, discuss how the techniques of humorous writing differ from those used in other media, such as movies, comic strips, stand-up comedy, and situation comedies. Create a chart, or other visual aid, in which you show how humor differs in these media.

 Go to **www.mirrorsandwindows.com** for more.

Rubrics for Writing Options

You can adapt this as a checklist for students to use as they write.

Creative Writing

☐ Does the letter follow the proper format?
☐ Does the letter present a humorous anecdote?
☐ Does the letter include vivid supporting details?

Persuasive Writing

☐ Does the writer take a clear position and appeal to both logic and emotion?
☐ Does the conclusion summarize the argument?

FISH CHEEKS

A Personal Essay by Amy Tan

Preview the Selection

At a Glance
Directed Reading
- Reading Level: Easy
- Difficulty Consideration: Vocabulary
- Ease Factor: Length

Objectives
Studying this lesson will enable students to
- use reading skills such as analyzing text structure
- define sensory details and explain how they enrich a story
- define the literary accomplishments of Amy Tan and explain how her Chinese-American background influences her writing
- appreciate an account of a formative learning experience

Launch the Lesson
Prior to reading "Fish Cheeks," ask students: "Has a family member or friend ever taught you a lesson about life? Were you able to perceive the wisdom of the lesson at the time, or did it take you a little while to understand what you had learned?" Have students share their experiences and insights as a class.

BEFORE READING

Build Background
Cultural Context A traditional Chinese holiday meal may include several kinds of fish (sometimes served whole), tofu, pickled vegetables, and rice. The New Year's holiday, and meal, is perhaps the most important in the Chinese calendar. For Chinese Christians, the Christmas holiday is also very important.

Reader's Context Different cultures in America have different foods and traditions on holidays. What are some traditional holiday foods and customs in your family? Do you think these traditions are important to follow, or will you abandon them when you are older?

Set Purpose
Previewing the title and the first two paragraphs of "Fish Cheeks" will help you to make predictions about what the narrator will experience and how she feels about this experience. Read to determine how accurate your predictions are.

Analyze Literature
Sensory Details Words and phrases that appeal to the five senses are **sensory details.** As you read "Fish Cheeks," notice the details that appeal to sight, sound, touch, taste, and smell.

Meet the Author
Amy Tan's parents came to the San Francisco Bay Area from China, and Tan was born in Oakland, California, in 1952. Although her parents wanted her to become a doctor, she began a writing career instead. Her first of many books, *The Joy Luck Club*, was published in 1989 and was made into a successful film in 1994. She continues to write fiction and nonfiction in San Francisco.

Use Reading Skills
Analyze Text Structure Writing is organized in different ways. Narrative writing is often organized chronologically, in the order or sequence in which events happen. When you read certain types of writing, such as a short story or an account of events in a person's life, keep track of the sequence of events. Use a sequence map to record what happens in "Fish Cheeks." In each box, describe key events in this essay.

Event 1: The author falls in love with the minister's son.

Event 2:

Event 3:

Event 4:

Preview Vocabulary
ap·pall·ing (ə pôl´ iŋ) *adj.,* inspiring disgust

rum·pled (rum´ pəld) *adj.,* wrinkled

pluck (plʉk) *v.,* pull off or out

FISH CHEEKS **317**

Words in Use

Preview Vocabulary
appalling, 319
rumpled, 319
pluck, 319

Common Core State Standards
Reading Literature
RL.1
Reading Informational
RI.5
Writing
W.2

FISH

Teach the Selection

Summary

The narrator's Chinese family invites the Caucasian minister's family to Christmas Eve dinner. The fourteen-year-old narrator is horrified. She has a crush on the minister's son and knows he will not appreciate her family's traditions. The narrator's mother prepares an elaborate Chinese meal; her relatives eat according to their custom. Most embarrassingly, her father belches at the end of the meal—a Chinese way of showing appreciation.

After the guests leave, the narrator's mother gives her a miniskirt, a gift for an American girl. She also says that the daughter may act American but must always remain Chinese inside. She says the only shame is to be ashamed of who she is. The narrator says that many years later she saw how wise and understanding her mother had been. She also reveals that all the foods served that night had been her favorite dishes.

The Mirrors & Windows questions at the end of the selection focus on the theme of diversity. Before they begin to read, ask students: Why do you think big U.S. cities have so many different immigrant neighborhoods?

CHEEKS

A Personal Essay by Amy Tan

I fell in love with the minister's son the winter I turned fourteen. He was not Chinese, but as white as Mary in the manger. For Christmas I prayed for this blond-haired boy, Robert, and a slim new American nose.

318

Program Resources

Planning and Assessment
Program Planning Guide, Selection Lesson Plan
E-Lesson Planner
Assessment Guide, Lesson Test
ExamView

Technology Tools
Interactive Student Text on CD
Visual Teaching Package
Audio Library
mirrorsandwindows.com

Meeting the Standards
Nonfiction: Unit 3, Directed Reading, pp. 57–61

Differentiating Instruction
English Language Learners, Analyze Text Structure, pp. 96–102

When I found out that my parents had invited the minister's family over for Christmas Eve dinner, I cried. What would Robert think of our shabby *Chinese* Christmas? What would he think of our noisy *Chinese* relatives who lacked proper American manners? What terrible disappointment would he feel upon seeing not a roasted turkey and sweet potatoes but *Chinese* food?

On Christmas Eve I saw that my mother had outdone herself in creating a strange menu. She was pulling black veins out of the backs of fleshy prawns.[1] The kitchen was littered with <u>appalling</u> mounds of raw food: A slimy rock cod[2] with bulging fish eyes that pleaded not to be thrown into a pan of hot oil. Tofu, which looked like stacked wedges of rubbery white sponges. A bowl soaking dried fungus back to life. A plate of squid, their backs crisscrossed with knife markings so they resembled bicycle tires.

And then they arrived—the minister's family and all my relatives in a clamor of doorbells and <u>rumpled</u> Christmas packages. Robert grunted hello, and I pretended he was not worthy of existence.

Dinner threw me deeper into despair. My relatives licked the ends of their chopsticks and reached across the table, dipping them into the dozens or so plates of food. Robert and his family waited patiently for platters to be passed to them. My relatives murmured with pleasure when my mother brought out the whole steamed fish. Robert grimaced.[3] Then my father poked his chopsticks just below the fish eye and <u>plucked</u> out the soft meat. "Amy, your favorite," he said, offering me the tender fish cheek. I wanted to disappear.

At the end of the meal my father leaned back and belched loudly, thanking my mother for her fine cooking. "It's a polite Chinese custom to show you are satisfied," explained my father to our astonished guests. Robert was looking down at his plate with a reddened face. The minister managed to muster up a quiet burp. I was stunned into silence for the rest of the night.

Robert grunted hello, and I pretended he was not worthy of existence.

After everyone had gone, my mother said to me, "You want to be the same as American girls on the outside." She handed me an early gift. It was a miniskirt in beige tweed. "But inside you must always be Chinese. You must be proud you are different. Your only shame is to have shame."

And even though I didn't agree with her then, I knew that she understood how much I had suffered during the evening's dinner. It wasn't until many years later—long after I had gotten over my crush on Robert—that I was able to fully appreciate her lesson and the true purpose behind our particular menu. For Christmas Eve that year, she had chosen all my favorite foods. ❖

---

1. **prawns.** Small shellfish that resemble shrimp
2. **rock cod.** Large, soft-finned fish that lives among rocks
3. **grimaced.** Twisted one's face to show disapproval or disgust

ap•pall•ing (ə pôl´ iŋ) *adj.*, inspiring disgust

rum•pled (rʉm´ pəld) *adj.*, wrinkled

pluck (plʉk) *v.*, pull off or out

What is it like to feel different from others? Would you have felt the way the author feels during dinner? How are those who seem different treated in our society?

Review the Selection

Find Meaning

1. (a) She knows Americans are not accustomed to the foods her mother is preparing. (b) *Fleshy, slimy, bulging fish eyes*, and *rubbery white*

2. She recognizes that Americans will think that licking chopsticks, reaching across the table, and serving a whole steamed fish are strange behaviors. When her father belches to show appreciation of the meal, she is "stunned into silence" by the guests' reactions.

3. Her mother gives her an early gift of a beige tweed miniskirt.

Make Judgments

4. She means that her daughter should not be ashamed of being Chinese. She should instead be ashamed of denying that she is Chinese.

5. It was to show pride in Chinese culture by treating American guests to a Chinese meal.

Analyze Literature

Sensory Details Sensory details referring to sight and touch include descriptions of raw fish, tofu, and dried fungus. The doorbell, a belch, and a burp appeal to sound. Rumpled packages, licking the ends of chopsticks, and poking chopsticks below the fish eye appeal to touch. Taste and smell are vaguely evoked in food descriptions.

Find Meaning

1. (a) Why does the author say that the mounds of food in the kitchen are appalling? (b) What other words express her disgust?
2. Why does she feel deeper despair during dinner?
3. What does the author's mother do to make her daughter feel better?

Analyze Literature

Sensory Details Amy Tan uses a variety of details that appeal to the senses. Use a chart, like the one to the right, to record the sensory details that Tan uses, beneath the sense to which they appeal.

Make Judgments

4. The author's mother says, "Your only shame is to have shame." What do you think she means?
5. The author says that later she was able to "fully appreciate...the true purpose behind our particular menu." What was that purpose?

Sight	Sound	Touch	Taste	Smell
"bulging fish eyes"				

Extend Understanding

Writing Options

Creative Writing Write a **dialogue** between the author as an adult and her mother in which each recalls the Christmas Eve dinner. Be sure to have each woman express her feelings about that time. With a friend, read the dialogue aloud for the class.

Expository Writing Write an **expository essay** in which you describe the problem the author confronts and how she overcomes it. At the end of your essay, tell whether you think the way in which the author overcame this problem is satisfactory. When you are finished, share your essay with the class.

Collaborative Learning

Hold a Small-Group Discussion In a small group, discuss whether or not the structure of Amy Tan's essay is effective. First decide what the structure is. Then think about possible alternative ways the essay could have been organized. Work with the group to plan an agenda that accomplishes your goals within the time allotted and make certain that everyone has a chance to contribute. Finally, organize your thoughts by creating a summary of the text as well as an overview of the material presented.

Lifelong Learning

Conduct Research All cultures have important holidays. Using a variety of sources, research a holiday in a culture different from your own. Create a list with the meaning of the holiday and elements such as food, decorations, displays, music, and celebrations.

Go to **www.mirrorsandwindows.com** for more.

Rubrics for Writing Options

You can adapt this as a checklist for students to use as they write.

Creative Writing

☐ Does the dialogue accurately present the characters' relationship?
☐ Does the dialogue clearly distinguish each person?
☐ Does the dialogue clearly express events described in "Fish Cheeks"?

Expository Writing

☐ Does the essay state the author's problem?
☐ Does the essay state how the author overcomes that problem?
☐ Does the essay state whether or not the way the author overcame the problem was satisfactory?

Grammar & Style

Fragments and Run-on Sentences

Fragments

A plate of squid, their backs crisscrossed with knife markings so they resembled bicycle tires.

—AMY TAN, "Fish Cheeks"

A sentence contains a subject and a verb and should express a complete thought. A **sentence fragment** is a phrase or clause that does not express a complete thought but has been punctuated as though it did. The above quote from "Fish Cheeks" is a fragment because it lacks a verb.

> **FRAGMENTS**
>
> *Made this the happiest Christmas I can remember.*
>
> *The fish and slabs of tofu piled on red and green plates.*

As a rule, sentence fragments should be avoided. However, for stylistic reasons, authors sometimes include sentence fragments in their work. Novelists and short story writers frequently use sentence fragments to make their characters' dialogue feel more like authentically spoken speech.

Run-on Sentences

A **run-on sentence** is made up of two or more sentences that have been run together as if they were one complete thought. A run-on sentence can confuse the reader about where a thought starts or ends. A run-on sentence is created when no end punctuation is used between two independent clauses.

> **RUN-ON**
>
> *I couldn't eat the wonderful dinner I was so embarrassed when my father belched.*

This sentence can be corrected by adding appropriate end punctuation or by adding an appropriate conjunction and a comma.

> **EXAMPLES**
>
> *I couldn't eat the wonderful dinner. I was so embarrassed when my father belched.*
>
> *I couldn't eat the wonderful dinner, and I was so embarrassed when my father belched.*

You can also correct run-on sentences by inserting a semicolon between two independent clauses. However, only use a semicolon if the two clauses are very closely related.

Sentence Improvement

Identify whether each selection below is a complete sentence, a fragment, or a run-on sentence. Then revise the run-ons and fragments to form one or more complete sentences.

1. The table with dishes, fish, and other seafood.
2. I was happy when my mother gave me the miniskirt.
3. My mother went to the kitchen I started to eat.
4. Across the living room and down the hall.
5. The steam rose from the rice the minister's son did not look up.
6. I learned to be proud of being me.
7. I could not finish eating my dinner.
8. With each plate on the table.
9. Underneath the ribbons and bows and beautiful wrapping paper.
10. My father left the table my mother looked up and smiled.

Sentence Improvement

These are possible answers. Actual student revisions will vary.

1. The table was covered with dishes, fish, and other seafood. (fragment)
2. Complete sentence
3. My mother went to the kitchen. I started to eat. (run-on sentence)
4. I walked across the living room and down the hall. (fragment)
5. The steam rose from the rice, and the minister's son did not look up. (run-on sentence)
6. Complete sentence
7. Complete sentence
8. We began with each plate on the table. (fragment)
9. It was the same old gift, underneath the ribbons and bows and beautiful wrapping paper. (fragment)
10. My father left the table. My mother looked up and smiled. (run-on sentence)

> For more information, see Grammar & Style Section 3.17, Writing Effective Sentences, in the Language Arts Handbook.

Program Resources

You will find additional lessons on Fragments and Run-on Sentences in the *Exceeding the Standards: Grammar & Style* resource.

KEY TERMS

Common Core State Standards

Language
L.4.1f

At a Glance
Directed Reading
"A Bittersweet Memoir"
- Reading Level: Moderate
- Difficulty Consideration: Length
- Ease Factor: Vocabulary

"Searching for January"
- Reading Level: Moderate
- Difficulty Consideration: Unfamiliar subject
- Ease Factor: Conversational tone

Objectives
Studying this lesson will enable students to
- compare literary selections of different genres
- use reading skills such as analyzing the author's perspective
- define *characterization* and learn to recognize both direct and indirect forms of characterization
- explore and compare the tributes to Roberto Clemente created by a biographer and a fiction writer
- enjoy two portrayals of a noted baseball player

Launch the Lesson
Note that the selection (as well as the related reading) pays tribute to someone for whom the author feels great admiration. Ask students to think about public figures they admire. Why do they admire them?

Before reading "Searching for January," ask students if they have ever wished they could talk to a hero, living or dead. If they could have a conversation with anyone, who would it be? Why?

A Bittersweet Memoir
A Biography by Jerry Izenberg

Searching for January
A Short Story by W. P. Kinsella

BEFORE READING

Build Background
Historical Context The subject of both Jerry Izenberg's biography and W. P. Kinsella's short story is Roberto Clemente, who was born in Puerto Rico and joined Major League Baseball in the 1950s. In 1954, he was drafted by the Pittsburgh Pirates and led the team to two World Series victories. He died in 1972 while flying supplies to earthquake victims in Nicaragua.

Reader's Context Who from the past or present do you most admire and why?

Set Purpose
Preview the illustrations and the quotations on the following pages to predict how each text will deal with Clemente's life and death.

Meet the Authors

Jerry Izenberg is a sportswriter and columnist for *The Star-Ledger* in Newark, New Jersey. He was born in 1930. Izenberg's many books include a history of the New York Giants and *Great Latin Sports Figures: Proud People*, from which his memoir of Roberto Clemente is taken.

W. P. Kinsella was born in 1935 in Edmonton, Alberta, a Canadian province. Kinsella has written numerous books about baseball and other topics. His book *Shoeless Joe* was made into the motion picture *Field of Dreams*.

Compare Literature: Characterization
The act of creating or describing a character is called **characterization.** Writers use three major techniques to create characters: showing what characters say, do, and think; showing what other characters say about them; and showing their physical features, dress, and personalities. Use a chart to record examples of characterization.

"A Bittersweet Memoir"	"Searching for January"
He was not a man who made friends casually.	

Preview Vocabulary
de•lin•e•ate (di lī´ nē āt´) v., describe

brace (brās) n., grove that provides shelter from wind

con•jec•ture (kən jek´ chər) v., predict; guess

lithe•ly (līth´ lē) adv., bending easily

Words in Use

"A Bittersweet Memoir"

Preview Vocabulary
delineate, 324
brace, 325
conjecture, 326

Selection Words
overseer, 327
undercurrent, 329

KEY TERMS
BIOGRAPHY, 322
SHORT STORY, 322
MEMOIR, 322
CHARACTERIZATION, 322
DIRECT CHARACTERIZATION, 339
INDIRECT CHARACTERIZATION, 339
NEWS ARTICLE, 339

Common Core State Standards
Reading Literature
RL.1

Reading Informational
RI.3

A Bittersweet Memoir

A Biography by Jerry Izenberg

"He was the greatest we ever had...maybe one of the greatest anyone ever had."

Pittsburgh Pirates outfielder Roberto Clemente in 1967.

Teach the Selection

Summary

Roberto Clemente (1934–1972) played baseball for the Pittsburgh Pirates from 1955 to 1972, when he died in a plane crash. Jerry Izenberg begins with his own trip to Puerto Rico, to the place where the crash occurred. He explains that Clemente was taking emergency supplies to Nicaragua after a devastating earthquake. He describes the last hours of Clemente's life and how people reacted to his disappearance. Then Izenberg chronicles Clemente's life, often quoting people who knew him. A beloved teacher, María Casares, describes his boyhood in Puerto Rico; others tell about his progress in baseball. Izenberg describes Clemente's successes and the challenges he faced trying to win people's respect and learning to live in a foreign culture. Near the end, Clemente's friend Willie Stargell says he believes Clemente would have agreed that he had lived a "full life." Izenberg finishes by saying Clemente "touched the hearts" of all different kinds of people.

MIRRORS & WINDOWS The Mirrors & Windows questions at the end of the selection focus on the theme of fame. Before students begin to read, ask: Who is the most famous sports figure in the world today?

Program Resources

Planning and Assessment
Program Planning Guide, Selection Lesson Plan
E-Lesson Planner
Assessment Guide, Lesson Test
ExamView

Technology Tools
Interactive Student Text on CD
Visual Teaching Package
Audio Library
mirrorsandwindows.com

Meeting the Standards
Nonfiction: Unit 3, Directed Reading, pp. 62–70

Differentiating Instruction
English Language Learners, Characterization, pp. 120–131

Use Reading Skills
Analyze Author's Perspective
Remind students that the author's perspective is the writer's viewpoint. Ask students what this short preface, presented in italics, tells them about Izenberg's perspective in the piece. (Students should glean that the author is *looking back,* both on Clemente's life and on his own feelings about Clemente.) **A**

Analyze Literature
Setting Remind students that setting is when and where a story happens. Note that often, as in this selection, an author describes the setting to help establish a mood (the emotion he or she wants people to feel as they read). Ask students to talk about the mood in this paragraph and the next one. (The dark, the rain, the poverty, and the rough waters of the ocean set a solemn mood.) **B**

Use Reading Skills
Main Idea and Supporting Details
Review the terms *main idea* and *supporting details.* Note that not every paragraph contains both a main idea and supporting details. Exceptions might include

- a short paragraph (it might serve as a transition or emphasize an idea by isolating it.)
- a dialogue paragraph (Taken together, lines of dialogue can include a main idea and supporting details.)

Ask students to find examples of such paragraphs in the selection. Have them identify whether they express a main idea or a supporting detail.

I saw him play so often. I watched the grace of his movements and the artistry of his reflexes from who knows how many press boxes. None of us really appreciated how pure an athlete he was until he was gone. What follows is a personal retracing of the steps that took Roberto Clemente from the narrow, crowded streets of his native Carolina to the local ball parks in San Juan and on to the major leagues. But it is more. It is a remembrance formed as I stood at the water's edge in Puerto Rico and stared at daybreak into the waves that killed him. It is all the people I met in Puerto Rico who knew him and loved him. It is the way an entire island in the sun and a Pennsylvania city in the smog took his death.... **A**

The record book will tell you that Roberto Clemente collected 3,000 hits during his major-league career. It will say that he came to bat 9,454 times, that he drove in 1,305 runs, and played 2,433 games over an eighteen-year span.

But it won't tell you about Carolina, Puerto Rico; and the old square; and the narrow, twisting streets; and the roots that produced him. It won't tell you about the Julio Coronado School and a remarkable woman named María Isabella Casares, whom he called "Teacher" until the day he died and who helped to shape his life in times of despair and depression. It won't tell you about a man named Pedron Zarrilla who found him on a country softball team and put him in the uniform of the Santurce club and who nursed him from promising young athlete to major-league superstar.

And most of all, those cold numbers won't begin to <u>delineate</u> the man Roberto Clemente was. To even begin to understand what this magnificent athlete was all about, you have to work backward. The search begins at the site of its ending.

The car moves easily through the predawn streets of San Juan. A heavy all-night rain has now begun to drive, and there is that post-rain sweetness in the air that holds the promise of a new, fresh, clear dawn. This is a journey to the site of one of Puerto Rico's deepest tragedies. This last says a lot. Tragedy is no stranger to the sensitive emotional people who make this island the human place it is.

Shortly before the first rays of sunlight, the car turns down a bumpy secondary road and moves past small shantytowns, where the sounds of the children stirring for the long **B**

de·lin·e·ate (di li′ nē āt′) *v.,* describe

324 **UNIT 3** NONFICTION

walk toward school begin to drift out on the morning air. Then there is another turn, between a <u>brace</u> of trees and onto the hardpacked dirt and sand, and although the light has not yet quite begun to break, you can sense the nearness of the ocean. You can hear its waves pounding harshly against the jagged rocks. You can smell its saltiness. The car noses to a stop, and the driver says, "From here you must walk. There is no other way." The place is called Puente Maldonado and the dawn does not slip into this angry place. It explodes in a million lights and colors as the large fireball of the sun begins to nose above the horizon.

"This is the nearest place," the driver tells me. "This is where they came by the thousands on that New Year's Eve and New Year's Day. Out there," he says, gesturing with his right hand, "out there, perhaps a mile and a half from where we stand. That's where we think the plane went down."

The final hours of Roberto Clemente were like this. Just a month or so before, he had agreed to take a junior-league baseball team to Nicaragua and manage it in an all-star game in Managua. He had met people and made friends there. He was not a man who made friends casually. He had always said that the people you wanted to give your friendship to were the people for whom you had to be willing to give something in return—no matter what the price. **C**

Two weeks after he returned from that trip, Managua, Nicaragua exploded into flames. The earth trembled and people died. It was the worst earthquake anywhere in the Western Hemisphere in a long, long time.

Back in Puerto Rico, a television personality named Luis Vigereaux heard the news and was moved to try to help the victims. He needed someone to whom the people would listen, someone who could say what had to be said and get the work done that had to be done and help the people who had to be helped.

"I knew," Luis Vigereaux said, "Roberto was such a person, perhaps the only such person who would be willing to help."

And so the mercy project, which would eventually claim Roberto's life, began. He appeared on television. But he needed a staging area. The city agreed to give him Sixto Escobar Stadium.

"Bring what you can," he told them. "Bring medicine...bring clothes...bring food... bring shoes...bring yourself and help us load. We need so much. Whatever you bring, we will use."

And the people of San Juan came. They walked through the heat and they drove cars and battered little trucks, and the mound of supplies grew and grew. Within two days, the first mercy planes left for Nicaragua.

Meanwhile, a ship had been chartered and loaded. And as it prepared to steam away, unhappy stories began to drift back from Nicaragua. Not all the supplies that had been flown in, it was rumored, were getting through. Puerto Ricans who had flown the planes had no passports, and Nicaragua was in a state of panic.

"We have people there who must be protected. We have black-market types that must not be allowed to get their hands on these supplies," Clemente told Luis Vigereaux. "Someone must make

He was not a man who made friends casually.

---

brace (brās) *n.*, grove that provides shelter from wind

(Opposite page) San Juan Harbor in Puerto Rico.

Teach the Selection

Analyze Literature
Foreshadowing Review the definition of *foreshadowing*—hinting at events that will happen later in the story. Ask students to point out details that might be considered foreshadowing. (One example is the information that Clemente would do anything for friends, "no matter what the price." This hints that he paid his life—the highest possible price—for his Nicaraguan friends.) **C**

Science Connection
Nicaragua's Earthquake The earthquake that struck Nicaragua on December 23, 1972, registered 6.2 on the Richter scale. It destroyed nearly the entire capital city of Managua. As many as 7,000 people died, and 15,000 were injured in a city with a total population of about 400,000. Because it was midsummer in the Southern Hemisphere and the terrain was dry, the fires ignited by the quake increased the damage. This was the most destructive earthquake to hit Central America in recorded history.

Research Skills

Find Images
To provide practice with finding images for reports and presentations, have students look for pictures relating to an aspect of the story (such as the Nicaragua earthquake). Discuss solid approaches to finding images online:

- One place to start is Google image search. It gathers pictures from all over the web. Students must remember only to use pictures from reliable websites.

- In general, the most reliable websites are government organizations (URLs ending in .gov), educational or nonprofit institutions (URLs ending in .edu or .org), and well-known businesses. One great source is the Library of Congress American Memory Collection.

Geography Connection

Distances The distance between San Juan, Puerto Rico, and Managua, Nicaragua, is around 1,400 miles—about the distance from Philadelphia, Pennsylvania, to Dallas, Texas. To get to Nicaragua, in Central America, from the island of Puerto Rico, Clemente would have flown the entire width of the Caribbean Sea, heading southwest. **A**

Analyze Literature

Tone Remind students that tone is the writer's attitude toward the subject matter and the reader. Tone is determined by the words chosen and by how sentences are presented in a piece. Draw students' attention to the fragments and short sentences in the description of Clemente's disappearance. How do they help express the writer's attitude? Model a response: "The short sentences create a dramatic tone by mirroring the tension of people who were waiting vainly to hear from the plane." **B**

---

sure—particularly before the ship gets there. I'm going on the next plane."

The plane they had rented was an old DC-7. It was scheduled to take off at 4:00 P.M. on December 31, 1972. Long before take-off time, it was apparent that the plane needed more work. It had even taxied onto **A** the runway and then turned back. The trouble, a mechanic who was at the airstrip that day conjectured, had to do with both port [left side] engines. He worked on them most of the afternoon.

The departure time was delayed an hour, and then two, and then three. Across town, a man named Rudy Hernandez, who had been a teammate of Roberto's when they were rookies in the Puerto Rican League and who had later pitched for the Washington Senators, was trying to contact Roberto by telephone. He had just received a five-hundred-dollar donation, and he wanted to know where to send it. He called Roberto's wife, Vera, who told him that Roberto was going on a trip and that he might catch him at the airport. She had been there herself only moments before to pick up some friends who were coming in from the States, and she had left because she was fairly sure that the trouble had cleared and Roberto had probably left already.

"I caught him at the airport and I was surprised," Rudy Hernandez told me. "I said I had this money for Nicaraguan relief and I wanted to know what to do with it. Then I asked him where he was going."

"Nicaragua," Clemente told him.

"It's New Year's Eve, Roberto. Let it wait."

"Who else will go?" Roberto told him. "Someone has to do it."

> "Who else will go?" Roberto told him. "Someone has to do it."

At 9 P.M., even as the first stirrings of the annual New Year's Eve celebration were beginning in downtown San Juan, the DC-7 taxied onto the runway, received clearance, rumbled down the narrow concrete strip, and pulled away from the earth. It headed out over the Atlantic and banked toward Nicaragua, and its tiny lights disappeared on the horizon.

Just ninety seconds later, the tower at San Juan International Airport received this message from the pilot: "We are coming back around."

Just that. **B**
Nothing more.
And then there was a great silence.

"It was almost midnight," recalls Rudy Hernandez, a former teammate of Roberto's. "We were having this party in my restaurant, and somebody turned on the radio and the announcer was saying that Roberto's plane was feared missing. And then, because my place is on the beach, we saw these giant floodlights crisscrossing the waves, and we heard the sound of the helicopters and the little search planes."

Drawn by a common sadness, the people of San Juan began to make their way toward the beach, toward Puente Maldonado. A cold rain had begun to fall. It washed their faces and blended with the tears.

They came by the thousands and they watched for three days. Towering waves boiled up and made the search virtually impossible. The U.S. Navy sent a team of expert divers into the area, but the battering of the waves defeated them too. Midway

con·jec·ture (kən jek´ chər) *v.*, predict; guess

Differentiated Instruction

Reading Proficiency

Less-proficient readers may have difficulty keeping track of the people mentioned in the selection. Suggest that, as they read, students write down each name and a brief description. Suggest also that they abbreviate Roberto Clemente's name so that they do not have to write it over and over in their notes. Example: "Rudy Hernandez—RC's teammate in Puerto Rican League."

through the week, the pilot's body was found in the swift-moving currents to the north. On Saturday bits of the cockpit were sighted.

And then—nothing else.

"I was born in the Dominican Republic," Rudy Hernandez said, "but I've lived on this island for more than twenty years. I have never seen a time or a sadness like that. The streets were empty, the radios silent, except for the constant bulletins about Roberto. Traffic? Forget it. All of us cried. All of us who knew him and even those who didn't, wept that week.

"Manny Sanguillen, the Pittsburgh catcher, was down here playing winter ball, and when Manny heard the news he ran to the beach and he tried to jump into the ocean with skin-diving gear. I told him, man, there's sharks there. You can't help. Leave it to the experts. But he kept going back. All of us were a little crazy that week.

"There will never be another like Roberto."

Who was he...I mean really?

Well, nobody can put together all the pieces of another man's life. But there are so many who want the world to know that it is not as impossible a search as you might think.

He was born in Carolina, Puerto Rico. Today the town has about 125,000 people, but when Roberto was born there in 1934, it was roughly one-sixth its current size.

María Isabella Casares is a schoolteacher. She has taught the children of Carolina for thirty years. Most of her teaching has been done in tenth-grade history classes. Carolina is her home and its children are her children. And among all of those whom she calls her own (who are all the children she taught), Roberto Clemente was something even more special to her.

"His father was an overseer on a sugar plantation. He did not make much money," she explained in an empty classroom at Julio Coronado School. "But then, there are no rich children here. There never have been. Roberto was typical of them. I had known him when he was a small boy because my father had run a grocery store in Carolina, and Roberto's parents used to shop there." **C**

There is this thing that you have to know about María Isabella Casares before we hear more from her. What you have to know is that she is the model of what a teacher should be. Between her and her students even now, as back when Roberto attended her school, there is this common bond of mutual respect. Earlier in the day, I had watched her teach a class in the history of the Abolition Movement in Puerto Rico. I don't speak much Spanish, but even to me it was clear that this is how a class should be, this is the kind of person who should teach, and these are the kinds of students such a teacher will produce.

With this as a background, what she has to say about Roberto Clemente carries much more impact. **D**

"Each year," she said, "I let my students choose the seats they want to sit in. I remember the first time I saw Roberto. He was a very shy boy and he went straight to the back of the room and chose the very last seat. Most of the time he would sit with his eyes down. He was an average student. But there was something very special about him. We would talk after class for hours. He wanted to be an engineer, you know, and perhaps he could have been. But then he began to play softball, and one day he came to me and said, 'Teacher, I have a problem.'

"He told me that Pedron Zarrilla, who was one of our most prominent baseball people, had seen him play, and that Pedron wanted him to sign a professional contract

History Connection

Puerto Rico One of the main reasons New World colonies such as Puerto Rico were valuable to European countries was that the tropical climate of the Caribbean allowed for cultivation of crops like sugarcane, used to make sugar and rum, both luxury goods. Because the native populations of the American colonies were sparse (and even more so after people began to contract diseases brought over by Europeans), Spain imported slaves from Africa to work the Caribbean plantations. Today, most Puerto Ricans are of mixed heritage, and have some combination of African, European, and indigenous ancestors. **C**

Analyze Literature

Style Remind students that an audience is the group of people for whom an author writes. Deciding who the audience is affects the style of the piece (that is, the way voice, tone, word choice, and sentence construction work together). Talk about who Izenberg considers his audience to be and challenge students to describe his style. (They should notice that he is writing for readers who do not necessarily know about Clemente. He uses an informal, conversational style and often explains specialized information.) **D**

Grammar Skills

Adjective Phrases and Clauses

Review the difference between a phrase and a clause. Explain that both can be used as adjectives to modify nouns. An adjective phrase often begins with a preposition (the people of San Juan), a participle (the man wearing black), or an infinitive (work to do). Often adjective clauses begin with a word such as *who, that, which,* or *when.*

Have students identify the adjective phrase or clause (underlined). Have them point out more examples from the reading.

1. the final hours of Roberto Clemente (phrase)

2. not a man who made friends casually (clause)

3. a television personality named Luis Vigereaux (phrase)

Analyze Literature

Flashback Remind students that a flashback is when a story's chronological sequence is interrupted to show something that happened earlier. An example is María Casares's description of how she encouraged Clemente to play professional baseball. (Note that her statement that she often thinks of that conversation illustrates another aspect of flashbacks.) Many people experience such flashes of memory as they go through life. Ask students if they have ever had this experience, too, and ask them to describe it. Have them review the selection and point out other flashbacks in the text. **A**

Use Reading Skills

Identify Sequence of Events
Encourage students to pause occasionally while reading and to go over the sequence of events they have just read. This will strengthen their comprehension. Model this process to give students an idea how to proceed: "What happened when his teacher had a back injury? Clemente carried her to the doctor himself and then paid for her treatment."

---

with the Santurce Crabbers. He asked me what he should do.

A "I have thought about that conversation many times. I believe Roberto could have been almost anything, but God gave him a gift that few have, and he chose to use that gift. I remember that on that day I told him, 'This is your chance, Roberto. We are poor people in this town. This is your chance to do something. But if in your heart you prefer not to try, then Roberto, that will be your problem—and your decision.'"

There was and there always remained a closeness between this boy-soon-to-be-a-man and his favorite teacher.

"Once, a few years ago, I was sick with a very bad back. Roberto, not knowing this, had driven over from Rio Piedras, where his house was, to see me."

"Where is the teacher?" Roberto asked Mrs. Casares' stepdaughter that afternoon.

"Teacher is sick, Roberto. She is in bed."

"Teacher," Roberto said, pounding on the bedroom door, "get up and put on your clothes. We are going to the doctor whether you want to or not."

"I got dressed," Mrs. Casares told me, "and he picked me up like a baby and carried me in his arms to the car. He came every day for fifteen days, and most days he had to carry me, but I went to the doctor and he treated me. Afterward, I said to the doctor that I wanted to pay the bill.

"'Mrs. Casares,' he told me, 'please don't start with that Clemente, or he will kill me. He has paid all your bills, and don't you dare tell him I have told you.'

"Well, Roberto was like that. We had been so close. You know, I think I was there the day he met Vera, the girl he later married. She was one of my students, too. I was working part-time in the pharmacy and he was already a baseball player by then, and one day Vera came into the store.

"'Teacher,' Roberto asked me, 'who is that girl?'

"'That's one of my students,' I told him. 'Now don't you dare bother her. Go out and get someone to introduce you. Behave yourself.'

"He was so proper, you know. That's just what he did, and that's how he met her, and they were married here in Carolina in the big church on the square."

On the night Roberto Clemente's plane disappeared, Mrs. Casares was at home, and a delivery boy from the pharmacy stopped by and told her to turn on the radio and sit down. "I think something has happened to someone who is very close with you, Teacher, and I want to be here in case you need help."

María Isabella Casares heard the news. She is a brave woman, and months later, standing in front of the empty crypt in the cemetery at Carolina where Roberto Clemente was to have been buried, she said, "He was like a son to me. This is why I want to tell you about him. This is why you must make people—particularly our people, our Puerto Rican children—understand what he was. He was like my son, and he is all our sons in a way. We must make sure that the children never forget how beautiful a man he was."

The next person to touch Roberto Clemente was Pedron Zarrilla, who owned the Santurce club. He was the man who discovered Clemente on the country softball team, and he was the man who signed him for a four-hundred-dollar bonus.

"He was a skinny kid," Pedron Zarrilla recalls, "but even then he had those large powerful hands, which we all noticed right away. He joined us, and he was nervous. But I watched him, and I said to myself, 'this kid can throw and this kid can run, and this kid can hit. We will be patient

---

Differentiated Instruction

Enrichment

Reading this tribute to one of Izenberg's heroes may inspire students to create a tribute to a hero of their own. Encourage them to choose a person of outstanding accomplishment—male or female—about whom they feel strongly, and to research and create the tribute. They may wish to focus on writing a biography, like the selection; they could also create a poster or multimedia presentation. Have students display their work on a "Heroes" board in the classroom.

Roberto Clemente slides home in a 1971 game against the Montreal Expos.

Teach the Selection

Use Reading Skills
Compare and Contrast Ask students to think back to the reading from *Off the Court* by Arthur Ashe (page 297). Working as a class, have students compare and contrast the two pieces. Write their ideas on the board in a two-column chart with one column labeled Similarities and the other labeled Differences. Similarities include the fact that both works tell how their subjects became professional athletes; both men were black and experienced racism. Differences include that Clemente's story is biography, while Ashe's is autobiography; Clemente grew up poor, while Ashe did not.

with him.' The season had been through several games before I finally sent him in to play."

Luis Olmo remembers that game. Luis Olmo had been a major-league outfielder with the Brooklyn Dodgers. He had been a splendid ballplayer. Today he is in the insurance business in San Juan. He sat in his office and recalled very well that first moment when Roberto Clemente stepped up to bat.

"I was managing the other team. They had a man on base and this skinny kid comes out. Well, we had never seen him, so we didn't really know how to pitch to him. I decided to throw him a few bad balls and see if he'd bite.

"He hit the first pitch. It was an outside fast ball, and he never should have been able to reach it. But he hit it down the line for a double. He was the best bad-ball hitter I have ever seen, and if you ask major-league pitchers who are pitching today, they will tell

you the same thing. After a while it got so that I just told my pitchers to throw the ball down the middle because he was going to hit it no matter where they put it, and at least if he decided not to swing we'd have a strike on him.

"I played in the big leagues. I know what I am saying. He was the greatest we ever had...maybe one of the greatest anyone ever had. Why did he have to die?"

Once Pedron Zarrilla turned him loose, there was no stopping Roberto Clemente. As Clemente's confidence grew, he began to get better and better. He was the one the crowd came to see out at Sixto Escobar Stadium.

"You know, when Clemente was in the lineup," Pedron Zarrilla says, "there was always this undercurrent of excitement in the ball park. You knew that if he was coming to bat, he would do something spectacular. You knew that if he was on first base, he was going to try to get to second base. You knew that if he was playing right field and there

A BITTERSWEET MEMOIR / SEARCHING FOR JANUARY **329**

Vocabulary Skills

Specialized Words
Explain that a dictionary should be the first resource students consult to look up unfamiliar words, but that sometimes specialized terms might not appear in a general-purpose dictionary. Their next choices include:
- Find a larger, more comprehensive dictionary.
- Consult an encyclopedia or reference book dedicated to the topic.
- Do online research (taking care to rely only on trustworthy websites).

Have each student compile a glossary of ten baseball terms from the selection. Have students share their finished glossaries and talk about the most helpful sources they found during their research.

Use Reading Strategies

Ask Questions Ask students to review this sentence and then paraphrase it. (The sentence begins on page 329.) Encourage them to pose questions to each other to interpret the sentence. ("You don't try to get home against Roberto Clemente's arm" means Clemente could throw the ball so far that any player who tried to run home from third base would be tagged out.) **A**

Use Reading Skills

Monitor Comprehension Point out that Izenberg acknowledges that readers who do not know much about baseball may have trouble following some of what he says. This cue is a good reminder to students to pause now, monitor comprehension, and reengage their focus on the material. Model questions students might ask themselves, such as "What is this passage about?" and "How does this information contribute to the story?" **B**

Analyze Literature

Figurative Language Write this sentence on the board and challenge students to identify the literary technique used in it (metaphor). Ask: "What is Izenberg saying?" (Izenberg compares Clemente to a diamond and his teammates to broken glass to say that Clemente's talent was rare and special, while theirs was common.) **C**

was a man on third base, then that man on third base already knew what a lot of men on third base in the majors were going to find out—you don't try to get home against **A** Roberto Clemente's arm.

"I remember the year that Willie Mays came down here to play in the same outfield with him for the winter season. I remember the wonderful things they did and I remember that Roberto still had the best of it.

"Sure I knew we were going to lose him. I knew it was just a matter of time. But I was only grateful that we could have him if only for that little time."

The major-league scouts began to make their moves. Olmo was then scouting, and he tried to sign him for the Giants. But it was the Dodgers who won the bidding war. The Dodgers had Clemente, but in having him, they had a major problem. He had to be hidden.

B This part takes a little explaining. Under the complicated draft rules that baseball used at that time, if the Dodgers were not prepared to bring Clemente up to their major-league team within a year (and because they were winning with proven players, they couldn't), then Clemente could be claimed by another team.

They sent him to Montreal with instructions to the manager to use him as little as possible, to hide him as much as possible, and to tell everyone he had a sore back, a sore arm, or any other excuse the manager could give. But how do you hide a **C** diamond when he's in the middle of a field of broken soda bottles?

In the playoffs that year against Syracuse, they had to use Clemente. He hit two doubles and a home run and threw a man out at home the very first try.

The Pittsburgh Pirates had a man who saw it all. They drafted him at the season's end.

And so Roberto Clemente came to Pittsburgh. He was the finest prospect the club had had in a long, long time. But the Pirates of those days were spectacular losers and even Roberto Clemente couldn't turn them around overnight.

"We were bad, all right," recalls Bob Friend, who later became a great Pirate pitcher. "We lost over a hundred games, and it certainly wasn't fun to go to the ball park under those conditions. You couldn't blame the fans for being noisy and impatient. Branch Rickey, our general manager, had promised a winner. He called it his five-year plan. Actually, it took ten."

When Clemente joined the club, it was Friend who made it his business to try to make him feel at home. Roberto was, in truth, a moody man, and the previous season hadn't helped him any.

"I will never forget how fast he became a superstar in this town," says Bob Friend. "Later he would have troubles because he was either hurt or thought he was hurt, and some people would say that he was loafing. But I know he gave it his best shot and he helped make us winners."

The first winning year was 1960, when the Pirates won the pennant and went on to beat the Yankees in the seventh game of the World Series. Whitey Ford, who pitched against him twice in that Series, recalls that Roberto actually made himself look bad on an outside pitch to encourage Whitey to come back with it. "I did," Ford recalls, "and he unloaded. Another thing I remember is the way he ran out a routine ground ball in the last game and when we were a little slow covering, he beat it out. It was something most people forget but it made the Pirates' victory possible."

The season was over. Roberto Clemente had hit safely in every World Series game. He had batted over .300. He had been a

Differentiated Instruction

English Language Learning

To give English learners practice at speaking, ask them to talk about Buck Canel's assessment of the effects of the language barrier on Clemente. Have they experienced the kinds of misunderstandings Canel describes on page 331? How have their experiences changed as their language skills have improved?

superstar. But when they announced the Most Valuable Player Award voting, Roberto had finished a distant third.

"I really don't think he resented the fact that he didn't win it," Bob Friend says. "What hurt—and in this he was right—was how few votes he got. He felt that he simply wasn't being accepted. He brooded about that a lot. I think his attitude became one of 'Well, I'm going to show them from now on so that they will never forget.'

"And you know, he sure did."

Roberto Clemente went home and married Vera. He felt less alone. Now he could go on and prove what it was he had to prove. And he was determined to prove it.

"I know he was driven by thoughts like that," explains Buck Canel, a newspaper writer who covers all sports for most of the hemisphere's Spanish language papers. "He would talk with me often about his feelings. You know, Clemente felt strongly about the fact that he was a Puerto Rican and that he was a black man. In each of these things he had pride.

"On the other hand, because of the early language barriers, I am sure that there were times when he *thought* people were laughing at him when they were not. It is difficult for a Latin-American ballplayer to understand everything said around him when it is said at high speed, if he doesn't speak English that well. But, in any event, he wanted very much to prove to the world that he was a superstar and that he could do things that in his heart he felt he had already proven."

In later years, there would be people who would say that Roberto was a hypochondriac (someone who *imagined* he was sick or hurt when he was not). They could have been right, but if they were, it made the things he did even more remarkable. Because I can testify that I saw him throw his body into

outfield fences, teeth first, to make remarkable plays. If he thought he was hurt at the time, then the act was even more courageous.

Matty Alou, Manny Mota, Roberto Clemente, and Willie Stargell, members of the 1966 Pittsburgh Pirates.

His moment finally came. It took eleven years for the Pirates to win a World Series berth again, and when they did in 1971, it was Roberto Clemente who led the way. I will never forget him as he was during that 1971 series with the Orioles, a Series that the Pirates figured to lose, and in which they, in fact, dropped the first two games down in Baltimore.

When they got back to Pittsburgh for the middle slice of the tournament, Roberto Clemente went to work and led this team. He was a superhero during the five games that followed. He was the big man in the Series. He was the MVP.[1] He was everything he had ever dreamed of being on a ball field.

---

1. **MVP.** Most Valuable Player

Teach the Selection

Use Reading Skills

Analyze Cause and Effect Remind students that a cause is an event that makes something else happen and a result is an effect. Point out that a narrative really consists of causes and effects—one thing leads to another and another and another. Have students point out causes and effects in the selection, phrasing their ideas in this way: "Because of [give cause], [describe effect]." Model an example: "Because Clemente did not win MVP in 1960, he resolved to prove that he deserved the title."

Analyze Literature

Characterization Discuss the idea that one of the author's primary purposes, or goals, in creating a biographical work like Izenberg's is to describe the subject's character. Ask students to point out details that contribute to the characterization of Roberto Clemente. Have them identify each as something Clemente says, thinks, or does ("indirect characterization") or as straight description of his personality ("direct characterization"). Sample responses include "I saw him throw his body into outfield fences" (indirect) and "If he thought he was hurt . . . the act was even more courageous" (direct). **D**

Writing Skills

Use References

Remind students that a thesaurus is a good tool for finding words—if they use it with care. A thesaurus groups words with similar meanings, but this doesn't mean the words in an entry are interchangeable. A writer must use personal knowledge, and perhaps consult a dictionary, to choose the right word.

Have students choose a paragraph from the selection. Then have them choose three or four words in that paragraph to replace with their own choices, using a thesaurus or picking synonyms they already know. Have students read their paragraphs to the class. Can classmates pick out which words are the replacements? How?

Answer: Students' reactions may center on the tragedy of a successful athlete's early death. They may use the words *brave*, *caring*, and *talented* to describe him. Fans admire and are curious about many sports figures, especially if the athletes play for a winning team.

Find Meaning

1. (a) He died in a plane crash.
(b) He was helping deliver supplies to victims of an earthquake.
2. Carolina, Puerto Rico
3. (a) She was a schoolteacher.
(b) When Clemente asked her what he should do about signing a baseball contract, she told him it was his "chance to do something," but if he preferred not to, it would be his problem and decision.

Make Judgments

4. (a) He was caring and unselfish, anxious to help those in need.
(b) They gathered because Clemente was their hero.
5. He was a great baseball player and a person with a strong connection to others and to his roots.
6. Most students will say the piece does a good job of describing Clemente and his impact on the world. It focuses on his character as well as his accomplishments.

Most important of all, the entire country saw him do it on network television, and never again—even though nobody knew it would end so tragically soon—was anyone ever to doubt his ability.

The following year, Clemente ended the season by collecting his three-thousandth hit. Only ten other men had ever done that in the entire history of baseball.

"It was a funny thing about that hit," Willie Stargell, his closest friend on the Pirates, explains. "He had thought of taking himself out of the lineup and resting for the playoffs, but a couple of us convinced him that there had to be a time when a man had to do something for himself, so he went on and played and got it. I'm thankful that we convinced him, because, you know, as things turned out, that number three thousand was his last hit.

"When I think of Roberto now, I think of the kind of man he was. There was nothing phony about him. He had his own ideas about how life should be lived, and if you didn't see it that way, then he let you know in so many ways, without words, that it was best you each go your separate ways.

"He was a man who chose his friends carefully. His was a friendship worth having. I don't think many people took the time and the trouble to try to understand him, and I'll admit it wasn't easy. But he was worth it.

"The way he died, you know, I mean on that plane carrying supplies to Nicaraguans who'd been dying in that earthquake, well, I wasn't surprised he'd go out and do something like that. I wasn't surprised he'd go. I just never thought what happened could happen to him.

"But I know this. He lived a full life. And if he knew at that moment what the Lord had decided, well, I really believe he would have said, 'I'm ready.'"

He was thirty-eight years old when he died. He touched the hearts of Puerto Rico in a way that few people ever could. He touched a lot of other hearts, too. He touched hearts that beat inside people of all colors of skin.

He was one of the proudest of The Proud People. ❖

What is your reaction to the life and death of Roberto Clemente? What words would you use to describe him? Many people enjoy reading about famous sports figures in books, magazines, and newspapers. Why do you think this is so?

Find Meaning

1. (a) How did Roberto Clemente die? (b) Why was Clemente going to Nicaragua?
2. Where did Clemente grow up?
3. (a) Who was María Isabella Casares? (b) What advice did she give Clemente?

Make Judgments

4. (a) What did Clemente's final actions reveal about him? (b) Why did people gather at Puente Maldonado by the thousands?
5. In what ways was Clemente a role model?
6. How well does "A Bittersweet Memoir" give readers an understanding of who Roberto Clemente was and how he changed the world? Explain your answer.

TEACHING NOTE

Self-Generated Questioning

Ask students to reflect on what they have learned. Ask: "What question raised by the selection would you really like answered?" Model a possible question: "What was the reaction in the United States to the news of Clemente's death?" Have individuals articulate a question, write it down, and then conduct research to find an answer. Finally, set aside time to have students present their questions and answers to the class.

Searching

for

January

A Short Story by W. P. Kinsella

Is this some local fisherman playing a cruel joke on a tourist?

333

Teach the Selection

Summary

As the narrator walks on a beach, a man comes to shore on a raft and says he is Roberto Clemente and that his plane crashed six days earlier. At first the narrator does not believe him; Clemente died fifteen years ago. Gradually, however, he is convinced the man is telling the truth. He must explain to Clemente that it is now 1987.

The men consider the implications of the situation. Clemente realizes that his wife and children will have aged, his teammates retired. Rather than face this, he returns to his raft, reasoning that if he made it to the future, surely he can get back to his own time. The narrator wishes him success, hoping that if Clemente changes history, it will be possible to see him play. Finally, the narrator wonders about leaving with Clemente, but it is too late.

The Mirrors & Windows questions at the end of the story focus on the theme of yearning for the past. Before students begin to read, ask: If you could visit a single moment in history, when and where would it be?

Words in Use

"Searching for January"

Preview Vocabulary
lithely, 334

Selection Words
bales, 335
ingenuity, 338
malfunction, 338
engulf, 338

TEACHING NOTE

Skim and Scan

Note that skimming and scanning are both useful quick-reading techniques. Explain that readers might *skim* to preview a text and learn the author's main ideas before they decide whether to read in detail. They might *scan* when they know the text has some information they need (for example, one scans the page of a dictionary to find the right word).

Common Core State Standards

Reading Literature
RL.1, RL.9

Analyze Literature

Fantasy Discuss the idea that fiction can be realistic (lifelike) or fantastical (having unreal, magical, or supernatural elements). Often authors combine realism and fantasy, as Kinsella does. Have students point out realistic and fantastical elements in the story. (They might note that Clemente was a real person and his portrayal seems true to life; the element of time travel is fantastical.)

Literary Connection

Arthurian Legend The medieval tales of King Arthur and his knights of the Round Table are collectively referred to as Arthurian legend. Scholars disagree over whether there was a real King Arthur. The stories have been passed on for centuries and continue to inspire writers. By using this reference, Kinsella compares Clemente to King Arthur, suggesting that the baseball player, too, was courageous, noble, and heroic. **A**

Use Reading Skills

Compare and Contrast Note that the two readings represent different *genres*, or types of literature. Ask students to identify each genre and to define the term. (The Izenberg article is biography, a nonfiction work about a person's life. The Kinsella piece is a short story, a brief fictional work.) Have students discuss similarities between the pieces.

The sand is white as salt but powdery as icing sugar, cool on my bare feet, although if I push my toes down a few inches, yesterday's heat lurks, waiting to surface with the sun.

It is 6:00 A.M. and I am alone on a tropical beach a mile down from our hotel. The calm ocean is a clear, heart-breaking blue. Fifty yards out a few tendrils of sweet, gray fog laze above the water; farther out the mist, water, and pale morning sky merge.

A It appears slowly out of the mist, like something from an Arthurian legend, a large, inflatable life raft, the depressing khaki and olive-drab of military camouflage. A man kneeling in front directs the raft with a paddle. He waves when he sees me, stands up and calls out in an urgent voice, but I can't make it out. As the raft drifts closer I can see that the lone occupant is tall and athletic-looking, dark-skinned, with a long jaw and flashing eyes.

"Clemente!" is the first word I hear clearly. "I am Clemente! The baseball player. My plane went down. Days ago! Everyone must think I am dead."

What he says registers slowly. Clemente! It has been fifteen years. Is this some local fisherman playing a cruel joke on a tourist?

"Yes," I call back, after pausing too long, scanning his features again. There is no question: it is Roberto Clemente. "I believe everyone does think you're dead."

"We crashed on New Year's Eve," he said. "I'm the only one who survived."

He steps <u>lithely</u> into the water, pulls the raft up on the beach, tosses the paddle back into the raft.

"Five days I've been out there," he says. "Give or take a day. I sliced up the other paddle with my pocket knife, made a spear. Caught three fish. Never thought I'd enjoy eating raw fish. But I was so hungry they tasted like they were cooked. By the way,

where am I?"

I tell him.

He thinks a minute.

"It's possible. We crashed at night on the way to Managua. The plane was carrying three times the weight it should have, but the need was so great. Supplies for the earthquake victims.

"You look so surprised," he says after a pause. "Have they called off the air search already, given us up for dead?" When I remain silent he continues. "Which way is your hotel? I must call my wife, she'll be so worried."

"I am surprised. More than surprised. You are Roberto Clemente, the baseball player?"

"Of course."

"You were lost at sea?"

"Until now."

"There's something not quite right."

"Like what?" says Clemente.

"Like what year do you think this is?"

"When we took off it was 1972, but New Year's Eve. We crashed in the ocean. It must be January fifth or sixth, maybe even the seventh, 1973. I haven't been gone so long that I'd lose track of the year."

"What if I told you that it was March 1987?"

"I'd laugh. Look at me! I'd be an old man in 1987. I'd be..."

"Fifty two. Fifty three in August."

"How do you know that?"

"I know a little about baseball. I was a fan of yours."

He smiles in spite of himself.

"Thank you. But 1987? Ha! And I don't like the way you said *was*. *Was* a fan of mine." He touches spread fingers to his chest. "These are the clothes I wore the night we crashed. Do I look like I've been wearing

> **lithe·ly** (līth′ lē) *adv.*, bending easily

Differentiated Instruction

Visual Learning

Students who respond best to visual methods may enjoy translating the short story into graphic novel form. Have students work alone or in groups on this project. They will need to decide which moments they want to illustrate, as well as which parts of the dialogue should be used. Encourage them to add flashbacks to scenes from Clemente's life or events the narrator describes, as well as thought balloons expressing images or dialogue that might occur in the characters' imaginations. Have students share their artwork with classmates.

them for fifteen years? Is this a fifteen-year growth of beard?" he asks, rubbing a hand across his stubbly chin. "A six-day beard would be my guess."

His eyes study me as if I were an umpire who just called an outside pitch strike three: my pale, tourist's skin, the slight stoop as if the weight of paradise is too much for me.

"Say, what are you doing out here alone at dawn?" Clemente says skeptically. "Are you escaped from somewhere?"

"No. But I think you may be. Believe me, it is 1987."

"Can't be. I can tell. I'm thirty-eight years old. I play baseball. See my World Series ring." He thrusts his hand toward me, the gold and diamonds glitter as the sun blushes above the horizon.

I dig frantically in my wallet. "Look!" I cry. "I'm from Seattle. Here's the 1987 Seattle Mariners schedule." I hold the pocket-sized schedule out for him to look at.

"Seattle doesn't have a team."

"They have a new franchise,[1] since 1977. Toronto came in the same year. Read the schedule."

He studies it for a moment.

"It's crazy, man. I've only been gone a few days."

We sit down on the sand, and I show him everything in my wallet: my credit cards, an uncashed check, my driver's license, coins, and bills.

"Try to remember when your plane went down. Maybe there's a clue there."

We walk slowly in the direction of the

hotel, but at the edge of the bay, where we would turn inland, Clemente stops. We retrace our steps.

"It was late in the night. The plane was old. It groaned and creaked like a haunted house. I was sitting back with the cargo—bales of clothes, medical supplies—when the pilot started yelling that we were losing altitude. We must have practically been in the water before he noticed. We hit the ocean a few seconds later, and I was buried under boxes and bales as the cargo shifted. A wooden box bounced off my head, and I was out for...a few seconds or a few minutes." He rubs the top of his head.

> "I yelled for the others but I don't know if they were alive or if they heard me."

"See, I still got the lump. And I bled some, too." He bends toward me so I can see the small swelling, the residue of dried blood clinging around the roots of his sleek, black hair.

"When I woke up I was in front of the emergency door, the cargo had rolled over me and I was snug against the exit. The plane must have been more than half submerged. There was this frightening slurping, gurgling sound. Then I realized my clothes were wet. The raft was on the wall right next to the door. I pulled the door open and the ocean flooded in. I set out the raft, inflated it, and took the paddles and the big water canteen off the wall. I yelled for the others but I don't know if they were alive or if they heard me. There was a mountain of cargo between me and the front of the plane.

"I climbed into the raft, paddled a few

---

1. **franchise.** Right or license granted to a group

Teach the Selection

Analyze Literature
Sensory Details Remind students that sensory details relate to one of the five senses (sight, sound, taste, touch, and smell). Draw their attention to Clemente's description of the accident. What sensory details help make the event seem real? Responses include the nighttime darkness and crowded space in the plane (sight); the plane's groaning and creaking, the pilot yelling, the slurping and gurgling (sound); and the feeling of hitting the water and being struck on the head (touch). **B**

Use Reading Skills
Identify Multiple Levels of Meaning Remind students that literary works often have multiple meanings—that is, symbolic meanings in addition to what the words literally say. Challenge them to identify possible levels of meaning in the story. (The story is not about Roberto Clemente really walking out of the ocean. Instead, it might be a fantasy that the narrator, a huge baseball fan, has as he walks on the beach during his vacation.)

Writing Skills

Monologue
Explain that a monologue is a speech in which one character (often in a play, but also in prose) explains his or her thoughts or feelings to another. It is a form of personal narrative, a story told from the speaker's point of view. Point out that Clemente's speech, beginning with "When I woke up" is an example.

Note that when a speech in a story goes on for more than one paragraph, it is punctuated differently: There are no quotation marks at the end of a paragraph if the speaker continues speaking in the next paragraph. Have students write a three- to five-paragraph personal narrative that includes a monologue. Remind them to correctly punctuate the speech.

Analyze Literature

Figurative Language Ask students to identify similes and metaphors as they read. You may wish to return to this page to review those ("strong as a bull," "They've been doormats for several seasons," "sand white as a bridal gown") as well as turns of phrase such as "Gone to hell in a handbasket" and "The earth wills out." Have volunteers suggest what these sayings mean.

History Connection

Puerto Rican Statehood Puerto Rico was ruled by Spain from 1509 until 1898, when the United States seized the territory during the Spanish American War. Over time, the United States instituted many social and economic programs there. In 1917, Puerto Ricans were granted U.S. citizenship, and the country was declared an independent commonwealth in 1952. It has its own constitution, leader (a governor), and legislature, but still operates under U.S. supervision. There has been a longstanding debate over whether Puerto Rico should become the fifty-first state. Most Puerto Ricans favor some sort of connection with the United States, rather than complete independence. So far, though, proposals in favor of statehood have been voted down in 1967, 1993, and 1998. **Ⓐ**

yards, and when I looked back the plane was gone. I've been drifting for five or six days, and here I am."

"I don't know where you've been, but you went missing New Year's Eve 1972. They elected you to the Baseball Hall of Fame in 1973, waived the five-year waiting period because you'd died a hero."

"Died?" Clemente begins a laugh, then thinks better of it. "What if I go back with you and call in?"

"You'll create one of the greatest sensations of all time."

"But, look at me, I'm thirty-eight years old, strong as a bull."

"But my wife, my family. Will they all be fifteen years older?"

"I'm afraid so."

"My kids grown up?"

"Yes."

"Maybe my wife has remarried?"

"I don't know, but it's certainly a possibility."

"But, look at me, I'm thirty-eight years old, strong as a bull. The Pirates need me in the outfield."

"I know."

"My teammates?"

"All retired."

"No."

"If I remember right, Bruce Kison was the last to go, retired last year."

"Willie Stargell?"

"Retired in 1982. He's still in baseball but not playing."

"Then I suppose everyone that played at the same time, they're gone too? Marichal? Seaver? Bench? McCovey? Brock? McCarver? Carlton?"

"Carlton's won over three hundred games, but he doesn't know when to quit. He's a marginal player in the American League. So is Don Sutton, though he's also won three hundred. Jerry Reuss is still hanging on, maybe one or two others. Hank Aaron broke Babe Ruth's home-run record, then a guy from Japan named Sadaharu Oh broke Hank Aaron's record."

"And my Pirates?"

"Gone to hell in a handbasket. They won the World Series in '78, Willie Stargell's last hurrah. They've been doormats for several seasons, will be again this year. Attendance is down to nothing; there's talk of moving the franchise out of Pittsburgh."

"They need Roberto Clemente."

"Indeed they do."

"And Nicaragua? The earthquake?"

"The earth wills out," I said. "The will of the people to survive is so strong....The earthquake is history now."

Ⓐ "And Puerto Rico? Is my home a state yet?"

"Not yet."

He looks longingly toward the path that leads to the hotel and town. We sit for a long time in that sand white as a bridal gown. He studies the artifacts of my life. Finally he speaks.

"If I walk up that path, and if the world is as you say—and I think I believe you—I will become a curiosity. The media will swarm

336 UNIT 3 NONFICTION

Differentiated Instruction

Auditory and Kinesthetic Learning

The reading includes promising ideas for dramatic skits or monologues. These include

- the first conversation between Clemente and the narrator on page 334 and the top of page 335
- Clemente's monologue on page 335, ending at the top of page 336
- the concluding dialogue beginning at the end of page 336 and finishing on page 337

Students may work individually or in pairs. Give students time to choose what they are going to do, adapt it for performance, and rehearse. Have them perform in the order in which their material appears in the reading.

over me unlike anything I've ever known. Religious fanatics will picnic on my blood. If I see one more person, I'll have no choice but to stay here."

"What are your alternatives?"

"I could try to pass as an ordinary citizen who just happens to look like Roberto Clemente did fifteen years ago. But if I become real to the world I may suddenly find myself white-haired and in rags, fifty-three years old."

"What about baseball?"

"I could never play again, I would give myself away. No one plays the game like Clemente."

"I remember watching you play. When you ran for a fly ball it was like you traveled three feet above the grass, your feet never touching. 'He has invisible pillows of angel hair attached to his feet,' my wife said one night, 'that's how he glides across the outfield.' **B**

"Perhaps you could go to the Mexican Leagues," I suggest. "Remember George Brunet, the pitcher? He's still pitching in the badlands and he's nearly fifty."

"I suffer from greed, my friend, from wanting to claim what is mine: my family, my home, my wealth. My choice is all or nothing."

Use Reading Strategies

Visualize Ask students to visualize the narrator's description of how Clemente ran across a ball field, including his wife's statement "He has invisible pillows of angel hair attached to his feet . . . that's how he glides across the outfield." Have students describe what this would look like, or have them give you examples of other sports figures who move like this. **B**

Make Connections

Give students a minute to study the photograph on this page. Ask them how it represents the mood of the story. You might also ask students how the photograph makes them feel.

Writing Skills

Audience

Remind students that when they write, it is critical to consider their audience—the person or group of people they want to read their work. They should answer such questions as

- Will the topic interest the targeted readers?
- How much do they already know about the topic? Can I use specialized terminology or should I provide background information?

- What is the audience's reading level? Are they beginning readers, experienced readers, or readers with special interests?

Have students consider Kinsella's audience. Ask: "For whom was Kinsella writing?"

Analyze Literature

Characterization Remind students to list instances of characterization on the charts they created before reading "A Bittersweet Memoir." Encourage the class to compare and contrast the character of Roberto Clemente as presented by Jerry Izenberg and W. P. Kinsella. Offer students opportunities to state which "Clemente" they like better or which they find more intriguing. Then probe to find out which details led them to make these choices.

Answer: Most students will have wished for this for a variety of reasons. Most will also agree that this is a fairly common feeling, especially when people are unhappy with their current situations.

"The nothing being?"

"To continue the search."

"But how?"

"I've searched a few days and already I've found 1987. Time has tricked me some way. Perhaps if I continue searching for January 1973, I'll find it."

"And if you don't?"

"Something closer then, a time I could accept, that would accept me."

"But what if this is all there is? What if you drift forever? What if you drift until you die?"

"I can't leap ahead in time. It's unnatural. I just can't."

"If you came back to baseball, Three Rivers Stadium would be full every night. You could make Pittsburgh a baseball city again. You'd have to put up with the media, the curious, the fanatics. But perhaps it's what you're destined to do."

"I am destined to be found, maybe even on this beach, but fifteen years in your past. I intend to be found. I'll keep searching for January."

He walked a few steps in the direction of the raft.

"Wait. I'll go and bring you supplies. I can be back in twenty minutes."

"No. I don't want to carry anything away from this time. I have five gallons of water, a bale of blankets to warm me at night, the ingenuity to catch food. Perhaps my footprints in the sand are already too much, who knows?"

He is wading in the clear water, already pushing the raft back into the ocean.

"If you find January...if the history I know is suddenly altered, I hope I went to see you play a few times. With you in the line-up the Pirates probably made it into the World Series in '74 and '75. They won their division those years, you know...you would have been the difference..."

I watch him drift. Trapped. Or am I trapped, here in 1987, while he, through some malfunction of the universe, is borne into timelessness? What if I were to accompany him?

"Wait!" I call. "There's something..."

But Clemente has already drifted beyond hearing. I watch as he paddles, his back broad and strong. Just as the mist is about to engulf him, as ocean, fog, and sky merge, he waves his oar once, holding it like a baseball bat, thrusting it at the soft, white sky. ❖

When have you wished to be in another place or time? Why did you feel that way? Why do you think most people have experienced this feeling in their lives?

Differentiated Instruction

Enrichment

Students may note that the disorientation the narrator feels in "Searching for January" is similar to the temporary disorientation experienced in "The Inn of Lost Time" in Unit 1. In this story, the narrator watches as Clemente anticipates what it would be like to lose years of his life and chooses not to. In the other story, characters fear they have already lost many years and struggle to regain them. Have students write a brief essay comparing and contrasting the characters' reactions to "time travel" in these two stories.

Review the Selections

Find Meaning

1. (a) Who appears out of the mist in front of the narrator? (b) What does this person shout to the narrator?

2. (a) How many years have passed since Clemente's plane went down? (b) How does the narrator prove what year it actually is?

Compare Literature

Characterization In *direct characterization,* an author or narrator makes direct statements about a character's personality. In *indirect characterization,* the writer reveals a character's personality through the character's words, thoughts, actions, appearance, or the words and thoughts of other characters. Review the descriptions that you recorded in your chart to answer these questions.

Make Judgments

3. What do Clemente's questions and statements reveal about his values?

4. Why does Clemente decide to go back to his raft?

1. What did Clemente look like?

2. Find an example of direct and indirect characterization of Clemente from Izenberg's biography or Kinsella's short story.

3. Which selection contains the most examples of Clemente's conversation, regardless of whether this conversation is fictional or not?

Extend Understanding

Writing Options

Creative Writing Imagine that the narrator in "Searching for January" reported his experience on the beach. Assume that you have interviewed the narrator, and write a brief **news article** about the incident. Use quotations from your imaginary interview and information you learned from reading the story.

Expository Writing In an **essay,** compare and contrast Clemente as presented in the biography and in the short story. First, use a graphic organizer to show the features you want to write about, such as appearance, character, achievements, and effect on others. You may organize your work either by examining how Clemente is presented first in one work and then in the other or by discussing each feature in turn. Share your work with the class.

Collaborative Learning

Create a Dialogue Imagine that the narrator of "Searching for January" runs into Clemente once again, after several more years have passed, and Clemente still hasn't changed. Working in pairs, create a dialogue between Clemente and the narrator of "Searching for January." Perform your dialogue for the class.

Media Literacy

Conduct Internet Research Evaluate the home pages of two or three sports organizations. Include in your evaluation how well the home page is organized, how current the information is, how easy it is to find information, and whether you find errors of any kind. Present your findings to the class.

Go to www.mirrorsandwindows.com for more.

Find Meaning

1. (a) A man paddling a camouflaged raft appears out of the mist. (b) The man shouts that he is Clemente and that his plane went down days ago.

2. (a) Fifteen years have passed. (b) The narrator shows Clemente a 1987 Seattle Mariners schedule, his credit cards, a check, and his driver's license. He also relates changes in the world of baseball.

Make Judgments

3. Clemente is concerned about what has happened to his family and his teammates, Puerto Rico, and his ability to play again if he becomes "real to the world." He feels a strong connection to his family, friends, country, and baseball.

4. He understands that if he suddenly reappears, he will "become a curiosity." Clemente wants to go where he feels he belongs.

Compare Literature

Characterization

1. In "A Bittersweet Memoir," Luis Olmo remembers him as a skinny kid. The narrator in "Searching for January" says he is "tall and athletic-looking, dark-skinned, with a long jaw and flashing eyes."

2. Examples will vary. Izenberg includes the most about other people's opinions, which constitute indirect characterization.

3. The short story contains more examples.

Rubrics for Writing Options

You can adapt this as a checklist for students to use as they write.

Creative Writing

☐ Does the article use information from the short story?

☐ Does the article include information from an imaginary interview?

☐ Does the article use quotations?

Expository Writing

☐ Does the essay compare and contrast Clemente as portrayed in the biography and in the short story?

☐ Is the essay organized effectively?

☐ Does the essay accurately present the facts about Clemente?

DIRECTED READING

At a Glance
Directed Reading
- Reading Level: Challenging
- Difficulty Consideration: Vocabulary
- Ease Factor: Introduction

Objectives
Studying this lesson will enable students to
- use reading skills such as context clues
- identify the purposes of introductions and conclusions
- recognize how writers and artists keep alive the stories of people from history
- appreciate a story about how a person won freedom

Launch the Lesson
Ask students to work in small groups. Give groups three minutes to jot down everything they know about the hair care business. Prompt them with words such as *color, cut, shop,* and *curl.* Then have representatives from each group take turns giving information from the group's discussion. When each group has taken two or three turns, tell students that now they will read "Madam C.J. Walker," a biography about a true pioneer in the hair care business.

Madam C. J. Walker
A Biography by Jim Haskins

BEFORE READING

Build Background
Historical Context Life for African Americans was very difficult during and just after Reconstruction, the period that followed the Civil War. Many white people refused to hire freed slaves or train them for careers other than farming or manual labor. Many African Americans became sharecroppers. A sharecropper provided farm labor in return for a share in the profits from the crop produced. But sharecroppers had to buy food and equipment from the landowner, and the share of the crop was typically not enough to pay for these things. Often sharecroppers were left with no money or even went into debt.

Reader's Context What goals do you have for your life? What obstacles might you face in achieving these goals?

Set Purpose
Preview the Historical Context and the first page of "Madam C. J. Walker." Predict how Madam Walker might have overcome the obstacles faced by African-American business owners.

Analyze Literature
Introduction and Conclusion An **introduction** to a literary work should capture the reader's attention and present the subject of the work. A **conclusion** should sum up the ideas presented in the piece and present a final analysis of the subject. As you read, pay close attention to the introduction and conclusion of this selection.

Meet the Author
Jim Haskins (1941–2005) wrote more than one hundred books in his lifetime. Many of his books tell the stories of famous African Americans, including Rosa Parks, Thurgood Marshall, and Colin Powell. He won the *Washington Post* Children's Book Guild Award for his nonfiction books for young people. Haskins was an English professor at the University of Florida.

Use Reading Skills
Context Clues Unlock the meaning of each word by using the context clues provided in the sentences.

1. Sheri withdrew from the class, with the <u>provision</u> that she could retake it.
2. We protested the decision to <u>segregate</u> students based on race.
3. The coach will try to <u>recruit</u> Gabriel for the basketball team.
4. Mia's <u>ambition</u> is to become a doctor.
5. The ancient Romans held <u>lavish</u> feasts with endless food.
6. The captain made the <u>astute</u> decision to return to port when he saw the storm.

Preview Vocabulary
pro•vi•sion (prə viˊ zhən) *n.,* arrangement made beforehand to deal with a certain need

seg•re•gate (segˊ ri gāt') *v.,* separate a race, class, or ethnic group from the rest of the population; set apart

re•cruit (ri krütˊ) *v.,* hire or engage the services

am•bi•tion (am biˊ shən) *n.,* drive to succeed

lav•ish (laˊ vish) *adj.,* abundant; rich

as•tute (ə stütˊ) *adj.,* possessing practical intelligence and the ability to make good decisions

---

Words in Use

Preview Vocabulary
provision, 342
segregate, 342
recruit, 345
ambition, 346
lavish, 346
astute, 346

Selection Words
sharecroppers, 342
salve, 344
avid, 346
hypertension, 346
rejuvenation, 347

Common Core State Standards
Reading Literature
RL.4

Reading Informational
RI.4

Madam C. J. Walker

A Biography by Jim Haskins

Then one night she had a dream.

341

Summary

Madam C. J. Walker, born Sarah Breedlove in 1867, was the daughter of former slaves. Sarah had little opportunity for schooling. She married young, and her husband was killed in a lynching when the couple's baby, Lelia, was just two. Sarah provided for her child by doing laundry for others. Later, a seemingly unfortunate situation, Sarah's discovery that her hair was falling out, became a turning point in her life. She created a remedy for the problem and began selling it and other hair care products. Sarah became known as Madam C. J. Walker, *Walker* being her second husband's name and *Madam* because she liked the sound of it. She became the first American woman to earn a million dollars.

The Mirrors & Windows questions at the end of the selection focus on the theme of helping others. Before students begin to read, ask: What have you done in the last week to help someone else get ahead?

Program Resources

Planning and Assessment
Program Planning Guide, Selection Lesson Plan
E-Lesson Planner
Assessment Guide, Lesson Test
ExamView

Technology Tools
Interactive Student Text on CD
Visual Teaching Package
Audio Library
mirrorsandwindows.com

Meeting the Standards
Nonfiction: Unit 3, Directed Reading, pp. 71–81

Differentiating Instruction
English Language Learners, Use Context Clues, pp. 120–131

Analyze Literature

Introduction Call attention to the introductory paragraph. Explain that an introduction gives an overview of what a selection will be about. Model using the introduction: "The introduction makes me wonder, 'How did Walker achieve success?'" Invite students to share questions the introduction inspires for them. **A**

Cultural Connection

Entrepreneurs Write the word *entrepreneur* on the board. Explain that the word comes from the French verb *entreprendre*, which means to undertake. Tell students that an entrepreneur is a person who starts and manages a business. An entrepreneur risks his or her money, time, and talent in hopes of making a profit. Point out that in the 1800s and early to mid-1900s, it was rare for a woman to be an entrepreneur. As students read, ask them to think about how Madam C. J. Walker fits the definition of an entrepreneur and which of her qualities allowed her to do something so unusual.

Use Reading Skills

Take Notes Suggest that students use a graphic organizer called a sequence chain to keep track of the major events. Tell them to sketch a series of horizontal rectangles connected with left and right arrows. Instruct them to write one key event in each rectangle and to record events in the order in which they happen. Have them include dates, when possible.

A Madam C. J. Walker was the first American woman to earn a million dollars. There were American women millionaires before her time, but they had inherited their wealth, either from their husbands or from their families. Madam Walker was the first woman to earn her fortune by setting up her own business and proving that women could be financially independent of men. The company she started in the early years of this century is still in operation today.

Madam C. J. Walker was born Sarah Breedlove on December 23, 1867. She grew up in the South under very racist conditions. Her parents, Owen and Minerva Breedlove, had been slaves until President Abraham Lincoln's Emancipation Proclamation and the Union victory in the Civil War had freed the slaves.

After the war, few <u>provisions</u> were made to help former slaves become independent. They did not receive money to help them get started in their new lives. They were uneducated, they had few skills except the ability to grow crops, and many were unaware of what freedom meant. Like the majority of former slaves, the Breedloves remained on the Burney family plantation in Delta, Louisiana. They had little choice but to stay on the same land where they had been slaves, only now they were sharecroppers.

Sharecroppers farm land for a landowner. In return, they receive a place to live and part of the crop. But since they must buy what they cannot grow from the landowner, when they harvest the crop they find themselves owing whatever is their share to the landowner anyway.

The Breedloves sharecropped cotton. Like her brothers and sisters, Sarah was working in the cotton fields by the time she was six. By the time she was seven, both her parents were dead, and she moved in with her older sister, Louvenia. A few years later, they moved across the river to Vicksburg, Mississippi.

Sarah had little schooling. Like other sharecroppers' children, she had a chance to go to school only when there were no crops to be planted or harvested, which totaled about four months out of the year. She also had little happiness in her childhood. Not only was she an orphan, but she also suffered at the hands of her sister's cruel husband. Sarah was just fourteen when she married a man named McWilliams to get away from her sister's household.

By the time Sarah got married, conditions in the South for blacks were actually worse than they had been during slavery. This was the time when Jim Crow laws were passed, <u>segregating</u> southern blacks from whites in nearly every area of life. It was the time when white supremacy groups like the Ku Klux Klan achieved their greatest power, and lynchings of blacks were common.

Sarah and her husband lived with the terror of being black as best they could. In

> **Madam C. J. Walker was the first American woman to earn a million dollars.**

pro·vi·sion (prə viˊ zhən) *n.*, arrangement made beforehand to deal with a certain need

seg·re·gate (segˊ ri gātˊ) *v.*, separate a race, class, or ethnic group from the rest of the population; set apart

---

Differentiated Instruction

Reading Proficiency

Work with students to begin recording events on their sequence chains. Model placing the first entry on the chain: "1867: birth of Sarah Breedlove." Help students identify the next event to add to the chain. Then have pairs work together to record events from the first page of the selection. Tell students to keep working on the chain as they read.

Visual Learning

Have students find a visual way to summarize what sharecroppers gained and gave up (or lost) in the sharecropping system. For example, a student might summarize in equation form: work + part of the crop = home + part of the crop.

1885 their daughter, Lelia, was born, and her parents dreamed of making a better life for their little girl. Then, when Lelia was two, McWilliams was killed by a lynch mob.[1]

Sarah was a widow at the age of twenty, and the sole support of a two-year-old daughter. She took in laundry to earn a living and was determined to leave the South. With Lelia, she made her way up the Mississippi River and settled in St. Louis, where she worked fourteen hours a day doing other people's laundry. She enrolled Lelia in the St. Louis public schools and was pleased that her daughter would get the education that had been denied to her. But she wanted more for her daughter and for herself.

Not long after they moved to St. Louis, Sarah McWilliams realized that her hair was falling out. She did not know why, but it is likely that the practice of braiding her hair too tightly was part of the cause. At the time, few hair-care products were available for black women. The ideal was straight, "white," hair, and to achieve this effect black women divided their hair into sections, wrapped string tightly around each section, and then twisted them. When the hair was later combed out, it was straighter. But this procedure pulled on the scalp and caused the hair to fall out.

The Coiffeur. Anne Goldthwaite. The Newark Museum, Newark, New Jersey.

Sarah was not the only black woman to suffer from hair loss. But she was one who refused to accept the idea that there was nothing she could do about it. For years she tried every hair-care product available. But nothing worked.

Then one night she had a dream. As she told the story many years later, in her dream "a black man appeared to me and told me what to mix up for my hair. Some of the remedy was grown in Africa, but I sent for it, mixed it, put it on my scalp, and in a few weeks my hair was coming in faster than it had ever fallen out." Sarah never publicly revealed[2] the formula of her mixture.

Sarah's friends remarked on what a full and healthy head of hair she had, and she gave some of her mixture to them. It worked on them, too, so she decided to sell it. She later said that she started her "Hair Grower" business with an investment of $1.50.

She had not been in business long when she received word that a brother who lived in Denver, Colorado, had died, leaving a wife and daughters. Her own daughter, Lelia, was attending Knoxville College, a private black college in Tennessee, and did not need her around all the time. Sarah decided to go to

---

1. **McWilliams...mob.** No documentation actually proves that he died this way.
2. **revealed.** Showed; made known

History Connection

Lynching Explain that the Ku Klux Klan was a secret group established after the Civil War. Its aim was to rid communities of African Americans. In the dark of night, members dressed in robes and hoods to disguise themselves and went about terrorizing black people. They even resorted to murder. They were responsible for many lynchings. Explain that a lynching is hanging a person accused of some wrongdoing without a legal trial. A *lynch mob* is the group of people who carry out the hanging. Over 3,400 African Americans were lynched between 1882 and 1951. **B**

Use Reading Skills

Context Clues Call attention to the word *sole*. Help students use the context clue *widow* to determine that *sole* means "only." **C**

Analyze Literature

Characterization Have students think back over what they have read. Ask: "What do we know so far about the kind of person Sarah Breedlove was?" Model a response: "She was a hard worker. I can tell because Haskins says she worked fourteen hours a day." Have students identify other qualities of Breedlove and match them with specific details from the biography. **D**

Primary and Secondary Sources

Point out that in writing about Madam Walker's life, Haskins may have used both primary and secondary sources. Primary sources are firsthand information, such as a letter written by Walker. Secondary sources contain information communicated by people who did not personally experience an event, but found out about it through others. A newspaper article would be a secondary source. Have students sort the following into primary and secondary sources: the notes Walker used to give a speech, the transcript of an interview with her, a book about her, an entry from her journal, a play about her, and an advertisement she wrote for her business.

Make Connections
Tell students that Madam C. J. Walker once said, "I got my start by giving myself a start." Have students explain what this quote means, and then ask them how the quote relates to what they have read so far about Walker. Invite students to tell about someone they know personally to whom this quote also applies and explain why he or she fits the quote.

Analyze Literature
Characterization Point out that Madam Walker and her second husband had some things in common as well as some differences of opinion. Have students use a Venn diagram to compare and contrast the knowledge and personalities of Madam C. J. Walker and her husband, C. J. Walker. Sketch a Venn diagram on the board. Label one circle "Madam C. J. Walker" and the other circle "C. J. Walker." Write "Both" where the circles overlap. Then model using the diagram by writing "no knowledge of advertising" in the circle for Madam Walker and "knowledge of mail order" in the circle for Mr. Walker. Ask students to propose more traits for you to record on the diagram. **Ⓐ**

Denver to live with her sister-in-law and nieces.

In Denver, Sarah began to sell her special haircare product and did well. But she realized she needed to advertise to get more customers. Six months after arriving in Denver, she married C. J. Walker, a newspaperman who knew a lot about selling by mail order. With his help, she began to advertise her product, first in black newspapers across the state and later in black newspapers nationwide, and to make more money.

But soon her marriage was in trouble. As Sarah Walker later said of her husband, **Ⓐ** "I had business disagreements with him, for when we began to make ten dollars a day, he thought that amount was enough and that I should be satisfied. But I was convinced that my hair preparations would fill a longfelt want, and when we found it impossible to agree, due to his narrowness of vision, I embarked in business for myself."

In addition to helping her learn about advertising, her marriage gave Sarah Breedlove McWilliams Walker the name she would use for the rest of her life—Madam C. J. Walker. The "Madam" part was an affectation,[3] but Sarah liked the way it sounded. She thought it would be good for

Advertisement showing Madam C. J. Walker's hair and skin products.

her business. By 1906 her business was so well that she was able to stop doing laundry for a living and devote all her time to her hair-care company. Her products by this time included "Wonderful Hair Grower," "Glossine" hair oil, "Temple Grower," and "Tetter Salve" for the scalp.

Madam Walker was very proud of being a woman, and she was convinced that she could make it in the business world without the help of men. Almost from the start she determined that her business would be run by women. In 1906 she put her twenty-one-year-old daughter, Lelia, in charge of her growing mail-order business. She herself started traveling throughout the South and East selling her preparations and teaching her methods of hair care. She was so successful that two years later she and Lelia moved to Pittsburgh, Pennsylvania, and started Lelia College, which taught the Walker System of hair care.

Once again, Lelia ran the business while her mother traveled thousands of miles to spread the word. Madam Walker realized that the normal outlets for her products—white department stores and pharmacies—

---

3. affectation. Artificial behavior meant to impress others

Auditory Learning
As Madam C. J. Walker, have students give talks promoting her Hair Grower product. To prepare, have them brainstorm words that would tap into their audience's concern about the problem and words that would excite people about the product.

Enrichment
Use a classroom computer, or send students to the library, to visit the Madam C. J. Walker website. This site has intriguing historical photographs and background about Walker's life and times.

were not open to her. These stores would not stock black products because they did not want black customers. In addition to advertising, mostly in black newspapers, Madam Walker had to depend on the institutions in the black communities, the black churches, and the black women's clubs.

Madam Walker's lectures on hair culture were widely attended. She was an excellent speaker and a commanding woman, nearly six feet tall, who was always beautifully dressed and coiffed.[4] She made a lasting impression wherever she went.

Her travels, and her personality, brought her into contact with many important black people. She joined the National Association of Colored Women **B** and through that organization met the educator Mary McLeod Bethune. She also met Ida B. Wells-Barnett, who worked for the right of women to vote, and against lynching in the South. She formed friendships with these women, who helped her spread the word about her business.

Although she lacked the formal education that most of these women had, Madam Walker never felt ashamed of her shortcomings[5] in that area. She taught herself as much as she could and was not afraid to ask someone to define a word she did not know or explain something she did not understand.

There were other black hair-care companies in business at this time. A couple of companies were owned by whites. But they stressed hair straightening. Madam

Walker emphasized hair care. Most of the products she developed were aimed at producing healthy hair, not straight hair. She did design a steel comb with teeth spaced far enough apart to go through thick hair, but its main purpose was not hair straightening.

Madam Walker also wanted black women to go into business. Why should they toil over hot laundry tubs and clean white people's houses when they could be in business for themselves? Helping other black women also helped the Walker Company, and with this goal in mind Madam Walker recruited and trained scores of women to use and sell Walker products. Many of them set up salons in their own homes. Others traveled door-to-door selling Walker products and demonstrating the Walker System. Madam Walker insisted that her agents sign contracts promising to abide by her strict standards of personal hygiene[6]—long before various states passed similar laws for workers in the cosmetics field. By 1910 the Walker Company had trained around 5,000 black female agents, not just in the United States but in England, France, Italy, and the West Indies. The company itself was taking in $1,000 a day, seven days a week.

That same year, Madam Walker's travels took her to Indianapolis, Indiana, a city that impressed her so much that she decided to

> **She was an excellent speaker and a commanding woman, nearly six feet tall, who was always beautifully dressed and coiffed.**

---

4. **coiffed.** Styled, specifically hair
5. **shortcomings.** Less than what is expected or required
6. **hygiene.** Cleanliness and sanitary practices

re·cruit (ri krüt´) v., hire or engage the services

Teach the Selection

History Connection

Walker's Peers Mary McLeod Bethune was born in 1875 to former slaves. Although it was a hardship, her family made it possible for her to go to school. She taught in a mission school for a time, and then in 1904 opened her own school. Bethune was especially concerned about educating girls. Her school grew rapidly and in time became the Bethune-Cookman College, which still exists.

Ida Bell Wells was also the daughter of slaves. She was born in 1862 and was college educated. At fourteen, Wells got a job teaching in a country school for African-American children. She was fired, however, when she wrote an article speaking out against the poor quality of schools for African Americans. This inspired her to begin working as a journalist. In 1892, three of her friends were lynched. This made her put her energies into speaking out against this horrible crime. She continued this campaign, along with working for the vote for black women, throughout her life. **B**

Analyze Literature

Tone Explain that tone is a writer's attitude toward the subject or the reader. Help students determine Haskins's attitude toward Madam C. J. Walker. Have students support their responses with information from the biography.

Vocabulary Skills

Restatements

Have students locate the sentence with the word *abide* in it. Read it aloud. Ask: "What is another word for *standard*?" (rule) "What did Walker want her workers to do?" (follow her rules) Then have students restate the sentence in their own words.

Have students find other words in the selection that are challenging for them or they think might be unfamiliar to other students. Guide them in using questions and restatements to clarify the meanings of those words.

Cultural Connection

Segregation Point out that when Walker was traveling around the country, segregation still existed. Therefore, Walker had to use separate facilities for transportation, lodging, and meals on her trips.

Use Reading Skills

Identify Sequence of Events
Provide time for students to finish their sequence chains (see the Skills lesson on page 342). Then, have them used the completed chains to summarize events that led to the success of Madam Walker.

Make Connections

Have students make a two-column chart showing in one column what Madam Walker accomplished and in the other the personal traits that allowed her to succeed. Then ask students to make a second chart. Have them think about something they care about deeply. In the first column have them list some things they would like to accomplish related to that interest. In the other column, have them list personal traits that they have or can develop to accomplish their goals.

Analyze Literature

Conclusion Call attention to the conclusion of the biography on page 347. Have students identify information that summarizes the main point of the selection.

---

move her headquarters there. She put a man in charge of her operations, which was a departure from her usual philosophy, but Freeman B. Ransom was, in her opinion, an unusual man.

She had met him in her travels when he was working as a train porter summers and during school vacations, while working his way through Columbia University Law School. He impressed her with his <u>ambition</u> and with his vision of progress for blacks. When he finished school, she put him in charge of her Indianapolis headquarters.

In 1913 Lelia moved from Pittsburgh to New York to expand the Walker Company's East Coast operations. Madam Walker built a <u>lavish</u> town house in Harlem at 108–110 West 136th Street and installed a completely equipped beauty parlor.

Lelia had become an <u>astute</u> businesswoman herself, although she did not have the drive of her mother. Lelia, who changed her name to A'Lelia, liked to enjoy the fruits of their success. The Walker town house soon became the "in" place for parties in Harlem, attended by wealthy and artistic people, black and white.

Madam Walker also enjoyed spending the money she made. In 1917 she built a $250,000 mansion on the Hudson River in upstate New York. She hired the black architect Vertner Tandy to design it and named it Villa Lewaro. She drove around in an electric car, dressed in the finest clothing, and was said to have spent $7,000 on jewelry in a single afternoon.

> ...Madam Walker insisted that the Madam C. J. Walker Company always be headed by a woman....

Madam Walker also gave generously to charity. She had a strong interest in education and took time out of her busy schedule to be tutored by Booker T. Washington, founder of Tuskegee Institute in Alabama. She became an avid reader of literature and American history. She encouraged her friend Mary McLeod Bethune and later gave money to Mrs. Bethune to establish her Daytona Normal and Industrial Institute for Negro Girls in Daytona, Florida. When the National Association of Colored Women decided to pay off the mortgage on the home of the late black abolitionist Frederick Douglass, Madam Walker made the largest single contribution.

Madam Walker did not have much of a private life. She spent her time thinking of new ways to increase her business. The friends she had were people who could help her.

By 1917 the years of traveling and overwork began to take their toll on her. She developed high blood pressure, and in 1918 her doctors warned her that she had to slow down. She turned over her responsibilities in the business to her daughter, to Freeman B. Ransom, and to other trusted associates, and retired to her mansion, Villa Lewaro. There, she tried to relax, but her mind was always on her business. She died quietly of kidney failure resulting from hypertension in May 1919.

> **am•bi•tion** (am biʹ shən) *n.*, drive to succeed
>
> **lav•ish** (laʹ vish) *adj.*, abundant; rich
>
> **as•tute** (ə stütʹ) *adj.*, possessing practical intelligence and the ability to make good decisions

---

Differentiated Instruction

English Language Learning

Explain, discuss, and practice using expressions and idioms from the selection, such as "put in charge of," "have the drive," and "fruits of their success."

Reading Proficiency

Remind students to add dates to their sequence chains whenever possible. Point out that sometimes they will have to figure out a date from context clues. For example, when Haskins says," That same year, Madam Walker's travels. . . ," they will need to look back a few sentences to see that the year was 1910.

In her will, Madam Walker left the bulk of her estate and the business to her daughter, A'Lelia. But she also provided generously for a variety of educational institutions run by black women, including $5,000 to Dr. Bethune's school. She established a trust fund for an industrial and mission school in West Africa and provided bequests[7] to Negro orphanages, old people's homes, and Negro YWCA branches. In addition, she made bequests to many friends and employees.

Also in her will, Madam Walker insisted that the Madam C. J. Walker Company always be headed by a woman, and her wishes were carried out. Her daughter, A'Lelia, became president of the company after her death and presided at the dedication of the new company headquarters in Indianapolis in 1927, fulfilling a long-held dream of her mother's.

Times have changed greatly since Madam C. J. Walker made her millions. Drugstores and department stores owned by both whites and blacks now stock hair- and skin-care products for black women. Many more companies, white and black, manufacture such products. In the midst of all that competition, the Walker Company is not as active as it once was, although it still sells some of the products Madam developed. The Walker Building is being renovated[8] as part of the rejuvenation of downtown Indianapolis. Now called the Madam Walker Urban Life Center, it houses professional offices and a cultural center.

Madam C. J. Walker, the daughter of former slaves, with little education, overcame the barriers of being black and a woman and succeeded beyond everyone's expectations but her own. ❖

---

7. **bequests.** Things handed down or passed on
8. **renovated.** Replaced worn and broken parts

 Madam C. J. Walker helped many African-American women escape poverty and become successful businesswomen. If you could do one thing to help others, what would you choose to do and why?

Find Meaning

1. (a) What inspired Madam Walker to develop her first haircare product? (b) What did she realize she needed to do to get more customers?
2. (a) How did Madam Walker's second husband help her business? (b) Name all the ways that Madam Walker reached possible buyers for her products. Why did she need to use all these methods to sell her products?
3. (a) What did Madam Walker and her second husband disagree about? (b) Why did Madam Walker think her company could do better? (c) What does this suggest about her personality?

Make Judgments

4. (a) What hardships did Madam Walker experience from childhood until the time she started her own business? (b) How did Madam Walker help others who faced similar difficulties? (c) In what ways did she make a difference so that others might not face such a struggle?
5. (a) How did Madam Walker deal with her lack of formal education? (b) What does this behavior say about her?
6. (a) How does the author describe the character of Madam Walker? (b) How did these character traits help her succeed in business?

MADAM C. J. WALKER **347**

Grammar Skills

Independent Clauses

Remind students that an independent clause can stand on its own as a sentence, and a sentence may contain one or more independent clauses.

For example, "Madam Walker was a millionaire." has one independent clause. "She developed her own hair care products, and she started a school" has two independent clauses. Have students identify the independent clauses in the following sentences:

1. Walker talked to other women about starting businesses, and they opened their own salons.
2. The Walker Company had five thousand workers by 1910.
3. Although she enjoyed spending money on herself, Madam Walker also gave a lot of money to charity.

Teach the Connection

Cultural Connection

Faith Ringgold Faith Ringgold learned to quilt from her great-great-grandmother, a former slave. Slave communities valued quilts not just for their warmth, but as ways to preserve memories, tell stories, and send messages about gaining freedom. Quilting today is usually considered a folk work, or "craft," but Ringgold's story quilts are fine art. This quilt is one of a series called "The French Collection." The series features a fictional character named Willa Marie Simone who goes to Paris to become an artist.

Analyze Literature

Introductions and Conclusions
Review the introduction (section 1). Have students state the information it gives and suggest why Ringgold included these ideas. After they read, have students describe the conclusion (section 12), its tie to the introduction, and its purpose.

TEACHING NOTE

Story Quilt

Encourage students to plan a story quilt like this one. Have them work in pairs or small groups. Urge them to identify the theme or meaning of Ringgold's quilt so that they can imitate it. They should choose a topic from social studies, history, or current events and create a sketch or collage that could be turned into a story quilt. Have them display their work on a class bulletin board.

In "Madam C. J. Walker," Jim Haskins tells the story of an African-American woman who built a successful business in spite of prejudice and discrimination. The following selection is from *The Sunflower Quilting Bee at Arles*, a story quilt by **Faith Ringgold** (b. 1930). Born in New York City, Ringgold began her career as a painter and is perhaps best known for her painted story quilts, which combine painting, quilted fabric, and storytelling. As you read, consider why the author has chosen to write about this group of women.

The Sunflower Quilting Bee at Arles

A Story Quilt by Faith Ringgold

1. The National Sunflower Quilters Society of America are having quilting bees in sunflower fields around the world to spread the cause of freedom. Aunt Melissa has written to inform me of this and to say: "Go with them to the sunflower fields in Arles.[1] And please take care of them in that foreign country, Willa Marie. These women are our freedom," she wrote.

2. Today the women arrived in Arles. They are Madame Walker, Sojourner Truth, Ida Wells, Fannie Lou Hamer, Harriet Tubman, Rosa Parks, Mary McLeod Bethune and Ella Baker, a fortress of African American women's courage, with enough energy to transform a nation piece by piece.

3. Look what they've done in spite of their oppression: Madame Walker invented the hair straightening comb and became the first self-made American-born woman millionaire. She employed over 3,000 people. Sojourner Truth spoke up brilliantly for women's rights during slavery, and could neither read nor write.

Ida Wells made an exposé of the horror of lynching in the South.

4. Fannie Lou Hamer braved police dogs, water hoses, brutal beatings, and jail in order to register thousands of people to vote. Harriet Tubman brought over 300 slaves to freedom in 19 trips from the South on the Underground Railroad during slavery and never lost a passenger. Rosa Parks became the mother of the Civil Rights Movement when she sat down in the front of a segregated bus and refused to move to the back.

5. Mary McLeod Bethune founded Bethune Cookman College and was special advisor to Presidents Harry Truman and Franklin Delano Roosevelt. Ella Baker organized thousands of people to improve the condition of poor housing, jobs, and consumer education. Their trip to Arles was to complete *The Sunflower Quilt*, an international symbol of their dedication to change the world.

---

1. **Arles.** City in France where Vincent van Gogh painted many of his famous sunflower paintings.

348 UNIT 3 NONFICTION

Words in Use

"The Sunflower Quilting Bee at Arles"
Selection Words
oppression, 348
exposé, 348
tormented, 350

Differentiated Instruction

Reading Proficiency
Explain that the quilt is about real people, but in a fictional setting. Point out that these people were not all alive at the same time. Ask students why they think Faith Ringgold put these people together.

Common Core State Standards

Reading Literature
RL.1, RL.9

Reading Informational
RI.5

History Connection

Sojourner Truth Tell students that Sojourner Truth gave a short, powerful speech in 1851 in which she highlighted the irony of promoting women's rights for white women, but not for black women. Students interested in the intersection of Civil Rights and women's rights might enjoy reading "Ain't I a Woman," which is widely available on the Internet.

Art Connection

Tell students that the text on these pages is actually writing on the surface of the quilt.

When Ringgold's "French Collection," including this story quilt, was exhibited in New York City in 1992, *The New York Times* published a review. The review said the quilts "mix art and politics." It refers to this quilt as a "tribute to female solidarity and individual struggle." Suggest to students that, as they study the image and read the text, they look for examples of both qualities. Model one possible response: "I see female solidarity because the women surround the quilt, and the man is off to the side."

Reading Skills

Identify the Main Idea and Supporting Details

Use a main idea and details organizer to help students comprehend the text. Ask them to draw a horizontal rectangle, to represent a table top, at the top of a sheet of paper. In it, have them write a sentence that states the main idea of the quilt and text. Then have them draw legs under the table top and write a supporting detail on each leg.

Use Reading Skills
Identify Author's Purpose Ask students to reread sections 7 and 8 and ask themselves, "Why did Ringgold tell these stories? Is her purpose here to persuade, to inform, or to convey a message about life? Why won't the figure of Van Gogh move?" Encourage volunteers to state and explain the author's purpose they infer.

Use Reading Skills
Use Context Clues Ask: "Based on information in sections 9 and 10, what does the word *piecing* mean?" (sewing quilt panels together). Then, ask if Ringgold is using the verb literally or figuratively. Draw attention to the last sentence of section 10, where the women say their "real art" is "making this world piece up right." **A**

Text-to-Text Connection
Answer: Both say she was the first American woman to earn a million dollars, she invented hair care products, including a "hair straightening" comb, and she created many jobs for black people. She contributed to African-American freedom by helping black people achieve financial freedom when most lived in poverty, showing that black women could be successful in business, and supporting black educational institutions that trained thousands of people to become financially self-sufficient.

6. The Dutch painter, Vincent van Gogh came to see the black women sewing in the sunflower fields. "Who is this strange looking man," they said. "He is un grand peintre," I told them, "though he is greatly troubled in his mind." He held a vase of sunflowers, no doubt une nature morte, a still life, for one of his paintings.

7. "He's the image of the man hit me in the head with a rock when I was a girl," Harriet said. "Make him leave. He reminds me of slavers." But he was not about to be moved. Like one of the sunflowers, he appeared to be growing out of the ground. Sojourner wept into the stitches of her quilting for the loss of her thirteen children mostly all sold into slavery.

8. One of Sojourner's children, a girl, was sold to a Dutch slaver in the West Indies who then took her to Holland. "Was that something this Dutch man might know something about? He should pay for all the pain his people has given us. I am concerned about you, Willa Marie. Is this a natural setting for a black woman?" Sojourner asked.

9. "I came to France to seek opportunity," I said. "It is not possible for me to be an artist in the States." "We are all artists. Piecing is our art. We brought it straight from Africa," they said. "That was what we did after a hard day's work in the fields to keep our sanity and our beds

warm and bring beauty into our lives. That was not being an artist. That was being alive."

10. When the sun went down and it was time for us to leave, the tormented little man just settled inside himself and took on the look of the sunflowers in the field as if he were one of them. The women were finished piecing now. "We need to stop and smell the flowers sometimes," **A** they said. "Now we can do our real quilting, our real art: making this world piece up right."

11. "I got to get back to that railroad," Harriet said. "Ain't all us free yet, no matter how many them laws they pass. Sojourner fighting for women's rights. Fannie for voter registration. Ella and Rosa working on civil rights. Ida looking out for mens getting lynch. Mary Bethune getting our young-uns' education, and Madame making money fixing hair and giving us jobs. Lord, we is sure busy."

12. "I am so thankful to my aunt Melissa for sending you wonderful women to me," I said. "Art can never change anything the way you have. But it can make a picture so everyone can see and know our true history and culture from the art. Some day I will make you women proud of me, too. Just wait, you'll see." "We see, Willa Marie," they said. "We see." ✤

TEXT ⟷ TEXT
TO
CONNECTION

Jim Haskins's biography and Faith Ringgold's story quilt describe the accomplishments of Madam C. J. Walker and other African-American women. Which of Madam Walker's accomplishments are mentioned in both works? Through these accomplishments, how has Madam Walker contributed to the cause of freedom for African Americans?

350   UNIT 3 NONFICTION

Differentiated Instruction

Enrichment
Have students work in two groups. Have one group learn more about Faith Ringgold at her website. Suggest that they view two other works (listed under Private Collections): "Dancing at the Louvre" and "Cotton Fields, Sunflowers, Black Birds and Quilting Bees." Have the other group learn more about Van Gogh at one of the websites that has a gallery of his works. Encourage them to search for "Paintings" and then "Sunflowers" to see some of the art he created at Arles. Have both groups prepare brief reports on what they learn, and set aside time for the groups to make presentations to the class.

Analyze Literature

Introduction and Conclusion Effective introductions capture the reader's attention and present the subject of the literary work. Effective conclusions sum up the important ideas in a work and present the author's final analysis of the subject. How does Haskins capture the reader's attention in his introduction? What main idea is presented? How are the ideas in the conclusion related to the ideas in the introduction? What is the final point that Haskins makes about Madam Walker's accomplishments? When you are finished, summarize the author's description of Madam Walker's accomplishments. Exchange your summary with a classmate. In a paragraph, evaluate your classmates summary for accuracy of the main ideas, supporting details, and overall meaning of the selection.

Extend Understanding

Writing Options

Creative Writing A **jingle** is a short song or slogan that advertises a product and is easy to remember. Write a jingle to be used in a radio advertisement for one of Madam Walker's haircare products. Your jingle can be spoken or sung. Use concise but catchy language. In small groups, perform your jingle for other group members and vote on the jingle that is the most memorable. Note that advertisements and other media will often influence its audience with words, images, and sounds. When you evaluate your jingles, also evaluate the various ways different types of media influence their audiences. Consider whether the most memorable jingle incorporated any of these same techniques.

Expository Writing Pretend that you are writing a **biography** of someone you admire for a website devoted to great Americans. Choose a person who is currently making important contributions to American society or an important person from American history. Include a summary of the person's life and contributions to American society, and at least one quote in his or her own words.

Critical Literacy

Analyze a Speech A **policy speech** attempts to persuade a listener to support a change in government policy and contains quotations from experts and arguments that address policy issues. Identify and read the text of a contemporary speech that addresses women's rights. Interpret the speaker's purpose by asking questions or making comments about the evidence presented. Finally, analyze the structure of the speech's central argument and identify the different types of evidence used to support the argument.

Media Literacy

Analyze Advertisements Advertising for products has grown immensely on the Internet. Evaluate a variety of product websites that exist as online advertisements. You can enter types of products or specific brand names into any search engine to find ads. What do you learn about the products from the advertisement? What—if any—important information is missing? What methods does the advertisement use to sell the products? Does the ad contain music or sound? If so, how might the sound techniques influence the audience? Report on your findings to your classmates.

Go to www.mirrorsandwindows.com for more.

Review the Selection

Analyze Literature

Introduction and Conclusion The author captures the reader's attention by saying that Madam Walker was the first American woman to earn a million dollars. The main idea is that Madam Walker worked hard—and alone—to achieve her success. The conclusion restates that despite facing many odds, Madam Walker succeeded in her life and business. The author's final analysis of Madam Walker's accomplishments is that she was more successful than others thought she would be, but she herself always expected to achieve great things. Student summary evaluations will vary.

Program Resources

For further instruction, refer students to the following extension activity: Media Literacy: Analyze Advertisements, *Exceeding the Standards: Extension Activities*, pp. 9–10.

Rubrics for Writing Options

You can adapt this as a checklist for students to use as they write.

Creative Writing

☐ Is the jingle memorable?

☐ Does the jingle clearly make the product memorable?

☐ Does the jingle use simple, catchy language?

Expository Writing

☐ Does the biography summarize the significant moments in the person's life and work?

☐ Does the biography include at least one quote in the person's own words?

☐ Does the biography explain a lasting contribution the person made to American society?

from Barrio Boy
A Memoir by Ernesto Galarza

The two of us walked south on Fifth Street one morning to the corner of Q Street and turned right. Half of the block was occupied by the Lincoln School. It was a three-story wooden building, with two wings that gave it the shape of a double-T connected by a central hall. It was a new building, painted yellow, with a shingled roof that was not like the red tile of the school in Mazatlán.[1] I noticed other differences, none of them very reassuring.

We walked up the wide staircase hand in hand and through the door, which closed by itself. A mechanical contraption screwed to the top shut it behind us quietly.

In a matter of seconds I had to decide whether she was a possible friend or a menace.

Up to this point the adventure of enrolling me in the school had been carefully rehearsed. Mrs. Dodson had told us how to find it and we had circled it several times on our walks. Friends in the *barrio*[2] explained that the director was called a principal, and that it was a lady and not a man. They assured us that there was always a person at the school who could speak Spanish.

Exactly as we had been told, there was a sign on the door in both Spanish and

1. **Mazatlán.** Seaport in western Mexico
2. ***barrio.*** Spanish-speaking, urban neighborhood (Spanish)

Ernesto Galarza (1905–1984) began his life near Tepic, Mexico. Due to the instability and social upheaval caused by the Mexican Revolution, Galarza's family migrated to the United States. After settling in Sacramento, California, they worked as farm laborers. Galarza spent much of the rest of his life working with various labor groups to help improve conditions for poor farmhands. In 1979 he was nominated for a Nobel Prize in Literature.

352

English: "Principal." We crossed the hall and entered the office of Miss Nettie Hopley.

Miss Hopley was at a roll-top desk to one side, sitting in a swivel chair that moved on wheels. There was a sofa against the opposite wall, flanked by two windows and a door that opened on a small balcony. Chairs were set around a table and framed pictures hung on the walls of a man with long white hair and another with a sad face and a black beard.

The principal half turned in the swivel chair to look at us over the pinch glasses crossed on the ridge of her nose. To do this she had to duck her head slightly as if she were about to step through a low doorway.

What Miss Hopley said to us we did not know but we saw in her eyes a warm welcome and when she took off her glasses and straightened up she smiled wholeheartedly, like Mrs. Dodson. We were, of course, saying nothing, only catching the friendliness of her voice and the sparkle in her eyes while she said words we did not understand. She signaled us to the table. Almost tiptoeing across the office, I maneuvered myself to keep my mother between me and the gringo lady. In a matter of seconds I had to decide whether she was a possible friend or a menace. We sat down.

Then Miss Hopley did a formidable thing. She stood up. Had she been standing when we entered she would have seemed tall. But rising from her chair she soared. And what she carried up and up with her was a buxom superstructure,[3] firm shoulders, a straight sharp nose, full cheeks slightly molded by a curved line along the nostrils, thin lips that moved like steel springs, and a high forehead topped by hair gathered in a bun. Miss Hopley was not a giant in body

but when she mobilized it to a standing position she seemed a match for giants. I decided I liked her.

She strode to a door in the far corner of the office, opened it and called a name. A boy of about ten years appeared in the doorway. He sat down at one end of the table. He was brown like us, a plump kid with shiny black hair combed straight back, neat, cool, and faintly obnoxious.

Miss Hopley joined us with a large book and some papers in her hand. She, too, sat down and the questions and answers began by way of our interpreter. My name was Ernesto. My mother's name was Henriqueta. My birth certificate was in San Blas. Here was my last report card from the Escuela Municipal Numero 3 para Varones of Mazatlán, and so forth. Miss Hopley put things down in the book and my mother signed a card.

As long as the questions continued, Doña Henriqueta could stay and I was secure. Now that they were over, Miss Hopley saw her to the door, dismissed our interpreter and without further ado took me by the hand and strode down the hall to Miss Ryan's first grade.

Miss Ryan took me to a seat at the front of the room, into which I shrank—the better to survey her. She was, to skinny, somewhat runty me, of a withering height when she patrolled the class. And when I least expected it, there she was, crouching by my desk, her blond radiant[4] face level with mine, her voice patiently maneuvering me over the awful idiocies of the English language.

During the next few weeks, Miss Ryan overcame my fears of tall, energetic teachers

---

3. **buxom superstructure.** Large body
4. **radiant.** Bright; lovely

BARRIO BOY **353**

Teach the Selection

Summary

The account begins as Ernesto and his mother enroll him in first grade. They have recently arrived from Mexico and do not speak English. Ernesto meets the principal, Miss Hopley, who is intimidating but kind. Then he is taken to class, taught by the equally intimidating and kind Miss Ryan. As time passes, Miss Ryan helps Ernesto and his classmates, who are from many countries, learn to read and speak English. The students learn to respect each other and be friends despite their differences. He ends by saying that at school he learned to be proud, both of being American and of his Mexican heritage.

MIRRORS & WINDOWS

The Mirrors & Windows questions at the end of the selection focus on the theme of alienation. Before students begin to read, ask: Do people ever come to enjoy feeling like outsiders? If so, why?

TEACHING NOTE

Frequently Confused Words

Write the words *principal* and *principle* on the board and ask students to define them. Have students think of other words people commonly confuse and misspell. Possibilities include *capital* and *capitol, loose* and *lose,* and *affect* and *effect.* Invite students to suggest ways of remembering the correct spellings for each set of words.

Words in Use

Selection Words
flanked, 353
maneuvered, 353
formidable, 353
mobilized, 353
obnoxious, 353
recitations, 354
foreign, 355

Teaching Words
instability, 352
upheaval, 352
migrated, 352
immigrants, 355

KEY TERMS
MEMOIR, 352
EDITORIAL, 355
PARAPHRASE, 355
MAIN IDEA, 355
THESIS, 355
OUTLINE, 355

Analyze Literature

Voice Tell students that voice is the way a writer uses language to express his or her personality and attitude. Ask students to describe Galarza's voice and to explain their answers. (His voice is friendly and casual with informal word choices and a conversational tone.)

Use Reading Skills

Identify Author's Purpose Explain that purpose is an author's reason for writing—how he or she wants to affect readers. Have students think about how Galarza's work personally affects them. Are they entertained? Do they learn something?

Make Connections

Encourage any students who have been in places where they did not speak the language to share their experiences.

Literary Connection

Mexican-American Stories In addition to Galarza's *Barrio Boy*, many works portray the Mexican-American experience. Students might enjoy Pam Muñoz Ryan's novel *Becoming Naomi León*, Gary Soto's autobiographical works *Living Up the Street* and *A Summer Life*, and Viola Canales's story collection *Orange Candy Slices and Other Secret Tales*.

Tribute to the American Working People (detail), 1951. Honoré D. Sharrer. Smithsonian American Art Museum, Washington, DC.

as she bent over my desk to help me with a word in the pre-primer. Step by step, she loosened me and my classmates from the safe anchorage[5] of the desks for recitations at the blackboard and consultations at her desk. Frequently she burst into happy announcements to the whole class. "Ito can read a sentence," and small Japanese Ito, squint-eyed and shy, slowly read aloud while the class listened in wonder: "Come, Skipper, come, Come and run." The Korean, Portuguese, Italian, and Polish first graders had similar moments of glory, no less shining than mine the day I conquered *butterfly*, which I had been persistently pronouncing in standard Spanish as boo-ter-flee. "Children," Miss Ryan called for attention. "Ernesto has learned how to pronounce butterfly!" And I proved it with a perfect imitation of Miss Ryan. From that celebrated success, I was soon able to match Ito's progress as a sentence reader with "Come, butterfly, come fly with me."

Like Ito and several other first graders who did not know English, I received private lessons from Miss Ryan in the closet, a narrow hall off the classroom with a door at each end. Next to one of these doors

Miss Ryan placed a large chair for herself and a small one for me. Keeping an eye on the class through the open door she read with me about sheep in the meadow and a frightened chicken going to see the king, coaching me out of my phonetic rut in words like *pasture, bow-wow-wow, hay,* and *pretty,* which to my Mexican ear and eye had so many unnecessary sounds and letters. She made me watch her lips and then close my eyes as she repeated words I found hard to read. When we came to know each other better, I tried interrupting to tell Miss Ryan how we said it in Spanish. It didn't work. She only said "oh" and went on with *pasture, bow-wow-wow,* and *pretty.* It was as if in that closet we were both discovering together the secrets of the English language and grieving together over the tragedies of Bo-Peep. The main reason I was graduated with honors from the first grade was that I had fallen in love with Miss Ryan. Her radiant, no-nonsense character made us either afraid not to love her or love her so we would not be afraid, I am not sure which. It was not only that we sensed she was with it, but also that she was with us.

Like the first grade, the rest of the Lincoln School was a sampling of the lower part of town where many races made their home. My pals in the second grade were Kazushi, whose parents spoke only Japanese; Matti, a skinny Italian boy; and Manuel, a fat Portuguese who would never get into a fight but wrestled you to the ground and just sat on you. Our assortment of nationalities included Koreans, Yugoslavs, Poles, Irish, and home-grown Americans.

Miss Hopley and her teachers never let us forget why we were at Lincoln: for those who

---

5. **anchorage.** Place for putting in a ship's anchor; secure place

Differentiated Instruction

Reading Proficiency

To help less-confident readers visualize events in the story, ask them to choose a descriptive passage and to draw it, using every detail provided. (You might suggest a picture of the school or a portrait of Miss Hopley.) Circulate as students work, asking them to show you how their pictures correspond to the text.

Enrichment

The reading may spark students' interest in bilingual education. Tell students there are different methods for helping nonnative English speakers learn. (Galarza describes a kind of "English immersion.") Students could research one of these methods or a topic such as the Bilingual Education Act of 1968.

were alien, to become good Americans; for those who were so born, to accept the rest of us. Off the school grounds we traded the same insults we heard from our elders. On the playground we were sure to be marched up to the principal's office for calling someone a wop, a chink, a dago, or a greaser. The school was not so much a melting pot as a griddle where Miss Hopley and her helpers warmed knowledge into us and roasted racial hatreds out of us.

At Lincoln, making us into Americans did not mean scrubbing away what made us originally foreign. The teachers called us as our parents did, or as close as they could pronounce our names in Spanish or Japanese. No one was ever scolded or punished for speaking in his native tongue on the playground. Matti told the class about his mother's down quilt, which she had made in Italy with the fine feathers of a thousand geese. Encarnación acted out how boys learned to fish in the Philippines. I astounded the third grade with the story of my travels on a stagecoach, which nobody else in the class had seen except in the museum at Sutter's Fort. After a visit to the Crocker Art Gallery and a collection of heroic paintings of the golden age of California, someone showed a silk scroll with a Chinese painting. Miss Hopley herself had a way of expressing wonder over these matters before a class, her eyes wide open until they popped slightly. It was easy for me to feel that becoming a proud American, as she said we should, did not mean feeling ashamed of being a Mexican.

 When have you felt like an outsider? How did people make you feel, welcome or unwelcome? Why should people be open to newcomers?

Analyze and Extend

1. Describe some of Miss Ryan's characteristics, including how she looks and behaves. How do these traits affect the narrator?
2. What do you think was the most valuable thing Galarza gained by attending Lincoln School? Support your claim with evidence from the text.
3. Briefly describe Galarza's purpose or purposes. For example, is he writing to entertain, to inform, to persuade, or for a combination of these purposes?

Persuasive Writing Imagine that you are writing a **newspaper editorial** about how centuries of immigration in the United States have influenced the national character. Describe how you think immigrants from all over the world have influenced what it means to be an American. Use direct quotations or paraphrases from *Barrio Boy* as support.

Collaborative Learning With a partner, discuss the importance of a strong education. Create a list of as many main ideas and details in support of your thesis as possible. Then use this list to create a formal outline. Each main idea in your outline should have at least three details that support it. Use your outline to give a presentation to the class.

 Go to www.mirrorsandwindows.com for more.

Answer: Many students will have felt like an outsider, such as on a first day at a new school. Their feelings of being welcome or unwelcome will vary. They will probably say it is good to welcome others, because this is how they would hope to be treated.

Analyze and Extend

1. Students might describe Miss Ryan as persistent, understanding, "radiant," "no-nonsense," tall, and blond. Her manner makes the narrator feel more comfortable.
2. Students may say Galarza gained the self-confidence that helped him succeed. Some may say he learned that becoming American "did not mean scrubbing away what made us originally foreign."
3. The purpose may be to inform and to persuade. Galarza informs readers about his experiences and those of others like him. He also tries to persuade them to accept newcomers.

Rubric for Persuasive Writing

You can adapt this as a checklist for students to use as they write.

☐ Does the editorial describe how immigration has affected the national character?

☐ Does the editorial include quotations and paraphrases from *Barrio Boy*?

Writing Skills

Personal Narrative

Remind students that a personal narrative is the story of a person's experiences. It is related to a personal essay (see page 281), but an essay focuses on the author's ideas about a specific topic, while a narrative gives an account of something that happened. A narrative usually presents events in chronological order.

Suggest that when students need to draft their own personal narratives, they use a time line to help keep the sequence of events straight and avoid leaving out key events. Have students think of an experience they might want to write about and create a time line to describe the order in which things happened.

Preview the Selection

At a Glance
Independent Reading
- Reading Level: Moderate
- Difficulty Considerations: Vocabulary and organization
- Ease Factor: Humor

Objectives
Reading this selection will enable students to do the following:
- read with developing fluency
- read silently with comprehension for a sustained period of time

Launch the Lesson
Ask students to think about the funniest thing that has ever happened to them. Would the story sound believable if it were written down? Can they think of ways to add details that would make the experience even funnier? Have students share their stories with classmates.

Independent Reading
Students who like "The Night the Bed Fell" might enjoy other humorous essays by Thurber. Other authors known for humorous works include Mark Twain, Robert Benchley, Dave Barry, Sarah Vowell, and David Sedaris.

TEACHING NOTE
Although this selection is presented in the student edition as an independent reading, teaching support has been provided should you choose to cover it in class.

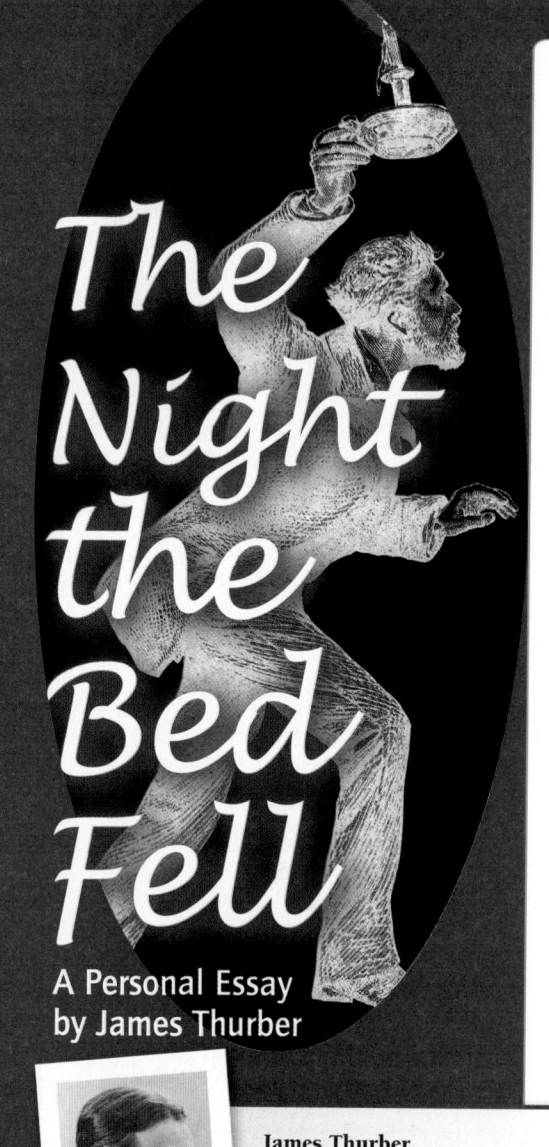

The Night the Bed Fell

A Personal Essay by James Thurber

James Thurber (1894–1961) is best known for the humorous stories, essays, and cartoons he wrote and drew for *The New Yorker* magazine. These works are frequently filled with "regular" people who find themselves caught in awkward or improbable situations.

Thurber was born in Columbus, Ohio. An accident left him almost completely blind at an early age. His injury prevented him from participating in sports as a young person and later from graduating from college. As a result, Thurber redirected his efforts into his writing. Today he is remembered as one of the greatest American humorists of the twentieth century.

The situation was finally put together like a gigantic jigsaw puzzle.

I suppose that the high-water mark of my youth in Columbus, Ohio, was the night the bed fell on my father. It makes a better recitation (unless, as some friends of mine have said, one has heard it five or six times) than it does a piece of writing, for it is almost necessary to throw furniture around, shake doors, and bark like a dog, to lend the proper atmosphere and verisimilitude[1] to what is admittedly a somewhat incredible tale. Still, it did take place.

It happened, then, that my father had decided to sleep in the attic one night, to be away where he could think. My mother opposed the notion strongly because, she said, the old wooden bed up there was unsafe: it was wobbly and the heavy headboard would crash down on father's head in case the bed fell, and kill him. There

1. **verisimilitude.** Appearance of being real

356

Program Resources

Planning and Assessment
Program Planning Guide, Selection Lesson Plan
E-Lesson Planner
Assessment Guide, Lesson Test
ExamView

Technology Tools
Interactive Student Text on CD
Visual Teaching Package
Audio Library
mirrorsandwindows.com

Meeting the Standards
Nonfiction: Unit 3, Independent Reading, pp. 89–94

Differentiating Instruction
Advanced Students, Independent Author Study, pp. 19–20

Common Core State Standards

Reading Literature
RL.1, RL.10

Reading Informational
RI.10

was no dissuading him, however, and at a quarter past ten he closed the attic door behind him and went up the narrow twisting stairs. We later heard ominous creakings as he crawled into bed. Grandfather, who usually slept in the attic bed when he was with us, had disappeared some days before. On these occasions he was usually gone six or eight days and returned growling and out of temper, with the news that the Federal Union was run by a passel[2] of blockheads and that the Army of the Potomac[3] didn't have a chance.

We had visiting us at this time a nervous first cousin of mine named Briggs Beall, who believed that he was likely to cease breathing when he was asleep. It was his feeling that if he were not awakened every hour during the night, he might die of suffocation. He had been accustomed to setting an alarm clock to ring at intervals until morning, but I persuaded him to abandon this. He slept in my room and I told him that I was such a light sleeper that if anybody quit breathing in the same room with me, I would wake instantly. He tested me the first night—which I had suspected he would—by holding his breath after my regular breathing had convinced him I was asleep. I was not asleep, however, and called to him. This seemed to allay[4] his fears a little, but he took the precaution of putting a glass of spirits of camphor[5] on a little table at the head of his bed. In case I didn't arouse him until he was almost gone, he said, he would sniff the camphor, a powerful reviver. Briggs was not the only member of his family who had his crotchets.[6] Old Aunt Melissa

Beall (who could whistle like a man, with two fingers in her mouth) suffered under the premonition[7] that she was destined to die on South High Street, because she had been born on South High Street and married on South High Street. Then there was Aunt Sarah Shoaf, who never went to bed at night without the fear that a burglar was going to get in and blow chloroform[8] under

---

2. **passel.** Large group
3. **Army of the Potomac.** Union Army during the Civil War
4. **allay.** Relieve
5. **spirits of camphor.** Strong-smelling medicinal liquid
6. **crotchets.** Unusual beliefs
7. **premonition.** Strong feeling about the future
8. **chloroform.** Chemical used in early medicine as an anesthetic

Summary

The narrator explains that he is going to tell the story of the night a bed fell on his father. The father decides to spend a night in the attic, even though the mother is afraid the bed will collapse and hurt him. The narrator begins to tell who is in the house that night, starting with his cousin Briggs, who has a phobia about dying in his sleep. Describing Briggs's eccentricity reminds the narrator of other relatives who aren't present but have similar odd behaviors. He describes them, too.

Returning to his topic, the narrator finishes telling who is in the house and where they are sleeping. Then he explains that his own bed, a rickety cot, falls on him during that night. The noise wakes his mother, who, convinced the father's bed has fallen, raises an alarm. One by one, everyone in the house wakes up and adds to the chaos. Finally, the father comes downstairs, uninjured. His bed never fell at all.

MIRRORS & WINDOWS The Mirrors & Windows questions at the end of the selection focus on the theme of storytelling. Before students begin to read, ask: What is the funniest story you can tell about your family?

Use Reading Skills

Read Aloud Some students may be best able to enjoy the selection by hearing it read aloud. Read it yourself or ask a confident and expressive student to present it to classmates. If possible, give the student advance warning so he or she can become familiar with the text.

Science Connection

Phobias Explain that a phobia is an exaggerated and often irrational fear. Many people have mild phobias that cause little trouble; a few have fears so acute that they must seek treatment. Phobias have specific names. For example, two of the narrator's aunts suffer from sclerophobia, fear of burglars. **A**

Make Connections

Ask students how they are affected by the author's detailed description of the layout of the house. (This may help them visualize the complicated events that follow, and it increases the humor by setting up a silly situation as if it were a serious setting such as a crime scene.) **B**

Use Reading Skills

Identify Sequence of Events To help students keep track of the sequence of events, and to give them practice in recognizing plot elements, have them sketch a plot diagram for the story (see page 6).

---

her door through a tube. To avert[9] this calamity—for she was in greater dread of anesthetics than of losing her household goods—she always piled her money, silverware, and other valuables in a neat stack just outside her bedroom, with a note reading: "This is all I have. Please take it and do not use your chloroform, as this is all I have." Aunt Gracie Shoaf also had a burglar phobia, but she met it with more fortitude.[10] She was confident that burglars had been getting into her house every night for forty years. The fact that she never missed any thing was to her no proof to the contrary. She always claimed that she scared them off before they could take anything, by throwing shoes down the hallway. When she went to bed she piled, where she could get at them handily, all the shoes there were about her house. Five minutes after she had turned off the light, she would sit up in bed and say "Hark!" Her husband, who had learned to ignore the whole situation as long ago as 1903, would either be sound asleep or pretend to be sound asleep. In either case he would not respond to her tugging and pulling, so that presently she would arise, tiptoe to the door, open it slightly and heave a shoe down the hall in one direction, and its mate down the hall in the other direction. Some nights she threw them all, some nights only a couple of pair.

But I am straying from the remarkable incidents that took place during the night that the bed fell on father. By midnight we were all in bed. The layout of the rooms and the disposition of their occupants is important to an understanding of what later occurred. In the front room upstairs (just under father's attic bedroom) were my mother and my brother Herman, who sometimes sang in his sleep, usually "Marching Through Georgia" or "Onward, Christian Soldiers." Briggs Beall and myself were in a room adjoining[11] this one. My brother Roy was in a room across the hall from ours. Our bull terrier, Rex, slept in the hall.

My bed was an army cot, one of those affairs which are made wide enough to sleep on comfortably only by putting up, flat with the middle section, the two sides which ordinarily hang down like the sideboards of a drop-leaf table. When these sides are up, it is perilous[12] to roll too far toward the edge, for then the cot is likely to tip completely over, bringing the whole bed down on top of one, with a tremendous banging crash. This, in fact, is precisely what happened about two o'clock in the morning. (It was my mother who, in recalling the scene later, first referred to it as "the night the bed fell on your father.")

Always a deep sleeper, slow to arouse (I had lied to Briggs), I was at first unconscious

9. **avert.** Avoid
10. **fortitude.** Strength
11. **adjoining.** Connecting to or positioned next to
12. **perilous.** Dangerous

Differentiated Instruction

Reading Proficiency

Less-confident readers may lose the thread of the narrative when Thurber digresses to talk about his two aunts, beginning on page 357 and continuing here. Point the passage out to students ahead of time. Ask them to think about people they know who get distracted while talking about one thing and end up talking about another. Note that Thurber is doing this on purpose, for comic effect.

English Language Learning

Draw students' attention to what Briggs says after he spills the camphor on page 359 (*ugf, ahfg, gugh*). Explain that these words are a type of onomatopoeia (words intended to imitate sounds). Tell students to pay attention to context if they encounter similar words in the future—context usually clarifies the meaning. Have students make up their own onomatopoetic words for sounds.

of what had happened when the iron cot rolled me onto the floor and toppled over on me. It left me still warmly bundled up and unhurt, for the bed rested above me like a canopy. Hence I did not wake up, only reached the edge of consciousness and went back. The racket, however, instantly awakened my mother, in the next room, who came to the immediate conclusion that her worst dread was realized: the big wooden bed upstairs had fallen on father. She therefore screamed, "let's go to your poor father!" It was this shout, rather than the noise of my cot falling, that awakened Herman, in the same room with her. He thought that mother had become, for no apparent reason, hysterical. "You're all right, Mamma!" he shouted, trying to calm her. They exchanged shout for shout for perhaps ten seconds: "Let's go to your poor father!" and "You're all right!" That woke up Briggs. By this time I was conscious of what was going on, in a vague way, but did not yet realize that I was under my bed instead of on it. Briggs, awakening in the midst of loud shouts of fear and apprehension, came to the quick conclusion that he was suffocating and that we were all trying to "bring him out." With a low moan, he grasped the glass of camphor at the head of his bed and instead of sniffing it poured it over himself. The room reeked of camphor. "Ugf, ahfg," choked Briggs, like a drowning man, for he had almost succeeded in stopping his breath under the deluge of pungent spirits. He leaped out of bed and groped toward the open window, but he came up against one that was closed. With his hand, he beat out the glass, and I could hear it crash and tinkle on the alleyway below. It was at this

juncture[13] that I, in trying to get up, had the uncanny sensation of feeling my bed above me! Foggy with sleep, I now suspected, in my turn, that the whole uproar was being made in a frantic endeavor to extricate[14] me from what must be an unheard-of and perilous situation. "Get me out of this!" I bawled. "Get me out!" I think I had the nightmarish belief that I was entombed in a mine. "Gugh," gasped Briggs, floundering in his camphor.

By this time my mother, still shouting, pursued by Herman, still shouting, was trying to open the door to the attic, in order to go up and get my father's body out of the wreckage. The door was stuck, however, and wouldn't yield. Her frantic pulls on it only added to the general banging and confusion. Roy and the dog were now up, the one shouting questions, the other barking.

Father, farthest away and soundest sleeper of all, had by this time been awakened by the battering on the attic door. He decided that the house was on fire. "I'm coming, I'm coming!" he wailed in a slow, sleepy voice—it took him many minutes to regain full consciousness. My mother, still believing he was caught under the bed,

---

13. **juncture.** Specific point in time
14. **extricate.** Release a person or thing from a complicated situation

Teach the Selection

Analyze Literature
Humor Ask students to think, as they read, about what makes a piece of writing funny. Have them pause whenever they laugh and ask themselves exactly what was so funny. Afterward, have students share their ideas with the group.

Analyze Literature
Exaggeration Tell students that the practice of exaggerating for literary effect is known as hyperbole. Have students point out examples of hyperbole in the selection. Model an example: "The mother and son shout at each other after the noise awakens them." **C**

Use Reading Skills
Compare and Contrast
Tell students that it is possible for an essay to be both personal and persuasive. Thurber often mixed forms by blending fiction into essays. Explain that "The Night the Bed Fell" comes from *My Life and Hard Times*, about his youth. Thurber added so many details that experts do not consider his accounts to be factual.

Ask students to point out details that seem characteristic of either fiction or personal essay. Possibilities include the author's assertion that the event "did take place" (essay), descriptions of characters like Gracie Shoaf, who throws shoes every night (fiction), and all the crazy events that happen after the narrator's bed falls (fiction).

Answer: Many students will have family members who tell stories. Students might say that sharing the stories reinforces a sense of community.

Analyze and Extend

1. (a) Most will say Thurber exaggerated; examples will vary.
(b) He probably exaggerated the truth for comic effect.
2. (a) Thurber writes in the first-person point of view. (b) This increases the excitement and humor.
3. Students should agree that the purpose is to entertain. Most will say Thurber was successful.

Rubric for Expository Writing

You can adapt this as a checklist for students to use as they write.

☐ Does the essay describe a humorous experience?

☐ Does the essay use dialogue, sensory details, and precise language?

☐ Does the essay describe what led up to the event and how it was resolved?

---

detected in his "I'm coming!" the mournful, resigned note of one who is preparing to meet his Maker. "He's dying!" she shouted.

"I'm all right!" Briggs yelled to reassure her. "I'm all right!" He still believed that it was his own closeness to death that was worrying mother. I found at last the light switch in my room, unlocked the door, and Briggs and I joined the others at the attic door. The dog, who never did like Briggs, jumped for him—assuming that he was the culprit in whatever was going on—and Roy had to throw Rex and hold him. We could hear father crawling out of bed upstairs. Roy pulled the attic door open, with a mighty jerk, and father came down the stairs, sleepy and irritable but safe and sound. My mother began to weep when she saw him. Rex began to howl. "What in the name of heaven is going on here?" asked father.

The situation was finally put together like a gigantic jigsaw puzzle. Father caught a cold from prowling around in his bare feet but there were no other bad results. "I'm glad," said mother, who always looked on the bright side of things, "that your grandfather wasn't here."

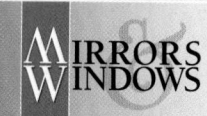

What stories does your family tell about things that happened to them in the past? Are there some stories that are told over and over again? Briefly describe these stories. Why do you think family members repeatedly share the same stories with each other?

Analyze and Extend

1. (a) Do you think Thurber exaggerated some of the events described in this essay? Which events? (b) Why might he have done this?
2. (a) From what point of view is this essay written? (b) How does this point of view affect it?
3. Briefly describe Thurber's purpose or purposes. Do you think he successfully fulfilled his purposes? Explain.

Descriptive Writing Think of a humorous event that has happened in your life. What led up to the event? How was it resolved? Write a brief **descriptive essay** in which you describe the event and the characters involved. Use dialogue, sensory details, and precise language. As you write, be aware of your audience. When you have finished, share your essay with a partner.

Critical Literacy In a small group, create a list of at least five questions you would like to ask Thurber about "The Night the Bed Fell." You might ask questions about specific characters, the events of the night he describes, or if the events actually occurred as he described them. After you have created your list, present your questions to the class.

Go to **www.mirrorsandwindows.com** for more.

Differentiated Instruction

Enrichment

Students may be interested in researching the life of James Thurber, both to learn more about him and to get a stronger sense of how much this account might have been fictionalized. Have students work in groups to research Thurber and present their findings to classmates.

For Your Reading List

The Forbidden Schoolhouse: The True and Dramatic Story of Prudence Crandall and Her Students
by Suzanne Jurmain

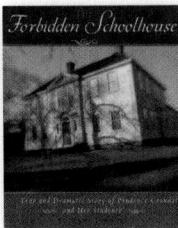

In 1831, a school for African-American girls opened in Canterbury, Connecticut. Prudence Crandall, the founder and operator of the school, was sympathetic to the antislavery movement. However, her school met with terrible resistance from the people of Canterbury. This work provides a stirring, and sometimes unsettling, view into a dark corner of America's past.

5,000 Miles to Freedom: Ellen and William Craft's Flight from Slavery
by Dennis Fradin and Judith Fradin

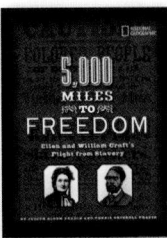

In 1848, Ellen Craft, a light-skinned African American, disguised herself as a white man and escaped with her husband to England. Years later, they returned to America to start their own school. The authors use primary sources, including Ellen's and William's letters and diaries, to enrich the story.

The Kidnapped Prince: The Life of Olaudah Equiano
by Ann Cameron

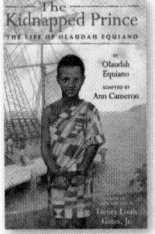

Olaudah Equiano was kidnapped by slave traders at the age of eleven from his home in Benin, Africa. After spending over ten years as a slave in England, the West Indies, and the United States, Equiano was able to buy his freedom. Cameron's book paints a compelling portrait of Equiano's life.

George Washington, Spymaster: How the Americans Outspied the British and Won the Revolutionary War
by Thomas B. Allen

Spying was a key part of the Revolutionary War, and according to Allen, it may have been central to America's victory over the British. This book includes maps and sample codes and provides a unique perspective from which to view the Revolutionary War.

Big Annie of Calumet: A True Story of the Industrial Revolution
by Jerry Stanley

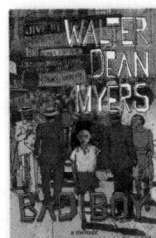

In 1913, the miners of Calumet, Michigan, went on strike to protest dangerous working conditions and terrible wages. Big Annie Clemenc, the wife of a miner, helped organize a women's group in support of the strike. The strike secured rights for workers in the face of extreme pressure from the mining company.

Bad Boy: A Memoir
by Walter Dean Myers

Walter Dean Myers's depiction of his life growing up in Harlem is exciting, heartbreaking, and vivid. After dropping out of high school and joining the military, he faced a seemingly gloomy future. Although this book describes the many difficult experiences Myers faced, it is, at its core, a celebration of the power to overcome.

Independent Reading

For Your Reading List
Independent Reading Activity

Help students link their reading to the unit theme, Experiencing the World. Ask how reading nonfiction can expand their horizons. You might try this as a library activity: Have each student identify either (a) the type of person who would be his or her exact opposite in at least two ways or (2) a foreign country he or she would like to visit for the first time. Then have students locate library books about the types of persons or places they identified. After allowing time for students to read these books independently, ask volunteers to describe, in two or three minutes, how this reading gave them an experience of the world.

▶ EMC E-Library

The EMC E-Library contains over twenty thousand pages of literary classics that students may read independently. An Electronic Library Guide provides teaching suggestions, enrichment activities, and reading strategy guidesheets.

TEACHING NOTE

Questioning

Have students use their independent readings to practice questioning skills. Ask each student to select a nonfiction piece and instruct them to prepare a list of questions they could ask either the author or another expert in the same field. Suggest that they devise ten total questions: five for clarification of the reading, and five for further evidence to support the writer's claims.

Program Resources

EMC Access Editions

For additional independent reading, you may wish to refer students to one of EMC's Access Edition titles such as Elisa Carbone's *Stealing Freedom.* Each Access Edition contains a thorough study apparatus, including background information, literal comprehension questions, footnotes, vocabulary definitions, critical thinking questions, and related projects and activities. An Assessment Manual offering worksheets and exams is available for each Access Edition.

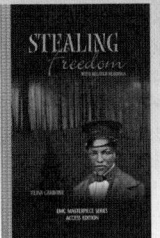

Common Core State Standards
Reading Literature
RL.10

Objectives

Participating in this lesson will help students write a cause-and-effect essay that

- has an interesting introduction with a clear thesis statement
- has a clear organizational pattern
- explains the relationship between effects and causes and uses cause-effect signal words and phrases
- uses details, facts, and examples to support explanations
- has a strong conclusion that sums up main points and restates the thesis

Launch the Lesson

To stimulate students' thinking about a cause-and-effect essay, have them brainstorm about current events. Ask: "What has dominated the news this week? What events caught your attention?" Choose one event, write it on the board, and ask students how they would go about investigating it to find its causes.

Program Resources

Additional writing workshops are available in the *Exceeding the Standards: Writing* resource.

Common Core State Standards

Writing
W.2, W.4, W.5, W.6, W.10

Writing Workshop

Expository Writing

Cause-and-Effect Essay

Reading and Writing

In this unit you read personal stories by and about famous people from all areas of life, including sports (Arthur Ashe and Roberto Clemente), entertainment (Bill Cosby), and literature (Julia Alvarez and James Thurber). These people weren't born famous, though they owe their fame in part to their experiences growing up. Our life experiences as young people often greatly affect who we become as adults. This is an example of a cause-and-effect relationship.

In this workshop you will learn how to write a **cause-and-effect essay.** In cause-and-effect writing, you analyze an event and the reasons it occurred, or you consider the relationship between an event and its results. As you approach the assignment, consider your goal and a strategy to help achieve that goal. Pay close attention to the writing rubric, a set of standards by which you judge your work and whether or not your cause-and-effect essay is successful. You will use this rubric in both drafting and revising your essay.

- **Assignment:** Write a cause-and-effect essay in which I examine the causes or results of a specific event.
- **Goal:** To explain a relationship between an event and why it occurred or what happened as a result.
- **Strategy:** To organize my points logically, and to use details and signal words to clearly indicate the cause-and-effect relationship.
- **Writing Rubric:** My cause-and-effect essay should include the following:

  - an interesting introduction with a thesis that presents my central idea
  - an explanation of the relationship between the effects and their causes
  - a clear organizational pattern
  - supporting details, facts, and examples
  - signal words and phrases
  - a strong conclusion that sums up my main points and restates my thesis

What Great Writers Do

Julia Alvarez recalls her life after coming back to the United States with her parents and how that experience influenced her growth as a writer. Note the effects her particular experience caused.

When I'm asked what made me into a writer, I point to the watershed experience of coming to this country. Not understanding the language, I had to pay close attention to each word—great training for a writer. I also discovered the welcoming world of the imagination and books. There, I sunk my new roots.

Words in Use

Teaching Words

watershed, 362
ecosystem, 363
manageable, 363
contributed, 363
circumstances, 363
indicate, 364
anticipated, 365
unnecessarily, 366

KEY TERMS

CAUSE-AND-EFFECT ESSAY, 362	**PUNCTUATION,** 364
THESIS, 362	**TRANSITION,** 364
ORGANIZATIONAL PATTERN, 362	**PEER REVIEW,** 365
TOPIC, 363	**ANNOTATION,** 365
THESIS STATEMENT, 363	**PROOFREAD,** 366
CAUSE-AND-EFFECT ORGANIZATION, 364	
INTRODUCTION, 364	
BODY, 364	
CONCLUSION, 364	

1. PREWRITE

Choosing Your Topic

Begin by brainstorming possible topics that interest you to write about. Consider topics in technology, art, science, nature, and history, to name a few. Then think of a particularly interesting outcome or event and the reasons it occurred or its results. For example, you might choose to write about how an oil spill affected Alaska's ecosystem, what the effects of a large-scale energy blackout were, or how John F. Kennedy's life experiences led to his becoming president. Answer the following questions to spark ideas:

1. What people, places, or events interest you most?
2. What major events have occurred lately? What caused them?
3. What recent events or issues have had surprising or unexpected effects?

Narrow Your Focus Once you decide on a topic, ask yourself if it is too broad to write about. Try to narrow your topic so that it is manageable but you still have enough to write about.

Too broad: How athletes achieve success

Appropriate: How circumstances in Arthur Ashe's life contributed to his success at tennis

Too narrow: How Ashe's height contributed to his success at tennis

Gathering Details

Once you narrow down a topic that interests you, begin gathering the details, facts, and examples that will illustrate your cause-and-effect relationship. A cause-and-effect chart can help you identify the causes that led to an event or outcome. Below is a cause-and-effect chart showing how childhood experiences shaped the life of tennis great Arthur Ashe.

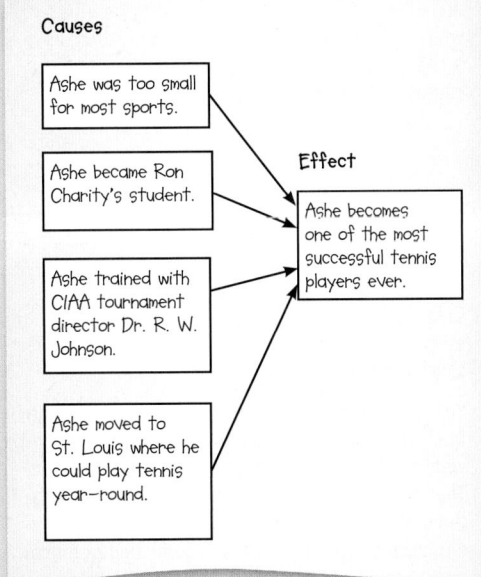

Causes

Ashe was too small for most sports.

Ashe became Ron Charity's student.

Ashe trained with CIAA tournament director Dr. R. W. Johnson.

Ashe moved to St. Louis where he could play tennis year-round.

Effect

Ashe becomes one of the most successful tennis players ever.

Deciding on Your Purpose

After you gather details about your topic, determine what cause-and-effect relationship you will explain in your essay. State the relationship clearly in a thesis statement.

A series of fortunate circumstances shaped Arthur Ashe's life as a tennis player.

Literary Connection

John McPhee Essay writing has made some people quite famous. Among contemporary nonfiction writers, John McPhee is known for essays that explain how something came to be—from the career of "Brand Inspector" to the entire surface of a continent. Many of his essays are collected in books. You might have students check the library for books by John McPhee and find at least one title that interests them.

Prewrite

Narrowing the Focus As students choose their topics, visit with them individually to help them pick subjects they can reasonably write about in the time available. This means considering not just the topic itself, but the resources available for student research.

Thesis Statement Remind students that a thesis statement has two parts: the topic and something particular about the topic. Demonstrate that the model in the book has a topic—Arthur Ashe—and a particular feature, his formative circumstances.

Have students work in pairs to test their thesis statements. Each student should read his or her statement, and then ask for feedback on whether it is narrow enough, interesting, and can be supported with details, facts, and examples.

Differentiated Instruction

English Language Learning

Explain the phrase *watershed experience* in the Alvarez quote (an experience that completely changes one's circumstances). Compare a watershed experience to the climax of a plot. Ask students if coming to this country was a watershed experience for anyone they know.

Reading Proficiency

Point out that, in Alvarez's last sentence, *sunk* is used as the past tense of *sink.* Tell students that the verb *sink* is like other irregular verbs whose tenses don't change with regular rules—such as *am, was,* and *have been*—and that its past tense can be either *sank* or *sunk.*

Draft

Organizing Ideas Be sure students have a clear organizational pattern in mind before they begin writing. For most students, the topic and thesis statement will lead to an easy choice. If a student has trouble choosing one of the patterns described in the text, suggest that he or she review previous decisions.

- Is the topic narrow enough?
- Is the thesis statement clear?
- Are details appropriate?

Modeling a Plan Assure students that they can draft their essays in whatever order feels natural to them. Model thinking through this process: "I know that three main factors led the school board to ask for a funding referendum: one, a need to hire new teachers; two, a need to renovate three elementary schools; and three, a need to replace revenue that used to come from taxes. I can write a paragraph about each factor. Then I can connect the factors to my thesis statement in the introduction: The ballot referendum is based on three pressing needs that current school funding cannot meet."

What Great Writers Do

The next project I'm thinking about is vague. It may be a short piece about geology, something to do with cretaceous extinction. What caused it when the dinosaurs disappeared? It's not as clear as people think. I might get into that subject.

JOHN MCPHEE

2. DRAFT

Organizing Ideas

When organizing your essay, use **cause-and-effect organization.** Determine which type of cause-and-effect order fits your topic. If you focus on an event and its causes, use effect-to-cause organization. If you focus on an event and its effects, use cause-to-effect organization. Review the organizational models here.

In some cases, a cause-and-effect chain may be the clearest way to organize your essay. Use a cause-and-effect chain if your cause leads to an effect, which in turn causes a new effect, and so on, as in a chain reaction. In a chain, be sure to state the causes and effects in the order they occur.

Effect-to-Cause	Cause-to-Effect
State the Effect	State the Cause
Cause 1 detail detail	Effect 1 detail detail
Cause 2 detail detail	Effect 2 detail detail
Cause 3 detail detail	Effect 3 detail detail

Cause → Effect (Cause) → Effect

Putting Your Thoughts on Paper

Like most essays, a cause-and-effect essay has three basic parts: introduction, body, and conclusion. Create a plan for your essay like the one here for an essay on Arthur Ashe. Refer to your cause-and-effect chart to get started.

You may want to draft your essay straight through from the beginning to the end, or you may prefer to write the body paragraphs before the introduction. There is no single way to draft your paper. During the drafting stage, concentrate on the content and organization. You will focus on correcting grammar, punctuation, and spelling at the editing and proofreading stage.

Introduction
- Briefly explain the cause-and-effect relationship between the circumstances of Ashe's life and his tennis achievements.

Body
- Each paragraph should focus on a cause that led to Ashe's achievement.
- Give details to explain the connection between the causes and the effect.

Conclusion
- Restate thesis statement.
- Sum up main points.

Making Connections

In your essay, use transitions and other signal words and phrases to identify cause-and-effect relationships. Be sure to use some variety in your choice of transition words. Here is a list of signal words and phrases that indicate cause-and-effect relationships.

after this	if	then
as a result	in order that	therefore
because	since	thus
consequently	so	while

Differentiated Instruction

Reading Proficiency

Review the cause-effect signal words and phrases with struggling readers. Use each word or phrase in a sentence, and have students tell you the causes and effects. Encourage them to use complete sentences.

EXAMPLES:
"<u>After</u> the fire, she was homeless." (Fire caused homelessness.)

"He won <u>as a result of</u> hard work." (Hard work caused winning.)

"She plants hundreds of bulbs <u>in order that</u> spring would be colorful." (Planting hundreds causes color.)

3. REVISE

Evaluating Your Draft

Once your draft is complete, review your writing. First, look over your own paper for strengths and weaknesses. Correct these as best you can. Then, exchange papers with a classmate, and conduct a **peer review.** Discuss ways to improve the drafts.

Below is the first part of an essay about Arthur Ashe. The annotations to the right indicate the reasons for the changes marked in the draft.

Revising Checklist

☐ Does the introduction present the cause-and-effect relationship clearly?

☐ Is the essay organized in a logical way?

☐ Is the relationship between causes and effects explained and supported?

☐ Does the essay include signal words?

Arthur Ashe's childhood experiences greatly impacted his life as a professional athlete. From his time on the court under Ron Charity's guidance to winning his first national title, ~~Arthur was surrounded by important people and experiences growing up. He became one of the best tennis players of all time.~~ *a series of fortunate circumstances shaped Arthur Ashe's life as a tennis player.*

Arthur Ashe was a small-framed boy growing up in Richmond, Virginia. *Because* he was so small, his father didn't want him to play contact sports. *So* Arthur spent a lot of time reading, swimming, and playing sports like baseball. As a boy, he used to sit on his back porch and watch the players on the courts outside his house. One player in particular caught Arthur's eye. His name was Ron Charity. Arthur liked watching Ron play, noting the way he hit the ball, how he returned serves and volleys, and how he anticipated shots. *One day, Ron saw Arthur and asked the seven-year-old if he'd like to learn to play tennis. Arthur accepted with an enthusiastic yes, and his career in tennis began.*

> *Revise introduction to present the cause-and-effect relationship clearly.*

> *Include signal words to indicate a cause-and-effect relationship between events.*

> *Add explanatory sentences to show how the details of the cause led to the effect.*

Revise

Evaluating a Draft Give students tips for delivering and receiving helpful criticism:

Delivering a Peer Review

- **Be focused.** Concentrate on content, organization, and style. Leave spelling and punctuation for the proofreading stage.
- **Be positive.** Respect the writer's feelings and genuine writing efforts.
- **Be specific.** Give the writer concrete ideas for improving his or her work.

Receiving a Peer Review

- **Be specific.** Tell your peer reviewer your specific concerns and questions.
- **Ask questions.** Make sure you understand your reviewer's comments.
- **Be selective.** Accept your reviewer's suggestions graciously, but you don't have to use all—or any—of them.

Evaluating Tone Remind students that a cause-effect essay is expository, so it should have a formal tone. As they review and revise their work, have them check for a consistent, formal tone.

Writing Skills

Facts, Details, and Examples

Review with students the differences among facts, details, and examples. Facts are statements that someone can prove. A detail is a specific piece of the whole. An example is something that demonstrates or illustrates a point. Point out that an item may fall into more than one category, such as being both a fact and a detail.

Use these sentences to help students recognize the three types of support.

1. Arthur trained with Bobby Johnson, the doctor's son. (fact; might also be a detail)
2. On the indoor courts Arthur also learned new approaches to serving and volleying. (example and detail)

Edit and Proofread

Students may want to use proofreader's marks when correcting their work. Refer them to the Language Arts Handbook, Writing Section 4.1, Proofreader's Symbols.

TEACHING NOTE

As students consider commonly confused words, point out that many such words are homophones—they sound alike. If you are going to have students read their essays aloud in class, advise them to be especially alert for homophones. Suggest that they try to use context clues to clarify which meaning they intend.

▶ **Publish and Present**

Before students begin their final versions, suggest that they read the Language Arts Handbook, Writing Section 4.1, Writing Follow-up.

4. EDIT AND PROOFREAD

Focus: Avoiding Wordiness

Wordy sentences make reading unnecessarily confusing and difficult. When you write, use only words necessary to make your meaning clear. To correct wordiness,

1. Replace a group of words with one word.

> Because ~~Due to the fact that~~ he was so small, his father didn't want him to play contact sports.

2. Delete a group of unnecessary or repetitive words.

> Ron saw Arthur and asked the seven-year-old if he'd like to learn to play ~~the game of~~ tennis.

As you edit your writing for wordiness, consider whether or not the words contribute to the meaning. Note that a long or complicated sentence is not necessarily wordy. Recall that varying sentence length creates rhythm and liveliness in writing.

Focus: Commonly Confused Words

Some common words can be confusing when you are writing. Review carefully your usage of words such as *their, there, they're,* and *excepted* and *accepted* when you revise your draft. If you are confused as to which word is correct, use a dictionary to find out which word has the meaning you're looking for.

> *accepted*
> Arthur ~~excepted~~ with an enthusiastic yes, and his career in tennis began.

Accepted is the correct word in this sentence. It means "agreed to." The word *excepted* means "left out" and would not make sense in the context of the sentence.

Proofreading

Quality Control The purpose of proofreading is to find errors in punctuation, grammar, capitalization, and spelling. You find and fix these errors when you edit your essay. Use proofreader's marks to highlight any errors. (See the Language Arts Handbook, section 4.1, for a list of proofreader's symbols.)

5. PUBLISH AND PRESENT

Final Draft

Final Steps Rewrite your essay to make a final draft. If it is handwritten, make sure the essay is neat and legible. If you are using a word processing program, double-space your paper and use a readable typeface or font. Whether you are submitting your work to your teacher or elsewhere, be sure to check presentation guidelines.

Differentiated Instruction

Auditory Learning

Have students help each other check for wordiness and sentence variety. Ask students to read a paragraph of their essays aloud to a partner, and have the partner respond to any wordiness or repetitive sentence structures. Students should also evaluate sentence lengths, noting how sentence variety affects the rhythm and liveliness of the writing.

English Language Learning

Students learning English will probably appreciate extra practice with commonly confused English words. When these students have completed their drafts, pair them with fluent native speakers as peer reviewers to help them identify and clarify any commonly confused words.

Student Model

Arthur Ashe and His Rise to Star Athlete
by Stewart Anthony

Arthur Ashe's childhood experiences greatly impacted his life as a professional athlete. From his time on the court under Ron Charity's guidance to winning his first national title, a series of fortunate circumstances shaped Arthur Ashe's life as a tennis player.

Arthur Ashe was a small-framed boy growing up in Richmond, Virginia. Because he was so small, his father didn't want him to play contact sports. So Arthur spent a lot of time reading, swimming, and playing sports like baseball. As a boy, he used to sit on his back porch and watch the players on the courts outside his house. One player in particular caught Arthur's eye. His name was Ron Charity. Arthur liked watching Ron play, noting the way he hit the ball, how he returned serves and volleys, and how he anticipated shots. One day, Ron saw Arthur and asked the seven-year-old if he'd like to learn to play tennis. Arthur accepted with an enthusiastic yes, and his career in tennis began.

Through Ron Charity, Arthur began learning the basics of tennis. Most of all, Arthur learned timing. "Timing," Arthur would later confirm, "is the most important element in tennis." Ron Charity could only take Arthur so far, however, and he introduced him to his next mentor, Dr. R. W. Johnson.

Dr. Johnson worked with young players, helping them develop their tennis abilities. It was a chance for Arthur to train and play against other good players for two weeks in the summer. Arthur trained with Bobby Johnson, the doctor's son. Arthur learned a lot under the Johnsons, especially the basics of good tennis play and standard tennis principles. He also learned more about the ways of the world at that time, especially the segregated South. Dr. Johnson's support helped Arthur maintain his focus, however, despite the injustices around him.

Dr. Johnson knew that if Arthur were to improve at tennis, he would need to play year round, something he couldn't do in Richmond. Therefore, in his senior year of high school, Arthur moved to St. Louis, Missouri, to live with Mr. Hudlin, Dr. Johnson's friend. There, Arthur could finish high school and continue training on Mr. Hudlin's backyard tennis courts and wooden indoor courts. Arthur's game improved and he eventually earned a scholarship to UCLA, one of the top tennis schools.

Arthur Ashe went on to become one of the most successful tennis players ever. Arthur seized his opportunities and, through hard work and great mentors, became a champion.

> *Presents the cause-and-effect relationship clearly in the introduction*

> *Presents causes to explain the effect*
>
> *Supports the thesis with details, including facts and examples*
>
> *Highlights the cause-and-effect relationships with signal words and phrases*
>
> *Avoids unnecessary wordiness*

> *Sums up the main points and restates the thesis*

Teach the Workshop

Student Model

Using the Model Direct students' attention to the model. Point out the side notes that identify the thesis statement, the body paragraphs, the signal words, and the conclusion. Some students might benefit from outlining the model to grasp the writer's organization and use of supporting material.

What Great Writers Do

Alaskan reporter, nature writer, and teacher Sherry Simpson provides insight into sources of inspiration. After reading this quote, ask students what it means to "draft off the thoughts and obsessions of others."

Annie Dillard is one of my favorite writers. She's an example of a nonfiction writer who can draft off the thoughts and obsessions of others. I like to tag along with biologists, to experience the benefit of their ability to name things. It's the same thing with the explorers. Reading about them is a great way to launch yourself imaginatively through facts.

Writing Skills

Jargon

Remind students that it is all right to use jargon—terms from a particular profession or activity—when a reader can use context clues to understand the terms. Point out sports and tennis jargon in the second paragraph of the model: *contact sports, serves, volleys,* and *shots.* Invite students to define these terms based on their reading of the model.

Put the following sentences on the board. Ask students to define the underlined jargon term based on context clues.

1. Elise cut into the stem, holding the sharp <u>scalpel</u> as if she were holding a paintbrush.
2. He determined his exact location using the map's <u>coordinates</u>.

Teach the Workshop

Objectives

Participating in this lesson will help students deliver an informative presentation with

- an attention-grabbing introduction and conclusion
- a clear organization that will appeal to a particular audience
- a clear, concise main idea and effective supporting details

Launch the Lesson

Ask volunteers to describe the most interesting informational speech they ever heard, and then have them describe the most boring speech they ever heard. As a class, come up with two or three differences between boring and interesting informative speeches. Write traits of interesting speeches on the board.

> For more information, see the Language Arts Handbook Section 7, Speaking & Listening.

Program Resources

To expand upon this workshop lesson, Giving and Actively Listening to Informative Presentations, see the *Exceeding the Standards: Speaking & Listening* resource.

Common Core State Standards

Speaking and Listening
SL.4, SL.5, SL.6

Giving and Actively Listening to Informative Presentations

You have probably explained how to do something, told facts about an event you've witnessed, or given directions to someone. These are all ways of presenting information. In this lesson, you will give an informative presentation to an audience. An effective **informative presentation** delivers factual information in an interesting and lively manner. When you give and actively listen to informative presentations, you share information and exchange ideas with your audience.

Planning an Informative Presentation

Choose a Topic Before you can develop your informative presentation, you must choose a topic. Your topic should be one you are interested in or familiar with. Be sure you can find enough information about your topic to give an effective presentation. You may want to begin with a broad topic and then narrow your topic to a more manageable one. For example, you might begin with a broad topic, such as television, and then narrow it down to the history of television, and then further still to television's early development.

Focus Your Idea Now that you have narrowed your topic, it's time to research and take notes. Use note cards to record your information. Each card should have one main idea and at least three supporting details. Use a highlighter so that you will be able to easily spot the main idea on each note card. Group your notes so that your strongest ideas are presented first.

Identify Your Audience Who will listen to what you have to say? Determine whether or not your audience will be familiar with your topic. This will determine the kind of language you will use. Your choice of using either technical and specialized words or simpler language in your presentation will depend on your audience and its knowledge of the topic. For example, you might avoid using terms such as *photoconductivity* or *cathode ray* when speaking to an audience that knows little about the science of television.

Effective Introductions and Closings From the start, you want to capture your audience's attention. Draw in your audience by making it a part of your presentation. Ask people to imagine, remember, think, or dream. You could open with a statement, such as *Imagine a world without television,* or a question, such as *Have you ever wondered how a television works?* Drawing in an audience makes people more attentive.

Words in Use

Teaching Words
technical, 368
specialized, 368
rephrasing, 369
nonverbal, 369
enunciation, 369

KEY TERMS

INFORMATIVE
  PRESENTATION, 368
AUDIENCE, 368
TOPIC, 368
MAIN IDEA, 368
FEEDBACK, 369
CHART, 369
GRAPH, 369
INTRODUCTION, 369
CONCLUSION, 369

You should also be mindful of your closing. An informative presentation should wrap up all the information you have just presented in a clear, clean, and simple way. Draw the audience back in by rephrasing your opening statement or answering the opening question. Leave your audience satisfied with the information you presented.

Evaluating Your Informative Presentation

Work with a partner or a small group and take turns rehearsing what you want to say. After each turn, provide constructive feedback to the speaker. When you give constructive feedback, be respectful, helpful, and polite. Offer praise, but also give ideas for improvement. Use the listening and speaking rubrics on this page to evaluate each informative presentation.

Delivering Your Informative Presentation

Your nonverbal cues are as important as your speaking ability. As you deliver your informative presentation, your main purpose is to deliver factual information. Unless movement is part of your presentation, try to stand still. Maintain eye contact with your audience. If you have charts, graphs, or other visual aids, be sure to present them in the most effective way. Consider how they specifically relate to the text of your presentation.

Listen Actively It is also important to be an active and effective listener. To listen actively and effectively, you should maintain eye contact with the speaker. Remain quiet and attentive, and ask questions when appropriate.

Speaking Rubric

Your informative presentation will be evaluated on the following elements:

Content

- ☐ attention-grabbing introduction and conclusion
- ☐ information organized to achieve a particular purpose and to appeal to a particular audience
- ☐ clear and concise main idea and adequate supporting details

Delivery and Presentation

- ☐ appropriate volume, enunciation, and eye contact
- ☐ effective nonverbal cues
- ☐ appropriate pacing

Listening Rubric

As a peer reviewer or audience member, you should do the following:

- ☐ listen quietly and attentively
- ☐ maintain eye contact with speaker
- ☐ ask appropriate questions
- ☐ (as peer reviewer) provide constructive feedback

Evaluating an Informative Presentation

Have students create a feedback checklist to use as they rehearse with their partners or small groups. This checklist should relate to the strength of their introductions, the clarity of the ideas and information expressed, and their ability to connect with the audience, as well as to both verbal and nonverbal aspects of their deliveries. Tell them to use the checklist consistently so that they can keep track of their improvements in different aspects of speaking.

Delivering an Informative Presentation

Remind students that like actors, they need to project their voices. This means that they need to effectively focus their voices. Students can establish an appropriate volume by rehearsing with a partner standing at the back of the classroom.

TEACHING NOTE

Extemporaneous Speeches
Invite students to give brief, extemporaneous speeches in small groups. Students should choose topics about which they already know a great deal. Tell them not to use notes, but instead to try grabbing attention with a strong introduction, two or three informative examples, and conclude with a simple summary of the main idea or message. Allow members of the group to quickly critique each person's speech.

Speaking & Listening Skills

Retell and Summarize

As students rehearse their presentations, encourage them to use the listening rubric. Also give them tips on active listening:

- Focus on the speaker, not on other listeners.
- Try not to think of questions as you listen; think of questions after the speaker finishes.
- Do not interrupt the speaker.

- Try to disregard the speaker's nonverbal communication.

As an exercise, challenge students in rehearsal groups to summarize the points each speaker makes. Have them write the main points on a note card. At the conclusion of a rehearsal session, ask students to give their note cards to each speaker, for the speaker to use in revising and improving his or her speech.

Objectives

Completing this lesson will enable students to

- write a response to literature based on a timed writing prompt
- answer standardized test questions that demonstrate revising and editing skills
- answer standardized questions that demonstrate the ability to make inferences from a reading

Timed Writing

Say that standardized tests often ask students to write a response to a prompt in a specified period of time. Give the following tips:

- Read the entire question carefully.
- Look for key words in the question that tell you what is expected.
- Underline these words or write them on your own note paper.
- Use the key words to make sure to answer all parts of the question.
- Organize. Allow time for planning, writing, and reviewing.
- Before you begin writing, create a rough outline of points to make.
- Write a clear introduction. This will help keep you on track as you write each paragraph.
- If you find yourself running out of time, state your remaining points and add a conclusion.
- Review your completed essay to see if you have answered all parts of the question.
- Proofread before you turn in your completed essay.

Common Core State Standards

Writing
W.2

Language
L.6.1e

Test Practice Workshop

Writing Skills

Expository Essay

Read the following short excerpt and the writing assignment. Before you begin writing, think carefully about what task the assignment is asking you to perform. Then create an outline to help guide your writing.

from *Alone Across the Arctic* by Pam Flowers

The desire to make this expedition didn't just appear suddenly, out of nowhere. When I look back, I can see it was part of a much larger dream that began when I was a kid growing up in Michigan.

I was eleven years old when a scientist came to my school to show slides and talk about Antarctica. I don't remember anything he said. But I clearly recall an image: a photograph of endless snow-covered mountains under a brilliant blue sky.

Immediately I knew I wanted to go to a place like that. The landscape was beautiful, so clean and empty. Best of all, there were no people. To a loner like me, it looked like the most perfect place imaginable.

Even back then, I spent most of my time alone. I didn't fit in well at school. My best friend was my dog, a German shepherd named Lady. Together we wandered the woods near my home, exploring for hours. I imagined ways we could survive in the wilderness—the food I would gather, the shelter I would build. I spent as many hours as possible outside with Lady.

I learned to love that time outdoors, alone with my dog. It became the source of my well-being. But I had no idea that someday I'd explore with my dogs for real in one of the harshest environments on Earth. I didn't expect to grow up to be an Arctic adventurer.

Assignment: What **caused** the narrator to make an expedition alone across the Arctic? Plan and write several paragraphs for an **expository essay** in which you state and support a **thesis** about the **causes** and **effects** of the narrator's decision. Include evidence from the passage to support your thesis.

Rubric for an Expository Essay

Have students use these criteria when evaluating their essays.

- ☐ Does the essay have an introduction that clearly states the thesis?
- ☐ Does the essay address causes and effects, and follow a clear organizational pattern?
- ☐ Does the essay use textual evidence to support the main ideas?
- ☐ Does the conclusion tie the body paragraphs to the thesis?

Revising and Editing Skills

Each blank indicates that a word has been omitted. Beneath the sentence are five words or sets of words. Choose the word or set of words that, when inserted in the sentence, *best* completes the sentence.

1. Disgusted, Mari ____ the ____ meat from the refrigerator and tossed it in the trash.
   - A. rebuffed...ominous
   - B. plucked...noisome
   - C. emulated...chaotic
   - D. incorporated...rumpled
   - E. forfeited...chaotic

2. The teacher was ____ by George's refusal to follow directions.
   - A. forfeited
   - B. incorporated
   - C. repressed
   - D. emulated
   - E. exasperated

3. Because they could not come to a compromise, Brad and Roland had reached ____.
   - A. a prerogative
   - B. an impasse
   - C. a conjecture
   - D. a prestige
   - E. a tedium

4. The vet explained that she had an effective ____ for the dog's troublesome ____ problems.
   - A. prerogative...ominous
   - B. conjecture...impasse
   - C. prosperity...preliminary
   - D. antidote...physiological
   - E. prestige...chaotic

5. The researchers' ____ that the planet was covered in ice could not be proved.
   - A. directive
   - B. conjecture
   - C. impasse
   - D. prestige
   - E. antidote

6. The unwanted visitor was ____ as he tried to enter.
   - A. plucked
   - B. incorporated
   - C. emulated
   - D. forfeited
   - E. rebuffed

7. The team was forced to ____ the game because of unsportsmanlike conduct.
   - A. delineate
   - B. repress
   - C. rebuff
   - D. exasperate
   - E. forfeit

8. I admire her because she measures ____ in terms of happiness rather than wealth.
   - A. impasse
   - B. locomotion
   - C. tedium
   - D. prosperity
   - E. prerogative

9. Grace's job was so filled with ____ that she would fall asleep at her desk.
   - A. tedium
   - B. directive
   - C. impasse
   - D. conjecture
   - E. antidote

Teach the Workshop

Revising and Editing Skills

1. B
2. E
3. B
4. D
5. B
6. E
7. E
8. D
9. A

Test-Taking Tips

Avoid Distractors Instruct students to watch out for distractors, incorrect answers that look right because they are partially correct. Distractors are usually based on common mistakes students make. Model a think-aloud showing how to detect distractors.

Question 4. I've already eliminated C and E, so my choice is now between A, B, and D. But I see that A and B are distractors, because although those answers could fit grammatically, they don't really make sense. So D is the correct answer.

> For more information, see the Language Arts Handbook Section 8, Test-Taking Skills.

Program Resources

For more study and practice with test-taking skills, see the *Exceeding the Standards: Test Practice* resource:
- Expository Essay Practice Test: Revising and Editing, pp. 8–9

Words in Use

Teaching Words

expedition, 370	impasse, 371
omitted, 371	conjecture, 371
rebuffed, 371	prestige, 371
ominous, 371	tedium, 371
emulated, 371	antidote, 371
forfeited, 371	aviator, 372
repressed, 371	tandem, 372
exasperated, 371	tethered, 372
prerogative, 371	perilous, 372

KEY TERMS

OUTLINE, 370	TONE, 373
NARRATOR, 370	POINT OF VIEW, 373
EXPOSITORY ESSAY, 370	FIRST-PERSON, 373
THESIS, 370	SECOND-PERSON, 373
CAUSE, 370	THIRD-PERSON, 373
EFFECT, 370	THIRD-PERSON
PERSONIFICATION, 373	LIMITED, 373
FORESHADOWING, 373	THIRD-PERSON
THEME, 373	OMNISCIENT, 373
CONFLICT, 373	BIOGRAPHY, 373
FIGURATIVE	AUTOBIOGRAPHY, 373
LANGUAGE, 373	MEMOIR, 373
PROTAGONIST, 373	

Tell students that reading comprehension questions give a short piece of writing and then ask several questions about it. The questions may ask students to figure out something based on information in the passage. Urge them to keep the following tips in mind:

- Read all the questions quickly.
- Read the passage with the questions in mind.
- Reread the first question carefully.
- Scan the passage, looking for key words. When you find a key word, slow down and read carefully.
- Answer the first question.
- Repeat this process to answer all the rest of the questions.

Reading Skills

Carefully read the following passage. Then, on a separate piece of paper, answer each question.

from "Flying" by Reeve Lindbergh

I always flew with my father, who had been a pioneer aviator in the 1920s and '30s. I think that he wanted to share his love for the air and for airplanes with his growing family, the way sports-minded fathers took their children to ball games on Saturdays and taught them to play catch afterward. My father took

5   his children to the airport instead and taught them to fly.

Though he was the pilot on these flights, he did not own the airplane. It was a sixty-five-horsepower Aeronca, with tandem cockpits, that he rented from a former bomber pilot whose name was Stanley. Stanley managed the airport, including the huge loaf-shaped hangar that served as a garage for repairs and

10   maintenance to the aircraft, and he leased out the group of small planes tethered near the building like a fleet of fishing boats clustered around a pier.

It was Stanley, most often, who stood in front of the airplane and waited for my father to shout "ConTACT!" from the cockpit window, at which time, Stanley gave the propeller a hefty downward shove that sent it spinning into

15   action and started the plane shaking and shuddering on its way. The job of starting the propeller was simple but perilous. My father had warned us many times about the danger of standing anywhere near a propeller in action. We could list almost as well as he did the limbs that had been severed from the bodies of careless individuals "in a split second" by a propeller's whirling force.

20   Therefore, each time that Stanley started the propeller, I would peer through its blinding whir to catch a glimpse of any pieces of him that might be flying through the air. Each time, I saw only Stanley, whole and smiling, waving us onto the asphalt runway with his cap in his hand and his hair blowing in the wind of our passing—"the propwash" my father called it.

25   My sister and my three brothers flew on Saturdays too. The older ones were taught to land and take off, to bank and dip, and even to turn the plane over in midair, although my second-oldest brother confessed that he hated this—it made him feel so dizzy. The youngest of my three brothers, only a few years older than me, remembers my father instructing him to "lean into the curve" as

30   the plane made a steep sideways dive toward the ground. My brother was already off balance, leaning away from the curve, and hanging on for dear life. For my sister, our father demonstrated "weightlessness" by having the plane climb steeply and then dive so sharply that for a moment she could feel her body straining upward against her seatbelt,

35   trying to fight free, while our father shouted out from the front seat that one of his gloves was actually floating in midair.

Differentiated Instruction

Reading Proficiency

Point out the spoken word "ConTACT!" in the reading and ask students why they think the writer used this format for the word. Remind students that writers may take liberties with spelling and punctuation to show that they are using words or phrases in a special way. Ask students to locate other words and phrases enclosed by quotation marks. Explain that these are not necessarily spoken words. Instead, the writer is indicating something special. Most students will understand "in a split second" and "lean into the curve." Tell them that "propwash" is a term for the wind that propellers (props) produce; "weightlessness" is in quotes because the word describes a feeling rather than a genuine absence of weight.

1. Based on the context, which of the following is the *best* definition of the word *pioneer* in line 1?
   A. an early farmer in the western United States
   B. one of the first people to explore a geographic area
   C. one of the first plants to grow in bare land
   D. a person who is one of the first to explore a new activity
   E. a person who traveled west in a covered wagon

2. The narrator's father differs from the fathers of other children because he
   A. doesn't like sports.
   B. doesn't spend time with his children.
   C. teaches his children to fly.
   D. likes football more than baseball.
   E. owns an airplane.

3. The phrase that begins on line 11 "like a fleet of fishing boats clustered around a pier" is an example of
   A. personification.
   B. foreshadowing.
   C. theme.
   D. conflict.
   E. figurative language.

4. Why does the narrator's father shout "ConTACT" in line 13?
   A. It orders Stanley to touch the plane.
   B. It tells Stanley to spin the propeller.
   C. It means the radio is turned on.
   D. It means "I've got the controls."
   E. It tells the narrator to take the controls.

5. In lines 20 and 21, the narrator expected
   A. Stanley to be chopped to pieces.
   B. the plane to shudder and shake.
   C. her father to yell "ConTACT."
   D. the plane to take off.
   E. the plane's engine to start.

6. What can you infer about how the narrator's brothers and sister felt about flying?
   A. They loved everything about it.
   B. They couldn't wait to learn more.
   C. They wanted to fly by themselves.
   D. They hated everything about flying.
   E. They didn't like some parts of it.

7. The protagonist of this passage is
   A. the father.
   B. the narrator.
   C. Stanley.
   D. the narrator's sister.
   E. the narrator's second-oldest brother.

8. What is the overall tone of the passage?
   A. frightened
   B. thrilled
   C. sad
   D. conversational
   E. angry

9. This story is written from which point of view?
   A. first-person
   B. second-person
   C. third-person
   D. third-person limited
   E. third-person omniscient

10. This passage is *best* described as
   A. a literary response.
   B. a biography.
   C. an autobiography or memoir.
   D. a persuasive essay.
   E. a review.

Teach the Workshop

Reading Skills

1. D
2. C
3. E
4. B
5. A
6. E
7. B
8. D
9. A
10. C

Test-Taking Skills

Eliminate Incorrect Responses

Point out to students that a key skill in working with multiple-choice questions is eliminating incorrect responses. Demonstrate this skill by modeling a think-aloud for one question in the Reading Skills section.

Question 3. I know that a comparison that uses the word *like* is a simile, but that is not one of the answer choices. Foreshadowing relates to plot and so does conflict, and themes usually aren't stated directly. That seems to eliminate B, C, and D. Personification is a kind of figurative language, like similes, so E is probably correct.

Select another question and have the class work as a group to eliminate the incorrect responses.

Unit 4 Visual Planning Guide

Planning and Assessment Tools

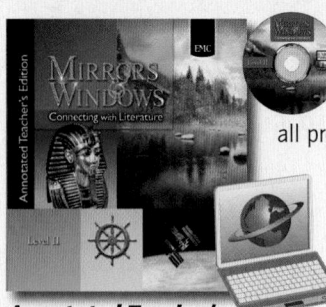

Annotated Teacher's Edition

Annotated Teacher's Edition
One location for accessing, previewing, and planning for use of all program resources.

EMC Launchpad
Desktop application for accessing, previewing, planning, posting, and grading all program resources. Post personal resources and lessons, and access the E-Lesson Planner, the E-Gradebook, and training modules for computer literacy.

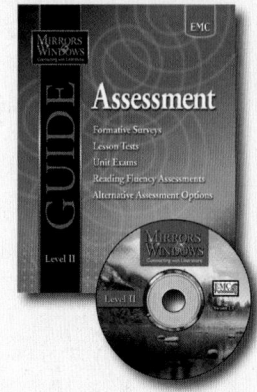

Assessment Guide and ExamView
A variety of assessments are available for this unit in print and electronic forms, including:
- Formative Survey
- Lesson Tests
- Unit Exams
- Alternative Assessment Options
- Reading Fluency Assessments

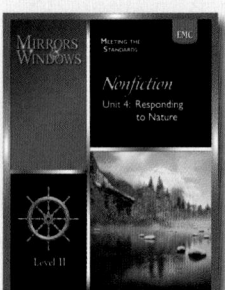

Meeting the Standards: Unit 4
In addition to lesson-by-lesson resources, *Meeting the Standards* includes the following unit-based resources:
- Unit Study Guide
- Practice Test
- Active Reading Model
- Selection Quizzes

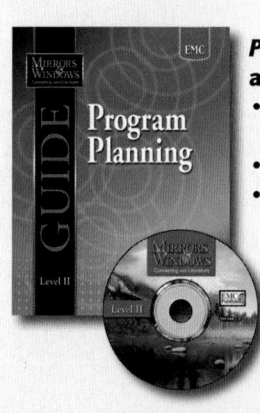

Program Planning Guide and E-Lesson Planner
- Lesson Plans for all the selections in the unit
- Core Standards-Based Selections
- Reading Log and Evaluation Forms

The E-Lesson Planner contains fully developed lesson plans and unit resources with an electronic calendar for editing lesson plans.

Technology Tools

Visual Teaching Package
This package contains unit-based lectures, games, art collections, and Writing Workshops in PowerPoint format; included within the EMC Launchpad.

Interactive Student Text on CD
The student textbook on CD includes highlighting, note-taking, bookmarking, and a direct link to the student website, in addition to everything in the student text.

Audio Library
Authentic, dramatic recordings with listening activities expand listening skills and offer additional support for developing readers and English Language Learners.

ETS Online Criterion-Based Essay Grader (Grades 9–12)
Students can use this ETS web-based tool to evaluate their essays online before submitting them for teacher review and final evaluation.

mirrorsandwindows.com
Student and teacher resources, support, references, technology tools, and state-specific standards are available at **mirrorsandwindows.com.** The website is customizable using the EMC Launchpad.

Unit-Based Resources

Exceeding the Standards Unit Resources

Each of the *Exceeding the Standards* resources provides fully developed lessons to help you extend the textbook lessons and to expand upon the themes and skills covered in the unit. You can also download these lessons from **mirrorsandwindows.com**.

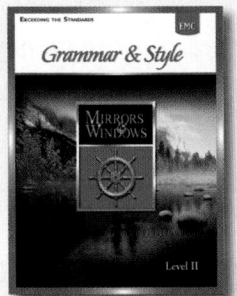

Grammar & Style
This resource contains:
- Three lessons on Complements, pp. 82–91
- Five lessons on Modifiers, pp. 92–112

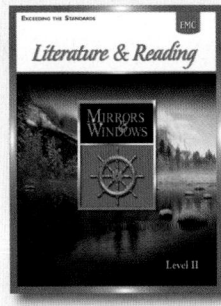

Literature & Reading
This resource contains:
- Analyze and Interpret Informational Text and Visual Media, pp. 8–10

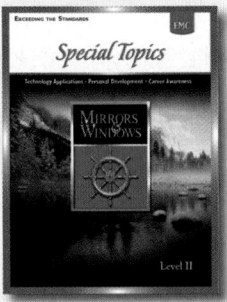

Special Topics
This resource contains:
- Lifelong Learning: Analyzing Yourself: Part 2, pp. 14–15
- Media Literacy: Designing a Website, pp. 16–17

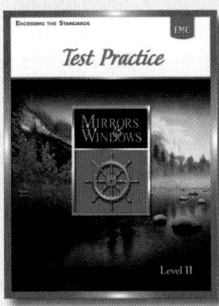

Test Practice
This resource contains:
- Descriptive Essay Practice Test: Reading, pp. 10–12

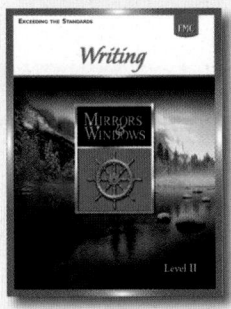

Writing
This resource contains:
- Expository Writing: Explain Using Cause and Effect, pp. 23–30

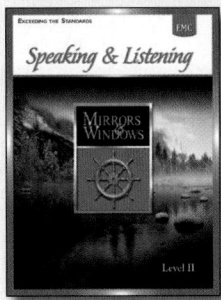

Speaking & Listening
This resource contains the following lesson to expand on the Viewing Workshop:
- Critical Viewing, pp. 10–12

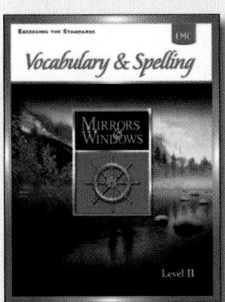

Vocabulary & Spelling
This resource contains:
- Four lessons on Context Clues, pp. 35–42
- One lesson on Denotation and Connotation, pp. 43–44.

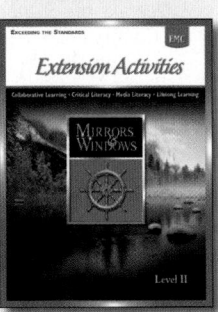

Extension Activities
This resource contains:
- Lifelong Learning: Researching Myths and Legends, p. 11
- Critical Literacy: Hold a Debate, pp. 12–13

Unit 4 Visual Planning Guide

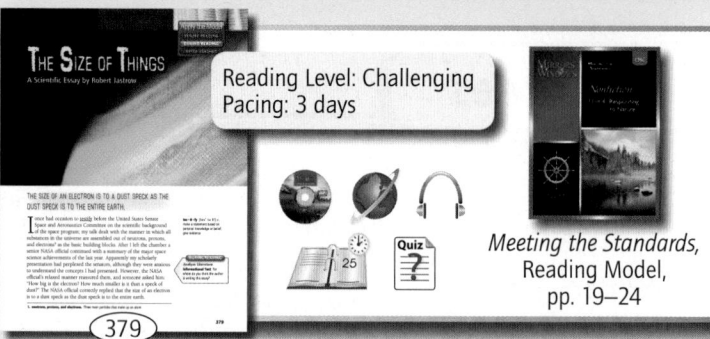

THE SIZE OF THINGS
A Scientific Essay by Robert Jastrow

Reading Level: Challenging
Pacing: 3 days

(379)

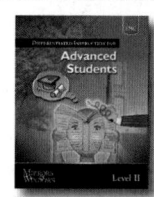

Meeting the Standards,
Reading Model,
pp. 19–24

National Audubon Society
The SIBLEY Guide to Birds
Written and illustrated by DAVID ALLEN SIBLEY

Reading Level: Easy
Pacing: 2 days

(391)

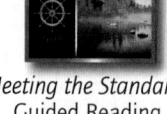

Meeting the Standards,
Guided Reading,
pp. 25–29

Advanced Students
Level II

Advanced Students,
Comparing Literature
Activity, pp. 21–22

Ships in the Desert
An Essay by Al Gore

Reading Level: Challenging
Pacing: 3 days

"We are creating a world that is hostile to wildness, that seems to prefer concrete, to natural landscapes."

(397)

Meeting the Standards,
Guided Reading,
pp. 30–35

Mute Dancers:
How to
Watch a
Hummingbird
A Scientific Essay
by Diane Ackerman

Hummingbirds have huge hearts and need colossal amounts of energy to fuel their flights...

Reading Level: Moderate
Pacing: 3 days

(409)

Meeting the Standards,
Compare Literature,
pp. 36–45

Developing Readers
Level II

Developing Readers,
Set Purpose,
pp. 28–30

THE FACE OF THE DEEP IS FROZEN
A Historical Essay by Jennifer Armstrong

The ship itself was a mess of snapped rigging and broken spars.

Reading Level: Challenging
Pacing: 3 days

(416)

Meeting the Standards,
Directed Reading,
pp. 46–52

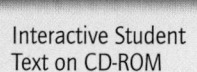 Interactive Student
Text on CD-ROM

 Selection
Lesson Plan

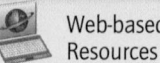 Web-based
Resources

Lesson-by-Lesson Resources

Hmong Storycloth

Reading Level: Moderate
Pacing: 3 days

Quiz

Meeting the Standards,
Directed Reading,
pp. 53–58

Developing Readers,
Take Notes, pp. 31–33

424

DUST BOWL PHOTOGRAPHS

Reading Level: Easy
Pacing: 2 days

Quiz

Meeting the Standards,
Directed Reading,
pp. 59–65

Advanced Students,
Critical Viewing
Activity, p. 23

432

Death in the Open

Reading Level: Challenging
Pacing: 1 day

Quiz

Meeting the Standards,
Independent Reading,
pp. 66–73

Advanced Students,
Author's Purpose
Analysis, p. 24

440

Astonishing Animals

Reading Level: Easy
Pacing: 1 day

Quiz

Meeting the Standards,
Independent Reading,
pp. 74–82

Advanced Students,
Visual Media Project,
pp. 25–26

443

 Lesson Test

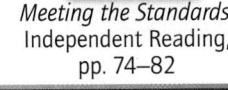 Audio Library

Unit 4 Scope & Sequence Guide

Selection or Feature	Genre	Reading Support/ Reading Level	Word Count	Reading Skill	Graphic Organizer	
Introduction to Informational Text and Visual Media pp. 376–377						
The Size of Things Robert Jastrow pp. 378–388	Scientific Essay	Guided Reading: Reading Model/ Challenging	2,317	Monitor Comprehension	Note-Taking Chart; K-W-L Chart	
Literature Connection: Achieving Perspective Pattiann Rogers pp. 386–387	Lyric Poem	Moderate	280			
from **The Sibley Guide to Birds** David Allen Sibley pp. 390–395	Visual Media	Guided Reading: Reading Model/Easy	233	Draw Conclusions	Details Web; Visual Media Chart	
Informational Text Connection: from **Wild Turkey** John James Audubon p. 394	Essay	Easy	448			
Ships in the Desert Al Gore pp. 396–406	Essay	Directed Reading/ Challenging	2,425	Analyze Main Idea and Supporting Details	Main Idea Map; Analogy Chart	
Informational Text Connection: I Am a Native of North America Chief Dan George pp. 403–405	Personal Essay	Easy	1,239			
Comparing Literature: Mute Dancers: How to Watch a Hummingbird Diane Ackerman pp. 408–414	Scientific Essay	Directed Reading/ Moderate	1,100		Sensory Details Chart	
The Hummingbird That Lived Through Winter William Saroyan pp. 408–414	Short Story	Directed Reading/ Moderate	897			
The Face of the Deep is Frozen Jennifer Armstrong pp. 415–422	Historical Essay	Directed Reading/ Challenging	2,066	Context Clues	Description Chart	
Literature Connection: Fire and Ice Robert Frost p. 421	Lyric Poem	Moderate	54			

GUIDED READING

DIRECTED READING

Literary Element	*Mirrors & Windows* Theme	Cross-Curricular Connection	Writing Options	Extension Activities
Purposes of Nonfiction Types of Informational Text Types of Visual Media				
Informational Text	Seeking Knowledge		Creative: Descriptive Paragraph Applied: List	Collaborative Learning: Give Complex Instructions Lifelong Learning: Borrowed Words
Visual Media	Observing Nature		Creative: Descriptive Paragraph Persuasive: Book Review	Collaborative Learning: Peer Review Lifelong Learning: Identify Birds
Analogy	Environmental Activism	Science Connection: *Global Warming*	Creative: Letter Expository: Problem-Solution Essay	Critical Literacy: Write a Proposal Media Literacy: Conduct Internet Research
Compare Literature: Description	Understanding Nature Helping Animals		Creative: Dialogue Expository: Critical Analysis	Critical Literacy: Analyze Adaptations Lifelong Learning: Research Myths and Legends
Description	Taking Risks		Creative: Journal Entry Expository: Literary Response	Lifelong Learning: Summarize an Incident Critical Literacy: Hold a Debate

Unit 4 Scope & Sequence Guide

	Selection or Feature	Genre	Reading Support/ Reading Level	Word Count	Reading Skill	Graphic Organizer	
DIRECTED READING	**Hmong Storycloth** Mee Vang pp. 424–431	Visual Media	Directed Reading/ Moderate		Sequence of Events	Timeline; Purpose Chart	
	Primary Source Connection: An Unforgettable Journey Maijue Xiong pp. 426–430	Autobiography	Challenging	2,405			
	Dust Bowl Photographs Arthur Rothstein pp. 432–439	Visual Media	Directed Reading/Easy		Activate Prior Knowledge	K-W-L Chart; Purpose Chart	
	Informational Text Connection: Dust Changes America Margaret Bourke-White pp. 436–438	Essay	Moderate	1,362			
INDEPENDENT READING	**Death in the Open** Lewis Thomas pp. 440–442	Scientific Essay	Independent Reading/ Challenging	1,086	Identify the Main Idea		
	Astonishing Animals Tim Flannery and Peter Schouten pp. 443–446	Visual Media	Independent Reading/ Easy	478	Draw Conclusions		

Unit 4 Language Arts Workshops

Grammar & Style	Vocabulary & Spelling	Writing	Speaking & Listening	Test Practice
Adjective and Adverb Clauses, p. 389 Simple and Compound Subjects, p. 407	Context Clues, p. 423	Descriptive Writing: Descriptive Essay, pp. 448–453	Critical Viewing, pp. 454–455	Writing Skills: Descriptive Essay, p. 456 Revising and Editing Skills, p. 457 Reading Skills: from "Beastly Behaviors" by Janine Benyus, pp. 458–459

Literary Element	*Mirrors & Windows* Theme	Cross-Curricular Connection	Writing Options	Extension Activities
Purpose	Preserving Memories		Creative: Descriptive Essay Expository: Historical Essay	Critical Literacy: Analyze a Speech Lifelong Learning: Research Southwest Asia
Purpose	Coping with Disaster	History Connection: *The New Deal*	Creative: Outline or Plot Diagram Applied: Interview Questions	Collaborative Learning: Trace a Migration Media Literacy: Visit the Library of Congress
Purpose	Dealing with Death		Expository: Literary Response	Critical Literacy: Hold a Panel Discussion
Visual Media	Reacting to Animals		Creative: Journal Entry	Lifelong Learning: Further Research

Unit 4 Building Vocabulary

The lists below identify the Words in Use and Key Terms within this unit. These words are listed at the bottom of the Teacher's Edition pages at the beginning of each lesson. Vocabulary development activities are provided in the *Meeting the Standards* unit book and in *Exceeding the Standards: Vocabulary & Spelling*.

WORDS IN USE

Preview Vocabulary

Preview Vocabulary are words taken from the sentences within each selection. These words are defined in the side margin or at the bottom of the pages on which they appear. The "Preview Vocabulary" section introduces these words in the Before Reading page preceding each selection.

benign, 410	consolidated, 417	iridescence, 409	transformation, 413
cache, 418	deduce, 380	peril, 401	unprecedented, 398
colossal, 409	diffuse, 381	perpetual, 409	void, 385
conclusively, 380	dire, 418	phenomenon, 399	
congeal, 417	erode, 417	testify, 379	

Selection Words

Selection Words are additional words from the reading that may be challenging but are not central to the selection and are not identified in the prereading section. These words can easily be learned using the story context, and they provide excellent practice for using content clues to find meaning without explicit instruction.

acute, 445	flock, 392	operetta, 410	spherical, 382
adrift, 437	floe, 417	outermost, 385	sponsored, 429
ancestry, 393	gale, 437	panhandle, 437	stable, 430
apparition, 401	hoarding, 405	peculiar, 443	stark, 438
bestir, 410	impenetrable, 382	perish, 421	strolling, 392
bribed, 427	inconceivably, 381	plight, 438	succulent, 410
catastrophe, 442	incongruous, 392	pretense, 386	suffice, 421
colliding, 386	inexorable, 400	prisms, 411	suspended, 412
commissioned, 436	inlet, 403	progeny, 441	tempest, 419
communal, 403	instinct, 394	prominent, 444	toil, 438
compelled, 418	integration, 405	refugee, 428	transient, 441
detestable, 442	interpenetrating, 386	rendered, 399	transition, 426
disintegration, 386	lateral, 444	ridicule, 405	translucent, 401
elliptical, 387	leisurely, 394	roost, 394	trawls, 443
erosion, 417	nuclear, 383	serenade, 410	underlying, 399
evoking, 440	obscure, 429	sifts, 436	upwelling, 440

Teaching Words

Teaching Words consist of vocabulary that is used in the directions about the lessons. Teaching words explain to students what to focus on within the selection, help establish the story context, clarify the meaning of literary terms, and define the goals or instructional purpose.

accurate, 388	communists, 424	enabled, 376	inverted, 449
advocate, 446	concise, 376	endure, 435	jargon, 376
aesthetically, 390	convey, 448, 454	erosion, 454	keen, 440
ancestors, 458	crazed, 457	evoke, 414	memorialize, 425
anecdote, 408	deafeningly, 449	evolutionary, 458	microscopic, 440
astute, 458	delve, 408	expedition, 415	misguided, 432
attributed, 408	depict, 454	formulate, 439	naturalists, 448
awareness, 396	destructiveness, 448	fumble, 393	objective, 376
awe, 458	diligently, 396	heirlooms, 424	paleontology, 446
barren, 415	dramatization, 422	heritage, 408	petrified, 449
clarification, 455	drought, 432	inappropriate, 435	phenomena, 376, 453
coincide, 455	ecosystem, 455	interference, 405	photojournalist, 432
collaborate, 388	elaboration, 455	intricate, 424	pictorial, 390

KEY TERMS

Key Terms are commonly referred to as *academic vocabulary.* These terms appear in the instructional material to teach the terminology that students need to acquire to understand literature. The repetition of the terms throughout the program ensures student mastery and provides a solid foundation for the continuing study of literature and language arts.

Objectives

Studying this unit will help students meet the following objectives:

- Connect the themes expressed in the selections to their own lives and to the world around them
- Identify common forms of nonfiction
- Understand different elements of nonfiction, including *informational text, visual media, analogy, description,* and *purpose*
- Understand variations of literary forms and authors' use of language to develop forms

Reading Strategies

Ask Questions
Clarify
Make Inferences
Make Predictions
Visualize

Reading Skills

Activate Prior Knowledge
Analyze Main Idea and Supporting Details
Context Clues
Determine Sequence of Events
Draw Conclusions
Monitor Comprehension

Literary Elements

Analogy
Description
Informational Text
Purpose
Visual Media

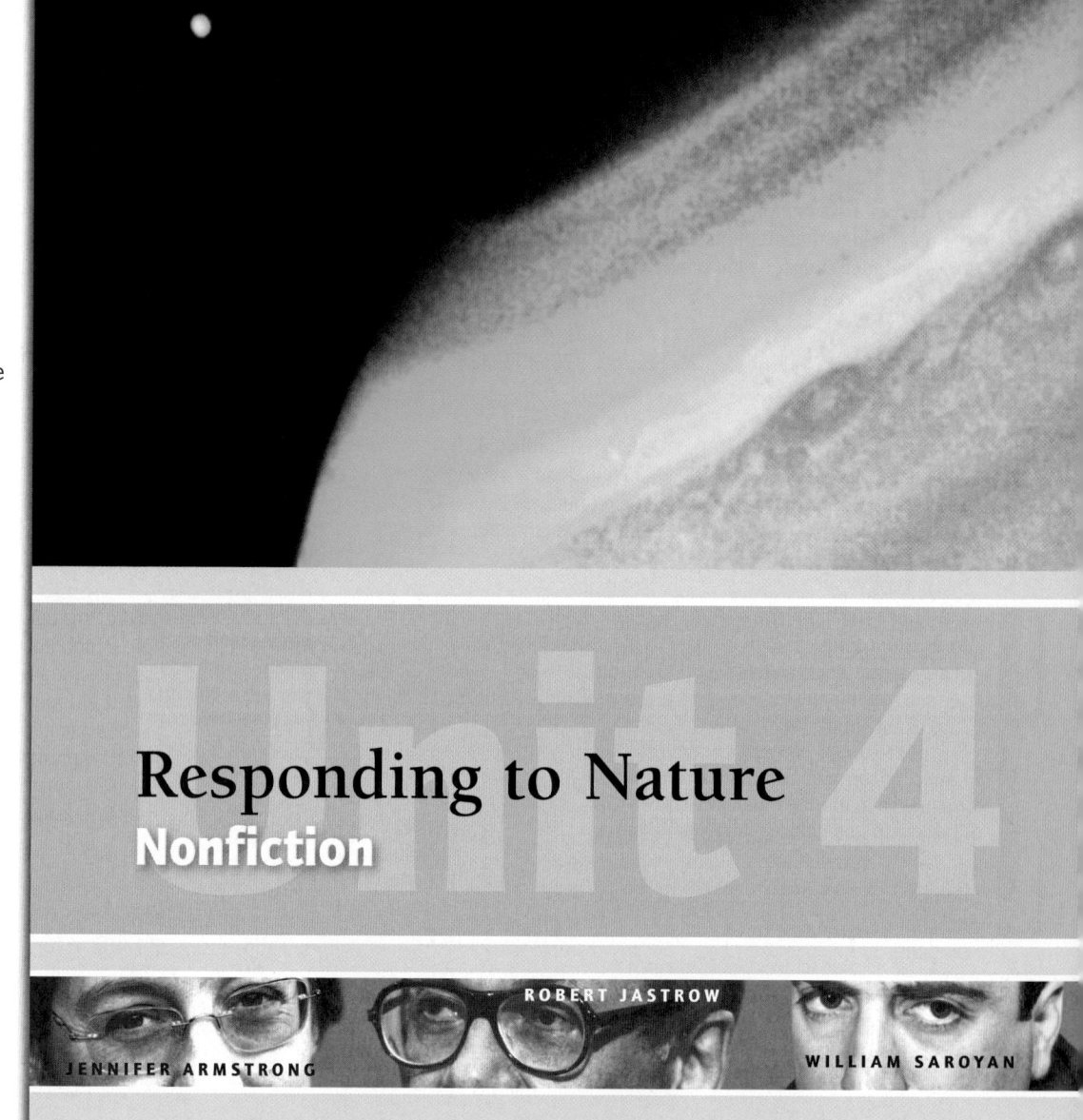

Responding to Nature
Nonfiction

ROBERT JASTROW

JENNIFER ARMSTRONG

WILLIAM SAROYAN

Launch the Unit

Have students work in small groups to create other questions that might relate to the unit theme. Suggest that they focus on how people respond and react to nature. Model this by proposing a question: "Why do thunderstorms always make me feel humble?" Have students write down their questions and keep the list. When you have completed the unit, revisit the lists of questions. Identify selections that provide insights about how to answer them.

> "...imagine that you can see the individual atoms in a kitchen table, and that each atom is the size of a grain of sand. On this scale of enlargement the table will be 2000 miles long."
>
> —ROBERT JASTROW, "The Size of Things"

Have you ever tried to imagine the size of an atom? In his article, scientist Robert Jastrow tries to describe the size of very small things, like the atom, and very large things, like the Milky Way Galaxy. One of the goals of informational texts is to present sometimes complicated information in a straightforward way. As you explore the texts and visuals in this unit, examine how authors and artists present their information.

AL GORE   DAVID ALLEN SIBLEY   TIM FLANNERY

375

Writing Options

Creative Writing
Descriptive Essay
Descriptive Paragraph
Dialogue
Journal Entry
Letter to the Editor
Outline
Plot Diagram

Applied Writing
Interview Questions
List of Jargon Terms

Expository Writing
Critical Analysis
Historical Essay
Literary Response
Problem-Solution Essay

Persuasive Writing
Book Review

Language Arts Workshops

Grammar & Style
Adjective and Adverb Clauses
Simple and Compound Subjects

Vocabulary & Spelling
Context Clues

Writing Workshop
Descriptive Essay

Viewing Workshop
Critical Viewing

Test Practice Workshop
Descriptive Essay
Reading Skills
Revising and Editing Skills

Program Resources

For a visual reminder of the unit-based resources available for Unit 4, Nonfiction, see pages 374A and 374B. As you introduce the unit, you may want to provide students with the Unit Study Guide, which is contained in the *Meeting the Standards* resource.

Teach the Genre

Introduction to Informational Text and Visual Media

Most students will have experienced informational text and visual media. Try to draw on their past experience as you teach this lesson. Encourage them also to explore the elements of informational text and visual media in the Before Reading and After Reading sections of each selection in Unit 4.

Launch the Lesson

From materials available in your classroom, gather one or more examples of informational text—a newspaper or magazine, a textbook, and a letter, memo, or instruction sheet—and several examples of visual media, such as newspaper photographs and a map or graph. Display them for students and ask: "What purpose do all of these things share?" Draw out the observation that the purpose of each item is to convey information. Then, ask students to speculate on why people would study these things in a literature class. Elicit the response that reading informational text will give them practice in analyzing and critical thinking. Suggest that studying informational text and visual media will also give them models they can imitate of effective prose and visual communication.

Program Resources

To help students explore literature on a deeper level, assign the following activity: Analyze and Interpret Informational Text and Visual Media, *Exceeding the Standards: Literature & Reading*, pp. 8–10.

Common Core State Standards

Speaking and Listening
SL.2, SL.3

Purposes of Nonfiction

In the previous unit, you read several types of nonfiction, including autobiography, biography, and essay. One of the characteristics shared by these types of nonfiction is a subjective approach, an emphasis on the writer's personal response to his or her subject. There are many other types of nonfiction, however, where the writer's approach to the subject is much more objective. To help understand this distinction, read the following passages. Both deal with the importance of space exploration. How do the two passages differ?

> The question I am most often asked is, "Where is the frontier now?" The answer should be obvious. Our frontier lies in outer space. The moon, the asteroids, the planets, these are mere stepping stones, where we will test ourselves, learn needful lessons, and grow in knowledge before we attempt those frontiers beyond our solar system.
>
> —LOUIS L'AMOUR, "The Eternal Frontier"

> Achieving spaceflight enabled humans to begin to explore the solar system and the rest of the universe, to understand the many objects and phenomena that are better observed from a space perspective, and to use for human benefit the resources and attributes of the space environment. All of these activities—discovery, scientific understanding, and the application of that understanding to serve human purposes—are elements of space exploration.
>
> —ENCYCLOPAEDIA BRITANNICA ONLINE, "Space Exploration"

The two passages differ in several ways, including the style of the writing, the tone, and the level of detail that is presented. Another major difference is in the basic purpose of the two passages. Louis L'Amour's essay does far more than simply relate the facts of space exploration. He

---

interprets these facts and uses them to support an idea he is hoping to persuade his reader to accept. By contrast, the basic purpose of the encyclopedia article is to present the facts about space exploration in a straightforward and objective way. An encyclopedia article is one common type of informational text.

Types of Informational Text

An **informational text** is a type of nonfiction whose basic purpose is to inform rather than to entertain or persuade. Among the most common types of informational texts are articles of various kinds. Here are a few of the most familiar.

News Article

A **news article** is an informational text about a particular topic, issue, event, or series of events. News articles can be found in newspapers, in magazines, and on Internet sites. Broadcast news stories on radio and television are also news articles. The main purpose of such articles is to convey information. This is particularly evident in the newspaper story, where the traditional structure is the "inverted pyramid." In a news story using this structure, the most important facts are presented first, followed by less important supporting details.

Science Article

A familiar type of news article is the **science article,** which offers information about a particular theory, scientific observation, or discovery. These articles are sometimes filled with a specialized vocabulary, or *jargon.* Writers who write about science for a mainstream audience, however, usually avoid terms with which most readers would be unfamiliar. Robert Jastrow's "The Size of Things" (page 378), for example, discusses the size of the universe in a way that is concise and easily understood.

Words in Use

Teaching Words
subjective, 376
objective, 376
enabled, 376
phenomena, 376
jargon, 376
concise, 376

KEY TERMS

Web Page

A **web page** is the basic unit of the World Wide Web, an organizational structure that includes a large part of what is offered on the Internet. One of the main purposes of web pages is to provide information. Web pages can contain links, or connections to other pages within the site or in completely different sites altogether. These connections are mostly in the form of "hotlinks" or "hyperlinks," which are addresses signaled by underlined or differently colored text.

Types of Visual Media

In addition to written language, information is conveyed through **visual media,** or pictorial or other graphic forms of communication. There is a wide variety of visual media, including photographs, illustrations, charts, diagrams, and maps.

Photograph

A **photograph** is an image typically created by light acting on a sensitive material. Photography is one of the primary visual methods of providing information. Like an informational text, a photograph needs to be "read" carefully. This might include identifying the overall subject, focusing in on specific details, and checking the title, label, caption, or other accompanying text. Photographers take photographs for a purpose. Arthur Rothstein's famous photographs of the Dust Bowl (page 432), for example, were taken to create a historical record and to inform viewers of the plight of poor farmers.

Illustration

An **illustration** is a photograph, drawing, or diagram that serves to make a concept clearer by providing a visual example. The illustrations in Tim Flannery and Peter Schouten's *Astonishing Animals: Extraordinary Creatures and the Fantastic Worlds They Inhabit* (page 443) help readers understand the strange animals that the text describes.

Chart

A **chart** is a visual representation of data that is intended to clarify, highlight, or put a certain perspective on the information presented. There are many types of charts, each with a different purpose. Here are some common examples:

- A *time line* shows the relative order of a series of events, such as dates in a period of history.
- A *flow chart* is a graphic representation of a process. For example, a flow chart might show how a bill becomes a law.
- A *pie chart* or *circle chart* shows the parts that make up the whole of something. For example, a pie chart might show the proportion of the world's fresh water on each continent.

Diagram

A **diagram** is an illustration that serves to explain a concept or process, and the arrangement and relationships among its various parts.

Map

A **map** is a representation, often on a flat surface such as a sheet of paper, of a geographic area that shows various significant features. These features vary with the purpose of the map. For example, a political map includes such features as the boundaries of countries and the locations of cities and towns. The map included in the entry from David Allen Sibley's *The Sibley Guide to Birds* (page 390) shows readers the specific range of a particular bird.

Speaking & Listening Skills

At a Glance
Guided Reading: Reading Model
- Reading Level: Challenging
- Difficulty Considerations: Concepts and vocabulary
- Ease Factor: Reading model

Objectives
Studying this lesson will enable students to
- use reading skills such as monitoring comprehension
- define *informational text* and recognize elements of this genre
- explain why Robert Jastrow has the expertise to write about matter
- appreciate an article about scale that helps them respond to nature

Launch the Lesson
Before reading "The Size of Things," ask students to suggest the smallest thing they can think of. As students name objects, keep asking if anyone can think of anything smaller. When they get to the smallest object they can think of, ask students if the object itself could be divided into even smaller pieces.

GUIDED READING

THE SIZE OF THINGS
A Scientific Essay by Robert Jastrow

Build Background
Scientific Context This essay deals with the concept of scale—in particular, things so small or so large that scientists must use mathematical formulas to estimate their sizes. Science is forty years advanced from the time Jastrow wrote this essay, but thinking about unimaginable sizes is as challenging today as it was in the 1960s.

Reader's Context Do you ever wonder what you are made of or where the universe ends? Read for some possible answers.

Set Purpose
Preview the essay by skimming it for unfamiliar terms. Skim the words in Preview Vocabulary and the footnotes on each page.

Analyze Literature
Informational Text An **informational text** is a type of nonfiction whose basic purpose is to inform rather than to entertain or persuade. Among the most common types of informational texts are articles and essays of various kinds. "The Size of Things" is a scientific essay, a type of informational text. As you read, discover what information Jastrow is presenting.

Meet the Author
Robert Jastrow (1925–2008) joined NASA, the National Aeronautics and Space Administration, when it formed in 1958. He was the first chair of its Lunar Exploration Committee. A theoretical physicist, Jastrow was perfect for the job. Scientists conduct experiments to test their ideas, and theoretical physicists are the scientists who recommend specific experiments for testing theories. At NASA, Jastrow helped establish the scientific goals for the *Apollo* trips to the Moon.

Use Reading Skills
Monitor Comprehension The author's purpose in this essay is to inform you, so try to keep track of new information on each page. You can use a note-taking chart like the one here. Record Jastrow's main ideas in the left-hand column, and use the right-hand column to list ideas and terms you would like to understand more fully. When you are done, try summarizing your notes at the bottom of the chart.

Main Ideas	Difficult Ideas and Terms
The electron is very small.	electron microscope

Summary of My Notes:

Preview Vocabulary
tes•ti•fy (tes′ tə fī′) *v.*, make a statement based on personal knowledge or belief; give evidence

con•clu•sive•ly (kən klü′ siv lē) *adv.*, in a way that ends debate or discussion

de•duce (di düs′) *v.*, infer

dif•fuse (di fyüs′) *adj.*, spread out loosely and widely

void (vôid) *n.*, emptiness

Words in Use

Preview Vocabulary
testify, 379
conclusively, 380
deduce, 380
diffuse, 381
void, 385

Selection Words
inconceivably, 381
impenetrable, 382
spherical, 382
nuclear, 383
outermost, 385

Teaching Words
theories, 378
accurate, 388
collaborate, 388

KEY TERMS
SCIENTIFIC ESSAY, 378
INFORMATIONAL TEXT, 378
AUTHOR'S PURPOSE, 378
SUMMARIZE, 378
SENSORY DETAIL, 385
ANALOGY, 388
BIOGRAPHY, 388

Common Core State Standards
Reading Informational
RI.1, RI.5, RI.8

THE SIZE OF THINGS

A Scientific Essay by Robert Jastrow

Apply the Model

BEFORE READING

DURING READING

AFTER READING

THE SIZE OF AN ELECTRON IS TO A DUST SPECK AS THE DUST SPECK IS TO THE ENTIRE EARTH.

I once had occasion to <u>testify</u> before the United States Senate Space and Aeronautics Committee on the scientific background of the space program; my talk dealt with the manner in which all substances in the universe are assembled out of neutrons, protons, and electrons[1] as the basic building blocks. After I left the chamber a senior NASA official continued with a summary of the major space science achievements of the last year. Apparently my scholarly presentation had perplexed the senators, although they were anxious to understand the concepts I had presented. However, the NASA official's relaxed manner reassured them, and someone asked him: "How big is the electron? How much smaller is it than a speck of dust?" The NASA official correctly replied that the size of an electron is to a dust speck as the dust speck is to the entire earth.

tes·ti·fy (tes´ tə fī′) v., make a statement based on personal knowledge or belief; give evidence

DURING READING

Analyze Literature
Informational Text For whom do you think the author is writing this essay? **A**

---
1. **neutrons, protons, and electrons.** Three main particles that make up an atom

379

Teach the Model

Summary
In "The Size of Things," physicist Robert Jastrow explains that all substances in the universe are made from the same three tiny building blocks—protons, neutrons, and electrons. Jastrow describes experiments scientists used to deduce the existence and size of atomic particles. He then explains various theories of how protons, neutrons, and electrons combine in different types of atoms. Atoms then combine and form molecules of different types of matter, which in turn form larger and larger objects, such as the planets, sun, and stars. The article offers several analogies to help readers visualize the relative sizes of objects and the spaces between them.

MIRRORS & WINDOWS The Mirrors & Windows questions at the end of the selection focus on the theme of seeking knowledge. Before they begin to read, ask students: What do you think of people who really enjoy science?

Analyze Literature
Informational Text *Answer:* He is writing for people like the senators, non-specialists who want to understand what makes up the universe. **A**

Program Resources

Planning and Assessment
Program Planning Guide, Selection Lesson Plan
E-Lesson Planner
Assessment Guide, Lesson Test
ExamView

Technology Tools
Interactive Student Text on CD
Visual Teaching Package
Audio Library
mirrorsandwindows.com

Meeting the Standards
Nonfiction: Unit 4, Reading Model, pp. 19–24

Make Connections
Answer: Students should show that they've thought about whether the "feeling" or "conviction" is enough evidence to suit them. Skepticism is a valid response. **Ⓐ**

Use Reading Skills
Monitor Comprehension *Answer:* He wanted to find the amount of electric charge an electron carries. **Ⓑ**

Analyze Literature
Tone Using this sentence as an example, have students analyze the tone the author uses and suggest how it relates to the audience for which he wrote the article. As students respond, they should use details from the text to support their conclusions. **Ⓒ**

TEACHING NOTE

Evaluate Sources
Explain that in research, people must determine when an article was written, as well as the credibility of the writer—especially in a field that changes as rapidly as science. For example, Pluto is no longer classified as a planet, but many astronomy books still list it as one.

Work with students to locate the copyright dates of a book, a magazine article, a newspaper article, and an Internet document.

Have students locate copyright dates for three selections in this book, as well as for two books and two magazine articles in your classroom.

---

con·clu·sive·ly
(kən klü′ siv lē) *adv.,* in a way that ends debate or discussion

> **DURING READING**
>
> **Make Connections**
> Are you convinced that the electron exists, based on this discussion so far? Why or why not? **Ⓐ**

> **DURING READING**
>
> **Use Reading Skills**
> **Monitor Comprehension**
> What did Millikan want to learn through this experiment? **Ⓑ**

de·duce (di düs′) *v.,* infer

The electron is indeed a tiny object. Its diameter is one 10-trillionth of an inch, a million times smaller than can be seen with the best electron microscope.[2] Its weight is correspondingly small; 10,000 trillion electrons make up one ounce. How can we be certain that such a small object exists? No one has ever picked up an electron with a pair of forceps[3] and said, "Here is one." The evidence for its existence is all indirect. During the 150 years from the late eighteenth century to the beginning of the twentieth century a great variety of experiments were carried out on the flow of electricity through liquids and gases. The existence of the electron was not proved <u>conclusively</u> by any single one of these experiments. However, the majority of them could be explained most easily if the physicist assumed that the electricity was carried by a stream of small particles, each bearing its own electrical charge. Gradually physicists acquired a feeling, bordering on conviction, that the electron actually exists.

The question now was, how large is the electron, and how much electric charge does each electron carry? The clearest answer to this question came from an American physicist, Robert Millikan, who worked on the problem at the University of Chicago in the first decades of the twentieth century. Millikan arranged a device, clever for its simplicity, in which an atomizer[4] created a mist of very fine droplets of oil just above a small hole in the top of a container. A small number of the droplets fell through the hole and slowly drifted to the bottom of the container. Millikan could see the motions of these droplets very clearly by illuminating them from the side with a strong light so that they appeared as bright spots against a dark background. Millikan discovered that some of these droplets carried a few extra electrons, which had been picked up in the atomizing process. By applying an electrical force to the droplets and studying their motions in response to this force, he could <u>deduce</u> the amount of electric charge carried by the electrons on each droplet. This charge turned out to be exceedingly minute.[5] As a demonstration of its minuteness, it takes an electric current equivalent to a flow of one million trillion electrons every second to light a 10-watt bulb. All this happened rather recently in the history of science. Millikan's first accurate measurements were completed in 1914. **Ⓒ**

---

2. **electron microscope.** Instrument that uses a beam of electrons to make an enlarged image of a very small object
3. **forceps.** Tongs
4. **atomizer.** Instrument that converts a liquid or solid to a fine mist or dust
5. **minute** (mī nüt′). Very small; tiny; infinitesimal

Differentiated Instruction

Reading Proficiency
Students may find the specialized vocabulary in a scientific article difficult. As students read through the article on their own, have them list unfamiliar terms that are not explained in the footnotes. Have them create a list of main ideas and concepts. Then have students form reading groups to compare terms and ideas and clarify difficult concepts.

English Language Learning
Jastrow uses English measurements, such as the inch and ounce, which may confuse students from cultures that use metric measurements. Explain that an inch is about 2.5 centimeters and an ounce is about 28 grams.

The tiny electron, and two sister particles, are the building blocks out of which all matter in the world is constructed. The sister particles to the electron are the proton and the neutron. They were discovered even more recently than the electron; the proton was identified in 1920 and the neutron was first discovered in 1932. These two particles are massive[6] in comparison with the electron—1840 times as heavy—but still inconceivably light by ordinary standards. The three particles combine in an amazingly simple way to form the objects we see and feel. A strong force of attraction[7] binds neutrons and protons together to form a dense, compact body called the nucleus, whose size is somewhat less than one-trillionth of an inch. Electrons are attracted to the nucleus and circle around it as the planets circle around the sun, forming a solar system in miniature.[8]

Together the electrons and the nucleus make up the atom.

The size of a typical atom is one hundred-millionth of an inch. To get a feeling for the smallness of the atom compared to a macroscopic[9] object, imagine that you can see the individual atoms in a kitchen table, and that each atom is the size of a grain of sand. On this scale of enlargement the table will be 2000 miles long.

The comparison of the atom with a grain of sand implies that the atom is a solid object. Actually, the atom consists largely of empty space. Each of the atoms that makes up the surface of a table consists of a number of electrons orbiting around a nucleus. The electrons form a diffuse shell around the nucleus, marking the outer boundary of the atom. The size of the atom is 10,000 times as great as the size of the nucleus at the center. If the outer shell of electrons in the atom were the size of the Astrodome that covers the Houston baseball stadium, the nucleus would be a ping-pong ball in the center of the stadium. That is the emptiness of the atom.

If most of the atom is empty space, why does a tabletop offer resistance when you push it with your finger? The reason is that the surface of the table consists of a wall of electrons, the electrons belonging to the outermost layer of atoms in the tabletop; the surface of your finger also consists of a wall of electrons; where they meet,

THE THREE PARTICLES COMBINE IN AN AMAZINGLY SIMPLE WAY TO FORM THE OBJECTS WE SEE AND FEEL. **D**

DURING READING

Use Reading Skills
Monitor Comprehension
How is an atom different from a grain of sand? **E**

dif·fuse (di fyüs′) *adj.*, spread out loosely and widely

---

6. **massive.** Containing a lot of matter or mass; dense
7. **strong force of attraction.** Particles in the nucleus of an atom stick together due to a force known in Jastrow's day as "the strong force." Today scientists know that the protons and neutrons consist of even smaller particles that stay together because of "the strong interaction."
8. **Electrons…forming a solar system in miniature.** This "planetary model" of the atom was popular in the 1960s. Scientists have found it impossible to determine the path of a single electron, so today they say that electrons form a cloud around the nucleus.
9. **macroscopic.** Visible to the naked eye

Science Connection
Planetary Model Comparing the movement of electrons around the nucleus to the movement of planets around the sun helps the layperson visualize atomic structure, but is not completely accurate. The attractive force that keeps the planets in orbit is gravity. The force that keeps electrons moving around the nucleus is electrical and can be either attractive or repulsive. Electrons do not move in circular orbits like the planets. In quantum theory, electrons have different amounts of energy that determine their position and movement. **D**

Use Reading Skills
Monitor Comprehension *Answer:* The grain of sand is solid; an atom is mostly empty space. **E**

Vocabulary Skills

Stressed and Unstressed Syllables
Remind students that some words, such as *minute* (a unit of time) and *minute* (very small), may be spelled the same, but (1) the vowels are pronounced differently; (2) the stressed syllable is different; and (3) the words act as different parts of speech and have different meanings.

Encourage students to use a dictionary to identify and label the stressed and unstressed syllables in

the following words. Students' marks will vary. Have English language learners practice speaking and producing these stressed and unstressed syllables by repeating these words with the class. Answers below show the main stress only.

1. atomizer (ATomizer)
2. infinitesimal (infiniTESimal)
3. macroscopic (macroSCOPic)
4. nuclear (NUclear)
5. cyclotron (CYclotron)

Use Reading Strategies

Visualize Suggest that students visualize the tabletop and their fingertips made up of thousands of tiny magnets. The north poles of the magnets in both the tabletop and their fingertip are facing one another, so they strongly repel one another. **A**

Use Reading Strategies

Clarify Ask students to suggest several synonyms for the word *massy* in Newton's description of the atom. Point out that mass is the amount of matter in an object. An object's weight is a measure of how strongly Earth's gravity pulls on the object's mass. **B**

Analyze Literature

Sensory Details Ask students what they think Rutherford meant when he said that atoms were "red or grey in color, according to taste." After they respond, remind students that atoms can't be seen, so are often shown as differently colored spheres in textbooks. **C**

Palomar Observatory on Palomar Mountain in California.

"IT WAS QUITE THE MOST INCREDIBLE EVENT THAT HAS EVER HAPPENED TO ME IN MY LIFE."

strong forces of electrical repulsion[10] prevent the electrons in your fingertip from pushing past the outermost electrons in the top of the table into the empty space within each atom. An atomic projectile[11] such as a proton, accelerated to high speed in a cyclotron,[12] could easily pass through these electrons, which are, after all, rather light and unable to hurl back a fast-moving object. But it would take more force than the pressure of the finger can produce to force them aside and penetrate the inner space of the atom. **A**

The concept of the empty atom is a recent development. **B** Isaac Newton described atoms as "solid, massy, hard, impenetrable, moveable particles." Through the nineteenth century, physicists continued to regard them as small, solid objects. Lord Rutherford, the greatest experimental physicist of his time, once said, "I was brought up to look at the atom as a nice hard fellow, red or grey in color, according to taste." **C** At the beginning of the twentieth century, J. J. Thomson, a British physicist and one of the pioneers in the investigation of the structure of matter, believed that the atom was a spherical plum pudding of positive electric charge in which negatively charged electrons were embedded like raisins. No one knew that the mass of the atom, and its positive charge, were concentrated in a small, dense nucleus at the center, and that the electrons circled around this nucleus at a considerable distance. But in 1911 Rutherford, acting on a hunch, instructed his assistant, Hans Geiger, and a graduate student named Marsden, to fire a beam of alpha particles[13] into a bit of thin gold foil. These alpha particles are extremely fast-moving atomic projectiles which should have penetrated the gold foil and emerged from the other side. Most of

---

10. **strong forces of electrical repulsion.** Like charges repel. If you try to join two bar magnets at their negative poles, for example, the poles will push each other apart.
11. **projectile.** Something forcefully propelled, like a bullet
12. **cyclotron.** Instrument that accelerates small particles (like electrons) using electric and magnetic fields
13. **alpha particles.** High-energy particles (radiation) that are ejected from an atomic nucleus at very high speeds

Differentiated Instruction

Enrichment

Some students may be interested in learning more about early theories of the atom, beginning with the first use of the word *atom* by the Greek philosopher Democritus, through J. J. Thomson's "plum pudding model," and to changes in the atomic model with the work of Millikan, Rutherford, and Bohr.

Have students make a time line showing how scientists' ideas about the atom have changed over the years. Students can share what they learn with the class.

them did, but Geiger and Marsden found that in a very few cases the alpha particles came out of the foil on the same side they had entered. Rutherford said later, "It was quite the most incredible event that has ever happened to me in my life. It was almost as incredible as if you fired a 15-inch shell at a piece of tissue paper and it came back and hit you."

Later Geiger told the story of the occasion on which Rutherford saw the meaning of the experiment. He relates: "One day [in 1911] Rutherford, obviously in the best of spirits, came into my room and told me that he now knew what the atom looked like and how to explain the large deflections[14] of the alpha particles." What had occurred, Rutherford had decided, was that now and then an alpha particle hit a massive object in the foil, which bounced it straight back. He realized that the massive objects must be very small since the alpha particles hit them so rarely. He concluded that most of the mass of the atom is concentrated in a compact body at its center, which he named the nucleus. Rutherford's discovery opened the door to the nuclear era.

Let us continue with the description of the manner in which the universe is assembled out of its basic particles. Atoms are joined together in groups to form molecules, such as water, which consists of two atoms of hydrogen joined to one atom of oxygen. Large numbers of atoms or molecules cemented together form solid matter. There are a trillion trillion atoms in a cubic inch of an ordinary solid substance, which is roughly the same as the number of grains of sand in all the oceans of the earth.

The earth itself is an especially large collection of atoms bound together in a ball of rock and iron 8000 miles in diameter,[15] weighing six billion trillion tons. It is one of nine planets, which are bound to the sun by the force of gravity. Together the sun and planets form the solar system. The largest of the planets is Jupiter, whose diameter is 86,000 miles; Mercury, the smallest, is 3100 miles across, one-third the size of the earth, and scarcely larger than the moon. All the planets are dwarfed by the sun, whose diameter is one million miles. The weight of the sun is 700 times greater than the combined weight of the nine planets. Like the atom, the solar system consists of a massive central body—the sun—surrounded by small, light objects—the planets—which revolve about it at great distances.

---

14. **deflections.** Turning or bending of radiation from a straight course
15. **diameter.** Length of a straight line through the center of a sphere

> **DURING READING**
>
> **Analyze Literature**
> **D** **Informational Text** What was Rutherford trying to express with this comparison?

> **DURING READING**
>
> **Use Reading Skills**
> **E** **Monitor Comprehension** In the phrases "nuclear energy" and "the nuclear era," what does the word *nuclear* mean?

Analyze Literature
Informational Text *Answer:* He was expressing his own amazement at an experience that he neither predicted nor expected. **D**

Use Reading Skills
Monitor Comprehension *Answer:* The word refers to the center of an atom; students may say it means *atomic.* **E**

Cultural Connection
Science Education When the Russians launched the Sputnik satellite in 1957, Americans lost their complacency about the nation's status in scientific and technological communities. Policymakers pressured the U.S. educational system, which had focused on "child-centered" approaches to learning, to shift to more rigid science and mathematics curricula in an effort to improve the scientific literacy of all Americans and regain the technological lead. Jastrow wrote this article during that period.

Science Connection
Light Years Students may ask how many miles are in a light year. The answer is approximately 5.9 trillion.

Reading Skills

Take Notes

Point out that the type of graphic organizer one chooses when reading depends on the organization of the writing. Discuss the organization of this text. Explain that, while it describes a sequence of events, it also describes the universe, building from the smallest to the largest objects. Suggest that students prepare an organizer that begins with the three basic particles of matter, and use arrows to show how they combine to form other matter.

Electrons Protons Neutrons

↓

Atoms

↓

Analyze Literature

Informational Text *Answer:* He makes an analogy between the galaxy and a pair of hats (the "double sombrero"). **Ⓐ**

Use Reading Skills

Monitor Comprehension *Answer:* The correct order is atom, planet, star, galaxy. **Ⓑ**

Analyze Literature

Analogy Remind students that an analogy is a comparison between two different things that highlights their similarities. After students read this paragraph, point out that Jastrow uses an orange, a grain of sand, cherry pits, and city blocks in an analogy to help readers understand the scale of the solar system. Ask students what property of those objects the author is comparing (size). Ask: "What properties of the objects are *not* comparable to objects in the solar system?" (Dissimilar properties are the specific colors, hardnesses, and compositions of the objects.) **Ⓒ**

The sun is only one among 200 billion stars that are bound together by gravity into a large cluster of stars called the galaxy. The stars of the galaxy revolve about its center as the planets revolve about the sun. The sun itself participates in this rotating motion, completing one circuit around the galaxy in 250 million years.

The galaxy is flattened by its rotating motion into the shape of a disk, whose thickness is roughly one-fiftieth of its diameter. Most of the stars in the galaxy are in this disk, although some are located outside it. A relatively small, spherical cluster of stars, called the nucleus of the galaxy,[16] bulges out of the disk at the center. The entire structure resembles a double sombrero[17] with the galactic nucleus as the crown and the disk as the brim. The sun is located in the brim of the sombrero about three-fifths of the way out from the center to the edge. When we look into the sky in the direction of the disk we see so many stars that they are not visible as separate points of light, but blend together into a luminous band stretching across the sky. This band is called Milky Way.

The stars within the galaxy are separated from one another by an average distance of about 36 trillion miles. In order to avoid the frequent repetition of such awkwardly large numbers, astronomical distances are usually expressed in units of the light year. A light year is defined as the distance covered in one year by a ray of light, which travels at 186,000 miles per second. The distance turns out to be six trillion miles; hence in these units the average distance between stars in the galaxy is five light years, and the diameter of the galaxy is 100,000 light years.

In spite of the enormous size of our galaxy, its boundaries do not mark the edge of the observable universe. The 200-inch telescope on Palomar Mountain[18] has within its range no less than 100 billion other galaxies, each comparable to our own in size and containing a similar number of stars. The average distance between these galaxies is one million light years. The extent of the visible universe, as it can be seen in the 200-inch telescope, is 15 billion light years.

An analogy will help to clarify the meaning of these enormous distances. Let the sun be the size of an orange; on that scale of sizes the earth is a grain of sand circling in orbit around the sun at a

---

DURING READING

Analyze Literature
Informational Text How does Jastrow help the reader visualize our galaxy? **Ⓐ**

DURING READING

Use Reading Skills
Monitor Comprehension
Place these in order from smallest to largest: star, planet, atom, galaxy. **Ⓑ**

16. **nucleus of the galaxy.** Center of a spiral galaxy like the Milky Way
17. **double sombrero.** The sombrero is a hat with a high crown and a very wide brim. Jastrow is suggesting that the galaxy's shape is like two sombreros placed base to base.
18. **200-inch telescope on Palomar Mountain.** The Hale Telescope on Palomar Mountain near San Diego, California, was the world's largest telescope from 1948 to 1976. It contains a mirror that is 200 inches across.

Visual Learning
You might wish to show students a segment of *Cosmos* or a documentary video about the universe that deals with scale, such as Nova's *The Elegant Universe*.

As students watch the film, have them focus on how the filmmaker helps viewers visualize vast differences in the sizes of objects or the distances among objects in space.

distance of 30 feet; the giant planet Jupiter, 11 times larger than the earth, is a cherry pit revolving at a distance of 200 feet or one city block; Saturn is another cherry pit two blocks from the sun; and Pluto, the outermost planet,[19] is still another sand grain at a distance of ten city blocks from the sun.

On the same scale the average distance between the stars is 2000 miles. The sun's nearest neighbor, a star called Alpha Centauri, is 1300 miles away. In the space between the sun and its neighbors there is nothing but a thin distribution of hydrogen atoms, forming a vacuum[20] far better than any ever achieved on earth. The galaxy, on this scale, is a cluster of oranges separated by an average distance of 2000 miles, the entire cluster being 20 million miles in diameter.

An orange, a few grains of sand some feet away, and then some cherry pits circling slowly around the orange at a distance of a city block. Two thousand miles away is another orange, perhaps with a few specks of planetary matter circling around it. That is the <u>void</u> of space. ❖

DURING READING

Use Reading Strategies
Clarify In the model Jastrow proposes, what fruit represents the sun and other stars? **D**

void (vôid) *n.*, emptiness

---

19. **Pluto, the outermost planet.** In 2006, astronomers decided that Pluto is not a planet.
20. **vacuum.** Space without any matter at all

If you wanted to know more about either atoms or the universe, whom could you ask? Do you think these topics are good for everyone to study, or just for people who are deeply interested in science?

Find Meaning

1. What does an atom contain?
2. (a) What makes up most of an atom (in terms of its volume)? (b) How is the structure of the universe like the structure of an atom?
3. (a) Why can't the force of your finger push apart the electrons on the top of a table? (b) How can a proton, which is billions of times smaller than a fingertip, push apart those same electrons?

Make Judgments

4. (a) Why do you think Jastrow includes information about people and events in history? (b) What did you learn from this information?
5. Jastrow worked as an astronomer, which is a space scientist. Why do you think he spends so much of this essay talking about atoms?
6. Identify several examples of sensory or descriptive detail in this essay. Explain why you think Jastrow's use of these techniques is or is not effective.
7. What kind of text organizational pattern does Jastrow use in the last seven paragraphs of this essay? Why does he use this pattern? What do you learn from it?

THE SIZE OF THINGS **385**

Teach the Model

Use Reading Strategies
Clarify *Answer:* Oranges represent the sun and other stars. **D**

You may want to ask students to write a journal entry or quick write, or divide students into discussion groups or lead a whole-class discussion about this question. *Answer:* Students should think of a knowledgeable person to consult. Most will say these things are good for everyone to learn.

Find Meaning
1. It contains protons, neutrons, electrons, and empty space.
2. (a) Empty space. (b) There are great distances among components.
3. (a) Electrons in the fingertip and electrons in the table push each other apart. (b) A proton can move at a higher speed, and therefore with a greater force, than a fingertip.

Make Judgments
4. (a) Jastrow may be trying to help readers relate to the scientists, or may be trying to show that ideas about the atom developed over a long time. (b) Answers will vary.
5. Students will probably say it is because atoms are the building blocks of everything.
6. Examples will vary. Students may say that the techniques are effective because they help people imagine very large and very small things.
7. Jastrow uses spatial organization to help the reader visualize the galaxy. This visualization can help the reader compare sizes and distances in the galaxy versus those in atoms.

Grammar Skills

Prepositional Phrases

Remind students that a prepositional phrase includes a preposition and the object of the preposition, along with any related adjectives and adverbs. For example, in the phrase "on the same scale," *on* is the preposition, *scale* is the object of the preposition, and "the same" modifies *scale.* Prepositional phrases can act as nouns, adjectives, and adverbs.

Have students identify and write down five prepositional phrases from this page. For each phrase, students should underline the preposition and circle the object of the preposition. Then have students tell whether the phrase is a noun, adjective, or adverb.

Teach the Connection

History Connection

Lyric Poetry In ancient Greek theater, when an actor expressed his own personal feelings, he sometimes sang the lines and accompanied himself on a lyre. The word *lyric* means "sung to the lyre." Because the words were more memorable than the music, they are all that remain of the early Greek plays. But the name *lyric poetry* still refers to personal expressions of feeling or thought, rather than to an attempt to tell a story (as in narrative poetry). **Ⓐ**

Analyze Literature

Lyric Poetry Tell students that lyric poetry has looser "rules" for the use of words and grammar than prose. Have students identify the simple subject and verb of the first sentence of the poem (galaxies are colliding). Ask students why they might not use the same type of sentence in a story or essay. **Ⓑ**

Make Connections

Ask students if they have ever reminded themselves about the size of the universe or the infinity of time to keep themselves from blowing small crises in their lives out of proportion. Invite students to share their experiences. **Ⓒ**

In "The Size of Things," Robert Jastrow tries to describe objects that are incredibly small and large. He uses descriptions and comparisons to help his readers imagine things they cannot see. **Pattiann Rogers** was born in 1940 in Joplin, Missouri. Her poetry often explores nature and the principles of science. As you read her poem, think about how her purpose and the literary elements she uses compare to those of Jastrow.

Achieving Perspective

Ⓐ A Lyric Poem by Pattiann Rogers

Straight up away from this road,
Away from the fitted particles of frost
Coating the hull of each chick pea,[1]
And the stiff archer bug making its way
5   In the morning dark, toe hair by toe hair,
Up the stem of the trillium,[2]
Straight up through the sky above this road right now,
Ⓑ The galaxies of the Cygnus A cluster
Are colliding with each other in a massive swarm
10   Of interpenetrating and exploding catastrophes.
Ⓒ I try to remember that.
And even in the gold and purple pretense
Of evening, I make myself remember
That it would take 40,000 years full of gathering
15   Into leaf and dropping, full of pulp splitting
And the hard wrinkling of seed, of the rising up
Of wood fibers and the disintegration of forests,
Of this lake disappearing completely in the bodies
Of toad slush and duckweed rock,
20   40,000 years and the fastest thing we own,
To reach the one star nearest to us.

---

1. chick pea. Seed about the size of a marble; also called garbanzo
2. trillium. Spring-blooming three-petalled flower

Words in Use

"Achieving Perspective"

Selection Words
colliding, 386
interpenetrating, 386
pretense, 386
disintegration, 386
elliptical, 387

Common Core State Standards

Reading Literature
RL.9

Differentiated Instruction

Reading Proficiency
Remind students that, when reading poetry, they should not stop at the end of each line unless the line ends in a period. Point out that the commas indicate separate phrases and clauses that are all part of a single sentence. Have students work together and take turns reading each sentence. After each sentence, they should stop and paraphrase or summarize the meaning of the sentence.

And when you speak to me like this,
I try to remember that the wood and cement walls
Of this room are being swept away now,
25 Molecule by molecule, in a slow and steady wind,
And nothing at all separates our bodies
From the vast emptiness expanding, and I know
We are sitting in our chairs
Discoursing[3] in the middle of the blackness of space.
30 And when you look at me
I try to recall that at this moment
Somewhere millions of miles beyond the dimness
Of the sun, the comet Biela,[4] speeding
In its rocks and ices, is just beginning to enter
35 The widest arc of its elliptical turn.[5] ❖

---

3. **Discoursing.** Expressing oneself in conversation
4. **Biela.** Comet discovered by Wilhelm von Biela in 1826
5. **widest arc of its elliptical turn.** An ellipse is an elongated
   circle. The widest arc would resemble one of the long sides of an
   oval racetrack.

TEXT ←→ TEXT CONNECTION

What feelings does this poem express? Think of how Robert Jastrow
might express the same feelings. What perspective do you think
Rogers's speaker is trying to achieve? All in all, which presentation
is easier to understand, that of Jastrow or Rogers? Be sure to
support your opinion with evidence from the texts.

Teach the Connection

Science Connection

Cygnus A The Cygnus A cluster mentioned in the poem appears from Earth to be a double galaxy in the constellation Cygnus (the swan), which is more than 600 million light years from Earth. Cygnus A is the most powerful source of radio waves in the known universe, emitting 10^{11} times more energy than the sun. At one time, astronomers believed that the energy was caused by the collision of the two galaxies, but that theory doesn't account for the huge output of energy. Some astronomers now believe the source may be a black hole between the galaxies.

Text-to-Text Connection

Answer: Students will probably say the poem expresses a feeling of smallness. They may say that Jastrow would try to express the same sense of being a small part of the universe, but in prose. They should recognize that Rogers's speaker is trying to achieve perspective in the context of daily life and a relationship with another person. They will probably say the speaker achieves perspective. Other opinions and preferences will vary.

Vocabulary Skills

Use a Dictionary

Point out that poets often select precise words to establish a specific tone or mood. Understanding subtle differences in meaning can enhance the reader's enjoyment and understanding of the poem. Encourage students to use dictionaries to look up the meanings of words alone and in phrases, such as *fitted particles of frost, interpenetrating, toad slush,* and *duckweed.*

Have students work in small groups to discuss why the poet might have chosen those specific words to create the tone and mood of the poem.

Review the Model

Analyze Literature

Informational Text Students may already know that atoms are made of smaller particles. They may also know that protons have a positive charge and electrons have a negative charge. They will probably know about the solar system, comets, stars, and galaxies. They will want to learn various things. Some may cite Jastrow's title, "The Size of Things," as something they expected to learn in the essay. What students learned from the essay will vary.

Lifelong Learning

Borrowed Words Student responses will vary slightly. The Latin phrase *bona fide* means "in good faith." The word *nemesis* comes from Greek and means one's rival or opponent. *RSVP* is an acronym that stands for the French phrase *"Répondez s'il vous plaît"* and means "reply please."

Analyze Literature

Informational Text Analyze Jastrow's essay with a K-W-L chart. In the first column, put something you already knew about atoms or space. In the center column, write something you want to learn about that topic. Scan the essay to remind yourself of information the article contains, and then, in the third column, write what you learned from the essay. When you are done, summarize what you learned in a single sentence. As a separate activity, write a full summary of the essay and exchange your summary with a classmate. Write an evaluation of their work based on the accuracy of the main ideas, supporting details, and the overall meaning of the essay.

What I Already Know	What I Want to Learn	What I Learned
That atoms are small and the universe is big		

Extend Understanding

Writing Options

Creative Writing Write a **descriptive paragraph** using an analogy. An analogy is a comparison of things that are alike in some ways but different in others. Imagine that you want to describe an atom to one of your state's senators. Then choose what to emphasize—such as the atom's size, its composition, the empty space it contains, or the number of atoms in a common object—and invent an analogy that will convey this to your senator.

Applied Writing Jargon is terminology about a specific topic that most people will not understand. Create a **list** of terms from this essay that you believe are jargon. When you have completed your list, draft a definition for each term in your own words. Use a dictionary or other reference material to help you find accurate and complete definitions. Also, using a dictionary, identify the proper syllabication, pronunciation, and part of speech for each word. Finally, consult a thesaurus to identify any alternate word options.

Collaborative Learning

Give Complex Instructions With a partner, take turns giving oral instructions to perform specific tasks, answer questions, or solve problems. Set a time limit for each speaker and switch when your time is up. Focus your instructions on researching or analyzing the selection or the literature connection.

Lifelong Learning

Borrowed Words "Achieving Perspective" uses the phrase "exploding catastrophes." The word *catastrophe* comes from the Greek word *katastrophē* and is one example of foreign words commonly used in the English language. Identify the meaning of the following foreign phrases and acronyms used in English: *bona fide, nemesis,* and *RSVP*. Note any other foreign words that you have encountered.

Go to **www.mirrorsandwindows.com** for more.

Rubrics for Writing Options

You can adapt this as a checklist for students to use as they write.

Creative Writing

☐ Does the paragraph attempt to describe the atom?
☐ Does the paragraph contain an analogy?
☐ Does the paragraph emphasize a specific aspect of the atom?

Applied Writing

☐ Does the list use jargon from the essay?
☐ Does the list contain both terms and definitions?
☐ Are the definitions accurate and complete?

Grammar & Style

Adjective and Adverb Clauses

Adjective Clauses

It is one of nine planets, which are bound to the sun by the force of gravity.

—ROBERT JASTROW, "The Size of Things"

In the sentence above, *which are bound to the sun by the force of gravity* is a clause that provides information about the noun *planets*. An **adjective clause** is a dependent clause that modifies a noun or pronoun. Adjective clauses follow the word they modify and are generally introduced with words such as *that, which, who, whom, whose, after, before, since, than, when, why,* and *where*.

When an adjective clause is **essential** to the meaning of a sentence, it should not be set off from the rest of the sentence with commas.

> EXAMPLE
>
> *This is the method that they used to measure the electron.*

When an adjective clause is **nonessential,** it is set off with commas.

> EXAMPLE
>
> *The senator, who had attended my lecture, asked about the size of an electron.*

Adverb Clauses

An **adverb clause** is a dependent clause that functions as an adverb. It modifies a verb, an adjective, or another adverb.

> EXAMPLE
>
> *The scientists knew the electron existed before they understood its size.*

In the sentence above, *before they understood its size* is a clause that modifies the verb *knew*. Adverb clauses often start with a subordinating conjunction such as *after, although, because, before, if, so that, unless, when, whether,* and *while*.

> EXAMPLE
>
> *Because electrons are so small,* they are difficult to measure.

When an adverb clause begins a sentence, it is set off by a comma.

Sentence Improvement

On a separate sheet of paper, correct the punctuation of the clauses in the following sentences. If a sentence has no punctuation errors, write *correct*. Next to each sentence, state whether the clause it contains is an adjective or adverb clause.

1. Millikan was the scientist, who measured the mass of the electron.
2. It was the most incredible event that ever happened to him.
3. Jupiter which has a diameter of 86,000 miles is the largest of the planets.
4. Scientists were unsure of the electron's existence before the experiments.
5. Because of the work of Rutherford and Geiger our understanding of the atom increased.

Sentence Improvement

1. Millikan was the scientist who measured the mass of the electron. Adjective
2. Correct; Adjective
3. Jupiter, which has a diameter of 86,000 miles, is the largest of the planets. Adjective
4. Correct; Adverb
5. Because of the work of Rutherford and Geiger, our understanding of the atom increased. Adverb

> For more information, see Grammar & Style Section 3.8, Modifiers, in the Language Arts Handbook.

TEACHING NOTE

Extra Practice

Each sentence below has both an adverb clause (single underscore) and an adjective clause (double underscore). Read each sentence aloud, and have students identify the two types of clauses.

1. After the detectives left, we burned the documents that made Nora seem guilty.
2. The man whose tree fell on the shed agreed to pay after we called the city.
3. Let's meet, unless you find a florist who will sell all the flowers you need.
4. Leon, who can't be with us in person, can participate because he has access to video-conferencing technology.

KEY TERMS

ADJECTIVE CLAUSE, 389
DEPENDENT CLAUSE, 389
NOUN, 389
PRONOUN, 389
ESSENTIAL, 389
NONESSENTIAL, 389
ADVERB CLAUSE, 389
SUBORDINATING CONJUNCTION, 389
PUNCTUATION, 389

Program Resources

You will find additional lessons on Adjective and Adverb Clauses in the *Exceeding the Standards: Grammar & Style* resource.

Common Core State Standards

Language
L.1

Preview the Model

At a Glance
Guided Reading: Reading Model
- Reading Level: Easy
- Difficulty Consideration: Vocabulary
- Ease Factors: Length and illustration

Apply the Model

BEFORE READING
DURING READING
AFTER READING

from *The Sibley Guide to Birds*

Visual Media by David Allen Sibley

GUIDED READING

Objectives
Studying this lesson will enable students to
- use reading skills such as drawing conclusions
- interpret visual media
- recognize the work of David Allen Sibley and John James Audubon
- compare visual descriptions and written descriptions

Launch the Lesson
Tell students they are about to read about two people who are famous for their observations of birds. Ask students to brainstorm for words they would use to describe birds they have seen, such as words describing size, shape, coloring, feathers, and sounds. Have them name some birds they can identify, such as robin or blue jay. Challenge them to describe these birds in words so that other people could recognize them. Finally, have students make sketches of the birds to accompany their descriptions. Ask the class to decide which descriptions are more helpful, the ones in words or those in drawings.

Build Background
Scientific Context Ornithologists are scientists who study birds, but there are many more birdwatchers than there are ornithologists. Birdwatchers spend hours looking for birds, and they keep careful records of birds they have seen. Birdwatchers use illustrated manuals called *field guides* to help identify birds. In 2000, ornithologist David Allen Sibley published a field guide that describes over eight hundred species of birds in North America. This entry is about one of those species.

Reader's Context Would you know a wild turkey if you saw one? You probably would. Imagine having this kind of book along with you in the woods and encountering a flock of birds. Study this entry to learn more about them.

Set Purpose
As you read this entry from *The Sibley Guide to Birds,* consider how the author conveys information in words and images. Which do you find more effective?

Analyze Literature
Visual Media In addition to written language, information can be conveyed through **visual media,** pictorial or other graphic forms of communication. There is a wide variety of visual media, including photographs, illustrations, charts, graphs, diagrams, and maps. Field guides, like *The Sibley Guide to Birds,* often contain both text and several different kinds of visual media. As you read this entry, examine how visual media and text interact to provide the reader with information.

Use Reading Skills
Draw Conclusions Use details from the entry to draw a conclusion about what traits can be used to distinguish the wild turkey from other birds. As you study the entry, record details with a web. Put details about the wild turkey in the outer ovals.

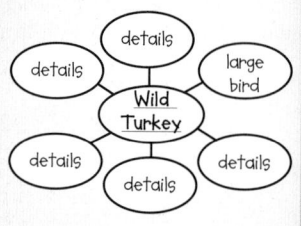

Meet the Author
David Allen Sibley (b. 1962) first started thinking about making a field guide in the 1970s. According to Sibley, "Birds are beautiful, in spectacular as well as subtle ways; their colors, shapes, actions, and sounds are among the most aesthetically pleasing in nature." Sibley lives in Concord, Massachusetts, and continues to write about and paint birds.

Words in Use

Selection Words
strolling, 392
flock, 392
incongruous, 392
ancestry, 393

Teaching Words
species, 390
pictorial, 390
aesthetically, 390
fumble, 393

KEY TERMS
FIELD GUIDE, 390
VISUAL MEDIA, 390
ILLUSTRATION, 395
REVIEW, 395

Common Core State Standards
Reading Informational
RI.1

NATIONAL AUDUBON SOCIETY

The

SIBLEY

Guide to Birds

Written and illustrated by
DAVID ALLEN SIBLEY

391

MIRRORS & WINDOWS

The Mirrors & Windows questions at the end of the selection focus on the theme of observing nature. Before students begin to read, ask: What is the most intriguing natural phenomenon you know of?

Science Connection

Recognizing Birds Drawings and photographs are essential to the science of ornithology, the study of birds. Bird watchers must recognize distinguishing features of different species in order to identify the birds in the field. Sibley's art is based on close observation, and shows details that may not be apparent even in close-up photographs of turkeys.

Independent Reading

Students who like reading about birds might enjoy other works by David Allen Sibley and John James Audubon. Many books of their writings and paintings are available.

Program Resources

Planning and Assessment
Program Planning Guide, Selection Lesson Plan
E-Lesson Planner
Assessment Guide, Lesson Test
ExamView

Technology Tools
Interactive Student Text on CD
Visual Teaching Package
Audio Library
mirrorsandwindows.com

Meeting the Standards
Nonfiction: Unit 4, Guided Reading, pp. 25–29

Differentiating Instruction
Advanced Students, Comparing Literature
  Activity, pp. 21–22

Teach the Model

Literary Connection

Page Layouts In Sibley's printed guide, the range map and the commentary appear on the same page as the illustrations. There is one page per bird species. Explain to students that the Sibley page is split in the textbook to allow for footnotes and During Reading questions.

Use Reading Skills

Draw Conclusions *Answer:* It suggests that their appearance is not what one would expect; their necks, heads, and legs seem too small for their bodies. **A**

Use Reading Skills

Draw Conclusions Remind students to fill in their detail webs about the turkey. Encourage them to use large pieces of paper and record as many details as they can find on the page from the field guide. Students may develop separate webs for males and females, but they should be prepared to identify distinctive traits that are common to both.

Analyze Literature

Visual Media *Answer:* The most striking differences are on the head and neck and in the male's display. **B**

Analyze Literature

Visual Media Ask students how the drawings and text interact to convey information. Model asking questions to interpret the interactions: "How would I interpret the drawing of a group without its label?"

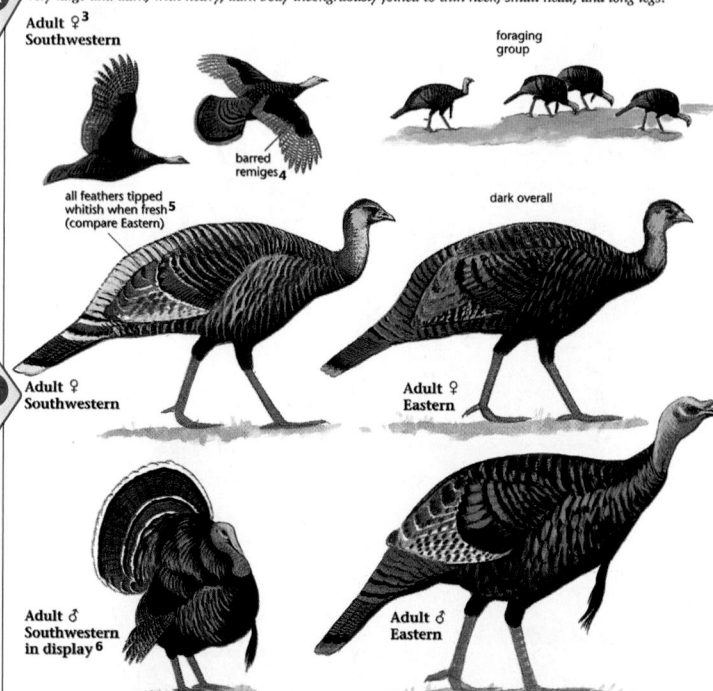

DURING READING

Use Reading Skills
Draw Conclusions What does the word *incongruously* suggest about these birds? Use a dictionary if you need help. **A**

DURING READING

Analyze Literature
Visual Media How can you interpret these drawings to tell a female from a male? **B**

WILD TURKEY
One of our largest birds, Wild Turkey is found in flocks in open woods with fields or clearings, usually in oak or beech woods. It is often seen strolling across open ground in flocks of up to 60.

Wild Turkey
Meleagris gallopavo[1]
♂ L 46" WS 64" WT 16.2 lb (7,400 g)[2]
♀ L 37" WS 50" WT 9.2 lb (4,200 g)
Very large and dark, with heavy, dark body incongruously joined to thin neck, small head, and long legs.

Adult ♀[3]
Southwestern

foraging group

barred remiges[4]

all feathers tipped whitish when fresh[5]
(compare Eastern)

dark overall

Adult ♀
Southwestern

Adult ♀
Eastern

Adult ♂
Southwestern
in display[6]

Adult ♂
Eastern

Voice: Male in display gives familiar descending gobble. Female gives loud, sharp *tuk* and slightly longer, whining *yike, yike* . . . repeated in slow series. Both sexes give a variety of other soft clucks and rolling calls.

---

1. ***Meleagris gallopavo.*** Scientific name for the wild turkey species
2. **L, WS, WT.** Abbreviations for *length, wingspan,* and *weight*
3. **♂ ♀.** Symbols for male and female
4. **remiges** (rē´ mi jēz'). Flight feathers, which are attached to wing bones
5. **all feathers...when fresh.** A fresh feather replaces a feather lost during molting.
6. **display.** Action of spreading tail and puffing out the chest to attract a mate

---

Differentiated Instruction

English Language Learning

Pair English learners with native speakers to review this page. Encourage both students to ask and answer questions about how common this bird is, where people can find it, and its role in American culture.

Auditory Learning

Sibley reproduces some turkey calls in the text—*tuk* and *yike, yike*. He also mentions "the familiar descending gobble." Have students practice making these sounds based on the text. Interested students can research turkey sounds on the Internet to see if they have reproduced them accurately.

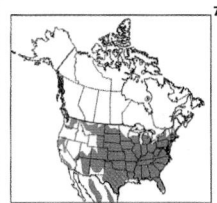

Southwestern populations have tail and uppertail coverts tipped pale buffy or whitish, creating a strikingly different appearance than the darker, rufous-tipped Eastern birds, but the change is broadly clinal.[9] Domestic turkeys, often escaped or released, average heavier than Wild Turkey and have white-tipped tail feathers similar to Southwestern birds. Furthermore, birds of mixed ancestry have been widely introduced, and the species is now found farther north and much farther west than ever before. ❖

DURING READING

Use Reading Skills
Draw Conclusions What do you think "birds of mixed ancestry" means? **C**

7. **(range map.)** The color on this map shows where wild turkeys live in North America.
8. **coverts** (kə´ vərts). Feathers that help streamline and insulate the bird
9. **rufous...clinal.** *Rufous* (rü´ fəs) refers to a yellowish-pink to orange color; *clinal* (klīn´ əl) is a characteristic, such as color, that changes gradually, usually in relation to a change in environment

 When have you taken the time to closely observe something in nature? How did it affect you? Why do you think people like to watch birds?

Find Meaning

1. (a) What are the two main types of wild turkey? (b) How can you tell the difference between them?
2. Which type of bird gobbles and when?
3. Reread the paragraph next to the map. (a) What is a domestic turkey? (b) Based on this paragraph, if you encountered a wild turkey in the woods, would you expect it to look exactly like one of these pictures? Why or why not?

Make Judgments

4. What elements of the description in this entry would help you most when identifying a wild turkey?
5. (a) How do you think Sibley chose the specific details about wild turkeys that appear in this entry? (b) What kinds of topics or pictures do you think he could add if he had more room?
6. This field guide includes advice on identifying birds. Sibley writes: "The first rule is simple: *Look at the bird.* Don't fumble with a book, because by the time you find the right picture, the bird will most likely be gone.... Watch what the bird does, watch it fly away, and only then try to find it in your book." Do you think this is realistic advice? Explain your answer.

THE SIBLEY GUIDE TO BIRDS **393**

Teach the Model

Use Reading Skills
Draw Conclusions *Answer:* They are combinations of wild and domestic (farm-raised) birds that have escaped or been released to the wild. **C**

 Answer: Students will have had different encounters with nature. They may say people are drawn to birds because birds are beautiful.

Find Meaning
1. (a) The main types are Southwestern and Eastern. (b) The differences are in feather colors and, presumably, location.
2. The male turkey gobbles during displays, when it is seeking a mate.
3. (a) A domestic turkey is raised on a farm. (b) The bird probably won't look exactly like one of the pictures. Details of appearance may differ based on geography and ancestry.

Make Judgments
4. Students may mention plumage, call, habitat, or behavior.
5. (a) He probably chose details that most clearly distinguish wild turkeys from other birds. (b) There could be more on turkey behavior, variations of feather color in birds of mixed ancestry, and juvenile birds.
6. This is realistic advice, because a person watching birds can't do two things at once and is likely to see more this way.

Speaking & Listening Skills

Visual Aids

Tell students that when they make presentations, they will often use visual aids. These both summarize complex topics and engage the audience's attention. Ask students to imagine they are going to give a presentation about your state bird to an enthusiastic audience. Then ask them to match each visual aid at left below to the type of information it would best convey.

graph — life cycle
poster — shape and color
map — population increase
photograph — nest locations

Teach the Connection

Use Reading Skills
Analyze Author's Perspective
Before students begin the essay, ask them to consider Audubon's perspective as he wrote it. Remind them that all writing reflects its author's perspective, or viewpoint. Note that Audubon probably had a distinctive perspective on such subjects as turkeys, pets, and hunting. Paying attention to word choice can help students analyze this. After they read, challenge students to point out passages that reflect Audubon's perspective.

Analyze Literature
Anecdote Tell students that an anecdote is usually a short narrative of a single incident. Unlike a short story, it does not have a complicated plot. Point out that Audubon's story about his pet turkey gives the animal a personality that Sibley's birds do not have. Have students answer Audubon's concluding questions from their own points of view. (Most will say the turkey remembered the particular dog.)

David Allen Sibley follows in the footsteps of **John James Audubon** (1785–1851). Son of a French sea captain, Audubon came to the United States in 1803 and began to study and paint birds. He eventually published his work in *Birds of America*. Several years later he published *Ornithological Biographies,* from which this excerpt is drawn.

from Wild Turkey

An Essay by John James Audubon

While at Henderson, on the Ohio in Kentucky, I had many wild birds. I had a fine male Turkey that I had raised from its youth, having caught it when it was two or three days old. It became so tame that it would follow any person who called it, and it was the favorite of the little village where I lived. Yet it would never roost with the tame Turkeys, but always slept at night on the roof of the house, where it remained until dawn.

When it was two years old, it began to fly to the woods. There it would remain for most of the day, returning home only when night came on. It kept this up until the following spring, when, several times, I saw it fly from its roosting place in the top of a tall cottonwood tree on the banks of the Ohio. There, after resting a while, it would sail to the opposite shore, where the river was nearly half a mile wide, and return towards night.

One morning I saw it fly off at a very early hour to the woods. I paid little attention. Several days passed, but the bird did not return. I was going towards some lakes near Green River to shoot when I saw a fine large gobbler cross the path before me and move leisurely along. Turkeys were in the best condition for eating at that season. I ordered Juno, my dog, to chase it and flush[1] it into the air. The dog hurried ahead, and, as it drew near the bird, I saw with great surprise that the Turkey did not run off. Juno was about to seize it, when suddenly she stopped and turned her head towards me. I ran to them, and you can guess my surprise when I saw that the creature was my own favorite bird, and discovered that it had recognized the dog and would not fly from it, although it would have run off from a strange dog at once.

A friend of mine who was looking for a deer he had wounded happened to come along. He put my bird on his saddle in front of him and carried it home for me.

The following spring the Turkey was accidentally shot when it was taken for a wild one. It was brought back to me when the hunter saw the red ribbon it wore around its neck.

How shall we explain the way my Turkey knew my dog at sight in the woods, after seeing it at home in the yard and grounds? Was it instinct? Reason? Memory? Or the act of an intelligent mind? ✣

---

1. flush. Force a bird out of hiding

394 UNIT 4 NONFICTION

Words in Use

from "Wild Turkey"

Selection Words
roost, 394
leisurely, 394
instinct, 394

Common Core State Standards

Reading Informational
RI.2

Differentiated Instruction

English Language Learning
Point out that words in English can be onomatopoetic; that is, a word can sound like its meaning. The word *gobbler* for the sound a turkey makes, and in turn as a synonym for the word *turkey,* is an example. Have English learners give examples of words in their native languages that sound like what they mean. Animal sounds are good examples of this kind of language.

TEXT ←TO→ TEXT
CONNECTION

Sibley's guide provides a lot of visual information, but it also describes the turkey's behavior and voice. How does Sibley's "Wild Turkey" entry help you visualize the turkey Audubon describes?

Analyze Literature

Visual Media Why do you think Sibley chose to convey some information visually instead of in written form? How might the use of visual media be more effective than language in this context? Create a three-column chart to examine Sibley's use of visual media. In the left column, list examples of illustrations, maps, or symbols. In the middle column, describe the author's purpose for including these. In the right column, briefly describe why this was or was not an effective use of visual media. Finally, write a paragraph that explains the difference between the theme presented in "Wild Turkey" and the author's purpose within "The Sibley Guide to Birds."

Example	Purpose	My Evaluation
illustration of foraging group	useful to bird-watchers in the field; person might actually see this	

Extend Understanding

Writing Options

Creative Writing Imagine that you have a friend who has never seen an image of a wild turkey. Look again at the illustrations of turkeys in this selection. What traits are most prominent? What characteristics do you find most interesting? Use the images and text from this selection to prompt a **descriptive paragraph** for your friend about the wild turkey. Be sure to describe all of the bird's most recognizable traits.

Persuasive Writing Suppose the manager of your local bookstore asks you to recommend some good nature books. Draft a one- or two-paragraph **book review** about *The Sibley Guide to Birds*. Give its purpose and describe any strengths and weaknesses you can name. Then conclude your review by stating whether or not you think the bookstore should carry the book.

Collaborative Learning

Peer Review Exchange your descriptive paragraph about the wild turkey with a partner. Take notes as you read each other's work. Your notes should praise the most effective elements of the paragraph but also specifically suggest how it might be improved. When you are done, share your feedback with your partner.

Lifelong Learning

Identify Birds Find a field guide for wild birds in your region and take it to a wildlife sanctuary, nature park, or other bird habitat. Use the photos and descriptions in the guide to identify as many birds as possible. Take notes on your overall experience and on how useful the guide was. Use your notes to write a one-page review for the publisher of the book. Include comments on the guide's strengths and weaknesses, such as descriptions that were confusing and photos that were particularly helpful. Offer suggestions for improving the guide in its next edition.

 Go to **www.mirrorsandwindows.com** for more.

Review the Model

Text-to-Text Connection

Answer: By providing actual pictures, the guide plants a picture of a turkey in the reader's mind. Readers can specifically picture an adult male turkey, like Audubon's turkey, because of Sibley's drawings. The guide further helps the reader imagine how the pet turkey walks and flies.

Analyze Literature

Visual Media The visuals are supposed to make it easy to identify bird species. Most will agree that the visuals in this selection were effective. Student paragraphs will vary but should accurately explain the differences between the theme and purpose of the two texts.

Rubrics for Writing Options

You can adapt this as a checklist for students to use as they write.

Creative Writing

☐ Does the paragraph describe the bird's most prominent traits?

☐ Does the paragraph convey the student's particular interests?

☐ Does the paragraph include information gathered from both images and text?

Persuasive Writing

☐ Does the review explain the field guide's purpose?

☐ Does the review identify strengths and weaknesses of the guide?

☐ Does the review conclude with a recommendation to the bookstore manager?

DIRECTED READING

At a Glance
Directed Reading
- Reading Level: Challenging
- Difficulty Considerations: Concepts, vocabulary, and sentence length
- Ease Factor: Vivid imagery

Objectives
Studying this lesson will enable students to
- use reading skills such as analyzing the main idea and supporting details
- define *analogy* and evaluate examples in the selection
- compare the perspectives that Al Gore and Chief Dan George hold regarding the environment
- appreciate literature that proposes solutions to a problem

Launch the Lesson
Prior to reading "Ships in the Desert," encourage students to examine the photograph on pages 396–397. Ask: "How does this picture relate to the title of the essay?" After students respond, tell them that the essay will explain why this ship is nowhere near a body of water.

Ships in the Desert

An Essay by Al Gore

BEFORE READING

Build Background
Scientific Context "Ships in the Desert" is a nonfiction essay from *Earth in the Balance: Ecology and the Human Spirit,* which Al Gore wrote while serving as a U.S. senator. Gore wanted to raise people's awareness about the environment, its problems, and possible solutions. In a healthy environment, plants, animals, air, soil, and water exist in a balanced relationship.

Reader's Context What environmental problem concerns you? How does it affect you now, or how may it affect you in the future?

Set Purpose
Use Build Background and the first paragraph to preview "Ships in the Desert." Based on your preview, what environmental changes do you think Al Gore will focus on in the essay?

Analyze Literature
Analogy An **analogy** is a comparison of things that are alike in some ways but different in others, for example, a *camel is a ship of the desert.* Writers use analogies to add interest and vitality to their writing, and also to explain difficult ideas in a way that makes them clear and vivid for readers. As you read "Ships in the Desert," think about the analogies Gore uses to describe environmental problems.

Meet the Author
Al Gore (b. 1948) became vice president of the United States in 1992, the same year that he published *Earth in the Balance: Ecology and the Human Spirit,* from which this essay is taken. As a former U.S. representative and senator, Gore was a leader in environmental awareness. As vice president, Gore worked diligently to fight environmental threats. In 2007, he shared the Nobel Peace Prize for his study of global warming.

Use Reading Skills
Analyze Main Idea and Supporting Details In nonfiction, writers usually have one central thought or message that they want to communicate to readers. All of the facts, details, and examples included in the text are specifically chosen to support and explain that main idea. Identifying supporting details as you read can help you draw conclusions about the writer's main idea. As you read "Ships in the Desert," use a web to keep track of details that can help you find the main idea.

Preview Vocabulary
un•pre•ce•dent•ed (ʉn' pre´ sə den' təd) *adj.,* unheard of; new

phe•nom•e•non (fi nä´ mə nän') *n.,* extremely unusual or extraordinary thing or occurrence

per•il (per´ əl) *n.,* danger, exposure to harm

396 UNIT 4 NONFICTION

Words in Use

Preview Vocabulary
unprecedented, 398
phenomenon, 399
peril, 401

Selection Words
rendered, 399
underlying, 399
inexorable, 400
translucent, 401
apparition, 401

Teaching Words
awareness, 396
vitality, 396
vivid, 396
diligently, 396
interference, 405

KEY TERMS
ESSAY, 396
ANALOGY, 396
MAIN IDEA, 396
SUPPORTING DETAIL, 396
PERSONAL ESSAY, 403

Common Core State Standards
Reading Informational
RI.1, RI.2, RI.3, RI.5, RI.8

Ships
in the
Desert

An Essay by Al Gore

We are creating a world that is hostile to wildness,
that seems to prefer concrete to natural landscapes.

397

Teach the Selection

Summary

A shrinking sea in the center of the Asian continent, mass deaths of starfish and dolphins, toxic wastes washing up on beaches—these and other troubling images of environmental change fill Gore's essay. According to Gore, each example underscores a crisis in the world's ability to maintain hospitable conditions for thousands of species. As thinning ice at the poles affects climate worldwide, so too do burning rain forests in the Amazon destroy habitats and oxygen-producing trees that could mitigate the effects of pollution from burning coal and oil.

The Mirrors & Windows questions at the end of the selection focus on the theme of environmental activism. Before students begin to read, ask: How have people changed the natural world in the years since you were born?

TEACHING NOTE

Problem-Solution Organization

Tell students that Gore will describe both problems and solutions in his essay. Note that persuasive writing can follow a problem-solution organization. In a problem-solution paragraph, the topic sentence states a problem; ensuing sentences offer solutions; and the concluding sentence emphasizes the need to address the problem with the solutions.

Program Resources

Planning and Assessment
Program Planning Guide, Selection Lesson Plan
E-Lesson Planner
Assessment Guide, Lesson Test
ExamView

Technology Tools
Interactive Student Text on CD
Visual Teaching Package
Audio Library
mirrorsandwindows.com

Meeting the Standards
Nonfiction: Unit 4, Guided Reading, pp. 30–35

Use Reading Strategies

Visualize Ask students to describe the scene Gore presents at the opening of the essay. Have them explain how the scene of the ships in the desert sand resembles the image of the fried egg. (In both, things are out of place.) **Ⓐ**

Use Reading Skills

Analyze Main Idea and Supporting Details Point to the third paragraph, and ask students to state the essay's main idea up to this point (the world has changed so that things seem out of place). Ask for one or two details that illustrate this main idea.

History Connection

Environmental Advocacy Many writers have championed the natural environment—Henry David Thoreau, John Muir, Aldo Leopold, and Rachel Carson are classic examples. Some scientists have written popular books about the impact people have on the environment. But few politicians publish books on environmental issues, as Al Gore has. You may wish to point out that supporting environmental policies can be risky for an elected official. Challenge students to explain why this is so.

I was standing in the sun on the hot steel deck of a fishing ship capable of processing a fifty-ton catch on a good day. But it wasn't a good day. We were anchored in what used to be the most productive fishing site in all of central Asia, but as I looked out over the bow, the prospects of a good catch looked bleak. Where there should have been gentle blue-green waves lapping against the side of the ship, there was nothing but hot dry sand—as far as I could see in all directions. The other ships of the fleet were also at rest in the sand, scattered in the dunes that stretched all the way to the horizon.

Ⓐ Oddly enough, it made me think of a fried egg I had seen back in the United States on television the week before. It was sizzling and popping the way a fried egg should in a pan, but it was in the middle of a sidewalk in downtown Phoenix. I guess it sprang to mind because, like the ship on which I was standing, there was nothing wrong with the egg itself. Instead, the world beneath it had changed in an unexpected way that made the egg seem—through no fault of its own—out of place. It was illustrating the newsworthy point that at the time Arizona wasn't having an especially good day, either, because for the second day in a row temperatures had reached a record 122 degrees.

As a camel walked by on the dead bottom of the Aral Sea, my thoughts returned to the unlikely ship of the desert on which I stood, which also seemed to be illustrating the point that its world had changed out from underneath it with sudden cruelty. Ten years ago the Aral was the fourth-largest inland sea in the world, comparable to the largest of North America's Great Lakes. Now it is disappearing because the water that used to feed it has been diverted in an ill-considered irrigation scheme to grow cotton in the desert. The new shoreline was almost forty

kilometers across the sand from where the fishing fleet was now permanently docked. Meanwhile, in the nearby town of Muynak the people were still canning fish—brought not from the Aral Sea but shipped by rail through Siberia from the Pacific Ocean, more than a thousand miles away.

I had come to the Aral Sea in August 1990 to witness at first hand the destruction taking place there on an almost biblical scale. But during the trip I encountered other images that also alarmed me. For example, the day I returned to Moscow from Muynak, my friend Alexei Yablokov, possibly the leading environmentalist in the Soviet Union, was returning from an emergency expedition to the White Sea, where he had investigated the mysterious and <u>unprecedented</u> death of several *million* starfish, washed up into a knee-deep mass covering many miles of beach. That night, in his apartment, he talked of what it was like for the residents to wade through the starfish in hip boots, trying to explain their death.

Later investigations identified radioactive military waste as the likely culprit in the White Sea deaths. But what about all of the other mysterious mass deaths washing up on beaches around the world? French scientists recently concluded that the explanation for

un·pre·ce·dent·ed (ʉn′ preʹ sə denʹ təd) *adj.*, unheard of; new

Differentiated Instruction

Visual Learning

Encourage visual learners to make drawings of the images Gore offers early in the essay (especially through the second full paragraph on page 399). Each student should choose a single image to draw. Ask students to try to convey the mood of the image in their drawings.

Reading Proficiency

Less-able readers may feel overwhelmed by the multiple locations Gore describes. Provide a globe or world map for the class, and encourage students to stop and find the places Gore visits. If possible, permit students to mark the sequence of Gore's travels on a wall map using markers or push pins and string.

the growing number of dead dolphins washing up along the Riviera was accumulated environmental stress, which, over time, rendered the animals too weak to fight off a virus. This same phenomenon may also explain the sudden increase in dolphin deaths along the Gulf Coast in Texas as well as the mysterious deaths of 12,000 seals whose corpses washed up on the shores of the North Sea in the summer of 1988. Of course, the oil-covered otters and seabirds of Prince William Sound a year later[1] presented less of a mystery to science, if no less an indictment[2] of our civilization.

As soon as one of these troubling images fades, another takes its place, provoking new questions. What does it mean, for example, that children playing in the morning surf must now dodge not only the occasional jellyfish but the occasional hypodermic needle washing in with the waves? Needles, dead dolphins, and oil-soaked birds—are all these signs that the shores of our familiar world are fast eroding, that we are now standing on some new beach, facing dangers beyond the edge of what we are capable of imagining?

With our backs turned to the place in nature from which we came, we sense an unfamiliar tide rising and swirling around our ankles, pulling at the sand beneath our feet. Each time this strange new tide goes out, it leaves behind the flotsam and jetsam[3] of some giant shipwreck far out at sea, startling images washed up on the sands of our time, each a fresh warning of hidden dangers that lie ahead if we continue on our present course.

My search for the underlying causes of the environmental crisis has led me to travel around the world to examine and study many of these images of destruction. At the very bottom of the earth, high in the Trans-Antarctic Mountains, with the sun glaring at midnight through a hole in the sky, I stood in the unbelievable coldness and talked with a scientist in the late fall of 1988 about the tunnel he was digging through time. Slipping his parka back to reveal a badly burned face that was cracked and peeling, he pointed to the annual layers of ice in a core sample dug from the glacier on which we were standing. He moved his finger back in time to the ice of two decades ago. "Here's where the U.S. Congress passed the Clean Air Act," he said. At the bottom of the world, two continents away from Washington, D.C., even a small reduction in one country's emissions had changed the amount of pollution found in the remotest and least accessible place on earth.

> Where there should have been gentle blue-green waves lapping against the side of the ship, there was nothing but hot dry sand...

But the most significant change thus far in the earth's atmosphere is the one that began with the industrial revolution early in the last century and has picked up speed ever since. Industry meant coal, and later oil, and we began to burn lots of it—bringing rising levels of carbon dioxide (CO_2), with its ability to trap more heat in the atmosphere and slowly warm the earth. Fewer than a hundred yards from the South Pole, upwind

1. **oil-covered otters...a year later.** The *Exxon-Valdez* tanker spilled eleven million gallons of oil in Prince William Sound, Alaska, in 1989.
2. **indictment.** Condemnation
3. **flotsam and jetsam.** Floating debris

---

phe·nom·e·non (fi nä´ mə nän') *n.*, extremely unusual or extraordinary thing or occurrence

Analyze Literature

Analogy Point out the comparisons Gore uses to describe encounters with environmental change. Explain that such comparisons, or analogies, describe situations in new ways. Ask for volunteers to describe the feeling of having surf "pulling at the sand beneath our feet." Ask others to describe any debris they have seen in a large body of water. Then ask: "Do 'the sands of our time' refer to real sand or to something else?" Select volunteers to identify other analogies in the essay and explain how they show a situation in a new way. **B**

Use Reading Skills

Identify Author's Purpose Have students consider the topics Gore has introduced so far. Then have them take turns making a statement of the author's purpose, such as "Gore's purpose is to entertain." Have the class choose one accurate statement.

History Connection

Machines and Pollution Tell students that dramatic environmental change began in England in the 1700s with the invention of machines for weaving. Over the following centuries, increased demand for energy to power machinery led to pollution of waterways, soil, and air. New methods of transportation powered by fossil fuels also added pollutants to the environment.

Grammar Skills

Types of Paragraphs

Remind students that writers use different types of paragraphs depending on their purpose for writing. For example, descriptive paragraphs can set a scene, create a mood, or appeal to a reader's senses. Narrative paragraphs can tell a story, relate a series of events, or tell about people's lives. Informative paragraphs present or explain an idea or a process. Persuasive paragraphs present an argument or suggest a course of action. Have students identify the types of paragraphs Gore uses on these pages.

Use Reading Skills

Analyze Main Idea and Supporting Details Have students select and outline two paragraphs from "Ships in the Desert" by identifying the topic sentence of each paragraph and listing the supporting details. Then have them sum up the main idea the two paragraphs express. Students can compare their outlines and discuss their statements of the main idea in small groups.

Science Connection

Midnight Sun Most of this page is about Gore's experiences at the North Pole. Explain that the "midnight sun" occurs during the summer at each pole, when the planet's tilt on its axis means that the sun never totally sets. Encourage students who understand the science behind this to sketch Earth's position at this time of year on the board. **(A)**

Science Connection

Global Warming Gore offers startling images such as those of the Aral Sea, burning rain forests, and thinning polar ice. These vivid descriptions startle the reader and draw attention to Gore's attitude of concern.

---

from the ice runway where the ski plane lands and keeps its engines running to prevent the metal parts from freeze-locking together, scientists monitor the air several times every day to chart the course of that inexorable change. During my visit, I watched one scientist draw the results of that day's measurements, pushing the end of a steep line still higher on the graph. He told me how easy it is—there at the end of the earth—to see that this enormous change in the global atmosphere is still picking up speed.

(A) Two and a half years later I slept under the midnight sun at the other end of our planet, in a small tent pitched on a twelve-foot-thick slab of ice floating in the frigid Arctic Ocean. After a hearty breakfast, my companions and I traveled by snowmobiles a few miles farther north to a rendezvous[4] point where the ice was thinner—only three and a half feet thick—and a nuclear submarine hovered in the water below. After it crashed through the ice, took on its new passengers, and resubmerged, I talked with scientists who were trying to measure more accurately the thickness of the polar ice cap, which many believe is thinning as a result of global warming. I had just negotiated an agreement between ice scientists and the U.S. Navy to secure the release of previously top secret data from submarine sonar tracks, data that could help them learn what is happening to the north polar cap. Now, I wanted to see the pole itself, and some eight hours after we met the submarine, we were crashing through that

ice, surfacing, and then I was standing in an eerily beautiful snowscape, windswept and sparkling white, with the horizon defined by little hummocks, or "pressure ridges" of ice that are pushed up like tiny mountain ranges when separate sheets collide. But here too, CO_2 levels are rising just as rapidly, and ultimately temperatures will rise with them—indeed, global warming is expected to push temperatures up much more rapidly in the polar regions than in the rest of the world. As the polar air warms, the ice here will thin;

SCIENCE ▶▶ CONNECTION

Global Warming The greenhouse effect is a naturally occurring process that maintains Earth's warm, life-sustaining temperature. Greenhouse gases (water vapor, carbon dioxide, nitrous oxide, and methane) trap some infrared radiation within the atmosphere. In the last one hundred years, concentrations of greenhouse gases have increased and Earth's temperature has risen by about one degree Fahrenheit. Nearly all scientists believe this is the result of human activities. They also believe that temperatures will continue to rise unless people change their behavior.

and since the polar cap plays such a crucial role in the world's weather system, the consequences of a thinning cap could be disastrous.

Considering such scenarios is not a purely speculative exercise. Six months after I returned from the North Pole, a team of scientists reported dramatic changes in the pattern of ice distribution in the Arctic, and a second team reported a still controversial

---

4. **rendezvouz** (rän′ di vü′). Meeting

TEACHING NOTE

Ask the Author

Have students form small groups to brainstorm questions they would like to ask Al Gore about "Ships in the Desert." Have groups exchange and review questions. Then have representatives from each group share novel questions with the class.

claim (which a variety of data now suggest) that, overall, the north polar cap has thinned by 2 percent in just the last decade. Moreover, scientists established several years ago that in many land areas north of the Arctic Circle, the spring snowmelt now comes earlier every year, and deep in the tundra[5] below, the temperature of the earth is steadily rising.

As it happens, some of the most disturbing images of environmental destruction can be found exactly halfway between the North and South poles—precisely at the equator in Brazil—where billowing clouds of smoke regularly blacken the sky above the immense but now threatened Amazon rain forest. Acre by acre, the rain forest is being burned to create fast pasture for fast-food beef; as I learned when I went there in early 1989, the fires are set earlier and earlier in the dry season now, with more than one Tennessee's worth of rain forest being slashed and burned each year. According to our guide, the biologist Tom Lovejoy, there are more different species of birds in each square mile of the Amazon than exist in all of North America—which means we are silencing thousands of songs we have never even heard.

But for most of us the Amazon is a distant place, and we scarcely notice the disappearance of these and other vulnerable species. We ignore these losses at our peril, however. They're like the proverbial[6] miners' canaries, silent alarms whose message in this **B** case is that living species of animals and plants are now vanishing around the world *one thousand times faster* than at any time in the past 65 million years.

To be sure, the deaths of some of the larger and more spectacular animal species now under siege do occasionally capture our attention. I have also visited another place along the equator, East Africa, where I

encountered the grotesquely horrible image of a dead elephant, its head mutilated by poachers who had dug out its valuable tusks with chain saws. Clearly, we need to change our purely aesthetic[7] consideration of ivory, since its source is now so threatened. To me, its translucent whiteness seems different now, like evidence of the ghostly presence of a troubled spirit, a beautiful but chill apparition, inspiring both wonder and dread.

A similar apparition lies just beneath the ocean. While scuba diving in the Caribbean, I have seen and touched the white bones of a dead coral reef. All over the earth, coral reefs have suddenly started to "bleach" as warmer ocean temperatures put unaccustomed stress on the tiny organisms that normally live in the skin of the coral and give the reef its natural coloration. As these organisms— nicknamed "zooks"—leave the membrane of the coral, the coral itself becomes transparent, allowing its white limestone skeleton to shine through—hence its bleached appearance. In the past, bleaching was almost always an occasional and temporary phenomenon, but repeated episodes can exhaust the coral. In the last few years, scientists have been shocked at the sudden occurrence of extensive worldwide bleaching episodes from which increasing numbers of coral reefs have failed to recover. Though dead, they shine more brightly than before, haunted perhaps by the same ghost that gives spectral[8] light to an elephant's tusk. **C**

But one doesn't have to travel around the world to witness humankind's assault on the earth. Images that signal the distress of our global environment are now commonly seen almost anywhere. A few miles from the

---

5. **tundra.** Flat, frozen, treeless land
6. **proverbial.** Widely referred to
7. **aesthetic.** Relating to beauty
8. **spectral.** Ghostly

per•il (perʹ əl) *n.,* danger; exposure to harm

Answer: Students will suggest various sacrifices or changes. They may say that although one person alone cannot save the planet, combined efforts of individuals around the globe can make a huge difference.

Find Meaning

1. (a) Diverting water for irrigation is draining the Aral Sea. (b) People often plan projects without analyzing their effects on the environment.

2. (a) The samples show reduced air pollution after passage of the Act. (b) This suggests that air pollution is a global phenomenon.

3. (a) He learned that an area the size of Tennessee burned each year, which made thousands of species extinct. (b) It demonstrates that species are vanishing a thousand times faster than at any time in the past sixty-five million years.

Make Judgments

4. (a) Humans can destroy nature and often fail to appreciate the complex natural world in which they live. (b) He thinks statistics will make his point persuasively.

5. (a) He would like people to be aware of how their actions affect the environment and to change their behavior accordingly. (b) Answers will vary, but any change of habits will be difficult.

Capitol, for example, I encountered another startling image of nature out of place. Driving in the Arlington, Virginia, neighborhood where my family and I live when the Senate is in session, I stepped on the brake to avoid hitting a large pheasant walking across the street. It darted between the parked cars, across the sidewalk, and into a neighbor's backyard. Then it was gone. But this apparition of wildness persisted in my memory as a puzzle: Why would a pheasant, let alone such a large and beautiful mature specimen, be out for a walk in my neighborhood? Was it a much wilder place than I had noticed? Were pheasants, like the trendy Vietnamese potbellied pigs, becoming the latest fashion in unusual pets? I didn't solve the mystery until weeks later, when I remembered that about three miles away, along the edge of the river, developers were bulldozing the last hundred acres of untouched forest in the entire area. As the woods fell to make way for more concrete, more buildings, parking lots, and streets, the wild things that lived there were forced to flee. Most of the deer were hit by cars; other creatures—like the pheasant that darted into my neighbor's backyard—made it a little farther.

Ironically, before I understood the mystery, I felt vaguely comforted to imagine that perhaps this urban environment, so similar to the one in which many Americans live, was not so hostile to wild things after all. I briefly supposed that, like the resourceful raccoons and possums and squirrels and pigeons, all of whom have adapted to life in the suburbs, creatures as wild as pheasants might have a fighting chance. Now I remember that pheasant when I take my children to the zoo and see an elephant or a rhinoceros. They too inspire wonder and sadness. They too remind me that we are creating a world that is hostile to wildness, that seems to prefer concrete to natural landscapes. We are encountering these creatures on a path we have paved— one that ultimately leads to their extinction. ✤

If you had to give up one thing or change your behavior in one way to save the environment, what would you give up or change? Do you think individual sacrifice and change can make enough of a difference?

Find Meaning

1. (a) Why is the Aral Sea disappearing? (b) What impression of human planning does this create?

2. (a) What effect did passage of the Clean Air Act have on ice core samples dug from polar glaciers? (b) What does this evidence suggest about air pollution?

3. (a) What alarming fact did the author learn about the rain forest on a 1989 visit to the Amazon? (b) Why does the author find this so alarming?

Make Judgments

4. (a) From the examples provided by the author, what conclusions can you draw about human beings' relationship with nature? (b) Why do you think the author provides statistics about the number of species lost each year?

5. (a) What attitudes and behaviors do you think the author would like people to change regarding the environment? (b) Which of these changes will probably be the most difficult for people to make?

Differentiated Instruction

Enrichment

Offer interested students an opportunity to report on the health of coral reefs in different parts of the world. Students should focus on the following questions:

- What is coral, and what is a coral reef?
- Where are some of the world's greatest coral reefs?
- How are coral reefs important to the human populations that live near them?

Encourage students to use pictures, drawings, and/ or maps in their reports.

In "Ships in the Desert," Al Gore bears witness to what he calls "humankind's assault on the earth." The following selection, "I Am a Native of North America," is a personal essay by **Chief Dan George** (1899–1981). Born in North Vancouver, British Columbia, Canada, George was given the tribal name Geswanouth Slaholt. At age sixty-two, after working a variety of odd jobs, George's son encouraged him to take over the part of a Native American character on a Canadian television series. For the next twenty years, George appeared in television, stage, and film productions, including the 1970 film *Little Big Man,* for which he received an Academy Award nomination. As you read, look for details that George uses to explain and support his main idea about modern society's attitudes toward nature.

I Am a Native of North America

A Personal Essay by Chief Dan George

In the course of my lifetime I have lived in two distinct cultures. I was born into a culture that lived in communal houses. My grandfather's house was eighty feet long. It was called a smoke house, and it stood down by the beach along the inlet. All my grandfather's sons and their families lived in this large dwelling. Their sleeping apartments were separated by blankets made of bull rush reeds, but one open fire in the middle served the cooking needs of all. In houses like these, throughout the tribe, people learned to live with one another; learned to serve one another; learned to respect the rights of one another. And children shared the thoughts of the adult world and found themselves surrounded by aunts and uncles and cousins who loved them and did not threaten them. My father was born in such a house and learned from infancy how to love people and be at home with them.

And beyond this acceptance of one another there was a deep respect for everything in nature that surrounded them. My father loved the earth and all its creatures. The earth was his second mother. The earth and everything it contained was a gift from See-see-am[1]...and the way to thank this great spirit was to use his gifts with respect.

I remember, as a little boy, fishing with him up Indian River and I can still see him as the sun rose above the mountain top in the early morning...I can see him standing by the water's edge with his arms raised above his head while he softly moaned..."Thank you, thank you." It left a deep impression on my young mind.

And I shall never forget his disappointment when once he caught me gaffing[2] for fish "just for the fun of it."

1. **See-see-am.** Name of a god in the Salish language
2. **gaffing.** A *gaff* is a pole with a large hook or spear on the end. *Gaffing* involves using a gaff to stab and catch a large fish.

Words in Use

"I Am a Native of North America"

Selection Words
communal, 403
inlet, 403
hoarding, 405
integration, 405
ridicule, 405

Explain that many European settlers feared and mistreated Native Americans. Ask students to evaluate Dan George's observation that brotherhood and love of creation are not part of the European mind-set. Ask: "To what extent do you agree or disagree with this viewpoint?" **A**

Analyze Literature

Repetition Tell students that persuasive writers often repeat points to strengthen the impression they make on readers. Ask students to locate repeated phrases on this page (most obvious are variations of "hard to understand" and "without love"). Then have them describe the effect of the repetition. Model a possible response: "I see that Chief Dan George has trouble understanding the predominant American culture. This makes me think he's completely different from most people I know."

"My Son," he said, "the Great Spirit gave you those fish to be your brothers, to feed you when you are hungry. You must respect them. You must not kill them just for the fun of it."

This then was the culture I was born into and for some years the only one I really knew or tasted. This is why I find it hard to accept many of the things I see around me.

I see people living in smoke houses hundreds of times bigger than the one I knew. But the people in one apartment do not even know the people in the next and care less about them.

It is also difficult for me to understand the deep hate that exists among people. It is hard to understand a culture that justifies the killing of millions in past wars, and is at this very moment preparing bombs to kill even greater numbers. It is hard for me to understand a culture that spends more on wars and weapons to kill, than it does on education and welfare to help and develop.

A It is hard for me to understand a culture that not only hates and fights its brothers but even attacks nature and abuses her. I see my white brother going about blotting out nature from his cities. I see him strip the hills bare, leaving ugly wounds on the face of mountains. I see him tearing things from the bosom of mother earth as though she were a monster, who refused to share her treasures with him. I see him throw poison in the waters, indifferent to the life he kills there; and he chokes the air with deadly fumes.

My white brother does many things well for he is more clever than my people but I wonder if he knows how to love well. I wonder if he has ever really learned to love at all. Perhaps he only loves the things that are his own but never learned to love the things that are outside and beyond him. And this is, of course, not love at all, for man must love all creation or he will love none of it. Man

must love fully or he will become the lowest of the animals. It is the power to love that makes him the greatest of them all...for he alone of all animals is capable of love.

Love is something you and I must have. We must have it because our spirit feeds upon it. We must have it because without it we become weak and faint. Without love our self-esteem weakens. Without it our courage fails. Without love we can no longer look out confidently at the world. Instead we turn inwardly and begin to feed upon our own personalities and little by little we destroy ourselves.

You and I need the strength and joy that comes from knowing that we are loved. With it we are creative. With it we march tirelessly. With it, and with it alone, we are able to sacrifice for others.

There have been times when we all wanted so desperately to feel a reassuring

---

Differentiated Instruction

Reading Proficiency

Ask students to describe the prior knowledge they have about Native American culture. Suggest that they read carefully to see if Chief Dan George adds information that changes what they know in any way. Encourage them to write down any insights they have as they read.

Auditory Learning

Chief Dan George had a career as an actor and spokesperson for the Native American people. Ask volunteers to assume the author's persona and read the selection aloud to the class. Some students may choose to learn parts of the essay by heart and perform it for classmates.

My culture did not prize the hoarding of private possessions; in fact, to hoard was a shameful thing to do among my people. The Indian looked on all things in nature as belonging to him and he expected to share them with others and to take only what he needed.

Everyone likes to give as well as receive. No one wishes only to receive all the time. We have taken much from your culture...I wish you had taken something from our culture...for there were some beautiful and good things in it.

Soon it will be too late to know my culture, for integration is upon us and soon we will have no values but yours. Already many of our young people have forgotten the old ways. And many have been shamed of their Indian ways by scorn and ridicule. My culture is like a wounded deer that has crawled away into the forest to bleed and die alone.

The only thing that can truly help us is genuine love. You must truly love us, be patient with us and share with us. And we must love you—with a genuine love that forgives and forgets...a love that forgives the terrible sufferings your culture brought ours when it swept over us like a wave crashing along a beach...with a love that forgets and lifts up its head and sees in your eyes an answering love of trust and acceptance.

This is brotherhood...anything less is not worthy of the name.

I have spoken. ❖

hand upon us...there have been lonely times when we so wanted a strong arm around us...I cannot tell you how deeply I miss my wife's presence when I return from a trip. Her love was my greatest joy, my strength, my greatest blessing.

I am afraid my culture has little to offer yours. But my culture did prize friendship and companionship. It did not look on privacy as a thing to be clung to, for privacy builds up walls and walls promote distrust. My culture lived in big family communities, and from infancy people learned to live with others.

TEXT →TO→ **TEXT**
CONNECTION

What different details does Al Gore's essay and Chief Dan George's personal essay use to illustrate the causes and effects of human interference with nature? What common message does each writer hope to communicate? Finally, explain the difference between the theme of "I am a Native of North America" and the author's purpose in "Ships in the Desert."

Use Reading Skills

Analyze Main Idea and Supporting Details When students complete their reading, have them briefly gather in four small groups. Have each group summarize the main idea Chief Dan George expresses about one of these topics:

1. The experience of growing up in a Native American culture
2. The character of the dominant culture Chief Dan George observes
3. Privacy and private possessions
4. Love

Use Reading Skills

Analyze Author's Perspective
Chief Dan George assumes the role of spokesperson for Native American culture. Have students discuss the kind of person they see behind the voice of the essay. To what extent is the chief's anger justified? To what extent is his sadness justified? Ask students if they agree with the chief's view that his culture is disappearing.

Text-to-Text Connection

Answer: Encourage students to use their lists of main ideas and their Venn diagrams to summarize details, causes and effects, and the messages of each author. Particularly encourage them to identify a message common to both writers and to explain the differences between the theme of Chief Dan George's personal essay and the purpose of Al Gore's essay.

Grammar Skills

Parts of Speech
Pause to quickly review the eight parts of speech with students:
A noun names a person, place, thing, or idea. A pronoun is used in place of a noun. A verb expresses action or a state of being. An adjective modifies a noun or pronoun. An adverb modifies a verb, an adjective, or another adverb. A preposition shows the relationship between its object and another word. A conjunction joins words or groups of words. An interjection expresses emotion.

Have students find an example of each part of speech in the end of the essay on this page.

Review the Selection

Analyze Literature

Analogy Gore's analogies often contain sensory details. His intent is to help us appreciate an idea or a phenomenon occurring on so large a scale or in so distant a location that we are unlikely to relate to it. For example, Gore describes finding ships in the desert and seeing an egg frying on a sidewalk. Both images help convey the complex idea that more and more things seem out of place in the natural world. The examples students use in their charts will vary. Make sure they grasp the things being compared. (It is often easy to get absorbed in the imagery of the analogy and miss the underlying idea.) Student summaries and peer evaluations will vary.

Analyze Literature

Analogy A writer's use of analogy helps to clarify complicated ideas and enhances the reader's overall understanding and appreciation of the text. Skim "Ships in the Desert," looking for analogies. Use a chart to record analogies you find and tell what the analogies compare. Then explain in one or two sentences how these analogies affect the author's message. As a separate activity, write a full summary of the essay and exchange your summary with a classmate. Write an evaluation of their work based on the accuracy of the main ideas, supporting details, and the overall meaning of the essay.

Example of Analogy	What Is Compared?	Effect
"ghostly presence of a troubled spirit"	ivory to a ghost	

Extend Understanding

Writing Options

Creative Writing Select one of the environmental disasters described in "Ships in the Desert," and write a **letter** to the editor of your local paper calling attention to the problem and stressing why, in your opinion, the problem needs to be resolved. Include in your letter at least one suggestion for how your community can contribute to the solution. Support your claims and opinions with evidence.

Expository Writing Al Gore provides a variety of vivid and startling images that "signal the distress of our global environment." Write a **problem-solution essay** in which you offer a solution to one of the problems he identifies. In the introductory paragraph, state the problem. In the body paragraphs, explain changes people can make to ease or resolve this problem. In the concluding paragraph, suggest what could happen in the future if such changes are not made. Use facts and details from "Ships in the Desert" to support your ideas. Share your work with the class.

Critical Literacy

Write a Proposal In small groups, select an environmental cause that interests you. Imagine that you are going to form a student group working for that cause. Write a proposal to an organization that might be willing to fund your cause, or write a proposal to your school, asking for permission to hold a fund-raiser. When you have finished, share your ideas with the class. You could then agree on volunteer activities to participate in as a class.

Media Literacy

Conduct Internet Research Use a search engine to find websites that discuss environmental issues. Narrow the list to ten websites that address one or two of the environmental problems discussed in "Ships in the Desert." Evaluate each site to determine the author's purpose, tone, bias, and credibility. To assess a site's credibility, distinguish between factual claims, opinions, and commonplace assertions or rhetorical fallacies (untruths or exaggerations).

 Go to **www.mirrorsandwindows.com** for more.

Rubrics for Writing Options

You can adapt this as a checklist for students to use as they write.

Creative Writing

☐ Does the letter clearly identify an environmental disaster?

☐ Does the letter clearly suggest at least one solution to the problem?

☐ Does the letter offer evidence to support claims and opinions?

Expository Writing

☐ Does the essay have a clear introduction that states one problem?

☐ Does the body of the essay clearly present possible solutions?

☐ Does the concluding paragraph express an idea of what could happen if humans do not solve the problem?

Grammar & Style

Simple and Compound Subjects

Simple Subjects

Instead, the world beneath it had changed in an unexpected way....

—AL GORE, "Ships in the Desert"

In a sentence, the **simple subject** is the key word or words in the subject of the independent clause. The simple subject is usually a noun or a pronoun and does not include any modifiers. The simple subject in the quotation above is the noun *world*.

> EXAMPLES
>
> *The camel is often called the ship of the desert.*
>
> *He was standing on the deck of a ship in the middle of the desert.*

Compound Subjects

Of course, the oil-covered otters and seabirds of Prince William Sound a year later presented less of a mystery to science....

—AL GORE, "Ships in the Desert"

A sentence may have more than one subject. A **compound subject** has two or more simple subjects that have the same predicate. The subjects are joined by the conjunction *and, either, or, neither, nor,* or *but*. In the quotation above, the compound subject is *otters and seabirds*.

If there are three or more subjects, commas should separate each. If there are only two subjects, or if a coordinating conjunction is used between every subject, commas should not be used.

> EXAMPLES
>
> *Neither my friend nor I contacted the city government about the recycling program.*
>
> *Juan, Mary Kay, and Jorge are members of the group that the teacher assigned to research environmental problems.*

Identifying Simple and Compound Subjects

On a separate sheet of paper, underline once the simple subjects in the following sentences. Underline twice any compound subjects.

1. His thoughts returned to his experiences at the equator.
2. The camels and their drivers kicked up sand as they passed by.
3. Neither scientists nor government officials have the complete picture of global warming.
4. We couldn't believe how much damage had been done.
5. Ten years ago, the Aral was the fourth-largest inland sea in the world.
6. During the trip, the scientists and I encountered other images that alarmed us.
7. They had investigated the mysterious and unusual death of several million starfish.
8. Needles, dead dolphins, and oil-soaked birds are all signs that the shores of our familiar world are fast eroding.
9. The earth's atmosphere began to change.
10. After a hearty breakfast, my companions and I traveled by snowmobile a few miles farther north.

Teach the Workshop

Identifying Simple and Compound Subjects

1. His <u>thoughts</u> returned to his experiences at the equator.
2. The <u>camels</u> and their <u>drivers</u> kicked up sand as they passed by.
3. Neither <u>scientists</u> nor government <u>officials</u> have the complete picture of global warming.
4. <u>We</u> couldn't believe how much damage had been done.
5. Ten years ago the <u>Aral</u> was the fourth-largest inland sea in the world.
6. During the trip, the <u>scientists</u> and <u>I</u> encountered other images that alarmed us.
7. <u>They</u> had investigated the mysterious and unusual death of several million starfish.
8. <u>Needles</u>, dead <u>dolphins</u>, and oil-soaked <u>birds</u> are all signs that the shores of our familiar world are fast eroding.
9. The earth's <u>atmosphere</u> began to change.
10. After a hearty breakfast, my <u>companions</u> and <u>I</u> traveled by snowmobile a few miles farther north.

> ▶ For more information, see Grammar & Style Section 3.1, The Sentence, in the Language Arts Handbook.

KEY TERMS

SIMPLE SUBJECT, 407
INDEPENDENT CLAUSE, 407
NOUN, 407
PRONOUN, 407
MODIFIER, 407
COMPOUND SUBJECT, 407
COMMA, 407
COORDINATING CONJUNCTION, 407

Program Resources

You will find additional lessons on Simple and Compound Subjects in the *Exceeding the Standards: Grammar & Style* resource.

Common Core State Standards

Language
L.3

At a Glance
Directed Reading
"Mute Dancers"
- Reading Level: Moderate
- Difficulty Considerations: Vocabulary and sentence length
- Ease Factor: Subject matter

"The Hummingbird That Lived Through Winter"
- Reading Level: Moderate
- Difficulty Consideration: Prior knowledge needed
- Ease Factor: Length

Objectives
Studying this lesson will enable students to
- compare literary selections of different genres on the same topic
- use reading strategies such as setting a purpose for reading
- define description and compare its effects in these selections
- describe literary accomplishments of Diane Ackerman and William Saroyan
- compare the ways people respond to nature

Launch the Lesson
If students have not had firsthand experience with hummingbirds, you may wish to show a videotape of a nature documentary featuring hummingbirds.

Ask students if they have ever helped a bird or other animal that was sick or injured. Invite students to state when they would or wouldn't try to help an animal in distress.

DIRECTED READING

Comparing Literature

Mute Dancers: How to Watch a Hummingbird
A Scientific Essay by Diane Ackerman

The Hummingbird That Lived Through Winter
A Short Story by William Saroyan

BEFORE READING

Build Background
Scientific Context Hummingbirds live only in the Americas. Just sixteen of more than three hundred species appear in the United States. The smallest birds on the planet, hummingbirds are also the only birds that can fly up, down, forward, backward, and sideways.

Reader's Context What lengths would you go to in order to save a sick or wounded animal?

Set Purpose
Preview the title and first few sentences of the essay and the story to make predictions about what you will learn.

Meet the Authors

Diane Ackerman (b. 1948) is a naturalist and a writer of poetry, essays, and books. *The Rarest of Rare* and *The Moon by Whale Light* are just two of numerous nonfiction works by Ackerman that delve into the mysteries of the natural world. "Mute Dancers: How to Watch a Hummingbird" was originally published in 1994 in *The New York Times Magazine.*

William Saroyan (1908–1981) was a prolific and versatile writer whose collected works include novels, short stories, plays, and poetry. Saroyan published his first book, *The Daring Young Man on the Flying Trapeze*, at the age of twenty-six. Born in Fresno, California, to Armenian parents, the author attributed much of his inspiration for writing to his Armenian heritage.

Compare Literature: Description
Writing that describes a character, object, or scene using sensory details is called **description.** In this essay and story, the authors use sensory details to help you see, hear, smell, taste, and feel what they are describing. Use a chart to record sensory details and their effects.

Sensory Details	Effect of Details
"fury of iridescence" →	

Preview Vocabulary
ir·i·des·cence (ir' ə de´ s'n[t]s) *n.,* show of rainbow colors that seem to shimmer and change when viewed from different angles

co·los·sal (kə lä´ səl) *adj.,* of a very large degree or amount

per·pet·u·al (pər pe´ chə wəl) *adj.,* going on forever

be·nign (bi nīn´) *adj.,* posing no threat

trans·for·ma·tion (tran[t]s fər mā´ shən) *n.,* change in composition, structure, or outward form and appearance

408 UNIT 4 NONFICTION

Words in Use

"Mute Dancers"

Preview Vocabulary	Selection Words	Teaching Words
iridescence, 409	bestir, 410	delve, 408
colossal, 409	operetta, 410	prolific, 408
perpetual, 409	serenade, 410	versatile, 408
benign, 410	succulent, 410	attributed, 408
	prisms, 411	heritage, 408
		unique, 408
		anecdote, 408
		evoke, 414

KEY TERMS
SCIENTIFIC ESSAY, 408
SHORT STORY, 408
DESCRIPTION, 408
SENSORY DETAIL, 408
DIALOGUE, 414
POINT OF VIEW, 414

Common Core State Standards
Reading Informational
RI.1

The Aztec God Quetzalcoatl with a Hummingbird (manuscript illustration), c. 1500. Aztec artist. Biblioteca Nazionale Centrale, Florence, Italy.

Mute Dancers: How to Watch a Hummingbird

A Scientific Essay
by Diane Ackerman

A lot of hummingbirds die in their sleep. Like a small fury of <u>iridescence</u>, a hummingbird spends the day at high speed, darting and swiveling among thousands of nectar-rich blossoms. Hummingbirds have huge hearts and need <u>colossal</u> amounts of energy to fuel their flights, so they live in a <u>perpetual</u> mania to find food. They tend to prefer red, trumpet-shaped flowers, in which nectar thickly oozes, and eat every 15 minutes or so. A hummingbird drinks with a W-shaped tongue, licking nectar up as a cat might (but faster). Like a tiny drum roll, its heart beats at 500 times a minute. Frighten a hummingbird and its heart can race to over 1,200 times a minute. Feasting and flying, courting and dueling, hummingbirds consume life at a fever pitch. No warm-blooded animal on earth uses more energy,

> *Hummingbirds have huge hearts and need colossal amounts of energy to fuel their flights...*

for its size. But that puts them at great peril. By day's end, wrung-out and exhausted, a hummingbird rests near collapse.

In the dark night of the hummingbird, it can sink into a zombielike state of torpor;[1] its breathing grows shallow and its wild heart slows to only 36 beats a minute. When dawn breaks on the fuchsia and columbine, hummingbirds must jump-start their hearts and fire up their flight muscles to raise their body temperature for another all-or-nothing day. That demands a colossal effort, which some can't manage. So a lot of hummingbirds die in their sleep.

---

1. torpor. Hibernation-like state during which there is no movement

---

ir·i·des·cence (ir' ə de´ s'n[t]s) *n.*, show of rainbow colors that seem to shimmer and change when viewed from different angles

co·los·sal (kə lä´ səl) *adj.*, of a very large degree or amount

per·pet·u·al (pər pe´ chə wəl) *adj.*, going on forever

409

Teach the Selection

Summary

This scientific essay provides information about some unusual characteristics of hummingbirds. The author describes the high-speed, risky lives of these tiny birds as they search for food and survive cold nights. She sprinkles the essay with personal remembrances of hummingbird encounters, as well as with historical references such as Aztec legends about the tiny birds and the role hummingbirds play in pollinating vanilla. The author closes by suggesting the best way to observe hummingbirds and explaining their brilliant colors.

MIRRORS & WINDOWS The Mirrors & Windows questions at the end of the selection focus on the theme of understanding nature. Before students begin reading, ask: Why do hummingbirds fascinate people?

Program Resources

Planning and Assessment
Program Planning Guide, Selection Lesson Plan
E-Lesson Planner
Assessment Guide, Lesson Test
ExamView

Technology Tools
Interactive Student Text on CD
Visual Teaching Package
Audio Library
mirrorsandwindows.com

Meeting the Standards
Nonfiction: Unit 4, Comparing Literature, pp. 36–45

Differentiating Instruction
Developing Readers, Set Purpose, pp. 28–30

Teach the Selection

Analyze Literature

Description Ask students to identify three examples of description the author uses to help readers visualize the appearance, attitude, and movement of hummingbirds. Model examples, such as "darting and swiveling" (page 409), "glittery," and "thuglike," which describe motion, appearance, and attitude.

Science Connection

Hearing Hummingbirds

Hummingbirds are not really "mute." They vocalize in a chattering chirp that is difficult for some people to hear because of its high pitch. The rapid vibrations of their wings create humming sounds, which vary by species because of different wing sizes and beats per second. A hummingbird can hover or fly in any direction because it can rotate its wings as humans rotate their wrists. Ⓐ

Use Reading Strategies

Ask Questions Have pairs of students briefly pause in their reading and think of questions they would like to ask about details or descriptions in the essay. Model one possible question: "What do various hummingbird movements mean to other birds?" Ⓑ

But most do bestir themselves. This is why, in American Indian myths and legends, hummingbirds are often depicted as resurrection birds, which seem to die and be reborn on another day or in another season. The Aztec[2] god of war was named Huitzilopochtli,[3] a compound word meaning "shining one with weapon like cactus thorn," and "sorcerer that spits fire." Aztec warriors fought, knowing that if they fell in battle they would be reincarnated as glittery, thuglike hummingbirds. The male birds were lionized for their ferocity in battle. And their feathers flashed in the sun like jewel-encrusted shields. Aztec rulers donned ceremonial robes of hummingbird feathers. As they walked, colors danced across their shoulders and bathed them in a supernatural light show.

Ⓐ While most birds are busy singing a small operetta of who and what and where, hummingbirds are virtually mute. Such small voices don't carry far, so they don't bother much with song. But if they can't serenade a mate, or yell war cries at a rival, how can they perform the essential dramas of their lives? They dance. Using body language, they spell out their intentions and moods just as bees, fireflies or hula dancers do. That means Ⓑ elaborate aerial ballets in which males twirl, joust, sideswipe and somersault. Brazen and fierce, they will take on large adversaries— even cats, dogs or humans.

My neighbor Persis once told me how she'd been needled by hummingbirds. When Persis lived in San Francisco, hummingbirds often attacked her outside her apartment building. From their perspective she was on *their* property, not the other way round, and

they flew circles around her to vex her away. My encounters with hummingbirds have been altogether more <u>benign</u>. Whenever I've walked through South American rain forests, with my hair braided and secured by a waterproof red ribbon, hummingbirds have assumed my ribbon to be a succulent flower and have probed my hair repeatedly, searching for nectar. Their touch was as delicate as a sweat bee's. But it was their purring by my ear that made me twitch. In time, they would leave unfed, but for a while I felt like a character in a Li'l Abner[4] cartoon who could be named something like "Hummer." In Portuguese, the word for hummingbird (*Beija flora*) means "flower kisser." It was the American colonists who first imagined the birds humming as they went about their chores.

> The feathers were ruffled and there was a bit of blood on the breast, but the bird still looked perky and alive.

Last summer, the historical novelist Jeanne Mackin winced to see her cat, Beltane, drag in voles, birds and even baby rabbits. Few things can compete with the blood lust of a tabby cat. But one day Beltane dragged in something rare and shimmery—a struggling hummingbird. The feathers were ruffled and there was a bit of blood on the breast, but the bird still looked perky and alive. So Jeanne fashioned a nest for it out of a small wire basket lined in gauze, and fed it sugar water from an eye dropper. To her

---

2. **Aztec** (az´ tek'). Powerful and highly advanced Native American civilization whose empire was located in central Mexico from the 1400s to the early 1500s
3. **Huitzilopochtli** (wēt' sē lə pōch´ tlē).
4. **Li'l Abner.** Newspaper comic strip created by cartoonist Al Capp in 1934

---

be•nign (bi nīn´) *adj.*, posing no threat

---

410 UNIT 4 NONFICTION

Differentiated Instruction

English Language Learning

Review the paragraph that describes Persis being "needled" by hummingbirds. Explain that *needle* is an idiom that means "to annoy or provoke." Ask students for examples of terms from their own languages that mean the same thing. Also, make sure students see the humor in the relationship between "needled" and the shape of the hummingbird's beak.

Enrichment

Have students locate several Internet sites that have recordings of hummingbird vocalizations and wing sounds and listen to the sounds. Then invite students to explain why the author might say that hummingbirds are "virtually mute."

amazement, as she watched, "it miscarried a little pearl." Hummingbird eggs are the size of coffee beans, and females usually carry two. So Jeanne knew one might still be safe inside. After a quiet night, the hummingbird seemed stronger, and when she set the basket outside at dawn, the tiny assault victim flew away.

It was a ruby-throated hummingbird that she nursed, the only one native to the East Coast. In the winter they migrate thousands of miles over mountains and open water to Mexico and South America. She may well have been visited by a species known to the Aztecs. Altogether, there are 16 species of hummingbirds in North America, and many dozens in South America, especially near the equator, where they can feed on a buffet of blossoms. The tiniest—the Cuban bee hummingbird—is the smallest warm-blooded animal in the world. About two and one-eighth inches long from beak to tail, it is smaller than the toe of an eagle, and its eggs are like seeds.

Hummingbirds are a New World phenomenon. So, too, is vanilla,[5] and their stories are linked. When the early explorers returned home with the riches of the West, they found it impossible, to their deep frustration, to grow vanilla beans. It took ages before they discovered why—that hummingbirds were a key pollinator of vanilla orchids—and devised beaklike splinters of bamboo to do the work of birds.

Now that summer has come at last, lucky days may be spent watching the antics of hummingbirds. The best way to behold them is to stand with the light behind you, so that the bird faces the sun. Most of the trembling colors aren't true pigments, but the result of light staggering through clear cells that act as prisms. Hummingbirds are iridescent for the same reason soap bubbles are. Each feather contains tiny air bubbles separated by dark spaces. Light bounces off the air bubbles at different angles, and that makes blazing colors seem to swarm and leap. All is vanity in the end. The male's shimmer draws a female to mate. But that doesn't matter much to gardeners, watching hummingbirds patrol the impatiens[6] as if the northern lights[7] had suddenly fallen to earth. ❖

---

5. **vanilla.** Fragrant flavoring often used in baking
6. **impatiens.** Plant with many red, pink, or white flowers
7. **northern lights.** Showy display of natural lights that appears in the night sky, also known as the aurora borealis (ə rôr´ ə bôr´ ē a´ ləs)

 How did this essay make you feel about hummingbirds? What details or descriptions most influenced these feelings? What makes the hummingbird unique?

Find Meaning

1. (a) Why does a hummingbird spend all day eating? (b) How does this affect its condition at night?
2. (a) Why don't hummingbirds sing? (b) According to the author, what do male hummingbirds do to attract mates or assert their power?

Make Judgments

3. (a) How would you describe the narrator's encounters with hummingbirds? (b) What does her description of these encounters suggest about her relationship with nature?
4. (a) Why do you think the author tells how Jeanne Mackin nursed a wounded hummingbird? (b) What do this anecdote and other examples in the essay reveal about the author's attitude toward hummingbirds?

Grammar Skills

Compound Words

Direct students' attention to hyphenated compound words in "Mute Dancers," such as *nectar-rich* and *trumpet-shaped.* Have students locate at least five other hyphenated compound words in the essay (*warm-blooded, wrung-out, jump-start, all-or-nothing, jewel-encrusted, ruby-throated*).

Point out that adjectives can be formed by adding -*like* to a noun; for example, *zombielike.* Have students locate two other examples of adjectives formed in this way in the text (*thuglike, beaklike*).

The Hummingbird That Lived Through Winter

A Short Story by William Saroyan

There was a hummingbird once which in the wintertime did not leave our neighborhood in Fresno, California.

I'll tell you about it.

Across the street lived old Dikran, who was almost blind. He was past eighty and his wife was only a few years younger. They had a little house that was as neat inside as it was ordinary outside—except for old Dikran's garden, which was the best thing of its kind in the world. Plants, bushes, trees—all strong, in sweet black moist earth whose guardian was old Dikran. All things from the sky loved this spot in our poor neighborhood, and old Dikran loved *them*.

One freezing Sunday, in the dead of winter, as I came home from Sunday School I saw old Dikran standing in the middle of the street trying to distinguish what was in his hand. Instead of going into our house to the fire, as I had wanted to do, I stood on the steps of the front porch and watched the old man. He would turn around and look upward at his trees and then back to the palm of his hand. He stood in the street at least two minutes and then at last he came to me. He held his hand out, and in Armenian[1] he said, "What is this in my hand?"

I looked.

"It is a hummingbird," I said half in English and half in Armenian. Hummingbird I said in English because I didn't know its name in Armenian.

"What is that?" old Dikran asked.

"The little bird," I said. "You know. The one that comes in the summer and stands in the air and then shoots away. The one with the wings that beat so fast you can't see them. It's in your hand. It's dying."

"Come with me," the old man said. "I can't see, and the wife's at church. I can feel its heart beating. Is it in a bad way? Look again once."

I looked again. It was a sad thing to behold. This wonderful little creature of summertime in the big rough hand of the old peasant. Here and pathetic, not suspended in

"It's in your hand. It's dying."

---

1. **Armenian.** Language spoken by the people dwelling chiefly in Armenia and in neighboring regions of Turkey and Azerbaijan

412

a shaft of summer light, not the most alive thing in the world, but the most helpless and heart-breaking.

"It's dying," I said.

The old man lifted his hand to his mouth and blew warm breath on the little thing in his hand which he could not even see. "Stay now," he said in Armenian. "It is not long till summer. Stay, swift and lovely."

We went into the kitchen of his little house, and while he blew warm breath on the bird he told me what to do.

"Put a tablespoon of honey over the gas fire and pour it into my hand, but be sure it is not too hot."

This was done.

After a moment the hummingbird began to show signs of fresh life. The warmth of the room, the vapor of the warm honey—and, well, the will and love of the old man. Soon the old man could feel the change in his hand, and after a moment or two the hummingbird began to take little dabs of the honey.

"It will live," the old man announced. "Stay and watch."

The <u>transformation</u> was incredible. The old man kept his hand generously open, and I expected the helpless bird to shoot upward out of his hand, suspend itself in space, and scare the life out of me—which is exactly what happened. The new life of the little bird was magnificent. It spun about in the little kitchen, going to the window, coming back to the heat, suspending, circling as if it were summertime and it had never felt better in its whole life.

> **trans·for·ma·tion** (tran[t]s fər mā′ shən) *n.*, change in composition, structure, or outward form and appearance

The old man sat on the plain chair, blind but attentive. He listened carefully and tried to see, but of course he couldn't. He kept asking about the bird, how it seemed to be, whether it showed signs of weakening again, what its spirit was, and whether or not it appeared to be restless; and I kept describing the bird to him.

When the bird was restless and wanted to go, the old man said, "Open the window and let it go."

"Will it live?" I asked.

"It is alive now and wants to go," he said. "Open the window."

I opened the window, the hummingbird stirred about here and there, feeling the cold from the outside, suspended itself in the area of the open window, stirring this way and that, and then it was gone.

"Close the window," the old man said.

We talked a minute or two and then I went home.

The old man claimed the hummingbird lived through that winter, but I never knew for sure. I saw hummingbirds again when summer came, but I couldn't tell one from the other.

One day in the summer I asked the old man.

"Did it live?"

"The little bird?" he said.

"Yes," I said. "That we gave the honey to. You remember. The little bird that was dying in the winter. Did it live?"

"Look about you," the old man said. "Do you see the bird?"

"I see humming*birds*," I said.

"Each of them is our bird," the old man said. "Each of them, each of them," he said swiftly and gently. ✤

When might humans be responsible for helping sick or wounded wild animals? When is it not appropriate to help?

Speaking & Listening Skills

Group Discussion Etiquette

Review etiquette for group discussions. Remind students that listeners and speakers play different roles.

- The speaker should present a point of view clearly and concisely and answer questions other group members may ask.

- Listeners should listen actively, ask questions, and provide polite, constructive feedback.
- Everyone should remember that expressions or body language provide nonverbal information and feedback as they speak or listen.

Ask students to apply discussion etiquette as they work in small groups to discuss the *Mirrors & Windows* questions at the end of the story.

Find Meaning

1. (a) Dikran is almost blind.
(b) Dikran only speaks Armenian and does not know the word *hummingbird*, so the narrator describes the bird's size and actions.
2. (a) Dikran blows warm breath on the bird. The narrator heats some honey and pours it into Dikran's hand for the bird. (b) The narrator is amazed at the bird's transformation.

Make Judgments

3. (a) Dikran recognizes that the bird is well enough to go and wants to be free. (b) It is deep and unselfish.
4. (a) By caring about one bird, they helped save the spirit of all the birds. (b) The presence of many healthy birds reminds them that it would be worthwhile to save any individual bird.

Compare Literature

Description

1. Ackerman uses such details as "fury of iridescence" and "feathers flashed in the sun like jewel-encrusted shields."
2. He has the narrator describe a hummingbird to Dikran with details such as the "little bird" that "stands in the air and then shoots away," and has "wings that beat so fast you can't see them."
3. Answers will vary. Students should give examples from the selections as evidence to support their answers.

AFTER READING

Find Meaning

1. (a) Why does Dikran ask the narrator, "What is this in my hand?" (b) Why doesn't Dikran understand the narrator at first? What does the narrator do to help Dikran understand?
2. (a) How do Dikran and the narrator help the hummingbird? (b) How does the hummingbird's gradual recovery affect the narrator?

Compare Literature

Description When a writer uses description, he or she uses sensory details to create vivid images that help readers visualize people, places, things, and ideas. Review sensory details in "Mute Dancer: How to Watch a Hummingbird" and "The Hummingbird That Lived Through Winter" that you recorded in your chart to answer these questions.

Make Judgments

3. (a) Why does Dikran tell the narrator to open the window and let the bird go? (b) What does this reveal about the kind of love Dikran has for birds and nature?
4. (a) What does Dikran mean when he tells the narrator that each of the hummingbirds he sees "is our bird"? (b) Why might it not matter if one of those is the one they saved?

1. What sensory details does Ackerman use to create a vivid picture of a hummingbird?
2. How does Saroyan evoke a clear image of the hummingbird in his short story?
3. Which details used to describe a hummingbird had the greatest impact on you? Why?

Extend Understanding

Writing Options

Creative Writing Use **dialogue** to write a conversation that old Dikran might have with his wife when she returns home about finding, helping, and releasing the hummingbird. When creating dialogue for Dikran, use details that help him describe what he heard, smelled, and touched as he and the narrator treated the bird. Also have him explain how the experience might have made him feel.

Expository Writing Write a **critical analysis** in which you analyze the first-person point of view used in both "Mute Dancer: How to Watch a Hummingbird" and "The Hummingbird That Lived Through Winter." Explain why this was the most effective point of view to use in the essay and the story. Provide at least one example from the essay and the story to support your ideas. Share your work with the class.

Critical Literacy

Analyze Adaptations Works of nonfiction are often changed or adapted into another medium or genre. Find an adaptation of an autobiography or a diary and describe the structural and substantive differences between the two. Consider comparing Anne Frank's *The Diary of a Young Girl* with a dramatic adaptation (film, play) of the book.

Lifelong Learning

Research Myths and Legends Form a small group to research myths and legends about hummingbirds. Find a myth or legend in which the hummingbird plays a major role. With your group members, decide on a way to retell the myth or legend. You can rewrite the story in your own words and retell it to the class, or you can present the myth or legend as a skit.

Go to **www.mirrorsandwindows.com** for more.

Program Resources

For further instruction, refer students to the following extension activity: Lifelong Learning: Research Myths and Legends, *Exceeding the Standards: Extension Activities*, p. 11.

Rubrics for Writing Options

You can adapt this as a checklist for students to use as they write.

Creative Writing

☐ Is the dialogue between Dikran and his wife?
☐ Does Dikran explain how he found and helped the hummingbird with the narrator's help?
☐ Do Dikran's words contain sensory details about his experience with the hummingbird?

Expository Writing

☐ Does the analysis show a clear understanding of first-person point of view?
☐ Does the analysis explain how the first-person point of view allows both narrators to share experiences and feelings with the reader?
☐ Does the analysis use examples to support ideas?

THE FACE OF THE DEEP IS FROZEN

A Historical Essay by Jennifer Armstrong

BEFORE READING

Build Background
Historical Context In August 1914, Ernest Shackleton and twenty-seven men sailed from England toward Antarctica on a mission to cross the barren continent. Their ship became trapped in ice in January of 1915, where it survived the Antarctic winter, but then it sank. The men were forced to camp on the ice and set out on foot. In August 1916, the men were rescued; every member of the expedition survived. This selection is from a book about the harrowing expedition.

Reader's Context Would you like to be an explorer? How would you balance the possible dangers with the potential thrills of doing something remarkable?

Set Purpose
Skim the reading quickly. Based on information in Build Background and the title, predict what will happen in this excerpt. Read to find out how accurate your prediction is.

Analyze Literature
Description An author portrays a character or a scene through **description**. Authors use **sensory details** to describe how things look, sound, smell, taste, or feel. The use of **precise words, imagery,** and **figurative language** in description is important in appealing to the reader's senses. As you read, notice how the author uses these devices to describe.

Meet the Author
Jennifer Armstrong (b. 1961) is an award-winning author of books for young readers. Her book *Shipwreck at the Bottom of the World: The Extraordinary True Story of Shackleton and the* Endurance tells the true tale of an incredible expedition. To write the book, Armstrong conducted months of research, which resulted in vivid descriptions of the explorers and how they survived the trip to Antarctica. Armstrong also writes fiction and science fiction.

Use Reading Skills
Context Clues Preview the vocabulary words from this selection in the sentences below. Try to determine the meaning of each word using the context clues in the sentences.

1. Students referred to the combined offices as the consolidated school district.
2. It can take only a few days of blowing desert sand to entirely erode the surface of a statue.
3. After a few hours in the refrigerator, fat began to congeal on top of the stew.
4. The family had no electricity, and by January their situation was dire.
5. They kept a supply of dried moose meat in a frozen outdoor cache.

Preview Vocabulary
con·sol·i·dat·ed (kən säˊ lə dā təd) *adj.*, joined together; compacted

e·rode (i rōdˊ) *v.*, wear away, usually through natural forces such as weather

con·geal (kən jēlˊ) *v.*, change from liquid to solid due to cold temperature

dire (dīˊ [ə]r) *adj.*, desperate; horrifying

cache (kash) *n.*, stored supply, often hidden

THE FACE OF THE DEEP IS FROZEN **415**

Summary

Beginning with a vivid description of the harsh and unwelcoming landscape of Antarctica, the author goes on to describe how the captain and crew of *Endurance* survived after the ship became trapped in ice. Ernest Shackleton and his twenty-seven men made difficult decisions as they prepared for a journey of 346 miles across the barren terrain that looked as if "a giant hand had smashed down onto the frozen face of the deep. . ." The story continues with a description of the first two days of the journey, as the men dragged twenty-foot boats behind them and covered less than two miles.

 The Mirrors & Windows questions at the end of the selection focus on the theme of taking risks. Before students begin reading, ask: What would you need to survive a night without shelter?

Critical Viewing

As students study the picture, have them describe the scene in their own words. Encourage students to use precise and vivid terms in their descriptions. Then have students use terms related to motion and body sensations to describe what it would be like to reach the ship from the place where the picture was taken.

THE FACE OF THE DEEP IS FROZEN

A Historical Essay by Jennifer Armstrong

The ship itself was a mess of snapped rigging and broken spars.

416

Program Resources

Planning and Assessment
Program Planning Guide, Selection Lesson Plan
E-Lesson Planner
Assessment Guide, Lesson Test
ExamView

Technology Tools
Interactive Student Text on CD
Visual Teaching Package
Audio Library
mirrorsandwindows.com

Meeting the Standards
Nonfiction: Unit 4, Directed Reading, pp. 46–52

The Antarctic contains ninety percent of the world's snow and ice, and there are more than eighty kinds of it. There's brash ice, pancake ice, bullet ice, green ice, frazil, nilas, breccia, shuga, slush ice, rotten ice, pressure ice, grease ice, ice dust, shorefast ice, ice flowers, ice haycocks, ice saddles, floes, calf bergs, growlers, and sastrugi, to name just a few. And when it comes to icebergs, there are whole family trees to study. In the family of tabular[1] bergs, there are domed, horizontal, blocky, tilted, and uneven bergs; in the tribe of rounded bergs, there are surrounded, well-rounded, and rounded bergs; and when it comes to irregular bergs, there are tabular remnant, pinnacled, pyramidal, drydock, castellate,[2] jagged, slab, and roof bergs.

Much of the ice on the continent of Antarctica[3] is actually a form of <u>consolidated</u> snow called firn. As snow accumulates, it begins to compact, forcing out the air between the snowflakes. Eventually, all the air is squeezed out, and the snow is a dense, heavy ice. This compression also makes much of the ice blue.

These masses of ice form glaciers that reach the edge of the continent, where every year 5,000 to 10,000 icebergs "calve," or break off, from the ice sheets into the surrounding ocean. Many icebergs are so large that they create their own weather systems. The largest iceberg ever recorded was one the size of Belgium (close to 12,000 square miles), spotted in 1956, and the most northerly iceberg reached twenty-six degrees south latitude in the Atlantic Ocean, in 1894. This is the latitude of Rio de Janeiro, in Brazil, just south of the Tropic of Capricorn.[4] As the icebergs drift, the seawater <u>erodes</u> them from below, until the berg abruptly topples over and continues its journey upside down. The erosion continues until the berg flips again, and then

again, and eventually it is eroded and melted away.

As the icebergs calve from the glaciers on the continent, they bring with them mineral deposits scraped up from the ground, and release these nutrients into the water. As they melt, the bergs also release atmospheric nutrients that have been trapped in the ice for centuries. It is this steady deposit of nutrients from icebergs that makes the waters of the Southern Ocean so rich and full of life.

(A) Of course, the ocean around the continent also turns to ice. Salt water freezes at a lower temperature than fresh water, around twenty-seven degrees Fahrenheit, depending on the concentration of salt and other minerals. As the water on the surface cools, it begins to condense, and individual ice crystals act as seeds, causing the water to <u>congeal</u> around them, squeezing the salt out into the water below. On the surface, the water seems to stiffen and turn greasy. This layer of thick, flexible ice is called nilas. If the nilas is disturbed by wind, the ice forms rounded discs called pancakes, which look something like white lily pads with their edges turned up. As the air temperature drops and the water continues to freeze, the pancakes mass together and harden into a single sheet, or ice field. Because the water forces out salt as it freezes, the water below the ice field is saturated with salt and

---

1. **tabular.** Having a flat surface
2. **castellate.** Built like a castle
3. **the continent of Antarctica.** Surrounding Earth's south pole, this landmass is twice the size of Australia. In winter, ice doubles its size.
4. **twenty-six degrees south latitude...Tropic of Capricorn.** The iceberg traveled very far north, into relatively warm waters.

con·sol·i·dat·ed (kən säˊ lə dā təd) *adj.*, joined together; compacted

e·rode (i rōdˊ) *v.*, wear away, usually through natural forces such as weather

con·geal (kən jēlˊ) *v.*, change from liquid to solid due to cold temperature

THE FACE OF THE DEEP IS FROZEN **417**

Analyze Literature

Description This account contains many unfamiliar terms that describe ice. Understanding these terms will help students visualize the setting. Have students read the first paragraph and skim the rest of the selection, noting unfamiliar words. Assign each type of ice to an individual or pair of students. (The author names twenty-one types.) Model the research process of locating a description and picture of *frazil* using an Internet image search. Then have students locate descriptions and pictures of their forms of ice. Have students share their descriptions and pictures before continuing the reading. **(A)**

Geography Connection

Antarctica Antarctica is the world's fifth-largest continent. Its land surface is over 5.5 million square miles, or ten percent of Earth's total land surface. The ice sheet overlaying the continent averages 6,500 feet thick and represents about ninety percent of the world's glacial ice. Antarctica has the world's lowest recorded temperature, −128.6 °F (−89.2 °C). There are few land plants, but the rich supply of fish offshore nourishes penguins and huge seabird colonies.

Vocabulary Skills

Jargon

Jargon is specialized vocabulary that members of a particular profession or group use. Jargon can make writing more specific and authentic, but can also make a story or article hard to read.

"The Face of the Deep Is Frozen" includes jargon related to exploration and geological processes that students may not understand. Terms include *stores,*

cache, erosion, calving, and *expedition.* Remind students to use context clues to uncover meaning. For instance, the action of *calving* is described in the words *break away.* Encourage students to look up jargon in the dictionary if context does not lead to understanding.

Use Reading Skills

Identify Text Organization Remind students that nonfiction may have different organizational structures, such as cause and effect, compare and contrast, spatial, and sequence of events. Model how to determine the structure of the first part of the reading: "The descriptions of ice, snow, and geography provide a setting. This segment has a spatial organization." Have small groups determine how Armstrong organizes the story once Shackleton and his men are introduced.

Use Reading Strategies

Make Inferences This is the first mention of dogs. Ask students to infer why an expedition to the Antarctic would include dogs. **A**

Analyze Literature

Theme Remind students that a theme is a general message an author wants to convey. Read aloud the first sentence of Shackleton's diary entry. Then invite students to analyze the diary entry and explain its theme. **B**

Analyze Literature

Description Point out the word *march* in the passage. Invite students to suggest other words that could describe the actions of the men, such as *move*, *walk*, or *travel*. Discuss together the author's reason for using the specific word *march* rather than one of the more general words. **C**

---

minerals, and the ice itself is clean enough to melt into drinking water.

This process of turning seawater into drinking water is important—it means that a shipwreck on the frozen sea does not *necessarily* mean certain death.

When the exhausted crew of *Endurance* gave up the battle against the pressure and abandoned the ship, the ice field around her was not a sight to inspire confidence. The ship itself was a mess of snapped rigging and broken spars.[5] Beside her on the ice was Dump Camp, a junk pile of most of the stores[6] and equipment the men had. The dogs milled around, straining at their tethers, snapping and snarling at one another. The crew staggered like dead men, utterly beaten from their labors, trying to pitch tents so they could crawl in to sleep. There were only eighteen sleeping bags, originally meant for the overland journey, and the men drew straws to see who would get them. The rest of the men had to make do with wool blankets. Tom Crean was suffering from snow blindness (a temporary condition that often affects polar travelers when they are exposed to the glare of sunlight on snow); he had to be helped into a tent. That night, the ice beneath the tents quivered as whales rubbed up against it from below.

"Though we have been compelled to abandon the ship, which is crushed beyond all hope of ever being righted, we are alive and well, and we have stores and equipment for the task that lies before us. The task is to reach land with all the members of the expedition," Shackleton wrote in his diary the next morning.

There were precious few options available to the Boss. Already the ship had drifted 1,000 miles north and west with the pack ice. The tip of South America was more than 2,000 miles away, and there was no way of reaching it on foot. They had ample food,

guns, matches, and dogs. But, after all, they were in the Antarctic, not Hyde Park in London. The circumstances were <u>dire</u>, to say the least.

After a quiet conference with Wild, Shackleton announced his plan to the crew: they would march across the frozen sea with two of the three lifeboats to Paulet Island, 346 miles to the northwest. To the best of Shackleton's knowledge, there was a <u>cache</u> of stores in a hut on Paulet Island from a 1902 Swedish expedition. What they would do once they reached this destination was not specified: it was enough to have a goal. He would plan the next step when they got there. But 346 miles is more than the distance between Boston and New York City, almost as far as from Los Angeles to San Francisco, about the entire width of Iowa. They would have to walk the whole way, hauling their gear and the two boats. The men knew they were doomed without the boats; eventually they would reach open water. They would need the boats, no matter how burdensome they were to drag over the ice. Shackleton gave the men a couple of days' rest. October 30 was the appointed day of departure.

In the meantime, there was much to get ready. Mrs. Chippy, the carpenter's cat, had to be shot, because without the protection of the ship the dogs would have eaten him. The youngest of the puppies, who were too small to pull with a team, also had to be killed. While McNeish and McLeod began fitting the lifeboats onto sledges,[7] the rest of the crew began sorting their equipment. The men were

---

5. **rigging and spars.** Ropes, wires, and pulleys that support the masts and control a boat's sails, plus the poles that support the rigging
6. **stores.** Supplies
7. **sledges.** Large sleds pulled by animals

dire (dī′ [ə]r) *adj.*, desperate; horrifying
cache (kash) *n.*, stored supply, often hidden

Differentiated Instruction

English Language Learning

Students learning English may have difficulty identifying the subject when a sequence of phrases or clauses is used to modify the noun in an independent clause. Model locating the subject of the independent clause in a sentence such as *The crew staggered like dead men, utterly beaten from their labors, trying to pitch tents so they could crawl in to sleep.* Suggest that students work in pairs to identify the subject in each sentence that begins a paragraph on these two pages.

given a two-pound limit on personal gear, which allowed them to keep only the items that were essential for survival—although the Boss did allow them to keep their diaries and their tobacco, and the doctors were allowed their medical supplies. In a dramatic gesture, Shackleton took his gold cigarette case and a handful of gold coins from his pocket and dropped them on the snow. Gold was useless for the task ahead.

He then opened the Bible inscribed to him by Queen Alexandra and ripped out a page from the Book of Job:[8]

Out of whose womb came the ice?
And the hoary frost of Heaven, who hath gendered it?[9]
The waters are hid as with a stone,
And the face of the deep is frozen.

Then he folded the page into a pocket and dropped the heavy Bible on the cigarette case and gold coins, showing the crew the route they must take. If they wanted to survive, they must travel light, harden their hearts against sentimental keepsakes, and trust that they could make do with the bare bones of equipment. Shackleton the improviser[10] believed that it was foolish to burden themselves with equipment for *every* possible emergency. As the day wore on, the pile of discards grew. Extra clothes, books, scientific instruments and specimens, chess sets, flags, lanterns, tools, sewing kits, lucky talismans, razors, barometers, combs, scissors, playing cards, dishes, silverware, photographs—each man added to the heap. Some of the men saved leather suitcases to use for boot repairs later on. Hussey kept his toothbrush, and Shackleton ordered him to keep the banjo, because they would need the comfort of music in the hard months ahead. Each man kept a spoon and a knife.

The journey was ready to begin at 2:00 P.M. on October 30 under heavy gray skies. It had already snowed on and off during the day, and it threatened to continue. That didn't pose much of a problem, but the road ahead did. If they only had to trek across 346 miles of flat ice field, the journey would have been bearable. But stretching ahead of them into the white horizon was a scene of utter devastation and chaos. It was as if a giant hand had smashed down onto the frozen face of the deep and broken it into a million shards.[11] Jagged floes tilted up at all angles. Pressure ridges reared up like wrinkles in a huge white blanket. If the sea had been frozen at the height of a tempest, and every storm-tossed wave locked into place, the scene could not have been more jumbled and uneven. There were 346 miles of *that* to cross—assuming the drift of the pack didn't change course and carry them helplessly in another direction.

On the lead sled went Shackleton, Wordie, Hussey, and Hudson, looking for the best route among the pressure ridges and tumbled ice floes. They were equipped with shovels, picks, and axes to chop a path through the chaos of ice. Behind them came the other dog teams pulling sleds that were each loaded with 900 pounds of stores and gear.

Bringing up the rear was the remainder of the crew pulling the boats on sledge runners. Loaded with food and equipment, the boats weighed in at more than a ton apiece. Fifteen men in harness dragged one boat at a time across the wet snow and over the ice, stopping every quarter mile to rest, before going back to haul the second boat forward. Shackleton was in constant anxiety

8. **Book of Job.** A Hebrew scripture. In the passage Shackleton saved, God is making a long speech to remind the man Job that a person is just one small part of creation.
9. **gendered it.** Given it identity
10. **improviser.** Inventor; one who responds creatively to new situations or makes something out of materials available at the time, without instructions
11. **shards.** Sharp broken pieces

History Connection
Finding Antarctica As early as the sixteenth century, explorers believed that a large continent existed in the south. They named it *Terra Australis Incognita*—the Unknown Southern Land. In 1772, Captain James Cook and his crew sailed near Antarctica, but high winds and ice forced them to leave. In 1821, American seal hunters led by Captain John Davis landed at Hughes Bay. They were on shore for less than an hour, but were the first humans known to have set foot on Antarctica.

Make Connections
Invite students to think of a time when they were worried about something that might happen in nature, such as a bad storm that might knock out electric power or a rainstorm when they were camping. How did they prepare themselves? How did the event turn out? Have students share their experiences in small groups.

Grammar Skills

Capitalization Rules
Review capitalization rules. Write the words *proper name* on the board. Invite students to add other types of words that should be capitalized, such as dates, specific places, personal titles, and the titles of books. Then have students locate and list each capitalized word—except the first word of every sentence—on this page next to its category, such as Boss (a personal title), Shackleton (a proper name), and Bible (a book title). Ask students to explain why the word *northwest* isn't capitalized.

Answer: Some students will relate to the experience, particularly if they have traveled far from home. Opinions will vary as to explorers' motivations.

Find Meaning

1. (a) The ship is stuck in the ice and breaking apart. (b) The first challenge was setting up tents and deciding who would sleep in them.

2. (a) The first step was to pull supplies and lifeboats across the ice to an island. (b) They made almost no forward progress. (c) The new plan was to drift on top of an ice floe.

3. (a) He dropped his gold cigarette case, gold coins, and his Bible. (b) They saved them to repair boots.

4. They stayed close together so the men would not be separated if the ice cracked apart beneath them.

Make Judgments

5. This material builds a feeling for the setting. It deepens understanding of difficulties the crew faced.

6. Having the goal gave the men something to focus on or strive for, as an alternative to dwelling on the dangers of their situation.

7. (a) He changes his plans after the first strategy proves ineffective. (b) It illustrates Shackleton's flexibility; he adapts his plans to changing circumstances. It may also suggest he doesn't really know what to do.

over continuing pressure in the ice. If a crack opened up between one team and another, the result could be disastrous. So he kept the men and sleds and boats close together, relaying forward one agonizing quarter mile at a time. Frequently, one of the dog teams had to be unharnessed from its sled and then hitched to a lifeboat to help the men drag it up and over a hummock or ridge.

After two hours of backbreaking labor, hauling the boats through wet, heavy snow, detouring around piles of broken floe, they were only one mile from *Endurance*. Soaked, and numb with fatigue, the men swallowed a hasty dinner and fell into their tents. It began to snow during the night. When the men resumed their burdens the next day, they had a new layer of heavy, wet slush to trudge through, and more wet snow was falling steadily. After another three hours and only an additional three quarters of a mile, the Boss called a halt. He and Worsley were

worried about damaging the boats as they knocked their way across the ice. They were getting nowhere.

At the moment they were on a very large, level floe, more than a half a mile in diameter. There wasn't another good, solid, flat floe in sight, and Shackleton felt they could not do better for a camping place. The men pitched their tents on the wet snow and crawled into their sleeping bags. Shackleton anxiously scouted ahead and found it impossible to advance.

Next morning, he announced that they would stay where they were and let the drifting pack carry them northward into a better position to make for Paulet Island. There was no alternative. Shackleton told Green to start adding large chunks of blubber to the crew's food. The thick seal fat that kept the animals warm would provide valuable calories in the men's diets and keep them from freezing. It was time to get used to it. ❖

Have you ever been in a situation where you "prepared for the worst and hoped for the best"? Why do you think people like Shackleton put themselves in such dangerous situations?

Find Meaning

1. (a) Why do the men abandon their ship? (b) What was the first challenge they faced then?

2. (a) What was the first step in Shackleton's plan? (b) Why did the crew abandon this plan? (c) What new plan did they adopt?

3. (a) What did Shackleton drop into the snow before setting off? (b) Why did some of the men save suitcases?

4. Why did Shackleton have the men pulling the boats keep them so close together?

Make Judgments

5. Why does Armstrong spend so many paragraphs describing ice, icebergs, and seawater?

6. As the crew sets out, Armstrong writes, "What they would do once they reached this destination was not specified: it was enough to have a goal." Why was having a goal enough?

7. (a) What does Shackleton do after the first day and a half on foot? (b) What does this suggest about his qualities as a leader?

Differentiated Instruction

Enrichment

Have students pretend they are journalists for a newspaper. Ask them to find more information on Ernest Shackleton and his expedition. Then have them write a one-page article on Shackleton and the expedition based on what they read and on other information they acquired during their research. Remind students that newspaper articles should focus on who, what, where, when, why, and how.

Jennifer Armstrong creates strong images of what it was like to be lost in a frozen world. **Robert Frost** (1874–1963) was a celebrated American poet who spent much of his life in New England. In this poem, the speaker compares fire and ice as ways the world might end. He also equates fire and ice to some particular human emotions. Which one does the speaker find harder to endure? As you read, think about how Frost's imagery compares to the images in "The Face of the Deep Is Frozen."

Fire and Ice

A Lyric Poem by Robert Frost

Some say the world will end in fire,
Some say in ice.
From what I've tasted of desire
I hold with those who favor fire.
But if it had to perish twice,
I think I know enough of hate
To say that for destruction ice
Is also great
And would suffice. ❖

TEXT ◀—▶ TEXT CONNECTION

How were the men of Shackleton's expedition prepared for the end of the world? What would they have thought of Frost's poem? Think also about how Frost equates fire with desire and ice with hate. Do you agree with those connections? Finally, explain the difference between the theme of "Fire and Ice" and Jennifer Armstrong's purpose for writing "The Face of the Deep is Frozen." Write your responses in your notebook.

FIRE AND ICE **421**

Teach the Connection

Use Reading Skills
Compare and Contrast Discuss the first sentence of the poem, focusing on ways in which either fire or ice could destroy the world. After students read the poem, point out that Frost compares desire to fire and hate to ice. Make a two-column chart on the board with the column headings *desire/fire* and *hate/ice*. Then have students list other words that describe each combination, such as *burning* for desire and fire, and *cold* or *hard* for hate and ice.

Analyze Literature
Poetry Review with students some differences between prose and poetry. Remind students that poetry creates a mood as much as it gives information. Have each student define prose and poetry in his or her own words and record the definitions in a journal.

Text-to-Text Connection
Answer: All the men with Shackleton were explorers and were prepared for danger. They probably were not expecting the world to end in a literal sense. Their responses to Frost's poem would have varied by individual. Many students will agree that desire is often characterized as a hot emotion and hatred as a cold one. Student views on the theme of "Fire and Ice" and the author's purpose in "The Face of the Deep is Frozen" will vary slightly.

Words in Use

"Fire and Ice"

Selection Words
perish, 421
suffice, 421

Speaking & Listening Skills

Person-to-Person Conversation
Set up a round-robin process so that students can practice reading and responding to this poem with several different classmates. Working in pairs, have one student read the poem aloud, and have the other student comment on the poem's meaning. Have one member of each pair then move to the group immediately to the right to repeat the process.

Common Core State Standards

Reading Literature
RL.9

Reading Informational
RI.1

Analyze Literature

Description Sensory details should include descriptions of the different kinds of ice, how ice forms, and how salt is squeezed out during the freezing process. Choices of precise words will vary; there are many examples. Figurative language includes personification in "the face of the deep" (although those are not Armstrong's words) and the image of a giant hand smashed onto the "frozen face of the deep."

Program Resources

For further instruction, refer students to the following extension activity: Critical Literacy: Hold a Debate, *Exceeding the Standards: Extension Activities*, pp. 12–13.

Analyze Literature

Description A writer's ability to describe events, settings, and characters depends on how well he or she chooses words and images. Make a three-column chart to record some of Armstrong's most effective word choices. Skim the selection, looking for images that affected you strongly. As you notice images, sort them into their proper columns on your chart.

Sensory Details	Precise Words	Figurative Language
Water seems to stiffen and turn greasy.	sentimental keepsakes	"like wrinkles in a huge white blanket"

Extend Understanding

Writing Options

Creative Writing Suppose that you are the leader of a ship's crew facing life or death in Antarctica. Write a one-paragraph **journal entry** about how you feel. Use sensory details, precise words, and figurative language as necessary to express your situation in a limited amount of space. This paper will be sent with the members of your party who are heading off to find help. Reread your paragraph to imagine how seeing it might affect your friends and family as they wait for your return.

Expository Writing How would you describe the mood of "The Face of the Deep Is Frozen"? Think about the setting. Then, in a one-paragraph **literary response,** explain how you think the setting affects the mood of the piece. Recall the author's use of sensory details to evoke the setting, and give an example or two in your paragraph.

Lifelong Learning

Summarize an Incident Use library resources to find out more about the expedition involving Shackleton and the crew of *Endurance*. You could find the book Armstrong wrote about it, encyclopedia articles, and videos or DVDs of dramatizations. Then prepare a poster for display in class that summarizes the incident. Consider using visual devices, such as photographs or time lines, to convey information in your poster.

Critical Literacy

Hold a Debate In a small group, review "The Face of the Deep Is Frozen" to specifically look for decisions that Ernest Shackleton made. Choose one decision that seems most clearly to have involved a difficult choice, and discuss the pros and cons. Then divide into two debate teams and conduct a ten-minute debate, with one side supporting Shackleton's decision and the other side criticizing it. When your debate is over, talk for a minute about why leaders have to make decisions like this one, and what qualities often characterize a good leader.

Go to **www.mirrorsandwindows.com** for more.

Rubrics for Writing Options

You can adapt this as a checklist for students to use as they write.

Creative Writing
- ☐ Did the student write as an explorer in uncertain circumstances?
- ☐ Does the entry include vivid descriptions and feelings?
- ☐ Is the entry no longer than one paragraph?

Expository Writing
- ☐ Is the response confined to one paragraph?
- ☐ Does the response describe both setting and mood?
- ☐ Does the response include at least one example of Armstrong's use of sensory detail?

Vocabulary & Spelling

Context Clues

Brazen and fierce, they will take on large adversaries—even cats, dogs or humans.

—DIANE ACKERMAN, "Mute Dancers: How to Watch a Hummingbird"

You can often figure out the meaning of a word from **context clues**: words, phrases, or sentences that provide information about the word. In the quote above, examples of hummingbirds' courage help you define the word *brazen*.

Sometimes you can determine a word's meaning by what it is **compared** to or **contrasted** with.

> EXAMPLE
>
> *Comparison*
>
> *The wings are <u>transparent</u>, like glass.*

> EXAMPLE
>
> *Contrast*
>
> *Some believed hummingbirds were <u>supernatural</u>, and not bound by nature's laws.*

You might be able to define a word by a writer's brief **definition** or **description** of it.

> EXAMPLE
>
> *Definition*
>
> *The hummingbirds drink <u>nectar</u>, a sweet fluid that comes from plants.*

> EXAMPLE
>
> *Description*
>
> *<u>Hummingbirds</u> are very small birds that drink from flowers and float soundlessly in the air.*

You may also be able to determine a word's meaning by a writer's use of **examples** or his or her **restatement** of the word with a synonym.

> EXAMPLE
>
> *Example*
>
> *The bird's <u>coverts</u>, such as the feathers that cover part of its wing, are brightly colored.*

> EXAMPLE
>
> *Restatement*
>
> *The hummingbird's <u>bill</u>, or beak, is very slender.*

Vocabulary Practice

For each of the following sentences, use context clues to define the underlined word.

1. In contrast to the sparrow's <u>drab</u> feathers, the hummingbird's brilliant, colorful feathers were a shock.
2. The <u>verdant</u> jungle was filled with unending lush green plants.
3. The flower's <u>crimson</u> petals were as bright and rich as cherries.
4. The bird's <u>plumule</u>, a kind of soft feather, was nearly colorless.
5. The feathers on the <u>pinion</u>, unlike the feathers on the inner part of the wing, are used to support the bird in flight.

Vocabulary Practice

1. *Drab* means "having a dull or uninteresting color."
2. *Verdant* means "green and lush."
3. *Crimson* means "deep red."
4. *Plumule* means "soft, downy feather."
5. *Pinion* means "outer wing."

> For more information, see Vocabulary & Spelling Section 2.1, Using Context Clues, in the Language Arts Handbook.

Program Resources

You will find additional lessons on Context Clues in the *Exceeding the Standards: Vocabulary & Spelling* resource.

KEY TERMS

TEACHING NOTE

Extra Practice

Each sentence below contains one of the types of context clues discussed in this lesson (see the list above the practice questions). Have students match the sentence to the type of context clue.

1. The painting's composition, or arrangement of all the parts, is quite bizarre. (restatement)
2. Eleanor's forensic skills, such as winning debates, set her apart from other girls. (example)
3. Alex excels at clog dancing, which is like tap dancing but with wooden shoes. (comparison)
4. The planet's orbit is an ellipse, an elongated circle that resembles an oval. (definition)
5. In contrast to lemonade, melonade is made with melons. (contrast)
6. Lyric poems are often memorable because they have a musical rhythm. (description)

Common Core State Standards

Language
L.4, L.5, L.6

Preview the Selection

At a Glance
Directed Reading
- Reading Level: Moderate
- Difficulty Consideration: Topic
- Ease Factors: Visual format and point of view

Objectives
Studying this lesson will enable students to
- use reading skills such as identifying a sequence of events
- evaluate author's purpose in visual media such as a storycloth
- compare visual and written narratives by two Laotian refugees
- appreciate true stories of emigration

Launch the Lesson
Define exile for students as a forced absence from one's country or home. Ask them to give you examples of modern-day and historical exiles. After you have heard several examples, ask students to discuss in small groups why people react strongly to being exiled.

MIRRORS & WINDOWS

The Mirrors & Windows questions at the end of the selection focus on the theme of preserving memories. Before students begin to read, ask: What allows art to communicate from generation to generation?

DIRECTED READING

BEFORE READING

Build Background
Historical Context The Hmong are an ethnic group from Asia. During the Vietnam War, the U.S. government organized thousands of Hmong soldiers to fight against Lao Communists, or Pathet Lao. In 1975 the Pathet Lao won the war. When they did, all the Hmong who had been fighting against the Communists became refugees. Many of them immigrated to the United States. Today there are large Hmong communities in California, Minnesota, and Wisconsin.

Reader's Context How does your family keep a record of its past? Do your parents keep photographs, paintings you did as a child, or family heirlooms? Why do you think people keep records of the past?

Set Purpose
The pictures in a storycloth can be read from top to bottom much like words on a page. As you look at the storycloth, try to determine the story that is being told.

Analyze Literature
Purpose A visual artist can have a purpose in a way similar to an author. What do you think is the **purpose** of this storycloth? For example, is it meant to inform, educate, persuade, or tell a story? As you look at the storycloth, try to determine the artist's reason for creating it.

Meet the Artist
This storycloth was created by **Mee Vang.** Vang, like many Hmong women, is skilled in an intricate and ancient form of embroidery known as *paj ntaub* (pronounced pahn-dow), or "flower cloth." Until the 1900s, the Hmong people had no written language and passed along stories either orally or through pictures. Vang's storycloth describes her family's flight from Laos to Thailand and then to the United States.

Use Reading Skills
Sequence of Events
The order in which events occur is referred to as a *sequence of events.* Fiction and narrative nonfiction are frequently arranged so that the earliest events are described first. As you examine the storycloth, try to determine the sequence of events. Storycloths can be "read" from top to bottom. Use a time line like the one below. List the earliest events at the top of the line.

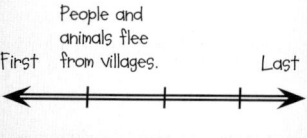

First — People and animals flee from villages. — Last

Words in Use

Teaching Words
communists, 424
refugees, 424
heirlooms, 424
intricate, 424
memorialize, 425
unacquainted, 431

KEY TERMS
VISUAL MEDIA, 424
PURPOSE, 424
SEQUENCE, 424
SENSORY DETAIL, 431
PRECISE LANGUAGE, 431

Common Core State Standards
Reading Informational
RI.5

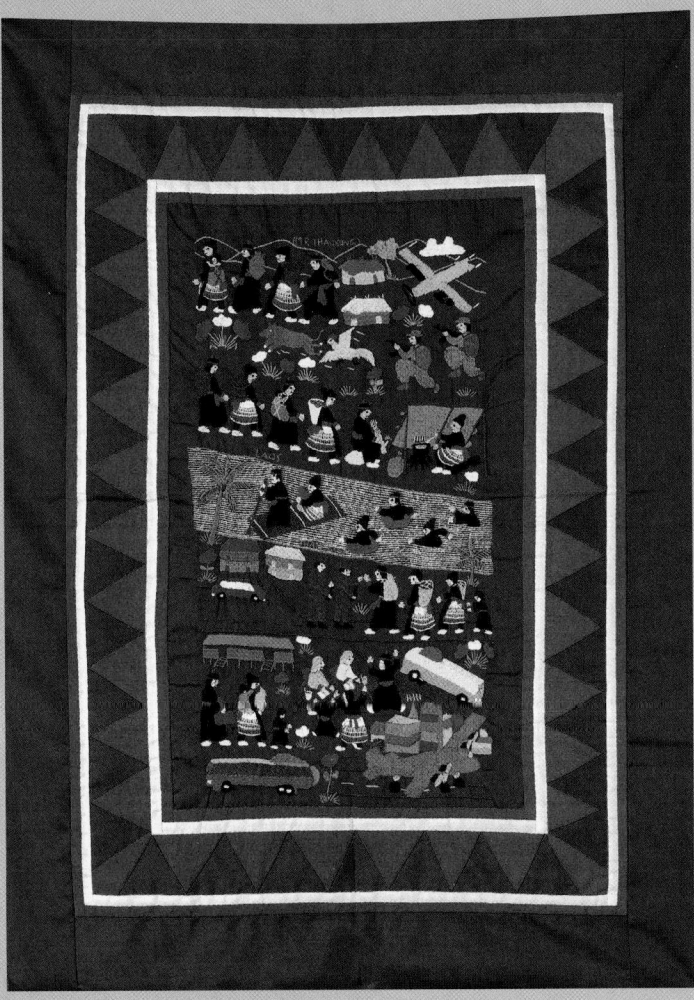

Use Reading Skills
Identify Sequence of Events Have students study the storycloth. Then, ask them to describe the beginning, middle, and ending of the story.

Analyze Literature
Identify Author's Purpose Ask students why they think Vang used this medium, or art form, to tell her story. Then ask if they have ever seen anything similar. For example, some may have seen quilts designed to commemorate an event. If you have taught Faith Ringgold's story quilt (page 348), encourage students to compare and contrast the purposes of the two works of art.

Answer: Students might keep journals, draw pictures, take photographs, or make scrapbooks. Some may say that the value of remembering negative experiences is to learn from them.

Find Meaning
1. They cross a river.
2. Thailand has roads, cars, and more modern-looking buildings, and no war is depicted there.

Make Judgments
3. She may be illustrating the effect of war on traditional village life.
4. These blondes could be Americans in their own country or people from a relief agency.

In what way might you try to memorialize an event in your life? Why might it be important to create something, such as a piece of art or writing, about a period of difficulty or struggle?

Find Meaning
1. How do the refugees depicted in this storycloth escape from Laos?
2. What are some of the differences you notice between the ways in which Laos and Thailand are depicted?

Make Judgments
3. Why do you think Vang included images of animals fleeing the village?
4. Who do you think the women sitting at the table near the bottom of the storycloth are?

HMONG STORYCLOTH **425**

Program Resources

Planning and Assessment
Program Planning Guide, Selection Lesson Plan
E-Lesson Planner
Assessment Guide, Lesson Test
ExamView

Technology Tools
Interactive Student Text on CD
Visual Teaching Package
Audio Library
mirrorsandwindows.com

Meeting the Standards
Nonfiction: Unit 4, Directed Reading, pp. 53–58

Differentiating Instruction
Developing Readers, Take Notes, pp. 31–33

Use Reading Skills

Identify Sequence of Events Have students define *autobiography*. Point out that Xiong uses first-person point of view. Explain that, like the storycloth, this work tells a story in chronological order. Have students make vertical time lines for Xiong's narrative that they can compare to their time lines for the storycloth.

Cultural Connection

Refugees Tell students that as of mid-2007, there were almost twenty-one million refugees around the world. Since 1951, the official international legal definition of a refugee has been "a person who has fled from and/or cannot return to their country" and who has a "well-founded fear of being persecuted for reasons of race, religion, nationality, membership of a particular social group, or political opinion." Suggest that students interested in learning more about refugees visit the website of the United Nations High Commissioner for Refugees (UNHCR), an international organization that tracks world trends, advises governments, and advocates for refugees.

PRIMARY SOURCE ▶▶ CONNECTION

In her storycloth, Mee Vang re-created her family's escape from Laos and the Pathet Lao. The family of **Maijue Xiong** (b. 1972), a writer and educator who lives in St. Paul, Minnesota, experienced events very similar to those Vang's family experienced. In the following autobiographical essay, Xiong describes how her family fled from Laos under extremely difficult and dangerous circumstances. As you read, compare and contrast Xiong's descriptions with Vang's storycloth.

An Unforgettable Journey

An Autobiography by Maijue Xiong

I was born in a small village called Muong Cha in Laos on April 30, 1972. At the time I was born, my father was a soldier actively fighting alongside the American Central Intelligence Agency against the Communists. Although a war was in progress, life seemed peaceful. We did not think of ever leaving Laos, but one day our lives were changed forever.

We found ourselves without a home or a Country and with a need to seek refuge in another country. This period of relocation involved a lot of changes, adjustments, and adaptations. We experienced changes in our language, customs, traditional values, and social status.[1] Some made the transition quickly; others have never fully adjusted. The changes my family and I experienced are the foundation of my identity today.

After Laos became a Communist country in 1975, my family, along with many others, fled in fear of persecution.[2] Because my father had served as a commanding officer for eleven years with the American Central

Intelligence Agency in what is known to the American public as the "Secret War," my family had no choice but to leave immediately. My father's life was in danger, along with those of thousands of others. We were forced to leave loved ones behind, including my grandmother who was ill in bed the day we fled our village. For a month, my family walked through the dense tropical jungles and rice fields, along rugged trails through many mountains, and battled the powerful Mekong River.[3] We traveled in silence at night and slept in the daytime. Children were very hard to keep quiet. Many parents feared the Communist soldiers would hear the cries of their young children; therefore, they drugged the children with opium to keep them quiet. Some parents even left those children who would not stop

---

1. **social status.** Position of a person in society, whether high, middle, or lower class
2. **persecution.** Act of injuring others or causing them to suffer, usually because of their beliefs
3. **Mekong River.** River in southeast Asia that forms part of the border between Laos and Thailand

Words in Use

"An Unforgettable Journey"

Selection Words
transition, 426
bribed, 427
refugee, 428
obscure, 429
sponsored, 429
stable, 430

Common Core State Standards

Speaking and Listening
SL.2, SL.3

crying behind. Fortunately, whenever my parents told my sisters and me to keep quiet, we listened and obeyed.

I do not remember much about our flight, but I do have certain memories that have been imprinted in my mind. It is all so unclear—the experience was like a bad dream: when you wake up, you don't remember what it was you had dreamed about but recall only those bits and pieces of the dream that stand out the most. I remember sleeping under tall trees. I was like a little ant placed in a field of tall grass, surrounded by a dense jungle with trees and bushes all around me—right, left, in the back, and in front of me. I also remember that it rained a lot and that it was cold. We took only what we could carry and it was not much. My father carried a sack of rice, which had to last us the whole way. My mother carried one extra change of clothing for each of us, a few personal belongings, and my baby sister on her back. My older sister and I helped carry pots and pans. My stepuncle carried water, dried meat, and his personal belongings.

From the jungles to the open fields, we walked along a path. We came across a trail of red ants and being a stubborn child, I refused to walk over them. I wanted someone to pick me up because I was scared, but my parents kept walking ahead. They kept telling me to hurry up and to step over the ants, but I just stood there and cried. Finally, my father came back and put me on his shoulders, along with the heavy sack of rice he was carrying. My dad said he carried me on his back practically all the way to Thailand.

I also recall a car accident we had. My father had paid a truckdriver to take my family and relatives to a nearby town. There were about fifteen of us in the truck. My father, along with the driver and my pregnant aunt, sat in front. The rest of us were in the bed of the truck. While going up a steep mountain, the truck got out of control and, instead of going uphill, started sliding downhill and off the road. Everyone was terrified, but with the help of God, the truck was stopped by a tree stump. Everyone panicked and scrambled out, except for my pregnant aunt who was trapped on the passenger's side because the door was jammed. The impact affected her so much that she could not crawl from her seat to the driver's side in order to get out. My father risked his life to save hers. The rest of us stood back and waited breathlessly as he

Our adventure did not end then—many nights filled with terror were yet to come.

tried to open the jammed door. He managed to free her just as the truck slid down the hill.

Our adventure did not end then—many nights filled with terror were yet to come. After experiencing many cold days and rainy nights, we finally saw Thailand on the other side of the Mekong River. My parents bribed several fishermen to row us across. The fishermen knew we were desperate, yet, instead of helping us, they took advantage of us. We had to give them all our valuables: silver bars, silver coins, paper money, and my mother's silver wedding necklace, which had cost a lot of money. When it got dark, the fishermen came back

Teach the Connection

Analyze Literature

Tone Remind students to pay attention to the language the narrator uses. Ask: "What does her language tell about her attitude? What does it tell about *her*?" Have students distinguish between the factual reporting of the first three paragraphs and the emotional content of the fourth paragraph, as when Xiong recounts her recollections of a "bad dream." Ⓐ

Use Reading Skills

Identify Author's Purpose Ask students to think about why the writer chose to tell her story. What connections can people today make with a story like this from the past? After they identify a purpose for the autobiography, have students discuss how the Hmong experience is similar to or different from other immigrant experiences today.

History Connection

Control of Laos Pathet Lao, which means "Land of Laos," first formed in the 1950s and was committed to the communist struggle against colonial occupation by France. After Laos gained independent status, however, years of civil struggle ensued. A coalition government was recognized in 1973, but after the fall of Vietnam and Cambodia to the communists in 1975, the coalition government collapsed and the Pathet Lao took control, forcing thousands to flee.

Grammar Skills

Dependent and Independent Clauses

Remind students that a dependent, or subordinate, clause must be attached to an independent, or main, clause. For example, in the sentence "When I left Laos, I was only three years old," the first clause is dependent—it cannot stand alone—and the second is independent.

Have students identify the independent and dependent clauses in the following sentences.
1. After we found him, we went inside and saw our mother mourning the baby's death.
2. Our relatives, whom we were leaving behind, walked my family from our house to the bus.
3. The first day was scary because I couldn't speak any English.

Use Reading Skills

Compare and Contrast Point out that although the sequence of events in this narrative is similar to that of the Hmong storycloth, there are several differences. Have students compare the stories section by section. For example, have them discuss how Xiong's description of her experience crossing the Mekong River differs from the scene portrayed in the storycloth. **A**

Make Connections

Ask students to discuss how they feel about the descriptions of violent events in Xiong's story. For example, she describes the death of her baby sister as a matter of fact, but says that it "still burns in my mind like a flame." Have students discuss what the expression conveys to them about the pain of losing a sister. **B**

Hmong refugee camp in Thailand.

A with a small fishing boat and took us across the river. The currents were high and powerful. I remember being very scared. I kept yelling, "We're going to fall out! We're going to fall into the river!" My mom tried to reassure me but I kept screaming in fear. Finally, we got across safely. My family, along with many other families, were picked up by the Thai police and taken to an empty bus station for the night.

After a whole month at this temporary refugee camp set up in the bus station, during which we ate rice, dried fish, roots we dug up, and bamboo shoots we cut down, and drank water from streams, we were in very poor shape due to the lack of nutrition. Our feet were also swollen from walking. We were then taken to a refugee camp in Nongkhai, where disease was rampant[4] and **B** many people got sick. My family suffered a loss: my baby sister, who was only a few months old, died. She had become very skinny from the lack of milk, and there was no medical care available. The memory of her

death still burns in my mind like a flame. On the evening she died, my older sister and I were playing with our cousins outside the building where we stayed. My father came out to tell us the sad news and told us to go find my stepuncle. After we found him, we went inside and saw our mother mourning the baby's death. Fortunately, our family had relatives around to support and comfort us.

Life in the refugee camp was very difficult. Rice, fish, vegetables, and water were delivered to the camp, but the ration for each family was never enough. Many times, the food my family received did not last until the next delivery. My parents went out to work in the fields to earn a little extra money to buy food. As a child, I did not understand why we had to work so hard and live so poorly.

When I left Laos, I was only three years old. I do not remember much of our life there, but my parents have told me that our family had been quite well off. We had our

---

4. **rampant.** Wild or unrestrained

Differentiated Instruction

Enrichment

Encourage pairs of students or small groups to learn the story of a group of refugees. Students can interview people they know, read books or articles from the library, or use the Internet. Direct them to answer the following questions:

1. Why did the refugees have to leave their homeland?

2. How did they make their escape?

3. Where did they find refuge?

4. What are they doing now?

Have students present their refugee experiences to the class. Ask the class to take notes and ask questions to generate ideas for further research.

own house, cattle, rice fields, and a garden where all our vegetables were grown. The money my father received for serving in the army was saved, for there was little need for money. We had enough to eat because we grew our own food. The poor life in the camp is the only life I can remember. I saw my parents' suffering, but I was too young to understand why life was so difficult. Only later did I realize that I and thousands of other young children were victims of a cruel war. Our family remained in Nongkhai for three agonizing years, with our fate uncertain and our future obscure.

Our family life in the camp was very unstable, characterized by deprivation[5] and neglect. My older sister and I were left alone for days while my parents were outside the camp trying to earn money to buy extra food. My parents fought a lot during this period, because we were all under such stress. They knew that if we remained in Thailand, there would be no telling what would become of us. We had to find a better life. Some people in the camp were being sponsored to go to the United States. The news spread that anyone who had served in the military with the CIA could apply to go to America. Since my stepuncle had already gone there two years earlier, he sponsored my family. Because my father had been in the military and we had a sponsor, it took only six months to process our papers when usually it took a year or more.

I can still recall the process of leaving the camp. Our relatives, whom we were leaving behind, walked my family from our house to the bus that was to take us to Bangkok. We boarded the bus with our few belongings. People hung out of the windows to touch loved ones for the last time. They cried, knowing they might never meet again. As the buses slowly made their way through the crowd, people ran after them calling out the names of their relatives. "Have a safe trip to your new home!" they shouted. "Don't forget us who are left behind! Please write and tell us about your new life!" Quickly the camp vanished out of sight...forever. The moments filled with laughter and tears shared with close friends and relatives were now just faint memories.

It took a full day to travel to Bangkok, where we stayed for four nights. The building we stayed in was one huge room. It was depressing and nerve-wracking. I especially remember how, when we got off the bus to go into the building, a small child about my age came up to my family to beg for food. I recall the exact words she said to my father, "Uncle, can you give me some food? I am hungry. My parents are dead and I am here alone." My dad gave her a piece of bread that we had packed for our lunch. After she walked away, my family found an empty corner and rolled out our bedding for the night. That night, the same child came around again, but people chased her away, which made me sad.

In the morning, I ran to get in line for breakfast. Each person received a bowl of rice porridge with a few strips of chicken in it. For four days, we remained in that building, not knowing when we could leave for the United States. Many families had been there for weeks, months, perhaps even years. On the fourth day, my family was notified to be ready early the next morning to be taken to the airport. The plane ride took a long time and I got motion sickness. I threw up a lot. Only when I saw my stepuncle's face after we landed did I know we had come to the end of our journey. We had come in search of a better life in the "land of giants."

On October 2, 1978, my family arrived at Los Angeles International Airport, where

5. **deprivation.** State of being in need

Teach the Connection

Make Connections
Have students describe the departure scene in their own words. Then invite students to share their own experiences of leaving friends or relatives behind when moving to a new place. Ask: "How did your experiences resemble this departure scene, if at all?" **C**

Use Reading Skills
Reread Ask students to pause to review the number of departures the narrator and her family have made up to this point in the story. Encourage them to make notes as they reread the selection to count the number of departures.

Cultural Connection
Child Refugees According to the UNHCR website, refugee children who are not with their parents (and not child soldiers) can be either unaccompanied or separated. An unaccompanied child has no adult caregiver whatsoever. A separated child may be with relatives, but has lost contact with his or her parents or primary caregivers. Both categories of children are at high risk for long-lasting emotional and physical damage. **D**

Grammar Skills

Direct Quotations
Point out to students that Xiong includes a few direct quotations in her story, such as when the child begs for food in the refugee camp. Remind students that direct quotations are capitalized as sentences and have quotation marks at the beginning and end of the words spoken. Also remind them that quotes are separated by a comma from the identification of the speaker.

Have students correctly punctuate and capitalize the following quotations.
1. My father said sadly your little sister has died.
2. Don't ask for food again cried the people.
3. The woman said that airplane will take you to America.

Analyze Literature

Theme Have students state a theme they think is shared by the Hmong storycloth and "An Unforgettable Journey." Model a possible response: "Both works portray struggles, so the theme might be that struggle changes a person." Themes could relate to struggle, the strength of family ties, and the desire for freedom.

Use Reading Skills

Analyze Author's Purpose Have students explain the purpose of Xiong's last paragraph. Ask: "Is this paragraph's purpose the same as the writer's overall purpose? Why or why not?" Suggest students consider what college graduation will mean to Xiong and to her family.

Use Reading Skills

Identify Sequence of Events Have students complete their time lines for this narrative. Ask them to highlight events that resemble events in the storycloth on page 425.

Text-to-Text Connection

Answer: Some students will find Xiong's descriptions more compelling than those in the storycloth, because the narrative contains more details and personal insights. Others will say the storycloth gave them an insight into Hmong culture that they could not have found in the narrative.

my uncle was waiting anxiously. We stayed with my uncle in Los Angeles for two weeks and then settled in Isla Vista because there were already a few Hmong families there. We knew only one family in Isla Vista, but later we met other families whom my parents had known in their village and from villages nearby. It was in Isla Vista that my life really began. My home life was now more stable. My mother gave

Hmong girl at a refugee camp in Thailand. The sign reads "Dangerous Area."

birth to a boy a month after we arrived in the United States. It was a joyous event because the first three children she had were all girls. (Boys are desired and valued far more than girls in Hmong culture).

I entered kindergarten at Isla Vista Elementary School. The first day was scary because I could not speak any English. Fortunately, my cousin, who had been in the United States for three years and spoke English, was in the same class with me. She led me to the playground where the children were playing. I was shocked to see so many faces of different colors. The Caucasian students shocked me the most. I had never seen people with blond hair before. The sight sent me to a bench, where I sat and watched everyone in amazement. In class, I was

introduced to coloring. I did not know how to hold a crayon or what it was for. My teacher had to show me how to color. I also soon learned the alphabet. This was the beginning of my lifelong goal to get an education...

Now that I am older, I treasure the long but valuable lessons my parents tried to teach us—lessons that gave me a sense of identity as a Hmong. "Nothing comes easy...," my parents always said. As I attempt to get a college education, I remember how my parents have been really supportive of me throughout my schooling, but because they never had a chance to get an education themselves, they were not able to help me whenever I could not solve a math problem or write an English paper. Although they cannot help me in my schoolwork, I know in my heart that they care about me and want me to be successful so that I can help them when they can no longer help themselves. Therefore, I am determined to do well at the university. I want to become a role model for my younger brother and sisters, for I am the very first member of my family to attend college. I feel a real sense of accomplishment to have set such an example. ❖

TEXT → TEXT CONNECTION In "An Unforgettable Journey" Maijue Xiong describes how she and her family encountered and overcame many obstacles, including hunger, sadness, and death. How does her description compare with the depiction of similar events in Vang's storycloth?

Differentiated Instruction

Enrichment

Interested students may find more information about Hmong émigrés to the United States and the communities they have established. Suggest that they start with the website for the national Hmong organization, founded in 1993, or write to the Hmong National Development Organization in Washington, D.C. They may present their findings to the class.

Analyze Literature

Purpose Artists, like authors, often have a purpose or multiple purposes when creating their work. For example, they might wish to inform, educate, or persuade. Re-examine Vang's storycloth and try to determine her purpose or purposes. Create a two-column chart. In the first column, create a list of details from the storycloth. Then, in the second column, list Vang's purpose or purposes.

Detail	Purpose
infants strapped to parents' backs	

Extend Understanding

Writing Options

Creative Writing Imagine that you are an art critic for a newspaper. Write a **descriptive essay** about Vang's storycloth. Describe the storycloth using sensory details and precise language. Be sure to include background information for readers unacquainted with the events depicted in the storycloth.

Expository Writing Using Vang's storycloth, Maijue Xiong's autobiography, and your own research, write a brief **historical essay** about the flight of the Hmong from Laos to Thailand. Describe the dangerous trek through jungles and across the Mekong River. Include details about the situation in the refugee camps and the ability of some refugees to escape to the United States. Use direct quotations from your research and "An Unforgettable Journey." Be sure you distinguish between factual claims, commonplace assertions, and opinions as you do your research. In your own essay, avoid using commonplace assertions, and support your opinions with facts and logical arguments.

Critical Literacy

Analyze a Speech A **policy speech** attempts to persuade a listener to support a change in government policy and contains quotations from experts and arguments that address policy issues. Identify and read the text of a contemporary speech that addresses refugee or immigration policies. Interpret the purpose by asking questions or making comments about the evidence presented. Finally, analyze the structure of the speech's central argument and identify the different types of evidence used to support the argument.

Lifelong Learning

Research Southeast Asia In groups of four or five, research Laos, Vietnam, or Cambodia. Use Internet or library resources to find out about the present political structure of the country you choose, its geography, its population, its languages, and any other important information. Divide tasks between group members and establish an agenda with clear goals and deadlines. Once you have completed your research, present your findings to the class. Be sure to set time limits for speakers and to take notes as other groups present their own research.

Go to **www.mirrorsandwindows.com** for more.

Analyze Literature

Purpose Students should recognize that the purpose of the storycloth is both to inform and to tell a story. The artist is informing her viewers of the plight of the Hmong during the war and offering a narrative about her family's experiences.

Rubrics for Writing Options

You can adapt this as a checklist for students to use as they write.

Creative Writing

☐ Does the essay accurately describe the content of the storycloth?

☐ Does the essay use sensory details and precise language?

☐ Does the essay include relevant background information?

Expository Writing

☐ Does the essay describe the Hmong's flight from Laos to Thailand?

☐ Does the essay include details about the refugee camps?

☐ Does the essay use direct quotations from student research and "An Unforgettable Journey"?

Preview the Selection

At a Glance
Directed Reading
- Reading Level: Moderate
- Difficulty Consideration: Topic
- Ease Factors: Visual format and imagery

Objectives
Studying this lesson will enable students to
- use reading skills such as activating prior knowledge
- practice determining the purpose of visual media
- describe the work of Arthur Rothstein and Margaret Bourke-White
- appreciate the historical value of photographs

Launch the Lesson
Have students work in pairs for one minute to define photojournalism based on their previous knowledge. Ask volunteers to offer some definitions to the class. Then tell students they are about to study the work of two famous photojournalists from the mid-twentieth century.

MIRRORS & WINDOWS

The Mirrors & Windows questions at the end of the selection focus on the theme of coping with disaster. Before students begin reading, ask: What natural disasters do we need to worry about in our hometown?

DIRECTED READING

BEFORE READING

Build Background
Historical Context As the nation sank into the Great Depression of the 1930s, eight years of drought, combined with misguided farming practices, eroded the Great Plains. When farmers tore out grasses to plant wheat, they removed roots that had held the soil in place. Without water, the topsoil dried out and blew away. The Dust Bowl stretched from Texas to the Dakotas and from Arkansas to Wyoming and New Mexico. It generated huge clouds of grit and eventually displaced over half a million people.

Reader's Context Does your family keep old photographs? Why do you think that is? What can old photographs offer you?

Set Purpose
As you look at the following images of the Dust Bowl, look at the difficulties the people in each photograph faced.

Analyze Literature
Purpose Is there a difference between photographs meant to tell a story—pictures by photojournalists or documentary photographers, for example—and other kinds? What do you think the purpose of these photographs is? For example, are they meant to inform, educate, or persuade? As you look at the photographs, try to determine the photographer's reason for taking them.

Meet the Photographer
In 1935, **Arthur Rothstein** (1915–1985) joined the Resettlement Administration, which became the Farm Security Administration in 1937. His job was to take photographs of the rural poor. Among Rothstein's most famous photographs are those of Dust Bowl farms and people in Gee's Bend, Alabama. After leaving the government, Rothstein worked for *Look* magazine and as a photographer during World War II.

Use Reading Skills
Activate Prior Knowledge You probably know something about the Great Depression and the Dust Bowl from studying American history. If you live in a state in the Great Plains or in a state to which Dust Bowl migrants relocated, you may know people who experienced these things firsthand. Before you study Rothstein's photographs, activate your prior knowledge using a K-W-L chart like this one.

What I Already Know	What I Want to Learn	What I Learn
The Dust Bowl destroyed farms.	Did people stay in the Dust Bowl?	

Words in Use

Teaching Words
drought, 432
misguided, 432
photojournalist, 432
endure, 435
inappropriate, 435
formulate, 439

KEY TERMS
VISUAL MEDIA, 432
PURPOSE, 432
ESSAY, 436
OUTLINE, 439
PLOT DIAGRAM, 439
EXPOSITION, 439
RISING ACTION, 439
CLIMAX, 439
FALLING ACTION, 439
RESOLUTION, 439

Common Core State Standards
Speaking and Listening
SL.2, SL.3

Playing on Farm, 1936. Arthur Rothstein.

433

Analyze Literature

Identify Author's Purpose Ask students to infer, based on Build Background and their prior knowledge, why Rothstein took the photograph on this page. Remind them that he worked for the government and had the assignment to document conditions of the rural poor. Model one approach to answering the question: "The title of the photo is 'Playing on Farm,' but this boy does not seem to be having any fun at all. I think Rothstein was trying to be sarcastic, and his purpose was to persuade people to help Dust Bowl farmers. He tries to do this by showing that playing was hard to do under the circumstances."

Use Reading Skills

Activate Prior Knowledge Ask students to share their prior knowledge about the Dust Bowl. Write their comments on the board. Suggest that they refer to the list on the board as they view the photos.

Literary Connection

John Steinbeck Tell students that John Steinbeck's famous novel *The Grapes of Wrath* chronicles the uprooting of an Oklahoma family (Okies) who head to California seeking a better life. Students may want to view the film based on the novel, which starred Henry Fonda as the leader of the Joad family.

Program Resources

Planning and Assessment
Program Planning Guide, Selection Lesson Plan
E-Lesson Planner
Assessment Guide, Lesson Test
ExamView

Technology Tools
Interactive Student Text on CD
Visual Teaching Package
Audio Library
mirrorsandwindows.com

Meeting the Standards
Nonfiction: Unit 4, Directed Reading, pp. 59–65

Differentiating Instruction
Advanced Students, Critical Viewing Activity, p. 23

Literary Connection

Oral Histories Tell students that even at the time, people knew that the Dust Bowl and Great Depression were events of historical proportions. Since the 1930s, many people have made an effort to learn what it was like to live during those times. The Library of Congress, many state historical societies and libraries, and academic institutions house collections of oral histories that describe personal experiences during the Dust Bowl. Some are written and some are in audio recordings. You might wish to offer students an opportunity to read or hear such stories as part of this lesson.

Use Reading Strategies

Clarify Encourage students to take time to identify and interpret details of the photographs. Model one approach using the top photograph: "I wonder why the smaller boy is behind his father and brother. Are they all hurrying, without taking time to stop and help each other? Is it because the storm is coming so fast? And look at that doorway. Can they get into this building if they want to? What would it be like in there?" Give students prompts as necessary to help them clarify what each photo depicts, and what Rothstein wanted the viewer to notice. For example, suggest that they focus on fences in each picture, or on animals.

Farmer and Sons Walking in the Face of a Dust Storm, 1936. Arthur Rothstein.

Dust Bowl Farmer Raising a Fence to Keep It from Being Buried under Drifting Sand, 1936. Arthur Rothstein.

434 UNIT 4 NONFICTION

Differentiated Instruction

Visual Learning

Have students carefully observe the land and sky around the main figures in the photographs. Suggest that they write a descriptive paragraph about either the land or the sky, and explain its effect on the impact of each photograph.

Enrichment

Ask students to interview a visual artist about the composition of these photographs. Have students work in teams to prepare questions and locate several people they might talk with. Help them set up an interview with appropriate supervision. After the students have conducted the interview, ask them to describe the strengths of Rothstein's compositions to the class.

Cows Huddling Next to a Windmill in the Dust Bowl, 1936. Arthur Rothstein.

How might a drought—a whole year without rain or snow—affect your region? Is there anything people can do to change the course of a natural disaster like a drought, or are natural disasters something people just have to endure?

Find Meaning

1. In *Farmer and Sons Walking in the Face of a Dust Storm,* what do you think the people are doing?
2. (a) In what ways is the title *Playing on Farm* an inappropriate title for this image? (b) Why do you think Rothstein chose this title?
3. What do the cows in *Cows Huddling Next to a Windmill in the Dust Bowl* suggest about what the land used to be?

Make Judgments

4. In *Dust Bowl Farmer Raising a Fence,* what does the landscape suggest about the challenges the farmer faces?
5. (a) Using sensory details, describe the storm depicted in *Farmer and Sons Walking in the Face of a Dust Storm.* How does the image make you feel? (b) Why do you think the photographer took this picture?
6. Imagine yourself as a member of the intended audience for these pictures in 1936. What would be your response?

DUST BOWL PHOTOGRAPHS **435**

Teach the Selection

Answer: Most regions would lose some crops or other plant life during a drought. Most natural disasters can't be prevented, but some students will observe that planning, such as earthquake preparedness measures and hurricane evacuation procedures, can mitigate their effects.

Find Meaning

1. They are seeking shelter.
2. (a) The boy seems to be holding a puppy, but there is no pleasure in his expression. He is in a strange place for playing. (b) He wanted to show how bleak farm life was.
3. The land used to have pasture for grazing.

Make Judgments

4. The challenges are insurmountable; he will have to raise the fence over and over and over.
5. (a) Students might use words like *dark, windy, suffocating, dry,* and *hot.* The image could evoke fear or panic. (b) Answers will vary.
6. Answers may range from concern for those affected by the Dust Bowl to experiencing a feeling of relief that the conditions are happening somewhere else in the country.

Speaking & Listening Skills

Oral Summary

Ask students what they think of when they hear the phrase "a picture is worth a thousand words." Point out that each of Rothstein's photographs expresses facts, opinions, and feelings that would take many words to describe.

Have students prepare oral summaries of the photographs. Instruct them to choose one photograph, and then make notes about its main message and the details that convey the message. Give them opportunities to rehearse their summaries in pairs. Then they can take turns delivering their summaries to the class.

DUST BOWL PHOTOGRAPHS **435**

Use Reading Strategies

Visualize Tell students to look for the images the author uses in this essay. Point out that Bourke-White, like Rothstein, was a photographer and therefore visually oriented. She was also a journalist and conveyed images through her words. Have students pick out two or three strong visual descriptions and explain their effects.

Analyze Literature

Figurative Language Point out Bourke-White's use of simile and hyperbole. For example, clouds creep up "like formless fog" or approach "like a tornado" and soil blows by "as a murky yellow haze." Hyperbole appears in the form of humorous tall-tale devices, as when Bourke-White quotes the locals as saying they just saw their uncle's "farm go by," and again when she relates the tale of the bachelor who used a storm to clean his pots and pans. Have volunteers tell how such figurative language affects them.

TEACHING NOTE

Comprehension Check

Bourke-White's prose is dense with imagery and sophisticated vocabulary. Have struggling readers pause after they read each paragraph to ask questions and determine the main idea. Check their comprehension. After they read the essay once in this fashion, ask a group to read it aloud, all the way through.

INFORMATIONAL TEXT ▶▶ CONNECTION

Arthur Rothstein took pictures of the Dust Bowl. Another prominent photojournalist of the 1930s was **Margaret Bourke-White** (1906–1971). She initially specialized in taking pictures of architecture and industrial operations. As her career developed, she traveled the world. In this essay, she describes a firsthand experience with the Dust Bowl. While you read, try to visualize what she describes.

Dust Changes America

An Essay by Margaret Bourke-White

Vitamin K they call it—the dust which sifts under the door sills, and stings in the eyes, and seasons every spoonful of food. The dust storms have distinct personalities, rising in formation like rolling clouds, creeping up silently like formless fog, approaching violently like a tornado. Where has it come from? It provides topics of endless speculation. Red, it is the topsoil from Oklahoma; brown, it is the fertile earth of western Kansas; the good grazing land of Texas and New Mexico sweeps by as a murky yellow haze. Or, tracing it locally, "My uncle will be along pretty soon," they say; "I just saw his farm go by."

The town dwellers stack their linen in trunks, stuff wet cloths along the window sills, estimate the tons of sand in the darkened air above them, paste cloth masks on their faces with adhesive tape, and try to joke about Vitamin K. But on the farms and ranches there is an attitude of despair.

By coincidence I was in the same parts of the country where last year I photographed the drought. As short a time as eight months ago there was an attitude of false optimism. "Things will get better," the farmers would say. "We're not as hard hit as other states.

The government will help out. This can't go on." But this year there is an atmosphere of utter hopelessness. Nothing to do. No use digging out your chicken coops and pigpens after the last "duster" because the next one will be coming along soon. No use trying to keep the house clean. No use fighting off that foreclosure[1] any longer. No use even hoping to give your cattle anything to chew on when their food crops have literally blown out of the ground.

It was my job to avoid dust storms, since I was commissioned by an airplane company to take photographs of its course from the air, but frequently the dust storms caught up with us, and as we were grounded anyway, I started to photograph them. Thus I saw five dust-storm states from the air and from the ground.

In the last several years there have been droughts and sand storms and dusters, but they have been localized, and always one state could borrow from another. But this year the scourge[2] assumes tremendous proportions. Dust storms are bringing

---

1. **foreclosure.** Taking of property because the person who borrowed money to buy it has not made payments
2. **scourge.** Punishment

Words in Use

"Dust Changes America"

Selection Words
sifts, 436
commissioned, 436
panhandle, 437
gale, 437
adrift, 437
plight, 438
stark, 438

Differentiated Instruction

Visual Learning

Students may better appreciate Bourke-White's descriptions if they think of them as photographs in words. Have students work in small groups to identify descriptions that have a photographic quality to them. Have artistic students sketch some of the images.

distress and death to 300,000 square miles; they are blowing over all of Kansas, all of Nebraska and Wyoming, strips of the Dakotas, about half of Colorado, sections of Iowa and Missouri, the greater part of Oklahoma, and the northern panhandle of Texas, extending into the eastern parts of New Mexico.

Last year I saw farmers harvesting the Russian thistle.[3] Never before had they thought of feeding thistles to cattle. But this prickly fodder[4] became precious for food. This year even the Russian thistles are dying out and the still humbler soap weed[5] becomes as vital to the farmer as the fields of golden grain he tended in the past. Last year's thistle-fed cattle dwindled to skin and bone. This year's herds on their diet of soap weed develop roughened hides, ugly growths around the mouth, and lusterless eyes.

Years of the farmers' and ranchers' lives have gone into the building up of their herds. Their herds were like their families to them. When AAA[6] officials spotted cows and steers for shooting during the cattle-killing days of last summer, the farmers felt as though their own children were facing the bullets. Kansas, a Republican state, has no love for the AAA. This year winds whistled over land made barren by the drought and the crop-conservation program. When Wallace[7] removed the ban on the planting of spring wheat he was greeted by cheers. But the wheat has been blown completely out of the ground. Nothing is left but soap weed, or the expensive cotton-seed cake,[8] and after that—bankruptcy.

The storm comes in a terrifying way. Yellow clouds roll. The wind blows such a gale that it is all my helper can do to hold my camera to the ground. The sand whips into my lens. I repeatedly wipe it away trying to snatch an exposure before it becomes completely coated again. The light becomes yellower, the wind colder. Soon there is no photographic light, and we hurry for shelter to the nearest farmhouse. Three men and a woman are seated around a dust-caked lamp, on their faces grotesque masks of wet cloth. The children have been put to bed with towels tucked over their heads. My host greets us: "It takes grit to live in this country." They are telling stories: A bachelor harnessed the sandblast which ripped through the keyhole by holding his pots and pans in it until they were spick and span. A pilot flying over Amarillo got caught in a sand storm. His motor clogged; he took to his parachute. It took him six hours to shovel his way back to earth. And when a man from the next county was struck by a drop of water, he fainted, and it took two buckets of sand to revive him.

The migrations of the farmer have begun. In many of the worst-hit counties 80 per cent of the families are on relief. In the open farm country one crop failure follows another. After perhaps three successive crop failures the farmer can't stand it any longer. He moves in with relatives and hopes for a job in Arizona or Illinois or some neighboring state where he knows he is not needed. Perhaps he gets a job as a cotton picker, and off he goes with his family, to be turned adrift again after a brief working period.

We passed them on the road, all their household goods piled on wagons, one lucky family on a truck. Lucky, because they had been able to keep their truck when the mortgage was foreclosed. All they owned in the world was packed on it; the children sat

---

3. **Russian thistle.** Prickly plant that American farmers normally treat as a weed
4. **fodder.** Food for livestock
5. **soap weed.** Plant whose leaves release a substance people can use as a detergent
6. **AAA.** Agricultural Adjustment Administration, a crop management program
7. **Wallace.** Henry A. Wallace, secretary of agriculture in the 1930s
8. **cotton-seed cake.** Lump made of cotton seeds after their oil is extracted

Teach the Connection

Critical Viewing

A larger image of this painting appears at the opening of Unit 4. Have students read the title of the painting, and then turn to page 375 and examine it. Ask students to compare the painting and Rothstein's photographs. Encourage each student to write a brief paragraph that describes the most striking image of the Dust Bowl he or she has seen. Suggest that they imitate the style Bourke-White uses in her essay.

History Connection

The New Deal *Answer:* Conserving soil was a first step in preventing spread of the Dust Bowl. The program educated people about how to reduce erosion under drought conditions. In this way, the program helped stem agricultural losses and stabilize the economy. **A**

Use Reading Skills

Identify Author's Purpose Some people say Bourke-White invented the field of photojournalism. Even without using photographs to support her writing, she has a clear viewpoint in her essay. Point out vivid words and phrases she uses, such as *scourge, distress, dwindled to skin and bone, cattle-killing days, terrifying, barren,* and *ripped*. Have students state the purpose behind her choice of such words to describe Dust Bowl scenes.

Text-to-Text Connection

Answer: Students will probably assign a menacing personality to the storm.

The New Deal When Franklin Delano Roosevelt became president in 1933, the national unemployment rate had reached nearly 25 percent. The country was counting on Roosevelt's administration to relieve the economic crisis. During his campaign, Roosevelt promised "a new deal for the American people." In his first one hundred days in office he launched programs to repair the economy. Among them were programs for revitalizing the farm economy. One new agency was the Soil Conservation Service, which offered specific programs to prevent the spread of the Dust Bowl. Why do you think this program was included as part of the New Deal? **A**

Drought Stricken Area, 1934. Alexandre Hogue. Dallas Museum of Art.

on a pile of bureaus topped with mattresses, and the sides of the truck were strapped up with bed springs. The entire family looked like a Ku Klux Klan[9] meeting, their faces done up in masks to protect them from the whirling sand.

Near Hays, Kansas, a little boy started home from school and never arrived there. The neighbors looked for him till ten at night, and all next day a band of two hundred people searched. At twilight they found him, only a quarter of a mile from home, his body nearly covered with silt. He had strangled to death. The man who got lost in his own ten-acre truck garden and wandered around choking and stifling for eight hours before he found his house considered himself lucky to escape with his life. The police and sheriffs are kept constantly busy with calls from anxious parents whose children are lost, and the toll is mounting of people who become marooned and die in the storms.

But the real tragedy is the plight of the cattle. In a rising sand storm cattle quickly become blinded. They run around in circles until they fall and breathe so much dust that they die. Autopsies show their lungs caked with dust and mud. Farmers dread the birth of calves during a storm. The newborn animals will die within twenty-four hours.

And this same dust that coats the lungs and threatens death to cattle and men alike, that ruins the stock of the storekeeper lying unsold on his shelves, that creeps into the gear shifts of automobiles, that sifts through the refrigerator into the butter, that makes housekeeping, and gradually life itself, unbearable, this swirling drifting dust is changing the agricultural map of the United States. It piles ever higher on the floors and beds of a steadily increasing number of deserted farmhouses. A half-buried plowshare, a wheat binder[10] ruffled over with sand, the skeleton of a horse near a dirt-filled water hole are stark evidence of the meager life, the wasted savings, the years of toil that the farmer is leaving behind him. ✤

---

9. **Ku Klux Klan.** Racist terrorist organization whose members wear pointed white hoods
10. **plowshare...wheat binder.** Farm implements; the plowshare cuts furrows in the soil and the wheat binder bundles cut grain into sheaves.

TEXT TO TEXT CONNECTION In her first paragraph, Margaret Bourke-White says dust storms have personalities. What personality would you give to the storm in Rothstein's *Farmer and Sons Walking in the Face of a Dust Storm?*

TEACHING NOTE

Self-Generated Questioning

Ask students to write three questions they would like to ask a survivor of the Dust Bowl. Encourage them to visualize a particular person—young, old, wealthy, poor—in their minds before drafting. Model a question: "When did you first know something was very, very wrong?" Then have students exchange questions and offer each other suggestions for making the questions better.

Analyze Literature

Purpose Re-examine Rothstein's photographs and try to determine his purpose or purposes. Create a two-column chart like this one for each photograph. In the first column, create a list of details from the photograph. Then, in the second column, list Rothstein's purpose or purposes.

Detail	Purpose
boy is carefully holding very small puppy	

Extend Understanding

Writing Options

Creative Writing Imagine you want to dramatize the plight of poor farmers to the president of the United States. Think of a short story you could write based on one of Rothstein's photographs. Focus first on determining the central conflict of the story. Then either **outline** the plot of your story, or use a **plot diagram** that shows the exposition, rising action, climax, falling action, and resolution.

Applied Writing Write a list of at least ten **interview questions** you would like to ask one of the people in Rothstein's photographs. Plan to use your interview to write a short article about life in the Dust Bowl. Formulate questions that you think will help you identify how your subject is coping with the effects of the drought and the bad economic situation.

Collaborative Learning

Trace a Migration In a small group, use library resources to research migrations during the Dust Bowl. Start with a specific place affected by the Dust Bowl, such as Oklahoma. Try to learn where people went and what circumstances greeted them in their new homes. Summarize what you learn to share with the class.

Media Literacy

Visit the Library of Congress Rothstein and many other photographers worked for the government during the 1930s and 1940s. Visit the Library of Congress's collection of related photographs online. You can see more pictures of rural America during the Dust Bowl and learn more about the photographers. Choose a page to recommend, and share the web address with the class.

 Go to **www.mirrorsandwindows.com** for more.

Analyze Literature

Purpose Students may list details of dress, posture, and expression in the people Rothstein pictures. For at least one photograph, they will probably note the dry, barren appearance of the land. Purposes will range from documentary to persuasive. For example, the detail of digging out fence posts might be intended to document the futility of farming in this area.

Rubrics for Writing Options

You can adapt this as a checklist for students to use as they write.

Creative Writing

☐ Does the outline or diagram include exposition, rising action, climax, falling action, and resolution?

☐ Will the story outlined or diagrammed dramatize the plight of poor farmers?

Applied Writing

☐ Does the list include at least ten questions?

☐ Do the questions address the concerns of a person living in the Dust Bowl?

☐ Would the questions elicit information about how the subject is coping with the situation?

Preview the Selection

At a Glance
Independent Reading
- Reading Level: Challenging
- Difficulty Considerations: Concepts and vocabulary
- Ease Factor: Imagery

Objectives
Reading this selection will enable students to do the following:
- read with developing fluency
- read silently with comprehension for a sustained period of time

Launch the Lesson
Tell students they will be reading "Death in the Open," an essay about death. Remind them that the topic is usually a very emotional one and that people often prefer not to talk about it. Point out that we use euphemisms for death, such as "pass away." If appropriate, ask students to offer additional euphemisms.

TEACHING NOTE
Although this selection is presented in the student edition as an independent reading, teaching support has been provided should you choose to cover it in class.

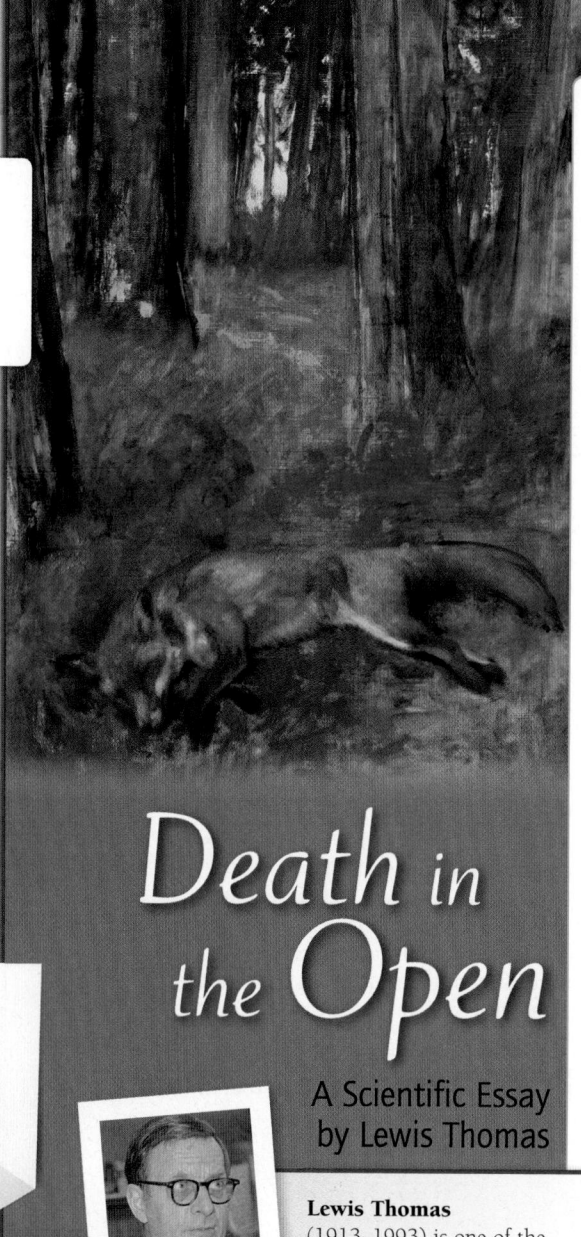

Death in the Open

A Scientific Essay
by Lewis Thomas

Lewis Thomas (1913–1993) is one of the best-known science writers of the last fifty years. Thomas had an extraordinary academic career, attending Princeton and Harvard, and he eventually became the dean of Yale Medical School.

As a doctor and biologist, Thomas displayed a wide-ranging and keen interest in the world, from the microscopic functions of the cell to the ways in which human society interacts with natural processes. His essays written for the *New England Journal of Medicine*, collected in *The Lives of a Cell*, were awarded the National Book Award in 1974.

440

It is the nature of animals to die alone.

Most of the dead animals you see on highways near the cities are dogs, a few cats. Out in the countryside, the forms and coloring of the dead are strange; these are the wild creatures. Seen from a car window they appear as fragments, evoking memories of woodchucks, badgers, skunks, voles, snakes, sometimes the mysterious wreckage of a deer.

It is always a queer shock, part a sudden upwelling of grief, part unaccountable amazement. It is simply astounding to see an animal dead on a highway. The outrage is more than just the location; it is the impropriety[1] of such visible death, anywhere. You do not expect to see dead animals in the open. It is the nature of animals to die alone, off somewhere, hidden. It is wrong to see them lying out on the highway; it is wrong to see them anywhere.

Everything in the world dies, but we only know about it as a kind of abstraction.[2] If you stand in a meadow, at the edge of a hillside, and look around carefully, almost everything you can catch sight of is in the process of dying, and most things will be dead long before you are. If it were not for

1. **impropriety.** Behavior or conduct considered impolite
2. **abstraction.** Generalized concept, or idea

(Above left) *Dead Fox Lying in the Undergrowth,* 1865. Edgar Degas. Musée des Beaux-Arts, Rouen, France.

Program Resources

Planning and Assessment
Program Planning Guide, Selection Lesson Plan
E-Lesson Planner
Assessment Guide, Lesson Test
ExamView

Technology Tools
Interactive Student Text on CD
Visual Teaching Package
Audio Library
mirrorsandwindows.com

Meeting the Standards
Nonfiction: Unit 4, Independent Reading, pp. 66–73

Differentiating Instruction
Advanced Students, Author's Purpose Analysis, p. 24

Common Core State Standards
Reading Informational
RI.1, RI.10

the constant renewal and replacement going on before your eyes, the whole place would turn to stone and sand under your feet.

There are some creatures that do not seem to die at all; they simply vanish totally into their own progeny. Single cells do this. The cell becomes two, then four, and so on, and after a while the last trace is gone. It cannot be seen as death; barring mutation, the descendants are simply the first cell, living all over again. The cycles of the slime mold[3] have episodes that seem as conclusive as death, but the withered slug, with its stalk and fruiting body, is plainly the transient tissue of a developing animal; the free-swimming amebocytes use this organ collectively in order to produce more of themselves.

There are said to be a billion billion insects on the earth at any moment, most of them with very short life expectancies by our standards. Someone has estimated that there are 25 million assorted insects hanging in the air over every temperate square mile, in a column extending upward for thousands of feet, drifting through the layers of the atmosphere like plankton.[4] They are dying steadily, some by being eaten, some just dropping in their tracks, tons of them around the earth, disintegrating as they die, invisibly. **(A)**

Who ever sees dead birds, in anything like the huge numbers stipulated by the certainty of the death of all birds? A dead bird is an incongruity,[5] more startling than an unexpected live bird, sure evidence to the human mind that something has gone wrong. Birds do their dying off somewhere, behind things, under things, never on the wing.

Animals seem to have an instinct for performing death alone, hidden. Even the largest, most conspicuous[6] ones find ways to conceal themselves in time. If an elephant **(B)**

missteps and dies in an open place, the herd will not leave him there; the others will pick him up and carry the body from place to place, finally putting it down in some inexplicably[7] suitable location. When elephants encounter the skeleton of an elephant out in the open, they methodically[8] take up each of the bones and distribute them, in a ponderous[9] ceremony, over neighboring acres.

It is a natural marvel. All of the life of the earth dies, all of the time, in the same volume as the new life that dazzles us each morning, each spring. All we see of this is the odd stump, the fly struggling on the porch floor of the summer house in October, the fragment on the highway. I have lived all my life with an embarrassment of squirrels in my backyard, they are all over the place, all year long, and I have never seen, anywhere, a dead squirrel.

I suppose it is just as well. If the earth were otherwise, and all the dying were done in the open, with the dead there to be looked at, we would never have it out of our minds. We can forget about it much of the time, or think of it as an accident to be avoided, somehow. But it does make the process of dying seem more exceptional than it really is, and harder to engage in at the times when we must ourselves engage.

In our way, we conform as best we can to the rest of nature. The obituary pages tell us of the news that we are dying away, while the birth announcements in finer print, off

---

3. **slime mold.** Protists that can join together to form a slug-like body
4. **plankton.** Organisms that float in bodies of water and serve as food for larger organisms
5. **incongruity.** Inconsistency
6. **conspicuous.** Obvious; noticeable
7. **inexplicably.** Unexplainably
8. **methodically.** Carefully; according to an exact procedure
9. **ponderous.** Slow and awkward

Summary

Lewis Thomas says the sight of death is unusual in nature. Animals have a way of concealing their dead. Thomas claims people focus only on deaths that affect them personally, and live unaware of the many beings that are always dying and being born. Thomas speculates that with the increase in human population, death will be more difficult to hide.

 The Mirrors & Windows questions at the end of the selection focus on the theme of dealing with death. Before students begin to read, ask: Where do insects go to die?

Science Connection

Life Spans Animal life spans vary widely. For example, some insects, such as the mayfly, live only a few days as adults; some tortoises can live to be well over a hundred and fifty years old. **(A)**

Analyze Literature

Tone Have students describe and give examples of Thomas's tone. Although Thomas writes matter-of-factly about death, he also uses vivid and precise words. Ask students how they respond to such phrases as "mysterious wreckage of a deer" (page 440) and "performing death alone." **(B)**

Words in Use

Selection Words
evoking, 440
upwelling, 440
progeny, 441
transient, 441
catastrophe, 442
detestable, 442

Teaching Words
keen, 440
microscopic, 440
speculation, 442

KEY TERMS
SCIENTIFIC ESSAY, 440
MAIN IDEA, 442
SUPPORTING DETAIL, 442
THESIS, 442

Answer: Answers will vary. Some will agree that animals do have an instinct for dying privately; some will claim that humans do, too.

Analyze and Extend

1. Both treat death as a private and, at times, secret event. Humans generally commemorate death in more complicated ways.

2. Students may say that elephants are governed by instinct. Others may say elephants commemorate death in a way similar to that of humans.

3. Most will agree that population growth or environmental changes will cause death to become more public.

Rubric for Expository Writing

You can adapt this as a checklist for students to use as they write.

☐ Does the response analyze and evaluate the main idea and supporting details?

☐ Does the opening paragraph state the main idea?

☐ Do the body paragraphs analyze the supporting details?

☐ Does the concluding paragraph restate the thesis?

---

at the side of the page, inform us of our replacements, but we get no grasp from this of the enormity[10] of scale. There are 3 billion of us on the earth, and all 3 billion must be dead, on a schedule, within this lifetime. The vast mortality, involving something over 50 million of us each year, takes place in relative secrecy. We can only really know of the deaths in our households, or among our friends. These, detached in our minds from all the rest, we take to be unnatural events, anomalies,[11] outrages. We speak of our own dead in low voices; struck down, we say, as though visible death can only occur for cause, by disease or violence, avoidably. We send off for flowers, grieve, make ceremonies, scatter bones, unaware of the rest of the 3 billion on the same schedule. All of that immense mass of flesh and bone and consciousness will disappear by absorption into the earth, without recognition by the transient[12] survivors.

Less than a half century from now, our replacements will have more than doubled the numbers. It is hard to see how we can continue to keep the secret, with such multitudes doing the dying. We will have to give up the notion that death is catastrophe, or detestable, or avoidable, or even strange. We will need to learn more about the cycling of life in the rest of the system, and about our connection to the process. Everything that comes alive seems to be in trade for something that dies, cell for cell. There might be some comfort in the recognition of synchrony,[13] in the information that we all go down together, in the best of company.

10. **enormity.** Great size
11. **anomalies.** Oddities
12. **transient.** Disappearing; short-lived
13. **synchrony.** Occurrences at the same time

Why do you think, so many animals die in private? Do you think animals have an instinct related to this? Do people?

Analyze and Extend

1. What similar attitudes do animals and people share about death? What are some differences in their attitudes?

2. Why do you think elephants act the way that they do about death?

3. Do you agree with Thomas's speculation that in the near future, death will take place in the open? Explain.

Expository Writing In a short essay, write a **literary response** to "Death in the Open." Analyze and evaluate Thomas's main idea and supporting details. In your opening paragraph, state what you believe his main idea to be and whether or not you agree with it. In your body paragraphs, analyze his supporting details and determine whether they effectively support his main idea. Your conclusion should restate your thesis.

Critical Literacy Hold a panel discussion about Thomas's essay in which you share your thoughts about Thomas's essay. Use the literary response that you wrote as the basis for your discussion. Present evidence in support of any claims you make, and listen attentively and respond respectfully to others' ideas.

Go to **www.mirrorsandwindows.com** for more.

442 **UNIT 4** NONFICTION

Reading Skills

Identify the Main Idea

Have students work in small groups to select a sentence from Thomas's essay that states the main idea of the piece, such as "Everything in the world dies, but we only know about it as a kind of abstraction." Then have them select four or five sentences that support the main idea, such as "It is the nature of animals to die alone, off somewhere, hidden." Have groups present their choice of main idea and supporting sentences as a cluster map, with the main idea in the center and the supporting sentences on spokes around the center.

Astonishing Animals

Visual Media by Tim Flannery and Peter Schouten

INDEPENDENT READING

Whip dragonfish
(Grammatostomias flagellibarba)

The deeper one ventures in the oceans, the stranger life becomes.
Many fish that inhabit the eternally dark ocean depths have highly exaggerated body parts, but none seems as extreme as the whip dragonfish. At twenty centimetres long, it has a barbel or 'beard' that extends a metre and a half from its chin. Just what it uses this pale, brown-speckled 'whip' for is unclear. Perhaps it trawls with its barbel, hoping to attract prey. But if so, how does it reach down with its mouth to swallow it before its prey darts off?

Many deep-sea creatures possess a variety of light-emitting organs known as photophores, and those of the whip dragonfish are peculiar. Only the male has a bright yellow light-emitting organ behind its eyes, the other light-emitting organs being a violet-purple colour in both sexes. These organs produce their light in a complex manner, for it is generated both by the action of particular bacteria that live in the luminescent[1] organs, as well as through chemical reactions produced by the fish itself.

---
1. **luminescent.** Light producing

443

Preview the Selection

At a Glance
Independent Reading
- Reading Level: Easy
- Difficulty Consideration: Vocabulary
- Ease Factors: Visual format and imagery

Objectives
Reading this selection will enable students to do the following:
- read with developing fluency
- read silently with comprehension for a sustained period of time
- interpret visual media

Launch the Lesson
Conduct a class brainstorming session on sea monsters. Gradually have students agree on a general description of sea monsters, noting two or three key features they must have. Then tell them they are about to encounter real creatures that may give them further creative ideas about mythical beasts.

▶ More by This Author
Students who like "Astonishing Animals" might enjoy Flannery and Schouten's *A Gap in Nature: Discovering the World's Extinct Animals.*

TEACHING NOTE
Although this selection is presented in the student edition as an independent reading, teaching support has been provided should you choose to cover it in class.

Program Resources

Planning and Assessment
Program Planning Guide, Selection Lesson Plan
E-Lesson Planner
Assessment Guide, Lesson Test
ExamView

Technology Tools
Interactive Student Text on CD
Visual Teaching Package
Audio Library
mirrorsandwindows.com

Meeting the Standards
Nonfiction: Unit 4, Independent Reading, pp. 74–82

Differentiating Instruction
Advanced Students, Visual Media Project, pp. 25–26

Common Core State Standards
Reading Informational
RI.1

Summary

Creatures that live in the dark depths of the oceans have many distinctive characteristics, including their own light sources. The whip dragonfish has a long "whip" that extends from its chin more than seventy times its body length. The wolftrap seadevil has its own built-in fishing pole, line, and lure. The Elsman's whipnose swims upside down with its lantern held in front, just above the ocean floor, possibly to lure worms from under the sea bottom.

 M&IRRORS WINDOWS The Mirrors & Windows questions at the end of the selection focus on the theme of reacting to animals. Before they begin reading, ask students: What, in your opinion, would make an animal "astonishing"?

Cultural Connection

Fishing Jargon The authors use some fishing terminology to describe the movements of these fish. Explain that *trawling* means dragging a line through the water to attract a *strike*. Define *lure* as artificial bait that a fisherman attaches to a fishing line. *Casting* is tossing a line toward a fish to attract it to the baited hook on the end of the line.

Wolftrap seadevil

(Lasiognathus saccostomus)

Also known as 'Regan's strainermouth', the scientific name of this seadevil means 'hairy jaws', and it has one of the worst overbites in nature. The first specimen found was a female just seven centimetres long, which was brought up from the depths of the Caribbean. It is now known to be widespread in the depths of the Pacific and Atlantic oceans. The wolftrap seadevil possesses a strangely raised lateral line system. In fish the lateral line, which runs the length of the body from gills to tail fin, is used to detect changes in water pressure. In this species it may be supersensitive. It also has prominent nostrils, which suggests a fine sense of smell.

The wolftrap seadevil is a true fisherman with a long, articulated fishing pole, line and lure. The lure is illuminated and has two hooked, tooth-like structures that may function as fish-hooks. It evidently snares tiny prey with its lure and hooks and whips them into the cavernous mouth. It may even, like a fly-fisherman, cast its lure towards prey.

Words in Use

Selection Words
- **trawls**, 443
- **peculiar**, 443
- **lateral**, 444
- **prominent**, 444
- **acute**, 445

Teaching Words
- **advocate**, 446
- **paleontology**, 446
- **renowned**, 446

KEY TERMS

VISUAL MEDIA, 443
HYPOTHESIS, 446
SENSORY DETAIL, 446
PRECISE LANGUAGE, 446

Elsman's whipnose
(Gigantactis elsmani)

Gigantactis means 'giant touching device' in Latin, in reference to the extraordinary nose-mounted fishing poles possessed by these curious anglerfish. As recently as 1968 fewer than thirty adult whipnoses of all species (of which there were then ten known) had been collected, and even today these large, predatory deepwater fish are little known. A chance encounter with a Japanese submersible[2] revealed that Elsman's whipnose swims upside down with its lantern in front of it, just above the ocean bottom, perhaps to lure worms from their burrows. It has weak eyes, which may be compensated by an acute sense of smell, the males in particular having prodigious[3] nostrils. ✤

---

2. **submersible.** Small boat or craft that travels underwater
3. **prodigious.** Very large

ASTONISHING ANIMALS **445**

ASTONISHING ANIMALS **445**

Answers: Many students will have found the animals strange or startling. Most will agree that people are likely to be amazed by these animals.

Analyze and Extend

1. The text suggests that the whip dragonfish uses its barbel to catch food. It might also use the barbel to attract a mate or scare off predators.

2. (a) Flannery says the whipnose swims upside down to attract worms for food. (b) Most will say the idea is reasonable. Students who have studied hypotheses in science class may note that it would be hard to test this idea, because to do so one would have to spend a lot of time at the ocean bottom.

3. (a) All three fish have gills, fins, unusually shaped mouths, and barbels. (b) Most of these traits are common to fish. The barbel is probably an adaptation that helps these fish acquire food.

Rubric for Creative Writing

You can adapt this as a checklist for students to use as they write.

☐ Does the journal entry adopt the voice of an undersea explorer?

☐ Does the journal entry accurately describe the animal?

☐ Does the journal entry include precise language and sensory details?

Tim Flannery (b. 1956) is a museum director, biologist, environmental advocate, and notable science writer. Born and raised in Australia, Flannery holds degrees in English literature, Earth science, and paleontology. He has held teaching positions at numerous universities, including Harvard, where he acted as Visiting Chair in Australian Studies.

Illustrator and painter **Peter Schouten** is a world-renowned wildlife artist. Born in Australia, Schouten was educated as a paleontologist. A self-trained artist, his first book of art led to a position as technical illustrator at the school of zoology at the University of New South Wales. He now works as a freelance wildlife illustrator.

How did you react to the animals depicted in this selection? Describe your reactions, both emotional and intellectual. How do you think most people would react to these animals?

Analyze and Extend

1. For what reason or reasons do you think the whip dragonfish has such a long barbel?

2. (a) What hypothesis is presented regarding the Elsman's whipnose's habit of swimming upside down? (b) Explain why you think this is a reasonable or unreasonable idea.

3. (a) What physical traits do all three fish share? (b) Why do you think they have these traits in common?

Creative Writing Imagine that you are a deep sea explorer. On an undersea mission, you discover one of the animals described and pictured in this selection. Write a **journal entry** about your discovery. Include sensory details and precise language, and list as many specific details about the animal as possible.

Lifelong Learning Using the Internet and the library, further research one of the animals depicted in this selection. Create a list of the facts that you gather, such as the animal's size, diet, and the year in which it was first discovered. Then use this list to create a short informative paragraph about the animal you researched.

 Go to www.mirrorsandwindows.com for more.

Differentiated Instruction

Enrichment

Students interested in undersea creatures may wish to learn more about the field of oceanography. They can explore various subfields or possible careers. The main subfields relate to other branches of science: geologists study the history and structure of the seafloor as well as sediments in the ocean; chemists study seawater; physicists study waves, tides, currents, weather, and light and sound in the ocean; and biologists study ocean life, ocean ecology, and how to feed people from the sea. Students might also wish to explore the ocean in literature, creating a bibliography of titles from *Moby Dick* to *The Old Man and the Sea* and *The Perfect Storm.*

Have students research their chosen subfields and present reports to the class or create an oceanography bulletin board in the classroom.

For Your Reading List

The New Way Things Work
by David Macaulay

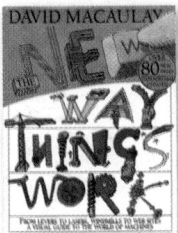

David Macaulay's *The New Way Things Work* exposes the secret inner workings of machines. Over the course of a few hundred pages, with drawings and text, Macaulay illustrates and describes how hundreds of machines, from parking meters to zippers, work. His drawings are always clear and often humorous, and his descriptions concise.

Pick Me Up
by Jeremy Leslie and David Roberts

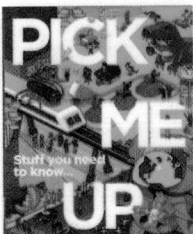

One part puzzle book, one part encyclopedia, *Pick Me Up* is all offbeat. This innovative text combines vivid illustrations, graphic aids, and fascinating tidbits. In the way that individual web pages are linked to hundreds of others, every page is distinct and loaded with cross-references that will send you flipping to other parts of the book.

Photography: An Illustrated History
by Martin W. Sandler

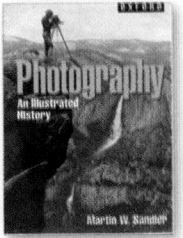

This book is a guide to the technical and creative innovations from the birth of photography to the digital age. From the daguerreotype to moving pictures and computers, every major innovation is accompanied with a photograph that illustrates what is being described in Sandler's thoughtful and extensive text. The book also covers the major fields of the art, such as fashion and war photography.

A Drop of Water
by Walter Wick

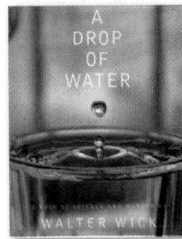

In *A Drop of Water*, photographer Walter Wick directs his camera to the study of the science and beauty of water. Through magnification and other techniques, Wick uses his camera to surprise the viewer with a new perspective on something we see every day. Each picture is accompanied by a paragraph describing the scientific principles at work in phenomena from a soap bubble to a droplet of rain.

Raptor! A Kid's Guide to Birds of Prey
by Christyna M. Laubach, René Laubach, and Charles W. G. Smith

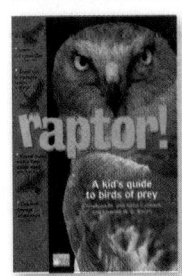

In this birding book for young people, the amazing lives of raptors—birds of prey such as owls, hawks, and eagles—are shown up close. Readers learn about the habits, food, behavior, and characteristics of these birds. Each entry includes information that will help with identification in the wild, along with numerous fascinating and informative exercises.

Universe
by Martin Rees (editor)

This nicely illustrated reference text provides a thoughtful and useful guide to the stars. Written by a team of astronomers who simply and carefully explain complicated topics, *Universe* is accessible to even the most science-challenged reader.

Independent Reading Activity

Help students link independent reading to the unit theme, Responding to Nature. Have students select a book from the list here or go to the library and find a similar nonfiction work that has many illustrations. They might also seek out books featuring microscopic images, fractal images, landscape photography, or aerial photography. When students have brought their selections to class, allow time for everyone to examine the books. Each student should then choose one image to which to respond. Ask students to write an essay of several paragraphs that describes the image and their thoughts and feelings about it. Students may read their essays to the class, exchange them with partners for feedback, or simply keep them in their journals or portfolios.

⊙ EMC E-Library

The EMC E-Library contains over twenty thousand pages of literary classics that students may read independently. An Electronic Library Guide provides teaching suggestions, enrichment activities, and reading strategy guidesheets.

Program Resources

EMC Access Editions

For additional independent reading, you may wish to refer students to one of EMC's Access Edition titles such as Gary Paulsen's *Hatchet*. Each Access Edition contains a thorough study apparatus, including background information, literal comprehension questions, footnotes, vocabulary definitions, critical thinking questions, and related projects and activities. An Assessment Manual offering worksheets and exams is available for each Access Edition.

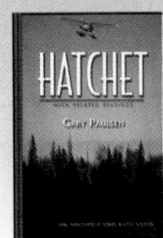

Common Core State Standards

Reading Informational
RI.10

Objectives

Participating in this lesson will help students write a descriptive essay that

- conveys a personal impression in its introduction
- has a clear organizational pattern
- uses figurative language and sensory details that create a picture, as well as strong verbs and active voice
- includes appropriate personal thoughts and feelings
- has a conclusion that summarizes and conveys a new insight

Launch the Lesson

Ask students to recall their most rewarding vacations, family trips, or school field trips to outdoor locations. Ask how they felt during the trip and what natural scene or object would most strongly evoke that feeling if they were to experience it again.

Additional writing workshops are available in the *Exceeding the Standards: Writing* resource.

What Great Writers Do

Ask students to read the quote from George Orwell. Then ask: "What does it mean for an image to be 'fresh'? Why would an old image, or a 'not-so-fresh' image, have less of an effect than a fresh image?" Elicit the observation that people will already be familiar with an old image, and their associations with it will reduce their ability to apply it to a new situation.

Writing Workshop

Descriptive Writing

Descriptive Essay

Reading and Writing

In this unit you have read essays on nature and the natural world. These essays were written by scientists, politicians, and naturalists. The writers described their views of the natural world around them. They wrote about subjects as diverse as the tiniest units of matter to humanity's destructiveness and Earth's resilience.

In this workshop, you will learn how to write a **descriptive essay.** The purpose of a descriptive essay is to present a piece of writing that creates a picture for the reader. Before writing a descriptive essay, determine your goal and a strategy to achieve it. The assignment summary here includes a writing rubric, that is, a set of standards by which you judge your work and whether or not your descriptive essay was successful. You will use this rubric in both drafting and revising your essay.

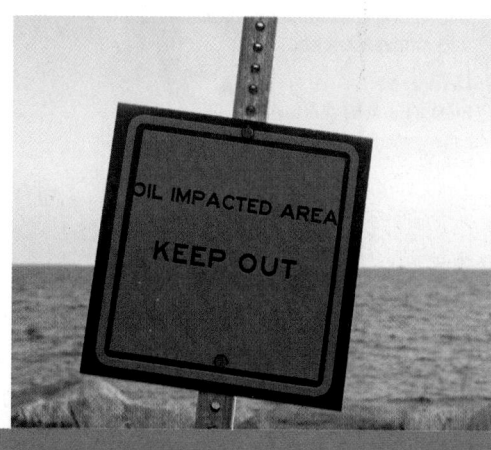

- **Assignment:** Write a descriptive essay in which I use sensory details and personal thoughts to give a response to nature.
- **Goal:** Convey my impression of a natural subject or event in a vivid way to bring it to life for my audience.
- **Strategy:** Include details that help the audience see, smell, taste, feel, or hear what I am describing, as well as my own thoughts and feelings.
- **Writing Rubric:** My descriptive essay should include the following:

  - an introduction that illustrates my impression of a natural subject or event
  - a clear organizational pattern appropriate to the subject or event I'm describing
  - figurative language and sensory details that create a picture for the reader
  - personal thoughts and feelings that help reinforce my overall impression
  - strong verbs and active voice
  - a conclusion that sums up my impression and adds insight

What Great Writers Do

George Orwell (1903–1950) was an essayist, novelist, and satirist. He wrote the novels Animal Farm *and* 1984. *Read his passage below about questions a writer should ask. How might this advice pertain to descriptive writing?*

A scrupulous writer, in every sentence that he writes, will ask himself at least four questions, thus: What am I trying to say? What words will express it? What image or idiom will make it clearer? Is this image fresh enough to have an effect?

Words in Use

Teaching Words

naturalists, 448
destructiveness, 448
resilience, 448
rubric, 448
convey, 448
vivid, 448
scrupulous, 448

inverted, 449
petrified, 449
deafeningly, 449
quiver, 450
phenomena, 453

KEY TERMS

DESCRIPTIVE ESSAY, 448	**SUBJECT,** 449	**PUNCTUATION,** 450
SUMMARY, 448	**ORGANIZATIONAL PATTERN,** 450	**PEER REVIEW,** 451
SENSORY DETAIL, 448	**CHRONOLOGICAL ORDER,** 450	**PASSIVE VOICE,** 452
AUDIENCE, 448	**SPATIAL ORDER,** 450	**ACTIVE VOICE,** 452
INTRODUCTION, 448	**INTRODUCTION,** 450	**VERB PHRASE,** 452
FIGURATIVE LANGUAGE, 448	**BODY,** 450	**ADJECTIVE,** 452
VERB, 448	**CONCLUSION,** 450	**ADVERB,** 452
IDIOM, 448		**PROOFREAD,** 452

Writing
W.2, W.4, W.5, W.6, W.10

1. PREWRITE

Choosing Your Topic

When you look around at the natural world, you see many things. Think about which subjects from nature fascinate, scare, inspire, or excite you. Specifically, what animals, outdoor spaces, land formations, or types of weather catch your interest? Try to focus on a particular moment or episode in your life when something from the natural world affected you strongly. Once you have a subject in mind, **narrow your focus.**

Below is how one student narrowed her focus. She created an inverted triangle with the broadest subject area first, narrowing it down to a more manageable subject. Keep in mind that any subject can work in a descriptive essay, as long as it is personally meaningful.

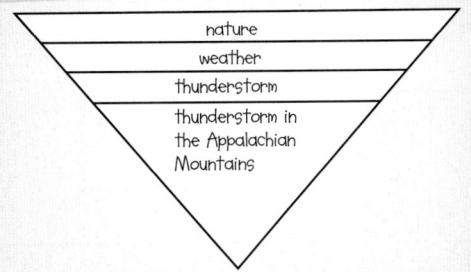

The writer began with the broad subject *nature* and narrowed that down to *weather*. *Weather* was further narrowed down to *thunderstorm,* and that subject further specified to focus on a *particular* thunderstorm that affected the writer personally.

Gathering Details

After you narrow your subject, begin gathering details. One way to gather sensory details is to create a word web. Here is a word web in which the writer recalls details about an especially frightening thunderstorm she experienced.

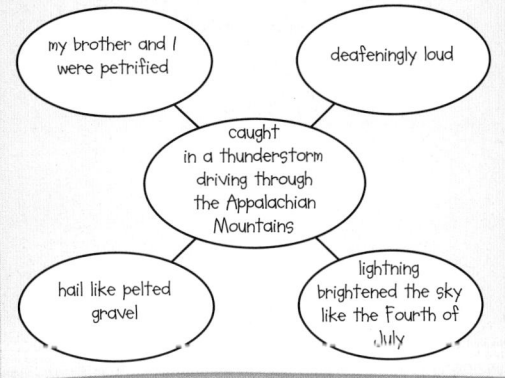

These are just a few details that the writer brought to mind about experiencing a thunderstorm. She used her five senses to remember how a specific thunderstorm made her feel.

Deciding on Your Purpose

Once you gather enough details for your essay, decide on your purpose for writing. For a descriptive essay, your purpose is to describe a subject or event with descriptive details and personal thoughts. Your details and thoughts should give your audience a clear picture of the subject or event and how it affected you. Create a thesis statement that reveals your impression of the subject or event. Note the example below.

> A thunderstorm can be one of the scariest and most beautiful things in nature to experience.

Teach the Workshop

Prewrite

Choosing a Topic Reinforce for students the value of choosing a topic that is personally meaningful. Tell them that writing from personal experience makes it easy to describe events and feelings. You might model a possible topic selection: "I love the ocean. I'm not sure why. I know I want to go back to the coast of Oregon. On spring vacation there ten years ago I saw whales. I will never forget that experience. I think I'll write about seeing gray whales from the beach in Oregon."

Deciding on a Purpose You might offer students alternative terms for "thesis statement" in this descriptive essay—for example, "controlling idea," "statement of purpose," or "main image." Help them settle on sentences that identify the topic and incorporate their personal reactions.

What Great Writers Do

What a loveliness a fire in a fireplace is to the man sitting there watching and listening, and what sweet whisperings of all manner of language come from the wood being consumed by the fire. In fire we may answer the question of life and art, how you die, do, live.

WILLIAM SAROYAN, Quoted in
The New York Times,
October 9, 2000

Writing Skills

Similes and Metaphors

Offer students practice creating similes and then turning them into metaphors. Remind them first that a simile is a comparison of two things using the word *like* or the word *as,* and a metaphor compares two things without using *like* or *as.* One thing is spoken of as if it is another thing.

Give students an example of a simile based on the word web: "Hail hit like pelted gravel." Model turning this into a metaphor: "The hail was pelted gravel." Then give them these similes and have them create metaphors.

- Insects buzzing like saws
- A field of sunflowers glittering like hundreds of Tinkerbell wands

When they are done, ask students to compare and contrast the effects of the statements as similes and as metaphors.

Draft

Organizing Ideas Help students distinguish between organization of the entire essay and organization of paragraphs. Explain that the overall essay may be chronological, but particular paragraphs may have chronological, spatial, compare-contrast, cause-effect, or order-of-importance organization. You may wish to give them more sample transition words and phrases:

- Order-of-importance — *first, most, least, greater, greatest*
- Compare-contrast — *also, both, however, in contrast, in the same way*
- Cause-effect — *as a result, because*

Spatial Order Models You can give students further practice with spatial order. Ask them to look for spatial order in the first two paragraphs of Annie Dillard's essay on page 258, in the last third of Robert Jastrow's essay earlier this unit, in the first stanza of Pattiann Rogers's poem on page 386, and at the beginning of Willam Saroyan's story on page 412.

2. DRAFT

Organizing Ideas

There are various ways you can organize data for your descriptive essay. You can present your information in one of two major **organizational patterns,** either in chronological order or by spatial order. In **chronological order,** you tell a series of events in the order in which they happened. In **spatial order,** you describe the parts of a scene in order of their location in space. Use spatial order to discuss the physical position or relationship between objects.

Chronological Order	Spatial Order
First Event ↓	1. Top ↕
Second Event ↓	Bottom
Third Event ↓	2. Left ←→ Right
Final Event	3. Near ←→ Far
Signal Words and Phrases first, next, then, after that, before, during, finally	**Signal Words and Phrases** behind, below, above, here, there, on the left, next to, in front of, inside

Putting Your Thoughts on Paper

An essay has three basic parts: an introduction, a body, and a conclusion. Create a plan for writing your descriptive essay like the one on the right. Use your word web.

You may want to write the body of your essay first and then write the introduction and conclusion. You can also write your essay all the way through from the introduction to the conclusion. There is no one correct way to write your essay. Your description should flow from one part to another, however, and be sure to include enough sensory details and personal thoughts to make your impression clear to the reader. For now, concentrate on content and organization. You will focus on grammar, punctuation, and spelling at the editing and proofreading stage.

Introduction
- Introduce the natural subject or event you will describe and your impression.

Body
- Organize by chronological or spatial order.
- Include sensory details in each paragraph.
- Include your personal thoughts and feelings that support your overall impression.

Conclusion
- Summarize your impression and add an insight.

Showing Instead of Telling

Remember that a goal of your descriptive essay is to help your audience picture what you are describing and share in the experience. Add descriptive details, such as sensory images and figurative language, to help your readers feel as if they are there. Consider the example.

Tell:
My brother was afraid.

Show:
My brother glanced at me, and I glanced at him. His face turned pale, and his eyes bulged wide. He clenched his seatbelt like a lifeline. I heard a low whimper as his bottom lip began to quiver.

450 UNIT 4 NONFICTION

Differentiated Instruction

Reading Proficiency and Visual Learning

Pair struggling readers with visual learners who can act as mentors and sketch artists. Have the visual learner elicit descriptions from the other student, and then sketch an appropriate organizational strategy. Encourage the mentor to offer creative suggestions about how to structure the essay.

Review results with both students before they return to individual work.

English Language Learners

You may wish to explain the word *insight.* An insight is a new perception or understanding of a situation. You might compare it to seeing things in a new way. (Other languages have words for this, such as the Spanish word *perspicacia*.)

3. REVISE

Evaluating Your Draft

Look over your draft for strengths and weaknesses. Correct weaknesses as best you can. After that, exchange papers with a classmate, and conduct a **peer review.** Then discuss ways you can improve your paper. The following is part of a student's descriptive essay. The annotations to the right indicate the reasons for the changes marked in the draft.

Revising Checklist

☐ Does the introduction illustrate my impression of a natural subject or event?

☐ Is the essay organized in a logical way?

☐ Do I use figurative language, sensory details, and active voice?

The worst thunderstorm I remember happened one summer on a drive back to Pennsylvania from a family trip to Georgia. ~~My grandparents live in Georgia.~~ We were cruising through the Appalachian Mountains when the storm hit. The mountains can be scary even in the best of weather. They are even scarier when you travel through them in a thunderstorm. *A thunderstorm can be one of the scariest and most beautiful things in nature to experience.*

Delete unrelated detail.

State the subject or event you will describe and your impression.

I remember that afternoon. I had fallen asleep in the car when ~~a storm woke me up.~~ *I awoke to the crash of thunder. The air felt thick and moist. It was dark outside, though it was only 3:30 in the afternoon. As I looked out the window, I saw lightning blaze through the shadowy sky, splitting off in random directions like a light show.* If it wasn't so scary, it might have been the most beautiful thing I'd ever seen! The lightning lit up the road and the entire side of the mountain. It felt like the Fourth of July.

Add descriptive details and figurative language to show instead of tell.

A loud clap of thunder ~~was heard~~ *shook the car* as heavy clouds rolled toward us. That's when I knew this was no ordinary rainstorm.

Replace passive voice with strong verbs in the active voice.

Revise

Evaluating a Draft Have students read the tips below for delivering and receiving constructive criticism. Then help them prepare for peer review with a warm-up.

Delivering Criticism

- **Be focused.** Concentrate on content, organization, and style. Leave spelling and punctuation for the proofreading stage.
- **Be positive.** Respect the writer's feelings and writing efforts.
- **Be specific.** Give concrete ideas for improving the essay.

Receiving Criticism

- **Ask questions.** Make sure you understand your reviewer's comments.
- **Be specific.** Ask your reviewer to clarify comments and suggestions.
- **Be selective.** Accept your reviewer's suggestions graciously. When you revise your essay, you can use just some—or none—of the suggestions.

Warm-up

Model poor criticism with these sentences, and have students suggest improvements:

"I don't like the way you described the tree." (Possible improvement: I think you could add detail about the tree's branches.)

"This reads like you don't care about writing well." (I'd be happy to help proofread your revised version.)

"I'm confused." (What did you mean when you said "the ball was flat"?)

Writing Skills

Revise

Tell students there are four main ways to revise a piece of writing. Give them the definitions below and ask volunteers for examples of times they used the technique. (You may model possible responses, as in the parentheses.)

1. Adding or expanding: Adding transitions or examples to connect ideas or make images more vivid ("I needed to add a transition sentence to connect seeing whales and my feeling of awe.")

2. Cutting or condensing: Deleting unrelated details, replacing wordy sentences with shorter ones, and eliminating repetitious modifiers

3. Replacing: Using active, concrete, vivid, and precise words instead of passive, abstract, boring, and imprecise words

4. Moving: Putting related images and ideas closer to each other

▶ **Edit and Proofread**
Students may want to use proofreader's marks when correcting their work. Refer them to the Language Arts Handbook, Writing Section 4.1, Proofreader's Symbols.

Recognizing Passive and Active Voice If you have told students "show, don't tell," you may wish to point out that passive voice almost always "tells" rather than "shows."

What Great Writers Do
Read aloud this quotation from Gish Jen, which offers an example of insight and an example of passive voice used well.

I walked past a reservoir in the spring and saw an ice island. This was gray-black and submerged enough that it could have been the reflection of a cloud, except that it was covered with birds. The birds were ankle deep in the cold water; pointing in all directions, they seemed, despite their concerted stares, to be scattered. The island was something I'd seen and admired every year, but when I looked at it this time, I saw that it was transitory yet permanent, that its islandness depended on the water, which would destroy it and create it again.

▶ **Publish and Present**
Before students begin their final versions, they might benefit from reading the Language Arts Handbook, Writing Section 4.1, Writing Follow-up.

4. EDIT AND PROOFREAD

Focus: Passive and Active Voice
Sometimes you may find yourself writing sentences that use the **passive voice.** Passive voice is the act of telling who or what *receives* the action in a sentence rather than showing who or what *performs* the action.

> **Passive Voice:**
>
> The road and the entire side of the mountain were lit up by the lightning.

> In **active voice** the subject performs the action:
>
> The lightning lit up the road and the entire side of the mountain.

Using the passive voice usually makes writing flat and less interesting. It can also create awkward sentences. To recognize passive voice, look for phrases after the action verb that begin with *by* or *by the.* Also watch out for verb phrases that use forms of the verb *be.* Look over your writing and try to rewrite passive sentences so that they are in active voice. Strong verbs in the active voice will make your descriptions clearer and more effective.

Focus: Adjectives and Adverbs
Adjectives and adverbs are descriptive words. Adjectives modify or tell more about nouns. They answer the questions *what kind, how many,* and *which one.* Adverbs modify verbs, adjectives, and other adverbs. They tell *how, when,* or *where* something happens. When you add adjectives and adverbs to your writing, you affect the meaning of the words they modify.

Adding adjectives and adverbs will enhance your descriptive essay and draw in your reader. Be careful not to overuse adjectives and adverbs, however, and lose the meaning of your writing.

> Rain fell.
>
> **Adding adjectives:**
>
> A hard, cold rain fell.
>
> **Adding adverbs:**
>
> Rain fell quickly and steadily.
>
> **Adding adjectives and adverbs:**
>
> A hard, cold rain fell quickly and steadily.

Proofreading
Quality Control The purpose of proofreading is to find errors in punctuation, grammar, capitalization, and spelling. You can always find and fix these errors as you revise your essay, but you should check for these errors specifically in the proofreading stage. Use proofreader's marks to highlight any errors and correct them. (See the Language Arts Handbook, section 4.1, for a list of proofreader's symbols.)

5. PUBLISH AND PRESENT

Final Draft
Rewrite your essay to make a final draft. If you wrote your essay by hand, make sure it is neat and legible. If you used a word processing program, double-space your paper and use a readable typeface or font. Be sure to check about any of your teacher's additional presentation guidelines.

Differentiated Instruction

Enrichment
Many scientists use passive voice to avoid implying that nonhumans can think or have motivations. However, most nature writers use active voice to involve readers in their narratives. Have students use their science textbooks to find an example of passive voice, and then rewrite that example using the active voice.

Reading Proficiency
Remind struggling readers that they are allowed to make choices about how they express themselves. Point out that passive voice is sometimes suitable. Similarly, they can choose which descriptions to enliven with additional adjectives and adverbs, and which to leave alone.

Student Model

A Drive to Remember
by Jamie Lee

The worst thunderstorm I remember happened one summer on a drive back to Pennsylvania from a family trip to Georgia. We were cruising through the Appalachian Mountains when the storm hit. The mountains can be scary even in the best of weather. They are even scarier when you travel through them in a thunderstorm. A thunderstorm can be one of the scariest and most beautiful things in nature to experience.

> *Introduces the natural event and the writer's impression of that event*

I remember that afternoon. I had fallen asleep in the car when I awoke to the crash of thunder. The air felt thick and moist. It was dark outside, though it was only 3:30 in the afternoon. As I looked out the window, I saw lightning blaze through the shadowy sky, splitting off in random directions like a light show. If it wasn't so scary, it might have been the most beautiful thing I'd ever seen! The lightning lit up the road and the entire side of the mountain. It felt like the Fourth of July.

A loud clap of thunder shook the car as heavy clouds rolled toward us. That's when I knew this was no ordinary rainstorm. The deafening sound of thunder made conversation impossible in the car. Yet my brother and I were so fascinated by the show outside our car window that neither of us wanted to talk anyway. Then it started to rain.

> *Organized logically, in chronological order*
>
> *Includes sensory details and figurative language that show instead of tell and help the reader share in the experience*
>
> *Includes personal thoughts and feelings that support and reinforce the overall impression of the event*

Gentle drops fell at first. Suddenly it seemed as though somebody had turned the water on full blast, and the rain crashed down in sheets. A hard, cold rain fell quickly and steadily. My brother glanced at me, and I glanced at him. His face turned pale, and his eyes bulged wide. He clenched his seatbelt like a lifeline. I heard a low whimper as his bottom lip began to quiver. I wondered how my dad could see the road. The rain tap-danced on the roof of the car like a thousand feet at once. Hail smacked against the roof like pelted gravel.

I felt the car slow to a crawl and finally stop along the shoulder of the road. Rain and hail pounded on the car, as if trying to get in with us. My little brother was shaking, and he hid his face inside his sweatshirt. I took his hand and he turned his face into my arm. Finally the noise seemed to ease and float away from us, taking its violence elsewhere. Though it was still raining, the sky wasn't as dark as before, and I knew that the sun was trying to break through the clouds. Dad started the car again, and we headed toward home.

Thunderstorms are one of nature's most fascinating and frightening events. They are necessary and natural phenomena, of course, but I plan to be in my own house the next time one hits!

> *Sums up the writer's impression and adds an insight*

Writing Skills

Review and Reflect on the Writing Process

Students have now completed several Writing Workshops and have offered each other constructive criticism. Have small groups meet to review and reflect on the writing process.

- First, Review the Process. Give students five minutes—one minute per step in the process—to list the easiest and hardest parts of each step.

(The steps are Prewriting, Drafting, Revising, Editing and Proofreading, and Publishing and Presenting.)

- Second, Reflect on the Process. Tell students to reach a consensus on three topics: the most enjoyable part of the process, the most difficult step (these could be the same), and the step on which they would most like to strengthen their skills. Let each group report results to the class.

Objectives

Participating in this lesson will help students plan and deliver a visual presentation that

- effectively employs visuals to enhance appeal
- is clear and well organized
- supports main ideas with evidence
- exhibits appropriate volume and pacing and effective nonverbal expression
- responds helpfully to audience questions

Launch the Lesson

Ask students to reminisce about grade-school "show and tell" presentations. Have them describe especially memorable events in which they or others presented an unexpected person or thing to the class. Tell them that now they will be able to craft more "educated" or "mature" presentations based on their advanced knowledge of informational text and visual media.

Cultural Connection

Public Speaking Tell students that public speaking is a skill with ancient roots. Ancient Greek and Roman orators are among the most famous historical figures. Currently, organizations such as Toastmasters International offer people experience and education in public speaking.

Viewing Workshop

Critical Viewing

How are you influenced by images when you watch television or read a web page, newspaper, or magazine? Do you evaluate the effectiveness of photographs, diagrams, illustrations, and charts? When you evaluate an image's meaning, purpose, or effectiveness, you are using **critical viewing** skills. In this workshop you will craft a presentation that uses visual aids to convey information.

Planning a Visual Presentation

Choose an Idea Do you have an interest in something you want to share with others? Might visual aids increase the clarity or effectiveness of your explanation? For example, you may be interested in the preservation of a natural habitat. A strictly verbal presentation may not be enough. Pictures, drawings, and real objects can help convey complicated ideas and bring your topic to life. Be sure to select a topic that will benefit from the use of visual aids.

Select Key Ideas and Visuals Once you select your topic, gather information about it. Use sources such as the Internet, books, magazines, and encyclopedias to begin taking notes. Along with your notes, which will lay the groundwork for the verbal part of your presentation, decide what kinds of visuals you will use to reinforce your main ideas or clarify the most difficult concepts in your presentation. Will photographs, drawings, diagrams, maps, or objects work best? Should you show pictures on poster board, on slides, or as part of a digital presentation? For example, if you were presenting the effects of housing developments on wetlands, you might include before-and-after photographs or illustrations that depict soil erosion.

Identify Your Audience What key ideas would you like your audience to learn from your presentation? Are these ideas very complicated? Do they require any special background knowledge or vocabulary? Determine whether your audience will have the background needed to understand any technical information or language. If you are presenting on a topic that requires a good deal of specialized knowledge, consider how you might make this topic accessible to a general audience.

Teaching Words

convey, 454
depict, 454
erosion, 454
coincide, 455
ecosystem, 455
clarification, 455
elaboration, 455

Auditory Learning

Offer students an opportunity to hear famous recorded speakers or speeches. Even a few minutes of listening can spark ideas, build confidence, and build (or reinforce) concept and language attainment. Collections of "greatest speeches" are available on the Internet and in tapes and CD format. Students may also watch speeches on DVDs to get ideas for nonverbal communication and visual aids

English Language Learning

English language learners will benefit from using visual supports to enhance and confirm their understanding of complex and elaborate spoken language. Ask students to explain how visual aids help them understand unfamiliar terminology and concepts.

Organize Your Visuals As you gather images, objects, or other visual aids for your presentation, try to determine how to use them in the most effective way. Make sure that you organize your visuals to coincide with your verbal presentation. If you are using photographs or drawings, you may want to set up a storyboard. Key each image to a different main idea in your presentation.

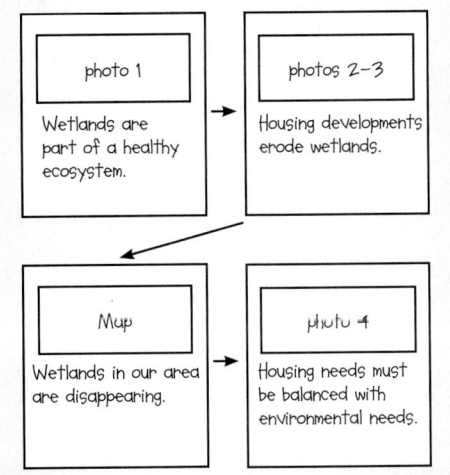

Evaluating Your Presentation

Work with a partner or group on your presentation. Take turns delivering your presentations. Consider how photographs, diagrams, illustrations, and graphs enhance the presentation's impact and improve clarity. Ask yourself: What do these images add? Provide constructive feedback about your peers' use of visual aids. Follow the speaking, listening, and viewing rubric on this page to evaluate the presentation.

Delivering Your Presentation

Insert cues into the notes, outline, or script to prompt you to present your visual aids at the appropriate moment. If you use photographs or art in your presentation, be sure you know the name of the artist or photographer, the title of the piece,

and the date it was created. Make sure your visuals are large enough and placed well for your audience to see them. When you refer to your visuals, point to them so that the audience can adjust its attention.

Listen Actively As an active listener, remember to be courteous to the speaker. Do not touch or handle visual aids without the speaker's permission. During the presentation, try to interpret the impact the images have on you. Ask questions when appropriate to clarify anything you find confusing, unclear, or in need of elaboration.

Speaking Rubric

Your presentation will be evaluated on the following elements:

Content
- ☐ visuals enhance appeal of presentation
- ☐ presentation is clear and well organized
- ☐ visuals are effectively used
- ☐ main ideas of presentation are supported with evidence

Delivery and Presentation
- ☐ appropriate volume and pacing
- ☐ appropriate responses to audience questions through clarification and elaboration
- ☐ effective nonverbal communication

Listening and Viewing Rubric

As a peer reviewer or audience member, you should do the following:

- ☐ listen quietly and attentively
- ☐ analyze the images presented
- ☐ ask appropriate questions
- ☐ (as peer reviewer) provide constructive feedback

Speaking & Listening Skills

Audience Questions

Tell students that as they rehearse their presentations, they can also practice responding to audience questions. Point out that speakers often pause to absorb a question and decide if it calls for giving a definition, elaborating with examples, or offering to seek additional information. Explain that speakers to not have to have answers for every imaginable question.

Read these questions to students and have them suggest the types of response that would be appropriate.

1. Where did you get this information?
2. How do you expect this situation to change?
3. How is this going to affect my family?
4. When will more information be available?

Writing Skills

Descriptive Essay

Objectives

Completing this lesson will enable students to

- write a descriptive essay based on a timed writing prompt
- answer standardized test questions that demonstrate revising and editing skills
- demonstrate the ability to make inferences from a reading by answering standardized questions

Timed Writing

Say that standardized tests often ask students to write a response to a prompt in a specified period of time. Give the following tips:

- Read the entire prompt carefully.
- Look for key words in the prompt that tell you what is expected.
- Underline these words or write them on your own notepaper.
- Use the key words to make sure you answer all parts of the question.
- Organize. Allow time for planning, writing, and reviewing.
- Before you begin writing, create a rough outline of points to make.
- Write a clear introduction. This will help keep you on track as you write each paragraph.
- If you find yourself running out of time, state your remaining points and add a conclusion.
- Review your completed essay to see if you have answered all parts of the question.
- Before you turn in your completed essay, take time to proofread.

Carefully read the following writing prompt. Before you begin writing, think carefully about what task the assignment is asking you to perform. Then create an outline to help guide your writing.

> In his essay "Ships in the Desert," Al Gore uses the analogy of an outgoing tide that leaves behind disturbing images in the sand. These images warn of dangers ahead if humans continue to "turn their backs on nature." What are some ways in which humans ignore nature as they go about their lives? What are some of the dangers that could arise if humans continue to do this?

In your essay, use descriptive and sensory language, as well as analogies, to describe several human actions that are having negative effects on nature. Use examples from Gore's essay, issues you have read or heard about, and evidence from your own life. As you write, be sure to:

> - Organize your essay in a logical and consistent way
> - Include introductory and concluding paragraphs
> - Introduce your position in the first paragraph
> - Support your main idea in each body paragraph

Rubric for a Descriptive Essay

Have students use these criteria when evaluating their essays.

- ☐ Is the essay on the topic of how humans ignore nature, and the implications of that practice?
- ☐ Does the essay clearly state a position in the first paragraph?
- ☐ Is the essay organized logically and consistently?
- ☐ Does each body paragraph support the main idea?
- ☐ Does the essay use descriptive language, sensory language, and analogies?
- ☐ Does the essay have a concluding paragraph?

Common Core State Standards

Language
L.4.1f, L.6.1e, L.6.2a

Revising and Editing Skills

In the following excerpt from the first draft of a student's paper, words and phrases are underlined and numbered. Alternatives to the underlined words and phrases appear in the right-hand column. Choose the one that *best* corrects any grammatical or style errors in the original. If you think that the original is error free, choose "NO CHANGE."

Some questions might also be asked about a section of the passage or the entire passage. These do not refer to a specific underlined phrase or word and are identified by a number in a box. Record your answers on a separate sheet of paper.

Because tornadoes are unpredictable they are
<u>1</u>
one of the deadliest forces in nature. Like a
crazed shopper at a department store sale, a
tornado races blindly across the countryside,
destroying homes and ending lives. How do I
know? I have lived through one. [2]

May 8, 1999, was an evening that I will never
forget. The breeze which was thick with moisture
<u>3</u>
carried the pleasant fragrance of freshly turned
earth and spring flowers. As we drove through
the countryside, my brother Darrell and I were
<u>4</u>
admiring a field of yellow and white daisies,
which danced like tiny ballerinas in the soft
breeze. The setting sun was brilliant on the
western horizon. Then dark clouds and wild
<u>5</u>
winds rolled in like ocean waves approaching the
beach. Within minutes, the entire landscape grew
silent the dancing daisies were now completely
still as rain began to spill from the sky. [6]

1. A. NO CHANGE
   B. Because tornadoes are unpredictable;
   C. Because tornadoes are unpredictable,
   D. Because tornadoes are unpredictable:

2. The first paragraph includes:
   A. visual media.
   B. dialect.
   C. internal conflict.
   D. an analogy.

3. A. NO CHANGE
   B. The breeze, which was thick with moisture,
   C. The breeze. Which was thick with moisture
   D. The breeze; which was thick with moisture;

4. A. NO CHANGE
   B. Darrell and me were admiring
   C. Darrell and me was admiring
   D. Darrell and I was admiring

5. This sentence contains:
   A. a nominative pronoun.
   B. a simple subject.
   C. a compound subject.
   D. the thesis statement.

6. The last sentence of this paragraph is:
   A. the topic sentence.
   B. the thesis.
   C. a fragment.
   D. a run-on.

Teach the Workshop

Revising and Editing Skills
1. C   4. A
2. D   5. C
3. B   6. D

Test-Taking Tip

Go Out of Order Tell students that in a Revising and Editing test, they should read the passage through once before attempting to answer any questions. However, once they have read the passage, they can approach the questions in several ways:

- First, they should read each question quickly to get an idea of the type of information they will have to consider.
- They may answer any general questions, such as Question 2 above, first.
- They can answer questions out of order.
- When they are through answering questions, they should review all of their answers to make sure they seem like the best.

> For more information, see the Language Arts Handbook Section 8, Test-Taking Skills.

Program Resources

For more study and practice with test-taking skills, see the *Exceeding the Standards: Test Practice* resource:
- Descriptive Essay Practice Test: Reading, pp. 10–12

Words in Use

Teaching Words
crazed, 457
evolutionary, 458
ancestors, 458
astute, 458
awe, 458
uncanny, 458
repulse, 458

KEY TERMS

Reading Comprehension Tests

Explain that reading comprehension tests give a short piece of writing and then ask several questions about it. The questions may ask students to figure out something based on information in the passage. Urge students to keep the following tips in mind:

- Begin by reading all the questions quickly.
- Read the passage with the questions in mind. If time permits, read the passage twice before answering any questions.
- Reread the first question carefully.
- Scan the passage, looking for key words. When you find a key word, slow down and read carefully.
- Answer the first question.
- Repeat this process to answer all the rest of the questions.

Reading Skills

Carefully read the following passage. Then, on a separate piece of paper, answer each question.

from "Beastly Behaviors" by Janine Benyus

It was no more than an evolutionary eyeblink ago that our apelike ancestors were crawling on their hands and knees in pursuit of big, dangerous, delicious animals. For five million years (99% of our time on Earth), our survival hinged on finding animals that we could eat. Stalking an animal meant knowing
5   everything about its habits: where it slept, where it drank its daily water, how fast it would run once it caught wind of us. By necessity, we became astute observers of our fellow creatures and learned a respect that comes with intense study of a subject. Although we've stepped further and further from the wild in our last 5,000 years of agriculture and industry, an ancient awe still stirs deep
10 within us. It's that to-the-bone shiver we feel when we see a wolf trot lightly from the woods or hear the thin song of a rising whale.

What is this uncanny ability animals have to amaze, delight, and at times, frighten or repulse us? Part attraction, part fear, and part admiration still make us curious about wild animals even though we no longer need them to fill our
15 stomachs. In this country alone, 115 million people pour through the turnstiles of zoos each year. That's more people than go to all the professional sporting events combined! Worldwide, 357 million people attended the 757 zoos listed in the *1984 International Zoo Yearbook*—the equivalent of all the people in the United States, Canada, France, and the United Kingdom. And it's not just
20 school groups either. For every wide-eyed child, there are three astonished adults rushing to the rail to see the dolphins leap.

These days, animals in zoos represent more than just a shadow of our ancestral past. They are the last ambassadors of a world that is rapidly becoming less and less wild. The red-alert sirens are screaming, and, for the
25 first time in history, we are admitting to our destructiveness and grappling to right the wrongs. Zoos that were once primarily amusement parks are now on the front lines of that fight, working to brighten the future for rare animals in their keeping. To track this sea change in the zoo world, we have to go back thousands of years, to the creation of the very first zoos.

Differentiated Instruction

English Language Learning

Students learning English will need help with the academic vocabulary used in standardized tests. Explain the following terms used in this workshop and advise students to become familiar with these terms.

prompt—cue, something to help one begin, 456. A "writing prompt" is usually a detailed paragraph of instruction.

position—opinion or point to be discussed, 456
evidence—facts that support an argument, 456

Help students internalize these academic terms by having them explain where they have encountered these words before or in what context they would expect to encounter them. Students should consider how these words are used in everyday life.

1. According to the author, why did early humans learn about the habits of animals?
   A. They were amazed and delighted by animals.
   B. They wanted to catch them for zoos.
   C. They wanted to catch them for food.
   D. They wanted to know everything about their environment.

2. Judging from the rest of the paragraph, what adjective in the first sentence provides the best clue about why humans were looking for animals?
   A. evolutionary
   B. apelike
   C. dangerous
   D. delicious

3. Based on the context, what is the meaning of *astute* in line 6?
   A. perceptive
   B. fearful
   C. unsure
   D. stupid

4. The sentence that begins in line 10 contains
   A. internal conflict.
   B. external conflict.
   C. dialect.
   D. sensory details.

5. The second paragraph
   A. appeals only to emotion.
   B. contains details that support the main idea.
   C. is mostly dialogue.
   D. uses many analogies.

6. When the author refers to zoos as "the last ambassadors of a world" in line 23, she is
   A. using visual media.
   B. using dialect.
   C. using analogy.
   D. using sensory details.

7. From the sentence in lines 26–28, what can you infer about the present role of zoos?
   A. Without zoos, some rare animals would disappear.
   B. Zoos are out-of-date and dangerous to the survival of animals.
   C. Zoos are more popular than amusement parks.
   D. Without zoos, rare animals would have a much better chance at survival.

8. The purpose of this passage is mainly
   A. to entertain.
   B. to tell a story.
   C. to instruct.
   D. to inform.

9. Based on the last paragraph, you can conclude that
   A. animals should only be kept in zoos.
   B. zoos have changed radically over time.
   C. keeping animals confined in zoos is hurting their survival.
   D. zoos have always had the same purpose.

10. What is the main idea of this passage?
    A. Though their purpose has changed over time, zoos help animals and inspire people.
    B. While zoos are good at inspiring people, they are cruel to animals.
    C. Zoos have always fought to protect animal habitats and the environment.
    D. Today's zoos are little more than amusement parks.

Teach the Workshop

Reading Skills

1. C
2. D
3. A
4. D
5. B
6. C
7. A
8. D
9. B
10. A

Test-Taking Skills

Eliminate Incorrect Responses

Tell students that a key skill in answering multiple-choice questions is eliminating incorrect responses. Model a think aloud for one question in the Reading Skills section.

Question 5. The second paragraph does not contain any quotation marks, so I doubt that the answer is C, dialogue. It also contains numbers, so I doubt that it "appeals only to emotion." That eliminates answer A. I need to read the paragraph again to see if it has more than one or two analogies. No—it doesn't. That eliminates answer D. The answer must be B.

Select another question and have the class work as a group to eliminate the incorrect responses.

Planning and Assessment Tools

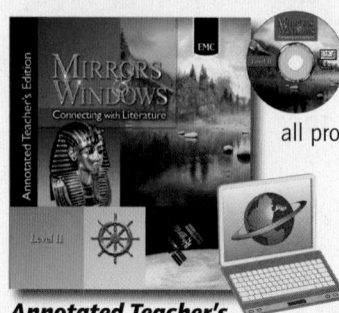

Annotated Teacher's Edition

Annotated Teacher's Edition
One location for accessing, previewing, and planning for use of all program resources.

EMC Launchpad
Desktop application for accessing, previewing, planning, posting, and grading all program resources. Post personal resources and lessons, and access the E-Lesson Planner, the E-Gradebook, and training modules for computer literacy.

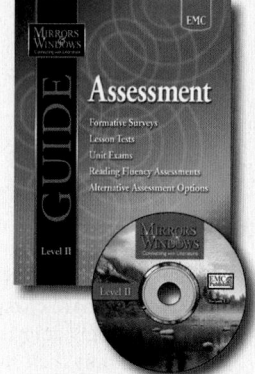

Assessment Guide and ExamView
A variety of assessments are available for this unit in print and electronic forms, including:
- Formative Survey
- Lesson Tests
- Unit Exams
- Alternative Assessment Options
- Reading Fluency Assessments

Meeting the Standards: Unit 5
In addition to lesson-by-lesson resources, *Meeting the Standards* includes the following unit-based resources:
- Unit Study Guide
- Practice Test
- Active Reading Model
- Selection Quizzes

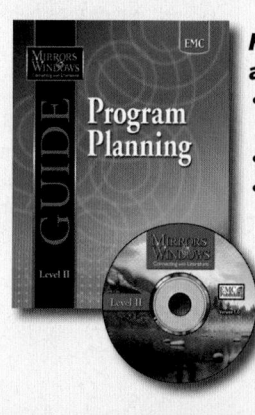

Program Planning Guide and E-Lesson Planner
- Lesson Plans for all the selections in the unit
- Core Standards-Based Selections
- Reading Log and Evaluation Forms

The E-Lesson Planner contains fully developed lesson plans and unit resources with an electronic calendar for editing lesson plans.

Technology Tools

Visual Teaching Package
This package contains unit-based lectures, games, art collections, and Writing Workshops in PowerPoint format; included within the EMC Launchpad.

Interactive Student Text on CD
The student textbook on CD includes highlighting, note-taking, bookmarking, and a direct link to the student website, in addition to everything in the student text.

Audio Library
Authentic, dramatic recordings with listening activities expand listening skills and offer additional support for developing readers and English Language Learners.

ETS Online Criterion-Based Essay Grader (Grades 9–12)
Students can use this ETS web-based tool to evaluate their essays online before submitting them for teacher review and final evaluation.

mirrorsandwindows.com
Student and teacher resources, support, references, technology tools, and state-specific standards are available at **mirrorsandwindows.com**. The website is customizable using the EMC Launchpad.

Exceeding the Standards Unit Resources

Each of the *Exceeding the Standards* resources provides fully developed lessons to help you extend the textbook lessons and to expand upon the themes and skills covered in the unit. You can also download these lessons from **mirrorsandwindows.com**.

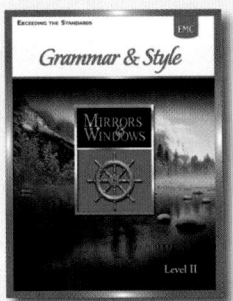

Grammar & Style
This resource contains:
- Three lessons on Prepositions and Conjunctions, pp. 113–122
- Three lessons on Interrupters, pp. 123–131

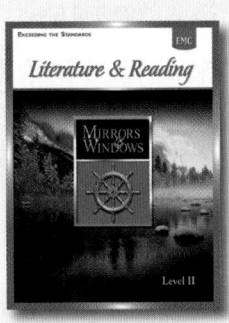

Literature & Reading
This resource contains one extended lesson:
- Deliver an Oral Interpretation of a Poem, pp. 11–13

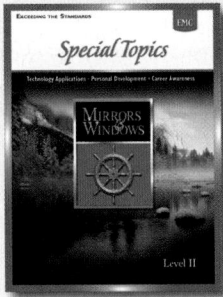

Special Topics
This resource contains:
- Lifelong Learning: Making Good Choices: Part 1, pp. 18–19
- Career Skills Development: Analyzing Your Skills and Values, pp. 20–21

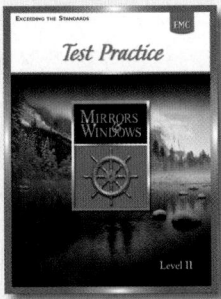

Test Practice
This resource contains:
- Expository Essay Practice Test: Timed Writing, p. 13

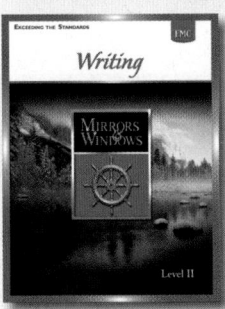

Writing
This resource contains:
- Descriptive Writing: Create an Analogy, pp. 31–38

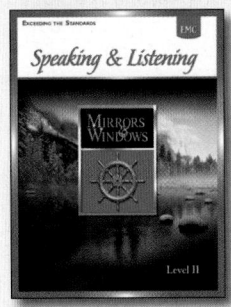

Speaking & Listening
This resource contains the following lesson to expand on the Speaking & Listening Workshop:
- Giving and Actively Listening to Expository Presentations, pp. 13–16

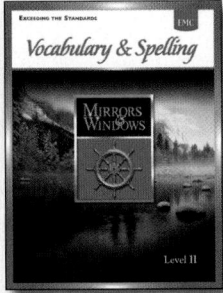

Vocabulary & Spelling
This resource contains:
- Four lessons on Prefixes, Roots, and Suffixes, pp. 47–54
- One lesson on Word Origins, pp. 55–57

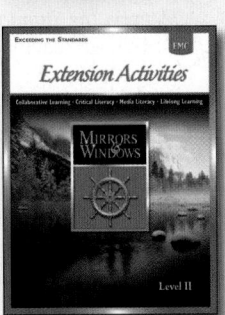

Extension Activities
This resource contains:
- Critical Literacy: Dramatic Reading, p. 14
- Media Literacy: Concrete Poetry, p. 15

Unit 5 Visual Planning Guide

Gold — A Lyric Poem by Pat Mora

467

Reading Level: Easy
Pacing: 1 day

Meeting the Standards,
Reading Model,
pp. 19–26

Developing Readers,
Set Purpose,
pp. 34–36

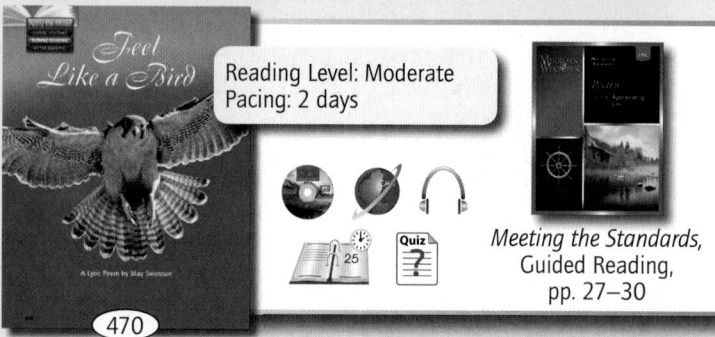

Feel Like a Bird — A Lyric Poem by May Swenson

470

Reading Level: Moderate
Pacing: 2 days

Meeting the Standards,
Guided Reading,
pp. 27–30

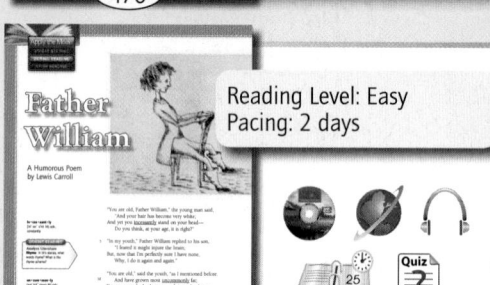

Father William — A Humorous Poem by Lewis Carroll

476

Reading Level: Easy
Pacing: 2 days

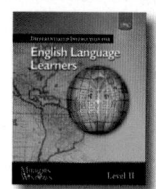

Meeting the Standards,
Guided Reading,
pp. 31–36

Advanced Students,
Author Study,
pp. 27–28

English Language Learners,
Text Organization,
pp. 132–138

Blackberry Eating — A Lyric Poem by Galway Kinnell

482

Reading Level: Moderate
Pacing: 1 day

Meeting the Standards,
Guided Reading,
pp. 37–41

Developing Readers,
Visualize, pp. 37–39

The Village Blacksmith — A Narrative Poem by Henry Wadsworth Longfellow

486

Reading Level: Moderate
Pacing: 2 days

Meeting the Standards,
Directed Reading,
pp. 42–47

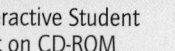 Interactive Student
Text on CD-ROM

 Selection
Lesson Plan

 Web-based
Resources

Lesson-by-Lesson Resources

492

Reading Level: Easy
Pacing: 2 days

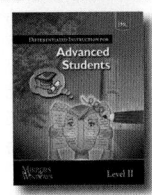
Meeting the Standards,
Directed Reading,
pp. 48–55

Advanced Students,
Cultural Context
Project, pp. 29–30

496

Reading Level: Moderate
Pacing: 2 days

Meeting the Standards,
Directed Reading,
pp. 56–63

503

Reading Level: Moderate
Pacing: 1 day

Meeting the Standards,
Directed Reading,
pp. 64–71

506

Reading Level: Easy; Moderate
Pacing: 2 days

Meeting the Standards,
Compare Literature,
pp. 72–79

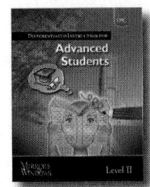
Advanced Students,
Lyric Poetry
Comparison, pp. 31–32

511

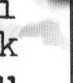
Reading Level: Moderate
Pacing: 1 day

Meeting the Standards,
Directed Reading,
pp. 80–86

 Lesson Test   🎧 Audio Library

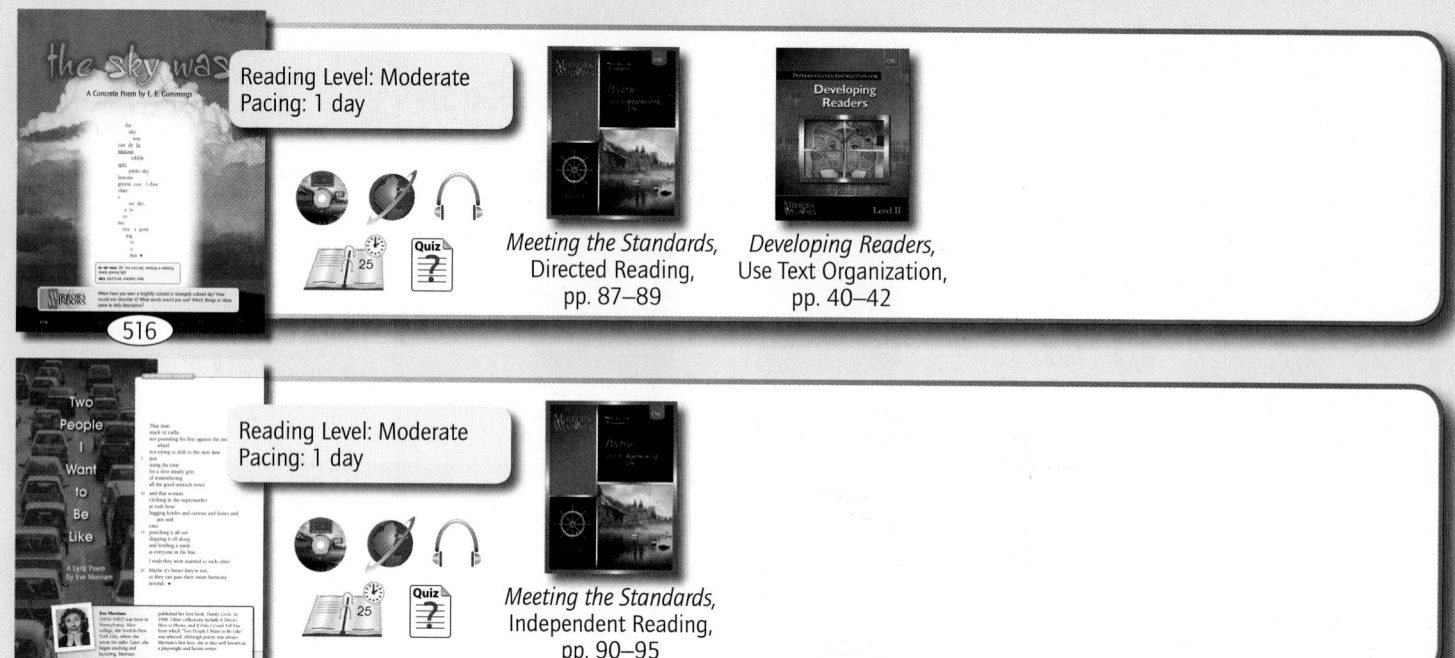

Reading Level: Moderate
Pacing: 1 day

Meeting the Standards,
Directed Reading,
pp. 87–89

Developing Readers,
Use Text Organization,
pp. 40–42

516

Reading Level: Moderate
Pacing: 1 day

Meeting the Standards,
Independent Reading,
pp. 90–95

518

Unit 5 Scope & Sequence Guide

Selection or Feature	Genre	Reading Support/ Reading Level	Word Count	Reading Skill	Graphic Organizer	
Introduction to Poetry pp. 462–463						
Understanding Imagery and Figurative Language p. 464						
Poetry Reading Model p. 465						
Gold Pat Mora pp. 466–468	Lyric Poem	Guided Reading: Reading Model/Easy	115	Identify Main Idea	Main Idea Map; Imagery Chart	
Feel Like a Bird May Swenson pp. 469–472	Lyric Poem	Guided Reading: Reading Model/ Moderate	104	Monitor Comprehension	Note-Taking Chart; Metaphor and Simile Chart	

GUIDED READING

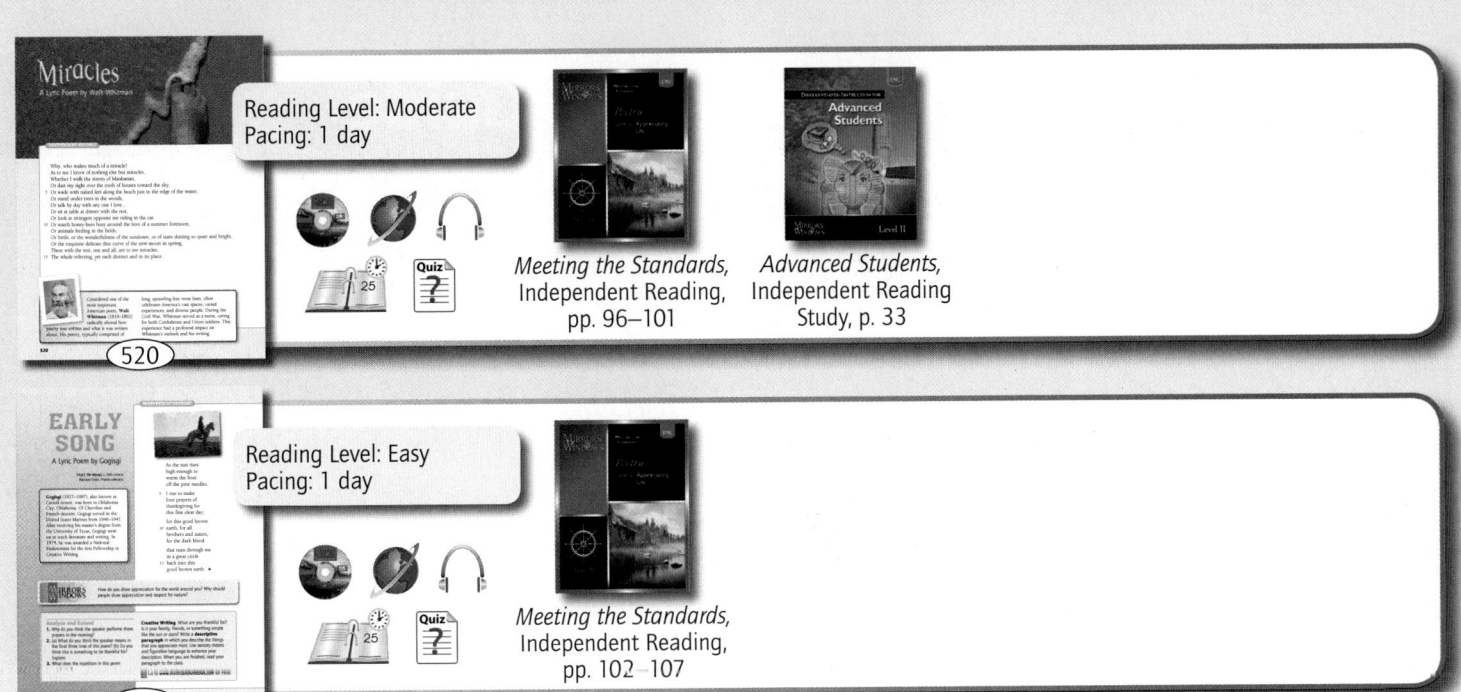

Reading Level: Moderate
Pacing: 1 day

Meeting the Standards,
Independent Reading,
pp. 96–101

Advanced Students,
Independent Reading
Study, p. 33

Reading Level: Easy
Pacing: 1 day

Meeting the Standards,
Independent Reading,
pp. 102–107

Literary Element	*Mirrors & Windows* Theme	Cross-Curricular Connection	Writing Options	Extension Activities
Types of Poetry Elements of Poetry				
What is Imagery? What is Figurative 　Language?				
Imagery	Home		Creative: Poem Expository: Critical Analysis	Collaborative Learning: Discuss 　Author's Purpose Lifelong Learning: Report on 　Desert Life
Metaphor and Simile	Inspiration		Creative: Descriptive Essay Expository: Literary 　Response	Lifelong Learning: Research Birds Media Literacy: Report on Birds in 　the Media

Unit 5 Scope & Sequence Guide

	Selection or Feature	Genre	Reading Support/ Reading Level	Word Count	Reading Skill	Graphic Organizer	
GUIDED READING	**Understanding Sound Devices,** pp. 473–474						
	Father William Lewis Carroll pp. 475–479	Humorous Poem	Guided Reading: Reading Model/Easy	278	Analyze the Effects of Form on Meaning	Form and Effect Chart	
	Blackberry Eating Galway Kinnell pp. 481–483	Lyric Poem	Guided Reading: Reading Model/ Moderate	95	Identify Author's Perspective	Perspective Chart; Alliteration Chart	
DIRECTED READING	**The Village Blacksmith** Henry Wadsworth Longfellow pp. 485–489	Narrative Poem	Directed Reading/ Moderate	302	Context Clues		
	Mother to Son Langston Hughes pp. 491–494	Lyric Poem	Directed Reading/Easy	112	Identify Main Idea	Main Idea Map; Repetition Chart	
	Under the Apple Tree Diana Rivera pp. 495–500	Lyric Poem	Directed Reading/ Moderate	88	Identify Multiple Levels of Meaning	Multiple Levels of Meaning Chart; Free Verse Chart	
	Informational Text Connection: from **The Botany of Desire** Michael Pollan pp. 498–499	Essay	Moderate	741			
	The Tropics in New York Claude McKay pp. 502–503	Lyric Poem	Directed Reading/ Moderate	99	Analyze Cause and Effect	Cause-and-Effect Chart; Rhyme Scheme Chart	
	Comparing Literature: Unfolding Bud Naoshi Koriyama pp. 505–509	Lyric Poem	Directed Reading/ Easy	74		Metaphor Chart	
	How to Eat a Poem Eve Merriam pp. 505–509	Lyric Poem	Directed Reading/ Moderate	72			
	Haiku Matsuo Bashō, Yosa Buson, and Kobayashi Issa pp. 510–514	Haiku	Directed Reading/ Moderate	36	Compare and Contrast	Comparative Chart; Imagery Chart	
	Informational Text Connection: from **Lost in Translation** Steven Harvey pp. 513–514	Essay	Moderate	489			

Literary Element	*Mirrors & Windows* Theme	Cross-Curricular Connection	Writing Options	Extension Activities
What Are Sound Devices? Rhyme Rhythm Onomatopoeia Alliteration, Consonance, and Assonance				
Rhyme	Character	Cultural Connection: *Wonderland*	Creative: Humorous Poem Descriptive: Character Sketch	Collaborative Learning: Discuss Hyperbole Critical Literacy: Perform a Role-Play
Alliteration	Associations		Creative: Narrative Essay Expository: Critical Analysis	Collaborative Learning: Discuss Alliteration Lifelong Learning: Write a Poem
Rhythm	Admirable Qualities		Creative: Short Story Expository: Critical Analysis	Critical Literacy: Conduct a Debate Media Literacy: Do Research
Repetition	Guidance		Creative: Monologue Narrative: Personal Narrative	Collaborative Learning: Discuss Challenges Critical Literacy: Dramatic Reading
Free Verse	Shared Experiences		Creative: Lyric Poem Persuasive: Newspaper Editorial	Lifelong Learning: Study Trees Media Literacy: List Poetry Sites
Rhyme Scheme	Homesickness		Creative: Personal Letter Expository: Expository Essay	Critical Literacy: Conduct a Television Interview Lifelong Learning: Research New Foods
Compare Literature: Metaphor	Appreciation		Creative: Descriptive Essay or Poem Expository: Persuasive Essay	Critical Literacy: Hold a Panel Discussion Lifelong Learning: Write a Biography
	Experiences			
Haiku	Inspiration		Creative: Advertisement Applied: Instructions	Media Literacy: Compare Translations Lifelong Learning: Origins of Haiku

Unit 5 Scope & Sequence Guide

	Selection or Feature	Genre	Reading Support/ Reading Level	Word Count	Reading Skill	Graphic Organizer	
DIRECTED READING	**the sky was** E.E. Cummings pp. 515–517	Concrete Poem	Directed Reading/ Moderate	37	Text Organization	Text Organization Chart; Details Web	
INDEPENDENT READING	**Two People I Want to Be Like** Eve Merriam pp. 518–519	Lyric Poem	Independent Reading/ Moderate	104	Identify the Main Idea		
INDEPENDENT READING	**Miracles** Walt Whitman pp. 520–521	Lyric Poem	Independent Reading/ Moderate	232	Analyze Text Organization		
INDEPENDENT READING	**Early Song** Gogisgi p. 522	Lyric Poem	Independent Reading/ Easy	60	Identify the Main Idea		

Unit 5 Language Arts Workshops

Grammar & Style	Vocabulary & Spelling	Writing	Speaking & Listening	Test Practice
Personal and Possessive Pronouns, p. 480 Nouns: Proper, Plural, Possessive, and Collective, p. 490 Reflexive and Intensive Pronouns, p. 501	Synonyms and Antonyms, p. 484	Expository Writing: Compare-and-Contrast Essay, pp. 524–529	Giving and Actively Listening to Expository Presentations, pp. 530–531	Writing Skills: Expository Essay, "Song" by Robert Browning, "The Gardener" (LXXXV) by Rabindranath Tagore, p. 532 Revising and Editing, p. 533 Reading Skills: "Silver" by Walter de la Mare, pp. 534–535

Literary Element	*Mirrors & Windows* Theme	Cross-Curricular Connection	Writing Options	Extension Activities
Concrete Poetry	Description		Creative: Concrete Poem Persuasive: Review	Collaborative Learning: Discuss Purpose Media Literacy: Concrete Poetry
Free Verse	Patience		Creative: Biography	Collaborative Learning: Discuss Personality Traits
Repetition	Miracles		Expository: Literary Response	Critical Literacy: Analyze and Discuss the Poem's Form
Repetition	Appreciation		Creative: Descriptive Paragraph	

Unit 5 Building Vocabulary

The lists below identify the Words in Use and Key Terms within this unit. These words are listed at the bottom of the Teacher's Edition pages at the beginning of each lesson. Vocabulary development activities are provided in the *Meeting the Standards* unit book and in *Exceeding the Standards: Vocabulary & Spelling*.

WORDS IN USE

Preview Vocabulary
Preview Vocabulary are words taken from the sentences within each selection. These words are defined in the side margin or at the bottom of the pages on which they appear. The "Preview Vocabulary" section introduces these words in the Before Reading page preceding each selection.

bellows, 487	incessantly, 476	sinewy, 487	tread, 497
benediction, 503	laden, 503	snipe, 471	unbidden, 482
brawny, 487	luminous, 516	splurge, 482	uncommonly, 476
crevice, 496	mystical, 503	spry, 516	wrought, 448
emerald, 496	sage, 477	supple, 477	
giddy, 471	scraggly, 497	trance, 496	

Selection Words
Selection Words are additional words from the reading that may be challenging but are not central to the selection and are not identified in the prereading section. These words can easily be learned using the story context, and they provide excellent practice for using content clues to find meaning without explicit instruction.

airs, 478	emblem, 499	immortal, 513	somersault, 476
boiled, 498	exquisite, 520	lattice, 513	spouting, 516
casements, 534	forenoon, 520	makeshift, 498	stalks, 482
catamaran, 498	fragrant, 532	meager, 513	swerved, 496
cote, 534	furiously, 496	ointment, 477	thatch, 534
deemed, 498	glimmer, 496	parson, 488	threshing, 487
delicate, 520	haltingly, 513	peculiar, 482	toiling, 488
despairing, 513	hastily, 497	ramshackle, 498	
distinct, 520	hence, 532	repose, 488	
edible, 516	hull, 498	shoon, 534	

Teaching Words
Teaching Words consist of vocabulary that is used in the directions about the lessons. Teaching words explain to students what to focus on within the selection, help establish the story context, clarify the meaning of literary terms, and define the goals or instructional purpose.

accessible, 485	compelling, 517	gloom, 473	mangoes, 502
admirable, 519	comprised, 520	gorge, 484	modify, 494
advocate, 466	consistent, 462, 473	guavas, 502	obvious, 521
altered, 520	contemporary, 505	hideaway, 500	papayas, 502
amateur, 500	contradict, 494	hybrid, 481	parson, 475
aphids, 524	convey, 473	impact, 473	peculiar, 483
bigotry, 494	cultivate, 481	indulge, 484	playwright, 505, 518
bilingual, 466	debris, 533	inhibit, 517	pollinate, 495
broad, 462	defy, 516	jargon, 530	pomes, 495
budding, 485	diametrically, 528	keen, 469	precise, 510
caricatures, 478	distinctions, 462	larvae, 524	prevalent, 502
chivalry, 528	elevate, 514	liberated, 508	prickly, 484
clarify, 509	evoke, 472, 502	lounged, 484	profound, 520
clergyman, 515	fungi, 524	manageable, 530	prosperity, 491

quirky, 478
radically, 520
regional, 466
reinforce, 489
representation, 463
rosaceae, 495

soot, 533
splurge, 484
sprawling, 520
stalks, 484
stencil, 517
tapestry, 478

traditions, 466
transcribe, 489
translate, 513
translation, 524
unbidden, 484
unimpressed, 507

unique, 463
virtuous, 475
vital, 519
vitality, 528
vivid, 469
wistful, 502

KEY TERMS

Key Terms are commonly referred to as *academic vocabulary*. These terms appear in the instructional material to teach the terminology that students need to acquire to understand literature. The repetition of the terms throughout the program ensures student mastery and provides a solid foundation for the continuing study of literature and language arts.

alliteration, 463, 474, 481, 500, 534
antonym, 484
apostrophe, 490
assonance, 474, 483, 500, 535
author's perspective, 481
author's purpose, 468, 505
biography, 509, 519
capitalization, 469, 491
cause and effect, 502
cause-and-effect order, 531
chronological order, 531
collective noun, 490
compare and contrast, 532
compare-and-contrast essay, 524
compare-and-contrast order, 531
comparison, 524
conclusion, 519, 524, 531
concrete poem, 462, 515
connotation, 484
consonance, 474, 483, 500, 534
consonant, 490
consonant blend, 484
context clue, 465, 485
contrast, 524
couplet, 462
denotation, 484
dialogue, 479
digraph, 484
drafting, 524
dynamic, 535
end rhyme, 473, 475, 502

expository essay, 532
expository presentation, 530
expository writing, 524
extended metaphor, 509, 535
figurative language, 463, 465, 495, 510, 515
figures of speech, 500
first-person point of view, 483
foot, 474
form, 521
free verse, 462, 495, 505, 521
haiku, 462, 510, 534
half rhyme, 473
hyperbole, 463, 479, 534
iamb, 474
image, 463, 495
imagery, 463, 466, 500, 510, 535
internal rhyme, 473, 475, 534
introduction, 531
introductory paragraph, 504
line, 462, 521
line break, 491
lyric, 462
lyric poem, 466, 469, 481, 491, 495, 502, 505, 520
lyric poetry, 521
main idea, 466, 491, 521
metaphor, 463, 469, 479, 483, 495, 505, 535
meter, 463, 474, 475, 485, 495, 505

monologue, 494
mood, 473
narrative, 462, 483
narrative poem, 485
onomatopoeia, 474, 534
organizational pattern, 527
outline, 468, 532
peer reviewer, 527
personal narrative, 494
personality trait, 519
personification, 463, 534
plural noun, 490
poem, 468
poetry, 462
point of view, 535
point-by-point, 527
possessive noun, 490
problem-and-solution order, 531
proper noun, 490
punctuation, 469, 491
quatrain, 462
renga, 510
repetition, 475, 491, 521, 535
review, 517
revising, 524
rhyme, 463, 473, 474, 475, 485, 521
rhyme scheme, 465, 500, 502, 505, 534, 573, 575
round, 535
sensory detail, 479, 483, 515
setting, 468

simile, 463, 468, 469, 479, 483, 495, 534
skim, 502, 505
slant rhyme, 463, 473
sonnet, 462
sound device, 463, 473, 483, 495
speaker, 462
stanza, 462, 466, 469, 485, 502, 521
stressed syllable, 474
structure, 475, 510, 515
subject-by-subject, 527
summarize, 468
summary, 524
syllable, 485, 510, 535
symbol, 463
synonym, 484
tanka, 510
tercet, 462
text organization, 515
text structure, 491
thesaurus, 484
thesis, 532
thesis statement, 524
third-person point of view, 483
tone, 462, 468, 473, 481, 510
transition, 524, 532
unstressed syllable, 474

Objectives

Studying this unit will enable students to

- connect the themes expressed in poems to their own lives and to the world around them
- understand different elements and forms of poetry, including *imagery, metaphor, simile, rhyme, rhyme scheme, alliteration, rhythm, repetition, free verse, haiku,* and *concrete poetry*

Reading Strategies

Ask Questions   Make Predictions
Clarify   Visualize
Make Inferences

Reading Skills

Analyze Cause and Effect
Analyze the Effects of Form on
  Meaning
Compare and Contrast
Context Clues
Identify Author's Perspective
Identify Main Idea
Identify Multiple Levels of Meaning
Monitor Comprehension
Text Organization

Literary Elements

Alliteration
Concrete Poetry
Figurative Language
Free Verse
Haiku
Imagery
Metaphor and Simile
Repetition
Rhyme and Rhyme Scheme
Rhythm
Sound Devices

Appreciating Life
Poetry
Unit 5

GALWAY KINNELL   CLAUDE McKAY   MAY SWENSON

Launch the Unit

Have small groups create questions that relate to the unit theme. Suggest that students focus on both general and specific ways of showing appreciation. Model this by proposing two questions: "How do people demonstrate that they appreciate nature?" and "What specific rituals in our community show that people appreciate each other?" Have groups list their questions. When you have completed the unit, revisit these lists. Identify selections that provide insights into how to answer them.

"Summer night—
even the stars
are whispering to each other."

— KOBAYASHI ISSA

Observing the world around you can help you appreciate life. In Kobayashi Issa's haiku—a kind of Japanese poetry—the speaker describes the beauty of the stars on a summer night. As you read the poems in this unit, try to visualize the portraits of the world that the poets create with language. Consider how each poet has a unique perspective on life.

E. E. CUMMINGS

LANGSTON HUGHES

WALT WHITMAN

461

Program Resources

For a visual reminder of the unit-based resources available for Unit 5, Poetry, see pages 460A and 460B. As you introduce the unit, you may want to provide students with the Unit Study Guide, which is contained in the *Meeting the Standards* resource.

Introduction to Poetry

Most students will have some experience with poetry. If you have English language learners in class, invite them to recite poems in their native languages so that the class can hear rhythm and rhyme. Try to draw on students' experience as you teach this lesson. Encourage them also to explore the elements of poetry in the Before Reading and After Reading sections of each selection in Unit 5.

Launch the Lesson

Read these lines—the first four lines of Shakespeare's Sonnet 34—aloud to students:

Why didst thou promise such a
    beauteous day,
And make me travel forth without my
    cloak,
To let base clouds o'ertake me in my
    way,
Hiding thy bravery in their rotten
    smoke?

Ask questions to generate some interpretation of these lines, such as: "What do you think has happened? Have you ever regretted counting on good weather? When else in life might a person have this feeling?" Tell students that experts read this sonnet (a poem by William Shakespeare that has fourteen lines in all) not as a complaint about the weather, but as a metaphor rebuking a friend who has betrayed the speaker's trust. Tell them they will explore such layers of meaning in this unit.

Introduction to Poetry

Don't be polite.

Bite in.

Pick it up with your fingers and lick the juice
    that may run down your chin.

It is ready and ripe now, whenever you are.

You don't need a knife or fork or spoon

or plate or napkin or tablecloth.

—EVE MERRIAM, "How to Eat a Poem"

How is this passage different from pieces of literature you have read in previous units? What about its shape and tone makes it unique? The above passage is not prose; it is poetry. The language of **poetry** is musical, and the word choices exact. Poets use imagery, metaphor, simile, and other kinds of figurative language, as well as sound devices such as rhyme and alliteration.

One of the major distinctions between poetry and prose is the use of the line. A **line** of poetry is a single row of words. In prose, sentences are the basic unit with which writers work. Poets, however, work with both the sentence and the line.

Stanzas are made up of lines in the same way that paragraphs are made up of sentences. In a poem, each stanza is separated from the next by a space. The number of lines in a stanza helps to determine the kind of stanza it is. Some of the most common kinds of stanzas include the *couplet,* which is a two-line stanza, the *tercet,* which is a three-line stanza, and the *quatrain,* which is a four-line stanza.

Types of Poetry

Lyric Poems and Narrative Poems

There are two main kinds of poetry: lyric and narrative. A **lyric** poem expresses the emotions of the poem's **speaker,** or narrator. Often lyric poetry focuses on a single moment, image, or idea.

Narrative poetry tells a story and is frequently longer than lyric poetry. Narrative poems can include many of the same literary elements as fiction, such as characters and plot. Edgar Allan Poe's "Annabel Lee" (page 547) and Alfred Noyes's "The Highwayman" (page 551) are both examples of narrative poetry.

Poetic Forms

Within these two broad categories, there are many different poetic forms. A poem's form is determined by its individual elements. Here is a list of some poetic forms:

- **Sonnet:** A sonnet is a fourteen-line poem that usually explores the theme of romantic love. Sonnets are rhymed and use a regular rhythm.

- **Haiku:** Originating in Japan, haikus are short three-line poems that describe a single image or scene from nature. Traditionally, the first and third lines of a haiku have five syllables, whereas the second line has seven.

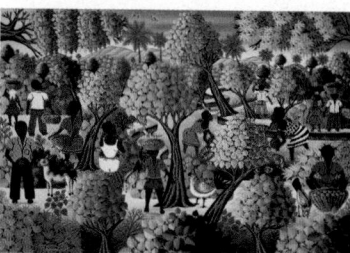

- **Concrete Poem:** A concrete poem is a poem that is shaped like the thing it describes. For example, if a poem describes a tree, the words on the page would be organized to visually resemble a tree.

- **Free Verse:** Free verse does not use consistent rhymes or rhythms. Free verse can take any shape and address any subject.

To help students explore literature on a deeper level, assign the following activity: Deliver an Oral Interpretation of a Poem, *Exceeding the Standards: Literature & Reading,* pp. 11–13.

Words in Use

Teaching Words
distinctions, 462
broad, 462
consistent, 462
unique, 463
representation, 463

KEY TERMS

TONE, 462	CONCRETE POEM, 462	SLANT RHYME, 463
POETRY, 462	FREE VERSE, 462	RHYTHM, 463
LINE, 462	FIGURATIVE LANGUAGE, 463	METER, 463
STANZA, 462		ALLITERATION, 463
COUPLET, 462	METAPHOR, 463	SYMBOL, 463
TERCET, 462	SIMILE, 463	
QUATRAIN, 462	HYPERBOLE, 463	
LYRIC, 462	PERSONIFICATION, 463	
SPEAKER, 462	IMAGE, 463	
NARRATIVE, 462	IMAGERY, 463	
SONNET, 462	SOUND DEVICE, 463	
HAIKU, 462	RHYME, 463	

Elements of Poetry

Every poem is unique, but most poems use some of the elements listed below. Knowing these elements will help you better understand poetry in general.

Figurative Language and Imagery

Nearly all poems use figurative language and imagery. **Figurative language** is anything written or spoken that is not meant to be taken literally. Figurative language includes metaphors and similes. A **metaphor** is a figure of speech in which one thing is spoken or written about as if it were another. For example, in Diana Rivera's poem "Under the Apple Tree" (page 495), the speaker uses a metaphor to describe a tree: "Branches are suns / that glimmer from within."

A **simile** also compares one thing to another, but it uses the word *like* or *as*. In "Under the Apple Tree," Rivera uses a simile to describe worms: "Earthworms insert themselves into the earth / like glossy, pink pins!"

Other common kinds of figurative language include hyperbole and personification. **Hyperbole** is an exaggeration used for effect or to make a point. **Personification** is a figure of speech in which something not human is described as if it were human. Rivera uses personification to describe apple blossoms: "here, under the apple tree, / where a crowd of petals close their eyes...."

An **image** is a concrete representation of an object or an experience. It is the vivid mental picture created in the reader's mind. When considered together, the images in a literary work are referred to as **imagery.**

Sound Devices

A **sound device** is any element that appeals to the reader's ear. Sound devices make poetry more exciting, more musical, and can affect a poem's meaning. Some of the most common sound devices used in poetry include rhyme, rhythm, and alliteration.

Rhyme is the repetition of sounds at the ends of words. For example, the word *soon* rhymes with *moon*. Sometimes a rhyme is not completely exact, like *step* and *stop*. This is called a **slant rhyme.**

Rhythm is the pattern of beats, or stressed syllables, in a line of poetry. If this pattern is regular, it is called **meter.**

Alliteration is the repetition of consonant sounds at the beginnings of words. For example, the repetition of the *b* sound in *bright blue bottle* is alliteration.

Meaning in Poetry

Finding meaning in poetry is slightly different from finding meaning in short stories or essays. Poems can have many different layers of meaning that make it difficult to identify a single main idea or purpose. In part, this is because poets express their ideas, experiences, and feelings with imagery, figurative language, and symbols. A **symbol** is a thing that stands for itself and something else. Some traditional symbols include doves for peace and owls for wisdom. Symbols can also be unique to a particular piece of literature, author, or culture.

Types of Poetry

Instead of reading through all the text on these pages at once, you could have students work in groups to hunt for and select good examples of each form and literary element introduced—sonnet, haiku, concrete poem, free verse, lyric poem, narrative poem, figurative language, symbol, and sound devices. Then, as you cover the material in this lesson, use students' examples to illustrate each item.

TEACHING NOTE

Enrichment

Have students with different learning styles collaborate on a creative translation of a short poem. Encourage pairs of students to select a single poem from this book or from classroom or library resources. The students should take turns reading the poem aloud to each other. Then the pair should decide on the medium into which they will translate the poem—dance, song, visual art, musical composition, and so on. Give students several days to put together their responses. Ask volunteers to present their work to the class.

Writing Skills

Maintain a Portfolio

Tell students that creating a personal portfolio of their own poems can help them improve as writers, as well as keep their work organized in case they must ever compile a selection for class. Urge them to choose a good method for storing their poems, such as a pocket folder with plenty of room. They should then regularly put their finished poems in it.

Urge them to put a date on every poem so they will know when they wrote it. By reviewing their portfolios now and then, students will see the progress they have made as poets. Other items to include are:

- notes with ideas for possible future poems
- rough drafts of finished poems
- written comments from teachers or peers about their poems

Common Core State Standards

Reading Literature
RL.4
Language
L.5

Understanding Imagery and Figurative Language

Reading strategies and skills that can help students understand imagery and figurative language include visualizing and making connections.

Use Reading Strategies

Visualize Because images are concrete, and almost always incorporate at least one sensory detail, encourage students to form pictures in their minds, as well as to imagine smells, sounds, feelings, and tastes relating to images. Tell students that reading poetry means taking time to experience imagery, even a few words or lines at a time.

Use Reading Skills

Activate Prior Knowledge Most readers find that poems evoke feelings and associations. Assure students that poets mean for this to happen. Encourage students to allow time as they read poems to experience the feelings, ideas, and images that come to them. Tell them they may refer to these things when they answer questions or write about the poems they read.

KEY TERMS

IMAGE, 464
IMAGERY, 464
SETTING, 464
CHARACTER, 464
MOOD, 464
FIGURATIVE LANGUAGE, 464
METAPHOR, 464
SIMILE, 464
PERSONIFICATION, 464
HYPERBOLE, 464

Understanding Imagery and Figurative Language

What Is Imagery?

An **image** is language that creates a concrete representation of an object or an experience. It is the vivid mental picture created in the reader's mind. When considered together, the images in a literary work are referred to as **imagery.**

In the passage on this page from Diana Rivera's poem "Under the Apple Tree," the poet uses sensory details and precise language to create the poem's imagery. For example, "where birds now nestle and sleep," "silver specks," and "fly through the glimmering blue" are all examples of imagery.

Writers can use imagery to create a setting or character, to express an idea or emotion, or to alter the mood or atmosphere of a piece of literature.

What Is Figurative Language?

Figurative language is writing or speech meant to be understood imaginatively instead of literally. Many writers use figures of speech to help readers see things in new ways. Some of the most common kinds of figurative language are metaphor, simile, personification, and hyperbole.

A **metaphor** is a figure of speech in which one thing is spoken or written about as if it were another. Metaphors invite the reader to make a comparison between these two things. A metaphor works because the things being compared have one or more qualities in common. A **simile** is like a metaphor. However, similes use the word *like* or *as* when making a comparison. For example, in the excerpt to the right, Rivera writes that the chirps "rise like tiny bells." The word *like* in this passage compares *chirping* to *tiny bells.*

When a writer uses **personification,** he or she is describing something that is not human as if it were. For example, in "Once by the Pacific" (page 544) Robert Frost describes the waves as if they could think and consciously act.

I like it
here
where birds now nestle and sleep,
where little, high-pitched,
    cricketed chirps
rise like tiny bells towards the
    ageless moon.

Here,
where insects,—silver specks—
fly through the glimmering blue.
—DIANA RIVERA, "Under the Apple Tree"

Hyperbole is exaggeration. Writers use hyperbole to make a point or to have an effect on the reader. Rivera calls the moon "ageless." This is an example of hyperbole. The moon is not ageless, but Rivera describes it in this way to make the point that the moon is very old.

Differentiated Instruction

English Language Learning

Remind English learners that images and figurative language emphasize details. Have them practice isolating details by listing five to ten details that strongly represent either themselves or individuals they're thinking of. Coach them to avoid big ideas, such as "nice," and focus on details, such as "cheerful voice."

Reading Proficiency

Point out that a poem's title may contribute to its meaning. For some poems in this book, skipping the title would deprive the reader of key information relating to images and figurative language in the poem. Suggest that students use the Table of Contents to skim titles in Units 5 and 6, reacting to whatever images the titles bring to mind.

Common Core State Standards

Language
L.5

Poetry Reading Model

Build Background

You need to apply two different types of background to read a poem effectively. One type is the poem's literary and historical context. Read the **Build Background** and **Meet the Author** features to get this information. The other type of background is the personal knowledge and experience you bring to your reading.

Set Purpose

Read the **Set Purpose** to decide what you want to get out of the poem. Before reading the poem, note how the lines are arranged.

Analyze Literature

Poets use different techniques in writing different poems. The **Analyze Literature** draws your attention to the type of poem or a literary element important to a particular poem.

Use Reading Skills

The **Use Reading Skills** feature will show you skills to help you get the most out of your reading. Learn how to apply skills such as determining author's purpose and using context clues. Identify a graphic organizer that will help you apply the skill before and while you read.

Use Reading Strategies

- **Ask questions** about things that seem significant or interesting.
- **Make predictions** about what's going to happen next. As you read, gather more clues to confirm or change your prediction.
- **Visualize** the images. Form pictures in your mind to help you see who or what the poet is describing.
- **Make inferences,** or educated guesses, about what is not stated directly.
- **Clarify,** or check that you understand, what you read. Reread any difficult parts.

Analyze Literature

What is the purpose of the poem, and what literary elements achieve that purpose? For example, how does imagery or rhyme add to the meaning? Note how these elements affect your understanding of the poem.

Make Connections

Notice where connections can be made between the poem and your life or the world outside the poem. What feelings or thoughts do you have while reading the poem?

Find Meaning

Recall the important details of the poem, such as the images, figurative language, and rhyme scheme. Use this information to **interpret,** or explain, the poem's meaning.

Make Judgments

- **Analyze** the poem by examining details and deciding what they contribute to the meaning.
- **Evaluate** the poem by making judgments about how the author creates meaning.

Analyze Literature

Review how the use of literary elements increases your understanding of the poem. For example, how might figurative language shape a poem's meaning?

Extend

Go beyond the text by exploring the poem's ideas through writing or other creative projects.

POETRY READING MODEL **465**

Use the Model

Introduce the Process

Use this page to show students the basic instruction provided for them before, during, and after reading most poems in Units 5 and 6.

"Gold" is an Active Reading Model. Side notes in these lessons prompt students to become more active readers by using reading strategies and skills, analyzing literature, and making connections. Students can apply the process they use to read "Gold" to other poems in Units 5 and 6.

For more information; see Reading Strategies and Skills, Section 1 in the Language Arts Handbook.

Before Reading Stress the distinction between the two types of background students need to apply, and encourage students to always set a specific purpose for reading.

During Reading Point out the side notes in "Gold": Analyze Literature and Use Reading Skills. Then show students the Mirrors & Windows questions on page 467. Explain that they will first respond to the poem personally, and then apply their insights to a broader issue.

After Reading Show students page 468. Tell them that "Find Meaning" questions will help them recall and interpret details. "Make Judgments" questions ask them to analyze a poem and evaluate how specific details contribute to its overall literary effect or meaning.

Speaking & Listening Skills

Listen to Recorded Poetry

Have students listen to the Audio Library recording of a poem in either Unit 5 or Unit 6.

To encourage students to respond to poems they hear, ask basic questions about the recorded poem and invite students to ask other questions.

- Who or what is the speaker in the poem?
- What is the speaker's initial attitude?
- What do we experience during the poem?

KEY TERMS

CONTEXT CLUE, 465
FIGURATIVE LANGUAGE, 465
RHYME SCHEME, 465

Common Core State Standards

Reading Literature
RL.1, RL.2
Speaking and Listening
SL.1

Gold

A Lyric Poem by Pat Mora

At a Glance

Guided Reading: Reading Model
- Reading Level: Easy
- Difficulty Considerations: None
- Ease Factors: Imagery and straightforward language

Objectives

Studying this lesson will enable students to

- use reading skills such as identifying the main idea
- define imagery and recognize how it is used in the poem
- define the literary accomplishments of Pat Mora and explain how home and nature influence her writing
- appreciate a lyric poem that celebrates feeling at home

Launch the Lesson

Prior to reading "Gold," ask students: "Do you ever sit and watch a landscape and the animals that live there? Is it beautiful? What else do you like to quietly observe?"

Summary

In "Gold," the speaker climbs the hills in a desert and sits among the rocks to watch the sun set. The speaker notices lizards, a rabbit, a sparrow, and a hawk, all beneath the backdrop of a golden sky.

GUIDED READING

Build Background

Literary Context Writers who celebrate, in their work, the geography, culture, and traditions of a particular area are known as regional writers. Mexican-American poet Pat Mora is a regional writer who expresses, through her poems and stories, her love of the American Southwest. In the poem "Gold," Mora describes a day in the desert.

Reader's Context Imagine that you are walking in the desert alone. What would you see? What feelings would you have about your surroundings?

Set Purpose

Previewing "Gold" will help you decide how to read and interpret the poem. Look at how the poem is structured, such as the length of the lines and stanzas. Try to determine how these structural elements affect the way in which you read and understand the poem.

Analyze Literature

Imagery The **imagery,** or mental pictures, in a poem often appeal to the reader's senses by describing how things look, sound, feel, taste, or smell. As you read "Gold," think about how the poet uses imagery to help you better visualize the landscape.

Use Reading Skills

Identify Main Idea To identify the main idea of "Gold," gather the details in a main idea map. Then examine the details to determine the overall message the poet wants to convey.

Meet the Author

Pat Mora (b. 1942), born in El Paso, Texas, is a Mexican-American writer of poetry, fiction, and nonfiction for adults and children. She has received many awards for her writing and is an advocate for bilingual literacy. Her writing is marked by strong imagery and often focuses on themes of cultural diversity, the Southwest, native traditions, and universal experiences.

Words in Use

Teaching Words
regional, 466
traditions, 466
advocate, 466
bilingual, 466

KEY TERMS
LYRIC POEM, 466
STANZA, 466
IMAGERY, 466
MAIN IDEA, 466
SETTING, 468
SIMILE, 468
POEM, 468
TONE, 468
SUMMARIZE, 468
AUTHOR'S PURPOSE, 468
OUTLINE, 468

Gold

A Lyric Poem by Pat Mora

When Sun paints the desert
with its gold,
I climb the hills.
Wind runs round boulders, ruffles
5 my hair. I sit on my favorite rock,
lizards for company, a rabbit,
ears stiff in the shade
of a saguaro.[1]
In the wind, we're all
10 eye to eye.

Sparrow on saguaro watches
rabbit watch us in the gold
of sun setting.
Hawk sails on waves of light, sees
15 sparrow, rabbit, lizards, me,
our eyes shining,
watching red and purple sand rivers
    stream down the hill.

I stretch my arms wide as the sky
like hawk extends her wings
20 in all the gold light of this, home. ❖

---

1. **saguaro** (sə gwär´ ə). Large cactus that grows in
the southwestern United States and in northern Mexico

> **DURING READING**
> **Analyze Literature**
> **Imagery** What do the images in this stanza help you see and feel? **A**

> **DURING READING**
> **Use Reading Skills**
> **Identify Main Idea** **B** What does the third stanza suggest about this poem's main idea?

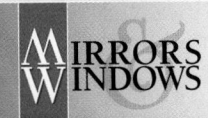
The speaker refers to the desert as "home." "Home" might be a place that makes us feel happy, hopeful, alive, and energized. What is a place that you might call "home"? What kinds of things make people feel most at home?

467

Teach the Model

Analyze Literature
Imagery Remind students that imagery creates the feeling of an experience. Have students point out words in "Gold" that relate to seeing.

Analyze Literature
Imagery *Answer:* They present the landscape washed with golden sunshine, the speaker sitting, animals nearby, and the feeling of the wind ruffling the speaker's hair. **A**

Use Reading Skills
Identify Main Idea Model beginning to infer the main idea: "The image of golden sunlight evokes warmth and comfort, feelings I associate with home."

Use Reading Skills
Identify Main Idea *Answer:* It suggests that the desert can be a happy home. **B**

MIRRORS & WINDOWS The Mirrors & Windows questions focus on the theme of home. Before students begin reading, ask: Where is the single place you most enjoy being? You may want to ask students to write a journal entry or quick write, or divide students into discussion groups or lead a whole-class discussion about this question. *Answer:* Students should say how the places they identify make them feel. Their general statements may include comfort, familiarity, and family.

Program Resources

Planning and Assessment
Program Planning Guide, Selection Lesson Plan
E-Lesson Planner
Assessment Guide, Lesson Test
ExamView

Technology Tools
Interactive Student Text on CD
Visual Teaching Package
Audio Library
mirrorsandwindows.com

Meeting the Standards
Poetry: Unit 5, Reading Model, pp. 19–26

Differentiating Instruction
Developing Readers, Set Purpose, pp. 34–36

Find Meaning

1. (a) It is in the desert. (b) The speaker often spends time here, as indicated by her "favorite rock."
2. The lizards are "company," creating a relaxed, friendly mood.
3. The speaker calls it home.

Make Judgments

4. It is watching the lizards.
5. (a) It describes sunset. (b) The speaker seems to describe how the sand reflects colors of the sunset.
6. (a) The speaker uses two similes. She compares the openness of her arms to the width of the sky, and her outstretched arms to the wings of a hawk in flight. (b) Both convey feelings of freedom and joy.

Analyze Literature

Imagery Charts should include sensory details the poet uses to create images of the desert, such as "Wind runs round boulders, ruffles my hair." Students should also recognize that these images convey the poet's love of nature and the way the desert instills in her feelings of freedom.

TEACHING NOTE

Lyric Poetry

Note that lyric poetry (verse that expresses an author's feelings and does not tell a story) usually differs from other kinds of writing because it is so personal. There may not be a message or argument. The poem may seem like a photograph or an expression of a state of mind.

Apply the Model

BEFORE READING
DURING READING
AFTER READING

Find Meaning

1. (a) What is the setting of this poem? (b) What does the fifth line tell you about the speaker's relationship with the setting?
2. What feeling is conveyed by the speaker's word choice in describing the lizards? Explain.
3. What does the speaker call the setting at the end of the poem?

Analyze Literature

Imagery Think about how the descriptive words and phrases used in the poem help to create images or mental pictures. List these images in the left column of a two-column chart. Then, in the right column of the chart, write about how each image affects you.

Make Judgments

4. In line 12, the speaker says the rabbit watches "us." In addition to the speaker, who or what is the rabbit watching?
5. (a) What time of day does the second stanza describe? (b) What do you think the speaker is describing in lines 17 and 18?
6. (a) List a simile that the speaker uses in the last stanza. (b) How would you describe the feeling that this simile creates?

Image	Effect
"Wind runs round boulders, ruffles my hair."	This sounds like a friendly wind.

Extend Understanding

Writing Options

Creative Writing Imagine that you have been asked to submit a **poem** for publication in a school magazine. Select a real or imaginary place where you would like to spend some time. Think about the sights, smells, sounds, textures, and tastes that you associate with this place. Then write a poem about the place you have chosen.

Expository Writing Write a short **critical analysis** in which you describe the main idea of Mora's poem. Examine the use of images, the setting, the speaker's descriptions, and the poem's tone. In the introduction of your analysis, summarize the poem and state what you believe the main idea to be. Then present evidence in support of your claims.

Collaborative Learning

Discuss Author's Purpose With a partner, discuss the author's purpose for writing "Gold." Consider what the poem does for you—does it inform you, entertain you, cause you to reflect on ideas, share a perspective, or persuade you to share a viewpoint? Collect evidence from the poem to support your claims. Then discuss your findings with a larger group.

Lifelong Learning

Report on Desert Life Research one of the desert animals or plants mentioned in "Gold." Use the Internet and library to gather information about your topic. Make an outline to organize your information and create a visual aid. Then, using your outline and visual aid, give a presentation to the class.

Go to www.mirrorsandwindows.com for more.

Rubrics for Writing Options

You can adapt this as a checklist for students to use as they write.

Creative Writing

☐ Does the poem focus on a specific place?
☐ Does the poem include vivid images and sensory details?

Expository Writing

☐ Does the analysis state the poem's main idea?
☐ Does the analysis include a brief summary of the poem?
☐ Does the student present evidence to support the main idea stated?

Feel Like a Bird

A Lyric Poem by May Swenson

Apply the Model
- BEFORE READING
- DURING READING
- AFTER READING

Preview the Model

At a Glance
Guided Reading: Reading Model
- Reading Level: Moderate
- Difficulty Considerations: Punctuation, capitalization, and diction
- Ease Factor: Length

Build Background

Literary Context May Swenson's poetry is known for its vivid imagery, clever word combinations, and unusual style elements, such as the nontraditional use of capital letters. Swenson once said that poetry is "based in a craving to get through the curtains of things as they appear, to things as they are, and then into the larger, wilder space of things as they are becoming."

Reader's Context Have you ever wanted to be like an animal? What animal?

Set Purpose

Preview the poem, paying attention to its structure; note the length of the lines, the length of the stanzas, and the use of punctuation and capitalization.

Analyze Literature

Metaphor and Simile Poets often use figures of speech to compare one thing to another. A **metaphor** is an unstated comparison between two unlike things that does not use the word *like* or *as*. A **simile** is a stated comparison between two things that uses the word *like* or *as*. As you read "Feel Like a Bird," look for examples of metaphor and simile and think about the effects these figures of speech create.

Use Reading Skills

Monitor Comprehension Taking notes as you read can help you monitor your comprehension of ideas that are stated in an unusual way. Use a note-taking chart as you read "Feel Like a Bird" to help you understand the meaning of the images that the poet presents.

> Before Reading:
> Set a purpose.
>
> I am going to determine what the speaker is saying about feeling like a bird.
>
> During Reading:
> Take notes.
>
> After Reading:
> Reflect on what has been learned.

Objectives

Studying this lesson will enable students to
- use reading skills such as monitoring comprehension
- define metaphor and simile and recognize how the poet uses them
- describe how the natural world influenced May Swenson's writing
- appreciate a playful poem that closely observes and celebrates birds

Launch the Lesson

Ask students to take time as they read "Feel Like a Bird" to think of their own images of birds. What similes and metaphors would they use to describe birds' appearance? How would they represent birds' actions?

MIRRORS & **W**INDOWS The Mirrors & Windows questions at the end of the poem focus on the theme of inspiration. Before students begin reading, ask: How often would you say you truly appreciate nature?

Meet the Author

May Swenson (1919–1989), born in Logan, Utah, was the oldest of ten children. Because her family spoke Swedish at home, she learned English as a second language. She won many awards for her poetry and was also a critic, editor, translator, and lecturer. Swenson's poems reflect her interest in nature and science. She had a keen eye for observing the world around her and developed a powerful way of describing what she observed.

Preview Vocabulary

snipe (snīp) *v.*, shoot from a hidden position; direct an attack

gid·dy (gi′ dē) *adj.*, feeling dizzy or unsteady

FEEL LIKE A BIRD **469**

Words in Use

Preview Vocabulary
snipe, 471
giddy, 471

Teaching Words
vivid, 469
keen, 469
evoke, 472

KEY TERMS

LYRIC POEM, 469
STANZA, 469
PUNCTUATION, 469
CAPITALIZATION, 469
METAPHOR, 469
SIMILE, 469

Common Core State Standards
Reading Literature
RL.1

Teach the Model

Summary
The poem imaginatively compares humans and birds.

Analyze Literature
Rhyme Although the poem is free verse—it does not have regular stanzas or meter (rhythm)—Swenson uses lots of rhymed words. Have students identify all the rhyming pairs (*understand/hand, Wing/thing, coat/boat, Air/there, sail/tail, Heap/leap,* and *Mate/Fate*).

Analyze Literature
Metaphor and Simile Have students pick one of Swenson's metaphors or similes and illustrate it, either drawing a picture or reproducing an existing image. Encourage them to try to convey exactly the idea that inspired Swenson to use that figure of speech.

▶ More About the Author
Explain that Swenson explored the way words look as well as what they mean. She often used unusual capitalization and sometimes crafted poems that form shapes on the page, a technique known as concrete poetry (see page 515). Her poem "Cardinal Ideograms" relates the shapes of written numbers (cardinal numbers) to images they evoke.

Feel Like a Bird

A Lyric Poem by May Swenson

470

Program Resources

Planning and Assessment
Program Planning Guide, Selection Lesson Plan
E-Lesson Planner
Assessment Guide, Lesson Test
ExamView

Technology Tools
Interactive Student Text on CD
Visual Teaching Package
Audio Library
mirrorsandwindows.com

Meeting the Standards
Poetry: Unit 5, Guided Reading, pp. 27–30

feel like A Bird
understand
he has no hand

instead A Wing
5   close-lapped
mysterious thing

in sleeveless coat
he halves The Air
skipping there
10 like water-licked boat

lands on star-toes
finger-beak in
feather-pocket
finds no Coin

15 in neat head like
seeds in A Quartered
Apple eyes join
<u>sniping</u> at opposites
stereoscope[1] The Scene
20 Before

close to floor <u>giddy</u>
no arms to fling
A Third Sail
spreads for calm
25 his tail

hand better
than A Wing?
to gather A Heap
to count
30 to clasp A Mate?

or leap
lone-free and mount
on muffled shoulders
to span A Fate? ❖

DURING READING

Analyze Literature
Metaphor and Simile What effect is created by the figures of speech used in lines 8–11? **A**

snipe (snīp) v., shoot from a hidden position; direct an attack

gid·dy (gi´ dē) adj., feeling dizzy or unsteady

DURING READING

Use Reading Skills
Monitor Comprehension What do you think the speaker is describing in this stanza? **B**

1. **stereoscope.** Instrument with two eyepieces that presents two photographs of a scene at slightly different angles; the combined image creates the illusion of depth so that the scene appears three-dimensional.

Poets and artists often gain inspiration from nature. What feelings and emotions do you associate with nature? Why do you think nature can have such a powerful effect on some people?

Teach the Model

Analyze Literature

Metaphor and Simile *Answer:* The metaphor "star-toes" compares the bird's toes to stars, which helps the reader visualize the shape of the bird's feet. The simile compares the bird's motion in flight to that of a boat "skipping" through water; this evokes an image of how the bird moves through the sky. **A**

Use Reading Skills

Monitor Comprehension Reassure students that their goal is not to find one correct "meaning" for the poem. Encourage them to use the tools they know to analyze what the poet might be saying. Also urge them to try to enjoy the imagery and wordplay.

Use Reading Skills

Monitor Comprehension *Answer:* The speaker is describing what a hand can do. **B**

Answer: Students may cite joy, serenity, excitement, danger, and wonder. They may say nature's beauty or vastness affects people.

Differentiated Instruction

Enrichment

One of Swenson's interests was riddle poems. Her books *Poems to Solve* and *More Poems to Solve* include a number of these. Other poets have written such poems, including Emily Dickinson and Robert Frost. Have students find a riddle poem, by Swenson or someone else, and share it with classmates.

English Language Learning

Point out terms likely to be unfamiliar, such as *close-lapped,* and talk students through using a dictionary to learn the meaning. Note that they will not find *close-lapped* under *close;* they must look up *lapped.* They must also consider context. In this case, *close-lapped* means wrapped up tightly (closely).

Review the Model

Find Meaning

1. (a) The speaker compares them to "seeds in A Quartered / Apple . . . sniping at opposites." (b) It helps the reader imagine how a bird's eyes, on opposite sides of its head, see the world in stereoscopic vision.

2. (a) The speaker asks which is better—a hand or a wing. (b) The speaker would probably claim that each has its benefits.

Make Judgments

3. Answers will vary. The comparisons reveal some of the speaker's feelings about both birds and people.

4. Although there are some drawbacks to being a bird, there are also wonders and joys, such as the freedom of flight, that humans can never know.

Analyze Literature

Metaphor and Simile Charts will vary. Similes include "like water-licked boat" and "neat head like / seeds in A Quartered / Apple eyes join / sniping at opposites." Metaphors include "star-toes" and "finger-beak."

Find Meaning

1. (a) In the fifth stanza, what image does the speaker use to describe the bird's eyes? (b) Why do you think Swenson chose this image?

2. (a) What question is the speaker asking in the final two stanzas? (b) How do you think the speaker would answer these questions?

Make Judgments

3. Why do you think the speaker compares birds and people?

4. To what conclusions about birds does the speaker come?

Analyze Literature

Metaphor and Simile How does the poet use metaphor and simile to help you better understand what she is describing? Use the first column of a figurative language chart to list the comparisons you find in the poem. In the second column, write down what is being compared in each example. Then, in the third column, describe what the metaphor or simile helps you envision.

Example of Metaphor or Simile	What Is Compared	What I Envision
in sleeveless coat / he halves The Air	wings to a coat without sleeves	a person in a sleeveless coat flapping their arms

Extend Understanding

Writing Options

Creative Writing Imagine that you want to describe a plant or animal. Write a one-paragraph **descriptive essay** about that plant or animal. Think about how your subject looks, feels, moves, smells, and sounds. Focus on the most striking images that occur to you. Include at least one metaphor or simile.

Expository Writing Lyric poetry describes the emotions of a speaker and does not tell a story. Write a one-page **literary response** to explore what makes "Feel Like a Bird" a lyric poem. Consider these questions: What does this poem reveal about the speaker's emotions? How does the speaker interpret or view the bird's behavior? Then share your work in small groups.

Lifelong Learning

Research Birds Reread "Feel Like a Bird" and try to picture the bird in your mind. What type of bird do you think the poem describes? What clues lead you to this conclusion? Browse through pictures and descriptions in a field guide for ideas. Create a list of three possible candidates.

Media Literacy

Report on Birds in the Media In small groups, brainstorm and make a list of movies, songs, television programs, poems, and stories that feature birds. What do the birds represent in the examples you found? What different emotions do they evoke? Discuss your views on these questions with the group.

Go to **www.mirrorsandwindows.com** for more.

Rubrics for Writing Options

You can adapt this as a checklist for students to use as they write.

Creative Writing

☐ Does the essay use striking images?

☐ Does the essay include one or more metaphors or similes?

☐ Does the essay clearly describe the subject using sensory details?

Expository Writing

☐ Does the response refer to the speaker's emotions and interpretations?

☐ Does the response use examples that show why "Feel Like a Bird" is a lyric poem?

Understanding Sound Devices

What Are Sound Devices?

Sound is one of the most noticeable things that distinguishes poetry from prose. Poetry is often musical, having rhythms, rhymes, and other sound devices. **Sound devices** are elements that writers use to appeal to the ears of listeners or readers. In what ways does the excerpt on this page from "The Village Blacksmith" appeal to your ear?

Sound devices can have a big impact on the mood and tone of a poem. Some sound devices might contribute to a lighthearted or humorous mood or tone. Others might help convey feelings of gloom or sadness. Also, sound devices can influence a poem's meaning by adding strength to a line or by suggesting the way in which a line is meant to be read.

Rhyme

Rhyme is the repetition of sounds at the ends of words. It is one of the most common sound devices used in poetry. For example, the word *tan* at the end of the second line in the excerpt from "The Village Blacksmith" rhymes with the word *can* in the fourth line. Because these words appear at the ends of their lines, the rhyme is referred to as an *end rhyme*. When a poem has a consistent pattern of end rhymes, it is said to have a **rhyme scheme.** You can identify the rhyme scheme by assigning a new letter to each new rhyme. For example:

His hair is crisp, and black, and long,	*a*
His face is like the tan;	*b*
His brow is wet with honest sweat,	*c*
He earns whate'er he can,	*b*

At times, a word in the middle of a line rhymes with either a word at the end of a line or a word in the middle of another line. This is called *internal rhyme.* In "The Village Blacksmith," Longfellow writes: "His brow is wet with honest sweat." Here, the word *wet* rhymes with the word *sweat,* which ends the line.

> His hair is crisp, and black, and
> long,
>   His face is like the tan;
> His brow is wet with honest sweat,
>   He earns whate'er he can,
> And looks the whole world in the
> face,
>   For he owes not any man.
>
> —HENRY WADSWORTH LONGFELLOW
> "The Village Blacksmith"

Also, rhymes are not always completely exact. Sometimes words are used, like the words *step* and *stop,* that only partially rhyme. If a rhyme is close, but not exact, it is called a *slant* or *half rhyme.* For example, in "Father William" (page 475) Lewis Carroll rhymes the word *brain* with *again.* Because this rhyme is not exact, it is a slant rhyme.

(continued)

Understanding Sound Devices

Reading skills that can help students understand sound devices include reading aloud and analyzing text structure.

Use Reading Skills

Read Aloud Tell students that poetry developed from oral traditions of reciting stories and singing songs. Urge them to always read a poem aloud, even if they can only whisper. Encourage them also to read a poem aloud several times so that they can adjust their tone, pace, and emphasis to best capture the poem's rhythm and rhyme.

Use Reading Skills

Analyze Text Structure Poets create rhythm and meaning with line length and stanza organization as well as with rhymes. Using one of the poems in this book, have students describe the line length, stanza structure, and punctuation. Model a possible description of "Father William" (page 476): "I see that the stanzas are four lines long, with alternating longer and shorter lines. There are quotation marks. The third line of some stanzas contains a dash and most of the second lines have semicolons. I wonder how those lines are supposed to sound?"

Words in Use

Teaching Words
impact, 473
convey, 473
gloom, 473
consistent, 473

KEY TERMS

Common Core State Standards

Reading Literature
RL.4

Analyze Literature

Rhythm Tap out the rhythm of the Longfellow lines and point out that the pattern is that of an unstressed syllable followed by a stressed syllable, repeated four times for one line and three times for the other line. Tell students that the first rhythm is iambic tetrameter and the second is iambic trimeter.

Literary Connection

Meter Tell students that meter has been part of poetry for thousands of years. Ancient Greek and Latin poems have characteristic meters, as do poems of other periods and cultures. There are six basic metrical feet: iamb, trochee, anapest, dactyl, spondee, and pyrrhic. Poets use the number of feet in a line to describe a poem's overall meter. For example, iambic pentameter is a line consisting of five (*penta-*) iambs. Shakespeare wrote in iambic pentameter. Give interested students an opportunity to further investigate the vocabulary of poetic meter.

Use Reading Skills

Read Aloud Have students work in groups of three or four. Let each group select a poem from this textbook and practice reading it aloud. Ask group members to take turns reading and listening for rhythm, onomatopoeia, alliteration, assonance, and consonance. Students should try to recognize elements of the English sound system, such as long and short vowels, consonant clusters, and silent letters.

Rhythm

The pattern of stressed and unstressed syllables in a line of poetry is its **rhythm.** Stressed syllables are referred to as beats. A regular and predictable pattern of stressed and unstressed syllables is called **meter.** Reading a poem aloud can help you better hear its rhythm and determine whether or not it is written in meter. For example, read these lines from "The Village Blacksmith" aloud.

His hair is crisp, and black, and long,

    His face is like the tan;

Can you hear the rhythm? Is the pattern of stressed and unstressed syllables regular and predictable? One way to help you determine whether a poem has a regular rhythm is by scanning it. Scanning is the process of marking / over stressed syllables, and ˘ over unstressed syllables.

His hair is crisp, and black, and long,

    His face is like the tan;

In this case the pattern is regular. These lines are metered. Every meter is made up of feet. A **foot** is a group of two or more stressed or unstressed syllables. There are different kinds of feet. In the above passage, the poem's meter is made up of feet called *iambs* (ī´ am[b]′z). An iamb contains a single unstressed syllable followed by a single stressed syllable. The first two words in the scanned lines above, *his hair,* make up a single iambic foot.

Onomatopoeia

When a writer uses a word or phrase that sounds like the thing it names, the writer is using **onomatopoeia.** Words like *pow, crash,* and *meow* are all examples of onomatopoeia. This device can add excitement and a layer of sensory experience to description.

Alliteration, Consonance, and Assonance

Writers sometimes repeat the same consonant or vowel sound in two or more nearby words. In Galway Kinnell's poem "Blackberry Eating" (page 481), for example, the *s* sound is repeated several times in a line: "I squeeze, squinch open, and splurge." When a consonant sound is repeated at the beginnings of words, as it is in Kinnell's poem, it is called **alliteration.**

If a consonant sound is repeated at the ends or in the middles of words, it is called **consonance.** When a writer repeats vowel sounds, it is called **assonance.** In "Blackberry Eating," Kinnell writes: "the fat, overripe, icy, black blackberries." In this line, the *i* sound is repeated in the words *overripe* and *icy,* and the *a* sound is repeated in *fat, black,* and *blackberries.*

Differentiated Instruction

Enrichment

Students who enjoy reading poetry aloud may enjoy exploring and performing some twentieth-century Caribbean dialect poetry or contemporary, reggae-influenced "dub poetry." They can also investigate poetry slams and performance poetry. Consider providing spoken-word recordings for class use; many collections are available. Some have recordings of the mid-twentieth-century poets in this book, such as Carl Sandburg, Robert Frost, and Elizabeth Bishop.

Father William

A Humorous Poem by Lewis Carroll

Preview the Model

At a Glance
Guided Reading: Reading Model
- Reading Level: Easy
- Difficulty Consideration: Vocabulary
- Ease Factors: Rhythm and humor

Build Background
Historical Context In the 1800s, English schoolchildren were often required to memorize a popular poem by Robert Southey (1774–1843) titled "Old Man's Comforts." In this poem, an old man, Father William, explains that he has good health and a cheerful attitude because he has lived a healthy, virtuous, and moral life. In *Alice's Adventures in Wonderland* (1865), Lewis Carroll poked fun at Southey's poem by having Alice recite "Father William."

Reader's Context How does it feel to be offered bad advice?

Set Purpose
Read "Father William" to determine how the rhyme contributes to the poem's mood.

Analyze Literature
Rhyme The repetition of sounds at the ends of words is called **rhyme.** *Internal rhyme* is the repetition of sounds within lines. *End rhyme* is the repetition of sounds at the ends of lines. A consistent pattern of end rhymes is called a *rhyme scheme.* Identify the rhyme scheme by assigning a new letter to each new rhyme. As you read "Father William," examine the use of rhyme.

Meet the Author
Lewis Carroll (1832–1898) is the pen name of Charles Lutwidge Dodgson, English mathematician, writer, and photographer. His father was a country parson, and he and his seven sisters and three brothers learned to entertain themselves by inventing games and telling stories. In addition to publishing academic works in the field of mathematics, Dodgson used his lively imagination to create humorous poems and stories, the most famous of which is *Alice's Adventures in Wonderland* (1865).

Use Reading Skills
Analyze the Effects of Form on Meaning The *form* of a poem involves its structure, meter, and rhyme scheme. The *structure* is the arrangement of lines and stanzas. The *meter* is the regular pattern of stressed and unstressed syllables in each line. *Rhyme* is the repetition of sounds at the ends of words. Create a two-column chart to help you analyze how each of these elements contributes to the meaning and tone of "Father William."

Form	Effect
Structure: Eight stanzas of four lines each	
Meter:	
Rhyme Scheme:	

Preview Vocabulary
in·ces·sant·ly (in′ se′ s′nt lē) *adv.,* constantly

un·com·mon·ly (ən′ kä′ mən lē) *adv.,* amazingly

sage (sāj) *n.,* wise man

sup·ple (sʉ′ pəl) *adj.,* flexible

Objectives
Studying this lesson will enable students to
- use reading skills such as analyzing the effects of form on meaning
- define rhyme and recognize its effect on tone
- define the literary accomplishments of Lewis Carroll
- appreciate a humorous poem

Launch the Lesson
Ask the class: "Have you ever asked someone so many questions at a time that the person lost patience? Can you see humor in the situation, now that you have some perspective?" Encourage students to keep their own experiences in mind as they read "Father William." Then have them share their thoughts.

The Mirrors & Windows questions at the end of the poem focus on the theme of a person's character. Before students begin reading, ask: Who's the silliest character you've encountered in your reading so far?

FATHER WILLIAM **475**

Words in Use

Preview Vocabulary
incessantly, 476
uncommonly, 476
sage, 477
supple, 477

Selection Words
somersault, 476
ointment, 477
airs, 478

Teaching Words
virtuous, 475
parson, 475
quirky, 478
tapestry, 478
caricatures, 478

KEY TERMS
RHYME, 475
INTERNAL RHYME, 475
END RHYME, 475
RHYME SCHEME, 475
STRUCTURE, 475
METER, 475
REPETITION, 475
SENSORY DETAIL, 479
METAPHOR, 479
SIMILE, 479
HYPERBOLE, 479
DIALOGUE, 479

Common Core State Standards
Reading Literature
RL.1, RL.4, RL.5

Speaking and Listening
SL.1

Summary

In "Father William," a young man asks his grandfather why he behaves so oddly in his old age. The father stands on his head, does back-somersaults, eats whatever he pleases, and balances an eel on his nose. The grandfather explains how he can still perform each task, but eventually scolds his nosey grandson and threatens to kick him down the stairs.

Analyze Literature

Rhyme *Answer:* The rhyming words are *son* and *none; brain* and *again* almost rhyme (see page 473). Taking other stanzas into account, the rhyme scheme is *a b a b.* **A**

Independent Reading

Students who like "Father William" might enjoy other humorous works by Lewis Carroll. Edward Lear, Ogden Nash, and Jack Prelutsky are all known for their humorous verse and might appeal to students as well.

TEACHING NOTE

Formal Speech

Students may be unfamiliar with the turns of phrase associated with extra-formal speech. Point out and explain

- *Why* (line 8) in this sense, an introductory word that expresses slight surprise at the information that follows
- *Pray* (line 12) in this sense, an introductory term that means, roughly, *please tell me*

Father William

A Humorous Poem
by Lewis Carroll

in·ces·sant·ly
(in' se´ s'nt lē) *adv.,*
constantly

> **DURING READING**
>
> **Analyze Literature**
> **Rhyme** In this stanza, what words rhyme? What is the rhyme scheme? **A**

un·com·mon·ly
(ən' kä´ mən lē) *adv.,*
amazingly

"You are old, Father William," the young man said,
   "And your hair has become very white;
And yet you <u>incessantly</u> stand on your head—
   Do you think, at your age, it is right?"

5   "In my youth," Father William replied to his son,
   "I feared it might injure the brain;
But, now that I'm perfectly sure I have none,
   Why, I do it again and again."

"You are old," said the youth, "as I mentioned before.
10   And have grown most <u>uncommonly</u> fat;
Yet you turned a back-somersault in at the door—
   Pray, what is the reason of that?"

476

Program Resources

Planning and Assessment
Program Planning Guide, Selection Lesson Plan
E-Lesson Planner
Assessment Guide, Lesson Test
ExamView

Technology Tools
Interactive Student Text on CD
Visual Teaching Package
Audio Library
mirrorsandwindows.com

Meeting the Standards
Poetry: Unit 5, Guided Reading, pp. 31–36

Differentiating Instruction
Advanced Students, Author Study, pp. 27–28
English Language Learners, Text Organization, pp. 132–138

Father William (manuscript illustration), 1865.
Lewis Carroll.

"In my youth," said the <u>sage</u>, as he shook his gray locks.
    "I kept all my limbs very <u>supple</u>
15 By the use of this ointment—one shilling[1] the box—
    Allow me to sell you a couple?"

"You are old," said the youth, "and your jaws are too weak
    For anything tougher than suet;[2]
Yet you finished the goose, with the bones and the beak—
20   Pray, how did you manage to do it?"

"In my youth," said his father, "I took to the law,
    And argued each case with my wife;
And the muscular strength, which it gave to my jaw
    Has lasted the rest of my life."

sage (sāj) *n.*, wise man

sup•ple (sʉ´ pəl) *adj.*, flexible

---

1. **shilling.** British coin
2. **suet.** Fat used in cooking

> **DURING READING**
> **Use Reading Skills**
> **Analyze Effects of Form on Meaning** How does repetition work to identify the speaker in each stanza for the reader? **B**

FATHER WILLIAM **477**

Teach the Model

Make Connections

Answer: Most would become annoyed after a few repetitions. **A**

Use Reading Skills

Analyze Effects of Form on Meaning To help students with their charts that analyze form and meaning (see page 475), explain that Carroll uses a lot of *anapestic meter* in the poem. Anapest is a three-syllable grouping of two unstressed syllables followed by one stressed syllable. For example: Yet you bal / anced an eel / on the end / of your nose—

Observe that anapestic meter, combined with rhyme, creates an artificial-sounding form that can enhance a poem's humorous effect.

Cultural Connection

Wonderland *Answer:* Answers will vary. Many will have read the books and found them strange or funny. Some students may be familiar with film adaptions. **B**

Answer: Most students will have found Father William strange or humorous. Some will argue that there are people similar to Father William, but none exactly like him, as his characteristics are exaggerated and bizarre.

> **DURING READING**
>
> **Make Connections**
> How do you think most parents would feel about being repeatedly reminded, "You are old"? **A**

25 "You are old," said the youth, "one would hardly suppose
     That your eye was as steady as ever;
   Yet you balanced an eel on the end of your nose—
     What made you so awfully clever?"

   "I have answered three questions, and that is enough,"
30   Said his father. "Don't give yourself airs!
   Do you think I can listen all day to such stuff?
     Be off, or I'll kick you downstairs!" ❖

CULTURAL ▶▶ CONNECTION

Alice Liddell photographed by Lewis Carroll.

Wonderland Lewis Carroll's *Alice's Adventures in Wonderland*, originally titled *Alice's Adventures Under Ground*, was first published in 1865. Carroll originally wrote the Alice stories for Alice Liddell, the daughter of the dean of the school at which Carroll taught. Alice's story became so popular that Carroll wrote a sequel, *Through the Looking-Glass, and What Alice Found There*. In the Alice stories, a young girl travels through a strange, illogical fantasy world populated by quirky characters. The story is a rich tapestry of games, riddles, word play, caricatures, parody, jokes, poems, and songs. The book has been translated into more than fifty languages and has been adapted for film and the theater. What do you already know about Alice? **B**

How did you respond to the character of Father William? Did you think he was foolish, intelligent, or strange? What people in the world remind you of Father William?

478 UNIT 5 POETRY

Differentiated Instruction

Enrichment

Students may wish to read the poem that inspired "Father William"; copies of Robert Southey's "The Old Man's Complaints" are available online. Define *parody* (a literary or performance piece that imitates another work in order to make fun of it) and explain that "Father William" is an example of it. Ask students to try a parody of their own by writing an extra verse for "Father William." Have them share their work with classmates.

Find Meaning

1. (a) Who is the speaker in the first stanza? (b) What is surprising about the information he conveys?

2. (a) Who is the speaker in the second stanza? (b) What does he reveal about his personality?

3. (a) What explanation does Father William give for the strength of his jaw? (b) What type of explanation is this? Explain.

Analyze Literature

Rhyme To describe a rhyme scheme, each rhyme is assigned a different lowercase letter. For example:

Jack be nimble	a
Jack be quick	b
Jack jump over	c
The candlestick	b

Make Judgments

4. What is unusual about the exchanges between father and son?

5. (a) List some of the comical images in "Father William." (b) Why do you think these images are comical?

6. (a) In what way does Father William's response to the last question differ from his other responses? (b) Why do you think he responds in this way?

The rhyme scheme of these lines is *abcb*.

Review "Father William," and determine the rhyme scheme of each stanza. On a separate sheet of paper, write out the rhyme scheme. Then discuss how the rhyme scheme affects the mood of the poem.

Extend Understanding

Writing Options

Creative Writing Try to write a **humorous poem** like "Father William." Brainstorm to come up with images, sensory details, metaphors, and similes. When drafting your poem, try to follow the rhyme scheme of "Father William." When you are done, read your poem to the class.

Descriptive Writing Use the poem to write a **character sketch** of Father William. Include details from the poem and at least one direct quotation to support your claims about Father William's character. In your conclusion, be sure to sum up Father William's character in a sentence or two. Then compare your sketch with a partner's sketch.

Collaborative Learning

Discuss Hyperbole With a partner, list examples of hyperbole, or exaggeration, in "Father William." Ask yourself: What purpose does hyperbole serve in this poem? How does hyperbole contribute to the tone? When you are finished, share your list and answers to the above questions with another group.

Critical Literacy

Perform a Role-Play In groups of two, practice reading the dialogue from this poem aloud. One partner should take on the role of Father William, the other of Father William's son. Correct yourself when you make mistakes and provide constructive feedback to your partner.

Go to www.mirrorsandwindows.com for more.

Find Meaning

1. (a) The speaker is Father William's son. (b) He says the father stands on his head.

2. (a) Father William is the speaker. (b) He really does stand on his head.

3. (a) It is strong because he used it to argue about law with his wife. (b) This is ridiculous, because talking would not strengthen muscles used for eating.

Make Judgments

4. The son asks about the father's weird actions and the father reacts as if the questions are normal.

5. (a) Comical images include an elderly man standing on his head, turning somersaults, eating a whole goose, and balancing an eel on his nose. (b) Most students will say that these feats would be physically impossible for an elderly, overweight man to accomplish.

6. (a) It is closer to what any parent might say. (b) The questions may have started annoying him.

Analyze Literature

Rhyme Students should identify the rhyme scheme as *a b a b*. They should note that this scheme emphasizes the singsong rhythm and adds to the lighthearted, comic mood.

Rubrics for Writing Options

You can adapt this as a checklist for students to use as they write.

Creative Writing

☐ Does the poem use the *a b a b* rhyme scheme?
☐ Does the poem have a humorous tone?
☐ Does the poem include metaphors, similes, images, and sensory details?

Descriptive Writing

☐ Does the sketch include details from the poem?
☐ Does the sketch include at least one direct quotation from the poem?
☐ Does the sketch sum up Father William's character in one or two sentences?

Personal and Possessive Pronouns

*"In my youth," Father William replied
to his son,
"I feared it might injure the brain...."*

—LEWIS CARROLL, "Father William"

A **personal pronoun** is used in place of a person or thing. In the quotation above, *my, his, I,* and *it* are all personal pronouns. Personal pronouns may be singular, plural, or possessive.

A **possessive pronoun** shows ownership or possession. Possessive pronouns may be singular or plural.

EXAMPLES

personal pronouns

singular	*I, me, you, he, she, it, him, her*
plural	*we, us, you, they, them*
possessive	*mine, yours, his, hers, ours, theirs, its*

Use personal pronouns to refer to yourself (first person), to refer to people to whom you are speaking (second person), and to refer to other people, places, and things (third person).

EXAMPLES

first person	*I, me, my, mine, we, us, our, ours*
second person	*you, your, yours*
third person	*he, him, his, she, her, hers, it, its, they, them, their, theirs*

Identifying Personal Pronouns in Literature

On a separate sheet of paper, copy and then underline the seven personal pronouns in the following passage.

"In my youth," said the sage, as he shook his gray locks.
"I kept all my limbs very supple
By the use of this ointment—one shilling the box—
Allow me to sell you a couple?"

Sentence Improvement

For each of the following sentences, choose the correct pronoun in parentheses.

1. (Him, His) son said, "(I, me) don't think (your, you) should stand on (your, yours) head."

2. (We, Our) friends think (it, its) makes you look foolish, and I agree with (their, they) opinion.

3. Father William said, "I don't care what (your, them) friends think."

4. (Their, Them) opinions are less important than (us, ours).

5. Arguing with (me, my) wife made my jaw strong, but (I, we) never changed (hers, her) mind about (my, mine) actions.

6. Father William was angry with (his, him) son.

7. (Their, They) were not very impressed with Father William and (his, him) tricks.

8. That is not (your, yours) to take.

9. (We, Our) laughter was very loud in (their, they) house.

10. (You, Your) answer to the question was silly.

TEACHING NOTE

Extra Practice

The following sentences are adapted from the student model in this unit's Writing Workshop. Read each sentence aloud, and have students correct your errors in pronoun usage. (Answers appear in parentheses.)

1. Harper Lee's *To Kill a Mockingbird* tells many stories, and all of <u>they</u> are very interesting, but <u>hers</u> novel has two major plots. (them, her)

2. Atticus Finch and <u>him</u> children stay in the reader's memory. (his)

3. Lee even calls <u>them</u> a "tired old town," almost as if <u>she</u> were a person. (it, it)

4. As Atticus says, "<u>Mine</u> never really know a man until <u>your</u> stand in <u>he</u> shoes and walk around in <u>they</u>." (You, you, his, them)

Blackberry Eating

A Lyric Poem by Galway Kinnell

Build Background

Scientific Context Several varieties of blackberries grow in the United States. Some are native to North America; others were brought from Europe. Berry breeders and farmers now cultivate many hybrid types of blackberries. Blackberries grow on vinelike bushes, many of which have sharp thorns. Although different varieties of blackberries ripen at different times, many are ready to eat in late summer. Berries ripen earlier in southern climates than they do in the north.

Reader's Context How would you describe the taste of blackberries?

Set Purpose

Preview the poem's first lines to help you determine the tone.

Analyze Literature

Alliteration The repetition of consonant sounds at the beginnings of words is called **alliteration.** Alliteration can have a big impact on a poem's tone and meaning. As you read, watch for examples of alliteration and try to determine the effect that they have.

Meet the Author

Galway Kinnell (b. 1927) was born in Providence, Rhode Island. In 1983, he received the Pulitzer Prize for *Selected Poems.* About writing poetry, Kinnell has said, "It's the poet's job to figure out what's happening within oneself, to figure out the connection between the self and the world, and to get it down in words that have a certain shape, that have a chance of lasting."

Use Reading Skills

Identify Author's Perspective An author's perspective is the attitude the author takes toward his or her subject. Authors carefully choose their words to express their perspective. Using a chart can help you determine Galway Kinnell's attitude about eating blackberries. In the first column, write words and phrases from the poem. In the second column, write about the attitudes that these words and phrases reveal.

Word Choices	Attitudes
fat, overripe, icy	

Preview Vocabulary

un·bid·den (ʊn' bĭ′ d'n) *adj.,* not asked or invited

splurge (splʊrj) *v.,* indulge oneself extravagantly or spend a lot of money

Preview the Model

At a Glance
Guided Reading: Reading Model
- Reading Level: Moderate
- Difficulty Considerations: Vocabulary and alliteration
- Ease Factor: Sensory details

Objectives

Studying this lesson will enable students to
- use reading skills such as identifying the author's perspective
- recognize alliteration
- explain how a poem connects the self and the world
- appreciate a poem inspired by an enjoyable experience

Launch the Lesson

Tell students that in the poem "Blackberry Eating," certain words come to the speaker's mind as he picks blackberries. Ask students if they have ever done an activity, like berry picking, that involves quiet, repetitive motion. Do ideas pop into their heads while they're doing these activities?

The Mirrors & Windows questions after the poem focus on the theme of feelings about foods. Before students begin reading, ask: Why do people get so excited about eating fruit right from the tree?

Words in Use

Preview Vocabulary	Selection Words	Teaching Words
unbidden, 482	peculiar, 482	cultivate, 481
splurge, 482	stalks, 482	hybrid, 481
		peculiar, 483

Common Core State Standards

Reading Literature
RL.1, RL.4
Writing
W.3
Speaking and Listening
SL.1

Teach the Model

Summary
A speaker shares the pleasure he feels when picking and eating blackberries.

Analyze Literature
Alliteration *Answer:* Alliterative words in lines 10–14 are *strengths, squinched, syllabled, squeeze, squinch, splurge, silent, startled,* and *September.* Students might also suggest *like, lettered, lumps, language,* and *late.* **A**

 Answer: Answers will vary.

Independent Reading
Students who like "Blackberry Eating" might enjoy other poems about blackberry picking, such as Sylvia Plath's "Blackberrying," Seamus Heaney's "Blackberry-picking," and Yusef Komunyakaa's "Blackberries."

TEACHING NOTE

Read Aloud
Invite students to read Kinnell's poem aloud. Have several volunteers read it through. Then, ask students to use reading aloud to explore some of the choices Kinnell made about punctuation. For example, ask a student to read line 2 as written. Then ask another student to read the same line without the comma after *icy.* Have students conduct the same experiment with lines 13 through 15, omitting different commas for different readings.

Apply the Model
BEFORE READING
DURING READING
AFTER READING

Picking Blackberries. William McGeorge. Eaton Gallery, London.

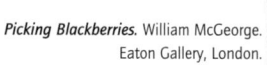

Blackberry Eating

A Lyric Poem by Galway Kinnell

I love to go out in late September
among the fat, overripe, icy, black blackberries
to eat blackberries for breakfast,
the stalks very prickly, a penalty
5 they earn for knowing the black art
of blackberry-making; and as I stand among them
lifting the stalks to my mouth, the ripest berries
fall almost <u>unbidden</u> to my tongue,
as words sometimes do, certain peculiar words
10 like *strengths* or *squinched,*
many-lettered, one-syllabled lumps,
which I squeeze, squinch open, and <u>splurge</u> well
in the silent, startled, icy, black language
of blackberry-eating in late September. ❖

un·bid·den (ʉn′ biʹ d'n) *adj.,* not asked or invited

DURING READING
Analyze Literature
Alliteration What examples of alliteration do you find in lines 10–14? **A**

splurge (splʉrj) *v.,* indulge oneself extravagantly or spend a lot of money

 What is your favorite food? What season, place, or person do you associate with that food? What words would you use to describe this food? Why do you think different people respond differently to foods?

482

Program Resources

Planning and Assessment
Program Planning Guide, Selection Lesson Plan
E-Lesson Planner
Assessment Guide, Lesson Test
ExamView

Technology Tools
Interactive Student Text on CD
Visual Teaching Package
Audio Library
mirrorsandwindows.com

Meeting the Standards
Poetry: Unit 5, Guided Reading, pp. 37–41

Differentiating Instruction
Developing Readers, Visualize, pp. 37–39

Find Meaning

1. (a) What are the blackberries like in late September? (b) What makes this time of year special for eating blackberries?

2. (a) According to the speaker, what do "certain peculiar words" do? (b) How are these words like blackberries?

Analyze Literature

Alliteration Alliteration may be used to establish a musical effect, to create a mood, or to emphasize certain words or ideas. Consonance and assonance are sound devices that can be used in similar ways. Reread the poem to identify examples of alliteration, consonance, and assonance. Use a chart to record these examples and to describe the effects of each on the poem.

Make Judgments

3. What does the phrase "squeeze, squinch open, and splurge" suggest to you? Explain.

4. (a) What sensory details does the writer use in the poem? (b) What overall effect do these details create?

Sound Device	Effect
alliteration: "black blackberries" ; "squeeze, squinch open"	

Extend Understanding

Writing Options

Creative Writing Think of a pleasurable experience you have had in nature. Create a list of all of the most important details from this experience. Then use this list to write a **narrative essay** that describes your experience.

Expository Writing Reread "Blackberry Eating" and consider how the first-person point of view influences the effectiveness of the poem's description. Ask yourself: How would this poem be different if the poet had used the third-person point of view? Write a **critical analysis** in which you discuss the effectiveness of the first-person point of view. Share your analysis with a partner once you have finished.

Collaborative Learning

Discuss Alliteration With a partner, discuss the use of sound devices in "Blackberry Eating." Using your sound devices two-column chart, explore the various examples of alliteration, assonance, and consonance that appear in this poem. Discuss the *overall* effect of these sound devices. Then share your findings with the class.

Lifelong Learning

Write a Poem Research three other common fruits or berries. Create a list of descriptive words, sensory details, metaphors, and similes for each. Once you have completed your list, choose the fruit or berry you find the most interesting and write a short poem about it.

Go to **www.mirrorsandwindows.com** for more.

Review the Model

Find Meaning

1. (a) They are "fat, overripe, icy, black." (b) Earlier in the year the berries might be small and underripe. In September they are just right.

2. (a) They fall, uninvited, on the speaker's tongue. (b) They mirror the way the blackberries easily fall off the stalks into the speaker's mouth.

Make Judgments

3. Most will say it suggests the delight the speaker takes in describing and eating blackberries.

4. (a) Sensory details include "fat, overripe," "black blackberries," "icy," "prickly," and "ripest." (b) The overall effect is to capture the essence of "blackberry eating in late September."

Analyze Literature

Alliteration Examples of alliteration: *black, blackberries, breakfast; prickly, penalty; strengths, squinched, syllabled, squeeze, splurge, silent, startled, September.* Examples of consonance: *late, September; blackberries, breakfast, stalks, prickly.* Examples of assonance: *fat, black; words, certain; black, language.* Students should see that the repetition creates a musical effect and helps emphasize certain ideas.

Rubrics for Writing Options

You can adapt this as a checklist for students to use as they write.

Creative Writing

☐ Does the essay describe a specific experience with nature?

☐ Does the narrative include precise language and sensory details?

Expository Writing

☐ Does the analysis discuss the effectiveness of the first-person point of view?

Teach the Workshop

Vocabulary Practice

These are sample answers. Other synonyms and antonyms are possible.

1. tasty; unsavory
2. awful; wonderful
3. victorious; unsuccessful
4. walked; ran
5. disappeared; appeared
6. glistening; dull
7. challenging; easy
8. chewy; soft
9. sugary; bitter
10. rapidly; slowly

Spelling Practice

1. <u>bl</u>ack<u>b</u>erries (blend/digraph)
2. <u>br</u>eak<u>f</u>ast (blends)
3. la<u>ng</u>uage (digraph/blend)
4. <u>pr</u>i<u>ckl</u>y (blend/digraph/blend)
5. <u>spl</u>urge (blends)
6. <u>squ</u>eeze (digraph)
7. <u>st</u>alks (blends)
8. <u>str</u>eng<u>ths</u> (blend/digraphs)

> For additional instruction on spelling rules, see the Vocabulary & Spelling Section 2.7, Spelling, in the Language Arts Handbook.

Program Resources

You will find additional lessons on Synonyms and Antonyms in the *Exceeding the Standards: Grammar & Style* resource.

Synonyms and Antonyms

I love to go out in late September among the fat, overripe, icy, black blackberries

—GALWAY KINNELL, "Blackberry Eating"

Synonyms are words that have the same, or nearly the same, meaning as another word. For example, the poet might have used the word *cold* or *freezing* in place of the word *icy* in the above lines from "Blackberry Eating." Writers will often choose a specific word instead of its synonym based on that word's connotation, or emotional association.

An **antonym** is a word that means the opposite of another word. In "Blackberry Eating," *early* is an antonym of *late, thin* is an antonym for *fat,* and *outside* is an antonym of *among.*

EXAMPLES

Word	Synonyms	Antonyms
unbidden	*uninvited*	*invited*
	unrequested	*requested*
	unasked	*asked*
	unexpected	*expected*
splurge (v)	*waste*	*save*
	indulge	*conserve*
	gorge	*preserve*
	misuse	*store*

A **thesaurus** is a useful reference for locating synonyms. Antonyms are also sometimes included.

When writing critically or creatively, it can be very useful to consult dictionaries and thesauruses. Finding the right word often involves understanding both denotations, or dictionary definitions, and connotations, or emotional associations. If you are unsure of a word's meaning, consult a dictionary. If you are looking for a word with an appropriate connotation, use a thesaurus.

Vocabulary Practice

Read the following sentences. Then, on a separate sheet of paper, write one synonym and one antonym for every underlined word.

1. The blackberries were juicy and so <u>delicious</u>.
2. There were very few blackberries on the bush; it was a <u>terrible</u> year for blackberries.
3. Last September, my family and I went on a <u>successful</u> blackberry picking expedition.
4. We <u>strolled</u> through the woods on our way to the lake.
5. The sun <u>vanished</u> behind the clouds as we lounged in the field.
6. The water was <u>shimmering</u> in the sunlight.
7. Which berry is the most <u>difficult</u> to pick?
8. That fruit has a very <u>tough</u> skin.
9. Blackberries have a very <u>sweet</u> flavor.
10. The fruit pickers were moving very <u>quickly</u>.

Spelling Practice

Consonant Blends and Digraphs

Consonant blends are clusters of consonants where each letter in the blend maintains its original sound, such as *br* or *cl. Digraphs* are two or three consonants that together make a new sound, such as *sh* or *th.* Be careful when spelling words with consonant blends or digraphs that you remember each letter in the grouping. Identify the consonant blends and digraphs in these words from "Blackberry Eating."

blackberries	splurge
breakfast	squeeze
language	stalks
prickly	strengths

Words in Use

Teaching Words

unbidden, 484
splurge, 484
indulge, 484
gorge, 484
lounged, 484
prickly, 484
stalks, 484

KEY TERMS

SYNONYM, 484
CONNOTATION, 484
ANTONYM, 484
THESAURUS, 484
DENOTATION, 484
CONSONANT BLEND, 484
DIGRAPH, 484

Common Core State Standards

Language
L.4, L.5, L.6

The Village Blacksmith

A Narrative Poem by Henry Wadsworth Longfellow

BEFORE READING

Build Background

Historical Context When Henry Wadsworth Longfellow wrote "The Village Blacksmith" around 1840, blacksmiths played a major role in towns and villages throughout America. The local blacksmith crafted nails, tools, wheels, and other objects made from iron and other metals. One of the blacksmith's most important jobs was making and fitting horseshoes. Since people relied on horses for almost all their transportation, as well as for farming and other heavy work, the blacksmith was a valuable and necessary member of the community.

Reader's Context Whom in your community do you admire for their hard work?

Set Purpose

Preview the number of lines in each stanza to determine how the poem is organized.

Analyze Literature

Rhythm The pattern of stressed syllables, or beats, that you hear when you read a line of poetry is called **rhythm.** Rhythm can give a poem its musical quality. A regular and predictable pattern of stressed and unstressed syllables is called meter. As you read "The Village Blacksmith," notice the number of syllables in each line and which syllables are stressed and unstressed.

Meet the Author

Henry Wadsworth Longfellow (1807–1882) was an American poet whose simple rhymes and basic American themes made his poetry extremely accessible and popular. Longfellow was among the first American poets to celebrate a young, budding American culture. The spreading chestnut tree and blacksmith shop, from the opening lines of the "The Village Blacksmith," stood along the route that Longfellow took each day to his teaching job at Harvard University in Cambridge, Massachusetts.

Use Reading Skills

Context Clues Preview the vocabulary words from this selection as they are used in the sentences below. Try to unlock the meaning of each word using the context clues provided in the sentences.

1. The wrestler's <u>sinewy</u> neck and arms were signs of his tremendous strength.
2. He went from scrawny to <u>brawny</u> by lifting weights.
3. As the blacksmith's young apprentice pumped the <u>bellows</u>, the fire began to roar.
4. Her life had been <u>wrought</u> by sacrifice and sorrow.

Preview Vocabulary

sin·ew·y (sin´ yü´ ē) *adj.*, powerful; strong, lean, and clearly displaying muscles and tendons

brawn·y (brô´ nē) *adj.*, muscular, strongly built

bel·lows (be´ lôz´) *n.*, device that expands and contracts to draw in and force out air, used to increase the intensity of a fire

wrought (rôt) *v.*, (archaic) past tense of *work*; created, shaped, or formed through hard work; formed by hammering, as on metal

Preview the Selection

At a Glance

Directed Reading

- Reading Level: Moderate
- Difficulty Considerations: Length and archaic vocabulary
- Ease Factors: Rhythm and rhyme

Objectives

Studying this lesson will enable students to

- use reading skills such as looking for context clues
- define and observe rhythm
- recognize Henry Wadsworth Longfellow and appreciate an iconic figure of early American life

Launch the Lesson

Explain that "The Village Blacksmith" paints a portrait of a tough-looking, hardworking man who also has a softer, emotional side. Ask them to think about people they know who might seem one way from the outside but reveal surprising qualities when you get to know them better. Invite students to talk about the people who come to mind.

The Mirrors & Windows questions after the poem focus on the theme of admirable qualities. Before students begin reading, ask: How would it feel to craft objects for a living? What skills would you need to do it?

THE VILLAGE BLACKSMITH **485**

Words in Use

Preview Vocabulary
sinewy, 487
brawny, 487
bellows, 487
wrought, 448

Selection Words
threshing, 487
parson, 488
toiling, 488
repose, 488

Teaching Words
accessible, 485
budding, 485
transcribe, 489
reinforce, 489

KEY TERMS
NARRATIVE POEM, 485
STANZA, 485
RHYTHM, 485
SYLLABLE, 485
METER, 485
CONTEXT CLUE, 485

Common Core State Standards

Reading Literature
RL.1, RL.4

The Village Blacksmith

A Narrative Poem by Henry Wadsworth Longfellow

Teach the Selection

Summary

In this poem, the speaker describes the village blacksmith, a strong, hardworking man. He works all week long, but goes to church on Sundays to hear his daughter sing in the choir and remember his mother. The speaker thanks the blacksmith for teaching the lesson that "our fortunes must be wrought."

Art Connection

The painter of this image, Jefferson David Chalfant, was born in Pennsylvania and spent most of his life in Wilmington, Delaware. He began painting without formal training, but did well enough to be able to travel to Paris and study for two years there. He is most famous for his still life paintings. If students like this image, encourage them to find more of Chalfant's paintings in the library or online.

Independent Reading

Students who like "The Village Blacksmith" might like other poems about workers, such as "The Solitary Reaper" by William Wordsworth and "The Ox Cart Man" by Donald Hall.

486

Program Resources

Planning and Assessment
Program Planning Guide, Selection Lesson Plan
E-Lesson Planner
Assessment Guide, Lesson Test
ExamView

Technology Tools
Interactive Student Text on CD
Visual Teaching Package
Audio Library
mirrorsandwindows.com

Meeting the Standards
Poetry: Unit 5, Directed Reading, pp. 42–47

Under a spreading chestnut tree
    The village smithy[1] stands;
The smith, a mighty man is he,
    With large and sinewy hands;
5 And the muscles of his brawny arms
    Are strong as iron bands.

His hair is crisp, and black, and long,
    His face is like the tan;
His brow is wet with honest sweat,
10   He earns whate'er he can,
And looks the whole world in the face,
    For he owes not any man.] **A**

Week in, week out, from morn till night,
    You can hear his bellows blow;
15 You can hear him swing his heavy sledge,[2]
    With measured beat and slow,
Like a sexton[3] ringing the village bell,
    When the evening sun is low.

And children coming home from school
20   Look in at the open door;
They love to see the flaming forge,[4]
    And hear the bellows roar,
And catch the burning sparks that fly
    Like chaff[5] from a threshing floor.

---

1. **smithy.** Blacksmith's workplace or shop
2. **sledge.** Heavy hammer, held and slung with two hands, used by blacksmiths to pound and shape metal; sledgehammer
3. **sexton.** Person in charge of taking care of a church and performing specific chores, such as ringing the church bell
4. **forge.** Furnace or very hot place where metal is heated so that it can be hammered and shaped; a blacksmith's shop
5. **chaff.** Outer covering or shell of grain seeds that is separated from the grain and discarded

> **sin•ew•y** (sin´ yü ē) *adj.*, powerful; strong, lean, and clearly displaying muscles and tendons
>
> **brawn•y** (brô´ nē) *adj.*, muscular, strongly built
>
> **bel•lows** (be´ lôz') *n.*, device that expands and contracts to draw in and force out air, used to increase the intensity of a fire

(Left) *The Blacksmith.* Jefferson David Chalfant. David David Gallery, Philadelphia.

THE VILLAGE BLACKSMITH **487**

Use Reading Skills

Use Context Clues Say that a way to understand a word from context is to try substituting another word for it, based on the available clues. Ask students how they would use context to figure out what *repose* means. (The word *night's* suggests something a person would do at night; fitting replacements might be *sleep* or *rest*.) Ⓐ

Use Reading Skills

Evaluate Author's Purpose Remind students that *purpose* is the answer to the question "Why did the author write this?" Have them suggest Longfellow's possible purpose for writing "The Village Blacksmith" (to celebrate the blacksmith, to teach readers a lesson about life, or to inspire).

MIRRORS & **W**INDOWS

Answer: Most students will probably admire his strength of body and spirit. Some will admire his determination and work ethic or his love and care for his family. These qualities suggest that the blacksmith is a hardworking, moral person. Most students will wish to possess these qualities.

---

25 He goes on Sunday to the church,
    And sits among his boys;
He hears the parson pray and preach,
    He hears his daughter's voice,
Singing in the village choir,
30   And it makes his heart rejoice.

It sounds to him like her mother's voice,
    Singing in Paradise!
He needs must think of her once more,
    How in the grave she lies;
35 And with his hard, rough hand he wipes
    A tear out of his eyes.

Toiling—rejoicing—sorrowing,
    Onward through life he goes;
Each morning sees some task begin,
40   Each evening sees it close;
Ⓐ Something attempted, something done,
    Has earned a night's repose.

Thanks, thanks to thee, my worthy friend,
    For the lesson thou hast taught!
45 Thus at the flaming forge of life
    Our fortunes must be <u>wrought</u>;
Thus on its sounding anvil[6] shaped
    Each burning deed and thought. ❖

---

6. **anvil.** Solid iron block where heated metal is placed to be hammered and shaped

wrought (rôt) *v.*, (archaic) past tense of *work*; created, shaped, or formed through hard work; formed by hammering, as on metal

MIRRORS & **W**INDOWS   Which of the blacksmith's traits and qualities do you find most admirable? Which of these qualities are most valued in today's world?

Differentiated Instruction

English Language Learning
With their relatively straightforward vocabulary, lines 25–30 are well suited to a translation project for students who speak other languages. Have them work to understand the stanza and then translate it into their own languages, trying to recreate the feeling of it. Assure them that they can change the details—Sunday church, the singing choir—to suit their own cultures. Have them read their work to the class. Encourage listeners to appreciate the sounds of the translation and ask: "Does the rhythm of the translation capture the feeling of Longfellow's poem?"

Find Meaning

1. (a) To what does the speaker compare the blacksmith and sound of the sledge in the third stanza? (b) What does this comparison suggest about the speaker's attitude toward the blacksmith?

2. What do the blacksmith's actions in church reveal about him?

Analyze Literature

Rhythm Scanning a poem helps you to determine if it has a regular rhythm. Scanning is the process of marking / over stressed syllables and �‿ over unstressed syllables. Read the poem aloud, listening for the rhythm created by stressed and unstressed syllables. Transcribe the first few lines. Then mark the stressed and unstressed syllables. For example, the third line of "The Village Blacksmith" looks like this when scanned.

Line	
3	˘ / ˘ / ˘ / ˘ / The smith, a mighty man is he,

Make Judgments

3. (a) What sensory details does the speaker provide in the first two stanzas to help you picture the blacksmith? (b) What do you think the speaker wants readers to understand about the blacksmith from these details?

4. Why does the speaker thank the blacksmith in the last stanza?

5. What do you think the blacksmith symbolizes for the speaker? Explain with examples from the poem.

Extend Understanding

Writing Options

Creative Writing Write a brief **short story** about the village blacksmith described in Longfellow's poem. Introduce a conflict, challenge, or problem for the blacksmith to solve. Reread "The Village Blacksmith" to find details that you can use to help you describe the setting and the blacksmith's character. Use your imagination to introduce additional details that develop the setting and characters.

Expository Writing Write a **critical analysis** that explores Longfellow's use of rhythm and rhyme in the "The Village Blacksmith." Explain the message that Longfellow communicates or reinforces through this use of rhythm and rhyme. Share your work with the class.

Critical Literacy

Conduct a Debate In a small group, conduct a debate about what the speaker means when he says "the lesson thou hast taught." Is the speaker referring to a lesson in blacksmithing? Has the speaker recently learned a specific lesson about life from the blacksmith? Be ready to back up your position with evidence from the poem.

Media Literacy

Do Research With a partner, research the bellows blacksmiths used during Longfellow's time. Use the library, the Internet, or both to find information. Write a description of how to operate this device. If possible, include a labeled sketch that identifies the parts of the bellows and shows how it works.

Go to www.mirrorsandwindows.com for more.

THE VILLAGE BLACKSMITH **489**

Find Meaning

1. (a) The speaker compares the man to a sexton and the sound to the church bell. (b) The speaker reveres the blacksmith and recognizes his role in the community.

2. He loves and enjoys his children. His daughter's voice reminds him of his dead wife, which makes him cry.

Make Judgments

3. (a) The speaker describes the blacksmith's sinewy hands, brawny arms strong as iron bands, long black hair, dark face, and sweaty brow. (b) Readers should see the blacksmith as powerful and hardworking.

4. The blacksmith taught him that the measure of character is not only work but also love of family, connection to community, and fully experiencing life's joys and sorrows.

5. He may symbolize ordinary Americans who face trials with strength, work hard, and are devoted to family and community. Be sure students give examples from the poem.

Analyze Literature

Rhythm The scanning should show that most lines alternate between iambic tetrameter and iambic trimeter. The poem begins with what is called a trochaic substitution, which means the very first foot is a trochee, / ˘.

/ ˘ / ˘ / ˘ /
Under a spreading chestnut tree
 ˘ / ˘ / ˘ /
 The village smithy stands;
˘ / ˘ / ˘ / ˘ /
The smith, a mighty man is he

Rubrics for Writing Options

You can adapt this as a checklist for students to use as they write.

Creative Writing

☐ Does the story include a conflict, challenge, or problem for the blacksmith to solve?

☐ Does the story use details from the poem to establish the setting and characters?

☐ Does the story contain additional details that develop setting, characters, and plot?

Expository Writing

☐ Does the analysis discuss Longfellow's use of rhythm and rhyme?

☐ Does the analysis explain the poem's message?

Recognizing Nouns

1. blacksmith (singular), family (collective), children's (plural possessive), voices (plural)
2. townspeople (plural), pastor's (singular possessive), sermons (plural)
3. Carl Peterson (proper), choir (collective), hymn (singular), honor (singular), mother's (singular possessive), birthday (singular)

> For more information, see Grammar & Style Section 3.3, Nouns, in the Language Arts Handbook.

TEACHING NOTE

Extra Practice

Each of these sentences has a collective noun. Have students tell you why the verb is either singular or plural in each case.
1. The committee <u>votes</u> tonight. (singular)
2. After I talked to the committee, they <u>had</u> a lot of questions. (plural)
3. The Girl Scout troop <u>is</u> going on an overnight trip to Canada. (singular)
4. I usually buy cookies from a Girl Scout when Susie's troop <u>is</u> selling them at the roller rink. (singular)
5. My class <u>loves</u> reading Shel Silverstein's poems. (singular)
6. The flock <u>competes</u> among itself for little corn kernels on the dusty ground. (singular)

Grammar & Style

Nouns: Proper, Plural, Possessive, and Collective

Proper and Plural Nouns

He goes on Sunday to the church,
And sits among his boys;

— HENRY WADSWORTH LONGFELLOW, "The Village Blacksmith"

A **proper noun** names a specific person, place, or thing and begins with a capital letter. In the above quote, *Sunday* is the name of a specific day of the week. Proper nouns include names, dates, places, and things.

If a noun represents more than one thing, it is a **plural noun.** In the lines from "The Village Blacksmith," *boys* is a plural noun formed by adding -s to the end of the word. Here are several other rules for forming plural nouns.

Rule	Examples
If a noun ends in *s, sh, ch, x,* or *z,* add -es.	pass/passes, dish/dishes, catch/catches, fox/foxes
If a noun ends in *o* preceded by a consonant, add -es.	hero/heroes
If a noun ends in *y* preceded by a consonant, change the *y* to *i* and add -es.	berry/berries
For some nouns that end in *f* or *fe,* change the *f* to *v* and add -es or -s.	loaf/loaves life/lives

Possessive Nouns

Nouns that show ownership are called **possessive nouns.** An apostrophe is used to form the possessive of nouns. To form the possessive of a singular noun, add an apostrophe and an -s to the end of the word.

> **EXAMPLE**
> *The blacksmith's muscles were very strong.*

If a plural noun does not end in *s,* add an apostrophe and an -s to the end of the word. If the plural noun ends with an *s,* add only an apostrophe.

> **EXAMPLES**
> *The children's school was only a block away.*
> *The boys' voices carried through the church.*

Collective Nouns

Collective nouns name groups that are made up of individuals. A collective noun is considered singular when the group acts together and plural when individuals within the group act independently.

> **EXAMPLES**
> **singular** *The* <u>choir</u> *sings for the service.*
> **plural** *The* <u>choir</u> *sing treble, alto, and bass.*

Recognizing Nouns

Rewrite each of the following sentences on a separate sheet of paper. Then underline the nouns in each, and write the kind of noun it is.

1. The blacksmith and his family listen to the children's voices.
2. The townspeople enjoyed discussing the pastor's sermons.
3. Carl Peterson asked the choir to sing a hymn in honor of his mother's birthday.

Program Resources

You will find additional lessons on Nouns: Proper, Plural, Possessive, and Collective in the *Exceeding the Standards: Grammar & Style* resource.

Common Core State Standards

Reading Literature
RL.2

Mother to Son

A Lyric Poem by Langston Hughes

BEFORE READING

Build Background

Historical Context The Harlem Renaissance of the 1920s and early 1930s was a culturally rich movement, centered in the Harlem district of New York City, where many African-American writers, musicians, and artists had settled. Works of the Harlem Renaissance, such as "Mother to Son," often reflect the struggles faced by African Americans who had fled the rural South searching for prosperity but frequently landed in poverty. At the same time, these works often celebrate the proud heritage of African Americans.

Reader's Context From which member of your family are you most likely to take advice? Why are you willing to listen to this person?

Set Purpose

Preview line lengths, line breaks, capitalization, punctuation, and repetition to see how ideas in the poem are organized. Read to determine how text structure affects the poem's meaning and emotional impact.

Analyze Literature

Repetition The repeated use of a word, group of words, or sound is **repetition.** Poets use repetition to emphasize and connect images, ideas, and feelings. As you read "Mother to Son," note the repeated words and ideas. Consider how this use of repetition unifies the poem and affects your understanding and appreciation of it.

Use Reading Skills
Identify Main Idea

The main idea of a poem is usually implied. Readers have to look at all the details in the poem, including specific word choices, and figure out what these details suggest. As you read "Mother to Son," use a web to keep track of details that can help you identify the main idea.

Meet the Author

Langston Hughes (1902–1967), a key figure in the Harlem Renaissance and twentieth-century literature, published his first stories and poems in his high school magazine. Hughes was born in Joplin, Missouri, and was just a toddler when his father left the family. For the remainder of his youth, Hughes was shuffled back and forth between his mother, Carrie, and his grandmother Mary Leary Langston, a proud but poor woman who probably was the inspiration for "Mother to Son."

Preview the Selection

At a Glance
Directed Reading
- Reading Level: Easy
- Difficulty Consideration: Nonstandard English
- Ease Factor: Informal tone

Objectives

Studying this lesson will enable students to
- use reading skills such as identifying the main idea
- define repetition and recognize its effect in the selection
- describe Langston Hughes and explain the influence of the Harlem Renaissance on his writing
- contemplate a poem about appreciating life despite hard times

Launch the Lesson

Ask several volunteers for generalizations about what parental advice is like. Do they always find it helpful? Do they feel that their parents' experiences are relevant? Try to elicit a few different responses and have some students give examples of parental advice they have received.

MIRRORS & WINDOWS The Mirrors & Windows questions after the poem focus on the theme of guidance. Before students begin reading, ask: What advice do you wish someone had given you before you started this school year?

Teaching Words
prosperity, 491
contradict, 494
modify, 494
bigotry, 494

KEY TERMS

Common Core State Standards
Reading Literature
RL.1, RL.5, RL.7
Speaking and Listening
SL.1

Summary

This poem describes life like a staircase. Instead of a "crystal stair," the speaker ascends a bare staircase filled with tacks, splinters, and torn boards. The speaker continues to climb, and explains that you mustn't sit down nor fall, but should keep moving.

Analyze Literature

Repetition In addition to repeating sounds, this poem has some repeating images. The mother turns corners and tells her son not to turn back; she keeps going in the dark, where there has been no light. She also repeats the word *climbin'*. Point out the repetitions to students and ask how they contribute to the main idea of the poem.

Use Reading Skills

Identify the Main Idea Ask students to read through the poem once, and then to offer their impressions of the main message this mother wants her son to get. Model a possible response: "Don't give up."

Independent Reading

Students who like "Mother to Son" might enjoy the poems "Choices" by Nikki Giovanni, "My Mother Enters the Workforce" by Rita Dove, and "my brothers" by Haki Madhubuti.

Mother to Son

A Lyric Poem by Langston Hughes

Mother Courage II, 1974. Charles Wilbert White. National Academy Museum, New York.

492

Program Resources

Planning and Assessment
Program Planning Guide, Selection Lesson Plan
E-Lesson Planner
Assessment Guide, Lesson Test
ExamView

Technology Tools
Interactive Student Text on CD
Visual Teaching Package
Audio Library
mirrorsandwindows.com

Meeting the Standards
Poetry: Unit 5, Directed Reading, pp. 48–55

Differentiating Instruction
Advanced Students, Cultural Context Project, pp. 29–30

Well, son, I'll tell you:
Life for me ain't been no crystal stair.
It's had tacks in it,
And splinters,
5   And boards torn up,
And places with no carpet on the floor—
Bare.
But all the time
I'se been a-climbin' on,
10 And reachin' landin's,
And turnin' corners,
And sometimes goin' in the dark
Where there ain't been no light.
So, boy, don't you turn back.
15 Don't you set down on the steps
'Cause you finds it kinder[1] hard.
Don't you fall now—
For I'se still goin', honey,
I'se still climbin',
20 And life for me ain't been no crystal stair. ✤

---

1. **kinder.** Kind of

If you had to ask an adult for advice about life, what person would you ask? What experiences and circumstances make that person the most likely one to offer you sound advice?

Teach the Selection

History Connection

McCarthyism One obstacle Langston Hughes faced in life was political persecution. After World War II, some people felt threatened by the popularity of communism. Senator Joseph McCarthy led an effort to rid the United States of communists. Many people, including artists, writers, and actors, were forced to testify before McCarthy's House Un-American Activities Committee. Many suspected "communist sympathizers" lost their jobs. Hughes testified in 1953. Luckily, the next year McCarthy was discredited, and Hughes continued his career.

Analyze Literature

Speaker Remind students that the speaker is the person whose voice they hear in a poem. Often, the speaker appears to be the poet, but this is not always the case. Ask the class to name the speaker in "Mother to Son" and explain the choice. (They should recognize the speaker as the mother, not the poet—at least partly because the poet is a man.)

Answer: Students should choose an adult they admire, respect, and trust. The person's experiences and circumstances will vary; be sure students give at least one example.

Differentiated Instruction

English Language Learning

Ask English learners whether their family members speak formally to each other, or if their conversation is relaxed. Note that most people speak informally with family and friends. Have students decide if the poem is formal or informal. Then confirm that the poem doesn't follow formal spelling and grammar rules. Help students "translate" it into words they can recognize. For example, "a-climbin'" translates into "climbing," and so on.

Reading Proficiency

Help students to see that in the poem, life is compared to a staircase. Remind them that this literary technique is called metaphor. Have them visualize the staircase. Ask a volunteer to sketch it on the board using input from others.

Find Meaning

1. (a) It has not been a crystal stair. (b) Her life has not been easy or filled with lovely things.
2. (a) Details include tacks, splinters, loose boards, and a bare floor. (b) Her life has been hard, with many obstacles and little comfort.

Make Judgments

3. (a) She tells him not to let difficulties stop him from having a full life. (b) She is speaking figuratively. In comparing life to a staircase, she means people should try to keep moving forward (upward).
4. Answers will vary. The son may have complained about his problems or asked her advice, or she may think he has given up on something too easily. Students may suggest she is alluding to Civil Rights obstacles African Americans have faced.
5. (a) Possible descriptions include proud, strong, and determined. (b) Her personality reflects the fact that her life was filled with obstacles. When she says she sometimes had to go in the dark, for instance, she may mean she had to find her own way, without guidance.

Analyze Literature

Repetition Examples include the repetition of "life for me ain't been no crystal stair" at the beginning and end, which emphasizes the speaker's message. The *And*s at the start of many lines evoke her many struggles. Student interpretations will vary.

Find Meaning

1. (a) What does the speaker say her life has not been? (b) What does the speaker want her son to understand about her life from this statement?
2. (a) What details does the speaker use in lines 3–7 to explain what her life has been like? (b) What do these details reveal?

Make Judgments

3. (a) What advice is the speaker giving her son in lines 14–17? (b) Is she speaking literally or figuratively when she says "don't you turn back"? Explain.
4. Why do you think the speaker feels the need to give her son advice?
5. (a) What adjectives would you use to describe the speaker's personality? (b) How have her experiences shaped her personality? Use details from the poem in your response.

Analyze Literature

Repetition Repetition in a poem affects its sound and the images that the poem brings to mind. Use a chart to analyze the use of repetition in "Mother to Son," and then briefly state how repetition influences your understanding and appreciation of the poem.

Example	Effect
"Life for me ain't been no crystal stair."	

Extend Understanding

Writing Options

Creative Writing Put yourself in the son's place as you reread "Mother to Son." How do the speaker's words make you feel? Do you agree with everything she says? Do you find her words encouraging and her advice necessary? Would you like to contradict or modify her opinions of you? Write a brief **monologue** in which you respond to the speaker. Tell her how you feel about what she has said and why you feel that way. Deliver your monologue to the class.

Narrative Writing The speaker in "Mother to Son" reminds her son that she has struggled to overcome many obstacles in her life. In a short **personal narrative,** identify a time in your life when you struggled with a serious challenge or difficulty. Explain what you did to face this challenge or difficulty. In your conclusion, explain how this experience changed you, what you learned from it, or both.

Collaborative Learning

Discuss Challenges With a partner, discuss the kinds of challenges the speaker in this poem might have faced. Consider who the speaker is and the setting in which she lived. Think about the indignities that people suffer because of poverty and racial bigotry. Ask yourself what character strengths the speaker had to possess or develop in order to survive her situation. Compare your ideas with those of other students.

Critical Literacy

Dramatic Reading Reading a poem aloud can give you a greater appreciation of its sound and sense. Reading aloud can also offer you an opportunity to dramatize the emotions the poem evokes in you. With a partner, practice reading "Mother to Son" aloud. As you read, self-correct any errors in pronunciation or delivery. When you are ready, perform your reading for the class.

 Go to **www.mirrorsandwindows.com** for more.

For further instruction, refer students to the following extension activity: Critical Literacy: Dramatic Reading, *Exceeding the Standards: Extension Activities*, p. 14.

Rubrics for Writing Options

You can adapt this as a checklist for students to use as they write.

Creative Writing

☐ Does the monologue adopt the son's point of view?
☐ Does the monologue respond specifically to what the speaker says in the poem?
☐ Does the monologue include emotional responses to the speaker's words?

Narrative Writing

☐ Does the narrative identify a challenge or difficulty the student faced?
☐ Does the narrative describe actions the student took to face or overcome this challenge?
☐ Does the narrative conclude by telling how the experience changed the student or the lessons it taught?

Under the Apple Tree

A Lyric Poem by Diana Rivera

Preview the Selection

At a Glance
Directed Reading
- Reading Level: Moderate
- Difficulty Consideration: Personification
- Ease Factor: Imagery

Objectives
Studying this lesson will enable students to
- use reading skills, such as identifying multiple levels of meaning
- define free verse and recognize an example of this literary technique
- describe Diana Rivera's work and use writing by Michael Pollan to deepen understanding of her poetry
- appreciate a poem that expresses enjoyment in the close observation of nature

Launch the Lesson
Prior to reading "Under the Apple Tree," name a tree students will know, one that is on or near your school grounds. Ask students what it would be like to sit under that tree for a long time. What would they see and hear? What would it make them think of?

Summary
A speaker describes sitting in an apple tree. The speaker describes its hollow belly, the bark, branches, and buds; the speaker also describes the surroundings, preferring to sit on the tree's rugged branch above the stone fences that separate pastures.

BEFORE READING

Build Background
Scientific Context The speaker in "Under the Apple Tree" has a close-up view of the natural world from under an apple tree. Apple trees belong to the *rosaceae*, or rose, family. In spring, white flowers that look like tiny roses appear on apple trees. Birds and insects pollinate the flowers, causing seeds to grow. The seeds grow into apples in about 140 to 170 days. Apples, like pears, are *pomes*—fleshy fruits consisting of an outer thickened fleshy layer and a central core with five or more seeds.

Reader's Context Where do you like to go to be alone? How do the characteristics of this special place affect your thoughts and view of the world?

Set Purpose
Look at the varied lengths of lines and stanzas in the poem and where sentences begin and end. As you read, decide how this organization affects the rhythm of the poem and the speed at which you read it.

Analyze Literature
Free Verse Poetry that attempts to follow the flow and patterns of regular speech is called **free verse**. Unlike more traditional forms of poetry, free verse does not conform to any strict line structure or to any definite rhyming pattern or meter. As you read "Under the Apple Tree," consider how the free verse form contributes to the poem's meaning.

Use Reading Skills
Identify Multiple Levels of Meaning In poetry, writers frequently use images, metaphors, similes, and sound devices to create multiple levels of meaning. By reading and rereading, you can better understand how these different levels contribute to the poem's overall effect. Use a chart like the one below to help you identify and analyze the effects of these different levels of meaning.

Images	Insects fly through the glimmering blue.
Figurative Language	
Character and Setting	

Preview Vocabulary
em•er•ald (em´ rəld) *adj.*, bright green

crev•ice (kre´ vəs) *n.*, narrow opening resulting from a split or crack

trance (trans) *n.*, stunned or dazed state

scrag•gly (skra´ g[ə]lē) *adj.*, uneven or ragged in growth or form

tread (tred) *v.*, walk on, along, or across; **trod** *past tense*

Meet the Author
Diana Rivera (b. 1954) was born and raised in Puerto Rico. She has studied art in Rome, Italy, and currently resides in Upper Grandview, New York, where she paints and writes. Rivera is the author of *Bird Language*, a collection of poetry published in 1994.

UNDER THE APPLE TREE **495**

Words in Use

Preview Vocabulary
emerald, 496
crevice, 496
trance, 496
scraggly, 497
tread, 497

Selection Words
swerved, 496
furiously, 496
glimmer, 496
hastily, 497

Teaching Words
rosaceae, 495
pollinate, 495
pomes, 495
hideaway, 500
amateur, 500

KEY TERMS
FREE VERSE, 495
METER, 495
METAPHOR, 495
SIMILE, 495
SOUND DEVICE, 495
FIGURATIVE LANGUAGE, 495
RHYME SCHEME, 500
ALLITERATION, 500
ASSONANCE, 500
CONSONANCE, 500
IMAGERY, 500
FIGURES OF SPEECH, 500

Common Core State Standards
Reading Literature
RL.1

Under the Apple Tree

A Lyric Poem by Diana Rivera

MIRRORS & WINDOWS

The Mirrors & Windows questions after the poem focus on the theme of shared experiences. Before students begin reading, ask: What happens when you really concentrate on something? Does this happen to everyone?

Use Reading Skills

Identify Multiple Levels of Meaning Tell students they may find it useful to create a chart to analyze the multiple levels of meaning in poetry. Draw a three-column chart on the board. Label the left column *Level*, and create four rows under it labeled *Literal Meaning, Images, Symbols,* and *Sound Devices.* Label the second column *Details* and the third column *Comments.* Tell students to copy the chart, and then to jot down details and their ideas in the corresponding places in these columns.

Analyze Literature

Free Verse Note that although free verse does not have regular rhyme or rhythm, its form—the line breaks, punctuation, and the like—still has an effect. Have students copy the first four stanzas of the selection as conventional sentences, adding punctuation. Compare the two versions and ask "What is lost in the copy?" (The poet's pauses and emphases have disappeared.)

The Apple Tree II, 1916. Gustav Klimt. Private collection.

I like it here,
under the apple tree,
knotty, with its hollow
belly

5　here
sitting on its branch
above stone fences that separate pastures,

taking life
here
10　with the sun that strokes
the sides of trees
casting its shadows on <u>emerald</u> hills.

I like it here,
entering the dark <u>crevice</u> of trunks,
15　studying the butterfly's tiny blue hearts
on powdery wings.

Like horses with their swerved necks,
I concentrate on grass.
Earthworms insert themselves into the earth
20　like glossy, pink pins!

Against the green, a yellow shrub
furiously sprouts
in a <u>trance</u> of burning stars.

Branches are suns
25　that glimmer from within
taking life
here, under the apple tree,
where a crowd of petals close their eyes,

em•er•ald (em´ rəld) *adj.,* bright green

crev•ice (kre´ vəs) *n.,* narrow opening resulting from a split or crack

trance (trans) *n.,* stunned or dazed state

496

Program Resources

Planning and Assessment
Program Planning Guide, Selection Lesson Plan
E-Lesson Planner
Assessment Guide, Lesson Test
ExamView

Technology Tools
Interactive Student Text on CD
Visual Teaching Package
Audio Library
mirrorsandwindows.com

Meeting the Standards
Poetry: Unit 5, Directed Reading, pp. 56–63

where <u>scraggly</u> layers of trunk
30   seem to slowly come apart.

At sunset the branch I sit
on snaps and coils.
The blue jay hastily darts, and disappears.

I like it
35   here
where birds now nestle and sleep,
where little, high-pitched, cricketed chirps
rise like tiny bells towards the ageless moon.

Here,
40   where insects,—silver specks—
fly through the glimmering blue.

Oh, but the mouse hides under the hay and
the cracks.
The horses <u>trod</u> down the pasture,
45   disappearing
like an impression of veils.

They say this apple tree is very old,
oh, but I like it here,
sitting on its rugged branch
50   above stone fences that separate
dark, sleepy pastures ❖

---

scrag•gly (skrag´ g[ə]lē) *adj.*, uneven or ragged in growth or form
tread (tred) *v.*, walk on, along, or across; **trod** *past tense*

What part of this experience is similar to an experience in your own life? Is the speaker sharing a purely personal experience, or does the poem also contain a more universal message?

Find Meaning

1. (a) How does the speaker personify, or give human characteristics to, the sun in the third stanza? (b) What does this tell you about how the speaker perceives the sun?
2. (a) What details does the speaker use to describe what happens at sunset? (b) What does the speaker do when sunset comes?

Make Judgments

3. (a) What happens to the horses near the end of the poem? (b) How does the poet use this image to help conclude the poem?
4. (a) How well do you think this poem captures the speaker's experience under the apple tree? (b) What, if anything, does the speaker reveal about herself or himself through the descriptions in this poem?

MIRRORS & WINDOWS

Answer: Students' own experiences will vary. While the speaker is definitely making a personal statement about a place he or she loves, quietly observing nature is an experience most people can appreciate.

Find Meaning

1. (a) The speaker says the sun "strokes" the trees and gives the hills shade, as if the sun has hands. (b) The speaker thinks of it as a gentle, positive force.
2. (a) The branch the speaker is sitting on coils and snaps, and a blue jay darts away and disappears. (b) The speaker continues watching the scene until it is nearly dark.

Make Judgments

3. (a) They disappear in the distance. (b) Their departure helps create an impression of the day's activities coming to a close.
4. (a) Most students will feel that the poem does a good job of capturing the speaker's observations, thoughts, and feelings. (b) Among the things the poem reveals are that the speaker loves this scene, enjoys closely observing nature, and is willing to sit still for a long time.

Differentiated Instruction

Reading Proficiency

Have students choose reading partners and take turns reading the poem aloud to each other. The listener should close his or her eyes and concentrate on the images that arise. After both students have read and listened, have them describe the vivid pictures the poem creates.

English Language Learning

Students may have difficulty with the poem's impressionistic nature. To help them, give step-by-step guidance. For example, note the first incidence of *here* and ask where the speaker means (under the apple tree). Ask how the speaker describes the tree (knotty, with a hollow belly). For the next stanza, ask where the speaker is (sitting on a branch), and so on.

Teach the Connection

Analyze Literature

Tone and Voice Remind students that tone is the attitude expressed toward a subject in a piece of writing, and voice is the way the writer uses language to reflect that attitude and help portray the speaker's personality. Ask students how they would describe Pollan's tone and voice in the selection. (Most will agree that his attitude toward the subject is one of respect for a remarkable person and that the voice is conversational and friendly.)

Geography Connection

Apple Growing People have cultivated apples for millennia; they were grown in Persia and Mesopotamia around 2,500 years ago. When Europeans came to America, they brought apple seeds with them. Now, apples grow in all fifty states. Thirty-six states produce apples commercially, most notably Washington, New York, Michigan, and California.

▶ More About the Author

In his writings, Michael Pollan explores how people and nature interact. His book *Second Nature* is about his experiences as a gardener. In *Omnivore's Dilemma,* he investigates the sources of the food we eat. Other books include *A Place of My Own* and *The Botany of Desire.*

In "Under the Apple Tree," the speaker provides a detailed description of nature as experienced from a perch on the branch of an apple tree. Although the speaker obviously appreciates the apple tree, the speaker never questions how it got there. The following excerpt from *The Botany of Desire: A Plant's-Eye View of the World* is by **Michael Pollan** (b. 1955). Pollan, an award-winning journalist and author of several critically acclaimed books, often writes about the connection between people and their environment. Raised on Long Island in New York, the author currently lives in San Francisco's Bay Area and is a professor of journalism at the University of California, Berkeley. As you read this passage, look for details that provide insight into how apple trees spread across the American landscape.

from **The Botany of Desire**

An Essay by Michael Pollan

If you happened to find yourself on the banks of the Ohio River on a particular afternoon in the spring of 1806—somewhere just to the north of Wheeling, West Virginia, say—you would probably have noticed a strange makeshift craft drifting lazily down the river. At the time, this particular stretch of the Ohio, wide and brown and bounded on both sides by steep shoulders of land thick with oaks and hickories, fairly boiled with river traffic, as a ramshackle armada[1] of keelboats and barges ferried settlers from the comparative civilization of Pennsylvania to the wilderness of the Northwest Territory.[2]

The peculiar craft you'd have caught sight of that afternoon consisted of a pair of hollowed-out logs that had been lashed together to form a rough catamaran, a sort of canoe plus sidecar.[3] In one of the dugouts lounged the figure of a skinny man of about thirty, who may or may not have been wearing a burlap coffee sack for a shirt and a tin pot for a hat. According to the man in Jefferson County who deemed the scene worth recording, the fellow in the canoe appeared to be snoozing without a care in the world, evidently trusting in the river to take him wherever it was he wanted to go. The other hull, his sidecar, was riding low in the water under the weight of a small mountain of seeds that had been carefully

---

1. **armada.** Fleet of ships
2. **Northwest Territory.** In the early days of American history, the large expanse of land that became Ohio, Indiana, Illinois, Michigan, Wisconsin, and part of Minnesota
3. **sidecar.** Separate place for a passenger to sit, attached to the side of a vehicle, or in this case, a canoe

Words in Use

from *The Botany of Desire*
Selection Words
makeshift, 498
boiled, 498
ramshackle, 498
peculiar, 498
catamaran, 498
deemed, 498
hull, 498
emblem, 499

Differentiated Instruction

Enrichment

Many writers have told the story of Johnny Appleseed. Have students use library or Internet resources to choose a version of the story that interests them and share what they learn with the class. Each presentation should involve a brief explanation of who wrote the version and why the student likes it, as well as a short reading from the account.

Common Core State Standards

Reading Literature
RL.1, RL.9

Reading Informational
RI.9

Language
L.6.1c

blanketed with moss and mud to keep them from drying out in the sun.

The fellow snoozing in the canoe was John Chapman, already well known to people in Ohio by his nickname: Johnny Appleseed. He was on his way to Marietta, where the Muskingum River pokes a big hole into the Ohio's northern bank, pointing straight into the heart of the Northwest Territory. Chapman's plan was to plant a tree nursery along one of that river's as-yet-unsettled tributaries, which drain the fertile, thickly forested hills of central Ohio as far north as Mansfield. In all likelihood, Chapman was coming from Allegheny County in western Pennsylvania, to which he returned each year to collect apple seeds, separating them out from the fragrant mounds of pomace[4] that rose by the back door of every cider mill. A single bushel of apple seeds would have been enough to plant more than three hundred thousand trees; there's no way of telling how many bushels of seed Chapman had in tow that day, but it's safe to say his catamaran was bearing several whole orchards into the wilderness.

The image of John Chapman and his heap of apple seeds riding together down the Ohio has stayed with me since I first came across it a few years ago in an out-of-print biography. The scene, for me, has the resonance[5] of myth—a myth about how plants and people learned to use each other, each doing for the other things they could not do for themselves, in the bargain changing each other and improving their common lot.

Ⓐ

Henry David Thoreau once wrote that "it is remarkable how closely the history of the apple tree is connected with that of man," and much of the American chapter of that story can be teased out of Chapman's story. It's the story of how pioneers like him helped domesticate the frontier by seeding it with Old World plants. "Exotics," we're apt to call these species today in disparagement,[6] yet without them the American wilderness might never have become a home. What did the apple get in return? A golden age: untold new varieties and half a world of new habitat.

As an emblem of the marriage between people and plants, the design of Chapman's peculiar craft strikes me as just right, implying as it does a relation of parity[7] and reciprocal[8] exchange between its two passengers. More than most of us do, Chapman seems to have had a knack for looking at the world from the plants' point of view—"pomocentrically,"[9] you might say. He understood he was working for the apples as much as they were working for him. Perhaps that's why he sometimes likened himself to a bumblebee, and why he would rig up his boat the way he did. Instead of towing his shipment of seeds behind him, Chapman lashed the two hulls together so they would travel down the river side by side. ❖

Ⓑ

---

4. **pomace.** Pulpy remains of apples or other fruits after they are smashed and pressed to extract juice
5. **resonance.** Ability to evoke an emotional response
6. **disparagement.** Criticism
7. **parity.** Equality
8. **reciprocal.** Mutual
9. **pomocentrically.** Made-up word meaning "from the fruit's unique viewpoint"

TEXT ⟷ TEXT CONNECTION

What is the main difference between the poem's speaker's relationship with nature and John Chapman's relationship with nature?

Analyze Literature
Free verse While free verse lacks formal elements, such as a consistent rhyme scheme or meter, that give poetry its traditional structure, free verse is still structured to enhance meaning. In "Under the Apple Tree," consider how the lengths of the lines emphasize the words on those lines. Also, how do sound devices, such as alliteration, assonance, and consonance, affect the poem's rhythm and meaning? Use a two-column chart to determine how these elements affect "Under the Apple Tree."

Element	Effect
Lines made up of the single word <u>here</u>	Emphasizes speaker's attachment to setting

Extend Understanding

Writing Options
Creative Writing A lyric poem expresses the personal feelings and thoughts of a speaker and does not tell a story. Write a **lyric poem** describing a secret hideaway that you have or can imagine. Your poem does not have to rhyme, but it should contain poetic elements, such as alliteration, assonance, consonance, imagery, and figures of speech. Revisit "Under the Apple Tree" and other lyric poems you have read for ideas about how to structure your poem.

Persuasive Writing Write a brief **newspaper editorial** in which you praise an element of nature. Introduce your topic in a lead sentence that will catch a reader's interest. In the body of your editorial, explain or describe your topic. Organize information so that your strongest arguments come first. End your editorial with a "call to action" in which you encourage readers to do or believe something. Share your editorial with the class.

Lifelong Learning
Study Trees Use library resources or the Internet to find information on the relationship between trees and the quality of life in neighborhoods. Keep a log to track the information you find and note sources. Look for answers to questions such as: How do trees affect air and water quality? What resources do trees provide for animals and humans? Use your findings to explain to a group of younger students why we need trees.

Media Literacy
List Poetry Sites Develop a list of at least five kids' amateur poetry sites. Include a review for each site. Critique each site by evaluating elements such as design, content, and ease of use. Finally, rank each site and use that ranking to organize your list. Before searching for the sites, create a list of criteria, or standards, by which to evaluate each element.

Go to www.mirrorsandwindows.com for more.

Rubrics for Writing Options
You can adapt this as a checklist for students to use as they write.

Creative Writing
☐ Does the poem describe a hideaway?
☐ Does the poem express the personal thoughts and feelings of the speaker?
☐ Does the poem contain poetic elements such as alliteration, assonance, consonance, imagery, or figures of speech?

Persuasive Writing
☐ Does the editorial praise an element of nature?
☐ Does the editorial begin with a lead sentence that captures the reader's interest?
☐ Does the editorial end with a call to action?

Grammar & Style

Reflexive and Intensive Pronouns

Reflexive Pronouns

Earthworms insert themselves into the earth

like glossy, pink pins!

—DIANA RIVERA, "Under the Apple Tree"

A **reflexive pronoun** refers back to a noun or pronoun previously used. It indicates that the subject has done something *to* or *for* itself. Reflexive pronouns are formed by adding the suffix *-self* or *-selves* to a pronoun. In the quotation above, *themselves* is a reflexive pronoun that refers back to the noun *earthworms*. Reflexive pronouns may be either singular or plural.

> **EXAMPLES**
>
> *myself, herself, himself, ourselves, yourself, yourselves, themselves*

The subject of a reflexive pronoun may be implied. A sentence such as "Don't *you* fool yourself" is often written, "Don't fool yourself." The subject (you) is implied. *Yourself* is a reflexive pronoun that refers back to the pronoun *you*.

Intensive Pronouns

Intensive pronouns are used to emphasize a noun or pronoun. In the sentence, "The author herself answered the questions," the word *herself* emphasizes that the author answered the questions rather than having someone else do it. Intensive pronouns don't indicate any action on the part of the noun or pronoun. They are typically added after the word they are intended to emphasize.

> **EXAMPLES**
>
> *The boys themselves were offering to help.*
>
> *I myself am going to send the package.*

Occasionally, an intensive pronoun is placed several words away from the noun or pronoun it emphasizes.

> **EXAMPLE**
>
> *I prefer sunny days myself.*

Identifying Reflexive and Intensive Pronouns

On a separate sheet of paper, rewrite the following sentences. Underline once each reflexive pronoun and the noun or pronoun to which it refers. Underline twice each intensive pronoun and the noun or pronoun to which it refers.

1. I reminded myself to be careful climbing the apple tree.
2. The tree itself provided plenty of shade.
3. Did you paint that picture yourself?
4. The scent of apple blossoms spreads itself across the landscape.
5. The birds hid themselves behind the branches.
6. We ourselves were getting sleepy.
7. You don't have to eat by yourself.
8. We ourselves are unhappy with the work.
9. Johnny Appleseed himself could not have predicted the outcome of his project.
10. He didn't seem capable of just being himself.

GRAMMAR & STYLE **501**

Teach the Workshop

Identifying Reflexive and Intensive Pronouns

1. I reminded myself to be careful climbing the apple tree.
2. The tree itself provided plenty of shade.
3. Did you paint that picture yourself?
4. The scent of apple blossoms spread itself across the landscape.
5. The birds hid themselves behind the branches.
6. We ourselves were getting sleepy.
7. You don't have to eat by yourself.
8. We ourselves are unhappy with the work.
9. Johnny Appleseed himself could not have predicted the outcome of his project.
10. He didn't seem capable of just being himself.

> For more information, see Grammar & Style Section 3.4, Pronouns, in the Language Arts Handbook.

Program Resources

You will find additional lessons on Pronouns in the *Exceeding the Standards: Grammar & Style* resource.

KEY TERMS

REFLEXIVE PRONOUN, 501
SUFFIX, 501
INTENSIVE PRONOUN, 501

TEACHING NOTE

Extra Practice

Have students identify the reflexive and intensive pronouns (underscored) in each pair of sentences below. Then have them tell you how the meanings of the sentences differ.

1. The battery had enough energy left to recharge itself.
2. The battery itself had enough energy left to recharge.
3. When Jada herself took the stage, we fell silent.
4. We fell silent when Jada took the stage herself.
5. Don't tell me the man found himself!
6. Don't tell me you found the man himself!

Student explanations will vary.

Preview the Selection

At a Glance
Directed Reading
- Reading Level: Moderate
- Difficulty Considerations: Vocabulary and setting
- Ease Factor: Sensory details

Objectives
Studying this lesson will enable students to
- use reading skills such as analyzing cause and effect
- define rhyme scheme and recognize its effect in the selection
- describe literary accomplishments of Claude McKay and explain his part in the Harlem Renaissance
- analyze a poem about longing

Launch the Lesson
Explain to students that in the early 1900s, food and other goods were being imported to U.S. cities from surrounding islands. Many island citizens also came to the U.S. during this time. As students read "The Tropics in New York," suggest that they consider how a new citizen might feel when reminded of their first home.

MIRRORS & WINDOWS The Mirrors & Windows questions after the poem focus on the theme of homesickness. Before students begin reading, ask: What objects can you see right now that remind you of home?

DIRECTED READING

BEFORE READING

Build Background
Cultural Context The speaker of "The Tropics in New York" is a Jamaican living in New York City in the 1920s. Situated in the Caribbean Sea, in the British West Indies, the island of Jamaica has a hot climate, suitable for growing a variety of tropical fruits and spices. In the early 1900s, Jamaica's economy relied heavily on the export of fruits, especially to the United States. Mangoes, papayas, and guavas would have been unfamiliar to many Americans. Yet, to Jamaican immigrants, these foods would have evoked memories of their tropical island home.

Reader's Context What foods remind you of home? What memories of home do you associate with these foods?

Set Purpose
Before you begin reading, skim the poem to identify the rhyme scheme and stanza lengths.

Analyze Literature
Rhyme Scheme When a rhyme appears at the end of a line of poetry, that rhyme is referred to as an *end rhyme*. When a poem has a consistent pattern of end rhymes, it is said to have a **rhyme scheme.** You can identify the rhyme scheme by assigning a new letter to each new rhyme. As you read "The Tropics in New York," note its rhyme scheme.

Meet the Author
Claude McKay (1890–1948), poet and novelist, lived for many years in the Harlem section of New York City. He was an influential figure in the early days of the Harlem Renaissance in the 1920s. McKay emigrated from Jamaica to the United States in 1912 at a time when racism was prevalent and violence against African Americans was common. While much of McKay's writing reflects the anger and frustration he experienced because of racism, some of his poems, such as "The Tropics in New York," have more wistful themes.

Use Reading Skills
Analyze Cause and Effect In poetry, writers use sensory language to describe personal and emotional responses to certain events. The event is the *cause*. The response is the *effect*. Understanding the cause-and-effect relationships in a poem can help you figure out its meaning and message. As you read "The Tropics in New York," use a chart to keep track of causes and effects.

Cause: Speaker sees bananas and other tropical fruit in the window.

Effect:

Preview Vocabulary
la • den (lād´ ən) *adj.,* weighed down

mys • ti • cal (mis´ ti kəl) *adj.,* having a spiritual quality; mysterious

ben • e • dic • tion (be' nə dik´ shən) *n.,* blessing

Words in Use

Preview Vocabulary
laden, 503
mystical, 503
benediction, 503

Teaching Words
mangoes, 502
papayas, 502
guavas, 502
evoked, 502
prevalent, 502
wistful, 502

KEY TERMS
LYRIC POEM, 502
SKIM, 502
RHYME SCHEME, 502
STANZA, 502
END RHYME, 502
CAUSE AND EFFECT, 502
INTRODUCTORY PARAGRAPH, 504

Common Core State Standards
Reading Literature
RL.1

Writing
W.2

Harvest Scene with Twelve People, c. 20th century. R. Mervilus. Private collection.

THE TROPICS IN NEW YORK

A Lyric Poem by Claude McKay

Bananas ripe and green, and ginger-root,
Cocoa in pods and alligator pears,[1]
And tangerines and mangoes and grapefruit,
Fit for the highest prize at parish[2] fairs,

5 Set in the window, bringing memories
Of fruit-trees <u>laden</u> by low-singing rills,[3]
And dewy dawns, and <u>mystical</u> blue skies
In <u>benediction</u> over nun-like hills.

My eyes grew dim, and I could no more gaze;
10 A wave of longing through my body swept,
And, hungry for the old, familiar ways,
I turned aside and bowed my head and wept. ❖

1. **alligator pears.** Avocados; the name given to the fruit by English people living in Jamaica
2. **parish.** One of twelve separate districts in Jamaica, each with its own local government
3. **rills.** Small brooks or streams

la•den (lād´ən) *adj.*, weighed down

mys•ti•cal (mis´ ti kəl) *adj.*, having a spiritual quality; mysterious

ben•e•dic•tion (be' nə dik´ shən) *n.*, blessing

When have you felt homesick for a place or missed someone, such as a relative or close friend? Why do you think homesickness and a longing for the past are frequent themes in literature and art?

503

Summary
The speaker in this poem sees a fruit in a city window and is reminded of his or her home. The vivid memory of home leaves the speaker in tears and longing for "the old, familiar ways."

Analyze Literature
Rhyme Scheme Ask students to listen for different kinds of rhymes in the poem. You may point out that in the second stanza, *memories* and *skies* create a slant rhyme.

Use Reading Skills
Analyze Cause and Effect Ask: "What does the window cause the speaker to remember?" (It reminds the speaker he is separated from the place he remembers.)

Answer: Most people have felt homesick or missed someone close to them; these are universal themes.

▶ More by This Author
Students who like "The Tropics in New York" might enjoy similar poems by McKay, such as "Outcast," "Home Thoughts," and "I Shall Return" or Derek Walcott's poem "Midsummer, Tobago."

Program Resources

Planning and Assessment
Program Planning Guide, Selection Lesson Plan
E-Lesson Planner
Assessment Guide, Lesson Test
ExamView

Technology Tools
Interactive Student Text on CD
Visual Teaching Package
Audio Library
mirrorsandwindows.com

Meeting the Standards
Poetry: Unit 5, Directed Reading, pp. 64–71

Review the Selection

Find Meaning

1. (a) The speaker is in New York City looking at tropical fruit in a window. (b) He could be walking past a home or store. Other answers are possible.
2. The speaker describes memories of a place where fruit trees grow near brooks, and where the sky seems to bless the hills.
3. (a) The speaker is weeping. (b) Looking at the fruit has created a longing for home.

Make Judgments

4. (a) In the beginning of the poem, the mood is colorful and appealing. In the middle, the mood seems dreamy. At the end, the mood is sad. (b) In the beginning, the speaker seems happy to think about his distant home, but by the end the speaker is weeping.
5. Answers will vary. Students may say that both can cause pain, or can cause a person to feel weak and disoriented.

Analyze Literature

Rhyme Scheme The rhyme scheme in the poem is *a b a b, c d c d, e f e f.* Answers will vary as to how the rhyme scheme affects tone and meaning. The orderly scheme may suggest that the speaker has his emotions under control, or that this is an experience he has had more than once.

Find Meaning

1. (a) Where does this poem take place? (b) What is the speaker doing?
2. What does the speaker describe in the second stanza?
3. (a) What is the speaker doing at the end of the poem? (b) What caused this situation?

Analyze Literature

Rhyme scheme How does the rhyme scheme in "The Tropics in New York" help to establish tone and convey meaning? Use a chart to identify the rhyme scheme in the poem. Then explain how the rhyme scheme contributes to the poem's tone and meaning.

Make Judgments

4. (a) How does the mood of the poem change from the beginning to the end? (b) How do the changes in the mood mirror the changes in the speaker's emotions?
5. In what ways is physical hunger like emotional hunger?

Lines	Rhyming Words	Rhyme Scheme
1–4	ginger-root grapefruit	
5–8		
9–12		

Extend Understanding

Writing Options

Creative Writing Imagine that you are the speaker in "The Tropics in New York." You grew up among family and friends on a small farm on the lush tropical island of Jamaica. Now you are living in an apartment in New York City. Write a **personal letter** back home. Tell about the fruit and the feelings that it evoked in you, and explain what you miss most about home and why.

Expository Writing Write an **expository essay** comparing and contrasting "Blackberry Eating" (page 481) and "The Tropics in New York." In the introductory paragraph, introduce the poems and their authors and provide a brief summary of each poem. In the body paragraphs, describe the poems' similarities and differences using evidence from each to support your ideas. Be sure to compare form, subject matter, and tone. In the concluding paragraph, restate your main points of comparison. Share your work with the class.

Critical Literacy

Conduct a Television Interview Pretend you are a television reporter and that your assignment is to interview the speaker in "The Tropics in New York." Keep in mind that an experienced reporter knows the importance of gathering background information and preparing a list of questions in advance of an interview. Create a set of questions to use during your interview. Then interview a partner who is pretending to be the speaker of this poem.

Lifelong Learning

Research New Foods Although many of the fruits and spices mentioned in "The Tropics in New York" were once considered new and exotic, today they are found in most supermarkets. Pizza, tacos, and egg rolls are other foods that were fairly recently brought to the United States. Learn about another food new to the United States. Organize the information you find and summarize your findings for the class.

MW Go to **www.mirrorsandwindows.com** for more.

Rubrics for Writing Options

You can adapt this as a checklist for students to use as they write.

Creative Writing

☐ Does the letter clearly identify the writer as the speaker of the poem?
☐ Does the letter describe the speaker's homesickness?
☐ Does the letter explain what the speaker misses most about home?

Expository Writing

☐ Does the essay summarize both poems?
☐ Does the essay identify and exemplify similarities and differences between the form, subject matter, and tone of the two poems?
☐ Does the conclusion restate the main points of comparison?

Comparing Literature

Unfolding Bud

A Lyric Poem by Naoshi Koriyama

How to Eat a Poem

A Lyric Poem by Eve Merriam

BEFORE READING

Build Background

Literary Context Both "Unfolding Bud" and "How to Eat a Poem" are free verse lyric poems. **Free verse** is poetry that does not use a regular rhyme scheme or meter. It originated in the late 1800s among French poets who wanted to use the rhythms of natural speech.

Reader's Context What images would you use to describe your favorite poem or song?

Set Purpose

Skim these poems to predict the authors' purposes. Then read to confirm or change your predictions.

Meet the Authors

Naoshi Koriyama, professor of English at Toyo University in Tokyo, Japan, has studied in the United States and has written some of his best-known work in English rather than in his native Japanese. In addition to writing his own work, he has translated the works of several contemporary Japanese poets into English.

 Eve Merriam (1916–1992) was born in Pennsylvania. After college, she lived in New York City, where she wrote for radio. Later, she began teaching and lecturing. Merriam published her first book, *Family Circle,* in 1946. Although poetry was always Merriam's first love, she is also well known as a playwright and fiction writer.

Compare Literature: Metaphor A

metaphor is a figure of speech in which one thing is spoken or written about as if it were another. The reader is invited to compare the qualities that these two things have in common. As you read the following poems, look for examples of metaphor. Use a two-column chart like the one below to keep track of the metaphors in each poem.

"Unfolding Bud"	"How to Eat a Poem"
poem and water–lily bud	

Preview the Selections

At a Glance
Directed Reading
"Unfolding Bud"
- Reading Level: Easy
- Difficulty Consideration: Metaphor
- Ease Factors: Vocabulary and length

"How to Eat a Poem"
- Reading Level: Moderate
- Difficulty Consideration: Poetic style
- Ease Factors: Simple, direct language

Objectives
Studying this lesson will enable students to
- use reading skills such as visualizing
- define metaphor and recognize it in two poems
- describe Naoshi Koriyama and Eve Merriam as writers
- appreciate two different approaches to reading poetry

Launch the Lesson
Explain that these two poems are about the act of reading poetry. Each is clearly by someone who knows about poetry and loves reading it. Ask students to consider how they feel about an activity they love. What advice would they give to people new to that activity? Model a possible response: "I love playing golf. I'd tell new golfers to enjoy walking in a beautiful setting, even if the game is hard to master." Have them share their ideas. Especially encourage students to speak who have differing points of view about the same activity.

DIRECTED READING

UNFOLDING BUD / HOW TO EAT A POEM **505**

Words in Use

Teaching Words
contemporary, 505
playwright, 505
unimpressed, 507
liberated, 508
clarify, 509

KEY TERMS
LYRIC POEM, 505
FREE VERSE, 505
RHYME SCHEME, 505
METER, 505
SKIM, 505
AUTHOR'S PURPOSE, 505
METAPHOR, 505
EXTENDED METAPHOR, 509
BIOGRAPHY, 509

Common Core State Standards
Reading Literature
RL.1

Teach the Selection

Summary

"Unfolding Bud" compares poetry to a water-lily bud. It explains that like a flower bud, a poem is not thought to be amazing until one discovers that it can unfold to reveal a "rich inner self."

The Mirrors & Windows questions at the end of the poem focus on the theme of developing an appreciation for something. Before students begin reading, ask: In nature, what are some examples of something unremarkable that turns into something magnificent?

Analyze Literature

Metaphor Tell students that comparing such different objects as a poem and a water lily makes for a powerful metaphor. Encourage students to aim for this kind of surprise effect in their own work.

Use Reading Skills

Compare and Contrast Challenge students to identify language in the poem that indicates a contrast or a comparison. (Contrasting language includes "One is amazed" / "One is not amazed." Language that stresses similarity includes the comparison "as tight-closed as a tiny bud" and use of the same words to describe both objects, such as *unfolding* and *richer/rich*.)

Unfolding Bud

A Lyric Poem by Naoshi Koriyama

506

Program Resources

Planning and Assessment
Program Planning Guide, Selection Lesson Plan
E-Lesson Planner
Assessment Guide, Lesson Test
ExamView

Technology Tools
Interactive Student Text on CD
Visual Teaching Package
Audio Library
mirrorsandwindows.com

Meeting the Standards
Poetry: Unit 5, Comparing Literature,
pp. 72–79

Differentiating Instruction
Advanced Students, Lyric Poetry Comparison,
pp. 31–32

One is amazed
By a water-lily bud
Unfolding
With each passing day,
5   Taking on a richer color
And new dimensions.

One is not amazed,
At a first glance,
By a poem,
10 Which is as tight-closed
As a tiny bud.

Yet one is surprised
To see the poem
Gradually unfolding,
15 Revealing its rich inner self,
As one reads it
Again
And over again. ❖

MIRRORS & WINDOWS When have you been unimpressed with something, like a piece of music or literature, and then later learned to love or admire it? Why do you think people's opinions change over time?

Find Meaning

1. (a) What experience is the speaker describing in the first stanza of "Unfolding Bud"? (b) What feelings does the speaker seem to have about this experience?

2. (a) In the second stanza, to what does the speaker compare a poem? (b) What does this description convey about the speaker's attitude toward poetry? Explain.

Make Judgments

3. (a) What experience does the speaker describe in the third stanza? (b) In what way has the speaker's attitude changed?

4. What words seem to tie the ideas in the first and third stanzas together?

UNFOLDING BUD / HOW TO EAT A POEM **507**

Teach the Selection

Answer: Students may suggest that first impressions are often inaccurate. They may also note that as people grow, gain experience, and mature, their tastes change.

Find Meaning

1. (a) The speaker is describing watching a water lily open from bud to full bloom. (b) The speaker is "amazed" by the experience.

2. (a) The speaker compares a poem to a tiny, tightly closed bud. (b) It suggests that the speaker's attitude was skeptical and implies that a poem's beauty is hidden from view at first glance. Further, it suggests that a reader must disassemble a poem slowly and in proper stages.

Make Judgments

3. (a) The experience is that each reading gradually reveals the meaning of the poem. (b) The speaker now appreciates the poem.

4. The word *surprised* in the third stanza mirrors *amazed* earlier. Stanzas 1 and 3 use *unfolding*, and the "rich inner self" in the third stanza recalls the "richer color" of the water lily in the first stanza.

Differentiated Instruction

Reading Proficiency

Point out that in "Unfolding Bud" Koriyama says reading poetry can be difficult and that the best way to approach a poem is to read it "Again/And over again." Encourage students to remember this and not to get frustrated if they don't understand a poem right away. To model the idea, ask several students to read the poem aloud. After each reading, pause for students to articulate their impressions.

Enrichment

Have students find photographs of water lilies online or at the library. Have them look for pictures that show various stages of the flower's development, from tight bud to open, richly colored bloom.

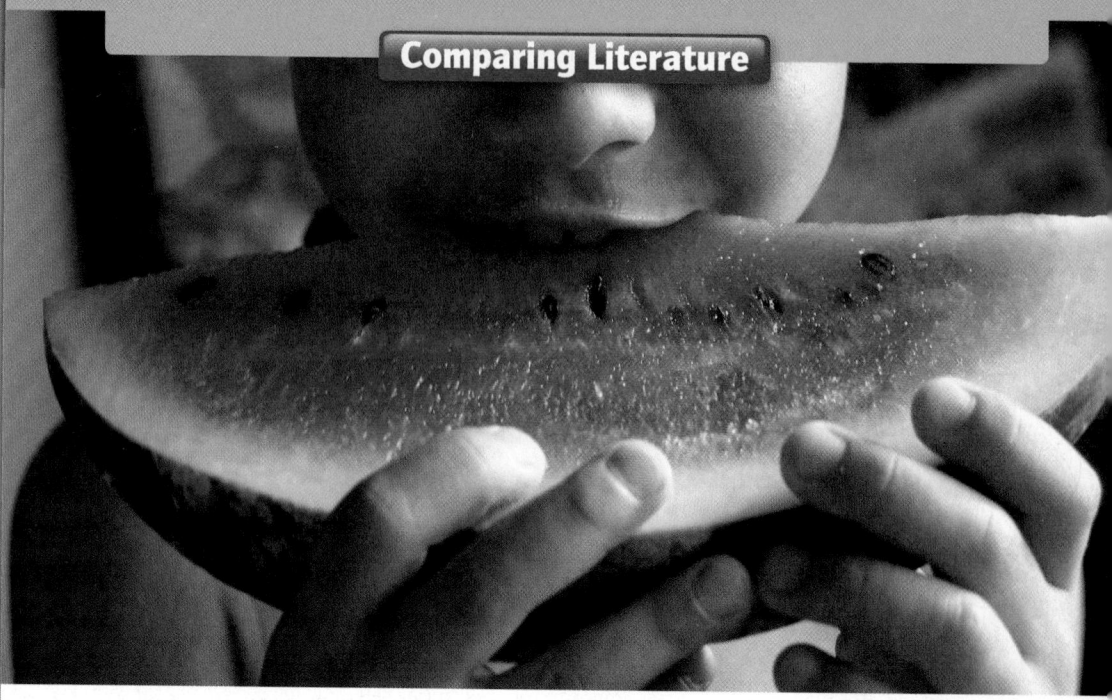

Comparing Literature

Teach the Selection

Summary

The poem advises readers on how to eat, or absorb, poetry. The main point is that there are no rules, nor special tools, needed to read poetry, but readers must fully immerse themselves.

Analyze Literature

Metaphor Note that while Merriam's metaphor compares poetry to ripe fruit, she does not name a specific fruit. Ask: "Why might this be?" (Leaving out this information allows readers to imagine a specific fruit.)

Use Reading Skills

Evaluate Author's Perspective
Ask: "How would you describe Merriam's perspective about her topic in this poem?" (She feels positive and enthusiastic about poetry. Students should cite the repeated encouragements and imagery of eating with gusto.)

The Mirrors & Windows questions focus on the theme of experiences. Before students begin reading, ask: How would it feel to read poetry without rules? *Answer:* Many students will have felt excited or liberated by music or art. Ask them to describe a specific piece and how it made them feel. Ideas about the reasons behind art's effects will vary.

How to Eat a Poem

A Lyric Poem
by Eve Merriam

Don't be polite.
Bite in.
Pick it up with your fingers and lick the juice
    that may run down your chin.
5 It is ready and ripe now, whenever you are.
You do not need a knife or fork or spoon
or plate or napkin or tablecloth.
For there is no core
or stem
10 or rind
or pit
or seed
or skin
to throw away. ❖

How might a piece of art, like a poem, song, or painting, make you feel liberated? How would you describe this experience? Why do you think the arts can have this effect on people?

508

Differentiated Instruction

English Language Learning

Students less familiar with English may not be aware of the multiple meanings of the word *rich*. Say that in addition to what may be its most common meaning ("wealthy"), *rich* has other meanings. When applied to color, it describes deep, vivid hues. In applying it to poetry, Merriam means not only "deep" and "vivid," but also "complex" and "full of meaning."

Common Core State Standards

Reading Literature
RL.1

Writing
W.1

Find Meaning

1. (a) What is unexpected about the title "How to Eat a Poem"? (b) What does the title suggest about the poem?

2. (a) What utensils does the speaker say you do not need while reading a poem? (b) What does not needing special tools or utensils suggest about reading poetry?

Compare Literature

Metaphor An *extended metaphor* in poetry is a comparison between two things that runs throughout a poem. Review the details from "Unfolding Bud" and "How to Eat a Poem" that you recorded in your chart to answer the following questions.

Make Judgments

3. To what type of food do you think Merriam is comparing poetry? Explain.

4. (a) What suggestions does Merriam give to a poetry reader? (b) How do these suggestions about "eating" translate into suggestions about "reading"?

1. What is the extended metaphor in each poem?

2. Based on the metaphor in "Unfolding Bud," how do you think Koriyama thinks people should approach reading poetry? Explain.

3. Based on the metaphor in "How to Eat a Poem," how do you think Merriam wants people to approach reading poetry? Explain.

Extend Understanding

Writing Options

Creative Writing Think about an activity such as a sport or a hobby that you enjoy. Write a short **descriptive essay** or a **poem** in which you use an extended metaphor to describe how you feel about the activity. Remember that your metaphor should extend through the entire course of your poem or essay. Once you have finished, share your work with the class.

Expository Writing Reread "Unfolding Bud" and "How to Eat a Poem," and evaluate the effectiveness of both poems' use of metaphor. Ask yourself: Which poem uses a more effective metaphor for poetry? Write a **persuasive essay** in which you state your position and defend it with evidence from these texts. Organize your essays so that your strongest evidence and arguments are presented first.

Critical Literacy

Hold a Panel Discussion With your classmates, form a panel to discuss the effectiveness of these two poems' use of metaphor. Always be prepared to clarify any statements you make and to present evidence in support of your claims. Be respectful of others' opinions, and actively listen to their arguments.

Lifelong Learning

Write a Biography Use the Internet and library to research the life of one of the poets in this lesson or another poet from the unit. Then write a brief biography. Include all of the vital details from that poet's life, such as his or her place and year of birth. Also, be sure to give the reader a sense of the poet's writing style.

Go to www.mirrorsandwindows.com for more.

Find Meaning

1. (a) The idea of eating a piece of writing is unexpected. (b) The title suggests that the poem will present unusual ideas in a playful way.

2. (a) You don't need a knife, fork, spoon, plate, napkin, or tablecloth. (b) A poem can be read anytime, anywhere, without any special equipment.

Make Judgments

3. She compares it to fruit. She describes it as "ripe," with juice that "runs down your chin."

4. (a) Merriam suggests that people read poetry without worrying about manners or rules. (b) Readers should simply read and experience poetry without worry.

Compare Literature

Metaphor

1. In "Unfolding Bud," the extended metaphor compares a poem to a water-lily bud. In "How to Eat a Poem," the extended metaphor compares a poem to a piece of fruit.

2. Koriyama thinks people should read and reread a poem carefully, looking for beauty hidden inside.

3. Merriam thinks people should read poetry with enthusiasm and gusto, without worrying about being careful or polite.

Rubrics for Writing Options

You can adapt this as a checklist for students to use as they write.

Creative Writing

☐ Does the essay or poem describe feelings about an activity the student enjoys?

☐ Does the essay or poem use an extended metaphor?

Expository Writing

☐ Does the essay state which poem uses a more effective metaphor?

☐ Does the essay include textual evidence?

☐ Does the essay include a logical organization of evidence, with the strongest argument presented first?

Preview the Selection

At a Glance
Directed Reading
- Reading Level: Moderate
- Difficulty Consideration: Structure
- Ease Factors: Brevity and vocabulary

Objectives
Studying this lesson will enable students to
- use reading skills such as comparing and contrasting
- define haiku and recognize various qualities and examples of this poetic form
- describe Matsuo Bashō, Yosa Buson, and Kobayashi Issa and explain their contributions to the haiku tradition
- appreciate haiku and the intricacies of constructing it

Launch the Lesson
Explain that haiku may contain only a few words but can have strong emotional and visual impact. Urge students not to rush while reading. Suggest that they pause to imagine having the experience described and try to create in themselves the calm, quiet feeling of the poems.

Summary
Three different haiku that reflect on nature.

haiku

Haiku by Matsuo Bashō, Yosa Buson, and Kobayashi Issa
translated by Robert Hass

BEFORE READING

Build Background
Historical Context Haiku is a poetic form that originated more than five hundred years ago in Japan. Originally associated with a traditional longer form known as the *tanka,* haiku gained popularity and evolved into its present form as a result of Matsuo Bashō, one of Japan's greatest poets. Many of the haiku that we associate with Bashō, though, are in fact the first three lines from longer poems known as *renga.*

Reader's Context When have you witnessed something startling or beautiful?

Set Purpose
Before you begin reading, examine these poems' structures. What characteristics do all three poems share? In what ways does the structure affect the meaning?

Analyze Literature
Haiku The poetic form known as **haiku** is very short and precise. It has five syllables in the first line, seven in the second line, and five in the third line. A traditional haiku presents a single, powerful image from the natural world. Because these three poems have been translated from Japanese into English, the traditional line lengths have been altered. As you read these poems, try to fully visualize each image.

Use Reading Skills
Compare and Contrast
Compare and contrast the elements in these poems to gain a better understanding of each one. Specifically, compare imagery, tone, structure, and use of figurative language. Use a table like the one below to help you.

	Issa	Bashō	Buson
Imagery			
Tone			
Structure			
Figurative Language			

Meet the Authors
Matsuo Bashō (1644–1694) was a haiku master and a teacher. In 1689 he grew restless, so he sold his house and began to travel. The result was his masterpiece *Narrow Road to the Far North.*

Yosa Buson (1716–1783) was born near Osaka, Japan. He earned his living as a painter but considered himself a poet.

Kobayashi Issa (1763–1827) was born in a small village in the mountains of Japan. Issa's poetry is filled with images of tiny creatures, especially mice, lice, and fleas.

Words in Use

Teaching Words
precise, 510
translate, 513
elevate, 514

KEY TERMS
HAIKU, 510
TANKA, 510
RENGA, 510
SYLLABLE, 510
IMAGERY, 510
TONE, 510
STRUCTURE, 510
FIGURATIVE LANGUAGE, 510

Common Core State Standards
Reading Literature
RL.1

haiku

Haiku by
Matsuo Bashō, Yosa Buson,
and Kobayashi Issa
translated by Robert Hass

Frog and Plum Tree, c. 19th century. Kishi Chikudo.

511

The Mirrors & Windows questions at the end of the poem focus on the theme of inspiration. Before students begin reading, ask: What does evening sound like?

Literary Connection

Japanese Poetry Tell students that *tanka* is a five-line form of Japanese poetry in which the first and third lines have five syllables and all other lines have seven. Tanka became popular around the ninth century. Then poets began to challenge each other by writing tanka in pairs. One came up with three lines, and the other added the last two. This collaboration was called *renga.* By the fifteenth century, renga had changed and there were many rules. In its standard form, renga has one hundred three-line verses with alternating syllable counts of seventeen and fourteen. The first verse has seventeen syllables and sets the scene. Many ancient haiku known today started as the first verse of renga.

Program Resources

Planning and Assessment
Program Planning Guide, Selection Lesson Plan
E-Lesson Planner
Assessment Guide, Lesson Test
ExamView

Technology Tools
Interactive Student Text on CD
Visual Teaching Package
Audio Library
mirrorsandwindows.com

Meeting the Standards
Poetry: Unit 5, Directed Reading, pp. 80–86

Use Reading Skills

Compare and Contrast Ask students to focus on setting and identify similarities and differences among the haiku. (All take place in nature; the first two involve water, while the third looks to the sky.)

Use Reading Skills

Analyze Effects of Form on Meaning Ask students to discuss the challenges of writing in such a concise, structured form. What sorts of topics and words can a writer choose? (Topics and language must be very precise.)

Answer: Personal responses and ideas about inspiration will vary.

Find Meaning

1. (a) It enters the water with a splash. (b) It could be ordinary, although it's surprising that the frog makes the "sound of water."
2. (a) It describes evening. (b) They capture stillness and coolness.

Make Judgments

3. (a) Personification appears.
(b) Encourage students to use sensory details to describe the effects.
4. Answers will vary. Ask students to explain their choices using specific examples.

> The old pond—
> a frog jumps in,
> sound of water. ❖
>
> —Matsuo Bashō

> Misty grasses,
> quiet waters,
> it's evening. ❖
>
> —Yosa Buson

> Summer night—
> even the stars
> are whispering to each other. ❖
>
> —Kobayashi Issa

 How did the images in each of these poems affect you? Why do you think artists often use the natural world as a subject and a source of inspiration?

Find Meaning

1. (a) How does the frog alter the setting in the Bashō haiku? (b) Does this change seem surprising, or ordinary? Explain.
2. (a) What time of day does Buson's haiku describe? (b) In what way are the images appropriate to this time of day?

Make Judgments

3. (a) What kind of figurative language appears in Issa's haiku? (b) Describe the effect that this figure of speech has on you.
4. Which haiku made the strongest impression on you? Explain.

512 UNIT 5 POETRY

Differentiated Instruction

Reading Proficiency

Less-confident readers may feel impatient with the brevity of haiku. To help them slow their contemplation of the poems, follow this procedure for one or more haiku: Ask three students to read the haiku aloud. Have them pause for an entire minute between each reading. Then have students copy each haiku and illustrate it. Encourage them to reread the poem to get the details right.

Enrichment

Haiku became popular in the English-speaking world during the 1960s. Have interested students use library or Internet resources to seek out haiku written by modern, English-speaking poets. Have them explain what appeals to them about the particular poems they choose.

In these haiku, the poets describe a single moment in the natural world. In the following excerpt from **Steven Harvey**'s book of personal essays, *Lost in Translation*, Harvey discovers how difficult it is to translate haiku. Harvey is a professor of English and the author of *Geometry of Lilies: Life and Death in an American Family*.

from Lost in Translation

An Essay by Steven Harvey

Armed with my book of Japanese kana[1] and her calculator-like word-finder, Junko and I sat at the dining room table and translated haiku—at least, we tried. I printed a transliterated[2] version of the haiku on the page in front of us and Junko read through it, her hand opening and closing as she counted off the syllables with her fingers.

"Yes, haiku," she said, when her fingers closed into a fist at the end of the five-syllable last line. She scratched the poison ivy under her eye and began writing English words above the Japanese. Over the word *ana* she wrote "hole" and over *ya* she wrote a colon.

"Haiku very boring," she said, opening her eyes wide as she always does when she is excited. "But if you see in your mind—is okay."

Above the syllable *no* she wrote " 's" but stumbled on the word in front of it. "Shoji," she whispered, "how say that." Eyes wide, she typed quickly into her word-finder. "Shoji like sliding door," she mumbled, "but...." Then she showed me the definition on her machine: "A sliding door with a piece of Japanese paper on a lattice."

"Not good for Sam," she added with a giggle. She brought her hand down in a mock karate chop and said, "Bam."

"That's for sure," I said.

She wrote "sliding door" and the word "then" above the long first word in the first line and "milky way" above the last word in the poem.

"Ama-no-gawa," I said in her language, haltingly, like a child—the word, not a word for me, but a plaything on my tongue.

"Mil-ky way," she answered. "Yes."

After a half hour of poking around at this text, our literal translation of Issa's immortal haiku looked like this:

> Then:
> Sliding door's hole's
> Milky Way.

We both examined the sheet for a while, not sure what to do next—this was our first experiment in translating haiku, and the results seemed, well, meager.

"Words and meaning are very different," she said, apologetically. "You must picture."

Despairing of any verbal solution, she drew a stick figure picture of a person under a window with a hole in the shade. Then she

---

1. **kana.** Japanese writing
2. **transliterated.** Written in the characters of a different alphabet

Teach the Connection

Use Reading Skills

Identify Author's Purpose Remind students that the purpose is the author's reason for writing a piece. Suggest that one purpose Harvey might have had in writing this essay was to teach. Ask students to tell what he might be trying to teach—such as how complex haiku are. Ask students to suggest and describe other possible purposes.

Literary Connection

Transliteration Expand on the footnote definition and reiterate that *transliteration* is the practice of writing a language in an alphabet different from its own. For example, Japanese is written in characters, but the sounds of the spoken characters can be transliterated to English. That way, English speakers can get a sense of how to say the Japanese words. (Emphasize that this is different from *translation*, which would reveal what the Japanese words mean.)

TEACHING NOTE

Write Legibly Using Cursive

Have students choose one of the haiku on page 512 to copy in cursive and illustrate. Encourage them to imagine that their work has been chosen for publication in an illustrated poetry magazine. (Those who prefer not to draw might wish to find appropriate images online and make a collage.) Display students' work in the classroom.

Words in Use

from *Lost in Translation*
Selection Words
lattice, 513
haltingly, 513
immortal, 513
meager, 513
despairing, 513

Research Skills

Find Examples

Create a class anthology of different Japanese poetic forms. Have students consult library or Internet resources to find other forms of Japanese poetry and report their findings to the class. Gradually create a master list of the forms for the anthology to include. Finally, have each student write his or her own poem in the chosen form. Collect students' work into a three-ring binder and make the anthology available for reference.

Common Core State Standards

Reading Literature
RL.1, RL.9

Analyze Literature

Haiku Note that what Junko says may not be a factual statement about haiku tradition. Ask students to look for clues in the text that might suggest she is mistaken. (She thinks haiku is "boring," so she may not be an expert in it. Her repeating "I *sure*" may also indicate uncertainty.) Ask students to research the idea that nighttime haiku always include moon imagery. **A**

Text-to-Text Connection

Answer: Harvey's experience suggests that some elements from the original poems might have been lost in the translation.

Analyze Literature

Haiku Students' charts will vary. The emotional states they describe should follow logically from the poems.

---

drew several lines from the hole to the man.

"Moonlight," she said, still drawing the lines—as if the figure were bathed in it. "Moonlight."

I looked back at her, puzzled, and pointed out that there was no mention of moon in the poem.

"Always moon in haiku—if night, always moon. I *sure*." She scratched the poison ivy

A again just under the rim of her glasses. "Every peoples in Japan know this shoji and this moon," she said. "I *sure*. Must picture moon."

She looked at me and opened her eyes wide again, as if I might look through them and see what she sees. For a moment we shared what is lost in translation. ❖

TEXT ← TO → TEXT CONNECTION What does Harvey's experience trying to translate haiku from Japanese into English suggest to you about the haiku you have just read?

AFTER READING

Analyze Literature

Haiku Haiku is known for its shortness and use of imagery. These images are intended to elevate the reader to a specific emotional state. What emotions did you experience while reading these three haiku? Use a two-column chart to describe the emotions you experienced.

Poem	My Response
Haiku by Buson	

Extend Understanding

Writing Options

Creative Writing Imagine that you are compiling a collection of haiku for a book. In order to make readers aware of your book, you will need to write an **advertisement.** Explain to readers why they should be excited about your collection and what they can expect to encounter in your book.

Applied Writing Write **instructions** for a photographer taking snapshots of the things described in one of the three poems. Include time of day, setting, and other elements necessary to capture the mood and content. If possible, exchange instructions with a classmate and try following the steps. Suggest revisions to the instructions based on your experience and results.

Media Literacy

Compare Translations Use the library to find collections of haiku. Look for different versions of the same poems. In what ways do the translations differ? What elements remain the same? Which translation do you like the best? Write down your responses to these questions along with the haiku and the translators of each.

Lifelong Learning

Origins of Haiku Using the library, research the history of haiku. Try to determine the cultural and historical surroundings in which haiku emerged. What was happening in the culture when poets began writing haiku? How has haiku changed over time? Write a summary of your findings.

Go to **www.mirrorsandwindows.com** for more.

Rubrics for Writing Options

You can adapt this as a checklist for students to use as they write.

Creative Writing

☐ Does the advertisement concisely describe the collection?

☐ Does the advertisement convey what readers should expect to find?

☐ Does the advertisement explain why readers should be excited about the collection?

Applied Writing

☐ Do the instructions clearly refer to one poem?

☐ Do the instructions include specific information about setting?

☐ Will the instructions help the photographer capture the poem's mood?

the sky was

A Concrete Poem by E. E. Cummings

BEFORE READING

Build Background

Literary Context One of the best known poets of the twentieth century, E. E. Cummings wrote during a time when literature was changing dramatically. Writers, especially poets, were taking bold new chances in the way they wrote. Cummings himself was known for his unique use of punctuation, spelling, and capitalization.

Reader's Context What have you tried to describe that seemed to resist description? How might figurative language and sensory details help express your ideas?

Set Purpose

Before you begin reading, preview the poem by examining its structure, the use of capitals and punctuation, and the poem's shape on the page. Consider how these elements affect the poem's meaning.

Analyze Literature

Concrete Poetry A **concrete poem,** or shape poem, is a poem with a shape that suggests the thing it describes. For example, the words in a concrete poem about a swan would be set on the page to physically resemble a swan. As you read "the sky was," try to determine what the shape of the poem suggests.

Meet the Author

Edward Estlin Cummings (1894–1962), the son of a distinguished clergyman, was born in Cambridge, Massachusetts. Cummings attended Harvard University, where he studied literature and classical and modern languages. During World War I, he volunteered to serve as an ambulance driver in France and was imprisoned by French authorities for writing letters that criticized the war. At the time of his death, Cummings was one of the most popular poets in the nation.

Use Reading Skills

Text Organization In poetry, the way in which a poem is organized is very important. Different kinds of organization are used for different kinds of poetry. In a concrete poem, the text is organized to create a visual effect. As you read the poem, try to determine how its shape influences your interpretation. Use a two-column chart like the one below to record details from the poem and their effects.

Details	Effects
the / sky / was	These lines seem like smoke trailing off.

Preview Vocabulary

lu·mi·nous (lü′ mə nəs) *adj.,* emitting or reflecting steady, glowing light

spry (sprī) *adj.,* energetic; lively

THE SKY WAS **515**

Preview the Selection

At a Glance

Directed Reading

- Reading Level: Moderate
- Difficulty Considerations: Structure and syntax
- Ease Factor: Intriguing shape

DIRECTED READING

Objectives

Studying this lesson will enable students to

- use reading skills such as considering text organization
- define concrete poetry and recognize how the selection is an example of this literary technique
- infer why E. E. Cummings experimented with language
- appreciate a concrete poem expressing enjoyment

Launch the Lesson

Explain that E. E. Cummings wrote many playful poems. Encourage students to note and enjoy the way he experiments not only with the shape of the poem, but also with word choice and arrangement, word divisions, and connotations.

 The Mirrors & Windows questions at the end of the poem focus on the theme of description. Before students begin reading, have them look out a window. Ask: What does the sky, right now, remind you of?

Words in Use

Preview Vocabulary	Selection Words	Teaching Words
luminous, 516	**edible,** 516	**clergyman,** 515
spry, 516	**spouting,** 516	**defy,** 516
		compelling, 517
		stencil, 517
		inhibit, 517

KEY TERMS

CONCRETE POEM, 515
FIGURATIVE LANGUAGE, 515
SENSORY DETAIL, 515
STRUCTURE, 515
TEXT ORGANIZATION, 515
REVIEW, 517

Common Core State Standards

Reading Literature
RL.1, RL.5

Summary

Cummings's poem describes the sky and possibly clouds, as well as smoke coming from a locomotive. The locomotive could be a train moving across the horizon, "spouting violets" into the pinky, color-filled sky.

Use Reading Skills

Analyze Text Organization Focus on the way Cummings breaks words apart (such as *can dy* and *lu / minous*). Ask: "How does this contribute to meaning?" (It pulls the words apart, making them look and sound wispy.)

Analyze Literature

Concrete Poetry E. E. Cummings was also a painter. Ask students how being a painter might have inspired him to create concrete poems.

Answer: Most students will have seen a remarkable sky. Descriptions will vary. Students might feel that not everything can be described. Ask them for specific examples.

TEACHING NOTE

Shape Poem

Explain that this poem is supposed to have a recognizable shape. Provide tracing paper or another means for students to trace an outline of the poem. Give students an opportunity to tell you what the outline looks like to them.

the sky was

A Concrete Poem by E. E. Cummings

```
        the
          sky
            was
    can  dy lu
    minous
              edible
    spry
              pinks shy
    lemons
    greens  coo  l choc
    olate
    s.
          un  der,
      a  lo
      co
      mo
        tive  s pout
          ing
            vi
              o
              lets ❖
```

lu·mi·nous (lü′ mə nəs) *adj.*, emitting or reflecting steady, glowing light

spry (sprī) *adj.*, energetic; lively

When have you seen a brightly colored or strangely colored sky? How would you describe it? What words would you use? Which things or ideas seem to defy description?

516

Program Resources

Planning and Assessment
Program Planning Guide, Selection Lesson Plan
E-Lesson Planner
Assessment Guide, Lesson Test
ExamView

Technology Tools
Interactive Student Text on CD
Visual Teaching Package
Audio Library
mirrorsandwindows.com

Meeting the Standards
Poetry: Unit 5, Directed Reading, pp. 87–89

Differentiating Instruction
Developing Readers, Use Text Organization, pp. 40–42

Find Meaning

1. (a) What appears *edible* to the speaker?
(b) What do you think the speaker means by this?
2. (a) What is introduced into the setting after the comma? (b) What is it doing?

Analyze Literature

Concrete Poetry For a poem to be concrete, it must physically resemble the thing that it describes. Some concrete poems are very precise; others are more abstract. What shape do you think "the sky was" is attempting to imitate? On a separate sheet of paper, draw what you think Cummings's poem is imitating. Then name the object that Cummings's poem resembles. Use a web to help create your drawing. In the outer ovals list details that suggest the object the poem describes.

Make Judgments

3. What images did you find most compelling in this poem? Explain.
4. In your opinion, how do sensory details affect the poem?

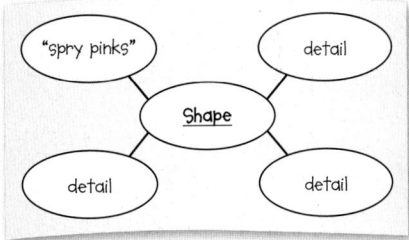

Extend Understanding

Writing Options

Creative Writing Think of an everyday object, such as a pencil or telephone. Think of images, sensory details, and figures of speech that could be used to describe that object. Then write a **concrete poem** about it. Remember, a concrete poem should physically resemble the thing that it describes. Try cutting out a stencil and using that to help guide you in creating your poem.

Persuasive Writing Imagine that you are the literary reviewer for a newspaper and have been asked to write a **review** of Cummings's poem. In your review, describe the elements that make this poem unique, such as its shape, lack of capitalization, and punctuation. Also, give your opinion of the poem. Once you have finished, share your review with a partner.

Collaborative Learning

Discuss Purpose With a partner, discuss Cummings's purpose for creating a poem with this unusual text structure. Ask yourself: What does this structure contribute to the poem's meaning? Does the structure inhibit or aid my understanding of the poem? As you discuss, create a list of your thoughts.

Media Literacy

Concrete Poetry Use the Internet and the library to find other examples of concrete poetry. John Hollander, George Herbert, and Lewis Carroll wrote some of the most famous examples of concrete poetry. Write a short description of at least two concrete poems. Then write a few sentences in which you compare and contrast the poems and state which you like better.

Go to **www.mirrorsandwindows.com** for more.

Two People I Want to Be Like

A Lyric Poem by Eve Merriam

That man
stuck in traffic
not pounding his fists against the steering
    wheel
not trying to shift to the next lane
5 just
using the time
for a slow steady grin
of remembering
all the good unstuck times

10 and that woman
clerking in the supermarket
at rush hour
bagging bottles and cartons and boxes and
    jars and
cans
15 punching it all out
slapping it all along
and leveling a smile
at everyone in the line.

I wish they were married to each other.

20 Maybe it's better they're not,
so they can pass their sweet harmony
around. ❖

Eve Merriam
(1916–1992) was born in Pennsylvania. After college, she lived in New York City, where she wrote for radio. Later, she began teaching and lecturing. Merriam published her first book, *Family Circle*, in 1946. Other collections include *It Doesn't Have to Rhyme,* and *If Only I Could Tell You,* from which "Two People I Want to Be Like" was selected. Although poetry was always Merriam's first love, she is also well known as a playwright and fiction writer.

518

When have you ever admired someone for his or her ability to stay cool under pressure? Why is patience such an admirable trait?

Analyze and Extend

1. (a) What about the two people's actions does the speaker admire? (b) What does the speaker's admiration suggest about him or her?

2. Why does the speaker wish that these two people were married?

3. How do you feel about the speaker's conclusion that it is better for these two people not be married to each other? Explain.

Creative Writing Imagine that you know one of the people described in this poem. Write a short **biography** about this person. Include vital information such as his or her age, occupation, and where he or she lives. Also, describe your subject's personality. Be sure to use some of the information from this poem when writing your biography. Once you have finished, share your biography with a classmate.

Collaborative Learning With a partner, discuss the personality traits of the two people described in this poem. Based on the poem's description, what do you admire about them? Do you think that they always display these traits? Why or why not? Take notes as you hold your discussion. When you are done, use your notes to present your thoughts to the class.

 Go to www.mirrorsandwindows.com for more.

Summary

The poem describes a man in traffic who is undisturbed by the inconvenience and a clerk in a busy supermarket who smiles at everyone in line. The speaker at first wishes the two were married then realizes it's better if they pass their "sweet harmony around."

 Answers: Answers will vary. Many students will admire this trait. They may also say patience shows self-control.

Analyze and Extend

1. (a) The speaker admires their ability to stay calm under pressure. (b) The speaker might have trouble keeping calm, or may often see people losing patience.

2. The speaker thinks their personalities are compatible.

3. Answers will vary.

Rubric for Creative Writing

You can adapt this as a checklist for students to use as they write.

☐ Does the biography include vital information?

☐ Does the biography describe the subject's personality?

☐ Does the biography use information from the poem?

Words in Use

Teaching Words
playwright, 518
admirable, 519
vital, 519

KEY TERMS
CONCLUSION, 519
BIOGRAPHY, 519
PERSONALITY TRAIT, 519

At a Glance
Independent Reading
- Reading Level: Moderate
- Difficulty Considerations: Line length and topic
- Ease Factor: Repetition

Objectives
Reading this selection will enable students to do the following:
- read with developing fluency
- read silently with comprehension for a sustained period of time

Launch the Lesson
Before students read the poem, talk about the word *miracle*. Have a volunteer read some dictionary definitions aloud. Ask: "What kind of event would you consider miraculous?"

The Mirrors & Windows questions after the poem focus on the theme of miracles. Before students begin reading, point out that many people don't believe in miracles. Ask: Do you think they're missing anything?

TEACHING NOTE

Although this selection is presented in the student edition as an independent reading, teaching support has been provided should you choose to cover it in class.

Miracles
A Lyric Poem by Walt Whitman

INDEPENDENT READING

Why, who makes much of a miracle?
As to me I know of nothing else but miracles,
Whether I walk the streets of Manhattan,
Or dart my sight over the roofs of houses toward the sky,
5 Or wade with naked feet along the beach just in the edge of the water,
Or stand under trees in the woods,
Or talk by day with any one I love...
Or sit at table at dinner with the rest,
Or look at strangers opposite me riding in the car.
10 Or watch honey-bees busy around the hive of a summer forenoon,
Or animals feeding in the fields,
Or birds, or the wonderfulness of the sundown, or of stars shining so quiet and bright,
Or the exquisite delicate thin curve of the new moon in spring;
These with the rest, one and all, are to me miracles,
15 The whole referring, yet each distinct and in its place.

Considered one of the most important American poets, **Walt Whitman** (1819–1892) radically altered how poetry was written and what it was written about. His poetry, typically comprised of long, sprawling free verse lines, often celebrates America's vast spaces, varied experiences, and diverse people. During the Civil War, Whitman served as a nurse, caring for both Confederate and Union soldiers. This experience had a profound impact on Whitman's outlook and his writing.

520

Program Resources

Planning and Assessment
Program Planning Guide, Selection Lesson Plan
E-Lesson Planner
Assessment Guide, Lesson Test
ExamView

Technology Tools
Interactive Student Text on CD
Visual Teaching Package
Audio Library
mirrorsandwindows.com

Meeting the Standards
Poetry: Unit 5, Independent Reading, pp. 96–101

Differentiating Instruction
Advanced Students, Independent Reading Study, p. 33

Common Core State Standards

Reading Literature
RL.10

To me every hour of the light and dark is a miracle,
Every cubic inch of space is a miracle,
Every square yard of the surface of the earth is spread with the same,
Every foot of the interior swarms with the same.

20 To me the sea is a continual miracle,
The fishes that swim—the rocks—the motion of the waves—the ships with men in them,
What stranger miracles are there? ❖

 MIRRORS & WINDOWS How is the world full of miracles, both big and small? Do you always feel this way about the world? What makes Whitman's perspective appealing?

Analyze and Extend

1. What do you think Whitman means by his question in the poem's first line: "Why, who makes much of a miracle?"
2. In your opinion, how does the poet's use of repetition affect the poem?
3. The final line of this poem is a rhetorical question, or a question used for effect and for which the answer should be obvious. How do you think Whitman would answer this question? Explain.

Expository Writing What is this poem's main idea? Do you agree with this idea completely? Do you agree partially? Do you disagree? Write a short **literary response** in which you analyze and evaluate the poem's main idea. State what you think the main idea is and provide textual evidence in support of your claim. Then evaluate the main idea, stating why you do or do not agree with it. Present evidence, either textual or otherwise, in support of your position.

Critical Literacy Hold a small-group discussion in which you analyze the form of this poem. Try to describe as many elements as you can. Use terms like *form, line, stanza, rhythm, repetition, lyric poetry,* and *free verse.* Once you have described as many elements as you can, discuss how the poem's form affects its meaning. For example, how do the long line lengths affect the poem's tone?

 Go to www.mirrorsandwindows.com for more.

Teach the Selection

Summary
The speaker of this poem wonders "Why, who makes much of a miracle?" The speaker believes that all things, people, places, objects, even small increments of space are miracles.

MIRRORS & WINDOWS *Answer:* Answers will vary. Students may feel Whitman's perspective is appealing because it makes the everyday world seem wonderful and astonishing.

Analyze and Extend
1. Students should understand that he means to suggest that miracles are commonplace.
2. Repetition helps create the sense that miracles are everywhere.
3. He would say that nothing could be more strange and miraculous than what he sees every day.

Rubric for Expository Writing
You can adapt this as a checklist for students to use as they write.

☐ Does the literary response state the poem's main idea and present evidence to support this statement?
☐ Does the response present the student's opinion of the main idea?
☐ Does the response present evidence in support of this opinion?

At a Glance
Independent Reading
- Reading Level: Easy
- Difficulty Consideration: Metaphor
- Ease Factor: Vocabulary

Objectives
Reading this selection will help students read with developing fluency.

Launch the Lesson
Gogisgi once said, "No one writes well unless he's in love . . ." Ask students to decide what kind of love Gogisgi expresses in this poem.

 MIRRORS & WINDOWS Before reading, ask students to think about what they are thankful for. *Answers:* Answers will vary.

Summary
This poem describes making four prayers of thanks for: the clear day; the good, brown earth; the speaker's people; and the blood in the speaker's veins.

Analyze and Extend
1. They set the tone for the day.
2. (a) The circulating blood refers to life, which ends in death. (b) Many will argue that this is.
3. It emphasizes cycles.

KEY TERMS
LYRIC POEM, 522
REPETITION, 522
SENSORY DETAIL, 522
FIGURATIVE LANGUAGE, 522

Common Core State Standards
Reading Literature
RL.1

EARLY SONG

A Lyric Poem by Gogisgi

(Right) *The Navajo*, c. 20th century. Maynard Dixon. Private collection.

Gogisgi (1927–1997), also known as Carroll Arnett, was born in Oklahoma City, Oklahoma. Of Cherokee and French descent, Gogisgi served in the United States Marines from 1946–1947. After receiving his master's degree from the University of Texas, Gogisgi went on to teach literature and writing. In 1974, he was awarded a National Endowment for the Arts Fellowship in Creative Writing.

As the sun rises
high enough to
warm the frost
off the pine needles,

5 I rise to make
four prayers of
thanksgiving for
this fine clear day,

for this good brown
10 earth, for all
brothers and sisters,
for the dark blood

that runs through me
in a great circle
15 back into this
good brown earth. ❖

MIRRORS & WINDOWS How do you show appreciation for the world around you? Why should people show appreciation and respect for nature?

Analyze and Extend
1. Why do you think the speaker performs these prayers in the morning?
2. (a) What do you think the speaker means in the final three lines of this poem? (b) Do you think this is something to be thankful for? Explain.
3. What does the repetition in this poem emphasize?

Creative Writing What are you thankful for? Is it your family, friends, or something simple like the sun or stars? Write a **descriptive paragraph** in which you describe the things that you appreciate most. Use sensory details and figurative language to enhance your description. When you are finished, read your paragraph to the class.

Go to www.mirrorsandwindows.com for more.

522

Program Resources

Planning and Assessment
Program Planning Guide, Selection Lesson Plan
E-Lesson Planner
Assessment Guide, Lesson Test
ExamView

Technology Tools
Interactive Student Text on CD
Visual Teaching Package
Audio Library
mirrorsandwindows.com

Meeting the Standards
Poetry: Unit 5, Independent Reading, pp. 102–107

For Your Reading List

The Invisible Ladder: An Anthology of Contemporary American Poems for Young Readers

by Liz Rosenberg

In this collection, Rosenberg has assembled a wide range of well-loved poets, such as Galway Kinnell, Nikki Giovanni, and Maxine Kumin. Accompanying each poem are contrasting photos of the poets when they were young and as adults. *The Invisible Ladder* also includes anecdotes from each poet describing how he or she first became interested in the craft.

Becoming Joe DiMaggio

by Maria Testa

This book tells the story of a boy named Joseph Paul and his passion for baseball. Over the course of two dozen brief poems, the reader learns about the challenges Joseph faces and the pleasure he derives from listening to baseball on the radio with his grandfather. As Joseph and his grandfather listen, they follow Joe DiMaggio's budding career, while the reader watches Joseph grow up.

I Am the Darker Brother: An Anthology of Modern Poems by African Americans

by Arnold Adoff

This edition of Adoff's classic collection of African-American verse has been updated to include twenty contemporary writers. Harlem Renaissance poets such as Langston Hughes and Countee Cullen, poets from earlier periods such as Paul Lawrence Dunbar, and later twentieth-century greats such as Gwendolyn Brooks are all represented.

War and the Pity of War

by Neil Philip

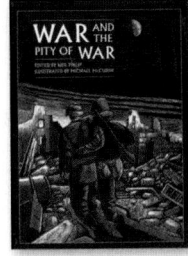

In this collection, poets both ancient and modern describe their wartime experiences. Each poem presents a perspective on war and is accompanied by a note that describes the era in which it was written and the war to which it refers. Powerful illustrations accompany each poem. Readers will be fascinated by the depictions of war across such a vast span of time and place.

Ancient Voices

by Kate Hovey

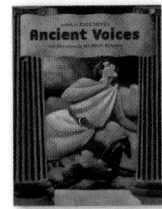

In this unique book, author Kate Hovey gives voice to the gods of Mount Olympus. The poems are divided into four themed sections and appear alongside interesting and often hilarious illustrations. Readers who are familiar with ancient mythology will appreciate the fresh perspective, while those who don't know the stories can find background information about the gods in the appendix.

The Dream on Blanca's Wall

by Jane Medina

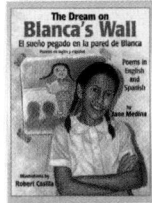

This book tells the story of a young girl, Blanca, who decides that she wants to become a teacher. Through twenty-four narrative free verse poems, the reader witnesses the obstacles Blanca faces as well as the support she receives from her teachers and her parents. The book also contains Spanish translations of the poems.

Independent Reading

Independent Reading Activity

Assign students to groups of four. Give each group eight minutes—two minutes per student—to share information on their favorite poems or poets in a discussion format. Prompt students to think of nursery rhymes and song lyrics—anything "poetic"—to choose their favorites. Then give each group two minutes to draw up a list of the key qualities a person should look for in a poem. Should it be how it sounds? The story it tells? How it makes a person feel? Have groups post their lists on a class bulletin board for everyone to consult when they begin seeking outside reading.

TEACHING NOTE

Group Discussion Behavior

Give students some guidelines for discussing poems, poets, and other types of literature in small groups.

- Agree on the topic and stick to it.
- Speak kindly.
- Do not interrupt; listen until each speaker has finished speaking.
- Try to make sure everyone has a chance to speak.
- Avoid generalizing from personal experience. Tell your story and then allow others to share.
- Be aware of your body language. Nonverbal communication can say just as much as words.

EMC E-Library

The EMC E-Library contains over twenty thousand pages of literary classics that students may read independently. An Electronic Library Guide provides teaching suggestions, enrichment activities, and reading strategy guidesheets.

Program Resources

EMC Access Editions

For additional independent reading, you may wish to refer students to one of EMC's Access Edition titles. Each Access Edition contains a thorough study apparatus, including background information, literal comprehension questions, footnotes, vocabulary definitions, critical thinking questions, and related projects and activities. An Assessment Manual offering worksheets and exams is available for each Access Edition.

Common Core State Standards

Reading Literature
RL.10

Objectives

Participating in this lesson will help students write a compare-and-contrast essay that has

- an introduction that sparks a reader's interest
- a solid thesis statement
- a clear organizational pattern
- transitions to indicate comparisons and contrasts
- an effective conclusion that restates the thesis

Launch the Lesson

Tell students that there are many practical reasons for learning to write a compare-and-contrast essay. One of the main reasons is to help people make choices. Ask for volunteers to tell you how comparing and contrasting can help a person make a choice, such as which of two movies to see on a weekend afternoon. Elicit the observation that by carefully comparing and contrasting, a person can make more informed and more satisfying choices.

Program Resources

Additional writing workshops are available in the *Exceeding the Standards: Writing* resource.

Writing Workshop

Expository Writing

Compare-and-Contrast Essay

Reading and Writing

In this unit, you read a translation of a famous haiku by the Japanese poet Bashō. Here are two more versions.

pond
frog
plop

—JAMES KIRKUP

The old pond
A frog jumped in,
Kerplunk!

—ALLEN GINSBERG

How are the three translations alike and different? To examine their similarities and differences involves making comparisons and contrasts, one of the most basic types of thinking used in studying literature. Much of the critical writing you will do in your literature classes and on standardized tests will ask you to make comparisons and contrasts.

In this workshop you will learn how to write a **compare-and-contrast essay**, a type of expository (or informational) writing that analyzes the similarities and differences between two or more related subjects. The following summary shows how you might sum up the assignment for a compare-and-contrast essay—what its goal is and how to go about it. This summary also includes a writing rubric, a set of standards by which to judge whether your compare-and-contrast essay is successful. You will use this rubric both in drafting and in revising your essay.

- **Assignment:** Write a compare-and-contrast essay in which I examine the similarities and differences between two subjects I choose.
- **Goal:** Make an overall point about these two subjects that will interest my audience.
- **Strategy:** Present evidence for this point by organizing details about my two subjects that clearly show how they are alike and different.
- **Writing Rubric:** My compare-and-contrast essay should include the following:
  - an introduction that sparks a reader's interest
  - a thesis statement that presents my overall point
  - a clear organizational pattern
  - transitions that indicate comparisons and contrasts
  - an effective conclusion that restates my thesis

What Great Writers Do

One approach to the compare-and-contrast essay is to show unexpected similarities. What basic point is Lewis Thomas making about ants and humans?

Ants are so much like human beings as to be an embarrassment. They farm fungi, raise aphids as livestock, launch armies into war, use chemical sprays to alarm and confuse enemies, capture slaves. The families of weaver ants engage in child labor, holding their larvae like shuttles to spin out the thread that sews the leaves together for their fungus gardens....They do everything but watch television.

Words in Use

Teaching Words

translation, 524
fungi, 524
aphids, 524
larvae, 524
diametrically, 528
vitality, 528
chivalry, 528

KEY TERMS

COMPARISON, 524
CONTRAST, 524
COMPARE-AND-CONTRAST
  ESSAY, 524
EXPOSITORY WRITING, 524
SUMMARY, 524
DRAFTING, 524
REVISING, 524

THESIS STATEMENT, 524
TRANSITION, 524
CONCLUSION, 524
ORGANIZATIONAL
  PATTERN, 527
SUBJECT-BY-SUBJECT, 527
POINT-BY-POINT, 527
PEER REVIEWER, 527

Common Core State Standards

Writing
W.2, W.4, W.5, W.6, W.10

Draft

Organizing Ideas Tell students that the details they collect may suggest their organizational pattern. For example, the details may make it clear that the items are similar in all but two key ways; this could dictate using a point-by-point organization to highlight the differences.

Planning and Transitions Suggest to students that they use transition words as they plan their essays. Model an example, using a point-by-point pattern to compare movies:

- Introduction: <u>Both</u> of these pirate movies feature superstar Smirk Small, <u>but</u> the appeal of the second movie is more universal for one big reason, its theme.
- Body paragraph 1: <u>Both</u> movies have pirates as the main characters.
- Body paragraph 2: The first movie is set on the pirate ship *Sally*. The second is set on the <u>same</u> ship.
- Body paragraph 3: The plot of the first movie is romantic. <u>In contrast,</u> the plot of the second movie is about overcoming evil pirates.
- Body paragraph 4: <u>Although</u> the movies are similar in many ways, the first has a theme of love <u>while</u> the second has a theme of justice.
- Conclusion: These two blockbuster movies are <u>like</u> each other in most ways. <u>However,</u> the second has a wider appeal because its theme is justice, <u>while</u> the theme of the first movie is love.

2. DRAFT

Organizing Ideas

Once you have chosen your subjects, gathered details, and created your thesis statement, you next need to decide how you want to organize your ideas. There are two basic **organizational patterns** for a compare-and-contrast essay. If you choose the **subject-by-subject** (or block) method, you present all the features of your first subject, then you present those same features about the second subject. If you choose the **point-by-point** method, you present each feature in turn, looking at the first subject, then at the second subject. Here is what these two organizational patterns look like.

Subject-by-Subject	Point-by-Point
novel plot characters setting theme **movie** plot characters setting theme	**plot** novel movie **characters** novel movie **setting** novel movie **theme** novel movie

Putting Your Thoughts on Paper

Any essay has three basic parts: an introduction, a body, and a conclusion. Create a plan for your compare-and-contrast essay, such as the one on the right comparing and contrasting the book and movie versions of *To Kill a Mockingbird*.

You might draft your essay straight through from the beginning to the end. Some writers prefer to begin with the body, however, leaving the introduction and conclusion until later. Whichever way you choose, your goal is to get all your ideas down on paper according to the plan you created. At the drafting stage, concentrate on content and organization, not on grammar, punctuation, and spelling. Focus on those details in the revising and proofreading stage.

Introduction
- Identify Harper Lee's novel <u>To Kill a Mockingbird</u> and the film based on it.
- Present my thesis statement.

Body
- Write one paragraph dealing with each feature— plot, character, setting, and theme.
- Compare and contrast the novel's and film's handling of each feature.

Conclusion
- Rephrase my thesis statement.
- Wrap up my essay.

Making Connections

When drafting your essay, make connections by using **transitions,** or words and phrases that clearly indicate comparisons and contrasts. Here are some examples of different types of transitions that can be helpful in a compare-and-contrast essay.

Transitions That Show Comparisons	Transitions That Show Contrasts
also *as* *both* *each* *just* *like*	*although* *but* *however* *in contrast* *yet* *while*

Differentiated Instruction

English Language Learning and Reading Proficiency

Give students practice with transition words for comparing and contrasting. Have students work in pairs. Provide each pair with a sheet of paper that has a mixed list of compare and contrast transition words and phrases, such as *by comparison, also, instead, unlike, another, yet, in the same way, similarly, likewise, in contrast, differently, on the other hand, both, also, although, however, too,* and *the same.* Have one student read half of the terms one by one, letting the other state whether each transition indicates comparison, contrast, or possibly either. Then have students switch roles and complete the list. Visit students as they work to monitor their comprehension and to offer assistance as necessary.

1. PREWRITE

Choosing Your Topic

In everyday life, we are always comparing and contrasting things—people we know, products we own, movies we see. You have material all around you. The point is to choose two subjects that will provide an interesting comparison. When you consider possible subjects, ask yourself if they fall into either of the following categories.

Apples and oranges? It is usually best to choose two subjects that are similar enough to make a fair comparison. Don't choose subjects that are so completely different in kind—such as a baseball team and a coin collection—that any comparison is really a stretch.

Peas in a pod? On the other hand, choose subjects that are different enough to make an interesting comparison. Don't choose subjects that are so alike that few people would be interested in their small differences, such as two different outlets of the same fast-food restaurant chain.

Gathering Details

Once you have chosen two subjects that you think will be interesting to compare and contrast, start organizing details. One way to do this is to make a chart. Here's a chart comparing and contrasting Harper Lee's novel *To Kill a Mockingbird* with the movie based on it. It lists features and details from both the novel and the movie.

Features	Novel	Movie
Plot	two major stories, several minor ones	focuses on two major stories; ignores minor plots
Characters	memorable characters	very fine performances
Setting	effective setting	not filmed on location; movie set seems authentic
Theme	importance of understanding	film expresses the same theme

Deciding on Your Purpose

When you have gathered details about your two subjects, review them to determine what the purpose of your compare-and-contrast essay is. Decide the basic point you are trying to make. This purpose is expressed in your **thesis statement.** An essay comparing and contrasting the book and movie versions of *To Kill a Mockingbird* might start with the following thesis statement:

> A good novel can be turned into a good movie by being faithful to the book's plot, characters, setting, and theme.

Teach the Workshop

Prewrite
Gathering Details Remind students that they do not have to use all the details they gather at this stage. In fact, they may learn some new things that cause them to revise their choice of topics. They may also start out being sure their topics are very different, for example, only to find out through gathering details that the topics are quite alike.

What Great Writers Do

Author Brian Garfield usually offers advice to suspense writers, but one of his rules applies to any kind of writing. As they decide on their topics, tell students that one successful writer says: "Don't write anything you wouldn't want to read." Make sure students know they should be interested in their topics before they begin.

TEACHING NOTE

Compare and Contrast
Give students some practice with the vocabulary of comparing and contrasting. Ask students to think about how they differ from their family members. Suggest starting a sentence with "I am different from everyone in my family because . . .". Then, ask students the way in which they most resemble everyone else in their families. Let several volunteers speak, and let everyone write down a similarity, beginning with "I am just like everyone else in my family because . . .".

Writing Skills

Using Graphic Organizers

Tell students that a common tool people use to compare and contrast is the Venn diagram. Students have probably used these organizers. Suggest that they use one as they gather details about their topic.

1. Draw two large circles that overlap by about one third.
2. At the top of one circle, write the name of one of the two things being compared.
3. Write the word *Both* at the top of the overlapping area.
4. Write the name of the other thing being compared at the top of the remaining circle.
5. Place distinctive details in each outer portions of the circles and shared details in the overlapping area.

Objectives

Studying this unit will enable students to

- connect the themes expressed in the selections to their own lives and to the world around them
- understand different forms and elements of poetry, including *lyric poetry, narrative poetry, meaning, the speaker, symbolism, tone, author's purpose, hyperbole,* and *irony*
- understand variations of literary forms and authors' use of language to develop forms

Reading Strategies

Ask Questions
Clarify
Make Inferences
Make Predictions
Visualize

Reading Skills

Analyze Main Idea and Supporting
  Details
Analyze Text Organization
Analyze Text Structure
Compare and Contrast
Evaluate Cause and Effect
Identify Multiple Levels of Meaning
Identify the Main Idea

Literary Elements

Author's Purpose
Hyperbole
Irony
Lyric Poetry
Narrative Poetry
Speaker
Symbolism
Tone

Unit 6

Searching Beneath the Surface
Poetry

CARL SANDBURG

ROBERT FROST

ALFRED NOYES

Launch the Unit

Have small groups create lists of other questions that relate to the unit theme. Experiment with concrete and abstract concepts. For example, suggest that some groups generate questions about what lies below the surface of sensory details, while other groups generate questions about meanings that underlie statements and actions. Model this by proposing two questions: "What does the red rose mean as a symbol?" and "What does it mean to have someone change your name for you?"

KEY TERMS

Key Terms are commonly referred to as *academic vocabulary*. These terms appear in the instructional material to teach the terminology that students need to acquire to understand literature. The repetition of the terms throughout the program ensures student mastery and provides a solid foundation for the continuing study of literature and language arts.

Unit 6 Building Vocabulary

The lists below identify the Words in Use and Key Terms within this unit. These words are listed at the bottom of the Teacher's Edition pages at the beginning of each lesson. Vocabulary development activities are provided in the *Meeting the Standards* unit book and in *Exceeding the Standards: Vocabulary & Spelling*.

WORDS IN USE

Preview Vocabulary

Preview Vocabulary are words taken from the sentences within each selection. These words are defined in the side margin or at the bottom of the pages on which they appear. The "Preview Vocabulary" section introduces these words in the Before Reading page preceding each selection.

aristocracy, 569	crochet, 559	high-strung, 559	shield, 578
ascend, 563	din, 545	intent, 545	tawny, 541
bear, 549	dusk, 541	peaked, 552	translucency, 559
brandish, 555	extraneous, 559	refrain, 554	writhe, 554
bygone, 569	hack, 578	saucy, 559	

Selection Words

Selection Words are additional words from the reading that may be challenging but are not central to the selection and are not identified in the prereading section. These words can easily be learned using the story context, and they provide excellent practice for using content clues to find meaning without explicit instruction.

ancestors, 569	comfy, 559	immaculately, 565	refugee, 586
banish, 584	disconcerting, 565	kinsmen, 549	spurred, 555
beams, 550	disconsolate, 565	note, 559	tawny, 553
bronzed, 586	dreary, 584	permeated, 559	torrent, 552
captive, 586	foreign, 586	perturbed, 565	
chilling, 549	highborn, 549	raiment, 565	

Teaching Words

Teaching Words consist of vocabulary that is used in the directions about the lessons. Teaching words explain to students what to focus on within the selection, help establish the story context, clarify the meaning of literary terms, and define the goals or instructional purpose.

allay, 604	dissensions, 604	innovators, 584	preceded, 590
beckoned, 598	drawbacks, 602	intermittently, 590	precise, 557
benefits, 602	emissions, 590	internment, 576	pursued, 539
billow, 567	entrap, 567	interpretation, 538	quarrels, 604
bizarre, 584	evident, 557	irrelevant, 596	Shakespearean, 544
bricklaying, 539	explicitly, 538	kooky, 575	solemn, 544
bulging, 598	forbade, 586	lateral, 590	subdue, 604
catastrophic, 590	forbidden, 562	nobility, 568	succinctly, 592
compelling, 594	fulfillment, 594	nonverbal, 601	symmetrical, 590
compelling, 602	fury, 544	notoriously, 584	unique, 538
concise, 594	genealogical, 568	opposed, 602	unofficial, 575
consensus, 592	genuinely, 592	outcome, 600	upheaval, 544
convey, 601	heritage, 587	pander, 567	vengeance, 604
criticism, 601	immigrants, 539, 576	particularly, 592	vivid, 576, 596
descent, 588	inadequate, 578	paternal, 604	wrangling, 604
discord, 604	inanimate, 598	Petrarchan, 546	wrath, 604
discouraged, 562	industrialism, 539	poet laureate, 568	

Literary Element	*Mirrors & Windows* Theme	Cross-Curricular Connection	Writing Options	Extension Activities
Hyperbole	Escaping Detection		Expository: Literary Analysis	Lifelong Learning: Locate and Read More of Dickinson's Poetry
Symbolism	Isolation		Creative: Diary Entry	Collaborative Learning: Discuss the Poem's Symbolism
Personification	Descriptions	Science Connection: *Mount Saint Helens*	Expository: Literary Analysis	Lifelong Learning: Create a Poster about Mount St. Helens
Mood	Fulfillment		Expository: Literary Analysis	Collaborative Learning: Discuss the Mood of this Poem

Unit 6 Scope & Sequence Guide

Selection or Feature	Genre	Reading Support/ Reading Level	Word Count	Reading Skill	Graphic Organizer	
I'm Nobody Emily Dickinson pp. 584–585	Lyric Poem	Independent Reading/ Easy	55	Summarizing		
Refugee Ship Lorna Dee Cervantes pp. 586–587	Lyric Poem	Independent Reading/ Easy	83	Analyze Author's Approach		
Loo Wit Wendy Rose pp. 588–590	Lyric Poem	Independent Reading/ Moderate	176	Draw Conclusions		
The Pasture Robert Frost pp. 591–592	Lyric Poem	Independent Reading/ Easy	78	Asking Questions		

INDEPENDENT READING

Unit 6 Language Arts Workshops

Grammar & Style	Vocabulary & Spelling	Writing	Speaking & Listening	Test Practice
Simple, Compound, Complex, and Compound-Complex Sentences, p. 543 Simple, Complete, and Compound Predicates, p. 571	Figurative Language, p. 561 Spelling by Syllables, p. 567	Narrative Writing: Personal Narrative, pp. 594–599	Giving and Actively Listening to Narrative Presentations, pp. 600–601	Writing Skills: Personal Essay, p. 602 Revising and Editing Skills, p. 603 Reading Skills: from *The Song of Hiawatha* by Henry Wadsworth Longfellow, pp. 604–605

Literary Element	*Mirrors & Windows* Theme	Cross-Curricular Connection	Writing Options	Extension Activities
Compare Literature: Narrative Poem	Grief	Cultural Connection: *Gothic Literature*	Creative: Narrative Poem Expository: Essay	Critical Literacy: Hold a Panel Discussion Lifelong Learning: Write a Literary Critique
	Actions			
Tone	First Impressions		Creative: Short Story Expository: Essay	Collaborative Learning: Consider the Author's Perspective Media Literacy: Draw the Images
Lyric Poetry	Reactions		Creative: Letter Expository: Personal Essay	Critical Literacy: List Questions Lifelong Learning: Research History
Author's Purpose	Ancestors		Creative: Biography Expository: Expository Paragraph	Critical Literacy: Hold a Panel Discussion Lifelong Learning: Research Your Ancestry
Symbol	Expressing Grief		Creative: Dream Poem Expository: Persuasive Paragraph	Collaborative Learning: Speaking and Listening Media Literacy: Wild Parrots
Hyperbole	Experiences	History Connection: *Japanese Internment*	Creative: Personal Letter Expository: Literary Response	Lifelong Learning: Research and Report Critical Literacy: Write a Dialogue
Irony	Familiar Feelings		Creative: Travel Brochure Expository: Compare-and-Contrast Essay	Collaborative Learning: Discuss and Speculate Media Literacy: Contrast Appearance and Reality

Evaluating Your Draft

When you revise, you identify strengths and weaknesses in your draft. You can evaluate your own writing. You can also work with a **peer reviewer.** Exchange essays with this partner and evaluate each other's work.

Below is part of a draft of a compare-and-contrast essay. The annotations indicate the reasons for changes.

Revising Checklist

☐ Does the introduction engage the reader?
☐ Does the thesis present the overall point?
☐ Is the essay organized in a logical way?
☐ Do I use transitions?

~~Some people think that no movie can be as good as the book it is based on.~~ *Can any movie be as good as the book it is based on? Consider Harper Lee's novel* To Kill a Mockingbird *and the 1962 film version.* The book won the 1961 Pulitzer Prize for fiction, and the movie was nominated for an Academy Award for Best Picture. ~~The movie's music is very good too.~~ A good novel can be turned into a good movie by being faithful to the book's plot, characters, setting, and theme.

Harper Lee's *To Kill a Mockingbird* tells many stories, but her novel has two major plots. The first is how three children, Scout and Jem Finch and their friend Dill Harris, try to find out about their strange neighbor Boo Radley. The second plot is how Jem and Scout's father, the lawyer Atticus Finch, defends a man named Tom Robinson. ~~The~~ *Although the* movie leaves out many stories, it focuses clearly on the two major plots.

> *Reword opening sentences to sharpen point.*

> *Delete a detail that is off the topic.*

> *Add the transitional word* although *to signal a contrast.*

Teach the Workshop

Revise

Evaluating a Draft Have students read the tips below for delivering and receiving constructive criticism. Then help them prepare for peer review by modeling good criticism.

Delivering Criticism

- **Be focused.** Concentrate on the introduction, the organization, and transitions. Leave spelling and punctuation for later.
- **Be positive.** Respect the writer's feelings and writing efforts.
- **Be specific.** Give concrete ideas for improving the essay.

Receiving Criticism

- **Ask questions.** Make sure you understand your reviewer's comments. Ask your reviewer to clarify comments and suggestions if necessary.
- **Be selective.** Accept your reviewer's time and suggestions graciously. When you revise your essay, you can use just some—or none—of the suggestions.

Modeling

Use the student model on this page to demonstrate appropriate criticism and suggestions. The first line, which has been crossed out, is: "Some people think that no movie can be as good as the book it is based on." Say: "I think I'm distracted by wondering which people think this, and how we know what they think. It's a good point, but can you make it more engaging? Maybe it would work better as a question."

Speaking & Listening Skills

Monitor Comprehension While Listening

You can use the peer review process as an opportunity for students to practice listening skills. Have each student read his or her draft aloud for a peer reviewer. Students may wish to hear the essays they are reviewing more than once. Tell reviewers to listen for these things as they monitor their own comprehension:

1. What does the introduction make you think? Do you want to learn more?
2. Does the organization make sense to you? Does your mind wander at any point? If so, where?
3. Do you understand how the items in the essay are alike and different? If not, what is confusing about the organization or transition words and phrases?

▶ Edit and Proofread

Students may want to use proofreader's marks when correcting their work. Refer them to the Language Arts Handbook, Writing Section 4.1, Proofreader's Symbols.

Using Commas If students have trouble reviewing their work for correct comma usage, refer them to the Grammar & Style review of Comma Use on page 162.

What Great Writers Do

In response to the question about Bruce Catton's use of the word *each*, students may be unsure whether it indicates a comparison or a contrast. Encourage them to read and think about the sentence in which the word appears. Catton is expressing a quality the two men have in common; both were perfect champions of their respective, and contrasting, causes. As indicted on page 526, *each* is generally used to indicate comparison.

▶ Publish and Present

Before students begin their final versions, they might benefit from reading the Language Arts Handbook, Writing Section 4.1, Writing Follow-up.

---

4. EDIT AND PROOFREAD

Focus: Transitions

The effective use of transitional words and phrases is a key element in a successful compare-and-contrast essay. In revising your draft, add transitions where needed to point out similarities and differences.

> Harper Lee created very memorable characters. Atticus Finch and his children, Dill, Boo Radley, Tom Robinson, and the others stay in the reader's memory. ~~The~~ *In the same way, the* actors create very memorable performances.

What Great Writers Do

In the last sentence, what does Bruce Catton indicate with the transitional word each?

> So Grant and Lee were in complete contrast, representing two diametrically opposed elements in American life. Grant was the modern man emerging; beyond him, ready to come on the stage, was the great age of steel and machinery, vitality. Lee might have ridden down from the age of chivalry, lance in hand. Each man was the perfect champion of his cause, drawing both his strengths and his weaknesses from the people he led.

Focus: Using Commas

In revising your draft, be aware of common punctuation errors, such as incorrect use of commas to set off words or phrases that interrupt sentences. Use two commas if the word or phrase falls in the middle of the sentence.

> Harper Lee's *To Kill a Mockingbird* tells many stories, and all of them are very interesting, but her novel has two major plots.

Use one comma if the word or phrase falls at the beginning or end of the sentence.

> Lee even calls it a "tired old town," almost like it was a person.

Proofreading

Quality Control The purpose of proofreading is to correct errors in grammar, punctuation, and spelling. You can pick out and fix these errors as you evaluate and revise your essay, but take time to focus on them during the proofreading stage. Use proofreader's marks to highlight any errors you find. (See the Language Arts Handbook, section 4.1, for a list of proofreader's symbols.)

5. PUBLISH AND PRESENT

Publishing and Presenting

Neatness Counts Make the finished version of your essay appealing to read. Handwritten papers should be neat and legible. If you are working on a word processor, double-space the lines of text and use a readable font, or typeface. Whether you are submitting your work to your teacher or elsewhere, be sure to follow any presentation guidelines.

Differentiated Instruction

Reading Proficiency

Review interrupters with students. Remind them that interrupters can be either words or phrases. They break the flow of a sentence. They are not bad; they often help clarify what a writer means. Encourage students to experiment with using some of their transition words as interrupters in sentences. Give them several examples, and then ask them to give you additional examples.

- The makeup in both movies was convincing, however.
- When I saw the second movie, however, I was not as impressed with the makeup as when I saw it the first time.

Student Model

Read the Book or See the Movie?
by Kathy Jeffers

Can any movie be as good as the book it is based on? Consider Harper Lee's novel *To Kill a Mockingbird* and the 1962 film version. The book won the 1961 Pulitzer Prize for fiction, and the movie was nominated for an Academy Award for Best Picture. A good novel can be turned into a good movie by being faithful to the book's plot, characters, setting, and theme.

Harper Lee's *To Kill a Mockingbird* tells many stories, and all of them are very interesting, but her novel has two major plots. The first is how three children, Scout and Jem Finch and their friend Dill Harris, try to find out about their strange neighbor Boo Radley. The second plot is how Jem and Scout's father, the lawyer Atticus Finch, defends a man named Tom Robinson. Although the movie leaves out many stories, it focuses clearly on the two major plots.

Harper Lee created very memorable characters. Atticus Finch and his children, Dill, Boo Radley, Tom Robinson, and the others stay in the reader's memory. In the same way, the actors create very memorable performances. Gregory Peck, who played Atticus, won the Oscar for Best Actor. Mary Badham, who played Scout, was nominated for Best Supporting Actress.

The setting of Harper Lee's novel, the small Alabama town of Maycomb in the 1930s, is a very important part of the effect she creates in her book. Maycomb is practically like a character. Lee even calls it a "tired old town," almost as if it were a person. The film version was not shot in Monroeville, Alabama, the town on which she based Maycomb. However, the movie set looks right.

The theme of *To Kill a Mockingbird* is the importance of understanding other people. As Atticus says, "You never really know a man until you stand in his shoes and walk around in them." In the novel, this theme is expressed through what the children learn about Boo Radley, Tom Robinson, and other people in Maycomb. Although it does not include many of the stories in the novel, the film still makes a powerful statement about the importance of understanding someone.

Although different in some details, the movie faithfully follows the novel's plot, characters, setting, and theme. Seeing the film version of *To Kill a Mockingbird* is not the same as reading the novel, but it is still very satisfying. The movie is as good a film as the book is a novel. So read the book *and* see the movie.

> *Identifies the specific subjects to be compared and contrasted*
>
> *Presents the thesis statement*

> *Provides details showing similarities and differences*

> *Summarizes the comparison and contrast*
>
> *Restates the thesis*

Student Model
Using the Model Direct students' attention to the model. Point out the side notes that identify the thesis statement, the body paragraphs with details, and the restatement of the thesis. Some students might benefit from outlining the model to grasp the writer's plan of organization and use of evidence.

Reviewing Transition Words and Phrases You may use the model to help students recognize compare-and-contrast transitions, including *all, but, although, in the same way, like, however, different,* and *not the same.*

Writing Skills

Use Management Time Lines

Tell students that analyzing a writing task will help them make decisions about how long they spend on any step in the process. Point out that sometimes they will have several weeks to produce an essay or a report; other times they will have several days or will have to write on demand, as on a test. In most circumstances, they will have to alter the time they spend prewriting or drafting. Ask students how they would manage their time in these situations:

- Your deadline for an article on school recycling is two days from today.
- A test asks you for a three-paragraph comparison of two classic fairy tales.
- You are entering a writing portfolio in a contest that is going to be judged next month.

Teach the Workshop

Objectives

Participating in this lesson will help students plan and deliver an expository presentation that

- draws the listener in with an effective introduction
- is clear, logical, and well-organized
- has well-researched content
- summarizes main ideas in its conclusion

Launch the Lesson

Ask students what kind of information they would like to hear from a poet. It could be one of the writers represented in this unit, or another poet they know. Have them try to identify two or three pieces of information that they genuinely would like to learn from someone who writes poetry as a profession. Then say they will learn about the possible structures and style of informational presentations in this lesson.

TEACHING NOTE

Expository Instruction

Tell students that most of the instruction they receive in school is a form of expository presentation. Have them articulate what they like best about learning from expository presentations. Encourage them to emulate these qualities as they prepare their own presentations.

> For more information, see the Language Arts Handbook Section 7, Speaking & Listening.

Giving and Actively Listening to Expository Presentations

Have you ever had something explained to you, such as how to solve a problem, how to operate a device, or the differences between two similar ideas? These are examples of expository presentations. In an **expository presentation,** you give facts and details about a topic. When you give and actively listen to an expository presentation, you share information about a topic.

There are different kinds of expository presentations. Some examples include *compare-and-contrast, cause-and-effect,* and *problem-and-solution* presentations.

Planning an Expository Presentation

Choose a Topic What will you present? What topics interest you? In an expository presentation, you give facts and details about a subject. What you discuss should be of interest to you and to your audience. Choose a subject that you find interesting and you know others will too. You might present on animals, sports, games, science—anything of your choosing.

Narrow Your Focus Now that you have a topic, narrow it to make it more manageable. You can use a chart to help narrow your topic. For instance, if you decided to discuss sports, you would need to choose a specific sport. Then you would need to narrow your topic further so that a specific aspect of that sport becomes the focus of your presentation. However, avoid narrowing your topic so much that you are left with little to discuss. Your chart might look like this.

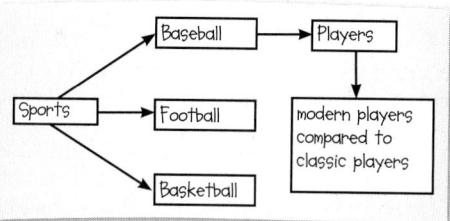

Identify Your Audience Now that you have identified and narrowed your topic, consider your audience. Your audience will determine much of what you say and how you say it. If you know that your audience is very familiar with your topic, try to introduce a new perspective or information with which they may not be familiar. If you know your topic is one your audience knows little about, avoid jargon and technical language.

Words in Use

Teaching Words
manageable, 530
jargon, 530

KEY TERMS

EXPOSITORY PRESENTATION, 530
INTRODUCTION, 531
CONCLUSION, 531
COMPARE-AND-CONTRAST ORDER, 531
CAUSE-AND-EFFECT ORDER, 531
CHRONOLOGICAL ORDER, 531
PROBLEM-AND-SOLUTION ORDER, 531

Common Core State Standards

Speaking and Listening
SL.4, SL.5, SL.6

Language
L.3, L.7.3a

Organize Your Information How will you organize what you want to say? All presentations should begin with an introduction and end with a conclusion that summarizes all of your main ideas. The kind of order you choose for the body of your presentation depends on your topic. For example, when comparing baseball players of today with those from a century ago, you would probably use **compare-and-contrast order.** To organize using this method, you would present all of the characteristics of one subject, and then those of another. Or you would present a single characteristic of one subject, compare it to that of your other subject, and so on.

Some other kinds of organization that you might find useful include cause-and-effect order, chronological order, and problem-and-solution order. In **cause-and-effect order,** you present one or more causes and one or more effects. In **chronological order,** you present events in the order that they occurred. In **problem-and-solution order,** you present problems and give solutions. Choose the order that best fits what you want to say.

Evaluating Your Expository Presentation

Working with your partner or in a small group, rehearse your presentation. Provide each other with constructive feedback through polite, respectful criticism and praise. Follow the speaking and listening rubrics on this page in your evaluations.

Delivering Your Expository Presentation

Nonverbal communication is an important part of listening and speaking. As you deliver your expository presentation, remember to make eye contact with the audience. In an expository essay, a key purpose is to clearly explain information to the listener. Therefore, speak loudly and clearly.

If you are using visual aids, such as graphs, charts, photographs, or multimedia, try to coordinate these materials with the content of your presentation. Also, avoid any unnecessary movements or gestures that might distract your audience.

Listen Actively It is also important to be an active, involved listener. Listen attentively by making eye contact and maintaining an engaged and respectful posture. Use the information in the presentation to ask relevant questions at the end of the speech or when prompted by the presenter.

Speaking Rubric

Your expository presentation will be evaluated on these elements:

Content
- ☐ an introduction that draws in the listener
- ☐ ideas clearly, logically, and consistently organized
- ☐ content well-researched and interesting
- ☐ conclusion that summarizes all main ideas

Delivery and Presentation
- ☐ maintains audience involvement
- ☐ good use of voice and nonverbal cues
- ☐ appropriate pacing

Listening Rubric

As a peer reviewer or audience member, you should do the following:

- ☐ listen quietly and attentively
- ☐ analyze any images that are presented
- ☐ ask appropriate questions
- ☐ (as peer reviewer) provide constructive feedback

Nonverbal Communication

Tell students that nonverbal communication can tell an audience more than the words they say. Also, different cultures have very different understandings of many nonverbal messages. Review the following elements of nonverbal communication with the class. Demonstrate some aspects of nonverbal communication yourself, and ask volunteers to demonstrate other aspects as appropriate. You might also wish to have students tell you what they think are positive and negative aspects of each element.

- Personal space: Maintain a comfortable distance from your audience.
- Posture: Sit or stand up straight, and lean slightly forward.
- Facial expression: A smile is the most engaging expression.
- Voice: Vary your tone, rhythm, volume, and pace.
- Gestures: Make gestures to punctuate a speech or to show visual aids; avoid unnecessary gestures. As a listener, nod to show that you understand or agree.
- Eye contact: Make "eye contact" with different parts of the audience.

Program Resources

To expand upon this workshop lesson, Giving and Actively Listening to Expository Presentations, see the *Exceeding the Standards: Speaking & Listening* resource.

Speaking & Listening Skills

Be Aware of Cultural Sensitivity

Remind students that nonverbal communication conveys much more than words. Caution them that different cultures interpret nonverbal "cues" differently. Point out that in Western cultures, it is respectful to meet someone's eyes, but in many other cultures it is considered disrespectful, rude, or worse to look another person directly in the eye. Ask students for other examples they know from personal experience. Tell them that whenever they can, they should learn what the audience members will expect in terms of such nonverbal cues as gestures and eye contact. One way to learn these things is to find a leader or representative of the audience and ask that person if the audience has expectations and sensitivities.

Teach the Workshop

Objectives

Completing this lesson will enable students to

- write a compare-and-contrast expository essay based on a timed writing prompt
- answer standardized test questions that demonstrate revising and editing skills
- answer standardized test questions that demonstrate the ability to infer from a reading

Timed Writing

Remind students that standardized tests often ask for a response to a prompt in a specified period of time. Give the following tips:

- Read the entire question carefully.
- Look for key words in the question that tell you what is expected.
- Underline these words or write them on your own notepaper.
- Use the key words to make sure to answer all parts of the question.
- Organize. Allow time for planning, writing, and reviewing.
- Before you begin writing, create a rough outline of points to make.
- Write a clear introduction. This will help keep you on track as you write each paragraph.
- If you find yourself running out of time, state your remaining points and add a conclusion.
- Review your completed essay to see if you have answered all parts of the question.
- Proofread before you turn in your completed essay.

Writing Skills

Expository Essay

Read the following short excerpts and the writing assignment that follows. Before you begin writing, think carefully about what task the assignment is asking you to perform. Then create an outline to help guide your writing.

"Song" by Robert Browning

The year's at the spring,
And day's at the morn;
Morning's at seven;
The hill-side's dew-pearled;
The lark's on the wing;
The snail's on the thorn;
God's in his Heaven—
All's right with the world!

"The Gardener" (LXXXV) by Rabindranath Tagore

Who are you, reader, reading my poems an hundred years hence?
 I cannot send you one single flower from this wealth of the spring,
one single streak of gold from yonder clouds.
 Open your doors and look abroad.
 From your blossoming garden gather fragrant memories of the
vanished flowers of an hundred years before.
 In the joy of your heart may you feel the living joy that sang one
spring morning, sending its glad voice across a hundred years.

Assignment: What do the two poems have in common? In what ways are they different? Plan and write several paragraphs for an **expository essay** in which you **compare** and **contrast** the poems. Use **transitions** that signal the organization of your essay. Include evidence from the poems to support your thesis.

Rubric for an Expository Essay

Have students use these criteria when evaluating their essays.

- ☐ Does the essay have both comparisons and contrasts, and do transitions signal a clear organizational pattern?
- ☐ Does the essay use evidence from the poems to support ideas?

Common Core State Standards

Writing
W.2

Language
L.6.1e

Revising and Editing Skills

The following sentences test your ability to recognize grammar and usage errors. Each sentence contains either a single error or no error at all. No sentence contains more than one error. The error, if there is one, is underlined and lettered. If the sentence contains an error, select the one underlined part that must be changed to make the sentence correct. If the sentence is correct, select choice E. In choosing answers, follow the requirements of standard written English.

1. The teacher invited <u>my</u> parents and <u>me</u> to the
            A   **B**
   art gallery <u>for</u> a showing of the paintings <u>she</u>
        C   **D**
   had done. <u>No error.</u>
              E

2. The <u>walls</u> of the gym, painted green and
        A
   trimmed with <u>yellow were</u> so far apart that our
               B
   <u>voices</u> created <u>echoes</u>. <u>No error.</u>
    C   **D**   **E**

3. The children excused <u>theirselves</u> from the
                  A
   table after <u>they</u> finished eating so <u>they</u> could
           B   **C**
   play with <u>their</u> new toys. <u>No error.</u>
         D   **E**

4. Last summer, <u>my parents</u>, brother, and <u>I</u>
            A   **B**
   visited the <u>cities</u> of Los Angeles and <u>San Diego</u>.
          C   **D**
   <u>No error.</u>
    E

5. <u>We</u> could not <u>believe</u> how bad the <u>boys</u>
   A   **B**   **C**
   behavior <u>had</u> become. <u>No error.</u>
         D   **E**

6. The <u>miners</u> faces were covered with soot after
      A
   <u>the</u> explosion, but <u>their</u> helmets and goggles
    B   **C**
   had protected <u>their</u> heads and eyes from
           D
   flying debris. <u>No error.</u>
            E

7. While the teacher <u>was</u> explaining Newton's
            A
   <u>laws</u> of motion, the class <u>were</u> startled when
    B   **C**
   she <u>broke</u> a board with her hand. <u>No error.</u>
       D   **E**

8. We <u>ourselves</u> spent almost an hour trying to
      A
   locate the <u>birds</u> nest so <u>we</u> could put back <u>its</u>
         B   **C**   **D**
   egg that had fallen to the ground. <u>No error.</u>
                        E

9. The <u>farmer's</u> <u>children</u>, in mud-covered
       A   **B**
   <u>overalls were</u> playing in the field with <u>their</u>
      C   **D**
   dog. <u>No error.</u>
       E

10. I am very proud of <u>me</u> because <u>I</u> got straight
                B   **C**
    A's on <u>my</u> report card. <u>No error.</u>
        D   **E**

Teach the Workshop

Revising and Editing Skills

1. E	**6.** A
2. B	**7.** C
3. A	**8.** B
4. E	**9.** C
5. C	**10.** B

Test-Taking Tip
Eliminate Incorrect Responses

Remind students that a key skill in working with multiple-choice questions is eliminating incorrect responses. Demonstrate this skill by modeling a think-aloud for one question on this page.

Question 5. Underlines A and B are the subject and predicate of a simple sentence, and they agree in number, so they are not errors. Underline C, "the boys," could be the object of the sentence, but it is followed by "behavior," so it must be an adjective. In that case, answer C is possible because this should be a possessive noun, boys'. D seems OK. So C must be the answer.

▶ For more information, see the Language Arts Handbook Section 8, Test-Taking Skills.

Program Resources

For more study and practice with test-taking skills, see the *Exceeding the Standards: Test Practice* resource:

- Expository Essay Practice Test: Timed Writing, p. 13

Reading Comprehension Tests

Tell students that reading comprehension questions give a short piece of writing and then ask several questions about it. The questions may ask students to figure out something based on information in the passage. Urge them to keep the following tips in mind:

- Skim all the questions quickly.
- Read the passage with the questions in mind.
- Reread the first question carefully.
- Find the portion of the passage to which the question refers. Slow down and read carefully.
- Answer the first question.
- Repeat this process to answer all the rest of the questions.

Reading Skills

1. D
2. C
3. A

Reading Skills

Carefully read the following passage. Then, on a separate piece of paper, answer each question.

"Silver" by Walter de la Mare

> Slowly, silently, now the moon
> Walks the night in her silver shoon;
> This way, and that, she peers, and sees
> Silver fruit upon silver trees;
> 5 One by one the casements catch
> Her beams beneath the silvery thatch;
> Couched in his kennel, like a log,
> With paws of silver sleeps the dog;
> From their shadowy cote the white breasts peep
> 10 Of doves in a silver-feathered sleep;
> A harvest mouse goes scampering by,
> With silver claws, and a silver eye;
> And moveless fish in the water gleam,
> By silver reeds in a silver stream.

1. Which of the following sound devices appears in line 1?
   A. onomatopoeia
   B. simile
   C. rhyme scheme
   D. alliteration
   E. internal rhyme

2. Which of the following kinds of figurative language appears in line 3?
   A. simile
   B. onomatopoeia
   C. personification
   D. hyperbole
   E. haiku

3. Which of the following sound devices appears in line 6?
   A. alliteration
   B. onomatopoeia
   C. consonance
   D. rhyme scheme
   E. simile

Differentiated Instruction

English Language Learning

Help students interpret the poem "Silver" by using the following definitions:

shoon — old-fashioned plural of *shoe;* shoes
casements — window frames
thatch — straw or other plant material used for a roof
cote — shed or pen for birds
reeds — tall grass

4. The phrase *like a log* in line 7 is an example of
   A. metaphor.
   B. simile.
   C. personification.
   D. onomatopoeia.
   E. assonance.

5. Which of the following represents the rhyme scheme in the first eight lines?
   A. *abababab*
   B. *aabbccdd*
   C. *abcabcab*
   D. *abbaccdd*
   E. *abbccaab*

6. How many beats, or stressed syllables, appear in line 8?
   A. 1
   B. 2
   C. 3
   D. 4
   E. 5

7. The description in line 14 is an example of
   A. hyperbole.
   B. a simile.
   C. a metaphor.
   D. personification.
   E. imagery.

8. The use of the word *silver* throughout this poem is an example of
   A. hyperbole.
   B. rhyme.
   C. simile.
   D. extended metaphor.
   E. repetition.

9. What is the overall mood of the passage?
   A. frightening
   B. humorous
   C. sad
   D. peaceful
   E. angry

10. Which of the following best describes this poem's point of view?
   A. first-person
   B. second-person
   C. third-person
   D. dynamic
   E. round

Teach the Workshop

Reading Skills
4. B
5. B
6. D
7. E
8. E
9. D
10. C

Test-Taking Skills

Avoid Distractors

Instruct students to watch out for distractors, incorrect answers that look right because they are partially correct. Distractors are usually based on common mistakes students make. Model a think-aloud showing how to detect distractors.

Question 1. I've already eliminated C because you can't find a rhyme scheme from a single line. The line doesn't have the word *like* or *as,* so there is no simile. That eliminates B. Nothing in the line is about sound, which eliminates option A. The answer must be either D or E.

Unit 6 Visual Planning Guide

Planning and Assessment Tools

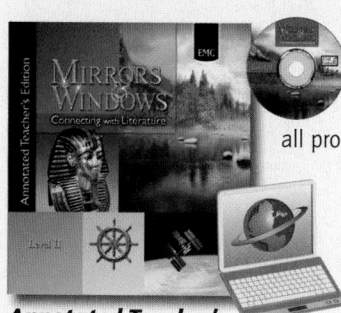

Annotated Teacher's Edition

Annotated Teacher's Edition
One location for accessing, previewing, and planning for use of all program resources.

EMC Launchpad
Desktop application for accessing, previewing, planning, posting, and grading all program resources. Post personal resources and lessons, and access the E-Lesson Planner, the E-Gradebook, and training modules for computer literacy.

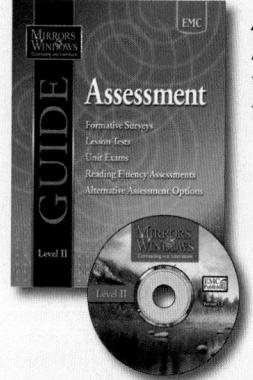

Assessment Guide and ExamView
A variety of assessments are available for this unit in print and electronic forms, including:
- Formative Survey
- Lesson Tests
- Unit Exams
- Alternative Assessment Options
- Reading Fluency Assessments

Meeting the Standards: Unit 6
In addition to lesson-by-lesson resources, *Meeting the Standards* includes the following unit-based resources:
- Unit Study Guide
- Practice Test
- Active Reading Model
- Selection Quizzes

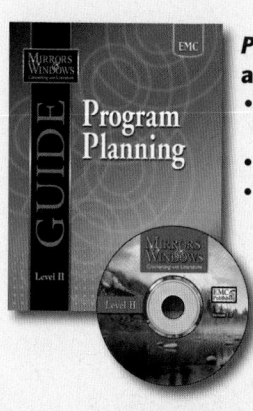

Program Planning Guide and *E-Lesson Planner*
- Lesson Plans for all the selections in the unit
- Core Standards-Based Selections
- Reading Log and Evaluation Forms

The E-Lesson Planner contains fully developed lesson plans and unit resources with an electronic calendar for editing lesson plans.

Technology Tools

Visual Teaching Package
This package contains unit-based lectures, games, art collections, and Writing Workshops in PowerPoint format; included within the EMC Launchpad.

Interactive Student Text on CD
The student textbook on CD includes highlighting, note-taking, bookmarking, and a direct link to the student website, in addition to everything in the student text.

Audio Library
Authentic, dramatic recordings with listening activities expand listening skills and offer additional support for developing readers and English Language Learners.

ETS Online Criterion-Based Essay Grader (Grades 9–12)
Students can use this ETS web-based tool to evaluate their essays online before submitting them for teacher review and final evaluation.

mirrorsandwindows.com
Student and teacher resources, support, references, technology tools, and state-specific standards are available at **mirrorsandwindows.com**. The website is customizable using the EMC Launchpad.

Unit-Based Resources

Exceeding the Standards Unit Resources

Each of the *Exceeding the Standards* resources provides fully developed lessons to help you extend the textbook lessons and to expand upon the themes and skills covered in the unit. You can also download these lessons from **mirrorsandwindows.com**.

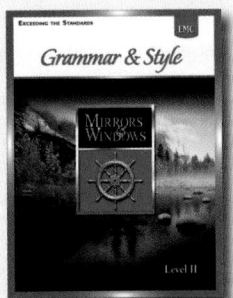

Grammar & Style
This resource contains:
- Four lessons on Phrases, pp. 132–143
- Three lessons on Clauses, pp. 144–154

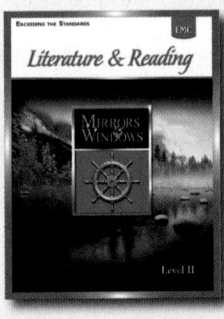

Literature & Reading
This resource contains:
- Analyze Poetry, pp. 14–16

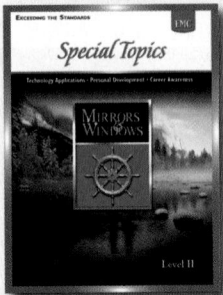

Special Topics
This resource contains:
- Lifelong Learning: Making Good Choices: Part 2, pp. 22–23
- Career Skills Development: Writing a Letter Requesting Job Information, pp. 24–25

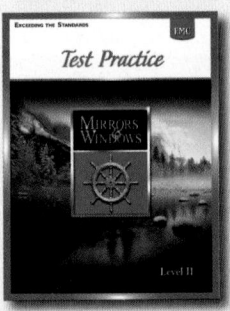

Test Practice
This resource contains:
- Personal Essay Practice Test: Revising and Editing, pp. 14–15

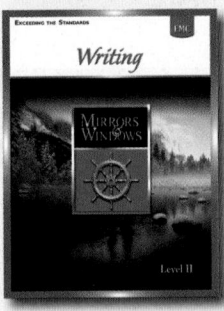

Writing
This resource contains:
- Descriptive Writing: Write a Descriptive Poem, pp. 39–46

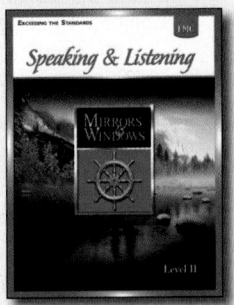

Speaking & Listening
This resource contains the following lesson to expand on the Speaking & Listening Workshop:
- Giving and Actively Listening to Narrative Presentations, pp. 17–18

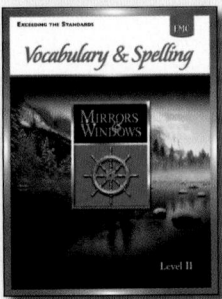

Vocabulary & Spelling
This resource contains:
- Two lessons on Homographs, Homophones, and Homonyms, pp. 58–63

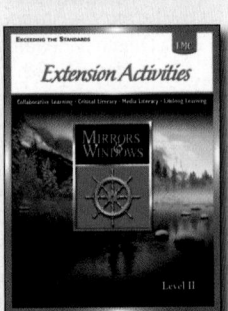

Extension Activities
This resource contains:
- Lifelong Learning: Write a Literary Critique, pp. 16–17
- Media Literacy: Draw the Images, p. 18

Unit 6 Visual Planning Guide

Reading Level: Moderate
Pacing: 2 days

Meeting the Standards,
Reading Model,
pp. 19–21

Developing Readers,
Visualize, pp. 43–45

540

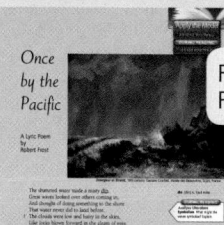

Reading Level: Moderate
Pacing: 1 day

Meeting the Standards,
Guided Reading,
pp. 22–25

545

Reading Level: Moderate;
Challenging   Pacing: 1 day

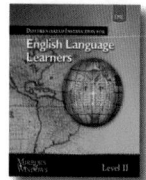

Meeting the Standards,
Compare Literature,
pp. 26–34

*English Language
Learners,* Mood,
pp. 139–145

548

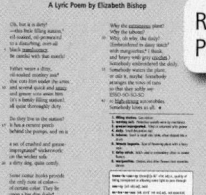
The Filling Station

Reading Level: Moderate
Pacing: 1 day

Meeting the Standards,
Directed Reading,
pp. 35–39

559

NAME GIVEAWAY

Reading Level: Easy
Pacing: 2 days

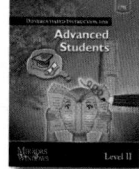

Meeting the Standards,
Directed Reading,
pp. 40–45

Advanced Students,
Historical Context
Project, pp. 39–40

563

Interactive Student
Text on CD-ROM

Selection
Lesson Plan

Web-based
Resources

Lesson-by-Lesson Resources

Reading Level: Easy
Pacing: 1 day

 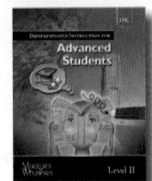

Meeting the Standards,
Directed Reading,
pp. 45–50

Advanced Students,
Cultural Connection
Activity, pp. 34–35

569

Reading Level: Easy
Pacing: 1 day

 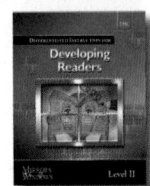

Meeting the Standards,
Directed Reading,
pp. 50–55

Developing Readers,
Take Notes, pp. 46–48

573

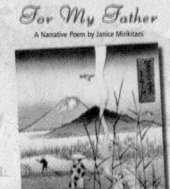

Reading Level: Moderate
Pacing: 1 day

 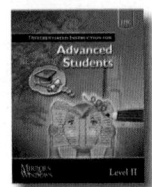

Meeting the Standards,
Directed Reading,
pp. 56–60

Advanced Students,
Character Analysis
Study, pp. 36–37

577

Reading Level: Easy
Pacing: 2 days

Meeting the Standards,
Directed Reading,
pp. 61–66

581

 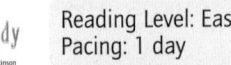

Reading Level: Easy
Pacing: 1 day

 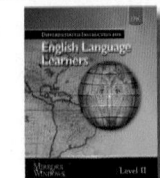

Meeting the Standards,
Independent Reading,
pp. 67–73

*English Language
Learners,* Compare and
Contrast, pp. 146–151

584

 Lesson Test   Audio Library

Reading Level: Easy
Pacing: 1 day

Meeting the Standards,
Independent Reading,
pp. 67–73

586

Reading Level: Moderate
Pacing: 1 day

Meeting the Standards,
Independent Reading,
pp. 74–80

Advanced Students,
Independent Reading
Project, p. 38

588

Unit 6 Scope & Sequence Guide

	Selection or Feature	Genre	Reading Support/ Reading Level	Word Count	Reading Skill	Graphic Organizer	
GUIDED READING	**Understanding Meaning in Poetry** p. 538						
	Theme in Yellow Carl Sandburg pp. 539–542	Lyric Poem	Guided Reading: Reading Model/ Moderate	70	Identify Multiple Levels of Meaning	Identify and Analyze Chart; Details Web	
	Once by the Pacific Robert Frost pp. 544–546	Lyric Poem	Guided Reading: Reading Model/ Moderate	121	Analyze Text Organization	Text Organization Chart; Symbolism Chart	

Reading Level: Easy
Pacing: 1 day

Meeting the Standards,
Independent Reading,
pp. 74–80

Literary Element	*Mirrors & Windows* Theme	Cross-Curricular Connection	Writing Options	Extension Activities
How Do Poems *Mean?* Speaker Symbolism				
Speaker	Autumn		Creative: Poem Expository: Literary Response	Collaborative Learning: Discuss Figurative Language Lifelong Learning: Research Pumpkins
Symbolism	Violence in Nature		Creative: Descriptive Paragraph Expository: Cause-and-Effect Essay	Collaborative Learning: Discuss Responses Lifelong Learning: Research the Sonnet

Unit 6 Scope & Sequence Guide

Selection or Feature	Genre	Reading Support/ Reading Level	Word Count	Reading Skill	Graphic Organizer	
Comparing Literature: Annabel Lee Edgar Allan Poe pp. 547–556	Narrative Poem	Directed Reading/ Moderate	315		Poetic/Story Elements Chart	
The Highwayman Alfred Noyes pp. 547–556	Narrative Poem	Directed Reading/ Challenging	1,025			
The Filling Station Elizabeth Bishop pp. 557–560	Lyric Poem	Directed Reading/ Moderate	180	Identify the Main Idea	Main Idea Map, Cluster Chart	
Name Giveaway Phil George pp. 562–566	Lyric Poem	Directed Reading/Easy	51	Analyze Text Organization	Text Organization Chart; T-Chart	
Primary Source Connection: from **An Indian Boy's Story** Ah-nen-la-de-ni pp. 564–565	Memoir	Moderate	863			
Ancestors Dudley Randall pp. 568–570	Lyric Poem	Directed Reading/Easy	100	Analyze Main Idea and Supporting Details	Main Idea Map; Author's Purpose Chart	
The Lost Parrot Naomi Shihab Nye pp. 572–575	Narrative Poem	Directed Reading/Easy	200	Compare and Contrast	Venn Diagram; Symbol Chart	
For My Father Janice Mirikitani pp. 576–579	Narrative Poem	Directed Reading/ Moderate	125	Analyze Text Structure	Text Structure Chart; Hyperbole Chart	
Money Order Janet S. Wong pp. 580–583	Narrative Poem	Directed Reading/Easy	44	Evaluate Cause and Effect	Cause and Effect Chart; Irony Chart	
Sisters Janet S. Wong pp. 580–583	Lyric Poem	Directed Reading/Easy	25			

"How dreary—to be—Somebody!
How public—like a Frog— "

—EMILY DICKINSON, "I'm Nobody"

What are authors trying to say with the images, symbols, and language they use? When you analyze a poem, you are searching beneath its surface to find meaning and discover themes. In Emily Dickinson's poem, "I'm Nobody," the author uses a variety of literary devices, including imagery, rhyme, and simile, to praise the privately lived life. As you read the poems in this unit, use your skills to find the meanings that lie just beneath the surface.

ELIZABETH BISHOP   EDGAR ALLAN POE   EMILY DICKINSON

537

Writing Options

Creative Writing

Biography	Narrative Poem
Descriptive Paragraph	Personal Letter
Diary Entry	Poem
Dream Poem	Short Story
Letter	Travel Brochure

Expository Writing

Analytical Essay	Expository Paragraph
Cause-and-Effect Essay	Literary Analysis
Compare-and-Contrast Essay	Literary Response
	Personal Essay

Persuasive Writing

Persuasive Paragraph

Language Arts Workshops

Grammar & Style

Simple, Compound, Complex, and Compound-Complex Sentences
Simple, Complete, and Compound Predicates

Vocabulary & Spelling

Figurative Language
Spelling by Syllables

Writing Workshop

Personal Narrative

Speaking & Listening Workshop

Narrative Presentation

Test Practice Workshop

Personal Essay
Reading Skills
Revising and Editing Skills

Program Resources

For a visual reminder of the unit-based resources available for Unit 6, Poetry, see pages 536A and 536B. As you introduce the unit, you may want to provide students with the Unit Study Guide, which is contained in the *Meeting the Standards* resource.

Understanding Meaning in Poetry

Reading strategies and skills that can help students understand meaning in poetry include asking questions, identifying multiple levels of meaning, and analyzing effects of form on meaning.

Use Reading Strategies

Ask Questions Encourage students to ask questions about every poem they read. To find meaning, the best questions may be *Why* questions. Why does the speaker repeat the sound of horses' hooves? Why do some lines contain just one word?

Use Reading Skills

Identify Multiple Levels of Meaning Have students tell you the difference between a denotation and a connotation. Students should recall that a connotation is an emotional association. Point out that for any word, the denotation and connotation represent at least two levels of meaning. Encourage students to re-read poems word by word to analyze denotations and potential connotations.

Use Reading Skills

Analyze Effects of Form on Meaning Note that poets make decisions about where to break lines, how to punctuate their thoughts, and how to group lines together. Poets also decide whether or not to title their poems. Urge students to consider how a poem is laid out as they interpret its meaning.

Literary Element

Understanding Meaning in Poetry

How Do Poems *Mean?*

Poems frequently challenge readers to imagine something in an unexpected way. Poets accomplish this with figurative language, sound devices, and imagery. Wendy Rose's poem "Loo-Wit" describes Mount Saint Helens, a mountain in southern Washington State that famously erupted in 1980, as if it were an old woman. Why do you think she makes this comparison? How does this comparison affect the way you think about the mountain?

Speaker

In short stories and novels, the voice that tells the story and describes the characters and setting is called the narrator. In poetry, the voice that narrates the poem is referred to as the **speaker.** The speaker sometimes participates in the action of the poem, using the first-person point of view. Other times, as in "Loo-Wit," the speaker narrates from the outside, using the third-person point of view.

The speaker's voice can be very much like the poet's voice, expressing beliefs or describing experiences similar to those of the poet. But you should never assume that a poem's speaker is the same as the poet. Often, the speaker is fictional. A speaker can be a person, an animal, an object, or an idea.

A poem's speaker sometimes explicitly states the theme, or central idea, of the poem. Generally, though, you must infer the theme by examining the tone, mood, description, and figurative language.

Symbolism

A **symbol** is a thing that stands for itself and something else. In "Loo-Wit," Mount Saint Helens is being used as a symbol. The mountain in the poem represents both the real mountain and the violence, beauty, and power of the natural world.

Some symbols are traditional, such as roses for love or doves for peace. Other symbols are unique to a piece of literature or author. In "Loo-Wit" the use of

She crouches
in the north,
her trembling
the source
of dawn.
Light appears
with the shudder
of her slopes,
the movement
of her arm.

—WENDY ROSE, "Loo-Wit"

Mount Saint Helens as a symbol is unique.

Symbols can be subjective, having more than one interpretation. It is not always clear how a writer intends a reader to interpret his or her use of a symbol. Always try to determine the theme, and consider how the poet's use of description, figures of speech, and symbols develops the theme.

538 UNIT 6 POETRY

To help students explore literature on a deeper level, assign the following activity: Analyze Poetry, *Exceeding the Standards: Literature & Reading*, pp. 14–16.

Common Core State Standards

Reading Literature
RL.5

Words in Use

Teaching Words
explicitly, 538
unique, 538
interpretation, 538

KEY TERMS

FIGURATIVE LANGUAGE, 538
SOUND DEVICE, 538
IMAGERY, 538
NARRATOR, 538
SPEAKER, 538
FIRST-PERSON POINT OF VIEW, 538
THIRD-PERSON POINT OF VIEW, 538
THEME, 538
TONE, 538
MOOD, 538
SYMBOL, 538
DESCRIPTION, 538

Theme in Yellow

A Lyric Poem by Carl Sandburg

At a Glance
Guided Reading: Reading Model
- Reading Level: Moderate
- Difficulty Consideration: Personification
- Ease Factors: Vocabulary and length

Build Background
Literary Context "Theme in Yellow" was published in 1916 in *Chicago Poems,* Sandburg's first major collection. Some considered his approach to poetry shocking; others found it refreshing. Most of Sandburg's poems are in the free verse form and use the everyday language of working people. His powerful voice celebrates the raw beauty of industrialism as well as America's landscape, music, and culture.

Reader's Context What is autumn like in your part of the country? What words would you use to describe it?

Set Purpose
Examine the poet's use of imagery. What mental picture does the poem create for you?

Analyze Literature
Speaker The **speaker** is the voice that speaks, or narrates, a poem. The speaker may or may not be the author. Poets often create characters in their poems. As you read "Theme in Yellow," try to determine who the speaker is. Is it a character in the poem, or is the speaker narrating from the outside?

Use Reading Skills
Identify Multiple Levels of Meaning In poetry, writers frequently use images, metaphors, similes, and sound devices to create multiple levels of meaning. By reading and rereading, you can better understand how these different levels affect each other and contribute to the poem's overall meaning. Use a chart like the one below to help you identify and analyze the effects of these different levels of meaning.

Images	golden cornfields at dusk
Figurative Language	
Characters, Setting	

Preview Vocabulary
taw·ny (tä´ nē) *adj.*, warm sandy color

dusk (dusk) *n.*, darker stage of twilight

Meet the Author
Carl Sandburg (1878–1967), the son of Swedish immigrants, grew up in Galesburg, Illinois. After the age of thirteen, he pursued his studies on and off while working at a variety of jobs, from bricklaying to house painting. After serving as a soldier during the Spanish-American War (1898), he briefly attended college, worked as a journalist, and became involved in politics. In addition to poetry, Sandburg is known for his biographies of Abraham Lincoln. He was awarded the Pulitzer Prize for *Abraham Lincoln: The War Years* (1939).

Objectives
Studying this lesson will enable students to
- use reading skills such as identifying multiple levels of meaning
- analyze a poem's speaker
- describe Carl Sandburg and explain his contributions to free verse
- analyze a poem about autumn told from a surprising point of view

Launch the Lesson
Ask students to brainstorm details about autumn that appeal to each of the five senses. Then have them read "Theme in Yellow" to find the details Sandburg uses to describe autumn in the poem.

 The Mirrors & Windows questions at the end of the poem focus on the theme of autumn. Before students begin reading, ask: What time of year do you think is yellowest?

Words in Use

Preview Vocabulary
tawny, 541
dusk, 541

Teaching Words
industrialism, 539
immigrants, 539
pursued, 539
bricklaying, 539

KEY TERMS
LYRIC POEM, 539
IMAGERY, 539
SPEAKER, 539
IMAGE, 539
METAPHOR, 539
SIMILE, 539
SOUND DEVICE, 539

Common Core State Standards
Reading Literature
RL.1

Teach the Model

Summary
"Theme in Yellow" is told from the joyful perspective of the pumpkins that decorate hills and cornfields. The pumpkins become jack-o'-lanterns with "terrible teeth" that don't truly frighten the children who circle around them.

Analyze Literature
Speaker Have students scan the poem. Ask them to identify the speaker's point of view (first person).

Use Reading Skills
Identify Multiple Levels of Meaning As students identify images, prompt them to analyze levels of meaning by asking themselves questions such as "How does this image make me feel?" and "What big idea might this stand for?"

More About the Author
Sandburg grew up in Illinois, where old-timers were proud of having known Abraham Lincoln. In the 1920s, he decided to write a biography of Lincoln for children, but his interest in the president was so deep that he ended up writing a two-volume biography for adults, *Abraham Lincoln: The Prairie Years* (1926). He published the Pulitzer Prize-winning *Abraham Lincoln: The War Years* in 1939.

Theme in Yellow

A Lyric Poem by Carl Sandburg

540

Program Resources

Planning and Assessment
Program Planning Guide, Selection Lesson Plan
E-Lesson Planner
Assessment Guide, Lesson Test
ExamView

Technology Tools
Interactive Student Text on CD
Visual Teaching Package
Audio Library
mirrorsandwindows.com

Meeting the Standards
Poetry: Unit 6, Reading Model, pp. 19–21

Differentiating Instruction
Developing Readers, Visualize, pp. 43–45

I spot the hills

With yellow balls in autumn.

I light the prairie cornfields

Orange and <u>tawny</u> gold clusters

5   And I am called pumpkins. **B**

On the last of October

When <u>dusk</u> is fallen

Children join hands

And circle round me

10 Singing ghost songs **C**

And love to the harvest moon;

I am a jack-o'-lantern

With terrible teeth

And the children know

15 I am fooling. ❖

DURING READING

Analyze Literature
Speaker Is this poem's speaker the author? Confirm or modify your answer as you read. **A**

taw • ny (tä′ nē) *adj.,* warm sandy color

dusk (dʉsk) *n.,* darker stage of twilight

DURING READING

Use Reading Skills
Identify Multiple Levels of Meaning What do the final four lines suggest about the speaker? **D**

Analyze Literature

Speaker *Answer:* No; in line 5, the speaker says "I am called pumpkins." **A**

Analyze Literature

Personification Ask students why Sandburg chose to use such an unusual speaker. Model a response: "By personifying a pumpkin, Sandburg forces me to view the changing season from a new perspective." **B**

Make Connections

Ask students how this image of the children affects their feelings about the speaker. What mood does it suggest? (The dancing children make the pumpkins seem meaningful or powerful. The mood seems festive.) **C**

Use Reading Skills

Identify Multiple Levels of Meaning *Answer:* Answers will vary. Students may say the lines show that the speaker likes the children and has a sense of humor. **D**

MIRRORS & WINDOWS

What do you like most about autumn? What do you like least about it? In what ways is autumn different from all the other seasons?

MIRRORS & WINDOWS

You may want to ask students to write a journal entry or quick write, or divide students into discussion groups or lead a whole-class discussion about this question. *Answer:* Personal responses will vary. Students may distinguish autumn by changing temperatures, leaves changing color, and various holidays.

THEME IN YELLOW **541**

Reading Skills

Identify Multiple Levels of Meaning

Tell students that the overall impression they gain from their first reading of a poem is its literal, or most obvious, meaning. Point out that rereading the poem several times will help them uncover additional levels of meaning.

Begin a cluster chart on the board, with "Theme in Yellow" in the center circle. For the first level of circles branching out from the center, have students suggest literal images from the poem, such as "prairie cornfields." For an outer ring of circles, have students suggest what each literal image might symbolize, such as "abundance." Note that an image can have different meanings for different readers, just as words have different connotations in different contexts. Finally, review and discuss the various levels of literal, symbolic, and cultural meanings that students have suggested.

Find Meaning

1. (a) The poem's speaker is a pumpkin. (b) By the end, the speaker is a jack-o'-lantern.

2. (a) The speaker mentions yellow, orange, and tawny gold. (b) They are associated with harvest and autumn.

Make Judgments

3. (a) They know that the speaker is not really scary or mean, but is only fooling. (b) The children are dancing and singing songs around the speaker without fear.

4. Students may say they were surprised the speaker was a pumpkin. Be sure they explain their answers.

Analyze Literature

Speaker Students may describe the speaker as proud, happy, silly, or mischievous. Details might include the poem's tone, the singing and dancing, or the speaker's claim to be "only fooling."

Find Meaning

1. (a) Who or what is this poem's speaker? (b) How does the speaker change by the end of the poem?

2. (a) What colors does the speaker mention in the poem? (b) Why might these colors be the most appropriate for this poem?

Analyze Literature

Speaker In poetry a speaker can be a person, place, or thing and may or may not express the thoughts of the poet. Use a web to determine the attitudes of the speaker. In the center oval, name the speaker. In each outer oval, write a detail that suggests a characteristic of the speaker. Then write a sentence describing the speaker's personality.

Make Judgments

3. (a) What does the speaker claim the children know? (b) In what ways do their actions support this claim?

4. How was the content of this poem surprising? Explain your answer.

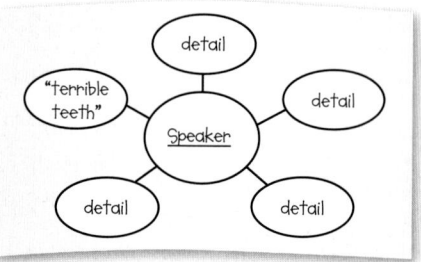

Extend Understanding

Writing Options

Creative Writing Write a **poem** about a favorite place from the perspective of an inanimate object that is a part of that place. Use sensory details and figurative language to help you describe the images and feelings you want your reader to understand.

Expository Writing Think about your reaction to "Theme in Yellow." How does it make you feel? Mood is the feeling or emotion that a writer creates in a work. List some words or phrases that describe the mood of the poem. Consider the speaker's choice of words and images, as well as the speaker's appearance. In a one-page **literary response,** analyze how the speaker affects the mood of "Theme in Yellow."

Collaborative Learning

Discuss Figurative Language Personification is a figure of speech in which an idea, animal, or thing is described as if it were a person. Form a small group, and brainstorm a list of other examples of personification you have encountered. What generalizations can you make about the items on your list?

Lifelong Learning

Research Pumpkins Is a pumpkin a fruit or a vegetable? How long have people been cultivating pumpkins? What are some of the most popular uses of pumpkins? How big do pumpkins grow? Use the Internet or the library to answer these and other questions about pumpkins. Organize your information into an illustrated pamphlet.

Go to **www.mirrorsandwindows.com** for more.

Rubrics for Writing Options

You can adapt this as a checklist for students to use as they write.

Creative Writing

☐ Does the poem describe a place?
☐ Is the speaker an inanimate object?
☐ Does the poem include sensory details and figurative language?

Expository Writing

☐ Does the response describe the mood of the poem?
☐ Does the response include examples that connect the speaker with the poem's mood?

Grammar & Style

Simple, Compound, Complex, and Compound-Complex Sentences

Simple Sentences

I spot the hills
With yellow balls in autumn.

—CARL SANDBURG, "Theme in Yellow"

Sentences are classified according to the types and number of clauses they contain. A **simple sentence** contains one independent clause and no subordinate clauses. Remember that a clause must have both a subject and verb. A simple sentence may have any number of phrases, a compound subject, or a compound verb. The quotation above is a simple sentence.

> EXAMPLE
> *The pumpkins grew all over the hills.*

In this simple sentence, the subject is *pumpkins* and the verb is *grew*.

Compound Sentences

I am a jack-o'-lantern
With terrible teeth
And the children know
I am fooling.

—CARL SANDBURG, "Theme in Yellow"

A **compound sentence** consists of two or more independent clauses joined with a comma and a coordinating conjunction, such as *and, but, or, nor, for, yet,* or *so*. In the above quotation, the independent clause *I am a jack-o'-lantern with terrible teeth* is joined to a second independent clause, *the children know I am fooling*, with the coordinating conjunction *and*. The quotation would be a good example of a compound sentence if the poet had used a comma before *and*.

> EXAMPLE
> *Not everyone loves jack-o'-lanterns, but carving them is fun.*

In this example, two independent clauses are joined by a comma and the coordinating conjunction *but*.

Complex Sentences

Combining an independent clause with at least one dependent clause makes a **complex sentence.**

> EXAMPLE
> *As the wind began to blow, the sky grew dark.*

Compound-Complex Sentences

A **compound-complex sentence** consists of a compound sentence with one or more dependent clauses.

> EXAMPLE
> *As the wind began to blow, the sky grew dark, and we ran for the shelter of the house.*

The sky grew dark, and we ran for the shelter of the house is a compound sentence. *As the wind began to blow* is a dependent clause.

Using Different Types of Sentences

Expand each of the following simple sentences into a compound, complex, or compound-complex sentence by adding one or more independent or dependent clauses. Then list the sentence type.

1. Jack-o'-lanterns are made from pumpkins.
2. The children joined hands to form a circle.
3. Jack-o'-lanterns aren't really scary.
4. Molly carved a funny face on her pumpkin.
5. The pumpkins looked like someone painted the hills with orange polka dots.

Using Different Types of Sentences

Answers may vary. Those below are examples. Make sure students correctly identify the types of sentences they create.

1. Jack-o'-lanterns are made from pumpkins, so they look like orange heads, but they have no bodies. (compound)
2. The children joined hands to form a circle, and then they danced around the pumpkins until they got dizzy and fell down. (compound-complex)
3. People try to carve ugly faces on pumpkins, but jack-o'-lanterns aren't really scary. (compound)
4. Molly carved a funny face on her pumpkin, but she really liked her brother's carving better because it looked like a monster. (compound-complex)
5. When the fall arrived, the pumpkins looked like someone painted the hills with orange polka dots, or like someone spilled a truckload of basketballs. (complex)

> ➤ For more information, see Grammar & Style Section 3.1, The Sentence, in the Language Arts Handbook.

Program Resources

You will find additional lessons on Simple, Complex, and Compound-Complex Sentences in the *Exceeding the Standards: Grammar & Style* resource.

KEY TERMS

SIMPLE SENTENCE, 543
INDEPENDENT CLAUSE, 543
SUBORDINATE CLAUSE, 543
SUBJECT, 543
VERB, 543
COMPOUND SENTENCE, 543
COMMA, 543
COORDINATING CONJUNCTION, 543
COMPLEX SENTENCE, 543
COMPOUND-COMPLEX SENTENCE, 543

Differentiated Instruction

English Language Learning

Evaluate the ability of your students to use a variety of connecting words and sentence lengths when they write and speak. To do so, ask them to apply the skills from this workshop to a short essay and presentation for the class that utilizes a variety of sentence lengths. The presentation can be on a topic of their choosing, but direct them to incorporate the lessons from the workshop. Correct any errors after the presentation.

Common Core State Standards

Language
L.1, L.6.3a

At a Glance
Guided Reading: Reading Model
- Reading Level: Moderate
- Difficulty Considerations: Style and personification
- Ease Factors: Imagery and length

Objectives
Studying this lesson will enable students to
- use reading skills such as analyzing text organization
- explore symbolism
- discuss Robert Frost and his use of traditional poetic form
- analyze a poem about nature's fury

Launch the Lesson
Before reading "Once by the Pacific," tell students that the speaker is in a dramatic storm. Ask students to think about how weather affects their emotions. For instance, how do they feel after a long stretch of rainy days?

The Mirrors & Windows questions after the poem focus on the theme of violence in nature. Before students begin reading, ask: When is the ocean most frightening?

Apply the Model
BEFORE READING
DURING READING
AFTER READING

Once by the Pacific
A Lyric Poem by Robert Frost

Build Background
Literary Context At a time when poets were moving toward free verse and themes of social upheaval, industrial life, and scientific discovery, Frost wrote using traditional poetic forms. He addressed themes of personal relationships, rural life, and nature. Even so, Frost's perspective was that of a modern man. He used simple language in well-crafted lines to express his frequently dark, ironic perspective on nature and society.

Reader's Context When have you ever experienced, firsthand, the fury of nature? In what ways can nature be both creative and destructive?

Set Purpose
Before you begin to read "Once by the Pacific," answer these questions: How many lines are in the poem? How many stanzas? What is the rhyme scheme?

Analyze Literature
Symbolism A **symbol** is a thing that represents itself and something else. As you read "Once by the Pacific," think about the various things being described. What might those things, including the setting, the characters, and their actions, represent?

Meet the Author
Robert Frost (1874–1963) was born in San Francisco but moved to New England at the age of eleven. He began writing poetry in high school. Frost supported himself and his family through a variety of occupations before achieving success with the publication in 1915 of two poetry collections. While Frost is widely known for poems that celebrate nature's beauty and peacefulness, much of his work, like "Once by the Pacific," is characterized by solemn reflections on life and death.

Use Reading Skills
Analyze Text Organization A *sonnet* is one of the most common poetic forms. A traditional Shakespearean, or English, sonnet is made up of one stanza with fourteen lines organized in three quatrains, or four-line sections, plus a final couplet, or two-line section. The rhyme scheme is *abab cdcd efef gg*. As you read "Once by the Pacific," use a two-column chart to determine how the poem's organization compares with that of a traditional sonnet.

Traditional Sonnet	"Once by the Pacific"
Number of lines:	Number of lines:
Rhyme scheme:	Rhyme scheme:
Stanza structure:	Stanza structure:

Preview Vocabulary
din (din) *n.,* loud noise

in·tent (in tent´) *n.,* purpose

Words in Use

Selection Words
din, 545
intent, 545

Teaching Words
upheaval, 544
fury, 544
solemn, 544
Shakespearean, 544
Petrarchan, 546

KEY TERMS
LYRIC POEM, 544
FREE VERSE, 544
THEME, 544
IRONIC, 544
STANZA, 544
RHYME SCHEME, 544
SYMBOLISM, 544
SYMBOL, 544

SONNET, 544
PERSONIFICATION, 546
COUPLET, 546
TONE, 546
MOOD, 546
MAIN IDEA, 546
RHYTHM, 546
IMAGE, 546

Common Core State Standards
Reading Literature
RL.1

Apply the Model
BEFORE READING
DURING READING
AFTER READING

Once by the Pacific

A Lyric Poem
by
Robert Frost

Downpour at Etretat, 19th century. Gustave Courbet. Musée des Beaux-Arts, Dijon, France.

The shattered water made a misty <u>din</u>.
Great waves looked over others coming in,
And thought of doing something to the shore
That water never did to land before.
5   The clouds were low and hairy in the skies,
Like locks blown forward in the gleam of eyes.
You could not tell, and yet it looked as if
The shore was lucky in being backed by cliff,
The cliff in being backed by continent;
10 It looked as if a night of dark <u>intent</u>
Was coming, and not only a night, an age.
Someone had better be prepared for rage.
There would be more than ocean-water broken
Before God's last *Put out the Light* was spoken. ✦

din (din) *n.,* loud noise

> **DURING READING**
> **Analyze Literature**
> **Symbolism** What might the waves symbolize? Explain **A**

in·tent (in tent´) *n.,* purpose

> **DURING READING**
> **Use Reading Skills**
> **Text Organization** What is this poem's rhyme scheme? **B**

Would you want to witness the scene being described by the poem's speaker? Why might this scene seem frightening to some people?

545

Teach the Model

Summary
The poem describes waves crashing onto a shore. The crashing could symbolize a great conflict that is unlikely to cease. While the waves keep coming, the shore is supported by cliffs, and the cliffs are supported by a continent.

Analyze Literature
Symbolism *Answer:* They could symbolize anger or confusion. **A**

Use Reading Skills
Analyze Text Organization Have students read "Use Reading Skills" on page 544. Point out that although "Once by the Pacific" could be a sonnet because it has fourteen lines, Frost does not follow the traditional form of the Shakespearean sonnet. Ask students what this break with tradition might signal about the poem's meaning.

Use Reading Skills
Text Organization *Answer:* It is *a a b b c c d d e e f f g g.* **B**

Answer: Some may want to witness the scene because it is dramatic and exciting. Others might say the situation seems dangerous.

Program Resources

Planning and Assessment
Program Planning Guide, Selection Lesson Plan
E-Lesson Planner
Assessment Guide, Lesson Test
ExamView

Meeting the Standards
Poetry: Unit 6, Guided Reading, pp. 22–25

Technology Tools
Interactive Student Text on CD
Visual Teaching Package
Audio Library
mirrorsandwindows.com

Review the Model

Find Meaning

1. (a) They are coming in toward the shore, thinking of "doing something" to it. (b) The mood is ominous and mysterious.

2. (a) The speaker says a night, and an age, of dark intent are coming. (b) Evidence includes low, hairy clouds and the sense that it was luck the shore had cliffs standing behind it.

Make Judgments

3. (a) The personification suggests a face in the sky. (b) The face seems malevolent. Gleaming eyes suggest intensity.

4. (a) The lines refer to ocean water as broken; in line 1 the water is shattered. (b) The phrase suggests violent destruction, possibly the end of the world.

Analyze Literature

Symbolism Students might mention the water, which could symbolize violence or impending destruction. They might also mention the shore or continent, which may represent humanity or stability.

Apply the Model

BEFORE READING
DURING READING
AFTER READING

Find Meaning

1. (a) According to the speaker, what are the waves doing? (b) What mood does the speaker's description of the waves create?

2. (a) What does the speaker say is coming? (b) What evidence does the speaker offer in support of this prediction?

Analyze Literature

Symbolism How does Frost use symbolism to convey meaning in this poem? Analyze symbols in the poem by listing the symbols in the left column. Then in the right column, write the meaning of the symbols or the ideas that they suggest to you.

Make Judgments

3. (a) What image is suggested by the personification in lines 5 and 6? (b) What traits does this image seem to convey? Explain.

4. (a) How does the last couplet refer back to the beginning of the poem? (b) What do the words *"Put out the Light"* suggest?

Symbol	Meaning
water	

Extend Understanding

Writing Options

Creative Writing Refer to the chart you created to analyze the symbolism in "Once by the Pacific." Think about each symbol you identified. What other symbols might represent the same thing? Record details about each new symbol that you imagine. Then choose one of your symbols and use it in a **descriptive paragraph.**

Expository Writing Reread Frost's poem. Try to determine, based on the setting, tone, mood, and other details, what caused the speaker to adopt the perspective in the poem. Write a brief **cause-and-effect essay** in which you state the speaker's outlook and determine the causes for that outlook. Use both direct quotations and paraphrases in support of your claims. At the end of your essay, restate your main idea.

Collaborative Learning

Discuss Responses How does this poem make you feel? Discuss your responses with a partner. Begin by brainstorming a list of adjectives that describe your feelings. What words, rhymes, rhythms, or images specifically influenced your reactions? What mental pictures did you imagine as you read the poem? Summarize the mood and its causes in one or two sentences.

Lifelong Learning

Research the Sonnet The two main types of sonnet are the Shakespearean, or English, sonnet and the Petrarchan, or Italian, sonnet. Research these different forms and collect examples of each type. What are the most common subjects of the sonnets you have collected? Present examples in support of your claims.

Go to **www.mirrorsandwindows.com** for more.

Rubrics for Writing Options

You can adapt this as a checklist for students to use as they write.

Creative Writing

☐ Does the descriptive paragraph include a symbol?

☐ Might the symbol represent the same concept or idea as one of the symbols in Frost's poem?

Expository Writing

☐ Does the essay present causes that might explain the speaker's outlook?

☐ Does the essay include paraphrases and direct quotations?

☐ Does the conclusion restate the main idea?

Annabel Lee
A Narrative Poem by Edgar Allan Poe

The Highwayman
A Narrative Poem by Alfred Noyes

Preview the Selections

At a Glance
Directed Reading
"Annabel Lee"
- Reading Level: Moderate
- Difficulty Considerations: Older English and vocabulary
- Ease Factors: Compelling story, fairy tale style

"The Highwayman"
- Reading Level: Challenging
- Difficulty Considerations: Many footnotes, adult concepts
- Ease Factors: Rhymes, suspenseful

BEFORE READING

Build Background
Literary Context Poetry that tells a story has ancient roots in the oral tradition. From Greek epics to English ballads, these works were often recited from memory and passed from one generation to another. Some tell exciting tales, such as *The Odyssey*, which relates the adventures of a Greek hero. Other narrative poems relate religious lessons, stories of idealized love, historical events, or personal experiences.

Reader's Context How would you react to a sudden dramatic change in your life?

Set Purpose
Preview these poems' rhyme schemes, rhythms, and text structures. Predict the effects of these elements on each poem.

Meet the Authors

Edgar Allan Poe (1809–1849) achieved fame as a writer of short stories, poetry, and literary criticism. His haunting poems dwell on melancholy themes and death. "Annabel Lee" was published in 1849, two years after the death of Poe's wife, Virginia.

Alfred Noyes (1880–1958) was born in Wolverhampton, England, and published his first collection of poems at the age of twenty-one. By the age of twenty-eight, he had published five more volumes of poetry. From 1914 to 1923, he taught in the United States.

Compare Literature: Narrative Poetry
A **narrative poem** is a poem that tells a story. Like a short story or a novel, it has characters, setting, plot, and point of view. Use a two-column chart to record the story elements and the poetic elements in "Annabel Lee" and "The Highwayman."

"Annabel Lee"

Poetic Elements	Story Elements
Rhyme Scheme	

Preview Vocabulary
bear (ber) *v.*, carry; **bore** *past tense*

peak·ed (pē´ kid) *adj.*, thin and drawn, as from sickness

writhe (rīth) *v.*, twist and turn

re·frain (ri frān´) *n.*, phrase or verse in a song or poem that is repeated throughout

bran·dish (bran´ dish) *v.*, wave threateningly

Objectives
Studying this lesson will enable students to
- analyze narrative poetry and compare two examples
- describe the literary accomplishments of Edgar Allan Poe and Alfred Noyes
- appreciate two poems about love that transcends death

Launch the Lesson
Tell students that the poems they are about to read tell stories of undying love. Ask them to recall famous love stories they know from literature, such as Romeo and Juliet. Ask what elements such stories share.

The Mirrors & Windows questions after the poem focus on the theme of grief. Before students begin reading, ask: Can death truly separate people who love each other?

Words in Use

"Annabel Lee"

Preview Vocabulary
bear, 549

Selection Words
highborn, 549
kinsmen, 549
chilling, 549
beams, 550

Teaching Words
recited, 547
idealized, 547
melancholy, 547
gothic, 550
ornate, 550
atypical, 550

KEY TERMS

Common Core State Standards
Reading Literature
RL.1

Teach the Selection

Summary

"Annabel Lee" describes the love one has for a young woman. The speaker believes that no other love could compare and believes that the angels in heaven are jealous. A wind chill kills the young Annabel Lee and she is placed in a tomb. The speaker, unable to sever their love, returns each night to lie down by her in the tomb.

Analyze Literature

Narrative Poetry Remind students that narrative poetry contains the plot elements of a conflict or problem, rising action, climax, and resolution.

Art Connection

The painting on this page is of a woman who drowned herself. The artist, G. F. Watts, was known for commenting on social issues through his paintings. According to most interpretations of this painting, the woman killed herself because of a doomed love. Watts believed it was unfair for women in this situation to feel that suicide was their only choice.

Ask students to imagine that this painting is very large, taking up almost one wall of your classroom. (Its actual size is close to four feet tall by seven feet wide.) Have them think silently for a minute about the mood of the painting. Point out that in the textbook, this painting goes with the poem they are about to read. Based on this and the above information about the painter, have students tell you what they expect the poem to be about.

Found Drowned, 1848–1850. George Frederick Watts. Watts Gallery, Compton, Surrey, Great Britain.

Annabel Lee

A Narrative Poem by Edgar Allan Poe

548

Program Resources

Planning and Assessment
Program Planning Guide, Selection Lesson Plan
E-Lesson Planner
Assessment Guide, Lesson Test
ExamView

Technology Tools
Interactive Student Text on CD
Visual Teaching Package
Audio Library
mirrorsandwindows.com

Meeting the Standards
Poetry: Unit 6, Compare Literature, pp. 26–34

Differentiating Instruction
English Language Learners, Mood,
   pp. 139–145

It was many and many a year ago,
   In a kingdom by the sea.
That a maiden there lived whom you may know
   By the name of Annabel Lee;
5 And this maiden she lived with no other thought
   Than to love and be loved by me.

I was a child and *she* was a child,
   In this kingdom by the sea;
But we loved with a love that was more than love—
10   I and my Annabel Lee—
With a love that the wingèd seraphs of heaven
   Coveted her and me.[1]   **A**

And this was the reason that, long ago,
   In this kingdom by the sea,
15 A wind blew out of a cloud, chilling
   My beautiful Annabel Lee;
So that her highborn kinsmen came
   And <u>bore</u> her away from me,
To shut her up in a sepulcher[2]
20   In this kingdom by the sea.

The angels, not half so happy in heaven,
   Went envying her and me—
Yes!—that was the reason (as all men know,
   In this kingdom by the sea)
25 That the wind came out of a cloud, by night,
   Chilling and killing my Annabel Lee.

But our love it was stronger by far than the love
   Of those who were older than we—
   Of many far wiser than we—
30 And neither the angels in heaven above
   Nor the demons down under the sea,
Can ever dissever[3] my soul from the soul
   Of the beautiful Annabel Lee:

---

1. **the wingèd seraphs...Coveted her and me.** The angels envied us.
2. **sepulcher.** Tomb or grave
3. **dissever.** Break; sever

---

bear (ber) *v.*, carry; **bore** *past tense*

35 For the moon never beams, without bringing me dreams
      Of the beautiful Annabel Lee;
    And the stars never rise, but I feel the bright eyes
      Of the beautiful Annabel Lee;
    And so, all the night-tide, I lie down by the side
    Of my darling—my darling—my life and my bride,
40   In her sepulcher there by the sea—
        In her tomb by the sounding sea. ❖

CULTURAL ▶▶ CONNECTION

Gothic Literature Edgar Allan Poe wrote during the Victorian Era (1837–1901) and was influenced by the revival of interest in Gothic art, architecture, and literature. The term *Gothic* originally described the heavy, ornate style of art and architecture popular in western Europe during the twelfth through the fifteenth century. *Gothic* later came to be applied to the genre of literature popularized by writers such as Horace Walpole (*The Castle of Otranto*, 1765) and Ann Radcliffe (*The Mysteries of Udolpho*, 1794). The typical Gothic novel is a dark tale of mystery and suspense that features lonely and foreboding settings, evil or mad characters, supernatural elements, and heightened emotion. In what ways does Poe's poem meet these criteria? **A**

Gothic Cathedral Seen through Ruins of a Castle, c. 1852. Carl Gustav Carus. Folkwang Museum, Essen, Germany.

What do you think about the way the speaker in the poem is coping with the death of his loved one? How is his reaction typical or atypical?

Find Meaning

1. (a) At what time in their lives were Annabel Lee and the speaker in love? (b) How much time has passed since then? Explain.
2. (a) What does the speaker say happened to Annabel Lee? (b) Whom does he blame? (c) What do you think really happened to her?

Make Judgments

3. In the fourth stanza, the speaker says, "Yes!—that was the reason...." What impression is created by the poet's use of the exclamation mark? Explain.
4. (a) What does the speaker do at the end of the poem? (b) What do you think he expects to happen?

550 UNIT 6 POETRY

Teach the Selection

Cultural Connection

Gothic Literature *Answer:* Students might cite the lonely and foreboding setting, and may also say the poem's brooding speaker seems unbalanced. **A**

Answer: Students may say the speaker's reaction is excessive, given that Annabel Lee died many years ago. Some might say he should try to work through his grief and move on with his life. Others may say he is dramatic and obsessive, or that he is simply very romantic. Opinions about how typical this reaction is will vary.

Find Meaning

1. (a) It was when they were very young. (b) A lot of time has passed, "many and many a year ago."
2. (a) The speaker says she died from a chill wind. (b) He blames angels who were jealous of their love. (c) It's likely that she died from a disease.

Make Judgments

3. The exclamation mark may create the impression that the speaker is unstable or is being melodramatic and is deluding himself about what happened and why.
4. (a) The speaker lies down in the tomb beside Annabel Lee. (b) He expects to die by her side.

Differentiated Instruction

English Language Learning

To provide additional help with language and sentence structure, read the poem aloud or play the recording from the Audio Library, stopping at the end of each stanza to paraphrase details. Help students fill in missing words. Encourage students to restate the information in their own words. This will help them remember what they have read and will also give them additional language practice.

550 UNIT 6 POETRY

The Highwaymen, c. 20th century. George Derville Rowlandson. Private collection.

The Highwayman[1]

A Narrative Poem by Alfred Noyes

---

1. **Highwayman.** Robber who preys on travelers on the highways

551

Teach the Selection

Summary

The highwayman loves Bess, the landlord's daughter. His promise to return the following night is overheard and troops arrive to hold Bess captive in order to trap the highwayman. Tied with a gun to her chest, Bess alerts the highwayman by shooting herself as he approaches. He is killed the following day.

MIRRORS & WINDOWS The Mirrors & Windows questions after the poem focus on the theme of realistic behavior. Before students begin reading, ask: Who is the most romantic literary character you know of? What characterizes a romantic person?

History Connection

Outlaws Through the ages, outlaws became idealized in popular culture. Robin Hood, known as a common robber in the fifteenth century, was transformed in ballads of the next century into a nobleman who stole from the rich to give to the poor. By the eighteenth century, highwaymen such as Dick Turpin held a kind of folk-hero status. Some were even praised for their polite behavior.

Alfred Noyes, always an avid reader, probably encountered these legends about outlaws growing up in Wales. He wrote "The Highwayman" in 1904, when he was just 24 years old.

Words in Use

"Highwayman"

Preview Vocabulary
peaked, 552
writhe, 554
refrain, 554
brandish, 555

Selection Words
torrent, 552
tawny, 553
spurred, 555

Common Core State Standards

Reading Literature
RL.1

Literary Connection
Ballad Tell students that a ballad is a narrative poem about love, death, or something supernatural. Ballads are often meant to be sung. One characteristic of ballads is called "incremental repetition," meaning that one or more lines repeat with small but significant changes. The changes move the plot along.

Use Reading Skills
Identify Structure Have students read aloud lines 4, 5, and 6, noting the cadence. Tell them to look and listen for repetition of these lines, with slight changes, as they continue to read the poem. Explain that such repetition is typical of the ballad style. **B**

Analyze Literature
Characterization Ask students to contrast the description of Tim the ostler with the earlier description of the highwayman. (The highwayman is well-dressed and dashing, while Tim is unkempt and has an air of madness.) **C**

PART ONE

A
> The wind was a torrent of darkness among the gusty trees.
> The moon was a ghostly galleon[2] tossed upon cloudy seas.
> The road was a ribbon of moonlight over the purple moor,[3]

B 5
> And the highwayman came riding—
>   Riding—riding—
> The highwayman came riding, up to the old inn door.

> He'd a French cocked hat on his forehead, a bunch of lace at his chin,
> A coat of the claret[4] velvet, and breeches of brown doeskin.
> They fitted with never a wrinkle. His boots were up to the thigh.
10
> And he rode with a jewelled twinkle,
>   His pistol butts a-twinkle,
> His rapier hilt[5] a-twinkle, under the jewelled sky.

> Over the cobbles he clattered and clashed in the dark inn yard,
> And he tapped with his whip on the shutters, but all was locked and barred;
15
> He whistled a tune to the window, and who should be waiting there
> But the landlord's black-eyed daughter,
>   Bess, the landlord's daughter,
> Plaiting a dark red love-knot[6] into her long black hair.

> And dark in the dark old inn yard a stable wicket[7] creaked
20
> Where Tim the ostler[8] listened. His face was white and <u>peaked</u>.
 C
> His eyes were hollows of madness, his hair like mouldy hay,
> But he loved the landlord's daughter,
>   The landlord's red-lipped daughter,
> Dumb[9] as a dog he listened, and he heard the robber say—

25
> "One kiss, my bonny[10] sweetheart, I'm after a prize tonight,
> But I shall be back with the yellow gold before the morning light;
> Yet, if they press me sharply, and harry[11] me through the day,
> Then look for me by moonlight,
>   Watch for me by moonlight,
30
> I'll come to thee by moonlight, though hell should bar the way."

---

2. **galleon.** Large sailing ship
3. **moor.** Flat, open land
4. **claret.** Purplish-red color
5. **rapier hilt.** Sword handle
6. **Plaiting a dark red love-knot.** Braiding a dark red ribbon
7. **wicket.** Small door or gate
8. **ostler.** Person who takes care of horses at an inn
9. **dumb.** Silent
10. **bonny.** Pretty; fine
11. **harry.** Torment; harass

peak·ed (pē´ kid) *adj.*, thin and drawn, as from sickness

Differentiated Instruction

Reading Proficiency
Have struggling readers skim through the poem to preview the footnotes. Say that becoming familiar with these definitions before reading will make for a smoother reading experience.

Auditory Learning
To help students appreciate the poem's strong rhythm, give them several opportunities to listen to fluent, dramatic readings of it. You also may wish to play a song based on this poem, or a similar ballad, to help students recognize musical elements of the language. Several folk artists have recorded abridged or adapted versions of Noyes's poem.

English Language Learning
Help students follow the plot of "The Highwayman." Use a plot diagram or time line if necessary.

He rose upright in the stirrups. He scarce could reach her hand,
But she loosened her hair in the casement.[12] His face burnt like a brand[13]
As the black cascade of perfume came tumbling over his breast;
And he kissed its waves in the moonlight,
35   (O, sweet black waves in the moonlight!)
Then he tugged at his rein in the moonlight, and galloped away to the west.

PART TWO

He did not come in the dawning. He did not come at noon;
And out of the tawny sunset, before the rise of the moon,
When the road was a gypsy's ribbon, looping the purple moor,
40 A red coat troop[14] came marching—
      Marching—marching—
King George's men came marching, up to the old inn door.

They said no word to the landlord. They drank his ale instead,
But they gagged his daughter, and bound her, to the foot of her narrow bed.
45 Two of them knelt at her casement, with muskets[15] at their side!
There was death at every window;
      And hell at one dark window;
For Bess could see, through her casement, the road that *he* would ride.

---

12. casement. Window frame
13. brand. Burning torch
14. red coat troop. Group of soldiers wearing red coats
15. muskets. Long-barreled firearms

ANNABEL LEE / THE HIGHWAYMAN **553**

Teach the Selection

Use Reading Skills
Identify Cause and Effect Have students explain why the highwayman has not arrived by morning. (Tim may have reported his activities to the authorities; he said he might be delayed if the authorities were following him.) **D**

Analyze Literature
Suspense Discuss with students the elements that build suspense in this stanza (the silent soldiers with their muskets; the image of Beth tied and gagged, staring through the window at the road; the descriptions of "death at every window" and "hell at one dark window"). **E**

Speaking & Listening Skills

Choral Reading
Have the class rehearse and perform a choral reading of "The Highwayman."
- Organize several groups and assign stanzas to different groups.
- To increase the dramatic effect, you may wish to have the entire class join in on stanzas 1, 3, and the last two stanzas.

- Give students ample practice time and tell them to pay special attention to their pacing.
- Encourage students to experiment with the pitch and volume of their voices.

During rehearsal, have students give each other feedback on the effectiveness of the techniques they are using. Students may enjoy performing their choral reading for another class.

ANNABEL LEE / THE HIGHWAYMAN **553**

Analyze Literature
Narrative Poetry Remind students that, like a story, a narrative poem has exposition, rising action, a climax, falling action, and a resolution. Ask students what plot element is played out in this passage (rising action). **Ⓐ**

Analyze Literature
Characterization Have students review lines 55–63 to analyze what they reveal about Bess. Ask them to describe her demeanor and state of mind. (Students may say that she was anxious but became calm and cool, and her actions show that she has a plan.) **Ⓑ**

Analyze Literature
Suspense Ask students what devices Noyes uses to heighten the suspense here (repetition of the sound of the horse's hooves and of the word *riding*, and the image of the approaching highwayman, unaware of the trap). **Ⓒ**

50	They had tied her up to attention,[16] with many a sniggering jest;[17]
	They had bound a musket beside her, with the muzzle beneath her breast!
	"Now, keep good watch!" and they kissed her. She heard the doomed man say—
	Look for me by moonlight;
	Watch for me by moonlight;
	I'll come to thee by moonlight, though hell should bar the way!

Ⓐ

55	She twisted her hands behind her, but all the knots held good!
	She <u>writhed</u> her hands till her fingers were wet with sweat or blood!
	They stretched and strained in the darkness, and the hours crawled by like years,
	Till, now, on the stroke of midnight,
	Cold, on the stroke of midnight,
60	The tip of one finger touched it! The trigger at last was hers!

Ⓑ

	The tip of one finger touched it. She strove no more for the rest!
	Up, she stood up to attention, with the muzzle beneath her breast.
	She would not risk their hearing; she would not strive again;
	For the road lay bare in the moonlight;
65	Blank and bare in the moonlight;
	And the blood of her veins in the moonlight, throbbed to her love's <u>refrain</u>.

	Tlot-tlot; tlot-tlot! Had they heard it: The horsehoofs ringing clear;
	Tlot-tlot, tlot-tlot, in the distance? Were they deaf that they did not hear?
	Down the ribbon of moonlight, over the brow of the hill,
70	The highwayman came riding—
	Riding—riding—
	The red-coats looked to their priming![18] She stood up, straight and still!

Ⓒ

	Tlot-tlot, in the frosty silence! *Tlot-tlot,* in the echoing night!
	Nearer he came and nearer. Her face was like a light.
75	Her eyes grew wide for a moment; she drew one last deep breath,
	Then her finger moved in the moonlight,
	Her musket shattered the moonlight,
	Shattered her breast in the moonlight and warned him—with her death.

---

16. tied her up to attention. Tied her to her bedpost, standing upright, with her hands at her sides
17. sniggering jest. Mocking joke
18. looked to their priming. Began to get their muskets ready to fire

> **writhe** (rīth) *v.,* twist and turn
>
> **re•frain** (ri frān´) *n.,* phrase or verse in a song or poem that is repeated throughout

Differentiated Instruction

Enrichment
Point out that Noyes makes extensive references to certain colors in "The Highwayman." Note that the highwayman wears a coat of *claret* velvet, and he loves the landlord's *black*-eyed daughter, who has long *black* hair.

Ask students to reread the poem to find all the references to the colors red and black leading up to the final image of the highwayman as he "lay in his blood on the highway." Then have students write a brief essay to interpret the poet's use of these visual images, supported with examples from the poem.

He turned. He spurred to the westward; he did not know who stood
80   Bowed, with her head o'er the musket, drenched with her own red blood!
Not till the dawn he heard it, and his face grew grey to hear
How Bess, the landlord's daughter,
        The landlord's black-eyed daughter,
Had watched for her love in the moonlight, and died in the darkness there.

85   Back, he spurred like a madman, shrieking a curse to the sky,
With the white road smoking behind him and his rapier <u>brandished</u> high.
Blood-red were his spurs in the golden noon, wine-red was his velvet coat;
When they shot him down on the highway,
        Down like a dog on the highway,
90   And he lay in his blood on the highway, with a bunch of lace at his throat.

And still of a winter's night, they say, when the wind is in the trees,
When the moon is a ghostly galleon tossed upon cloudy seas,
When the road is a ribbon of moonlight over the purple moor,
A highwayman comes riding—
95   *Riding—riding—*
A highwayman comes riding, up to the old inn door.

D

Over the cobbles he clatters and clangs in the dark inn yard.
He taps with his whip on the shutters, but all is locked and barred.
He whistles a tune to the window, and who should be waiting there
100   *But the landlord's black-eyed daughter,*
        Bess, the landlord's daughter,
Plaiting a dark red love-knot into her long black hair. ❖

bran·dish (bran´ dish) *v.*, wave threateningly

Would you describe the actions of the characters in "Annabel Lee" and "The Highwayman" as romantic, tragic, noble, or foolish? Do you think the characters behave like people from real life?

ANNABEL LEE / THE HIGHWAYMAN **555**

Teach the Selection

Use Reading Skills
Retell Sequence of Events Invite students to use their own words to retell the events from the arrival of the red coats at the inn to the death of the highwayman.

Analyze Literature
Narrative Poetry Have students compare the last two stanzas of the poem to stanzas 1 and 3. When they have noted the similarities and differences, point out that Noyes uses this repetition to create the feeling of an old ballad. **D**

Answer: Answers will vary, but all these terms describe some aspects of the characters and their actions. Many students will claim that the characters seem tragic. Most will agree that the characters seem too dramatic or idealized to be real.

Reading Skills

Compare and Contrast
Tell students that both of these poems, "Annabel Lee" and "The Highwayman," have been sung by folk musicians (Joan Baez and Loreena McKennitt, respectively) and have inspired many other products of popular culture. Divide the class into two groups, one for each poem. Have each group find five websites that refer to its poem. Then ask groups to rank the sites from most reliable (# 1) to least (# 5) reliable, based on these factors:

- Who sponsors the site, and what other things does the organization or individual sponsor?
- Does the site seem up to date, and how easy or difficult is it to tell?
- Does the site seem objective or subjective?

Review the Selections

Find Meaning

1. This helps show passage of time and separates exposition from action.
2. (a) He will commit a robbery and will soon return. (b) Bess loves him, which she shows by her actions.
3. (a) They set a trap for the highwayman by tying Bess up. (b) Tim probably informed them.

Make Judgments

4. His grief may have caused him to return to the inn, perhaps to seek revenge for Bess's death.
5. Their love transcends death.

Compare Literature

Narrative Poetry

1. Both couples are very much in love but are separated by death; Annabel Lee dies of an illness, while Beth's death is due to the choice she makes. Both men express anger and despair after their loved ones die. Both settings are remote and lonely.
2. (a) Answers will vary. (b) The mood of "Annabel Lee" is created by images such as the lonely grave by the sea. The mood of "The Highwayman" is created by images such as the red love-knot, the moonlight, the blood, and the sound of the galloping horse.
3. Poe uses internal and end rhyme, and he varies the end rhyme, breaking up the rhythm for a natural effect. He uses repetition for dramatic effect. Noyes uses a regular rhyme pattern and rhythm that emphasize suspense and drama.

Comparing Literature

Find Meaning

1. Why do you think the poet divided the poem into two parts?
2. (a) What does the highwayman tell Bess he is going to do? (b) How does Bess feel about the highwayman? How do you know this?
3. (a) What do the red coats do when they arrive at the inn? (b) How do you think they knew the highwayman would come there?

Compare Literature

Narrative Poetry Narrative poetry tells a story using rhyme, rhythm, and repetition as well as literary elements common to prose fiction. Review the charts that you created as you read "Annabel Lee" and "The Highwayman" to answer the following questions.

Make Judgments

4. Why do you think the highwayman decides to go back to the inn when he learns what happened to Bess instead of taking the opportunity to escape?
5. What do the last two stanzas suggest about Bess and the highwayman?

1. In what ways are the characters and settings in "Annabel Lee" and "The Highwayman" alike? In what ways are they different?
2. (a) How would you describe the mood of each poem? (b) What images create this mood?
3. What effect does each poet create through the use of rhyme, rhythm, and repetition?

Extend Understanding

Writing Options

Creative Writing Think of an exciting incident in your own life or in someone else's that would make a good subject for a **narrative poem.** Before you begin to write your poem, decide what point of view you will use. Would the action be more effectively told from the first- or third-person point of view? Once you have finished, share your poem with the class.

Expository Writing Recall what you know about the character traits of the women depicted in the two poems. What do their actions say about them? Which one would you prefer to meet? In a short **essay,** compare and contrast Annabel Lee and Bess, explaining which one you would choose to meet and why. Then compare your choice with the choices your classmates made.

Critical Literacy

Hold a Panel Discussion Which form of poetry do you prefer—narrative or lyric? With a small group, discuss the merits of each type. In what situations might you prefer to read or listen to a narrative poem? Might some topics, moods, or themes be better suited to lyric poems? Might some be better suited to narrative poems? Be sure to support your claims with evidence.

Lifelong Learning

Write a Literary Critique Research the careers and works of Edgar Allan Poe and Alfred Noyes. Locate and study another poem by each writer. Then write a paragraph that discusses how the poems that you studied fit into the poets' larger bodies of work. Consider each poem's tone, the cultural environment in which it was written, and the author's biography. When you are finished, share your research with the class.

Go to www.mirrorsandwindows.com for more.

Program Resources

For further instruction, refer students to the following extension activity: Lifelong Learning: Write a Literary Critique, *Exceeding the Standards: Extension Activities*, pp. 16–17.

Rubrics for Writing Options

You can adapt this as a checklist for students to use as they write.

Creative Writing

☐ Does the poem include narrative elements such as characters, setting, and plot?
☐ Does the poem use a consistent point of view?

Expository Writing

☐ Does the essay include character traits of both subjects?
☐ Does the essay state which character the student would prefer to meet?
☐ Does the essay compare and contrast the two women?

The Filling Station

A Lyric Poem by Elizabeth Bishop

Build Background

Literary Context Elizabeth Bishop published only five volumes of poetry during her lifetime. She tended to devote herself to perfecting each single piece, working and reworking it, rather than quickly moving on to the next poem. The care she took is evident in her precise and detailed observations. She also traveled widely, and her work often reflects her interest in geography. "The Filling Station," which first appeared in her 1965 book *Questions of Travel,* is one such poem.

Reader's Context What can you learn about people by carefully examining the spaces they inhabit?

Set Purpose

Preview the poem's six stanzas, noting the punctuation and the lengths of lines. Consider how these elements influence the way in which you read the poem.

Analyze Literature

Tone A writer's or speaker's attitude toward his or her subject is **tone.** A piece of literature can have many different tones. For example, it could be humorous, serious, angry, or ironic. Elements that contribute to tone include word choice, connotation, figurative language, sentence structure, images, and dialogue. Tone in poetry is also affected by rhyme and rhythm. As you read "The Filling Station," try to determine the poem's tone or tones.

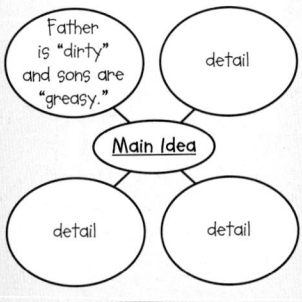

Meet the Author

Elizabeth Bishop (1911–1979) lost her parents at a young age and was raised by relatives in New England and Nova Scotia. After graduating from Vassar College, she traveled in Europe and Africa and then lived in places as varied as Florida, California, Mexico, and Brazil. Bishop won many awards during her lifetime, including the 1956 Pulitzer Prize for Poetry. She also wrote short stories, translated Portuguese literature, and loved to paint.

Use Reading Skills

Identify the Main Idea

When reading a poem, it is often necessary to infer the main idea. Pay attention to details, such as the tone, mood, and direct statements made by the speaker. Use a main idea map like the one below to help you determine the main idea in "The Filling Station."

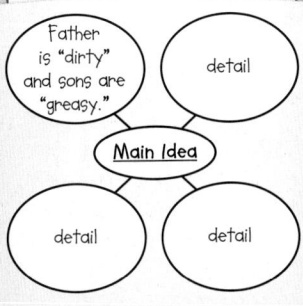

Preview Vocabulary

trans•lu•cen•cy (tran[t]s lü´ s'nt sē) *n.,* quality of being transparent or allowing some light to pass through

sau•cy (sô sē) *adj.,* bold

ex•tra•ne•ous (ek strā´ nē əs) *adj.,* not essential; not a part of the main idea

cro•chet (krō´shā´) *n.,* needlework made by interlocking loops of thread using a hooked needle

high-strung (hī´ strʉŋ´) *adj.,* nervous; extra sensitive

At a Glance
Directed Reading
- Reading Level: Moderate
- Difficulty Consideration: Vocabulary
- Ease Factor: Sensory details

Objectives

Studying this lesson will enable students to

- use reading skills such as identifying the main idea
- explore tone
- describe Elizabeth Bishop and appreciate the vivid images she creates
- analyze a poem to find meaning below the surface of an ordinary place

Launch the Lesson

Point out that nationwide chains are rapidly replacing family-owned grocery stores, hardware stores, and gas stations. Discuss how this affects the character of neighborhoods. Ask students to name some advantages and disadvantages of this trend, such as the advantage, or disadvantage, of predictability.

 The Mirrors & Windows questions after the poem focus on the theme of first impressions. Before students begin reading, ask: What place can you think of that is nicer than you would guess from how it looks on the outside?

Words in Use

Preview Vocabulary
translucency, 559
saucy, 559
extraneous, 559
crochet, 559
high-strung, 559

Selection Words
permeated, 559
comfy, 559
note, 559

Teaching Words
evident, 557
precise, 557

KEY TERMS

Common Core State Standards
Reading Literature
RL.1, RL.2

Summary

The speaker describes a filling station, noting that everything is soaked in oil and dirt, yet also notices a doily-covered stool and a potted plant. It is clear that someone cares for these things. The poem finishes with "Somebody loves us all."

Analyze Literature

Tone Suggest to students that reading the poem aloud will help them "hear" the speaker's tone.

Literary Connection

Irony Tell students that irony is a contrast between what one expects and what actually happens. Verbal irony exists when a person says one thing but means something else. Situational irony exists when a situation turns out to be just the opposite of what we expect. Have students try to find examples of irony in this poem.

History Connection

ESSO ESSO is a brand name of the Exxon Mobil Corporation. In 1973, the name *Exxon* replaced ESSO in the United States, except that in certain states one station still carries the ESSO name to protect trademark rights. The ESSO brand name is still used today in other countries.

558

The Filling Station

A Lyric Poem by Elizabeth Bishop

Oh, but it is dirty!
—this little filling station,[1]
oil-soaked, oil-permeated
to a disturbing, over-all
5 black translucency.
Be careful with that match!

Father wears a dirty,
oil-soaked monkey suit[2]
that cuts him under the arms,
10 and several quick and saucy
and greasy sons assist him
(it's a family filling station),
all quite thoroughly dirty.

Do they live in the station?
15 It has a cement porch
behind the pumps, and on it

a set of crushed and grease-
impregnated[3] wickerwork;
on the wicker sofa
20 a dirty dog, quite comfy.

Some comic books provide
the only note of color—
of certain color. They lie
upon a big dim doily[4]
25 draping a taboret[5]
(part of the set), beside
a big hirsute begonia.[6]

Why the extraneous plant?
Why the taboret?
30 Why, oh why, the doily?
(Embroidered in daisy stitch[7]
with marguerites,[8] I think,
and heavy with gray crochet.)
Somebody embroidered the doily.
35 Somebody waters the plant,
or oils it, maybe. Somebody
arranges the rows of cans
so that they softly say:
ESSO—SO—SO—SO
40 to high-strung automobiles.
Somebody loves us all. ❖

---

1. **filling station.** Gas station
2. **monkey suit.** Protective overalls worn by mechanics
3. **grease-impregnated.** Filled or saturated with grease
4. **doily.** Small decorative mat
5. **taboret.** Stool or small side table, often shaped like a drum
6. **hirsute begonia.** Type of flowering plant with a hairy stem
7. **daisy stitch.** Stitch used in embroidery, often to create flowers
8. **marguerites.** Daisies; also other flowers that resemble daisies

---

trans•lu•cen•cy (tran[t]s lü´ s'nt sē) *n.*, quality of being transparent or allowing some light to pass through

sau•cy (sô sē) *adj.*, bold

ex•tra•ne•ous (ek strā´ nē əs) *adj.*, not essential; not a part of the main idea

cro•chet (krō´shā´) *n.*, needlework made by interlocking loops of thread using a hooked needle

high-strung (hī´ struŋ´) *adj.*, nervous; extra sensitive

How might your initial impression of something change? Do you think a person's willingness to change his or her mind is a good or bad trait?

THE FILLING STATION **559**

Teach the Selection

Analyze Literature
Tone Ask students what this stanza reveals about the speaker's attitude. Point out language that contributes to the tone, such as "Oh, but it is dirty!" and note the exclamation points. **A**

Analyze Literature
Diction Ask students what the wording and phrasing suggest about the speaker's age, education, and social class. Model a response: "Language such as *saucy* and *quite thoroughly* tends to be used by older, well-educated, well-to-do people." **B**

Make Connections
Ask students how these details affect their ideas about the people who live here. **C**

Analyze Literature
Imagery Point out that the poem's imagery appeals to sight and touch. Ask what the color provided by the comic books might signify. (There is more here than meets the eye.) **D**

Use Reading Skills
Identify Main Idea Ask students how the last line of the poem helps express its main idea. (Expressions of love can be found in the most unexpected places.) **E**

Answer: Most will agree that such willingness is a positive trait.

Differentiated Instruction

English Language Learning
In addition to previewing vocabulary words, have students preview the footnotes and the following words and expressions:
permeated – passed into or through and affected every part of, 559
wickerwork – thin, flexible twigs or pieces of wood woven together like a basket to make furniture, 559
comfy – comfortable, 559

Reading Proficiency
Have students practice reading the poem aloud with the goal of achieving a conversational flow. Encourage them to pause for punctuation, not for line breaks, and point out that the third stanza breaks in the middle of a sentence.

Review the Selection

Find Meaning

1. (a) It is from comic books. (b) The rest of the station is black, gray, and brown from dirt and grease.

2. (a) Repeated words include *dirty*, *oil-soaked*, and *greasy*. (b) The repetition emphasizes the griminess of the scene.

Make Judgments

3. Students may say the line "Be careful with that match!" and the quip about the begonia are humorous.

4. Most students will conclude that the poet's attitude is positive. They may note the way the poet stops calling the scene dirty and greasy and begins pointing out pleasant details.

Analyze Literature

Tone Summaries of the tone will vary. Students should note that Bishop writes with refined, educated words that create a formal tone. The limited use of contractions contributes to the formality. She uses specialized terms such as *doily, taboret, hirsute begonia,* and *marguerites,* as well as sophisticated vocabulary like *translucency* and *extraneous.*

Program Resources

For further instruction, refer students to the following extension activity: Media Literacy: Draw the Images, *Exceeding the Standards: Extension Activities*, p. 18.

Find Meaning

1. (a) What is the only "note of color" in the filling station? (b) How does this note of color compare with the rest of the filling station?

2. (a) What are some of the most frequently repeated words in the poem? (b) What effect does Bishop achieve through this repetition?

Analyze Literature

Tone Images, figurative language, and word choice can all help establish tone. Idiom, or language used by a particular class or group, can also influence tone. For example, only a speaker knowledgeable about furniture would choose to say *taboret*; others might just say *stool*. Collect details from the poem that contribute to the tone. Then write a sentence that you think best describes the tone.

Make Judgments

3. Which parts of this poem do you find humorous? Explain.

4. Is the poet's overall attitude toward the scene positive or negative? Explain your answer using examples from the poem.

Sentence:

Extend Understanding

Writing Options

Creative Writing Imagine that you are one of the people Elizabeth Bishop encounters at the filling station. Write a very brief **short story** from that character's point of view, giving your account of the poet's visit to the filling station. Use sensory details to give readers a feeling for how you experience the place, and include dialogue and descriptive details to flesh out the characters. Share your story with the class.

Expository Writing In "The Filling Station," the speaker describes reactions to a filling station, noting the different surprising objects there. In literature, the difference between appearance and reality is referred to as irony. In a short **essay,** analyze the role irony plays in the poem. Provide at least three examples from the poem, explaining why they are ironic and how they express the speaker's feelings or the tone of the piece.

Collaborative Learning

Consider the Author's Perspective Working in a small group, talk about the author's perspective in the poem. As part of the discussion, you may wish to take into account both what you have learned about Bishop's life and the evidence in the poem itself. Be sure to take notes as you discuss. Present your ideas, and the reasons for them, to the class.

Media Literacy

Draw the Images An image is a vivid mental picture created in a reader's mind by language. When considered all together, the images in a literary work are referred to as imagery. Draw some of the images that came to mind as you read "The Filling Station." Exchange your pictures with a classmate. Ask him or her to look at your drawings and to describe the images he or she sees. How are these descriptions like or unlike the images you meant to represent?

Go to www.mirrorsandwindows.com for more.

Rubrics for Writing Options

You can adapt this as a checklist for students to use as they write.

Creative Writing

☐ Is the story narrated from the point of view of a character at Bishop's filling station?

☐ Does the story include sensory details and dialogue?

☐ Does the story relate the events of the poem from a different perspective?

Expository Writing

☐ Does the essay demonstrate an understanding of irony?

☐ Does the essay analyze the role irony plays in this poem?

☐ Does the essay analyze at least three examples of irony from the poem?

Vocabulary & Spelling

Figurative Language

Somebody

arranges the rows of cans

so that they softly say:

ESSO-SO-SO-SO

to high-strung automobiles.

—ELIZABETH BISHOP, "The Filling Station"

Figurative language is language that expresses more than literal meaning through imaginative or poetic use of words. Poets often use figurative language to help the reader visualize. In the quotation above, Bishop uses an **idiom,** an expression that means something other than what the words literally mean. The expression *high-strung* is an idiom that means "extremely nervous" or "sensitive." *Easy as pie* and *facing the music* are common idioms.

An **analogy** is an extended comparison between two different things. For example, in "The Filling Station," the speaker compares the care someone took in embroidering a doily to demonstrating love.

Two other common types of figurative language are metaphor and simile. A **metaphor** is a comparison between two seemingly unrelated things.

> **EXAMPLE**
> *The stars were flickering white moths.*

A **simile** is a comparison between two seemingly unrelated things that uses the word *like* or *as*.

> **EXAMPLE**
> *The boys ate like wild animals.*

Vocabulary Practice

Identify the type of figurative language in each example from "The Highwayman."

1. The wind was a torrent of darkness among the gusty trees.
2. Her face was like a light.
3. With the white road smoking behind him....
4. Down like a dog on the highway....
5. When the road was a gypsy's ribbon, looping the purple moor....
6. The moon was a ghostly galleon tossed upon cloudy seas.
7. ...his hair like mouldy hay....
8. His face burnt like a brand....
9. ...he spurred like a madman....
10. ...the hours crawled by like years....

Spelling Practice

Words with Vowel Combinations

Vowel combinations can be tricky in spelling because the same pair of letters can be pronounced in different ways. Review this list of spelling words from "The Filling Station" to see different vowel combinations. Try to group the words according to the sound produced by the vowel combination.

automobiles	greasy
certain	heavy
daisy	saucy
embroidered	soaked
extraneous	thoroughly

Vocabulary Practice

Judge student answers based on the definition you have taught for idiom. Native speakers generally understand common idioms, but English learners do not. Also, because an analogy is an extended comparison—by its nature taking more than a single phrase or sentence—this practice set does not include one.

1. metaphor
2. simile
3. idiom (also metaphor)
4. simile
5. metaphor
6. metaphor
7. simile
8. simile
9. simile
10. idiom (also simile)

TEACHING NOTE

Listening Skills

Ask students to read the words from the Spelling Practice list aloud. English language learners should both listen to and speak these words trying to recognize the vowel combinations within these newly acquired words.

> For additional instruction on spelling rules, see the Vocabulary & Spelling Section 2.7, Spelling, in the Language Arts Handbook.

Program Resources

You will find additional lessons on Figurative Language in the *Exceeding the Standards: Vocabulary & Spelling* resource.

TEACHING NOTE

Extra Practice

For each phrase below, have students write a sentence that uses the form of figurative language in parentheses. Students' sentences will vary; use this opportunity to make sure they understand these types of figurative language.

1. running to catch a bus (metaphor)
2. a deep swimming pool (simile)
3. lemonade and chocolate cookies (metaphor)
4. hearing thunder (idiom)
5. a father's smile (simile)

KEY TERMS

FIGURATIVE LANGUAGE, 561

IDIOM, 561

ANALOGY, 561

METAPHOR, 561

SIMILE, 561

Common Core State Standards

Language

L.5, L.6

A Lyric Poem by Phil George

Preview the Selection

At a Glance
Directed Reading
- Reading Level: Easy
- Difficulty Consideration: Topic
- Ease Factor: Vocabulary

Objectives
Studying this lesson will enable students to
- use reading skills to analyze and understand text organization
- identify elements of a lyric poem
- connect literature to social studies
- synthesize content from different texts

Launch the Lesson
Prior to reading "Name Giveaway," ask students how they would feel if someone told them they needed to change their names. Ask: "What factors might determine whether or not you would agree to the change?"

MIRRORS & WINDOWS The Mirrors & Windows questions after the poem focus on the theme of reacting to an offense. Before students begin reading, ask: Does anyone ever call you by the wrong name? If so, how does it feel?

Summary
The speaker describes being renamed by a school teacher.

DIRECTED READING

BEFORE READING

Build Background
Cultural Context In the late 1800s and early 1900s, the U.S. government forced Native Americans to send their children to church- or government-sponsored schools. These schools required the students to conform to the language, dress, and religion of white people. Native Americans were forced to take English given names. Translations of Native Americans' traditional names were forbidden or strongly discouraged. Government or church officials assigned everyone new names, such as James Peterson and Mary Smith.

Reader's Context To what degree is your name part of who you are? Why?

Set Purpose
Before you begin reading, examine the poem's structure. Watch for patterns in stanza and line length. Consider how these elements influence your interpretation of the poem.

Analyze Literature
Lyric Poetry A **lyric poem** expresses the emotions of the poem's speaker and focuses on a single moment, image, or idea. Lyric poetry is often musical and, unlike narrative poetry, does not tell a story. As you read "Name Giveaway," identify the elements that make this a lyric poem.

Meet the Author
Phil George (b. 1946) was born in Seattle, Washington. He attended Gonzaga University in Spokane, Washington, and the Institute of American Indian Arts in Santa Fe, New Mexico. George's poetry has been published in several anthologies, and he also produced and narrated the video recording *A Season of Grandmothers* for the Public Broadcasting Service. He is a champion Traditional Plateau dancer and is a member of the Seven Drums religion.

Use Reading Skills
Analyze Text Organization A *couplet* is a pair of lines that forms a unit in a poem. In "Name Giveaway," each couplet forms a single stanza. Use a two-column chart to note the idea or emotion expressed in each couplet.

Couplet	Ideas or Emotions
first	
second	
third	

Preview Vocabulary
as·cend (ə send´) *v.*, move upward; rise

Words in Use

Preview Vocabulary
ascend, 563

Teaching Words
forbidden, 562
discouraged, 562

KEY TERMS
LYRIC POEM, 562
STANZA, 562
NARRATIVE POETRY, 562
COUPLET, 562
MEMOIR, 564

Common Core State Standards
Reading Literature
RL.1
Reading Informational
RI.9

NAME GIVEAWAY

A Lyric Poem by Phil George

That teacher gave me a new name...again.
　　She never even had feasts or a giveaway!

Still I do not know what "George" means;
　　and now she calls me: "Phillip."

　TWO SWANS <u>ASCENDING</u> FROM STILL WATERS
must be a name too hard to remember. ✤

as·cend (ə send´) *v.*, move upward; rise

 How would you react if you were in the speaker's situation? Would you be angry, sad, or indifferent? How do you think most people would react?

Find Meaning

1. (a) What does the teacher do to the speaker? (b) What does the speaker suggest the teacher should have done?
2. What does the speaker dislike about the name "George"?

Make Judgments

3. (a) What was the speaker's name before the teacher renamed him? (b) How is this name different from "George" or "Phillip"?
4. What feeling do you think the original name inspired in the speaker?

563

Use Reading Strategies

Make Inferences Ask students how the speaker feels about the teacher, and what details support their inference. (The speaker is annoyed. Use of "<u>That</u> teacher" instead of "<u>My</u> teacher" signals disapproval.)

Analyze Literature

Lyric Poetry Ask students what the reversed indentation in the last couplet might signify (such as a long pause, or extra emphasis).

 Answer: Students may say they would feel indignant or disoriented. Most people would be angry.

Find Meaning

1. (a) The teacher gives him a new name. (b) She should have celebrated giving him the name.
2. He doesn't know its meaning.

Make Judgments

3. (a) It was Two Swans Ascending from Still Waters. (b) It is descriptive.
4. It probably created pride and hope, and a positive mental image.

Program Resources

Planning and Assessment
Program Planning Guide, Selection Lesson Plan
E-Lesson Planner
Assessment Guide, Lesson Test
ExamView

Technology Tools
Interactive Student Text on CD
Visual Teaching Package
Audio Library
mirrorsandwindows.com

Meeting the Standards
Poetry: Unit 6, Directed Reading, pp. 40–45

Differentiating Instruction
Advanced Students, Historical Context Project, pp. 39–40

Summary

The excerpt describes the experience of a young Native American boy who left his reservation to attend a government contract school. His initial excitement is replaced with homesickness when he discovers that the school is not what he imagined. He is bathed roughly by other Native Americans, his hair is cut, and he is given a new name. This final loss makes him feel that he has lost a part of himself.

Analyze Literature

Characterization Ask what details the author uses to convey his opinion of the Government agent. (For example, the phrase "honey-tongued" has a negative connotation, suggesting that the agent is not to be trusted.) **A**

Cultural Connection

Lacrosse Lacrosse originated as a Native American stickball game known as *baggataway*. Early French settlers called the game "lacrosse" because of the long curved stick, or *crosse,* used to move the ball across the field. To Native Americans, lacrosse had a spiritual significance; it was used to settle disputes and also in training for war. Many versions of the game developed, and today it is played around the world. **B**

PRIMARY SOURCE ▶▶ CONNECTION

In the lyric poem "Name Giveaway," Phil George muses about how he feels when his teacher gives him a new name. In the following excerpt from a memoir, **Ah-nen-la-de-ni** describes his experiences in a government school for Indians. After he finished school, Ah-nen-la-de-ni became a nurse.

from **An Indian Boy's Story**

A Memoir by Ah-nen-la-de-ni

A When I was thirteen a great change occurred, for the honey-tongued agent of a new Government contract Indian school appeared on the reservation, drumming up boys and girls for his institution. He made a great impression by going from house to house and describing, through an interpreter, all the glories and luxuries of the new place, the good food and teaching, the fine uniforms, the playground and its sports and toys.

All that a wild Indian boy had to do, according to the agent, was to attend this school for a year or two, and he was sure to emerge there from with all the knowledge and skill of the white man....

I had, up to this time, been leading a very happy life, helping with the planting, trapping, fishing, basket making and playing **B** all the games of my tribe—which is famous at lacrosse—but the desire to travel and see new things and the hope of finding an easy way to much knowledge in the wonderful school outweighed my regard for my home and its joys, and so I was one of the twelve boys who in 1892 left our reservation to go to the Government contract school for Indians, situated in a large Pennsylvania city and known as the Institute.

Till I arrived at the school I had never heard that there were any other Indians in the country other than those of our reservation, and I did not know that our tribe was called Mohawk. My people called themselves "Ga-nien-ge-ha-ga," meaning "People of the Beacon Stone," and Indians generally they termed "On-give-hon-we," meaning "Real-men" or "Primitive People."

My surprise, therefore, was great when I found myself surrounded in the school yard by strange Indian boys belonging to tribes of which I had never heard, and when it was said that my people were only the "civilized Mohawks," I at first thought that "Mohawk" was a nickname and fought any boy who called me by it.

I had left home for the school with a great deal of hope, having said to my mother:

Words in Use

from *An Indian Boy's Story*
Selection Words
disconcerting, 565
perturbed, 565
raiment, 565
immaculately, 565
disconsolate, 565

Differentiated Instruction

Enrichment
Have students work together in small groups to research what life was like for the Mohawk or other Native American groups in the late 1800s. Suggest that they focus on topics such as language, daily life, art, trade, and recreation. Some students may wish to find more information on boarding schools such as the one Ah-nen-la-de-ni attended. Ask students to present their findings to the class.

"Do not worry. I shall soon return to you a better boy and with a good education!" Little did I dream that that was the last time I would ever see her kind face. She died two years later, and I was not allowed to go to her funeral.

The journey to Philadelphia had been very enjoyable and interesting. It was my first ride on the "great steel horse," as the Indians called the railway train, but my frame of mind changed as soon as my new home was reached.

The first thing that happened to me and to all other freshly caught young redskins when we arrived at the institution was a bath of a particularly disconcerting sort. We were used to baths of the swimming variety, for on the reservation we boys spent a good deal of our time in the water, but this first bath at the institution was different. For one thing, it was accompanied by plenty of soap, and for another thing, it was preceded by a haircut that is better described as a crop.

The little newcomer, thus cropped and delivered over to the untender mercies of larger Indian boys of tribes different from his own, who laughingly attacked his bare skin with very hot water and very hard scrubbing brushes, was likely to emerge from the **C** encounter with a clean skin but perturbed mind. When, in addition, he was prevented from expressing his feelings in the only language he knew, what wonder if some rules of the school were broken.

After the astonishing bath the newcomer was freshly clothed from head to foot, while the raiment in which he came from the reservation was burned or buried. Thereafter he was released by the torturers, and could be seen sidling about the corridors like a lonely crab, silent, sulky, immaculately clean and most disconsolate.

After my bath and reclothing and after having had my name taken down in the records I was assigned to a dormitory, and began my regular school life, much to my dissatisfaction. The recording of my name was accompanied by a change which, though it might seem trifling to the teachers, was very important to me. My name among my own people was "Ah-nen-la-de-ni," which in English means "Turning crowd" or "Turns the crowd," but my family had had the name "La France" bestowed on them by the French some generations before my birth, and at the institution my Indian name was discarded, and I was informed that I was henceforth to be known as Daniel La France.

It made me feel as if I had lost myself. I had been proud of myself and my possibilities as "Turns the crowd," for in spite of their civilized surroundings the Indians of our reservation in my time still looked back to the old warlike days when the Mohawks were great people, but Daniel La France was to me a stranger and a nobody with no possibilities. It seemed as if my prospect of a chiefship had vanished. I was very homesick for a long time. ✤

TEXT → TEXT CONNECTION

Both Phil George's poem and Ah-nen-la-de-ni's memoir describe the experience of being given a new name. What does the memoir add to your understanding of the poem? Would the poem serve as a good summary of the experience described in the memoir?

Review the Selection

Independent Reading

Students who like "Name Giveaway" might enjoy reading fiction about Native Americans in Virginia, such as Driving Hawk Sneve's short story collection *Grandpa Was a Cowboy & an Indian and Other Stories.*

Analyze Literature

Lyric Poetry The speaker's names are Two Swans Ascending from Still Waters, which he feels comfortable with; George, which puzzles him; and Phillip, which annoys him.

Analyze Literature

Lyric Poetry A lyric poem expresses the emotions of the poem's speaker, or narrator, and focuses on a single moment, image, or idea. Use a chart to sort out the name changes in "Name Giveaway" and the speaker's feelings about each of his names. In the left column, list, in order, the names given to the speaker. In the right column, write how the speaker felt about each name.

Names	Feelings
George	puzzled

Extend Understanding

Writing Options

Creative Writing The speaker in "Name Giveaway" and Ah-nen-la-de-ni both had strong reactions when their teachers changed their names, yet they went along with the name changes. Imagine that you are a friend of Ah-nen-la-de-ni and that you want to write a **letter** to tell his teacher how he feels about the name change. In the letter, explain why she should stop changing her students' names. Provide solid reasons and examples, and use a polite, knowledgeable tone. Remember to use a business-letter format for your letter.

Expository Writing How do you feel about your own name? What do you like or dislike about it? Would you change it if you could? If so, what would you change it to? Why? Write a brief **personal essay** explaining to your family how you feel about your own name. Give reasons why you would or would not like to change your name. In your concluding paragraph, restate the main idea of your essay.

Critical Literacy

List Questions Imagine that you were given the opportunity to interview Phil George about his life and work. Use the library to research information about him. As you take notes during the research process, record questions you would like to ask the poet. Then meet with a small group to compile the most interesting questions or the questions most necessary for holding a successful interview.

Lifelong Learning

Research History With a partner, research the history of Native American schools. Brainstorm a list of questions about the schools. Where were they located? When were they established? Who ran the schools? What was the reason for having separate schools for Native Americans? Why did Native Americans send their children to these schools? Record the information that you uncover and share your findings with the class.

Go to **www.mirrorsandwindows.com** for more.

Rubrics for Writing Options

You can adapt this as a checklist for students to use as they write.

Creative Writing
☐ Does the letter follow the proper format?
☐ Does the letter have a polite, knowledgeable tone?
☐ Does the letter say why students' names should not be changed?

Expository Writing
☐ Does the essay express personal feelings?
☐ Does the essay offer details and reasons?
☐ Does the concluding paragraph restate the main idea?

Vocabulary & Spelling

Spelling by Syllables

That teacher gave me a new name...
again.

—PHIL GEORGE, "Name Giveaway"

How many syllables does the word *again* have? A syllable is a part of a word that contains a single vowel sound. All words have at least one syllable. Understanding how to break words into syllables can help you sound out unfamiliar words and spell them correctly.

There is no single correct way to divide syllables, or syllabicate, and sometimes you will see the same word divided two different ways. There are some general guidelines, however, that will help you syllabicate many words. Here are some of them. *V* stands for vowel and *C* stands for consonant.

Pattern 1: VCV If a word contains a consonant between two vowels, and the first vowel is long, you should break the word after the first vowel. If the vowel is short, break after the consonant.

> EXAMPLES
> *so-lo*
> *cab-in*

Pattern 2: VCCV If a word contains two consonants together, you should usually break the word between the two consonants.

> EXAMPLE
> *mud-dy*

Pattern 3: VV If a word contains two vowels and both vowels are pronounced, divide the word between the two vowels.

> EXAMPLE
> *cli-ent*

Pattern 4: Prefixes A prefix always forms a separate syllable.

> EXAMPLE
> *un-lock*

Pattern 5: Suffixes A suffix forms a syllable if it contains a vowel.

> EXAMPLE
> *sense-less*

The suffix *-y* follows the VCCV rule.

> EXAMPLE
> *hear-ty*

Spelling Practice

Exercise A
Write each of the following words, separating syllables with hyphens. Check your answers by looking up the words in a dictionary. Identify the words' part of speech and pronunciation.

1. billow
2. hammer
3. triumph
4. decline
5. prefer
6. warmly

Exercise B
Determine the meaning of the following words by looking them up and noting where their prefixes and suffixes originated (Greek, Latin, etc.). Then, break the words into their proper syllables.

1. antibody
2. unpublished
3. hyperbole
4. physics
5. universe
6. transfer

Preview the Selection

At a Glance

Directed Reading

- Reading Level: Easy
- Difficulty Considerations: None
- Ease Factors: Vocabulary and topic

Objectives

Studying this lesson will enable students to

- use reading skills such as analyzing main idea and supporting details
- explore author's purpose
- describe Dudley Randall and analyze his use of free verse
- analyze a poem about ancestry

Launch the Lesson

Prior to reading "Ancestors," ask students to imagine that they could choose any person from history to be one of their ancestors. Whom would they choose? Why?

MIRRORS & WINDOWS

The Mirrors & Windows questions after the poem focus on the theme of ancestors. Before students begin reading, ask: What did your most memorable ancestor do for a living?

Summary

The speaker of this poem wonders why most people think of their ancestors as kings or princes. He notes that he is just as proud of his own ancestor, who was a swineherd.

Common Core State Standards

Reading Literature
RL.1, RL.2

Writing
W.2, W.10

DIRECTED READING

BEFORE READING

Build Background

Cultural Context Dudley Randall reached the height of his influence during the most active years of the Civil Rights movement. He devoted his career to promoting African-American poets and often wrote about racial themes. His famous poem "The Ballad of Birmingham" is about the racially motivated bombing of an Alabama church. "Ancestors" addresses a less dramatic topic: the genealogical research among people who want to learn about their cultural heritage. In the poem, he pokes gentle fun at people's tendency to claim they descend from nobility.

Reader's Context What do you know about your ancestors?

Set Purpose

Before you begin reading, try to determine whether "Ancestors" is a free verse poem or if it is written in a form you recognize.

Analyze Literature

Author's Purpose An **author's purpose,** or aim, is his or her goal for writing a piece of literature. For example, an author may write to inform, to persuade, or to entertain. Writers may also have multiple purposes. The author's purpose is different from theme, or the work's central idea. As you read "Ancestors," think about why Randall might have written the poem—what was his purpose?

Meet the Author

A dedicated poet from childhood, **Dudley Randall** (1914–2000) published his first poems at thirteen. Following high school, he supported his writing by working at the Ford Motor Company and then as a mail carrier in Detroit, his hometown. After serving in World War II, he earned a degree and became a librarian. In 1965, Randall founded the Broadside Press and promoted the era's most promising African-American poets. Among other honors, he was named poet laureate of Detroit in 1981.

Use Reading Skills

Analyze Main Idea and Supporting Details To identify the main idea of "Ancestors," gather details in a main idea map. Then examine the details to determine the author's overall message.

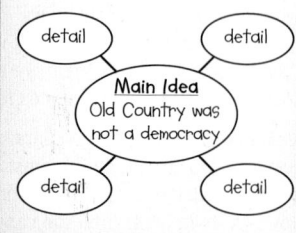

detail | detail

Main Idea
Old Country was
not a democracy

detail | detail

Preview Vocabulary

ar•is•toc•ra•cy (aˊ rə stäˊ krə sē) *n.*, noble or privileged class; government by people who belong to the noble class

by•gone (bīˊ gôn) *adj.*, long ago; in the distant past

Words in Use

Preview Vocabulary
aristocracy, 569
bygone, 569

Selection Words
ancestors, 569

Teaching Words
genealogical, 568
nobility, 568
poet laureate, 568

KEY TERMS

LYRIC POEM, 568
FREE VERSE, 568
AUTHOR'S PURPOSE, 568
MAIN IDEA, 568
POINT OF VIEW, 570
BIOGRAPHY, 570
CHRONOLOGICAL ORDER, 570
STANZA, 570

Ancestors

A Lyric Poem by Dudley Randall

Why are our ancestors
always kings or princes
and never the common people?

Was the Old Country a democracy
5   where every man was a king?
Or did the slavecatchers
take only the <u>aristocracy</u>
and leave the fieldhands
laborers
10   streetcleaners
garbage collectors
dishwashers
cooks
and maids
15   behind?

My own ancestor
(research reveals)
was a swineherd[1]
who tended the pigs
20   in the Royal Pigstye
and slept in the mud
among the hogs.

Yet I'm as proud of him
as of any king or prince
25   dreamed up in fantasies
of <u>bygone</u> glory. ❖

---

1. swineherd. Person who tends pigs

ar·is·toc·ra·cy (a' rə stä´ krə sē) *n.*, noble or
privileged class; government by people who belong to
the noble class

by·gone (bī´ gôn') *adj.*, long ago; in the distant past

Why is it important to know about your ancestors? How much does it
matter to you what kind of people your ancestors were? How do most
people feel about their ancestors?

569

Cultural Connection

Genealogy Many Americans can
research their family histories using
public records such as census data.
For African Americans whose
ancestors were enslaved, however,
records go back only as far as 1870.
New possibilities are opening up as
scientists learn how to trace lineage
through DNA.

Use Reading Skills

Analyze Text Organization Ask
students why Randall presents these
occupations as a long list. How does
the visual effect of this organization
relate to the speaker's message?
(It emphasizes the ordinary
occupations.) **A**

Use Reading Skills

**Analyze Main Idea and
Supporting Details** Have students
state the main idea of "Ancestors"
and cite details that support it.

Answer:
Students
may say
knowing
about ancestors—whatever their
status—can give people
perspective on their own lives.

Independent Reading

Students who like "Ancestors" might
also enjoy poems by Langston Hughes
such as "The Negro Speaks of Rivers"
and "Dreams."

Program Resources

Planning and Assessment
Program Planning Guide, Selection Lesson Plan
E-Lesson Planner
Assessment Guide, Lesson Test
ExamView

Technology Tools
Interactive Student Text on CD
Visual Teaching Package
Audio Library
mirrorsandwindows.com

Meeting the Standards
Poetry: Unit 6, Directed Reading, pp. 45–50

Differentiating Instruction
Advanced Students, Cultural Connection
Activity, pp. 34–35

Review the Selection

Find Meaning

1. (a) The ancestor came from Africa. (b) Students may say they inferred this from the word *slavecatchers*.
2. (a) The speaker did research. (b) The speaker's use of *dreamed up* and *fantasies of bygone glory* imply that royal ancestry is fabricated.

Make Judgments

3. (a) The speaker mentions fieldhands, laborers, street cleaners, garbage collectors, dishwashers, cooks, and maids.
(b) This list emphasizes that there are many more average people in the world than members of royalty.
4. (a) These questions undermine the notion of large numbers of royal ancestors. (b) These are questions the speaker may answer in the poem. The speaker would probably answer *no* to the last two.

Analyze Literature

Author's Purpose Students might identify the purpose as to persuade or to inform, and the theme as "People should take as much pride in common ancestors as they would in royal ones." Most students will say Randall communicated his ideas effectively.

Find Meaning

1. (a) From where did the speaker's ancestor come? (b) What led you to this conclusion?
2. (a) How did the speaker find out about his or her ancestor? (b) How does the speaker suspect that people have discovered their royal ancestry?

Analyze Literature

Author's Purpose The author's purpose is the reason for writing. The theme is the main message the author hopes to convey to readers. Create a chart identifying the purpose and theme of "Ancestors." Finally, provide an evaluation of how well Dudley Randall succeeded in his goals, from your own point of view as a reader.

Make Judgments

3. (a) What are some of the occupations the speaker mentions in this poem? (b) In what way does the speaker's use of this list reinforce the poem's main idea?
4. (a) The speaker begins by asking three questions in a row. What effect do these questions create? (b) What sort of answers do you think the speaker expects to receive?

Purpose	Theme
persuade	

My Evaluation:

Extend Understanding

Writing Options

Creative Writing Imagine that you have been commissioned to write a **biography** of the speaker's ancestor. Tell the story of the swineherd in chronological order so that the earliest events are told first. Use specific details. For example, be sure to include the place and year of his birth, his occupation, and other vital details. Also include at least one anecdote about the person.

Expository Writing In the last stanza of the poem, the speaker says of his or her ancestor, "I'm as proud of him / as of any king or prince...." Write an **expository paragraph** in which you explain why the speaker might feel this way. Use details from the poem, as well as your own analysis of the issues Randall raises in the poem, to support your thesis.

Critical Literacy

Hold a Panel Discussion Hold a panel discussion to explore the risks and benefits of knowing about ancestry. Agree beforehand who will moderate, or lead the discussion, and decide what points of view the participants will represent. Be sure that you always present evidence in support of your claims, and listen respectfully to other viewpoints.

Lifelong Learning

Research Your Ancestry Investigate your own roots or the roots of someone you admire by doing genealogical research. Talk to your parents, grandparents, and other relatives. Investigate genealogical websites. Use your findings to draw a family tree that goes back at least three generations. Include photos or hand-drawn portraits, as well as brief interesting facts, if desired. Display the family tree in your classroom.

Go to **www.mirrorsandwindows.com** for more.

Rubrics for Writing Options

You can adapt this as a checklist for students to use as they write.

Creative Writing

☐ Does the biography follow chronological order?
☐ Does the biography include specific details about the ancestor's life?
☐ Does the biography include at least one anecdote?

Expository Writing

☐ Does the paragraph explain why the poem's speaker feels this way?
☐ Does the paragraph include details from the poem to support the thesis?
☐ Does the paragraph include the student's analysis of the issues Randall raises?

Grammar & Style

Simple, Complete, and Compound Predicates

Simple and Complete Predicates

My own ancestor…
was a swineherd
who tended the pigs….

—DUDLEY RANDALL, "Ancestors"

The **simple predicate** is the key verb or verb phrase that tells what the subject does, has, or is. The **complete predicate** includes the verb and all the words that modify it. In the quotation above, *was* is the simple predicate and *was a swineherd who tended the pigs* is the complete predicate.

In the following examples, a vertical line separates the subject from the complete predicate. The simple predicate, or verb, is underlined.

> EXAMPLES
>
> Ancestors | <u>are</u> people from whom we descend.
>
> All the members of my family | <u>have sung</u> their hearts out.

Compound Predicates

Or did the slavecatchers
take only the aristocracy
and leave the fieldhands….

—DUDLEY RANDALL, "Ancestors"

A **compound predicate** has two or more simple predicates, or verbs, that share the same subject. The verbs are connected by the conjunction *and, or,* or *but.* In the quotation above, *take* and *leave* share the subject, *slavecatchers.*

> EXAMPLES
>
> She | <u>traced</u> her ancestors and <u>created</u> a family tree.
>
> My grandfather | <u>met</u>, <u>proposed to</u>, and <u>married</u> my grandmother within a month.

Identifying Simple, Complete, and Compound Predicates

On a separate sheet of paper, rewrite each sentence and draw a vertical line between the complete subject and predicate. Then underline once the simple predicate. Underline twice each compound predicate.

1. One of my ancestors bought land and built houses for all his children.
2. Jamal found addresses for all his cousins and sent them invitations to a family reunion.
3. My grandmother and great-aunt have never agreed.
4. Today would have been my great-grandfather's one hundredth birthday.
5. The first members of our family to arrive here lived, worked, and died within five miles of this house.
6. Many people in my family built their own homes.
7. My father returned from my grandparents' house and told us all about the trip.
8. His youngest sister called home that night.
9. Many of Tom's ancestors lived and worked in Dublin.
10. Carrie walked to the library and spoke with the librarian.

KEY TERMS

SIMPLE PREDICATE, 571
VERB PHRASE, 571
COMPLETE PREDICATE, 571
COMPOUND PREDICATE, 571
CONJUNCTION, 571

Program Resources

You will find additional lessons on Simple, Complete, and Compound Predicates in the *Exceeding the Standards: Grammar & Style* resource.

Common Core State Standards

Language
L.7.1c

Preview the Selection

At a Glance
Directed Reading
- Reading Level: Easy
- Difficulty Considerations: None
- Ease Factor: Vocabulary

Objectives
Studying this lesson will enable students to
- use reading skills such as compare and contrast
- analyze symbols
- describe Naomi Shihab Nye and discuss how she expresses her observations
- appreciate a poem about loss and hope

Launch the Lesson
Tell students they are about to read about a boy who is devastated by the loss of his parrot. Ask students to think of how they would comfort a friend who suffered such a loss.

MIRRORS & WINDOWS The Mirrors & Windows questions after the poem focus on the theme of expressing grief. Before students begin reading, ask: How can writing help a person cope with change?

▶ More by This Author
Students who like "The Lost Parrot" might enjoy reading more of Nye's poems in *Words Under the Words*.

DIRECTED READING

BEFORE READING

Build Background
Scientific Context "The Lost Parrot" is about a boy who is trying to write a poem describing a bird he once had as a pet. *Parrot* is the general term for a varied group of birds, including cockatoos, macaws, and parakeets, that typically live in warm habitats, such as tropical rain forests. More commonly, the term *parrot* is used to refer to large birds with colorful feathers, strong beaks, and fleshy tongues that enable them to mimic words and even sentences.

Reader's Context At some time or other, most of us have lost something or someone we particularly valued. How did you react to your loss at the time?

Set Purpose
Skim through the poem quickly to get a general sense of what it is about. Read to find out who Carlos is and what he is like.

Analyze Literature
Symbol A **symbol** is a thing that stands for both itself and something else. Some traditional symbols include the dove for peace and the lion for courage. Writers also create symbols of their own to represent personal meanings. As you read "The Lost Parrot," decide what the bird might symbolize.

Meet the Author
Naomi Shihab Nye is an award-winning Arab-American poet. Born in 1952 to an American mother and a Palestinian father, she began to write poetry as a child and had her first poems published when she was seven. Her family later moved to San Antonio, which is still her home. After college, she worked as a poet in the schools, encouraging students to explore the material of their own lives through words. "The Lost Parrot" grew out of this experience.

Use Reading Skills
Compare and Contrast
When you compare and contrast, you try to determine what is similar and what is different between two or more things. As you read the poem, compare and contrast the speaker and Carlos. What traits do they share? What makes them different from one another? Use a Venn diagram like the one below.

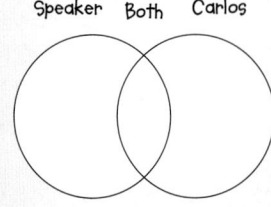

Words in Use

Teaching Words
kooky, 575
unofficial, 575

KEY TERMS

Common Core State Standards
Reading Literature
RL.1
Writing
W.1, W.10

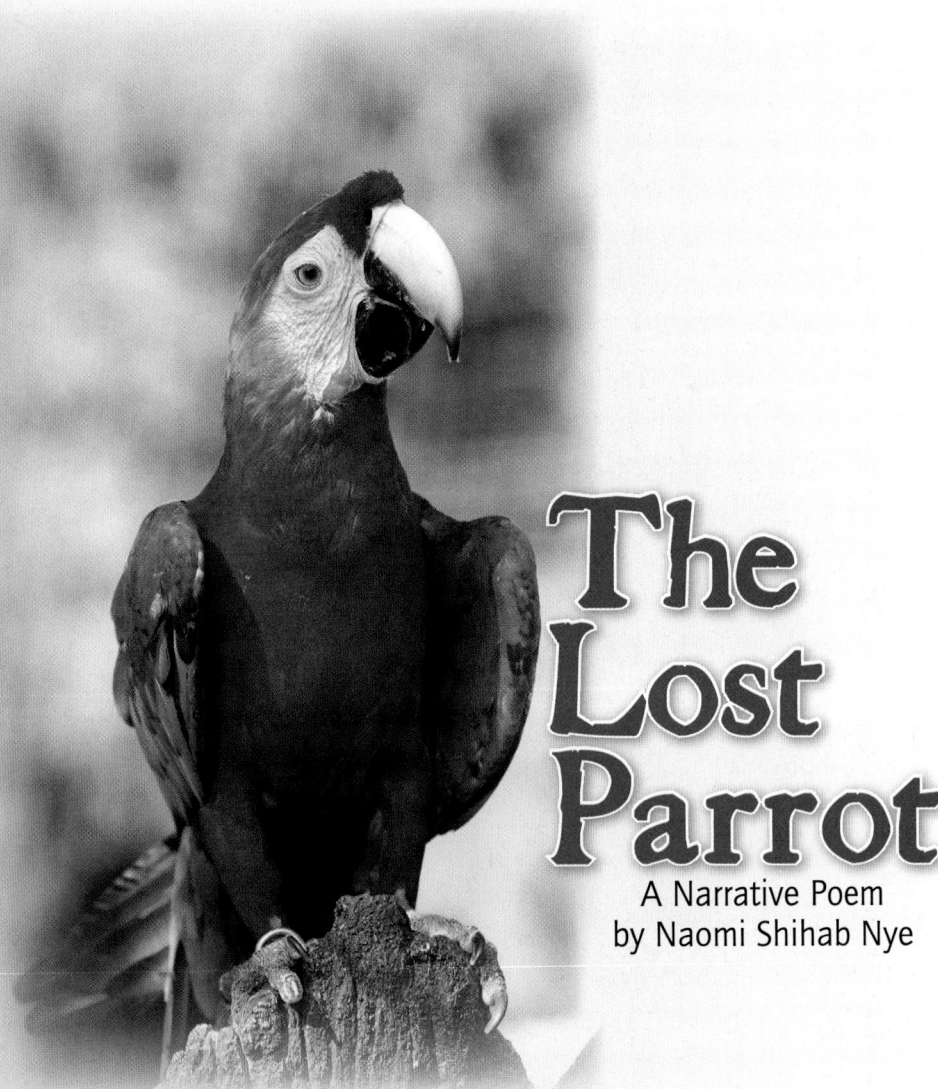

The Lost Parrot

A Narrative Poem
by Naomi Shihab Nye

Carlos bites the end of his pencil
He's trying to write a dream-poem, but waves at me, frowning

    I had a parrot

He talks slowly, like his voice travels far
5 to get out of his body

    A dream-parrot?

Teach the Selection

Summary
The poem describes a young boy named Carlos trying to write poetry for his class. The subject of his work is a lost parrot. The speaker wonders about losing things we love or things that inspire us.

Science Connection
Wild Parrots Flocks of wild parrots have become established in several parts of the United States. Scientists believe these flocks consist of birds that were caught in the wild and escaped during shipment. They don't think the flocks are pet birds that escaped from their owners, because pet birds are not likely to have survival skills such as finding food and water and avoiding predators. Wild-caught birds have these skills and can thrive in the warm climates of Florida, California, and Texas.

Analyze Literature
Characterization Ask students what lines 1–5 reveal about Carlos. (He is nervous and unhappy. The way his voice is described suggests that he is depressed.)

TEACHING NOTE

Text Structure
Draw students' attention to the unconventional structure of "The Lost Parrot," noting the indents, line breaks, and spacing. Explain that free verse allows the poet to create a structure that helps convey the message or theme.

Read through the poem with students, stopping to discuss how Nye's structural choices affect meaning.

Program Resources

Planning and Assessment
Program Planning Guide, Selection Lesson Plan
E-Lesson Planner
Assessment Guide, Lesson Test
ExamView

Technology Tools
Interactive Student Text on CD
Visual Teaching Package
Audio Library
mirrorsandwindows.com

Meeting the Standards
Poetry: Unit 6, Directed Reading, pp. 50–55

Differentiating Instruction
Developing Readers, Take Notes, pp. 46–48

Analyze Literature

Narrative Poetry Ask students to identify narrative elements in the poem. Have them focus on setting, characters, and conflict.

Use Reading Skills

Compare and Contrast Ask students to compare the teacher's attitude about the parrot with the class's attitude. (The class is bored with the parrot, but the teacher wants Carlos to write more about it.) **A**

Use Reading Skills

Analyze Effects of Form on Meaning Point out the extra spaces between words in line 24 and ask what feeling Nye conveys with these spaces. (They convey halting speech; it's possible that losing his parrot is so painful, Carlos can barely speak about it.) **B**

Analyze Literature

Symbol Have students discuss whether the parrot is a meaningful symbol in this poem. Most will say it's a good symbol because it is beautiful and elusive; it has flown away into the unknown, yet it may return. Conclude by asking what the bird symbolizes.

 Answer: Students might suggest that any act of personal expression can help people deal with change or loss.

No, a real parrot!
Write about it

He squirms, looks nervous, everyone else is almost finished
10   and he hasn't started

    It left
    What left?
    The parrot

He hunches over the table, pencil gripped in fist,
15   shaping the heavy letters
Days later we will write story-poems, sound-poems,
but always the same subject for Carlos

    It left

A   He will insist on reading it and the class will look puzzled
  20 The class is tired of the parrot

    Write more, Carlos
    I can't

    Why not?

B   I don't know   where   it went

25 Each day when I leave he stares at the ceiling
Maybe he is planning an expedition
into the back streets of San Antonio
armed with nets and ripe mangoes
He will find the parrot nesting in a rain gutter
30 This time he will guard it carefully, make sure it stays

Before winter comes and his paper goes white
in all directions

Before anything else he loves
gets away ❖

 When have you tried to use art, such as writing or drawing, to help cope with a loss or a change in your life? Why might creative acts help people deal with loss or change?

Differentiated Instruction

Reading Proficiency

Reading the poem aloud will help students appreciate how free verse develops a dramatic impact. Model a dramatic reading of the poem, or have students listen to the recording in the Audio Library. Then divide the class into mixed-ability groups of four students. Allow each group to divide up the poem for an oral reading. Less-confident readers may prefer to have fewer lines. Remind students to pause where a pause is indicated by spacing or punctuation. Have them practice reading their lines with expression and dramatic emphasis. Then have each group perform a dramatic reading of the poem for the class.

Find Meaning

1. (a) What is Carlos trying to write a poem about? (b) What are the only words he is able to write? (c) Why do you think he is unable to write more?

2. (a) What does the speaker imagine Carlos is planning? (b) Why does the speaker think Carlos wants to do this?

Analyze Literature

Symbol Symbols can be either traditional—such as a lamb for innocence—or personal, created by a writer to express some special meaning. In this poem, does the parrot function as a traditional symbol or a personal symbol? What do you think the parrot represents to Carlos? What do you think the bird represents to the speaker? Record your thoughts in a two-column chart.

Make Judgments

3. (a) What words and phrases does the speaker use to describe Carlos? (b) How would you sum up the speaker's description of Carlos?

4. What impression of the speaker do you get from this poem?

5. What is being compared in lines 31–32, "Before winter comes and his paper goes white / in all directions"?

6. Why do you think the parrot is so important to Carlos?

Symbol	Meaning
Parrot	

Extend Understanding

Writing Options

Creative Writing According to Naomi Shihab Nye, the images on which a dream poem is based can occur during either sleep or daydreams. She notes, "These can be kooky things, impossible things, wished-for things." She also urges students to "stay in the dream," and not conclude their poems by stating that they woke up. Use Nye's guidelines to write a **dream poem** of your own.

Persuasive Writing Poet William Stafford has described Naomi Shihab Nye as "a champion of the literature of encouragement." Use information from both Meet the Author and "The Lost Parrot" to write a **persuasive paragraph** supporting this view of Nye. Begin your paragraph with a thesis statement, and end it with a summary of all your paragraph's main points. Then exchange your paragraph with a partner.

Collaborative Learning

Speaking and Listening People experience many types of loss throughout life. Family members and friends die; homes and possessions are destroyed by storms, fires, and other disasters. People deal with these losses in very different ways. With other students, have a discussion exploring the effectiveness of various strategies for coping with loss.

Media Literacy

Wild Parrots The award-winning 2003 documentary *The Wild Parrots of Telegraph Hill* presents the fascinating experiences of Mark Bittner, who became the unofficial caretaker of flocks of wild parrots living around San Francisco. Working with a group of classmates, view the film and discuss how the film explores the relationship between Bittner and these birds.

Go to **www.mirrorsandwindows.com** for more.

Review the Selection

Find Meaning

1. (a) Carlos is trying to write about a parrot. (b) He can only write "It left." (c) He is overcome by sadness.

2. (a) The speaker imagines Carlos is planning an expedition to find his lost parrot. (b) Carlos might want to find the parrot so he can take better care of it this time.

Make Judgments

3. (a) Carlos bites the end of his pencil, frowns, speaks slowly, squirms, looks nervous, hunches over the table, and stares at the ceiling. (b) Carlos is shy, insecure, and capable of strong feelings.

4. The speaker is a creative, sympathetic, imaginative teacher.

5. Answers will vary. Students may say the lines compare paper and snow. Winter could endanger the bird, and thinking of the bird in danger makes Carlos unable to write about it—his paper stays white.

6. Carlos has lost something he loves.

Analyze Literature

Symbol In this poem, the parrot functions as a personal symbol. To Carlos, the parrot might represent lost happiness. To the speaker, it might represent something basic and mysterious about Carlos himself.

Rubrics for Writing Options

You can adapt this as a checklist for students to use as they write.

Creative Writing

☐ Does the poem "stay in the dream"?

☐ Does the poem include kooky, impossible, or "wished-for" things?

Persuasive Writing

☐ Does the paragraph support Stafford's view of Nye?

☐ Does the paragraph begin with a thesis statement?

☐ Does the paragraph end with a summary of main points?

For My Father

A Narrative Poem by Janice Mirikitani

Preview the Selection

At a Glance
Directed Reading
- Reading Level: Moderate
- Difficulty Considerations: Figurative language and background
- Ease Factor: Vocabulary

Objectives
Studying this lesson will enable students to
- use reading skills such as analyzing text structure
- identify hyperbole
- describe Janice Mirikitani and discuss her use of strong emotions in her work
- appreciate a poem about harsh realities

Launch the Lesson
Tell students they will be reading "For My Father," a narrative poem about someone who had a difficult childhood. Ask students why they think people write poetry that expresses painful emotions. Then, ask why people might read this kind of poetry.

▶ More by This Author
Students who like "For My Father" might be interested in *Ayumi: A Japanese American Anthology*, Mirikitani's collection of writing and graphics from four generations of Japanese Americans.

BEFORE READING

Build Background
Historical Context Near the turn of the twentieth century, many Japanese immigrants made a living as strawberry farmers, especially on the rich farmlands of California, Washington, and Oregon. World War II and the bombing of Pearl Harbor led to the internment of thousands of Japanese Americans and immigrants by the U.S. government. Most Japanese-American strawberry farmers did not return to farming after World War II.

Reader's Context What memories do you have from your early childhood that are impossible to forget? Why are they so vivid in your mind?

Set Purpose
Look at the structure, or the way the words are arranged on the page, in this poem. What can you predict about the poem? Revise your prediction as you read.

Analyze Literature
Hyperbole Exaggeration used for effect is called **hyperbole.** For example, saying someone ate a mountain of spaghetti is an exaggeration. Its effect might be to make someone smile, or to make someone understand that overeating is taking place. As you read "For My Father," identify uses of hyperbole and their effects on you.

Meet the Author
Janice Mirikitani (b. 1942) spent the first years of her life in an internment camp. Her family, along with thousands of other Japanese Americans, most of whom were U.S. citizens, had been interned against their will after Japan's attack on Pearl Harbor during World War II. In her poetry, Mirikitani often expresses her anger regarding this experience, as well as strong themes of family and her Japanese-American identity.

Use Reading Skills
Analyze Text Structure
When you read a poem, ask yourself why it takes a particular form or arrangement on the page. Think about how the author may want the poem to be viewed or read and why. As you read "For My Father," use an organizer like this one to sum up the effect of each stanza.

Structure	Effect
stanza 2: four lines	describes child's thoughts

Preview Vocabulary
hack (hak) *v.*, chop or cut forcefully

shield (shēld) *v.*, protect, guard, or defend against

Words in Use

Preview Vocabulary	Teaching Words
hack, 578	**immigrants,** 576
shield, 578	**internment,** 576
	vivid, 576
	inadequate, 578

KEY TERMS
NARRATIVE POEM, 576
HYPERBOLE, 576
STANZA, 576
TONE, 579
THESIS, 579

Common Core State Standards
Reading Literature
RL.1, RL.5

For My Father

A Narrative Poem by Janice Mirikitani

577

Summary

The speaker's father came from Japan and grows strawberries for a living. Unable to buy strawberries, the speaker steals them and is punished by his or her father. Yet the man sells strawberries to white families even though the children point at the speaker's eyes. The speaker is frustrated that he or she is unable to touch their father's strength.

MIRRORS & WINDOWS

The Mirrors & Windows questions after the poem focus on the theme of experiences. Before students begin reading, ask: Which of your parents' past experiences do you know a lot about? How did you learn what you know?

Cultural Connection
Traditional Fatherhood

Traditionally in Japanese culture, the father was expected to work long hours to support his family. Although the father spent little time with them, he exercised a great deal of authority over family members and took responsibility for their behavior. The father was a strict authority figure. To maintain that authority, he kept a certain distance from the family.

Program Resources

Planning and Assessment
Program Planning Guide, Selection Lesson Plan
E-Lesson Planner
Assessment Guide, Lesson Test
ExamView

Technology Tools
Interactive Student Text on CD
Visual Teaching Package
Audio Library
mirrorsandwindows.com

Meeting the Standards
Poetry: Unit 6, Directed Reading, pp. 56–60

Differentiating Instruction
Advanced Students, Character Analysis Study, pp. 36–37

Teach the Selection

Analyze Literature

Hyperbole Have students explain the image the speaker creates of the father through exaggeration. (He is burdened by the weight of having left his cultural heritage behind, only to face the indignities of internment.) **A**

Use Reading Skills

Analyze Text Structure Ask students what shift is indicated by indentation of the second stanza. (The speaker shifts from describing the father to telling about something the children did.)

Analyze Literature

Identify Multiple Levels of Meaning When they are done reading, ask students whose tears are referred to in the last line. (They may be the tears of the children or of the father.) **B**

Answer: Most will say parents' experiences affect how they act toward other people, including their children.

History Connection

Japanese Internment *Answer:* Answers will vary. Students may say that this information helps them feel more empathy toward the father. **C**

A
He came over the ocean
carrying Mt. Fuji[1]
on his back/Tule Lake[2] on his chest
<u>hacked</u> through the brush
5   of deserts
and made them grow
strawberries

        we stole berries
        from the stem
10   we could not afford them
        for breakfast

his eyes held
nothing
as he whipped us
15 for stealing.

the desert had dried
his soul.

wordless
he sold
20 the rich,
full berries
to hakujines[3]
whose children
pointed at our eyes

25   they ate fresh
        strawberries
        with cream.

Father,
I wanted to scream
30 at your silence.
Your strength
was a stranger
I could never touch.

iron
35 in your eyes
to <u>shield</u>
the pain
to shield desert-like wind
from patches
40 of strawberries
grown
from
tears. ✤

B

---

1. **Mt. Fuji.** Sacred mountain in Japan; a symbol of Japan
2. **Tule Lake.** Camp in Arkansas where Japanese-American people were interned from 1942–1946
3. **hakujines.** Japanese term meaning Caucasians

hack (hak) *v.*, chop or cut forcefully
shield (shēld) *v.*, protect, guard, or defend against

HISTORY ▶▶ CONNECTION

Japanese Internment When Japan bombed Pearl Harbor in Hawaii during World War II, the U.S. government reacted by officially entering the war. The government also began rounding up Japanese Americans in the United States and interning, or imprisoning, them in camps against their will. Tule Lake was the largest of all these internment camps, and life there was harsh. Japanese Americans were crammed into poor housing and received inadequate food and medical care. In addition, like the Japanese Americans who were interned in other camps, they lost everything they had. How does this affect your understanding of the speaker's father? **C**

 What kinds of difficulties have your parents faced? How can parents' experiences affect the lives of their children?

Differentiated Instruction

Reading Proficiency

Students may find it difficult to read the poem fluently, because it lacks standard sentence punctuation and capitalization. Tell students that in "For My Father," sometimes punctuation clues will tell them where the sentences end, and sometimes the extra space that signals the end of a stanza will tell them where to pause.

Have students take turns reading portions of the poem aloud. Point out that lines 34–43 make up a sentence fragment; guide students to rephrase them as a complete sentence (it could begin "Iron is in your eyes" or "There is iron in your eyes," for example).

Find Meaning

1. Who is the speaker of this poem?
2. What does the father do that makes the speaker so angry?
3. (a) Who do you think the "we" are in stanza 2? (b) Who are "they" in stanza 6?

Analyze Literature

Hyperbole Where did you find hyperbole as you read the poem? What effect did it have on you as a reader? Make a chart like this one to record two or more examples of hyperbole from the poem and to reflect on the emotions or reactions they caused. Then explain how the hyperbole helped you understand the father, the speaker, or the situation better.

Hyperbole	Effect
hacked	sounds angry

Make Judgments

4. (a) Why do you think the father in this poem behaves so harshly to the speaker? (b) How does the speaker feel about it now?
5. In the middle of the poem, the speaker makes a shift in who he or she is addressing. What are the effects of this shift on the reader?
6. This is a short poem—it has just 113 words. How well does the author characterize the father in this short space? Explain.

Extend Understanding

Writing Options

Creative Writing What would you like to say to a parent or older person about an experience from your past? Write a **personal letter** to someone you are close to about your own experience.

Expository Writing In a few words, sum up your personal response to this poem. Then think about how your response would have been different if the poem had been written in a less emotional tone or with less hyperbole. Write a **literary response** in which you evaluate the difference. Be sure to begin with a clear thesis that states your opinion. Use evidence, such as details, quotes, and examples from the poem to support your opinion.

Lifelong Learning

Research and Report Mt. Fuji is Japan's largest and most majestic mountain. It has been the inspiration of writers, artists, and poets for hundreds of years, and serves as a symbol of Japan throughout the world. Research the mountain, its landscapes, geography, climate, and neighboring inhabitants. Prepare a report for your class, including visual aids.

Critical Literacy

Write a Dialogue Imagine that the father in this poem read the poem and now wants to respond to the speaker. What do you think he might say to the speaker? How might the speaker reply? Create and write the dialogue you imagine taking place between the speaker and the father. Use natural, everyday language and clearly convey the feelings of each person.

Go to www.mirrorsandwindows.com for more.

FOR MY FATHER **579**

Review the Selection

Find Meaning

1. The speaker is a Japanese American who lived on a strawberry farm with an immigrant father.
2. He whips the children for stealing strawberries that he grows to sell to white people. He is unapproachable.
3. (a) "We" are the father's children. (b) "They" are the white children.

Make Judgments

4. (a) Students may say the father is harsh because of his hard life. He is full of pain, but he stays distant to hide his pain and appear strong. (b) In addition to expressing anger, the speaker seems disappointed and sad.
5. The shift gives the reader insight into the real source of the speaker's anger and frustration—the father's emotional distance.
6. The author creates a strong characterization through well-chosen words.

Analyze Literature

Hyperbole Students may cite *hacked, deserts, eyes held nothing, whipped, dried his soul, iron,* and *grown from tears.* Students should understand the speaker's anger and sadness, the father's coldness, and the harsh, inhospitable land in which he worked.

Rubrics for Writing Options

You can adapt this as a checklist for students to use as they write.

Creative Writing

☐ Does the letter relate a past experience?
☐ Is the letter personal rather than businesslike?

Expository Writing

☐ Does the response evaluate the difference between the poem as it is and what it might be if it were less emotional?
☐ Does the response have a clear thesis?
☐ Does the response include evidence from the poem, such as details, quotes, and examples, to support the thesis?

At a Glance
Directed Reading
- Reading Level: Easy
- Difficulty Considerations: Irony and metaphor
- Ease Factors: Length and vocabulary

Objectives
Studying this lesson will enable students to
- use reading skills such as evaluating cause and effect
- analyze irony
- describe the literary accomplishments of Janet Wong and discuss her use of imagery
- appreciate two poems about family relationships

Launch the Lesson
Tell students that "Money Orders" and "Sisters" are about tensions or resentments among family members. Ask students how they would deal with a relative who is inconsiderate.

Summary
The speaker's family lives off of little to provide for distant relatives, who live more extravagantly.

KEY TERMS
IRONY, 580
CAUSE AND EFFECT, 580
COMPARE AND CONTRAST, 583
THESIS STATEMENT, 583

Money Order and Sisters
Poems by Janet S. Wong

BEFORE READING

Build Background
Cultural Context Both of the poems you are about to read use food imagery typical of Asian and Asian-American dishes: rice, fish, tofu, and ginger. Rice is the most important staple of the Asian diet, and variations of fish and rice or salt fish and rice are typical main dishes. Tofu and ginger are common ingredients in the cuisine of China, Korea, and other Asian countries.

Reader's Context Do you have any relatives you have never met? What do you know about them? What do you think they know about you?

Set Purpose
Read the titles of the poems and preview the illustrations that accompany them. What can you predict about the content of each poem? Revise your prediction after you read the first stanza of each poem.

Analyze Literature
Irony The contrast between what is expected and what actually happens is **irony**. Often you can identify irony in literature by noticing outcomes to situations that seem to be the opposite of what you, as a reader, expected. This type of irony is called situational irony. As you read "Money Order" and "Sisters," look for examples of irony.

Meet the Author
Janet S. Wong was born in Los Angeles, California, in 1962 to a Korean mother and a Chinese father. Although Wong was educated as an attorney and has practiced law, she has made her reputation as an author of children's poetry. Her poems often use simple words and forms, as well as dashes of humor or irony, to present insight into issues of Asian-American identity. Wong lives on Bainbridge Island, Washington, with her husband and son. The following poems are taken from Wong's collection *A Suitcase of Seaweed and Other Poems*.

Use Reading Skills
Evaluate Cause and Effect When you evaluate cause and effect, you are looking for a logical relationship between a cause, or causes, and one or more effects. When you read poetry, you often have to infer causes and effects. As you read "Money Order," use an organizer like this one to identify causes and effects that you can infer from the poem.

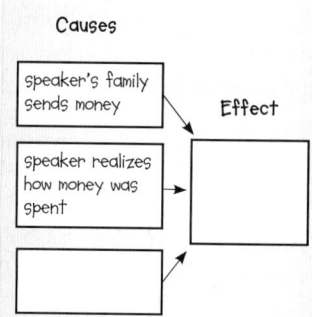

Causes

| speaker's family sends money |
| speaker realizes how money was spent |

Effect

Program Resources

Planning and Assessment
Program Planning Guide, Selection Lesson Plan
E-Lesson Planner
Assessment Guide, Lesson Test
ExamView

Technology Tools
Interactive Student Text on CD
Visual Teaching Package
Audio Library
mirrorsandwindows.com

Meeting the Standards
Poetry: Unit 6, Directed Reading, 61–66

Common Core State Standards

Reading Literature
RL.7

Money Order

A Narrative Poem by Janet S. Wong

We eat salt fish[1] and rice,
night after night after night,
to save some money
to send
5 to cousins
I never have seen

who used our money last year
to buy a color TV,
so they could watch
10 rich Americans
eating
steak and potatoes. ❖

A

B

---

1. **salt fish.** Fish that has been preserved with salt; salt fish is a cheaper alternative to fresh fish

581

The Mirrors & Windows questions after the poem focus on the theme of familiar feelings. Before students begin reading, ask: Which emotion is harder to manage, resentment or jealousy?

Use Reading Skills

Evaluate Cause and Effect Ask students what causes the family to eat salt fish and rice every night. (They are trying to save money to send to distant family members.) **A**

Analyze Literature

Irony Point out the situational irony in this stanza. Say that it seems the cousins need the money less than the speaker's family, because they use the money to buy a color TV. **B**

Use Reading Skills

Compare and Contrast To help students better understand the situational irony, ask them to compare and contrast what each branch of the family believes about the other branch. Then describe the probable reality of the situation. (The speaker's family believes that the cousins are struggling and need financial help. The cousins believe that the speaker's family is well-to-do. The reality seems to be that the speaker's family is struggling, while the cousins are living comfortably.)

Grammar Skills

Infinitive Phrases

Explain that an infinitive is a verb form preceded by the word *to*, such as *to eat, to walk,* or *to cry.* (Emphasize that it is a verb form, not a type of prepositional phrase.) An infinitive phrase is a sentence part made up of an infinitive and all of its modifiers and complements. Sometimes the *to* is left out of an infinitive phrase; instead, it is understood.

Infinitive phrases can function as nouns, adjectives, or adverbs. Point out the infinitive phrases in "Money Order" as examples. Then ask students to complete each of these sentences with an infinitive phrase that uses the verb in parentheses.

1. She doesn't like having _____ every night. (eat)
2. Her cousins like _____. (watch)
3. Her cousins don't need _____. (use)

Sisters

A Lyric Poem by Janet S. Wong

She calls me tofu[1]
because I am so soft,
easily falling apart.

I wish I were tough
and full of fire, like ginger[2]—
like her. ❖

---

1. **tofu.** White-colored, protein-rich but bland-tasting food made from soybeans
2. **ginger.** Root that is usually sliced, diced, or grated to give a strong, spicy flavor and aroma to a dish

MIRRORS & WINDOWS What feelings are expressed in these poems that you have felt too? Why might these be common feelings?

Summary

The speaker would like to be tougher, like his or her sister.

Analyze Literature

Symbol Point out that the speaker interprets the tofu comparison negatively. Ask students to suggest adjectives with positive connotations that describe tofu (such as *versatile, adaptable, tender,* and *delicate*).

Use Reading Skills

Compare and Contrast Ask students to compare and contrast tofu and ginger as foods. Ask: "Which is more nourishing and adaptable?" (Opinions may vary. Most will say ginger has a distinctive taste that is hard to change, while tofu goes with a variety of flavors.)

MIRRORS & WINDOWS *Answer:* Students may have felt resentful or inadequate. Students may say these are common feelings because people naturally compare themselves to others.

Common Core State Standards

Reading Literature
RL.1

Differentiated Instruction

Reading Proficiency

Note that "Money Order" is one long sentence. To help students process the information in the poem, read aloud two or three lines at a time, stopping to ask questions and paraphrase. For example, stop after line 3 and ask, "Why are they trying to save money?" Then read lines 4–6 to answer the question. When you read lines 7 and 8, back up to line 5, if necessary, to clarify that the antecedent for *who* is *cousins.*

Work with students to express each main idea in the poem as a separate sentence. Then read the entire poem aloud in an exasperated tone of voice to help students understand how the rush of words helps express the speaker's feelings.

Find Meaning

1. In "Money Order," who is the speaker referring to with the use of "we"?
2. In "Money Order," where do you think the cousins live?
3. What do you learn about the speaker in "Sisters"?

Analyze Literature

Irony Several details help create the irony in "Money Order." For example, the cousins probably think of the speaker's family as rich, but what is really true? The cousins may also have a vision of the speaker's family living like the Americans on television live. Use a chart to record details from the poem that are ironic, and explain how they suggest the opposite of what may be true.

Make Judgments

4. How does the speaker in "Money Order" feel about sending money to her cousins?
5. (a) What does the title "Money Order" refer to? (b) Why is it a good title for the poem?
6. (a) In "Sisters," how are the sisters different? (b) How are they alike?

Detail	Irony
eating salt fish and rice	

Extend Understanding

Writing Options

Creative Writing Travel brochures often make places seem fabulous—even if the picture they paint is not always accurate. Make a **travel brochure** that tells about your own city or town. Instead of presenting only the best things about your town, however, be as realistic about it as you can. Be as truthful as you would be to good friends or relatives who are thinking about moving there.

Expository Writing What makes you different from other members of your family? What traits do you share with siblings, parents, grandparents, aunts, or uncles? Write a **compare-and-contrast** essay in which you describe the traits that you share with members of your family and the things that make you unique. Be sure to include a thesis statement and support.

Collaborative Learning

Discuss and Speculate The speakers in both "Money Order" and "Sisters" see themselves in comparison to others. In a small group, discuss whether people always define or view themselves, at least in some ways, in comparison with others. Is it possible for us to define ourselves outside the context of those around us? Brainstorm a list of reasons that support your group's decision.

Media Literacy

Contrast Appearance and Reality One reason for the popularity of so-called "reality" television shows may be that many media images are so far from reality. With a partner, discuss the difference between how reality is portrayed in television shows, ads, games, magazines, and so on, and how you see yourself, your own life, and the lives of others around you. Come up with at least three contrasts. Cite specific ads, shows, movies, or other works on which you based each contrast.

 Go to **www.mirrorsandwindows.com** for more.

Review the Selections

Find Meaning

1. The speaker could be referring to the speaker and family, Asian Americans, and/or recent immigrants
2. They live in the place from which the speaker's family emigrated.
3. The speaker is female; she is soft and fragile, but would prefer to be tough and fiery.

Make Judgments

4. The speaker feels resentful.
5. (a) It refers to the way the money is sent to the cousins. (b) Accept any logical explanation. To the speaker, sending money is a kind of "order" that cannot be disobeyed; also, the word *order* suggests a progression, in which some family members emigrate first, sending money home to help others come next.
6. (a) One is soft and falls apart easily; the other is tough and full of fire. One calls the other a name; the other is quiet. One appears to be satisfied with who she is; the other is not. (b) They are alike because they compare each other to foods.

Analyze Literature

Irony Students may list details such as eating salt fish and rice while, ironically, the cousins may think they eat steak and potatoes; depriving themselves of tasty food while the cousins splurge by buying a color TV; and thinking their cousins need their money, while the cousins treat it as a windfall.

Rubrics for Writing Options

You can adapt this as a checklist for students to use as they write.

Creative Writing

☐ Does the travel brochure present a realistic view?

☐ Is the travel brochure intended to help people accurately evaluate the town or city as a possible home?

Expository Writing

☐ Does the essay compare and contrast the writer and his or her family members?

☐ Does the essay include a thesis statement and support?

Preview the Selection

At a Glance
Independent Reading
- Reading Level: Easy
- Difficulty Consideration: Metaphor
- Ease Factor: Length

Objectives
Reading this selection will enable students to do the following:
- read with developing fluency
- read silently with comprehension

Launch the Lesson
Ask students whether they would like to be famous. Then have them read to find out if they agree with the opinion the poem expresses.

Summary
The speaker reflects on being "nobody." The poem could be read as a celebration of obscurity and privacy.

 The Mirrors & Windows questions after the poem focus on the theme of escaping detection. Before students begin reading, ask: What advantages do introverts have over extroverts?

TEACHING NOTE
Although this selection is presented in the student edition as an independent reading, teaching support has been provided should you choose to cover it in class.

La Grande Guerre, 1964.
René Magritte. Private collection.

I'm Nobody

A Lyric Poem
by Emily Dickinson

I'm Nobody! Who are you?
Are you—Nobody—too?
Then there's a pair of us!
Don't tell! they'd banish us—you know!

How dreary—to be—Somebody!
How public—like a Frog—
To tell your name—the livelong June—
To an admiring Bog![1] ❖

---

1. **bog.** Marsh or swamp

In her own time, **Emily Dickinson**'s use of punctuation and syntax was considered bizarre. However, she is now considered one of the greatest innovators in American poetry. Dickinson was born in Amherst, Massachusetts, in 1830 and rarely strayed beyond its borders. She was notoriously secretive and published very few poems in her own lifetime. After Dickinson's death in 1886, "corrected" versions of her collected poems appeared, in which her lines were changed to suit the tastes of the day. Not until 1955 were Dickinson's poems finally published in their original unedited state.

584

Program Resources

Planning and Assessment
Program Planning Guide, Selection Lesson Plan
E-Lesson Planner
Assessment Guide, Lesson Test
ExamView

Technology Tools
Interactive Student Text on CD
Visual Teaching Package
Audio Library
mirrorsandwindows.com

Meeting the Standards
Poetry: Unit 6, Independent Reading, pp. 67–73

Differentiating Instruction
English Language Learners, Compare and Contrast, pp. 146–151

Common Core State Standards
Reading Literature
RL.10

When have you felt it was better to be unseen or unnoticed? Why did you feel this way? When might being "somebody" have its disadvantages?

Analyze and Extend

1. In the opening stanza, to whom do you think the speaker is directing these questions? Explain.
2. What do you think the speaker means by the statement, "they'd banish us—you know!"
3. (a) In the second stanza, to what does the speaker compare being "Somebody"?
   (b) What do you think the speaker's attitude toward "Somebodies" is?

Expository Writing Tone is the author's or speaker's attitude toward his or her subject. What do you think the tone of this poem is? Is it humorous? Is it angry? Write a **literary** **analysis** in which you analyze the poem's tone. Include a thesis statement, and support your claims with evidence from the text. When you are finished, compare your response with that of a partner.

Lifelong Learning Use the library to locate and read more of Emily Dickinson's poetry. *The Poems of Emily Dickinson,* edited by Thomas H. Johnson, contains all 1,775 of her poems. Read several poems and try to locate common themes, topics, and stylistic elements such as rhyme and rhythm. Write a paragraph in which you describe Dickinson's style and her common subjects and themes.

Go to www.mirrorsandwindows.com for more.

I'M NOBODY **585**

Teach the Selection

Analyze Literature
Hyperbole Ask students what the exaggeration in line 4 reveals about the speaker's attitude.

Use Reading Skills
Summarize Have volunteers summarize the main idea of the poem in their own words.

 Answer: Personal responses will vary. "Somebodies" may have a greater burden of expectations.

Analyze and Extend
1. The speaker is directing the questions to the reader, using second-person pronouns.
2. There is general prejudice against those who prefer a private life.
3. (a) The speaker compares it to being a frog. (b) The speaker is dismissive or critical of them.

Rubric for Expository Writing
You can adapt this as a checklist for students to use as they write.

☐ Does the analysis describe the poem's tone?
☐ Does the analysis include a thesis statement?
☐ Does the analysis include evidence from the poem?

Words in Use

Selection Words
banish, 584
dreary, 584

Teaching Words
bizarre, 584
innovators, 584
notoriously, 584

KEY TERMS
LYRIC POEM, 584
PUNCTUATION, 584
STANZA, 585
TONE, 585
THESIS STATEMENT, 585
THEME, 585
RHYME, 585
RHYTHM, 585

Refugee Ship

A Lyric Poem by Lorna Dee Cervantes

Provence Kitchen, 20th century. Josephine Trotter. Private collection.

Like wet cornstarch, I slide
past my grandmother's eyes. Bible
at her side, she removes her glasses.
The pudding thickens.
5 Mama raised me without language,

I'm orphaned from my Spanish name.
The words are foreign, stumbling
on my tongue. I see in the mirror
my reflection: bronzed skin, black hair.

10 I feel I am a captive
aboard the refugee ship.
The ship that will never dock.
El barco que nunca atraca.[1] ❧

---

1. *El barco...atraca.* The ship that never docks (Spanish)

Lorna Dee Cervantes was born in San Francisco in 1954. When she was a young person, her parents forbade her and her brother from speaking Spanish in the house. Throughout her life, she has been active in civil rights and political movements, including the American Indian Movement. In 1981, she won the American Book Award for *Emplumada,* her first collection of poems. Cervantes has also been awarded grants for poetry from the National Endowment for the Arts, the Paterson Prize for Poetry, and the Latino Literature Award.

586

Preview the Selection

At a Glance
Independent Reading
- Reading Level: Easy
- Difficulty Consideration: Topic
- Ease Factor: Vocabulary

Objectives
Reading this selection will enable students to do the following:
- read with developing fluency
- read silently with comprehension

Launch the Lesson
Ask: "Why do you think people care about feeling connected to their cultural heritage?" Allow time for a brief discussion.

Use Reading Strategies
Clarify Point out the image of wet cornstarch in line 1 and explain that cornstarch is used in pudding (line 4). Ask students to suggest what these images mean.

 MIRRORS & WINDOWS The Mirrors & Windows questions after the poem focus on the theme of isolation. Before students begin reading, ask: What about your heritage means the most to you?

TEACHING NOTE
Although this selection is presented in the student edition as an independent reading, teaching support has been provided should you choose to cover it in class.

Common Core State Standards
Reading Literature
RL.10

Program Resources

Planning and Assessment
Program Planning Guide, Selection Lesson Plan
E-Lesson Planner
Assessment Guide, Lesson Test
ExamView

Technology Tools
Interactive Student Text on CD
Visual Teaching Package
Audio Library
mirrorsandwindows.com

Meeting the Standards
Poetry: Unit 6, Independent Reading, pp. 67–73

MIRRORS & WINDOWS When have you felt cut off from your past or from your family? How did you respond to these feelings? How important is it for people to hold on to their heritage?

Analyze and Extend

1. Explain what you think the speaker means by the comparison made in the opening two lines of the poem.
2. (a) From what is the speaker orphaned? (b) What do you think this means?
3. Is a refugee ship an appropriate symbol for the speaker's situation? Why or why not?

Creative Writing Imagine that you are the speaker in this poem. How would it feel to be in this situation? Write a **diary entry** in the speaker's voice about your feelings. Use information from the poem to help you describe these feelings and your relationship with your mother and grandmother. Title your diary entry "Refugee Ship."

Collaborative Learning Gather in small groups and discuss what the "refugee ship" symbolizes. Does it symbolize the speaker's feelings? Her relationship with her family? Her relationship with her heritage? Be specific. One person in your group should act as secretary and record your discussion and your conclusions about the meaning of this symbol. When you are done, share your thoughts with the class.

 Go to www.mirrorsandwindows.com for more.

Summary

The speaker explains that his or her mother raised them "without language" and they feel orphaned from their "Spanish name." Using the image of a ship that never docks, the speaker expresses the feeling of being removed from one culture, but unable to move into another.

Analyze Literature

Voice Ask students to analyze the word choice, sentence structure, and tone to describe the speaker's voice.

Answer: Answers will vary. Most will say it is good to know and appreciate one's heritage.

Analyze and Extend

1. The speaker goes unnoticed.
2. (a) The speaker is orphaned from his or her Spanish name. (b) The speaker feels disconnected from his or her cultural heritage.
3. It conveys the sense of feeling adrift or lost.

Rubric for Creative Writing

You can adapt this as a checklist for students to use as they write.

☐ Does the diary entry express the speaker's feelings and describe relationships?
☐ Does the diary entry use information from the poem?

Words in Use

Selection Words	TeachingWords
foreign, 586	**forbade,** 586
bronzed, 586	**heritage,** 587
captive, 586	
refugee, 586	

KEY TERMS

Preview the Selection

At a Glance
Independent Reading
- Reading Level: Moderate
- Difficulty Considerations: Topic and imagery
- Ease Factor: Vocabulary

Objectives
Reading this selection will enable students to do the following:
- read with developing fluency
- read silently with comprehension

Launch the Lesson
Ask students what they know about famous volcanic eruptions. Tell them Loo-Wit is a Native American name for Mount Saint Helens in Washington State.

MIRRORS & WINDOWS The Mirrors & Windows questions after the poem focus on the theme of how we describe things. Before students begin reading, ask: What makes natural disasters disastrous?

TEACHING NOTE
Although this selection is presented in the student edition as an independent reading, teaching support has been provided should you choose to cover it in class.

Common Core State Standards

Reading Literature
RL.10

Loo Wit

A Lyric Poem
by Wendy Rose

The way they do
this old woman
no longer cares
what others think
5 but spits her black tobacco
any which way
stretching full length
from her bumpy bed.
Finally up
10 she sprinkles
ashes on the snow,
cold buttes[1]
promising nothing
but the walk
15 of winter.
Centuries of cedar
have bound her
to earth,
huckleberry ropes
20 lay prickly
on her neck.
Around her
machinery growls,
snarls and ploughs
25 great patches
of her skin.
She crouches
in the north,
her trembling
30 the source
of dawn.

---
1. buttes. Steep hills with flat tops

Wendy Rose was born in California in 1948. Her father was of Hopi descent and her mother was Miwok, a Native American tribe with traditional lands in Northern California. Much of Rose's verse explores issues of tribal identity and Rose's search for her own personal identity. The poem examines a violent natural catastrophe from a distinctly Native American perspective. As Rose has said, "For everything in this universe there is a song to accompany its existence."

588

Program Resources

Planning and Assessment
Program Planning Guide, Selection Lesson Plan
E-Lesson Planner
Assessment Guide, Lesson Test
ExamView

Technology Tools
Interactive Student Text on CD
Visual Teaching Package
Audio Library
mirrorsandwindows.com

Meeting the Standards
Poetry: Unit 6, Independent Reading, pp. 74–80

Differentiating Instruction
Advanced Students, Independent Reading Project, p. 38

Light appears
with the shudder
of her slopes,
35 the movement
of her arm.
Blackberries unravel,
stones dislodge.
It's not as if
40 they weren't warned.

She was sleeping
but she heard
the boot scrape,
the creaking floor,
45 felt the pull of the blanket
from her thin shoulder.
With one free hand
she finds her weapons
and raises them high;
50 clearing the twigs
from her throat
she sings, she sings,
shaking the sky
like a blanket about her
55 Loo-Wit[2] sings and sings and sings! ❖

---

2. **Loo-Wit.** Mount Saint Helens; this mountain, situated
in southern Washington State, erupted in 1980. It was
the most catastrophic volcanic event in the recorded
history of North America.

MIRRORS & WINDOWS

How would you describe a natural disaster? How might figurative language
and sensory details enhance your description? When might a straightforward
description using facts and figures be more effective?

Teach the Selection

Summary
This poem describes the eruption of
Mount Saint Helens (Loo-Wit) as an
old woman lying in bed who awakens
to lash out at the annoyances around
her (such as the machinery that
ploughs her skin or the ropes at her
neck). She shakes them loose, clears
her throat and sings.

Use Reading Strategies
Clarify Suggest that students use
visualization to clarify what is meant
by "the source of dawn" (page 588)
and the light that "appears with the
shudder of her slopes." (Lava shooting
from the volcano creates a light like
dawn.) **A**

Analyze Literature
Personification Ask students what
the old woman stands for in the
poem. What event do her actions
signal? (She personifies the volcano,
and her actions signal the beginning
of an eruption, as the volcano
awakens and begins to spit out ash.)

 Answer:
Using
figurative
language
and sensory details would convey
the drama of an event and the
feelings people have as they
witness it. Facts and figures would
give impressive supporting details
in a work of literature.

Words in Use

Teaching Words
descent, 588
symmetrical, 590
preceded, 590
emissions, 590
lateral, 590
intermittently, 590
catastrophic, 590

KEY TERMS
LYRIC POEM, 588
FIGURATIVE LANGUAGE, 589
SENSORY DETAIL, 589
PERSONIFICATION, 590

Independent Reading

Students who like "Loo Wit" might enjoy reading *Between Earth & Sky: Legends of Native American Sacred Places* by Joseph Bruchac.

Science Connection

Mount Saint Helens *Answer:* Warnings include belching gases and tremors. In the poem, such warnings could be the fact that the old woman "spits her black tobacco." She is "trembling," there is a "shudder of her slopes," and her arm "dislodges stones." **A**

Analyze and Extend

1. (a) The speaker compares it to an old woman. (b) It is effective because the volcano has existed for a long time and has a lot of experience.

2. The speaker may be saying the volcano is irritated by machinery that is clearing parts of its sides. Loo-Wit may also be irritable because her sleep has been disturbed. As a personified mountain, she can cause an eruption just to announce her presence and power.

3. Most will say the eruption shows how triumphant the mountain is.

Rubric for Expository Writing

You can adapt this as a checklist for students to use as they write.

☐ Does the analysis focus on the use of personification?
☐ Does the analysis include evidence from the text?

SCIENCE ▶▶ CONNECTION

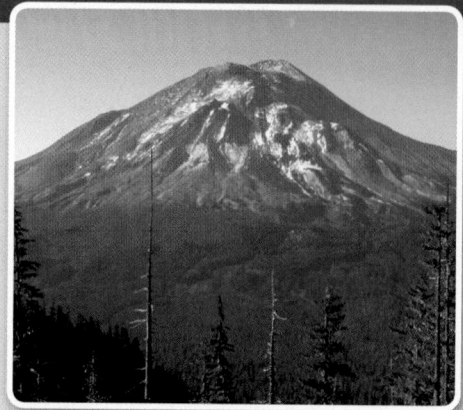

Mount Saint Helens Before 1980, Mount Saint Helens had a symmetrical cone that is now largely gone. The eruption was preceded by two months of localized earthquakes and emissions of steam. Then on the morning of May 18, 1980, the volcano erupted for nine hours, beginning with a gigantic lateral explosion that devastated more than 150 square miles, flattening forests and blocking rivers. Mount Saint Helens continued to erupt intermittently for the next three days, destroying vast amounts of wildlife and leaving fifty-seven people dead. Spewed sixteen miles into the air, volcanic ash spread over large areas of the Northwest, bringing midday darkness, disrupting travel, and causing widespread economic damage. In "Loo Wit," the speaker says, "It's not as if they weren't warned." What form might these "warnings" have taken? **A**

Analyze and Extend

1. (a) To what does the speaker compare Loo-Wit? (b) In what ways is this an effective comparison?

2. The speaker claims that around Loo-Wit "machinery growls, / snarls and ploughs / great patches / of her skin." Why do you think the speaker claims that this caused the eruption?

3. What do you think the speaker means by the poem's final line?

Expository Writing This poem uses personification, in which nonhuman things are given human characteristics. How does personification make this poem more effective?

Write a **literary analysis** of Rose's use of personification. Be sure to support your claims with evidence from the text. Then exchange your response with a classmate and discuss your reactions.

Lifelong Learning The eruption of Mount Saint Helens was catastrophic. The effects of the blast could be felt around the world. Tons of ash and rock were thrown far into the air. Use a library database to locate books about this eruption and its aftermath. Record the most interesting information you locate. Then use this material to create a poster with images and facts, and present it to the class.

Go to **www.mirrorsandwindows.com** for more.

Differentiated Instruction

Enrichment

Have two groups research and report on different aspects of Mount Saint Helens. One group can research Native American legends associated with the volcano. Ask them to give a dramatic presentation of the story of Loo-Wit to the class. The other group can research and prepare a picture-prompt essay on the scientific aspects of the 1980 Mount Saint Helens eruption. Suggest that they include a current image from Volcano Cam at the U.S. Forest Service's website. To locate this, students can use the keyword "volcano cam" in a web search engine.

INDEPENDENT READING

The Pasture

A Lyric Poem
by Robert Frost

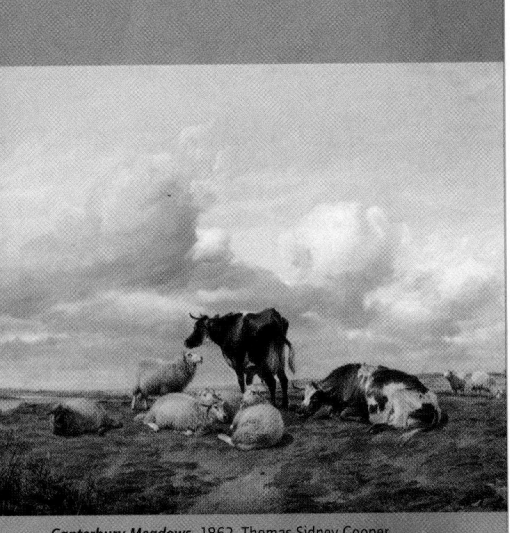

Canterbury Meadows, 1862. Thomas Sidney Cooper.
Art Gallery of New South Wales, Sydney, Australia.

I'm going out to clean the pasture spring;
I'll only stop to rake the leaves away
(And wait to watch the water clear, I may):
I sha'n't[1] be gone long.—You come too.

I'm going out to fetch the little calf
That's standing by the mother. It's so young,
It totters when she licks it with her tongue.
I sha'n't be gone long.—You come too. ❖

---

1. sha'n't. Shall not

Robert Frost (1874–1963) was born in San Francisco, but he moved to New England at the age of eleven. The quiet, rural landscape of New England profoundly affected his development as a poet. Frost supported himself and his family through a variety of occupations before achieving success with the publication in 1915 of two poetry collections. Frost won four Pulitzer Prizes for Poetry and earned a reputation as one of America's greatest poets.

591

Preview the Selection

At a Glance
Independent Reading
- Reading Level: Easy
- Difficulty Consideration: Topic
- Ease Factors: Vocabulary and length

Objectives
Reading this selection will enable students to do the following:
- read with developing fluency
- read silently with comprehension

Launch the Lesson
Before reading "The Pasture," ask students to consider the pros and cons of living on a farm. What would they enjoy most about such a life? What would they dislike?

Summary
The speaker in the poem describes going out to the pasture and fetching a calf, while imploring: "You come too."

The Mirrors & Windows questions after the poem focus on the theme of fulfillment. Ask students: When is work actually fun to do?

Use Reading Strategies
Ask Questions Encourage students to ask questions that help them form a mental picture of lines 1–4. Model a possible question: "Why would the speaker watch the water clear?"

Program Resources

Planning and Assessment
Program Planning Guide, Selection Lesson Plan
E-Lesson Planner
Assessment Guide, Lesson Test
ExamView

Technology Tools
Interactive Student Text on CD
Visual Teaching Package
Audio Library
mirrorsandwindows.com

Meeting the Standards
Poetry: Unit 6, Independent Reading, pp. 74–80

Common Core State Standards

Reading Literature
RL.10

Analyze Literature

Mood Ask students to state the mood of the poem, and then to identify images and language that contribute to it. Possibilities include the calf with its mother, the old-fashioned use of "sha'n't," and the gentle invitation to "come too."

 Answer: Answers will vary. Some students may find physical labor satisfying; others may feel most satisfied when their work seems to have a great purpose.

Analyze and Extend

1. (a) It is *abbc deec.* (b) It emphasizes the concrete, sensory images.
2. (a) Students may say it is happy and tranquil. (b) The tone seems friendly and signals that one of the author's purposes is to share a pleasant experience.
3. Both involve working with nature.

Rubric for Expository Writing

You can adapt this as a checklist for students to use as they write.

☐ Does the analysis focus on repetition in the poem?
☐ Does the analysis include a thesis statement?
☐ Does the analysis include evidence from the poem?

 Describe a time when you genuinely enjoyed your work. What kinds of work are particularly fulfilling?

Analyze and Extend

1. (a) What is this poem's rhyme scheme? (b) How does rhyme affect the poem?
2. (a) Describe this poem's tone. (b) In what ways does the tone help you identify the author's purpose?
3. How are the tasks that the speaker describes in this poem similar?

Expository Writing What words or phrases are repeated in this poem? Why do you think these particular words or phrases are repeated? Write a brief **literary analysis** in which you analyze the use of repetition. Before you begin writing, draft a thesis statement that succinctly states the main idea of your analysis. Support your thesis with evidence from the poem.

Collaborative Learning Gather in small groups to discuss the mood of this poem. Try to come to a consensus in your group about what you believe the mood to be. Then try to determine what most contributes to the mood. Also, try to determine to whom the speaker is speaking, and how the speaker influences the mood. Write down your thoughts and your evidence. When you have finished, share your conclusions with the class.

 Go to **www.mirrorsandwindows.com** for more.

Words in Use

Teaching Words
genuinely, 592
particularly, 592
succinctly, 592
consensus, 592

KEY TERMS
LYRIC POEM, 591
RHYME SCHEME, 592
TONE, 592
AUTHOR'S PURPOSE, 592
REPETITION, 592
THESIS STATEMENT, 592
MOOD, 592

For Your Reading List

Poetry for Young People: William Carlos Williams

by Christopher MacGowan

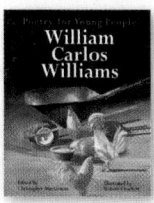

Many poems in this volume celebrate the unexpected beauty of ordinary things, whether they be a red wheelbarrow, a rotten apple, or broken pieces of green glass. The simple language and clear imagery of Williams's poems transformed American poetry and presented unusual insights into the places and things around us.

Laughing Out Loud, I Fly: Poems in English and Spanish

by Juan Felipe Herrera

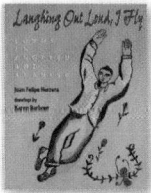

Herrera's poems express his memories of the people, places, and foods of his childhood, all in joyful, vivid language: "I am a monkey cartoon or a chile *tamal,* crazy / with paisley patches, infinite flavors cinnamon & / banana ice cream, it's 3 in the afternoon...." His poems, reprinted in Spanish and English, describe the joy and confusion of growing up between two cultures.

I Am Wings: Poems About Love

by Ralph Fletcher

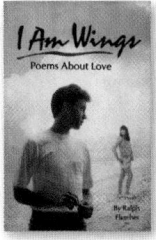

Written from the viewpoint of an infatuated young man, these short, easily understood poems about love form a kind of short story. Moving from attraction at the high school lockers in "First Look" through soaring early love in "I Am Wings" to falling out of love and becoming ready for a new love interest in "Seeds," these thirty-three free verse poems are gentle in tone.

Remember the Bridge: Poems of a People

by Carole Boston Weatherford

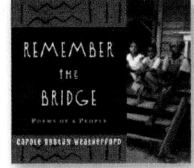

Four hundred years of African-American history are represented in these poems by Carole Boston Weatherford, including portraits of Africans who were kidnapped and sold into slavery as well as African-American farmers, craftspeople, storytellers, artists, and civil rights activists. Weatherford's words, along with dramatic drawings and photos of these individuals, immortalize their contributions to African-American freedom.

Poetry for Young People: Walt Whitman

by Jonathan Levin

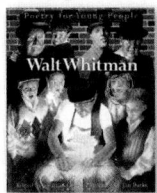

This collection features some of Whitman's most well-known poems—"I Hear America Singing," "Song of Myself"— and two poems about Abraham Lincoln: "O Captain! My Captain!" and "When Lilacs Last in the Dooryard Bloom'd." This illustrated volume provides a wonderful introduction to the work of a poet who was one of the first truly American voices in poetry.

A Wreath for Emmett Till

by Marilyn Nelson

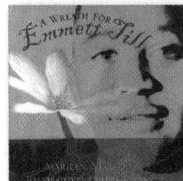

The death of Emmett Till, a fourteen-year-old black boy who was murdered in Mississippi, inspired Nelson to write a series of sonnets commemorating his life and tragic death. Another inspiration is Shakespeare's *Hamlet,* where Ophelia sadly recites the meanings of various flowers after her father's death. Throughout her poems, Nelson names the flowers she would like to weave into a wreath in memory of Till, whose death helped spark the Civil Rights movement.

FOR YOUR READING LIST **593**

Independent Reading

Independent Reading Activity

Use independent reading of a narrative poem to have students practice articulating emotional responses. Either assign a narrative poem yourself or encourage students to locate narrative poems in the library and select one. There are many recordings of classic narrative poems; tell students they may read the selected poem to themselves or listen to a recording.

As an out-of-class assignment, have students read or listen to the poem and pay attention to the feelings they have as the narrative unfolds. Suggest that they read or listen to the poem several times. After the first time, they should start making notes of how they feel. Then they may develop their notes either into a personal narrative of the listening experience or an objective description of what a reasonable reader might expect to feel as he or she reads or hears the poem. Steer students to use concrete details to describe emotions. Encourage them to keep their responses in a journal.

⊳ EMC E-Library

The EMC E-Library contains over twenty thousand pages of literary classics that students may read independently. An Electronic Library Guide provides teaching suggestions, enrichment activities, and reading strategy guidesheets.

Program Resources

EMC Access Editions

For additional independent reading, you may wish to refer students to one of EMC's Access Edition titles. Each Access Edition contains a thorough study apparatus, including background information, literal comprehension questions, footnotes, vocabulary definitions, critical thinking questions, and related projects and activities. An Assessment Manual offering worksheets and exams is available for each Access Edition.

Common Core State Standards

Reading Literature
RL.10
Language
L.4.3b

Teach the Workshop

Objectives

Participating in this lesson will help students write a personal narrative that

- grabs a reader's attention
- is organized by sequence of events
- includes descriptive detail as well as personal thoughts and feelings
- makes an event's significance clear in a compelling conclusion

Launch the Lesson

Ask students what makes an autobiography or a memoir especially powerful. Is it the descriptive detail? Or is it how easily a reader can relate to the author? Remind them of personal narratives they have read for this class, such as those by Annie Dillard in Unit 3 and by Maijue Xiong in Unit 4. Tell them that now they will have an opportunity to tell their own stories in short narratives.

Program Resources

Additional writing workshops are available in the *Exceeding the Standards: Writing* resource.

Narrative Writing

Personal Narrative

Reading and Writing

In this unit, you read poems from poets such as Carl Sandburg, Robert Frost, Emily Dickinson, and Dudley Randall about looking beneath the surface. With concise and elegant words, these poets were able to share engaging stories and compelling feelings with their readers.

You will sometimes need to describe an event or series of events from your own life in writing. When you tell a story about yourself, it is important to express your ideas and the events that occurred clearly and in a way that will interest your reader. By using a variety of techniques, such as figurative language, sensory details, characters, and plot, you will be able to tell a compelling story about yourself.

In this workshop you will learn how to write a **personal narrative.** A personal narrative is a true story told by the person it happened to. To complete the assignment, create a goal and determine your strategy to achieve it. This summary includes a writing rubric—a set of standards by which you will judge your work. You will use this rubric in both drafting and revising your essay.

Assignment: Write a personal narrative in which I tell about a meaningful event in my life.

Goal: Show the significance of the event to my audience.

Strategy: Include descriptive language as well as my own thoughts and feelings about the event.

Writing Rubric: My personal narrative should include the following:

- an opening that grabs the reader's attention
- important events told in sequence
- descriptive details as well as personal thoughts and feelings
- a compelling conclusion that makes the significance of the event clear to the audience

What Great Writers Do

Robert Frost used simple language to reveal deep meaning. In his poetry, he explored the relationship of individuals to each other and to nature. The following is what he said about writing poetry.

A poem begins with a lump in the throat, a home-sickness or a love-sickness. It is a reaching-out toward expression; an effort to find fulfillment. A complete poem is one where the emotion has found its thought and the thought has found the words.

Words in Use

Teaching Words

concise, 594
compelling, 594
fulfillment, 594
vivid, 596
irrelevant, 596
bulging, 598
inanimate, 598
beckoned, 598

KEY TERMS

SERIES OF EVENTS, 594
SENSORY DETAIL, 594
CHARACTER, 594
PLOT, 594
PERSONAL NARRATIVE, 594
WORD WEB, 595
CHRONOLOGICAL ORDER, 596
CAUSE-EFFECT ORDER, 596

PROBLEM-AND-SOLUTION ORDER, 596
PROOFREAD, 596
TRANSITION, 596
ADJECTIVE, 596
PEER REVIEW, 597
ANNOTATION, 597
CONCLUSION, 597
FIGURATIVE LANGUAGE, 598
SIMILE, 598

METAPHOR, 598
HYPERBOLE, 598
PERSONIFICATION, 598
APOSTROPHE, 598
SINGULAR POSSESSIVE NOUN, 598
PLURAL POSSESSIVE NOUN, 598
CONTRACTION, 598

Common Core State Standards

Writing
W.3, W.4, W.5, W.6, W.10

1. PREWRITE

Choosing Your Topic

Since a personal narrative is about an event from your own life, think about events that have affected you strongly. You may want to categorize events using a chart. Look at the chart below created by a student.

Strange	Scary	Exciting	Funny
seeing our town after a tornado	stuck in an elevator	my first roller-coaster ride	playing a trick on my dad
knowing my uncle was getting married before he said so	lost in a store	winning a championship basketball game	learning to square dance
finding a skeleton key that doesn't fit anything	being home alone for the first time	skiing downhill for the first time	sliding down a muddy hill

This student began with four categories: *strange, scary, exciting,* and *funny*. He chose events in his life that could fit into these categories. From these events, he will choose one event to write about in a personal narrative.

Gathering Details

Now that you have chosen an event to write about, it's time to explore it further. Ask yourself key questions about the event: *Who was there? When did it happen? Where did it happen? What time of day was it? Was the weather important? What did I see, hear, taste, touch, or smell? How did I feel about what happened? Why is the event significant or memorable to me?*

Use a word web to further explore the event. Write the event in the center of the web. In the ovals leading from the center, write key words that can help trigger memories of the event.

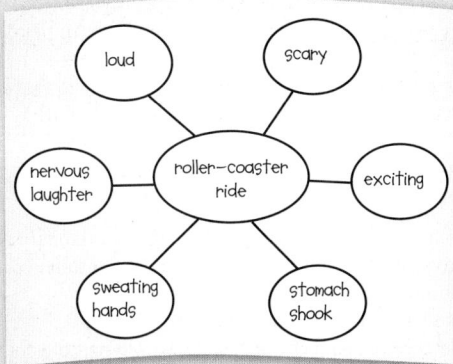

Deciding on Your Purpose

After you choose a topic and gather details, determine your purpose. You might be writing to entertain your audience. You may also want to teach a lesson or give an explanation. Keep in mind that no matter what your topic is, part of your purpose is to show your audience why the event was or is so memorable to you.

Prewrite

Brainstorm Topics Draw attention to the student chart on this page. Suggest other adjectives students might use as categories of personal experiences: *awe-inspiring, spooky, infuriating,* and *thrilling,* for example. Give students several minutes to choose some categories and write down anything that comes to mind. If a student gets stuck, pair him or her with a partner and have them interview each other to identify interesting life events.

TEACHING NOTE

Personal Narrative

Make sure students understand what *narrative* means. It is writing that tells a story. Remind them that the person telling a short story or novel is the *narrator,* and that poems that tell stories are called *narrative poems.* Therefore, writing a personal narrative is similar to writing a short story. The main difference is that the characters, settings, and events in the personal narrative are real instead of imaginary.

Reading Skills

Identify Author's Approach

Tell students they should consider writers they admire as they think about their topics and purposes. Ask students to review the reading they have done in class so far this year for the sole purpose of identifying two or three excellent narratives. Then, tell them to use the following questions to evaluate the selections they identify:

1. What was the writer's purpose?
2. Do I want to achieve a similar purpose?
3. What techniques does this writer use that I would like to imitate?
4. Can I use these techniques in my own personal narrative?

Draft

Grabbing Attention To inspire students to draft good first lines for their narratives, give them some examples. Remind them that they can draft a first line with plenty of sensory details, and then edit it to have the greatest possible impact. Read aloud the following opening lines.

"When I was nearly thirteen, my brother Jem got his arm badly broken at the elbow." (Harper Lee, *To Kill a Mockingbird*)

"It was 7 minutes after midnight. The dog was lying on the grass in the middle of the lawn in front of Mrs. Shears' house. Its eyes were closed." (Mark Haddon, *The Curious Incident of the Dog in the Night-Time*)

Elaborating Suggest to students that if they are concerned about having too many or too few details, they can read their drafts aloud. Even if they do this alone—as opposed to with a listener—they will hear sections that are too brief or sections that go on for too long.

TEACHING NOTE

Visualize

Sketch a plot diagram on the board. Remind students that a narrative tells a story, and have them summarize the main parts of a plot.

---

2. DRAFT

Organizing Ideas

You will want to organize your writing in an order that is interesting and logical. Most narratives are written in sequence, or **chronological order.** Other possible orders include **cause-effect order** and **problem-and-solution order.** Whichever order you choose, make sure it makes sense for the kind of personal narrative you want to tell.

> **Chronological Order**
> 1. first event
>   details
> 2. next event
>   details
> 3. final event
>   details

Putting Your Thoughts on Paper

A personal narrative should grab a reader's attention right from the beginning. It is your story, so remember to tell what happened from your point of view. Use sensory details so that your reader hears, sees, feels, smells, and tastes everything that you did. Include your own thoughts and feelings as you describe the event. Wrap up your personal narrative with a sentence or two that makes clear the significance or effect of the event.

You may want to write your draft straight through from beginning to end so that you get the story down. At first, concentrate on content and organization. You can then go back and add descriptive and personal details to each part of your draft to help your audience connect with your experience. Mechanical details, such as spelling, grammar, and punctuation, will be the focus of the editing and proofreading stages.

> **Introduction**
> - grab the reader's attention with an interesting question or a surprising statement
> - hint at the significance or effect of the event
>
> **Body**
> - tell the complete story
> - include descriptive language and personal details
> - use smooth transitions from one paragraph to the next
>
> **Conclusion**
> - write a compelling ending that wraps up the narrative and tells how things worked out
> - explain how the experience affected or changed you and why it is meaningful

Elaborating

Improve your narrative writing by adding details, examples, or transitions to connect ideas. Often a single adjective, sensory detail, or vivid verb can make your description clearer and more colorful.

As you narrate events, you may have a tendency to wander or give details that are irrelevant to your story. Read each sentence carefully. Ask yourself if the sentence is relevant to the story you are trying to tell. If the sentence does not enhance your story, delete it.

Differentiated Instruction

Reading Proficiency

Review possible organizational patterns with students. Chronological order is illustrated in the text on this page and on page 450. (Page 450 also shows spatial order.) Cause-and-effect order is illustrated on page 364. In problem-solution order, a writer states a problem and then offers possible solutions, or describes a solution and then lists the problems it solves. Model planning a personal narrative with a problem-solution order: "I was stuck at school with no way home but to walk fifteen miles, which just wasn't practical. I solved the problem by borrowing a large, sturdy plastic wash tub and using it to skate down hills. Was that ever a trip!"

3. REVISE

Evaluating Your Draft

Once your draft is complete, review what you have written to determine your narrative's strengths and weaknesses. Check that your organization and ideas are clear. For the best evaluation, have a **peer review.** Exchange papers with a classmate. Have the classmate read what you have written, and then discuss ways to improve your paper. Use the Revising Checklist as a guide. Below is the beginning of a personal narrative. The annotations to the right indicate the reasons for the changes marked in the draft.

There is one day in my life that I'll never forget. *That day marked the beginning of a quest for me—to ride every roller coaster in the world! I'm only thirteen now, but I will do it one day.* Here's how it all started.

I was only a kid, seven years old, when my brothers Luis and Miguel persuaded my parents that I was old enough (and tall enough) to experience the thrill of the roller coaster called the Monster. I was four when I first saw it. I begged, pleaded, and cried to be allowed to ride it, but my father said no. I clearly was not tall enough at four years old. *Disappointed, I was determined to grow enough by next year.* Next year turned into three years until I was finally tall enough to ride the Monster.

I moved slowly along with my brothers in the line that snaked its way closer and closer to the front. *Luis pointed at the triple loops, angles, turns, and steep plunges as the riders screamed and hollered.* Some scared people left the line. ~~I hate waiting in lines.~~ I couldn't wait to be up there! Finally, we reached the front.

> *Hint at the significance of the event in the introduction.*

> *Add personal thoughts and feelings.*

> *Add sensory details.*

> *Take out unnecessary details.*

Teach the Workshop

Revise

Evaluating a Draft The checklist refers to chronological order; remind students to check their narratives for a clear organization, be it chronological, cause-effect, or problem-solution. Also emphasize that the conclusion must convey why this event was personally significant. If a student has trouble discerning whether or not the significance comes through, suggest that he or she think of a theme for the narrative, and try stating it in the conclusion.

When students have done as much as they can in the available time, suggest that they conduct a peer review. Be sure they understand the rubric.

Allow ample time for students to read the narrative they receive to review. Schedule peer review exchanges when each student will have several minutes to deliver his or her review, and when each writer will have time to thoughtfully absorb the comments and ask questions for clarification.

What Great Writers Do

Assure students that an event's significance may become clear only during writing and revision. As reporter and essayist Sherry Simpson remarks,

As so often happens, I didn't know exactly what I thought until I began writing.

Speaking & Listening Skills

Retell and Summarize Points

Use the peer review process as an opportunity for students to practice listening skills. Ask reviewers to have their partners read their narratives aloud. Tell reviewers to use the Revising Checklist on this page as a rubric for listening. In addition, after listening, have each reviewer summarize the narrative he or she heard, and retell the significance of the event in his or her own words.

Edit and Proofread

Figurative Language Exercise If students wish to add figurative language, offer them this warm-up:

1. Write a simile about feeling powerful.

2. Write a metaphor comparing yourself to a cloud.

3. Use hyperbole to exaggerate your response to an irritating phone call.

4. Personify your school desk.

Apostrophe Exercise Ask students to identify incorrect apostrophe usage in these sentences:

1. Theres' a place I love to visit.

2. It was the viruses's fault.

3. Why did it wave it's arms?

4. A few weeks ago, I read a story called "Papas' Parrot."

▶ **Proofreading Marks** Refer students to the Language Arts Handbook, Writing Section 4.1, Proofreader's Symbols.

▶ **Publish and Present**

Before students begin their final versions, they might benefit from reading the Language Arts Handbook, Writing Section 4.1, Writing Follow-up.

4. EDIT AND PROOFREAD

Focus: Figurative Language

Figurative language brings color and originality to writing. The right figurative language can make an ordinary story or event come alive for the reader. Review the various types of figurative language and examples to make your own writing more effective.

Figurative Language	Examples
A **simile** is a comparison of two unlike things that are alike in at least one way. A simile uses the word *like* or *as* in the comparison.	I was as eager as a race horse.
A **metaphor** is a comparison of two unlike things without use of like or as. A metaphor says something is another thing.	We inched higher up the mountain of steel.
Hyperbole is exaggeration used for effect.	My mouth was open, and my eyes were bulging out of their sockets.
Personification occurs when human traits are used to describe animals, ideas, or inanimate objects.	The Monster beckoned, and I couldn't ignore it.

Focus: Apostrophes

Apostrophes are used to show possession. Pay careful attention to the use of apostrophes in your writing: *Miguel's hat, the boys' laughter.*

Remember these rules about using apostrophes in possessives in your writing.

Rule 1. To form the singular possessive noun, add an apostrophe and the letter s to the end of the noun: *Tony's father, the coaster's wheels.*

Rule 2. To form the plural possessive noun, write it in its plural form and add the apostrophe after the s: *the girls' hats, the puppies' noses.* For a noun whose plural form does not end in s, add an apostrophe and s to the end: *children's laughter, men's shoes.*

Apostrophes are also used in contractions, such as *don't, didn't, won't, should've, wouldn't, she's,* and *it's.* Note that the possessive form of it is *its; it's* is a contraction for *it is.*

Proofreading

Quality Control The purpose of proofreading is to catch errors in grammar, capitalization, spelling, and punctuation. You can find and fix these errors as you evaluate and revise your narrative. You may also correct these errors as you look for them specifically in a line-by-line reading of your paper. Use proofreader's marks to highlight any errors. See the Language Arts Handbook, section 4.1, for a list of proofreader's marks.

5. PUBLISH AND PRESENT

Final Draft

Now that you have taken your narrative through the revising and editing stages, make a final draft. Make sure your narrative is clean and free of errors. If it is handwritten, make sure the narrative is neat and legible. If you are using a word processing program, double-space your paper and use a readable typeface or font. Be sure to check that you have followed any additional presentation guidelines.

Differentiated Instruction

English Language Learning

Use this opportunity to gauge progress among English learners. Have them show you their editing and proofreading to see how well they have absorbed spelling and grammar lessons you have given. Take time to correct and discuss any consistent problems in these areas before students prepare final drafts.

Enrichment

Offer confident writers the opportunity to proofread each other's work. Encourage them to practice using proofreader's marks.

Student Model

A Thrill of a Ride
by Anthony Garcia

There is one day in my life that I'll never forget. That day marked the beginning of a quest for me—to ride every roller coaster in the world! I'm only thirteen now, but I will do it one day. Here's how it all started.

> *Draws in the reader and introduces the significance of the events*

I was only a kid, seven years old, when my brothers Luis and Miguel persuaded my parents that I was old enough (and tall enough) to experience the thrill of the roller coaster called the Monster. I was four when I first saw it. The Monster beckoned, and I couldn't ignore it. I begged, pleaded, and cried to be allowed to ride it, but my father said no. I clearly was not tall enough at four years old. Disappointed, I was determined to grow enough by next year. Next year turned into three years until I was finally tall enough to ride the Monster.

I moved slowly along with my brothers in the line that snaked its way closer and closer to the front. My jaws ached from the grin stuck to my face. Luis pointed at the triple loops, angles, turns, and steep plunges as the riders screamed and hollered. Some scared people left the line. I couldn't wait to be up there! Finally, we reached the front.

As I took the seat next to Miguel, the ride operator stared at me for a moment. I thought he was going to tell me I was still too short to ride on the Monster, but he just shrugged and locked me into my seat. I was as eager as a race horse. I remember Miguel whispering to me, "Okay, little bro?" I just nodded, still grinning, and gripped the bar in front of me. The operator then pushed a handle, and the car jerked forward.

> *Is organized in chronological order*
>
> *Elaborates on the events through figurative language, sensory details, and personal thoughts and feelings*

My heart was pounding as we first started rolling. We crept up a small climb and slid down a short drop first. My stomach jumped a little, but it wasn't anything I couldn't handle. Then I was pushed back in the seat as we inched higher up the mountain of steel. I remember every *click-click* of the track as the car continued its climb. When it reached the top, it hesitated only a second, and then we were off. We raced down, climbed back up and whooshed through spins, dips, and curls. My mouth was open and my eyes were bulging out of their sockets, anticipating each new thrill the ride had to offer. After one last corkscrew curl, the car slowed toward the starting block and stopped with a jerk. It was over.

My brothers were doubled over with laughter as I, still wide-eyed and opened-mouth, shakily got off the coaster. Then I stopped and looked back at the Monster. My brothers stopped too and looked at me.

I turned to them, grinned, and said, "Let's do it again!"

> *Wraps up the narrative and reveals the significance of the event to the writer*

Writing Skills

Refer to Prewriting Plan

When students have submitted their final narratives, ask them to take several minutes to review the writing process. Have them focus on the prewriting tools they used to choose a topic, gather details, and decide on a purpose. Ask them to answer the questions at right, keeping the responses in their journals for future reference.

1. What led you to choose the event about which you wrote?
2. As you wrote your draft, did you find that you had plenty of details to choose from, or did you have to add more?
3. How did your purpose change as you wrote and revised your draft, if at all?
4. What would you do differently the next time you get ready to write a personal narrative?

Objectives

Participating in this lesson will help students deliver narrative presentations that

- use chronological order
- include characters, setting, and action
- convey ideas through description
- use the voice to portray feelings
- are loud and clear
- employ effective nonverbal cues

Launch the Lesson

Ask several volunteers to read aloud Bill Cosby's personal essay "Was Tarzan a Three-Bandage Man?" on pages 314–315. Ask the class if they can imagine Cosby reading this as a personal narrative. Remind them that professional speakers and comedians often use personal narratives in their work. Say that now they will have a chance to practice their own skills delivering personal narratives.

> For more information, see the Language Arts Handbook Section 7, Speaking & Listening.

KEY TERMS

NARRATIVE	ORDER, 600
PRESENTATION, 600	FEEDBACK, 601
TOPIC, 600	TONE OF VOICE, 601
SETTING, 600	CHARACTER, 601
CHRONOLOGICAL	SETTING, 601

Speaking & Listening Workshop

Giving and Actively Listening to Narrative Presentations

Have you ever told a story about your life? Have you ever told a story to entertain your friends or family? Have you ever told a story as a means of providing others with information? When you tell a story, you are giving a narrative presentation. In a **narrative presentation,** you describe events from your life or the lives of others. When you give and actively listen to a narrative presentation, you share information about yourself with others.

Planning a Narrative Presentation

Choose a Story To give an effective narrative presentation, you need to first think about a specific event or series of events that you witnessed or in which you participated. Was the event strange, funny, happy, sad, or serious? Brainstorm to come up with a list of possible topics for your narrative presentation. Under each topic, write details related to it, such as the setting, the people involved, and the outcome.

Take Notes Once you have decided on a story to tell, try to jog your memory of the event. Talk to others who were present or perform research to fill in any gaps in your knowledge of the setting or people involved. If you have photographs, you may want to examine them to recall significant details.

> **Topic:**
> playing a funny joke on my dad
>
> **Details:**
> fishing in our big green canoe
> sunny July afternoon
> hooked a fake fish to the end of his line
> we laughed the entire ride home

Organize Your Story Narratives are most frequently told in chronological order. When you tell a story in chronological order, you give the events in the order in which they happened. Use a time line to organize your presentation. List all of the most significant events from left to right on the time line.

To expand upon this workshop lesson, Giving and Actively Listening to Narrative Presentations, see the *Exceeding the Standards: Speaking & Listening* resource.

Differentiated Instruction

English Language Learning

Pair English learners with confident students in storytelling partnerships. Allow time for each student to tell the other a story about his or her life. When partners finish, ask them to write down one or two qualities of a good narrative presentation. When all pairs have finished, have students give you some highlights from their notes.

Words in Use

Teaching Words

outcome, 600
criticism, 601
convey, 601
nonverbal, 601

Identify Your Audience Now that you have identified and organized the story that you are going to tell, consider your audience. Your audience will determine much of what you say and how you say it. If you know that your audience is very familiar with the details of your story, try to introduce a new perspective or information with which they may not be familiar. If you know your story is one with which they are likely to be unfamiliar, try to include as much description and background information as possible.

Evaluating Your Narrative Presentation

Working with a partner or in a small group, rehearse your narrative presentation. Then provide constructive feedback to your partner on what he or she did well and what could be improved. Constructive feedback means that you are respectful and polite whether you give criticism or praise. Follow the listening and speaking rubrics on this page in order to evaluate each oral summary.

Delivering Your Narrative Presentation

Convey dramatic effects through your tone of voice as well as your facial expression. If you are expressing surprise, show surprise in your voice and eyes. If you are expressing fear, show fear in your voice as well as in your movements and facial expressions. Keep your audience interested and entertained. Use gestures as an aid, but do not let them become a distraction from your speech. Remember to speak loudly and clearly. If your story is humorous, pause during moments of laughter.

Listen Actively Listening actively is just as important as being an effective speaker. Pay attention to what the speaker says, and react politely. Do not be a distraction by talking to others during the presentation. Ask questions when appropriate.

Speaking Rubric

Your presentation will be evaluated on these elements:

Content

☐ events are ordered chronologically

☐ narrative includes characters, setting, and action

☐ description used to convey ideas

Delivery and Presentation

☐ speaks loud and clear

☐ uses effective nonverbal cues

☐ uses voice to portray feeling

Listening Rubric

As a peer reviewer or audience member, you should do the following:

☐ listen quietly and attentively

☐ maintain eye contact with the speaker

☐ ask appropriate questions

☐ (as peer reviewer) provide constructive feedback

Teach the Workshop

Preparing for Presentations

Give students opportunities to practice their presentations alone and with peer reviewers. Offer these tips:

- Work within a range of times, such as two to five minutes. Try to find the best length for your narrative.
- Decide whether to use dialogue in the narration, and if you do use dialogue, decide how to indicate different speakers.
- Develop main characters carefully and minor characters quickly. Try to find a brief way to say a lot about each character and his or her role in the narrative.

TEACHING NOTE

Analyze a Speaker's Verbal and Nonverbal Messages

Use recorded poetry to give students practice analyzing a speaker's tone. Choose from various anthologies. For example, *Poetry Speaks* contains recordings of numerous poets, including Tennyson reading "The Charge of the Light Brigade" (see Unit 7). The series *Voice of the Poet* includes recordings of Elizabeth Bishop, Robert Frost, Langston Hughes, and E. E. Cummings. Choose a poem and give a copy to each student. Let students read the poem and form an impression of its meaning. Then have students listen to a recording of the poem and respond to the tone. Ask them whether the tone met their expectations, and if not, how it differed from what they expected. Finally, ask how the tone affected the meaning of the poem.

Writing Skills

Effective Transitions

Students will probably want to have notes for reference as they present their narratives. Tell students that one effective way to cue themselves in public speaking is with transition phrases. Give them these guidelines:

- First, record the main events of the narrative in order.
- Second, pick one or two words that will trigger a memory of each main event.
- Third, write the event trigger words in order on a large note card. Make sure your handwriting is large and neat enough to read in a hurry.
- Finally, write transition words before and/or after each event to cue yourself if you need a reminder.

Common Core State Standards

Speaking and Listening
SL.6

Objectives

Completing this lesson will enable students to

- write a personal essay based on a timed writing prompt
- answer standardized test questions that demonstrate revising and editing skills
- answer standardized test questions that demonstrate the ability to infer from a reading

Timed Writing

Say that standardized tests often ask students to write a response to a prompt in a specified period of time. Give the following tips:

- Read the entire prompt carefully.
- Look for key words in the prompt that tell you what is expected.
- Underline these words or write them on your own notepaper.
- Use the key words to make sure you follow all the instructions.
- Organize. Allow time for planning, writing, and reviewing.
- Before you begin writing, create a rough outline of points to make.
- Write a clear introduction. This will help keep you on track as you write each paragraph.
- If you find yourself running out of time, state your remaining points and add a conclusion.
- Review your completed essay to see if you have responded completely to the instructions.
- Proofread before you turn in your completed essay.

Test Practice Workshop

Writing Skills

Personal Essay

Carefully read the following writing prompt. Before you begin writing, think carefully about what task the assignment is asking you to perform. Then create an outline to help guide your writing.

> In Emily Dickinson's poem "I'm Nobody," the speaker suggests that it's better to be "nobody" than "somebody." What are some of the benefits and drawbacks of being a "nobody" as opposed to a "somebody"? How do you feel about the speaker's claims?

Relate a story from your own life that reflects or challenges the theme of Dickinson's poem. In your narrative, use descriptive, sensory, and figurative language, as well as examples from the poem. Concentrate on writing a compelling opening and closing for your story. As you write, be sure to:

- Organize your narrative in a logical and consistent way
- Include introductory and concluding paragraphs
- Introduce your position in the first paragraph
- Support your main idea in each body paragraph

Rubric for a Personal Essay

Make sure students understand that they should follow the instructions *below* the first tinted box in order to respond to the questions *inside* the box. Have students use these criteria to evaluate their essays.

☐ Does the introductory paragraph include my position on the theme of Dickinson's poem?

☐ Does the essay relate a personal story that supports my position?

☐ Is the essay organized logically and consistently?

☐ Does each body paragraph support the position I took in the introduction?

☐ Does the essay use descriptive, sensory, and figurative language?

☐ Does the essay have a concluding paragraph?

Common Core State Standards

Language
L.6.1e

Revising and Editing Skills

In the following excerpt from the first draft of a student's paper, words and phrases are underlined and numbered. Alternatives to the underlined words and phrases appear in the right-hand column. Choose the one that *best* corrects any grammatical or style errors in the original. If you think that the original is error-free, choose "NO CHANGE."

Some questions might also be asked about a section of the passage or the entire passage. These do not refer to a specific underlined phrase or word and are identified by a number in a box. Record your answers on a separate sheet of paper.

In the words of Archibald MacLeish, "A poem should not mean, but be." What does MacLeish mean? [1] I was hiking in Glacier National Parks forests last summer. [2] I was stunned by a scene that took my breath away. Craggy snow-topped mountains speared the sky and cradled an [3] impossibly smooth lake. The reflections in the lake perfectly mirrored the trees and mountains [4] rising above it. At that moment, I didn't think about what the scene meant. I just experienced it. [5] Similarly, my first thought when reading a good poem is not about its meaning. I simply experience it, letting my minds eye wander along with the poem's images. [6]

1. The second sentence of this paragraph is a
   A. simple sentence.
   B. compound sentence.
   C. complex sentence.
   D. compound-complex sentence.

2. A. NO CHANGE
   B. I was hiking, in Glacier National Parks forests, last summer.
   C. I was hiking; in Glacier National Parks forests last summer.
   D. I was hiking in Glacier National Park's forests last summer.

3. The sentence beginning *Craggy snow-topped mountains* has a
   A. simple predicate.
   B. compound predicate.
   C. complex predicate.
   D. compound-complex predicate.

4. A. NO CHANGE
   B. lake mirrored perfectly the trees
   C. lake, perfectly mirroring the trees
   D. lake perfectly mirror the trees

5. The sentence *I just experienced it* is a
   A. simple sentence.
   B. compound sentence.
   C. complex sentence.
   D. compound-complex sentence.

6. A. NO CHANGE
   B. mind's eye wander along with the poem's
   C. minds eye wander along with the poems
   D. minds eye wander, along with the poem's

Words in Use

Teaching Words

benefits, 602	quarrels, 604
drawbacks, 602	subdue, 604
opposed, 602	allay, 604
compelling, 602	vengeance, 604
paternal, 604	dissensions, 604
wrath, 604	discord, 604
wrangling, 604	

KEY TERMS

NARRATIVE, 602	COMPLEX PREDICATE, 603	CONFLICT, 605
DESCRIPTIVE LANGUAGE, 602	COMPOUND-COMPLEX PREDICATE, 603	RHYTHM, 605
SENSORY LANGUAGE, 602		LYRIC POEM, 605
FIGURATIVE LANGUAGE, 602	POINT OF VIEW, 605	CONCRETE POEM, 605
MAIN IDEA, 602	THIRD-PERSON OMNISCIENT, 605	HAIKU, 605
SIMPLE SENTENCE, 603		NARRATIVE POEM, 605
COMPOUND SENTENCE, 603	SYMBOLISM, 605	ONOMATOPOEIA, 605
COMPLEX SENTENCE, 603	METAPHOR, 605	CONSONANCE, 605
COMPOUND-COMPLEX SENTENCE, 603	SIMILE, 605	ANALOGY, 605
	RHYME, 605	REPETITION, 605
SIMPLE PREDICATE, 603	CHARACTERIZATION, 605	ALLITERATION, 605
COMPOUND PREDICATE, 603	PLOT, 605	

Reading Comprehension Tests

Remind students that reading comprehension tests give a short piece of writing and then ask several questions about it. The questions often ask students to interpret the passage. Urge students to keep the following tips in mind:

- Begin by skimming all the questions.
- Read the passage with the questions in mind. If time permits, read the passage twice before answering any questions.
- Reread the first question carefully.
- Locate the portion of the passage to which the question refers. Read it slowly and carefully.
- Answer the first question.
- Repeat this process to answer all the rest of the questions.

Reading Skills

Carefully read the following passage. Then on a separate piece of paper, answer each question.

from *The Song of Hiawatha* by Henry Wadsworth Longfellow

...Gitche Manito, the mighty,
The creator of the nations,
Looked upon them with compassion,
With paternal love and pity;
5   Looked upon their wrath and wrangling
But as quarrels among children,
But as feuds and fights of children!

Over them he stretched his right hand,
To subdue their stubborn natures,
10   To allay their thirst and fever,
By the shadow of his right hand;
Spake to them with voice majestic
As the sound of far-off waters,
Falling into deep abysses,
15   Warning, chiding, spake in this wise:

"O my children! my poor children!
Listen to the words of wisdom,
Listen to the words of warning,
From the lips of the Great Spirit,
20   From the Master of Life, who made you!

"I have given you lands to hunt in,
I have given you streams to fish in,
I have given you bear and bison,
I have given you roe and reindeer,
25   I have given you brant and beaver,
Filled the marshes full of wild-fowl,
Filled the rivers full of fishes:
Why then are you not contented?
Why then will you hunt each other?

30   "I am weary of your quarrels,
Weary of your wars and bloodshed,
Weary of your prayers for vengeance,
Of your wranglings and dissensions;
All your strength is in your union,
35   All your danger is in discord;
Therefore be at peace henceforward,
And as brothers live together..."

Differentiated Instruction

English Language Learning

Students learning English will need help with the academic vocabulary used in standardized tests. Explain the following terms used in this workshop: *prompt*—cue, something to help one begin, 602. A "writing prompt" is usually a detailed paragraph of instruction.

outline—short summary or description, usually arranged as a series of key points, 602
position—opinion or point to be discussed, 602

1. Based on the first stanza, the narrator's point of view is:
   A. first-person.
   B. second-person.
   C. third-person limited.
   D. third-person omniscient.

2. Which of the following kinds of figurative language appears in line 5?
   A. symbolism
   B. metaphor
   C. simile
   D. alliteration

3. The sensory language in lines 12–14 mostly contributes to which of the following elements?
   A. rhyme
   B. characterization
   C. plot
   D. conflict

4. Which of the following describes the rhythm of the poem's second stanza?
   A. / ˘ / ˘ / ˘ /˘
   B. ˘ ˘ ˘ / ˘ ˘ ˘ /
   C. / ˘ ˘ ˘ / ˘ ˘ ˘
   D. ˘ / / / ˘ / / /

5. This passage is an example of which type of poetry?
   A. lyric
   B. concrete
   C. haiku
   D. narrative

6. *Warning* and *chiding* in line 15 contain
   A. alliteration.
   B. metaphor.
   C. onomatopoeia.
   D. consonance.

7. Lines 21–27 contain
   A. metaphor and simile.
   B. analogy and symbolism.
   C. repetition and alliteration.
   D. rhyme and alliteration.

8. Based on the context, what is the most likely meaning of *brant* in line 25?
   A. a Native-American tribe
   B. a type of bird or animal
   C. a type of tree or plant
   D. food and clothing

9. Which of the following literary devices is absent in Longfellow's poem?
   A. rhythm
   B. rhyme
   C. repetition
   D. alliteration

10. What can you infer about the audience to whom Gitche Manito is speaking?
    A. They are warlike and unfriendly toward one other.
    B. They are part of a large family.
    C. They are Gitche Manito's brothers and sisters.
    D. They are all members of the same tribe.

Teach the Workshop

Reading Skills
1. D
2. D
3. B
4. A
5. D
6. D
7. C
8. B
9. B
10. A

Test-Taking Skills

Eliminate Incorrect Responses

Tell students that a key skill in answering multiple-choice questions is eliminating incorrect responses. Model a think-aloud for one question on this page.

Question 5. A concrete poem has a recognizable shape, and a haiku is only three lines long. That eliminates choices B and C. I know a lyric poem expresses an emotion and a narrative poem tells a story. This poem has a third-person point of view, so I think it is narrative, which eliminates answer A. The answer must be D.

Select another question and have the class work as a group to eliminate the incorrect responses.

Unit 7 Visual Planning Guide

Planning and Assessment Tools

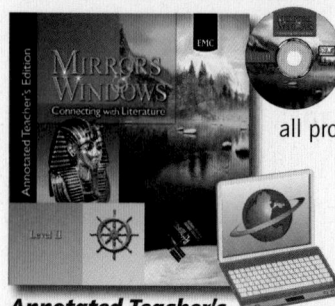

Annotated Teacher's Edition

Annotated Teacher's Edition
One location for accessing, previewing, and planning for use of all program resources.

EMC Launchpad
Desktop application for accessing, previewing, planning, posting, and grading all program resources. Post personal resources and lessons, and access the E-Lesson Planner, the E-Gradebook, and training modules for computer literacy.

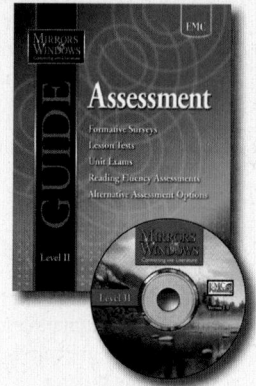

Assessment Guide and ExamView
A variety of assessments are available for this unit in print and electronic forms, including:
- Formative Survey
- Lesson Tests
- Unit Exams
- Alternative Assessment Options
- Reading Fluency Assessments

Meeting the Standards: Unit 7
In addition to lesson-by-lesson resources, *Meeting the Standards* includes the following unit-based resources:
- Unit Study Guide
- Practice Test
- Active Reading Model
- Selection Quizzes

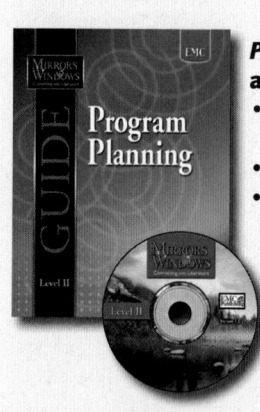

Program Planning Guide and *E-Lesson Planner*
- Lesson Plans for all the selections in the unit
- Core Standards-Based Selections
- Reading Log and Evaluation Forms

The E-Lesson Planner contains fully developed lesson plans and unit resources with an electronic calendar for editing lesson plans.

Technology Tools

Visual Teaching Package
This package contains unit-based lectures, games, art collections, and Writing Workshops in PowerPoint format; included within the EMC Launchpad.

Interactive Student Text on CD
The student textbook on CD includes highlighting, note-taking, bookmarking, and a direct link to the student website, in addition to everything in the student text.

Audio Library
Authentic, dramatic recordings with listening activities expand listening skills and offer additional support for developing readers and English Language Learners.

ETS Online Criterion-Based Essay Grader (Grades 9–12)
Students can use this ETS web-based tool to evaluate their essays online before submitting them for teacher review and final evaluation.

mirrorsandwindows.com
Student and teacher resources, support, references, technology tools, and state-specific standards are available at **mirrorsandwindows.com**. The website is customizable using the EMC Launchpad.

Unit-Based Resources

Exceeding the Standards Unit Resources

Each of the *Exceeding the Standards* resources provides fully developed lessons to help you extend the textbook lessons and to expand upon the themes and skills covered in the unit. You can also download these lessons from **mirrorsandwindows.com**.

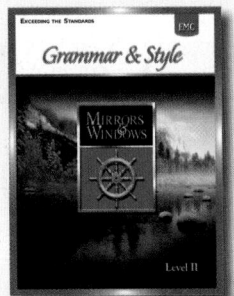

Grammar & Style
This resource contains:
- Seven lessons on Punctuation, pp. 156–172
- Five lessons on Capitalization, pp. 173–185

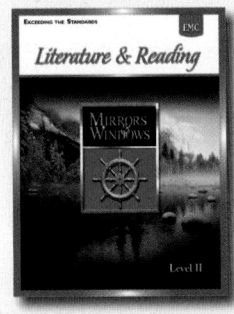

Literature & Reading
This resource contains:
- Dramatize an Original Script, pp. 17–20

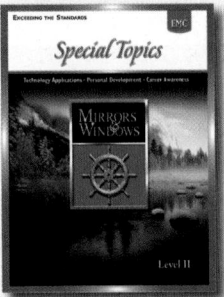

Special Topics
This resource contains:
- Lifelong Learning: Setting Goals: Part 1, pp. 26–27
- Career Skills Development: Writing an Ad for Bestworkerqualities.com, pp. 28–30

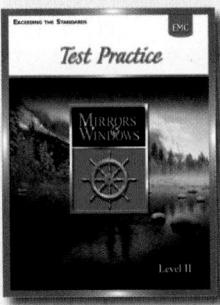

Test Practice
This resource contains:
- ACT Practice Test, pp. 16–19

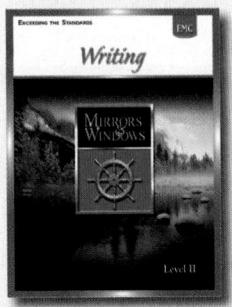

Writing
This resource contains:
- Narrative Writing: Write Dialogue, pp. 47–55

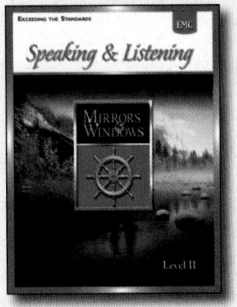

Speaking & Listening
This resource contains the following lesson to expand on the Speaking & Listening Workshop:
- Giving and Actively Listening to Persuasive Presentations, pp. 19–22

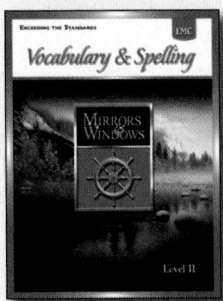

Vocabulary & Spelling
This resource contains:
- Two lessons on Reference Materials, pp. 64–67
- One lesson on Synonyms and Antonyms, pp. 68–69

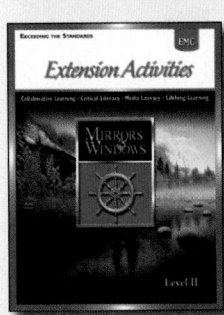

Extension Activities
This resource contains one extended lesson for each of the following:
- Collaborative Learning: Analyze the Story, p. 19
- Critical Literacy: Perform Reader's Theater, pp. 20–21

Unit 7 Visual Planning Guide

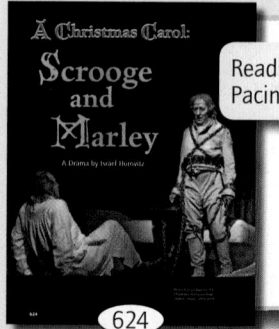

A Defenseless Creature
A Drama by Neil Simon, based on a story by Anton Chekhov

612

Reading Level: Moderate
Pacing: 3 days

 25 Quiz ?

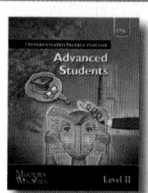

Meeting the Standards,
Reading Model,
pp. 19–27

A Christmas Carol:
Scrooge and Marley
A Drama by Israel Horovitz

624

Reading Level: Challenging
Pacing: 3 days

25 Quiz ?

Meeting the Standards,
Directed Reading,
pp. 28–33

Advanced Students,
Historical Context
Project, pp. 41–42

A Christmas Carol:
Scrooge and Marley
ACT 2
SCENE 1

645

Reading Level: Challenging
Pacing: 4 days

25 Quiz ?

Meeting the Standards,
Directed Reading,
pp. 34–42

606C   **UNIT 7** DRAMA

 Interactive Student
Text on CD-ROM

25 Selection
Lesson Plan

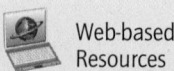 Web-based
Resources

Lesson-by-Lesson Resources

670

Reading Level: Challenging
Pacing: 3 days

Meeting the Standards,
Directed Reading, pp.
43–48

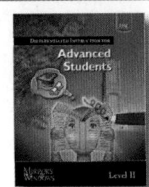

Advanced Students,
Communication
Analysis, p. 43

688

Reading Level: Easy;
Challenging Pacing: 2 days

Meeting the Standards,
Directed Reading,
pp. 49–58

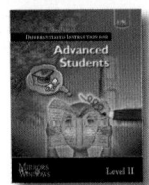

Advanced Students,
Literature Comparison,
p. 44

694

Reading Level: Challenging
Pacing: 2 days

Meeting the Standards,
Independent Reading,
pp. 59–68

Developing Readers,
Use Text Organization,
pp. 49–51

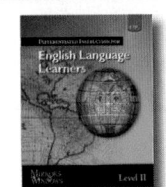

*English Language
Learners,* Cause and
Effect, pp. 152–174

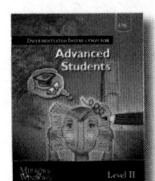

Advanced Students,
Media Study, p. 45

Quiz
? Lesson Test   ∩ Audio Library

Unit 7 Scope & Sequence Guide

Selection or Feature	Genre	Reading Support/ Reading Level	Word Count	Reading Skill	Graphic Organizer	
Introduction to Drama pp. 608–609						
Drama Reading Model p. 610						
A Defenseless Creature Neil Simon pp. 611–621	Drama	Guided Reading: Reading Model / Moderate	2,352	Identify Cause and Effect	Cause-and-Effect Chart; Drama Chart	
A Christmas Carol: Scrooge and Marley Act I Israel Horovitz pp. 623–644	Drama	Directed Reading/ Challenging	7,293	Draw Conclusions	Drawing Conclusions Chart; Plot Diagram	
Informational Text Connection: from What Jane Austen Ate and Charles Dickens Knew Daniel Pool pp. 642–643	Essay		548			
A Christmas Carol: Scrooge and Marley Act 2 Israel Horowitz pp. 645–667	Drama	Directed Reading/ Challenging	8,526			
Primary Source Connection: from A Christmas Carol John Leech pp. 665–666	Illustrations					
Let Me Hear You Whisper Paul Zindel pp. 669–686	Drama	Directed Reading/ Challenging	5,234	Distinguish Between Major and Minor Details	Details Chart; Dialogue Chart	
Informational Text Connection: from Going Ape Over Language Natalie Rosinsky pp. 683–685	Article		1,223			
Comparing Literature: St. Crispian's Day Speech William Shakespeare pp. 687–692	Dramatic Monologue	Directed Reading/Easy	234		Diction Chart	
The Charge of the Light Brigade Alfred, Lord Tennyson pp. 687–692	Narrative Poem	Directed Reading/ Challenging	277			

GUIDED READING

DIRECTED READING

Literary Element	*Mirrors & Windows* Theme	Cross-Curricular Connection	Writing Options	Extension Activities
Dramatic Forms Elements of Drama				
Drama	Manipulation		Creative: Scene Expository: Literary Analysis	Media Literacy: Summarize a Play Collaborative Learning: Analyze a Character
Plot	Misery	History Connection: *Industry and Reform*	Creative: Business Letter Persuasive: Review	Collaborative Learning: Analyze the Story Critical Literacy: Compare Versions
	Helping Others		Creative: Diary Entry Expository: Expository Essay	Lifelong Learning: Research Religious Holidays Critical Literacy: Perform a Scene
Dialogue	Ethics		Creative: Journal Entry Expository: Critical Analysis	Lifelong Learning: Write a Research Report Critical Literacy: Perform Reader's Theatre
Compare Literature: Diction	Motivation		Creative: Narrative Poem Expository: Expository Paragraph	Lifelong Learning: Research Shakespeare Critical Literacy: Recite a Monologue
	Following Orders	Cultural Connection: *Crimean War*		

Unit 7 Scope & Sequence Guide

Unit 7 Language Arts Workshops

Grammar & Style	Vocabulary & Spelling	Writing	Speaking & Listening	Test Practice
Verbals: Participles, Gerunds, and Infinitives, p. 622	Using Dictionaries and Thesauruses, p. 668	Persuasive Writing: Persuasive Essay, pp. 710–715	Giving and Actively Listening to Persuasive Presentations, pp. 716–717	Writing Skills: Persuasive Essay, p. 718
Punctuation: Dashes, Semicolons, and Colons, p. 693				Revising and Editing Skills, p. 719
				Reading Skills: from *The Ugly Duckling* by A.A. Milne, pp. 720–721

Literary Element	*Mirrors & Windows* Theme	Cross-Curricular Connection	Writing Options	Extension Activities
Mood	Reaching Unfair Conclusions		Expository: Literary Analysis	Critical Literacy: Role-play Characters from the Screenplay

Unit 7 Building Vocabulary

The lists below identify the Words in Use and Key Terms within this unit. These words are listed at the bottom of the Teacher's Edition pages at the beginning of each lesson. Vocabulary development activities are provided in the *Meeting the Standards* unit book and in *Exceeding the Standards: Vocabulary & Spelling*.

WORDS IN USE

Preview Vocabulary
Preview Vocabulary are words taken from the sentences within each selection. These words are defined in the side margin or at the bottom of the pages on which they appear. The "Preview Vocabulary" section introduces these words in the Before Reading page preceding each selection.

abundance, 629	blunder, 690	intercede, 659	terminate, 676
analysis, 671	compulsion, 646	lamentation, 633	venture, 654
apprehensively, 673	compulsory, 672	odious, 649	wane, 653
bleak, 626	destitute, 629	reel, 691	worldly, 632

Selection Words
Selection Words are additional words from the reading that may be challenging but are not central to the selection and are not identified in the prereading section. These words can easily be learned using the story context, and they provide excellent practice for using content clues to find meaning without explicit instruction.

atmosphere, 674	etiquette, 642	literally, 642	revelers, 647
battery, 691	exhibition, 642	memorable, 683	sabers, 691
confidentially, 645	impropriety, 627	mischievously, 684	seething, 645
contemplates, 673	incense, 647	mourner, 625	solitary, 626
decapitated, 675	infinity, 694	nebulae, 694	sundered, 691
deducted, 615	intelligible, 695	nervous disorder, 614	superstition, 694
dimension, 694	interspecies, 683	perplexed, 616	tolls, 626
dismal, 627	intimidated, 697	plague, 618	transfixed, 695
efficient, 671	lavish, 646	portable, 696	
encased, 613	linguist, 685	reflective, 695	

Teaching Words
Teaching Words consist of vocabulary that is used in the directions about the lessons. Teaching words explain to students what to focus on within the selection, help establish the story context, clarify the meaning of literary terms, and define the goals or instructional purpose.

adequate, 634	critical, 686	incorporated, 708	profound, 720
allied, 691	demonstrate, 613	industrialized, 623	prolific, 611
annotations, 712	descends, 608	influence, 710	prominent, 621, 641
anticipate, 711	dictating, 608	inspirational, 687	reform, 634
aspire, 718	discharge, 694	interpretation, 609	revenue, 665
attributed, 710	distinct, 623	mishaps, 608	sanitation, 634
bombarded, 691	diverse, 623	notable, 692	singled, 708
cavalry, 691	endure, 608	ornate, 687	sitcom, 608
chancellor, 720	enhance, 666	paratrooper, 694	sonography, 718
collaboration, 608	envisions, 608	perception, 634	species, 669
comic sketches, 611	faultily, 720	persistence, 611	supportive, 712
commentary, 708	flourished, 623	poet laureate, 687	tactic, 689
conscious, 608	futile, 691	potential, 712	textile, 634
conservation, 669	generate, 708	prehistoric, 608	tragic flaw, 608
constructive, 717	habitat, 669	premiered, 611	ultimately, 608
context, 721	hornrimmed, 720	prestigious, 623	vignettes, 611
controversial, 716	impact, 714	productions, 608	

KEY TERMS

Key Terms are commonly referred to as *academic vocabulary*. These terms appear in the instructional material to teach the terminology that students need to acquire to understand literature. The repetition of the terms throughout the program ensures student mastery and provides a solid foundation for the continuing study of literature and language arts.

act, 609, 667
active listening, 717
adjective, 622, 714
adverb, 622, 714
anecdote, 717
antagonist, 609
article, 622
audience, 712
capitalization, 714
cast, 609, 623
cast of characters, 611, 669
cause, 611
character, 623, 667, 686, 692, 719
climax, 609, 623, 721
comedies, 719
comedy, 608
comparative form, 714
conclusion, 710
conflict, 609, 623, 721
counterargument, 712, 716, 718
definitions, 668
diagram, 667
dialogue, 609, 611, 623, 669, 719
diction, 687
dictionary, 668
direct object, 622

drama, 608, 611, 719
effect, 611
etymology, 668
evidence, 710
exposition, 623, 721
expository essay, 710
fallacy, 717
falling action, 623, 721
fragment, 719
generalization, 717
gerund, 622
grammar, 714
Greek tragedy, 721
illustrate, 665
infer, 689
infinitive, 622
introduction, 710
major detail, 669
minor detail, 669
modifier, 622
monologue, 609, 692, 721
mood, 623, 667
motive, 686
narration, 669, 692
noun, 622
object of a preposition, 622
order of importance, 712
organizational pattern, 710

parallel, 714
participle, 622
past participle, 622
peer review, 713
persuasive essay, 710, 718
persuasive presentation, 716
persuasive technique, 718
play, 608
playwright, 608
plot, 609, 623, 667, 692, 721
positive form, 714
predicate nominative, 622
prepositional phrase, 622
present participle, 622
pronoun, 622
pronunciation, 668
proofreading, 714
prop, 686
protagonist, 609
punctuation, 714
rhetorical device, 718
resolution, 623, 721
rising action, 623, 721
rubric, 710, 717
run-on, 719
scene, 609, 621, 667, 692, 719
screenplay, 608, 694
script, 609

scriptwriter, 694
semicolon, 719
sensory, 667
set, 609
setting, 611, 623, 669, 686, 719
Shakespearean drama, 721
skim, 687
spelling, 714
stage direction, 609, 611, 623, 667, 669, 719
stanza, 692
straight drama, 608, 721
subject, 622
subject-verb agreement, 719
summary, 621, 686
superlative form, 714
synonyms, 66
thesaurus, 668
thesis, 667, 686, 710, 718
thesis statement, 621, 708
tone, 617, 667
topic, 711, 716
tragedies, 719
tragedy, 608, 721
verb, 622
verbal, 622

Objectives

Studying this unit will help students meet the following objectives:

- Connect the themes expressed in the selections to their own lives and to the world around them
- Identify common forms of drama
- Understand different elements of drama, including *plot, characters, dialogue, script, scenery, stage directions, dramatic monologue,* and *diction*
- Understand variations of literary forms and authors' use of language to develop forms

Reading Strategies

Ask Questions
Clarify
Make Inferences
Make Predictions
Visualize

Reading Skills

Distinguish Between Major and Minor Details
Draw Conclusions
Identify Cause and Effect

Literary Elements

Dialogue
Diction
Drama
Plot

Unit 7
Facing Challenges
Drama

ISRAEL HOROVITZ

WILLIAM SHAKESPEARE

NEIL SIMON

Launch the Unit

Place students into small groups and have them read the quotation and introductory paragraph on page 607. Ask groups to develop additional questions about when, how, and why individuals learn new "people skills," as Ebenezer Scrooge has to do. Model a possible question: "When do children learn not to criticize adults?" or "How can people incorporate the attitude of 'innocent until proven guilty' into daily life?" Have groups keep their questions. After you complete the unit, return to the questions and try to answer them as a class.

Writing Options

Creative Writing

Business Letter   Narrative Poem

Diary Entry   Scene

Journal Entry

Expository Writing

Critical Analysis

Expository Essay

Expository Paragraph

Literary Analysis

Persuasive Writing

Review

Language Arts Workshops

Grammar & Style

Verbals: Participles, Gerunds, and Infinitives

Punctuation: Dashes, Semicolons, and Colons

Vocabulary & Spelling

Using Dictionaries and Thesauruses

Writing Workshop

Persuasive Essay

Speaking & Listening Workshop

Persuasive Presentations

Test Practice Workshop

Persuasive Essay

Revising and Editing Skills

Reading Skills

"I present him to you: Ebenezer Scrooge....The cold within him freezes his old features, nips his pointed nose, shrivels his cheek...."

—ISRAEL HOROVITZ, *A Christmas Carol: Scrooge and Marley*

Have you ever faced a challenge? In Israel Horovitz's play *A Christmas Carol: Scrooge and Marley*, Ebenezer Scrooge must learn late in life to treat other people with warmth, kindness, and respect. As you read the drama in this unit, consider how the characters face and resolve conflicts. How can you relate their struggles to your own life?

ALFRED, LORD TENNYSON   PAUL ZINDEL   ROD SERLING

607

Program Resources

For a visual reminder of the unit-based resources available for Unit 7, Drama, see pages 606A and 606B. As you introduce the unit, you may want to provide students with the Unit Study Guide, which is contained in the *Meeting the Standards* resource.

Teach the Genre

Launch the Lesson

Read aloud these lines—the opening sentence of a soliloquy from Shakespeare's *Hamlet:*

To be, or not to be: that is the question:
Whether 'tis nobler in the mind to suffer
The slings and arrows of outrageous fortune,
Or to take arms against a sea of troubles,
And by opposing, end them?

Explain that these are the thoughts of Hamlet, a prince who must decide how to handle an onslaught of problems. In the play *Hamlet,* one event after another challenges his mental and emotional well-being. Tell students that Hamlet reveals his thoughts and emotions in dialogue with other characters and in monologues called soliloquies. Tell them they will learn about facing challenges from the dramatic characters in this unit.

Non-Western Drama

Students may have encountered forms of drama from non-Western traditions. If so, ask them to describe what they have seen. Possibilities include Indian and East Asian puppet theatre, Japanese no and kabuki theater, Chinese opera, and ceremonial drumming and dancing performances from many cultures.

"The bell tolls and I must take my leave. You must stay a while with Scrooge and watch him play out his scroogey life. It is now the story: the once-upon-a-time."

—ISRAEL HOROVITZ, *A Christmas Carol: Scrooge and Marley*

The art of performance has been around since the beginnings of human history. Modern theater can trace its roots back to prehistoric dance rituals, Native American healing ceremonies, African storytellers, and dramatic productions of the ancient Greeks, to name a few. A **drama** is a piece of literature that is written to be performed for an audience.

Dramatic Forms

Plays for the Theater

A play is a type of drama written for the stage. The playwright envisions how the story will take shape and includes specifics such as actors' locations on stage and details about props and sets. Unlike a piece of fiction, a playwright's finished script is not the final step. A director will use the script, in collaboration with actors, to make the story come alive on stage.

Screenplays and Television Scripts

Dramas are not always performed on stage. When you go to the movie theater or watch a sitcom on television, you are watching a different kind of drama. Screenplays and television scripts are dramas written to be acted out on film and shown to an audience on screen. In addition to stage directions dictating how an actor should speak or move, for example, screenplays and television scripts usually state how a scene should be filmed. You will see this in Rod Serling's screenplay, "The Monsters Are Due on Maple Street" (page 694).

Drama versus Fiction

Drama and fiction share many elements, such as plot, characters, dialogue, and setting. However, playwrights are faced with additional challenges.

A typical play usually lasts a few hours, and all the action and plot development must take place within that time frame. Playwrights must always be conscious of time, the size of the stage, and an audience's ability to endure and immediately understand what is taking place.

Types of Drama

Most modern Western theater descends from the style of the theatrical productions of the ancient Greeks.

- **Tragedy:** There is usually a heroic protagonist, or main character, who is ultimately destroyed by a tragic flaw within him- or herself.

- **Comedy:** The plot often involves a series of mishaps and humorous situations. Comedies typically have happy endings.

- **Straight Drama:** Most modern plays fall into this category, characterized by realistic characters and situations. Elements of tragedy or comedy may be involved, but usually not in extremes.

Program Resources

To help students explore literature on a deeper level, assign the following activity: Dramatize an Original Script, *Exceeding the Standards: Literature & Reading,* pp. 17–20.

Common Core State Standards

Reading Literature
RL.3

Words in Use

Teaching Words

prehistoric, 608
envisions, 608
collaboration, 608
sitcom, 608
dictating, 608
conscious, 608
endure, 608
descends, 608

productions, 608
ultimately, 608
tragic flaw, 608
mishaps, 608
interpretation, 609

KEY TERMS

PLAY, 608	CAST, 609
DRAMA, 608	DIALOGUE, 609
PLAYWRIGHT, 608	MONOLOGUE, 609
SCREENPLAY, 608	SCRIPT, 609
TRAGEDY, 608	STAGE DIRECTION, 609
COMEDY, 608	ACTS, 609
STRAIGHT DRAMA, 608	SCENE, 609
PLOT, 609	SET, 609
CONFLICT, 609	
CLIMAX, 609	
PROTAGONIST, 609	
ANTAGONIST, 609	

Elements of Drama

A drama, in its simplest form, is a story like any other piece of fiction. Unlike fiction, drama is composed of various theatrical elements that allow the story to be performed and brought to life.

Plot

Just as in novels and short stories, the **plot** introduces a drama's central conflict, or struggle, develops it through rising action, and resolves it after the climax.

Characters

The characters are the individuals who take part in the action of a drama. As in fiction, the **protagonist** is the most important character. Sometimes, another character takes on the role of the **antagonist,** who engages in conflict with the protagonist. Together, all of the characters form the drama's **cast.** The cast is usually listed at the beginning of a script, and it is the actions of and interactions among these characters that reveal the drama's plot.

Dialogue

In a drama, plot is mostly revealed through physical action and **dialogue,** or conversation between characters. Because of the performance format of drama, there is little room for narrative description as there is in most fiction. Thus, the audience learns the thoughts and feelings of characters, as well as the context for the story line, through what the characters do and say to each other. Sometimes, information is presented to the audience through the speech of one character. This is called a **monologue.** William Shakespeare's "St. Crispian's Day Speech" (page 687) from his play *Henry V* is an example of a monologue.

Script

A **script** is a drama's actual text. It includes character names, setting, stage directions, and dialogue. **Stage directions** appear before and after lines of dialogue, and they indicate how a character should say a certain line, what facial expressions to make, what gestures to use, and so on. Directions telling actors how and where to stand, move, or enter and exit the stage usually refer to this grid:

Up Right	Up Center	Up Left
Right Center	Center	Left Center
Down Right	Down Center	Down Left

Audience

The parts of the stage are described from the actors' point of view, looking out at the audience.

Just as a novel is sometimes divided into chapters, a script is usually divided into **acts** and **scenes.** Many plays have two or three acts, and each act is made up of a number of scenes.

Scenery

The scenery of a drama is called the **set.** The set includes the setting of each scene, the stage design, the lighting, and the props, or movable objects used by the characters. The playwright or screenwriter usually includes notes about stage design and the setting of each scene, but it is ultimately up to the production's director to interpret the scenery as he or she wishes.

Interpretations and Culture

A playwright's script may always read the same on paper, but the playwright's words are only the beginning. Each interpretation and performance breathes new life into a drama. Today, the classic plays of the ancient Greeks are still being performed around the world. A drama becomes something new in each theater, with each cast or director, and in each culture or time period in which it is performed and received.

Introduce the Process

Use this page to show students the basic instruction provided for them before, during, and after reading most dramas in Unit 7.

"A Defenseless Creature" is an Active Reading Model. Side notes in the lesson prompt students to become more active readers by using reading strategies and skills, analyzing literature, and making connections. Students can apply the process they use to read "A Defenseless Creature" to other selections in Unit 7.

For more information, see Reading Strategies and Skills, Section 1 in the Language Arts Handbook.

Before Reading Stress the two types of background students need to apply, and encourage students to always set a purpose for reading.

During Reading Point out the side notes on page 613: Analyze Literature and Use Reading Skills. Then show students the Mirrors & Windows questions on page 620. Explain that through these questions they will first respond to the drama personally, and then apply their insights to a broader issue.

After Reading Show students page 621. Tell them that "Find Meaning" questions will help them recall and interpret details. "Make Judgments" questions ask them to analyze a play and evaluate how specific details contribute to its overall literary effect and meaning.

Drama Reading Model

BEFORE READING

Build Background

You need to apply two types of background to read a drama effectively. One type is the drama's literary and historical context. Read the **Build Background** and **Meet the Author** features to get this information. The other type of background is the personal knowledge and experience you bring to your reading.

Set Purpose

A playwright presents characters and scenes to say something about life. Read **Set Purpose** to decide what you want to get out of the drama.

Analyze Literature

A playwright uses literary techniques, such as plot and dialogue, to create meaning. The **Analyze Literature** feature draws your attention to a key literary element in the drama.

Use Reading Skills

The **Use Reading Skills** feature will show you skills to help you get the most out of your reading. Learn how to apply skills such as drawing conclusions and summarizing. Identify a graphic organizer that will help you apply the skill before and while you read.

DURING READING

Use Reading Strategies

- **Ask questions** about things that seem significant or interesting.
- **Make predictions** about what's going to happen next. As you read, gather more clues to confirm or change your prediction.
- **Visualize** the drama. Form pictures in your mind to help you see the characters, actions, and settings.
- **Make inferences,** or educated guesses, about what is not stated directly.
- **Clarify,** or check that you understand, what you read. Reread any difficult parts.

Analyze Literature

What literary elements stand out? Are the characters vivid and interesting? Is there a strong central conflict? As you read, consider how these elements affect your enjoyment and understanding of the drama.

Make Connections

Notice where connections can be made between the drama and your life or the world outside the drama. What feelings or thoughts do you have while reading the drama?

AFTER READING

Find Meaning

Recall the important details of the drama, such as the sequence of events and characters' names. Use this information to **interpret,** or explain, the meaning of the drama.

Make Judgments

- **Analyze** the text by examining details and deciding what they contribute to the meaning.
- **Evaluate** the text by making judgments about how the author creates meaning.

Analyze Literature

Review how the use of literary elements increases your understanding of the story. For example, if the author uses monologue, how does it help to shape the drama's meaning?

Extend Understanding

Go beyond the text by exploring the drama's ideas through writing or other creative projects.

610 UNIT 7 DRAMA

Differentiated Instruction

Reading Proficiency

Use drama to help students develop fluency. After choosing a play or excerpt, gather readers and give them a frame of reference for reading. For example, you could say that Paul Zindel's *Let Me Hear You Whisper* is about a woman whose job comes to upset her. Pair students for cooperative reading. Have them skim the play or excerpt and read the stage directions, and then give pairs time to read aloud. Help them give each other appropriate encouragement and feedback. Pairs may read the selection more than once. After they have read enough to feel comfortable with the dialogue, gather a group for a reading.

A Defenseless Creature

A Drama by Neil Simon, based on a story by Anton Chekhov

Apply the Model
BEFORE READING
DURING READING
AFTER READING

GUIDED READING

Build Background

Literary Context "A Defenseless Creature" is from a play entitled *The Good Doctor* by Neil Simon. *The Good Doctor* consists of a series of vignettes adapted from stories written by Russian author Anton Chekhov. Born in 1860, Chekhov began writing comic sketches for humorous journals to support his family and himself as he studied medicine. By 1888, his stories had achieved great popularity. Chekhov went on to become one of Russia's greatest playwrights and was influential in developing the modern short story.

Reader's Context How can persistence convince people to help you even if your request is unreasonable?

Set Purpose

Skim the stage directions in *italic type*. What do you think the mood of the play will be?

Analyze Literature

Drama A story intended to be performed by actors for an audience is called a **drama,** or play. A dramatic script usually includes a cast of characters, a description of the setting, dialogue, and stage directions. As you read "A Defenseless Creature" identify details in the dialogue and stage directions that provide information about the characters.

Meet the Author

Neil Simon (b. 1927) began writing for radio and television comedians while still in his teens. His first play, *Come Blow Your Horn,* was written in 1960. Since then, the prolific author has written dozens of hit Broadway shows and screenplays including *Sweet Charity, Barefoot in the Park,* and *The Odd Couple.* In 1973, *The Good Doctor,* with "A Defenseless Creature" as one of its most popular vignettes, premiered in New York.

Use Reading Skills

Identify Cause and Effect As you read a dramatic script, identify cause-and-effect relationships created by stage directions, dialogue, and characters' actions. Determine the reasons, or *causes,* something exists or occurs, as well as the results, or *effects.* Record your ideas in a chart.

Cause	Effect
Kistunov is suffering from gout.	Loud noises bother him.

Preview Vocabulary

in•ca•pac•i•tat•ed (in' kə pa´ sə tāt' ed) *adj.,* unable to engage in normal activities; disabled

com•po•sure (kəm pō´ zhər) *n.,* calmness of mind or appearance

pe•ti•tion (pə ti´ shən) *n.,* formal request

del•i•cate•ly (del´ i kət lē) *adv.,* carefully; cautiously

ar•dent (är´ dənt) *adj.,* warmth of feeling characterized by eager support

prov•o•ca•tion (präv' ə kā´ shən) *n.,* something that calls forth an action or emotion

Preview the Model

At a Glance
Guided Reading: Reading Model
- Reading Level: Moderate
- Difficulty Considerations: Vocabulary and characterizations
- Ease Factor: Humor

Objectives
Studying this lesson will enable students to
- use reading skills such as identifying cause and effect
- define drama and recognize elements of drama in the selection
- describe some of Neil Simon's literary accomplishments
- appreciate a humorous play based on a short story by Anton Chekhov

Launch the Lesson
Ask students for examples of slapstick humor in movies, television shows, and plays that they have seen. If students are unfamiliar with the term *slapstick,* explain that it refers to humor that relies on physical actions and ridiculous situations. As students read "A Defenseless Creature," tell them to note elements that might qualify it as slapstick.

Words in Use

Preview Vocabulary	Selection Words	Teaching Words
incapacitated, 613	encased, 613	vignettes, 611
composure, 614	nervous disorder, 614	comic sketches, 611
petition, 615	deducted, 615	persistence, 611
delicately, 616	perplexed, 616	prolific, 611
ardent, 617	plague, 618	premiered, 611
provocation, 618		demonstrate, 613
		prominent, 621

Common Core State Standards

Reading Literature
RL.1

Summary

When Mr. Kistunov, a bank official, welcomes a woman into his office, his nerves are already on edge from a painful case of gout. The Woman wants the bank to pay her sick husband's overdue wages. To justify this strange request, the Woman catalogs a list of personal and bizarre misfortunes. Kistunov reasonably points out to the Woman that her husband's employer, not the bank, is responsible for his lost wages, but the shrewish female persists. Pained by her prolonged histrionics, the exhausted Kistunov sees only one way to get rid of the Woman. He orders his assistant to give her the money she wants.

The Mirrors & Windows questions at the end of the selection focus on the theme of manipulation. Before students begin reading ask: How does it feel to be relentlessly pestered?

Critical Viewing

Tell students that a caricature is a drawing that exaggerates a person's traits. Have students think about these questions as they study the caricature.

- Why are the woman and dog looking at the man this way?
- What features of the man and woman are exaggerated?
- Is the caricature funny? Why or why not?

Apply the Model
BEFORE READING
DURING READING
AFTER READING

A Drama by Neil Simon, based on a story by Anton Chekhov

A Defenseless Creature

An Old Woman and Her Dog Startled. Thomas Rowlandson. Private collection.

612

Program Resources

Planning and Assessment
Program Planning Guide, Selection Lesson Plan
E-Lesson Planner
Assessment Guide, Lesson Test
ExamView

Technology Tools
Interactive Student Text on CD
Visual Teaching Package
Audio Library
mirrorsandwindows.com

Meeting the Standards
Drama: Unit 7, Reading Model, pp. 19–27

"I'm about to lose my mind. The hair is coming out of my head."

The lights come up on the office of a bank official, KISTUNOV. *He enters on a crutch; his right foot is heavily encased in bandages, swelling it to three times its normal size. He suffers from the gout[1] and is very careful of any mishap which would only intensify his pain. He makes it to his desk and sits. An* ASSISTANT, *rather harried,[2] enters.*

ASSISTANT. [*With volume.*] Good morning, Mr. Kistunov!

KISTUNOV. Shhh! Please....Please lower your voice.

ASSISTANT. [*Whispers.*] I'm sorry, sir.

KISTUNOV. It's just that my gout is acting up again and my nerves are like little firecrackers. The least little friction can set them off.

ASSISTANT. It must be very painful, sir.

KISTUNOV. Combing my hair this morning was agony.

ASSISTANT. Mr. Kistunov.

KISTUNOV. What is it, Pochatkin?

ASSISTANT. There's a woman who insists on seeing you. We can't make head or tail out of her story, but she insists on seeing the directing manager. Perhaps if you're not well—

KISTUNOV. No, no. The business of the bank comes before my minor physical ailments. Show her in, please...quietly. [*The* ASSISTANT *tiptoes out. A* WOMAN *enters. She is in her late forties, poorly dressed. She is of the working class. She crosses to the desk, a forlorn look on her face. She twists her bag nervously.*] Good morning, madame. Forgive me for not standing, but I am somewhat <u>incapacitated</u>. Please sit down.

WOMAN. Thank you.

She sits.

KISTUNOV. Now, what can I do for you?

WOMAN. You can help me, sir. I pray to God you can help. No one else in this world seems to care....

---

1. **gout.** Condition that causes painful swelling of the joints, especially of the feet and hands
2. **harried.** Overwhelmed by problems

Teach the Model

Analyze Literature
Drama Point out that stage directions often provide details about the physical appearance of the setting and characters. Ask students what these stage directions explain about the setting and characters. (The play takes place in the office of Kistunov, a bank official. Kistunov's right foot is bandaged, he's in extreme pain, and something or someone has agitated his Assistant.) **A**

Science Connection
Gout Gout is a very painful condition that often affects the large joint of the big toe, but can also affect knee, wrist, and ankle joints. Uric acid is a waste product of digestion that normally dissolves in the blood and leaves the body via the kidneys. Gout occurs when the body either produces too much uric acid or fails to excrete enough. When uric acid builds up, sharp crystals can form in or around a joint, leading to inflammation, swelling, tenderness, and pain. Men are more likely to get gout than women. **B**

Analyze Literature
Drama *Answer:* He is a bank official using a crutch because of gout. **C**

Use Reading Skills
Identify Cause and Effect *Answer:* He believes the good of the bank is more important than his own discomfort. **D**

Differentiated Instruction

English Language Learning
Students learning English may need help with the following words:
intensify—make worse, 613
forlorn—sad and hopeless, 613
inkling—an idea based on clues, 614
recuperating—recovering one's health, 614
lunatic—a totally unreasonable person, 614

Reading Proficiency
Emphasize the value of reading *all* parts of the play, including stage directions, speaker tags, and dialogue. Have struggling students read the play as they listen to an oral reading. You can read aloud, or you can ask proficient readers to volunteer. You may also be able to locate a DVD of *The Good Doctor,* the Neil Simon play of which this is a part.

Teach the Model

Use Reading Skills
Identify Cause and Effect What effect does the Woman's wail have on Kistunov? What else is contributing to this effect? (Kistunov is in pain and his nerves are on edge. The Woman's wail worsens his pain, so he winces and grits his teeth.) **A**

Use Reading Skills
Identify Cause and Effect *Answer:* Kistunov suspects that the Woman's own irritating nature caused the husband's nervous disorder. **B**

Analyze Literature
Tone Ask students to describe the tone of the play so far. What details contribute to this tone? Model a response: "The Woman's wails and screams are comical. Kistunov's verbal responses to the Woman (for example, 'I have an inkling') add an ironic twist. I would say the tone so far is comically ironic." **C**

Analyze Literature
Humor Point out that when the woman says her sister has been dizzy for a month, she is probably exaggerating. Writers often use exaggeration to create humor. **D**

A *She begins to cry, which in turn becomes a wail—the kind of wail that melts the spine of strong men.* KISTUNOV *winces and grits his teeth in pain as he grips the arms of his chair.*

KISTUNOV. Calm yourself, madame. I *beg* of you. Please calm yourself.

WOMAN. I'm sorry. [*She tries to calm down.*]

KISTUNOV. I'm sure we can sort it all out if we approach the problem sensibly and quietly....Now, what exactly is the trouble?

WOMAN. Well, sir....It's my husband. Collegiate Assessor[3] Schukin. He's been sick for five months....Five agonizing months.

KISTUNOV. I know the horrors of illness and can sympathize with you, madame. What's the nature of his illness?

WOMAN. It's a nervous disorder. Everything grates on his nerves. If you so much as touch him he'll scream out— [*And without warning, she screams a loud bloodcurdling scream that sends* KISTUNOV *almost out of his seat.*] How or why he got it, nobody knows.

C

DURING READING

**Use Reading Skills
Identify Cause and
Effect** What does Kistunov
think causes the husband's
nervous disorder? **B**

com•po•sure
(kəm pō´ zhər) *n.,* calmness
of mind or appearance

KISTUNOV. [*Trying to regain his* <u>composure</u>.] I have an inkling....Please go on, a little less descriptively, if possible.

WOMAN. Well, while the poor man was lying in bed—

KISTUNOV. [*Braces himself.*] You're not going to scream again, are you?

WOMAN. Not that I don't have cause....While he was lying in bed these five months, recuperating, he was dismissed from his job—for no reason at all.

KISTUNOV. That's a pity, certainly, but I don't quite see the connection with our bank, madame.

WOMAN. You don't know how I suffered during his illness. I nursed him from morning till night. Doctored him from night till morning. Besides cleaning my house, taking care of my children, feeding our dog, our cat, our goat, my sister's bird, who was sick....

KISTUNOV. The bird was sick?

D **WOMAN.** My sister! She gets dizzy spells. She's been dizzy a month now. And she's getting dizzier every day.

KISTUNOV. Extraordinary. However—

WOMAN. I had to take care of her children and her house and her cat and her goat, and then her bird bit one of my children, and so our

---

3. Collegiate Assessor. Civil service rank in Imperial Russia

---

Differentiated Instruction

English Language Learning
Students learning English may benefit from an explanation of the following idiomatic expressions in the play:

grates on his nerves—annoys someone, 614
(about) to crack—to become mentally ill, 615

pack of (troubles)—a great number of, 615
lose my mind—become crazy, 615–616
making headway—making progress, 616
man of your word—person who can be trusted, 616
sink/sank in—become/became understandable, 617
skin and bones—very thin, 618

"Yes, well, you've certainly had your pack of troubles, haven't you? But I don't quite see—"

cat bit her bird, so my oldest daughter, the one with the broken arm, drowned my sister's cat, and now my sister wants my goat in exchange, or else she says she'll either drown my cat or break my oldest daughter's other arm— **E**

KISTUNOV. Yes, well, you've certainly had your pack of troubles, haven't you? But I don't quite see—

WOMAN. And then, I went to get my husband's pay, they deducted twenty-four rubles[4] and thirty-six kopecks.[5] For what? I asked. Because, they said, he borrowed it from the employees' fund. But that's impossible. He could never borrow without my approval. I'd break his arm....Not while he was sick, of course....I don't have the strength. I'm not well myself, sir. I have this racking cough that's a terrible thing to hear—

She coughs rackingly[6]—so rackingly that KISTUNOV *is about to crack.* **F**

KISTUNOV. I can well understand why your husband took five months to recuperate. But what is it you want from me, madame?

WOMAN. What rightfully belongs to my husband—his twenty-four rubles and thirty-six kopecks. They won't give it to me because I'm a woman, weak and defenseless. Some of them have laughed in my face, sir....Laughed! [*She laughs loud and painfully.* KISTUNOV *clenches[7] everything.*] Where's the humor I wonder, in a poor, defenseless creature like myself? **G**

She sobs.

KISTUNOV. None....I see none at all. However, madame, I don't wish to be unkind, but I'm afraid you've come to the wrong place. Your <u>petition</u>, no matter how justified, has nothing to do with us. You'll have to go to the agency where your husband was employed.

WOMAN. What do you mean? I've been to *five* agencies already and none of them will even listen to my petition. I'm about to lose my

---

4. **rubles.** Units of Russian money
5. **kopecks.** Hundredths of a ruble
6. **rackingly.** With heaves of painful effort
7. **clenches.** Holds or grips tightly

pe•ti•tion (pə ti´ shən) *n.,* formal request

A DEFENSELESS CREATURE **615**

A DEFENSELESS CREATURE **615**

Drama *Answer:* The stage directions tell the actor portraying the Woman to pull out a clump of her hair. Then they say for her to throw it on Kistunov's desk, for Kistunov to hand it back to her, and for her to put the clump back in her hair. Such bizarre action contributes to the wacky mood. **A**

▶ More About the Author

Anton Chekhov, who died of complications from tuberculosis when he was forty-four, wrote more than seven hundred short stories during his relatively brief career. Most of his stories offer a view of the ridiculous and sometimes tragic side of human nature. They also reveal Chekhov's keen ability to portray all Russians, from nobles to peasants, with wit and sensitivity. Later in his career, Chekhov penned a number of successful plays including *The Seagull,* published in1896, *Uncle Vanya,* published in 1897, and *Cherry Orchard,* published in 1904. Today, most literary analysts consider Chekhov the father of the modern short story and the modern drama.

Use Reading Skills

Identify Cause and Effect Ask students why Kistunov feels qualified to understand the husband's suffering. (Both suffer because of the Woman.) **B**

"Are you saying you won't believe my husband is sick? Here! Here is a doctor's certificate."

DURING READING

Analyze Literature
Drama How do the stage directions in this dialogue contribute to the play's mood? **A**

del·i·cate·ly
(del´ i kət lē) *adv.,* carefully; cautiously

mind. The hair is coming out of my head. [*She pulls out a handful.*] Look at my hair. By the fistful. [*She throws a fistful on his desk.*] Don't tell me to go to another agency!

KISTUNOV. [*Delicately and disgustedly, he picks up her fistful of hair and hands it back to her. She sticks it back in her hair.*] Please, madame, keep your hair in its proper place. Now listen to me carefully. This-is-a-bank. A bank! We're in the banking business. We bank money. Funds that are brought here are banked by us. Do you understand what I'm saying?

WOMAN. What are you saying?

KISTUNOV. I'm saying that I can't help you.

WOMAN. Are you saying you can't help me?

KISTUNOV. [*Sighs deeply.*] I'm trying. I don't think I'm making headway.

WOMAN. Are you saying you won't believe my husband is sick? Here! Here is a doctor's certificate. [*She puts it on the desk and pounds it.*] There's the proof. Do you still doubt that my husband is suffering from a nervous disorder?

KISTUNOV. Not only do I not doubt it, I would swear to it.

WOMAN. Look at it! You didn't look at it!

B **KISTUNOV.** It's really not necessary. I know full well how your husband must be suffering.

WOMAN. What's the point in a doctor's certificate if you don't look at it?! LOOK AT IT!

KISTUNOV. [*Frightened, quickly looks at it.*] Oh, yes….I see your husband is sick. It's right here on the doctor's certificate. Well, you certainly have a good case, madame, but I'm afraid *you've still come to the wrong place.* [*Getting perplexed.*] I'm getting excited.

WOMAN. [*Stares at him.*] You lied to me. I took you as a man of your word and you lied to me.

KISTUNOV. I? LIE? WHEN?

Differentiated Instruction

Enrichment

Students who find humor in the exchanges between Kistunov and the Woman because of miscommunication probably appreciate nuances in the English language. These students may enjoy working in pairs to present the classic "Who's on First" baseball routine to the class. Have students use the library or the Internet to find the script. They can also listen—online—to audio versions of the routine performed by Bud Abbot and Lou Costello, the comics who made it famous. Provide time for students to learn and practice the routine before they present it to the class. For more about "Who's on First," see the Literary Connection note on page 617.

WOMAN. [*Snatches the certificate.*] When you said you read the doctor's certificate. You couldn't have. You couldn't have read the description of my husband's illness without seeing he was fired unjustly. [*She puts the certificate back on the desk.*] Don't take advantage of me just because I'm a weak, defenseless woman. Do me the simple courtesy of reading the doctor's certificate. That's all I ask. Read it, and then I'll go.

KISTUNOV. But I read it! What's the point in reading something twice when I've already read it once?

WOMAN. You didn't read it carefully.

KISTUNOV. I read it in detail!

WOMAN. Then you read it too fast. Read it slower.

KISTUNOV. I don't have to read it slower. I'm a fast reader.

WOMAN. Maybe you didn't absorb it. Let it sink in this time.

KISTUNOV. [*Almost apoplectic.*[8]] I absorbed it! It sank in! I could pass a test on what's written here, but it doesn't make any difference because it has nothing to do with our bank!

WOMAN. [*She throws herself on him from behind.*] Did you read the part where it says he has a nervous disorder? Read that part again and see if I'm wrong.

KISTUNOV. THAT PART? OH, YES! I SEE YOUR HUSBAND HAS A NERVOUS DISORDER. MY, MY, HOW TERRIBLE! ONLY *I CAN'T HELP YOU! NOW PLEASE GO!* [*He falls back into his chair, exhausted.*]

WOMAN. [*Crosses to where his foot is resting.*] I'm sorry, Excellency. I hope I haven't caused you any pain.

KISTUNOV. [*Trying to stop her.*] Please, don't kiss my foot. [*He is too late—she has given his foot a most <u>ardent</u> embrace. He screams in pain.*] Aggghhh! Can't you get this into your balding head? If you would just realize that to come to us with this kind of claim is as strange as your trying to get a haircut in a butcher shop.

WOMAN. You can't get a haircut in a butcher shop. Why would anyone go to a butcher shop for a haircut? Are you laughing at me?

KISTUNOV. Laughing! I'm lucky I'm breathing....Pochatkin!

WOMAN. Did I tell you I'm fasting? I haven't eaten in three days. I want to eat, but nothing stays down. I had the same cup of coffee

---

8. **apoplectic.** Bursting with anger

> **DURING READING**
>
> **Analyze Literature**
> **Drama** What is the tone of Kistunov's dialogue here? How can you tell?
> **C**

ar·dent (är′ dənt) *adj.*, warmth of feeling characterized by eager support

A DEFENSELESS CREATURE **617**

Grammar Skills

Adverb Phrases
Remind students that an adverb phrase can modify a verb, an adjective, or another adverb. An adverb phrase answers the question *when? where? why? how?* or *how much?* Prepositional and infinitive phrases can function as adverbs. For example:

The Woman's husband suffered <u>from a nervous disorder,</u> probably caused <u>by her behavior.</u>

In the following sentences, have students identify the adverb phrases (underscored).
1. Kistunov was frightened <u>by the Woman's outrageous behavior</u> in his office.
2. She demanded that Kistunov look closely <u>at the doctor's certificate</u>.
3. She accused Kistunov of lying <u>to her</u>, which added <u>to his confusion.</u>

Science Connection

False Illnesses Munchausen syndrome is a medical condition in which people attempt to get attention by faking the symptoms of real diseases. Some people with this condition will even injure themselves to get medical attention. Munchausen syndrome is not the same as hypochondria. True hypochondriacs are convinced that they are ill, while people with Munchausen know that they are not. It's extremely likely that the Woman is fabricating her own physical ailments to gain sympathy. **Ⓐ**

Analyze Literature

Motivation Ask students to explain the motivation behind Kistunov's response to the Woman's threat that she is going to faint. (He is frustrated because he hasn't been able to communicate with her; he's angry because while she claims to be defenseless, she's clearly not; and he's in agony from his foot. At this point, he would probably like to strangle her.) **Ⓑ**

Use Reading Skills

Read Aloud To have students appreciate the antipathy that Kistunov feels for the Woman at this point, have them read aloud this passage, using appropriate oral expression to capture his outrage. **Ⓒ**

---

three times today.

KISTUNOV. [*With his last burst of energy, screams.*] POCHATKIN!

prov•o•ca•tion
(präv' ə kā´ shən) *n.,*
something that calls forth an action or emotion

Ⓐ **WOMAN.** I'm skin and bones. I faint at the least <u>provocation</u>….Watch. [*She swoons to the floor.*] Did you see? You saw how I just fainted? Eight times a day that happens.

The ASSISTANT *finally rushes in.*

ASSISTANT. What is it, Mr. Kistunov? What's wrong?

KISTUNOV. [*Screams.*] GET HER OUT OF HERE! Who let her in my office?

ASSISTANT. You did, sir. I asked you and you said, "Show her in."

KISTUNOV. I thought you meant a human being, not a lunatic with a doctor's certificate.

WOMAN. [*To* POCHATKIN.] He wouldn't even read it. I gave it to him, he threw it back in my face….You look like a kind person. Have pity on me. You read it and see if my husband is sick or not.

She forces the certificate on POCHATKIN.

ASSISTANT. I *read* it, madame. Twice!

KISTUNOV. Me too. I had to read it twice too.

ASSISTANT. You just showed it to me outside. You showed it to *everyone*. We *all* read it. Even the doorman.

WOMAN. You just looked at it. You didn't read it.

KISTUNOV. Don't argue. Read it, Pochatkin. For God's sake, read it so we can get her out of here

ASSISTANT. [*Quickly scans it.*] Oh, yes. It says your husband is sick. [*He looks up; gives it to her.*] Now will you please leave, madame, or I will have to get someone to remove you.

KISTUNOV. Yes! Yes! Good! Remove her! Get the doorman and two of the guards. Be careful, she's strong as an ox.

WOMAN. [*To* KISTUNOV.] If you touch me, I'll scream so loud they'll hear it all over the city. You'll lose all your depositors. No one will come to a bank where they beat weak, defenseless women….I think I'm going to faint again….

Ⓑ
Ⓒ **KISTUNOV.** [*Rising.*] WEAK? DEFENSELESS? You are as defenseless as a charging rhinoceros! You are as weak as the King of the Jungle![9] You are a plague, madame! A plague that wipes out all that crosses

---

9. **King of the Jungle.** Lion

Differentiated Instruction

Visual Learning

Have visual learners make collages to analyze the characters of Kistunov and the Woman. For each collage, have students write the character's name (Kistunov or the Woman) in the center of a large piece of paper. Then have them surround the name with descriptive words, sketches, and pictures cut from magazines that capture the character's personality. When they are done, ask students to explain how their collages illustrate techniques of characterization.

"DEFENSELESS? You are as defenseless as a charging rhinoceros!"

your path! You are a raging river that washes out bridges and stately homes! You are a wind that blows villages over mountains! It is women like you who drive men like me to the condition of husbands like yours!

WOMAN. Are you saying you're not going to help me?

KISTUNOV. Hit her, Pochatkin! Strike her! I give you permission to knock her down. Beat some sense into her!

WOMAN. [*To* POCHATKIN.] You hear? You hear how I'm abused? He would have you hit an orphaned mother. Did you hear me cough? Listen to this cough.

She "racks" up another coughing spell.

ASSISTANT. Madame, if we can discuss this in my office—

He takes her arm.

WOMAN. Get your hands off me....Help! Help! I'm being beaten! Oh, merciful God, they're beating me!

ASSISTANT. I am not beating you. I am just holding your arm.

KISTUNOV. Beat her, you fool. Kick her while you've got the chance. We'll never get her out of here. Knock her senseless!

He tries to kick her, misses and falls to the floor.

WOMAN. [*Pointing an evil finger at* KISTUNOV, *she jumps on the desk and punctuates each sentence by stepping on his desk bell.*] A curse! A curse on your bank! I put on a curse on you and your depositors! May the money in your vaults turn to potatoes! May the gold in your cellars turn to onions! May your rubles turn to radishes, and your kopecks to pickles....

KISTUNOV. STOP! Stop it, I beg of you!...Pochatkin, give her the money. Give her what she wants. Give her anything—only get her out of here!

WOMAN. [*To* POCHATKIN.] Twenty-four rubles and thirty-six kopecks....Not a penny more. That's all that's due me and that's all I want.

DURING READING

Make Connections
How would you have responded to the Woman?

DURING READING

Use Reading Strategies
Make Predictions What do you think the Woman's actions will cause Kistunov to do?

A DEFENSELESS CREATURE **619**

Reading Skills

Identify Author's Perspective
Point out that Neil Simon's close adaptation of Anton Chekhov's short story suggests that Simon shared Chekhov's perspective, or view, about what his audiences wanted. Have students answer these questions to make inferences about the authors' perspectives.

- How do you think Chekhov's readers responded to the characters and events in his story?

- How do you think most audiences respond to the characters and events in Simon's play?
- Assuming these responses are what both writers intended, what can you infer about Chekhov's and Simon's viewpoints toward their audiences? What can you infer about their perspectives on the absurdities of human nature?

Analyze Literature

Drama *Answer:* The play concludes with Kistunov beginning "to go mad." Kistunov hits the leg that is causing him great pain, which shows that any pain is better than having the Woman return. This is a sign of his madness. **A**

MIRRORS & WINDOWS

You may want to ask students to write a journal entry or quick write, or divide students into discussion groups or lead a whole-class discussion about this question.
Answer: Students will have had different experiences. Some students may say they agreed, because it was easier or less aggravating than having to constantly deal with the nagging person. Most people don't like to be nagged and might give in just to get peace.

"She's coming back....She's coming back...."

ASSISTANT. Come with me, I'll get you your money.

WOMAN. And another ruble to get me home. I'd walk but I have very weak ankles.

KISTUNOV. Give her enough for a taxi, anything, only get her out.

WOMAN. God bless you, sir. You're a kind man. I remove the curse. [*With a gesture.*] Curse be gone! Onions to money, potatoes to gold—

KISTUNOV. [*Pulls on his hair.*] REMOVE HERRRR! Oh, God, my hair is falling out!

He pulls some hair out.

WOMAN. Oh, there's one other thing, sir. I'll need a letter of recommendation so my husband can get another job. Don't bother yourself about it today. I'll be back in the morning. God, bless you, sir....

She leaves.

DURING READING

Analyze Literature
Drama How do the actions indicated in these stage directions help conclude this play?
A

KISTUNOV. She's coming back....She's coming back....[*He slowly begins to go mad and takes his cane and begins to beat his bandaged leg.*] She's coming back....She's coming back....

Dim-out. ❖

MIRRORS & WINDOWS

When has anyone ever caused you to agree to something unreasonable, just because he or she kept nagging you or making your life unpleasant? Why did you agree? Why might most people act in a similar way?

620   **UNIT 7** DRAMA

Differentiated Instruction

Enrichment

Students might like to stage a production of "A Defenseless Creature" for classmates, family, and the rest of the school. Point out that, depending on how elaborate a production they want to produce, they will need a cast, a director, and a stage crew responsible for set design, lighting, background music, costumes, and programs.

Other students might be interested in adapting a short story as a play. They can choose a story that they have read and discussed in class or a story by a favorite writer. Suggest that they use "A Defenseless Creature" as a model for formatting their script.

Review the Model

Find Meaning

1. (a) It is the bank official's office. (b) The Woman shouldn't be making her request at a bank.

2. (a) She wanted him to pay a claim that her husband made to his employer. (b) She should request money from the employer; the bank has nothing to do with the problem.

3. The Woman is driving Kistunov insane and he wants her to leave.

Make Judgments

4. (a) The mood is humorous. (b) The Woman's ridiculous explanation and behavior and her building conflict with Kistunov establish the mood.

5. (a) The Woman is dramatic, unreasonable, and stubborn. (b) She overwhelms Kistunov's attempts to reason with her, and he goes against his own good sense and agrees to pay her just to get rid of her.

6. (a) The title is ironic because the Woman is anything but defenseless. (b) Students' titles should be consistent with the characters and the plot.

Analyze Literature

Drama Students should add other examples of dialogue and stage directions to the chart that show the humor in the bizarre interaction between the Woman and Kistunov. Although Kistunov starts off apparently sane, the Woman's bizarre behavior and unreasonable demands drive him to act irrationally.

Find Meaning

1. (a) What is the setting of the play? (b) In what way is the setting important to the plot?

2. (a) Why did the Woman come to see Kistunov? (b) Why does Kistunov tell her that she came to the wrong place?

3. Why does Kistunov tell his Assistant to give the Woman the money?

Analyze Literature

Drama Reading a drama is different from reading a story. Everything you learn about the setting, characters, and plot is revealed through dialogue spoken by the actors, their actions, or details in the stage directions. Use a chart to analyze how the author uses dialogue and stage directions to create humor in the play.

Dialogue	Stage Directions
	Describe funny actions such as pulling out hair and screaming

Make Judgments

4. (a) What is the overall mood of the play? (b) What details help establish this mood?

5. (a) What are the Woman's most prominent character traits? (b) How do these traits affect her relationship with Kistunov?

6. (a) Why did the author call this play "A Defenseless Creature"? (b) What title would you give the play? Why?

Extend Understanding

Writing Options

Creative Writing Imagine that you are in charge of producing a show for your classmates. Write a brief **scene** for a humorous play. Be sure to include a cast of characters, setting, dialogue, and stage directions. Use "A Defenseless Creature" as a model for your scene.

Expository Writing Write a brief **literary analysis** of "A Defenseless Creature" that focuses on the tone of the play. Begin your analysis with a thesis statement. Use evidence from the play to support your analysis. Describe the effect of the play's tone on the audience.

Media Literacy

Summarize a Play While "A Defenseless Creature" is adapted from a story by Anton Chekhov, Chekhov is best known as a playwright. Locate one of Chekhov's plays in the school library or on the Internet. Use these resources to write a summary of the play.

Collaborative Learning

Analyze a Character In small groups, analyze the character of the defenseless Woman. Use evidence from the play to discuss her characteristics. Then write a short character sketch. Share your sketch with the class.

Go to www.mirrorsandwindows.com for more.

A DEFENSELESS CREATURE **621**

Rubrics for Writing Options

You can adapt this as a checklist for students to use as they write.

Creative Writing

☐ Does the scene portray a humorous event?

☐ Does the scene include a cast of characters, a description of the setting, dialogue, and stage directions?

☐ Does the scene contain characters and events that students will find entertaining?

Expository Writing

☐ Does the analysis begin with a thesis statement about the play's tone?

☐ Does the analysis use evidence from the play to support the thesis?

☐ Does the analysis describe the possible effects of the tone on the audience?

Teach the Workshop

Identifying Participles, Gerunds, and Infinitives

1. Learning—gerund; to change—infinitive
2. Meeting—participle; unfailing—participle
3. pleading—gerund; to work—infinitive; penny-pinching—participle
4. arriving—gerund; to satisfy—infinitive
5. Placing—participle; roasted—participle; cooked—participle; to eat—infinitive

> For more information, see Grammar & Style Section 3.11, Phrases, in the Language Arts Handbook.

Program Resources

You will find additional lessons on Verbals: Participles, Gerunds, and Infinitives in the *Exceeding the Standards: Grammar & Style* resource.

KEY TERMS

VERBAL, 622	PREDICATE
MODIFIER, 622	NOMINATIVE, 622
PARTICIPLE, 622	OBJECT OF A
GERUND, 622	PREPOSITION,
INFINITIVE, 622	622
ADJECTIVE, 622	NOUN, 622
PRESENT	ADVERB, 622
PARTICIPLE, 622	PREPOSITIONAL
PAST	PHRASE, 622
PARTICIPLE, 622	PRONOUN, 622
VERB, 622	ARTICLE, 622
SUBJECT, 622	
DIRECT OBJECT, 622	

Verbals: Participles, Gerunds, and Infinitives

Verbals

Verbals are verb forms that act as identifiers or modifiers. There are three different forms of verbals: participles, gerunds, and infinitives.

Participles

"...Scrooge! A squeezing, wrenching, grasping, scraping, clutching, covetous old sinner!"

—ISRAEL HOROVITZ,
A Christmas Carol: Scrooge and Marley

Participles are verb forms that act as adjectives. There are two kinds of participles: *present participles and past participles*. Present participles, such as the ones in the quotation above, end in *-ing*. Most past participles end in *-ed*. Though they are verb forms, participles act as modifiers.

EXAMPLE

Scrooge put on his <u>sleeping</u> cap and crawled into bed.

Gerunds

"What are you doing, Cratchit? Acting cold, are you?"

—ISRAEL HOROVITZ,
A Christmas Carol: Scrooge and Marley

Gerunds are action nouns formed by adding *-ing* to verbs. In the above quotation, the word *acting* is a gerund. Gerunds can act as the subject, direct object, predicate nominative, or object of a preposition in a sentence.

EXAMPLE

<u>Eating</u> took time away from business.

Both participles and gerunds end in *-ing*. To tell whether the word is a participle or a gerund, determine how the word is used in a sentence. When it is used as an adjective, it is a participle. When it is used as a noun, it is a gerund.

Infinitives

"Next you'll be asking to replenish your coal from my coal-box, won't you?"

—ISRAEL HOROVITZ,
A Christmas Carol: Scrooge and Marley

Infinitives are formed by adding the word *to* to a verb. Infinitives can act as nouns, adjectives, or adverbs in a sentence. In the quotation above, *to replenish* is an infinitive.

EXAMPLE

Bob wanted <u>to collect</u> what Scrooge owed him.

Don't confuse infinitives with prepositional phrases beginning with *to*. In a prepositional phrase, *to* is followed by a noun, pronoun, or article rather than a verb.

Identifying Participles, Gerunds, and Infinitives

Write the verbals in the following sentences. Then label each one *participle, gerund,* or *infinitive.*

1. Learning how people really felt about him seemed to change Scrooge.
2. Meeting the beggars, Scrooge explained his unfailing disregard for the poor.
3. His nephew's pleading didn't seem to work on the penny-pinching Scrooge.
4. Bob learned that arriving early was one way to satisfy Scrooge.
5. Placing the roasted goose and cooked vegetables on the table, she invited the guests to eat.

TEACHING NOTE

Extra Practice

Reinforce the difference between prepositional phrases and infinitives. Have students identify the infinitives (underlined).

1. Seeing the movie *To Kill a Mockingbird* always makes me want <u>to read</u> the book again.
2. We went to the theater <u>to watch</u> the movie.
3. After the film we went out <u>to eat</u>.

Reinforce the difference between participles and gerunds. Have students identify the participles (underlined).

4. Over <u>piping</u> hot pie, we started debating the ending of the film.
5. I stopped Roger from putting the <u>drinking</u> glass in the sink.
6. Of all the <u>conniving</u>, nasty things she said, that one is making me angriest.

Common Core State Standards

Language
L.1

A Christmas Carol: Scrooge and Marley

A Drama by Israel Horovitz

BEFORE READING

Build Background

Cultural Context *A Christmas Carol* by Charles Dickens, the novel on which Israel Horovitz based this play, reflects the social and economic conditions that existed in industrialized London in the 1840s. The city then had two separate and distinct personalities. On the one hand, the English upper classes flourished and prospered. On the other hand, the lower classes struggled for survival in the midst of extreme poverty and shameful living and working conditions.

Reader's Context Do you think that wealth automatically brings happiness and that poverty equals misery? Explain.

Set Purpose

Read the title, cast or list of characters, and description of setting. What do you think the mood of the play will be?

Analyze Literature

Plot As with a work of fiction, the **plot** of a drama consists of five parts. These parts include the *exposition,* in which the characters and setting are introduced, the *rising action,* in which the conflict is introduced, the *climax,* which is the story's turning point, the *falling action,* in which the conflict moves toward resolution, and the *resolution.* As you read *A Christmas Carol: Scrooge and Marley,* think about how these plot elements work together to create an interesting and suspenseful story.

Meet the Author

Israel Horovitz (b. 1939) had his first play, *The Comeback,* produced when he was eighteen years old. Since then he has written dozens of plays, acclaimed for their diverse subject matter and sharp dialogue. In 1979, the year that *A Christmas Carol* was published, Horovitz founded the prestigious Gloucester Stage Company in Massachusetts, where he was artistic director until 2006.

Use Reading Skills

Draw Conclusions

When reading a dramatic script, you will encounter dialogue and stage directions. They let readers imagine the setting, characters, and actions. Use the dialogue and stage directions to draw conclusions about the setting, the traits and attitudes of characters, and the nature of the central conflict.

Details	Conclusions
Jacob Marley's ghost speaks in a cackling voice while eerie music plays in the background.	

Preview Vocabulary

bleak (blēk) *adj.,* windy; cold; raw

des•ti•tute (des´ tə tüt') *adj.,* without money or other basic necessities for survival; extremely poor

abun•dance (ə bʉn´ dən[t]s) *n.,* wealth; riches; surplus of money and possessions

world•ly (wʉr[ə]ld´ lē) *adj.,* of or related to this world

lam•en•ta•tion (la' mən tā´ shən) *n.,* expression of sorrow or regret

A CHRISTMAS CAROL, ACT 1 **623**

Preview the Selection

At a Glance
Directed Reading
- Reading Level: Challenging
- Difficulty Considerations: Vocabulary and setting
- Ease Factor: Familiar, interesting story

Objectives

Studying this lesson will enable students to

- use reading skills such as drawing conclusions
- define plot and recognize the conflict that drives the plot
- describe the literary accomplishments of Israel Horovitz
- appreciate a play based on a classic story by Charles Dickens

Launch the Lesson

Have students share what they know about the story of *A Christmas Carol* and the character of Scrooge. Then write the following sentence on the board: "He is being such a scrooge."

Ask volunteers to read the sentence and replace the word *scrooge* with a synonym. You might repeat this activity after students have read Act 1 of the play and learned more about Scrooge's character.

KEY TERMS

CAST, 623	**FALLING ACTION,** 623
SETTING, 623	
MOOD, 623	**RESOLUTION,** 623
PLOT, 623	**DIALOGUE,** 623
EXPOSITION, 623	**STAGE DIRECTION,** 623
RISING ACTION, 623	
CLIMAX, 623	**CHARACTER,** 623
	CONFLICT, 623

Words in Use

Preview Vocabulary	Selection Words	Teaching Words	
bleak, 626	**mourner,** 625	**industrialized,** 623	**sanitation,** 634
destitute, 629	**solitary,** 626	**distinct,** 623	**reform,** 634
abundance, 629	**tolls,** 626	**flourished,** 623	**perception,** 634
worldly, 632	**dismal,** 627	**diverse,** 623	**prominent,** 641
lamentation, 633	**impropriety,** 627	**prestigious,** 623	
		textile, 634	
		adequate, 634	

Common Core State Standards

Reading Literature
RL.1

Summary

Ebenezer Scrooge has spent the better part of his life pursuing money at the expense of love, family, and happiness. One Christmas Eve, Scrooge gets the chance to redeem himself and salvage the remainder of his life when three ghosts present him with disturbing visions of his past, present, and future. In the opening scene of Act 1, the ghost of Scrooge's dead business partner, Jacob Marley, introduces the audience to Scrooge, who is disgusted by the fuss people make over Christmas. That evening, the first ghost, the Ghost of Christmas Past, visits Scrooge and takes him on a painful emotional journey.

 The Mirrors & Windows questions at the end of the selection focus on the theme of misery. Before students begin reading the play, ask: Do you think some people are born with negative attitudes, or does every unhappy person get that way through experience?

A Christmas Carol:

Scrooge and Marley

A Drama by Israel Horovitz

Photos from productions of *A Christmas Carol* by Goodman Theatre, Chicago, 2003–2006.

624

Program Resources

Planning and Assessment
Program Planning Guide, Selection Lesson Plan
E-Lesson Planner
Assessment Guide, Lesson Test
ExamView

Technology Tools
Interactive Student Text on CD
Visual Teaching Package
Audio Library
mirrorsandwindows.com

Meeting the Standards
Drama: Unit 7, Directed Reading, pp. 28–42

Differentiating Instruction
Advanced Students, Historical Context Project, pp. 41–42

THE PEOPLE OF THE PLAY

JACOB MARLEY, a spectre[1]
EBENEZER SCROOGE, not yet dead, which is to say still alive
BOB CRATCHIT, Scrooge's clerk
FRED, Scrooge's nephew
THIN DO-GOODERS
PORTLY DO-GOODERS
SPECTRES (various), carrying money-boxes
THE GHOST OF CHRISTMAS PAST
FOUR JOCUND[2] TRAVELERS
A BAND OF SINGERS
A BAND OF DANCERS
LITTLE BOY SCROOGE
YOUNG MAN SCROOGE
FAN, Scrooge's little sister
THE SCHOOLMASTER
SCHOOLMATES
FEZZIWIG, a fine and fair employer
DICK, young Scrooge's co-worker
YOUNG SCROOGE
A FIDDLER
MORE DANCERS
SCROOGE'S LOST LOVE
SCROOGE'S LOST LOVE'S DAUGHTER
SCROOGE'S LOST LOVE'S HUSBAND
THE GHOST OF CHRISTMAS PRESENT
SOME BAKERS
MRS. CRATCHIT, Bob Cratchit's wife
BELINDA CRATCHIT, a daughter
MARTHA CRATCHIT, another daughter
PETER CRATCHIT, a son
TINY TIM CRATCHIT, another son
SCROOGE'S NIECE, Fred's wife
THE GHOST OF CHRISTMAS FUTURE, a mute Phantom
THREE MEN OF BUSINESS
DRUNKS, SCOUNDRELS
WOMEN OF THE STREETS
A CHARWOMAN
MRS. DILBER
JOE, an old second-hand goods dealer
A CORPSE, very like Scrooge
AN INDEBTED FAMILY

ADAM, a young boy
A POULTERER
A GENTLEWOMAN
SOME MORE MEN OF BUSINESS

THE PLACE OF THE PLAY

Various locations in and around the City of London, including SCROOGE'S *Chambers and Offices; the* CRATCHIT *Home;* FRED'S *Home;* SCROOGE'S *School;* FEZZIWIG'S *Offices;* OLD JOE'S *Hide-a-Way.*

THE TIME OF THE PLAY

The entire action of the play takes place on Christmas Eve, Christmas Day, and the morning after Christmas, 1843.

(A)

ACT I
— SCENE I —

Ghostly mist in auditorium. A single spotlight on JACOB MARLEY. *He is ancient; awful, dead-eyed. He speaks straight out to auditorium.*

MARLEY. [*Cackle-voiced.*] My name is Jacob Marley and I am dead. [*He laughs.*] Oh, no, there's no doubt that I am dead. The register of my burial was signed by the clergyman, the clerk, the undertaker...and by my chief mourner...Ebenezer Scrooge...[*Pause; remembers.*] I am dead as a door-nail.

A spotlight fades up on SCROOGE, *in his counting-house,[3] counting.*

Lettering on the window behind SCROOGE *reads:* "SCROOGE AND MARLEY, LTD." *The spotlight is tight on* SCROOGE'S *head and shoulders. We shall not yet see into the offices and setting. Ghostly music continues, under.* MARLEY *looks across at* SCROOGE; *pitifully. After a moment's pause.*

(B)

1. **spectre.** Ghost, ghostly presence
2. **jocund.** High-spirited or merry
3. **counting-house.** Office where financial end of a business is handled

---

Use Reading Skills

Draw Conclusions Ask students if they know what the expression *keep your nose to the grindstone* means. If necessary, explain that it means to work extremely hard, continuously. Have students use their knowledge of that expression and what they learn about Scrooge in this speech to figure out what Marley means when he calls Scrooge "England's most tightfisted hand at the grindstone." (Scrooge makes the people he employs work long hours even though he doesn't pay them well.) **Ⓐ**

Analyze Literature

Plot Ask students to explain what role Marley plays in the exposition of the plot. (He sets the stage for the action to begin. He introduces the main character, Scrooge, and describes his personality, including character flaws that will probably contribute to conflict.) **Ⓑ**

Ⓐ **MARLEY.** [*Contd.*] I present him to you: Ebenezer Scrooge...England's most tightfisted hand at the grindstone, Scrooge! A squeezing, wrenching, grasping, scraping, clutching, covetous, old sinner! Secret, and self-contained, and solitary as an oyster. The cold within him freezes his old features, nips his pointed nose, shrivels his cheek, stiffens his gait; makes his eyes red, his thin lips blue; and speaks out shrewdly in his grating voice. Look at him. Look at him...

SCROOGE counts and mumbles.

SCROOGE. They owe me money and I will collect. I will have them jailed if I have to. They owe me money and I will collect what is due me.

MARLEY moves toward SCROOGE, two steps. The spotlight stays with him.

Ⓑ **MARLEY.** [*Disgusted.*] He and I were partners for I don't know how many years. Scrooge was my sole executor, my sole administrator, my sole assign, my sole residuary legatee,[4] my sole friend and my sole mourner. But Scrooge was not so cut up by the sad event of my death, but that he was an excellent man of business on the very day of my funeral, and solemnized it with an undoubted bargain. [*Pauses again in disgust.*] He never painted out my name from the window. There it stands, on the window and above the warehouse door: Scrooge and Marley. Sometimes people new to our business call him Scrooge and sometimes they call him Marley. He answers to both names. It's all the same to him. And it's cheaper than painting in a new sign, isn't it? [*Pauses; moves closer to SCROOGE.*] Nobody has ever stopped him in the street to say, with gladsome looks, "My dear Scrooge, how are you? When will you come to see me?" No beggars implored him to bestow a trifle,[5] no children ever ask him what it is o'clock, no man or woman now, or ever in his life, not once, inquire the way to such and such a place.

MARLEY stands next to SCROOGE now. They share, so it seems, a spotlight.

MARLEY. [*Contd.*] But what does Scrooge care of any of this? It is the very thing he likes! To edge his way along the crowded paths of life, warning all human sympathy to keep its distance.

A ghostly bell rings in the distance. MARLEY moves away from SCROOGE now. As he does, he "takes" the light: SCROOGE has disappeared into the black void beyond. MARLEY walks, talking directly to the audience. Pauses.

MARLEY. [*Contd.*] The bell tolls and I must take my leave. You must stay a while with Scrooge and watch him play out his scroogey life. It is now the story: the once-upon-a-time. Scrooge is in his counting-house. Where else? Christmas eve and Scrooge is busy in his counting-house. It is cold, <u>bleak</u>, biting weather outside: foggy withal:[6] and if you listen closely, you can hear the people in the court go wheezing up and down, beating their hands upon their breasts, and stamping their feet upon the pavement stones to warm them...

The clocks outside strike three.

MARLEY: [*Contd.*] Only three! and quite dark outside already: it has not been light all day this day.

This ghostly bell rings in the distance again. MARLEY looks about him. Music in. MARLEY flies away.

---

4. **executor...legatee.** Legal terms referring to the person left in charge of a deceased person's estate and carrying out the instructions of the will
5. **bestow a trifle.** Give a small gift
6. **withal.** In addition

bleak (blēk) *adj.*, windy; cold; raw

Vocabulary Skills

Extend Vocabulary

Point out that the play includes theater-related terms, such as *fade out* and *crossfade*. Some of these terms may be familiar and some may not. Students can extend their vocabulary of stage terms by looking up unfamiliar words and phrases in a standard dictionary or a dictionary of theatrical terms, and by reading other plays.

Students can use their library's card catalog and the Internet to find plays that interest them. You might also encourage students to look for plays that are adaptations of classic novels and stories, such as *Treasure Island* by Robert Louis Stevenson, adapted by Marjorie Ann York and *The Million-Pound Bank Note* by Mark Twain, dramatized by Walter Anthony Hackett. Urge students to keep a list of new theater terms from all sources.

— SCENE 2 —

Christmas music in, sung by a live chorus, full. At conclusion of song, sound fades under and into distance. Lights up in set: offices of SCROOGE AND MARLEY, LTD. SCROOGE *sits at his desk, at work. Near him is a tiny fire.*

His door is open and in his line of vision, we see SCROOGE'S *clerk,* BOB CRATCHIT, *who sits in a dismal tank of a cubicle, copying letters. Near* CRATCHIT *is a fire so tiny as to barely cast a light: perhaps it is one pitifully glowing coal?* CRATCHIT *rubs his hands together, puts on a white comforter and tries to heat his hands around his candle.* SCROOGE'S *nephew enters, unseen.*

SCROOGE. What are you doing, Cratchit? Acting cold, are you? Next you'll be asking to **(C)** replenish your coal from my coal-box, won't you? Well, save your breath, Cratchit! Unless you're prepared to find employ elsewhere!

NEPHEW. [*Cheerfully; surprising* SCROOGE.] A Merry Christmas to you, Uncle! God save you! **(D)**

SCROOGE. Bah! Humbug![7]

NEPHEW. Christmas a "humbug," Uncle? I'm sure you don't mean that.

SCROOGE. I do! Merry Christmas? What right do you have to be merry? What reason have you to be merry? You're poor enough!

NEPHEW. Come, then. What right have you to be dismal? What reason have you to be morose?[8] You're rich enough.

SCROOGE. Bah! Humbug!

NEPHEW. Don't be cross, Uncle.

SCROOGE. What else can I be? Eh? When I **(E)** live in a world of fools such as this? Merry Christmas? What's Christmas time to you but a time of paying bills without any money; a time for finding yourself a year older, but not an hour richer. If I could work my will, every idiot who goes about with "Merry Christmas"

on his lips, should be boiled with his own pudding, and buried with a stake of holly through his heart. He should!

NEPHEW. Uncle!

SCROOGE. Nephew! You keep Christmas in your own way and let me keep it in mine.

NEPHEW. Keep it! But you don't keep it, Uncle.

SCROOGE. Let me leave it alone, then. Much good it has ever done you!

NEPHEW. There are many things from which I have derived good, by which I have not profited, I daresay. Christmas among the rest. But I am sure that I always thought of Christmastime, when it has come round—as a good time: the only time I know of when men and women seem to open their shut-up hearts freely and to think of people below them as if they really were fellow passengers to the grave, and not another race of creatures bound on other journeys. And therefore, Uncle, though it has never put a scrap of gold or silver in my pocket, I believe that it has done me good, and that it will do me good; and I say, God bless it!

The CLERK *in the tank applauds, looks at the* **(F)** *furious* SCROOGE *and pokes out his tiny fire, as if in exchange for the moment of impropriety.* SCROOGE *yells at him.*

SCROOGE. [*To the* CLERK.] Let me hear another sound from you and you'll keep your Christmas by losing your situation. [*To the* NEPHEW.] You're quite a powerful speaker, sir. I wonder you don't go into Parliament.[9]

NEPHEW. Don't be angry, Uncle. Come! Dine with us tomorrow.

SCROOGE. I'd rather see myself dead than see myself with your family!

---

7. **humbug.** Old-fashioned expression meaning "nonsense"
8. **morose.** Negative; bad-tempered
9. **Parliament.** Highest body of the legislature in England made up of the House of Commons and the House of Lords

A CHRISTMAS CAROL, ACT 1 **627**

Teach the Selection

Use Reading Strategies

Make Inferences Ask students what they can infer about the history of the relationship between Scrooge and his Nephew. (The Nephew has made previous attempts to befriend Scrooge, but Scrooge has never responded favorably.) **Ⓐ**

Make Connections

Ask students to put themselves in the Nephew's place. Do they think they could have remained as good-natured as the Nephew in the same circumstances? (Some students may say that they would have gotten angry and stormed off. Others might say that because it was Christmas, they would not have let Scrooge spoil their cheerful spirit.) **Ⓑ**

NEPHEW. But, why? Why?

SCROOGE. Why did you get married?

NEPHEW. Because I fell in love.

SCROOGE. That, sir, is the only thing that you have said to me in your entire lifetime which is even more ridiculous than "Merry Christmas"! [*Turns from* NEPHEW.] Good afternoon.

NEPHEW. Nay, Uncle, you never came to see me before I married either. Why give it as a reason for not coming now?

SCROOGE. Good afternoon, Nephew!

Ⓐ **NEPHEW.** I want nothing from you; I ask nothing of you: why cannot we be friends?

SCROOGE. Good afternoon!

Ⓑ **NEPHEW.** I am sorry with all my heart, to find you so resolute.[10] But I have made the trial in homage to Christmas, and I'll keep my Christmas humor to the last. So A Merry Christmas, Uncle!

SCROOGE. Good afternoon!

NEPHEW. And A Happy New Year!

SCROOGE. Good afternoon!

NEPHEW. [*He stands facing* SCROOGE.] Uncle, you are the most...[*Pauses.*] no, I shan't. My Christmas humor is intact [*Pause.*] God bless you, Uncle...[NEPHEW *turns and starts for the door, he stops at* CRATCHIT'*s cage.*] Merry Christmas, Bob Cratchit.

CRATCHIT. Merry Christmas to you, sir, and a very, very happy New Year.

SCROOGE. [*Calling across to them.*] Oh, fine, a perfection, just fine...to see the perfect pair of you: husbands, with wives and children to support...my clerk there earning fifteen shillings a week...and the perfect pair of you, talking about a Merry Christmas! [*Pauses.*] I'll retire to Bedlam!

NEPHEW. [*To* CRATCHIT.] He's impossible!

---

10. **resolute.** Determined

Grammar Skills

Parallelism

Tell students that writers use parallelism to make sentences flow smoothly. Parallelism is repeating the form of words, phrases, or whole sentences. As an example, point to Marley's repetition of the words *I am dead* in his first speech and his repeated use of *-ing* words (*squeezing, wrenching, grasping, scraping, clutching*) to describe Scrooge in his second speech.

Have students revise these sentences so that they have parallel structure.
1. His goal was to work hard, to make huge profits, and getting rich. (. . . and to get rich.)
2. He made enemies of friends and family, of his employees, and neighbors, too. (. . . and of neighbors, too.)

CRATCHIT. Oh, mind him not, sir. He's getting on in years, and he's alone. He's noticed your visit. I'll wager your visit has warmed him.

NEPHEW. Him? Uncle Ebenezer Scrooge? Warmed? You are a better Christian than I am, sir. **C**

CRATCHIT. [Opening the door for NEPHEW; two DO-GOODERS enter, as NEPHEW exits.] Good day to you, sir, and God bless.

NEPHEW. God bless...

One man who enters is portly, the other thin. Both are pleasant.

CRATCHIT. Can I help you, gentlemen?

THIN MAN. [Carrying papers and books; looks around CRATCHIT to SCROOGE.] Scrooge and Marley's, I believe. Have I the pleasure of addressing Mr. Scrooge, or Mr. Marley?

SCROOGE. Mr. Marley has been dead these seven years. He died seven years ago this very night.

PORTLY MAN. We have no doubt his liberality[11] is well represented by his surviving partner...[Offers his calling card.]

SCROOGE. [Handing back the card; unlooked at.] Good afternoon.

THIN MAN. This will take but a moment, sir...

PORTLY MAN. At this festive season of the year, Mr. Scrooge, it is more than usually desirable that we should make some slight provision[12] for the poor and destitute, who suffer greatly at the present time. Many thousands are in want of common necessities; hundreds of thousands are in want of common comforts, sir.

SCROOGE. Are there no prisons?

PORTLY MAN. Plenty of prisons.

SCROOGE. And aren't the Union workhouses still in operation?

THIN MAN. They are. Still. I wish that I could say that they are not.

SCROOGE. The Treadmill[13] and the Poor Law[14] are in full vigor then?

THIN MAN. Both very busy, sir.

SCROOGE. Ohhh, I see. I was afraid, from what you said at first that something had occurred to stop them from their useful course. [Pauses.] I'm glad to hear it.

PORTLY MAN. Under the impression that they scarcely furnish Christian cheer of mind or body to the multitude, a few of us are endeavoring to raise a fund to buy the Poor some meat and drink and means of warmth. We choose this time, because it is a time, of all others, when Want is keenly felt, and Abundance rejoices. [Pen in hand; as well as notepad.] What shall I put you down for, sir?

SCROOGE. Nothing!

PORTLY MAN. You wish to be left anonymous?

SCROOGE. I wish to be left alone! [Pauses; turns away; turns back to them.] Since you ask me what I wish, gentlemen, that is my answer. I help to support the establishments that I have mentioned: they cost enough: and those who are badly off must go there.

THIN MAN. Many can't go there; and many would rather die.

SCROOGE. If they would rather die, they had better do it, and decrease the surplus

---

11. **liberality.** Generous behavior and attitude; charity
12. **provision.** Thing provided
13. **Treadmill.** Mechanical device used in English prisons on which prisoners were forced to walk at an incline, six to eight hours a day
14. **Poor Law.** England's Old Poor Law, passed in 1601, offered relief to the poor, especially those unable to work because of old age or physical disabilities. The Poor Law Amendment, passed in 1834, made it impossible for people to collect relief outside of workhouses, or poorhouses, which were known for their harsh, shameful conditions. **D**

des·ti·tute (des´ tə tüt') adj., without money or other basic necessities for survival; extremely poor

abun·dance (ə bʉn´ dən[t]s) n., wealth; riches; surplus of money and possessions

---

Cultural Connection

Forgiveness Values When the Nephew remarks to Cratchit, "You are a better Christian than I," he is referring to Cratchit's ability to forgive Scrooge and recognize a basic goodness in him. Christianity is the foundation of religions that follow the teachings of Jesus Christ, who taught that all humans, as children of God, are basically good and deserve love and forgiveness. **C**

Analyze Literature

Setting Remind students that *A Christmas Carol: Scrooge and Marley* is set in London in the 1840s, when entire families, including children, were sentenced to live in workhouses and debtor's prisons. It didn't matter if people were sick or disabled, or that these places were not fit for human habitation. If people couldn't meet their financial obligations, this was their fate. Ask students how knowing these details about the setting affects their understanding of the characters and the plot. (It sets the stage for events in the play, such as the Do-Gooders' request for money, that emphasize Scrooge's miserly traits. It also helps readers understand why Bob Cratchit wants to keep his job and, therefore, puts up with Scrooge's abuse.) **D**

Differentiated Instruction

Visual Learning

Some students may benefit from creating a time line that shows the sequence of events in each scene of Act 1 of the play. Students can use words and illustrations to show the order in which characters are introduced and main events occur. Students can then refer to their time lines to retell each scene of Act 1 in their own words, as an aid during class discussions about the characters and plot and as a study tool for tests and written responses about the play. Encourage students to continue filling in time lines as they read Act 2.

▶ More About the Author

Dickens wrote *A Christmas Carol* mostly to honor the courageous spirit of the poor, of which he had firsthand knowledge: His own family was thrown into debtor's prison when Dickens was a boy because his father couldn't pay the family's bills. Dickens also wanted to condemn the indifference toward the poor displayed by the wealthy, privileged members of Victorian society in the 1800s. **A**

Use Reading Skills

Draw Conclusions Ask students what they think Cratchit squeezes into the man's hand. (He gives the man money for the poor.) **B**

Analyze Literature

Protagonist and Antagonist

Remind students that a protagonist is the main character of a story who struggles to overcome an internal or external conflict. An antagonist is a character who opposes the protagonist and adds to the conflict. In most literary works, the protagonist is a basically good person with a character flaw that leads to a conflict, and the antagonist is often a villain. In *A Christmas Carol: Scrooge and Marley*, Scrooge is the protagonist. Ask students how Scrooge compares to other protagonists in stories they have read. (At this point in the play, although Scrooge is the main character, he seems like a villain.) **C**

---

population. Besides—excuse me—I don't know that.

THIN MAN. But you might know it!

SCROOGE. It's not my business. It's enough for a man to understand his own business, and not to interfere with other people's. Mine occupies me constantly. Good afternoon, gentlemen! [SCROOGE *turns his back on the gentlemen and returns to his desk.*]

A **PORTLY MAN.** But, sir, Mr. Scrooge...think of the poor.

SCROOGE. [*Turns suddenly to them. Pauses.*] Take your leave of my office, sirs, while I am still smiling.

The THIN MAN *looks at the* PORTLY MAN. *They are undone. They shrug. They move to door.* CRATCHIT *hops up to open it for them.*

THIN MAN. Good day, sir. [*To* CRATCHIT.] A Merry Christmas to you, sir...

CRATCHIT. Yes. A Merry Christmas to both of you...

PORTLY MAN. Merry Christmas...

B CRATCHIT *silently squeezes something into the hand of the* THIN MAN.

THIN MAN. What's this?

CRATCHIT. Shhhh...

CRATCHIT *opens the door; wind and snow whistle into the room.*

THIN MAN. Thank you, sir, thank you.

CRATCHIT *closes the door and returns to his workplace.* SCROOGE *is at his own counting table. He talks to* CRATCHIT *without looking up.*

SCROOGE. It's less of a time of year for being merry, and more a time of year for being loony...if you ask me.

CRATCHIT. Well, I don't know, sir...[*The clock's bell strikes 6 o'clock.*] Well there it is, eh, sir?

SCROOGE. Saved by six bells, are you?

CRATCHIT. I must be going home...[*He snuffs out his candle and puts on his hat.*] I hope you have a...very very lovely day tomorrow, sir.

SCROOGE. Hmmm. Oh, you'll be wanting the whole day tomorrow, I suppose?

CRATCHIT. If quite convenient, sir.

SCROOGE. It's not convenient, and it's not fair. If I was to stop half-a-crown for it, you'd think yourself ill-used, I'll be bound?

CRATCHIT *smiles faintly.*

CRATCHIT. I don't know, sir...

SCROOGE. And yet, you don't think me ill-used, when I pay a day's wages for no work.

CRATCHIT. It's only but once a year...

SCROOGE. A poor excuse for picking a man's pocket every 25th of December! But I **C** suppose you must have the whole day. Be here all the earlier the next morning!

CRATCHIT. Oh, I will, sir. I will. I promise you. And, sir...

SCROOGE. Don't say it, Cratchit.

CRATCHIT. But let me wish you a...

SCROOGE. Don't say it, Cratchit. I warn you...

CRATCHIT. Sir!

SCROOGE. Cratchit!

CRATCHIT *opens the door.*

CRATCHIT. All right, then, sir...well... [*Suddenly.*] Merry Christmas, Mister Scrooge!

And he runs out the door, shutting same behind him. SCROOGE *moves to his desk; gathering his coat, hat, etc. A* BOY *appears at his window...*

BOY. [*Singing.*] "Away in a manger..."

SCROOGE *seizes his ruler and whacks at the image of the* BOY *outside. The* BOY *leaves.*

SCROOGE. Bah! Humbug! Christmas! Bah! Humbug! [*He shuts out the light.*]

Differentiated Instruction

Auditory Learning

Many students will benefit from hearing Scene 2 read aloud. Assign pairs or groups of three students the conversations between or among

- Scrooge and Nephew,
- Nephew and Cratchit,
- Scrooge, Thin Man, and Portly Man, and
- Scrooge and Cratchit.

Encourage students to discuss the characters' personalities and their motivations (what they want and are trying to communicate). Tell students to use their understanding of the characters to read aloud with appropriate feeling and expression. Have students read each conversation in the order it occurs in the scene. If possible, record the readings so students may play them back for greater understanding.

A NOTE ON THE CROSSOVER, FOLLOWING SCENE 2

D

SCROOGE *will walk alone to his rooms from his offices. As he makes a long slow cross of the stage, the scenery should change, Christmas music will be heard, various people will cross by* SCROOGE, *often smiling happily.*

There will be occasional pleasant greetings tossed at him. SCROOGE, *in contrast to all, will grump and mumble. He will snap at passing boys, as might an old horrid hound.*

In short, SCROOGE's *sounds and movements will define him in contrast from all other people who cross the stage: he is the misanthrope, the malcontent, the miser.*[15] *He is* SCROOGE.

This statement of SCROOGE's *character, by contrast to all other characters, should seem comical to the audience.*

During SCROOGE's *crossover to his rooms, snow should begin to fall. All passers-by will hold their faces to the sky, smiling, allowing snow to shower them lightly.* SCROOGE, *by contrast, will bat at the flakes with his walking-stick, as might an insomniac swat at a sleep-stopping, middle-of-the-night swarm of mosquitoes. He will comment on the blackness of the night, and, finally, reach his rooms and his encounter with the magical spectre:* MARLEY, *his eternal mate.*

— SCENE 3 —

SCROOGE. No light at all...no moon...that is what is at the center of a Christmas Eve: dead black: void...

SCROOGE *puts his key in the door's keyhole. He has reached his rooms now. The door knocker changes and is now* MARLEY's *face. A musical sound; quickly: ghosty.* MARLEY's *image is not at all angry, but looks at* SCROOGE *as did the old* MARLEY *look at* SCROOGE. *The hair is curiously stirred; eyes wide open, dead: absent of focus.* SCROOGE *stares*

wordlessly here. The face, before his very eyes, does deliquesce:[16] *it is a knocker again.* SCROOGE *opens the door and checks the back of same, probably for* MARLEY's *pigtail. Seeing nothing but screws and nuts,* SCROOGE *refuses the memory.*

SCROOGE. [*Contd.*] Pooh, pooh!

The sound of the door closing resounds throughout the house as thunder. Every room echoes the sound. SCROOGE *fastens the door and walks across the hall to the stairs, trimming his candle as he goes: and then he goes slowly up the staircase. He checks each room: sitting room, bedroom, lumber-room.*[17] *He looks under the sofa, under the table: nobody there. He fixes his evening gruel on the hob;*[18] *changes his jacket.* SCROOGE *sits near the tiny low-flamed fire, sipping his gruel. There are various pictures on the walls: all of them now show likenesses of* MARLEY. SCROOGE *blinks his eyes.*

SCROOGE. [*Contd.*] Bah! Humbug!

SCROOGE *walks in a circle about the room. The pictures change back into their natural images. He sits down at the table in front of the fire. A bell hangs overhead. It begins to ring, of its own accord. Slowly, surely, begins the ringing of every bell in the house. They continue ringing for nearly half a minute.* SCROOGE *is stunned by the phenomenon. The bells cease their ringing all at once. Deep below* SCROOGE, *in the basement of the house, there is the sound of clanking, of some enormous chain being dragged across the floors; and now up the stairs. We hear doors flying open.*

SCROOGE. [*Contd.*] Bah still! Humbug still! This is not happening! I won't believe it!

MARLEY's GHOST *enters the room. He is horrible to look at: pigtail, vest, suit as usual, but he drags an enormous chain now, to which is fastened cashboxes, keys, padlocks, ledgers,*

---

15. **misanthrope...miser.** Person who dislikes humanity, is dissatisfied, and is greedy
16. **deliquesce.** Dissolve or melt away
17. **lumber-room.** Spare room
18. **gruel...hob.** Refers to cooking a thin soup over an open fire

Analyze Literature

Setting Have students explain how the setting changes from Scene 2 to Scene 3 as described in the Crossover. (It changes from Scrooge's offices to the street where snow falls, music plays, and the joyful Christmas revelers sharply contrast Scrooge, who is aware only of darkness as he reaches the door to his rooms.) **D**

Analyze Literature

Drama Have students point out details in the stage directions at the beginning of Scene 3 that add suspense and suggest something terrible is about to happen to Scrooge. (They may note Marley's image in the knocker, the ghosty music, the thunderous sound of the door closing, Scrooge moving slowly through the house, checking each room, the likenesses of Marley in all the pictures, the ringing bells, the clanking chain, the doors flying open, and the appearance of the horrible ghost of Marley.)

Writing Skills

Review

Have students write a review of a play, a movie, or a television program they have seen recently. The review should summarize the story and evaluate the use of specific dramatic elements. Point out that every genre, or form, of literature has its own distinctive literary elements. For drama, these elements include asides, a cast, monologues, scenes, a script, a set, and stage directions.

Before students begin to write, provide samples of reviews from newspapers and magazines. You might also want to have students submit the title of the work they plan to review for your approval. Have students share their completed reviews with the class.

Use Reading Skills

Analyze Cause and Effect Ask students why Scrooge asks, "Who are you?" (He doesn't recognize Marley, probably because in life Marley didn't look so horrible, and because Scrooge knows Marley is dead, so he doesn't expect to see him sitting in his rooms.) **Ⓐ**

Use Reading Skills

Draw Conclusions Ask students why Scrooge thinks Marley appears. What does he mean when he says "there's more of gravy than of grave" about Marley? (Scrooge suggests that his nerves are easily affected. He probably means that something he ate earlier, maybe something that had gravy on it, is upsetting his stomach and causing him to imagine things.) **Ⓑ**

Analyze Literature

Symbols Point out that writers often use symbols to stand for ideas that are not easy to picture. Ask students what the chain and its attachments symbolize. (The chain symbolizes Marley's slavish devotion to work and money.) **Ⓒ**

Use Reading Strategies

Clarify If students are puzzled by Marley's reference to seven Christmas Eves ago, suggest that they go back to page 629 and reread Scrooge's reply when the Thin Man asks if he is addressing Mr. Scrooge or Mr. Marley. **Ⓓ**

---

deeds, and heavy purses fashioned of steel. He is transparent. If possible, we should now, in faithfulness to Dickens' story, be able to see that MARLEY has no bowels. MARLEY stands opposite the strickened SCROOGE.

SCROOGE. [Contd.] How now! What do you want of me?

MARLEY. Much!

Ⓐ **SCROOGE.** Who are you?

MARLEY. Ask me who I was.

SCROOGE. Who were you then?

MARLEY. In life, I was your business partner: Jacob Marley.

SCROOGE. I see...can you sit down?

MARLEY. I can.

SCROOGE. Do it then.

MARLEY. I shall. [MARLEY sits opposite SCROOGE, in the chair across the table at the front of the fireplace.] You don't believe in me.

SCROOGE. I don't.

MARLEY. Why do you doubt your senses?

Ⓑ **SCROOGE.** Because every little thing affects them. A slight disorder of stomach makes them cheat. You may be an undigested bit of beef, blot of mustard, a crumb of cheese, a fragment of an underdone potato. There's more of gravy than of grave about you, whatever you are!

There is a silence between them. SCROOGE is made nervous by it. He picks up a toothpick.

SCROOGE. [Contd.] Humbug! I tell you: humbug!

MARLEY opens his mouth and screams a ghostly, fearful scream. The scream echoes about each room of the house. Bats fly, cats screech, lightning flashes. SCROOGE stands and walks backwards against the wall. MARLEY stands and screams again. This time, he takes his head and lifts it from his shoulders. His head continues to scream. MARLEY's face again appears on every

picture in the room: all screaming. SCROOGE, on his knees before MARLEY.

SCROOGE. [Contd.] Mercy! Dreadful apparition,[19] mercy! Why, O! why do you trouble me so?

MARLEY. Man of the <u>worldly</u> mind, do you believe in me, or not?

SCROOGE. I do. I must. But why do spirits such as you walk the earth? And why do they come to me?

MARLEY. It is required of every man that the spirit within him should walk around among his fellow-men, and travel far and wide; and if that spirit goes not forth in life, it is condemned to do so after death [MARLEY screams again: a tragic scream from his ghosty bones.] I wear the chain I forged in life. I **Ⓒ** made it link by link, and yard by yard. Is its pattern strange to you? Or would you know, you, Scrooge, the weight and length of the strong coil you bear yourself? It was full and **Ⓓ** heavy and long as this, seven Christmas Eves ago. You have labored on it, since. It is a ponderous[20] chain.

Terrified that a chain will appear about his body, SCROOGE spins and waves the unwanted chain away. None, of course, appears. Sees MARLEY watching him dance about the room. MARLEY watches SCROOGE; silently.

SCROOGE. Jacob. Old Jacob Marley, tell me more. Speak comfort to me, Jacob.

MARLEY. I have none to give. Comfort comes from other regions, Ebenezer Scrooge, and is conveyed by other ministers, to other kinds of men. A very little more, is all that is permitted to me. I cannot rest, I cannot stay, I cannot linger anywhere...[He moans again.] my spirit never walked beyond our counting-house—

---

19. apparition. Ghost-like presence
20. ponderous. Slow and awkward from great weight

---

world•ly (wʉr[ə]ld´ lē) *adj.*, of or related to this world

Differentiated Instruction

English Language Learning

Students learning English may struggle with sentences that contain examples of formal or archaic English, for example, "goes not forth," "hard upon me," and "shun the path I tread." Have students work with fluent partners who can translate these sentences into English that more closely mirrors contemporary speech.

Reading Proficiency

Some students may need a reminder that the play is based on the book *A Christmas Carol* by Charles Dickens. This will help them make sense of the phrase "in faithfulness to Dickens' story" in the stage directions on this page.

mark me!—in life my spirit never roved beyond the narrow limits of our money-changing hole; and weary journeys lie before me!

SCROOGE. But you were always a good man of business, Jacob.

MARLEY. [*Screams word "business"; a flashpot explodes with him.*] BUSI-NESS!!! Mankind was my business. The common welfare was my business; charity, mercy, forbearance,[21] benevolence, were, all, my business.

SCROOGE is quaking.

MARLEY. [*Contd.*] Hear me, Ebenezer Scrooge! My time is nearly gone!!

SCROOGE. I will, but don't be hard upon me. And don't be flowery, Jacob! Pray!

MARLEY. How is it that I appear before you in a shape that you can see, I may not tell. I have sat invisible beside you many and many a day. That is no light part of my penance. I am here tonight to warn you that you have yet a chance and hope of escaping my fate. A chance and hope of my procuring, Ebenezer.

SCROOGE. You were always a good friend to me. Thank'ee!

MARLEY. You will be haunted by Three Spirits.

SCROOGE. Would that be the chance and hope you mentioned, Jacob?

MARLEY. It is.

SCROOGE. I think I'd rather not.

MARLEY. Without their visits, you cannot hope to shun the path I tread. Expect the first one tomorrow, when the bell tolls one.

SCROOGE. Couldn't I take 'em all at once, and get it over, Jacob?

MARLEY. Expect the second on the next night at the same hour. The third upon the next night when the last stroke of twelve has ceased to vibrate. Look to see me no more. Others may, but you may not. And look that,

for your own sake, you remember what has passed between us!

MARLEY places his head back upon his shoulders. He approaches the window, and beckons to SCROOGE to watch. Outside the window, spectres fly by, carrying money-boxes and chains. They make a confused sound of <u>lamentation</u>*. MARLEY, after listening a moment, joins into their mournful dirge. He leans to the window and floats out into the bleak, dark night. He is gone.*

SCROOGE. [*Rushing to the window.*] Jacob! No, Jacob! Don't leave me! I'm frightened!

He sees that MARLEY has gone. He looks outside. He pulls the shutter closed, so that the scene is blocked from his view. All sound stops. After a pause, he re-opens the shutter and all is quiet, as it should be on a Christmas Eve. Carolers carol out of doors, in the distance. SCROOGE closes the shutter and walks down the stairs. He examines the door by which MARLEY first entered.

SCROOGE. [*Contd.*] No one here at all! Did I imagine all that? Humbug! [*He looks about the room.*] I did imagine it. It only happened in my foulest dream-mind, didn't it? An undigested bit of...

Thunder and lightning in the room, suddenly.

SCROOGE. [*Contd.*] Sorry! Sorry!

There is silence again. The lights fade out.

— SCENE 4 —

Christmas music, choral, "Hark the Herald Angels Sing," sung by an onstage choir of children. Above, SCROOGE, in his bed, dead to the world, asleep, in his darkened room. It should appear that the choir is singing somewhere

---

21. forbearance. Patience

lam·en·ta·tion (la′ mən tā′ shən) *n.*, expression of sorrow or regret

A CHRISTMAS CAROL, ACT 1 **633**

Teach the Selection

Use Reading Skills
Draw Conclusions Ask students what Marley has learned in death that he apparently did not understand in life. (He has learned that making the world a better place for all human beings should have meant more to him than making money.) **E**

Analyze Literature
Plot Ask students to explain the significance of Marley's appearance. How does it affect Scrooge? What does it do to move the story forward? (Marley's appearance helps Scrooge recognize what could happen if he continues to live just for work and money. It also foreshadows what will happen next in the story.) **F**

Use Reading Skills
Analyze Cause and Effect Ask students to explain what causes the thunder and lightning and why Scrooge says "Sorry! Sorry!" (Scrooge causes the thunder and lightning when he tries to use an upset stomach to explain Marley's visit. He says "Sorry!" because he knows that he has angered the fates that sent Marley to him.) **G**

Reading Skills

Monitor Comprehension
Point out that stage directions are instructions that tell the actors, members of the stage crew, and the director, who is responsible for blocking each scene, what to do. Explain that *blocking* refers to the planned movements and groupings of actors on the stage.

Have students select a scene from Act 1 of the play to block. They can sketch the blocking in a series of frames to show the different positions of the actors on the stage at different times in the scene, or they can enlist the aid of other students to act out the blocking. Remind students to follow the instructions in the stage directions when creating their blocking plan.

A CHRISTMAS CAROL, ACT 1 **633**

Teach the Selection

Analyze Literature
Drama Have students explain what the stage directions and Marley's speech indicate about his current role in the play. (The stage directions tell the actor playing Marley to speak directly to the audience. The stage directions and Marley's lines indicate that he is acting as narrator and commentator in the play.) **A**

Analyze Literature
Foreshadowing Remind students that foreshadowing hints at what will happen later. Ask students what Marley's dialogue may foreshadow. (It may be foreshadowing the change Scrooge undergoes after the Three Spirits visit him.) **B**

History Connection
Industry and Reform *Answer:* Some may say this makes Scrooge seem less like a villain and more a product of his time. **C**

---

outside of the house. When the singing is ended, the choir should fade out of view and MARLEY *should fade into view, in their place.*

A **MARLEY.** [*Directly to audience.*] From this point forth…I shall be quite visible to you, but invisible to him. [*Smiles.*] He will feel my presence nevertheless, for, unless my senses fail me completely, we are—you and I—witness to the changing of a miser: that one, my partner in life, in business, and in eternity: that one: Scrooge. [*Moves to staircase, below* SCROOGE.] See him now. He endeavors to pierce the darkness with his ferret eyes. [*To audience.*] See him, now. He listens for the hour.

The bells toll. SCROOGE *is awakened and quakes as the hour approaches one o'clock, but the bells stop their sound at the hour of twelve.*

SCROOGE. [*Astonished.*] Midnight! Why this isn't possible. It was past two when I went to bed. An icicle must have gotten into the clock's works! I couldn't have slept through the whole day and far into another night. It isn't possible that anything has happened to the sun, and this is twelve at noon. [*He runs to window; unshutters same; it is night.*] Night, still. Quiet, normal for the season, cold. It is certainly not noon. I cannot in any way afford to lose my days. Securities come due, promissory notes, interest on investments: these are things that happen in the daylight! [*He returns to his bed.*] Was this a dream?

MARLEY *appears in his room. He speaks to the audience.*

B **MARLEY.** You see? He does not, with faith,

believe in me fully, even still! Whatever will it take to turn the faith of a miser from money to men?

SCROOGE. Another quarter and it'll be one and Marley's ghosty friends will come. [*Pauses; listens.*] Where's the chime for one?

Ding, dong.

SCROOGE. [*Contd.*] A quarter past!

Repeats.

SCROOGE. [*Contd.*] Half-past!

Repeats.

HISTORY ▶▶ CONNECTION

Industry and Reform The Industrial Revolution of the late eighteenth century made England the world's first industrial nation. Factories and textile mills drew huge numbers of peasants to cities in search of work. Without adequate housing or sanitation, however, living conditions were miserable breeding grounds for disease. Factory owners and businesspeople grew wealthy, while the poor, including children, labored long hours for little pay. By the mid-nineteenth century, several reform efforts limited the workday for women and children under thirteen but did little to improve pay or working conditions. How does this information shape your perception of Scrooge? **C**

SCROOGE. [*Contd.*] A quarter to it! But where's the heavy bell of the hour one? This is a game in which I lose my senses! Perhaps, if I allowed myself another short doze.

MARLEY. Doze, Ebenezer, doze.

A heavy bell thuds its one ring: dull and definitely one o'clock. There is a flash of light. SCROOGE *sits up, in a sudden. A hand draws back the curtains by his bed. He sees it.*

Differentiated Instruction

Enrichment
A staging of *A Christmas Carol: Scrooge and Marley* would include many background sounds, such as tolling bells, a mournful dirge, thunder and lightning, and Christmas music. Students interested in sound design might enjoy researching this topic further.

- Students can contact music colleges to learn about courses students take to earn a degree in sound design engineering.
- They can contact members of sound design crews for local and professional theaters to learn more about their responsibilities and the tools they use to create sound.
- They can use the Internet to learn more about the history of sound design in theater and film.

SCROOGE. A hand! Who owns it? Hello!

Ghosty music again, but of a new nature to the play. A strange figure stands before SCROOGE— like a child, yet at the same time like an old man: white hair, but unwrinkled skin; long, muscular arms, but delicate legs and feet. Wears white tunic; lustrous belt cinches waist. Branch of fresh green holly in its hand, but has its dress trimmed with fresh summer flowers. Clear jets of light spring from the crown of its head. Holds cap in hand. The SPIRIT is called PAST.

SCROOGE. [*Contd.*] Are you the Spirit, Sir, whose coming was foretold to me?

PAST. I am.

MARLEY. Does he take this to be a vision of his green grocer?[22]

SCROOGE. Who, and what are you?

PAST. I am the Ghost of Christmas Past.

SCROOGE. Long past?

PAST. Your past.

SCROOGE. May I ask, please, sir, what business you have here with me?

PAST. Your welfare.

SCROOGE. Not to sound ungrateful, sir, and really, please do understand that I am plenty obliged for your concern, but, really, kind spirit, it would have done all the better for my welfare to have been left alone altogether, to have slept peacefully through this night.

PAST. Your reclamation,[23] then. Take heed!

SCROOGE. My what?

PAST. [*Motioning to SCROOGE and taking his arm.*] Rise! Fly with me! [*He leads SCROOGE to the window.*]

SCROOGE. [*Panicked.*] Fly, but I am a mortal and cannot fly!

PAST. [*Pointing to his heart.*] Bear but a touch of my hand here and you shall be upheld in more than this!

SCROOGE touches the SPIRIT's heart and the lights dissolve into sparkly flickers. Lovely crystals of music are heard. The scene dissolves into another, Christmas music again.

— SCENE 5 —

SCROOGE and the GHOST OF CHRISTMAS PAST walk together across an open stage. In the background, we see a field that is open; covered by a soft, downy snow: a country road.

SCROOGE. Good Heaven! I was bred in this place. I was a boy here!

SCROOGE freezes, staring at the field beyond. MARLEY's ghost appears beside him; takes SCROOGE's face in his hands, and turns his face to the audience.

MARLEY. You see this Scrooge: stricken by feeling. Conscious of a thousand odors floating in the air, each one connected with a thousand thoughts, and hopes, and joys, and cares long, long forgotten. [*Pause.*] This one—this—Scrooge—before your very eyes, returns to life, among the living. [*To audience, sternly.*] You'd best pay your most careful attention. I would suggest rapt.

There is a small flash and puff of smoke and MARLEY is gone again.

PAST. Your lip is trembling, Mr. Scrooge. And what is that upon your cheek?

SCROOGE. Upon my cheek? Nothing...a blemish on the skin from the eating of overmuch grease...nothing...[*Suddenly.*] Kind Spirit of Christmas Past, lead me where you will, but quickly! To be stagnant[24] in this place is, for me, unbearable!

PAST. You recollect the way?

---

22. **green grocer.** Person who sells fresh fruits and vegetables
23. **reclamation.** Recovery
24. **stagnant.** Unmoving

Teach the Selection

Analyze Literature
Drama Ask students to explain the purpose and value of these stage directions. (They describe the Ghost of Christmas Past. They provide specific details for the stage crew responsible for music, costumes, and lighting. **D**

Use Reading Skills
Draw Conclusions Ask students how Scrooge probably feels when he touches the Spirit's heart. (He probably feels frightened and curious, yet trusting.) **E**

Analyze Literature
Mood Ask students to identify the mood at the end of Scene 4 and details that contribute to this mood. (Such details as the Ghost touching his heart and his gentle, encouraging dialogue, the sparkly flickers, and the lovely crystals of music create a hopeful, loving, uplifting mood.) **F**

Analyze Literature
Plot Have students explain where the Ghost of Christmas Past takes Scrooge and why this matters. (The Ghost takes Scrooge to the place he grew up. This is the first step in Scrooge's deliverance from the same fate as Marley.) **G**

Writing Skills

Character Sketch
Tell students that a character sketch describes a character in a story. Ask students to write a one-paragraph character sketch of Marley, Scrooge, Cratchit, or Scrooge's nephew Fred. Character sketches should include
- sensory details that describe the character's appearance and/or traits
- an explanation of the character's role

- additional insight based on an understanding of the character.

Before they begin, remind students that a well-constructed paragraph has a topic sentence that states the main idea, body sentences that support the topic sentence and help explain the main idea, and a closing sentence that brings the paragraph to a satisfactory conclusion.

Analyze Literature

Characterization Ask students what this scene reveals about Scrooge's childhood memories of Christmas. Are they surprised by Scrooge's reaction to the visions of his childhood? (Scrooge apparently has happy memories of Christmas. His weepy response to the scenes will surprise most students.) **A**

Use Reading Skills

Draw Conclusions Ask students why they think the Ghost of Christmas Past insists that Scrooge look at the boy. (The Ghost wants Scrooge to understand how his past contributed to his development into an unhappy, mean old man.) **B**

Analyze Literature

Plot Ask students why Scrooge's remark that he should have given something to the boy singing a Christmas Carol matters in the plot. (It shows that Scrooge is changing.) **C**

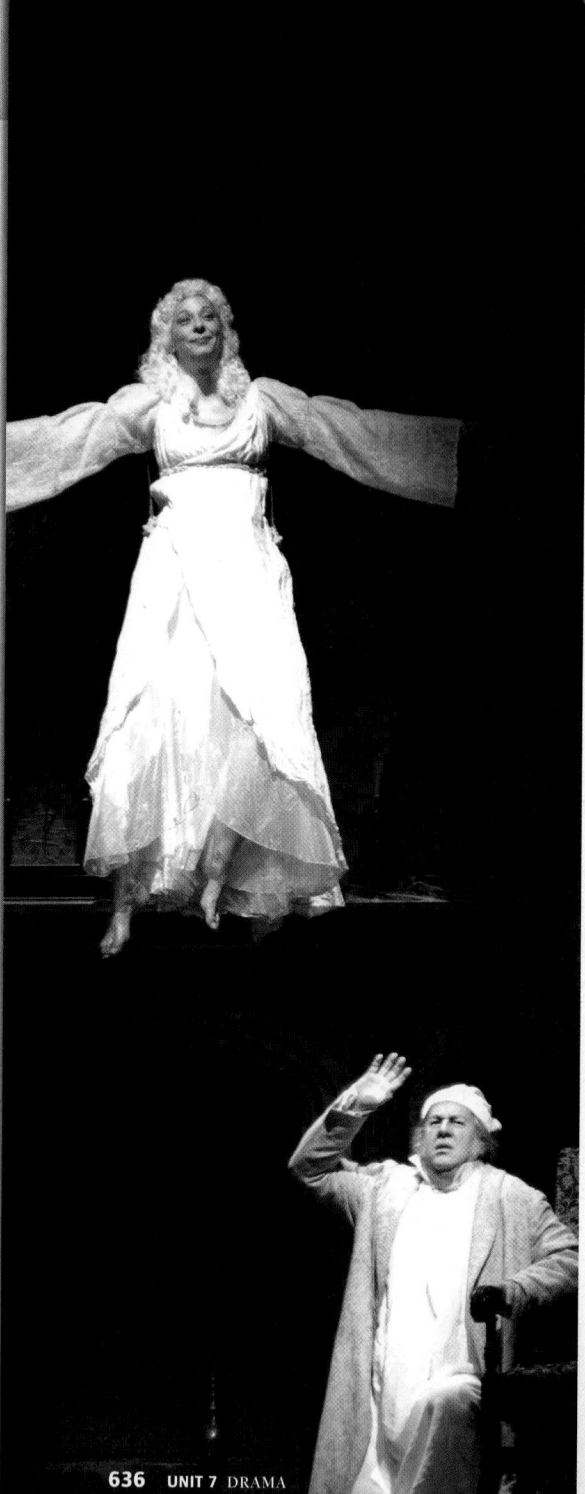

636 UNIT 7 DRAMA

SCROOGE. Remember it! I would know it blindfolded! My bridge, my church, my winding river! [*Staggers about, trying to see it all at once. He weeps again.*]

PAST. These are but shadows of things that have been. They have no consciousness of us.

Four jocund travelers enter; singing a Christmas song in four-part harmony—"God Rest Ye Merry Gentlemen." **A**

SCROOGE. Listen! I know these men! I know them! I remember the beauty of their song!

PAST. But, why do you remember it so happily? It is Merry Christmas that they say to one another! What is Merry Christmas to you, Mr. Scrooge! Out upon Merry Christmas, right? What good has Merry Christmas ever done you, Mr. Scrooge?

SCROOGE. [*After a long pause.*] None. No good. None...[*He bows his head.*]

PAST. Look, you, sir, a school ahead. The schoolroom is not quite deserted. A solitary child, neglected by his friends, is left there still.

SCROOGE *falls to the ground; sobbing as he sees, and we see, a small boy, the* YOUNG SCROOGE, *sitting and weeping, bravely, alone at his desk: alone in a vast space, a void.*

SCROOGE. I cannot look on him! **B**

PAST. You must, Mr. Scrooge, you must.

SCROOGE. It's me. [*Pauses; weeps.*] Poor boy. He lived inside his head...alone...[*Pauses; weeps.*] poor boy. [*Pauses; stops his weeping.*] I wish...[*Dries his eyes on his cuff.*] ah! it's too late!

PAST. What is the matter?

SCROOGE. There was a boy singing a Christmas Carol outside my door last night. I should like to have given him something: that's all. **C**

PAST. [*Smiles; waves his hand to* SCROOGE.] Come. Let us see another Christmas.

Grammar Skills

Predicate Adjectives

Remind students that a predicate adjective completes a sentence by describing the subject. The predicate adjective comes after a linking verb and answers *Who?* or *What?* about the subject. For example: "In spite of the holiday season, Scrooge was <u>grumpy</u> and <u>miserable</u>."

Have students identify the predicate adjectives (underscored) in the following sentences.

1. At times, his gruff behavior seemed <u>comical</u>, which made the audience laugh.
2. The actor appeared <u>ancient</u>, but in reality, he was <u>quite young</u>.
3. The streets were <u>dirty</u> and smelled rotten.
4. From a distance, the bells sounded <u>eerie</u>.

Lights out on little boy. A flash of light. A puff of smoke. Lights up on older boy.

SCROOGE. Look! Me, again! Older now! [*Realizes.*] Oh, yes still alone.

The boy—a slightly older SCROOGE—*sits alone in a chair, reading. The door to the room opens and a young girl enters. She is much, much younger than this slightly older* SCROOGE. *She is, say, six, and he is, say, twelve.* ELDER SCROOGE *and the* GHOST OF CHRISTMAS PAST *stand watching the scene, unseen.*

FAN. Dear, dear brother, I have come to bring you home.

BOY. Home, little Fan?

FAN. Yes! Home, for good and all! Father is so much kinder than he ever used to be, and home's like heaven! He spoke so gently to me one dear night when I was going to bed that I was not afraid to ask him; once more if you might come home, and he said "yes"...you should; and sent me in a coach to bring you. And you're to be a man and are never to come back here, but first, we're to be together all the Christmas long, and have the merriest time in the world.

BOY. You are quite a woman, little Fan!

Laughing; she drags at BOY, *causing him to stumble to the door with her. Suddenly we hear a mean and terrible voice in the hallway, Off. It is the* SCHOOLMASTER.

SCHOOLMASTER. Bring down Master Scrooge's travel box at once! He is to travel!

FAN. Who is that, Ebenezer?

BOY. O! Quiet, Fan. It is the Schoolmaster, himself!

The door bursts open and into the room bursts with it the SCHOOLMASTER.

SCHOOLMASTER. Master Scrooge?

BOY. Oh, Schoolmaster, I'd like you to meet my little sister, Fan, sir...

Two boys struggle on with SCROOGE's *trunk.*

FAN. Pleased, sir. [*She curtsies.*]

SCHOOLMASTER. You are to travel, Master Scrooge.

SCROOGE. Yes, sir. I know, sir...

All start to exit, but FAN *grabs the coattail of the mean old* SCHOOLMASTER.

BOY. Fan!

SCHOOLMASTER. What's this?

FAN. Pardon, sir, but I believe that you've forgotten to say your goodbye to my brother, Ebenezer, who stands still now awaiting it...[*She smiles, curtsies, lowers her eyes.*] Pardon, sir.

SCHOOLMASTER. [*Amazed.*] I...uh...harumph... uhh...well, then...[*Outstretches hand.*] Goodbye, Scrooge.

BOY. Uh, well, goodbye, Schoolmaster...

Lights fade out on all but BOY *looking at* FAN; *and* SCROOGE *and* PAST *looking at them.*

SCROOGE. Oh, my dear, dear little sister, Fan...how I loved her.

PAST. Always a delicate creature, whom a breath might have withered, but she had a large heart.

SCROOGE. So she had.

PAST. She died a woman, and had, as I think, children.

SCROOGE. One child.

PAST. True. Your nephew.

SCROOGE. Yes.

PAST. Fine, then. We move on, Mr. Scrooge. That warehouse, there? Do you know it?

SCROOGE. Know it? Wasn't I apprenticed[25] there?

PAST. We'll have a look.

---

25. **apprenticed.** Learned a trade by practical experience under a skilled worker

---

Use Reading Strategies

Make Inferences Have students speculate about why Scrooge was sent away to school. Do they think that Scrooge was happy about the decision? (Most students will infer that Scrooge probably did something that upset his father, who, according to Fan, wasn't so kind. The fact that Scrooge was weeping and alone shows he wasn't happy about it.) **D**

Analyze Literature

Character Ask students to describe Fan and her relationship with Scrooge. (Fan is Scrooge's younger sister. She is bold and fiercely loyal to Scrooge, whom she clearly loves.) **E**

TEACHING NOTE

Self-Generated Questioning

Post four or five large pieces of paper on walls around the classroom. Divide students into groups, and assign each group a piece of paper. Ask each group to write on its sheet of paper as many questions about the play as possible. Model a question: "Could this play be performed without a set?" As a class, determine which questions are "recall" level and which require higher-level thinking. Score one point for each recall question and two points for each higher-level question. Encourage students to answer the recall questions on their own. If possible, set aside time to discuss the higher-level questions as a class.

Reading Skills

Compare and Contrast

Remind students that the characters, setting, and plot of this play are based on the same elements of Dickens's *A Christmas Carol.* A written work that is reworked and presented in a different form is called an adaptation. Point out that not all adaptations remain as faithful to the original written work as does Horovitz's dramatic adaptation of Dickens's story. In many adaptations, settings change, new characters are added, and plots get new twists.

Have students identify examples of adaptations of written works that have been made into movies, plays, or television shows. Ask students who are familiar with the written works to explain how closely the adaptations stick to the originals.

Use Reading Skills

Sequence of Events Ask students where the Ghost of Christmas Past takes Scrooge after they leave Fan. (They go to the warehouse where Scrooge, as a young man, was an apprentice to Fezziwig.)

Use Reading Strategies

Visualize Have students use the details in the stage directions to form a mental picture of this scene. Ask them what this image conveys about the character of Fezziwig. (Fezziwig was a generous, happy family man, who shared his joy and good fortune with everyone he knew.) **A**

▶ More About the Author

Charles Dickens, who was hardly affluent at the time, paid the publication costs for *A Christmas Carol* out of his own pocket. In addition, so that the book would be affordable to as many people as possible, Dickens set a nominal fee of five shillings as the sale price. The book was released just before Christmas in December of 1843. In spite of its low price, some people made unauthorized copies of it. As a result, although *A Christmas Carol* was hugely popular and sold well, Dickens did not make much of a profit.

They enter the warehouse. The lights crossfade with them, coming up on an old man in Welsh wig: Fezziwig.

Scrooge. Why, it's old Fezziwig! Bless his heart; it's Fezziwig, alive again!

[Fezziwig *sits behind a large, high desk, counting. He lays down his pen; looks at the clock: seven bells sound.*] Quittin' time...

Fezziwig. Quittin' time...[*He takes off his waistcoat and laughs; calls off.*] Yo ho, Ebenezer! Dick!

Dick Wilkins *and* Ebenezer Scrooge—*a young man version—enter the room.* Dick *and* Ebenezer *are* Fezziwig's *apprentices.*

Scrooge. Dick Wilkins, to be sure! My fellow-'prentice! Bless my soul, yes. There he is. He was very much attached to me, was Dick. Poor Dick! Dear, dear! **A**

Fezziwig. Yo ho, my boys. No more work tonight. Christmas Eve, Dick...Christmas, Ebenezer!

They stand at attention in front of Fezziwig; *laughing.*

Fezziwig. [*Contd.*] Hilli-ho! Clear away, and let's have lots of room here! Hilli-ho, Dick! Chirrup, Ebenezer!

The young men clear the room, sweep the floor, straighten the pictures, trim the lamps, etc. The space is clear now. A Fiddler *enters, fiddling.*

Fezziwig. [*Cont'd.*] Hi-ho, Matthew! Fiddle away...where are my daughters?

The Fiddler *plays. Three young daughters of* Fezziwig, *followed by six young male suitors, are dancing to the music. All employees come in: workers, clerks, housemaids, cousins, the baker, etc. All dance. Full number wanted here. Throughout the dance, food is brought into the*

Differentiated Instruction

Kinesthetic Learning

Some students might benefit from participating in role-playing sessions in which they pantomime Scrooge's reactions and emotional responses at pivotal moments in the play. Encourage students to select key exchanges in Act 1 that help develop Scrooge's character and advance the plot. Students can work alone or in small groups. Point out to students that they can use stage directions as well as their own insights into Scrooge's character to prepare and practice their pantomimes. Ask volunteers to read aloud each passage as students present their pantomimes to the rest of the class.

feast. It is "eaten" in dance, by the dancers. EBENEZER *dances with all three of the daughters, as does* DICK*. They compete for the daughters, happily, in the dance.* FEZZIWIG *dances with his daughters.* FEZZIWIG *dances with* DICK *and* EBENEZER*. The music changes:* MRS. FEZZIWIG *enters. She lovingly scolds her husband. They dance. She dances with* EBENEZER*, lifting him and throwing him about. She is enormously fat. When the dance is ended, they all dance off, floating away, as does the music.* SCROOGE *and the* GHOST OF CHRISTMAS PAST *stand alone now. The music is gone.*

PAST. It was a small matter, that Fezziwig made those silly folks so full of gratitude.

SCROOGE. Small!

PAST. Shhh!

Lights up on DICK *and* EBENEZER*.*

DICK. We are blessed, Ebenezer, truly, to have such a master as Mr. Fezziwig!

YOUNG SCROOGE. He is the best, best, the very and absolute best! If ever I own a firm of my own, I shall treat my apprentices with the same dignity and the same grace. We have learned a wonderful lesson from the master, Dick!

DICK. Ah, that's a fact, Ebenezer. That's a fact!

PAST. Was it not a small matter, really? He spent but a few pounds of his mortal money on your small party. Three or four pounds, perhaps. Is that so much that he deserves such praise as you and Dick so lavish now?

SCROOGE. It isn't that! It isn't that, Spirit. Fezziwig had the power to make us happy or unhappy; to make our service light or burdensome; a pleasure or a toil. The happiness he gave is quite as great as if it cost him a fortune.

PAST. What is the matter?

SCROOGE. Nothing particular.

PAST. Something, I think.

SCROOGE. No, no. I should like to be able to say a word or two to my clerk just now! That's all!

EBENEZER enters the room and shuts down all the lamps. He stretches and yawns. The GHOST OF CHRISTMAS PAST *turns to* SCROOGE*; all of a sudden.*

PAST. My time grows short! Quick!

In a flash of light, EBENEZER *is gone, and in his place stands an* OLDER SCROOGE*, this one a man in the prime of his life. Beside him stands a* YOUNG WOMAN *in a mourning dress. She is crying. She says to the* MAN*, with hostility.*

WOMAN. It matters little...to you, very little. Another idol has displaced me.

MAN. What idol has displaced you?

WOMAN. A golden one.

MAN. This is an even-handed dealing of the world. There is nothing on which it is so hard as poverty; and there is nothing it professes to condemn with such severity as the pursuit of wealth!

WOMAN. You fear the world too much. Have I not seen your nobler aspirations fall off one by one, until the master-passion, Gain, engrosses[26] you? Have I not?

SCROOGE. No!

MAN. What then? Even if I have grown so much wiser, what then? Have I changed towards you?

WOMAN. No...

MAN. Am I?

WOMAN. Our contract is an old one. It was made when we were both poor and content to be so. You are changed. When it was made, you were another man.

MAN. I was not another man: I was a boy.

---

26. **engrosses.** Takes all the attention

Teach the Selection

Use Reading Skills

Draw Conclusions Ask students to think about what Young Scrooge says and what they know about how the elder Scrooge treats his clerk. Ask: "What conclusion can you draw from this?" (The elder Scrooge forgot the lesson he learned from Fezziwig. Somewhere along the line, money and profit became more important to him than treating others with dignity.) **B**

Analyze Literature

Theme Remind students that the theme of a story is the message about life that the author wants readers to get. Ask them to identify one theme in the play, based on what they have read so far and what Scrooge says here. (Love and kindness are riches that people should nurture and share.) **C**

Use Reading Skills

Draw Conclusions Ask students what Scrooge would probably say to his clerk if he had the chance. (He might wish Cratchit Merry Christmas. He might tell him not to worry about taking the day off.) **D**

Analyze Literature

Drama Have students explain the purpose of these stage directions. (They move the plot forward by changing the scene; they introduce an older, successful Scrooge and the Young Woman; they show that the woman is angry with Scrooge.) **E**

Reading Skills

Compare and Contrast

To prepare for the Skills lesson panel discussion on teacher page 641, or for the Collaborative Learning activity on student page 644, have students research different adaptations of Dickens's *A Christmas Carol.* Tell them to use a variety of media in their research, including videos of film and stage productions, books, magazine and newspaper plot summaries, photographs, and sound recordings.

Students can use the library and Internet to identify different resources. Suggest that they keep track of their resources in a chart with the following headings: Videos, Books, Magazines, Photos, and Sound Recordings. Many English language learners will find that listening to and deriving meaning from a variety of media will help them build and reinforce concept and language attainment.

Literary Connection

Victorian Authors The Victorian era (1837–1901) produced many successful British novelists. Among Dickens's contemporaries were William Makepeace Thackeray and the Brontë sisters—Emily, Anne, and Charlotte. Later Victorian novelists greatly influenced by Dickens include Thomas Hardy and George Elliot. A common theme in much Victorian literature is the great disparity between the comfortable and often extravagant lifestyles of the middle and upper classes and the intolerable conditions that characterized the lifestyle of the impoverished and lower classes.

Analyze Literature

Plot Students should notice that the elder Scrooge and the Man (Young Scrooge) repeat the same words. Have students explain how these lines highlight Scrooge's inner struggle. (His desire for money and success led him, as a young man, to abandon everyone who loved him and whom he loved. He now realizes the value of what he gave up.) **A**

Use Reading Strategies

Clarify Students may need to reread the entire conversation between the Man (Young Scrooge) and the Woman to understand the history of their relationship and why she leaves him. Encourage them to ask questions about anything that is still unclear.

WOMAN. Your own feeling tells you that you were not what you are. I am. That which promised happiness when we were one in heart is fraught[27] with misery now that we are two...

SCROOGE. No!

WOMAN. How often and how keenly I have thought of this, I will not say. It is enough that I have thought of it, and can release you...

SCROOGE. [*Quietly.*] Don't release me, madame...

MAN. Have I ever sought release?

WOMAN. In words. No. Never.

MAN. In what then?

WOMAN. In a changed nature; in an altered spirit. In everything that made my love of any worth or value in your sight. If this has never been between us, tell me, would you seek me out and try to win me now? Ah, no!

SCROOGE. Ah, yes!

MAN. You think not?

WOMAN. I would gladly think otherwise if I could, heaven knows! But if you were free today, tomorrow, yesterday, can even I believe that you would choose a dowerless[28] girl—you who in your very confidence with her weigh everything by Gain; or, choosing her, do I not know that your repentance and regret would surely follow? I do; and I release you. With a full heart, for the love of him you once were.

SCROOGE. Please, I...I...

MAN. Please, I...I...

WOMAN. Please. You may—the memory of what is past half makes me hope you will—have pain in this. A very, very brief time, and you will dismiss the memory of it, as an unprofitable dream, from which it happened well that you awoke. May you be happy in the life that you have chosen for yourself.

SCROOGE. No!

WOMAN. Yourself...alone...

SCROOGE. No!

WOMAN. Goodbye, Ebenezer...

SCROOGE. Don't let her go!

MAN. Goodbye.

A **SCROOGE.** No! [*She exits.* SCROOGE *goes to* YOUNGER MAN*: himself.*] You fool! Mindless loon! You fool!

27. **fraught.** Affected
28. **dowerless.** Lacking a dowry—the gift of goods or money a woman brings to a marriage

---

Differentiated Instruction

Enrichment

Encourage students to work independently or with classmates to write a dramatic adaptation of a scene from a favorite short story or novel. Provide these guidelines.

- Select a scene with at least two characters, including the main character, so that you have an opportunity for dialogue that helps reveal the characters' personalities.

- Select a scene that is interesting or exciting and that helps develop the plot.
- Include a list of characters, setting descriptions, and stage directions.
- Use *A Christmas Carol: Scrooge and Marley* as a model for formatting the script.

MAN. [*To exited* WOMAN.] Fool. Mindless loon. Fool…

SCROOGE. Don't say that! Spirit, remove me from this place.

PAST. I have told you these were shadows of the things that have been. They are what they are. Do not blame me, Mr. Scrooge.

SCROOGE. Remove me! I cannot bear it!

The faces of all who appeared in this scene are now projected for a moment around the stage: enormous, flimsy, silent.

SCROOGE. [*Contd.*] Leave me! Take me back! Haunt me no longer!

There is a sudden flash of light: a flare. The GHOST OF CHRISTMAS PAST *is gone.* SCROOGE *is, for the moment, alone onstage. His bed is turned down, across the stage. A small candle burns now in* SCROOGE's *hand. There is a child's cap in his other hand. He slowly crosses the stage to his bed, to sleep.* MARLEY *appears behind* SCROOGE, *who continues his long, elderly cross to bed.* MARLEY *speaks directly to the audience.*

MARLEY. Scrooge must sleep now. He must surrender to the irresistible drowsiness caused by the recognition of what was. [*Pauses.*] The cap he carries is from ten lives past: his boyhood cap…donned atop a hopeful hairy head…askew, perhaps, or at a rakish angle. Doffed now in honor of regret. Perhaps even too heavy to carry in his present state of weak remorse…

SCROOGE *drops the cap. He lies atop his bed. He sleeps. To audience.*

MARLEY. [*Contd.*] He sleeps. For him, there's even more trouble ahead. [*Smiles.*] For you? The play house tells me there's grog[29] and cider, both hot, as should be your anticipation for the spectres Christmas Present and Future, for I promise you both. [*Smiles again.*] So, I pray you hurry back to your seats refreshed and ready for a miser—to turn his coat of gray into a blazen Christmas holly-red.

A flash of lightning. A clap of thunder. Bats fly. Ghosty music. MARLEY *is gone.*

CURTAIN

[ACT 2 *continues on page 645.*]

---

29. **grog.** Warm drink

 Have you ever been miserable when you should have been happy? Why do you think some people are able to maintain a cheerful outlook on life while others, like Scrooge, seem miserable?

Find Meaning

1. (a) Where and when does each of the scenes in Act 1 take place? (b) In what way is the setting important to the plot?
2. (a) Who is Jacob Marley? (b) How does his role change from Scene 1 to Scene 3?
3. Why does Scrooge find it difficult to understand his nephew's enthusiasm for Christmas?

Make Judgments

4. (a) What is the overall mood of Act 1? (b) What details in Scene 1 help to establish this mood?
5. (a) What is Scrooge's most prominent character trait? (b) How does this trait affect his relationships with other characters in the play?
6. Based on Act 1, describe the conflict in this play.

A CHRISTMAS CAROL, ACT 1 **641**

Speaking & Listening Skills

Panel Discussion

Divide the class into teams and have each team prepare a panel discussion on the merits or shortcomings of various adaptations of *A Christmas Carol,* including Israel Horovitz's play. Provide time for teams to research and collect information. Tell students how much time each team will have to present ideas. Offer these additional guidelines:

- Use note cards to organize ideas.
- Decide on the order in which team members will present ideas.
- Have speakers speak loudly and clearly.
- Have listeners note any questions they have.
- Allow time for questions at the end of the presentations.

The action in *A Christmas Carol: Scrooge and Marley* takes place in London in the mid-1800s. Factories and mills of that time produced a great deal of smoke, and the city was filled with noises and smells associated with horses, unrefrigerated food, and thousands of people going about their daily lives. As you read the description from an essay by **Daniel Pool,** think about what it would have been like for the Cratchits and others living in London at that time.

from What Jane Austen Ate and Charles Dickens Knew

An Essay by Daniel Pool

The fog in London was very real. Just why it was the color it was no one has ever been able to ascertain[1] for sure, but at a certain time of the year—it was worst in November—a great yellowness reigned everywhere, and lamps were lit inside even during the day. In November, December, and January the yellow fog extended out some three or four miles from the heart of the city, causing "pain in the lungs" and "uneasy sensations" in the head. It has been blamed in part on the coal stoves. At eight o'clock in the morning on an average day over London, an observer reported the sky began to turn black with the smoke from thousands of coal fires, presumably for morning fires to warm dining rooms and bedrooms and to cook breakfast. Ladies going to the opera at night with white shawls returned with them gray. It has been suggested that the black umbrella put in its appearance because it did not show the effects of these London atmospherics.[2] The fog was so thick, observed a foreigner at mid-century, that you could take a man by the hand and not be able to see his face, and

A

people literally lost their way and drowned in the Thames. In a very bad week in 1873 more than 700 people above the normal average for the period died in the city, and cattle at an exhibition suffocated to death.

There were problems underfoot as well as in the air. One hundred tons of horse manure dropped on the streets of London each day, and a report to Parliament said that "strangers coming from the country frequently describe the streets of London as smelling of dung like a stable-yard." Originally, many streets were not paved; by mid-century, however, the dust from the pulverized[3] stone with which London streets were paved coated furniture in good weather and turned to mud when it rained. An etiquette book advised gentlemen to walk on the outside of the pavement when accompanying a lady to ensure that they walked on the filthiest part of it, and every major street had a crossing sweeper like Jo in

---
1. **ascertain.** Find out
2. **atmospherics.** Elements used to create a specific mood
3. **pulverized.** Broken into particles

Words in Use

from "What Jane Austen Ate and Charles Dickens Knew"
Selection Words
literally, 642
exhibition, 642
etiquette, 642

Bleak House, who for a penny swept the street before you made your way across it on rainy days so your boots did not become impossibly filthy. Nor was the Thames any better. London sewage, some 278,000 tons daily at mid-century, as well as pollutants from the factories along the river's banks, was dumped untreated into the water, presumably helping to fuel the cholera[4] epidemics that swept the city in the early part of the century. The smell was bad enough in the summer of 1858 to cause Parliament to end its session early.

There was what we would surely call noise pollution, too—the incessant sound of wheels and horses' hooves clacking over the pavement, the click of women's pattens[5] on the sidewalks in the rain, the bell of the muffin man, and the cries of the street peddlers selling such items as dolls, matches, books, knives, eels, pens, rat poison, key rings, eggs, and china, to say nothing of the German bands, the itinerant[6] clarinet players, and the hurdy-gurdies.[7] ❖

---

4. **cholera.** Infectious and often fatal disease
5. **pattens.** Shoes with raised soles
6. **itinerant.** Traveling from place to place
7. **hurdy-gurdies.** Instruments with a droning sound that are played with a crank

TEXT ←→ TEXT CONNECTION

There is little suggestion of these grim and dirty conditions in *A Christmas Carol: Scrooge and Marley.* How might some of the conditions described in this selection be portrayed in a play? Which would be difficult or impossible to suggest?

Tower Bridge from Cherry Garden Pier, c. 1900. Charles Edward Dixon. Private collection.

WHAT JANE AUSTEN ATE AND CHARLES DICKENS KNEW **643**

AFTER READING

Analyze Literature

Plot The plot in a piece of fiction or drama can be broken up into five parts: *exposition, rising action, climax, falling action,* and *resolution.* Begin a plot diagram for *A Christmas Carol: Scrooge and Marley,* noting the part or parts of the plot that appear in each scene. For each plot part you identify, write the scene number on your diagram; in addition, include a brief description of the action that occurred during that part of the plot. Add to the plot diagram as you read Act 2.

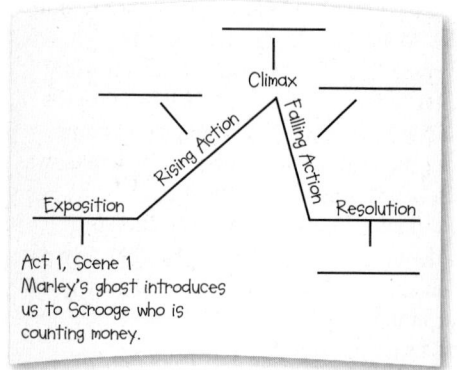

Act 1, Scene 1
Marley's ghost introduces us to Scrooge who is counting money.

Extend Understanding

Writing Options

Creative Writing Imagine that you are in charge of raising money for a local charity. Write a **business letter** to Scrooge asking for a sizable donation. Be sure to use the proper form for a business letter and appropriately polite language in your letter.

Persuasive Writing Pretend you are a member of the school drama club. Write a **review** of Act 1 of *A Christmas Carol: Scrooge and Marley* for your next meeting. Begin by providing a brief summary of the story and characters. Then evaluate the setting, characterization, mood, dialogue, and stage directions. Use evidence from the play to support your evaluations. Conclude by giving your opinion of the play and telling why you think the drama club should or should not put on this play for the school. Share your work with the class.

Collaborative Learning

Analyze the Story In small groups, discuss why the story of *A Christmas Carol* has remained so popular for so many years. Consider the main themes, the traits and flaws of the characters, and the conflicts that drive the characters and the plot. Prepare for the discussion by reading a summary or watching a film of the original version of *A Christmas Carol* by Charles Dickens.

Critical Literacy

Compare Versions Find and read the first chapter of *A Christmas Carol* by Charles Dickens. Compare and contrast the original story to the dramatic adaptation by Israel Horovitz. Note how each writer reveals characters and conflicts through description, narration, and dialogue. What elements of the story are the same? What elements are different? Create a Venn diagram to show the similarities and differences between the two versions. Then use the diagram to help you explain the reasons for the differences between the versions.

 Go to **www.mirrorsandwindows.com** for more.

A Christmas Carol: Scrooge and Marley

ACT 2
— SCENE 1 —

Lights. Choral music is sung. Curtain. SCROOGE, in bed; sleeping, in spotlight. We cannot yet see the interior of his room. MARLEY, opposite, in spotlight equal to SCROOGE's. MARLEY laughs. He tosses his hand in the air and a flame shoots from it, magically, into the air. There is a thunder clap, and then another; a lightning flash, and then another. Ghostly music plays under. Colors change. MARLEY's spotlight has gone out and now reappears, with MARLEY in it, standing next to the bed and the sleeping SCROOGE. MARLEY addresses the audience directly.

MARLEY. Hear this snoring Scrooge! Sleeping to escape the nightmare that is his waking day. What shall I bring to him now? I'm afraid nothing would astonish old Scrooge now. Not after what he's seen. Not a baby boy, not a rhinoceros, nor anything in between would astonish Ebenezer Scrooge just now. I can think of nothing…[*Suddenly.*] that's it! Nothing! [*He speaks confidentially.*] I'll have the clock strike one and, when he awakes expecting my second messenger, there will be no one…nothing. Then I'll have the bell strike twelve. And then one again…and then nothing. Nothing…[*Laughs.*] nothing will-astonish him. I think it will work.

The bell tolls one. SCROOGE leaps awake.

SCROOGE. One! One! This is it: time! [*Looks about the room.*] Nothing!

The bell tolls midnight.

SCROOGE. [*Contd.*] Midnight! How can this be? I'm sleeping backwards.

One again.

SCROOGE. [*Contd.*] Good heavens! One again! I'm sleeping back and forth! [*A pause. SCROOGE looks about.*] Nothing! Absolutely nothing!

Suddenly, thunder and lightning. MARLEY laughs and disappears. The room shakes and glows. There is suddenly spring like music. SCROOGE makes a run for the door.

MARLEY. Scrooge!

SCROOGE. What?

MARLEY. Stay you put!

SCROOGE. Just checking to see if anyone is in here.

Lights and thunder again: more music. MARLEY is of a sudden gone. In his place sits the GHOST OF CHRISTMAS PRESENT—to be called in the stage directions of the play, PRESENT—Center of room. Heaped up on the floor to form a kind of throne, are turkeys, geese, game, poultry, brawn,[1] great joints of meat, suckling pigs, long wreaths of sausages, mince-pies, plum puddings, barrels of oysters, red hot chestnuts, cherry-cheeked apples, juicy oranges, luscious pears, immense twelfth cakes, and seething bowls of punch, that make the chamber dim with their delicious steam. Upon this throne sits PRESENT, glorious to see. He bears a torch, shaped as a Horn of Plenty.[2] SCROOGE hops out of the door, and then peeks back again into his bedroom. PRESENT calls to SCROOGE.

PRESENT. Ebenezer Scrooge. Come in, come in! Come in and know me better!

---

1. **brawn.** Pig's or calf's head
2. **Horn of Plenty.** Goat's horn filled with flowers and fruit to suggest prosperity

A CHRISTMAS CAROL, ACT 2 **645**

Words in Use

Preview Vocabulary	Selection Words	Teaching Words
compulsion, 646	confidentially, 645	revenue, 665
odious, 649	seething, 645	enhance, 666
wane, 653	lavish, 646	
venture, 654	revelers, 647	
intercede, 659	incense, 647	

KEY TERMS
ILLUSTRATE, 665
PLOT, 667
ACT, 667
SCENE, 667
DIAGRAM, 667
SENSORY, 667
TONE, 667
MOOD, 667
CHARACTER, 667
STAGE DIRECTION, 667
THESIS, 667

Analyze Literature

Sequence of Events Ask students to describe the time frame of the visits from Jacob Marley, the Ghost of Christmas Past, and the Ghost of Christmas Present. (Marley appears when Scrooge arrives home on Christmas Eve. Although Scrooge says that he "went forth last night," the Ghosts of Christmas Past and Present both appear to him that same Christmas Eve after he goes to bed. Students should recognize that all the visits occur the same night.) **Ⓐ**

Analyze Literature

Character Remind students that a dynamic character undergoes a change during a story. Ask students how they can tell that Scrooge is a dynamic character. (He says that the lesson of last night is already working, suggesting that he is changing.) **Ⓑ**

Scrooge. Hello. How should I call you?

Present. I am the Ghost of Christmas Present. Look upon me.

Present is wearing a simple green robe. The walls around the room are now covered in greenery, as well. The room seems to be a perfect grove now: leaves of holly, mistletoe and ivy reflect the stage lights. Suddenly, there is a mighty roar of flame **Ⓐ** *in the fireplace and now the hearth burns with a lavish, warming fire. There is an ancient scabbard girdling³ the* Ghost's *middle, but without sword. The sheath is gone to rust.*

Present. [*Contd.*] You have never seen the like of me before?

Scrooge. Never.

Present. You have never walked forth with younger members of my family; my elder brothers born on Christmases Past?

Scrooge. I don't think I have. I'm afraid I've not. Have you had many brothers, Spirit?

Present. More than eighteen hundred.

Scrooge. A tremendous family to provide for!

Present stands.

Scrooge. [*Contd.*] Spirit, conduct me where you will. I went forth last night on <u>compulsion</u>, and learnt a lesson which is working now. Tonight, if you have aught⁴ to teach me, let me profit by it. **Ⓑ**

Present. Touch my robe.

---

3. girdling. Surrounding with a belt
4. aught. Anything

com·pul·sion (kəm pəl′ shən) *n.,* irresistible impulse to perform an act

Reading Skills

Activate Prior Knowledge

Point out that good readers use prior knowledge to understand why events happen and why characters behave as they do. Prior knowledge may come from real-life experiences and from what they learned earlier in a story.

For example, as students begin to read Act 2 of *A Christmas Carol: Scrooge and Marley,* suggest that they can use prior knowledge to think about

- what they have learned about the characters and events in Act 1,
- what they know about how real-life people react when frightened, and
- what they know from reading and seeing other versions of *A Christmas Carol.*

SCROOGE *walks cautiously to* PRESENT *and touches his robe. When he does lightning flashes, thunder claps, music plays.*

Blackout.

— SCENE 2 —

PROLOGUE

MARLEY *stands spotlit. He speaks directly to the audience.*

MARLEY. My ghostly friend now leads my living partner through the city's streets.

Lights up on SCROOGE *and* PRESENT.

MARLEY. [*Contd.*] See them there and hear the music people make when the weather is severe, as it is now.

Winter music. Choral group behind scrim,[5] *sings. When the song is done and the stage is re-set, the lights will fade up on a row of shops, behind the singers. The choral group will hum the song they have just completed and mill about the streets, carrying their dinners to the bakers' shops restaurants. They will, perhaps, sing about being poor at Christmastime, whatever.*

PRESENT. These revelers, Mr. Scrooge, carry their own dinners to their jobs, where they will work to bake the meals the rich men and women of this city will eat as their Christmas dinners. Generous people these...to care for the others, so...

PRESENT *walks among the choral group and a sparkling incense falls from his torch on to their baskets, as he pulls the covers off of the baskets. Some of the choral group become angry with each other.*

MAN #1. Hey, you, watch where you're going.

MAN #2. Watch it yourself, mate!

PRESENT *sprinkles them directly, they change.*

MAN #1. I pray go in ahead of me. It's

Christmas. You be first!

MAN #2. No, no, I must insist that YOU be first!

MAN #1. All right, I shall be, and gratefully so.

MAN #2. The pleasure is equally mine, for being able to watch you pass, smiling.

MAN #1. I would find it a shame to quarrel on Christmas Day...

MAN #2. As would I.

MAN #1. Merry Christmas then, friend!

MAN #2. And a Merry Christmas straight back to you!

Church bells toll. The choral group enters the buildings; the shops and restaurants; they exit the stage, shutting their doors closed behind them. All sound stops. SCROOGE *and* PRESENT *are alone again.*

SCROOGE. What is it you sprinkle from your torch?

PRESENT. Kindness.

SCROOGE. Do you sprinkle your kindness on any particular people or on all people?

PRESENT. To any person kindly given. And to the very poor most of all.

SCROOGE. Why to the very poor most?

PRESENT. Because the very poor need it most. Touch my heart...here, Mr. Scrooge. We have another journey.

SCROOGE *touches the* GHOST's *heart and music plays, lights change color, lightning flashes, thunder claps. A choral group appears on the street, singing Christmas carols.*

— SCENE 3 —

MARLEY *stands spotlit in front of a scrim on which is painted the exterior of* CRATCHIT's *four-roomed house. There is a flash and a clap and*

---

5. scrim. Sheer fabric used on stage to hide a scene until it is lit

Teach the Selection

Analyze Literature

Setting Have students tell you where and when Scene 3 takes place. (It takes place in the dining room of Bob Cratchit's home, on Christmas Day, probably just before Christmas dinner.) **Ⓐ**

Use Reading Skills

Draw Conclusions Ask students what Scrooge's questions about Cratchit's home and children suggest about Scrooge's relationship with his clerk. (It was strictly business. He obviously never cared enough to ask Cratchit about his family, and he never visited his home.) **Ⓑ**

Use Reading Strategies

Make Inferences Ask students what Present hopes Scrooge will learn from watching the Cratchits. (Present probably hopes Scrooge will learn that although Cratchit has little money, he has a source of joy and optimism in his family.) **Ⓒ**

Analyze Literature

Drama Have students explain what the stage directions reveal about Tiny Tim. (He is small enough for his father to carry him on his shoulder. His legs are in iron braces, indicating he has an illness or serious physical disability that prevents him from walking without crutches.) **Ⓓ**

Ⓐ *MARLEY is gone. The lights shift color again, the scrim flies away, and we are in the interior of the CRATCHIT family home. SCROOGE is there, with the SPIRIT [PRESENT], watching MRS. CRATCHIT set the table, with the help of BELINDA CRATCHIT and PETER CRATCHIT, a baby, pokes a fork into the mashed potatoes on his high-chair's tray. He also chews on his shirt collar.*

SCROOGE. What is this place, Spirit?

PRESENT. This is the home of your employee, Mr. Scrooge. Don't you know it?

Ⓑ SCROOGE. Do you mean Cratchit, Spirit? Do you mean this is Cratchit's home?

PRESENT. None other.

SCROOGE. These children are his?

PRESENT. There are more to come presently.

SCROOGE. On his meager earnings! What foolishness!

PRESENT. Foolishness, is it?

SCROOGE. Wouldn't you say so? Fifteen shillings a week's what he gets!

Ⓒ PRESENT. I would say that he gets the pleasure of his family, fifteen time a week times the number of hours in a day! Wait, Mr. Scrooge. Wait, listen and watch. You might actually learn something.

MRS. CRATCHIT. What has ever got your precious father then? And your brother, Tiny Tim? And Martha wasn't as late last Christmas by half an hour!

MARTHA opens the door, speaking to her mother as she does.

MARTHA. Here's Martha, now, Mother!

She laughs. The CRATCHIT CHILDREN squeal with delight.

BELINDA. It's Martha, Mother! Here's Martha!

PETER. Marthmama, Marthmama! Hullo!

BELINDA. Hurrah! Martha! Martha! There's such an enormous goose for us, Martha!

MRS. CRATCHIT. Why, bless your heart alive, my dear, how late you are!

MARTHA. We'd a great deal of work to finish up last night, and had to clear away this morning, Mother.

MRS. CRATCHIT. Well, never mind so long as you are home. Sit ye down before the fire, my dear, and have a warm, Lord bless ye!

BELINDA. No, no! There's Father coming. Hide, Martha, hide!

MARTHA giggles and hides herself.

MARTHA. Where? Here?

PETER. Hide, hide!

BELINDA. Not there! THERE!

Ⓓ *MARTHA is hidden. BOB CRATCHIT enters, carrying TINY TIM atop his shoulder. He wears a threadbare and fringeless comforter hanging down in front of him. TINY TIM carries small crutches and his small legs are bound in an iron frame brace.*

BOB AND TINY TIM. Merry Christmas.

BOB. Merry Christmas my love, Merry Christmas, Peter; Merry Christmas, Belinda. Why, where is Martha?

MRS. CRATCHIT. Not coming.

BOB. Not coming? Not coming upon Christmas Day?

MARTHA. [*Pokes head out.*] Ohhh, poor Father. Don't be disappointed.

BOB. What's this?

MARTHA. 'Tis I!

BOB. Martha! [*They embrace.*]

TINY TIM. Martha! Martha!

MARTHA. Tiny Tim!

TINY TIM is placed in MARTHA's arms. BELINDA and PETER rush him off-stage.

BELINDA. Come, brother! You must come hear the pudding singing in the copper.

Differentiated Instruction

Reading Proficiency

To prevent students from losing track of what is happening in the story, have them stop at the following points in Act 2 to retell in their own words what they have just read.

- At the end of Scenes 1, 2, and 3
- In Scene 4, after the Ghost of Christmas Present leaves
- In Scene 4, after Scrooge sees his own gravestone
- At the end of Scene 4
- In Scene 5, after Scrooge parts from the Portly Man
- At the end of the play

If students have trouble recalling details or have not understood something, they can reread and ask for additional help from classmates or you.

TINY TIM. The pudding? What flavor have we?

PETER. Plum! Plum!

TINY TIM. Oh, Mother! I love plum!

The CHILDREN exit the stage, giggling.

MRS. CRATCHIT. And how did little Tim behave?

BOB. As good as gold, and even better. Somehow he gets thoughtful sitting by himself so much, and thinks the strangest things you ever heard. He told me, coming home, that he hoped people saw him in the church, because he was a cripple, and it might be pleasant to them to remember upon Christmas Day, who made lame beggars walk and blind men see. [*Pauses.*] He has the oddest ideas sometimes, but he seems all the while to be growing stronger and more hearty...one would never know.

Hears TIM's crutch on floor outside door.

PETER. The goose has arrived to be eaten!

BELINDA. Oh, mama, mama, it's beautiful.

MARTHA. It's a perfect goose, Mother!

TINY TIM. To this Christmas goose, Mother and Father, I say...[*Yells.*] Hurrah! Hurrah!

OTHER CHILDREN. [*Copying TIM.*] Hurrah! Hurrah!

The family sits round the table. BOB and MRS. CRATCHIT serve the trimmings, quickly. All sit; all bow heads, all pray.

BOB. Thank you, dear Lord, for your many gifts...our dear children; our wonderful meal; our love for one another; and the warmth of our small fire—[*Looks up at all.*] A merry Christmas to us, my dear: God bless us!

ALL. [*Except TIM.*] Merry Christmas! God bless us!

TINY TIM. [*In a short silence.*] God bless us every one.

All freeze. Spotlight on PRESENT and SCROOGE.

SCROOGE. Spirit, tell me if Tiny Tim will live.

PRESENT. I see a vacant seat...in the poor chimney corner, and a crutch without an owner, carefully preserved. If these shadows remain unaltered by the future, the child will die.

SCROOGE. No, no, kind Spirit! Say he will be spared!

E **PRESENT.** If these shadows remain unaltered by the future, none other of my race will find him here. What then? If he be like to die, he had better do it, and decrease the surplus population.

SCROOGE bows his head. We hear BOB's voice speak SCROOGE's name.

BOB. Mr. Scrooge...

F **SCROOGE.** Huh? What's that? Who calls?

BOB. [*His glass raised in a toast.*[6]] I'll give you Mr. Scrooge, the Founder of the Feast!

SCROOGE. Me, Bob? You toast me?

PRESENT. Save your breath, Mr. Scrooge. You can't be seen or heard.

MRS. CRATCHIT. The Founder of the Feast, indeed! I wish I had him here, that miser Scrooge. I'd give him a piece of my mind to feast upon, and I hope he'd have a good appetite for it!

BOB. My dear! Christmas Day!

MRS. CRATCHIT. It should be Christmas Day, I am sure, on which one drinks the health of such an odious, stingy, unfeeling man as Scrooge...

SCROOGE. Oh, Spirit, must I?

MRS. CRATCHIT. You know he is, Robert! Nobody knows it better than you do, poor fellow!

G
H

---

6. **toast.** Drink to honor a person

o·di·ous (ō′ dē əs) *adj.,* hateful or disgusting

A CHRISTMAS CAROL, ACT 2 **649**

Analyze Literature

Motivation Ask students what motivates Cratchit's toast to Scrooge. (Cratchit is motivated by a generous spirit that makes him grateful for everything he has.) **A**

Use Reading Skills

Identify Cause and Effect Have students describe Scrooge's reaction to the toast. Ask: "Why does the toast have this effect on him?" (He seems both surprised and touched. He may feel guilty about how badly he treated Cratchit and others in the past.) **B**

Literary Connection

Carols Charles Dickens hoped people would share his story the way they shared carols. A carol is a religious song, often associated with Christmas. Dickens used a musical scheme to tell *A Christmas Carol.* Instead of chapters, he divided the story into five staves. A stave, or staff, is the name of the five lines on which a composer places notes. It is also a stanza or verse of poetry. As in poetry or musical verses, each of the five staves of *A Christmas Carol* has its own message. At the same time, each stave contributes to the overall joyful message of the story.

A **Bob.** This is Christmas Day, and I should like to drink to the health of the man who employs me and allows me to earn my living and our support and that man is Ebenezer Scrooge...

Mrs. Cratchit. I'll drink to his health for your sake and the day's, but not for his sake...a Merry Christmas and a Happy New Year to you, Mr. Scrooge, wherever you may be this day!

Scrooge. Just here, kind madam...out of sight, out of sight...

Bob. Thank you, my dear. Thank you.

B **Scrooge.** Thank you, Bob...and Mrs. Cratchit, too. No one else is toasting me...not now...not ever. Of that I am sure...

Bob. Children...

All. Merry Christmas to Mr. Scrooge.

Bob. I'll pay you six-pence, Tim, for my favorite song.

Tiny Tim. Oh, Father, I'd so love to sing it, but not for pay. This Christmas goose—this feast—you and Mother, my brother and sisters close with me: that's my pay—

Bob. Martha, will you play the notes on the lute, for Tiny Tim's song.

Belinda. May I sing, too, Father?

Bob. We'll all sing.

650 UNIT 7 DRAMA

Differentiated Instruction

Visual and Auditory Learning

Students may benefit from watching a film adaptation of *A Christmas Carol* to reinforce their understanding of the characters and the sequence of events. Select an adaptation that stays faithful to Dickens's story.

- Have students read a scene from the Horovitz's play and write down questions that they have about the characters or events.

- Then have students watch the corresponding scene in the film to see if it answers their questions.
- Provide time to discuss any questions about a particular scene that remain unanswered after viewing the film, especially if the questions interfere with students' overall enjoyment and comprehension of the play.

They sing a song about a tiny child lost in the snow, probably from Wordsworth's[7] poem. TIM sings the lead vocal; all chime in for the chorus. Their song fades under, as the GHOST OF CHRISTMAS PRESENT speaks.

PRESENT. Mark my words, Ebenezer Scrooge. I do not present the Cratchits to you because they are a handsome, or brilliant family. They are not handsome. They are not brilliant. They are not well-dressed, or tasteful to the times. Their shoes are not even water-proofed by virtue of money or cleverness spent. So when the pavement is wet, so are the insides of their shoes and the tops of their toes. These are the Cratchits, Mr. Scrooge. They are not highly special. They are happy, grateful, pleased with one another, contented with the time and how it passes. They don't sing very well, do they? But, nonetheless, they do sing...[*Pauses.*] think of that, Scrooge. 15 shillings a week and they do sing...hear their song until its end.

SCROOGE. I am listening.

The chorus sings full volume now, until...the song ends here.

SCROOGE. [*Contd.*] Spirit, it must be time for us to take our leave. I feel in my heart that it is...that I must think on that which I have seen here...

PRESENT. Touch my robe again...

SCROOGE touches PRESENT's robe. The lights fade out on the CRATCHITS, who sit, frozen, at the table. SCROOGE and PRESENT in a spotlight now. Thunder, lightning, smoke. They are gone.

— SCENE 4 —

MARLEY appears in single spotlight. A storm brews. Thunder and lightning. SCROOGE and PRESENT "fly" past. The storm continues, furiously, and, now and again, SCROOGE and PRESENT will zip past in their travels. MARLEY will speak straight out to the audience.

MARLEY. The Ghost of Christmas Present, my co-worker in this attempt to turn a miser, flies about now with that very miser, Scrooge, from street to street, and he points out partygoers on their way to Christmas parties. If one were to judge from the numbers of people on their way to friendly gatherings, one might think that no one was left at home to give anyone welcome...but that's not the case, is it? Every home is expecting company and...[*He laughs.*] Scrooge is amazed.

SCROOGE and PRESENT zip past again. The lights fade up around them. We are in the NEPHEW's home, in the living room, PRESENT and SCROOGE stand watching the NEPHEW: FRED and his WIFE, fixing the fire.

SCROOGE. What is this place? We've moved from the mines!

PRESENT. You do not recognize them?

SCROOGE. It is my nephew!...and the one he married...

MARLEY waves his hand and there is a lightning flash. He disappears.

FRED. It strikes me as soooo funny, to think of what he said...that Christmas was a humbug, as I live! He believed it!

WIFE. More shame for him, Fred!

FRED. Well, he's a comical old fellow, that's the truth.

WIFE. I have no patience with him.

FRED. Oh, I have! I am sorry for him; I couldn't be angry with him if I tried. Who suffers by his ill whims? Himself, always...

SCROOGE. It's me they talk of, isn't it, Spirit?

FRED. Here, wife, consider this. Uncle Scrooge takes it into his head to dislike us, and he won't come and dine with us. What's the consequence?

---

7. **Wordsworth.** William Wordsworth was a famous English poet of the late eighteenth and early nineteenth centuries.

Writing Skills

Assess Length

Tell students that it is useful to know how long a writing assignment should be so that they know how much information to gather and organize before they start to write. Sometimes a writing prompt will specify length. When an assignment is less specific—for example, if they are asked to write a "brief" paragraph or essay—here are some points they can keep in mind.

- A brief paragraph is generally six to eight sentences long. This includes an opening sentence (usually the topic sentence), body sentences, and a closing sentence.
- A brief essay is usually five to seven paragraphs long. This includes an introductory paragraph, three to five middle supporting paragraphs, and a closing paragraph.

Use Reading Skills

Draw Conclusions Ask: "Why does Fred have a hard time turning away from Scrooge?" Model a possible response: "Fred realizes that for all his uncle's riches, Scrooge has little to comfort him. Scrooge also reminds him of his mother, so turning away from Scrooge would be like turning away from his mother." **A**

Use Reading Strategies

Ask Questions Encourage students to work in pairs and ask themselves this: Why does Fred say Scrooge has given them "plenty of merriment" when, in fact, Scrooge has been so nasty to Fred? (Fred is being sarcastic. He and his wife may find Scrooge's eccentric behavior funny.) **B**

Use Reading Strategies

Make Inferences Ask students why Scrooge has a sudden urge to talk to his nephew and niece. Ask: "What do you think he wants to say to them?" (He may feel that his time is running out. He probably wants to apologize to them, and perhaps wish them a Merry Christmas.) **C**

WIFE. Oh...you're sweet to say what I think you're about to say, too, Fred...

FRED. What's the consequence? He don't lose much of a dinner by it, I can tell you that!

WIFE. Ooooooo, Fred! Indeed, I think he loses a very good dinner...ask my sisters, or your lecherous bachelor friend, Topper...ask any of them. They'll tell you what old Scrooge, your uncle, missed: a dandy meal!

FRED. Well, that's something of a relief, wife. Glad to hear it!

He hugs his WIFE. *They laugh. They kiss.*

FRED. [*Contd.*] The truth is, he misses much yet. I mean to give him the same chance every year, whether he likes it or not, for I pity him. Nay, he is my only uncle and I feel for the old miser...but, I tell you, wife: I see my dear and perfect mother's face on his own wizened[8] cheeks and brow: brother and sister they were, and I cannot erase that from each view of him I take...

WIFE. I understand what you say, Fred, and I am with you in your yearly asking. But he never will accept, you know. He never will.

FRED. Well, true, wife. Uncle may rail at Christmas till he dies. I think I shook him some with my visit yesterday...[*Laughing.*] I refused to grow angry...no matter how nasty he became...[*Whoops.*] It was HE who grew angry, wife!

They both laugh now.

SCROOGE. What he says is true, Spirit.

FRED AND WIFE. Bah humbug!

FRED. [*Embracing his* WIFE.] There is much laughter in our marriage, wife. It pleases me. You please me.

WIFE. And you please me, Fred. You are a good man...

They embrace.

WIFE. [*Contd.*] Come now. We must have a look at the meal...our guests will soon arrive...my sisters, Topper...

FRED. A toast first...[*He hands her a glass.*] A toast to Uncle Scrooge...[*Fill their glasses.*]

WIFE. A toast to him?

FRED. Uncle Scrooge has given us plenty of merriment, I am sure, and it would be ungrateful not to drink to his health. And I say...Uncle Scrooge!

WIFE. [*Laughing.*] You're a proper loon, Fred...and I'm a proper wife to you...[*She raises her glass.*] Uncle Scrooge! [*They drink. They embrace. They kiss.*]

SCROOGE. Spirit, please, make me visible! Make me audible! I want to talk with my nephew and my niece!

Calls out to them. The lights that light the room and FRED *and* WIFE *fade out.* SCROOGE *and* PRESENT *are alone spotlit.*

PRESENT. These shadows are gone to you now, Mr. Scrooge. You may return to them later tonight in your dreams. [*Pauses.*] My time grows short, Ebenezer Scrooge. Look you on me. Do you see how I've aged?

SCROOGE. Your hair has gone grey! Your skin, wrinkled! Are spirits' lives so short?

PRESENT. My stay upon this globe is very brief. It ends tonight.

SCROOGE. Tonight?

PRESENT. At midnight. The time is drawing near! [*Clock strikes 11:45.*] Hear those chimes? In a quarter hour, my life will have been spent! Look, Scrooge, man, look you here.

Two gnarled baby dolls are taken from PRESENT'*s skirts.*

SCROOGE. Who are they?

PRESENT. They are Man's children, and they

---

8. wizened. Shrunken or wrinkled

Differentiated Instruction

Kinesthetic Learning

Encourage students to enact the last part of Scene 3, in which Scrooge and the Ghost of Christmas Present observe Bob Cratchit and his wife discussing and then toasting Scrooge, and the first part of Scene 4 in which they observe Fred and his Wife discussing and then toasting Scrooge. After students reenact these scenes, they should be able to recognize and describe the similarities between these events.

cling to me, appealing from their fathers. The boy is Ignorance; the girl is Want. Beware them both, and all of their degree,[9] but most of all beware this boy, for I see that written on his brow which is doom, unless the writing is erased.

He stretches out his arms. His voice now amplified: lowly and oddly.

SCROOGE. Have they no refuge or resource?

PRESENT. Are there no prisons? Are there no workhouses?

Twelve chimes.

PRESENT. [*Contd.*] Are there no prisons? Are there no workhouses?

A PHANTOM, *hooded, appears in dim light.*

PRESENT. [*Contd.*] Are there no prisons? Are there no workhouses?

PRESENT *begins to deliquesce.* SCROOGE *calls after him.*

SCROOGE. Spirit, I'm frightened! Don't leave me! Spirit!

PRESENT. Prisons? Workhouses? Prisons? Workhouses...

He is gone. SCROOGE *is alone now with the* PHANTOM, *who is, of course, the* GHOST OF CHRISTMAS FUTURE. *The* PHANTOM *is shrouded in black. Only its outstretched hand is visible from under his ghostly garment.*

SCROOGE. Who are you, Phantom? Oh, yes, I think I know you! You are, are you not, the Spirit of Christmas Yet to Come?

No reply.

SCROOGE. [*Contd.*] And you are about to show me the shadows of the things that have not yet happened, but will happen in time before us. Is that not so, Spirit?

The PHANTOM *allows* SCROOGE *a look at his face. No other reply wanted here. A nervous giggle here.*

SCROOGE. [*Contd.*] Oh, Ghost of the Future, I fear you more than any Spectre I have seen! But, as I know that your purpose is to do me good, and as I hope to live to be another man from what I was, I am prepared to bear you company.

FUTURE *does not reply, but for a stiff arm, hand and finger set, pointing forward.*

SCROOGE. [*Contd.*] Lead on, then, lead on. The night is waning fast, and it is precious time to me. Lead on, Spirit!

FUTURE *moves away from* SCROOGE *in the same rhythm and motion employed at its arrival.* SCROOGE *falls into the same pattern, a considerable space apart from the* SPIRIT. *In the space between them,* MARLEY *appears. He looks to* FUTURE *and then to* SCROOGE. *He claps his hands. Thunder and lightning.* THREE BUSINESSMEN *appear, spotlighted singularly. Thus, six points of the stage should now be spotted in light.* MARLEY *will watch this scene from his position.*

FIRST BUSINESSMAN. Oh, no, I don't know much about it either way, I only know he's dead.

SECOND BUSINESSMAN. When did he die?

FIRST BUSINESSMAN. Last night, I believe.

SECOND BUSINESSMAN. Why, what was the matter with him? [*He uses snuff here; sneezes, etc.*] I thought he'd never die, really...

FIRST BUSINESSMAN. [*Yawning.*] God knows, God knows...

THIRD BUSINESSMAN. What has he done with his money?

SECOND BUSINESSMAN. I haven't heard. Have you?

FIRST BUSINESSMAN. Left it to his Company,

9. **all of their degree.** People of their status or position

wane (wān) *v.,* approach an end

A CHRISTMAS CAROL, ACT 2 **653**

Teach the Selection

Analyze Literature

Theme Ask students what message Present conveys to Scrooge here. (Humans are responsible for the poverty that exists in the world, and choosing to remain ignorant about the needs of others will lead to the downfall of all humankind.) **D**

Analyze Literature

Flashback Remind students that a flashback recalls an earlier event in a story. Ask what earlier event these questions recall. Why does Present keep repeating them? (Scrooge callously asked these questions in Act 1 when the Do-Gooders asked for a donation. Present repeats them to emphasize Scrooge's previous callousness in light of Scrooge's growing awareness.) **E**

Use Reading Strategies

Make Inferences Ask students why they think Future is silent and shrouded. (Being silent and shrouded makes Future mysterious, just as the future is.) **F**

Analyze Literature

Drama Ask students: "What are the businessmen discussing? How do the stage directions help convey the men's feelings toward their subject?" (They are casually discussing the death of a colleague. The snuff use and the yawning suggest that they are not sad about the person's death.) **G**

Research Skills

Graphic Organizers

Remind students that they can use graphic organizers to take notes while reading and doing research, and to organize information after they have finished reading or researching. Graphic organizers make the gathered information easy to read and use for a variety of tasks.

Display or sketch on the board some common graphic organizers: table, T-chart, Venn diagram,

time line, flow chart, and cluster diagram or web. Ask which ones students might use to compare and contrast the visits of the three Ghosts in *A Christmas Carol.* The most likely choice is a three-column table or chart, although students might also suggest using a modified Venn diagram with three circles arranged in a triangle.

Teach the Selection

Use Reading Strategies

Clarify Students may not be familiar with the expression the businessman use, "money to money." Have them offer possible meanings. (It refers to the seeming ease with which those who have plenty of money earn or get more money.) **Ⓐ**

Use Reading Skills

Draw Conclusions Ask students whose funeral they think the men are discussing. (Most will say Scrooge's.) **Ⓑ**

Ⓐ perhaps. Money to Money: you know the expression...

THIRD BUSINESSMAN. He hasn't left it to me. That's all I know...

FIRST BUSINESSMAN. [*Laughing.*] Nor to me... [*Looks at* SECOND BUSINESSMAN.] you, then? You got his money???

SECOND BUSINESSMAN. [*Laughing.*] Me, me, his money? Nooooo!

They all laugh.

Ⓑ **THIRD BUSINESSMAN.** It's likely to be a cheap funeral, for upon my life, I don't know of a living soul who'd care to <u>venture</u> to it. Suppose we make up a party and volunteer?

SECOND BUSINESSMAN. I don't mind going if a lunch is provided, but I must be fed, if I make one.

FIRST BUSINESSMAN. Well, I am the most disinterested among you, for I never wear black gloves, and I never eat lunch. But I'll offer to go, if anybody else will. When I come to think of it, I'm not all sure that I wasn't his most particular friend; for we used to stop and speak whenever we met. Well, then...bye, bye!

SECOND BUSINESSMAN. Bye, bye...

THIRD BUSINESSMAN. Bye, bye...

> **ven•ture** (ven[t]′ shər) *v.,* undertake the risks and dangers of an action

Differentiated Instruction

Reading Proficiency

Using a classroom tape recorder, have volunteers make audio recordings of the conversation between the businessmen, and of the conversation between Old Joe and the two women. (These may be especially difficult for less-able readers to follow.) Make sure students understand that the circumstances surrounding both conversations are intentionally vague, not vague because students have missed something. Recordings should include the dialogue as well as the stage directions.

Struggling readers can listen to the recordings as they read along in the text. They also can play back the recordings if they wish to reread either or both conversations.

They glide offstage in three separate directions. Their lights follow them.

SCROOGE. Spirit, why did you show me this? Why do you show me businessmen from my streets as they take the death of Jacob Marley. That is a thing past. You are future!

JACOB MARLEY *laughs a long, deep laugh. There is a thunder clap and lightning flash, and he is gone.* SCROOGE *faces* FUTURE, *alone on stage now.* FUTURE *wordlessly stretches out his arm-hand-and-finger-set, pointing into the distance. There, above them,* DRUNKS *and* SCOUNDRELS *and* WOMEN OF THE STREETS *"fly" by, half-dressed and slovenly.* [N.B.[10] *There could be a dance number here, showing the seamier[11] side of London city life.*] *When the scene has passed, a woman enters the playing area. She is almost at once followed by a second woman; and then a man in faded black; and then, suddenly, an old man, who smokes a pipe. The old man scares the other three. They laugh, anxious.*

FIRST WOMAN. Look here, old Joe, here's a chance! If we haven't all three met here without meaning it!

OLD JOE. You couldn't have met in a better place. Come into the parlor. You were made free of it long ago, you know; and the other two an't strangers. [*He stands; shuts a door. Shrieking.*] We're all suitable to our calling. We're well matched. Come into the parlor. Come into the parlor...[*They follow him.* SCROOGE *and* FUTURE *are now in their midst, watching; silent. A truck[12] comes in on which is set a small wall with fireplace and a screen of rags, etc. All props for the scene.*] Let me just rake this fire over a bit...[*He does. He trims his lamp with the stem of his pipe. The* FIRST WOMAN *throws a large bundle on to the floor. She sits beside it, crosslegged; defiantly.*]

FIRST WOMAN. What odds then? What odds, Mrs. Dilber? Every person has a right to take care of themselves. HE always did!

MRS. DILBER. That's true indeed! No man more so!

FIRST WOMAN. Why, then, don't stand staring as if you was afraid, woman! Who's the wiser? We're not going to pick holes in each other's coats, I suppose?

MRS. DILBER. No, indeed! We should hope not!

FIRST WOMAN. Very well, then! That's enough. Who's the worse for the loss of a few things like these? Not a dead man, I suppose?

MRS. DILBER. [*Laughing.*] No, indeed!

FIRST WOMAN. If he wanted to keep 'em after he was dead, the wicked old screw, why wasn't he natural in his lifetime? If he had been, he'd have had somebody to look after him when he was struck with Death, instead of lying gasping out his last there, alone by himself.

MRS. DILBER. It's the truest word that was ever spoke. It's a judgment on him.

FIRST WOMAN. I wish it were a heavier one, and it should have been, you may depend on it, if I could have laid my hands on anything else. Open that bundle, old Joe, and let me know the value of it. Speak out plain. I'm not afraid to be the first, nor afraid for them to see it. We knew pretty well that we were helping ourselves; before we met here, I believe. It's no sin. Open the bundle, Joe.

FIRST MAN. No, no, my dear! I won't think of letting you be the first to show what you've... earned...earned from this. I throw in mine. [*He takes a bundle from his shoulder; turns it upside down and empties its contents out on to the floor.*] It's not very extensive, see...seals... a pencil case...sleeve buttons....

10. **N.B.** Abbreviation for *nota bene*, meaning "take special note"
11. **seamier.** More unpleasant or rough
12. **truck.** Small cart on which scenery can move onstage and offstage

A CHRISTMAS CAROL, ACT 2 **655**

Teach the Selection

Analyze Literature
Motivation Ask students why Marley laughs. (He's laughing because he knows it's not *his* death the men are discussing.) **C**

Use Reading Strategies
Ask Questions Students may question who or what Old Joe is. Have them refer to "The People of the Play" on page 625 to refresh their memories. **D**

Use Reading Strategies
Visualize Ask students to visualize the scene with Old Joe. Ask: "How does this help you understand what is happening and how Scrooge might feel as he watches?" (Students may say the scene helps them realize the characters are selling a dead man's things, things they stole from him. Like Scrooge, students can see how crass and unfeeling the characters are about the dead man.) **E**

Analyze Literature
Characterization Ask students to point out details in speech patterns that help characterize Old Joe and the others. (Students may point out that the clipped words [keep 'em], slang [old screw], and improper English [speak out plain] establish them as shady or low-class characters.) **F**

Grammar Skills

Compound Subjects
Point out that a compound subject is made up of two or more simple subjects with the same predicate. Compound subjects are joined with *and, either, or, neither, nor,* or *but.*

Ask students to identify the simple subjects (underscored) that make up the compound subject in each sentence.

1. Loud thunderclaps and bright bolts of lightning startled the audience.
2. After a moment, darkness and an eerie silence enveloped the stage.
3. Neither Scrooge, Marley, nor the Ghost of Christmas Future was visible.

Cultural Connection

Adaptations There are countless stage, radio, and film versions of *A Christmas Carol.* Every Christmas season seems to produce new adaptations. Early versions, including a 1939 radio production starring Orson Welles and Lionel Barrymore and a 1951 film version starring Alastair Sim, adhered closely to Dickens's story. Some more recent adaptations take liberties with the characters and story line. In 1970, Albert Finney starred in a musical film titled *Scrooge.* Humorous versions include the 1962 animated movie *Mr. Magoo's Christmas Carol* and the 1992 film *The Muppets' Christmas Carol.*

Make Connections

Ask students how the attitude of these characters toward the dead man (whom students probably know to be Scrooge) makes them feel about him. (Some will feel sorry for Scrooge, especially because he is witnessing their behavior. Others may say that because of Scrooge's past behavior, their attitudes are understandable.) **Ⓐ**

Use Reading Skills

Draw Conclusions Ask students why they think Scrooge reacts so emotionally here. (He may recognize the calico shirt as his and be reacting to the idea of his own death, or because he is changing, he shows extreme sympathy and compassion for the dead man.) **Ⓑ**

MRS. DILBER. Nice sleeve buttons, though...

FIRST MAN. Not bad, not bad...a brooch[13] there...

OLD JOE. Not really valuable, I'm afraid...

FIRST MAN. How much, old Joe?

OLD JOE. [*Writing on the wall with chalk.*] A pitiful lot, really. Ten and six and not a sixpence more!

FIRST MAN. You're not serious!

OLD JOE. That's your account and I wouldn't give another sixpence if I was to be boiled for not doing it. Who's next?

MRS. DILBER. Me! [*Dumps out contents of her bundle.*] Sheets, towels, silver spoons, silver sugar-tongs...some boots...

OLD JOE. [*Writing on wall.*] I always give too much to the ladies. It's a weakness of mine and that's the way I ruin myself. Here's your total comin' up...two pounds-ten...if you asked me for another penny, and made it an open question, I'd repent being so liberal and knock off half a-crown.

FIRST WOMAN. And now do MY bundle, Joe.

OLD JOE. [*Kneeling to open knots on her bundle.*] So many knots, madam...[*He drags out large curtains; dark.*] What do you call this? Bed curtains!

FIRST WOMAN. [*Laughing.*] Ah, yes, bed curtains!

OLD JOE. You don't mean to say you took 'em down, rings and all, with him lying there?

FIRST WOMAN. Yes, I did, why not?

OLD JOE. You were born to make your fortune and you'll certainly do it. **Ⓐ**

FIRST WOMAN. I certainly shan't hold my hand, when I can get anything in it by reaching it out, for the sake of such a man as he was, I promise you, Joe. Don't drop that lamp oil on those blankets, now!

OLD JOE. His blankets?

FIRST WOMAN. Whose else's do you think? He isn't likely to catch cold without 'em, I daresay.

OLD JOE. I hope that he didn't die of anything catching? Eh?

FIRST WOMAN. Don't you be afraid of that. I ain't so fond of his company that I'd loiter about him for such things if he did. Ah! You may look through that shirt till your eyes ache, but you won't find a hole in it, nor a threadbare place. It's the best he had, and a fine one, too. They'd have wasted it, if it hadn't been for me.

OLD JOE. What do you mean "They'd have wasted it?"

FIRST WOMAN. Putting it on him to be buried in, to be sure. Somebody was fool enough to do it, but I took it off again [*She laughs, as do they all, nervously.*] If calico[14] ain't good enough for such a purpose, it isn't good enough then for anything. It's quite as becoming to the body. He can't look uglier than he did in that one! **Ⓑ**

SCROOGE. [*A low-pitched moan emits from his mouth; from the bones.*] OOOOOOOooooooO OOOOooooOOOOOOOOOooooOOOOOO ooooooOO!

OLD JOE. One pound six for the lot.

He produces a small flannel bag filled with money. He divvies it out. He continues to pass around the money as he speaks. All are laughing.

OLD JOE. [*Contd.*] That's the end of it, you see! He frightened every one away from him while he was alive, to profit us when he was dead! Hah ha ha!

ALL. HAHAHAHAhahahahahahah!

SCROOGE. OOOOOoOOOoooOOOoooOOOo ooOOoooOOoooOOOooo! [*He screams at them.*] Obscene demons! Why not market the

---

13. **brooch.** Ornament held by a pin and worn near the neck
14. **calico.** Inexpensive cotton fabric

Differentiated Instruction

Enrichment

Students interested in theater production might enjoy learning more about the process and costs of producing a play such as *A Christmas Carol: Scrooge and Marley,* or any of the other plays in this unit. Encourage students to use the Internet and the library to get general information on the production process, productions costs, and how these costs are covered. In addition, students can get more real-life, hands-on information by interviewing heads of drama departments at area schools and the managers of community and professional theater companies. Invite students to share with the class what they learn about producing a play.

corpse itself, as sell its trimming??? [*Suddenly.*] Oh, Spirit, I see it, I see it! This unhappy man—this stripped-bare corpse could very well be my own. My life holds parallel! My life ends that way now!

Scrooge backs into something in the dark behind his spotlight. Scrooge *looks at* Future, *who points to the corpse.* Scrooge *pulls back the blanket: The corpse is, of course,* Scrooge, *who screams. He falls aside the bed; weeping.*

Scrooge. [*Contd.*] Spirit, this is a fearful place. In leaving it, I shall not leave its lesson, trust me. Let us go!

Future *points to the corpse.*

Scrooge. [*Contd.*] Spirit, let me see some tenderness connected with a death, or that dark chamber, which we just left now, Spirit, will be forever present to me.

Future *spreads his robes again. Thunder and lightning. Lights up in the* Cratchit *home setting.* Mrs. Cratchit *and her daughters, sewing.*

Tiny Tim's voice. [*Off.*] And He took a child and set him in the midst of them.

Scrooge. [*Looking about the room; to* Future.] Huh? Who spoke? Who said that?

Mrs. Cratchit. [*Puts down her sewing.*] The color hurts my eyes. [*Rubs her eyes.*] That's better. My eyes grow weak sewing by candlelight. I shouldn't want to show your father weak eyes when he comes home...not for the world! It must be near his time...

Peter. [*In corner, reading. Looks up from book.*] Past it, rather. But I think he's been walking a bit slower than usual these last few evenings, Mother.

Mrs. Cratchit. I have known him walk with...[*Pauses.*] I have known him walk with Tiny Tim upon his shoulder and very fast indeed...

Peter. So have I, Mother! Often!

Daughter. So have I!

Mrs. Cratchit. But he was very light to carry and his father loved him so, that it was no trouble—no trouble.

Bob, *at door.*

Silent Night, 1891. Viggo Johansen. Hirschsprungske Samling, Copenhagen, Denmark.

Mrs. Cratchit. [*Contd.*] And there is your father at the door.

Bob Cratchit *enters. He wears a comforter. He is cold, forlorn.*

Peter. Father!

Bob. Hello, wife, children...

The Daughter *weeps; turns away from* Cratchit.

Bob. [*Contd.*] Children! How good to see you all! And you, wife. And look at this sewing! I've no doubt, with all your industry; we'll have quilt to set down upon our knees in church on Sunday!

Mrs. Cratchit. You made the arrangements today, then, Robert, for the...service...to be on Sunday.

Teach the Selection

Analyze Literature

Plot Have students explain what happens when Scrooge looks at the corpse. (He recognizes himself. He falls down weeping, probably for his death and the life he wasted.) **C**

Use Reading Strategies

Make Predictions Ask students to predict where Future will take Scrooge next. Then ask: "What clues did you use to make this prediction?" (Students may predict that Future will take Scrooge to the time of Tiny Tim's death. Clues include the fact that Scrooge asked the spirit to let him "see some tenderness connected with a death," and then Tiny Tim's voice is heard.) **D**

Analyze Literature

Mood Ask students to describe the mood in the Cratchit house. Then ask: "How does it compare to the mood in Scene 3?" (In Scene 3, the mood was happy; here it is sad.)

Use Reading Skills

Use Context Clues Have students explain the meaning of the word *arrangements* here. (It refers to funeral plans.) **E**

Speaking & Listening Skills

Nonverbal Communication

Point out that people often communicate with nonverbal clues. Note that in *A Christmas Carol,* the Ghost of Christmas Future never speaks or uses his voice in any way. Instead, he points. Remind students that gestures, such as pointing, and facial expressions are nonverbal clues. To fully understand and appreciate what is happening during a play, the audience has to recognize and interpret nonverbal clues that different characters use on stage.

Ask students to skim the stage directions in Scene 4 of Act 2 for examples of nonverbal clues used by different characters. Have them select examples to pantomime for the class. Ask the class to interpret and "translate" the clues.

Use Reading Skills

Draw Conclusions Ask students why they think Cratchit is so appreciative of how Scrooge's nephew treated him. (Cratchit, by nature, appreciates all kindnesses extended him. He also may be comparing Scrooge's nephew to Scrooge and realizing that even though they were related, the nephew was not like Scrooge in any way.) **Ⓐ**

Analyze Literature

Character Ask students if Cratchit is a dynamic or static character, and to explain their responses. (Cratchit is a static character. At the beginning of the story and at the end, he is positive, happy, and kind. Some students may point out that Cratchit is saddened by Tiny Tim's death [page 657]. His step is slowed; "He is cold, forlorn." Remind them that a static character, in contrast to a dynamic character, does not change as a result of the story's events. Cratchit's sadness occurs in the possible future that Scrooge sees, but his essential nature does not, in reality, change.)

Bob. The funeral. Oh, well, yes, yes, I did. I wish you could have gone. It would have done you good to see how green a place it is. But you'll see it often, I promised him that I would walk there on Sunday, after the service. [*Suddenly.*] My little, little child! My little child!

All Children. [*Hugging him.*] Oh, Father…

Bob. [*He stands.*] Forgive me. I saw Mr. Scrooge's nephew, who you know I'd just met once before, and he was so wonderful to me, wife…he is the most pleasant-spoken gentleman I've ever met…he said "I am heartily sorry for it and heartily sorry for your good wife. If I can be of service to you in any way, here's where I live." And he gave me this card.

Ⓐ Peter. Let me see it!

Bob. And he looked me straight in the eye, wife, and said, meaningfully, "I pray you'll come to me, Mr. Cratchit, if you need some help. I pray you do." Now it wasn't for the sake of anything that he might be able to do for us, so much as for his kind way. It seemed as if he had known our Tiny Tim and felt with us.

Mrs. Cratchit. I'm sure that he's a good soul.

Bob. You would be surer of it, my dear, if you saw and spoke to him. I shouldn't be at all surprised; if he got Peter a situation.**¹⁵**

Mrs. Cratchit. Only hear that, Peter!

Martha. And then, Peter will be keeping company with someone and setting up**¹⁶** for himself!

Peter. Get along with you!

Bob. It's just as likely as not, one of these days, though there's plenty of time for that, my dear. But however and whenever we part from one another, I am sure we shall none of us forget poor Tiny Tim—shall we?—or this first parting that was among us?

All Children. Never, Father, never!

Bob. And when we recollect how patient and mild he was, we shall not quarrel easily among ourselves, and forget poor Tiny Tim in doing it.

All Children. No, Father, never!

Little Bob. I am very happy, I am, I am, I am very happy.

Bob *kisses his little son, as does* Mrs. Cratchit, *as do the other children. The family is set now in one sculptural embrace. The lighting fades to a gentle pool of light, tight on them.*

Scrooge. Spectre, something informs me that our parting moment is at hand. I know it, but I know not how I know it.

Future *points to the other side of the stage. Lights out on* Cratchits. Future *moves slowing, gliding.* Scrooge *follows.* Future *points opposite.* Future *leads* Scrooge *to a wall and a tombstone. He points to the stone.*

Scrooge. [*Contd.*] Am I that man those ghoulish parasites so gloated over? [*Pauses.*] Before I draw nearer to that stone to which you point, answer me one question. Are these the shadows of things that will lie or, the shadows of things that MAY be, only?

Future *points to the gravestone.* Marley *appears in light. He points to grave as well. Gravestone turns front and grows to ten feet high. Words upon it:* Ebenezer Scrooge. *Much smoke billows now from the grave. Choral music here.* Scrooge *stands looking up at gravestone.* Future *does not at all reply in mortals' words, but points once more to the gravestone. The stone undulates**¹⁷** and glows. Music plays, beckoning* Scrooge, Scrooge *reeling in terror.*

Scrooge. [*Contd.*] Oh, no, Spirit! Oh, no, no!

---

15. situation. Job
16. keeping company…setting up. Dating and going out on his own
17. undulates. Moves in waves

Differentiated Instruction

Reading Proficiency

Struggling readers may stumble over phrases such as *sculptural embrace* and *ghoulish parasites*. Tell students that when they come to a difficult word or phrase, they can try different strategies:

• Use context clues to guess the meaning. If the meaning makes sense in the sentence, they can keep on reading.

• Skip over the word or phrase and keep reading.

• Ask for help if not understanding the word or phrase keeps them from reading on.

FUTURE's *finger still pointing.*

SCROOGE. [*Contd.*] Spirit! Hear me! I am not the man I was. I will be the man I would have been but for this intercourse. Why show in this, if I am past all hope?

FUTURE *considers* SCROOGE's *logic. His hand wavers.*

SCROOGE. [*Contd.*] Oh, Good Spirit, I see by your wavering hand that your good nature <u>intercedes</u> for me and pities me. Assure me that I yet may change these shadows that you have shown me by an altered life!

FUTURE's *hand trembles; pointing has stopped.*

SCROOGE. [*Contd.*] I will honor Christmas in my heart and try to keep it all the year. I will live in the Past, the Present, and the Future. The Spirits of all Three shall strive within me. I will not shut out the lessons that they teach. Oh, tell me that I may sponge away the writing that is upon this stone! **C**

SCROOGE *makes a desperate stab at grabbing* FUTURE's *hand. He holds it firm for a moment, but* FUTURE, *stronger than* SCROOGE, *pulls away.* SCROOGE *is on his knees, praying.*

SCROOGE. [*Contd.*] Spirit, dear Spirit, I am praying before you. Give me a sign that all is possible. Give me a sign that all hope for me is not lost. Oh, Spirit, kind Spirit, I beseech thee: give me a sign... **D**

FUTURE *deliquesces, slowly, gently. The* PHANTOM's *hood and robe drop gracefully to the ground in a small heap. Music in. There is nothing in them. They are mortal cloth. The* SPIRIT *is elsewhere.* SCROOGE *has his sign.* SCROOGE *is alone. Tableau.*[18] *The lights fade to black.*

— SCENE 5 —

The end of it. MARLEY, *spotlighted, opposite* SCROOGE, *in his bed, spotlighted.* MARLEY *speaks to audience, directly.*

B **MARLEY.** [*He smiles at* SCROOGE.] The firm of Scrooge and Marley is doubly blessed: two misers turned; one, alas, in Death, too late; but the other miser turned in Time's penultimate[19] nick. Look you on my friend, Ebenezer Scrooge...

SCROOGE. [*Scrambling out of bed; reeling in delight.*] I will live in the Past, in the Present, and in the Future! The Spirits of all Three shall strive within me! **E**

MARLEY. [*He points and moves closer to* SCROOGE's *bed.*] Yes, Ebenezer, the bedpost is your own. Believe it! Yes, Ebenezer, the room is your own. Believe it!

SCROOGE. Oh, Jacob Marley! Wherever you are, Jacob, know ye that I praise you for this! I praise you...and heaven...and Christmas time! [*Kneels facing away from* MARLEY.] I say it to ye on my knees, old Jacob, on my knees! [*He touches his bed curtains.*] Not torn down. My bed curtains are not at all torn down! Rings and all, here they are! They are here: I am here: the shadows of things that would have been, may now be dispelled. They will be, Jacob! I know they will be! [*He chooses clothing for the day. He tries different pieces of clothing and settles, perhaps, on a dress suit, plus a cape of the bed clothing: something of color.*] I am light as a feather, I am happy as an angel, I am as merry as a schoolboy. I am as giddy as a drunken man! [*Yells out window and then out to audience.*] Merry Christmas to everybody! Merry Christmas to everybody! A Happy New Year to all the world! Hallo here! Whoop! Whoop! Hallo! Hallo! I don't know what day of the month it is! I don't care! I don't know anything! I'm quite a baby! I don't care! I don't care a fig! I'd much rather

---

18. tableau. Motionless person or group
19. penultimate. Next to the last—the last being death

in·ter·cede (in' tər sēd´) *v.,* come between to cause a change

---

Use Reading Strategies

Visualize Have students use the dialogue to visualize Scrooge here. Ask: "How does this dialogue help you understand Scrooge's character?" (Students should recognize that Scrooge has undergone a complete transformation from a miserable miser to a happy, excited human being.) Then ask students how Scrooge's attitude toward Christmas has changed, and how they know. (He says "Whoop!" suggesting he's happy that it's Christmas Day.) **A**

Use Reading Skills

Use Context Clues Ask students to use context clues to tell you what the word *prize* means here. (It means the best and the biggest.) **B**

Use Reading Skills

Draw Conclusions Ask students: "Who will probably receive this turkey, and why?" (Some may say the Cratchit family. Others may say Scrooge's nephew or another family. Be sure they explain their choices.) **C**

Analyze Literature

Simile Have students tell you what effect this simile has on them. **D**

---

be a baby than be an old wreck like me or Marley! (Sorry, Jacob, wherever ye be!) Hallo! Hallo there!

Church bells chime in Christmas Day. A small boy, named ADAM, *is seen now as a light fades up on him.*

SCROOGE. [*Contd.*] Hey, you, boy! What's today? What day of the year is it?

ADAM. Today, sir? Why, it's Christmas Day!

SCROOGE. It's Christmas Day, is it? Whoop! Well, I haven't missed it after all, have I? The Spirits did all they did in one night. They can do anything they like, right? Of course they can! Of course they can!

A **ADAM.** Excuse me, sir?

SCROOGE. Huh? Oh, yes, of course, what's your name, lad?

SCROOGE *and* ADAM *will play their scene from their own spotlights.*

ADAM. Adam, sir.

SCROOGE. Adam! What a fine, strong name! Do you know the poulterer's[20] in the next street but one, at the corner?

ADAM. I certainly should hope I know him, sir!

B **SCROOGE.** A remarkable boy! An intelligent boy! Do you know whether the poulterer's have sold the prize turkey that was hanging up there? I don't mean the little prize turkey, Adam, I mean the big one!

ADAM. What, do you mean the one they've got that's as big as me?

SCROOGE. I mean, the turkey the size of Adam: that's the bird!

ADAM. It's hanging there now, sir.

C **SCROOGE.** It is? Go and buy it! No, no, I am absolutely in earnest and buy it and tell 'em to bring it here, so that I may give them directions to where I want it delivered, as a gift. Come back here with the man, Adam,

and I'll give you a shilling. Come back here with him in less than five minutes, and I'll give you half-a-crown!

ADAM. Oh, my, sir! Don't let my brother in on this.

ADAM *runs offstage.* MARLEY *smiles.*

D **MARLEY.** An act of kindness is like the first green grape of summer: one leads to another and another and another. It would take a queer man indeed to not follow an act of kindness with an act of kindness. One simply whets the tongue for more...the taste of kindness is too too sweet. Gifts—goods—are lifeless. But the gift of goodness one feels in the giving is full of life. It...is...a...wonder.

Pauses; moves closer to SCROOGE, *who is totally occupied with his dressing and arranging of his room and his day. He is making lists, etc.* MARLEY *reaches out to* SCROOGE.

ADAM. [*Calling, off.*] I'm here! I'm here!

ADAM *runs on with a man, who carries an enormous turkey.*

ADAM. [*Contd.*] Here I am, sir. Three minutes flat! A world record! I've got the poultryman and he's got the poultry! [*He pants, out of breath.*] I have earned my prize, sir, if I live...

He holds his heart, playacting. SCROOGE *goes to him and embraces him.*

SCROOGE. You are truly a champion, Adam...

MAN. Here's the bird you ordered, sir.

SCROOGE. Oh, my, MY!!! Look at the size of that turkey, will you! He never could have stood upon his legs, that bird! He would have snapped them off in a minute, like sticks of sealingwax! Why you'll never be able to carry that bird to Camden-Town.[21] I'll give you money for a cab...

MAN. Camden-Town's where it's goin', sir?

---

20. **poulterer.** Person who sells chickens, turkeys, and geese
21. **Camden-Town.** Area of North London

Differentiated Instruction

English Language Learning

A Christmas Carol is one of the most familiar holiday stories in the English language. Invite English learners to share familiar holiday stories from their own cultures, focusing on characters and what they symbolize. Students can also share facts about their traditional holidays, including but not limited to Christmas observances.

Use Reading Skills
Draw Conclusions Ask students why they think Scrooge wants to remain anonymous. (He truly understands that giving for the sake of giving is its own reward. He does not need to be recognized for his generosity.) **E**

Analyze Literature
Character Have students explain how kindness has affected Scrooge. (It has made him giddy and lightened his spirit.)

Make Connections
Ask students to name other villainous characters in their reading experience who undergo such a complete transformation as Scrooge does in *A Christmas Carol*. (Responses will vary depending on books and stories students have read.)

SCROOGE. Oh, I didn't tell you? Yes, I've written the precise address down just here on this...[*Hands paper to him.*] Bob Cratchit's house. Now he's not to know who sends him this. Do you understand me? Not a word...[*Handing out money and chuckling.*]

MAN. I understand, sir, not a word.

SCROOGE. Good. There you go then...this is for the turkey...[*Chuckle.*] and this is for the taxi. [*Chuckle.*]...and this is for your world-record run, Adam.

ADAM. But I don't have change for that, sir.

SCROOGE. Then keep it, my lad. It's Christmas!

ADAM. [*He kisses* SCROOGE's *cheek, quickly.*] Thank you, sir. Merry, Merry Christmas! [*He runs off.*]

MAN. And you've given me a bit overmuch here, too, sir...

SCROOGE. Of course I have, sir. It's Christmas!

MAN. Oh, well, thanking you, sir, I'll have this bird to Mr. Cratchit and his family in no time, sir. Don't you worry none about that. Merry Christmas to you, sir, and a very happy New Year, too...

The man exits. SCROOGE *walks in a large circle about the stage, which is now gently lit. A chorus sings Christmas music far in the distance. Bells*

A CHRISTMAS CAROL, ACT 2 **661**

Main Idea and Supporting Details

Remind students that in writing a paragraph or essay, they should keep the main idea in mind.
- In a paragraph, they usually state the main idea in a topic sentence. All other sentences should contain details that support or help explain that main idea.
- In an essay, they will give the main idea in a thesis statement in the opening paragraph. The remaining paragraphs contain details that support and explain the thesis statement.
- They may imply a main idea. Then, all the details combined convey the main idea.

Have students check a previous writing assignment to be sure it has a clear main idea and relevant supporting details.

Use Reading Strategies

Make Inferences Ask students what they think Scrooge whispers into the man's ear. (He is probably making a generous donation.) **A**

Analyze Literature

Drama Have students explain the purpose of these stage directions. Ask: "What do the stage directions reveal about Scrooge's inner feelings?" (These directions show that Scrooge is both excited and nervous about how his nephew and niece will receive him. They suggest that he's unsure of himself.) **B**

Make Connections

Ask students what they would be thinking in the nephew and niece's place. (They would probably be wondering why Scrooge is there and why he seems so cheerful. They might be thinking Scrooge has gone completely crazy.) **C**

TEACHING NOTE
Ask the Author

Divide the class into pairs of students, and have each pair review the selection together. Encourage them to skim and scan it page by page. Suggest that pairs stop at the end of every scene and write down questions they still have about the setting, characters, events, and author's purpose and perspective. Model a question: "Why did Horovitz include the scene with Old Joe?"

Then ask pairs to share some of their questions with the class. Have students note which questions they think still need answers. Talk as a class about where one could go to find those answers.

---

chime as well, far in the distance. A GENTLEWOMAN *enters and passes.* SCROOGE *is on the streets now.*

SCROOGE. Merry Christmas, madam...

WOMAN. Merry Christmas, sir...

The PORTLY BUSINESSMAN *from the first act enters.*

SCROOGE. Merry Christmas, sir.

PORTLY MAN. Merry Christmas, sir.

SCROOGE. Oh, you! My dear sir! How do you do? I do hope that you succeeded yesterday! It was very kind of you. A Merry Christmas.

PORTLY MAN. Mr. Scrooge?

A **SCROOGE.** Yes, Scrooge is my name though I'm afraid you may not find it very pleasant. Allow me to ask your pardon. And will you have the goodness to— [*He whispers into the man's ear.*]

PORTLY MAN. Lord bless me! My dear Mr. Scrooge, are you serious!?!

SCROOGE. If you please. Not a farthing less. A great many back-payments are included in it, I assure you. Will you do me that favor?

PORTLY MAN. My dear sir, I don't know what to say to such munifi—[22]

SCROOGE. [*Cutting him off.*] Don't say anything, please. Come and see me. Will you?

PORTLY MAN. I will! I will! Oh, I will, Mr. Scrooge! It will be my pleasure!

SCROOGE. Thank'ee, I am much obliged to you. I thank you fifty times. Bless you!

B PORTLY MAN *passes offstage.* SCROOGE *now comes to the room of his* NEPHEW *and* NIECE. *He stops at the door, begins to knock on it, loses his courage, tries again, loses his courage again, tries again, fails again, and then backs off and runs at the door, causing a tremendous bump against it. The* NEPHEW *and* NIECE *are startled.* SCROOGE, *poking head into room.*

SCROOGE. Fred!

NEPHEW. Why, bless my soul! Who's that?

NEPHEW AND NIECE. [*Together.*] How now? Who goes?

SCROOGE. It's I. Your Uncle Scrooge.

NIECE. Dear heart alive!

SCROOGE. I have come to dinner. May I come in, Fred?

C **NEPHEW.** May you come in???!!! With such pleasure for me you may, Uncle!!! What a treat!

NIECE. What a treat, Uncle Scrooge! Come in, come in!

They embrace a shocked and delighted SCROOGE. FRED *calls into the other room.*

NEPHEW. Come in here, everybody, and meet my Uncle Scrooge! He's come for our Christmas party!

Music in. Lighting here indicates that day has gone to night and gone day again. It is early, early morning. SCROOGE *walks alone from the party exhausted, to his offices, opposite side of the stage. He opens his offices. The offices are as they were at the start of the play.* SCROOGE *seats himself with his door wide open so that he can see into the tank, as he awaits* CRATCHIT, *who enters, head down, full of guilt.* CRATCHIT *starts writing almost before he sits.*

SCROOGE. What do you mean by coming in here at this time of day, a full eighteen minutes late, Mr. Cratchit? Hallo, sir? Do you hear me?

BOB. I am very sorry, sir. I am behind my time.

SCROOGE. You are? Yes, I certainly think you are. Step this way, sir, if you please...

BOB. It's only but once a year, sir...it shall not be repeated. I was making rather merry yesterday and into the night.

---

22. **munifi—.** Short for *munificence*, which means "great generosity"

Grammar Skills

Misplaced Modifiers

Tell students that misplaced modifiers are placed so far away from the words they modify that they seem to modify the wrong word.
incorrect: They sat by the fire waiting for guests patiently to arrive.
correct: While patiently waiting for guests to arrive, they sat by the fire.

correct: They sat by the fire and waited patiently for guests to arrive.

Have students identify the misplaced modifier in each sentence (underscored) and then correct the sentence.

1. The children sang holiday songs while waiting for dinner <u>in loud voices.</u>
2. Father played the piano <u>full of joy</u> as family and friends gathered around.

A CHRISTMAS CAROL, ACT 2 **663**

History Connection

Victorian Christmases In the early days of Victorian England, Christmas was not widely celebrated. The general populace had little money or energy to expend on frivolities and what had, over the centuries, become a secular festival. Interest in Christmas traditions was slightly renewed after Queen Victoria displayed a decorated Christmas tree that she had imported from Germany. However, it was the 1843 publication of *A Christmas Carol,* in which Dickens recalled the joyful parties and family celebrations of the past, that went farthest in renewing widespread interest in the Christmas season.

Analyze Literature

Plot Ask students what they think is the climax of the plot of *A Christmas Carol: Scrooge and Marley.* Allow them to discuss the question in small groups, and then tell them to keep their ideas in mind for future reference.

Speaking & Listening Skills

Active Listening

Have students work in pairs to improvise a conversation between two characters in *A Christmas Carol: Scrooge and Marley.* Encourage students to be creative and think beyond the action of the play so that they are not simply reworking existing play dialogue.

Tell students to apply the following listening skills during their improvisations.

- Face the speaker and make eye contact.
- Be attentive and show interest in what the speaker is saying.
- Note the speaker's tone, volume, and body language, and respond appropriately.
- Wait until it's your turn to speak.

Use Reading Skills

Identify Cause and Effect Ask students what Cratchit realizes and why he is astounded. (He realizes that Scrooge has been joking and has just given him a raise. This is totally out of character for Scrooge.) **A**

Answer: Students may say that they can help others by being kind and friendly, or giving of their time or energy.

Find Meaning

1. (a) Kindness sprinkles from the torch. (b) Anyone can receive it.

2. (a) Fred feels sorry for his uncle. (b) He missed a good meal.

3. (a) He thinks they're talking about Marley. (b) He sees his tombstone.

Make Judgments

4. (a) Present repeats many of the words Scrooge used, such as "Are there no prisons? No workhouses?" (b) Students may say Scrooge sees Tiny Tim as a real person. Before, "the poor" were faceless people.

5. (a) They stole them from Scrooge's house after he died. (b) Because Scrooge had no friends, there was no one to get him ready for burial or watch over his things.

6. Answers may include "friends and family are more important than money" or "money doesn't necessarily bring happiness."

SCROOGE. Now, I'll tell you what, Cratchit. I am not going to stand this sort of thing any longer. And therefore...[*He stands and pokes his finger into* BOB's *chest.*] I am...about...to... raise...your salary.

A **BOB.** Oh, no, sir, I...[*Realizes.*] what did you say, sir?

SCROOGE. A Merry Christmas, Bob...[*He claps* BOB's *back.*] A merrier Christmas, Bob, my good fellow than I have given you for many a year. I'll raise your salary and endeavor to assist your struggling family and we will discuss your affairs this very afternoon over a bowl of smoking bishop,²³ Bob! Make up the fires and buy another coal scuttle before you dot another i, Bob. It's too damned cold in this place! We need warmth and cheer, Bob Cratchit! Do you hear me? DO...YOU... HEAR...ME?

BOB CRATCHIT *stands, smiles at* SCROOGE. BOB CRATCHIT *faints. Blackout. As the main lights black out, a spotlight appears on* SCROOGE, *another on* MARLEY. *He talks directly to the audience.*

MARLEY. Scrooge was better than his word. He did it all and infinitely more; and to Tiny Tim, who did NOT die, he was a second father. He became as good a friend, as good a master, as good a man, as the good old city knew, or any other good old city, town, or borough in the good old world. And it was always said of him that he knew how to keep Christmas well, if any man alive possessed the knowledge. [*Pauses.*] May that be truly said of us, and all of us: And so, as Tiny Tim observed...

TINY TIM. [*Atop* SCROOGE's *shoulder.*] God Bless Us, Every One...

Lights up on chorus, singing final Christmas Song. SCROOGE *and* MARLEY *and all spirits and other characters of the play join in.*

The play has ended. ❖

---

23. **smoking bishop.** Warm drink made with wine and citrus fruit

---

Have you, like Scrooge, ever found great happiness in helping others or in changing your attitude toward life and other people? In what ways can others be helped without money or material things?

Find Meaning

1. (a) What does Present sprinkle from his torch? (b) Who receives Present's gift?

2. (a) How does Fred feel about his uncle? (b) What does Fred's wife say that Scrooge missed?

3. (a) Whose death does Scrooge think the three businessmen are discussing? (b) How does he find out about his own death?

Make Judgments

4. (a) How does Present make Scrooge think about the way he has acted in the past? (b) Why do you think seeing Tiny Tim changes the way Scrooge feels?

5. (a) How did Mrs. Dilber and the other people get the goods they are selling to Old Joe? (b) Why were they able to do this? Explain your answer.

6. What is the theme of *A Christmas Carol: Scrooge and Marley?* Use details to support your answer.

Differentiated Instruction

Enrichment

Students might enjoy presenting a mock debate about Charles Dickens. Assign students or teams one of these positions to debate.

- Charles Dickens was a talented, skilled writer who gained popularity because he crafted timeless stories with vivid characters and interesting plots.

- Charles Dickens was not a true literary artist. He wrote sentimental stories that he knew would appeal to a large number of readers.

Provide time for students to research their positions. Set aside class time for students to conduct their debate. At the end, have the rest of the class vote on who they think won the debate.

Dickens wrote and personally published *A Christmas Carol: A Ghost Story of Christmas* because his earlier works were not selling well, he was in debt, and his wife was expecting their fifth child. Dickens's expectations of quick revenue were not realized, however, because he had commissioned **John Leech,** a well-known London artist, to illustrate the book with hand-colored etchings and wood engravings.

from **A Christmas Carol**

Illustrations by John Leech

Marley's Ghost, 1843. John Leech. Dickens House Museum, London.

A CHRISTMAS CAROL **665**

Teach the Connection

▷ About the Illustrator

Illustrator and cartoonist John Leech (1817–1864) gained fame for his contributions to *Punch*, the London magazine that published 3,600 of his humorous drawings and cartoons. At age sixteen, Leech had attended medical school, where his anatomical drawings so impressed his teachers that they hired him to paint portraits. When family financial problems forced Leech to leave medical school, he decided to pursue a career as an artist. While much of Leech's work was humorous, many of his cartoons and drawings also revealed his views on the key political issues of Victorian times.

Leech met Charles Dickens while working for the publication *Bentley's Miscellany*, where Dickens worked as an editor. Besides drawing the illustrations for *A Christmas Carol*, Leech also acted in Dickens's amateur theatrical productions.

Use Reading Skills

Summarize Point out that both *A Christmas Carol: Scrooge and Marley* and Leech's illustrations recreate characters first developed by Charles Dickens. Ask students to list what they've learned from both sources about how artists adapt material (for example, by visualizing characters), and to synthesize their notes into a one-paragraph summary.

Reading Skills

Identify Cause and Effect

Remind students that Charles Dickens was greatly disturbed by the disparity between the classes in Victorian England, and was also angered by the insensitive treatment of the poor. Dickens wrote *A Christmas Carol* as a social criticism of the times.

Have students select another drama in this unit. Ask them to use the library and the Internet to find and read articles and reviews that explain more about the play, the playwright, and the context in which the play was written. For example, they might learn that the playwright, like Dickens, was inspired to comment on a particular social trend. Invite them to share what they learn with the class.

Common Core State Standards

Writing
W.2

Teach the Connection

Use Reading Strategies

Ask Questions Encourage students to ask themselves questions about the setting and characters in each illustration. Model some possible questions: "Where does this scene take place?" "How does Leech's use of light and darkness affect the mood?" Encourage students to use the answers to formulate an opinion of how effective the illustrations are.

Analyze Literature

Characterization Ask students to point out details in each illustration that reveal the personalities of Ebenezer Scrooge, Jacob Marley, and the spirits of Present and Future. Their responses should imply an understanding of these characters in the play and how Leech captured their individuality. For example, in the illustration on page 665 they might point out the pinched features and frown on Scrooge's face that reveal his crotchety disposition.

Text-to-Text Connection

Answer: Answers will vary. Many students will say the clothing and details of the setting are consistent with what they imagined. Students may claim that these images helped them better visualize the characters.

Scrooge's Third Visitor, 1843. John Leech. Dickens House Museum, London.

The Last of the Visitors, 1843. John Leech. Dickens House Museum, London.

TEXT ←TO→ TEXT CONNECTION In what ways do these illustrations accurately reflect the way you imagined the characters and setting of this play? In what ways do they enhance your understanding of the play?

Differentiated Instruction

Visual Learning

Visual learners can use details in the Leech illustrations to recall the visits by Jacob Marley and the spirits in *A Christmas Carol: Scrooge and Marley,* and to explain the role of each spirit's visit in the development of the plot and its resolution.

Kinesthetic and Visual Learning

To enrich students' appreciation of the illustrations and help them focus on the content, have them recreate the illustrations by posing silently and motionless in a series of tableaus. Depending on time and resources, students can add props and wear appropriate costumes to make their tableaus more precisely mirror the illustrations.

Analyze Literature

Plot Return to the plot diagram you began at the end of Act 1. What part or parts of the plot took place in Act 2? For each plot part you identify, write the act and scene number on your diagram. In addition, include a brief description of the action that occurred during that part of the plot.

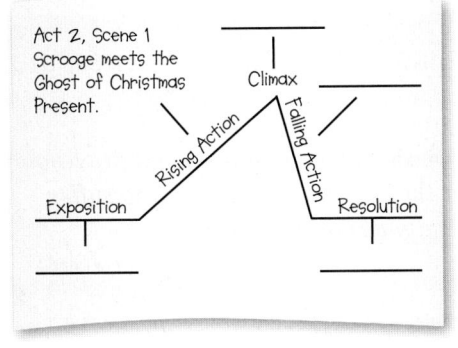

Act 2, Scene 1
Scrooge meets the Ghost of Christmas Present.

Exposition
Rising Action
Climax
Falling Action
Resolution

Analyze Literature

Plot Students should identify the first scenes of Act 2 as rising action, Scrooge learning that Tiny Tim will die and/or seeing his own tombstone as the climax, the scene where he gets the turkey and talks to people in a friendly manner as falling action, and the final scene as the resolution.

Extend Understanding

Writing Options

Creative Writing Write a **diary entry** as if you were Scrooge. Describe a key event of the past few days. Include sensory information about what you saw, heard, touched, and smelled. As you write, match Scrooge's tone, mood, and attitude about life, money, and people.

Expository Writing In a play, you can learn about a character from stage directions as well as from what characters say and do. In a short **expository essay,** compare and contrast the characters of Scrooge and Marley. State your main point in your thesis, and support it with evidence from the play. Include information about Scrooge's and Marley's physical appearance, attitude, and other aspects of their personalities.

Lifelong Learning

Research Religious Holidays Use the Internet or library resources to research the history and practices associated with holidays from different cultures, such as Ramadan or Passover. Share your findings with the class in an oral report. Use visuals, examples, or other nonverbal media to enliven your presentation.

Critical Literacy

Perform a Scene In small groups, practice and perform a scene from Act 2 of *A Christmas Carol: Scrooge and Marley.* Carefully read the stage directions and gather any props or set decorations. Choose one group member to be the "director." Hold a few rehearsals before performing the scene for the class.

 Go to **www.mirrorsandwindows.com** for more.

Rubrics for Writing Options

You can adapt this as a checklist for students to use as they write.

Creative Writing

☐ Does the diary entry describe a key event?
☐ Does the entry include sensory details?
☐ Does the entry express Scrooge's mood and tone about life, money, and people?

Expository Writing

☐ Does the essay compare and contrast Scrooge and Marley?
☐ Does the essay have a thesis statement that is supported by evidence?
☐ Does the essay include information about the physical appearance and attitudes of the two characters?

Teach the Workshop

Vocabulary Practice

Answers will vary based on the references a student uses. (This also applies to the Extra Practice questions below.)

1. meaning: exposed, barren, cold, grim; synonyms: gloomy, dismal
2. meaning: ample quantity, plenty; synonyms: affluence, profusion
3. meaning: relating to the world rather than to spiritual things; synonyms: sophisticated, practical
4. meaning: act of mourning or crying out; synonyms: lament, complaint, elegy
5. meaning: produced in abundance; synonyms: profuse, lush, luxuriant
6. meaning: irresistible urge; synonyms: obligation, craving
7. meaning: deserving hatred or repugnance; synonyms: hateful, foul, disgusting, repulsive
8. meaning: (v) to risk or attempt, (n) undertaking involving risk; synonyms: try, gamble, enterprise
9. meaning: intervene between parties; synonyms: mediate, interpose
10. meaning: wave, rise and fall; synonyms: fluctuate, waver, oscillate

> For more information, see Vocabulary & Spelling Section 2.3, Using a Dictionary, in the Language Arts Handbook. Refer to Section 2.7, Spelling, for additional instruction on spelling rules.

Using Dictionaries and Thesauruses

...we should make some slight provision for the poor and destitute, who suffer greatly at the present time.

—ISRAEL HOROVITZ, *A Christmas Carol: Scrooge and Marley*

Context clues suggest the meaning of the word *destitute* in the above quotation. However, to learn the exact definition of the word, you can look in a dictionary.

A **dictionary** is a reference source that provides one or more **definitions,** or meanings, of a word. Dictionaries also provide the **pronunciation** of the word—or the way the word is usually spoken—and a word's etymology. A word's **etymology** is its history or origin, including the root or base words from which it is formed. Etymology is usually provided for the simplest present-tense form of the word.

EXAMPLE

des · ti · tute (des´ tə tüt) *adj.* without money or other basic necessities for survival; extremely poor

[Latin *destituere* meaning "to abandon, deprive"]

A **thesaurus** is a reference source that contains synonyms rather than definitions. Synonyms are words that have the same, or nearly the same, meaning as another word. Synonyms are clues to a word's meaning.

EXAMPLE

destitute: *adj.* PENNILESS: poor, impoverished, distressed

Review the Terms

dictionary: a reference source that provides meanings and other information about words

definition: the meaning of a word

pronunciation: the way a word is usually spoken

etymology: the history or origin of a word

thesaurus: a reference containing synonyms for many words

Vocabulary Practice

Use a dictionary to list the meaning of each word below from *A Christmas Carol: Scrooge and Marley.* Then use a thesaurus to list two synonyms for each word.

1. bleak
2. abundance
3. worldly
4. lamentation
5. lavish
6. compulsion
7. odious
8. venture
9. intercede
10. undulate

Spelling Practice

Silent Letters

Silent letters can pose a problem in spelling unless you are familiar with the word or can recognize a common form. For instance, if you know that the *b* in *comb* is silent, you will know how to pronounce *lamb* when you see it and may be able to remember to spell it with the silent letter. Group these words from the excerpt from *A Christmas Carol* by patterns in their silent letters.

answers	doubt	lightly
assign	fastens	listen
business	indebted	whistle
daughter	knocker	wrenching

Program Resources

You will find additional lessons on Using Dictionaries and Thesauruses in the *Exceeding the Standards: Vocabulary & Spelling* resource.

Common Core State Standards

Language
L.4, L.6

Let Me Hear You Whisper

A Drama by Paul Zindel

At a Glance
Directed Reading
- Reading Level: Challenging
- Difficulty Considerations: Vocabulary, length, and topic
- Ease Factor: Suspense

BEFORE READING

Build Background
Scientific Context Dolphins fascinate humans, and as a result, the field of scientific research on dolphins is large. Researchers study dolphin intelligence as well as their complex social relationships and their communication system. Some of this research is aimed at training dolphins for useful tasks such as locating and retrieving objects. However, much of today's research is aimed at conservation of the species and its habitat.

Reader's Context Think of a time you felt a connection with an animal. What were your feelings? What about the animal caused them?

Set Purpose
Read the play's cast of characters and its setting. Predict what types of tasks Helen may have to do in her new job.

Analyze Literature
Dialogue Conversation involving two or more characters is called **dialogue.** Plays are mostly made up of dialogue and stage directions. In fiction, narration helps tell the story. In a play, there is usually no narration, so dialogue and characters' actions are the tools the playwright uses to tell the story. Stage directions tell how the character is supposed to speak and what he or she should be doing while delivering the lines.

Meet the Author
Paul Zindel (1936–2003) was interested in both science and writing as a child. He wrote his first play in high school. As a college student, he majored in chemistry but was also inspired by his creative writing teacher. Zindel taught high school science before becoming a full-time writer. As a writer, he created numerous plays and young adult novels. His first young adult novel was *The Pigman*.

Use Reading Skills
Distinguish Between Major and Minor Details Authors include many details to make their writing rich and believable. Major details are the keys to understanding a story. Minor details enhance a story but are not necessarily important to remember. You can use a chart to help you distinguish between these two types. When you complete the chart, consider how these details fit together.

Major Details:	Minor Details:
Helen has a new job in a lab.	The reception desk is in the hall.

Preview Vocabulary
a·nal·y·sis (ə naˊ lə səs) *n.*, act of separating something into its parts to examine them

com·pul·so·ry (kəm pᴜlˊ sə rē) *adj.*, required by a law or rule

ap·pre·hen·sive·ly (aˊ pri hen[t]ˊ siv lē) *adv.*, in a way that shows fear or caution

ter·mi·nate (tᴜrˊ mə nātʹ) *v.*, end

Objectives
Studying this lesson will enable students to
- use reading skills such as distinguishing between major and minor details
- define dialogue and recognize its effects in the selection
- describe the work of Paul Zindel and explain how his early interests may have affected his writing
- appreciate a story about a woman and a dolphin overcoming challenges

Launch the Lesson
Prior to reading "Let Me Hear You Whisper," have students give several examples of human-animal "communication." Many may suggest that having a dog come when called is communication. Have students compare such stimulus-response behavior with two-way communication, such as a conversation, between people. Point out that two-way communication is rare between humans and animals.

Words in Use

Preview Vocabulary	Selection Words	Teaching Words
analysis, 671	efficient, 671	conservation, 669
compulsory, 672	contemplates, 673	species, 669
apprehensively, 673	atmosphere, 674	habitat, 669
terminate, 676	decapitated, 675	critical, 686

Common Core State Standards
Reading Literature
RL.1

Teach the Selection

Summary

Helen is a new employee in a laboratory that conducts strange experiments involving mammals. She befriends a dolphin and is shocked to learn that the scientists plan to dissect the dolphin's brain because it hasn't "talked." She urges the dolphin to talk to them as it does to her, but the dolphin refuses and asks her for help. After Helen's failed attempt to rescue the dolphin, it does indeed "talk" for the scientists, and they plead with Helen to keep working for them. But having discovered their real purpose, Helen refuses and threatens to report them for animal cruelty.

The Mirrors & Windows questions at the end of the selection focus on the theme of ethics. Before students begin reading the play, ask: When was the last time you refused to do something because you thought it was unfair?

Let Me Hear You

Whisper

A Drama by Paul Zindel

"You will do best not to become fond of the subject animals."

670

Program Resources

Planning and Assessment
Program Planning Guide, Selection Lesson Plan
E-Lesson Planner
Assessment Guide, Lesson Test
ExamView

Technology Tools
Interactive Student Text on CD
Visual Teaching Package
Audio Library
mirrorsandwindows.com

Meeting the Standards
Drama: Unit 7, Directed Reading, pp. 43–48

Differentiating Instruction
Advanced Students, Communication Analysis, p. 43

CHARACTERS

HELEN *A little old cleaning lady who lives alone in a one-room apartment and spends most of her spare time feeding stray cats and dogs. She has just been hired to scrub floors in a laboratory that performs rather strange experiments with dolphins.*

MISS MORAY *A briskly efficient custodial supervisor who has to break Helen in to her new duties at the laboratory. She has a face that is so uptight she looks like she either throws stones at pigeons or teaches Latin.*

DR. CROCUS *The dedicated man of science who devises and presides over the weird experiments.*

MR. FRIDGE *Assistant to Dr. Crocus. He is so loyal and uncreative that if Dr. Crocus told him to stick his head in the mouth of a shark, he'd do it.*

DAN *A talky janitor, also under Miss Moray's control, who at every chance ducks out of the Manhattan laboratory for a beer at the corner bar.*

A DOLPHIN *The subject of an experiment being performed by Dr. Crocus.*

SETTING: *The action takes place in the hallway, laboratory and specimen room of a biology experimentation association located in Manhattan near the Hudson River.*

TIME: *The action begins with the night shift on Monday and ends the following Friday.*

ACT 1

SCENE 1

DR. CROCUS and MR. FRIDGE are leaving the laboratory where they have completed their latest experimental tinkering with a dolphin, and they head down a corridor to the elevator. The elevator door opens and MISS MORAY emerges with HELEN.

MISS MORAY. Dr. Crocus. Mr. Fridge. I'm so

Ⓐ glad we've run into you. I want you to meet Helen.

HELEN. Hello.

DR. CROCUS and MR. FRIDGE nod and get on elevator.

MISS MORAY. Helen is the newest member of our Custodial Engineering Team.

MISS MORAY and HELEN start down the hall.

MISS MORAY. Dr. Crocus is the guiding heart here at the American Biological Association Development for the Advancement of Brain Analysis. For short, we call it "Abadaba."

HELEN. I guess you have to.

They stop at a metal locker at the end of the hall.

MISS MORAY. This will be your locker and your key. Your equipment is in this closet.

HELEN. I have to bring in my own hangers, I suppose.

MISS MORAY. Didn't you find Personnel pleasant?

HELEN. They asked a lot of crazy questions.

MISS MORAY. Oh, I'm sorry. [*Pause.*] For instance.

HELEN. They wanted to know what went on in my head when I'm watching television in my living room and the audience laughs. They asked if I ever thought the audience was laughing at *me.*

MISS MORAY. [*Laughing.*] My, oh my! [*Pause.*] What did you tell them?

HELEN. I don't have a TV.

MISS MORAY. I'm sorry.

HELEN. I'm not.

MISS MORAY. Yes. Now, it's really quite simple. That's our special soap solution. One tablespoon to a gallon of hot water, if I may suggest.

> **a·nal·y·sis** (ə na′ lə səs) *n.,* act of separating something into its parts to examine them

Teach the Selection

Use Reading Skills
Distinguish Between Major and Minor Details Invite a volunteer to read aloud the character description of Helen. Point out that the playwright probably considers these to be major details of her character. Ask students why they think the author included information about Helen feeding stray cats and dogs. Have them predict what might happen to Helen in the story based on this, and how she might respond. Ⓐ

Analyze Literature
Characterization Point out that Zindel uses figurative language and some judgmental phrases to describe some of his characters in the "Characters" list. He also provides details that may seem irrelevant. After they read the dialogue on this page, ask students to tell you how the character descriptions influenced the way they understood the scene. (They may already have formed opinions about which characters they are going to like and dislike.)

Differentiated Instruction

Reading Proficiency
Work with students to preview the descriptions of the play's characters and setting. Have students sum up each character in their own words. Point out that the dolphin is listed as a character. Have students predict what this might mean in terms of the dialogue in the play.

Visual Learning
Direct students' attention to the picture. Have each students make up three questions that require making an inference or drawing a conclusion based on something in the picture. Model a question: "Where is this animal?" Have students exchange questions and answer the questions they receive.

Science Connection

Marine Mammals Some people think of dolphins as fish, but they are mammals called *cetaceans*—a group that includes whales, dolphins, and porpoises. Mammals breathe air, give birth to live young, produce milk, and have at least some hair on their bodies. The word *cetacean* derives from Latin and Greek words meaning "large sea creature or monster." Dolphins have cone-shaped teeth, beaks, and curved or hooked dorsal fins. Many zoos and aquariums have bottlenose dolphins. People have misnamed the largest dolphin, the orca, "killer whale."

Use Reading Skills

Use Context Clues Ask students to use context clues to figure out the meaning of the word *natatorium.* Have students use a dictionary to check their ideas. (A natatorium is an indoor swimming pool.) **A**

HELEN *is busy running water into a pail which fits into a metal stand on wheels.*

MISS MORAY. I'll start you in the laboratory. We like it done first. The specimen room is next, and finally the hallway. By that time we'll be well toward morning, and if there are a few minutes left, you can polish the brass strip. [*She points to brass strip which runs around the corridor, halfway between ceiling and floor.*] Ready? Fine.

They start down the hall, MISS MORAY *thumbing through papers on a clipboard.*

MISS MORAY. You were with one concern for fourteen years, weren't you? Fourteen years with Metal Climax Building. That's next to the Radio City Music Hall, isn't it, dear?

HELEN. Uh-huh.

MISS MORAY. They sent a marvelous letter of recommendation. My! Fourteen years on the seventeenth floor. You must be very proud. Why did you leave?

HELEN. They put in a rug.

MISS MORAY *leads* HELEN *into the laboratory, where* DAN *is picking up.*

MISS MORAY. Dan, Helen will be taking Marguerita's place. Dan is the night porter[1] for the fifth through ninth floors.

DAN. Hiya!

HELEN. Hello. [*She looks around.*]

MISS MORAY. There's a crock on nine you missed, and the technicians on that floor have complained about the odor.

HELEN *notices what appears to be a large tank of water with a curtain concealing its contents.*

HELEN. What's that?

MISS MORAY. What? Oh, that's a dolphin, dear. But don't worry about anything except the floor. Dr. Crocus prefers us not to touch either the equipment or the animals.

HELEN. Do you keep him cramped up in that all the time?

A **MISS MORAY.** We have a natatorium for it to exercise in, at Dr. Crocus's discretion.[2]

HELEN. He looks really cramped.

MISS MORAY *closes a curtain which hides the tank.*

MISS MORAY. Well, you must be anxious to begin. I'll make myself available at the reception desk in the hall for a few nights in case any questions arise. Coffee break at two and six A.M. Lunch at four A.M. All clear?

HELEN. I don't need a coffee break.

MISS MORAY. Helen, we all need Perk-You-Ups. All of us.

HELEN. I don't want one.

MISS MORAY. They're <u>compulsory</u>. [*Pause.*] Oh, Helen, I know you're going to fit right in with our little family. You're such a nice person. [*She exits.*] [HELEN *immediately gets to work, moving her equipment into place and getting down on her hands and knees to scrub the floor.* DAN *exits.* HELEN *gets in a few more rubs, glances at the silhouette of the dolphin's tank behind the curtain, and then continues. After a pause, a record begins to play.*]

RECORD. "Let me call you sweetheart,

I'm in love with you.

Let me hear you whisper

That you love me, too."

HELEN'S *curiosity makes her open the curtain and look at the dolphin. He looks right back at her. She returns to her work, singing "Let Me Call You Sweetheart" to herself, missing a word here and there; but her eyes return to the dolphin. She*

---

1. **porter.** Janitor
2. **discretion.** Freedom to choose or make a decision

---

com·pul·so·ry (kəm pǔl´ sə rē) *adj.*, required by a law or rule

---

Reading Skills

Draw Conclusions

Tell students that getting a good sense of the characters at the beginning of a play will help them interpret the characters' motivations and actions in later scenes. Encourage students to review the dialogue and stage directions on this page with the goal of deepening their understanding of the characters. Model this process with the lines in which Miss Moray introduces Helen to Dr. Crocus and Mr. Fridge on page 671. Point out that the men seem uninterested in Helen. One might infer that they think their employees—at least on the custodial staff—are not worth their time.

Have small groups of students make inferences about the characters from the remaining dialogue on this page. Have them keep track of their inferences for later review.

Faraday's Magnetic Laboratory, 1852. Harriet Jane Moore. The Royal Institution, London.

Science Connection
Dolphin Communication A dolphin is as unlikely to produce "words" through its blowhole as humans are to produce accurate dolphin whistles with their vocal chords. Bottlenose dolphins communicate mainly through a large variety of high-pitched whistles, squeals, and sound pulses that come from their blowholes. Dolphins form different sounds by moving air through sacs beneath the blowhole, causing tissue structures in the area to vibrate like a trumpet player's lips. This produces clicks and whistles, which are often too high for the human ear to hear. Dolphins recognize one another through these whistles as easily as humans recognize the sounds of other people's voices.

becomes uncomfortable under his stare and tries to ease her discomfort by playing peek-a-boo with him. There is no response and she resumes scrubbing and humming. The dolphin lets out a bubble or two and moves in the tank to bring his blowhole to the surface.

DOLPHIN. Youuuuuuuuuuuu.

HELEN *hears the sound, assumes she is mistaken, and goes on with her work.*

DOLPHIN. Youuuuuuuuuuuu.

HELEN *has heard the sound more clearly this time. She is puzzled, contemplates a moment, and then decides to get up off the floor. She closes the curtain on the dolphin's tank and leaves the laboratory. She walks the length of the hall to* MISS MORAY, *who is sitting at a reception desk near the elevator.*

MISS MORAY. What is it, Helen?

HELEN. The fish is making some kinda funny noise.

MISS MORAY. Mammal, Helen. It's a mammal.

HELEN. The mammal's making some kinda funny noise.

MISS MORAY. Mammals are supposed to make funny noises.

HELEN. Yes, Miss Moray.

HELEN *goes back to the lab. She continues scrubbing.*

DOLPHIN. Youuuuuuuuuuuu.

She <u>apprehensively</u> approaches the curtain and

> **ap•pre•hen•sive•ly** (a' pri hen[t]′ siv lē) *adv.*, in a way that shows fear or caution

Differentiated Instruction

English Language Learning
Have students skim the page and identify unfamiliar or difficult words. Provide definitions and context sentences for words they identify. Also explain these terms:
specimen—individual organism used as an example of the whole population, 671
recommendation—expression of good opinion, 672
technician—person skilled in a procedure, 672

silhouette—dark image against a lighter background, 672.

Enrichment
Have interested students learn and perform "Let Me Call You Sweetheart" for the class.

Analyze Literature

Characters Point out that Dan is a supporting character in the play. As they read Dan's dialogue, have students suggest why the author included him and what he contributes to the play. (He does not seem to have strong opinions, so he counterbalances Helen's worry. Dan also provides exposition.) **Ⓐ**

TEACHING NOTE

Ask an Expert

Divide the class into small groups, and have the groups brainstorm and jot down questions they would like to ask an expert about communicating with animals. Model a question: "How do people train captive dolphins?" Instruct each group to pass its questions to another group. Have students in the receiving groups imagine that they are scientists engaged in research. They should carefully consider and attempt to answer the questions they receive. Finally, have the groups share some of their questions and answers with the class.

---

opens it. Just then DAN *barges in. He goes to get his reaching pole, and* HELEN *hurriedly returns to scrubbing the floor.*

DAN. Bulb out on seven.

HELEN. What do they have that thing for?

DAN. What thing?

HELEN. That.

DAN. Yeah, he's something, ain't he? [*Pause.*] They're tryin' to get it to talk.

HELEN. Talk?

Ⓐ **DAN.** Uh-huh, but he don't say nothing. They had one last year that used to laugh. It'd go "heh heh heh heh heh heh heh." Then they got another one that used to say "Yeah, it's four o'clock." Everybody took pictures of that one. All the magazines and newspapers.

HELEN. It just kept saying "Yeah, it's four o'clock"?

DAN. Until it died of pneumonia. They talk outta their blowholes, when they can talk that is. Did you see the blowhole?

HELEN. No.

DAN. Come on and take a look.

HELEN. I don't want to look at any blowhole.

DAN. Miss Moray's at the desk. She won't see anything.

HELEN *and* DAN *go to the tank. Their backs are to the lab door and they don't see* MISS MORAY *open the door and watch them.*

DAN. This one don't say anything at all. They been playing the record every seven minutes for months, and it can't even learn a single word. Don't even say "Polly want a cracker."

MISS MORAY. Helen?

HELEN *and* DAN *turn around.*

MISS MORAY. Helen, would you mind stepping outside a moment?

HELEN. Yes, Miss Moray.

DAN. I was just showing her something.

MISS MORAY. Hadn't we better get on with our duties?

DAN. All right, Miss Moray.

MISS MORAY *guides* HELEN *out into the hall, and puts her arm around her as though taking her into her confidence.*

MISS MORAY. Helen, I called you out here because…well, frankly, I need your help.

HELEN. He was just showing me…

MISS MORAY. Dan is an idle-chatter breeder. How many times we've told him, "Dan, this is a scientific atmosphere you're employed in and we would appreciate a minimum of subjective[3] communication." So—if you can help, Helen—and I'm sure you can, enormously—we'd be so grateful.

HELEN. Yes, Miss Moray.

MISS MORAY *leads* HELEN *back to the lab.*

MISS MORAY. Now, we'll just move directly into the specimen room. The working conditions will be ideal for you in here.

HELEN *looks ready to gag as she looks around the specimen room. It is packed with specimen jars of all sizes. Various animals and parts of animals are visible in their formaldehyde baths.*

MISS MORAY. Now, you will be responsible not only for the floor area but the jars as well. A feather duster—here—is marvelous.

MISS MORAY *smiles and exits. The sound of music and voice from beyond the walls floats over.*

RECORD. "Let me call you sweetheart…"

HELEN *gasps as her eyes fall upon one particular jar in which is floating a preserved human brain. The lights go down, ending Act 1, Scene 1.*

---

3. **subjective.** Based on personal feelings and opinions rather than facts

Speaking & Listening Skills

Dramatic Effect

Have students think about what they "hear" in their minds as they read dialogue. Ask: "How do you hear the characters' voices?" Point out that actors delivering these lines would adopt a characteristic volume, stress, inflection, pacing, and enunciation for each character.

Assign students to small groups and have them decide how each character in Scene 1 sounds. Then have groups assign roles and read dialogue aloud. Challenge groups to read characters' speeches in different ways. When groups are satisfied with their readings, have them take turns presenting their scenes to the class. Then discuss which vocal qualities most probably portray the characters as the playwright intended.

SCENE 2

It is the next evening. HELEN *pushes her equipment into the lab. She opens the curtain so she can watch the dolphin as she works. She and the dolphin stare at each other.*

HELEN. Youuuuuuuuuuuu. [*She pauses, watches for a response.*] Youuuuuuuuuuuu. [*Still no response. She turns her attention to her scrubbing for a moment.*] Polly want a cracker? Polly want a cracker? [*She wrings out a rag and resumes work.*] Yeah, it's four o'clock. Yeah, it's four o'clock. Polly want a cracker at four o'clock?

She laughs at her own joke, then goes to the dolphin's tank and notices how sad he looks. She reaches her hand in and just touches the top of his head. He squirms and likes it.

HELEN. Heh heh heh heh heh heh heh heh heh.

MISS MORAY *gets off the elevator and hears the peculiar sounds coming from the laboratory. She puts her ear against the door.*

HELEN. Heh heh heh heh heh…

MISS MORAY. [*Entering.*] Look how nicely the floor's coming along! You must have a special rinsing technique.

HELEN. Just a little vinegar in the rinse water.

MISS MORAY. You brought the vinegar yourself. Just so the floors…they are sparkling, Helen. Sparkling! [*She pauses—looks at the dolphin, then at* HELEN.] It's marvelous, Helen, how well you've adjusted.

HELEN. Thank you, Miss Moray.

MISS MORAY. Helen, the animals here are used for experimentation, and….Well, take Marguerita. She had fallen in love with the mice. All three hundred of them. She seemed shocked when she found out Dr. Crocus was…using…them at the rate of twenty or so a day in connection with electrode implanting. She noticed them missing after a while and when I told her they'd been decapitated, she seemed terribly upset.

HELEN. What do you want with the fish—mammal?

MISS MORAY. Well, dolphins may have an intelligence equal to our own. And if we can teach them our language—or learn theirs—we'll be able to communicate.

HELEN. I can't understand you.

MISS MORAY. [*Louder.*] Communicate! Wouldn't it be wonderful?

HELEN. Oh, yeah….They chopped the heads off three hundred mice? That's horrible.

MISS MORAY. You're so sensitive, Helen. Every laboratory in the country is doing this type of work. It's quite accepted.

HELEN. Every laboratory cutting off mouse heads!

MISS MORAY. Virtually….

HELEN. How many laboratories are there?

MISS MORAY. I don't know. I suppose at least five thousand.

HELEN. Five thousand times three hundred… that's a lot of mouse heads. Can't you just have one lab chop off a couple and then spread the word?

MISS MORAY. Now, Helen—this is exactly what I mean. You will do best not to become fond of the subject animals. When you're here a little longer you'll learn…well…there are some things you just have to accept on faith.

MISS MORAY *exits, leaving the lab door open for* HELEN *to move her equipment out.*

DOLPHIN. Whisper….[HELEN *pauses a moment.*] Whisper to me. [*She exits as the lights go down, ending the scene.*]

Grammar Skills

Ellipses

"Five thousand times three hundred . . . that's a lot of mouse heads!"
Tell students that an ellipsis is a series of three spaced points. The plural is *ellipses*. Writers use ellipses for two main reasons:

- to indicate a pause in the sentence. The ellipsis creates a longer pause than a comma, giving the reader more time to think about what was said

previously. The ellipsis in the quotation above emphasizes the first part of the sentence.
- to show that material has been left out. The dolphin says *Whisper . . .* and then *Whisper to me.*

Have students locate other examples of ellipses in the play and figure out why an ellipsis was used in each case.

Using Reading Skills

Distinguish Between Major and Minor Details Direct students' attention to the stage direction that begins "Helen is dumbfounded. . . ." Have students decide what parts of the information in the stage direction are major details (Helen looks dumfounded and the dolphin is desperate), and which are minor details (Miss Moray exits and Helen picks up her equipment). **A**

Make Connections

Point out the words *terminate* (underscored) and *kill* on this page. Remind students that words with the same literal meaning can have different emotional effects on people. Have students suggest words that have the literal meaning "to cause the death of" such as *kill, murder, terminate, euthanize, sanction, slaughter, execute, sacrifice,* and *exterminate.* Ask students to monitor the way each word makes them feel, and to think of contexts in which they might use each word. **B**

SCENE 3

It is the next evening. HELEN *goes from her locker to the laboratory.*

DOLPHIN. Hear….

HELEN. What?

DOLPHIN. Hear me….

DAN *barges in with his hamper, almost frightening* HELEN *to death. He goes to the dolphin's tank.*

DAN. Hiya fella! How are ya? That reminds me. Gotta get some formaldehyde jars set up by Friday. If you want anything just whistle.

He exits. HELEN *goes to the tank and reaches her hand out to pet the dolphin.*

HELEN. Hear. [*Pause.*] Hear.

DOLPHIN. Hear.

HELEN. Hear me.

DOLPHIN. Hear me.

HELEN. That's a good boy.

DOLPHIN. Hear me….

HELEN. Oh, what a pretty fellow. Such a pretty fellow.

MISS MORAY *enters.*

MISS MORAY. What are you doing, Helen?

HELEN. I…uh….

MISS MORAY. Never mind. Go on with your work.

MISS MORAY *surveys everything, then sits on a stool.* DAN *rushes in with large jars on a wheeled table.*

DAN. Scuse me, but I figure I'll get this formaldehyde set up tonight.

MISS MORAY. Very good, Dan.

HELEN. [*Noticing the dolphin is stirring.*] What's the formaldehyde for?

MISS MORAY. The experiment series on…the dolphin will…<u>terminate</u> on Friday. That's

why it has concerned me that you've apparently grown…fond…of the mammal.

HELEN. They're gonna kill it?

DAN. Gonna sharpen the handsaws now. Won't have any trouble getting through the skull on this one, no, sir. [*He exits.*]

HELEN. What for? Because it didn't say anything? Is that what they're killing it for?

MISS MORAY. Helen, no matter how lovely our intentions, no matter how lonely we are and how much we want people or animals… to like us…we have no right to endanger the genius about us. Now, we've spoken about this before.

A HELEN *is dumbfounded as* MISS MORAY *exits.* HELEN *gathers her equipment and looks at the dolphin, which is staring desperately at her.*

DOLPHIN. Help. [*Pause.*] Please help me.

HELEN *is so moved by the cries of the dolphin she looks ready to burst into tears as the lights go down, ending Act 1.*

ACT 2

The hall. It is the night that the dolphin is to be dissected. Elevator doors open and HELEN *gets off, nods, and starts down the hall.* MISS MORAY *comes to* HELEN *at closet.*

MISS MORAY. I hope you're well this evening.

HELEN. When they gonna kill it?

B **MISS MORAY.** Don't say kill, Helen. You make it sound like murder. Besides, you won't have to go into the laboratory at all this evening.

HELEN. How do they kill it?

MISS MORAY. Nicotine mustard, Helen. It's very humane. They inject it.

HELEN. Maybe he's a mute.

---

ter·mi·nate (tʉrʹ mə nāt') *v.,* end

Differentiated Instruction

Enrichment

Tell students that animal experimentation is a source of controversy among many people. Invite interested students to research both sides of the issue. What are laboratory animals used for? Why do scientists feel this is necessary? Are there any alternatives? What are the arguments against animal experimentation? Have students prepare a poster or PowerPoint presentation listing the major arguments on both sides of the issue. Invite students to use their displays to explain their findings to the class, and then lead a class discussion of the issue.

MISS MORAY. Do you have all your paraphernalia?[4]

HELEN. Some human beings are mute, you know. Just because they can't talk we don't kill them. **C**

MISS MORAY. It looks like you're ready to open a new box of steel wool.

HELEN. Maybe he can type with his nose. Did they try that?

MISS MORAY. Now, now, Helen—

HELEN. Miss Moray, I don't mind doing the lab.

MISS MORAY. Absolutely not! I'm placing it off limits for your own good. You're too emotionally involved.

HELEN. I can do the lab, honest. I'm not emotionally involved.

MISS MORAY. [*Motioning her to the specimen-room door.*] Trust me, Helen. Trust me.

HELEN. [*Reluctantly disappearing through the door.*] Yes, Miss Moray.

MISS MORAY *stations herself at the desk near the elevator and begins reading her charts.* HELEN *slips out of the specimen room and into the laboratory without being seen. The lights in the lab are out and moonlight from the window casts eerie shadows.*

DOLPHIN. Help.

HELEN *opens the curtain. The dolphin and she look at each other.*

DOLPHIN. Help me.

HELEN. You don't need me. Just say something to them. Anything. They just need to hear you say something….You want me to tell 'em? I'll tell them. I'll just say I heard you say "Help." [*Pauses, then speaks with feigned cheerfulness.*] I'll go tell them.

DOLPHIN. Noooooooooooooooo.

HELEN *stops. Moves back toward tank.*

HELEN. They're gonna kill you!

DOLPHIN. Plaaaaan.

HELEN. What?

DOLPHIN. Plaaaaaaaan.

HELEN. Plan? What plan?

DAN *charges through the door and snaps on the light.*

DAN. Uh-oh. Miss Moray said she don't want you in here.

HELEN *goes to* DR. CROCUS's *desk and begins to look at various books on it.*

HELEN. Do you know anything about a plan?

DAN. She's gonna be mad. What plan?

HELEN. Something to do with….[*She indicates the dolphin.*]

DAN. Hiya, fella!

HELEN. About the dolphin….

DAN. They got an experiment book they write in.

HELEN. Where?

DAN. I don't know.

HELEN. Find it and bring it to me in the animals' morgue.[5] Please.

---

4. **paraphernalia.** Assorted pieces of equipment used for a specific purpose
5. **morgue.** Place where bodies are kept

LET ME HEAR YOU WHISPER, ACT 2 **677**

Teach the Selection

Analyze Literature
Personification Remind students that one type of personification is attributing human characteristics to animals. Ask if they think Helen is using personification when she compares mute humans to mute animals. Have students explain their reasoning. **C**

Science Connection
Dolphin Intelligence Many people argue that judging animal intelligence based on whether an animal can behave like humans is unrealistic, because an animal's "intelligence" evolved in a very different environment. Experiments have shown that dolphins are self-aware—they recognize their reflections as themselves rather than behaving as if reflections are other creatures. Self-awareness is just one type of "intelligence." Other types are declarative (understanding symbolic representations of things and events), procedural (understanding how things work and how to manipulate them), and social (understanding activities and identities of others). Dolphins demonstrate all of these abilities. They are also very good at imitating other mammals, which takes strong learning and memory skills. Among mammals, only people imitate the voices and behaviors of others as well as dolphins.

Reading Skills

Take Notes

Have students outline the plot of *Let Me Hear You Whisper* by creating either a sequence-of-events graphic organizer or a plot diagram. Remind students that the plot diagram includes A. introduction; B. rising action; C. climax; D. falling action; and E. resolution.

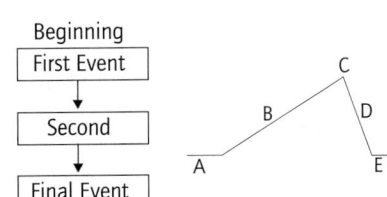

Use Reading Strategies

Clarify Have students work with a partner to paraphrase Miss Moray's line about ladyfingers. Encourage students to use a dictionary to look up the words *confectionery* and *macabre*. Then remind students that irony is an unexpected contrast. Point out the irony that Miss Moray thinks the name of a pastry is macabre, but doesn't seem to find the experiments on animals macabre. **Ⓐ**

Analyze Literature

Mood Point out that there have been instances of humor in the dialogue throughout the play. Ask students why an author might inject humor into a story that deals with a serious subject such as animal experimentation. (A writer might use this technique to temporarily lighten the mood, and to heighten the seriousness of an issue by placing it in contrast with something trivial or lighthearted.)

DAN. I'll try. I'll try, but I got other things to do, you know.

HELEN *slips out the door and makes it safely back into the specimen room.* DAN *rummages through the desk and finally finds the folder. He is able to sneak into the specimen room.*

DAN. Here.

HELEN *grabs the folder and starts going through it.* DAN *turns and is about to go back out into the hall when he sees that* MISS MORAY *has stopped reading.* HELEN *skims through more of the folder. It is a bulky affair. She stops at a page discussing uses of dolphins.* MISS MORAY *gets up from the desk and heads for the specimen-room door.*

> # "I don't like lazy selfish people, mammals or animals."

DAN. She's coming.

HELEN. Maybe you'd better hide. Get behind the table. Here, take the book.

DAN *ducks down behind one of the specimen tables, and* HELEN *starts scrubbing away.* MISS MORAY *opens the door.*

MISS MORAY. Perk-You-Up time, Helen. Tell Dan, please. He's in the laboratory.

HELEN *moves to the lab door, opens it, and calls into the empty room.*

HELEN. Perk-You-Up time.

MISS MORAY. Tell him we have ladyfingers.[6]

HELEN. We have ladyfingers.

Ⓐ **MISS MORAY.** Such a strange thing to call a confectionery, isn't it? It's almost macabre.

HELEN. Miss Moray….

MISS MORAY. Yes, Helen?

HELEN. I was wondering why they wanna talk with….

MISS MORAY. Now now now!

HELEN. I mean, supposing dolphins *did* talk?

MISS MORAY. Well, like fishing, Helen. If we could communicate with dolphins, they might be willing to herd fish for us. The fishing industry would be revolutionized.

HELEN. Is that all?

MISS MORAY. All? Heavens, no. They'd be a blessing to the human race. A blessing. They would be worshipped in oceanography. Checking the Gulf Stream…taking water temperatures, depth, salinity readings. To say nothing of the contributions they could make in marine biology, navigation, linguistics![7] Oh, Helen, it gives me the chills.

HELEN. It'd be good if they talked.

MISS MORAY. God's own blessing.

DAN *opens the lab doors and yells over* HELEN'S *head to* MISS MORAY.

DAN. I got everything except the head vise. They can't saw through the skull bone without the head vise.

MISS MORAY. Did you look on five? They had it there last week for…what they did to the St. Bernard.

From the laboratory, music drifts out. They try to talk over it.

DAN. I looked on five.

MISS MORAY. You come with me. It must have been staring you in the face.

---

6. **ladyfingers.** Small finger-shaped cakes
7. **linguistics.** Study of languages

Differentiated Instruction

Reading Proficiency

Have less-able readers read the dialogue and stage directions aloud in small groups, with each group member taking the part of one of the characters or reading the stage directions. Encourage students to read with expression.

Auditory and Kinesthetic Learning

Invite interested pairs of students to perform a portion of the play that contains dialogue between Helen and the dolphin. Challenge students to imagine what a dolphin might sound like if it tried to speak human words through its blowhole (rather than using vocal chords as a human does). Encourage students to act out the dolphin's movements as well as Helen's.

DAN *and* MISS MORAY *get on the elevator.*

MISS MORAY. We'll be right back, Helen.

The doors close and HELEN *hurries into the laboratory. She stops just inside the door, and it is obvious that she is angry.*

DOLPHIN. Booooooooook.

HELEN. I looked at your book. I looked at your book all right!

DOLPHIN. Booooooooook.

HELEN. And you want to know what I think? I don't think much of you, that's what I think.

DOLPHIN. Booooooooook.

HELEN. Oh, shut up. Book book book book book. I'm not interested. You eat yourself silly—but to get a little fish for hungry humans is just too much for you. Well. I'm going to tell 'em you can talk.

The dolphin moves in the tank, lets out a few warning bubbles.

HELEN. You don't like that, eh? Well, I don't like lazy selfish people, mammals or animals.

The dolphin looks increasingly desperate and begins to make loud blatt and beep sounds. He struggles in the tank.

HELEN. Cut it out—you're getting water all over the floor.

DOLPHIN. Booooooooook!

HELEN *looks at the folder on the desk. She picks it up, opens it, closes it, and sets it down again.*

HELEN. I guess you don't like us. I guess you'd die rather than help us….

DOLPHIN. Hate.

HELEN. I guess you do hate us….

She returns to the folder.

HELEN. [*Reading.*] Military implications… war…plant mines in enemy waters…deliver atomic warheads…war…nuclear torpedoes…

attach bombs to submarines…terrorize enemy waters…war….They're already thinking about ways to use you for war. Is that why you can't talk to them? [*Pause.*] What did you talk to me for? [*Pause.*] You won't talk to them, but you…you talk to me because…you want something…there's something…I can do?

DOLPHIN. Hamm….

HELEN. What?

DOLPHIN. Hamm….

HELEN. Ham? I thought you ate fish.

DOLPHIN. [*Moving with annoyance.*] Ham… purrrr.

HELEN. Ham…purrrr? I don't know what you're talking about.

DOLPHIN. [*Even more annoyed.*] Ham…purrrr.

HELEN. Ham…purrrr. What's a purrrr?

Confused and scared, she returns to scrubbing the hall floor just as the doors of the elevator open, revealing MISS MORAY, DAN, *and* MR. FRIDGE. DAN *pushes a dissection table loaded with shiny instruments toward the lab.*

MISS MORAY. Is the good doctor in yet?

MR. FRIDGE. He's getting the nicotine mustard on nine. I'll see if he needs assistance.

MISS MORAY. I'll come with you. You'd better leave now, Helen. It's time. [*She smiles and the elevator doors close.*]

DAN. [*Pushing the dissection table through the lab doors.*] I never left a dirty head vise. She's trying to say I left it like that.

HELEN. Would you listen a minute? Ham… purrrr. Do you know what a ham…purrrr is?

DAN. The only hamper I ever heard of is out in the hall. [HELEN *darts to the door, opens it, and sees the hamper at the end of the hall.*]

HELEN. The hamper!

Use Reading Skills

Compare and Contrast Ask students to compare and contrast Helen's attitude toward the dolphin at this point in the play to her attitude when she was repeating words to try to make the dolphin talk. (She now talks to the dolphin like another person, rather than as an animal she's trying to train.) **B**

Analyze Literature

Character Review the definitions of protagonist and antagonist. Remind students that there may be more than one of each. Have students suggest which character or characters in *Let Me Hear You Whisper* act as protagonist. (They may see both Helen and the dolphin as protagonists.) Then, ask students which character or characters act as antagonist for each of the protagonists. Have students explain their answers.

Make Connections

Invite students to think about the fact that only Helen seems concerned about the dolphin's survival. Ask why they think the other characters place such a low priority on the dolphin's life. Have students explain their thinking about each character.

Dialogue

Remind students that dialogue provides insight into characters. Compare and contrast the ways in which Dan, Helen, and Miss Moray speak. For example, you wouldn't expect Dan to say, "Is the good doctor in yet?" Tell students that dialogue should sound natural and convincing.

Have students work in small groups to write two pages of dialogue that include all the characters in the play. Suggest students begin by thinking up a situation in which all the characters might appear. Each student in the group might pretend to be a different character and then carry on a conversation. Students can write down what they naturally say, and then revise their dialogue to make it flow smoothly.

Cultural Connection

Protecting Animals During the 1860s, it was common to see horse-driven carts hauling coal to New York City residents. The horses were often emaciated, and were whipped by their drivers. Henry Bergh, a European diplomat in the United States, was determined to prevent such mistreatment of animals. Bergh studied England's Royal Society for the Prevention of Cruelty to Animals, founded in 1840. He persuaded a number of dignitaries to sign his "Declaration of the Rights of Animals" and convinced the New York State legislature to authorize a charter for a society to protect animals. This was the beginning of the ASPCA—the American Society for the Prevention of Cruelty to Animals.

DAN. Kazinski left the high-altitude chamber dirty once, and I got blamed for that, too. [*He exits.*]

HELEN. [*Rushing to the dolphin.*] You want me to do something with the hamper. What? To get it? To put...you want me to put you in it? But what'll I do with you? Where can I take you?

DOLPHIN. Sea....

HELEN. See? See what?

DOLPHIN. Sea....

HELEN. I don't know what you're talking about. They'll be back in a minute. I don't know what to do!

DOLPHIN. Sea...sea....

HELEN. See?...The sea! That's what you're talking about! The river...to the sea!

She darts into the hall and heads for the hamper. Quickly she pushes it into the lab, and just as she gets through the doors unseen, MISS MORAY *gets off the elevator.*

MISS MORAY. Helen? [*She starts down the hall. Enters the lab. The curtain is closed in front of the tank.*]

MISS MORAY. Helen? Are you here? Helen?

She sees nothing and is about to leave when she hears movement behind the curtain. She looks down and sees HELEN's *shoes.* MISS MORAY *moves to the curtain and pulls it open. There is* HELEN *with her arms around the front part of the dolphin, lifting it a good part of the way out of the water.*

MISS MORAY. Helen, what do you think you're hugging?

HELEN *drops the dolphin back into the tank.*

MR. FRIDGE. [*Entering.*] Is anything wrong, Miss Moray?

MISS MORAY. No...nothing wrong. Nothing at all. Just a little spilled water.

HELEN *and* MISS MORAY *grab sponges from the lab sink and begin to wipe up the water around the tank.* DR. CROCUS *enters and begins to fill a hypodermic syringe while* MR. FRIDGE *expertly gets all equipment into place.* DAN *enters.*

MR. FRIDGE. Would you like to get an encephalogram[8] during the death process, Dr. Crocus?

DR. CROCUS. Why not?

MR. FRIDGE *begins to implant electrodes in the dolphin's head. The dolphin commences making high-pitched distress signals.*

MISS MORAY. Come, Helen. I'll see you to the elevator.

MISS MORAY *leads her out to the hall.* HELEN *gets on her coat and kerchief.*

MISS MORAY. Frankly, Helen, I'm deeply disappointed. I'd hoped that by being lenient with you—and heaven knows I have been—you'd develop a heightened loyalty to our team.

HELEN. [*Bursting into tears and going to the elevator.*] Leave me alone.

MISS MORAY. [*Softening as she catches up to her.*] You really are a nice person, Helen. A very nice person. But to be simple and nice in a world where great minds are giant-stepping the micro- and macrocosms, well—one would expect you'd have the humility to yield in unquestioning awe. I truly am very fond of you, Helen, but you're fired. Call Personnel after nine A.M.

As MISS MORAY *disappears into the laboratory, the record starts to play.*

RECORD. "Let me call you sweetheart, I'm in love with you. Let me hear you whisper...."

The record is roughly interrupted. Instead of getting on the elevator, HELEN *whirls around and barges into the lab.*

---

8. encephalogram. X-ray picture of the brain

Differentiated Instruction

Enrichment

Tell students that *Let Me Hear You Whisper* was made into a movie as well as being performed as a play. Have interested students find out more about how *Let Me Hear You Whisper* was staged. Have them answer such questions as: Was an actual dolphin used in either the stage version or the movie? If so, would keeping a dolphin in a small tank during production constitute cruelty? Have students share what they find out with the class.

"You're a coward, that's what you are."

HELEN. Who do you think you are? [*Pause.*] Who do you think you *are*? [*Pause.*] I think you're a pack of killers, that's what I think.

MISS MORAY. Doctor. I assure you this is the first psychotic outbreak she's made. She did the entire brass strip….

HELEN. I'm tired a being a nice person, Miss Moray. I'm going to report you to the ASPCA,[9] or somebody, because…I've decided I don't like you cutting the heads off mice and sawing through skulls of St. Bernards… and if being a nice person is just not saying anything and letting you pack of butchers run around doing whatever you want, then I don't want to be nice anymore. [*Pause.*] You gotta be very stupid people to need an animal to talk before you know just from looking at it that it's saying something…that it knows what pain feels like. I'd like to see you all with a few electrodes in your heads. Being nice isn't any good. [*Looking at dolphin.*] They just kill you off if you do that. And that's being a coward. You gotta talk back. You gotta speak up against what's wrong and bad, or you can't ever stop it. At least you've gotta try. [*She bursts into tears.*]

MISS MORAY. Nothing like this has ever happened with a member of the Custodial Engineering….Helen, dear….

HELEN. Get your hands off me. [*Yelling at the dolphin.*] You're a coward, that's what you are. I'm going.

DOLPHIN. Loooooooooveeeeeeeee.

Everyone turns to stare at the dolphin.

DOLPHIN. Love.

DR. CROCUS. Get the recorder going.

---

9. **ASPCA.** American Society for the Prevention of Cruelty to Animals

LET ME HEAR YOU WHISPER, ACT 2 **681**

Answer: Students might say that they would discuss the problem with someone they trust, such as a parent, and then make a decision they could live with.

Find Meaning

1. (a) She doesn't like it. (b) He would probably say his work will help humans.

2. Miss Moray wants the people she supervises to do what they are told no matter what. Helen wants to do a good job, but isn't willing to be part of something she thinks is wrong.

3. (a) Both are against using animals for war-related purposes. (b) Many answers are possible. Among them, Helen protests by speaking up about her feelings; the dolphin protests by not speaking up.

Make Judgments

4. Opinions will vary. She takes her job seriously, obeys all the procedures, and tries to be caring and positive with her employees.

5. Answers will vary. Helen did her work well and was a hard worker, but was not well matched to her job.

6. She may be right, because she won't be part of something she believes wrong. Some may say she should have stayed and tried to protect the dolphin.

HELEN *pats the dolphin, exits. The laboratory becomes a bustle of activity.*

DOLPHIN. Love….

DR. CROCUS. Is the tape going?

MR. FRIDGE. Yes, Doctor.

DOLPHIN. Love.

DR. CROCUS. I think that woman's got something to do with this. Get her back in here.

MISS MORAY. Oh, I fired her. She was hugging the mammal…and….

DOLPHIN. Love.

DR. CROCUS. Just get her. [*To MR. FRIDGE.*] You're sure the machine's recording?

MISS MORAY. Doctor, I'm afraid you don't understand. That woman was hugging the mammal….

DR. CROCUS. Try to get another word out of it. One more word….

MISS MORAY. The last thing in the world I want is for our problem in Custodial Engineering to….

DR. CROCUS. [*Furious.*] Will you shut up and get that washwoman back in here?

MISS MORAY. Immediately, Doctor.

She hurries out of the lab. HELEN *is at the end of the hall waiting for the elevator.*

MISS MORAY. Helen? Oh, Helen? Don't you want to hear what the dolphin has to say. He's so cute! Dr. Crocus thinks that his talking might have something to do with you. Wouldn't that be exciting? [*Pause.*] Please, Helen. The doctor….

HELEN. Don't talk to me, do you mind?

MISS MORAY. It was only in the heat of argument that I…of course, you won't be discharged. All right? Please, Helen, you'll embarrass me….

The elevator doors open and HELEN *gets on to face* MISS MORAY. *She looks at her a moment and then lifts her hand to press the button for the ground floor.*

MISS MORAY. Don't you dare…Helen, the team needs you, don't you see? You've done so well—the brass strip, the floors. The floors have never looked so good. Ever. Helen, please. What will I do if you leave?

HELEN. Why don't you get a rug?

HELEN *helps slam the elevator doors in* MISS MORAY's *face as the lights go down, ending the play.* ❖

Imagine you have a job that requires you to do something you do not believe is right or that makes you uncomfortable. How would you handle the situation? When is it acceptable to refuse an order?

Find Meaning

1. (a) What is Helen's opinion about the way animals are treated in the lab? (b) How might Dr. Crocus respond to her opinion?
2. How do Helen and Miss Moray differ?
3. (a) How are Helen and the dolphin alike? (b) How are they different?

Make Judgments

4. Is Miss Moray a good supervisor? Explain.
5. Do you think Helen is a good employee? Why or why not?
6. Is Helen right to leave her job at the end of the play? Why or why not?

TEACHING NOTE

Self-Generated Questioning

Pair up students and then divide the play into as many sections as there are pairs of students. Assign each pair to review a section of the play and to write down any questions that arise during their review. Collect the questions and arrange them all on the board (in writing or by using tape) in these categories:

- Stage Directions
- Dialogue
- Theme

When you can devote ten or fifteen minutes to the activity, as a class go over the play section by section, looking for answers to the questions.

Let Me Hear You Whisper is about a dolphin that speaks. While the selection is fiction, it is true that dolphins have a language of whistles that they use to communicate with each other. Other animals also use language. In fact, some apes have been taught to use a form of human language. The following article, "Going Ape Over Language," by **Natalie Rosinsky** describes how a chimpanzee named Washoe learned to communicate with humans. As you read the article, think about the differences between the treatment of animals in the play and in the article.

from Going Ape Over Language

An Article by Natalie Rosinsky

Humans talking with apes? Such conversations were once found only in fables, or in science fiction like *Planet of the Apes*. But, since the 1960s, scientists have "gone ape" over other methods of interspecies communication.

Great apes physically cannot produce the consonants or some vowel sounds of human speech. So, instead of spoken language, researchers are using American Sign Language (ASL) and technology to teach human language to other primates.

A Chimpanzee Named Washoe

In 1966, Dr. Allen Gardner and his wife, Beatrix, began teaching ASL to a year-old female chimpanzee named Washoe. They taught Washoe by "cross-fostering" her—that is, treating her like a deaf human child. Washoe had a stimulating[1] environment filled with toys and attentive human companions who used ASL to "discuss" daily activities. In those first years, one important topic of conversation was—of course—potty training! Dr. Roger Fouts, an early companion, and his wife, Debbi, have now spent more than 30 years with "Project Washoe." In 1992, the Foutses founded the Chimpanzee and Human Communication Institute at Central Washington University, where Washoe lives with an adoptive family of four other ASL-using chimpanzees.

Washoe is the most "talkative" member of this group, with an ASL vocabulary of 240 signs. She often "translates" spoken words she understands into ASL. Washoe signs correctly even when an object is out of sight—signaling "DOG," for example, whenever she hears canine barking. She also accurately puts together short "sentences"— signing "ROGER TICKLE WASHOE" when this is what has occurred. If she does not know the sign for an item, Washoe creatively yet logically "renames" it. She called her first candy bar a "CANDY BANANA?"

Yet emotion, not just logic, has filled some of Washoe's most memorable conversations with humans. Washoe had

---

1. **stimulating.** Causing a feeling of interest or excitement

Cultural Connection

Sign Language American Sign Language (ASL) is a complete language in which people communicate through hand shape, position, and movement; body movements; gestures; facial expressions; and other visual cues. For example, a question is indicated by raising the eyebrows and widening the eyes. Like any other language, ASL has its own rules for grammar, punctuation, and sentence order, and also includes regional "slang" and jargon.

Make Connections

Ask students what they would think and how they would act in response to Koko's actions when she was caught eating the crayon. Ask: "Does Koko know the difference between right and wrong? Is there any other explanation for her behavior?" **Ⓐ**

TEACHING NOTE

Generate Questions

Locate a video of Washoe and/or another chimpanzee using sign language, or other experiments in interspecies communication. For example, PBS has several shows from *Nova* and *Scientific American Frontiers* related to animal communication. Before showing the video, explain the general topic and encourage students to make a list of questions they would like to see answered. As they watch the video, students should activate their prior knowledge enough to listen for answers to their questions. When the video is over, discuss with students any information that surprised them, as well as any new questions the program stimulated.

Claudine Andre, director of the "Lola ya bonobo" park in the Democratic Republic of the Congo, plays with bonobos.

already had two unsuccessful pregnancies when she learned that a caregiver's baby had died. The chimpanzee looked groundward, then directly into the woman's eyes, and signed "CRY" while touching the woman's cheek just below her eye. Later that day, Washoe wouldn't let her caregiver go home without further consolation,[2] signing "PLEASE PERSON HUG."

Researchers are also excited by the chimpanzees' use of ASL among themselves. Washoe, her adoptive son Loulis, and other family members have been videotaped having ASL conversations on their own about games, food, and "housecleaning." Birthday parties and holiday celebrations are other "hot" topics of conversation. The chimpanzees have even been observed "talking to themselves," much as a human might mutter under her breath. When Loulis mischievously ran away with one of her favorite magazines, an **Ⓐ**

annoyed Washoe signed "BAD, BAD, BAD" to herself.

It is Loulis's use of ASL, though, that may be most significant. In a planned experiment, researchers avoided signing in Loulis's presence during his first five years. Yet Loulis—like deaf human children—learned ASL by watching and imitating his adoptive mother and other family members! Chimpanzees, it seems, not only can learn human language, but also can transmit it to others.

A Gorilla Named Koko

Koko, a female lowland gorilla, began learning ASL in 1972, when she was one year old. Her teacher, Dr. Francine Patterson, provided her with a gorilla companion in 1976, when three-year-old Michael joined them at the official start of the Gorilla Foundation.

Koko has a working vocabulary of 1,000 signs and understands 2,000 spoken words. Michael—before his unexpected death last year—used 600 signs to communicate. Both gorillas, like Washoe, have shown creativity and logic in naming unknown objects. It was obvious to Koko that a face mask is an "EYE HAT," while Michael had no difficulty at all in titling his painting (yes, gorillas paint) of a bouquet of flowers "STINK"! Koko has even used ASL to "talk" herself out of trouble. When a trainer caught her eating a crayon, Koko signed "LIP" and pretended to be applying lipstick! Koko also likes to joke using ASL, calling herself an "ELEPHANT" after pointing to a long tube held out in front of her like that animal's trunk.

---

2. consolation. Comfort expressed to someone who is upset or sad

English Language Learning

Students learning English may have difficulty with some of the proper names in this selection, such as Washoe, Fouts, Chimpanzee and Human Communication Institute, Loulis, Kanzi, Yerkes, Savage-Rumbaugh, and Noam Chomsky. Suggest that students first identify the names as people, places, or things and then work with fluent speakers to pronounce the names.

Reading Proficiency

Have less-capable readers work in pairs to take turns reading paragraphs from the article. After each paragraph, tell the reader to demonstrate comprehension by paraphrasing or summarizing the content.

Koko has also used ASL to express sadness and some complex ideas. She mourned the death of her kitten, named All Ball, by repeatedly signing "SAD." When asked when gorillas die, Koko signed "TROUBLE OLD." When she was then asked what happens to gorillas after they die, Koko answered "COMFORTABLE HOLE." With Dr. Patterson as an interpreter, Koko has even participated in on-line, computerized "chats"!

A Bonobo Named Kanzi

Kanzi, a male bonobo[3] born in 1980, speaks a different human language than Washoe and Koko. He communicates in "Yerkish," a visual code invented by researchers at Georgia State University and the Yerkes Primate Research Center. "Yerkish" is a set of several hundred geometric symbols called "lexigrams," each representing a verb, noun, or adjective. These lexigrams are placed on an adapted computer keyboard, which bonobos learn to use while learning the meanings of the lexigrams. Kanzi communicates by computer! (Outdoors, Kanzi points to lexigrams on a carry-around tagboard.)

Kanzi, who also understands more than 1,000 spoken English words, first learned Yerkish by watching humans train his mother. Like a silent toddler who astonishes parents by first speaking in complete sentences, two-year-old Kanzi amazed researchers on the day he first "spoke" Yerkish by using most of the lexigrams taught to his mother. By the age of six, he had a Yerkish vocabulary of 200 lexigrams. According to Dr. Sue Savage-Rumbaugh, Kanzi and other bonobos construct logical sentences in Yerkish and even use the lexigram for "later" to discuss future activities.

Aping Their Betters?

Linguist Noam Chomsky insists that human beings are the only primates neurologically capable of language. Some other scientists, including MIT's Dr. Steven Pinker, share this view. They conclude that "Project Washoe" and similar research prove only that apes can be trained, and that they will imitate the behavior of trainers just for rewards or approval. These critics maintain that investigators, along with animal rights activists, have misinterpreted the results of these researchers because they want to believe that apes can "talk."

But there are answers to these objections. The private signing done by chimpanzees is evidence that apes use language for more than rewards or approval. And the technology used to teach "Yerkish" to bonobos lessens the possibly questionable element of imitation in this and similar research. Furthermore, as Dr. Sue Savage-Rumbaugh notes, comprehension and visual cues between humans are themselves part of a broader definition of language. It may be unfair to define language for apes only in the narrowest sense. Lastly, current research into how apes communicate among themselves in the wild is reshaping our views of them. Geographically separated groups of bonobos have their own "dialects" of communicative gestures and sounds. And bonobos already may communicate symbolically among themselves, smashing plants and placing them at particular angles as "road signs." ✤

---

3. **bonobo.** Ape that looks and behaves much like a chimpanzee

---

Text-to-Text Connection

Answer: In Zindel's play, scientists want the dolphin to speak human words through its blowhole. They want to use the dolphin to help them win a war. The scientists in Rosinsky's article realize that chimps can't speak aloud, but want to study how they think and whether they can learn a language and communicate with their bodies and/or with a computer. Helen probably would have enjoyed working for the Gardners because of their respect for animals.

Analyze Literature

Dialogue Helen is a hard-working woman with a strong sense of right and wrong. Miss Moray is a nervous woman who is committed to doing her job exactly right. Dan is a friendly man who would rather talk than work. Students should cite specific dialogue to support their conclusions.

Program Resources

For further instruction, refer students to the following extension activity: Critical Literacy: Perform Reader's Theater, *Exceeding the Standards: Extension Activities*, pp. 20–21.

TEXT ←TO→ TEXT CONNECTION

Both Zindel's play and Rosinsky's article address scientists who study animal language. How does the form of communication differ between the two selections? What are the differences between the use of animals? Contrast the purposes for study in the two selections. Do you think Helen's character would have been willing to work for the Gardners?

AFTER READING

Analyze Literature

Dialogue Paul Zindel uses dialogue to reveal the traits of the characters in the play. Revisit some of the lines of dialogue spoken by Helen, Miss Moray, and Dan. Decide what the characters' words show about them. Use a chart to record your findings and interpretations. Use the ideas in your chart to write a summary statement about each character.

Character	What the Character Says	What the Dialogue Shows about the Character
Helen	"Some human beings are mute, you know. Just because they can't talk we don't kill them."	

Extend Understanding

Writing Options

Creative Writing Recall your thoughts from Build Background about a connection you have had with an animal. Use the experience of reading the previous selections to help you think more deeply about your connection to that animal. Write a **journal entry** about this connection. Include factual information and personal thoughts and feelings.

Expository Writing Analyze how Paul Zindel used dialogue in *Let Me Hear You Whisper.* Revisit the play to get more ideas about how dialogue reveals character traits and motives. Also, analyze how Zindel uses dialogue to advance the plot. Write a **critical analysis** of Zindel's use of dialogue. Include a thesis statement, and give examples from the play to support your points.

Lifelong Learning

Write a Research Report Use books, science magazines, and the Internet to research what scientists have learned about the intelligence of dolphins. What can dolphins do? What can't they do? Compare and contrast their intelligence with that of other animals. How are their abilities similar to human abilities? Try to include some visuals such as charts, tables, or graphic organizers in your report.

Critical Literacy

Perform Reader's Theater In small groups, choose a scene from the play to perform, and assign a role to each group member. Be creative in your interpretation of the characters, setting, and props. Rehearse your scene repeatedly as a group, and perform it for the class.

Go to www.mirrorsandwindows.com for more.

Rubrics for Writing Options

You can adapt this as a checklist for students to use as they write.

Creative Writing

☐ Does the journal entry address the topic of a special connection with an animal?

☐ Does the entry include feelings as well as factual information?

Expository Writing

☐ Does the analysis address how dialogue reveals character traits and motives?

☐ Does the analysis discuss how dialogue moved the plot along?

☐ Does the analysis include supporting examples from the play?

St. Crispian's Day Speech
A Dramatic Monologue by William Shakespeare

The Charge of the Light Brigade
A Narrative Poem by Alfred, Lord Tennyson

BEFORE READING

Build Background
Historical Context Shakespeare's "St. Crispian's Day Speech," from the play *Henry V*, recalls the battle in the French village of Agincourt. There King Henry V, who ruled England from 1413 to 1422, staged a victorious battle in 1415. "The Charge of the Light Brigade" by Alfred, Lord Tennyson memorializes the 1854 Battle of Balaklava during the Crimean War.

Reader's Context What traits do successful leaders share?

Set Purpose
Skim both texts to help make predictions about the purpose and attitude of the speaker in each selection.

Meet the Authors

William Shakespeare (1564–1616) was born and educated in the small village of Stratford-on-Avon. Shakespeare moved to London where he worked as an actor and a playwright. He became part owner of London's famed Globe Theater in 1599, at which *Henry V* was performed.

Alfred, Lord Tennyson (1809–1892) was appointed England's poet laureate by Queen Victoria in 1850. In "The Charge of the Light Brigade," which contains some of the most frequently quoted lines of his poetry, Tennyson recounts the story of a poorly planned military attack that cost hundreds of British soldiers their lives.

Compare Literature: Diction
In literature, **diction** is part of a writer's overall style. It refers to the writer's word choice. The diction in a piece of literature can be formal or informal, ornate or plain, outdated or modern, and so on. To help you identify and describe the diction of each text, use a chart to record examples of words and phrases that suggest a specific diction.

"St. Crispian's Day Speech"	Effect of Diction
ne'er	
a-bed	

Preview Vocabulary
blun·der (blun´ dər) *v.*, make a serious error in judgment; make a thoughtless mistake

reel (rēl) *v.*, stumble as the result of a hard hit

At a Glance
Directed Reading
"St. Crispian's Day Speech"
- Reading Level: Easy
- Difficulty Consideration: Subject matter
- Ease Factor: Straightforward sentence structure

"The Charge of the Light Brigade"
- Reading Level: Challenging
- Difficulty Considerations: Sentence structure, subject matter
- Ease Factor: Repetition

Objectives
Studying this lesson will enable students to
- compare literary selections of different genres
- use reading skills such as drawing conclusions and making connections
- define diction and compare its effects in two literary works
- recognize some literary accomplishments of William Shakespeare and Alfred, Lord Tennyson
- recognize techniques leaders use to inspire soldiers before battle

Launch the Lesson
Have students discuss their beliefs about war. Is war ever justified? If so, under what circumstances? Would students be willing to die for their country in a war? Encourage all students to participate in the discussion, and to respect the ideas and opinions of others.

Words in Use

Teaching Words
poet laureate, 687
ornate, 687
inspirational, 687
tactic, 689
allied, 691
futile, 691
cavalry, 691
bombarded, 691
notable, 692

KEY TERMS
SKIM, 687
DICTION, 687
INFER, 689
STANZA, 692
NARRATIVE, 692
PLOT, 692
CHARACTER, 692
SCENE, 692
MONOLOGUE, 692

Common Core State Standards
Reading Literature
RL.1

The Mirrors & Windows questions at the end of the monologue focus on the theme of motivation. Before students begin reading ask: What motivates soldiers who know they have a slim chance of success?

History Connection

Agincourt The Battle of Agincourt took place during the Hundred Years' War between England and France. Despite overwhelming odds, a highly disciplined English army led by Henry V and consisting of about six thousand troops outmaneuvered and defeated a French army of anywhere from eighteen thousand to thirty thousand troops.

Analyze Literature

Diction Ask students what effect the repetition of *shall* (in lines 5, 10, 12, 17, 18, 20, 23, 24, and 26) has on the diction of the speech. (It makes it commanding and forceful.)

Use Reading Skills

Draw Conclusions After they read, ask students what conclusions they can draw about Henry's military leadership qualities. (He recognizes that his troops need encouragement; he understands how to rouse his troops by appealing to their patriotism and pride; he plans to fight alongside them.)

St. Crispian's Day Speech

A Dramatic Monologue
by William Shakespeare

Sir Laurence Olivier as Henry V in a 1944 film version of Shakespeare's play.

This day is call'd the feast of Crispian:[1]
He that outlives this day, and comes safe home,
Will stand a' tiptoe when this day is named,
And rouse him at the name of Crispian.
5 He that shall live this day, and see old age,

---

1. **feast of Crispian.** Christian holiday celebrated on October 25, honoring Crispin and Saint Crispian, two brothers martyred for their religious beliefs in the third century

688

Program Resources

Planning and Assessment
Program Planning Guide, Selection Lesson Plan
E-Lesson Planner
Assessment Guide, Lesson Test
ExamView

Technology Tools
Interactive Student Text on CD
Visual Teaching Package
Audio Library
mirrorsandwindows.com

Meeting the Standards
Drama: Unit 7, Directed Reading, pp. 49–58

Differentiating Instruction
Advanced Students, Literature Comparison, p. 44

Will yearly on the vigil feast his neighbors,
And say, "To-morrow is Saint Crispian."
Then will he strip his sleeve and show his scars,
And say, "These wounds I had on Crispin's day."
10   Old men forget; yet all shall be forgot,
But he'll remember with advantages
What feats he did that day. Then shall our names,
Familiar his mouth as household words,
Harry the King, Bedford and Exeter,
15   Warwick and Talbot, Salisbury and Gloucester,[2]
Be in their flowing cups freshly rememb'red.
This story shall the good man teach his son;
And Crispin Crispian shall ne'er go by,
From this day to the ending of the world,
20   But we in it shall be remembered—
We few, we happy few, we band of brothers;
For he to-day that sheds his blood with me
Shall be my brother; be he ne'er so vile,
This day shall gentle his condition;
25   And gentlemen in England, now a-bed,
Shall think themselves accurs'd they were not here;
And hold their manhoods cheap whiles any speaks
That fought with us upon Saint Crispin's day. ✤

2. **Bedford...Gloucester.** Bedford, Exeter, Warwick, Talbot, Salisbury, and
Gloucester were English nobility and members of King Henry's entourage.

If you had doubts about engaging in a battle, what effect would an
inspirational speech such as Henry's have on you? Is it fair of military
leaders to urge troops into battle when they know their chances of success
are slim?

Find Meaning

1 (a) When does Henry give the St. Crispian's
Day speech? (b) What is his main purpose for
giving this speech?
2. (a) What does Henry believe the men who
survive the battle will say and feel on the
anniversary of the battle? (b) What can you
infer about Henry's understanding of human
nature from these remarks?

Make Judgments

3. (a) Why do you think Henry mentions his own
name and the names of several English
noblemen? (b) In your opinion, is this a wise
tactic?
4. Of all the reasons Henry gives for joining him
in battle, which one would you have found
most convincing? Why?

ST. CRISPIAN'S DAY SPEECH / THE CHARGE OF THE LIGHT BRIGADE   **689**

Teach the Selection

Answer:
Some might
say that
since Henry
himself was willing to go into
battle, it was fair of him to expect
his troops to follow him. Some
students would hesitate to
engage in any conflict when the
odds were so obviously against
them. Others might say that
Henry's speech would instill a
strong sense of patriotism that
could eliminate their doubts.

Find Meaning

1. (a) He gives it on St Crispian's
Day, right before he leads his troops
into battle. (b) He hopes to inspire his
army to fight valiantly.
2. (a) They will feel exceptionally proud
and will boast of their wounds and their
actions in battle. (b) He realizes that the
men will relish the idea of becoming
legendary heroes.

Make Judgments

3. (a) He wants his troops to realize
how noble their actions will seem to
everyone at home. (b) Student
opinions will vary.
4. Most students will say having
Henry refer to them as a band of
brothers would convince them. Others
may say they would be convinced by
Henry's comments that those who do
not fight "think themselves accurs'd"
and "hold their manhoods cheap."

Differentiated Instruction

Reading Proficiency
Students may benefit from hearing a summary of
this speech before they begin reading. You might
also ask an older student who is interested in
theater to prepare a dramatic interpretation of the
speech. Then ask students to read through the
dramatic monologue on their own.

English Language Learning
Point out the following words and expressions.
rouse—make (someone) emotional, 688
vigil—the night before, 689
feats—deeds; accomplishments, 689
band—group, 689
vile—terrible, 689
gentle—raise to a level of nobility, 689
accurs'd—accursed, meaning horrible, 689

ST. CRISPIAN'S DAY SPEECH / THE CHARGE OF THE LIGHT BRIGADE   **689**

Teach the Selection

MIRRORS & WINDOWS The Mirrors & Windows questions at the end of the poem focus on the theme of following orders. Before students begin reading, ask: Why do military experts consider it crucial for soldiers to always follow orders?

Literary Connection

Effects of Rhyme Tennyson's rhyme scheme changes from stanza to stanza. The rhyme is sometimes exact, as in *Brigade* and *dismayed,* in stanza 2, and sometimes slant, as in *Brigade* and *said* in stanza 1 and *blunder'd* and *hundred* in stanza 2 (see student page 473 for more on rhyme). In stanzas 4 through 6, the battle heats up, and the rhyme becomes more regular: *bare, air,* and *there; smoke* and *broke; wondered* and *sundered: shell, fell, well,* and *Hell,* and *fade, made,* and *Brigade.* This increases the tempo and adds to the suspense.

Use Reading Strategies

Clarify If this structure confuses students, have them reread the lines and try to rephrase them. For example, they could reword these lines as, "The soldiers didn't know someone had made a big mistake." **A**

The Charge of the Light Brigade

A Narrative Poem by Alfred, Lord Tennyson

1
Half a league,[1] half a league,
Half a league onward,
All in the valley of Death
    Rode the six hundred.
5 "Forward, the Light Brigade![2]
Charge for the guns!" he said:
Into the valley of Death
Rode the six hundred.

2
"Forward, the Light Brigade!"
10 Was there a man dismayed?
A Not though the soldier knew
    Someone had <u>blundered</u>:
Theirs not to make reply,
Theirs not to reason why,
15 Theirs but to do and die,
Into the valley of Death
    Rode the six hundred.

3
Cannon to right of them,
Cannon to left of them,
20 Cannon in front of them
    Volleyed[3] and thundered;
Stormed at with shot and shell,
Boldly they rode and well,
Into the jaws of Death,
25 Into the mouth of Hell
    Rode the six hundred.

---

1. **league.** Measure of distance equal to about three miles
2. **Light Brigade.** A *brigade* is a unit of troops. The term *light* was assigned to the British brigade because the soldiers carried only swords into battle.
3. **volleyed.** Fired or discharged (weapons) all at once

blun·der (blŭn´ dər) *v.,* make a serious error in judgment; make a thoughtless mistake

(Above) *Balaclava, 1889,* c. 19th century. John Charlton. Blackburn Museum and Art Gallery, Lancashire, United Kingdom.

690

Words in Use

"The Charge of the Light Brigade"

Preview Vocabulary
blunder, 690
reel, 691

Selection Words
sabers, 691
battery, 691
sundered, 691

Common Core State Standards

Reading Literature
RL.1, RL.7, RL.9
Writing
W.2, W.10

CULTURAL ▶▶ CONNECTION

Crimean War During the Crimean War (1853–1856), the allied forces of Great Britain, France, Turkey, and Sardinia fought against the forces of the Russian Empire. Much of the fighting took place on Crimea, a peninsula in the Black Sea that is now the Ukraine. On October 25, 1854, a British brigade of more than six hundred soldiers staged a brave but futile assault on a Russian encampment near the town of Balaklava. The British cavalry, moving under confused and mistaken orders from two rival British officers, was bombarded by cannon fire on three sides. When the skirmish ended, nearly two hundred and fifty English soldiers were dead or wounded. The battle itself had no major significance to the outcome of the war. **B**

4

Flashed all their sabers bare,
Flashed as they turned in air,
Sab'ring the gunners there,
30 Charging an army, while
      All the world wondered:
Plunged in the battery smoke
Right through the line they broke:
Cossack[4] and Russian
35 <u>Reeled</u> from the saber stroke
      Shattered and sundered.
Then they rode back, but not,
      Not the six hundred.

----

4. Cossack. Soldier in the Russian cavalry unit known as Cossacks

reel (rēl) *v.*, stumble as the result of a hard hit

5

Cannon to right of them,
40 Cannon to left of them,
Cannon behind them
      Volleyed and thundered;
Stormed at with shot and shell,
While horse and hero fell,
45 They that had fought so well
Came through the jaws of Death,
Back from the mouth of Hell,
All that was left of them,
      Left of six hundred.

6

50 When can their glory fade?
O the wild charge they made!
      All the world wondered.
Honor the charge they made!
Honor the Light Brigade,
55   Noble six hundred! ❖

What is your opinion of the British soldiers, knowing that the orders to charge were a mistake? Do soldiers really have no right "to make reply" or "to reason why," and no choice but "to do and die"?

ST. CRISPIAN'S DAY SPEECH / THE CHARGE OF THE LIGHT BRIGADE **691**

Teach the Selection

Cultural Connection
Crimean War *Answer:* Most students will say the public reaction would be largely negative. **B**

Analyze Literature
Repetition Have students describe the repetition in stanzas 3 and 5 and tell what the repetition emphasizes. (In stanza 3, the soldiers are all alive and riding bravely into battle. In stanza 5, only a few survivors are left to return. The repetitions emphasize the loss.)

Analyze Literature
Diction Ask students which words in the poem most helped them understand the ultimate fate of the Light Brigade. (They may point out "the valley of Death," "Someone had blundered," "the jaws of Death," and "the mouth of Hell.")

Make Connections
Ask students which part of the poem was most exciting or suspenseful for them. (They will probably choose stanza 3 or 4, as the men engage in battle.)

MIRRORS & WINDOWS Some may say the soldiers were brave because they charged into battle knowing there was a good possibility they would die. Others might say following a leader blindly into battle is foolish. Most will know that soldiers who don't obey orders will be punished.

Differentiated Instruction

English Language Learning
Help students understand the following words.
brigade—large body of troops, 690
cannon—big gun, 690
volleyed—propelled or discharged an object into the air, 690
gunners—soldiers who operate or aim guns, 691

Enrichment
Interested students can work in groups to research the Crimean War. Suggest that students look for answers to these questions:
- Why was Russia so interested in controlling the Black Sea?
- Why did England, France, and Sardinia want to stop Russia?
- What were major events in the war?
- What was the outcome of the war?

Find Meaning

1. (a) The troop of six hundred cavalry soldiers rode into battle knowing that they were facing death. (b) Repetition emphasizes this idea and adds to the tone of doom.

2. (a) They feel dismayed. (b) They have been commanded to do so, and it is their duty to continue no matter what they think.

Make Judgments

3. (a) The speaker admires the soldiers. (b) He thinks the rest of the world will probably feel the same.

4. He wanted to commemorate the battle and honor the members of the Light Brigade as heroes. He probably wanted to make sure the public remembered why they died.

Compare Literature

Diction

1. Some examples include "this day is call'd," "comes safe home," "feast his neighbors," "Be in their flowing cups freshly rememb'red," and "be he ne'er so vile."

2. Some examples include "Half a league, half a league, / Half a league onward," "Into the valley of Death / Rode the six hundred," "Theirs not to make reply," and "Reeled from the saber stroke / Shattered and sundered."

3. Answers will vary. The diction in both is somewhat old-fashioned and elevated or heroic sounding.

Find Meaning

1. (a) What is the meaning of the lines "Into the valley of Death / Rode the six hundred"? (b) Why are these lines repeated at the ends of the first, second, and third stanzas and echoed at the ends of the remaining stanzas?

2. (a) How do the troops feel as they ride into battle? (b) Aware of the probable outcome, why do the members of the Light Brigade continue the assault?

Compare Literature

Diction Diction is a part of a writer's overall style. It refers to the writer's word choice. When choosing words, writers consider how the words will sound and what images the words will evoke in the reader's mind. Review the words and phrases from "St. Crispian's Day Speech" and "The Charge of the Light Brigade" that you recorded in your diction chart to answer the following questions.

Make Judgments

3. (a) How does the speaker feel about the British soldiers who participated in this battle? (b) How does the speaker think the rest of the world will feel about them?

4. Tennyson may have begun writing this poem to attack the mistake made by the commanding officers at Balaklava. In the end, what do you think Tennyson's goal was?

1. What words and phrases in "St. Crispian's Day Speech" most helped you to describe the diction?

2. What words and phrases in "The Charge of the Light Brigade" most helped you to describe the diction?

3. Describe the diction in both texts. How does each poem's diction compare?

Extend Understanding

Writing Options

Creative Writing Write a **narrative poem** that uses the same subject as Tennyson's poem. Do research to learn more about the events surrounding the Battle of Balaklava and the people involved. Consider writing your poem from a new point of view, for example, from the point of view of one of the soldiers or perhaps one of the leaders.

Expository Writing Write an **expository paragraph** comparing and contrasting the speakers in "St. Crispian's Day Speech" and "The Charge of the Light Brigade." Discuss similarities and differences in the speakers' tone and purposes. Provide examples to support your claims.

Lifelong Learning

Research Shakespeare To understand the context of "St. Crispian's Day Speech," learn more about the play from which it is taken. Use the library to research the plot, characters, and notable scenes from *Henry V.* Present your findings to the class as an oral report.

Critical Literacy

Recite a Monologue With a partner, practice reciting Shakespeare's "St. Crispian's Day Speech." Provide feedback about your partner's delivery, including tone of voice, clarity, and facial expressions. When you feel you are ready, perform the monologue for the class.

Go to **www.mirrorsandwindows.com** for more.

Rubrics for Writing Options

You can adapt this as a checklist for students to use as they write.

Creative Writing

☐ Does the poem tell a story about the Battle at Balaklava?

Expository Writing

☐ Does the paragraph compare and contrast the speakers?

☐ Does the paragraph examine the speakers' tones and purposes?

☐ Does the paragraph contain examples to support the ideas?

Grammar & Style

Punctuation: Dashes, Semicolons, and Colons

Dashes

But we in it shall be remembered—

We few, we happy few, we band of
brothers

— WILLIAM SHAKESPEARE, "St. Crispian's Day Speech"

A **dash,** like the one that ends the first line in the quotation above, is used to show a sudden break or change in thought. Note that a dash is longer than a hyphen. Dashes sometimes replace other marks of punctuation, such as periods, semicolons, or commas. In the quotation above, the dash provides a dramatic pause.

> EXAMPLE
>
> *Today, you will fight a great battle—a battle that will be remembered forever.*

Semicolons

Old men forget; yet all shall be
forgot....

— WILLIAM SHAKESPEARE, "St. Crispian's Day Speech"

A **semicolon** joins two closely related independent clauses. The semicolon signals a pause that is longer than a comma's pause but shorter than that of a period.

> EXAMPLE
>
> *The soldiers are preparing themselves; they will be ready for battle.*

Conjunctions such as *and, but, so, or, nor, for,* and *yet* can also be used to combine two related independent clauses. A semicolon can be used in place of the comma and the conjunction.

Using a semicolon instead of a comma and a coordinating conjunction adds emphasis to the second clause.

> EXAMPLES
>
> *The opposing army is much larger, <u>and</u> it will probably defeat Henry and his troops.*
>
> *The opposing army is much larger; it will probably defeat Henry and his troops.*

Colons

A **colon** introduces a list of items. Colons are also used between numbers that tell hours and minutes and after the greeting in a business letter.

> EXAMPLE
>
> *You will be remembered for three things: your courage, your boldness, and your bravery.*

Understanding Dashes, Semicolons, and Colons

Rewrite the following sentences, correcting the punctuation where necessary. If no changes are needed, write *correct.*

1. This is your greatest challenge; my band of brothers.
2. People often forget: you will not be forgotten.
3. The story blends these elements drama, adventure, and excitement.
4. We shall be remembered—we few, we happy few.
5. The battle draws close we are prepared.
6. Everyone will honor you; those who shed their blood with me shall be my brothers.
7. His troops were ready with their weapons; swords, shields, and spears.

At a Glance
Independent Reading
- Reading Level: Challenging
- Difficulty Considerations: Length, vocabulary, and science concepts
- Ease Factor: Exciting plot

Objectives
Reading this selection will enable students to do the following:
- read with developing fluency
- read silently with comprehension for a sustained period of time

Launch the Lesson
Have students work in small groups to write a definition of the phrase *twilight zone*. Tell them to use what they know about the old TV program and their own common sense to compose the definition. Then have them compare their definitions with the narrator's definition at the beginning of Act 1.

MIRRORS **&** **W**INDOWS The Mirrors & Windows questions at the end of the play focus on the theme of reaching unfair conclusions. Before students begin reading, ask: How can gossip harm a person?

TEACHING NOTE
Although this selection is presented in the student edition as an independent reading, teaching support has been provided should you choose to cover it in class.

Common Core State Standards
Reading Literature
RL.10

INDEPENDENT READING

CHARACTERS

NARRATOR
FIGURE ONE
FIGURE TWO

RESIDENTS OF MAPLE STREET

STEVE BRAND
CHARLIE'S WIFE
MRS. GOODMAN
MRS. BRAND
TOMMY
WOMAN
DON MARTIN
SALLY (*Tommy's Mother*)
MAN ONE
MAN TWO
PETE VAN HORN
CHARLIE
LES GOODMAN

The Monsters Are Due on Maple Street

A Screenplay by Rod Serling

694

Rod Serling (1924–1975) is one of the best-known television writers of all time. His sometimes frightening, often strange, and always amazing program *The Twilight Zone* changed the face of prime-time television. Born in Syracuse, New York, Serling served as a paratrooper in World War II. Soon after his discharge from the military, Serling attended Antioch College in Ohio, where he studied literature and worked part time as a scriptwriter. By the age of thirty-one, Serling had already won an Emmy for his work in television. The following screenplay originally aired on March 4, 1960, during the first season of *The Twilight Zone*.

–ACT I–

Fade in on a shot of the night sky. The various nebulae and planet bodies stand out in sharp, sparkling relief, and the camera begins a slow pan across the Heavens.

NARRATOR'S VOICE. There is a fifth dimension beyond that which is known to man. It is a dimension as vast as space, and as timeless as infinity. It is the middle ground between light and shadow—between science and

---

Program Resources

Planning and Assessment
Program Planning Guide, Selection Lesson Plan
E-Lesson Planner
Assessment Guide, Lesson Test
ExamView

Technology Tools
Interactive Student Text on CD
Visual Teaching Package
Audio Library
mirrorsandwindows.com

Meeting the Standards
Drama: Unit 7, Independent Reading, pp. 59–68

Differentiating Instruction
Developing Readers, Use Text Organization, pp. 49–51
English Language Learners, Cause and Effect, pp. 152–174
Advanced Students, Media Study, p. 45

superstition. And it lies between the pit of man's fears and the summit of his knowledge. This is the dimension of imagination. It is an area which we call The Twilight Zone.

The camera has begun to pan down until it passes the horizon and is on a sign which reads "Maple Street." Pan down until we are shooting down at an angle toward the street below. It's a tree-lined, quiet residential American street, very typical of the small town. The houses have front porches on which people sit and swing on gliders, conversing across from house to house. STEVE BRAND *polishes his car parked in front of his house. His neighbor,* DON MARTIN, *leans against the fender watching him. A Good Humor man rides a bicycle and is just in the process of stopping to sell some ice cream to a couple of kids. Two women gossip on the front lawn. Another man waters his lawn.*

NARRATOR'S VOICE. Maple Street, U.S.A., late summer. A tree-lined little world of front porch gliders, hop scotch, the laughter of children, and the bell of an ice cream vendor.

There is a pause and the camera moves over to a shot of the Good Humor man and two small boys who are standing alongside, just buying ice cream.

NARRATOR'S VOICE. At the sound of the roar and the flash of light it will be precisely 6:43 P.M. on Maple Street.

At this moment one of the little boys, TOMMY, *looks up to listen to a sound of a tremendous screeching roar from overhead. A flash of light plays on both their faces and then it moves down the street past lawns and porches and rooftops and then disappears.*

Various people leave their porches and stop what they're doing to stare up at the sky.

STEVE BRAND, *the man who's been polishing his car, now stands there transfixed, staring upwards. He looks at* DON MARTIN, *his neighbor from across the street.*

STEVE. What was that? A meteor?

DON. [*Nods.*] That's what it looked like. I didn't hear any crash though, did you?

STEVE. [*Shakes his head.*] Nope. I didn't hear anything except a roar.

MRS. BRAND. [*From her porch.*] Steve? What was what?

STEVE. [*Raising his voice and looking toward porch.*] Guess it was a meteor, honey. Came awful close, didn't it?

MRS. BRAND. Too close for my money! Much too close.

The camera pans across the various porches to people who stand there watching and talking in low tones.

NARRATOR'S VOICE. Maple Street. Six-forty-four P.M. on a late September evening. [*A pause.*] Maple Street in the last calm and reflective moment...before the monsters came!

The camera slowly pans across the porches again. We see a man screwing a light bulb on a front porch, then getting down off the stool to flick the switch and finding that nothing happens.

Another man is working on an electric power mower. He plugs in the plug, flicks on the switch of the power mower, off and on, with nothing happening.

Through the window of a front porch, we see a woman pushing her finger back and forth on the dial hook. Her voice is indistinct and distant, but intelligible and repetitive.

Teach the Selection

Summary

Early one evening, a roar overhead and a flash of light disturb the quiet calm of Maple Street. At first, people think a meteor has landed nearby. However, when the electricity goes out and none of their cars or other machines work, they begin to suspect something else. Their fears build when fourteen-year-old Tommy suggests that the events are just like a story he read in which creatures from outer space, looking like humans, move into a neighborhood to prepare for an invasion.

Soon neighbors are eyeing each other with suspicion. Violence erupts and an innocent man is shot. As chaos reigns on Maple Street, figures sit in a spacecraft, viewing the spectacle from a distance. Calmly, they discuss how easy it is to get humans to destroy themselves.

Use Reading Skills

Author's Purpose Ask students how they think Serling wants the setting to contribute to his overall message. (He probably wants readers and viewers to understand that this street and these people are ordinary. What is about to happen here could happen on any street in the United States.) **A**

Analyze Literature

Mood Ask students how the narrator's dialogue affects the mood of the opening scene. (It adds suspense and an ominous feeling.) **B**

Words in Use

Selection Words
nebulae, 694
dimension, 694
infinity, 694
superstition, 694
transfixed, 695
reflective, 695
intelligible, 695
portable, 696
intimidated, 697

Teaching Words
paratrooper, 694
discharge, 694
singled, 708
incorporated, 708
commentary, 708
generate, 708

KEY TERMS
SCRIPTWRITER, 694
SCREENPLAY, 694
THESIS STATEMENT, 708

Use Reading Strategies

Ask Questions Students may question who the Voices are and what purpose they have in the play. Encourage students to reread the dialogue and stage directions that come before the Voices. Students should recognize that the Voices belong to unidentified people on the street. They should determine from what the Voices say that their purpose is to echo or emphasize the people's problem: Maple Street has mysteriously lost all its power. **A**

Use Reading Skills

Analyze Cause and Effect Ask students why the portable radio should be broadcasting. What effect does its failure have on the people? (A portable radio works by battery, so it should work without electrical power. The fact that it isn't working makes people fear that something worse than a simple power failure has occurred.) **B**

Analyze Literature

Characterization Ask students for their first impressions of Steve. (They may say he seems level-headed and not easy to alarm. He also seems like a kind person.) **C**

WOMAN. Operator, operator, something's wrong on the phone, operator!

MRS. BRAND *comes out on the porch and calls to* STEVE.

MRS. BRAND. [*Calling.*] Steve, the power's off. I had the soup on the stove and the stove just stopped working.

WOMAN. Same thing over here. I can't get anybody on the phone either. The phone seems to be dead.

We look down on the street as we hear the voices creep up from below, small, mildly disturbed voices highlighting these kinds of phrases:

A **VOICES.**

Electricity's off.

Phone won't work.

Can't get a thing on the radio.

My power mower won't move, won't work at all.

Radio's gone dead!

PETE VAN HORN, *a tall, thin man, is seen standing in front of his house.*

VAN HORN. I'll cut through the back yard… See if the power's still on on Floral Street. I'll be right back!

He walks past the side of his house and disappears into the back yard.

The camera pans down slowly until we're looking at ten or eleven people standing around the street and overflowing to the curb and sidewalk. In the background is STEVE BRAND'S *car.*

STEVE. Doesn't make sense. Why should the power go off all of a sudden, and the phone line?

DON. Maybe some sort of an electrical storm or something.

CHARLIE. That don't seem likely. Sky's just as blue as anything. Not a cloud. No lightning. No thunder. No nothing. How could it be a storm?

WOMAN. I can't get a thing on the radio. Not even the portable.

The people again murmur softly in wonderment and question.

CHARLIE. Well, why don't you go downtown and check with the police, though they'll probably think we're crazy or something. A little power failure and right away we get all flustered and everything.

B **STEVE.** It isn't just the power failure, Charlie. If it was, we'd still be able to get a broadcast on the portable.

There's a murmur of reaction to this. STEVE *looks from face to face and then over to his car.*

C **STEVE.** I'll run downtown. We'll get this all straightened out.

He walks over to the car, gets in it, turns the key. Looking through the open car door, we see the crowd watching him from the other side. STEVE *starts the engine. It turns over sluggishly[1] and then just stops dead. He tries it again and this time he can't get it to turn over. Then, very slowly and reflectively, he turns the key back to "off" and slowly gets out of the car.*

The people stare at STEVE. *He stands for a moment by the car, then walks toward the group.*

STEVE. I don't understand it. It was working fine before…

---

1. **sluggishly.** Inactively; slowly moving

Differentiated Instruction

Reading Proficiency

Provide time for students to preview the title, list of characters, and first couple of pages. Point out that because this is a television script, stage directions often use the expression "we see," which refers to what will appear on TV screens. The stage directions also contain camera terms, such as:

fade in—gradually go from total darkness to full brightness, 694

pan—move a camera across a scene to capture it all, 695

long shot—filmed from a long distance, 701

close-up—filmed from very near, 701

medium shot—filmed from a slight distance, 702

angle—the position of the camera, such as high angle or low angle, 705.

DON. Out of gas?

STEVE. [*Shakes his head.*] I just had it filled up.

WOMAN. What's it mean?

CHARLIE. It's just as if…as if everything had stopped. [*Then he turns toward* STEVE.] We'd better walk downtown. [*Another murmur of assent[2] at this.*]

STEVE. The two of us can go, Charlie. [*He turns to look back at the car.*] It couldn't be the meteor. A meteor couldn't do this.

He and CHARLIE *exchange a look, then they start to walk away from the group.*

We see TOMMY, *a serious-faced fourteen-year-old in spectacles who stands a few feet away from the group. He is halfway between them and the two men, who start to walk down the sidewalk.*

TOMMY. Mr. Brand…you better not!

STEVE. Why not?

TOMMY. They don't want you to.

STEVE *and* CHARLIE *exchange a grin, and* STEVE *looks back toward the boy.* **D**

STEVE. Who doesn't want us to?

TOMMY. [*Jerks his head in the general direction of the distant horizon.*] Them!

STEVE. Them?

CHARLIE. Who are them?

TOMMY. [*Very intently.*] Whoever was in that thing that came by overhead.

STEVE *knits his brows for a moment, cocking his head questioningly. His voice is intense.*

STEVE. What?

TOMMY. Whoever was in that thing that came over. I don't think they want us to leave here.

STEVE *leaves* CHARLIE *and walks over to the boy. He kneels down in front of him. He forces his voice to remain gentle. He reaches out and holds the boy.*

STEVE. What do you mean? What are you talking about?

TOMMY. They don't want us to leave. That's why they shut everything off.

STEVE. What makes you say that? Whatever gave you that idea?

WOMAN. [*From the crowd.*] Now isn't that the craziest thing you ever heard? **E**

TOMMY. [*Persistently but a little intimidated by the crowd.*] It's always that way, in every story I ever read about a ship landing from outer space.

WOMAN. [*To the boy's mother,* SALLY, *who stands on the fringe of the crowd.*] From outer space, yet! Sally, you better get that boy of yours up to bed. He's been reading too many comic books or seeing too many movies or something.

SALLY. Tommy, come over here and stop that kind of talk.

STEVE. Go ahead, Tommy. We'll be right back. And you'll see. That wasn't any ship or anything like it. That was just a…a meteor or something. Likely as not—[*He turns to the group, now trying to weight his words with an optimism he obviously doesn't feel but is desperately trying to instill in himself as well as the others.*] No doubt it did have something to do with all this power failure and the rest of it. Meteors can do some crazy things. Like sunspots.

---

2. assent. Agreement

Speaking & Listening Skills

Inflection

Explain to students that *inflection* refers to the way a speaker changes his or her voice. It may include raising or lowering the voice, speeding up or slowing down, pausing, and stressing a phrase, a word, or even a single vowel sound.

Play audio recordings of Rod Serling's introduction to *The Twilight Zone* and have students analyze the inflection of Rod Serling's voice, using the items above as criteria. Ask students how Serling's inflection affects the meaning of the words. You can find audio recordings of *The Twilight Zone* introductions on the Internet, through the National Public Radio website.

Science Connection

Astronomical Causes Steve's theory that a meteor or sunspot is responsible for what has happened is more scientific, and therefore less alarming, than Tommy's theory.

- Meteors—sometimes called shooting stars—are bright lights that streak across the sky when objects called meteorites explode or vaporize in Earth's atmosphere.

- Sunspots appear as dark spots on the face of the sun. They are surrounded by magnetic fields and constantly change size. Scientists study sunspots to learn more about the behavior of the sun and to find out, for example, if it's possible to prevent power outages caused by solar activity.

698 UNIT 7 DRAMA

Grammar Skills

Sentence Fragments

Remind students that natural speech often contains sentence fragments, which are incomplete thoughts that lack a subject, a verb, or both. Explain that writers include fragments in dialogue to make the dialogue sound natural and to make the characters more believable.

Point out the fragments in Charlie's dialogue on page 696: "Not a cloud. No lighting. No thunder. No nothing." Ask students to compare that to "There isn't a cloud. There isn't any lighting or thunder. There is nothing." Students should recognize that the fragments are more natural sounding and also more appropriate for the character and the situation. Have students find other examples of fragments on these pages.

DON. [Picking up the cue.] Sure. That's the kind of thing—like sunspots. They raise Cain[3] with radio reception all over the world. And this thing being so close—why, there's no telling the sort of stuff it can do. [He wets his lips, smiles nervously.] Go ahead, Charlie. You and Steve go into town and see if that isn't what's causing it all.

STEVE and CHARLIE *again walk away from the group down the sidewalk. The people watch silently.*

TOMMY *stares at them, biting his lips, and finally calling out again.*

TOMMY. Mr. Brand!

The two men stop again. TOMMY *takes a step toward them.*

TOMMY. Mr. Brand...please don't leave here.

STEVE *and* CHARLIE *stop once again and turn toward the boy. There's a murmur in the crowd, a murmur of irritation and concern as if the boy were bringing up fears that shouldn't be brought up; words which carried with them a strange kind of validity that came without logic but nonetheless registered and had meaning and effect. Again we hear a murmur of reaction from the crowd.*

TOMMY *is partly frightened and partly defiant as well.*

TOMMY. You might not even be able to get to town. It was that way in the story. Nobody could leave. Nobody except—

STEVE. Except who?

TOMMY. Except the people they'd sent down ahead of them. They looked just like humans. And it wasn't until the ship landed that—

The boy suddenly stops again, conscious of the parents staring at them and of the sudden hush of the crowd.

SALLY. [*In a whisper, sensing the antagonism[4] of the crowd.*] Tommy, please son...honey, don't talk that way—

MAN ONE. That kid shouldn't talk that way...and we shouldn't stand here listening to him. Why this is the craziest thing I ever heard of. The kid tells us a comic book plot and here we stand listening—

STEVE *walks toward the camera, stops by the boy.*

STEVE. Go ahead, Tommy. What kind of story was this? What about the people that they sent out ahead?

TOMMY. That was the way they prepared things for the landing. They sent four people. A mother and a father and two kids who looked just like humans...but they weren't.

There's another silence as STEVE *looks toward the crowd and then toward* TOMMY. *He wears a tight grin.*

STEVE. Well, I guess what we'd better do then is to run a check on the neighborhood and see which ones of us are really human.

There's laughter at this, but it's a laughter that comes from a desperate attempt to lighten the atmosphere. It's a release kind of laugh. The people look at one another in the middle of their laughter.

CHARLIE. There must be somethin' better to do than stand around makin' bum jokes about it. [*Rubs his jaw nervously.*] I wonder if

---

3. **raise Cain.** Cause trouble
4. **antagonism.** Hostility; open opposition

Teach the Selection

Analyze Literature
Characterization Ask students what the details in the stage directions and dialogue suggest about Tommy. Have them support their answers with evidence from the play. (Tommy hesitates and bites his lip before calling out. This suggests he is nervous. It also shows he believes so strongly in what he is saying that he's willing to risk interfering. He says *please*, which suggests he is earnest.) Ⓐ

Use Reading Strategies
Make Predictions Ask students how they think the crowd will react to Tommy's story. (Some may predict that most people will laugh at Tommy's crazy ideas. Others may predict that because the people are already nervous, some will wonder if Tommy's ideas could be possible.) Ⓑ

Analyze Literature
Mood Invite students to describe the mood of the crowd. (Its mood is uneasy, slightly paranoid, and increasingly fearful.) Ⓒ

Research Skills

Evaluate Sources
Remind students that most people would not consider science fiction a useful source of factual information. When doing research, students should be able to evaluate their sources for accuracy, timeliness, completeness, and reliability. Have students explain whether the following sources would be useful for a report on meteorites.

- An article on meteors in a current issue of *Science* magazine
- An Internet article written by a member of a UFO (Unidentified Flying Objects) club
- An interview with an astronomy professor at a local college
- A website hosted by the National Aeronautics and Space Administration (NASA)
- A book about meteors published in 1956

Use Reading Skills

Analyze Cause and Effect Ask students why the people are "wildly, frightened" and what effect this growing fear has on them, especially Charlie and Don. (Goodman's car has apparently started on its own. People are startled and suspicious. Don and Charlie become belligerent and want to confront Goodman for an explanation.) **A**

Use Reading Strategies

Visualize Have students visualize the people heading across the street. Tell them to picture their facial expressions and body gestures. Ask: "What about this image tells you that they have become a mob?" (Students may picture angry, wild expressions and imagine the people waving their arms or making fists. Be sure students understand what a mob is.) **B**

Use Reading Strategies

Make Inferences Ask students why the group pauses and then walks slowly. (Steve has called them a mob. At this point, they have not yet lost all control. Some students may interpret their actions as deliberate and menacing.) **C**

Floral Street's got the same deal we got. [*He looks past the houses.*] Where is Pete Van Horn anyway? Didn't he get back yet?

Suddenly there's the sound of a car's engine starting to turn over.

We look across the street toward the driveway of LES GOODMAN'*s house. He's at the wheel trying to start the car.*

SALLY. Can you get it started, Les? [*He gets out of the car, shaking his head.*]

GOODMAN. No dice.

He walks toward the group. He stops suddenly as behind him, inexplicably and with a noise that inserts itself into the silence, the car engine starts up all by itself. GOODMAN *whirls around to stare toward it.*

The car idles roughly, smoke coming from the exhaust, the frame shaking gently. GOODMAN'*s eyes go wide, and he runs over to his car.*

The people stare toward the car.

MAN ONE. He got the car started somehow. He got his car started!

A *The camera pans along the faces of the people as they stare, somehow caught up by this revelation and somehow, illogically, wildly, frightened.*

WOMAN. How come his car just up and started like that?

SALLY. All by itself. He wasn't anywheres near it. It started all by itself.

DON *approaches the group, stops a few feet away to look toward* GOODMAN'*s car and then back toward the group.*

DON. And he never did come out to look at that thing that flew overhead. He wasn't even interested. [*He turns to the faces in the group,*

his face taut and serious.] Why? Why didn't he come out with the rest of us to look?

CHARLIE. He always was an oddball. Him and his whole family. Real oddball.

DON. What do you say we ask him?

B *The group suddenly starts toward the house. In this brief fraction of a moment they take the first step toward performing a metamorphosis*[5] *that changes people from a group into a mob. They begin to head purposefully across the street toward the house at the end.* STEVE *stands in front of them. For a moment their fear almost turns their walk into a wild stampede, but* STEVE'*s voice, loud, incisive, and commanding, makes them stop.*

STEVE. Wait a minute…wait a minute! Let's not be a mob!

C *The people stop as a group, seem to pause for a moment, and then much more quietly and slowly start to walk across the street.* GOODMAN *stands alone facing the people.*

GOODMAN. I just don't understand it. I tried to start it and it wouldn't start. You saw me. All of you saw me.

And now, just as suddenly as the engine started, it stops and there's a long silence that is gradually intruded upon by the frightened murmuring of the people.

GOODMAN. I don't understand. I swear…I don't understand. What's happening?

DON. Maybe you better tell us. Nothing's working on this street. Nothing. No lights, no power, no radio. [*And then meaningfully.*] Nothing except one car—yours!

---

5. metamorphosis. Change in form or nature

TEACHING NOTE

Self-Generated Questioning

Have students form several groups, and urge them to develop as many questions as they can about the play up to this point. Model some possible questions: "Why don't people stop and listen to each other?" "What's so bad about Goodman that people turn on him so easily?" Have representatives from each group read some of the questions. Record the questions on the board or on an overhead. Then place a star next to each question students consider critical to understanding the play, and two stars next to each question they consider hard to answer. As you proceed with the play, take breaks as a class to discuss questions in each set.

The people pick this up and now their murmuring becomes a loud chant filling the air with accusations and demands for action. Two of the men pass DON *and head toward* GOODMAN, *who backs away, backing into his car and now at bay.*

GOODMAN. Wait a minute now. You keep your distance—all of you. So I've got a car that starts by itself—well, that's a freak thing, I admit it. But does that make me some kind of a criminal or something? I don't know why the car works—it just does!

This stops the crowd momentarily and now GOODMAN, *still backing away, goes toward his front porch. He goes up the steps and then stops to stand facing the mob.*

We see a long shot of STEVE *as he comes through the crowd.*

STEVE. [*Quietly.*] We're all on a monster kick, Les. Seems that the general impression holds that maybe one family isn't what we think they are. Monsters from outer space or something. Different than us. Fifth columnists[6] from the vast beyond. [*He chuckles.*] You know anybody that might fit that description around here on Maple Street? **D**

GOODMAN. What is this, a gag or something? This a practical joke or something?

We see a close-up of the porch light as it suddenly goes out. There's a murmur from the group.

GOODMAN. Now I suppose that's supposed to incriminate[7] me! The light goes on and off. That really does it, doesn't it? [*He looks around the faces of the people.*] I just don't

understand this—[*He wets his lips, looking from face to face.*] Look, you all know me. We've lived here five years. Right in this house. We're no different from any of the rest of you! We're no different at all. Really…this whole thing is just…just weird—

WOMAN. Well, if that's the case, Les Goodman, explain why—[*She stops suddenly, clamping her mouth shut.*]

GOODMAN. [*Softly.*] Explain what?

STEVE. [*Interjecting.*] Look, let's forget this—

CHARLIE. [*Overlapping him.*] Go ahead, let her talk. What about it? Explain what?

WOMAN. [*A little reluctantly.*] Well… sometimes I go to bed late at night. A couple of times…a couple of times I'd come out on the porch and I'd see Mr. Goodman here in the wee hours of the morning standing out in front of his house…looking up at the sky. [*She looks around the circle of faces.*] That's right, looking up at the sky as if…as if he were waiting for something. [*A pause.*] As if he were looking for something. **E**

There's a murmur of reaction from the crowd again.

We cut suddenly to a group shot. As GOODMAN *starts toward them, they back away frightened.*

GOODMAN. You know really…this is for laughs. You know what I'm guilty of? [*He laughs.*] I'm guilty of insomnia. Now what's the penalty for insomnia? [*At this point the laugh, the humor, leaves his voice.*] Did you

6. **Fifth columnists.** Citizens who support the goals of an invading army
7. **incriminate.** Show proof of involvement in a crime

Cultural Connection

TV in the Sixties Most television shows in 1960, the year "The Monsters Are Due on Maple Street" aired, were not science fiction. Among the most popular programs that year were shows about the Wild West, such as *Maverick, Cheyenne, Wyatt Earp, Bonanza, Stagecoach West, The Westerner,* and *Gunsmoke.* Popular family shows included *The Donna Reed Show, The Adventures of Ozzie and Harriett,* and *My Three Sons.*

Analyze Literature

Irony Ask students to explain the irony in Steve's comments about monsters from outer space and the fifth columnists. (He is trying to be funny to lighten a tense situation. However, he's probably right.) **D**

Analyze Literature

Plot Ask: "How do the Woman's accusations about Goodman relate to the main conflict in the play?" (After a roar and a flash of light, Maple Street has mysteriously lost power. Fueled by fear that is sparked by Tommy's story, residents begin to suspect each other of being aliens. This is the main conflict in the play. The Woman's insinuation that Goodman is waiting for a spaceship is the result of the growing suspicion and fear among neighbors.) **E**

Dramatic Reading

Divide students into small groups and have each group select a portion of the play for a dramatic reading. Tell groups to discuss what is going on in their scene and the reactions and feelings of the characters in that scene. Remind students to consult the stage directions for information that will help them understand the characters' attitudes and motivation in the scene.

Provide time for students to practice reading the scene. Encourage them to evaluate each other's delivery of the dialogue. When groups are ready, have them present their dramatic readings for the class.

Use Reading Skills

Draw Conclusions Have students tell you why the people are standing watch outside Les Goodman's house. (They suspect him of being from outer space. They may want to make sure he doesn't try to contact the invaders from the spaceship or try to escape.) **Ⓐ**

Use Reading Strategies

Clarify Ask students what Charlie means when he says, "these aren't normal circumstances." Model a response: "He means that looking up at the sky wouldn't be such a big deal if it weren't possible that some of the neighbors are space aliens posing as a people." **Ⓑ**

Make Connections

Ask students if they think Goodman's reaction is justified. How do they think they would respond in a similar situation? (Most will feel that Goodman is justly defending his family and property. Some will say they would react just like Goodman. Others might say they aren't sure how they would react, but they wouldn't threaten to cause any more trouble.) **Ⓒ**

---

hear what I said? I said it was insomnia. [*A pause as he looks around, then shouts.*] I said it was insomnia! You fools. You scared, frightened rabbits, you. You're sick people, do you know that? You're sick people—all of you! And you don't even know what you're starting because let me tell you…let me tell you—this thing you're starting—that should frighten you. As God is my witness…you're letting something begin here that's a nightmare!

—Act 2—

We see a medium shot of the Goodman *entry hall at night. On the side table rests an unlit candle.* Mrs. Goodman *walks into the scene, a glass of milk in hand. She sets the milk down on the table, lights the candle with a match from a box on the table, picks up the glass of milk, and starts out of scene.*

Mrs. Goodman *comes through her porch door, glass of milk in hand. The entry hall, with table and lit candle, can be seen behind her.*

Ⓐ *Outside, the camera slowly pans down the sidewalk, taking in little knots of people who stand around talking in low voices. At the end of each conversation they look toward* Les Goodman's *house. From the various houses we can see candlelight but no electricity, and there's an all-pervading quiet that blankets the whole area, disturbed only by the almost whispered voices of the people as they stand around. The camera pans over to one group where* Charlie *stands. He stares across at* Goodman's *house.*

We see a long shot of the house. Two men stand across the street in almost sentry-like poses. Then we see a medium shot of a group of people.

Sally. [*A little timorously.*[8]] It just doesn't seem right, though, keeping watch on them. Why…he was right when he said he was one of our neighbors. Why, I've known Ethel Goodman ever since they moved in. We've been good friends—

Charlie. That don't prove a thing. Any guy who'd spend his time lookin' up at the sky early in the morning—well, there's something wrong with that kind of person. There's something that ain't legitimate. Maybe under normal circumstances we could let it go by, **Ⓑ** but these aren't normal circumstances. Why, look at this street! Nothin' but candles. Why, it's like goin' back into the dark ages or somethin'!

Steve *walks down the steps of his porch, walks down the street over to* Les Goodman's *house, and then stops at the foot of the steps.* Goodman *stands there, his wife behind him, very frightened.*

Ⓒ **Goodman.** Just stay right where you are, Steve. We don't want any trouble, but this time if anybody sets foot on my porch, that's what they're going to get—trouble!

Steve. Look Les—

Goodman. I've already explained to you people. I don't sleep very well at night sometimes. I get up and I take a walk and I look up at the sky. I look at the stars!

Mrs. Goodman. That's exactly what he does. Why this whole thing, it's…it's some kind of madness or something.

Steve. [*Nods grimly.*] That's exactly what it is—some kind of madness.

---

8. timorously. Shyly

Auditory Learning

Some students may benefit from listening to an audio recording of the play as they read along. Alternatively, you can read aloud short sections of the play while students follow along silently in their books. After reading each section, stop to clarify any vocabulary words or ideas that confuse students.

Reading Proficiency

Point out the ellipses in the dialogue and explain that sometimes ellipses stand for words left out. However, in dialogue ellipses show natural pauses or hesitant speech, such as when someone is confused or excited.

CHARLIE'S VOICE. [*Shrill, from across the street.*] You best watch who you're seen with, Steve! Until we get all this straightened out, you ain't exactly above suspicion yourself.

STEVE. [*Whirling around toward him.*] Or you, Charlie. Or any of us, it seems. From age eight on up!

WOMAN. What I'd like to know is—what are we gonna do? Just stand around here all night?

CHARLIE. There's nothin' else we can do! [*He turns back looking toward* STEVE *and* GOODMAN *again.*] One of 'em'll tip their hand.[9] They got to.

STEVE. [*Raising his voice.*] There's something you can do, Charlie. You could go home and keep your mouth shut. You could quit strutting around like a self-appointed hanging judge and just climb into bed and forget it.

CHARLIE. You sound real anxious to have that happen, Steve. I think we better keep our eye on you too!

DON. [*As if he were taking the bit in his teeth, takes a hesitant step to the front.*] I think everything might as well come out now. [*He turns toward* STEVE.] Your wife's done plenty of talking, Steve, about how odd you are!

CHARLIE. [*Picking this up, his eyes widening.*] Go ahead, tell us what she's said.

We see a long shot of STEVE *as he walks toward them from across the street.*

STEVE. Go ahead, what's my wife said? Let's get it all out. Let's pick out every idiosyncrasy[10] of every single man, woman, and child on the street. And then we might as well set up some kind of kangaroo court.[11]

How about a firing squad at dawn, Charlie, so we can get rid of all the suspects? Narrow them down. Make it easier for you.

DON. There's no need gettin' so upset, Steve. It's just that…well…Myra's talked about how there's been plenty of nights you spent hours down in your basement workin' on some kind of radio or something. Well, none of us have ever seen that radio—

By this time STEVE *has reached the group. He stands there defiantly close to them.*

CHARLIE. Go ahead, Steve. What kind of "radio set" you workin' on? I never seen it. Neither has anyone else. Who you talk to on that radio set? And who talks to you?

STEVE. I'm surprised at you, Charlie. How come you're so dense all of a sudden? [*A pause.*] Who do I talk to? I talk to monsters from outer space. I talk to three-headed green men who fly over here in what look like meteors.

STEVE's *wife steps down from the porch, bites her lip, calls out.*

MRS. BRAND. Steve! Steve, please. [*Then looking around, frightened, she walks toward the group.*] It's just a ham radio[12] set, that's all. I bought him a book on it myself. It's just a ham radio set. A lot of people have them. I can show it to you. It's right down in the basement.

STEVE. [*Whirls around toward her.*] Show them nothing! If they want to look inside our house—let them get a search warrant.

---

9. **tip their hand.** Expose themselves; accidentally reveal information
10. **idiosyncrasy.** Odd character trait
11. **kangaroo court.** Unjust or unofficial court
12. **ham radio.** Noncommercial two-way radio

Use Reading Skills

Analyze Cause and Effect Have students pause in their reading. Ask: "What has happened to the residents of Maple Street, and why?" (They have been frightened out of their senses. Because of their mounting fear, they now all suspect one another.) **D**

Analyze Literature

Stereotype Have students explain how Steve's description of the aliens fits the stereotype of invaders from outer space, and how that stereotype was probably formed. (Beings from outer space are often depicted with green skin and bizarre features. They come to Earth with "evil intentions." This image has been popularized in stories, comic books, movies, and television.) **E**

History Connection

Space Travel Space exploration in the late 1950s and early 1960s changed people's view of Earth and what lay beyond its boundaries. With humans traveling into space, the idea of visitors from other worlds traveling to Earth, while not probable, seemed less impossible. Science fiction writers echoed this new fear of alien invaders in films such as *Invasion of the Body Snatchers* and television programs such as *The Twilight Zone*.

Vocabulary Skills

Idioms

Remind students that they use idioms in their ordinary speech all the time. To make characters' speech sound as realistic and natural as possible, playwrights often use idioms in dialogue. Remind students that an idiom is an expression that has a meaning beyond the literal meaning of the individual words. For example, when Steve asks Charlie why he's suddenly "so dense," he's really asking him why he's being so stubborn and refusing to think reasonably.

Have students find and interpret other idioms in the play. Some idioms they might identify are: "too close for my money," "cut through (the back yard)," "all straightened out," "you better not," "no dice," and "nothing of the sort."

Use Reading Skills

Use Context Clues Remind students that they can use synonyms and antonyms as context clues. Have students find a synonym and an antonym in the surrounding text that suggest the meaning of *menace*. (Students can use *dangerous* and *safe* to figure out that a menace is someone or something dangerous to others.) **Ⓐ**

Use Reading Strategies

Visualize Have students visualize this scene. What do they hear, see, and feel? (Sounds are the clickety-clack of footsteps and a woman crying out. A shadowy figure walks toward the people as a woman grabs her son. They should feel tension and fear.) **Ⓑ**

Use Reading Skills

Draw Conclusions Ask students who they think the shadowy figure is. (It is probably a neighbor, because that makes sense, but it could be a stranger or, as the people believe, a creature from outer space.) **Ⓒ**

CHARLIE. Look, buddy, you can't afford to—

STEVE. [*Interrupting.*] Charlie, don't tell me what I can afford! And stop telling me who's dangerous and who isn't and who's safe and who's a menace. [*He turns to the group and shouts.*] And you're with him, too—all of you! You're standing here all set to crucify—all set to find a scapegoat[13]—all desperate to point some kind of a finger at a neighbor! Well now look, friends, the only thing that's gonna happen is that we'll eat each other up alive—

He stops abruptly as CHARLIE *suddenly grabs his arm.*

CHARLIE. [*In a hushed voice.*] That's not the only thing that can happen to us.

Cut to a long shot looking down the street. A figure has suddenly materialized in the gloom and in the silence we can hear the clickety-clack of slow, measured footsteps on concrete as the figure walks slowly toward them. One of the women lets out a stifled cry. The young mother grabs her boy as do a couple of others.

TOMMY. [*Shouting, frightened.*] It's the monster! It's the monster!

Another woman lets out a wail and the people fall back in a group, staring toward the darkness and the approaching figure.

We see a medium group shot of the people as they stand in the shadows watching. DON MARTIN *joins them, carrying a shotgun. He holds it up.*

DON. We may need this.

STEVE. A shotgun? [*He pulls it out of* DON's *hand.*] Good Lord—will anybody think a thought around here? Will you people wise up? What good would a shotgun do against—

Now CHARLIE *pulls the gun from* STEVE's *hand.*

CHARLIE. No more talk, Steve. You're going to talk us into a grave! You'd let whatever's out there walk right over us, wouldn't yuh? Well, some of us won't!

He swings the gun around to point it toward the sidewalk. The dark figure continues to walk toward them.

---

13. **scapegoat.** Person, group, or thing that is unfairly blamed

---

Differentiated Instruction

Reading Proficiency

Some students may need to reread the portion of Act 1 in which Van Horn volunteers to check the power on Floral Street. Encourage them to refresh their memories of what happened earlier in the play, and be sure they understand why Van Horn suddenly appears out of the darkness.

English Language Learning

English learners may struggle with some of the vocabulary in the stage directions, especially adverbs such as *intently, questioningly, desperately, illogically,* and *purposefully.* Suggest that students note which words create problems and have them use a dictionary or work with a partner to find meanings. Students should then write a paragraph that correctly uses these newly acquired words.

STEVE. [*Slowly looks up.*] It's Pete Van Horn.

DON. [*In a hushed voice.*] Pete Van Horn! He was just gonna go over to the next block to see if the power was on—

WOMAN. You killed him, Charlie. You shot him dead!

CHARLIE. [*Looks around at the circle of faces, his eyes frightened, his face contorted.*] But...but I didn't know who he was. I certainly didn't know who he was. He comes walkin' out of the darkness—how am I supposed to know who he was? [*He grabs* STEVE.] Steve—you know why I shot! How was I supposed to know he wasn't a monster or something? [*He grabs* DON *now.*] We're all scared of the same thing. I was just tryin' to...tryin' to protect my home, that's all! Look, all of you, that's all I was tryin' to do. [*He looks down wildly at the body.*] I didn't know it was somebody we knew! I didn't know—

There's a sudden hush and then an intake of breath. We see a medium shot of the living room window of CHARLIE's *house. The window is not lit, but suddenly the house lights come on behind it.*

WOMAN. [*In a very hushed voice.*] Charlie... Charlie...the lights just went on in your house. Why did the lights just go on?

DON. What about it, Charlie? How come you're the only one with lights now?

GOODMAN. That's what I'd like to know. [*A pause as they all stare toward* CHARLIE.]

GOODMAN. You were so quick to kill, Charlie, and you were so quick to tell us who we had to be careful of. Well, maybe you had to kill. Maybe Peter there was trying to tell us something. Maybe he'd found out something and came back to tell us who there was amongst us we should watch out for—

The group stands there, fearful, apprehensive, mothers clutching children, men standing in front of wives. CHARLIE *slowly raises the gun. As the figure gets closer and closer he suddenly pulls the trigger. The sound of it explodes in the stillness. There is a long angle shot looking down at the figure, who suddenly lets out a small cry, stumbles forward onto his knees and then falls forward on his face.* DON, CHARLIE, *and* STEVE *race forward over to him.* STEVE *is there first and turns the man over. Now the crowd gathers around them.*

D

E

Grammar Skills

Apostrophes
Remind students to use apostrophes to form the possessive of nouns and to form contractions. For example,

Possessive: The lights went on in Charlie's house.

Contraction: Charlie swore he didn't know what was happening.

Have students add the missing apostrophes.

1. The residents of Maple Street couldnt recognize the truth. (couldn't)
2. Tommys story wasnt believable, yet the days events have made everyone nervous. (Tommy's, wasn't, day's)
3. Accusations have fueled the peoples anger. (people's)
4. A mans dead body is on the sidewalk, but whos really to blame? (man's, who's)

Analyze Literature
Characterization Have students tell you how Charlie's role has changed. (He has changed from accuser to accused.) **A**

Use Reading Skills
Author's Purpose Ask students what they think Serling wants readers and viewers to understand about fear. (He probably wants them to understand that fear can make people act irrationally and violently.) **B**

Analyze Literature
Motivation Ask students why Charlie says he knows who the monster is. (He wants to divert the crowd's anger and keep them from attacking him.) **C**

Use Reading Strategies
Make Inferences Have students infer why Charlie accuses Tommy. (Tommy started the story about invaders from outer space. Charlie probably doesn't really believe it's Tommy, but because Tommy started the story, maybe the crowd will turn on Tommy and leave Charlie alone.) **D**

CHARLIE *backs away from the group, his eyes wide with fright.*

CHARLIE. No…no…it's nothing of the sort! I don't know why the lights are on. I swear I don't. Somebody's pulling a gag or something.

He bumps against STEVE, *who grabs him and whirls him around.*

STEVE. A gag? A gag? Charlie, there's a dead man on the sidewalk and you killed him! Does this thing look like a gag to you?

CHARLIE *breaks away and screams as he runs toward his house.*

A **CHARLIE.** No! No! Please!

A man breaks away from the crowd to chase CHARLIE.

B *We see a long angle shot looking down as the man tackles* CHARLIE *and lands on top of him. The other people start to run toward them.* CHARLIE *is up on his feet, breaks away from the other man's grasp, lands a couple of desperate punches that push the man aside. Then he forces his way, fighting, through the crowd to once again break free, jumps up on his front porch. A rock thrown from the group smashes a window alongside of him, the broken glass flying past him. A couple of pieces cut him. He stands there perspiring, rumpled, blood running down from a cut on the cheek. His wife breaks away from the group to throw herself into his arms. He buries his face against her. We can see the crowd converging on the porch now.*

VOICES.

It must have been him.

He's the one.

We got to get Charlie.

Another rock lands on the porch. Now CHARLIE *pushes his wife behind him, facing the group.*

C **CHARLIE.** Look, look I swear to you…it isn't me…but I do know who it is…I swear to you, I do know who it is. I know who the monster is here. I know who it is that doesn't belong. I swear to you I know.

GOODMAN. [*Shouting.*] What are you waiting for?

WOMAN. [*Shouting.*] Come on, Charlie, come on.

MAN ONE. [*Shouting.*] Who is it, Charlie, tell us!

DON. [*Pushing his way to the front of the crowd.*] All right, Charlie, let's hear it!

CHARLIE'S *eyes dart around wildly.*

CHARLIE. It's…it's…

MAN TWO. [*Screaming.*] Go ahead, Charlie, tell us.

D **CHARLIE.** It's…it's the kid. It's Tommy. He's the one!

There's a gasp from the crowd as we cut to a shot of SALLY *holding her son* TOMMY. *The boy at first doesn't understand and then, realizing the eyes are all on him, buries his face against his mother.*

SALLY. [*Backs away.*] That's crazy! That's crazy! He's a little boy.

WOMAN. But he knew! He was the only one who knew! He told us all about it. Well, how did he know? How could he have known?

The various people take this up and repeat the question aloud.

VOICES.

How could he know?

Differentiated Instruction

Auditory and Kinesthetic Learning
Some students may develop a deeper grasp of the final collapse of the crowd if they hear that portion of the play read aloud. Ask for volunteers to reenact the play, from the point when Charlie says "Look, look I swear to you . . ." until Don says, "It's Charlie. He's the one." Tell readers to use appropriate oral and nonverbal expression, using the stage directions as a guide.

Who told him?

Make the kid answer.

Don. It was Charlie who killed old man Van Horn.

Woman. But it was the kid here who knew what was going to happen all the time. He was the one who knew!

We see a close-up of Steve.

Steve. Are you all gone crazy? [*Pause as he looks about.*] Stop. **E**

A fist crashes at Steve's *face, staggering him back out of the frame of the picture.*

There are several close camera shots suggesting the coming of violence. A hand fires a rifle. A fist clenches. A hand grabs the hammer from Van Horn's *body, etc. Meanwhile, we hear the following lines.*

Don. Charlie has to be the one—Where's my rifle—

Woman. Les Goodman's the one. His car started! Let's wreck it.

Mrs. Goodman. What about Steve's radio— He's the one that called them—

Mrs. Goodman. Smash the radio. Get me a hammer. Get me something.

Steve. Stop—Stop—

Charlie. Where's that kid—Let's get him.

Man One. Get Steve—Get Charlie—They're working together.

The crowd starts to converge around the mother, who grabs the child and starts to run with him. The crowd starts to follow, at first walking fast, and then running after him.

We see a full shot of the street as suddenly Charlie's *lights go off and the lights in another house go on. They stay on for a moment, then*

from across the street other lights go on and then off again.

Man One. [*Shouting.*] It isn't the kid…it's Bob Weaver's house.

Woman. It isn't Bob Weaver's house. It's Don Martin's place.

Charlie. I tell you it's the kid.

Don. It's Charlie. He's the one.

We move into a series of close-ups of various people as they shout, accuse, scream, interspersing these shots with shots of houses as the lights go on and off, and then slowly in the middle of this nightmarish morass[14] of sight and sound the camera starts to pull away, until once again we've reached the opening shot looking at the Maple Street sign from high above.

The camera continues to move away until we dissolve to a shot looking toward the metal side of a space craft, which sits shrouded in darkness. An open door throws out a beam of light from the illuminated interior. Two figures silhouetted against the bright lights appear. We get only a vague feeling of form, but nothing more explicit than that.

Figure One. Understand the procedure now? Just stop a few of their machines and radios and telephones and lawn mowers…throw them into darkness for a few hours, and then you just sit back and watch the pattern. **F**

Figure Two. And this pattern is always the same?

Figure One. With few variations. They pick the most dangerous enemy they can find… and it's themselves. And all we need do is sit back…and watch.

Figure Two. Then I take it this place…this

---

14. **morass.** Complicated or bewildering situation

Teach the Selection

Analyze Literature
Characterization Challenge students to explain what Steve's character has represented throughout the play. (He has consistently represented reason and calm.) **E**

Analyze Literature
Irony Challenge students to explain the irony in the final twist of the plot. (People feared that a spaceship had landed in their neighborhood. That fear was correct, but ironically, the aliens didn't do anything. The people destroyed themselves.) **F**

Analyze Literature
Stereotype Point out that Maple Street fits the stereotype of a suburban neighborhood at the beginning of the play. Have students describe it, and then have them tell how the events in the story challenge that stereotype. (Maple Street is at first quiet and serene, an apparently ideal suburban neighborhood where children play safely in the street and neighbors are friends. At the end of the play, the neighbors no longer trust each other; one has shot and killed another; fear and bigotry have taken over; and no one feels safe.)

Reading Skills

Compare and Contrast
Point out to students that a play script and a screenplay are similar in format and design. For example, both begin with a list of characters. Have students identify similarities between the screenplay for "The Monsters Are Due on Maple Street" and the script for one of the other dramas in this unit, such as "A Defenseless Creature" by Neil Simon or *Let Me Hear You Whisper* by Paul Zindel. Suggest that students record the similarities in a list. Ask students how having read other scripts helped them know how to read the screenplay for "The Monsters Are Due on Maple Street."

Cultural Connection

Fallout Shelters By the early 1960s, the United States and the former Soviet Union were in the midst of the Cold War. Fear that the Soviets would drop a nuclear bomb on the United States resulted in a general paranoia. Some people responded by building fallout shelters—enclosed spaces that supposedly would protect people from radioactive fallout after a nuclear explosion. **A**

Answer: Answers will vary. Many will say prejudice or ignorance causes people to reach such conclusions.

Analyze and Extend

1. (a) He is singled out because he takes late-night walks and his car starts by itself. (b) He is singled out because he is different.

2. (a) Many would have tried harder to establish the facts of the situation. (b) Most would feel frightened.

3. Students may say this screenplay is an indictment of prejudice.

Rubric for Expository Writing

You can adapt this as a checklist for students to use as they write.

☐ Does the analysis include a thesis statement?

☐ Does the analysis include evidence from the screenplay?

☐ Does the analysis describe the impact of the surprise ending?

Maple Street…is not unique.

FIGURE ONE. [*Shaking his head.*] By no means. Their world is full of Maple Streets. And we'll go from one to the other and let them destroy themselves. One to the other…one to the other…one to the other—

Now the camera pans up for a shot of the starry sky and over this we hear the NARRATOR'S VOICE.

A **NARRATOR'S VOICE.** The tools of conquest do not necessarily come with bombs and

A explosions and fallout. There are weapons that are simply thoughts, attitudes, prejudices—to be found only in the minds of men. For the record, prejudices can kill and suspicion can destroy and a thoughtless frightened search for a scapegoat has a fallout all its own for the children…and the children yet unborn. [*A pause.*] And the pity of it is… that these things cannot be confined to…The Twilight Zone! ❖

 How do you think the characters felt being unfairly judged or threatened? Why do people sometimes reach unfair or dangerous conclusions?

Analyze and Extend

1. (a) Why is Les Goodman singled out in the first act? (b) What does this suggest?

2. (a) In what ways would you have acted differently from the residents of Maple Street? (b) In what ways would you have acted or felt the same?

3. Serling often incorporated social and political commentary into his work. Describe the social or political comment that this screenplay makes.

Expository Writing What is the effect of the ending of this screenplay? Does it lessen or enhance the overall impact of the screenplay? How does it affect the theme? Write a short

literary analysis of "The Monsters Are Due on Maple Street" in which you analyze and evaluate the conclusion. Be sure to include a thesis statement and evidence from the text in support of your claims. When you are finished, present your paper to the class.

Critical Literacy Gather into small groups to role-play characters from the screenplay. One member should act as a reporter, while others should choose the characters they would like to play. As a group, generate a list of questions that the reporter will ask. Then act out interviews based on these questions.

Go to **www.mirrorsandwindows.com** for more.

Differentiated Instruction

Enrichment

Encourage students to work independently or with classmates to write a one-act screenplay for an episode of *The Twilight Zone.*

- Suggest that students view several episodes of *The Twilight Zone,* which are readily available on videotape and DVD.
- Tell students to notice how Serling used the elements of science fiction to address problems faced by ordinary Americans.

- Encourage students to think of a problem plaguing people today and to use that problem as a starting point for the story.
- Students can use "The Monsters Are Due on Maple Street" as a guide for formatting the screenplay.

For Your Reading List

The Jumbo Book of Drama
by Deborah Dunleavy

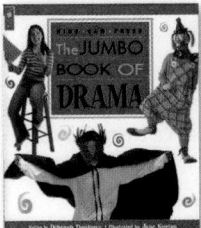

This book is an introduction to all aspects of the theater, including drama, comedy, and tragedy. Dunleavy has broken the book up into four "Acts." Act 1 introduces physical movement; Act 2 focuses on the uses of the voice; Act 3 investigates comedy and tragedy; and Act 4 looks at other aspects of the theater, such as directing, lights, set design, and costumes. Dunleavy has also included many engaging activities, exercises, and scripts for young actors.

Plays from Hispanic Tales
by Barbara Winther

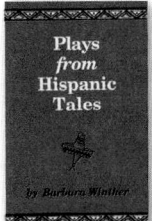

These one-act plays are based on Hispanic folk tales and legends, including trickster tales, a ghost story, and tales on the themes of honor and honesty. These clever and lively tales come from Aztec and Mayan culture, South and Central America, Spain, and the Caribbean. An introduction to each play gives background information on the story and how it fits into Hispanic folklore.

Shakespeare's Theater
by Jacqueline Morley

Full-color illustrations of Shakespeare's Globe Theatre dominate this book about the origins of English theater. Key elements in each picture are magnified with inset illustrations. Quotes from Shakespeare's plays and detailed color artwork throughout enhance this fascinating look at Elizabethan theater.

Plays of Black Americans: The Black Experience in America, Dramatized for Young People
by Sylvia E. Kamerman

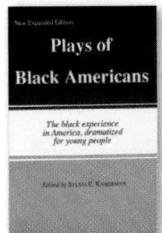

This collection of eleven plays, including plays about Martin Luther King, Jr., Langston Hughes, Abraham Lincoln, and the abolitionist movement, focuses on important moments in African-American history. These short plays offer a creative and unusual way of presenting the contributions of famous individuals to American history.

Greek Theatre
by Stewart Ross

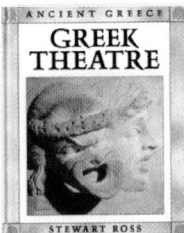

This introduction to ancient Greek theater opens with the preparations for a performance of *Oedipus the King*. A description of the early history of Greek drama follows and includes theater festivals, set design, actors and choruses, and biographical sketches of Greek playwrights. Color photographs of ancient sites and artifacts illustrate the text.

Seattle Children's Theatre: Six Plays for Young Audiences
by Marisa Smith

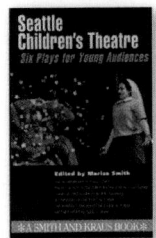

These plays focus on young people searching for their places in the world. Plays include a work based on the memoirs of Joyce Simmons—a Native American woman who was forced to leave her family and attend an off-reservation boarding school—and an adaptation of the classic story *Anne of Green Gables*.

Independent Reading Activity

Dramas are provocative readings for student Literature Circles. Create groups of five or six students, in combinations you think will have fruitful discussions. Ask each group to choose a short drama from one of the collections here or from another collection. They may wish to consult a librarian. Allow ample time for students to collaborate on their group choices.

When a group has chosen its play, help members locate enough copies for everyone to read. Give groups a week to read the play outside of class. Then allow Literature Circles to meet during class. Encourage them to devise a focus question for their discussions, or prompt them with this question: "How is the play relevant to daily life in the modern world?"

See the Skills lesson below for how students can establish their own rules of etiquette. Tell students to reflect on their experiences once they conclude the group discussion.

▶ EMC E-Library
The EMC E-Library contains over twenty thousand pages of literary classics that students may read independently. An Electronic Library Guide provides teaching suggestions, enrichment activities, and reading strategy guidesheets.

Program Resources

EMC Access Editions
For additional independent reading, you may wish to refer students to one of EMC's Access Edition titles such as Mildred D. Taylor's *Roll of Thunder, Hear My Cry*. Each Access Edition contains a thorough study apparatus, including background information, literal comprehension questions, footnotes, vocabulary definitions, critical thinking questions, and related projects and activities. An Assessment Manual offering worksheets and exams is available for each Access Edition.

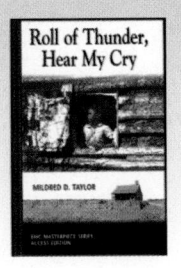

Common Core State Standards
Reading Literature
RL.10
Reading Informational
RI.10

Objectives

Participating in this lesson will help students write a persuasive essay that has

- an effective introduction
- a clear thesis statement
- a clear and logical organizational pattern
- evidence that supports the thesis
- an effective conclusion that restates the thesis and adds an insight

Launch the Lesson

Tell students to imagine they have to prepare for a debate on the following resolution: "The school day should start and end two hours later than it does right now." Divide the class into two groups, one arguing for the resolution and one arguing against it. Ask groups to brainstorm for three minutes on arguments they would use to win people to their side. Then convene the class and ask volunteers to explain whether it was easy or difficult to come up with arguments. After several comments from students, tell the class that now they will learn how to draft convincing arguments to win people over, that is, to persuade.

Program Resources

Additional writing workshops are available in *Exceeding the Standards: Writing.*

Common Core State Standards

Writing
W.1, W.4, W.5, W.6, W.10

Writing Workshop

Persuasive Writing

Persuasive Essay

Reading and Writing

In Shakespeare's "St. Crispian's Day Speech," King Henry tries to persuade his troops that they will be seen as heroes for their participation in the battle of Agincourt. In your own life, you have probably tried to persuade parents, family members, teachers, or friends to agree with a point of view or to take a specific action.

In this workshop, you will learn how to write a persuasive essay. This is an expository essay in which you try to convince your audience to do or believe something. In a **persuasive essay,** you can appeal to the logic and emotion of your audience, use persuasive techniques, and address opposing viewpoints in a counterargument. The following summary includes a rubric, that is, a set of standards by which you judge your work to determine whether or not you were successful in the final product. You will use the rubric in both drafting and revising your essay.

Assignment: Write a persuasive essay in which I try to win others to my point of view.

Goal: To present my topic clearly and convincingly to my audience.

Strategy: Present evidence for my point of view through persuasive techniques.

Writing Rubric: My persuasive essay should include the following:

- an introduction that grabs the reader's attention, that includes a question or a quotation, or that connects to a common human experience
- a thesis statement in the introduction that clearly presents my argument or point of view
- a clear and logical organizational pattern
- evidence, such as reasons, facts, and examples, to support my thesis
- an effective conclusion that restates my thesis and adds a final insight

What Great Writers Do

William Shakespeare, (1564–1616), was a well-known English dramatist and the author of plays such as Romeo and Juliet, Hamlet, *and* Othello. *Many sayings are attributed to him. Here is what he said about the power of words to influence. How might this saying apply to your own persuasive writing?*

"Strong words make strong reasons."

Words in Use

Teaching Words

attributed, 710
influence, 710
anticipate, 711
potential, 712
supportive, 712
annotations, 712
impact, 714

KEY TERMS

EXPOSITORY ESSAY, 710
PERSUASIVE ESSAY, 710
RUBRIC, 710
INTRODUCTION, 710
THESIS, 710
ORGANIZATIONAL PATTERN, 710
EVIDENCE, 710
CONCLUSION, 710
TOPIC, 711
ORDER OF IMPORTANCE, 712
COUNTERARGUMENT, 712
AUDIENCE, 712

PEER REVIEW, 713
PARALLEL, 714
ADJECTIVE, 714
ADVERB, 714
POSITIVE FORM, 714
COMPARAGIVE FORM, 714
SUPERLATIVE FORM, 714
PROOFREADING, 714
PUNCTUATION, 714
GRAMMAR, 714
CAPITALIZATION, 714
SPELLING, 714

1. PREWRITE

Choosing Your Topic

A persuasive essay should be on a topic about which you feel strongly. Consider your school or community. What kinds of local issues affect you? What would you change? Is there something that might change that you would want to remain the same? Ask yourself questions to choose an appropriate and interesting topic for your persuasive essay.

1. Does this topic interest a lot of people?
2. How do I feel about this topic?
3. Can I find enough information on the topic?
4. Is this topic debatable?

The answers to these questions will help you determine if you can and should write about a particular topic. Use the questions to explore a variety of topics.

Gathering Information

Once you have your topic, gather details about it. For instance, if your topic is on the use of cell phones in school, gather facts and examples to support your position. Finding out as much information as possible on your topic will help strengthen your position and help you anticipate counterarguments. Note that your original position on the topic may change as you gather more and more information. This is acceptable. Just be sure that you have enough evidence to support your position. You may want to use a graphic organizer like this one to help you write.

Cell Phones in School

Pros	Cons
• helpful in an emergency	• distracting
• keeps parents informed of students' whereabouts	• some students use them to play games or cheat
• convenient	•
•	

Keep in mind that if your pros and cons are nearly equal in number, you may not be able to make a strong argument. Revise your topic as necessary to make sure you can argue convincingly for one side or the other.

Determining Your Thesis Statement

Once you choose a topic and gather enough information, determine your thesis. Your purpose is to persuade your audience of your position, so be sure your thesis is an opinion statement that can be supported logically. See the example below.

It is important that students be allowed to have cell phones in school, as long as they use them responsibly.

Prewrite

Choosing a Topic Caution students to avoid these pitfalls in choosing topics for their essays:

- Don't argue facts. You don't need to persuade people that "cancer is dangerous" or "clean water is important." Search for controversial topics instead.
- Don't argue about preferences. People like different things; they have different tastes. People who prefer milk chocolate, for example, may see your point about how good dark chocolate is, but they will still prefer milk chocolate.
- Don't argue about emotions and beliefs. These things are usually too deep and too personal to analyze.

Anticipating Counterarguments

Reinforce the point that gathering information will help students anticipate counterarguments. Explain that acknowledging alternative views is an element of effective persuasion. As they review the information they gather on their topics, urge students to imagine actual arguments people could make against their positions. Encourage them to make notes on how they could respond to such arguments. (This will be explored in further detail on page 712.)

Reading Skills

Determine Importance of Details

Have students review the Writing Rubric on page 710, focusing on the first bullet. Tell them that as they gather details on their topics, they should remember what they need the details to do, such as to provide a quote for a strong introduction. Ask students to jot down one detail about their topics for each of these purposes:

1. An attention-grabbing fact or statistic
2. An intriguing question
3. An engaging quotation
4. A common human experience

Draft

Organizing Ideas Students may also wish to explore using cause-and-effect, compare-and-contrast, or problem-solution organization patterns. These strategies have been covered earlier in the book. For example, you can refer to teacher page 397 for a short discussion of problem-solution organization, and point students to page 406 for an exercise in writing a problem-solution essay.

Putting Thoughts on Paper Tell students that one strategy for beginning a persuasive essay is to establish rapport with the reader. They can achieve this by establishing some common ground—a point on which most people agree. Model this technique: "I'm going to write an essay arguing that all our schools should teach music. I know some people think music instruction should be optional. I'll open with a quote: 'To paraphrase Henry Wadsworth Longfellow, Music is the language of humanity.'"

What Great Writers Do

Encourage students to be careful to support their claims with logical arguments. Thomas Jefferson wrote:

In a republican nation, whose citizens are to be led by reason and persuasion and not by force, the art of reasoning becomes of first importance.

---

2. DRAFT

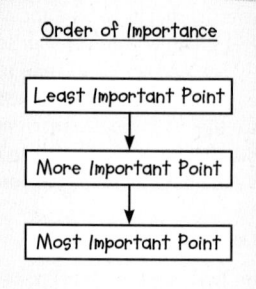

Organizing Ideas

Review the information you gathered to write your essay. Organize your ideas to make your meaning clear and to present a convincing argument to your audience. A logical organization pattern for a persuasive essay is **order of importance.** For example, you might state your most important point first to draw in your reader. Or you might choose to begin with a less important point and save your strongest point for the end. Stating your most important point last leaves your audience with a strong impression of your argument. Determine which order better fits your argument.

Order of Importance

- Least Important Point
  ↓
- More Important Point
  ↓
- Most Important Point

Putting Your Thoughts on Paper

An essay has three basic parts: an introduction, a body, and a conclusion. Create a plan for your persuasive essay like the one on the right. Use your organizational plan as you begin drafting.

Begin with an effective introduction. Remember, you want to grab your reader's attention right away. The opening of your essay should make your reader want to pay close attention to what you have written about the topic. As you draft your essay, remember it is only the first draft. Write your thoughts and refine them later. Record your main ideas and supporting evidence and organize these ideas in a logical and effective way. You can fix errors in grammar, spelling, and punctuation later.

Introduction
- Grab the reader's attention right away with an interesting opener.
- State the position in a clear thesis.

Body
- In the topic sentence of each body paragraph, state a reason or main point.
- In supporting sentences, give supporting evidence.
- Anticipate and respond to counterarguments.

Conclusion
- Restate the thesis in a new way.
- Add an insight.

Addressing Counterarguments

In persuasive essays, writers use various techniques to convince an audience of their point of view or position on a topic. One method is to anticipate potential counterarguments and to respond to them. When a writer does this, he or she shows that both sides of the argument have been considered. The writer should show through supportive facts and details why his or her point of view should be seen as the correct one.

When addressing a counterargument, keep your audience in mind. Try to anticipate opposing points, address them, and point out the flaws in those arguments. Keep your tone respectful, but make your position clear. Your goal is to show your audience that your position is the most logical one.

Differentiated Instruction

Enrichment

Several approaches to teaching persuasive writing refer to the ancient art of rhetoric, or using language to please and persuade. One foundation of rhetoric is called the "three appeals": *logos, ethos,* and *pathos.* These Greek words refer to reason, to credibility of the speaker, and to emotion. Have students explore the three terms using the library and Internet resources. Then ask them to summarize for the whole class what they learned and how it applies to writing a persuasive essay.

3. REVISE

Evaluating Your Draft

Read over your draft and note strengths and weaknesses. Correct these as best you can. To get a better evaluation, conduct a **peer review** with a classmate. Have him or her look over what you have written and discuss ways you can improve your paper. Use the Revising Checklist.

Below is part of a draft. The annotations to the right indicate the reasons for the revisions.

Revising Checklist

☐ Does the introduction grab the reader's attention?

☐ Does the thesis present the argument?

☐ Is there a clear organizational pattern?

☐ Is the thesis supported with evidence?

Imagine you are at school after hours. Practice ran long, and the last bus has gone. You have no phone. No one has a phone. The school is locked and it's getting late. What do you do? By now, most of the school knows about the new rule the school board is considering that would ban all cell phone use for students. If passed, this decision would make the school less safe for students. The school board is making a ~~ridiculous~~ hasty decision based on a few minor incidents. *It is important that students be allowed to have cell phones in school, as long as they use them responsibly.*

Many students are involved in after-school activities. Though the school has a reliable bus service, sometimes activities run long. The buses run on a schedule, and if students miss the final bus, they are stuck. *With a cell phone, students can call a parent or other adult to pick them up or give them permission to go to a friend's house.* Cell phones offer that convenience and that added protection. Parents feel better knowing that their children can keep in touch.

> *Grab the audience's attention in the introduction.*

> *Maintain a respectful tone.*

> *Include a clear thesis statement.*

> *Use reasons and evidence to support the argument.*

Revise

Evaluating a Draft Give students the following tips for delivering and receiving constructive criticism.

Delivering Criticism

- **Be focused.** Concentrate on the introduction, the organization, and transitions. Leave spelling and punctuation for later.
- **Be positive.** Respect the writer's feelings and writing efforts.
- **Be specific.** Give concrete ideas for improving the essay.

Receiving Criticism

- **Ask questions.** Make sure you understand your reviewer's comments. Ask your reviewer to clarify comments and suggestions if necessary.
- **Be selective.** Accept your reviewer's time and suggestions graciously. When you revise your essay, you can use just some — or none — of the suggestions.

TEACHING NOTE

Defining Persuasive Techniques

Provide students with a list of persuasive techniques, including any you have covered in class such as analogy, appeals to authority, and hyperbole. Then ask students to work in pairs and assign each pair a technique to define. Ask each pair to turn its definition into a question. Model this format: "What persuasive technique involves exaggerating to make a point?"

Gather as a class. Have each pair ask its question, and have the rest of the class name the persuasive technique that answers the question.

Writing Skills

Rhetorical Devices

An Internet search can yield scores of rhetorical devices. Students are already familiar with those that are also figures of speech and sound devices, such as hyperbole, metaphor, personification, simile, and various types of repetition. Have students identify the "rhetorical device" in each of these sentences and say how it might be persuasive.

1. Without music our children will lose the full range of their voices. (hyperbole)
2. Music soothes the fearful and cheers the lonely. (personification)
3. Babies smile at music, toddlers smile at music, children smile at music, commuters smile at music, and grandparents smile at music. (repetition)

⊳ Edit and Proofread

Students may want to use proofreader's marks when correcting their work. Refer them to the Language Arts Handbook Writing Section 4.1, Proofreader's Symbols.

What Great Writers Do

Tell students that diction—the choice of words—is considered a rhetorical device. Share this statement by novelist Joseph Conrad and ask if they agree or disagree, and why:

He who wants to persuade should put his trust not in the right argument, but in the right word. The power of sound has always been greater than the power of sense.

⊳ Publish and Present

Before students begin their final versions, they might benefit from reading the Language Arts Handbook Writing 4.1, Writing Follow-up.

4. EDIT AND PROOFREAD

Focus: Parallel Structure

When sentences or parts of a sentence are **parallel,** they have the same grammatical structure. For example, all verbs are in the same tense. Parallel structure makes ideas clearer and can add impact or emphasis to your writing. Note the correction below.

> **Not parallel:**
> Whether a student walks to school, rides the bus, or will get a ride, a cell phone can come in handy.

> **Corrected:**
> Whether a student walks to school, rides the bus, or <u>gets</u> a ride, a cell phone can come in handy.

Reread your draft and edit it to make like ideas parallel. In persuasive writing, parallel structure is an effective way to emphasize points and help make them memorable to your audience.

Focus: Comparative and Superlative

There are three forms of adjectives and adverbs: positive, comparative, and superlative. The form of an adjective or adverb is often changed to show the degree to which a certain quality is present.

In the sentence *Cell phones are an important part of life*, the word *important* is used in the **positive form.** It focuses on one thing—cell phones—without comparing them to anything else.

To use the **comparative form,** two things need to be compared, as in *Cell phones are more important than gym shoes.* Cell phones and gym shoes are being compared. The word *more* is used with the word *important* to show this comparison.

The **superlative form** compares three or more things, such as in *Cell phones are the most important items a student can carry.* The use of the word *most* with the word *important* compares cell phones with everything else a student can carry.

Most adjectives and adverbs that have one syllable, and some that have two syllables, form their comparative and superlative degrees by adding *-er* or *-est.* Other two-syllable modifiers and all modifiers of more than two syllables use *more* and *most.*

Proofreading

Correct Final Errors The purpose of proofreading is to find errors you have made in punctuation, grammar, capitalization, and spelling. Use proofreader's marks to highlight any errors. (See the Language Arts Handbook, section 4.1, for a list of proofreader's symbols.)

5. PUBLISH AND PRESENT

Final Draft

Submit Your Work Rewrite your essay to make a final draft. If it is handwritten, make sure the essay is neat and legible. If you are using a word processing program, double-space your paper and use a readable font or typeface. Whether you are submitting your work to your teacher or someone else, be sure to check about presentation guidelines.

Differentiated Instruction

Auditory Learning

Set up peer review partnerships that pair auditory learners with other readers. Have the students read their drafts to each other, and then brainstorm about sound devices that could make the arguments more memorable. Encourage both students to incorporate sound devices into their final drafts.

English Language Learning

Ask students to give an oral presentation of their persuasive essays. English language learners should pay particular attention to the grammatical structures they used within their essays.

Student Model

Cell Phones for Students
by Kyla Weatherspoon

Imagine you are at school after hours. Practice ran long, and the last bus has gone. You have no phone. No one has a phone. The school is locked and it's getting late. What do you do? By now, most of the school knows about the new rule the school board is considering that would ban all cell phone use for students. If passed, this decision would make the school less safe for students. The school board is making a hasty decision based on a few minor incidents. Cell phones are important to our health and welfare. It is important that students be allowed to have cell phones in school, as long as they use them responsibly.

> *Includes an attention-grabbing opener*
>
> *States the position in a clear thesis*

Many students are involved in after-school activities. Though the school has a reliable bus service, sometimes activities run long. The buses run on a schedule, and if students miss the final bus, they are stuck. With a cell phone, students can call a parent or other adult to pick them up or give them permission to go to a friend's house. Cell phones offer that convenience and that added protection. Parents feel better knowing that their children can keep in touch.

Cell phones are also good to have in case of an emergency. Whether a student walks to school, rides the bus, or gets a ride, a cell phone can come in handy. Things can happen when you least expect them. We live in a state that gets a lot of snow in the winter. Sometimes buses get stuck or break down due to the weather. Having a cell phone allows students to call for help or let a parent or guardian know they will not be returning home on time. If there is a problem at school, many parents appreciate a call from their children telling them that they are okay. If there is an emergency at home, parents can leave a text or voice message for their children and let them know any change of plans.

> *States main points in a logical order*
>
> *Includes reasons, facts, and examples to support the argument*

Cell phones can be distracting during class, and some students use them to play games or even cheat on tests. Yet, instead of banning cell phone use entirely, the school board could make and enforce rules regarding when and where cell phones can be used. This would prevent the negative uses of cell phones, while allowing them to keep students safe.

> *Responds to a counterargument*
>
> *Maintains a respectful tone*

Banning cell phones altogether seems like the wrong direction to take. If used responsibly, cell phones can keep students safe. Before the school board makes a decision that could have negative consequences, it should consider a plan that works for everyone.

> *Sums up main points and adds additional insight*

Teach the Workshop

Objectives

Participating in this lesson will help students deliver persuasive presentations that

- open and close strongly
- promote a solid viewpoint
- use valid arguments
- present ideas clearly
- employ persuasive techniques convincingly
- incorporate effective pacing, volume, and nonverbal expression

Launch the Lesson

Enthusiastically tell students how much they will enjoy this workshop, using phrases such as "You're going to love this," "This is going to be so fun," and "You won't want to stop being persuasive." Pause, and then ask students how convincing you were. Lead them to observe that to be persuaded, an audience has to have more to go on than the speaker's enthusiasm. Tell students they will learn more about persuasive presentations now.

For additional details about persuasive techniques and rhetorical devices, see the teacher notes for the Writing Workshop on pages 710–715.

> For more information, see the Language Arts Handbook, Section 7, Speaking & Listening.

Speaking & Listening Workshop

Giving and Actively Listening to Persuasive Presentations

Think of a time when you discussed a controversial issue with a friend or family member. Did you take a position that others disagreed with? How did you try to convince others that your position was correct? In a **persuasive presentation,** you try to influence an audience's beliefs about an issue. When you give and actively listen to persuasive presentations, you participate in an exchange of ideas and attempt to gain support for your perspective.

Planning a Persuasive Presentation

Choose a Topic What particular topic do you feel strongly about? Is there more than one perspective on this topic or issue? Is it controversial? Take time to think through a topic you would like to discuss with an audience. For example, do you feel strongly about the building of a new gymnasium? Should a dog park be built in your neighborhood? Do you think your district should have year-round school or a shorter school week? Select a topic that is of interest to you and about which you can present evidence in support of your claims.

Examine Both Sides Once you select an issue to present, consider as many different perspectives on the issue as possible. Try to anticipate objections to your position that others may raise when you give your presentation. These objections are known as **counterarguments.** Once you have established some counterarguments, consider how you will address them. It may be helpful to make a chart. For example, look at this chart on the issue of a new park.

The Need for a Park

Counterargument	Response
Too many kids in area	Young people good for the community
Dangerous activity	Safe place to play
Young children on equipment	Minimum age limit
Park not regulated	Rules and regulations enforced

Program Resources

To expand upon this workshop lesson, Giving and Actively Listening to Persuasive Presentations, see the *Exceeding the Standards: Speaking and Listening* resource.

Words in Use

Teaching Words
controversial, 716
constructive, 717

KEY TERMS

PERSUASIVE PRESENTATION, 716	FALLACY, 717
	GENERALIZATION, 717
TOPIC, 716	RUBRIC, 717
ANECTDOTE, 717	ACTIVE LISTENING, 717
COUNTERARGUMENT, 716	

Evaluate Evidence and Audience During your presentation, you must appear knowledgeable about your topic. Introduce facts, anecdotes, quotations, and other research in support of your opinions. As you present this information, avoid jargon, or specialized vocabulary with which your audience may not be familiar. Be prepared to answer questions about the information you present.

Avoid Fallacies A **fallacy** is an untruth, an exaggeration of the truth, or an example of faulty logic. A persuasive presentation may present facts, but it is your opinion and interpretation of those facts that you use to convince others. Be careful of using generalizations. When you use words such as *all, everyone, no one,* and *anybody,* you are making a generalization. Generalizations are often misleading. Examine your presentation prior to delivering it and eliminate these kinds of statements.

Evaluating Your Persuasive Presentation

Work with a partner or a peer group to evaluate your persuasive presentations. Provide feedback to each other on what was done well and what still needs work. Continue to be constructive in your comments, offering helpful criticism in a polite and respectful way. Follow the listening and speaking rubrics on this page in order to evaluate each persuasive presentation.

Delivering Your Persuasive Presentation

Begin your presentation with a strong opener. You might begin with a question, a quotation, a visual demonstration, or an interesting anecdote or fact. Sometimes the repetition of a key word or phrase can help keep your audience involved with the main idea of your presentation.

Close with a brief powerful statement to leave your audience something to think about long after you have ended your presentation. You want your point of view to become the point of view of your audience.

Active Listening Active listening is just as important as effective speaking. Pay attention to what the speaker says and react politely, asking questions when appropriate.

Speaking Rubric

Your presentation will be evaluated on these elements:

Content
- ☐ ideas were clearly presented
- ☐ viewpoint was easily understood
- ☐ valid arguments were presented
- ☐ strong opening and closing were included

Delivery and Presentation
- ☐ convincing persuasive techniques
- ☐ effective nonverbal expression
- ☐ appropriate volume and pacing

Listening Rubric

As a peer reviewer or audience member, you should do the following:

- ☐ listen quietly and attentively
- ☐ maintain eye contact with speaker
- ☐ ask appropriate questions
- ☐ (as peer reviewer) provide constructive feedback

Evaluating an Audience

Emphasize the value of developing rapport with an audience. (You can define *rapport* as a relationship based on understanding and sharing the same concerns.) Point out that people are persuaded when they identify with a speaker who has a particular point of view. For a concrete demonstration of relating to different listeners, ask students how they would present their arguments to each of these audiences:
- a group of restaurant workers
- their aunts and uncles
- high-school students
- classmates in a math class

What Great Speakers Do

Dean Rusk, the U.S. Secretary of State under Presidents Kennedy and Johnson, once said:

One of the best ways to persuade others is with your ears—by listening to them.

Rehearsing a Speech

Give students opportunities to practice their presentations alone and with peer reviewers. Offer these tips:
- Set a time limit, such as four or five minutes.
- Make sure your arguments are memorable. This may mean editing explanations and adding repetition or figurative language.
- Ask for feedback. If a listener is not persuaded, find out why.

Differentiated Instruction

Reading Proficiency

Encourage struggling readers to choose topics for which they can use interviews to gather information. Ask them what people are talking about, what gets people worked up, and how they could learn more about the two sides to a hot issue. Prompt students to write out two or three questions that will elicit responses on the topic, and tell them also to work out a note-taking plan before they conduct their interviews. Encourage them to use a graphic organizer, like the one on this page, to record the opinions they hear.

Common Core State Standards

Speaking and Listening
SL.3, SL.4, SL.6

Persuasive Essay

Teach the Workshop

Objectives

Completing this lesson will enable students to

- write a persuasive essay based on a timed writing prompt
- answer standardized test questions that demonstrate revising and editing skills
- answer standardized questions that demonstrate the ability to make inferences from a reading

Timed Writing

Say that standardized tests often ask students to write a response to a prompt in a specified period of time. Give the following tips:

- Read the entire prompt carefully.
- Look for key words in the prompt that tell you what is expected.
- Underline these words or write them on your own notepaper.
- Use the key words to make sure you follow all the instructions.
- Organize. Allow time for planning, writing, and reviewing.
- Before you begin writing, create a rough outline of points to make.
- Write a clear introduction. This will help keep you on track as you write each paragraph.
- If you find yourself running out of time, state your remaining points and add a conclusion.
- Review your completed essay to see if you have responded completely to the instructions.
- Proofread before you turn in your completed essay.

Read the following short excerpt and the writing assignment that follows. Before you begin writing, think carefully about what task the assignment is asking you to perform. Then create an outline to help guide your writing.

from *Braille: The Early Life of Louis Braille* by Lola H. and Coleman A. Jennings

CHARACTERS: LOUIS BRAILLE, a young blind boy who wants to learn to read
BARBIER: Inventor of sonography, a system that represents sounds with dots and dashes punched in paper

LOUIS. I am honored to meet the inventor of sonography.
BARBIER. Ahhh! Then, you have learned my system…and you find it helpful?
LOUIS. [*Hesitantly.*] I think it is a good beginning, Captain…You have done the blind a great service with your invention. But it's very complicated…Each sound is written with too many dots and dashes. It's hard to feel them. And when you write, punching so many dots makes writing very slow…
BARBIER. [*Getting angry.*] This is a note-making system. You don't need periods, commas, and question marks when you write short messages.
LOUIS. But sir, we need a system that we can use for books, too.
BARBIER. Since when have the blind needed to read books? [*Crossing to* PIGNIER.] Are these the hopes you encourage in this school, Headmaster Pignier? I thought you were here to teach trades to the blind. [*To* LOUIS.] Is there anything else?
LOUIS. [*Reluctantly.*] I…can't find a way to write numbers so we can do arithmetic.
BARBIER. [*Exploding.*] I suppose now you want to be bookkeepers! Foolish child, you do sums in your head. Any number too large for that is not for the blind to be concerned with. Good day, young man! [*Starts to exit.*]

Assignment: Barbier believed that the blind should accept their limitations and not aspire to the same things "normal" people do. Plan and write a **persuasive essay** in which you state and support a **thesis** about the value of encouraging all people to succeed. Include **persuasive techniques** and **rhetorical devices**, as well as **counterarguments**.

Rubric for a Persuasive Essay

Make sure students understand that they should follow the instructions *below* the blue rule. Have students use these criteria to evaluate their essays.

- ☐ Does the thesis statement convey a viewpoint about encouraging people to succeed?
- ☐ Do the body paragraphs support the thesis?
- ☐ Does the essay address counterarguments?
- ☐ Does the essay employ persuasive techniques and rhetorical devices?

Common Core State Standards

Writing
W.1

Language
L.4.1f, L.4.3b, L.6.1e

Revising and Editing Skills

The following passage is a draft of a student's essay. The passage contains grammatical and other errors that require correction. Some questions require you to correct specific sentences. Others ask you to identify parts of the essay or to improve the overall organization. Answer each question on a separate sheet of paper.

(1) Drama is a literary form involve dialogue that characters perform. (2) A script contains dialogue spoken by the characters, as well as stage directions. (3) The written text of a drama is called a *script*. (4) One purpose of a script's stage directions is to state clearly what actors should do. (5) Stage directions often include descriptions of the setting; descriptions of the characters' appearance; and directions on how a character should act or move. (6) Stage directions are useful for three things—to visualize a scene, to stage a drama, and to instruct actors. (7) There are two main types of drama. (8) Comedies are humorous plays that end happily. (9) Tragedies, in which the central characters meet an unhappy or disastrous end.

1. Which of the following is the *best* revision of sentence 1?
   A. Drama is a literary form; involve dialogue that characters perform.
   B. Drama is a literary form involving dialogue that characters perform.
   C. Drama is a literary form, involve dialogue that characters perform.
   D. Drama is a literary form to involve dialogue that characters perform.
   E. Drama is a literary form: involve dialogue that characters perform.

2. What change should be made to sentence 2 to improve the paragraph's organization?
   A. Sentence 2 could be moved to the end of the paragraph.
   B. Sentence 2 could be removed.
   C. Sentence 2 could be moved after sentence 3.
   D. Sentence 2 could be moved after sentence 6.
   E. Sentence 2 could be moved to the start of the paragraph.

3. The semicolons in sentence 5 should be replaced with
   A. hyphens.
   B. periods.
   C. dashes.
   D. commas.
   E. colons.

4. The dash in sentence 6 should be replaced with a
   A. hyphen.
   B. period.
   C. semicolon.
   D. question mark.
   E. colon.

5. What error appears in sentence 9?
   A. The sentence is a run-on.
   B. The sentence is a fragment.
   C. The sentence uses incorrect end punctuation.
   D. The sentence lacks a semicolon.
   E. The sentence lacks subject-verb agreement.

6. What change could be made to improve the overall organization of the paragraph?
   A. Move sentence 5 to a separate paragraph.
   B. Move sentence 1 to the end of the paragraph.
   C. Move sentence 2 to a separate paragraph.
   D. Remove sentence 3.
   E. Move sentences 7, 8, and 9 to a separate paragraph.

Teach the Workshop

Revising and Editing Skills
1. B   4. E
2. C   5. B
3. D   6. E

Test-Taking Tip
Preview Questions Tell students that when they take a revising and editing test, it is a good idea to refresh their memories about the skills they will have to use. One way is to study the passage provided before they preview the questions. Use this test as an example. Ask students to read the paragraph and decide how well organized it is. Give students time to note the order in which they would put the numbered sentences for a better organization. Then ask: "What errors did you see right away?" Have students record the number of each sentence that has one or more errors. Finally, have students answer the sample test questions. Afterward, ask them whether activating prior knowledge helped them feel better prepared for the test.

> For more information, see the Language Arts Handbook, Section 8, Test-Taking Skills.

Program Resources

For more study and practice with test-taking skills, see the *Exceeding the Standards: Test Practice* resource:
• ACT Practice Test, pp. 16–19

Words in Use

Teaching Words
sonography, 718
aspire, 718
chancellor, 720
hornrimmed, 720
profound, 720
faultily, 720
context, 721

KEY TERMS

PERSUASIVE ESSAY, 718	**SETTING,** 719	**EXPOSITION,** 721
THESIS, 718	**CHARACTER,** 719	**RISING ACTION,** 721
PERSUASIVE TECHNIQUE, 718	**SCENE,** 719	**RESOLUTION,** 721
REHETORICAL DEVICE, 718	**COMEDIES,** 719	**CLIMAX,** 721
COUNTERARGUMENT, 718	**TRAGEDIES,** 719	**FALLING ACTION,** 721
DRAMA, 719	**SEMICOLON,** 719	**TRAGEDY,** 721
DIALOGUE, 719	**RUN-ON,** 719	**SHAKESPEAREAN DRAMA,** 721
STAGE DIRECTION, 719	**FRAGMENT,** 719	**STRAIGHT DRAMA,** 721
	SUBJECT-VERB AGREEMENT, 719	**GREEK TRAGEDY,** 721
	PLOT, 721	
	MONOLOGUE, 721	
	CONFLICT, 721	

Reading Comprehension Tests

Remind students that reading comprehension tests give a short piece of writing and then ask several questions about it. The questions often ask students to interpret the passage. Urge students to keep the following tips in mind:

- Begin by skimming all the questions.
- Read the passage with the questions in mind. If time permits, read the passage twice before answering any questions.
- Reread the first question carefully.
- Locate the portion of the passage to which the question refers. Read it slowly and carefully.
- Answer the first question.
- Repeat this process to answer all the rest of the questions.

Reading Skills

Carefully read the following passage. Then on a separate piece of paper, answer each question.

from *The Ugly Duckling* by A. A. Milne

CHARACTERS
THE KING
THE QUEEN
THE PRINCESS CAMILLA
5   THE CHANCELLOR
DULCIBELLA
PRINCE SIMON
CARLO

[*The scene is the Throne Room of the Palace; a*
10 *room of many doors, or, if preferred, curtain-*
openings: simply furnished with three thrones for
Their Majesties and Her Royal Highness the
PRINCESS CAMILLA—*in other words, with three*
handsome chairs. At each side is a long seat:
15 *reserved, as it might be, for His Majesty's*
Council (if any), but useful, as today, for other
purposes. The KING *is asleep on his throne with a*
handkerchief over his face. He is a king of any
country from any storybook, in whatever
20 *costume you please. But he should be wearing his*
crown.]

A VOICE. [*Announcing.*] His Excellency the
Chancellor! [*The* CHANCELLOR, *an elderly man*
in hornrimmed spectacles, enters, bowing. The
25 KING *wakes up with a start and removes the*
handkerchief from his face.]

KING. [*With simple dignity.*] I was thinking.
CHANCELLOR. [*Bowing.*] Never, Your Majesty,
was greater need for thought than now.
30 KING. That's what I was thinking. [*He*
struggles into a more dignified position.] Well,
what is it? More trouble?
CHANCELLOR. What we might call the old
trouble, Your Majesty.
35 KING. It's what I was saying last night to the
Queen. "Uneasy lies the head that wears a
crown," was how I put it.
CHANCELLOR. A profound and original

thought, which may well go down to
40 posterity.
KING. You mean it may go down well with
posterity. I hope so. Remind me to tell you
some time of another little thing I said to
Her Majesty: something about a fierce light
45 beating on a throne. Posterity would like
that, too. Well, what is it?
CHANCELLOR. It is in the matter of Her Royal
Highness's wedding.
KING. Oh…yes.
50 CHANCELLOR. As Your Majesty is aware, the
young Prince Simon arrives today to seek
Her Royal Highness's hand in marriage. He
has been traveling in distant lands and, as I
understand, has not—er—has not—
55 KING. You mean he hasn't heard anything.
CHANCELLOR. It is a little difficult to put this
tactfully, Your Majesty.
KING. Do your best, and I will tell you
afterwards how you got on.
60 CHANCELLOR. Let me put it this way. The
Prince Simon will naturally assume that Her
Royal Highness has the customary—so
customary as to be, in my own poor
opinion, slightly monotonous—has what
65 one might call the inevitable—so inevitable
as to be, in my opinion again, almost
mechanical—will assume, that she has the,
as I think of it, faultily faultless, icily regular,
splendidly—
70 KING. What you are trying to say in the
fewest words possible is that my daughter is
not beautiful.
CHANCELLOR. Her beauty is certainly elusive,
Your Majesty.

Differentiated Instruction

English Language Learning

Students will appreciate knowing that the King's two "statements for posterity" allude to things famous people already said. (The first alludes to Shakespeare's *Henry IV, Part II,* and the second to Tennyson's *Idylls of the King.*) Milne intends the allusions to be humorous; the king is offering these borrowed statements as original thoughts. Students may also need help with some of the adjectives in the excerpt.

dignified—proper and respectable, 720
customary—normal or traditional, 720
monotonous—boring and repetitive, 720
inevitable—impossible to avoid, 720
mechanical—done without thinking, 720
elusive—hard to find or hard to catch, 720

1. Lines 1–8 are an example of
   A. plot.
   B. setting.
   C. cast list.
   D. stage directions.
   E. dialogue.

2. Lines 9–21 are an example of
   A. setting.
   B. monologue.
   C. dialogue.
   D. stage directions.
   E. cast list.

3. What is the tone of the exchange between the King and the Chancellor in lines 27–33?
   A. humorous
   B. angry
   C. serious
   D. sad
   E. solemn

4. Lines 33–40 are an example of
   A. setting.
   B. monologue.
   C. dialogue.
   D. stage directions.
   E. cast list.

5. Based on the context, what does the word *posterity* in line 40 mean?
   A. the past
   B. future generations
   C. books
   D. present day
   E. friends

6. What is the tone of lines 50–55?
   A. jolly
   B. peaceful
   C. self-assured
   D. angry
   E. hesitant

7. Based on the context, what does the word *tactfully* in line 57 mean?
   A. quiet
   B. full of confusion
   C. full of humor
   D. showing meanness
   E. showing sensitivity

8. What conflict is introduced in this passage?
   A. the Chancellor's anger
   B. the King's restlessness
   C. the Princess's disappearance
   D. the arrival of the Prince
   E. the Chancellor's plot against the King

9. This excerpt is most likely drawn from the
   A. exposition.
   B. rising action and resolution.
   C. rising action and climax.
   D. climax.
   E. falling action and resolution.

10. Which of the following *best* describes this play?
    A. tragedy
    B. Shakespearean drama
    C. comedy
    D. straight drama
    E. Greek tragedy

Teach the Workshop

Reading Skills

1. C
2. D
3. A
4. C
5. B
6. E
7. E
8. D
9. A
10. C

Test-Taking Skills

Choose the Best Answer

Tell students that a key skill in answering multiple-choice questions is deciding which is the *best* answer available. Note that many times, they will be able to think of good answers to a question. However, not all of those answers will be offered as choices. Model this skill using a question from the sample.

Question 8. The question asks for the conflict introduced in the passage. I think the conflict is that the prince will expect to see a beautiful princess, but the princess is not beautiful. That is not one of the possible answers, though. Of the options offered, the best, or closest, is answer D.

Unit 8 Visual Planning Guide

Planning and Assessment Tools

Annotated Teacher's Edition

Annotated Teacher's Edition
One location for accessing, previewing, and planning for use of all program resources.

EMC Launchpad
Desktop application for accessing, previewing, planning, posting, and grading all program resources. Post personal resources and lessons, and access the E-Lesson Planner, the E-Gradebook, and training modules for computer literacy.

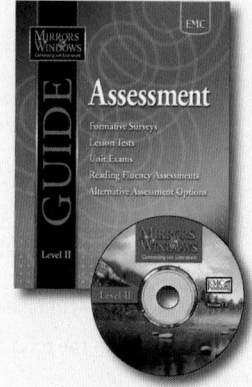

Assessment Guide and ExamView
A variety of assessments are available for this unit in print and electronic forms, including:
- Formative Survey
- Lesson Tests
- Unit Exams
- Alternative Assessment Options
- Reading Fluency Assessments

Meeting the Standards: Unit 8
In addition to lesson-by-lesson resources, *Meeting the Standards* includes the following unit-based resources:
- Unit Study Guide
- Practice Test
- Active Reading Model
- Selection Quizzes

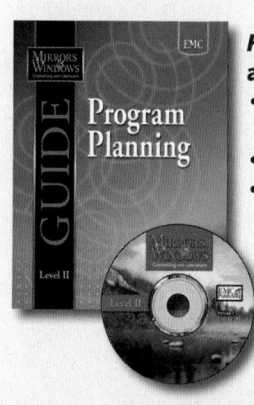

Program Planning Guide and *E-Lesson Planner*
- Lesson Plans for all the selections in the unit
- Core Standards-Based Selections
- Reading Log and Evaluation Forms

The E-Lesson Planner contains fully developed lesson plans and unit resources with an electronic calendar for editing lesson plans.

Technology Tools

Visual Teaching Package
This package contains unit-based lectures, games, art collections, and Writing Workshops in PowerPoint format; included within the EMC Launchpad.

Interactive Student Text on CD
The student textbook on CD includes highlighting, note-taking, bookmarking, and a direct link to the student website, in addition to everything in the student text.

Audio Library
Authentic, dramatic recordings with listening activities expand listening skills and offer additional support for developing readers and English Language Learners.

ETS Online Criterion-Based Essay Grader (Grades 9–12)
Students can use this ETS web-based tool to evaluate their essays online before submitting them for teacher review and final evaluation.

mirrorsandwindows.com
Student and teacher resources, support, references, technology tools, and state-specific standards are available at **mirrorsandwindows.com**. The website is customizable using the EMC Launchpad.

Unit-Based Resources

Exceeding the Standards Unit Resources

Each of the *Exceeding the Standards* resources provides fully developed lessons to help you extend the textbook lessons and to expand upon the themes and skills covered in the unit. You can also download these lessons from **mirrorsandwindows.com**.

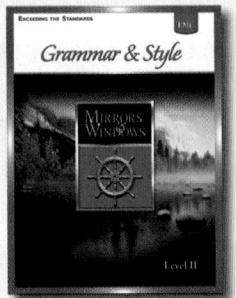

Grammar & Style
This resource contains:
- Five lessons on Common Usage Problems, pp. 186–200
- Three lessons on Building Effective Sentences, pp. 201–210

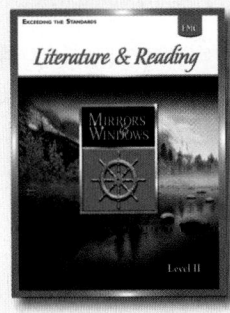

Literature & Reading
This resource contains:
- Read and Discuss Folklore, Superstition, and Science, pp. 21–23

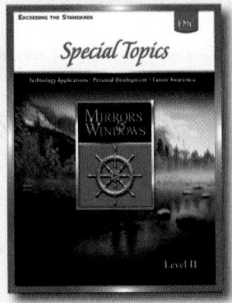

Special Topics
This resource contains:
- Lifelong Learning: Setting Goals: Part 2, pp. 31–32
- Career Skills Development: Conducting an Internet Job Search, pp. 33–35

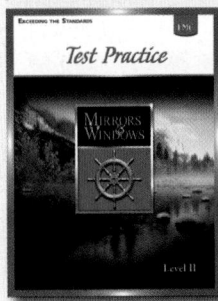

Test Practice
This resource contains:
- SAT Practice Test, pp. 20–23

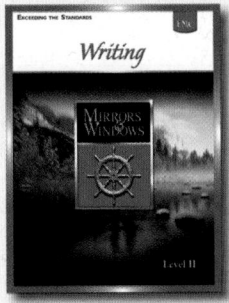

Writing
This resource contains:
- Narrative Writing: Write a Fable, pp. 56–64

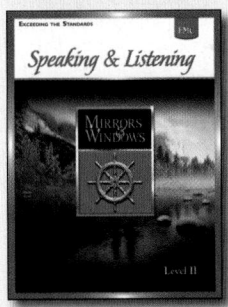

Speaking & Listening
This resource contains the following lesson to expand on the Speaking & Listening Workshop:
- Giving and Actively Listening to Research Presentations, pp. 23–25

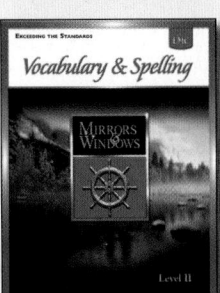

Vocabulary & Spelling
This resource contains :
- Three lessons on Collecting and Choosing Your Words, pp. 71–78

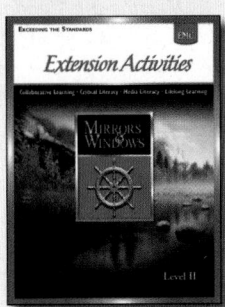

Extension Activities
This resource contains one extended lesson for each of the following:
- Lifelong Learning: Find a Myth, pp. 22–23
- Collaborative Learning: Discuss the Message, p. 24

Unit 8 Visual Planning Guide

(728)

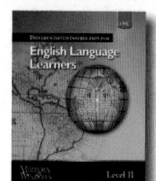

Reading Level: Moderate
Pacing: 2 days

Meeting the Standards, Reading Model, pp. 19–27

Developing Readers, Make Connections, pp. 52–54

English Language Learners, Monitor Comprehension, pp. 175–183

---

(734)

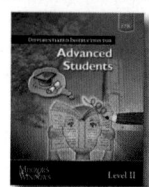

Reading Level: Moderate
Pacing: 1 day

Meeting the Standards, Guided Reading, pp. 28–33

Advanced Students, Cultural Connection Analysis, p. 46

---

(739)

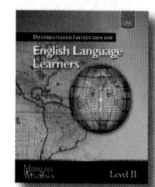

Reading Level: Moderate
Pacing: 3 days

Meeting the Standards, Directed Reading, pp. 34–39

English Language Learners, Cause and Effect, pp. 184–192

---

(748)

Reading Level: Moderate
Pacing: 3 days

Meeting the Standards, Directed Reading, pp. 40–45

---

(758)

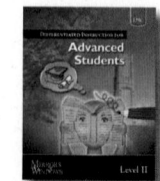

Reading Level: Easy
Pacing: 1 day

Meeting the Standards, Directed Reading, pp. 46–50

Advanced Students, Author/Theme Study, p. 47

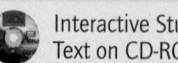 Interactive Student Text on CD-ROM

 Selection Lesson Plan

 Web-based Resources

Lesson-by-Lesson Resources

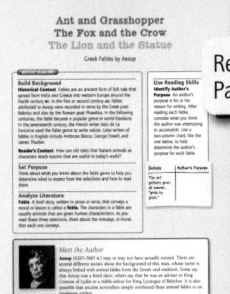

Ant and Grasshopper
The Fox and the Crow
The Lion and the Statue
Greek Fables by Aesop

765

Reading Level: Easy
Pacing: 1 day

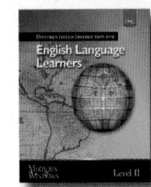

Meeting the Standards,
Directed Reading,
pp. 51–55

English Language Learners, Author's
Purpose, pp. 193–199

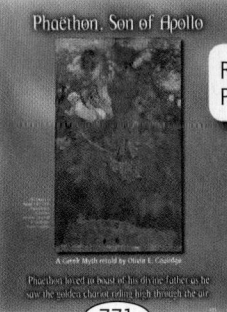

Phaëthon, Son of Apollo

A Greek Myth retold by Olivia E. Coolidge

771

Reading Level: Moderate
Pacing: 2 days

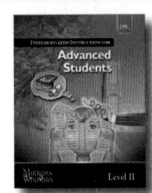

Meeting the Standards,
Directed Reading,
pp. 56–61

Advanced Students,
Comparison of Myths,
p. 48

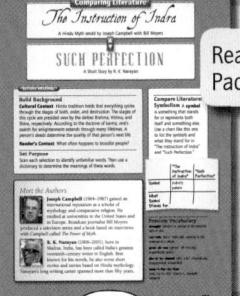

The Instruction of Indra

SUCH PERFECTION

777

Reading Level: Challenging
Pacing: 3 days

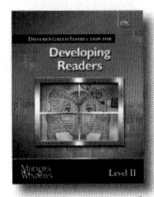

Meeting the Standards,
Compare Literature,
pp. 62–71

Developing Readers,
Set Purpose,
pp. 55–57

Amaterasu *A Japanese Myth retold by Carolyn Swift*

787

Reading Level: Moderate
Pacing: 1 day

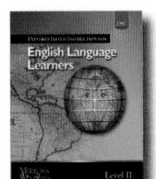

Meeting the Standards,
Directed Reading,
pp. 72–77

Developing Readers,
Take Notes, pp. 58–60

English Language Learners,
Draw Conclusions,
pp. 200–208

Aunty Misery
A Puerto Rican Folk Tale retold by Judith Ortiz Cofer

793

Reading Level: Easy
Pacing: 1 day

Meeting the Standards,
Directed Reading,
pp. 78–82

 Lesson Test

Audio Library

Reading Level: Easy
Pacing: 2 days

Meeting the Standards,
Independent Reading, pp. 82–88
Advanced Students, Independent
Reading Study, pp. 49–50

796

Reading Level: Moderate
Pacing: 1 day

*Meeting the
Standards,*
Independent
Reading, pp. 89–94

803

Reading Level: Easy
Pacing: 1 day

Meeting the Standards,
Independent Reading,
pp. 95–96

805

Unit 8 Scope & Sequence Guide

	Selection or Feature	Genre	Reading Support/ Reading Level	Word Count	Reading Skill	Graphic Organizer	
GUIDED READING	**Introduction to Folk Literature,** pp. 724–725						
	Folk Literature Reading Model, p. 726						
	Persephone and Demeter Ingri and Edgar Parin d' Aulaire pp. 727–732	Greek Myth	Guided Reading: Reading Model / Moderate	1,114	Monitor Comprehension	K-W-L Chart; Myth Chart	
	Eshu Judith Gleason pp. 733–737	Yoruban Folk Tale	Guided Reading: Reading Model / Moderate	826	Identify the Main Idea	Main Idea Map; Folk Tale List	
DIRECTED READING	**The Secret Name of Ra** Geraldine Harris pp. 738–745	Egyptian Myth	Directed Reading/ Moderate	1,306	Analyze Cause and Effect	Cause-and-Effect Chart; Motivation Chart	
	Literature Connection: from ***Akhenaton's Hymn to the Sun*** John A. Wilson pp. 743–744	Hymn	Moderate	288			
	Tsali of the Cherokees Alice Lee Marriott pp. 747–756	Oral History	Directed Reading/ Moderate	2,876	Identify Author's Purpose	Author's Purpose Chart; Motivation Chart	
	Informational Text Connection: Moving West: A Native American Perspective Christine Graf p. 755	Magazine Article	Easy	316			

Reading Level: Easy
Pacing: 1 day

Meeting the Standards, Independent Reading, pp. 97–98

807

Reading Level: Easy
Pacing: 1 day

Meeting the Standards, Independent Reading, pp. 99–100

815

Literary Element	*Mirrors & Windows* Theme	Cross-Curricular Connection	Writing Options	Extension Activities
Myths Folk Tales and Fables				
Myth	Powerful Emotions		Creative: Retelling Persuasive: Persuasive Speech	Lifelong Learning: Find a Myth Critical Literacy: Greek Myth
Folk Tale	Quarreling		Creative: Flyer Expository: Critical Analysis	Collaborative Learning: Discuss a Role of the Trickster Lifelong Learning: Research the History of Nigeria
Motivation	Trickery	History Connection: *Ancient Egypt*	Creative: Myth Expository: Summary	Collaborative Learning: Examine Motivation Lifelong Learning: Learn About the Nile
Motivation	Homeland	Social Studies Connection: Indian Removal	Creative: News Article Expository: Literary Analysis	Lifelong Learning: Dig into History Critical Literacy: Plan an Interview

Unit 8 Scope & Sequence Guide

Selection or Feature	Genre	Reading Support/ Reading Level	Word Count	Reading Skill	Graphic Organizer	
We Are All One Laurence Yep pp. 757–763	Chinese Folk Tale	Directed Reading/ Easy	1,670	Sequence of Events	Timeline; Conflict Organizer	
Ant and Grasshopper/ The Fox and the Crow/ The Lion and the Statue Aesop pp. 765–769	Greek Fables	Directed Reading/ Easy	524	Identify Author's Purpose	Author's Purpose Chart; Fable Chart	
Phaëthon, Son of Apollo Olivia E. Coolidge pp. 770–775	Greek Myth	Directed Reading/ Moderate	1,503	Draw Conclusions	Drawing Conclusions Chart; Details Map	
Comparing Literature: The Instruction of Indra Joseph Campbell pp. 777–785	Hindu Myth	Directed Reading/ Challenging	1,312	Compare Literature: Symbol	Symbolism Chart	
Such Perfection R.K. Narayan pp. 777–785	Short Story	Directed Reading/ Moderate	1,640			
Amaterasu Carolyn Swift pp. 786–791	Japanese Myth	Directed Reading/ Moderate	1,060	Draw Conclusions	Drawing Conclusions Chart; Details Map	
Aunty Misery Judith Ortiz Cofer pp. 792–795	Puerto Rican Folk Tale	Directed Reading/ Easy	668	Analyze Cause and Effect	Cause-and-Effect Chart; Simile Chart	
The Force of Luck Rudolfo A. Anaya pp. 796–802	Southwestern Folk Tale	Independent Reading/Easy	3,366	Use Context Clues		
How the Snake Got Poison Zora Neale Hurston pp. 803–804	African-American Folk Tale	Independent Reading/ Moderate	443	Identify the Main Idea		
The Rabbits Who Caused All the Trouble James Thurber pp. 805–806	Fable	Independent Reading/Easy	1,645			
Rabbit and the Tug of War Michael Thompson pp. 807–814	Graphic Folk Tale	Independent Reading/Easy	434			
from **Ella Enchanted** Gail Carson Levine pp. 805–806	Novel based on Fairy Tale	Independent Reading/Easy	1,159			

Left vertical labels: **DIRECTED READING** / **INDEPENDENT READING**

Unit 8 Language Arts Workshops

Grammar & Style	Vocabulary & Spelling	Writing	Speaking & Listening
Misplaced Modifiers, p. 764 Dangling Modifiers, p. 776	Homographs, Homophones, and Homonyms, p. 746	Expository Writing: Research Report, pp. 820–827	Giving and Actively Listening to Research Presentations, pp. 828–829

Literary Element	*Mirrors & Windows* Theme	Cross-Curricular Connection	Writing Options	Extension Activities
Conflict	Oneness		Creative: Descriptive Paragraph Expository: Literary Response	Critical Literacy: Hold a Debate Lifelong Learning: Magical Animals
Fable	Good Advice		Creative: Fable Persuasive: Editorial	Critical Literacy: Create a Drama Lifelong Learning: Research Fables
Allegory	Overconfidence	Science Connection: *Solar Models*	Creative: Business Letter Expository: Literary Analysis	Critical Literacy: Write a Character Sketch Lifelong Learning: Compare Myths
	Learning		Creative: Taking Notes Expository: Expository Paragraph	Collaborative Learning: Discuss Meaning Lifelong Learning: Compare Hinduism and Buddhism
	Creativity and Destruction			
Characterization	Envy	Cultural Connection: *Shintoism*	Creative: Biography Applied: Instructions	Lifelong Learning: Summarize Stories Media Literacy: Evaluate Websites
Simile	Cheating Death		Creative: Poem Expository: Expository Paragraph	Collaborative: Discuss the Message Critical Literacy: Hold a Panel Discussion
Theme	Luck		Expository: Critical Analysis	Critical Literacy: Hold a Debate
Folk Tale	Opportunity		Expository: Critical Analysis	Lifelong Learning: Research a Poisonous Snake
Fable, Satire	Persecution		Creative: Alternative Morals	Collaborative Learning: Group Discussion
Trickster tale	Deception		Creative: Original Trickster Tale	Lifelong Learning: Research Mvskoke Creek People
Parody	Disobedience		Expository Writing: Critical Essay	Critical Literacy: Perform Story Scene

Test Practice

Writing Skills: Research Report, pp. 830
Revising and Editing Skills, p. 831
Reading Skills: from "Why the Owl Has Big Eyes," pp. 832–833

Unit 8 Building Vocabulary

The lists below identify the Words in Use and Key Terms within this unit. These words are listed at the bottom of the Teacher's Edition pages at the beginning of each lesson. Vocabulary development activities are provided in the *Meeting the Standards* unit book and in *Exceeding the Standards: Vocabulary & Spelling*.

WORDS IN USE

Preview Vocabulary

Preview Vocabulary are words taken from the sentences within each selection. These words are defined in the side margin or at the bottom of the pages on which they appear. The "Preview Vocabulary" section introduces these words in the Before Reading page preceding each selection.

abyss, 740	deference, 772	gnarled, 794	precipitous, 774
amber, 774	deity, 740	grandiose, 779	radiant, 731
askew, 753	disillusioned, 781	grumble, 788	regretfully, 760
astonishing, 736	dissolve, 760	implore, 772	retaliate, 736
avenging, 730	dissuade, 773	inevitable, 794	root, 729
barren, 730	drivel, 740	larva, 759	sole, 740
cleft, 729	drought, 779	manifestation, 781	sulkily, 750
cosmic, 779	encroaching, 748	militia, 751	taunt, 794
courteous, 734	exalted, 740	missionary, 749	wearily, 761
cunning, 740	fondness, 790	omen, 760	

Selection Words

Selection Words are additional words from the reading that may be challenging but are not central to the selection and are not identified in the prereading section. These words can easily be learned using the story context, and they provide excellent practice for using content clues to find meaning without explicit instruction.

adjoining, 734	dismal, 729	internal, 806	poplar, 729, 774
amidst, 784	divine, 779	jesting, 800	probability, 805
bran, 798	envoys, 741	keerful, 804	prosperous, 796
chanted, 790	eternity, 779	mawnin', 803	quench, 814
civilize, 805	festivity, 743	mixed-blood, 748	radiant, 773
coaxed, 748	flourish, 744	modestly, 796	respective, 796
cock, 789	hearth, 793	mouf, 803	skeered, 804
comrades, 772	honorable, 796	novelty, 799	squandered, 797
consent, 729	hospitality, 793	ointment, 774	subtle, 782
consoled, 798	illuminate, 799	ornament, 803	undertone, 782
constellation, 780	immensity, 803	perceive, 743	vacant, 783
consulting, 800	immortal, 779	persist, 808	varmints, 803
crevice, 729	industry, 734	pester, 808	whoop, 810
crotchety, 780	infinite, 735	pilgrim, 793	writhed, 782

Teaching Words

Teaching Words consist of vocabulary that is used in the directions about the lessons. Teaching words explain to students what to focus on within the selection, help establish the story context, clarify the meaning of literary terms, and define the goals or instructional purpose.

academic, 828	comprehensive, 821	deities, 733	Egyptology, 738
acclaimed, 770	consensus, 795	depict, 733	elaborate, 826
anthropologist, 733	considerate, 829	derived, 725	emerging, 738
arrogant, 833	constructive, 829	descended, 786	episode, 747
aspect, 732	contemporary, 725	devotion, 827	ethnographer, 807
astronomers, 773	convey, 737, 765, 770	displaced, 751	ethnologist, 747
authority, 831	counterparts, 831	dispossessed, 747	exhibit, 742
barren, 724	courteous, 829	divine, 742, 789	exploits, 770
celestial, 773	criteria, 791	dominated, 792	fertile, 741
civilizations, 727	deceit, 831	effectiveness, 795	flourish, 727, 738

forcibly, 751
generalizations, 770
generation, 724, 733
generous, 833
ghetto, 805
guile, 831
hieroglyphics, 824
incorporate, 828
insights, 795, 796
internal, 791
inundation, 813
millennium, 741

mischievous, 833
mummification, 826
mythological, 725
optimistic, 795
otherworldly, 725
pantheon, 727
paraphrase, 830
perspective, 821
pessimistic, 795
pharaoh, 826
phenomena, 727
pogram, 805

phenomenon, 791
popularized, 792
practitioner, 733
prominent, 747
reaped, 757
relevant, 769
reliability, 791
relics, 789
relocate, 754
reputable, 821
revered, 770
rubric, 820, 829

shrine, 789
sophisticated, 741
stationary, 773
supernatural, 724, 727, 733
sustained, 741
sustainer, 738
time line, 757
transition, 826
vain, 724
vanquished, 738
verified, 821

KEY TERMS

Key Terms are commonly referred to as *academic vocabulary*. These terms appear in the instructional material to teach the terminology that students need to acquire to understand literature. The repetition of the terms throughout the program ensures student mastery and provides a solid foundation for the continuing study of literature and language arts.

allegory, 770, 833
anonymous, 725
author's purpose, 747, 765
biography, 770, 791
cause, 738
cause and effect, 792
cause-and-effect order, 822
character flaw, 770
character sketch, 775
character trait, 775
character, 727, 737, 738, 769, 770, 786, 792
characterization, 732, 733, 786
chronological order, 791, 822, 829
citation, 824
cite, 828
clause, 764, 776
comma, 776
compare and contrast, 785
comparison-and-contrast order, 822, 829
complex sentence, 831
compound sentence, 831
compound-complex sentence, 831
conclusion, 786
conflict, 736, 757, 775, 833
coordinating conjunction, 824
correlative conjunction, 824
costume, 769
creation myth, 724
dangling modifier, 776, 831
dependent clause, 824

description, 733
dialect, 804
dialogue, 732, 733, 769
direct quotation, 824, 828
drama, 769, 833
effect, 738
epic poem, 833
essay, 803
fable, 725, 765, 805, 833
first-person point of view, 833
folk tale, 725, 733, 757, 765, 792, 796, 803
genre, 757, 765, 770, 833
graphic tale, 807
Greek myth, 727
hero, 770
hero myth, 724
historical fiction, 770
homograph, 746
homonym, 746
homophone, 746
imagery, 732
independent clause, 824
introduction, 822
irony, 802
k-w-l chart, 727
legend, 724, 747
main character, 757
main idea, 733
major character, 747
metaphor, 795
minor character, 747
misplaced modifier, 764, 817
mood, 786

moral, 725, 765, 792, 806
moral lesson, 770
motivated, 786
motivation, 738, 747
myth, 724, 727, 737, 738, 747, 757, 770, 786, 830
nature myth, 724
noun, 776
novel, 796, 803
oral history, 724, 747
oral tradition, 724, 757
origin myth, 724, 727
paraphrase, 824, 828
peer review, 823
phrase, 764
play, 796, 803
plot, 733, 738, 747
poem, 795
poetry, 795
point by point order, 829
predicate, 824
primary source, 821
problem-and-solution order, 829
prop, 769
prose, 765, 795
quest, 724, 757
quotation, 764, 776
research presentation, 828
research report, 820
revise, 823
run-on sentence, 831
satire, 765, 806
scan, 777
secondary source, 821

second-person point of view, 833
sensory language, 795
sequence of events, 757
set, 769
setting, 727, 745, 786, 792, 796
short story, 796, 803
simile, 833
simple sentence, 824, 831
skim, 727, 745
source, 828
stage direction, 769
subject, 824
subject-verb agreement, 831
subordinate clause, 776
subordinating conjunction, 824
summarize, 737, 824
summary, 745, 769, 828
symbol, 777, 833
symbolism, 785
theme, 738, 756, 770, 775, 795, 796, 802
third-person limited point of view, 819
third-person omniscient point of view, 833
third-person point of view, 791
title, 757, 770
tone, 733, 804
topic, 828
trickster, 733, 833
trickster character, 725
trickster tale, 725, 807
verse, 765

UNIT 8 OVERVIEW Folk Literature

Objectives

Studying this unit will help students meet the following objectives:

- Connect the themes expressed in the selections to their own lives and to the world around them
- Identify common forms and elements of literature from the oral tradition, including *myth, folk tale, oral history, fable, allegory, motivation, conflict, symbol, characterization,* and *simile*
- Understand variations of literary forms and authors' use of language to develop forms

Reading Strategies

Ask Questions
Clarify
Make Inferences
Make Predictions
Visualize

Reading Skills

Analyze Cause and Effect
Draw Conclusions
Identify Author's Purpose
Identify the Main Idea
Monitor Comprehension
Sequence of Events

Literary Elements

Allegory
Characterization
Conflict
Folk Tale
Motivation
Myth
Simile
Symbol

Seeking Wisdom
Folk Literature

Unit 8

JUDITH ORTIZ COFER   LAURENCE YEP   JUDITH GLEASON

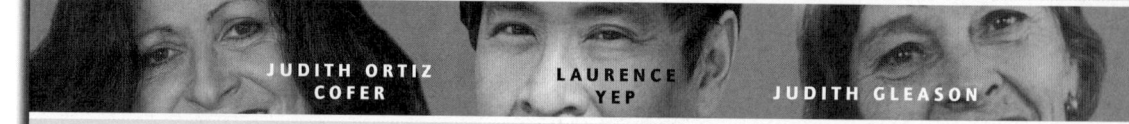

Launch the Unit

Ask students to read the introductory quotation and text on page 723. Then ask students to think for a minute of stories they have heard since they were children about how to behave. On a fresh sheet of paper, have each student write down one lesson they learned about how to behave, and note which story taught that lesson.

Place students into groups of four or five. Have students in each group exchange their sheets of paper. Challenge students to state the lesson they receive and identify a different story that teaches the same lesson. When groups begin to wind down, reconvene as a class and ask volunteers to name some of the lessons their groups discussed.

722 **UNIT 8** FOLK LITERATURE

"He could never bear to be beaten, even if he must risk his life in some rash way to win."

—OLIVIA E. COOLIDGE, "Phaëthon, Son of Apollo"

Think of some of your favorite stories. What lessons do they teach? In Olivia E. Coolidge's retelling of the Greek myth "Phaëthon, Son of Apollo," Phaëthon insists on driving his father's chariot, even though he is not ready. Phaëthon's pride leads to disaster. As you read the tales, fables, and myths in this unit, try to determine what wisdom each story offers.

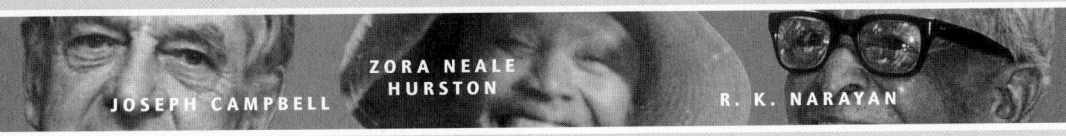

JOSEPH CAMPBELL   ZORA NEALE HURSTON   R. K. NARAYAN

Writing Options

Creative Writing

Biography	Myth
Business Letter	News Article
Descriptive	Notes
Paragraph	Poem
Fable	Retelling
Flyer	

Applied Writing

Instructions

Expository Writing

Critical Analysis	Literary Analysis
Expository	Literary Response
Paragraph	Summary

Persuasive Writing

Editorial
Persuasive Speech

Language Arts Workshops

Grammar & Style

Misplaced Modifiers
Dangling Modifiers

Vocabulary & Spelling

Homographs, Homophones, and Homonyms

Writing Workshop

Research Report

Speaking & Listening Workshop

Research Presentations

Test Practice Workshop

Research Report
Revising and Editing Skills
Reading Skills

723

Program Resources

For a visual reminder of the unit-based resources available for Unit 8, Folk Literature, see pages 722A and 722B. As you introduce the unit, you may want to provide students with the Unit Study Guide, which is contained in the *Meeting the Standards* resource.

Teach the Genre

Teach the Genre

Launch the Lesson

Read these lines—the opening sentence of L. Frank Baum's *The Wonderful Wizard of Oz*—aloud to students:

Dorothy lived in the midst of the great Kansas prairies, with Uncle Henry, who was a farmer, and Aunt Em, who was the farmer's wife.

Ask students if they know the story of Dorothy and the Wizard of Oz. Many will have seen the 1939 movie on television. Have one or two volunteers summarize the plot. Point out that Dorothy's story is a quest, which is a common type of story in folk literature. In a quest, the hero (or heroine) searches for something. Magical creatures help in the search, and the hero receives magical tools to overcome obstacles along the way. Tell students they will learn more about quests and other traditional storytelling forms in this unit.

Art Connection

Point out the photograph on this page. Tell students it shows a model of the Trojan horse. Have students use library or Internet resources to find the story of the Trojan horse, part of the legendary Trojan war. (Students will have to distinguish this from the Trojan horse type of malicious computer program.) Have volunteers share the story with the class.

Long before people invented writing, they were telling stories, reciting poetry, and singing songs about their beliefs, dreams, and experiences. Much of this material formed part of the **folk literature,** the works, ideas, or customs of a culture passed by word of mouth from generation to generation. Eventually, many of these stories, poems, and songs were written down and have become part of world literature. Works in folk literature or the *oral traditions* of peoples around the world include myths, legends, folk tales, fairy tales, and fables.

Myths

What is happening in the following passage?

> Demeter ran about searching for her lost daughter, and all nature grieved with her. Flowers wilted, trees lost their leaves, and the fields grew barren and cold. In vain did the plow cut through the icy ground; nothing could sprout and nothing could grow while the goddess of the harvest wept. People and animals starved and the gods begged Demeter again to bless the earth. But she refused to let anything grow until she had found her daughter.

> — INGRI AND EDGAR PARIN D'AULAIRE,
> "Persephone and Demeter"

In this passage, nothing will grow because the goddess of the harvest has lost her child. The passage is part of a Greek myth. A **myth** is a traditional story that usually presents supernatural events involving gods and heroes.

The myths of the classical world, which includes both the Greeks and the Romans, are usually the most well known to Western audiences. However, nearly all cultures have created their own body of myths, gods, and goddesses.

Types of Myths

There are many kinds of myths. Three common and widespread types are creation myths, origin myths, and hero myths. A *creation myth* tells how the world and human beings came to exist. An *origin myth,* or nature myth, is a story that explains objects or events in the natural world. Ingri and Edgar Parin d'Aulaire's "Persephone and Demeter" (page 727) is a Greek origin myth. A *hero myth* tells of the deeds and adventures of a hero. The plots of hero myths often involve battles with monsters and the adventurous journeys known as *quests.* Olivia Coolidge's "Phaëthon, Son of Apollo" (page 770) is a Greek hero myth. A type of story related to the myth is the legend. A *legend* is a traditional story that is popularly thought of as historical but lacks evidence to verify that the events occurred. Stories about the Trojan War and King Arthur are legends.

Replica of the legendary Trojan Horse. During the Trojan War, Greek soldiers hid in the horse to enter the city of Troy secretly.

Many legends begin as *oral histories,* or stories that are passed from generation to generation orally. Oral histories are not written down and may change with time, often gaining or losing plot or other story elements. "Tsali of the Cherokees" (page 747) is an example of oral history.

Program Resources

To help students explore literature on a deeper level, assign the following activity: Read and Discuss Folklore, Superstition, and Science, *Exceeding the Standards: Literature & Reading,* pp. 21–23.

Words in Use

Teaching Words
generation, 724
barren, 724
vain, 724
supernatural, 724
contemporary, 725
derived, 725
mythological, 725
otherworldly, 725

KEY TERMS

ORAL TRADITION, 724
MYTH, 724
CREATION MYTH, 724
ORIGIN MYTH, 724
HERO MYTH, 724
NATURE MYTH, 724
QUEST, 724
LEGEND, 724

ORAL HISTORY, 724
FOLK TALE, 725
ANONYMOUS, 725
TRICKSTER TALE, 725
TRICKSTER CHARACTER, 725
FABLE, 725
MORAL, 725

The Value of Myths

Every early culture around the world created its own myths. Learning about these myths can help you better understand the cultures that produced them. Examining myths provides an effective way to compare and contrast the beliefs and values of different cultures. Understanding myths can also help you better understand your own culture. Characters, events, and ideas from myths often appear in contemporary literature. Words derived from mythological characters and places also appear in modern English. Becoming familiar with myths from around the world will help you identify these references in other works and in everyday life.

The Little Mermaid (illustration), c. 1900. Eddie J. Andrews.

Folk Tales and Fables

Folk tales are stories passed by word of mouth from generation to generation. Although the term *folk tale* is often used to refer to any type of story in folk literature, it also refers specifically to stories that could have taken place anywhere and at any time and that are considered anonymous (created by an unknown person). "Hansel and Gretel" and "Little Red Riding Hood" are two well-known folk tales. Folk tales, like myths, can be filled with supernatural events and creatures. Often, seemingly regular people will encounter magical beings or go on adventures that introduce them to otherworldly places and characters.

Trickster Tales

One common type of folk tale is the **trickster tale.** The trickster character, which can be a human or an animal with speech and other human traits, has two sides. Tricksters frequently cause trouble, but they are also clever and creative. Judith Gleason's "Eshu" (page 733), a Yoruban folk tale, is an example of a trickster tale. Like myths, folk tales sometimes offer explanations for features of the natural world. Zora Neale Hurston's retelling of the African-American folk tale, "How the Snake Got Poison" (page 803), is an example of such a folk tale.

Fables

A **fable** is a brief story that frequently includes animal characters and a moral. The stories of the ancient Greek writer known as Aesop are the most famous fables in Western literature. "The Fox and the Crow" (page 765) is one of Aesop's fables.

Little Red Riding Hood (illustration), c. 19th century. Charles Robinson.

Introduction to the Oral Tradition

Reinforce definitions for students as necessary. Affirm that categories of the oral tradition overlap.

myth story with supernatural beings that tells about creation, origins, and/or heroes

legend story presented as history but not likely to be true

folk tale story passed by word of mouth

fairy tale story for children about imaginary beings, often teaching a lesson as well

fable story that teaches a lesson, often with animal characters

You do not have to cover this entire introduction at one time. As students prepare to read selections in the unit, encourage them to return to these pages to learn about the different genres of the oral tradition.

Differentiated Instruction

English Language Learning

Use this opportunity to invite English learners to share elements of their own oral traditions. Pair English learners with fluent speakers. Have partners work together to translate a folk tale, fable, or myth from the English learner's heritage into English. Invite partners to create a display that tells the story in words and artwork.

Enrichment

Have interested students find examples of classic and contemporary quest stories. Ask each student to identify the standard components of a quest, name an example, and show how the example includes all the standard components.

Common Core State Standards

Reading Literature
RL.5

Use the Model

Introduce the Process

Use this page to show students the basic instruction provided for them before, during, and after reading most selections in Unit 8.

"Persephone and Demeter" and "Eshu" are Active Reading Models. Side notes in these lessons prompt students to become more active readers by using reading strategies and skills, analyzing literature, and making connections. Students can apply the process they use to read these stories to other selections in Unit 8.

For more information, see Reading Strategies and Skills, Section 1 in the
.

Before Reading Stress the two types of background students need to apply, and encourage students to always set a purpose for reading.

During Reading Point out the side notes on page 729: Use Reading Skills and Make Connections. Then show students the Mirrors & Windows questions on page 731. Explain that they will first respond to a story personally, and then apply their insights to a broader issue.

After Reading Show students page 732. Tell them that "Find Meaning" questions will help them recall and interpret details. "Make Judgments" questions ask them to analyze a selection and evaluate how specific details contribute to its overall literary effect and meaning.

Folk Literature Reading Model

BEFORE READING

Build Background
Apply two types of background to read myths, fables, and folk tales effectively. One type is the story's literary and cultural context. Read the **Build Background** and **Meet the Author** features to get this information. The other type of background is the personal knowledge and experience you bring to your reading.

Set Purpose
Folk literature presents characters and actions to say something about life. Read **Set Purpose** to decide what you want to get out of the story.

Analyze Literature
Folk literature includes literary techniques, such as plot and setting, to create meaning. The **Analyze Literature** feature draws your attention to key literary elements.

Use Reading Skills
The **Use Reading Skills** feature will show you skills to help you get the most out of your reading. Identify a graphic organizer to help you apply the skill before and while you read.

DURING READING

Use Reading Strategies
- **Ask questions** about things that seem significant or interesting.
- **Make predictions** about what's going to happen next. As you read, gather more clues to confirm or change your prediction.
- **Visualize** the story. Form pictures in your mind to help you see the characters, actions, and settings.
- **Make inferences,** or educated guesses, about what is not stated directly.
- **Clarify,** or check that you understand, what you read. Reread any difficult parts.

Analyze Literature
What literary elements stand out? Are the characters vivid and interesting? Is there a lesson or moral? As you read, consider how these elements affect your enjoyment and understanding of the story.

Make Connections
Notice where connections can be made between the story and your life or another story, myth, or legend. What feelings or thoughts do you have while reading the story?

AFTER READING

Find Meaning
Recall the important details of the story, such as the sequence of events and character traits. Use this information to help **interpret,** or explain, the meaning of the story.

Make Judgments
- **Analyze** the text by examining details and deciding what they contribute to the meaning.
- **Evaluate** the text by making judgments about how the author creates meaning.

Analyze Literature
Review how the use of literary elements increases your understanding of the story. For example, if the story includes dialogue, how does it help shape the story's meaning?

Extend Understanding
Go beyond the text by exploring the story through writing or other creative projects.

726 UNIT 8 FOLK LITERATURE

Differentiated Instruction

Enrichment

During Reading questions in the text's Active Reading Models often ask students to "make connections" by responding to events and characters or by relating those elements to their own experience and knowledge. As students read the myths, folk tales, and other stories in this unit, invite them to keep a log of connections. Have them prepare a three-column chart with the

headings shown here. For each selection, have them enter at least one overall response and one example of a way in which the story relates to their lives.

Title	My Overall Response(s)	How It Relates to Me

Persephone and Demeter

A Greek Myth retold by Ingri and Edgar Parin d'Aulaire

Apply the Model

BEFORE READING
DURING READING
AFTER READING

GUIDED READING

Preview the Model

At a Glance
Guided Reading: Reading Model
- Reading Level: Moderate
- Difficulty Consideration: Vocabulary
- Ease Factor: Length

Build Background
Cultural Context As long as nine thousand years ago, civilizations existed in the lands around the Aegean Sea, in present-day Greece and Turkey. Architecture and arts such as sculpture, pottery, and music flourished in these societies. The literature of that time was passed on by word of mouth, and many stories were told about the Greek pantheon of gods and goddesses.

Reader's Context Think about your own relationships. What friend or family member cheers you up? What qualities make that person so special?

Set Purpose
Preview the vocabulary words and footnotes. Then skim for other unfamiliar words and look them up.

Analyze Literature
Myth A traditional story that usually presents supernatural events involving gods and heroes is called a **myth.** There are many different kinds of myths. An *origin myth*, like "Persephone and Demeter," is a story that explains the existence of things or events in the natural world. As you read "Persephone and Demeter," determine what real-world phenomena it explains.

Use Reading Skills
Monitor Comprehension
One good method for monitoring your comprehension is to pose questions about the text. As you read, ask yourself: What have I learned about Greek myth? To what characters, events, settings, and ideas have I been introduced? Use a K-W-L chart to record your ideas.

What I Know	What I Want to Know	What I Learned
Persephone and Demeter were Greek goddesses.		

Objectives
Studying this lesson will enable students to
- use reading skills such as monitoring comprehension
- define myth and recognize the elements of the selection that identify it as myth
- define the literary accomplishments of Ingri d'Aulaire and Edgar Parin d'Aulaire and explain the role they played in exposing English-speaking readers to myths and folklore of various cultures
- appreciate a myth about the origin of the seasons

Launch the Lesson
Tell students that the myth "Persephone and Demeter" shows gods reacting in very different ways to the emotion of love. Ask them to think about their own reactions to strong emotions. As they read, have them consider what they would do if they were Demeter or if they were Hades.

Meet the Authors

Authors and illustrators **Ingri d'Aulaire** (1904–1980) and **Edgar Parin d'Aulaire** (1898–1986) met in Germany. Ingri was from a large Norwegian family. Edgar, the son of two artists, grew up in Switzerland. The couple moved to the United States in 1929 and collaborated on their first children's book two years later. The collections of Greek and Norse myths that they published in the 1960s remain popular today.

Preview Vocabulary
yawn·ing (yô´ niŋ) *adj.,* wide open

root (rüt) *v.,* dig in the ground

cleft (kleft) *n.,* space made when something breaks open

a·veng·ing (ə venj´ iŋ) *adj.,* taking revenge or punishing someone for something

bar·ren (ber´ ən) *adj.,* unable to reproduce or bear fruit; desolate

ra·di·ant (rā´ dē ənt) *adj.,* shining bright

TEACHING NOTE

Listening Skills
It would be helpful for English language learners to hear the vocabulary words spoken aloud. Read the words aloud or ask students to say them aloud as a class. English language learners should listen to these words and try to recognize elements of the English sound system such as consonant and vowel sounds within them.

PERSEPHONE AND DEMETER **727**

Words in Use

Preview Vocabulary	Selection Words	Teaching Words
root, 729	**consent,** 729	**civilizations,** 727
cleft, 729	**crevice,** 729	**flourished,** 727
avenging, 730	**dismal,** 729	**pantheon,** 727
barren, 730	**poplars,** 729	**supernatural,** 727
radiant, 731		**phenomena,** 727
		aspect, 732

KEY TERMS
MYTH, 727
SKIM, 727
ORIGIN MYTH, 727
GREEK MYTH, 727
CHARACTER, 727
SETTING, 727
K-W-L CHART, 727
CHARACTERIZATION, 732
IMAGERY, 732
DIALOGUE, 732

Common Core State Standards

Reading Literature
RL.1

PERSEPHONE AND DEMETER **727**

Teach the Model

Summary

Hades, god of the underworld, falls in love with Persephone, daughter of the harvest goddess, Demeter. He knows that Demeter would never agree to a marriage, so he kidnaps the girl, takes her to his kingdom, and makes her his queen.

Demeter searches frantically for Persephone. The earth falls into constant winter. Finally, Demeter learns what happened and goes to the leader of the gods, Zeus. She threatens never again to let the earth flourish if her daughter is not freed.

At Zeus's command, Hades releases Persephone, but as she is about to go, his gardener reveals that she ate a few pomegranate seeds. Tasting this food of the dead has doomed her to return. From then on, Persephone lives six months with Hades and six months with Demeter. When she is with her mother, the earth produces bountiful crops. When she is below, it grows cold.

The Mirrors & Windows questions at the end of the selection focus on the theme of powerful emotions. Before students begin reading, ask: How much should a person be ruled by emotions?

Persephone and Demeter

The Rape of Persephone by Hades, c. 19th century. English School. Bibliothèque des Arts Décoratifs, Paris.

A Greek Myth retold by Ingri and Edgar Parin d'Aulaire

At the reins stood grim Hades.

728

Program Resources

Planning and Assessment
Program Planning Guide, Selection Lesson Plan
E-Lesson Planner
Assessment Guide, Lesson Test
ExamView

Technology Tools
Interactive Student Text on CD
Visual Teaching Package
mirrorsandwindows.com

Meeting the Standards
Folk Literature: Unit 8, Reading Model,
    pp. 19–27

Differentiating Instruction
Developing Readers, Make Connections,
    pp. 52–54
English Language Learners, Monitor
    Comprehension, pp. 175–183

P ersephone grew up on Olympus[1] and her gay laughter rang through the brilliant halls. She was the daughter of Demeter, goddess of the harvest, and her mother loved her so dearly she could not bear to have her out of her sight. When Demeter sat on her golden throne her daughter was always on her lap; when she went down to earth to look after her trees and fields, she took Persephone. Wherever Persephone danced on her light feet, flowers sprang up. She was so lovely and full of grace that even Hades,[2] who saw so little, noticed her and fell in love with her. He wanted her for his queen, but he knew that her mother would never consent to part with her, so he decided to carry her off.

One day as Persephone ran about in the meadow gathering flowers, she strayed away from her mother and the attending nymphs.[3] Suddenly, the ground split open and up from the yawning crevice came a dark chariot drawn by black horses. At the reins stood grim Hades. He seized the terrified girl, turned his horses, and plunged back into the ground. A herd of pigs rooting in the meadow tumbled into the cleft, and Persephone's cries for help died out as the ground closed again as suddenly as it had opened. Up in the field, a little swineherd[4] stood and wept over the pigs he had lost, while Demeter rushed wildly about in the meadow, looking in vain for her daughter, who had vanished without leaving a trace.

With the frightened girl in his arms, Hades raced his snorting horses down away from the sunlit world. Down and down they sped on the dark path to his dismal underground palace. He led weeping Persephone in, seated her beside him on a throne of black marble, and decked her with gold and precious stones. But the jewels brought her no joy. She wanted no cold stones. She longed for warm sunshine and flowers and her golden-tressed[5] mother.

Dead souls crowded out from cracks and crevices to look at their new queen, while ever more souls came across the Styx[6] and Persephone watched them drink from a spring under dark poplars. It was the spring of Lethe,[7] and those who drank from its waters forgot who they were and what they had done on earth.

---

1. **Olympus.** Mountain in what is now Thessaly, Greece, where the ancient Greeks believed most gods lived
2. **Hades.** God of the underworld; sometimes the name *Hades* is used for the underworld itself
3. **nymphs.** Minor female goddesses who live in natural spots like forests or trees, rivers, and streams
4. **swineherd.** Person who keeps or tends pigs
5. **golden-tressed.** Having golden hair (tresses); blond
6. **Styx.** Main river of the underworld, which surrounds it and separates it from the world of the living
7. **Lethe.** River of forgetfulness

Differentiated Instruction

English Language Learning
Point out and explain these expressions:
gay—emphasize that in older works, this simply means joyful or happy, 729
yawning crevice—wide opening in the ground, 729
in vain—hopelessly, without success, 729
laden—fully loaded, 731

Reading Proficiency
Struggling readers may be distracted by the Greek names of the gods and the words for some concepts in the myth. Using a dictionary, encyclopedia, or the Internet, obtain necessary pronunciations and review these pronunciations with students. To help them become more comfortable with the words, have them take turns reading aloud passages from the selection. Students should self-correct their pronunciation using these resources.

Analyze Literature

Imagery Draw attention to this sentence. Ask: "What is the name of the literary technique used to describe Persephone's heart? Do you find it effective?" (The figure of speech is metaphor—the heart is compared to ice. Most students will find this evocative.) **A**

Use Reading Skills

Monitor Comprehension *Answer:* She is goddess of the harvest and has the power to cause plants to grow or to die, depending on her mood. **B**

Use Reading Skills

Monitor Comprehension *Answer:* She meets Triptolemus, who tells her that his brother saw the kidnapping. **C**

Use Reading Skills

Draw Conclusions Remind students that a conclusion is a reasoned judgment based on available information. Ask: "What details allow Demeter to conclude that Hades kidnapped Persephone?" (Students should note Triptolemus's testimony that the ground swallowed up the pigs and a girl screamed. Demeter already knew Persephone was in the area and, as a goddess, she knows Hades has the power to arise from below ground.) **D**

a·veng·ing (ə venj´ iŋ) *adj.*, taking revenge or punishing someone for something

Rhadamanthus, a judge of the dead, dealt out punishment to the souls of great sinners. They were sentenced to suffer forever under the whips of the <u>avenging</u> Erinyes.[8] Heroes were led to the Elysian fields,[9] where they lived happily forever in never-failing light.

Around the palace of Hades there was a garden where whispering poplars and weeping willows grew. They had no flowers and bore no fruit and no birds sang in their branches. There was only one tree in the whole realm of Hades that bore fruit. That was a little pomegranate[10] tree. The gardener of the underworld offered the tempting pomegranates to the queen, but Persephone refused to touch the food of the dead.

A Wordlessly she walked through the garden at silent Hades' side and slowly her heart turned to ice.

Above, on earth, Demeter ran about searching for her lost daughter, and all nature grieved with her. Flowers wilted, trees lost their leaves, and the fields grew <u>barren</u> and cold. In vain did the plow cut through the icy ground; nothing could sprout and nothing could grow while the goddess of the harvest wept. People and animals starved and the gods begged Demeter again to bless the earth. But she refused to let anything grow until she had found her daughter.

bar·ren (ber´ ən) *adj.*, unable to reproduce or bear fruit; desolate

> **DURING READING**
> **Use Reading Skills**
> **Monitor Comprehension** Why does Demeter's grief have an effect on nature? **B**

Bent with grief, Demeter turned into a gray old woman. She returned to the meadow where Persephone had vanished and asked the sun if he had seen what had happened, but he said no, dark clouds had hidden his face that day. She wandered around the meadow and after a while she met a youth whose name was Triptolemus. He told her that his brother, a swineherd, had seen his pigs disappear into the ground and had heard the frightened screams of a girl.

> **DURING READING**
> **Use Reading Skills**
> **Monitor Comprehension** How does Demeter find out what happened to Persephone? **C**

D Demeter now understood that Hades had kidnapped her daughter, and her grief turned to anger. She called to Zeus[11] and said that she would never again make the earth green if he did not command Hades to return Persephone. Zeus could not let the world

---

8. **Erinyes.** Three spirits of punishment
9. **Elysian fields.** Paradise
10. **pomegranate.** Round, red fruit with a hard rind
11. **Zeus.** King of the Greek gods

Differentiated Instruction

Enrichment

Note the other characters from Greek mythology who play supporting roles in this myth (such as Rhadamanthus, the Erinyes, Triptolemus, Zeus, and Hermes). Encourage students to choose one of these characters and seek out other myths in which the character plays a central role. Have students present their findings to classmates.

Auditory Learning

Have a group of students create a television talk show-style performance about this story. Have them choose roles—one should be the host, others can be characters from the myth, and some can play psychologists, experts on the laws of the gods, or other such roles. Have the host ask questions and moderate the discussion. Encourage students to play their roles as dramatically as they wish.

perish and he sent Hermes[12] down to Hades, bidding him to let Persephone go. Even Hades had to obey the orders of Zeus, and sadly he said farewell to his queen.

Joyfully, Persephone leaped to her feet, but as she was leaving with Hermes, a hooting laugh came from the garden. There stood the gardener of Hades, grinning. He pointed to a pomegranate from which a few of the kernels were missing. Persephone, lost in thought, had eaten the seeds, he said. **E**

Then dark Hades smiled. He watched Hermes lead Persephone up to the bright world above. He knew that she must return to him, for she had tasted the food of the dead.

When Persephone again appeared on earth, Demeter sprang to her feet with a cry of joy and rushed to greet her daughter. No longer was she a sad old woman, but a <u>radiant</u> goddess. Again she blessed her fields and the flowers bloomed anew and the grain ripened.

> **ra·di·ant** (rā´ dē ənt)
> *adj.*, shining bright

"Dear child," she said, "never again shall we be parted. Together we shall make all nature bloom." But joy soon was changed to sadness, for Persephone had to admit that she had tasted the food of the dead and must return to Hades. However, Zeus decided that mother and daughter should not be parted forever. He ruled that Persephone had to return to Hades and spend one month in the underworld for each seed she had eaten.

Every year, when Persephone left her, Demeter grieved, nothing grew, and there was winter on earth. But as soon as her daughter's light footsteps were heard, the whole earth burst into bloom. Spring had come. As long as mother and daughter were together, the earth was warm and bore fruit.

> **DURING READING**
>
> **Analyze Literature**
> **Myth** What is one natural phenomenon this myth attempts to explain? **F**

Demeter was a kind goddess. She did not want mankind to starve during the cold months of winter when Persephone was away. She lent her chariot, laden with grain, to Triptolemus, the youth who had helped her to find her lost daughter. She told him to scatter her golden grain over the world and teach men how to sow it in spring and reap it in fall and store it away for the long months when again the earth was barren and cold. ❖

---

12. Hermes. Messenger god

 MIRRORS & WINDOWS

When have you, like Demeter, experienced an emotion that changed your outlook on life? Was the emotion positive or negative? In what ways can emotions be both destructive and constructive?

PERSEPHONE AND DEMETER **731**

Science Connection

Pomegranates Pomegranates figure in much ancient literature, including the Bible. Tell students unfamiliar with the fruit that a pomegranate is about the size of a large orange, with leathery red skin enclosing creamy pulp filled with clusters of tiny seeds, each surrounded by juicy, bright red flesh. **E**

Analyze Literature

Myth Remind students that myths have supernatural elements and discuss the meaning of *supernatural* (literally, "beyond or more than natural," such as things having to do with gods, demons, or spirits). Ask: "What supernatural elements are in this myth?" (They include the god characters, the spirits of the dead, and Demeter's power over nature.)

Analyze Literature

Myth *Answer:* It explains the seasons. It also explains the origins of agriculture and describes the afterlife. **F**

 MIRRORS & WINDOWS

You may want to ask students to write a journal entry or quick write, or divide students into discussion groups or lead a whole-class discussion about this question. *Answer:* Students' assessments of emotions will vary. They might argue that positive emotions, such as love, can cause people to act foolishly or selflessly. Emotions like anger can goad people into fighting injustice or inspire them to acts of violence.

Compare and Contrast

Remind students that one of the best ways to organize their ideas when they must compare and contrast topics is with a Venn diagram. Note that this graphic organizer works for two or three topics. (You may demonstrate by drawing two-, three-, and four-circle Venn diagrams. Show students that the four-circle version is not only too crowded, but also does not provide space for similarities shared only by the two circles positioned across from each other.) For practice, draw a large two-circle Venn diagram on the board and label the circles *Winter* and *Summer*. Work as a class to compare and contrast details about these two seasons as students read "Persephone and Demeter."

Find Meaning

1. (a) It is dark and dismal, crowded with the souls of the dead. Only one plant in the garden bears fruit, and there are no flowers. (b) The world above is filled with light. As long as Demeter is happy, the earth is filled with flowers and fruit.

2. Erinyes punish sinners. Heroes go to live in the Elysian fields.

3. (a) She is distraught, looks everywhere for her daughter, begins to appear old, and ignores her responsibilities. (b) Most students will agree that anger and sadness are realistic responses to losing a child.

Make Judgments

4. Students may suggest that Hades has no idea how to make someone else happy. They may also note that, as a powerful god, he might feel he should not have to appeal to anyone else to get what he wants.

5. (a) Answers will vary. Some may say that it is unfair to mortals, who played no part in the kidnapping. (b) Some students may suggest having Persephone spend less time with Hades or even letting her return to earth full time. Some might want to punish Hades for kidnapping her.

Analyze Literature

Myth The myth answers such questions as What makes plants grow? Why do we have seasons? What happens after you die? How did people learn to cultivate grain?

Apply the Model

BEFORE READING
DURING READING
AFTER READING

Find Meaning

1. (a) What is it like in the underworld? (b) How is this different from the world above?

2. According to the myth, what happens to great sinners after they die? To heroes?

3. (a) How does Demeter react when Persephone is kidnapped? (b) In what ways is this similar to how a human mother would react?

Analyze Literature

Myth What aspects of the natural world and human experience are explained in the myth "Persephone and Demeter"? Create a two-column chart to document your ideas. In the first column, write the questions people might have had about their world, and in the second, write the details from the story that help to answer those questions.

Make Judgments

4. What do you think Hades's decision to kidnap Persephone says about his personality?

5. (a) Does Persephone's schedule at the end of the story seem fair to you? (b) How would you have settled the problem if you were Zeus?

Real-world Question	Myth's Explanation
What makes plants grow?	

Extend Understanding

Writing Options

Creative Writing Imagine that you are a storyteller and you must recite the story of Persephone and Demeter. Write a **retelling** of the myth using modern characterizations, language, and imagery. Add dialogue to develop the characters. Recite your modernized myth to your classmates.

Persuasive Writing In "Persephone and Demeter," the goddess Demeter must appeal to Zeus to help save her daughter. Put yourself in Demeter's place and write a short **persuasive speech** to deliver to Zeus. A successful persuasive argument begins with a statement of the writer's position, followed by three or more reasons supporting that position.

Lifelong Learning

Find a Myth Choose an aspect of nature that is explained in "Persephone and Demeter." Then find a myth from another culture that explains the same thing. What are the similarities? The differences? Share your findings with the class.

Critical Literacy

Greek Myth Prepare a presentation about another Greek myth. Choose a myth that has something in common with "Persephone and Demeter." For example, you may wish to choose a myth that features Persephone. You could also focus on a different retelling of the same story. In your presentation, describe traits common to both myths. Which story do you prefer? Why?

Go to **www.mirrorsandwindows.com** for more.

Program Resources

For further instruction, refer students to the following extension activity: Lifelong Learning: Find a Myth, *Exceeding the Standards: Extension Activities*, pp. 22–23.

Rubrics for Writing Options

You can adapt this as a checklist for students to use as they write.

Creative Writing

☐ Does the retelling include the characters and plot elements from the myth?

☐ Does the retelling use dialogue?

Persuasive Writing

☐ Does the speech address Zeus from Demeter's point of view?

☐ Does the speech state a position and support it with evidence?

Eshu

A Yoruban Folk Tale retold by Judith Gleason

Preview the Model

At a Glance
Guided Reading: Reading Model
- Reading Level: Moderate
- Difficulty Considerations: Context and confusing ending
- Ease Factor: Dialogue

Build Background

Cultural Context The Yoruba people live primarily in southwestern Nigeria, an area they settled about a thousand years ago. According to Yoruban tradition, Earth and heavens were created by a supreme being, Oludumare. Below him were several hundred minor deities, or Orisha, and among the most powerful of those was Eshu. He was not only a trickster—a traditional figure of mischief—but also the messenger who carried news from Earth to Oludumare.

Reader's Context When has a foolish argument threatened one of your friendships? How did you resolve the situation?

Set Purpose

Preview "Eshu," looking for unfamiliar terms. Write down any words and phrases you would like to investigate further.

Analyze Literature

Folk Tale Stories passed by word of mouth from generation to generation are **folk tales.** They often depict everyday activities and the adventures of common people. In addition, folk tales sometimes include gods and other supernatural characters. As you read, think about how "Eshu" depicts daily life in this community.

Meet the Author

Anthropologist **Judith Gleason** (b. 1929) is an expert in Yoruba culture. Since 1960, she has been a practitioner of Santeria—a religion that evolved among Yoruban slaves in Cuba. Her books include the novel *Agotime: Her Legend* and an anthology of African praise poems, *Leaf and Bone*. The story of Eshu appeared in *Orisha: The Gods of Yorubaland.*

Use Reading Skills

Identify the Main Idea
The main idea, or theme, is what the author wants you to know or think after reading a work. The main idea is often not stated outright. Readers need to examine supporting details of the dialogue, tone, description, plot, and characterization to identify the main idea. Create a main idea map to help you determine the main idea of "Eshu."

Eshu's cap is red on one side, black on the other. — detail — Main Idea — detail — detail

Preview Vocabulary

cour•te•ous (kʉr´ tē əs) *adj.,* polite; well mannered

re•tal•i•ate (ri ta´ lē āt´) *v.,* respond to an action by doing a similar thing back, usually in a negative sense, such as repaying one injury by inflicting another

as•ton•ish•ing (ə stä´ ni shiŋ) *adj.,* amazing; very surprising

ESHU **733**

Objectives

Studying this lesson will enable students to
- use reading skills such as identifying the main idea
- define folk tale and recognize the selection as an example
- describe Judith Gleason's role in popularizing African folk tales
- appreciate a folk tale featuring a trickster character

Launch the Lesson

As students prepare to read "Eshu," ask them to think about what causes people to be friends. Ask: "Whom do you think of as your best friends, and can you explain why?" Give students a moment to think; do not ask them to name their best friends aloud. Then discuss as a class the various reasons for calling someone a best friend.

Words in Use

Preview Vocabulary	Selection Words	Teaching Words
couteous, 734	adjoining, 734	deities, 733
retaliate, 736	industry, 734	generation, 733
astonishing, 736	infinite, 735	depict, 733
		supernatural, 733
		anthropologist, 733
		practitioner, 733
		convey, 737

KEY TERMS

TRICKSTER, 733
FOLK TALE, 733
MAIN IDEA, 733
DIALOGUE, 733
TONE, 733
DESCRIPTION, 733
PLOT, 733
CHARACTERIZATION, 733
CONFLICT, 736
SUMMARIZE, 737
CHARACTER, 737
MYTH, 737

Common Core State Standards

Reading Literature
RL.1, RL.2

Speaking and Listening
SL.1

Teach the Model

Summary

Two village men are such good friends that their chief has given them adjacent farm plots. One day, Eshu the trickster walks along the path between their plots. He is wearing a hat that is red on one side and black on the other, carrying his stick at his back rather than his chest as is customary, and holding his pipe at the back of his head.

At the end of the day, the friends begin to wonder about the passerby and soon realize they have different impressions. One says he was going into town, while the other says he was leaving. One says his hat was red; the other says black. They start to argue, and the fight escalates into physical violence. At last, they declare their friendship over. Their chief, sad to hear this, switches their farm plots so they are far apart. Finally, he makes a puzzling pronouncement.

The Mirrors & Windows questions at the end of the selection focus on the theme of quarreling. Before students begin reading, ask: What starts most arguments among friends?

Use Reading Strategies

Visualize *Answer:* They are right next to each other. The path to the village runs between them. **A**

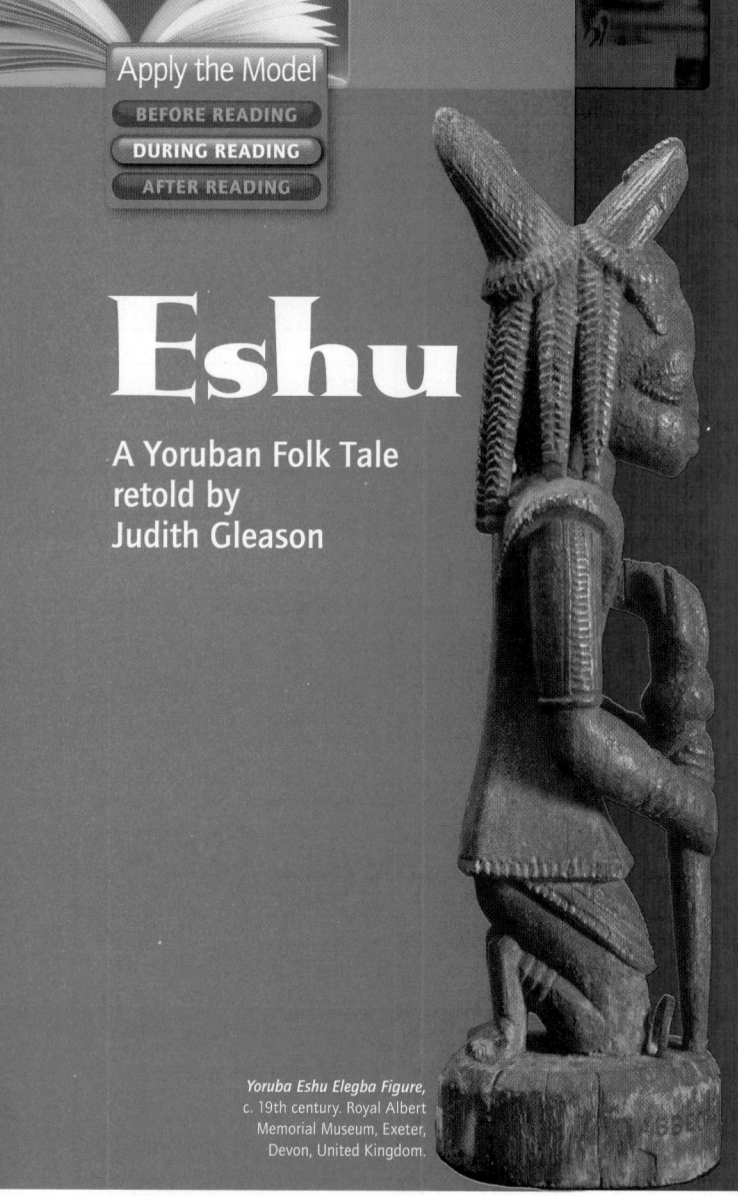

Eshu

A Yoruban Folk Tale
retold by
Judith Gleason

There were two friends who loved each other like yam porridge and pepper soup.

Yoruba Eshu Elegba Figure, c. 19th century. Royal Albert Memorial Museum, Exeter, Devon, United Kingdom.

DURING READING

Use Reading Strategies
Visualize Picture the two friends' work plots. How are they arranged? **A**

cour·te·ous (kʉr´ tē əs) *adj.*, polite; well mannered

There were two friends who loved each other like yam porridge and pepper soup. Whenever they went out, they wore identical cloths. Their farm plots, thanks to the chief's respect for their friendship, were adjoining. The path to and from the village was all that divided them as they worked, and all day long they called across <u>courteous</u> greetings:

734

Program Resources

Planning and Assessment
Program Planning Guide, Selection Lesson Plan
E-Lesson Planner
Assessment Guide, Lesson Test
ExamView

Technology Tools
Interactive Student Text on CD
Visual Teaching Package
Audio Library
mirrorsandwindows.com

Meeting the Standards
Folk Literature: Unit 8, Guided Reading, pp. 28–33

Differentiating Instruction
Advanced Students, Cultural Connection Analysis, p. 46

"Good-day my very special friend, I hope the sun is not beating too hard upon your shoulders."

"Not at all, my dear age-mate; I salute you for working so steadily in the heat."

"May your soil yield even finer crops than mine."

"My compliments upon your new wife; may she bring forth sons to commend your industry."

"Salutations on the coming cool of the evening."

"May the sun not deceive you into lingering too late in the field."

And so on, as weaver bird[1] converses with weaver bird, these friends continued to embroider their amity.[2]

Until one day an old man walked down the path between them. It was Eshu. He was wearing a pointed cap, black on one side and red on the other. He held his pipe to the nape of his neck[3] and slung his stick over his shoulder so that it dangled down his back instead of over his chest as he usually carried it. The two friends answered his greeting, then went on with their work and thought no more about him until, late in the afternoon as they prepared to go home, one of them said, "I wonder what business that old man had in our village?"

"Whatever it was, he must have completed it quickly," said the other.

"How do you know?"

"Because he left before noon, don't you remember? Long before our wives brought out our dinners."

"True, he passed by midmorning," said the other, "but he was heading into the village, not out of it."

"Nonsense," said his friend, "he was going in the opposite direction, up country, not towards the village as you said. Perhaps you've confused him with another. This traveler was an old, old man with a stick slung over his shoulder. You know, the one who used to wear a black cap."

"Don't take that tone with me. I know precisely who he is, and today he looked exactly the same and, as always, his face was following his pipe bowl into our village."

"You looked at his pipe, but I saw his feet. For all we know, he may have been puffing through a hole in the back of his neck; but this much is clear: That old man in his brand new red hat was leaving our village farther and farther behind him."

---

1. **weaver bird.** Type of bird known for being very social and for making elaborate hanging nests by interweaving grasses and other fibers
2. **embroider their amity.** Increase their friendship
3. **nape of his neck.** Back of his neck

> **DURING READING**
>
> **Analyze Literature**
> **Folk Tale** What have you learned so far about daily life in this setting? **B**

C

"I wonder what business that old man had in our village?"

Teach the Model

Analyze Literature
Folk Tale *Answer:* The setting is rural and the people are agricultural. **B**

Use Reading Skills
Identify the Main Idea Encourage students to use visualization as they consider the main idea. For example, as the friends begin to fight here, have readers take time to visualize the details provided earlier about Eshu's appearance. That way, they will better understand why the two men disagree. **C**

Analyze Literature
Folk Tale Talk about the etymology of the term *folk tale.* Explain that *folk* comes from the Old English word for "common people," so that a folk tale is a story told by the common people. Have students brainstorm other terms that include *folk* and consider what they mean (examples include *folk music,* music of the people; *Volkswagen,* car for the people; *folklore,* traditional beliefs and stories).

TEACHING NOTE

Word Study Notebook
Suggest that students collect new vocabulary words in a word study notebook. This can be a notepad where they write down words and definitions. Encourage students to keep these notebooks at hand whenever they read. Briefly talk about sources of words other than books. Note that if students are assigned to keep track of how many words they collect, they can start a word log— an ongoing tally of the number of words in their notebooks.

Differentiated Instruction

English Language Learning
English learners may wonder if the sentence fragment that opens the ninth paragraph is an error. Acknowledge that it is a fragment. Explain that writers sometimes use fragments to add emphasis. Note how this one emphasizes that the men's friendship is about to change.

Reading Proficiency
Because comprehension of the story hinges on understanding how Eshu looks to the two friends, have students focus on the paragraph that describes his appearance. Ask them to draw a portrait of Eshu using all the details provided. Have students compare their drawings—did they all include everything the story describes?

Teach the Model

Use Reading Skills

Identify the Main Idea *Answer:* Answers will vary. Some may say that the absurdity of the argument suggests that petty squabbles should not ruin friendships. **Ⓐ**

Use Reading Strategies

Make Inferences *Answer:* The chief is both reasonable and intuitive. He makes a point of not interfering in other people's business. **Ⓑ**

Geography Connection

Nigeria Nigeria, where most Yoruba live, is on the western coast of Africa. It is the most heavily populated country on the continent. There are many other groups there besides the Yoruba—hundreds of different languages are spoken in the country. Nigeria's position near the equator (at the south, it's about six degrees north) means that the climate is hot year-round, and the ground is quite fertile. Most Nigerians support themselves through farming.

MIRRORS & WINDOWS

Answer: Students may say the fight was caused by something silly. Others may accept the blame or insist the other person is to blame. Students may suggest that some personalities are more compatible than others.

---

re·tal·i·ate (ri tal´ē āt´) *v.*, respond to an action by doing a similar thing back, usually in a negative sense, such as repaying one injury by inflicting another

DURING READING

Use Reading Skills
Identify the Main Idea
What does this friend's claim that he always thought the other was "a little mad" suggest about the main idea? **Ⓐ**

as·ton·ish·ing (ə stä´ ni shiŋ) *adj.*, amazing; very surprising

DURING READING

Use Reading Strategies
Make Inferences What does the chief's response to the quarrel tell you about his character? **Ⓑ**

"How absurd to talk about backwards pipe-smoking. You're just trying to throw me off the track."

"Not at all. There are infinite possibilities in this world, which only a clod like you would fail to consider. For example, it's perfectly possible, although unlikely, that the sun won't set this evening. What I saw I saw, without error, and you, too stubborn to admit your lack of observation, your lack of imagination, <u>retaliate</u> by accusing me of playing with the facts just to get a wedge under your bulk. Why shouldn't a man buy a hat of a different color? And why shouldn't he invent a new way of smoking? I've half a mind to cut a hole in the back of my neck just to show you it can be done."

"And stop the sun, I suppose. I've always thought you a little mad, and now I'm convinced of it. Some witch is eating you. You ought to go to a doctor—"

"So that's it! I don't care what you think. You're impossible. I can't imagine why I ever found you good company. Your stupid face revolts me. I can't stop myself," he said, hitting his friend over the head with his hoe.

"So you admit you're mad, mad enough to pick a fight with me. Well I accept the challenge. Crazy or not, there's but one way to deal with unreasonable aggressors." And with that he threw his one-time friend flat on his back.

"Crude, evil-tempered man," said the other, "flat-footed rhinoceros, illegitimate offspring of a mortar and pestle.[4] Begone. I don't care how late it is. I wouldn't walk home at midnight with you. Our friendship is finished. Dead. No words will ever pass between us again."

When the chief heard of the <u>astonishing</u> quarrel between these two whose loyalty he had always supposed more durable than that of other men, he sighed deeply and went off to perform a sacrifice to Eshu. The next time village council met, he reallocated[5] the land so that henceforth the former friends would work at opposite corners of the communal tract. Then, holding up an old hoe for all to see, he said, mysteriously, "The sacrifice that iron refused to make is what's eating him." ❖

---

4. **mortar and pestle.** Device for pulverizing herbs
5. **reallocated.** Reassigned

MIRRORS & WINDOWS

Think of a time when you had a quarrel with a close friend or family member. What caused this conflict? Why are some friendships stronger than others?

Differentiated Instruction

Enrichment

Other versions of the story of Eshu and the two friends progress quite differently from this one. (Eshu returns and speaks to the friends, for instance.) Students may be interested in comparing different versions. Have them use library or Internet resources to find alternative tellings of the tale and have them report their findings to classmates.

Auditory and Kinesthetic Learning

Students may enjoy preparing a performance of "Eshu" for the class. Have them work in a group of five (four actors to play the two friends, Eshu, and the chief, plus a student director). Encourage them to play up the visual humor as well as the verbal humor in the dialogue.

Find Meaning

1. (a) How exactly does Eshu trick the two friends? (b) What does his success suggest about their friendship?

2. What does the chief say at the end of the tale?

Analyze Literature

Folk Tale Folk tales often depict everyday activities and the adventures of common people. These stories offer insights into the culture from which they come. What have you learned about Yoruban culture and everyday life from this folk tale? Create a list of details from the folk tale that help paint a picture of Yoruban culture. Then write a sentence that summarizes what you know.

Make Judgments

3. Why do you think Eshu acts the way he does?

4. (a) Which parts of the folk tale do you find funny? (b) How might humor help convey the main idea?

> Yoruban Culture
>
> 1. Agricultural community
>
> 2.
>
> 3.
>
> My Summary:

Extend Understanding

Writing Options

Creative Writing Imagine that you are gardening in one of the plots right next to the two friends in "Eshu." Concerned about the harm Eshu can cause, you decide to write a **flyer** to give passersby, warning them about his tricks. Use library resources or the Internet to find other Yoruban stories that feature the trickster god Eshu. Distribute copies of the flyer to classmates.

Expository Writing Can you think of a better solution than the one the chief devised? Write a brief **critical analysis** about the problem solving that occurs in "Eshu." Begin by stating your opinion of the chief's actions. Then briefly describe and discuss the problems the characters face and suggest your own solutions.

Collaborative Learning

Discuss the Role of the Trickster Working in a small group, discuss why Eshu behaves the way he does in the folk tale. What motivates him? You may wish to read folk tales and myths from other traditions that feature tricksters, for example, Anansi the spider in Ashanti folklore and Loki in Norse mythology.

Lifelong Learning

Research the History of Nigeria Research Nigeria's history. Begin by consulting a general reference work. Then, as a class, brainstorm specific topics related to the country's history. Choose a topic that interests you and research it in greater depth. Create a multimedia presentation, and present your report to the class.

W Go to www.mirrorsandwindows.com for more.

Find Meaning

1. (a) He wears a hat that is red on one side and black on the other, and holds his pipe and stick at the back of his body instead of the front. (b) The friendship was not very sturdy.

2. He makes a mysterious pronouncement about sacrifice while holding up a hoe.

Make Judgments

3. Answers will vary. Some will say Eshu enjoys causing trouble. Others will say that the farmers must have offended him in some way.

4. (a) Funny aspects might include the flowery compliments the two friends pay to each other, the image of Eshu in his costume, the language in the escalating argument, and the way the two men hit each other. (b) The humor may transmit the main idea by making the story engaging.

Analyze Literature

Folk Tale Details should include the fact that farming is part of daily life and the people work their own garden plots on communal land; the community is ruled by a chief, and there is also a community council; and it is customary for the wives to bring the men their meals in the field. Student summaries will vary.

Rubrics for Writing Options

You can adapt this as a checklist for students to use as they write.

Creative Writing

☐ Does the flyer include details that suggest the writer witnessed the events in this story?

☐ Does the flyer mention other problems Eshu has caused?

☐ Does the flyer provide a persuasive argument for why readers should beware of the trickster?

Expository Writing

☐ Does the analysis state a clear opinion?

☐ Does the analysis describe the problems presented in the story?

☐ Does the analysis offer solutions to the problems described?

At a Glance
Directed Reading
- Reading Level: Moderate
- Difficulty Consideration: Vocabulary
- Ease Factor: Length

Objectives
Studying this lesson will enable students to

- use reading skills such as analyzing cause and effect
- define motivation and recognize how this literary technique is used in connection with characters
- describe literary accomplishments of Geraldine Harris
- appreciate an Egyptian myth about a power struggle between the gods

Launch the Lesson
Before students begin reading "The Secret Name of Ra," ask them to think about the title of the selection. Are they intrigued by the idea of a secret name? What do they think the name might do? Who is Ra—do they already know? Have them examine the pictures and the display quote, then begin the story.

KEY TERMS
MYTH, 738
MOTIVATION, 738
CHARACTER, 738
CAUSE, 738
EFFECT, 738
PLOT, 738
THEME, 738
SETTING, 745
SUMMARY, 745
SKIM, 745

Common Core State Standards
Reading Literature
RL.1

DIRECTED READING

The Secret Name of Ra

An Egyptian Myth retold by Geraldine Harris

BEFORE READING

Build Background
Cultural Context While ancient Egyptians worshipped a large number of gods, the sun god, Ra, was the most important. He was both creator and sustainer of the world. As an agricultural people, the Egyptians worshipped the power of the sun to make crops flourish. Each day Ra traveled across the sky in his bark canoe, and at night he traveled through the underworld, where he vanquished a giant serpent before emerging on the other side of the world.

Reader's Context When have you given your trust to someone you should not have? What was the outcome?

Set Purpose
Preview Build Background, as well as the vocabulary, footnotes, and artwork with the reading. Try to predict what this story will be about.

Analyze Literature
Motivation A force that moves a character to think, feel, or behave a certain way is called a **motivation.** You might expect the gods in "The Secret Name of Ra" to have very different reasons for their actions than humans. However, Egyptian gods possess many human qualities. As you read, try to determine the motivations of both Isis and Ra.

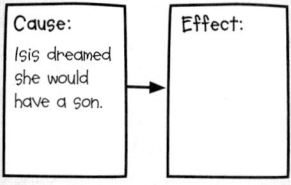

Meet the Author

Geraldine Harris (b. 1951) teaches Egyptology at Oxford University in England and has published both fiction and nonfiction. Her creative writing, which includes the four-novel Seven Citadels series for young readers, is strongly influenced by her knowledge of folklore and mythology. Harris has also published a number of books about ancient Egyptian mythology and culture.

Use Reading Skills
Analyze Cause and Effect A *cause* is an action or event that makes something else happen. Any action or event that results from a cause is an *effect*. By analyzing the causes and effects, you will better understand the plot, characters, and theme of a story. As you read, create a cause-and-effect chart for "The Secret Name of Ra."

Cause:		Effect:
Isis dreamed she would have a son.	→	

Preview Vocabulary
sole (sōl) *adj.*, only

ex·alt·ed (ig zōlt´ ed) *adj.*, held in high regard

cun·ning (kʉ´ niŋ) *adj.*, clever or tricky

de·i·ty (dē´ə tē) *n.*, god or goddess

driv·el (driv´ əl) *v.*, drool

a·byss (ə bis´) *n.*, bottomless pit; something too deep to measure

---

Words in Use

Preview Vocabulary	Selection Words	Teaching Words	
sole, 740	**envoys,** 741	**sustainer,** 738	**sophisticated,** 741
exalted, 740		**flourish,** 738	
cunning, 740		**vanquished,** 738	**divine,** 742
deity, 740		**emerging,** 738	**exhibit,** 742
drivel, 740		**Egyptology,** 738	
abyss, 740		**fertile,** 741	
		millennium, 741	
		sustained, 741	

The Secret Name of Ra

Detail depicting the deceased led by Horus before Osiris, c. 1250 BC. British Museum, London.

An Egyptian Myth retold by Geraldine Harris

Ra gave a scream that was heard through all creation.

739

Teach the Selection

Summary

The goddess Isis dreams that one day she will have a son, Horus. Desiring to make Horus the most powerful god, she decides to steal the power of the Sun God and Sole Creator, Ra. Ra is getting old, but he is protected by a secret name and cannot be harmed by anything he has created. Isis follows him and obtains a bit of his saliva when it drops on the ground. Mixing the saliva and earth into clay, she forms a serpent and uses magic to bring it to life.

As Ra is passing by, the serpent bites him, and because it uses his own power (his saliva) against him, he is instantly in agony. He summons the other gods, hoping that they can help him. Isis offers to use her powerful magic, and Ra, unaware that she betrayed him, welcomes her help.

Isis tells him that unless he reveals his secret name, he cannot be cured. Ra is reluctant, but his pain and fear are so great that he gives in. Isis rejoices, knowing that one day her son will take over Ra's throne.

MIRRORS & WINDOWS The Mirrors & Windows questions at the end of the selection focus on the theme of trickery. Before students begin reading, ask: Under what circumstances, if any, would it be wise to use trickery?

Program Resources

Planning and Assessment
Program Planning Guide, Selection Lesson Plan
E-Lesson Planner
Assessment Guide, Lesson Test
ExamView

Technology Tools
Interactive Student Text on CD
Visual Teaching Package
Audio Library
mirrorsandwindows.com

Meeting the Standards
Folk Literature: Unit 8, Directed Reading, pp. 34–39

Differentiating Instruction
English Language Learners, Cause and Effect, pp. 184–192

Use Reading Skills

Analyze Cause and Effect Note that a good way of identifying cause-and-effect relationships is to ask *why* questions: The questions identify effects, and the answers state causes. Model a question and answer, then have students suggest others. (For example, "Why can't anything in creation harm Ra?" "Because his secret name protects him.")

Analyze Literature

Symbol Remind students that a symbol represents both itself and something else. Focusing on this sentence, have them look up *crossroads;* note that it means both an intersection of roads and, more symbolically, a critical point. Ask how the crossroads is a fitting symbol in this case. (Students should see that when Ra is bitten at the crossroads, he stops being all-powerful and becomes vulnerable.) **A**

Analyze Literature

Diction Explain that diction is a writer's or speaker's choice of words. The goal is to use the words that best express ideas for the desired audience. Ask students to point out words that they find exceptionally effective in the selection and to explain why they chose them.

Ra, the Sole Creator was visible to the people of Egypt as the disc of the sun, but they knew him in many other forms. He could appear as a crowned man, a falcon or a man with a **A** falcon's head and, as the scarab beetle[1] pushes a round ball of dung in front of it, the Egyptians pictured Ra as a scarab pushing the sun across the sky. In caverns deep below the earth were hidden another seventy-five forms of Ra: mysterious beings with mummified bodies[2] and heads consisting of birds or snakes, feathers or flowers. The names of Ra were as numerous as his forms; he was the Shining One, The Hidden One, The Renewer of the Earth, The Wind in the Souls, The Exalted One, but there was one name of the Sun God which had not been spoken since time began. To know this secret name of Ra was to have power over him and over the world that he had created.

Isis longed for such a power. She had dreamed that one day she would have a marvellous falcon-headed son called Horus and she wanted the throne of Ra to give to her child. Isis was the Mistress of Magic, wiser than millions of men, but she knew that nothing in creation was powerful enough to harm its creator. Her only chance was to turn the power of Ra against himself and at last Isis thought of a cruel and cunning plan. Every day the Sun God walked through his kingdom, attended by a crowd of spirits and lesser deities, but Ra was growing old. His eyes were dim, his step no longer firm and he had even begun to drivel.

One morning Isis mingled with a group of minor goddesses and followed behind the King of the Gods. She watched the face of Ra until she saw his saliva drip onto a clod of earth. When she was sure that no-one was taking any notice of her, she scooped up the earth and carried it away. Isis mixed the earth with the saliva of Ra to form clay and

modelled a wicked-looking serpent. Through the hours of darkness she whispered spells over the clay serpent as it lay lifeless in her hands. Then the cunning goddess carried it to a crossroads on the route which the Sun God always took. She hid the serpent in the long grass and returned to her palace.

The next day Ra came walking through his kingdom with the spirits and lesser deities crowding behind him. When he approached the crossroads, the spells of Isis began to work and the clay serpent quivered into life. As the Sun God passed, it bit him in the ankle and crumbled back into earth. Ra gave a scream that was heard through all creation.

His jaws chattered and his limbs shook as the poison flooded through him like a rising Nile. "I have been wounded by something deadly," whispered Ra. "I know that in my heart, though my eyes cannot see it. Whatever it was, I, the Lord of Creation, did not make it. I am sure that none of you would have done such a terrible thing to me, but I have never felt such pain! How can this have happened to me? I am the Sole Creator, the child of the watery abyss. I am the god with a thousand names, but my secret name was only spoken once, before time began. Then it was hidden in my body so that no-one should ever learn it and be able to

1. **scarab beetle.** Dung beetle; this insect was held sacred by ancient Egyptians, who saw it as a symbol both of the sun god and of the continued existence of the soul after death.
2. **mummified bodies.** Bodies that have been preserved for burial by removing the internal organs, treating them with special substances, and wrapping them in cloth to keep them from decaying

sole (sōl) *adj.,* only
ex·alt·ed (ig zōlt´ ed) *adj.,* held in high regard
cun·ning (kʉ´ niŋ) *adj.,* clever or tricky
de·i·ty (dē´ə tē) *n.,* god or goddess
driv·el (driv´ əl) *v.,* drool
a·byss (ə bis´) *n.,* bottomless pit; something too deep to measure

Differentiated Instruction

Enrichment

Students may be interested in exploring stories about one of the many gods and goddesses in the selection. Have them use library or Internet resources to research the deity, then prepare a poster featuring the god or goddess. Display the posters in the classroom.

English Language Learners

English learners may benefit from a review of appositives. Remind them that an appositive is a noun, pronoun, or noun phrase placed next to another noun or noun phrase to modify it. The paragraph on page 741 listing the gods who came to see Ra contains many examples. Work through it to help students identify and understand the appositives and what they modify.

work spells against me. Yet as I walked through my kingdom something struck at me and now my heart is on fire and my limbs shake. Send for the Ennead![3] Send for my children! They are wise in magic and their knowledge pierces heaven."

HISTORY ▶▶ CONNECTION

Ancient Egypt Although most of North Africa is desert, the fertile lands of the Nile River valley made it possible for a thriving civilization to develop in ancient Egypt during the third millennium BC. Sustained by increasingly sophisticated agricultural practices, Egyptians were free to explore architecture, the arts, and the sciences. Much of what they achieved can still be seen today. During most of its history, ancient Egypt was ruled by a series of all-powerful kings called pharaohs. A pharaoh, as the earthly embodiment of a god, was responsible for maintaining *ma'at,* or "divine order," in the kingdom. What role do you think this concept of *ma'at* plays in "The Secret Name of Ra"? **B**

Messengers hurried to the great gods and from the four pillars of the world came the Ennead: Shu and Tefenet, Geb and Nut, Seth and Osiris, Isis and Nephthys. Envoys traveled the land and the sky and the watery abyss to summon all the deities created by Ra. From the marshes came frog-headed Heket, Wadjet the cobra goddess and the fearsome god, crocodile-headed Sobek. From the deserts came fiery Selkis, the scorpion goddess, Anubis the jackal, the guardian of the dead and Nekhbet the vulture goddess. From the cities of the north came warlike Neith, gentle cat-headed Bastet, fierce lion-headed Sekhmet and Ptah the god of crafts. From the cities of the south came Onuris, the divine huntsman and ram-headed Khnum with Anukis his wife and

Satis his daughter. Cunning Thoth and wise Seshat, goddess of writing; virile Min and snake-headed Renenutet, goddess of the harvest, kindly Meskhenet and monstrous Taweret, goddesses of birth—all of them were summoned to the side of Ra.

The gods and goddesses gathered around the Sun God, weeping and wailing, afraid that he was going to die. Isis stood among them beating her breast and pretending to be as distressed and bewildered as all the other frightened deities.

"Father of All," she began, "whatever is the matter? Has some snake bitten you? Has some wretched creature dared to strike at his Creator? Few of the gods can compare with me in wisdom and I am the Mistress of Magic. If you will let me help you, I'm sure that I can cure you." **C**

Ra was grateful to Isis and told her all that had happened. "Now I am colder than water and hotter than fire," complained the Sun God. "My eyes darken. I cannot see the sky and my body is soaked by the sweat of fever."

"Tell me your full name," said cunning Isis. "Then I can use it in my spells. Without that knowledge the greatest of magicians cannot help you."

"I am the maker of heaven and earth," said Ra. "I made the heights and the depths,

---

3. **Ennead.** Literally, a group of nine; in Egyptian mythology, the most ancient group of nine gods

Writing Skills

Summarizing
Review the principles behind summarizing for students, and note that one good way to create a summary is to
- break the work down into several sections,
- summarize each section, and
- review the section summaries in order to create an overall summary.

Suggest that students consider using a summary chart or separate note cards for each section summary to keep their ideas organized. Have students use one of these methods when they do the Expository Writing assignment on page 745, and have them turn in their working notes along with their summaries so that they can receive feedback.

Answer: Answers will vary. Some students will cite selfish reasons; others will claim they tricked another person for a greater cause; and some will argue that tricks are never acceptable.

Find Meaning

1. (a) They include The Shining One, The Hidden One, The Renewer of the Earth, The Wind in the Souls, and The Exalted One. (b) He is very powerful and holds a central place in Egyptian religious life.

2. (a) She plans to injure him. Then she will tell him that only his secret name can cure him. (b) She appears ambitious, clever, and ruthless.

3. (a) She makes a serpent using Ra's saliva. (b) It turns his own power against him. Nothing that Ra created can be used against him; only something already within him — his saliva — will be effective.

Make Judgments

4. Ra knows she is a god and a great magician.

5. (a) Ra is old and frail. Isis is duplicitous and ambitious. (b) Some may suggest that Egyptians would feel closer to gods who felt the same emotions as they felt. Also, mistakes and quarrels of the gods could explain bad things that happen in the world.

I set horizons at east and west and established the gods in their glory. When I open my eyes it is light; when I close them it is dark. The mighty Nile floods at my command. The gods do not know my true name but I am the maker of time, the giver of festivals. I spark the fire of life. At dawn I rise as Khepri, the scarab and sail across the sky in the Boat of Millions of Years.[4] At noon I blaze in the heavens as Ra and at evening I am Ra-atum, the setting sun."

"We know all that," said Isis. "If I am to find a spell to drive out this poison, I will have to use your secret name. Say your name and live."

"My secret name was given to me so that I could sit at ease," moaned Ra, "and fear no living creature. How can I give it away?"

Isis said nothing and knelt beside the Sun God while his pain mounted. When it became unbearable, Ra ordered the other gods to stand back while he whispered his secret name to Isis. "Now the power of the secret name has passed from my heart to your heart," said Ra wearily. "In time you can give it to your son, but warn him never to betray the secret!"

> "My secret name was given to me so that I could sit at ease... and fear no living creature. How can I give it away?"

Isis nodded and began to chant a great spell that drove the poison out of the limbs of Ra and he rose up stronger than before. The Sun God returned to the Boat of Millions of Years and Isis shouted for joy at the success of her plan. She knew now that one day Horus her son would sit on the throne of Egypt and wield the power of Ra. ❖

---

4. Boat of Millions of Years. Name often used in Egyptian texts for the boat in which Ra sailed across the sky during the day and through the underworld at night

---

Think of a time you tricked someone in order to get something you wanted very badly. How did you justify your actions to yourself or others? Is there ever a time when it is acceptable to trick others?

Find Meaning

1. (a) What are some of the names of Ra? (b) What do these names suggest about his place in ancient Egyptian religious life?

2. (a) What is Isis's plan for learning Ra's secret name? (b) What does her plan reveal about her character?

3. (a) What does Isis create to harm Ra? (b) Why is this object able to hurt him?

Make Judgments

4. Why did Ra trust Isis?

5. (a) Egyptian deities have both human and divine qualities. What human qualities do Ra and Isis have? (b) Why might these gods exhibit human traits?

Differentiated Instruction

Reading Proficiency

Remind students to monitor comprehension as they read. Encourage them to pause every two or three paragraphs and to ask themselves if they understand what is happening. If not, they should read that section again.

Visual Learning

Students may enjoy creating a picture book based on "The Secret Name of Ra." Ask them to choose scenes to illustrate and to simplify the text that accompanies the pictures. Their goal is to tell the whole story, keeping in mind that the audience for a picture book is children who cannot yet read or who have just learned to read. Have students share their work with classmates.

In "The Secret Name of Ra," the sun god has become a failing old man and Isis plots to replace him. The hymn, or song of praise, excerpted here comes from a time when an Egyptian pharaoh attempted something similar. Akhenaton and his queen Nefertiti ruled Egypt during the fourteenth century BC. They ordered their people to abandon the old gods. Instead, they were to worship a single sun god, the formerly minor deity Aton. In the end, the change didn't catch on. The people returned to their old ways after Akhenaton's death. It is unlikely that Akhenaton wrote the hymn himself, although it is sometimes attributed to him.

from **Akhenaton's Hymn to the Sun**

A Hymn translated by John A. Wilson

> When thou settest[1] in the western horizon,
> The land is in darkness as if in death.
> Men sleep in a room with heads wrapped up,
> And no eye sees another.
> 5 Though all their goods under their heads be stolen,
> Yet would they not perceive it.
> Every lion comes forth from his den,
> And all creeping things sting.
> Darkness is a shroud[2] and the earth is still,
> 10 For he who made them rests in his horizon.
>
> At daybreak, when thou risest[3] on the horizon,
> When thou shinest as the sun disk by day,
> Thou drivest away darkness and givest thy rays;
> Then the Two Lands[4] are in daily festivity:
> 15 Men awake and stand upon their feet,
> For thou hast[5] raised them up.
> They wash their bodies and take their clothing,
> Their arms raised in praise at thy appearing.
> And all the world, they do their work....

---

1. **thou settest.** You set
2. **shroud.** Cloth used to wrap a body before burial
3. **thou risest.** You rise
4. **Two Lands.** Upper and Lower Egypt, regions that were at war for centuries, until they were united around 3,000 BC by a king named Menes
5. **thou hast.** You have

AKHENATON'S HYMN TO THE SUN **743**

Analyze Literature
Sensory Details Remind students that sensory details relate to the senses (sight, sound, taste, touch, and smell). Writers use them to create vivid descriptions in a literary work. Challenge students to identify sensory details in "Akhenaton's Hymn" and tell which sense they describe. Answers include "darkness as if in death" and "goods under their heads" (sight); "heads wrapped up," "sting," and "they wash their bodies" (touch).

Analyze Literature
Metaphor Remind students that in a metaphor, one thing is written about as if it is another. Ask students to identify metaphors in the selection. (Darkness is compared to a shroud in line 9, and the sun god is compared to a person's lifetime in line 33.)

Science Connection
The Sun Note that it was logical for the ancient Egyptians and other people in antiquity to attribute great power to sun gods. Explain that the sun, the star around which the earth revolves, is the source of the energy that supports life. This energy works in many ways, such as keeping the atmosphere warm; powering photosynthesis in plants; and causing water to evaporate.

Words in Use

from "Akhenaton's Hymn to the Sun"
Selection Words
perceive, 743
festivity, 743
flourish, 744

Common Core State Standards
Reading Literature
RL.9

Use Reading Skills

Paraphrase Remind students that paraphrasing means putting things into their own words. Challenge them to rephrase lines from the poem, translating the old-fashioned diction into familiar modern words and word order. For example, they might express "How manifold it is / What thou hast made!" as "You have made so many different kinds of things!"

Use Reading Strategies

Ask Questions Ask students how access to modern technology might have changed this poet's perception of the impact of the sun's setting. (The invention of electric lighting allows people to go on with their lives after dark.) **A**

Text-to-Text Connection

Answer: Students may point out that the sun in "Akhenaton's Hymn to the Sun" is the maker of all things and what drives away the "creeping things" that sting. In "The Secret Name of Ra" the personification of the sun, Ra, is the creator. Egyptians seem to have associated the sun with fertility and nature.

---

20   How manifold[6] it is,
     What thou hast made!
     It is hidden from the face of man.
     Thou sole god, without thy like,
     Thou didst create the world after thy desire,
25   Whilst[7] thou wert alone:
     All mankind, cattle and wild beasts,
     Whatever goes by foot upon the earth,
     Whatever flies on high with wings....
     The world came into being by thy hand,
30   According as thou didst make them all.
     When thou hast risen they live,
A When thou settest then they die.
     Thou art lifetime thy own self,
     For we live only through thee.
35   Eyes are fixed on beauty until thou settest,
     All work is laid aside when thou settest in the west.
     But when thou risest again,
     Then everything is made to flourish.... ❖

---

6. manifold. Having many different forms, features, or parts
7. whilst. While

TEXT TO TEXT CONNECTION Although "The Secret Name of Ra" and "Akhenaton's Hymn to the Sun" feature different sun gods, both provide a sense of how much ancient Egyptians revered the sun. Based on details from both works, why do you think this is so?

744 UNIT 8 FOLK LITERATURE

Differentiated Instruction

English Language Learning and Reading Proficiency

Both English learners and less-confident readers may benefit from focusing on the archaic language in the poem. Review the verb ending *–est,* used throughout. Explain that this is an old-fashioned ending for present-tense second-person singular verbs. It follows the subject *thou,* meaning "you."

So, for example, "thou settest," is the same as "you set." Irregular forms also used in the selection are *thou hast* ("you have") and *thou wert* ("you were"). Another older word form students will encounter is the possessive pronoun *thy,* or "your."

Analyze Literature

Motivation When you read, analyzing characters' motivations gives you a deeper understanding of the story and a better sense of the people the writer has worked to portray. Make a three-column chart in which you track the motivations of Ra and Isis and relate that information to their personality traits and behaviors.

Character	Traits and Behaviors	Motivation
Ra	getting old	

Extend Understanding

Writing Options

Creative Writing Use what you learned from reading "The Secret Name of Ra" to create your own short Egyptian **myth.** Use Geraldine Harris's retelling as your model. Include characters, settings, and themes that appear in her myth.

Expository Writing A summary retells the main ideas of a text. A summary should be shorter than the original and use different words. Write a **summary** of "The Secret Name of Ra." Cover all the key details of the plot, setting, and characters. When you are done, read your summary to the class.

Collaborative Learning

Examine Motivation With a partner, discuss why Ra would have a secret name that held such power over him. Skim "The Secret Name of Ra" to look for possible answers to this question. Seek out other versions of the same myth to see if they provide additional guidance. Present your ideas to the class and solicit more ideas.

Lifelong Learning

Learn About the Nile Research the Nile to learn how the river affected the lives of the ancient Egyptians. Possible topics to investigate include the agricultural practices that evolved along its shores, gods and goddesses that were associated with the Nile, and the settlements built near it. Prepare and deliver a presentation on your findings for the class.

 Go to **www.mirrorsandwindows.com** for more.

Analyze Literature

Motivation Answers will vary. Students may suggest that Ra's motivations include the desire to make the pain stop and protect his secret name. They may say that Isis wishes to win power.

Rubrics for Writing Options

You can adapt this as a checklist for students to use as they write.

Creative Writing

☐ Does the myth use characters, settings, and themes from "The Secret Name of Ra"?

☐ Does the myth use Geraldine Harris's retelling as a model?

Expository Writing

☐ Does the summary present the main ideas from the myth?

☐ Does the summary include plot, setting, and characters?

☐ Is the summary significantly shorter than the original?

Vocabulary & Spelling

Homographs, Homophones, and Homonyms

Isis mixed the earth with the saliva of Ra to form clay....

—GERALDINE HARRIS, "The Secret Name of Ra"

English contains many words that are spelled alike but pronounced differently—such as *lead* (to guide) and *lead* (the metal). It also includes words that are pronounced alike but spelled differently—such as *hear* and *here*—and words that are both spelled and pronounced alike but have completely different meanings. For example, *form* in the above quotation can mean "an appearance," "a category," "a printed document," or the verb "to shape." These types of easily confused words are known as homographs, homophones, and homonyms.

Homographs and Homophones

Homographs are words that have the same spelling but have different meanings and different pronunciations.

> EXAMPLE
>
> **produce** (prə düs´) *v.*, make
>
> **produce** (prō´ düs) *n.*, products grown on a farm, especially fruit and vegetables

Homophones are words that are pronounced the same but differ in spelling and meaning.

> EXAMPLE
>
> **bare** (ber) *adj.*, without covering
>
> **bear** (ber) *v.*, support; hold up

Other common examples include *to, two,* and *too;* and *their, they're,* and *there.*

Homonyms

Homonyms are words that are both homographs and homophones—that is, they are spelled and pronounced alike but have different and unrelated meanings. For example, the word *fine* can refer to a penalty or to a feeling of well being.

Use context clues to determine the meaning of multiple meaning words. First, determine the word's part of speech. Then, decide which meaning makes sense in context.

Vocabulary Practice

On a separate sheet of paper, choose the correct spelling to complete each sentence.

1. ...the Sun God walked (threw, through) his kingdom....
2. ...all of them were summoned to the (side, sighed) of Ra.
3. They are wise in magic and (there, their, they're) knowledge pierces heaven.

Spelling Practice
Homophones

The following words from "The Secret Name of Ra" have homophones, or words that sound the same, but have different spellings and meanings. Write a homophone for each word in the list below.

for	sail	through
great	so	to
knew	sole	warn
know	son	
or	there	

Tsali of the Cherokees

An Oral History by Norah Roper, as told to Alice Lee Marriott

BEFORE READING

Build Background

Historical Context The Trail of Tears is a prominent, painful episode in Cherokee history. In the mid-1800s, thousands of Cherokee from the southeastern United States were dispossessed of their land by the U.S. government and forced to march to a region called Indian Territory. There they joined similarly relocated Choctaw, Chickasaw, Creek, and Seminole tribes.

Reader's Context Imagine what it would feel like if strangers arrived and forced your family from its property. Read to learn about a time when that was a common experience for Native Americans.

Set Purpose

As you read, try to determine how oral histories differ from legends and myths. What elements might oral histories and these other genres share?

Analyze Literature

Motivation A force that moves a character to think, feel, or behave in a certain way is called a **motivation.** A character's motivations can often be determined by analyzing his or her actions. As you read "Tsali of the Cherokees," try to determine what motivates the major and the minor characters and how these motivations affect the plot.

Use Reading Skills

Identify Author's Purpose An author's purpose is his or her reason for writing. For example, writers may write to inform, to entertain, or to persuade. A writer may also have more than one purpose. As you read this oral history, try to identify the author's purpose for recording and retelling this story. Use a two-column chart to help.

Details	Author's Purpose
Chiefs acted unfairly	

Preview Vocabulary

en·croach·ing (in krōch´ iŋ) *adj.,* trespassing; creeping slowly into a territory with the object of stealing it

mis·sion·ary (mi´ shə ner' ē) *n.,* person sent to other countries or remote areas to spread a religion and, sometimes, to care for people

sulk·i·ly (sʉl´ kə lē) *adv.,* moodily silent

mi·li·tia (mə li´ shə) *n.,* citizens' army

a·skew (ə skyü´) *adj.,* out of line; crooked

Meet the Author

Alice Lee Marriott (1910–1992) was an ethnologist, or a person who studies cultural history and practices such as rituals and medicine. Ethnologists often collect oral histories, which are unwritten stories recounted by the descendants of people who originally experienced the events. Alice Lee Marriott was a longtime resident of Oklahoma and recorded this oral history from a Cherokee named Norah Roper, granddaughter of Tsali.

At a Glance
Directed Reading
- Reading Level: Moderate
- Difficulty Consideration: Vocabulary
- Ease Factors: Sympathetic narrator and plot

Objectives

Studying this lesson will enable students to
- use reading skills such as identifying an author's purpose
- define motivation and analyze its use in the selection
- describe the work of Alice Lee Marriott and Christine Graf, and recognize how their backgrounds influence their writing
- compare an oral history to a magazine article
- observe ways in which people respond to pressures that test their limits

Launch the Lesson

Prior to reading "Tsali of the Cherokees," ask students to tell you some things they know about how white settlers treated Native Americans. After they give several examples, say they are about to read a firsthand account of such treatment.

Words in Use

Preview Vocabulary	Selection Words	Teaching Words
encroaching, 748	mixed-blood, 748	prominent, 747
missionary, 749	coaxed, 748	episode, 747
sulkily, 750		dispossessed, 747
militia, 751		ethnologist, 747
askew, 753		displaced, 751
		forcibly, 751
		relocate, 754

KEY TERMS

Common Core State Standards

Reading Literature
RL.1

Reading Informational
RI.6

Teach the Selection

Summary

Many descriptions of the western movement of settlers in this country are told from the perspective of people of European ancestry. "Tsali of the Cherokees" tells part of that story from the point of view of people who were mistreated and displaced during the settlers' westward migration. Tsali and his family farmed two hills and a valley in western Georgia. Soon after white people discovered gold in the hills, Tsali and the other Cherokee were surprised to learn that some of their chiefs had agreed to forfeit their land. Although Tsali, who like other Indians did not share the white man's obsession with gold, at first hoped the white people would want the valley but not the hills, missionaries insisted that the whites wanted all the land. Ultimately separated from each other and forced from their land, Tsali's family members and other Cherokees' lives changed forever.

MIRRORS & WINDOWS The Mirrors & Windows questions at the end of the selection focus on the theme of homeland. Before students begin reading, ask: What would it be like to return to the homeland of your ancestors? Would you choose to go, or would you have to be forced to live there?

Reenactment of the Trail of Tears 150 years after the forced relocation of the Cherokee.

Tsali of the Cherokees

An Oral History by Norah Roper, as told to Alice Lee Marriott

They knew that their tribal chiefs traveled back and forth to the white man's place called Washington more often than they used to do. They knew that when the chiefs came back from that place, there were quarrels in the tribal council.

Up in the hills and the back country, where the *Ani Keetoowah*—the true Cherokees—lived, word of the changes came more slowly than the changes themselves came to the valley Cherokees. Many of the hill people never left their farm lands, and those who did went only to the nearest trading post and back. Few travelers ever came into the uplands, where the mists of the Smokies[1] shut out the <u>encroaching</u> world.

So, when the news came that some of the chiefs of the Cherokees had touched the pen, and put their names or their marks on a paper, and agreed by doing so that this was no longer Cherokee country, the *Ani Keetoowah* could not believe what they heard. Surely, they said to each other, this news must be false. No Cherokee—not even a mixed-blood—would sign away his own and his people's lands. But that was what the chiefs had done.

Then the word came that the chiefs were even more divided among themselves and that not all of them had touched the pen. Some were not willing to move away to the

---

1. **Smokies.** Great Smoky Mountains, part of the Appalachian range in North Carolina and Tennessee

en·croach·ing (in krōch' iŋ) *adj.*, trespassing; creeping slowly into a territory with the object of stealing it

748

Program Resources

Planning and Assessment
Program Planning Guide, Selection Lesson Plan
E-Lesson Planner
Assessment Guide, Lesson Test
ExamView

Technology Tools
Interactive Student Text on CD
Visual Teaching Package
Audio Library
mirrorsandwindows.com

Meeting the Standards
Folk Literature: Unit 8, Directed Reading, pp. 40–45

new lands across the Mississippi and settle in the hills around Fort Gibson, Oklahoma.

"Perhaps we should hang on," the *Ani Keetoowah* said to one another. "Perhaps we will not have to go away after all." They waited and hoped, although they knew in their hearts that hope is the cruelest curse on mankind.

One of the leaders of the *Ani Keetoowah* was Tsali. The white men had trouble pronouncing his name, so they called him "Charley" or "Dutch." Tsali was a full blood, and so were his wife and their family. They were of the oldest *Keetoowah* Cherokee blood and would never have let themselves be ashamed by having half-breed relatives.

Tsali and his four sons worked two hillsides and the valley between them, in the southern part of the hill country. Tsali and his wife and their youngest son lived in a log house at the head of the hollow. The others had their own homes, spread out along the hillsides. They grew corn and beans, a few English peas, squashes and pumpkins, tobacco and cotton, and even a little sugar cane and indigo.[2] Tsali's wife kept chickens in a fenced run away from the house.

The women gathered wild hemp[3] and spun it; they spun the cotton, and the wool from their sheep. Then they wove the thread into cloth, and sometimes in winter when their few cattle and the sheep had been cared for and the chickens fed and there was not much else to do, the men helped at the looms,[4] which they had built themselves. The women did all the cutting and the making of garments for the whole family.

Tsali and his family were not worldly rich, in the way that the chiefs and some of the Cherokees of the valley towns were rich. They had hardly seen white man's metal money in their lives. But Tsali's people never lacked for food, or good clothing, or safe shelter.

(A) The missionaries seldom came into the uplands then. Tsali took his sons and their wives, and his own wife, to the great dance ground where the seven *Keetoowah* villages gathered each month at the time of the full moon. There they danced their prayers in time to the beating of the women's terrapin-shell[5] leg rattles, around and around the mound of packed white ashes on top of which bloomed the eternal fire that was the life of all the Cherokees.

> "There's no hope this time. The lands have all been sold.... You'll have to go west."

The occasional missionaries fussed over the children. They gave them white men's names, so that by Tsali's time everyone had an Indian name and an English one. The Cherokees listened to the missionaries politely, for the missionaries were great gossips, and the Cherokees heard their news and ignored the rest of their words.

"You will have to go soon," said one white preacher to Tsali. "There's no hope this time. The lands have all been sold, and the Georgia troopers are moving in. You'll have to go west." **(C)**

"We'll never leave," Tsali answered. "This is our land and we belong to it. Who could take it from us—who would want it? It's hard even for us to farm here, and we're used to

---

2. **indigo.** Plant used to make a blue dye
3. **hemp.** Plant with tough stems whose fibers can be woven into rope and cloth
4. **looms.** Machines for weaving fabric from fibers or threads
5. **terrapin-shell.** Turtle shell

---

mis·sion·ary (mi′ shə ner′ ē) *n.,* person sent to other countries or remote areas to spread a religion and, sometimes, to care for people

---

Teach the Selection

Use Reading Skills

Identify Author's Purpose Have students pause in their reading after the first five paragraphs and recall what they have read. Ask: "What was the purpose of including this information in the oral history?" Lead students to observe that the first several paragraphs give historical, cultural, and geographical background for understanding what is to come. You might also draw students' attention to the tone of these paragraphs, which prepares the reader for the main character's disappointment. **(A)**

Use Reading Strategies

Make Inferences Remind students that this selection is part of an oral history—the actual memories of a member of the Cherokee nation. Invite students to make inferences about why Cherokees might say ". . . hope is the cruelest curse on mankind." After they respond, ask students when they think hope is useful and when it can become a "curse." Encourage them to explain their answers. **(B)**

Use Reading Skills

Identify Author's Purpose Discuss the author's purpose in shifting from third-person point of view to dialogue at this point in this selection. (The dialogue makes the story more immediate.) **(C)**

Differentiated Instruction

English Language Learning
Use this selection to help English learners practice recognizing singular, plural, and possessive pronouns. Have students make columns on a sheet of paper for different types of pronouns—singular, plural, and possessive. Tell students to work individually or with partners to identify and list such pronouns as *they, their, those, his, him, it,* and *themselves* in the proper columns. Then work with students to identify the gender of each pronoun.

Use Reading Strategies

Clarify Remind students to ask questions as they read to clarify, or make clear, what is happening, why it is happening, and how it is happening. Encourage them to ask about what is actually happening, what might happen, how events relate, the deep meaning of an action, or how an event relates to the theme of the selection. Model asking several types of questions about these pages: "Why does Tsali think white people would want the valley land?" "Why was Tsali so confident when he first talked with the missionaries?" **Ⓐ**

Science Connection

Panning for Gold Rains wash gold from rock into streams and rivers. Because gold is denser than sand and rock, it settles to the bottom and may be separated by a process called panning. A person can mix several handfuls of gold-bearing sand or gravel with water in a pan with shallow sides. Swirling the contents of the pan makes the lighter materials wash over the side, leaving small chunks of gold behind.

Analyze Literature

Motivation Remind students that a character's motivations explain his or her actions. Ask: "What motivates the trader to warn Tsali not to say anything about the gold on his land? Is he concerned with Tsali's well being?" (The trader wants to have Tsali's gold for himself.) **Ⓑ**

Ⓐ hill farming. The white men wouldn't want to come here—they'll want the rich lands in the valleys, if the lowland people will give them up."

"They want these hills more than any other land," the missionary said. He sounded almost threatening. "Don't you see, you poor ignorant Indian? They are finding gold—gold, man, gold—downstream in the lower *Keetoowah* country. That means that the source of the gold is in the headwaters of the rivers that flow from here down into the valleys. I've seen gold dust in those streams myself."

"Gold?" asked Tsali. "You mean this yellow stuff?" And he took a buckskin pouch out of the pouch that hung from his sash, and opened it. At the sight of the yellow dust the pouch contained, the missionary seemed to go a little crazy.

"That's it!" he cried. "Where did you get it? How did you find it? You'll be rich if you can get more."

"We find it in the rivers, as you said," Tsali replied. "We gather what we need to take to the trader. I have this now because I am going down to the valley in a few days, to get my wife some ribbons to trim her new dress."

"Show me where you got it," the missionary begged. "We can all be rich. I'll protect you from the other white men, if you make me your partner."

"No, I think I'd better not," said Tsali thoughtfully. "My sons are my partners, as I was my father's. We do not need another partner, and, as long as we have our old squirrel guns, we do not need to be protected. Thank you, but you can go on. We are better off as we are."

The missionary coaxed and threatened, but Tsali stood firm. In the end, the white man went away, without any gold except a pinch that Tsali gave him, because the

missionary seemed to value the yellow dust even more than the trader did.

Then it was time to go to the trading post. When Tsali came in the store, the trader said to him, "Well, Chief, glad to see you. I hear you're a rich man these days."

"I have always been a rich man," Tsali answered. "I have my family and we all have our good health. We have land to farm, houses to live in, food on our tables, and enough clothes. Most of all, we have the love in our hearts for each other and our friends. Indeed, you are right. We are very rich."

"That's one way of looking at it," said the trader, "but it isn't what I was thinking about. From what I hear, there's gold on your land. You've got a gold mine."

"A gold man?" repeated Tsali. "I never heard of a gold man."

"No!" shouted the trader. "A gold mine, I said. A place where you can go and pick up gold."

"Oh, that!" Tsali exclaimed. "Yes, we have some places like that on our land. Here's some of the yellow dust we find there."

And he opened the pouch to show the trader. The trader had seen pinches of Tsali's gold dust before, and taken it in trade, without saying much about it. Now he went **Ⓑ** as crazy as the missionary. "Don't tell anybody else about this, Charley," he whispered, leaning over the counter. "We'll just keep it to ourselves. I'll help you work it out, and I'll keep the other white men away. We'll all be rich."

"Thank you," said Tsali, "but I don't believe I want to be rich that way. I just want enough of this stuff to trade you for ribbons and sugar."

"Oh, all right," answered the trader <u>sulkily</u>, "have it your own way. But don't blame me if you're sorry afterwards."

---

sulk·i·ly (sŭl′ kə lē) *adv.*, moodily silent

Reading Skills

Take Notes

Remind students that they can take notes in many different ways. Review the use of outlines, as well as different types of graphic organizers. Ask student volunteers to show the class examples of several graphic organizers, such as story strips, Venn diagrams, main idea maps, and time lines.

Encourage students to skim the text before taking notes and to use signal words, such as *first, next, on the other hand,* and *one example is* to decide on text organization. Then students can choose a form of note-taking that works best for the selection.

"I won't blame anybody," said Tsali, and bought his ribbon.

A month later, when the Georgia <u>militia</u> came riding up the valley to Tsali's house, the missionary and the trader were with them. The men all stopped in front of the house, and Tsali's wife came out into the dogtrot, the open-ended passage that divided the two halves of the house and made a cool breezeway where the family sat in warm weather. She spoke to the men. **C**

signed it over to the government, and now it's open for settlement. One or the other of these two gentlemen will probably claim it."

"They can't do that!" Amanda protested. "It's our land—nobody else's. The chiefs had no right to sign it away. My husband's father worked this place, and his father before him. This is our home. This is where we belong."

"No more," said the captain. "You belong in the removal camps[6] down by the river, with the rest of the Indians. They're going to

---

SOCIAL STUDIES ▶▶ CONNECTION

Indian Removal From almost the moment they arrived on this continent, white settlers regularly took and traded Native American lands. As Native Americans were displaced by ever larger numbers of white settlers, the U.S. government began to forcibly remove tribes to "Indian Territory"—what is now the state of Oklahoma. Today, Oklahoma has the highest Native American population of any state. This population includes members of the Choctaw, Creek, Seminole, Cherokee, and Chickasaw tribes. How does this information affect your understanding of Tsali? **D**

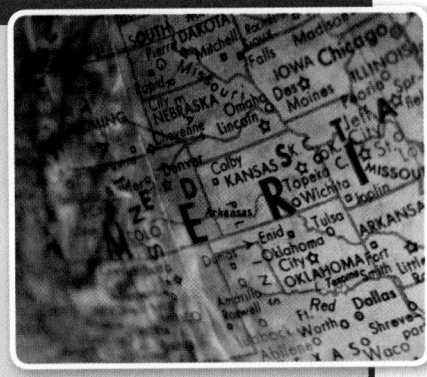

"Won't you come in and sit down?"

"Where's the old man?" the militia captain asked.

"Why, he's working out in the fields," said Amanda. "Sit down and have a cool drink of water while I send the boy for him."

"Send the boy quickly," the captain ordered. "We'll wait in our saddles and not trouble to get down."

"All right, if you'd rather not," Amanda said. "Do you mind telling me why you're here?"

"We're here to put you off this place," said the captain. "Haven't you heard? This isn't Cherokee land any more; the chiefs

start shipping the Cherokees west tomorrow morning."

Amanda sat down on the bench in the dogtrot with her legs trembling under her. "All of us?" she asked.

"Every one of you."

"Let me call my son and send him for his daddy," Amanda said. **E**

"Hurry up!"

Amanda went into the house, calling to the boy, who was just fourteen and had been

---

6. **removal camps.** Temporary residences for people forced from their own property

---

mi·li·tia (mə li´ shə) *n.*, citizens' army

Teach the Selection

Use Reading Skills
Use Context Clues Have students find the word *dogtrot* (line 8) and read the sentence in which it falls. Then have them tell you the kind of context clue provided to define it (definition). **C**

Social Studies Connection
Indian Removal *Answer:* Students will probably note that Tsali's experience was not unique. They may also say that moving like this challenged tribal identity as well as personal and family well-being. **D**

Analyze Literature
Characterization Remind students that dialogue helps readers understand characters. Have students report what the dialogue between Amanda and the militia captain tells them about each character. (She is cordial and he is businesslike, then brutally frank.) **E**

Make Connections
Invite students to imagine that they and a group of friends "discover" an island where people already live and raise crops. As they wander around the island, they realize that there are deposits of gold and gemstones on the land. The people themselves don't value these things. Ask students if they would want the gold and gemstones for themselves and, if so, what they would do to obtain them.

Differentiated Instruction

Kinesthetic Learners
Invite several students to prepare and perform an enactment of the conversation among Tsali, the missionary, and the trader. Ask students to collaborate and choose roles. Encourage them to find one student to direct the enactment, offering feedback during rehearsals and cueing the actors as

necessary during the performance. Urge the students to take time to explore their characters' motivations. When students are ready, have them perform the conversation for the class. Ask audience members to interpret and describe the characters' motivations based on the performance.

Cultural Connection

Cherokee Society The Cherokees were far from the "ignorant savages" many white people portrayed. In 1820, they had adopted a system of government similar to that of the United States, with a senate, a house of representatives, and an elected chief. In 1827, they drafted a constitution, writing it in their native language, "Talking Leaves," which was invented by Sequoyah, a tribal member. The Cherokees adopted Western agricultural methods and had churches, roads, and public schools. Literacy was widespread. In 1828, they published the first Native American newspaper, the *Cherokee Phoenix.*

Analyze Literature

Motivation Ask students to explain what motivated Amanda and the other women to wait in the house. (Many will say the women trusted that Tsali and his sons would devise a plan for dealing with the white men. Some may say the women waited because they hoped the white men would just go away.)

standing, listening, behind the door. She gave him his father's old squirrel gun, and he sneaked his own blowgun and darts and slid out the back of the house. Amanda went back to the dogtrot and sat and waited. She sat there and waited, while the missionary, the trader, and the captain quarreled about which of their wives should cook in her kitchen. She let them quarrel and hoped her men were all right.

Tsali and his older sons were working the overhill corn field, when the boy came panting up and told them what had happened.

"Is your mother all right?" Tsali asked.

"She was when I left," the boy answered.

"We'll hide in the woods till they're gone," Tsali told his older sons. "If they find us, they'll have to kill us to put us off this land."

"What about the women?" the oldest son asked.

"They'll be all right," Tsali answered. "Your mother's a quick-thinking woman; she'll take care of them. If we can hide in the caves by the river till dark, we'll go back then and get them."

They slipped away into the woods, downhill to the river, taking the boy with them, although he offered to go back and tell the white men he couldn't find his father.

All afternoon Amanda waited. Her daughters-in-law saw the strange men and horses in front of the big house and came to join her. At dusk, the captain gave up and ordered his men to make camp in the front yard. "We'll wait here until the men come back," he said.

With the white men camped all around the house, the women went into the kitchen and barred all the doors. It was a long time before the campfires made from the fence pickets ceased to blaze and began to smolder. It was a longer time until the women heard

it—a scratch on the back door, so soft and so light that it would have embarrassed a mouse. Amanda slid back the bar, and Tsali and his sons slipped into the darkened room. There was just enough moonlight for them to make out each other's shapes.

"We came to get you," Tsali said. "Come quickly. Leave everything except your knives. Don't wait a minute."

Amanda and her daughters-in-law always wore their knives at their belts, so they were ready. One at a time, Tsali last, the whole family crept out of their home and escaped into the woods.

> **They slipped away into the woods, downhill to the river, taking the boy with them. . . .**

In the morning, when the white men stretched and scratched and woke, the *Ani Keetoowah* were gone.

It was spring, and the weather was warm, but the rain fell and soaked the Cherokees. They had brought no food, and they dared not fire a gun. One of the daughters-in-law was pregnant, and her time was close. Amanda was stiff and crippled with rheumatism.[7] They gathered wild greens, for it was too early for berries or plums, and the men and boy trapped small animals and birds in string snares the women made by pulling out their hair and twisting it.

Day by day, for four weeks, the starving family listened to white men beating through the woods. The Cherokees were tired and cold and hungry, but they were silent. They even began to hope that in time the white men would go away and the Indians would be safe.

---

7. rheumatism. Chronic, painful joint inflammation

Vocabulary Skills

Denotation and Connotation

Remind students that denotation is the literal meaning of a word, while connotation is an emotion attached to the word. Model several examples, such as *thin-slender-skinny* and *inexpensive-cheap-cut-rate.* Explain that authors may use connotations to convey a character's attitude, to suggest motivations, and to influence the reader's thinking.

Point to where the missionary addresses Tsali as "you poor ignorant Indian" in the first full paragraph on page 750. Ask why the author chose those words instead of *unfortunate* (poor) and *uninformed* (ignorant.) Then ask: "How do the connotations affect your perceptions of the missionary and his motivations?"

It was not to be. One trooper brought his dog, and the dog caught the human scent. So the dog, with his man behind him, came sniffing into the cave, and Tsali and his family were caught before the men could pick up their loaded guns.

The militiamen shouted, and other white men came thudding through the woods. They tied the Cherokee men's hands behind them and bound them all together along a rope. The militiamen pushed Tsali and his sons through the woods. The women followed, weeping.

At last they were back at their own house, but they would not have recognized it. The troopers had plundered the garden and trampled the plants they didn't eat. The door from the kitchen into the dogtrot hung <u>askew</u>, and the door to the main room had been wrenched off its hinges. Clothes and bedding lay in filthy piles around the yard. What the militiamen could not use, they ruined. **A**

"Oh, my garden!" cried Amanda, and, when she saw the scattered feathers, "Oh, my little hens!"

"What are you going to do with us?" Tsali demanded.

"Take you down to the river. The last boat is loading today. There's still time to get you on it and out of here."

"I—will—not—go," Tsali said quietly. "You—nor you—nor you—nobody can make me go."

"Our orders are to take all the Cherokees. If any resist, shoot them."

"Shoot me, then!" cried Tsali. The captain raised his rifle.

Cherokee woman carrying her child in Raleigh, North Carolina, in 1946.

"Stop!" Amanda screamed. She stepped over beside her husband. "If you shoot, shoot us both," she ordered. "Our lives have been one life since we were no older than our boy here. I don't want to go on living without my husband. And I cannot leave our home any more than he can. Shoot us both."

The four sons stepped forward. "We will die with our parents," the oldest one said. "Take our wives to the boat, if that is the only place where they can be safe, but we stay here." He turned to his wife and the other young women. **B**

"That is my order as your husband," Tsali's son said. "You must go away to the west and make new lives for yourselves while

a·skew (ə skyü′) *adj.*, out of line; crooked

Use Reading Skills

Author's Purpose Direct attention to the third paragraph. Ask students what the author's purpose was in including the details about the house. (These details show how destructive the white men were.) **A**

Analyze Literature

Motivation Ask: "Why does Tsali speak so quietly when he refuses to take the boat away from his home?" (He is so serious, and perhaps so angry, that he speaks softly, slowly, and clearly.) **B**

Make Connections

Point out that, throughout history, some people have been willing to die rather than give up their beliefs or lose their independence. Ask students if there is anything they value that they would be willing to protect so strongly. Invite students to explain their reasoning.

TEACHING NOTE

Reflect on History

Ask students to reflect on their reading and note which parts of the oral history generated the most questions for them. Encourage them to return to the selection, mark those parts with sticky notes, and write down their questions. Create groups and ask each group to develop two questions about the oral history that they would like to ask someone who knows Cherokee history. Discuss as a class how you could go about finding answers.

Grammar Skills

Dangling and Misplaced Modifiers

Explain that the placement of modifiers helps a reader figure out what a sentence means. In the sentence, "One trooper brought his dog, and the dog caught the human scent" it is clear that the dog caught the scent. In "Catching the scent of the humans, the trooper followed the dog into the cave," it appears that the trooper caught the scent.

Tell students that a misplaced modifier is too far from the word it modifies.

Ask students to tell you why this sentence is confusing and how to improve it: "Tsali demanded that the soldiers leave angrily." (It is unclear whether Tsali or the soldiers are angry. Placing the word *angrily* right after the word *Tsali* makes the sentence clear.)

Answer: Students will have had a range of relocation experiences, from recent times to stories of past generations. Most will realize that their families came from elsewhere, and different families or generations have assimilated to different degrees. Opinions will vary about how closely families should identify with current or past locations.

Find Meaning

1. (a) He finds it useful for trading, but otherwise uninteresting. (b) The other men equate gold with wealth. (c) It suggests a conflict of values.
2. (a) The chiefs disagree among themselves, but some sign away rights to Cherokee lands. (b) He cannot believe they did this.
3. (a) He does not want to leave his home. (b) He is shot.

Make Judgments

4. They feel more important than the Cherokee and show little respect.
5. Opinions will vary, but students will point out that the sons honored their father by staying.
6. Students' descriptions of their feelings will vary. Most will be upset to some degree.

---

you are still young enough to do so." The wives sobbed and held out their arms, but the husbands turned their backs on the women. "We will stay with our parents," all the young men said.

The young boy, too, stood with his brothers, beside his father. "Let this boy go," Tsali said to the white men. "He is so young. A man grows, and plants his seed, and his seed goes on. This is my seed. I planted it. My older sons and I have had our chances. They will leave children, and their names will never be forgotten. But this boy is too young. His seed has not ripened for planting yet. Let him go, to care for his sisters, on the way to the west."

"Very well," said the captain. "He can't do much harm if he does live." He turned to two militiamen. "Take the boy and the young women away," he ordered. "Keep them going till they come to the boats, and load them on board."

The young women and the boy, stunned and silenced, were driven down the road before they could say goodbye, nor would the trooper let them look back. Behind them, as they started on the long main road, they heard the sound of the shots. ❖

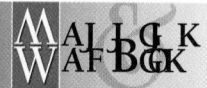

When was the last time your family had to relocate? Should families define themselves by where they have lived in past generations, or should they identify themselves only with where they live today?

Find Meaning

1. (a) What is Tsali's attitude about the gold on his land? (b) How does his attitude differ from the attitudes of the missionary and the trader? (c) What does this difference suggest?
2. (a) What do the Cherokee chiefs do? (b) How does Tsali respond to their actions?
3. (a) Why does Tsali refuse to go west? (b) What is the result of his refusal?

Make Judgments

4. What do the soldiers' actions suggest about their feelings for the Cherokee?
5. What is your opinion about Tsali's sons' decision to stay with their parents?
6. Describe your feelings about Tsali's decision to stay on his land.

Differentiated Instruction

Enrichment

Students may want to read more about the causes of misunderstanding between the Cherokees and white people. Encourage students to conduct research on Cherokee history, and then to write a personal essay about how misunderstandings between people with different values and beliefs affect their lives. Ask them to include any implications they think these observations have in modern society.

In "Tsali of the Cherokees," Alice Lee Marriott retells the story of one family's experience during the removal of the Cherokee from Georgia. In the following article by history and social studies writer **Christine Graf,** the reasons for this removal and its effects on the Cherokee are described. As you read, use the information this article presents to better understand the story of Tsali.

(Above) *The Trail of Tears,* 1942. Robert Lindneux. The Granger Collection, New York.

Moving West: A Native American Perspective

A Magazine Article by Christine Graf

Wouldn't it be wonderful to discover gold on your land? Well, when gold was discovered on land where Cherokee Indians lived in Georgia, it wasn't wonderful at all—at least, not for them.

By the 1800s, white settlers had already taken most of the Cherokee land. The Cherokees were left with only a small section of western Georgia. When gold was discovered there in 1828, whites wanted this last part of Cherokee land, too. Through an act of Congress called the Indian Removal Act, President Andrew Jackson ordered the Cherokees to leave. Dozens of other American Indian tribes had already been forced from their land.

In May 1838, army troops began forcing the Cherokees from their homes. The Cherokees were imprisoned in forts, then forced to walk almost 1,000 miles into Oklahoma. This terrible, forced migration became known as the Trail of Tears. Four thousand Cherokees died as a result.

American Indians faced other difficulties as more and more settlers moved west. Contact with white people meant exposure to new diseases. In 1837 alone, tens of thousands of Indians died of smallpox, a disease carried into Indian land by white fur traders.

In many parts of the West, settlers took over traditional Indian hunting and farming lands. They killed most of the buffalo the Indians needed for food, clothes, tipis, and more. "When the buffalo went away, the hearts of my people fell to the ground, and they could not lift them up again," said Crow Indian Plenty Coups.

By the late 1800s, thousands of tribes had been forced by the government to give up their land. Some fought back against army attacks. Sadly, they were no match for the United States Army and couldn't save their land. Instead, they were forced to live on reservations (land set aside for them). Their lives were never the same. ❖

MOVING WEST **755**

Teach the Connection

History Connection

Cherokee Legal Status After the passage of the Indian Removal Act in 1830, the Cherokee Nation asked the Supreme Court for a ruling that would void all Georgia laws dealing with Cherokee land. They claimed that the Cherokees were an independent nation that did not fall under the white man's Constitution and laws, and said that the purpose of Georgia's laws was "to annihilate the Cherokees as a political society." The Supreme Court refused to rule, saying that the Cherokee Nation was neither a state nor a foreign nation, but a "domestic dependent nation," so the Supreme Court had no jurisdiction over it.

Analyze Literature

Tone After students have read the article, ask them to describe its tone. Prompt them to consider the audience for which Graf was writing, any bias apparent in the article, and the examples Graf chose to support her thesis statement in the first paragraph. Then ask: "Which tone do you prefer, the tone of the oral history or the tone of the article?" Encourage students to support their preferences with examples from the two pieces.

Grammar Skills

Phrases

Give students practice identifying prepositional and infinitive phrases in the text. Model identifying phrases in a sentence such as "By the late 1800s, thousands of tribes had been forced by the government to give up their land." Identify the subject and verb in the sentence and then point out that "by the late 1800s" and "by the government" are prepositional phrases. Remind students that an infinitive phrase begins with *to* followed by a verb, as in "to give up." Have students work in pairs to locate and identify other phrases in the article.

Common Core State Standards

Reading Literature
RL.9

Text-to-Text Connection

Answer: Opinions will vary. Students should recognize that the white men would have taken the land one way or another. Indians who sold their land got something for it, while those who refused to sell lost everything.

Analyze Literature

Motivation Be sure students list motivations for they key characters in the oral history. Remind them to record details from the text to support the motivations they list. They will use this chart in the Expository Writing activity under Extend Understanding.

TEXT ← TO → TEXT
CONNECTION

Some Cherokee agreed to sell their land to the white settlers, but most did not. Was it wise for them to sell their land? How does reading this account affect the way you interpret "Tsali of the Cherokees"?

AFTER READING

Analyze Literature

Motivation What motivated Tsali? What motivated his wife and sons? What motivated the soldiers, the missionary, and the trader? Use a two-column chart to record details about each of the characters to determine what motivated their actions.

Details	Motivation
"missionary seemed to go a little crazy"	Tsali's gold

Extend Understanding

Writing Options

Creative Writing It is the winter of 1839, and you are a budding writer in northern Alabama. You have been hearing about a forced march of Cherokees, something the federal government has ordered so that white people can search for gold on native land. Investigate and write a **news article** about the forced march in three or four paragraphs. Each paragraph should have just two or three sentences. When you are done, exchange articles with a classmate and act as each other's editor.

Expository Writing Write a **literary analysis** of Tsali's character. Use the chart you created to analyze character motivation in "Tsali of the Cherokees" to help you form and support your thesis. Ask yourself: Why did Tsali choose to stay on his land? What does he value? How does he interact with others? At the end of your analysis, be sure to restate your thesis. When you are finished, share your analysis with the class.

Lifelong Learning

Dig Into History The Indian Removal Act of 1830 was just one of many government actions that affected Native Americans. Find out more about President Jackson's life and political career, the laws and treaties related to native people during Jackson's presidency, and the national mood that permitted Jackson to order relocation of the tribes. Summarize what you learn with a poster you could display in class.

Critical Literacy

Plan an Interview Suppose you had an opportunity to meet a survivor who walked the Trail of Tears. Prepare some interview questions you can ask this person as part of an oral history of the migration. With no more than ten questions, try to draw out stories about what the experience was like. Write your questions in a way that will allow you to learn both facts and feelings from the person you interview.

Go to **www.mirrorsandwindows.com** for more.

Rubrics for Writing Options

You can adapt this as a checklist for students to use as they write.

Creative Writing

☐ Is the news article about the forced march of Cherokees?

☐ Are there three or four paragraphs, and does each paragraph have two or three sentences?

Expository Writing

☐ Does the analysis refer to the motivation chart prepared for Analyze Literature?

☐ Does the analysis focus on the character of Tsali and explore his motivation in detail?

☐ Does the analysis include a thesis, which is restated at the end?

We Are All One

A Chinese Folk Tale retold by Laurence Yep

BEFORE READING

Build Background

Literary Context Like folk tales everywhere, Chinese folk tales began as part of folk literature. These stories were told by parents and grandparents to reinforce the values and traditions of their culture while also providing entertainment. A popular theme in both folk tales and myths is the quest, in which the main character goes on a journey to solve a problem. Along the way, the character encounters obstacles and is either helped or hindered by characters or animals that have magical powers.

Reader's Context How does it make you feel to do a favor for someone with no expectation of reward? Have you ever reaped an unexpected reward from doing a good deed?

Set Purpose

Before you begin, read the title of the selection and consider the selection's genre. Use these clues to predict what will happen in the folk tale.

Analyze Literature

Conflict The **conflict** in a piece of fiction is the struggle between a character and him- or herself, another character, society, or nature. As you read "We Are All One," identify the central conflict of the story, and note the other obstacles that the main character overcomes along the way.

Meet the Author

Laurence Yep (b. 1948) grew up in San Francisco. As a boy, he enjoyed reading fantasy and science fiction stories about children who traveled to strange places. Yep writes for children and young adults and has won many awards for his novels and story collections. Books he has written include *Dragonwings*, *Child of the Owl*, and *Sea Glass*.

Use Reading Skills
Sequence of Events
Using a graphic organizer can help you keep track of the sequence of events, or the order in which things happen, in a story. As you read "We Are All One," use a time line to keep track of the key events in the story.

First   Last

Man offers
reward

Preview Vocabulary

lar•va (lär´ və) *n.*, early wingless form of a newly hatched insect; **larvae** (lär´ vī) *n. pl.*

re•gret•ful•ly (ri gret´ fə lē) *adv.*, with a sense of loss or sorrow

o•men (ō´ mən) *n.*, prophetic sign

dis•solve (di zälv´) *v.*, melt; reduce to liquid form

wea•ri•ly (wir´ ə lē) *adv.*, tiredly

Preview the Selection

At a Glance
Directed Reading
- Reading Level: Easy
- Difficulty Consideration: Setting
- Ease Factors: Manageable segments and dialogue

Objectives

Studying this lesson will enable students to
- use reading skills such as determining the sequence of events
- define conflict and recognize conflict in the selection
- describe some literary accomplishments of Laurence Yep
- appreciate a Chinese folk tale

Launch the Lesson

Tell students they are about to read "We Are All One," a tale in which a poor man is able to save a rich one, and in which simple, genuine goodness is rewarded. Ask them to consider this in light of what they have learned about folk tales by and about regular people.

Words in Use

Preview Vocabulary	Teaching Words
larva, 759	reaped, 757
regretfully, 760	time line, 757
omen, 760	
dissolve, 760	
wearily, 761	

KEY TERMS

Common Core State Standards
Reading Literature
RL.1

Summary

A rich man has a painful eye disease and cannot find a cure, no matter how much he spends on doctors. At last he offers a reward to anyone who cures him. Hearing this, a kind old candy peddler remembers that his mother knew of a magic herb that cures eye troubles.

The next day, the peddler sets off to find the herb. On his way, he helps some ants whose nest is being flooded by a stream. Later, as he naps, he dreams of the ant city and its queen, who thanks him for saving her kingdom. She offers to help him in his search, though she doesn't know about the herb.

The next day the peddler saves a centipede from a bird. Later, the centipede tells him where to find a magic bead that will cure the eye ailment. With the help of the ants, the peddler gets the bead and cures the rich man, who is so grateful that he doubles his reward. The good peddler and his family live happily ever after.

MIRRORS & WINDOWS The Mirrors & Windows questions at the end of the selection focus on the theme of oneness. Before they read, ask students: If you were gathering people with whom you feel a sense of oneness, who would they be?

We Are All One

A Chinese Folk Tale retold by Laurence Yep

758

Program Resources

Planning and Assessment
Program Planning Guide, Selection Lesson Plan
E-Lesson Planner
Assessment Guide, Lesson Test
ExamView

Technology Tools
Interactive Student Text on CD
Visual Teaching Package
Audio Library
mirrorsandwindows.com

Meeting the Standards
Folk Literature: Unit 8, Directed Reading, pp. 46–50

Differentiating Instruction
Advanced Students, Author/Theme Study, p. 47

*...he gave away as
much as he sold, so he
was always poor.*

Long ago there was a rich man with a disease in his eyes. For many years, the pain was so great that he could not sleep at night. He saw every doctor he could, but none of them could help him.

"What good is all my money?" he groaned. Finally, he became so desperate that he sent criers[1] through the city offering a reward to anyone who could cure him.

Now in that city lived an old candy peddler. He would walk around with his baskets of candy, but he was so kind-hearted that he gave away as much as he sold, so he was always poor.

When the old peddler heard the announcement, he remembered something his mother had said. She had once told him about a magical herb that was good for the eyes. So he packed up his baskets and went back to the single tiny room in which his family lived.

When he told his plan to his wife, she scolded him, "If you go off on this crazy hunt, how are we supposed to eat?"

Usually the peddler gave in to his wife, but this time he was stubborn. "There are two baskets of candy," he said. "I'll be back before they're gone."

The next morning, as soon as the soldiers opened the gates, he was the first one to leave the city. He did not stop until he was deep inside the woods. As a boy, he had often wandered there. He had liked to pretend that the shadowy forest was a green sea and he was a fish slipping through the cool waters.

As he examined the ground, he noticed ants scurrying about. On their backs were larvae like white grains of rice. A rock had fallen into a stream, so the water now spilled into the ant's nest.

"We're all one," the kind-hearted peddler said. So he waded into the shallow stream and put the rock on the bank. Then with a sharp stick, he dug a shallow ditch that sent the rest of the water back into the stream.

Without another thought about his good deed, he began to search through the forest. He looked everywhere; but as the day went on, he grew sleepy. "Ho-hum. I got up too early. I'll take just a short nap," he decided, and lay down in the shade of an old tree, where he fell right asleep.

In his dreams, the old peddler found himself standing in the middle of a great city. Tall buildings rose high overhead. He couldn't see the sky even when he tilted back his head. An escort of soldiers marched up to him with a loud clatter of their black lacquer armor. "Our queen wishes to see you," the captain said. **A**

The frightened peddler could only obey and let the fierce soldiers lead him into a shining palace. There, a woman with a high crown sat upon a tall throne. Trembling, the old peddler fell to his knees and touched his forehead against the floor.

But the queen ordered him to stand. "Like the great Emperor Yü of long ago, you tamed the great flood. We are all one now.

---

1. **criers.** People who shouted news throughout the town

lar•va (lär´ və) *n.,* early wingless form of a newly hatched insect; **larvae** (lär´ vī) *n. pl.*

Analyze Literature

Theme Remind students that the theme is the main idea of a literary work. Suggest that one way to go about identifying theme is to look for repeated phrases or for events that follow similar patterns. Ask: "Based on this page, how would you describe the theme of the story, and why? ("We are all one" is the theme; students should point to the title and repetition of this statement when the peddler helps the ants.) Encourage students to look for repetition and any changes to the theme as they read the rest of the story.

Science Connection

Lacquer and Exoskeletons Explain that lacquer is a shiny, hard varnish made of tree resin that Chinese craftsmen use to make decorative objects. Show students pictures of an ant and a lacquerware object, and note how the shiny ant resembles the lacquer. Explain that insects like ants do not have an internal, bony skeleton. Instead, their bodies are supported and protected by a rigid outer shell called an exoskeleton. **A**

Differentiated Instruction

Enrichment

Tell students that a quest, like the old peddler's quest for the cure, is a common theme in literature and folklore. Have students use library resources to seek out another folk tale that features a quest and prepare a presentation comparing it to "We Are All One."

Reading Proficiency

Remind less-confident readers that pausing to make predictions as they read can deepen their interest in a story. Assure them that their predictions don't have to be correct; they can compare them to actual outcomes later. To model a prediction, pause after the first paragraph and ask: "What will the rich man do? I predict he will send for a famous magician to heal him."

Analyze Literature

Setting Remind students that to make the description of a setting more vivid, authors often use sensory details (details that relate to sight, hearing, sound, touch, or smell). Challenge students to identify the sensory details Yep uses to set scenes in his tale. Examples include the ant city's tall buildings and the green temple roof that is barely visible in the twilight (sight), as well as the nighttime coldness (touch).

Use Reading Skills

Determine Sequence of Events Remind students that a good way to keep track of the sequence of events is to be alert to time-related words and phrases. Have students point out sentences that use such words. Examples include "He stumbled through the growing darkness <u>until</u> he reached a ruined temple" and "<u>The next day</u>, he reached the house of the rich man" (page 762).

You have only to ask, and I or any of my people will come to your aid."

The old peddler cleared his throat. "I am looking for a certain herb. It will cure any disease of the eyes."

The queen shook her head <u>regretfully</u>. "I have never heard of that herb. But you will surely find it if you keep looking for it."

And then the old peddler woke. Sitting up, he saw that in his wanderings he had come back to the ants' nest. It was there he had taken his nap. His dream city had been the ants' nest itself.

"This is a good <u>omen</u>," he said to himself, and he began searching even harder. He was so determined to find the herb that he did not notice how time had passed. He was surprised when he saw how the light was fading. He looked all around then. There was no sight of his city—only strange hills. He realized then that he had searched so far he had gotten lost.

Night was coming fast and with it the cold. He rubbed his arms and hunted for shelter. In the twilight, he thought he could see the green tiles of a roof.

He stumbled through the growing darkness until he reached a ruined temple. Weeds grew through cracks in the stones and most of the roof itself had fallen in. Still, the ruins would provide some protection.

As he started inside, he saw a centipede[2] with bright orange skin and red tufts of fur along its back. Yellow dots covered its sides like a dozen tiny eyes. It was also rushing into the temple as fast as it could, but there was a bird swooping down toward it.

The old peddler waved his arms and shouted, scaring the bird away. Then he put down his palm in front of the insect. "We are all one, you and I." The many feet tickled his skin as the centipede climbed onto his hand.

Inside the temple, he gathered dried leaves and found old sticks of wood and soon he had a fire going. The peddler even picked some fresh leaves for the centipede from a bush near the temple doorway. "I may have to go hungry, but you don't have to, friend."

He wanted to run from the temple, but he couldn't even get up.

Stretching out beside the fire, the old peddler pillowed his head on his arms. He was so tired that he soon fell asleep, but even in his sleep he dreamed he was still searching in the woods. Suddenly he thought he heard footsteps near his head. He woke instantly and looked about, but he only saw the brightly colored centipede.

"Was it you, friend?" The old peddler chuckled and, lying down, he closed his eyes again. "I must be getting nervous."

"We are one, you and I," a voice said faintly—as if from a long distance. "If you go south, you will find a pine tree with two trunks. By its roots, you will find a magic bead. A cousin of mine spat on it years ago. <u>Dissolve</u> that bead in wine and tell the rich man to drink it if he wants to heal his eyes."

The old peddler trembled when he heard the voice, because he realized that the centipede was magical. He wanted to run

---

2. centipede. Wormlike insect that has numerous body segments, each with a pair of legs

re·gret·ful·ly (ri gret´ fə lē) *adv.*, with a sense of loss or sorrow

o·men (ō´ mən) *n.*, prophetic sign

dis·solve (di zälv´) *v.*, melt; reduce to liquid form

Differentiated Instruction

Enrichment

Point out the reference in the story to Emperor Yü at the end of page 759, and explain that he is said to have saved China from floods. Have interested students use library and Internet resources to learn as much as they can about the Yü legend and share what they learn in class.

Visual Learning

Challenge students to create an illustration of the scene or image in the story that is most evocative to them. When they have finished their drawings (they could also choose to make a painting or collage), have them explain why they chose this subject.

from the temple, but he couldn't even get up. It was as if he were glued to the floor.

But then the old peddler reasoned with himself: If the centipede had wanted to hurt me, it could have long ago. Instead, it seems to want to help me.

So the old peddler stayed where he was, but he did not dare open his eyes. When the first sunlight fell through the roof, he raised one eyelid cautiously. There was no sign of the centipede. He sat up and looked around, but the magical centipede was gone.

He followed the centipede's instructions when he left the temple. Traveling south, he kept a sharp eye out for the pine tree with two trunks. He walked until late in the afternoon, but all he saw were normal pine trees.

A <u>Wearily</u> he sat down and sighed. Even if he found the pine tree, he couldn't be sure that he would find the bead. Someone else might even have discovered it a long time ago.

But something made him look a little longer. Just when he was thinking about turning back, he saw the odd tree. Somehow his tired legs managed to carry him over to the tree, and he got down on his knees. But the ground was covered with pine needles and his old eyes were too weak. The old peddler could have wept with frustration, and then he remembered the ants.

He began to call, "Ants, ants, we are all one."

---

wea•ri•ly (wir´ ə lē) *adv.*, tiredly

Analyze Literature

Motivation Remind students that a character's reason for doing things is called motivation. Ask students for their ideas about why the peddler doesn't flee from the centipede. What are his motivations? (Students should note both that the centipede's magic physically prevented the man from getting up and that he reasons that the centipede must want to help him.) **A**

WE ARE ALL ONE **761**

Reading Skills

Identify Text Structure

Review the elements that make up the plot of a story (see pages 6–7). Note that not every one of these elements always appears—some stories, for example, do not offer exposition; some end right at the climax and do not have a resolution. Acknowledge also that it can be difficult to decide how to assign some plot elements. Ask students to try to identify the climax of "We Are All One." (Although some students may feel that the dream of the ant queen or the talk with the centipede is the high point, help them see that the moment just before the man calls the ants—when he almost gives up his quest—is the climax because it is the point when he is closest to failing.)

Analyze Literature

Conflict Remind students that characters usually experience one of two kinds of conflict, external or internal. In external conflicts, characters struggle against forces outside of themselves. In an internal conflict, the opposition comes from within; it is often an emotion, such as doubt or longing. Ask students to identify the type of conflict in the selection. (It is external conflict.)

Analyze Literature

Plot Remind students that the resolution is the point at which the main conflict in a story is settled. Have them identify the resolution in this story. (The peddler's quest finally ends when the magic bead cures the rich man's ailment.)

Answer: Answers will vary. Students should give examples related to their lives and to contemporary society.

Almost immediately, thousands of ants came boiling out of nowhere. Delighted, the old man held up his fingers. "I'm looking for a bead. It might be very tiny."

Then, careful not to crush any of his little helpers, the old man sat down to wait. In no time, the ants reappeared with a tiny bead. With trembling fingers, the old man took the bead from them and examined it. It was colored orange and looked as if it had yellow eyes on the sides.

There was nothing very special about the bead, but the old peddler treated it like a fine jewel. Putting the bead into his pouch, the old peddler bowed his head. "I thank you and I thank your queen," the old man said. After the ants disappeared among the pine needles, he made his way out of the woods.

The next day, he reached the house of the rich man. However, he was so poor and ragged that the gatekeeper only laughed at him. "How could an old beggar like you help my master?"

The old peddler tried to argue. "Beggar or rich man, we are all one."

"Beggar or rich man, we are all one."

But it so happened that the rich man was passing by the gates. He went over to the old peddler. "I said anyone could see me. But it'll mean a stick across your back if you're wasting my time."

The old peddler took out the pouch. "Dissolve this bead in some wine and drink it down." Then, turning the pouch upside down, he shook the tiny bead onto his palm and handed it to the rich man.

The rich man immediately called for a cup of wine. Dropping the bead into the wine, he waited a moment and then drank it down. Instantly the pain vanished. Shortly after that, his eyes healed.

The rich man was so happy and grateful that he doubled the reward. And the kindly old peddler and his family lived comfortably for the rest of their lives. ❖

 How might you reflect the peddler's belief that "We are all one" in your own life? How would the world be different if everyone practiced this philosophy?

Differentiated Instruction

English Language Learning

Discuss the idea that some words have more than one meaning, focusing on *great,* which appears several times in the selection. Explain that, while in casual conversation, *great* usually means "really good" or "fantastic," it has other meanings, which can be either slightly or very different. Discuss the different uses of the word in the text:

the pain was so great — here, *great* means "extreme" or, essentially, "terrible," 759

a great city — in this case it means "very large," 759

the great emperor Yü — very noble, 759

the great flood — immense, 759

Find Meaning

1. (a) What is the setting of this story? (b) How is the setting important to the plot?

2. (a) What does the old candy peddler decide to do to help the rich man? (b) Why do you think he decides to do this?

3. (a) What good deed does the peddler perform for the ants? (b) What does he say as he does this? (c) What does he mean by this?

Analyze Literature

Conflict As the peddler goes on his journey, he encounters several obstacles that prevent him from completing his task. List each obstacle the peddler encounters, and note how the problem was solved. Then review all the obstacles and determine the story's main conflict.

Make Judgments

4. Why does the peddler think his dream of the ants' nest is a good omen?

5. Why is the peddler more frightened by the centipede than by the ants?

6. (a) How do the ants help the peddler? (b) What inspires the peddler to ask the ants for help?

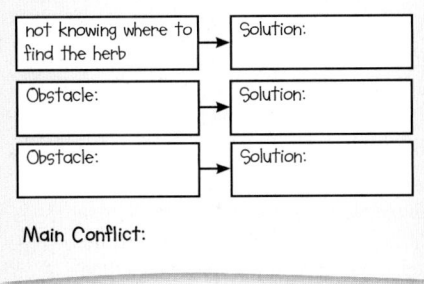

Extend Understanding

Writing Options

Creative Writing Review the dream sequence in which the ants are described as soldiers in shining black armor. Using this passage as a model, write a **descriptive paragraph** in which you personify an animal. Use the animal's habitat and natural appearance as the basis for your imagined humanlike description.

Expository Writing Write a **literary response** in which you analyze and evaluate the theme of "We Are All One." First, describe the theme, restating it in your own words. Then, provide evidence that supports your claim. Finally, state whether or not you agree with the theme of the folk tale.

Critical Literacy

Hold a Debate As a class, debate the notion that "we are all one." Do you agree with it or disagree with it? If a national government adopted this concept as a guiding principle, what kinds of policies might the government implement? How would the world be different if everyone believed that "we are all one"?

Lifelong Learning

Magical Animals Animals that have magical or unusual powers are fairly common in folk tales. In a small group, brainstorm a list of other stories in which the main character encounters magical animals. Do some animals appear more frequently in these tales than others? If so, what might explain this? How do they interact with humans? Present your findings to the class.

Go to www.mirrorsandwindows.com for more.

WE ARE ALL ONE **763**

Find Meaning

1. (a) The setting is a long-ago, faraway place. (b) In the modern world, the rich man's disease would be cured by medicine rather than by magic, so the setting is essential to the believability of the plot.

2. (a) He decides to hunt for a magical herb to cure the disease. (b) Because he gives away as much candy as he sells, it's likely that he decides to help out of kindness.

3. (a) He saves their nest from being flooded. (b) He says "We're all one." (c) He means that all living things are connected and anything that benefits one creature benefits all.

Make Judgments

4. Students may say it is because the ant queen pledges her help and urges him to keep looking for the herb.

5. The ants' message came in a dream, but he hears the centipede while awake, so he concludes that it is magical, which frightens him.

6. (a) They find the bead under the tree. (b) His dream of the ant queen inspires him.

Analyze Literature

Conflict Obstacles include not knowing where to find the herb, the flooded ants' nest, the centipede being attacked by a bird, and the rich man's servant, who tries to turn the peddler away. Students should determine that the main conflict is the peddler's quest to find the cure and give it to the rich man, in spite of the obstacles.

Rubrics for Writing Options

You can adapt this as a checklist for students to use as they write.

Creative Writing

☐ Does the paragraph describe an animal as if it has human characteristics?

☐ Does the description reflect the animal's actual appearance and habits?

Expository Writing

☐ Does the response identify the theme?

☐ Does the response provide evidence to support its claims?

☐ Does the response include an opinion of the theme?

Correcting Misplaced Modifiers

These are sample answers.

1. Lying beside the fire, the old peddler pillowed his head on his arms.

2. In the wine, dissolve the bead that you find near a pine tree.

3. Looking up, the peddler saw a bird swooping toward a caterpillar.

4. In the cave burned a small fire that the peddler had built.

5. As it was getting dark, the peddler saw the odd tree.

6. The announcement posted on the wall included information about the rich man.

7. The ants crawling from their nest looked up at the peddler.

8. The queen in her crown spoke with the peddler.

9. The rich man waited at his table for the peddler.

10. From her throne, the queen called her army when the peddler asked for help.

11. Over the peddler's head flew a bird watching the earth.

12. The rich man drinking his wine yelled at his guard.

13. Pine trees dropping needles to the ground glimmered in the sunlight.

14. Up the peddler's leg crawled an ant, clenching a bead in its mouth.

15. Speaking to the peddler, the magic centipede moved around the temple.

> For more information, see Grammar & Style Section 3.13, Common Usage Problems, in the Language Arts Handbook.

Grammar & Style

Misplaced Modifiers

When the old peddler heard the announcement, he remembered something his mother had said.

—LAURENCE YEP, "We Are All One"

Misplaced modifiers are phrases and clauses that confuse the meaning of a sentence. A **misplaced modifier** is located so far from the word it should modify that it appears to be modifying an inappropriate word.

For example, in the quotation above, the phrase *When the old peddler heard the announcement* modifies the verb *remembered*. Consider the following reworking of the above quotation.

INCORRECT

He remembered something his mother had said when the old peddler heard the announcement.

Now the placement of the phrase *when the old peddler heard the announcement* makes it appear to modify the verb *said*.

To correct misplaced modifiers, move the modifier closer to the word it modifies.

INCORRECT

He noticed ants scurrying around <u>when he examined the ground</u>.

In this example, it sounds as if the ants scurried because he examined the ground. To correct this error, move the modifier.

CORRECT

When he examined the ground, he noticed ants scurrying around.

Correcting Misplaced Modifiers

Rewrite each sentence so that the underlined phrase or clause modifies the underlined word.

1. The old <u>peddler</u> pillowed his head on his arms <u>lying beside the fire</u>.

2. Dissolve the <u>bead</u> in the wine <u>that you find near a pine tree</u>.

3. The <u>peddler</u> saw a bird swooping toward a caterpillar <u>looking up</u>.

4. A small <u>fire</u> burned in the cave <u>that the peddler had built</u>.

5. The peddler <u>saw</u> the odd tree <u>as it was getting dark</u>.

6. The <u>announcement</u> included information about the rich man <u>posted on the wall</u>.

7. The <u>ants</u> looked up at the peddler <u>crawling from their nest</u>.

8. The <u>queen</u> spoke with the peddler <u>in her crown</u>.

9. The <u>rich man</u> waited for the peddler <u>at his table</u>.

10. When the peddler asked for help, the <u>queen</u> called her army <u>from her throne</u>.

11. A <u>bird</u> flew over the peddler's head <u>watching the earth</u>.

12. The <u>rich man</u> yelled at his guard <u>drinking his wine</u>.

13. <u>Pine trees</u> glimmered in the sunlight <u>dropping needles to the ground</u>.

14. An <u>ant</u> crawled up the peddler's leg <u>clenching a bead in its mouth</u>.

15. The <u>magic centipede</u> moved around the temple <u>speaking to the peddler</u>.

KEY TERMS

MISPLACED MODIFIER, 764
PHRASE, 764
CLAUSE, 764
QUOTATION, 764

Program Resources

You will find additional lessons on Misplaced Modifiers in the *Exceeding the Standards: Grammar & Style* resource.

Common Core State Standards

Language
L.1, L.7.1c

Ant and Grasshopper
The Fox and the Crow
The Lion and the Statue

Greek Fables by Aesop

At a Glance
Directed Reading
- Reading Level: Easy
- Difficulty Consideration: Clarity of morals
- Ease Factor: Length

BEFORE READING

Build Background
Historical Context Fables are an ancient form of folk tale that spread from India and Greece into western Europe around the fourth century BC. In the first or second century AD, fables attributed to Aesop were recorded in verse by the Greek poet Babrius and also by the Roman poet Phaedrus. In the following centuries, the fable became a popular genre in world literature. In the seventeenth century, the French writer Jean de La Fontaine used the fable genre to write satires. Later writers of fables in English include Ambrose Bierce, George Orwell, and James Thurber.

Reader's Context How can old tales that feature animals as characters teach lessons that are useful in today's world?

Set Purpose
Think about what you know about the fable genre to help you determine what to expect from the selections and how to read them.

Analyze Literature
Fable A brief story, written in prose or verse, that conveys a moral or lesson is called a **fable.** The characters in a fable are usually animals that are given human characteristics. As you read these three selections, think about the message, or moral, that each one conveys.

Use Reading Skills
Identify Author's Purpose An author's purpose is his or her reason for writing. After reading each fable, consider what you think the author was attempting to accomplish. Use a two-column chart, like the one below, to help determine the author's purpose for each fable.

Details	Author's Purpose
The ant gathers grain all summer, "grain by grain."	

Objectives
Studying this lesson will enable students to
- use reading skills such as identifying the author's purpose
- define fable and recognize how the three readings are examples of this genre
- describe the ancient fables credited to a figure named Aesop and recognize their influence on later works of literature
- appreciate entertaining stories of lessons learned

Launch the Lesson
Note that in the fables students are about to read, one character teaches another a lesson of some kind. Ask students to think about a time when they themselves have been taught a lesson. Could they tell about that experience in the form of a fable? Have students share their ideas with the class.

Meet the Author
Aesop (620?–560? BC) may or may not have actually existed. There are several different stories about the background of this man, whose name is always linked with animal fables from the Greek oral tradition. Some say that Aesop was a freed slave; others say that he was an adviser to King Croesus of Lydia or a riddle-solver for King Lycurgus of Babylon. It is also possible that ancient storytellers simply attributed these animal fables to an imaginary author.

AESOP'S FABLES **765**

Words in Use

Teaching Words
conveys, 765
relevant, 769

KEY TERMS

Common Core State Standards
Reading Literature
RL.1
Reading Informational
RI.6

Summary

A grasshopper spends the summer enjoying himself while the ant works to store food for the winter. One cold day, the grasshopper begs the ant for some food, but she refuses to give it to him.

A fox sees a crow that has found a piece of cheese. The fox pays the crow elaborate compliments and, last of all, asks her to sing for him. When she opens her mouth to sing, the cheese falls and the fox grabs it, advising her never to trust flatterers.

A man wants to prove that humans are stronger than lions. He shows a live lion a statue of Hercules killing a lion. The live lion is not convinced, because the statue was sculpted by a man.

The Mirrors & Windows questions at the end of the selection focus on the theme of good advice. Before students begin reading, ask: What is one very simple lesson, such as "waste not, want not," that you remember nearly every day?

Analyze Literature

Fable Have students place a sheet of paper over the second half of each fable before they begin reading. Tell them to pause after reading the first half and make predictions. What will happen next? What will the moral be? After they finish reading, ask if their predictions were correct.

The Ant and the Grasshopper, c. 20th century. Edward Bawden. Chelmsford Museums, Essex, United Kingdom.

Ant and Grasshopper

Aesop's Fable retold by James Reeves

All summer the ant had been working hard, gathering a store of corn for the winter. Grain by grain she had taken it from the fields and stowed it away in a hole in the bank, under a hawthorn bush.

One bright, frosty day in winter Grasshopper saw her. She was dragging out a grain of corn to dry it in the sun. The wind was keen, and poor Grasshopper was cold.

"Good morning, Ant," said he. "What a terrible winter it is! I'm half dead with hunger. Please give me just one of your corn grains to eat. I can find nothing, although I've hopped all over the farmyard. There isn't a seed to be found. Spare me a grain, I beg."

"Why haven't you saved anything up?" asked Ant. "I worked hard all through the summer, storing food for the winter. Very

glad I am too, for as you say, it's bitterly cold."

"I wasn't idle last summer, either," said Grasshopper.

"And what did you do, pray?"

"Why, I spent the time singing," answered Grasshopper. "Every day from dawn till sunset I jumped about or sat in the sun, chirruping to my heart's content."

"Oh you did, did you?" replied Ant. "Well, since you've sung all summer to keep yourself cheerful, you may dance all winter to keep yourself warm. Not a grain will I give you!"

And she scuttled off into her hole in the bank, while Grasshopper was left cold and hungry. ✤

766

Program Resources

Planning and Assessment
Program Planning Guide, Selection Lesson Plan
E-Lesson Planner
Assessment Guide, Lesson Test
ExamView

Technology Tools
Interactive Student Text on CD
Visual Teaching Package
Audio Library
mirrorsandwindows.com

Meeting the Standards
Folk Literature: Unit 8, Directed Reading, pp. 51–55

Differentiating Instruction
English Language Learners, Author's Purpose, pp. 193–199

Fox and Crow. Bibliothèque Nationale, Paris.

The Fox and the Crow

Aesop's Fable retold by Joseph Jacobs

A Fox once saw a Crow fly off with a piece of cheese in its beak and settle on a branch of a tree. "That's for me, as I am a Fox," said Master Reynard, and he walked up to the foot of the tree.

"Good day, Mistress Crow," he cried. "How well you are looking today: how glossy your feathers; how bright your eye. I feel sure your voice must surpass that of other birds, just as your figure does; let me hear but one song from you that I may greet you as the Queen of Birds."

A The Crow lifted up her head and began to caw her best, but the moment she opened her mouth the piece of cheese fell to the ground, only to be snapped up by Master Fox. "That will do," said he. "That was all I wanted. In exchange for your cheese I will give you a piece of advice for the future—

Do not trust flatterers." ✤

Use Reading Skills
Compare and Contrast Have students choose two fables to compare and contrast. Suggest that they use a Venn diagram to organize their ideas. Have students find a partner who analyzed the same two fables and exchange ideas.

Use Reading Strategies
Clarify Remind students that a good way to make sure they understand a written passage is to paraphrase it, or use their own words to explain what it is about. Ask them to focus on the last sentence of "The Lion and the Statue." Ask: "Can you clarify the meaning?" (The lion means that a human sculptor is likely to express the human point of view, which, in this case, is that people are more powerful than lions.) **A**

Answer: Responses will vary. Students should support their answers with reasons.

The Lion and the Statue
Aesop's Fable retold by Joseph Jacobs

A Man and a Lion were discussing the relative strength of men and lions in general. The Man contended that he and his fellows were stronger than lions by reason of their greater intelligence. "Come now with me," he cried, "and I will soon prove that I am right." So he took him into the public gardens and showed him a statue of Hercules overcoming the Lion and tearing his mouth in two.

"That is all very well," said the Lion, "but proves nothing, **A** for it was a man who made the statue." ❖

Emperor Commodus as Hercules, AD 191–192. Unknown artist. Musei Capitolini, Rome.

How have you applied a moral lesson from one of these fables? Which fable offers the most useful advice for people today? Why is it important advice?

Differentiated Instruction

Reading Proficiency
The use of articles (*a* and *the*) before the proper nouns in the last two fables is not conventional and could confuse struggling readers. Review proper nouns and note the following:
- All characters in these fables are called by descriptive names (Ant, Grasshopper, Fox, Crow, Lion, Man).

- When a title is part of a name, it is also capitalized (Master Reynard, Mistress Crow).
- In conventional modern English, proper nouns would not be preceded by articles, as in the last two fables. Explain that this is a special style for these stories. It is a bit old-fashioned and may reflect the time when they were first published, or may be intended to evoke the sense that the fables are very old.

Find Meaning

1. (a) Why does Ant refuse to help Grasshopper? (b) Do you agree with Ant's decision? Why or why not?

2. (a) In "The Fox and the Crow," what goal does the Fox achieve? (b) How does the Fox achieve this goal?

3. (a) What do the characters argue about in "The Lion and the Statue"? (b) Why does the man want the Lion to see the statue?

Analyze Literature

Fable How well do the events in each fable support the moral? How do the characters and the events help you remember and understand the lesson conveyed? Use a chart to paraphrase, or restate in your own words, the moral of each fable. Then write a brief evaluation of that moral.

Make Judgments

4. What human character trait does the Crow exhibit that causes her to be tricked by the Fox?

5. In "Ant and Grasshopper," what adjectives would you use to describe the character traits of each animal?

6. In your own words, describe the moral of "The Lion and the Statue."

	Moral	My Evaluation
"Ant and Grasshopper"	The fruits of labor only go to those who work hard for them.	
"The Fox and the Crow"		
"The Lion and the Statue"		

Extend Understanding

Writing Options

Creative Writing Write a modern **fable** for young children. Remember that a fable should convey a straightforward moral lesson. Decide on a lesson that you think is important for young children to learn, and think of a plot that might teach that lesson. Be sure to include animal characters that have human traits. State the moral at the end of your fable.

Persuasive Writing Write an **editorial** to post on a class website. In your editorial, support one of the morals from the fables. Choose the moral that you think is the most useful. Determine why you think this lesson is relevant. Then use these reasons to back up your claims.

Critical Literacy

Create a Drama With a partner, select one of these fables to rewrite as a short drama. Make a list of the characters; write descriptions of the set, costumes, and props; and write the dialogue and stage directions. Rehearse your play several times before you perform it for your class.

Lifelong Learning

Research Fables Use the library or the Internet to find fables from a variety of cultures. On note cards, write brief summaries of at least four fables. Include the moral of each fable. Present your summaries to the class. Then, as a class, compare the fables and morals you have collected. Discuss similarities and differences. Post the note cards in a class display, organizing them according to culture.

 Go to **www.mirrorsandwindows.com** for more.

Find Meaning

1. (a) By helping, Ant would endanger her own survival.
(b) Responses may vary. Students who agree may say that Grasshopper will never become responsible and industrious if someone just gives him what he needs.

2. (a) The Fox gets the cheese.
(b) The Fox pretends to admire the Crow's voice and persuades her to sing a song for him. When she opens her mouth to sing, she drops her cheese and the Fox picks it up.

3. (a) They argue about who is stronger, a lion or a man. (b) The man thinks the statue will prove men are stronger than lions.

Make Judgments

4. The Crow exhibits vanity.

5. Students may describe the Grasshopper as carefree, irresponsible, and lazy; they may describe the Ant as industrious, responsible, and smart.

6. Answers should be along the lines of "Always consider the source of claims of superiority."

Analyze Literature

Fable Students' paraphrases and evaluations will vary. Check that paraphrases are accurate.

Rubrics for Writing Options

You can adapt this as a checklist for students to use as they write.

Creative Writing

☐ Does the fable include animal characters with human traits?

☐ Does the fable convey a straightforward lesson and conclude with a moral?

Persuasive Writing

☐ Does the editorial identify the moral from one of these fables?

☐ Does the editorial provide reasons or examples to support the moral?

Phaëthon, Son of Apollo

A Greek Myth retold by Olivia E. Coolidge

At a Glance

Directed Reading

- Reading Level: Moderate
- Difficulty Considerations: Background and names
- Ease Factors: Description and suspense

Objectives

Studying this lesson will enable students to

- use reading skills such as drawing conclusions
- define allegory and recognize how it is used in the selection
- describe literary accomplishments of Olivia Coolidge
- appreciate a Greek myth about how pride and foolishness lead to a hero's downfall

Launch the Lesson

Explain that this myth, "Phaëthon, Son of Apollo," examines the effects of human weaknesses, such as pride. Ask students to think, as they read, about their own experiences with the emotions they encounter in the story.

BEFORE READING

Build Background

Cultural Context The heroes of ancient Greece were highly revered. A hero might have one parent who was a god and one who was a human, or a hero might simply be a person with exceptional attributes, such as beauty or strength. Many heroes were known for their bold and daring exploits. Both gods and heroes had character flaws similar to those of ordinary humans, and these flaws often led to their downfall.

Reader's Context When have you done something that others warned was dangerous? Why did you do it?

Set Purpose

Before you begin to read, look at the artwork that accompanies the story, think about the title and genre, and use these clues to predict the theme or message that the myth conveys.

Analyze Literature

Allegory A story that has a symbolic meaning in addition to its literal meaning is an **allegory.** Often, allegorical stories offer moral lessons. As you read "Phaëthon, Son of Apollo," think about the underlying meanings related to the characters and events.

Use Reading Skills

Draw Conclusions

Allegories convey truths or generalizations about human behavior or experience. As you read "Phaëthon, Son of Apollo," use a two-column chart to collect evidence and draw conclusions about the theme or message of the allegory.

Evidence	Conclusion
Phaëthon always had to be the first and best at everything, and he would take any risk to win.	

Preview Vocabulary

def·er·ence (de´ fə rən[t]s) *n.,* respectful yielding

im·plore (im plōr´) *v.,* beg

dis·suade (di swäd´) *v.,* deter a person from a course of action by persuasion

pre·cip·i·tous (pri si´ pə təs) *adj.,* very steep

am·ber (am´ bər) *adj.,* yellowish red; *n.,* hardened sap

Meet the Author

Olivia E. Coolidge (1908–2006) was born in London, England. She graduated from Oxford University in 1931 and went on to earn a master's degree. The first book she published was *Greek Myths* in 1949, which she wrote for children and young adults. She later published collections of Roman and Egyptian myths as well as biographies and historical fiction. Coolidge is acclaimed for her accurate portrayals of historical subjects and for her ability to bring ancient and mythical worlds to life.

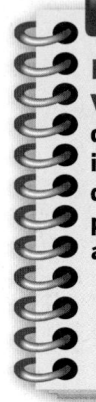

Words in Use

Preview Vocabulary
deference, 772
implore, 772
dissuade, 773
precipitous, 774
amber, 774

Selection Words
comrades, 772
radiant, 773
ointment, 774
poplar, 774

Teaching Words
revered, 770
exploits, 770
acclaimed, 770
convey, 770
generalizations, 770
astronomers, 773
celestial, 773
stationary, 773

KEY TERMS

MYTH, 770
HERO, 770
CHARACTER FLAW, 770
GENRE, 770
ALLEGORY, 770
MORAL LESSON, 770
BIOGRAPHY, 770
HISTORICAL FICTION, 770
CHARACTER TRAIT, 775
CONFLICT, 775
THESIS, 775
CHARACTER SKETCH, 775

Common Core State Standards

Reading Literature
RL.1

Phaëthon, Son of Apollo

The Chariot of Apollo, 1907–1910. Odilon Redon. Fitzwilliam Museum, University of Cambridge, United Kingdom.

A Greek Myth retold by Olivia E. Coolidge

Phaëthon loved to boast of his divine father as he saw the golden chariot riding high through the air.

771

Teach the Selection

Summary

Phaëthon, son of the sun god Apollo and a mortal, Clymene, is proud and boastful about his heritage. Most people like him anyway because he is so handsome and noble, but one youth, Epaphos, scorns his claims. Phaëthon demands proof of who his father is from Clymene, and she tells him to go to Apollo's eastern palace and talk to the god in person.

Apollo instantly recognizes Phaëthon and offers to do anything to help him. Phaëthon asks to drive the sun chariot. Apollo tries to talk his son out of the idea, but Phaëthon is determined.

As soon as he sets off in the chariot, he loses control. The horses race wildly off course and set the ground on fire. To save the earth, Zeus kills Phaëthon with a lightning bolt. Clymene and her daughters find and bury his body, mourning so deeply that the gods, in pity, change them into poplar trees.

MIRRORS & WINDOWS The Mirrors & Windows questions at the end of the selection focus on the theme of overconfidence. Before students begin reading, ask: Who was the last person you saw overestimate his or her abilities?

Program Resources

Planning and Assessment
Program Planning Guide, Selection Lesson Plan
E-Lesson Planner
Assessment Guide, Lesson Test
ExamView

Technology Tools
Interactive Student Text on CD
Visual Teaching Package
Audio Library
mirrorsandwindows.com

Meeting the Standards
Folk Literature: Unit 8, Directed Reading, pp. 56–61

Differentiating Instruction
Advanced Students, Comparison of Myths, p. 48

"Let me drive the chariot of the sun

Geography Connection
Ethiopia Ethiopia is a country on what is called the horn of eastern Africa. It has been home to humans for eight thousand years or more, and was a powerful trading center known to ancient Greek travelers as the kingdom of Aksum. **(A)**

Analyze Literature
Setting To help students understand how descriptions of setting can contribute to a story, focus on the passage about Apollo's magnificent palace. Ask: "How does this setting enhance the story?" (Students should agree that the palace, with its many bright and shining elements, adds to the brightness and power of Apollo's character. It also emphasizes how bold Phaëthon is.) **(B)**

Though Apollo always honored the memory of Daphne she was not his only love. Another was a mortal, Clymene,[1] by whom he had a son named Phaëthon.[2] Phaëthon grew up with his mother, who, since she was mortal, could not dwell in the halls of Olympus[3] or in the palace of the sun. **(A)** She lived not far from the East in the land of Ethiopia, and as her son grew up, she would point to the place where Eos,[4] goddess of the dawn, lighted up the sky and tell him that there his father dwelt. Phaëthon loved to boast of his divine father as he saw the golden chariot riding high through the air. He would remind his comrades of other sons of gods and mortal women who, by virtue of their great deeds, had themselves become gods at last. He must always be first in everything, and in most things this was easy, since he was in truth stronger, swifter, and more daring than the others. Even if he were not victorious, Phaëthon always claimed to be first in honor. He could never bear to be beaten, even if he must risk his life in some rash way to win.

Most of the princes of Ethiopia willingly paid Phaëthon honor, since they admired him greatly for his fire and beauty. There was one boy, however, Epaphos,[5] who was rumored to be a child of Zeus[6] himself. Since this was not certainly proved, Phaëthon chose to disbelieve it and to demand from Epaphos the <u>deference</u> that he obtained from all others. Epaphos was proud too, and one day he lost his temper with Phaëthon and turned on him, saying, "You are a fool to believe all that your mother tells you. You are all swelled up with false ideas about your father."

Crimson with rage, the lad rushed home to his mother and demanded that she prove to him the truth of the story that she had often told. "Give me some proof," he <u>implored</u> her, "with which I can answer this insult of Epaphos. It is a matter of life and death to me, for if I cannot, I shall die of shame."

"I swear to you," replied his mother solemnly, "by the bright orb of the sun itself that you are his son. If I swear falsely, may I never look on the sun again, but die before the next time he mounts the heavens. More than this I cannot do, but you, my child, can go to the eastern palace of Phoebus Apollo— it lies not far away—and there speak with the god himself."

The son of Clymene leaped up with joy at his mother's words. The palace of Apollo was indeed not far. It stood just below the eastern horizon, its tall pillars glistening with bronze and gold. Above these it was white with gleaming ivory, and the great doors were flashing silver, embossed with pictures of earth, sky, and sea, and the gods that dwelt therein. Up the steep hill and the bright steps climbed Phaëthon, passing unafraid through the silver doors, and stood in the presence of the sun. Here at last he was forced to turn away his face, for Phoebus sat in state on his golden throne. It gleamed with emeralds and precious stones, while on the head of the god was a brilliant diamond crown upon which no eye could look undazzled. **(B)**

Phaëthon hid his face, but the god had recognized his son, and he spoke kindly,

---

1. **Clymene** (klim´ ə nē).
2. **Phaëthon** (fā´ ə tän).
3. **Olympus.** In Greek mythology, the home of the gods
4. **Eos** (e´ äs).
5. **Epaphos** (ep´ ə fəs).
6. **Zeus.** Ruler of the gods, associated with the thunderbolt; he controlled thunder, lightning, and rain.

---

def•er•ence (de´ fə rən[t]s) *n.*, respectful yielding
im•plore (im plōr´) *v.*, beg

---

772 **UNIT 8** FOLK LITERATURE

Differentiated Instruction

Reading Proficiency
Less-confident readers may have some trouble with the rather formal language and tone of the selection. Have them read portions aloud, then paraphrase them in a more conversational style. For example: "Ask of me whatever thing you wish to prove your origin to men, and you shall have it." (Ask for whatever you want to prove I'm your father, and I'll give it to you.)

Enrichment
Students may wish to investigate the story of Apollo and Daphne, mentioned in the opening sentence of the myth. Have them research the story online or at the library and create a presentation about it for the class.

across the heavens for one day," he said.

asking him why he had come. Then Phaëthon plucked up courage and said, "I come to ask you if you are indeed my father. If you are so, I beg you to give me some proof of it so that all may recognize me as Phoebus'[7] son."

SCIENCE ▶▶ CONNECTION

Solar Models While ancient peoples told myths such as the story of Phaëthon to help explain the rising and setting of the sun, ancient astronomers were carefully observing the movements of the celestial bodies and forming theories about the universe. About AD 150, Egyptian scientist Claudius Ptolemy theorized that the Earth was at the center of the universe. According to Ptolemy's model, the Earth is stationary and the planets, sun, and moon move slowly around it. However, this Earth-centered, or *geocentric*, theory left many questions unanswered. It wasn't until the sixteenth century that Polish astronomer Nicolaus Copernicus began to establish the basis for the sun-centered, or *heliocentric*, universe. Though stories such as "Phaëthon, Son of Apollo" are scientifically unsound, why might they still be useful?

(Above) *Portrait of Polish Astronomer Nicolas Copernicus*, c. 1933. **C**

The god smiled, being well pleased with his son's beauty and daring. He took off his crown so that Phaëthon could look at him, and coming down from his throne, he put his arms around the boy, and said, "You are indeed my son and Clymene's, and worthy to be called so. Ask of me whatever thing you wish to prove your origin to men, and you shall have it."

Phaëthon swayed for a moment and was dizzy with excitement at the touch of the

god. His heart leaped; the blood rushed into his face. Now he felt that he was truly divine, unlike other men, and he did not wish to be counted with men any more. He looked up for a moment at his radiant father. "Let me drive the chariot of the sun across the heavens for one day," he said.

Apollo frowned and shook his head. "I cannot break my promise, but I will <u>dissuade</u> you if I can," he answered. "How can you drive my chariot, whose horses need a strong hand on the reins? The climb is too steep for you. The immense height will make you dizzy. The swift streams of air in the upper heaven will sweep you off your course. Even the immortal gods could not drive my chariot. How then can you? Be wise and make some other choice."

The pride of Phaëthon was stubborn, for he thought the god was merely trying to frighten him. Besides, if he could guide the sun's chariot, would he not have proved his right to be divine rather than mortal? For that he would risk his life. Indeed, once he had seen Apollo's splendor, he did not wish to go back and live among men. Therefore, he insisted on his right until Apollo had to give way.

When the father saw that nothing else would satisfy the boy, he bade the Hours

---

7. **Phoebus** (fē´ bəs). Another name for Apollo

dis•suade (di swād´) *v.*, deter a person from a course of action by persuasion

---

Science Connection
Solar Models *Answer:* Many will note that the story offers fairly true depictions of human emotions and a useful moral.

Use Reading Skills
Draw Conclusions Remind students that they can draw conclusions by interpreting text details in light of their own knowledge. As students read Apollo's warning and Phaëthon's insistence on driving the chariot, ask what they think will happen, and why. (Based on the description of Phaëthon's flawed character, Apollo's status as a powerful god, and the strong objections Apollo raises, things will not turn out well if Phaëthon drives the chariot.)

Literary Connection
Apollo Apollo, son of Zeus and Leto, was a prominent Greek god. His twin sister, Artemis, was goddess of the hunt. Apollo was associated with many aspects of life, including music, poetry, and medicine. He controlled the Oracle at Delphi, where the faithful went to ask advice and hear prophecies. After the fifth century BC, the god's most powerful aspect was as Phoebus Apollo, the sun god (*phoebus* means "bright").

Grammar Skills

Inverted Sentences
Explain that in an inverted sentence, the subject comes after the verb.

- Many questions are inverted sentences (Who was Phaëthon?)
- Many inverted sentences begin with *here* or *there* (There sat Apollo on his throne).
- Many begin with an adverb phrase (To the east stood Apollo's palace). Note that this structure can create a more formal tone.

Challenge students to find examples of inverted sentences in the selection, such as

- If I swear falsely, may I never look on the sun again . . . (inverting "I may" to "may I")
- Up the steep hill and the bright steps climbed Phaëthon . . . (inverting "Phaëthon climbed" to "climbed Phaëthon") You might also ask students to create inverted sentences from some other material in the story.

Use Reading Strategies

Visualize Draw attention to the phrase "rosy-fingered Dawn." Ask: "What image does this evoke?" Explain that this is a traditional *epithet* (phrase used in place of or in addition to a name). It began with the Greek author Homer, who used it more than twenty times (Greek for "rosy-fingered" is *rhododactylos*). **A**

Analyze Literature

Allegory Explain that in allegory, characters often symbolize moral qualities or ideas. Note that Dawn and the Hours are already called by names that reflect ideas. Ask students if they can think of the quality associated with Phaëthon. (Phaëthon symbolizes pride.)

Cultural Connection

Amber Amber forms when tree resin, usually from pines, fossilizes. It is usually a shade of yellow, and the most valuable types are transparent. Amber has long been considered valuable; people use it for jewelry and as a charm for good luck or good health. Maybe because it was found in an area believed to be where Phaëthon fell, the Greeks explained its source as being the tears of the Phaëthon's mother and sisters after they became poplars. **B**

Answer: Students may refer to the way pride and overconfidence can distort people's perceptions.

---

bring forth his chariot and yoke the horses. The chariot was of gold and had two gold-rimmed wheels with spokes of silver. In it there was room for one man to stand and hold the reins. Around the front and sides of it ran a rail, but the back was open. At the end of a long pole there were yokes for the four horses. The pole was of gold and shone with precious jewels: the golden topaz, the bright diamond, the green emerald, and the flashing ruby. While the Hours were yoking **A** the swift, pawing horses, rosy-fingered Dawn hastened to the gates of heaven to draw them open. Meanwhile Apollo anointed his son's face with a magic ointment, that he might be able to bear the heat of the fire-breathing horses and the golden chariot. At last Phaëthon mounted the chariot and grasped the reins, the barriers were let down, and the horses shot up into the air.

At first the fiery horses sped forward up the accustomed trail, but behind them the chariot was too light without the weight of the immortal god. It bounded from side to side and was dashed up and down. Phaëthon was too frightened and too dizzy to pull the reins, nor would he have known anyway whether he was on the usual path. As soon as the horses felt that there was no hand controlling them, they soared up, up with fiery speed into the heavens till the earth grew pale and cold beneath them. Phaëthon shut his eyes, trembling at the dizzy, precipitous height. Then the horses dropped down, more swiftly than a falling stone, flinging themselves madly from side to side in panic because they were masterless.

Phaëthon dropped the reins entirely and clung with all his might to the chariot rail. Meanwhile as they came near the earth, it dried up and cracked apart. Meadows were reduced to white ashes, cornfields smoked and shriveled, cities perished in flame. Far and wide on the wooded mountains the forests were ablaze, and even the snowclad Alps were bare and dry. Rivers steamed and dried to dust. The great North African plain was scorched until it became the desert that it is today. Even the sea shrank back to pools and caves, until dried fishes were left baking upon the white-hot sands. At last the great earth mother called upon Zeus to save her from utter destruction, and Zeus hurled a mighty thunderbolt at the unhappy Phaëthon, who was still crouched in the chariot, clinging desperately to the rail. The dart cast him out, and he fell flaming in a long trail through the air. The chariot broke in pieces at the mighty blow, and the maddened horses rushed snorting back to the stable of their master, Apollo.

Unhappy Clymene and her daughters wandered over the whole earth seeking the body of the boy they loved so well. When they found him, they took him and buried him. Over his grave they wept and could not be comforted. At last the gods in pity for their grief changed them into poplar trees, **B** which weep with tears of amber in memory of Phaëthon. ✤

> **pre‧cip‧i‧tous** (pri si′ pə təs) *adj.,* very steep
> **am‧ber** (am′ bər) *adj.,* yellowish red; *n.,* hardened sap

Think of a time when you overestimated your abilities. What happened? Why do you think people misjudge themselves in this way?

Differentiated Instruction

English Language Learning

Review words and phrases to clarify their meanings for English language learners. Examples include the following:

dwelt — (a variant of *dwelled*) lived, 772
by virtue of — because of, 772
paid . . . honor — respected, 772
all swelled up — full of pride (in this case, unjustified pride), 772

plucked up courage — tried to act brave, 773
divine — godlike, one of the gods, 773
bade — commanded, 773
anointed — rubbed, applied to, 774
dashed — knocked around, flung, 774
with all his might — with all his strength, 774
utter — (adjective) complete, 774

Find Meaning

1. What does Phaëthon's behavior with his friends reveal about his character?

2. (a) Who is Phaëthon's father? (b) Why does Phaëthon want everyone to know who his father is?

3. (a) What does Phaëthon request of his father? (b) Why does he ask for this?

Analyze Literature

Allegory Allegories typically present a moral lesson. What is the theme, or message, of "Phaëthon, Son of Apollo"? Use a theme map to gather details from this story. List the main characters and their traits, the story's central conflict, and the way this conflict is resolved. Then think about what these details suggest about the story's theme.

Make Judgments

4. (a) Why does Apollo agree to Phaëthon's request? (b) Should he have refused? Why or why not?

5. (a) At what point would most people have recognized the danger involved in driving the chariot? (b) Why do you think Phaëthon failed to recognize this?

Extend Understanding

Writing Options

Creative Writing Imagine that your crops were lost as a result of Phaëthon's ride. Write a **business letter** to Apollo to complain about his management of the sun. Cite reasons for your dissatisfaction. Offer some suggestions for how to correct the problem. Be sure to use an appropriate and respectful tone.

Expository Writing Using your theme map, write a brief **literary analysis** of "Phaëthon, Son of Apollo." At the start of your analysis, state the theme of this myth in a thesis. Then support your claims with reasons and evidence from the text. At the end of your response, restate what you believe the theme to be, and sum up your main points.

Critical Literacy

Write a Character Sketch In small groups, collect and discuss information about Phaëthon's personality. Begin by listing his reasons for wanting to drive his father's chariot. Then determine what this list suggests about his character. Use the information you collect to write a brief character sketch of Phaëthon.

Lifelong Learning

Compare Myths Use library resources or the Internet to locate another retelling of this myth. Compare and contrast the two retellings. Do they both express the same theme? In what ways are the retellings alike? In what ways are they different? Create a Venn diagram to show how these retellings are both similar and different.

Go to www.mirrorsandwindows.com for more.

Find Meaning

1. Phaëthon is strong, swift, and daring, but he is also competitive, boastful, proud, and dishonest.

2. (a) Apollo is his father. (b) He wants to make them pay more respect to him.

3. (a) Phaëthon asks Apollo to allow him to drive the chariot of the sun across the sky. (b) He thinks that by doing this he will prove to everyone that he should be thought of as a god rather than as a mortal.

Make Judgments

4. (a) Apollo has given his word and feels that he must not break a promise. (b) Answers will vary. Some students may say he could have made Phaëthon go through training before driving the chariot.

5. (a) Most people would probably have heeded Apollo's warnings or at least seen how dangerous the fire-breathing horses were. (b) Phaëthon could only think of the glory he expected to gain from his daring feat.

Analyze Literature

Allegory Students' theme statements should be supported by the details they list. Most will say one theme of the story is that great pride can be dangerous.

Rubrics for Writing Options

You can adapt this as a checklist for students to use as they write.

Creative Writing

☐ Does the letter follow the proper format?

☐ Does the letter cite reasons for the dissatisfaction?

☐ Does the letter offer suggestions?

☐ Does the letter use an appropriate tone?

Expository Writing

☐ Does the analysis state the theme of the myth?

☐ Does the analysis include evidence and reasons?

☐ Does the analysis end with a restatement of the theme and sum up main points?

Understanding Dangling Modifiers

These are sample answers.

1. He received answers from his mother, but questions about his father remained.

2. It was easy to guess that something would happen to him, because he was poorly behaved.

3. Phaëthon anointed his face with magic ointment so the sun would not burn him.

4. The sky was filled with light as he dived and soared.

5. As he fell near the earth, meadows were reduced to white ashes.

6. He acted superior to other children, but endured a terrible end.

7. The chariot fell to earth as he cried out in fear.

8. After he left his home, his attention turned to the sun.

9. The other children laughed while he spoke with his mother.

10. The chariot rose and fell as he called to the horses.

> For more information, see Grammar & Style Section 3.13, Common Usage Problems, of the Language Arts Handbook.

Program Resources

You will find additional lessons on Dangling Modifiers in the *Exceeding the Standards: Grammar & Style* resource.

Grammar & Style

Dangling Modifiers

Crimson with rage, the lad rushed home to his mother....

—OLIVIA E. COOLIDGE, "Phaëthon, Son of Apollo"

Dangling modifiers confuse the reader. A **dangling modifier** seems to modify nothing because the word it should modify does not appear in the sentence.

A reader assumes that an introductory phrase or clause will modify the first noun after the comma. For example, imagine a sentence similar to the quotation above.

> **INCORRECT**
> *Crimson with rage, the fence kept him away from us.*

The sentence is confusing because it appears that *the fence* was crimson with rage.

To correct dangling modifiers, reword the sentence. The sentence often becomes clear when the modified word or words is added.

> **CORRECT**
> *Crimson with rage, <u>he</u> was kept away from us by the fence.*

By expanding the dangling phrase into a full subordinate clause, you can also eliminate dangling modifiers.

> **INCORRECT**
> <u>*Falling toward the earth*</u>, *many fields were burned.*

> **CORRECT**
> <u>*As Phaëthon fell toward the earth*</u>, *he burned many fields.*

By changing the dangling phrase *Falling toward the earth* into the full subordinate clause *As Phaëthon fell toward the earth*, the dangling modifier is eliminated.

Understanding Dangling Modifiers

On a separate sheet of paper, revise each sentence to correct the dangling modifier.

1. Receiving answers from his mother, questions about his father remained.

2. Poorly behaved, it was easy to guess that something would happen to him.

3. Anointing his face with a magic ointment, the sun wouldn't burn Phaëthon.

4. Diving and soaring, the sky was filled with light.

5. Falling near the earth, meadows were reduced to white ashes.

6. Acting superior to other children, a terrible end was endured.

7. Crying out in fear, the chariot fell to earth.

8. After leaving his home, the sun grabbed his attention.

9. While speaking with his mother, laughter of the other children could be heard.

10. Calling to the horses, the chariot rose and fell.

KEY TERMS

DANGLING MODIFIER, 776
CLAUSE, 776
NOUN, 776
COMMA, 776
QUOTATION, 776
SUBORDINATE CLAUSE, 776

Common Core State Standards

Language
L.7.1c

The Instruction of Indra

A Hindu Myth retold by Joseph Campbell with Bill Moyers

SUCH PERFECTION

A Short Story by R. K. Narayan

BEFORE READING

Build Background

Cultural Context Hindu tradition holds that everything cycles through the stages of birth, order, and destruction. The stages of this cycle are presided over by the deities Brahma, Vishnu, and Shiva, respectively. According to the doctrine of karma, one's search for enlightenment extends through many lifetimes. A person's deeds determine the quality of that person's next life.

Reader's Context What often happens to boastful people?

Set Purpose

Scan each selection to identify unfamiliar words. Then use a dictionary to determine the meanings of these words.

Meet the Authors

Joseph Campbell (1904–1987) gained an international reputation as a scholar of mythology and comparative religion. He studied at universities in the United States and in Europe. Broadcast journalist Bill Moyers produced a television series and a book based on interviews with Campbell called *The Power of Myth.*

R. K. Narayan (1906–2001), born in Madras, India, has been called India's greatest twentieth-century writer in English. Best known for his novels, he also wrote short stories and stories based on Hindu mythology. Narayan's long writing career spanned more than fifty years.

Compare Literature: Symbolism

A **symbol** is something that stands for or represents both itself and something else. Use a chart like this one to list the symbols and what they stand for in "The Instruction of Indra" and "Such Perfection."

	"The Instruction of Indra"	"Such Perfection"
Symbol	Indra's palace	
What Symbol Stands for		

Preview Vocabulary

drought (draút) *n.*, period of dry weather; lack of rain

cos•mic (käz´ mik) *adj.*, relating to the universe as a whole

gran•di•ose (gran´ dē ōs´) *adj.*, magnificent; grand

dis•il•lu•sioned (dis´ ə lü´ zhənd) *adj.*, disappointed; dissatisfied

man•i•fes•ta•tion (ma' nə fə stā´ shən) *n.*, example; instance

Preview the Selection

At a Glance
Directed Reading
"The Instruction of Indra"
- Reading Level: Challenging
- Difficulty Considerations: Setting, concepts, and vocabulary
- Ease Factor: None

"Such Perfection"
- Reading Level: Moderate
- Difficulty Considerations: Cultural and religious background
- Ease Factor: Description, simple narrative

Objectives

Studying this lesson will enable students to
- compare literary selections of different genres
- use reading skills such as monitoring comprehension
- define symbolism and analyze its use in the selections
- describe literary accomplishments of Joseph Campbell and R. K. Narayan
- appreciate stories about gaining greater wisdom

Launch the Lesson

Tell students that in "The Instruction of Indra," each decision Indra makes turns out to have an impact on those around him. Encourage them to think about how their own actions affect others, and consider how much they typically weigh this when they make decisions.

Before reading "Such Perfection" encourage students to think about their own experiences of beauty. Ask: "Have you ever seen anything *perfectly* beautiful? What was it?"

THE INSTRUCTION OF INDRA / SUCH PERFECTION **777**

Words in Use

"The Instruction of Indra"

Preview Vocabulary	Selection Words	Teaching Words
drought, 779	**immortal,** 779	**deities,** 777
cosmic, 779	**eternity,** 779	**respectively,** 777
grandiose, 779	**divine,** 779	**doctrine,** 777
disillusioned, 781	**crotchety,** 780	**karma,** 777
manifestation, 781	**constellation,** 780	**enlightenment,** 777
		comparative, 777

KEY TERMS
SCAN, 777
SYMBOL, 777
SYMBOLISM, 785
COMPARE AND CONTRAST, 785

Common Core State Standards
Reading Literature
RL.1

Summary

After defeating a monster, Indra decides to build a palace that befits his magnificence. His ideas about the palace grow ever more fantastic. Fearing the work will go on forever, his carpenter complains to Brahma.

The next day, a blue-black boy arrives and tells Indra about the many Indras he has seen in his long life. An army of ants goes past and, at Indra's insistence, the boy reveals that each one is an Indra reincarnated at the lowest level. An old yogi arrives. He has a disc of hair on his chest, but half the hairs are gone. He explains that each time an Indra dies, another chest hair falls.

Shaken by this news of his mortality, Indra abandons his palace. He resolves to leave his comfortable life to become a yogi. Now his wife, Indrani, is upset and complains to the priest of the gods, who reminds Indra that he embodies the Brahma and should honor that privilege. Indra realizes that it is best to face his responsibilities to society and to his family rather than run from them.

The Mirrors & Windows questions at the end of the myth focus on the theme of learning. Before students start to read, ask: At what age do you think people realize their experiences and desires are not unique?

The Instruction of Indra

A Hindu Myth retold by Joseph Campbell with Bill Moyers

"Indras before you, I have seen them come and go, come and go.

778

Program Resources

Planning and Assessment
Program Planning Guide, Selection Lesson Plan
E-Lesson Planner
Assessment Guide, Lesson Test
ExamView

Technology Tools
Interactive Student Text on CD
Visual Teaching Package
mirrorsandwindows.com

Meeting the Standards
Folk Literature: Unit 8, Compare Literature, pp. 62–71

Differentiating Instruction
Developing Readers, Set Purpose, pp. 55–57

There is a wonderful story in one of the Upanishads[1] about the god Indra.[2] Now, it happened at this time that a great monster had enclosed all the waters of the earth, so there was a terrible <u>drought</u>, and the world was in a very bad condition. It took Indra quite a while to realize that he had a box of thunderbolts and that all he had to do was drop a thunderbolt on the monster and blow him up. When he did that, the waters flowed, and the world was refreshed and Indra said, "What a great boy am I."

So, thinking, "What a great boy am I," Indra goes up to the <u>cosmic</u> mountain, which is the central mountain of the world, and decides to build a palace worthy of such as he. The main carpenter of the gods goes to work on it, and in very quick order he gets the palace into pretty good condition.

But every time Indra comes to inspect it, he has bigger ideas about how splendid and <u>grandiose</u> the palace should be. Finally, the carpenter says, "My god, we are both immortal, and there is no end to his desires. I am caught for eternity." So he decides to go to Brahma, the creator god, and complain.

Brahma sits on a lotus,[3] the symbol of divine energy and divine grace. The lotus grows from the navel of Vishnu, who is the sleeping god, whose dream is the universe. So the carpenter comes to the edge of the great lotus pond of the universe and tells his story to Brahma. Brahma says, "You go home.

I will fix this up." Brahma gets off his lotus and kneels down to address sleeping Vishnu. Vishnu just makes a gesture and says something like, "Listen, fly, something is going to happen."

Next morning, at the gate of the palace that is being built, there appears a beautiful blue-black boy with a lot of children around him, just admiring his beauty. The porter at the gate of the new palace goes running to Indra, and Indra says, "Well, bring in the boy." The boy is brought in, and Indra, the king god, sitting on his throne, says, "Young man, welcome. And what brings you to my palace?"

"Well," says the boy with a voice like thunder rolling on the horizon, "I have been told that you are building such a palace as no Indra before you ever built."

And Indra says, "Indras before me, young man—what are you talking about?"

The boy says, "Indras before you. I have seen them come and go, come and go. Just think, Vishnu sleeps in the cosmic ocean, and the lotus of the universe grows from his navel. On the lotus sits Brahma, the creator. **A**

Engraving of Indra mounted on his elephant, c. 1880.

---

1. **Upanishads.** Indian philosophical and religious writings
2. **Indra.** Chief god of ancient India
3. **lotus.** Pink or white water lily used as a religious symbol in Hinduism

drought (draŭt) *n.*, period of dry weather; lack of rain

cos·mic (käz´ mik) *adj.*, relating to the universe as a whole

gran·di·ose (gran´ dē ōs´) *adj.*, magnificent; grand

Analyze Literature

Symbolism Ask: "What symbols are used in this sentence? What do they suggest about mortality and time?" (Water droplets and grains of sand symbolize the Brahma's lives. This emphasizes how vast time is and what a small part of it is allotted to each living being.) **A**

Analyze Literature

Character Remind students that a character is a participant in the action of a literary work and can be static (unchanging during the story), dynamic (changed by the events), flat (one-dimensional), or round (a complex personality). Ask students how they would characterize Indra using these distinctions. (Most will say round and dynamic.)

God with Three Faces, Brahma, c. 11th century. Musée Guimet, Paris.

Brahma opens his eyes, and a world comes into being, governed by an Indra. Brahma closes his eyes, and a world goes out of being. The life of a Brahma is four hundred and thirty-two thousand years. When he dies, the lotus goes back, and another lotus is formed, and another Brahma. Then think of the galaxies beyond galaxies in infinite space, each a lotus, with a Brahma sitting on it, opening his eyes, closing his eyes. And Indras? There may be wise men in your court who would volunteer to count the drops of water in the oceans of the world or the grains of sand on the beaches, but no one would count those Brahmin, let alone those Indras."

While the boy is talking, an army of ants parades across the floor. The boy laughs when he sees them, and Indra's hair stands on end, and he says to the boy, "Why do you laugh?"

The boy answers, "Don't ask unless you are willing to be hurt."

Indra says, "I ask. Teach." (That, by the way, is a good Oriental idea: you don't teach until you are asked. You don't force your mission down people's throats.)

And so the boy points to the ants and says, "Former Indras all. Through many lifetimes they rise from the lowest conditions to highest illumination.[4] And then they drop their thunderbolt on a monster, and they think, 'What a good boy am I.' And down they go again."

While the boy is talking, a crotchety old yogi[5] comes into the palace with a banana leaf parasol. He is naked except for a loincloth,[6] and on his chest is a little disk of hair, and half the hairs in the middle have all dropped out.

The boy greets him and asks him just what Indra was about to ask. "Old man, what is your name? Where do you come from? Where is your family? Where is your house? And what is the meaning of this curious constellation of hair on your chest?"

"Well," says the old fella, "my name is Hairy. I don't have a house. Life is too short for that. I just have this parasol. I don't have a family. I just meditate on Vishnu's feet, and think of eternity, and how passing time is. You know, every time an Indra dies, a world disappears—these things just flash by like that. Every time an Indra dies, one hair drops out of this circle on my chest. Half the hairs are gone now. Pretty soon they will all be gone. Life is short. Why build a house?"

Then the two disappear. The boy was Vishnu, the Lord Protector,[7] and the old yogi

---

4. **illumination.** Highest level of spiritual understanding
5. **yogi.** Hindu holy man, one who practices a spiritual path, or yoga
6. **loincloth.** Cloth worn about the waist and upper thighs
7. **Vishnu, the Lord Protector.** In Hindu belief, one of the appearances of Vishnu on Earth was as Krishna, frequently pictured as a beautiful blue-black youth

Differentiated Instruction

English Language Learning

Campbell uses many colloquial terms in telling the story. Point these out. Examples include
in very quick order—very quickly, 779
by the way—way of saying that information is worth noting but not necessarily on topic, 780
fella—a casual pronunciation of *fellow*, 780

was Shiva, the creator and destroyer of the world, who had just come for the instruction of Indra, who is simply a god of history but thinks he is the whole show.

Indra is sitting there on the throne, and he is completely <u>disillusioned</u>, completely shot. He calls the carpenter and says, "I'm quitting the building of this palace. You are dismissed." So the carpenter got his intention. He is dismissed from the job, and there is no more house building going on.

Indra decides to go out and be a yogi and just meditate on the lotus feet of Vishnu. But he has a beautiful queen named Indrani. And when Indrani hears of Indra's plan, she goes to the priest of the gods and says, "Now he has got the idea in his head of going out to become a yogi."

"Well," says the priest, "come in with me, darling, and we will sit down, and I will fix this up."

So they sit down before the king's throne, and the priest says, "Now, I wrote a book for you many years ago on the art of politics. You are in the position of the king of the gods. You are a <u>manifestation</u> of the mystery

of Brahma in the field of time. This is a high privilege. Appreciate it, honor it, and deal with life as though you were what you really are. And besides, now I am going to write you a book on the art of love so that you and your wife will know that in the wonderful mystery of the two that are one, the Brahma is radiantly present also."

And with this set of instructions, Indra gives up his idea of going out and becoming a yogi and finds that, in life, he can represent the eternal as a symbol, you might say, of the Brahma.

So each of us is, in a way, the Indra of his own life. You can make a choice, either to throw it all off and go into the forest to meditate, or to stay in the world, both in the life of your job, which is the kingly job of politics and achievement, and in the love life with your wife and family. Now, this is a very nice myth, it seems to me. ❖

---

dis·il·lu·sioned (dis' ə lü' zhənd) *adj.*, disappointed; dissatisfied

man·i·fes·ta·tion (ma' nə fə stā' shən) *n.*, example; instance

---

In your own words, explain the lessons that Indra learned. How important are such lessons in your own life? How are these lessons relevant to people living in today's world?

Find Meaning

1. (a) What problem does Indra solve by using a thunderbolt? (b) What might you infer about Indra from the fact that it took him "quite a while to realize" that he could use the thunderbolts?
2. (a) Why does Indra decide to build a palace? (b) Based on Indra's actions, what do you think of him?

Make Judgments

3. In what ways do you find the arguments of the beautiful blue-black boy and the old yogi compelling?
4. (a) Why does Indrani go to see the priest? (b) Do you agree with the priest's advice to Indra? Explain.

Differentiated Instruction

Enrichment
Students may wish to learn more about Indra's battle with the monster. Tell them the monster was a dragon named Vritra. Have students use library or Internet resources to locate and read a version of this story. Afterward, have students gather in small groups to describe and compare the versions they found.

Reading Proficiency
Students may benefit from listening to an audiotape or watching the DVD of Campbell telling this story.

SUCH PERFECTION

A Short Story by R. K. Narayan

A sense of great relief filled Soma as he realized that his five years of labor were coming to an end. He had turned out scores of images in his lifetime, but he had never done any work to equal this. He often said to himself that long after the Deluge[1] had swept the earth this Nataraja[2] would still be standing on His pedestal.

No other human being had seen the image yet. Soma shut himself in and bolted all the doors and windows and plied[3] his chisel[4] by the still flame of a mud lamp, even when there was a bright sun outside. It made him perspire unbearably, but he did not mind it so long as it helped him to keep out prying eyes. He worked with a fierce concentration and never encouraged anyone to talk about it.

After all, his labors had come to an end. He sat back, wiped the perspiration off his face and surveyed his handiwork with great satisfaction. As he looked on he was overwhelmed by the majesty of this image. He fell prostrate[5] before it, praying, "I have taken five years to make you. May you reside in our temple and bless all human beings!" The dim mud flame cast subtle shadows on the image and gave it an undertone of rippling life. The sculptor stood lost in this vision. A voice said, "My friend, never take this image out of this room. It is too perfect...." Soma trembled with fear. He looked round. He saw a figure crouching in a dark corner of the room—it was a man. Soma dashed forward and clutched him by the throat. "Why did you come here?" The other writhed under the grip and replied, "Out of admiration for you. I have always loved your work. I have waited for five years...."

"How did you come in?"

"With another key while you were eating inside...."

Soma gnashed his teeth. "Shall I strangle you before this God and offer you as sacrifice?" "By all means," replied the other, "if it will help you in any way...but I doubt it. Even with a sacrifice you cannot take it

---

1. **Deluge.** In Hindu mythology, every 4,320,000 years humanity is destroyed by a flood and is then re-created.
2. **Nataraja.** Form of the Hindu god Shiva, also known as Lord of the Dance, whose dancing sets in motion the destruction of the world
3. **plied.** Worked with
4. **chisel.** Wedgelike tool used for shaping wood or stone
5. **prostrate.** Stretched out with face on the ground in humility

782

Words in Use

"Such Perfection" Selection Words
subtle, 782
undertone, 782
writhed, 782
vacant, 783
amidst, 784

"THIS PERFECTION, THIS GOD, IS NOT FOR MORTAL EYES.

out. It is too perfect. Such perfection is not for mortals." The sculptor wept. "Oh, do not say that. I worked in secrecy only for this perfection. It is for our people. It is a God coming into their midst. Don't deny them that." The other prostrated before the image and prayed aloud, "God give us the strength to bear your presence...."

This man spoke to people and the great secret was out. A kind of dread seized the people of the village. On an auspicious[6] day, Soma went to the temple priest and asked, "At the coming full moon my Nataraja must be consecrated.[7] Have you made a place for him in the temple?" The priest answered, "Let me see the image first...." He went over to the sculptor's house, gazed on the image and said, "This perfection, this God, is not for mortal eyes. He will blind us. At the first chance of prayer before him, he will dance...and we shall be wiped out...." The sculptor looked so unhappy that the priest added, "Take your chisel and break a little toe or some other part of the image, and it will be safe...." The sculptor replied that he would sooner crack the skull of his visitor. The leading citizens of the village came over and said, "Don't mistake us. We cannot give your image a place in our temple. Don't be angry with us. We have to think of the safety of all the people in the village....Even now if you are prepared to break a small finger..."

"Get out, all of you," Soma shouted. "I don't care to bring this Nataraja to your temple. I will make a temple for him where he is. You will see that it becomes the greatest temple on earth...." Next day he pulled down a portion of the wall of the room and constructed a large doorway opening on the street. He called Rama, the tom-tom beater, and said, "I will give you a silver coin for your trouble. Go and proclaim

in all nearby villages that this Nataraja will be consecrated at the full moon. If a large crowd turns up, I will present you with a lace shawl."

At the full moon, men, women and children poured in from the surrounding villages. There was hardly an inch of space vacant anywhere. The streets were crammed with people. Vendors of sweets and toys and flowers shouted their wares, moving about in the crowd. Pipers and drummers, groups of persons chanting hymns, children shouting in joy, men greeting each other—all this created a mighty din. Fragrance of flowers and incense hung over the place. Presiding over all this there was the brightest moon that ever shone on earth.

The screen which had covered the image parted. A great flame of camphor was waved in front of the image, and bronze bells rang. A silence fell upon the crowd. Every eye was fixed upon the image. In the flame of the circling camphor Nataraja's eyes lit up. His limbs moved, his ankles jingled. The crowd was awe-stricken. The God pressed one foot on earth and raised the other in dance. He destroyed the universe under his heel, and smeared the ashes over his body, and the same God rattled the drum in his hand and by its rhythm set life in motion again....Creation, Dissolution and God attained a meaning now; this image brought it out...the bells rang louder every second. The crowd stood stunned by this vision vouchsafed[8] to them.

At this moment a wind blew from the east. The moon's disc gradually dimmed. The wind gathered force, clouds blotted out the moon; people looked up and saw only pitchlike darkness above. Lightning flashed, thunder roared and fire poured down from the sky. It

6. **auspicious.** Giving promise of success or good fortune
7. **consecrated.** Made sacred; dedicated
8. **vouchsafed.** Granted

was a thunderbolt striking a haystack and setting it ablaze. Its glare illuminated the whole village. People ran about in panic, searching for shelter. The population of ten villages crammed in that village. Another thunderbolt hit a house. Women and children shrieked and wailed. The fires descended with a tremendous hiss as a mighty rain came down. It rained as it had never rained before. The two lakes, over which the village road ran, filled, swelled and joined over the road. Water flowed along the streets. The wind screamed and shook the trees and the homes. "This is the end of the world!" wailed the people through the storm.

The whole of the next day it was still drizzling. Soma sat before the image, with his head bowed in thought. Trays and flowers and offerings lay scattered under the image, dampened by rain. Some of his friends came wading in water, stood before him and asked, "Are you satisfied?" They stood over him like executioners and repeated the question and added, "Do you want to know how many lives have been lost, how many homes washed out and how many were crushed by the storm?"

"No, no, I don't want to know anything," Soma replied. "Go away. Don't stand here and talk."

"God has shown us only a slight sign of his power. Don't tempt Him again. Do something. Our lives are in your hands. Save us, the image is too perfect."

A After they were gone he sat for hours in the same position, ruminating.[9] Their words still troubled him. "Our lives are in your hands." He knew what they meant. Tears gathered in his eyes. "How can I mutilate this image? Let the whole world burn, I don't care. I can't touch this image." He lit a lamp

before the God and sat watching. Far off the sky rumbled. "It is starting again. Poor human beings, they will all perish this time." He looked at the toe of the image. "Just one neat stroke with the chisel, and all troubles will end." He watched the toe, his hands trembled. "How can I?" Outside, the wind began to howl. People were gathering in front of his house and were appealing to him for help.

Soma prostrated before the God and went out. He stood looking at the road over which the two lakes had joined. Over the eastern horizon a dark mass of cloud was rolling up. "When that cloud comes over, it will wash out the world. Nataraja! I cannot mutilate your figure, but I can offer myself as a sacrifice if it will be any use...." He shut his eyes and decided to jump into the lake. He checked himself. "I must take a last look at the God before I die." He battled his way through the oncoming storm. The wind shrieked. Trees shook and trembled. Men and cattle ran about in panic.

He was back just in time to see a tree crash on the roof of his house. "My home," he cried, and ran in. He picked up his Nataraja from amidst splintered tiles and rafters. The image was unhurt, except for a little toe which was found a couple of yards off, severed by a falling splinter.

"God himself has done this to save us!" people cried.

The image was installed with due ceremonies at the temple on the next full moon. Wealth and honors were showered on **B** Soma. He lived to be ninety-five, but he never touched his mallet and chisel again. ✦

9. **ruminating.** Meditating or reflecting

If you were in Soma's place, would you destroy the statue? Why do you think destroying a beautiful thing might be difficult?

AFTER READING

Find Meaning

1. Why do people fear Nataraja?
2. (a) What does the priest suggest that Soma should do to his image of Nataraja? (b) Why does he want Soma to do this?

Compare Literature

Symbolism Writers use symbolism to convey a message that is greater than the literal meaning contained in a story. Review the symbolism in "The Instruction of Indra" and "Such Perfection" and answer the following questions.

Make Judgments

3. Why do you think Soma refuses to change his sculpture of Nataraja?
4. (a) When does the god finally decide to save the people? (b) What do you think caused him to make this decision?

1. In "The Instruction of Indra," what do the ants symbolize?
2. What does the disk on the yogi's chest symbolize?
3. In "Such Perfection," what different things does the statue symbolize?

Find Meaning

1. His dancing can trigger destruction of the universe.
2. (a) He wants Soma to make a small chip or imperfection in the image. (b) He fears the image is so perfect that it will come alive and dance, destroying everyone.

Make Judgments

3. Soma has worked so hard to make his image perfect that he cannot bring himself to damage it.
4. (a) The god decides after Soma offers himself as a sacrifice. (b) Soma's demonstration of selflessness shows he is not motivated so much by pride as by simple love of perfection and reverence for the god.

Compare Literature
Symbolism

1. The ants symbolize former Indras that have had to start the cycle of rebirth from the bottom.
2. It symbolizes impermanence.
3. The statue symbolizes perfection, the god Nataraja, and destruction.

Extend Understanding

Writing Options

Creative Writing In this story, Indra learns some lessons. Imagine that you are **taking notes** for him so that he will not forget what he has learned. Jot down the lessons that he should draw from his experiences. Also, write down meaningful and relevant quotations from the different characters Indra encounters.

Expository Writing Write an **expository paragraph** in which you compare and contrast the symbols in "The Instruction of Indra" and "Such Perfection." Refer to the chart you made at the start of this lesson. In what ways are the symbols alike? In what ways do they differ? Share your paragraph with the class.

Collaborative Learning

Discuss Meaning In small groups, discuss your ideas about the theme of "The Instruction of Indra." What generalizations can you make about the character of Indra? What lessons can the reader learn from this story? How might these lessons relate to your own life? After discussing the story, write down your interpretation of its theme. Support your claims with evidence from the text.

Lifelong Learning

Compare Hinduism and Buddhism India is the birthplace of two major Eastern religions, Hinduism and Buddhism. With a partner, research the history of these religions. What geographic locations are associated with Hinduism? With Buddhism? What are the main principles and beliefs of each religion? In what ways are they similar and different? Organize your information and prepare a brief written report that compares and contrasts the two religions.

 Go to **www.mirrorsandwindows.com** for more.

Rubrics for Writing Options

You can adapt this as a checklist for students to use as they write.

Creative Writing

☐ Do the notes identify the lessons Indra should learn?
☐ Do the notes include meaningful, relevant quotations?

Expository Writing

☐ Does the paragraph compare and contrast the symbols from both selections?
☐ Does the paragraph explain what the different symbols represent?
☐ Does the paragraph agree with information in the chart of symbols?

Preview the Selection

At a Glance
Directed Reading
- Reading Level: Moderate
- Difficulty Consideration: Setting
- Ease Factor: Sympathetic characters

Objectives
Studying this lesson will enable students to
- use reading skills such as drawing conclusions
- define characterization and recognize how it is achieved in the selection
- describe some literary accomplishments of Carolyn Swift
- appreciate a Japanese myth about troubles among the gods

Launch the Lesson
Tell students this story focuses partly on the difficult relationship between a brother and sister. Ask students who have siblings to think, after they read, about whether they've ever had a fight similar to the one between Amaterasu and Susanoo. (If you wish, after the class has read the story, offer these students a chance to tell what happened and how the conflict was resolved.)

DIRECTED READING

BEFORE READING

Build Background
Historical Context Japan's mountainous geography led to the development of small independent villages. In the years around AD 150, a priestess named Himiko united many of these villages under her rule and established contact and trade with China. Around AD 200, the Yamato people of central Japan gained control over most of the country. The Yamato rulers claimed to be descended from the sun goddess, Amaterasu, a claim that Japanese emperors continued to make into the twentieth century.

Reader's Context How do you react when you feel that someone has been unfair to you?

Set Purpose
Previewing the images and quotes that accompany "Amaterasu" will help you make predictions about the setting, characters, and mood. Read to determine how accurate your predictions are.

Analyze Literature
Characterization The act of creating or describing a character is called **characterization.** Writers use three major techniques to create a character: showing what characters say, do, and think; showing what other characters say about them; and showing what physical features, dress, and personality the characters display. As you read, note how these elements help to develop the characters in "Amaterasu."

Meet the Author
Carolyn Swift (1923–2002) was born in London and moved to Ireland in 1946, where she cofounded the Pike Theatre. She was an actor and a director before she began writing full-time. In addition to writing plays, Swift wrote many books for young people, including two series of novels known as the Bugsy and Robbers series. She has also written many retellings of myths.

Use Reading Skills
Draw Conclusions As you read, gather evidence to draw conclusions about the myth's characters. What motivates them? How are they influenced by the setting and other characters? Do they represent something other than themselves? Use a two-column chart to record details from the story and your conclusions.

Details	My Conclusions
Susanoo complains about everything, even when he is made god of the sea.	

Preview Vocabulary
grum·ble (grɐm´ bəl) v., mumble unhappily

fond·ness (fän[d]´ nəs) n., affection; having a liking

Words in Use

Preview Vocabulary
grumble, 788
fondness, 790

Selection Words
cock, 789
chanted, 790

Teaching Words
descended, 786
relics, 789
divine, 789
shrine, 789
phenomenon, 791
internal, 791
reliability, 791
criteria, 791

KEY TERMS
MYTH, 786
SETTING, 786
CHARACTER, 786
MOOD, 786
CHARACTERIZATION, 786
CONCLUSION, 786
MOTIVATED, 786
BIOGRAPHY, 791
THIRD-PERSON POINT OF VIEW, 791
CHRONOLOGICAL ORDER, 791

Common Core State Standards
Reading Literature
RL.1

Amaterasu

A Japanese Myth
retold by Carolyn Swift

Amaterasu Appearing from the Cave, 1882. Taiso Yoshitoshi. Private collection.

Without the sun's heat the land became very cold
and nothing grew in field or forest.

787

Teach the Selection

Summary

Susanoo, son of the Lord of the Heavens and the Lady of the Underworld, is always complaining. He is made god of the sea but is unhappy because his sister Amaterasu is goddess of the sun, which he thinks is better. Exasperated, his father finally asks Susanoo to leave heaven.

When Susanoo visits Amaterasu to say good-bye, the siblings get into a fight. Susanoo gets so angry that he destroys the rice fields, and Amaterasu, frightened, hides in a cave. The sunless world grows dark and cold; evil spirits run wild.

The good spirits decide they must do something. After much deliberation, they invent the mirror, because Amaterasu likes looking at her reflection. They use crowing roosters to draw her to the mouth of the cave, and then a mirror to lure her all the way out. After their plan succeeds, the spirits remember that Susanoo caused the trouble. They cut off his ponytail and eject him from heaven.

MIRRORS & WINDOWS The Mirrors & Windows questions at the end of the selection focus on the theme of envy. Before students begin reading, ask: Do you know any siblings who are jealous of each other? What is that like?

Program Resources

Planning and Assessment
Program Planning Guide, Selection Lesson Plan
E-Lesson Planner
Assessment Guide, Lesson Test
ExamView

Technology Tools
Interactive Student Text on CD
Visual Teaching Package
Audio Library
mirrorsandwindows.com

Meeting the Standards
Folk Literature: Unit 8, Directed Reading,
   pp. 72–77

Differentiating Instruction
Developing Readers, Take Notes, pp. 58–60
English Language Learners, Draw Conclusions,
   pp. 200–208

Teach the Selection

Use Reading Skills

Take Notes Explain that, while students may regularly take notes on nonfiction, especially for textbook assignments, it can also be helpful to take notes on stories. Notes can refresh their memories later about major characters, themes, and plot elements. To get students started, ask them to take notes on "Amaterasu." Afterward, have them share their notes with a small group. What did they write down and why? Can they learn helpful note-taking ideas from others in the group?

Use Reading Skills

Draw Conclusions Remind students that a conclusion is a judgment based on the information available, including a reader's own knowledge about life. Ask what kinds of conclusions they might draw about Susanoo's bad attitude, based on the information in this paragraph. (A lot of young people would be unhappy about being separated from their mothers, and this could be part of the problem. Some may say that Susanoo's constant complaining shows this is just his natural temperament.) **A**

...he found himself facing the drawn bow of a fierce-looking warrior.

Back in the mists of time there lived a boy called Susanoo. His father and mother were the first people on earth, but then his father became Lord of the Heavens and his mother Lady of the Underworld.

A Susanoo himself lived with his brothers and sisters on the bridge which linked heaven and earth, but he was always complaining. He complained about not being able to visit his mother, even though his father explained to him that if he once went to the underworld he would never be able to come back, and he complained even more when his sister Amaterasu was given the jewelled necklace of heaven and made goddess of the sun, while he was given only corals and made god of the sea. Finally his father became sick of his constant moanings and groanings.

"I don't want to see your face around Heaven any more," he told him. "You have the whole earth and sea to play around in so there's no need for you to make all our lives a misery up here."

"Oh, all right," Susanoo <u>grumbled</u>, "but first I must say goodbye to Amaterasu."

So off he stumped to look for her. Being in a bad mood, he shook every mountain he passed so that rocks crashed down the slopes, and he stamped his feet so that the earth quaked. Hearing all the noise, Amaterasu was frightened. She took up her bow and arrow so that, when her younger brother arrived, he found himself facing the drawn bow of a fierce-looking warrior.

"You can put that thing down," he told her. "I come in peace."

"Prove it," she said suspiciously, not taking her eyes off him.

Susanoo handed her his sword. She took it from him and broke it into three pieces. Then, before he could complain, she blew on them and turned them into three beautiful little girls.

"One day these three little daughters of mine will bring new life into the world," she told him, "while your sword could only have brought death."

"I can do better than that!" Susanoo boasted. "Give me the necklaces you're wearing."

So Amaterasu unclasped the five necklaces and gave them to her brother. Then he blew on them and turned them into five little boys.

 ...the world was suddenly plunged into darkness.

"Now I have five sons," he said.

"They were made out of my necklaces so they should be my sons!" Amaterasu snapped.

"But your daughters were made from my sword," Susanoo argued.

"That's different!" Amaterasu told him.

At that Susanoo lost his temper. He tore

---

grum • ble (grŭm′ bəl) v., mumble unhappily

Differentiated Instruction

English Language Learning

Explain idioms in the selection for English learners. For example

I come in peace—my reason for coming is peaceful, 788

in the first place—first, before anything else, 789

put their heads together—worked together to solve a problem, 789

in vain—without success, 790

Reading Proficiency

Use the vivid verbs in the myth as the basis for vocabulary review. Point out sentences featuring action verbs and have students demonstrate what they describe. For example, for the sentence " 'Oh, all right,' Susanoo <u>grumbled</u>," have a student speak the dialogue as described (grumblingly). For "So off he stumped to look for her," have a student demonstrate this walk.

up all the rice fields that Amaterasu had been carefully ripening and caused such destruction that the frightened goddess ran and hid in a cave, blocking the entrance with a large stone.

Because Amaterasu was the sun goddess, this meant that the world was suddenly plunged into darkness. Without the sun's heat the land became very cold and nothing grew in field or forest. Worse still, the evil spirits took advantage of the darkness to get up to all sorts of wickedness. It was a disaster. Something had to be done, so all the good spirits gathered together in a dry river bed to try to decide what to do.

"We must tempt Amaterasu to come out of the cave," said one.

"And block up the entrance the minute she does, so she can't go back into it again," added another.

"But what would tempt her to come out?" asked a third.

"We must put everything she likes most outside," replied the first.

"And what does she like most?" the third asked.

"Seeing her sunny face reflected in the lake," answered a fourth. **C**

"But we can't bring the lake up to the cave!" objected the third.

"Then we must make something that will reflect her face the way the lake does and put that outside the cave," suggested a fifth.

"I don't know what we could make that would do that," the third grumbled, "and

anyway, how will she know it's there unless we can get her to come out of the cave in the first place?"

At that they all looked thoughtful. No one spoke for a while.

"I know!" the second suddenly shouted in triumph. "She always used to come out every morning as soon as she heard the cock crow. We must get all the cocks to crow outside the cave."

So they all put their heads together to try to think what would reflect the sun like the waters of the lake. After trying all sorts of

CULTURAL ▶▶ CONNECTION

Shintoism In Shinto, the ancient native religion of Japan, Amaterasu is the goddess of the sun. Until 1946, Japanese emperors were considered to be gods descended from Amaterasu. It is said that when the first emperor, Jimmu, took power in 660 BC, Amaterasu gave him holy relics known as the Imperial Regalia as proof of his divine authority. The Imperial Regalia include the sacred mirror, the sacred sword, and the curved jewels. The mirror and the jewels were used to lure Amaterasu from the cave where she hid from her brother's rage. The sword was presented to Amaterasu by Susanoo to acknowledge his submission. Today, the mirror is believed to be in Amaterasu's shrine in Ise, Japan, and the jewels are kept at the Imperial Palace in Tokyo. The sword was lost in battle in 1185. How does this information affect your reading of the myth? **B**

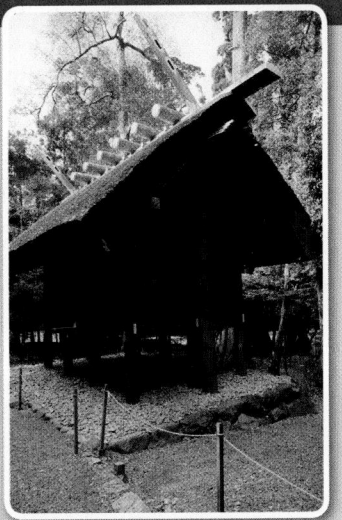
Amaterasu's shrine in Ise, Japan.

Teach the Selection

Cultural Connection

Shintoism *Answer:* Answers will vary. It may make the myth seem more real. **B**

Analyze Literature

Characterization Note that dialogue is a very effective way to depict character. Have students carefully read the conversation on this page among the good spirits. Ask: "Does this dialogue reveal anything about the individual personalities of the spirits?" (Most spirits are trying hard to find a solution. The third spirit, however, is doubtful and questions the others' proposals without offering fresh ideas.)

Literary Connection

Vanity Explain that before mirrors were invented or widely available, people would have been able to look at their reflections on the surface of calm water, as Amaterasu did. Note that in this myth the goddess's vanity works in her favor. In Greek mythology, however, vanity is dangerous. Because he angers the gods, the beautiful Narcissus is doomed to fall in love with his reflection in the water. After his death, the flower named for him springs up in the spot where he sat. Have students investigate the details of the Narcissus story, and then discuss it as a class. **C**

Reading Skills

Identify Text Organization

Note that "Amaterasu" makes use of a type of organization that is also associated with persuasive writing. In problem-solution organization, the writer first describes the details of a problem, then proposes possible solutions. Have students identify the problems involved in the story, then list the solutions. These might include the following:

- Problem: While Amaterasu hides in a cave, the earth suffers in cold and darkness.
- Solution: Lure Amaterasu out with crowing roosters and a mirror.
- Problem: Susanoo is a troublemaker.
- Solutions: Cut off his pigtail and banish him from heaven.

Analyze Literature

Tone Remind students that tone is a writer's attitude toward the subject or the reader. Ask them to focus on the image of the goddess tap-dancing on an overturned tub. Ask: "What sort of tone does this establish?" (The comical image creates a light tone.) **A**

Analyze Literature

Motivation Note that motivation is a force that causes a character to think, feel, or behave in a certain way. Draw attention to the series of actions Amaterasu performs as she leaves the cave. Ask what motivates each action. (Possible motivations include curiosity about the noises, jealousy and then rage that there might be another sun goddess, and delight at the sight of her reflection.) **B**

Answer: Responses will vary. Some may say that being god of the sea is nothing to complain about and they would be happy with the situation. Many will say that jealousy makes people act dishonestly or cruelly.

things in vain, they finally managed to invent a mirror, or looking-glass. This they hung from the branch of a japonica tree[1] immediately opposite the cave and, knowing Amaterasu's <u>fondness</u> for jewellery, they hung

> "If Susanoo had stayed out of heaven when his father told him to, this would never have happened!"

jewelled necklaces from the other branches.

When all was ready, they gathered outside the cave with every cock they could find. First they chanted prayers. Then they gave the signal and all the cocks began to crow. Not satisfied with that, everyone present began to sing and dance, led by the goddess Ama no Uzume[2] doing a tap-dance on an upturned tub.

Wondering what all the noise was about, Amaterasu peeped out of the cave and at once saw her own face reflected in the mirror. She had never seen a looking-glass

before, so she thought the people must have found another sun to replace her and ran from the cave in a rage. The others immediately stretched ropes across the mouth of the cave to stop her from going back into it again, but there was no need. By then she had discovered that it was her own shining face looking back at her. She was delighted by this and by the necklaces, as well as the singing and dancing for, truth to tell, she had begun to feel lonely in her cave. So once more the sun's bright rays lit the earth and the trees and flowers and rice began to grow again in its heat. Then everyone suddenly remembered the cause of all the trouble.

"If Susanoo had stayed out of heaven when his father told him to, this would never have happened!" they shouted angrily, and went off in a body to look for him. When they found him, they cut off his pigtail as punishment and threw him out of heaven by force. ❖

---

1. **japonica tree.** Any tree, shrub, or plant associated with the Far East
2. **Ama no Uzume.** Goddess of dawn and mirth

fond•ness (fän[d]′ nəs) *n.*, affection; having a liking

 If you were in Susanoo's place, how would you feel about being chosen as god of the sea rather than god of the sun? In what ways can jealousy ruin friendships?

Differentiated Instruction

Auditory and Kinesthetic Learning

"Amaterasu" is well suited for adaptation as a performance. Have interested students choose roles, work together to create a script, rehearse, and perform for classmates or another class.

Enrichment

Students may be interested in investigating other myths about sun gods and goddesses. Have students do research to find the names of other sun deities—for example, Helios or Phoebus Apollo (Greek), Sol Invictus (Roman), Ra (Egyptian), Utu (Mesopotamian), and Surya (Hindu)—and then read a myth featuring that deity and make a presentation to the class.

Find Meaning

1. (a) What does Susanoo complain about? (b) Why do you think Susanoo complains so much?
2. (a) What does Amaterasu do with Susanoo's sword? (b) What does her action indicate about her character?
3. (a) Why does Amaterasu hide in the cave? (b) Why are the good spirits concerned about Amaterasu's staying in the cave?

Analyze Literature

Characterization How does the writer create the character of Amaterasu? Remember that characterization makes use of direct description, words, actions, and the character's internal states. Use a web to organize what you have learned about the goddess. In each outer circle, list a detail from the myth that helps you understand Amaterasu's character.

Make Judgments

4. What do Susanoo's actions indicate about his character?
5. (a) What plan do the good spirits develop to draw Amaterasu out of the cave? (b) Why does Amaterasu not mind being tricked?
6. What natural phenomenon might this story attempt to explain?

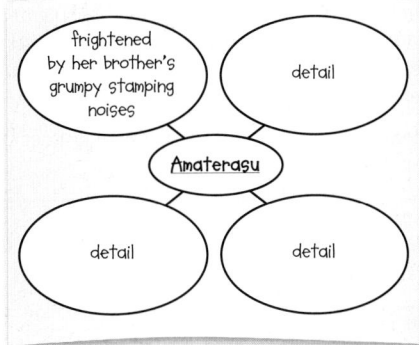

Extend Understanding

Writing Options

Creative Writing Imagine that you have been asked to write a brief **biography** of Amaterasu. Use the library or Internet to supplement the information you have learned about her from this myth. Maintain a consistent third-person point of view, and relate her biography in chronological order.

Applied Writing When Susanoo frightened Amaterasu, she fled into a cave and hid, causing disaster in the world. Imagine that Amaterasu has fled into the cave again. If she isn't persuaded to come out, crops won't grow and people will starve. Write a set of logically ordered **instructions** for how to lure Amaterasu out again.

Lifelong Learning

Summarize Stories In this myth, the good spirits trick Amaterasu into coming out of the cave. What happens after that? Use the Internet to read more stories about Amaterasu. Write summaries of the end of this myth and of one of the stories you find. Share one of your summaries with the class.

Media Literacy

Evaluate Websites Locate and review several websites that provide information about Japanese culture and history. Evaluate the websites for reliability and quality, explaining the criteria on which you based your evaluation. For example, does the information seem accurate, complete, current, and well written? Write a brief paragraph for each website you visit.

Go to www.mirrorsandwindows.com for more.

AMATERASU **791**

Review the Selection

Find Meaning

1. (a) He cannot visit his mother and he was only given the seas to rule. (b) Some may say he is spoiled and selfish. Others may sympathize with his having been separated from a parent or may suggest he envies Amaterasu.
2. (a) She makes three daughters out of the broken sword. (b) Some students may say it shows that she values life. Others may note that she destroyed Susanoo's property and suggest she could have been motivated by sibling rivalry.
3. (a) She is frightened by Susanoo's anger. (b) Without the sun, the earth gets cold and dark, plants don't grow, and evil spirits cause trouble.

Make Judgments

4. He has a quick temper, is competitive, and is destructive when he is angry.
5. (a) They decide to get her attention by having cocks crow, and then draw her outside with a mirror. (b) She was getting lonely inside the cave. Also, she is excited by the mirror.
6. Amaterasu's disappearance might explain an eclipse or darkness caused by storm clouds. Susanoo's tantrum might represent an earthquake.

Analyze Literature

Characterization Charts will vary. Check that information in the webs is accurate.

Rubrics for Writing Options

You can adapt this as a checklist for students to use as they write.

Creative Writing

☐ Does the biography include facts about Amaterasu?
☐ Does the biography use chronological organization?
☐ Does the biography use a consistent third-person point of view?

Applied Writing

☐ Do the instructions include all of the steps necessary to draw Amaterasu from the cave? (Instructions may repeat the earlier strategy or reflect a new plan.)
☐ Do the instructions follow a logical order?

DIRECTED READING

At a Glance
Directed Reading
- Reading Level: Easy
- Difficulty Considerations: None
- Ease Factors: Length and style

Objectives
Studying this lesson will enable students to
- use reading skills such as analyzing cause and effect
- define simile and recognize how similes contribute to a story
- name literary accomplishments of Judith Ortiz Cofer and explain how her Puerto Rican heritage influences her writing
- appreciate a folk tale about how misery became a part of life

Launch the Lesson
Before students read "Aunty Misery," tell them that two major characters in the story are Misery and Death. Have them think about the sort of personalities they would expect these characters to have. Ask them to keep their ideas in mind as they read and compare them to the way the story turns out.

Aunty Misery
A Puerto Rican Folk Tale retold by Judith Ortiz Cofer

BEFORE READING

Build Background
Literary Context The folk tales of Puerto Rico are heavily influenced by Spanish culture, which has dominated the island for hundreds of years. Like the fables popularized by Aesop, "Aunty Misery" includes elements of magic, trickery, and a stated lesson or moral. Details such as setting and character names reflect the island culture of Puerto Rico.

Reader's Context If you could have just one wish granted, what would it be?

Set Purpose
Preview the title and skim the text to learn the setting. Read to determine the lesson the folk tale conveys.

Analyze Literature
Simile A **simile** is a comparison between two unlike things that uses *like* or *as*. Writers use similes to create vivid images and to stimulate the reader's imagination. As you read "Aunty Misery," look for the author's use of similes and pay attention to how they help you visualize what is being described.

Meet the Author
Judith Ortiz Cofer (b. 1952) was born in Puerto Rico. Although her family moved to the United States in 1956, they kept close ties with Puerto Rico. The award-winning writer credits her *abuela*, grandmother, for her storytelling gifts. "When my abuela sat us down to tell a story, we learned something from it, even though we always laughed." Cofer's poetry, essays, and novels frequently explore themes related to Puerto Rican culture.

Use Reading Skills
Analyze Cause and Effect A *cause* is an action or event that makes something else happen. Any action or event that results from a cause is an *effect*. One cause may have several effects, and an effect may become the cause of other events. Use a chart to keep track of causes and effects in "Aunty Misery."

Cause: children steal fruit → Effect:

Preview Vocabulary
taunt (tänt) *v.*, mock; jeer at

gnarled (när[ə]ld) *adj.*, misshapen

in·ev·i·ta·ble (i ne´ və tə bəl) *n.*, unavoidable situation

Words in Use

Preview Vocabulary
taunt, 794
gnarled, 794
inevitable, 794

Selection Words
pilgrim, 793
hearth, 793
hospitality, 793

Teaching Words
dominated, 792
popularized, 792
insights, 795
effectiveness, 795
optimistic, 795
pessimistic, 795
consensus, 795

KEY TERMS
FOLK TALE, 792
MORAL, 792
SETTING, 792
CHARACTER, 792
CAUSE AND EFFECT, 792
THEME, 795
PROSE, 795
POETRY, 795
POEM, 795
METAPHOR, 795
SENSORY LANGUAGE, 795

Study of Three Pears, c. 20th century.
Ashton Hinrichs. Private collection.

Aunty Misery

A Puerto Rican Folk Tale retold by Judith Ortiz Cofer

This is a story about an old, a very old woman who lived alone in her little hut with no other company than a beautiful pear tree that grew at her door. She spent all her time taking care of this tree. The neighborhood children drove the old woman crazy by stealing her fruit. They would climb her tree, shake its delicate limbs, and run away with armloads of golden pears, yelling insults at *la Tía Miseria,* Aunty Misery, as they called her.

They would climb her tree, shake its delicate limbs, and run away with armloads of golden pears....

One day, a traveler stopped at the old woman's hut and asked her for permission to spend the night under her roof. Aunty Misery saw that he had an honest face and bid the pilgrim come in. She fed him and made a bed for him in front of her hearth. In the morning the stranger told her that he would show his gratitude for her hospitality by granting her one wish.

"There is only one thing that I desire," said Aunty Misery.

793

Teach the Selection

Summary

Aunty Misery is constantly enraged by the way the local children steal fruit from her pear tree. One day a stranger comes to her door asking for a place to stay the night, and she takes him in. Next morning, he offers to grant her a wish. She asks that anyone who climbs the pear tree be trapped until she gives permission for the person to come down.

After that, it takes only a short time for the children to learn to leave her pears alone. Many years pass. Then another stranger arrives at Aunty Misery's door. He says that he is Death, come to take her away.

Aunty Misery asks him first to fetch her some pears to take with her, so he climbs the tree and is trapped. Without Death, the world is very different. People whose jobs depend on illness and death complain, as do those who feel ready to die. At last, Aunty Misery makes Death promise to leave her alone, then sets him free.

The Mirrors & Windows questions at the end of the selection focus on the theme of cheating death. Before students begin reading, ask: What would the world be like if death were optional?

Program Resources

Planning and Assessment
Program Planning Guide, Selection Lesson Plan
E-Lesson Planner
Assessment Guide, Lesson Test
ExamView

Technology Tools
Interactive Student Text on CD
Visual Teaching Package
Audio Library
mirrorsandwindows.com

Meeting the Standards
Folk Literature: Unit 8, Directed Reading, pp. 78–82

Analyze Literature

Repetition Ask students what they notice about this sentence (it echoes the description of how the children got stuck in the tree) and have them talk about the effect of the repetition. (Being stuck the same way makes Death as helpless as the children; the repetition shows how strong Aunty Misery is, since her power affects Death and children equally.) **A**

Use Reading Skills

Analyze Cause and Effect Point to this paragraph about the effects of Death being trapped. Ask: "What else might happen if people stopped dying?" (Students may note that the world would become overpopulated or that people would feel free to behave recklessly.) **B**

Answer: Answers will vary. Some may say Aunty Misery's actions would lessen the suffering. Students might also echo some of the complaints expressed in the story.

"Ask, and it shall be yours," replied the stranger, who was a sorcerer in disguise.

"I wish that anyone who climbs up my pear tree should not be able to come back down until I permit it."

"Your wish is granted," said the stranger, touching the pear tree as he left Aunty Misery's house.

And so it happened that when the children came back to <u>taunt</u> the old woman and to steal her fruit, she stood at her window watching them. Several of them shimmied up the trunk of the pear tree and immediately got stuck to it as if with glue. She let them cry and beg her for a long time before she gave the tree permission to let them go on the condition that they never again steal her fruit, or bother her.

Time passed and both Aunt Misery and her tree grew bent and <u>gnarled</u> with age. One day another traveler stopped at her door. This one looked untrustworthy to her, so before letting him into her home the old woman asked him what he was doing in her village. He answered her in a voice that was dry and hoarse, as if he had swallowed a desert: "I am Death, and I have come to take you with me."

Thinking fast Aunty Misery said, "All right, but before I go I would like to pluck some pears from my beloved tree to remember how much pleasure it brought me in this life. But I am a very old woman and cannot climb to the tallest branches where the best fruit is. Will you be so kind as to do it for me?"

With a heavy sigh like wind through a tomb, Señor Death climbed the pear tree. **A** Immediately he became stuck to it as if with glue. And no matter how much he cursed and threatened, Aunty Misery would not allow the tree to release Death.

Many years passed and there were no deaths in the world. The people who make their living from death began to protest **B** loudly. The doctors claimed no one bothered to come in for examinations or treatments anymore, because they did not fear dying; the pharmacists' business suffered too because medicines are, like magic potions, bought to prevent or postpone the <u>inevitable</u>; priests and undertakers were unhappy with the situation also, for obvious reasons. There were also many old folks tired of life who wanted to pass on to the next world to rest from miseries of this one.

La Tía Miseria was blamed by these people for their troubles, of course. Not wishing to be unfair, the old woman made a deal with her prisoner, Death: if he promised not ever to come for her again, she would give him his freedom. He agreed. And that is why there are two things you can always count on running into in this world: Misery and Death: *La miseria y la muerte.* ❖

"I am Death, and I have come to take you with me."

---

taunt (tänt) *v.*, mock; jeer at
gnarled (när[ə]ld) *adj.*, misshapen
in·ev·i·ta·ble (i ne´ və tə bəl) *n.*, unavoidable situation

For what reasons would you appreciate Aunty Misery's actions? Why might they upset you? Do you think that a world without death would be a good or bad thing?

Differentiated Instruction

Enrichment

Tell students that it is common in folk tales and fairy tales for a character to be granted wishes; sometimes the story hinges on the disasters caused by a poorly thought-out wish. Have students use library or Internet resources to seek out another tale that involves granting wishes and present their findings to the class.

Reading Proficiency

Remind students that they can increase their comprehension by pausing as they read to ask questions and consider answers. Model some questions students might ask (urge them to use the five Ws, *who, what, when, where,* and *why*). Examples include "Why do the children call the woman Aunty Misery?" and "Where is Death going to take the woman?"

Find Meaning

1. (a) What do the children do to annoy the old woman? (b) Why do you think they call her Aunty Misery?

2. (a) Why does the sorcerer grant a wish to Aunty Misery? (b) What does Aunty Misery's wish reveal about her?

Analyze Literature

Simile How do the similes in this selection help to create mental images? Use the first column of a chart to list the similes that you find in "Aunty Misery." In the second column, write down the comparison being made by the simile. In the third column, describe the effect of the simile or what it adds to the story.

Simile	Comparison	Effect
"stuck to it as if with glue"	compares the children stuck in the tree to things stuck with glue	

Make Judgments

3. What does Aunty Misery's behavior toward the first traveler reveal about her?

4. What lesson about life does this folk tale convey?

Extend Understanding

Writing Options

Creative Writing Themes explored in prose can also be explored in poetry. Write a **poem** about Aunty Misery, her pear tree, and Death. You may wish simply to retell the story, or you may want to express your own feelings about the story. Use simile, metaphor, and sensory language in your poem.

Expository Writing A story's theme, or message, often gives readers new insights about life or human nature. Write a brief **expository paragraph** to explore the theme of "Aunty Misery." Describe the theme in your own words, and evaluate its effectiveness. Is "Aunty Misery" a story you would enjoy telling to a friend? What truth does this story reveal? Explain.

Collaborative Learning

Discuss the Message Is the message of "Aunty Misery" optimistic, or hopeful, or is it pessimistic, or gloomy? Discuss this question in small groups, citing examples from the story to support your opinion. Share your thoughts with the class.

Critical Literacy

Hold a Panel Discussion Did Aunty Misery make a good decision or a bad decision when she let Death out of the pear tree? List the effects of each course of action. Hold a panel discussion to consider the question and try to reach a general consensus on this topic. Present evidence in support of your opinions and be respectful of other points of view.

 Go to www.mirrorsandwindows.com for more.

AUNTY MISERY **795**

Find Meaning

1. (a) They steal pears from her tree. (b) They may call her this because she seems unhappy, since they always see her when she is chasing them away from her pear tree.

2. (a) She has been kind to him; she gave him food and shelter. (b) Answers will vary. Some may say she foresees Death's visit. Others might say that she is only trying to protect her fruit at that point.

Make Judgments

3. Answers will vary. Many will say it shows she is not all bad.

4. It explains why death and misery are always in the world.

Analyze Literature

Simile Check that students correctly list similes from the story. Examples include "as if with glue," "dry and hoarse as if he had swallowed a desert," and "like wind through a tomb."

After students have made their simile charts, you might ask them to come up with alternative similes for each image. For example, to replace *he became stuck to it as if with glue,* students might suggest *he became stuck to it like a magnet on steel.*

Program Resources

For further instruction, refer students to the following extension activity: Collaborative Learning: Discuss the Message, *Exceeding the Standards: Extension Activities*, p. 24.

Rubrics for Writing Options

You can adapt this as a checklist for students to use as they write.

Creative Writing

☐ Does the poem refer to the events described in "Aunty Misery"?

☐ Does the poem include similes, metaphors, and sensory language?

Expository Writing

☐ Does the paragraph describe the theme of the folk tale?

☐ Does the paragraph evaluate the theme?

AUNTY MISERY **795**

Preview the Selection

At a Glance
Independent Reading
- Reading Level: Easy
- Difficulty Consideration: Length
- Ease Factors: Simple language and compelling plot

Objectives
Reading this selection will enable students to do the following:
- read with developing fluency
- read silently with comprehension for a sustained period of time

Launch the Lesson
Have students think about luck before they read "The Force of Luck." Ask: "Do people experience good or bad luck only by chance? Can attitude or actions affect a person's luck sometimes?"

TEACHING NOTE
Although this selection is presented in the student edition as an independent reading, teaching support has been provided should you choose to cover it in class.

Taos Countryside,
1999. Patti Mollica.
Private collection.

The Force of Luck

A Southwestern Folk Tale retold by Rudolfo A. Anaya

Rudolfo A. Anaya (b. 1937) often draws on the themes and settings of the American Southwest to create his stories. His works, including short stories, plays, and novels, offer insights into the Hispanic cultural life of this region. Born in Pastura, New Mexico, Anaya moved throughout the state during his youth. "The Force of Luck" is a retelling of a traditional oral folk tale of the American Southwest.

*O*nce two wealthy friends got into a heated argument. One said that it was money which made a man prosperous, and the other maintained that it wasn't money, but luck, which made the man. They argued for some time and finally decided that if only they could find an honorable man then perhaps they could prove their respective points of view.

One day while they were passing through a small village they came upon a miller who was grinding corn and wheat. They paused to ask the man how he ran his business. The miller replied that he worked for a master and that he earned only four bits a day, and with that he had to support a family of five.

The friends were surprised. "Do you mean to tell us you can maintain a family of five on only fifteen dollars a month?" one asked.

"I live modestly to make ends meet," the humble miller replied.

The two friends privately agreed that if they put this man to a test perhaps they could resolve their argument.

"I am going to make you an offer," one of them said to the miller. "I will give you two hundred dollars and you may do whatever you want with the money."

"But why would you give me this money when you've just met me?" the miller asked.

"Well, my good man, my friend and I have a long standing argument. He contends that it is luck which elevates a man to high position,

796

Program Resources

Planning and Assessment
Program Planning Guide, Selection Lesson Plan
E-Lesson Planner
Assessment Guide, Lesson Test
ExamView

Technology Tools
Interactive Student Text on CD
Visual Teaching Package
Audio Library
mirrorsandwindows.com

Meeting the Standards
Folk Literature: Unit 8, Independent Reading, pp. 82–88

Differentiating Instruction
Advanced Students, Independent Reading Study, pp. 49–50

Common Core State Standards
Reading Literature
RL.10
Speaking and Listening
SL.1

"The first fish my husband catches will be yours."

and I say it is money. By giving you this money perhaps we can settle our argument. Here, take it, and do with it what you want!"

So the poor miller took the money and spent the rest of the day thinking about the strange meeting which had presented him with more money than he had ever seen. What could he possibly do with all this money? Be that as it may, he had the money in his pocket and he could do with it whatever he wanted.

When the day's work was done, the miller decided the first thing he would do would be to buy food for his family. He took out ten dollars and wrapped the rest of the money in a cloth and put the bundle in his bag. Then he went to the market and bought supplies and a good piece of meat to take home.

On the way home he was attacked by a hawk that had smelled the meat which the miller carried. The miller fought off the bird but in the struggle he lost the bundle of money. Before the miller knew what was happening the hawk grabbed the bag and flew away with it. When he realized what had happened he fell into deep thought.

"Ah," he moaned, "wouldn't it have been better to let that hungry bird have the meat! I could have bought a lot more meat with the money he took. Alas, now I'm in the same poverty as before! And worse, because now those two men will say I am a thief! I should have thought carefully and bought nothing. Yes, I should have gone straight home and this wouldn't have happened!"

So he gathered what was left of his provisions[1] and continued home, and when he arrived he told his family the entire story.

When he was finished telling his story

his wife said, "It has been our lot[2] to be poor, but have faith in God and maybe someday our luck will change."

The next day the miller got up and went to work as usual. He wondered what the two men would say about his story. But since he had never been a man of money he soon forgot the entire matter.

Three months after he had lost the money to the hawk, it happened that the two wealthy men returned to the village. As soon as they saw the miller they approached him to ask if his luck had changed. When the miller saw them he felt ashamed and afraid that they would think that he had squandered the money on worthless things. But he decided to tell them the truth and as soon as they had greeted each other he told his story. The men believed him. In fact, the one who insisted that it was money and not luck which made a man prosper took out another two hundred dollars and gave it to the miller.

"Let's try again," he said, "and let's see what happens this time."

The miller didn't know what to think. "Kind sir, maybe it would be better if you put this money in the hands of another man," he said.

"No," the man insisted, "I want to give it to you because you are an honest man, and if we are going to settle our argument you have to take the money!"

The miller thanked them and promised to do his best. Then as soon as the two men left he began to think what to do with the money so that it wouldn't disappear as it had the first time. The thing to do was to take the money

---

1. **provisions.** Food or supplies
2. **lot.** Fate

Teach the Selection

Summary
Two men debating about whether wealth is due to luck or money decide to see if giving a poor miller money will make him prosper. The miller buys meat, but an eagle, trying to steal the meat, takes the rest of the money. The miller tells the two men, and they give him more money. This time he stashes it in a jar of bran, then learns that his wife traded the bran for clay. Again, the miller explains to the men. As they part company, one of them gives the miller a lump of lead.

Soon his neighbor needs lead for fishing lures. The miller gives it to him and receives a fish in return. Inside is a glassy object. A jeweler and his wife recognize this as a diamond and try to buy it, but the miller, suspicious, resists until they offer a hundred thousand dollars. He can now build his own mill, and when he next sees the two men, he is rich. He and the men find an eagle's nest with the lost money in it, then recover the money-filled jar of bran by accident. The two men are pleased but still can't decide how to settle the debate.

 The Mirrors & Windows questions at the end of the selection focus on the theme of luck. Before students begin reading, ask: Is there such a thing as a lucky life?

Words in Use

Selection Words

prosperous, 796
honorable, 796
respective, 796
modestly, 796
squandered, 797
bran, 798
consoled, 798

illuminate, 799
novelty, 799
consulting, 800
jesting, 800

Teaching Words

insights, 796

KEY TERMS

FOLK TALE, 796
THEME, 796
SETTING, 796
SHORT STORY, 796
PLAY, 796
NOVEL, 796
IRONY, 802
THESIS, 802

Cultural Connection

Setting Although the folk tale does not give much detail about setting, Anaya usually sets his stories in New Mexico, where he has lived his entire life. A clue that the setting is the Southwest is the wife's purchase of clay for the house. Because wood is scarce in this area, people build houses out of adobe, bricks made of clay and straw. The brick walls are coated with a smooth layer of more clay, which can contain lime to make it white. (Perhaps the wife bought lime, since she mentions whitewashing. Otherwise the clay would be reddish). Some native groups in the New World used this construction method, but the Spanish also brought it when they settled the Southwest. **Ⓐ**

Analyze Literature

Character and Stereotype Explain that a stereotype is an oversimplified idea about something. When applied to a character, it means an assessment based on what "that kind of person" is like, rather than on the individual. Sometimes an author uses stereotyped characters on purpose, as symbols. In this case, a character in the story talks about the miller as a stereotype. Ask students to identify the stereotypes expressed about the miller. (They should note the statement that the poor are honest because they don't have enough money to get into trouble. They might also note his assumption that anyone poor is bound to gamble.) **Ⓑ**

---

straight home. He took out ten dollars, wrapped the rest in a cloth, and headed home.

When he arrived his wife wasn't at home. At first he didn't know what to do with the money. He went to the pantry where he had stored a large earthenware jar filled with bran. That was as safe a place as any to hide the money, he thought, so he emptied out the grain and put the bundle of money at the bottom of the jar, then covered it up with the grain. Satisfied that the money was safe he returned to work.

That afternoon when he arrived home from work he was greeted by his wife.

Ⓐ "Look, my husband, today I bought some good clay with which to whitewash³ the entire house."

"And how did you buy the clay if we don't have any money?" he asked.

"Well, the man who was selling the clay was willing to trade for jewelry, money, or anything of value," she said. "The only thing we had of value was the jar full of bran, so I traded it for the clay. Isn't it wonderful, I think we have enough clay to whitewash these two rooms!"

The man groaned and pulled his hair.

"Oh, you crazy woman! What have you done? We're ruined again!"

"But why?" she asked, unable to understand his anguish.

"Today I met the same two friends who gave me the two hundred dollars three months ago," he explained. "And after I told them how I lost the money they gave me another two hundred. And I, to make sure the money was safe, came home and hid it inside the jar of bran—the same jar you have traded for dirt! Now we're as poor as we were before! And what am I going to tell the two men? They'll think I'm a liar and a thief for sure!"

"Let them think what they want," his wife said calmly. "We will only have in our lives what the good Lord wants us to have. It is our lot to be poor until God wills it otherwise."

So the miller was consoled and the next day he went to work as usual. Time came and went, and one day the two wealthy friends returned to ask the miller how he had done with the second two hundred dollars. When the poor miller saw them he was afraid they would accuse him of being a liar and a spendthrift.⁴ But he decided to be truthful and as soon as they had greeted each other he told them what had happened to the money.

Ⓑ "That is why poor men remain honest," the man who had given him the money said. "Because they don't have money they can't get into trouble. But I find your stories hard to believe. I think you gambled and lost the money. That's why you're telling us these wild stories."

"Either way," he continued, "I still believe that it is money and not luck which makes a man prosper."

"Well, you certainly didn't prove your point by giving the money to this poor miller," his friend reminded him. "Good evening, you luckless man," he said to the miller.

"Thank you, friends," the miller said.

"Oh, by the way, here is a worthless piece of lead I've been carrying around. Maybe you can use it for something," said the man who believed in luck. Then the two men left, still debating their points of view on life.

Since the lead was practically worthless, the miller thought nothing of it and put it in his jacket pocket. He forgot all about it until he arrived home. When he threw his jacket

---

3. **whitewash.** Paint with a mixture used to whiten walls
4. **spendthrift.** Person who is wasteful with money

Differentiated Instruction

English Language Learning

Review idioms from the selection to increase English learners' familiarity with them.

heated argument—lively debate, 796
make ends meet—earn enough to survive, 796
Be that as it may—expression that implies acceptance but also dismissal, essentially, "while that may be true . . ." , 797
man of money—wealthy man, 797

by the way—expression that means the information is extra, outside the main point, 798
thought nothing of it—didn't pay attention, 798
it so happened—expression used in storytelling to introduce what happened next, 799
couldn't believe his eyes—could not believe what he was seeing, 800
fair and square—completely fairly, 800

on a chair he heard a thump and he remembered the piece of lead. He took it out of the pocket and threw it under the table. Later that night after the family had eaten and gone to bed, they heard a knock at the door.

"Who is it? What do you want?" the miller asked.

"It's me, your neighbor," a voice answered. The miller recognized the fisherman's wife. "My husband sent me to ask you if you have any lead you can spare. He is going fishing tomorrow and he needs the lead to weight down the nets."

The miller remembered the lead he had thrown under the table. He got up, found it, and gave it to the woman.

"Thank you very much, neighbor," the woman said. "I promise you the first fish my husband catches will be yours."

"Think nothing of it," the miller said and returned to bed. The next day he got up and went to work without thinking any more of the incident. But in the afternoon when he returned home he found his wife cooking a big fish for dinner.

"Since when are we so well off we can afford fish for supper?" he asked his wife.

"Don't you remember that our neighbor promised us the first fish her husband caught?" his wife reminded him. "Well this was the fish he caught the first time he threw his net. So it's ours, and it's a beauty. But you should have been here when I gutted him! I found a large piece of glass in his stomach!"

"And what did you do with it?"

"Oh, I gave it to the children to play with," she shrugged.

When the miller saw the piece of glass he noticed it shone so brightly it appeared to illuminate the room, but because he knew nothing about jewels he didn't realize its value and left it to the children. But the bright glass was such a novelty that the children were soon fighting over it and raising a terrible fuss.

Now it so happened that the miller and his wife had other neighbors who were jewelers. The following morning when the miller had gone to work the jeweler's wife visited the miller's wife to complain about all the noise her children had made.

Three Fishes, 1997. David Brayne. Private collection.

"We couldn't get any sleep last night," she moaned.

"I know, and I'm sorry, but you know how it is with a large family," the miller's wife explained. "Yesterday we found a beautiful piece of glass and I gave it to my youngest one to play with and when the others tried to take it from him he raised a storm."

Analyze Literature

Folk Tale Remind students that a folk tale is a story passed down by word of mouth from generation to generation. It may take a variety of forms, but usually some of the characters are everyday people and the setting is general, rather than specific—both qualities of this story. Elements of folk tales that do not appear in this story are talking animal characters, god characters, a supernatural element, and explanation of the origins of natural phenomena. Have students browse through the unit, noting the different qualities of the folk tales in it.

Make Connections

Draw attention to the miller's decision to go to work the next day. Ask: "Is this what you would have done if you found you were suddenly rich? What does this say about the miller's character?" **A**

The jeweler's wife took interest. "Won't you show me that piece of glass?" she asked.

"But of course. Here it is."

"Ah, yes, it's a pretty piece of glass. Where did you find it?"

"Our neighbor gave us a fish yesterday and when I was cleaning it I found the glass in its stomach."

"Why don't you let me take it home for just a moment. You see, I have one just like it and I want to compare them."

"Yes, why not? Take it," answered the miller's wife.

So the jeweler's wife ran off with the glass to show it to her husband. When the jeweler saw the glass he instantly knew it was one of the finest diamonds he had ever seen.

"It's a diamond!" he exclaimed.

"I thought so," his wife nodded eagerly. "What shall we do?"

"Go tell the neighbor we'll give her fifty dollars for it, but don't tell her it's a diamond!"

"No, no," his wife chuckled, "of course not." She ran to her neighbor's house. "Ah yes, we have one exactly like this," she told the miller's wife. "My husband is willing to buy it for fifty dollars—only so we can have a pair, you understand."

"I can't sell it," the miller's wife answered. "You will have to wait until my husband returns from work."

That evening when the miller came home from work his wife told him about the offer the jeweler had made for the piece of glass.

"But why would they offer fifty dollars for a worthless piece of glass?" the miller wondered aloud. Before his wife could answer they were interrupted by the jeweler's wife.

"What do you say, neighbor, will you take fifty dollars for the glass?" she asked.

"No, that's not enough," the miller said cautiously. "Offer more."

"I'll give you fifty thousand!" the jeweler's wife blurted out.

"A little bit more," the miller replied.

"Impossible!" the jeweler's wife cried, "I can't offer any more without consulting my husband." She ran off to tell her husband how the bartering was going, and he told her he was prepared to pay a hundred thousand dollars to acquire the diamond.

He handed her seventy-five thousand dollars and said, "Take this and tell him that tomorrow, as soon as I open my shop, he'll have the rest."

When the miller heard the offer and saw the money he couldn't believe his eyes. He imagined the jeweler's wife was jesting with him, but it was a true offer and he received the hundred thousand dollars for the diamond. The miller had never seen so much money, but he still didn't quite trust the jeweler.

"I don't know about this money," he confided to his wife. "Maybe the jeweler plans to accuse us of robbing him and thus get it back."

"Oh no," his wife assured him, "the money is ours. We sold the diamond fair and square—we didn't rob anyone."

A "I think I'll still go to work tomorrow," the miller said. "Who knows, something might happen and the money will disappear, then we would be without money and work. Then how would we live?"

So he went to work the next day, and all day he thought about how he could use the money. When he returned home that afternoon his wife asked him what he had decided to do with their new fortune.

"I think I will start my own mill," he

Differentiated Instruction

Reading Proficiency

Have students form small groups. Ask them to read the story one page at a time, pausing at the end of each page to predict what might happen next and to discuss their predictions with the group. At the end, allow students time to share their impressions of the story as a whole. Who made the most correct predictions? What did they like best about the story and why?

Enrichment

Let students investigate other folk tales from the Southwest. Have them use library resources to find anthologies and then choose a story to read. Ask them to share their discoveries with the class and answer these questions: What does the story have in common with "The Force of Luck"? What are the differences?

answered, "like the one I operate for my master. Once I set up my business we'll see how our luck changes."

The next day he set about buying everything he needed to establish his mill and to build a new home. Soon he had everything going.

Six months had passed, more or less, since he had seen the two men who had given him the four hundred dollars and the piece of lead. He was eager to see them again

> ## "Once I set up my business we'll see how our luck changes."

and to tell them how the piece of lead had changed his luck and made him wealthy.

Time passed and the miller prospered. His business grew and he even built a summer cottage where he could take his family on vacation. He had many employees who worked for him. One day while he was at his store he saw his two benefactors[5] riding by. He rushed out into the street to greet them and ask them to come in. He was overjoyed to see them, and he was happy to see that they admired his store.

"Tell us the truth," the man who had given him the four hundred dollars said. "You used that money to set up this business."

The miller swore he hadn't, and he told them how he had given the piece of lead to his neighbor and how the fisherman had in return given him a fish with a very large diamond in its stomach. And he told them

how he had sold the diamond.

"And that's how I acquired this business and many other things I want to show you," he said. "But it's time to eat. Let's eat first then I'll show you everything I have now."

The men agreed, but one of them still doubted the miller's story. So they ate and then the miller had three horses saddled and they rode out to see his summer home. The cabin was on the other side of the river where the mountains were cool and beautiful. When they arrived the men admired the place very much. It was such a peaceful place that they rode all afternoon through the forest. During their ride they came upon a tall pine tree.

"What is that on top of the tree?" one of them asked.

"That's the nest of a hawk," the miller replied.

"I have never seen one; I would like to take a closer look at it!"

"Of course," the miller said, and he ordered a servant to climb the tree and bring down the nest so his friend could see how it was built. When the hawk's nest was on the ground they examined it carefully. They noticed that there was a cloth bag at the bottom of the nest. When the miller saw the bag he immediately knew that it was the very same bag he had lost to the hawk which fought him for the piece of meat years ago.

"You won't believe me, friends, but this is the very same bag in which I put the first two hundred dollars you gave me," he told them.

"If it's the same bag," the man who had doubted him said, "then the money you said the hawk took should be there."

---

5. **benefactors.** People who provide financial support

Analyze Literature

Theme Remind students that the theme is the main idea in a literary work. Although it may not be stated outright, readers can infer it using clues in the text. Ask students to point out possible clues to the folk tale's theme. (Students may note such details as the title, which suggests luck is the most powerful factor in what happens, or the miller's shrewd bargaining skills, which, in contrast to luck, bring him a large amount of money for the diamond.)

TEACHING NOTE

Self-Generated Questioning

Ask students to consider what could have happened differently in the story. Have them come up with "what if" questions based on the story, such as "What if the miller hadn't been an honest man?" and "What if the eagle hadn't stolen the money?" Then challenge students to write their own versions of the tale based on one of their questions. When they are done, have pairs of students read their work to each other.

Grammar Skills

Compound-Complex Sentences

Remind students that a compound-complex sentence contains two or more independent clauses and one or more subordinate clauses. Point out some examples of compound-complex sentences in the text, and challenge students to find more. Here are some examples with subordinate clauses underlined.

- She ran off to tell her husband <u>how the bartering was going</u>, and he told her [that] <u>he was prepared to pay a hundred thousand dollars to acquire the diamond</u>. (Note that the word *that* is implied in this subordinate clause, a noun clause serving as a direct object.)
- His business grew and he even built a summer cottage <u>where he could take his family on vacation</u>.

Answer: Answers will vary. Many will feel that luck has played a role in their lives. Some might say luck has only a marginal effect on most people's lives.

Analyze and Extend

1. (a) The miller loses the money. (b) It starts a chain of events that leads the miller to great wealth.

2. (a) It causes the miller to come into possession of a diamond. (b) The money the miller received all seemed to lead to naught.

3. Answers will vary. Make sure students reasonably defend their positions.

Rubric for Expository Writing

You can adapt this as a checklist for students to use as they write.

☐ Does the analysis examine the story's use of irony?

☐ Does the analysis describe which events in the story are ironic?

☐ Does the analysis describe the effect of irony on the theme?

"No doubt about that," the miller said. "Let's see what we find."

The three of them examined the old, weatherbeaten bag. Although it was full of holes and crumbling, when they tore it apart they found the money intact. The two men remembered what the miller had told them and they agreed he was an honest and honorable man. Still, the man who had given him the money wasn't satisfied. He wondered what had really happened to the second two hundred he had given the miller.

They spent the rest of the day riding in the mountains and returned very late to the house.

As he unsaddled their horses, the servant in charge of grooming and feeding the horses suddenly realized that he had no grain for them. He ran to the barn and checked, but there was no grain for the hungry horses. So he ran to the neighborhood granary and there he was able to buy a large clay jar of bran. He carried the jar home and emptied the bran into a bucket to wet it before he fed it to the horses. When he got to the bottom of the jar he noticed a large lump which turned out to be a rag covered package. He examined it and felt something inside. He immediately went to give it to his master who had been eating dinner.

"Master," he said, "look at this package which I found in an earthenware jar of grain which I just bought from our neighbor!"

The three men carefully unraveled the cloth and found the other one hundred and ninety dollars which the miller had told them he had lost. That is how the miller proved to his friends that he was truly an honest man.

And they had to decide for themselves whether it had been luck or money which had made the miller a wealthy man! ✣

How is luck important in your life? How has luck helped you get to where you are today? For most people, how might luck play a role in their lives?

Analyze and Extend

1. (a) In what ways is the hawk attack an unlucky event? (b) How is it lucky?

2. (a) What effect does the piece of lead have on the miller? (b) Why is this surprising?

3. In your opinion, was it luck or money that made the miller a wealthy man? Explain.

Expository Writing In literature, something is considered ironic if it defies the expectations of the reader. Write a brief **critical analysis** of the use of irony in "The Force of Luck." Which events are ironic? How does the use of irony affect your appreciation of the story? How does the use of irony affect the theme? State your position in a thesis, and support it with evidence.

Critical Literacy Gather into small groups, and hold a debate about "The Force of Luck." Was it luck or money that had the greatest impact on the miller's fate? Half of the group should adopt one position, and half should adopt the other. Present evidence from the story in support of your claims. Be respectful of others' opinions.

Go to **www.mirrorsandwindows.com** for more.

Writing Skills

Thesis Statements

Remind students that a thesis statement conveys the topic of a piece of writing. In persuasive writing, it describes the position the author supports. In expository writing, it gives the process or concept to be explained. Narrative writing, such as this story, might not have a thesis statement. The message, or theme, is implied.

Ask: "Imagine the two rich men engaged in debate. If you asked them to give a thesis statement for this story, what would they say?" (One would say money makes a man prosperous, while the other would say luck makes him prosperous.) Then ask: "What do you think the author of the story wants us to conclude?" Have students explain their answers.

Well, when God made de snake he put him in de bushes to ornament de ground. But things didn't suit de snake so one day he got on de ladder and went up to see God. "Good mawnin', God."

"How do you do, Snake?"

"Ah ain't so many, God, you put me down there on my belly in de dust and everything trods upon me and kills off my generations. Ah ain't got no kind of protection at all."

> But things didn't suit de snake so one day he got on de ladder and went up to see God.

God looked off towards immensity and thought about de subject for a while, then he said, "Ah didn't mean for nothin' to be stompin' you snakes lak dat.

"You got to have some kind of a protection. Here, take dis poison and put it in yo' mouf and when they tromps on you, protect yo'self."

So de snake took de poison in his mouf and went on back.

So after awhile all de other varmints went up to God.

"Good evenin', God."

"How you makin' it, varmints?"

"God, please do somethin' 'bout dat snake. He' layin' in de bushes there wid

How the Snake Got Poison

An African-American Folk Tale retold by Zora Neale Hurston

Zora Neale Hurston (1891–1960) retold a number of traditional African-American folk tales, like "How the Snake Got Poison," in books such as *Mules and Men* and *Go Gator and Muddy the Water*. Throughout her life, Hurston also wrote many other works, including short stories, novels, plays, and essays. She is perhaps best known for her novel *Their Eyes Were Watching God*.

803

Preview the Selection

At a Glance
Independent Reading
- Reading Level: Moderate
- Difficulty Consideration: Dialect
- Ease Factor: Humor

Objectives
Reading this selection will enable students to do the following:
- read with developing fluency
- read silently with comprehension for a sustained period of time

Launch the Lesson
Tell students they are going to read a folk tale in which God does his best to make all his creatures happy. Ask them to think about what such an accommodating deity might indicate about the religious beliefs of the culture that created the tale.

 The Mirrors & Windows questions at the end of the folk tale focus on the theme of opportunity. Before students begin reading, ask: What is the least powerful animal you know? Which animal is most powerful?

TEACHING NOTE
Although this selection is presented in the student edition as an independent reading, teaching support has been provided should you choose to cover it in class.

Program Resources

Planning and Assessment
Program Planning Guide, Selection Lesson Plan
E-Lesson Planner
Assessment Guide, Lesson Test
ExamView

Technology Tools
Interactive Student Text on CD
Visual Teaching Package
Audio Library
mirrorsandwindows.com

Meeting the Standards
Folk Literature: Unit 8, Independent Reading, pp. 89–94

Common Core State Standards
Reading Literature
RL.10

Summary

God originally meant the snake to be ornamental, so he didn't give it arms or legs. Because of this, other creatures keep stepping on it. Unhappy, the snake asks for a way to defend itself, so God gives it poison. Soon the other animals complain that the snake kills anyone who rustles its bush. The snake counters that it can't tell enemies from friends. God gives the snake a rattle for its tail.

 Answer: Answers will vary. Many will say equal opportunity is in everyone's best interest.

Analyze and Extend

1. (a) It is being trampled on and needs a way to defend itself. (b) God gives the snake poison. This makes other animals complain that the snake kills indiscriminately.

2. Achieving it can be hard. Helping one being may harm another.

3. (a) and (b) Answers will vary.

Rubric for Expository Writing

You can adapt this as a checklist for students to use as they write.

☐ Does the analysis address tone, dialect, and content and how they relate to the tale's cultural source?

☐ Does the analysis contain evidence to support its claims?

☐ Does the end restate the main idea and key points?

---

poison in his mouf and he's strikin' everything dat shakes de bush. He's killin' up our generations. Wese skeered to walk de earth."

So God sent for de snake and tole him:

"Snake, when Ah give you dat poison, Ah didn't mean for you to be hittin' and killin' everything dat shake de bush. I give you dat poison and tole you to protect yo'self when they tromples on you. But you killin' everything dat moves. Ah didn't mean for you to do dat."

De snake say, "Lawd, you know Ah'm down here in de dust. Ah ain't got no claws to fight wid, and Ah ain't got no feets to git me out de way. All Ah kin see is feets comin' to trample me. Ah can't tell who my enemy is and who is my friend. You gimme dis protection in my mouf and Ah uses it."

God thought it over for a while then he says:

"Well, snake, I don't want yo' generations all stomped out and I don't want you killin' everything else dat moves. Here take dis bell and tie it to yo' tail. When you hear feets comin' you ring yo' bell and if it's yo' friend, he'll be keerful. If it's yo' enemy, it's you and him."

So dat's how de snake got his poison and dat's how come he got rattles.

Biddy, biddy, bend my story is end.

Turn loose de rooster and hold de hen.

 "When you hear feets comin' you ring yo' bell and if it's yo' friend, he'll be keerful."

MIRRORS & WINDOWS When have you felt that you needed a slight advantage over others? In what ways was the situation fair or unfair? Why should everyone have an equal opportunity to succeed?

Analyze and Extend

1. (a) Why does the snake ask God for help? (b) What happens as a result of its request?

2. What do the varmints' complaints suggest about the difficulties associated with fairness?

3. (a) In what ways is God's solution at the end of the story a good one? (b) In what ways might it be a bad one?

Expository Writing Write a brief **critical analysis** of the tone, dialect, and content of this story. How do these elements relate to or reflect the culture from which this folk tale is derived?

As you write, present evidence from the story in support of your claims. At the end of your analysis, restate the main idea and sum up the most important points.

Lifelong Learning Using the Internet, identify and research a kind of poisonous snake. Learn as much information as you can, focusing on the most vital details, such as its life span, diet, and the region in which it lives. Also, try to determine the threat level it poses to humans. Then present your findings to the class.

Go to www.mirrorsandwindows.com for more.

Words in Use

Selection Words

ornament, 803
mawnin', 803
immensity, 803
mouf, 803
varmints, 803
skeered, 804
keerful, 804

KEY TERMS

FOLK TALE, 803
SHORT STORY, 803
NOVEL, 803
PLAY, 803
ESSAY, 803
TONE, 804
DIALECT, 804

The Rabbits Who Caused All the Trouble

A Fable by James Thurber

Within the memory of the youngest child there was a family of rabbits who lived near a pack of wolves. The wolves announced that they did not like the way the rabbits were living. (The wolves were crazy about the way they themselves were living, because it was the only way to live.) One night several wolves were killed in an earthquake and this was blamed on the rabbits, for it is well known that rabbits pound on the ground with their hind legs and cause earthquakes. On another night one of the wolves was killed by a bolt of lightning and this was also blamed on the rabbits, for it well known that lettuce-eaters cause lightning. The wolves threatened to civilize the rabbits if they didn't behave, and the rabbits decided to run away to a desert island. But the other animals, who lived at a great distance, shamed them, saying, "You must stay where you are and be brave. This is no world for escapists.[1]

If the wolves attack you, we will come to your aid, in all probability." So the rabbits continued to live near the wolves and one day there was a terrible flood which drowned a great many wolves. This was blamed on the rabbits, for it is well known that carrot-

---

1. **escapists.** Those who wish to escape from reality

American wit **James Thurber** (1894–1961) is well known for his cartoons and humorous stories, including fables like this one. (See page 356 for more about Thurber.) "**The Rabbits Who Caused All the Trouble**" appeared in *The New Yorker* magazine in 1939. In 1940, it was included in his book *Fables for Our Time*. At the time

Thurber wrote his tale, the Nazi party, led by Adolf Hitler, had risen to power in Germany by blaming Jewish people for many of the nation's problems. Jews all over Europe were being forced into ghettos and concentration camps and killed in massacres called pogroms. More than six million Jews died before the Allied nations, including U.S., Russian, and British forces, defeated Hitler in 1945. As you read, decide whether Thurber intended his fable as a comment on Nazism in Europe.

805

Preview the Selection

At a Glance
Independent Reading
- Reading Level: Easy
- Difficulty Considerations: Ironic tone; symbolic meaning
- Ease Factor: Length; simple plot

Objectives
Reading this selection will enable students to do the following:
- read with developing fluency
- read silently with comprehension for a sustained period of time

Launch the Lesson
Ask students to give the definition of a fable and recall fables they have read or heard. (See pages 765–769.) Explain that this story is a modern fable.

The Mirrors & Windows questions at the end of the selection focus on why people fail to help when injustice occurs. Before students begin reading, ask: "When have you seen someone being mistreated while others stood by and did nothing to stop it?"

TEACHING NOTE
Although this selection is presented in the student edition as an independent reading, teaching support has been provided should you choose to cover it in class.

Program Resources

Planning and Assessment
Program Planning Guide, Selection Lesson Plan
E-Lesson Planner
Assessment Guide, Lesson Test
ExamView

Technology Tools
Interactive Student Text on CD
Visual Teaching Package
Audio Library
mirrorsandwindows.com

Meeting the Standards
Folk Literature: Unit 8, Independent Reading

Common Core State Standards
Reading Literature
RL.10
Writing
W.3, W.10
Speaking and Listening
SL.1

Summary

A pack of wolves blames a rabbit family for causing natural disasters. The rabbits plan to flee, but the other animals urge them to be brave. The wolves imprison the rabbits and eat them.

 Answer: Fear and prejudice often play a role. During the Holocaust, some Germans feared being targeted by the Nazis if they helped Jews, but others shared Hitler's anti-Semitic feelings.

Analyze and Extend

1. (a) The wolves are intolerant of the rabbits' lifestyle. (b) They blame the rabbits for causing earthquakes, lightning, and floods by pounding the ground and eating lettuce and carrots.
2. (a) The rabbits are imprisoned and eaten. (b) The other animals fail to aid them.
3. (a) It is a humorous tale that criticizes the way humans scapegoat and persecute certain cultures or ethnic groups in society. (b) It also condemns those who fail to intervene.

Rubric for Creative Writing

You can adapt this as a checklist for students to use as they write.
☐ Does the moral sum up the main message of the story?
☐ Does it offer a lesson or advice to the reader?
☐ Is it expressed in one sentence?

---

nibblers with long ears cause floods. The wolves descended on the rabbits, for their own good, and imprisoned them in a dark cave, for their own protection.

When nothing was heard about the rabbits for some weeks, the other animals demanded to know what had happened to them. The wolves replied that the rabbits had been eaten and since they had been eaten the affair was a purely internal matter. But the other animals warned that they might possibly unite against the wolves unless some reason was given for the destruction of the rabbits. So the wolves gave them one. "They were trying to escape," said the wolves, "and, as you know, this is no world for escapists."

Moral: Run, don't walk, to the nearest desert island. ❖

 Why do you think others choose not to become involved when they see that a person or group of people is being mistreated?

Analyze and Extend

1. (a) What do the wolves dislike about the rabbits? What troubles do the wolves blame on the rabbits? (b) What reasons do the wolves give for blaming the rabbits?
2. (a) What happens to the rabbits? (b) What blame do the other animals have in what happens to the rabbits, and why?
3. **Satire** is humorous writing intended to point out human failings. (a) What makes this fable satirical? (b) What type of human behavior is Thurber criticizing?

Creative Writing A fable is a tale with a moral, or lesson. Reread the story "The Rabbits Who Caused All the Trouble" and come up with several alternative morals to the story. Share your ideas with others in your class.

Collaborative Learning Form groups to discuss Thurber's fable and how it relates to history and/or current events. Who might the wolves represent in human society past and present? Who might the rabbits represent? You may conduct research to find examples.

 Go to www.mirrorsandwindows.com for more.

Words in Use

Selection Words
civilize, 805
probability, 805
internal, 806

Teaching Words
ghetto, 805
pogrom, 805

Key Terms
FABLE, 805
MORAL, 806
SATIRE, 806

RABBIT
and the
TUG of WAR

As told by Michael Thompson with art by Jacob Warrenfeltz

It is told that one day Rabbit was going along his usual way...

...when he spied two Buffalo lying on opposite sides of a dusty hill...

...and he got an idea.

THOMPSON

Michael Thompson is a high-school English teacher from the Mvskoke (Muskogee) Creek people of Oklahoma. **Jacob Warrenfeltz** is a comic book artist who lives in Maryland. They collaborated to create this graphic version of "**Rabbit and the Tug of**

War," a Native American trickster tale, for the book *Trickster: Native American Tales*. The rabbit is a trickster figure in the folklore of many Native American groups. This story was taken from the Mvskoke tradition. It is an old tale which was first written down in the early 1900s by ethnographer John Swanton.

807

Preview the Selection

At a Glance
Independent Reading
- Reading Level: Easy
- Difficulty Considerations: None
- Ease Factor: Illustrations

Objectives
Reading this selection will enable students to do the following:
- read with developing fluency
- read silently with comprehension for a sustained period of time

Launch the Lesson
Ask students to give the definition of a trickster tale and recall trickster tales they have read. (See page 725 for a definition and page 734 for an example.) Explain that this is a graphic version of a trickster tale.

TEACHING NOTE
Although this selection is presented in the student edition as an independent reading, teaching support has been provided should you choose to cover it in class.

Program Resources

Planning and Assessment
Program Planning Guide, Selection Lesson Plan
E-Lesson Planner
Assessment Guide, Lesson Test
ExamView

Technology Tools
Interactive Student Text on CD
Visual Teaching Package
Audio Library
mirrorsandwindows.com

Meeting the Standards
Folk Literature: Unit 8, Independent Reading

Common Core State Standards
Reading Literature
RL.4, RL.10
Writing
W.3, W.7, W.10

Summary

Rabbit challenges two Buffalo to a tug-of-war, but then tricks them into pulling against each other. The Buffalo are angry at the trick and forbid Rabbit from drinking in their waterhole. However, the thirsty Rabbit tricks them a second time by borrowing the shoes of a Deer. The nearsighted Buffalo, seeing the tracks, think Rabbit is a Deer and allow him to drink. Rabbit boasts, "That's the way to trick them twice."

The Mirrors & Windows questions at the end of the selection focus on how it feels to be tricked or to trick someone. Before they read, ask students whether they enjoy practical jokes, and why.

Reading Strategies

Use Context Clues Remind students that they can use context clues to determine the meanings of unfamiliar words. For example, students will not know the meaning of the word *Hensci*, used by the Rabbit when he greets the Buffalo. However, they should be able to figure out from the context that it is a word of greeting. In fact, the word means "Hello" in the Mvskoke Creek language.

808   UNIT 8 FOLK LITERATURE

Words in Use

Selection Words
persist, 808
pester, 808
whoop, 810
quench, 814

Teaching Words
ethnographer, 807

Key Terms

GRAPHIC TALE, 807
TRICKSTER TALE, 807

...and carried it across the hill, first to one Buffalo, then to the other, and he positioned himself at the center.

Next he got a big strong grapevine...

When he was ready, he gave a loud whoop...

...and the two Buffalo began to pull hard against each other.

Analyze Literature

Personification Personification is a figure of speech in which something nonhuman is described as if it were human. Ask students to explain how the animals are personified in this tale. For instance, the animals can speak and laugh, make fun of others, participate in a game, lend property, and punish others (as the Buffalo do by forbidding access to the water hole). Students may debate about what behavior animals are capable of. For instance, can animals in nature play tricks on one another? If so, how?

History Connection

American Bison American bison, also known as buffalo, were hunted nearly to extinction in the 1800s as settlers from Europe populated the continent. While Native Americans hunted bison for meat, European hunters killed them for their hides and left the meat to rot. Sale of the hides was profitable, and many buffalo hides were exported to Europe. The U.S. Army also encouraged buffalo hunting as a way to weaken the Native American peoples who depended on the bison for food. By the end of the century, the bison had nearly disappeared. Due to conservation efforts since then, the buffalo population is today estimated at 350,000, compared to an estimated 60 to 100 million in the mid-1800s.

RABBIT AND THE TUG OF WAR **809**

Commonly Confused Words

Lay and *lie* are commonly confused. *Lay* is a transitive verb, meaning it must have an object. *Lie* is intransitive, meaning it does not have an object. (Examples: *Lay* the book on the desk. *Lie* down.) Adding to the confusion, the past tense of *lay* is *laid*. The past tense of *lie* is *lay*. Present and past participles are: *lay—laying, laid; lie—lying, lain.*

1. The Buffalo were (laying, lying) on opposite sides of the hill.
2. They (lay, laid) there all day.
3. They had (laid, lain) there every day for years.
4. Rabbit will (lie, lay) the grapevine between them.

THE RABBITS WHO CAUSED ALL THE TROUBLE **809**

Analyze Literature

Character Ask students to describe the characters of the Rabbit, Buffalo, and Deer in the story based on their words and actions. For instance, they may note that the Buffalo are prideful, as the Buffalo tells the Rabbit, "I don't bother with little things like you." You may have them create a character chart for each animal.

Analyze Literature

Trickster Tale Remind students that trickster tales are stories that feature a human or an animal with human characteristics who plays tricks on others. Ask them to read the Yoruba trickster tale "Eshu" on page 733 and compare and contrast it with "Rabbit and the Tug of War." How are Eshu and the Rabbit similar?

Independent Reading

Students who enjoy "Rabbit and the Tug of War" might like to read the other stories included in the book *Trickster: Native American Tales.*

Differentiated Instruction

Auditory Learning

Stories like this one are from the oral tradition, meaning they were traditionally told aloud, not read in a book. Have students work in pairs to read the story aloud, or go around the room and have one student read each frame.

English Language Learning

Point out the words *snort* and *whoop* and explain that these are examples of words that sound like what they mean. Other examples of onomatopoeic words include *buzz, click,* and *pop.* Ask English language learners to give examples of words in their language that sound like what they mean. See if other students can guess the meanings of the foreign words based on their sound.

After a long time, when the two Buffalo were both nearly worn out and all the whooping had stopped, they began to think that something was wrong...

...so they walked around the hill and met.

They said, "Rabbit has made big fun of us. Because of this, we will no longer let him drink at our waterhole. Let him die of thirst, for all we care."

Teach the Selection

Analyze Literature

Graphic Tale Point out to students that in a graphic novel or tale, the pictures are just as important as the words. Ask students: How do the pictures help you understand the story? Which frames show how Rabbit set up his trick? Which frames help show the emotions and attitudes of the characters? Point out the two frames that have no captions. What is being shown in these frames?

Reading Strategies

Make Predictions Remind students that active readers make predictions as they read. Ask students to make a prediction about what the Rabbit will do next, now that the Buffalo plan to block his way to the waterhole.

Grammar Skills

Ellipses

Explain to students that the punctuation mark made of three dots (...) is known as an ellipsis (plural *ellipses*). Ellipses can be used to indicate a break in a sentence or a thought, as in this story. They indicate to the reader that the sentence is not complete, but will be continued in the next frame. Ellipses can also be used in the following cases:

- In dialogue to show where speech or thought trails off or is interrupted: "If only I could..." she began, shaking her head sadly.
- In a quoted passage to show where material has been left out. If the material is left out at the end of a sentence, the period is added after the ellipsis: "Four score and seven years ago our fathers brought forth...a new nation, conceived in Liberty...."

Teach the Selection

Analyze Literature

Oral Tradition Point out the phrases used to open and close the story: "It is told that..." and "That's how they tell it." These phrases are reminders that the story comes from the oral tradition, in which stories are passed by word of mouth from generation to generation. This story was passed down for generations by the Mvskoke Creek people of the southeastern United States.

History Connection

Mvskoke Nation Mvskoke (also Muscogee, or Creek) people originally lived in the Deep South of the U.S., in present-day Georgia, Tennessee, and Alabama. They lived in villages along river valleys, each village led by a *mico* or chief. Women elders also had power in Mvskoke society, as the tribe was matrilineal, which meant that clan membership was passed down through the women. After the Indian Removal Act of 1830, most Mvskoke were relocated to reservations in Oklahoma. Many Mskoke people today live in Florida, Oklahoma, Alabama, and Georgia.

Vocabulary Skills

Commonly Confused Words

Lend and *borrow* are commonly confused words. To *lend* or *loan* something is to give it to someone else with the expectation that it will be returned. The past tense of *lend* is *lent*. To *borrow* something is to take something from someone else, with the intention of returning it later. It is incorrect in English to say, for instance, "Can you borrow me that pen?" Have students choose the correct answer for each and come up with three example sentences of their own.

1. Rabbit asked if he could (borrow, lend) Deer's shoes.
2. Deer (lent, borrowed) her shoes to Rabbit.

Teach the Selection

Science Connection

American bison, or buffalo, have an acute sense of smell and hearing, but their eyesight is poor. Other animals, such as the eagle, have excellent eyesight. Rabbits have good long-distance eyesight but poor eyesight at close range. Ask students to theorize why senses in different animals evolved differently. They should be able to conclude that as a herbivore, the buffalo does not need good eyesight to find prey, while the eagle needs good vision to spot prey on the ground. The rabbit needs good long-distance eyesight to escape predators coming from a distance, but close vision is not crucial for rabbits' survival.

Analyze Literature

Theme and Folk Tale A **theme** is a central message or perception about life that is revealed through a literary work. **Folk tales** often teach lessons. Ask students what the theme or lesson of this story might be. Examples may include: "Cleverness beats strength" or "Beware of a challenge that looks too easy."

Grammar Skills

Punctuation in Dialogue

In dialogue, quotation marks are used to enclose the words being spoken. End punctuation such as commas or periods must be placed inside the quotation marks. Tag lines such as "he said" or "she said" are added to make clear who is speaking. Have students punctuate the following lines of dialogue, being sure to capitalize where needed to form a new sentence.

1. I will trick these Buffalo said the Rabbit to himself.
2. Can I borrow your shoes asked the Rabbit.
3. Yes you may said the Deer here you go.
4. I can't believe he tricked us again exclaimed the Buffalo.

So Rabbit quenched his thirst.

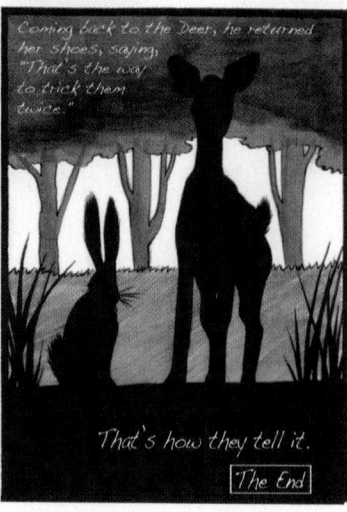

Coming back to the Deer, he returned her shoes, saying, "That's the way to trick them twice."

That's how they tell it.

The End

MIRRORS & WINDOWS

Answer: Many people enjoy tricking others, but are annoyed when they themselves are tricked.

Analyze and Extend

1. (a) The Rabbit tricks them into a tug-of-war. Each Buffalo believes he is competing against the Rabbit, while actually tugging against the other Buffalo. The Rabbit tricks them again by wearing the Deer's shoes to sneak down to the water hole. (b) The Buffalo are easily tricked because they are so proud and confident of their strength. They also have poor eyesight.

2. Responses will vary, but most students will see the Rabbit as a hero.

3. Responses will vary, but the pictures may help students visualize the action.

Rubric for Creative Writing

You can adapt this as a checklist for students to use as they write.

☐ Does the trickster tale involve a human or animal who plays tricks on others?

☐ Is it written in clear chronological order?

☐ Is the dialogue in the story punctuated correctly?

☐ If written as a graphic tale, are the illustrations easy to interpret and do they relate well to the captions?

MIRRORS & WINDOWS

Recall a funny trick you played on a friend or family member, or a time when a trick was played on you. How did you feel in each case?

Analyze and Extend

1. (a) What trick does the Rabbit play on the two Buffalo? How does he trick them a second time? (b) Why do you think the Buffaloes fall for Rabbit's tricks?

2. Tricksters are common figures in folklore. On the one hand they cause trouble, but they are also clever and creative. Do you see the Rabbit as a hero or a villain in this tale? Explain.

3. A **graphic tale** is one that is told through pictures. How do the pictures add to the story?

Creative Writing A **trickster tale** is a tale that involves a human or animal that plays tricks on others. Common tricksters include the rabbit, the fox, and the spider of African folklore. Find other examples of trickster tales. Then write your own original trickster tale. You may use an unexpected person or animal as your trickster.

Lifelong Learning Conduct research to find out more about the Mvskoke Creek people. Where is their homeland? What types of animals did they hunt? Create a map showing the major Native American groups in each part of the continental U.S.

Go to **www.mirrorsandwindows.com** for more.

Writing Skills

Chronological Order

Remind students that when writing a story, they should be sure the events are in chronological order—that is, in the order they occur. Connecting words and phrases like "Suddenly," "Several hours later," and "The next day" should be used to help readers understand the time flow.

If students break out of chronological order by using flashbacks or flash forwards, the time of the event should be clearly labeled with key words like "Years earlier," or "Ten years later." The correct verb tense (past perfect or future) must also be used to show the shift in time. Flashbacks and flash forwards should be used sparingly, as too many shifts in time can be confusing for the reader.

from

Ella Enchanted

A Novel by Gail Carson Levine

Chapter One

"My gift is obedience. Ella will always be obedient. Now stop crying, child."

That fool of a fairy Lucinda did not intend to lay a curse on me. She meant to bestow a gift. When I cried inconsolably through my first hour of life, my tears were her inspiration. Shaking her head sympathetically at Mother, the fairy touched my nose. "My gift is obedience. Ella will always be obedient. Now stop crying, child."

I stopped.

Father was away on a trading expedition as usual, but our cook, Mandy, was there. She and Mother were horrified, but no matter how they explained it to Lucinda, they couldn't make her understand the terrible things she'd done to me. I could picture the argument: Mandy's freckles standing out sharper than usual, her frizzy gray hair in disarray, and her double chin shaking with anger; Mother still and intense, her brown curls damp from labor, the laughter gone from her eyes.

I couldn't imagine Lucinda. I didn't know what she looked like.

American author **Gail Carson Levine** (b. 1947) grew up in Manhattan, New York. She worked as a welfare administrator for many years before becoming a successful writer of books for young adults. *Ella Enchanted*, first published in 1997, was Levine's first book. The novel is based on the popular fairy tale *Cinderella,* but with lots of humorous twists. *Ella Enchanted* received a Newbery Honor in 1998 and was made into a movie in 2004.

Preview the Selection

At a Glance
Independent Reading
- Reading Level: Easy
- Difficulty Considerations: Vocabulary
- Ease Factor: Interesting plot

Objectives
Reading this selection will enable students to do the following:
- read with developing fluency
- read silently with comprehension for a sustained period of time

Launch the Lesson
Ask students to recall fairy tales that involve a magic spell or curse. For instance, Sleeping Beauty is cursed by a bad fairy, so that she is doomed to die when her finger is pricked by a spindle. Another fairy modifies the curse so that she will not die but will fall into a deep sleep, to be awakened by true love's kiss. Students should read to find out what spell or curse is bestowed on Ella, the heroine of this story.

TEACHING NOTE
Although this selection is presented in the student edition as an independent reading, teaching support has been provided should you choose to cover it in class.

815

Program Resources

[Planning and Assessment
Program Planning Guide, Selection Lesson Plan
E-Lesson Planner
Assessment Guide, Lesson Test
ExamView

Technology Tools
Interactive Student Text on CD
Visual Teaching Package
Audio Library
mirrorsandwindows.com

Meeting the Standards
Folk Literature: Unit 8, Independent Reading

Common Core State Standards
Reading Literature
RL.1, RL.9, RL.10
Writing
W.2, W.10

Summary

At her birth, Ella is placed under a fairy's spell that makes her always obedient. While the fairy intended to bestow a gift, Ella's obedience is really a curse because she is forced to obey any direct order, even if harmful to herself. When told to eat cake at her fifth birthday, she eats herself sick, unable to stop. Ella is forced to help with kitchen chores and is taken advantage of by a playmate. She learns to creatively defy orders and to keep her curse a secret.

The Mirrors & Windows questions at the end of the selection ask when it is a good idea to disobey an order. Before reading, you may ask students to think of a time when they rebelled against an order from a parent or other authority figure.

Reading Strategies

Use Context Clues Remind students to use context clues to determine the meanings of unfamiliar words. Model the technique using the word *bestow* as an example: "What do you normally do with a gift? You *give* a gift, so *bestow* must mean *give*." Have students use context clues to come up with the meanings of other unfamiliar words in the selection.

She wouldn't undo the curse.

My first awareness of it came on my fifth birthday. I seem to remember that day perfectly, perhaps because Mandy told the tale so often.

" For your birthday," she'd start, "I baked a beautiful cake. Six layers."

Bertha, our head maid, had sewn a special gown for me. "Blue as midnight with a white sash. You were small for your age even then, and you looked like a china doll, with a white ribbon in your black hair and your cheeks red from excitement."

In the middle of the table was a vase filled with flowers that Nathan, our manservant, had picked.

We all sat around the table. (Father was away again.) I was thrilled. I had watched Mandy bake the cake and Bertha sew the gown and Nathan pick the flowers.

Mandy cut the cake. When she handed me my piece, she said without thinking, "Eat."

The first bite was delicious. I finished the slice happily. When it was gone, Mandy cut another. That one was harder. When it was gone, no one gave me more, but I knew I had to keep eating. I moved my fork into the cake itself.

"Ella, what are you doing?" Mother said.

"Little piggy." Mandy laughed. "It's her birthday, Lady. Let her have as much as she wants." She put another slice on my plate.

I felt sick, and frightened. Why couldn't I stop eating?

Swallowing was a struggle. Each bite weighed on my tongue and felt like a sticky mass of glue as I fought to get it down. I started crying while I ate.

Mother realized first. "Stop eating, Ella," she commanded.

I stopped.

Anyone could control me with an order. It had to be a direct command, such as "Put on a shawl," or "You must go to bed now." A wish or a request had no effect. I was free to ignore "I wish you would put on a shawl," or "Why don't you go to bed now?" But against an order I was powerless.

If someone told me to hop on one foot for a day and a half, I'd have to do it. And hopping on one foot wasn't the worst order I could be given. If you commanded me to cut off my own head, I'd have to do it.

I was in danger at every moment.

As I grew older, I learned to delay my obedience, but each moment cost me dear—in breathlessness, nausea, dizziness, and other complaints. I could never hold out for long. Even a few minutes were a desperate struggle.

I had a fairy godmother, and Mother asked her to take the curse away. But my fairy godmother said Lucinda was the only one who could remove it. However, she also said it might be broken someday without Lucinda's help.

But I didn't know how. I didn't even know who my fairy godmother was.

Instead of making me docile, Lucinda's curse made a rebel of me. Or perhaps I was that way naturally.

Words in Use

Selection Words

bestow, 815
inconsolably, 815
inspiration, 815
sympathetically, 815
disarray, 815
nausea, 816

evade, 817
smugly, 817
rash, 817
ogre, 818

Teaching Words

welfare, 815
heroine, 818

Key Terms

FAIRY TALE, 815
PARODY, 818
DIALOGUE, 818

Instead of making me docile,[1] Lucinda's curse made a rebel of me. Or perhaps I was that way naturally.

Mother rarely insisted I do anything. Father knew nothing of my curse and saw me too infrequently to issue many commands. But Mandy was bossy, giving orders almost as often as she drew breath. Kind orders or for-your-own-good orders. "Bundle up, Ella." Or "Hold this bowl while I beat the eggs, sweet."

I disliked these commands, harmless as they were. I'd hold the bowl, but move my feet so she would have to follow me around the kitchen. She'd call me minx[2] and try to hem me in with more specific instructions, which I would find new ways to evade. Often, it was a long business to get anything done between us, with Mother laughing and egging each of us on by turn.

We'd end happily—with me finally choosing to do what Mandy wanted, or with Mandy changing her order to a request.

When Mandy would absentmindedly give me an order I knew she didn't mean, I'd say, "Do I have to?" And she'd reconsider.

When I was eight, I had a friend, Pamela, the daughter of one of the servants. One day she and I were in the kitchen, watching Mandy make marchpane.[3] When Mandy sent me to the pantry for more almonds, I returned with only two. She ordered me back with more exact instructions, which I followed exactly, while still managing to frustrate her true wishes.

Later, when Pamela and I retreated to the garden to devour the candy, she asked why I hadn't done what Mandy wanted straight off.

"I hate when she's bossy," I answered.

Pamela said smugly, "I always obey my elders."

"That's because you don't have to."

"I do have to, or Father will slap me."

"It's not the same as for me. I'm under a

---

1. **docile.** Easily taught or directed; obedient
2. **minx.** A girl or young woman who is considered overly bold
3. **marchpane.** Marzipan, a candy made from almond paste

Answer: It is a good idea to disobey an order when it is unjust or could lead to harm.

Analyze and Extend

1. (a) Ella receives the gift of obedience. (b) It is actually a curse because it forces her to obey any command she is given, whether reasonable or not.

2. (a) Ella eats too much cake on her birthday because she is told "Eat" and cannot stop eating until commanded to stop. She must help with kitchen chores even when she does not wish to, and a playmate takes advantage of her. (b) She learns to creatively defy orders and to keep her curse a secret from everyone.

3. The story contains fairies and magic, but uses humor to lightly make fun of fairy tale conventions. For instance, the idea that fairy tale heroines are always sweet and obedient is parodied, as Ella is literally obedient to a fault.

Rubric for Expository Writing

You can adapt this as a checklist for students to use as they write.

☐ Does the critical essay compare and contrast Ella with the typical fairy tale heroine?

☐ Does the essay have a clear thesis statement?

☐ Does the essay include specific examples to support the thesis statement?

---

spell." I enjoyed the importance of the words. Spells are rare. Lucinda was the only fairy rash enough to cast them on people.

"Like Sleeping Beauty?"

"Except I won't have to sleep for a hundred years."

"What's your spell?"

I told her.

"If anybody gives you an order, you have to obey? Including me?"

I nodded.

"Can I try it?"

"No." I hadn't anticipated this. I changed the subject. "I'll race you to the gate."

"All right, but I command you to lose the race."

"Then I don't want to race."

"I command you to race, and I command you to lose."

We raced. I lost.

We picked berries. I had to give Pamela the sweetest, ripest ones. We played princesses and ogres. I had to be the ogre.

An hour after my admission, I punched her. She screamed, and blood poured from her nose.

Our friendship ended that day. Mother found Pamela's mother a new situation far from our town of Frell.

After punishing me for using my fist, Mother issued one of her infrequent commands: never to tell anyone about my curse. But I wouldn't have anyway. I had learned caution. ❖

When is it a good idea to disobey an order?

Analyze and Extend

1. (a) What "gift" does Ella receive from the fairy Lucinda? (b) Why is this gift really a curse?

2. (a) What problems does the curse create for Ella? (b) How does she learn to deal with the curse?

3. A **parody** is a piece of writing that imitates another work in order to make fun of it. Explain why this selection can be considered a parody of fairy tales. What elements of a fairy tale does it have, and how does it put a humorous twist on fairy tales?

Expository Writing Heroines in fairy tales are usually presented to be beautiful, sweet-tempered, and obedient. Write a **critical essay** examining Ella's character. How is she similar and/or different from the typical fairy tale heroine?

Critical Literacy In small groups, choose a scene from the story to perform in front of the class. You may use the dialogue from the story and ad lib your own lines as you wish. Alternately, you may create an original skit showing problems Ella might encounter in life as a result of her curse.

 Go to **www.mirrorsandwindows.com** for more.

Writing Skills

Using a Graphic Organizer

Before they begin writing, you may ask students to create a two-column chart as a graphic organizer to contrast the characteristics of Ella with those of the typical fairy tale heroine.

Fairy Tale Heroine
- beautiful
- obedient
- uncritical
- gentle and helpless; needs rescue

Ella
- her appearance is not emphasized, although at age five she is described as looking like "a china doll"
- obedient, but not by choice; in fact, she is rebellious
- has her own opinions; calls Lucinda a "fool" and says she hates Mandy's bossiness
- defends herself by punching a playmate in the nose

Horse Hooves and Chicken Feet: Mexican Folktales
by Neil Philip

The folk tales in this collection describe a fascinating world of magical creatures and supernatural events, where a boy outsmarts a great magician, a witch transforms seven brothers into seven blue oxen, and a mysterious shadow rescues a man from drowning. The collection includes colorful, vibrant illustrations inspired by Mexican folk art.

Beowulf
by Michael Morpurgo

The epic of Beowulf, Britain's oldest epic poem, tells the story of a courageous young warrior who battles dreadful creatures, including the monster Grendel and a powerful dragon. The poem was composed around AD 800. Battles and action scenes are illustrated throughout with bold and dramatic paintings by Michael Foreman.

The Four Corners of the Sky
by Steve Zeitlin

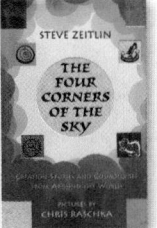

This collection of stories from many different cultures describes ancient beliefs about the creation of the world. Stories include Egyptian, Greek, Hebrew, Incan, Indian, and Chinese accounts of creation, with background information about each culture and its beliefs. Also included are illustrations of designs and artifacts from each culture.

Peace Walker: The Legend of Hiawatha and Tekanawita
by C. J. Taylor

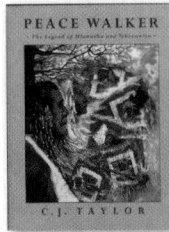

Author C. J. Taylor draws upon her Mohawk ancestry to present the story of the Iroquois Confederacy, one of the world's great democracies, and the peace walker, Hiawatha. The legend describes how Chief Hiawatha and Chief Tekanawita united to defeat the cruel Chief Atotahara, bringing peace and unity to their nations.

The Legend of Lord Eight Deer: An Epic of Ancient Mexico
by John M. D. Pohl

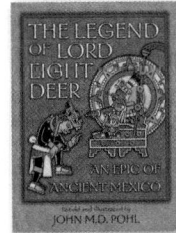

This epic story of the Mixtec people of Mexico describes the journey of Lord Eight Deer to the gates of the Sun God. The story was recorded in pictographs more than five hundred years ago. The author's bold and powerful illustrations are based on the images in the original Mixtec source. This dramatic story presents a picture of one of the last great civilizations of early Mexico.

The Story of King Arthur and His Knights
by Howard Pyle

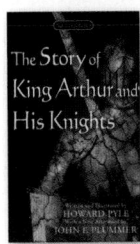

Master storyteller Howard Pyle retells the legend of King Arthur, the knights of the round table, and the court of Camelot in a lively and accessible style. Discover the legend that inspired great works of literature by many famous authors, including Alfred, Lord Tennyson; Sir Thomas Malory; and T. H. White.

Independent Reading Activity
Help students link their reading to the unit theme, Seeking Wisdom. Ask how literature from the oral tradition can help readers learn, grow confident, and make wise decisions. You might try this as an in-class activity: Have students read silently one or two tales from a single tradition for at least twenty minutes. Then have students identify what wisdom the tale or tales can impart to a contemporary American reader.

> ### EMC E-Library
> The EMC E-Library contains over twenty thousand pages of literary classics that students may read independently. An Electronic Library Guide provides teaching suggestions, enrichment activities, and reading strategy guidesheets.

Use Reading Skills
Summarize Tell students that stories from the oral tradition provide opportunities to practice summarizing skills. Ask students to choose a folk tale, myth, or legend from their independent reading and summarize its plot, characters, and setting.

Ask students to write one or two sentences about the theme, or main message, of the story. When students have completed their summaries, post them in a "recommended reading" display.

Program Resources

EMC Access Editions
For additional independent reading, you may wish to refer students to one of EMC's Access Edition titles such as Stephen Crane's *The Red Badge of Courage*. Each Access Edition contains a thorough study apparatus, including background information, literal comprehension questions, footnotes, vocabulary definitions, critical thinking questions, and related projects and activities. An Assessment Manual offering worksheets and exams is available for each Access Edition.

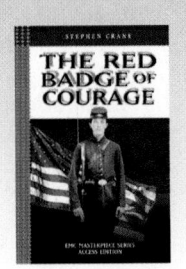

Common Core State Standards
Reading Literature
RL.10

Objectives

Participating in this lesson will help students write a research report that

- clearly introduces a purpose and thesis
- uses a clear organizational pattern and effective transitions
- supports the thesis with quoted, paraphrased, and summarized information from multiple sources
- effectively summarizes main points in a conclusion
- lists all sources cited

Launch the Lesson

Have students take out a clean sheet of paper or a blank note card. Give them two minutes to write down the most interesting topic they have ever researched. Tell them that they can consider informal research, such as reading an article with a catchy title or asking questions about a new piece of technology, as well as school research assignments. Collect the papers or cards and shuffle them. Read out the topics (students should remain anonymous) and ask for class reactions. When you determine you have read enough, tell students they will have a chance to write up some exciting research in this workshop.

Program Resources

Additional writing workshops are available in the *Exceeding the Standards: Writing* resource.

Research Report

Reading and Writing

In this unit, you have read myths and folk tales. In earlier times, myths and folk tales were created to explain mysteries of nature or how something came to be. Today, we do research to find out about the world around us, past and present.

In this unit, you will learn how to write an effective **research report.** In a research report, a writer uses multiple sources to find out information about a topic. You may sum up the assignment by creating a goal and deciding how to go about writing. Use the writing rubric, or set of standards by which you will judge your work, as a guide and to determine whether or not you were successful. You will use this rubric in both drafting and revising your report.

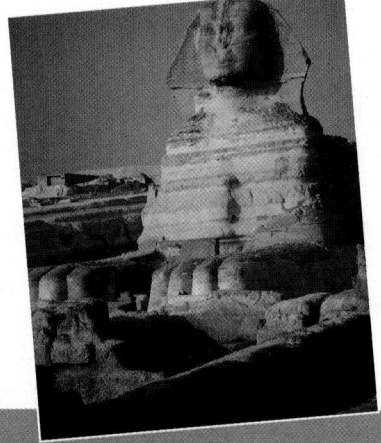

- **Assignment:** Write an effective research report on a topic of my choosing.
- **Goal:** Thoroughly research my topic and write an interesting report that answers my questions about the topic.
- **Strategy:** Use a variety of sources to research the topic and present my information to an audience in a clear and logically organized way.
- **Writing Rubric:** My research report should include the following:
  - an introduction that clearly states my purpose and thesis
  - a clear organizational pattern with effective transitions
  - quoted, paraphrased, and summarized information from multiple sources that supports my thesis
  - an effective conclusion that sums up my main points
  - a list of sources cited in my report

What Great Writers Do

Gail Gibbons is a writer of children's nonfiction books. In an interview, she gave the following advice to teachers about assigning topics for student writers. Consider Gibbons's advice as you consider topics of your own.

Tell [students] to write what they find exciting and interesting in their lives or something they're really curious about themselves. If they don't follow that route, they're going to write a very boring thing.

Words in Use

Teaching Words

rubric, 820
comprehensive, 821
reputable, 821
verified, 821
perspective, 821
hieroglyphics, 824
pharaoh, 826
elaborate, 826
transition, 826
mummification, 826
inundation, 827
devotion, 827

KEY TERMS

Common Core State Standards

Writing
W.2, W.4, W.5, W.6, W.7

Choosing and Narrowing Your Topic

You have read many different forms of literature about varied topics from varied time periods in this book. Which selections or issues caused you to see your world in a different way? What sparked your interest or made you curious? Did any particular topic or issue leave you wanting to know more? Perhaps you have questions that haven't yet been answered. Use your questions and curiosity to guide you in selecting a topic and conducting your research.

First, brainstorm topics of interest. Use a cluster chart to narrow your topic. State your general topic in the center of the cluster chart, and identify interesting aspects of the topic in the outer parts. Then, decide on the aspect you find most engaging.

Remember to narrow your focus so that it is manageable for a research paper, but do not make it so narrow that you won't be able to find enough information to write about.

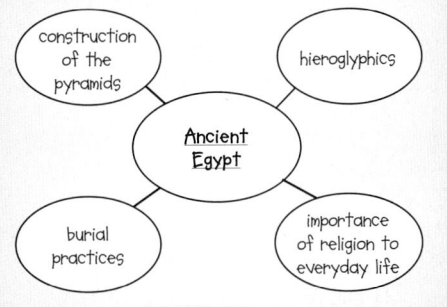

Gathering Information

Primary and Secondary Sources Use at least four different sources of information in your report. Try to include both primary and secondary sources for the most comprehensive and accurate perspective on your topic. **Primary sources** are firsthand accounts recorded by people who personally witnessed an event or situation. Primary sources include letters, journals, and historical documents. **Secondary sources** are accounts that explain or give information about a person, event, or topic but that rely on material from other sources rather than firsthand accounts. Secondary sources include encyclopedias, newspaper articles, and most books.

Evaluate Sources When researching material, make sure your information is accurate and current. Are your facts and statistics up to date? Check that Internet articles come from reputable sources and can be verified. Use information from several different types of sources and be sure that the authors are experts or professionals in their fields.

Make a list of questions you want to answer about your topic to guide your research. Use your questions to keep your research focused. Consider one student's questions about how religion affected everyday life of the ancient Egyptians.

> 1. What was the purpose of religion in Egyptian life?
> 2. How did the ancient Egyptians view death?
> 3. How did religion affect Egyptian daily life?

Deciding On Your Purpose

Use your questions to develop a thesis stating your topic and perspective. You may wish to do some research before settling on a thesis. See the example below.

> For the ancient Egyptians, religion was a part of their everyday lives.

Teach the Workshop

Prewrite

Gather Information Suggest that students use a graphic organizer to plan their research. It should have columns for primary and secondary sources. In their initial explorations of secondary sources, such as encyclopedias, they will probably read about primary sources they would like to consult.

Students can develop their organizers to keep track of source credibility. For example, they can note a source's date and the background of its author.

Thesis Statement Encourage students to take time to craft a succinct thesis statement. Point out that this statement will guide their writing and revising. It should identify the topic and what the research will reveal about it. Also point out that as they conduct research, they may want to refine their thesis statements.

What Great Researchers Do

Pioneering scientist Barbara McClintock loved research. Tell students to have fun gathering information, just as she did:

I was just so interested in what I was doing I could hardly wait to get up in the morning and get at it. One of my friends, a geneticist, said I was a child, because only children can't wait to get up in the morning to get at what they want to do.

Brainstorm

Remind students that brainstorming is a way of generating a lot of ideas without stopping to analyze them. Organize students into small groups based on similar interests, reading levels, or other appropriate factors. Provide these guidelines, and allow groups to brainstorm for five minutes about interesting research topics. Have each group decide on a way to record its ideas before it begins. When groups finish, encourage individual members to note any great ideas they want to pursue.
1. For the first round of ideas, go around the group and let everyone speak. Then, start generating new ideas based on the first round.
2. Do not comment on any idea. Just record it.
3. Repetition is OK.

Draft

Organizing Information Tell students to record as much information about each source they use as possible. This means including author information; the year of publication, the date, or the edition; a volume number or page number; and even where a quotation begins and ends on a page. Assure them that although they may not use all of this information in a Works Cited list, they may need it to retrace their steps and confirm the accuracy of their sources. Suggest that they also check their note cards before they "put away" a source, to make sure they have all the information they need.

Summarize the Steps Make sure students understand that they should
1. Keep detailed notes of their research.
2. Organize their notes by topic.
3. Write an outline from their organized set of notes.

Point out that students can annotate their outlines with reference to sources they plan to use.

2. DRAFT

Organizing Your Information

Organize Sources Keep track of your research and sources using note cards. Use a different note card for each source you use. Write the source information on the card. In the upper right or left corner, number each card. This will help you keep track of which information came from which sources, and it will help you later in writing your Works Cited list.

Take Notes As you research your sources and take notes, write the main idea or guiding question at the top of each note card. Then quote the supporting detail exactly (using quotation marks) or paraphrase it in your own words, listing the page number or numbers where you found it. Write the number on the upper corner of the card that corresponds to the number on the source card. Use a new card for each new piece of information.

1

Jim R. Eddy, Ancient Egypt, Thomson Gale, Farmington Hills, 2005.

1

What is the purpose of religion?

Eddy, Ancient Egypt

p. 26 "Religious duties and responsibilities were at the heart of the Egyptian life and civilization. Each community and region in Egypt had its own god or set of gods."

Putting Your Thoughts on Paper

Before you begin writing, sort your note cards by main idea. Consider the best order for presenting your ideas. You might choose **chronological order, cause-and-effect order,** or **comparison-and-contrast order,** to name a few. Make sure the order you choose makes sense for the ideas you are presenting. Use transitions that make your organization clear to your audience and your ideas easy to follow.

Create an outline to organize your main ideas and research into manageable chunks. Make sure to include your introduction, body, and main ideas. Make sure each body paragraph has a main idea and support. For more complex ideas, you may need several body paragraphs. Nonetheless, make sure each paragraph has a main idea and support. The main ideas and details in your outline will become your topic sentences and supporting sentences in your draft.

From your outline, you can begin writing your report. Use your notes and outline to write a first draft. Concentrate on content and organization.

The Ancient Egyptians and Their Gods

I. Introduction: Religion was a part of everyday life for the ancient Egyptians.

II. The Beginnings
   A. Where Egypt is located
   B. Records of ancient life

III. Land of the Gods
   A. Major gods and goddesses
      1. Ra
      2. Osiris and Isis
   B. Minor gods
      1. Bes
      2. Tawaret

IV. Life on Earth
   A. Pharaohs
   B. The Nile River

V. Conclusion: Ancient Egyptians lived their religion every day.

Differentiated Instruction

Kinesthetic Learning

Offer kinesthetic learners the chance to arrange their material on part of the board or on a large sheet of paper. The paper can hang on the wall or lie on a tabletop. Invite students to use this space to organize their notes into categories, to experiment with putting their notes in different sequences, and to map their reports using time lines, cluster charts, and other organizers. When students are satisfied with how they have laid out their notes, encourage them to draw or otherwise record their work before erasing it or taking it down.

3. REVISE

Evaluating Your Draft

Once your draft is complete, review what you have written for strengths and weaknesses. Correct errors as best you can, revising the organization or adding details. Then conduct a **peer review.** Exchange papers with a classmate and have him or her review your draft and discuss ways to improve it. Use the Revising Checklist as a guide.

Below is part of a research report on ancient Egypt. The annotations to the right indicate the reasons for the changes marked in the draft.

Revising Checklist

☐ Does the introduction clearly state the purpose and thesis of the report?

☐ Is there a clear organizational pattern?

☐ Is the thesis supported with information from multiple sources?

☐ Are sources clearly cited?

Egypt has one of the oldest civilizations in the world. The ancient Egyptians believed in many gods and goddesses. *While we may worship on Fridays, Saturdays, or Sundays in accordance with our religious beliefs, for the ancient Egyptians, religion was a part of their everyday lives.*

> Add a thesis statement to give the paper a purpose.

Beginnings

Ancient Egypt rose out of the desert along the Nile River. While other tribal groups were still in the hunter-gatherer stage of existence, the ancient Egyptians found no need to move about or follow prey in order to survive. The Nile River gave them everything they needed (*Eddy 7*). Yet, as with most ancient cultures, the ways of the world were a mystery to the ancient Egyptians. Why did the sun rise and set? Why were there sandstorms? Made the river flood? Who made them? *Ancient Egyptians contemplated and tried to explain these and other questions about their existence.*

> Cite the source for paraphrased information.

> Add a sentence to explain how information relates to the thesis.

Revise

Evaluating a Draft Remind students to check for a clear organization and good transitions as they review their own work. When they have done as much as they can in the available time, suggest that they conduct a peer review. Be sure they understand the rubric.

Allow ample time for reviewers to read the report they receive. Schedule peer review exchanges when each student will have several minutes to deliver his or her review, and when each writer will have time to thoughtfully absorb the comments and ask questions for clarification.

Citation Styles Instruct students to use the citation style you prefer. The one in the model gives an author and page number. If you wish, teach students how to use footnotes.

What Great Researchers Do

Assure students that they may make major changes as they revise. They can reorganize their material and pause to conduct further research. Tell them that Albert Einstein said:

If we knew what it was we were doing, it would not be called research, would it?

Writing Skills

Avoid Plagiarism

Remind students to avoid plagiarism, using another person's words as if they are one's own. Point out that plagiarism is not always intentional. A writer can forget where he or she heard something and can unintentionally repeat a source's exact words.

The revising step is an excellent place to check for potential plagiarism. Counsel peer reviewers to be alert to it. As they read, they should question sentences that sound as if they were written by someone other than the author of the report. Tell students that it is better to cite too many sources than too few. They can always combine citations or omit unnecessary supporting details at the editing stage.

Edit and Proofread
Students may want to use proofreader's marks when correcting their work. Refer them to page 895 of the Language Arts Handbook, Writing Section 4.1, Proofreader's Symbols.

Editing
Remind students of the goal of editing their reports: to ensure clarity and to ensure accuracy. This means that they can remove unnecessary information, add missing information, and reorganize.

Publish and Present
Before students begin their final version, they might benefit from reading the Language Arts Handbook, Writing Section 4.1, Writing Follow-up.

4. EDIT AND PROOFREAD

Focus: Paraphrasing and Summarizing
As you gather research, you will need to quote, paraphrase, or summarize the information from other sources in your report. Whether you quote the material directly or restate the ideas in your own words, give credit to the original source.

Direct Quotation: Quote the author's exact words when the phrasing is particularly effective.

Paraphrase: To paraphrase is to restate someone else's ideas. A paraphrase can include both main ideas and supporting details. Most of your research will be paraphrased.

Summarize: To summarize, you only state someone else's main ideas in your own words. You may wish to summarize a complicated idea to provide your readers with basic information.

Look at the example below to see how a student paraphrased ideas about hieroglyphics.

> The ancient scribes wrote in a picture style called hieroglyphics. Without a code, this writing was almost impossible to understand. It wasn't until 1822 when a Frenchman named Jean Champollion broke the code and the history of the ancient Egyptian people was revealed (Caselli 4).

Note how a citation immediately follows the paraphrased material and precedes the end punctuation. Full source information is listed in a Works Cited list at the end of the report.

Focus: Conjunctions
Your sentences should flow smoothly in your paragraphs. Use conjunctions to combine sentences to make your writing smoother. Review the three kinds of conjunctions.

Coordinating conjunctions are *and, but, or, nor, so, for,* and *yet.* Use them to combine subjects, predicates, and simple sentences of *equal* importance.

Correlative conjunctions are words used in pairs to join parts of a sentence. *Both/and, either/or, neither/nor,* and *not only/but also* are common correlative conjunctions. Both parts of the sentence must be of *equal* importance and structure.

Subordinating conjunctions introduce dependent clauses in sentences. These clauses cannot stand alone. That is, they do not make a complete thought by themselves. Subordinating conjunctions connect them to independent clauses.

> **While** the ancient Egyptians had major gods, they also had minor or local gods.

Proofreading
Quality Control The purpose of proofreading is to find errors you have made in the mechanics and grammar of your paper. You can find and fix these errors as you evaluate and revise your report. You should also look for them specifically at the proofreading stage. Use proofreader's marks to highlight any errors. (See the Language Arts Handbook, section 4.1, for a list of proofreader's symbols.)

5. PUBLISH AND PRESENT

Final Draft
Now that you have edited and proofread your report, rewrite it to make a final draft for presentation. If you are using a word processing program, double-space your paper and use a readable typeface or font. Be sure to check any guidelines for presenting the final paper. Make sure any quoted, paraphrased, or summarized information is properly cited.

Differentiated Instruction

English Language Learning
Have English learners show you their editing and proofreading to see how well they have absorbed spelling and grammar lessons you have given. Evaluate how their vocabularies have grown or changed as a result of recent reading. Take time to correct and discuss any consistent problems in these areas before students prepare final drafts of their reports.

Reading Proficiency
To help students understand the lesson, tell them what the assignment will be and show them the student model. Point out that the lesson is organized into five steps. Then have students read and summarize the instructions for each step before they begin the assignment.

Student Model

The Ancient Egyptians and Their Gods
by Randy Scott

Egypt has one of the oldest civilizations in the world. The ancient Egyptians believed in many gods and goddesses. While we may worship on Fridays, Saturdays, or Sundays in accordance with our beliefs, for the ancient Egyptians, religion was a part of their everyday lives.

> *States topic and purpose clearly in the introduction*

Beginnings

Ancient Egypt rose out of the desert along the Nile River. While other tribal groups were still in the hunter-gatherer stage of existence, the ancient Egyptians found no need to move about or follow prey in order to survive. The Nile River gave them everything they needed (Eddy 7). Yet, as with most ancient cultures, the ways of the world were a mystery to the ancient Egyptians. Why did the sun rise and set? Why were there sandstorms? Who made the river flood? Who made them? Ancient Egyptians contemplated and tried to explain these and other questions about their existence.

> *Includes titles to serve as transitions for each section and point out the main ideas*

Once the Egyptians figured out a system of writing, they began to keep records of their legends, myths, and beliefs about life. The ancient scribes wrote in a picture style called hieroglyphics. Without a code, this writing was almost impossible to understand. It wasn't until 1822 when a Frenchman named Jean Champollion broke the code and the history of the ancient Egyptian people was revealed (Caselli 4).

> *Paraphrases information from sources and includes proper citation*

Land of the Gods

The ancient Egyptians believed in many gods. Some were personal house gods, but there were also major gods that everyone knew about. Some of these principal gods included Ra, the sun god who became the most important god. He was also known as Atum (Ra-Atum) and Amun (Amun-Ra), the creator god. Ra was the father of Shu, the air, and Tefnut, the moon goddess and wife of Shu. To the ancient Egyptians, intermarriage between gods and goddesses was acceptable. For example, Shu and Tefnut had two children, Nut, the sky goddess, and Geb, the Earth. It was Shu's job to keep Nut and Geb apart, but Nut and Geb loved each other and together had four children, Osiris, Isis, Seth (or Set), and Nephthys. Isis and Osiris had a son, Horus.

The gods of the ancient Egyptians had specific forms that signified their roles in Egyptian society. Usually the gods were shown with the head or body of an animal to represent their power, such as a falcon,

Using Section Titles

Point out the title of the student model on page 811 (The Ancient Egyptians and Their Gods). Then have a volunteer read aloud the three section titles, or headings, in the student model (Beginnings, Land of the Gods, and Life on Earth). Ask: "Based on the title, what can you infer from each of these section titles about the material that follows?" After several students have responded, ask: "How do you think the writer chose these section titles?"

Challenge students to use their outlines to draft several section titles for their research reports. Note that a good section title gives clues about what will follow. (You may wish to say that "Beginnings" in the student model is least effective in this regard.) Have students write down their report titles and section titles on a note card. Invite students to exchange note cards, and then try to determine what each research paper is about based on the information on the card.

What Great Writers Do

Zora Neal Hurston wrote,

Research is formalized curiosity. It is poking and prying with a purpose.

Student Model CONTINUED

hawk, or ibis head, the body of a lion or a hippopotamus, or even the head of a crocodile. Anything the image of a god carried or wore was a part of that god's power.

> *States the main idea in a topic sentence followed by supporting sentences*

For the ancient Egyptians, the gods did not live in far-off places and look down upon them. Their gods were a part of their everyday existence. In some stories, Ra was the first pharaoh. In these ancient tales, he took the form of a man and ruled over the land of Egypt. In other stories, Ra's grandson Osiris was the true first pharaoh. It was he who taught the ancient Egyptians how to farm and cultivate their fields. He later became ruler of heaven and the underworld (McCall 16). Isis, Osiris's sister and wife, was the most powerful goddess. When Osiris was killed through the treachery of his brother Seth, Isis made sure that her son Horus—and not the evil Seth—would become the next pharaoh after Osiris (Ardagh 19).

While the ancient Egyptians had major gods, they also had minor or local gods. One of these was Bes, protector of the home and god of family life. He was also the god of children, pleasure, music, and dance (Broyles 27). Tawaret was a god who protected women in childbirth. Ancient Egyptians usually kept shrines in their homes to honor these minor gods and seek their blessings.

Ancient Egyptians were deeply concerned about the afterlife. They created elaborate tales of what happened to a body and its spirit after a person died. If you go to modern Egypt today, you can see monuments to their strong beliefs in the afterlife. Pyramids, tombs, and temples all concern the transition between life on earth and life after death. A person's life was judged once he or she left earth and traveled to the underworld. The Egyptians learned the art of mummification and removed the important organs, such as the heart and liver, from the body before burial. These organs were put into jars, and the judge of the underworld, the god Anubis, would weigh a person's heart against a feather on the scales on Ma'at, the god of balance and order. This idea reflects the ancient Egyptian belief in the sense of balance. The ancient Egyptians believed a person needed to live a good life on earth in order to enjoy a pleasant afterlife.

Life on Earth

The central figure in the everyday life of ancient Egyptians was the pharaoh. For the everyday Egyptian, the pharaoh symbolized god on earth. In fact, he was regarded as a god, and to the people of Egypt, he became Horus, their greatest pharaoh. It was through him that the land

TEACHING NOTE

Ask the Author

After students have read the model, have them gather in groups of three or four. Ask each group to generate five questions they would like to ask the model author, either about the content of the report or about the process he used to write it. Model some possible questions: "What kind of power could a hippopotamus represent?" and

"How did the writer decide which details to leave out?"

Have groups write their questions on a sheet of paper. Collect the sheets and read the questions aloud one by one. For each question, have students suggest either an answer or a source they could consult to find an answer.

would be rewarded with the ability to sustain itself, and that ability came from the inundation, or flooding, of the Nile River (Watson 7).

Egypt is surrounded by desert. Rain rarely falls there, and the life of ancient Egyptians depended on the flooding from the Nile River. When it flooded, rich soil would wash up on the shores, allowing the people to plant crops and sustain themselves. The flooding had to be just right, though. Too much water and the crops could not be planted at the right time of year. Too little flooding and the people would have a poor yield or no crops at all. The main job of the pharaoh was to make sure the flooding happened on time and just right. He had to please the gods to make sure his people did not starve in times of need.

Unlike many modern people, the Egyptians lived their religion every day through their devotion to their gods and goddesses. Their daily lives depended on the life-giving waters of the Nile River and the power of the pharaoh. To the ancient Egyptian, life and death were closely linked, and what one did on the earth mattered greatly once one left it.

Sums up main ideas and restates thesis in the conclusion

Works Cited

Ardagh, Philip. *Ancient Egyptian Myths and Legends.* Chicago: World Book, Vol. 2, 2002. Print.

Broyles, Janell. *Egyptian Mythology.* New York: The Rosen Publishing Group, 2006. Print.

Caselli, Morley. *Egyptian Myths.* Lincolnwood: Peter Bedrick Books, 1999. Print.

Eddy, Jim R. *Ancient Egypt.* Farmington Hills: Thomson Gale, 2005. Print.

McCall, Henrietta. *Gods and Goddesses in the Daily Life of Ancient Egyptians.* Columbus: McGraw-Hill Children's Publishing, 2002. Print.

Watson, John. "An Overview of the Ancient Egyptian Religion." Web. 13 June 2009. <http://www.touregypt.net/featurestories/religion.htm>.

Includes Works Cited with sources in alphabetical order and in correct form

Concluding the Report

Have students compare the concluding paragraph to the introductory paragraph on page 811. Have them identify the restated thesis ("Egyptians lived their religion every day"). Then ask them to connect other statements in the conclusion to the main ideas of sections or paragraphs in the body of the report.

Works Cited

Tell students that the terms *bibliography* and *works cited* are often used interchangeably. Note that different teachers and different schools prefer different styles for citing sources. Encourage students to always ask for instructions about citing sources before they begin gathering data for a research report. That way, they can be sure to record all the necessary information as they take notes from their sources.

Research Skills

Multiple Sources

Direct students to the Writing Rubric on page 806. Point out that the third item includes the phrase "information from multiple sources." Ask: "What would be some advantages of writing a report based on five or six primary and secondary sources rather than on a single encyclopedia article?" Draw out the response that multiple sources allow a writer to learn more about a topic and avoid conveying the bias that a single source might have.

Have students review the Works Cited list on page 813. Ask them to describe the sources this writer used, based on information in the citations.

Teach the Workshop

Objectives

Participating in this lesson will help students deliver research presentations that

- have strong introductions and conclusions
- follow clear organization
- cover material in depth
- support ideas with evidence
- incorporate photographs or objects
- demonstrate appropriate volume, pacing, eye contact, and nonverbal expression

Launch the Lesson

Ask the class to describe a recent display of research in the school, such as a science fair, an informational bulletin board, or results of school elections. Then ask: "What makes for a good research presentation?"

Students will probably respond by describing informational displays. Encourage them to observe what makes such displays clear and interesting. Then tell them they will be able to incorporate these qualities in spoken research presentations.

Program Resources

To expand upon this workshop lesson, Giving and Actively Listening to Research Presentations, see the *Exceeding the Standards: Speaking & Listening* resource.

▶ More more information, see the Language Arts Handbook Section 7, Speaking & Listening.

Giving and Actively Listening to Research Presentations

Throughout your academic career, you will be asked to give presentations that require research. This research may be done at the library, online, or through interviews. In a **research presentation,** you orally present information you have gathered about a specific topic. When you give and actively listen to a research presentation, you share the information you learned with others.

Planning a Research Presentation

Prepare Your Topic When selecting a topic on which to present, consider the kinds of sources that will be available to you. Ask yourself: Is this topic too narrow? Too broad? Will I be able to find an adequate number of reliable sources to support my claims? However, you may be using a research paper as the basis of your presentation. If this is the case, you should not simply give a reading of your paper. Look it over and decide which points you want to stress in your presentation.

Select Key Points If you are using a written report, make a summary of what you want to say. Review the outline you made or notes you took during the prewriting stage of your paper. If you are beginning from scratch, use several different sources. Incorporate paraphrased information and direct quotations from these sources. Be sure to cite sources as you present.

Make note cards on which you list all of the key points you want to make during your presentation. Use these note cards as a guide. For example, the following is a set of partial notes that one student made. Notice that the student indicates where to present visual aids.

> **Facts on Frogs**
>
> Introduction
> - Found on every continent except Antarctica
> - At least 3,900 species of frogs in the world
> - Frogs and toads closely related
>
> Life Cycle (diagram A)
> - begins life as fertilized egg
> - tadpole
> - tadpole with legs
> - froglet
> - frog

Words in Use

Teaching Words
academic, 828
incorporate, 828
constructive, 829
rubrics, 829
considerate, 829
courteous, 829

KEY TERMS

Common Core State Standards

Speaking and Listening
SL.4, SL.5, SL.6

Identify Your Audience Even though your audience may know something about your topic, it is unlikely that they have done as much research as you. Consider the different ways you can expand on what they already know. Also, make sure that your topic is appropriate and the information you present is clear and reliable. Be prepared to answer questions about your topic.

Organize Your Speech Remember, you are giving an oral presentation of your research. You are not reading word for word from a research paper you have written. Organize your notes in a way that fits your research and is comfortable for you. If you are describing a series of events, chronological order will suit your presentation best. If you are giving facts, organize your presentation point by point. You may also want to consider cause-and-effect order, problem-and-solution order, or comparison-and-contrast order. Find an order that best suits the materials you are presenting.

Evaluating Your Research Presentation

Work with a partner or small group to evaluate your research presentations. Offer constructive feedback on the subject, organization, and delivery of the material. Remember to be helpful and respectful in your criticism and praise. Follow the speaking and listening rubrics on this page to evaluate each research presentation.

Delivering Your Research Presentation

Prior to your presentation, organize any pictures, objects, or other visual media you want to include. Make sure you have marked in your notes when to show these pictures or objects. Remember to maintain eye contact with your audience. Refer to your notes, but don't read them word for word. Avoid unnecessary movements if they are not part of what you are trying to say. Speak loudly and clearly enough to be heard and understood.

Active Listening When listening to a research presentation, be a considerate and courteous audience member. Give the speaker your undivided attention. Remain quiet and respectful, and ask questions at the appropriate time.

Speaking Rubric

Your presentation will be evaluated on these elements:

Contents
- [ ] clear organization of material
- [ ] strong introduction and conclusion
- [ ] in-depth presentation of material
- [ ] ideas supported with evidence

Delivery and Presentation
- [ ] appropriate volume and pacing
- [ ] appropriate use of photographs or objects
- [ ] good eye contact with audience
- [ ] effective use of nonverbal expression

Listening Rubric

As a peer reviewer or audience member, you should do the following:

- [ ] listen quietly and attentively
- [ ] maintain eye contact with speaker
- [ ] ask appropriate questions
- [ ] (as peer reviewer) provide constructive feedback

Teach the Workshop

Relate to an Audience
Most students will be making their presentations to classmates or other peers in a school setting. Invite students to think specifically about experiences they have shared with the audience they will address. Point out that they can use shared experiences to make connections with an audience and hold its attention. Model one possibility: "We have all read Al Gore's article called 'Ships in the Desert,' so I can assume the audience knows people change the environment. I can add a quote or two from that article when I talk about irrigation."

Peer Reviews
Give students opportunities to practice their research presentations alone and with peer reviewers. Suggest that before they give feedback, peer reviewers write down one new thing they learned from a presentation. They can incorporate this item into their positive comments.

TEACHING NOTE
Visual Aids
The rubric calls for "appropriate use of photographs or objects." Give students some guidance on appropriate visuals such as:
- Photographs or paintings of the subject.
- Maps or representations of people and places.
- Graphics with appropriate, dramatic data.

During peer reviews, have students describe to each other two visuals that could accompany their presentations.

Differentiated Instruction

Reading Proficiency
Have students review research reports they have written during the school year. Ask each student to choose a written report and develop it into an oral presentation. Tell students that the goal is to select points to emphasize. Give students time to read their reports and highlight information they want to convey. They may then create an outline and/or note cards from which to speak.

Assess students' ability to recognize main ideas and supporting details in their written reports. On an individual basis, help students summarize and paraphrase information. You might also ask students to show how they determine the relative importance of details. Give remedial instruction to students struggling with the skills.

Teach the Workshop

Objectives

Completing this lesson will enable students to

- write a research report based on a timed writing prompt
- answer standardized test questions that demonstrate revising and editing skills
- answer standardized questions that demonstrate the ability to make inferences from a reading

Timed Writing

Remind students that standardized tests often require writing a response to a prompt in a specified period of time. Give the following tips:

- Read the entire prompt carefully.
- Look for key words in the prompt that tell you what is expected.
- Underline these words or write them on your own notepaper.
- Use the key words to make sure you follow all the instructions.
- Organize. Allow time for planning, writing, and reviewing.
- Before you begin writing, create a rough outline of points to make.
- Write a clear introduction. This will help keep you on track as you write each paragraph.
- If you find yourself running out of time, state your remaining points and add a conclusion.
- Review your completed essay to see if you have responded completely to the instructions.
- Proofread before you turn in your completed essay.

Writing Skills

Research Report

Carefully read the following writing prompt. Before you begin writing, think carefully about what task the assignment is asking you to perform. Then create an outline to help guide your writing.

> In this unit, you have read several myths about Greek gods, such as Persephone, Demeter, and Apollo. In many cultures, gods are wise beings. However, many of the gods in Greek myths show human failings such as foolishness and envy. How do the gods that you have read about demonstrate human failings?

Write a research report in which you examine the personalities of gods from the myths in this unit. Discuss the qualities present in their personalities and the ways these characters are like or unlike humans. Gather your information from at least three myths. In your essay, use both paraphrases and direct quotations. As you write, be sure to:

- Organize your report in a logical and consistent way
- Include introductory and concluding paragraphs
- Introduce your main idea in the first paragraph
- Support your main idea in each body paragraph

Rubric for a Research Report

Make sure students understand that they should use the myths in this textbook as the sources for their research. Give students these criteria to evaluate their reports.

- ☐ Does the first paragraph introduce the report and state the main idea?
- ☐ Does each body paragraph support the main idea?
- ☐ Is the report organized logically and consistently?
- ☐ Does the report have a concluding paragraph?

Common Core State Standards

Reading Informational
RI.2, RI.6

Writing
W.1, W.3, W.6

Revising and Editing Skills

In the following excerpt from the first draft of a student's paper, words and phrases are underlined and numbered. Alternatives to the underlined words and phrases appear in the right-hand column. Choose the one that *best* corrects any grammatical or style errors in the original. If you think that the original is error-free, choose "NO CHANGE."

Some questions might also focus on a section of the passage or the entire passage. These do not refer to a specific underlined phrase or word and are identified by a number in a box. Record your answers on a separate sheet of paper.

Greek myths evolved over many centuries, culture influenced their development. $\boxed{1}$ The gods, goddesses, and heroes that populate these myths also mirror cultural beliefs. <u>Having great authority, the people saw them as all-powerful.</u>
<u>2</u>
The most important <u>figures in early Greek myths</u>
<u>3</u>
<u>was</u> very powerful males, such as Uranos and Kronos. The best-known leader of the <u>Greek gods</u>
<u>was Zeus, who threw</u> thunderbolts across the sky
<u>4</u>
to demonstrate his power. Although goddesses with some godlike powers <u>also lived on Mount</u>
<u>Olympus they</u> often got the better of their male
<u>5</u>
counterparts through guile or deceit. $\boxed{6}$

1. Which of the following errors appears in the first sentence?
   A. run-on sentence
   B. misplaced modifier
   C. dangling modifier
   D. lack of subject-verb agreement

2. A. NO CHANGE
   B. Because the gods had great authority, the people saw them as all powerful.
   C. People, having great authority, were all-powerful.
   D. Having great authority; the people saw them as all-powerful.

3. A. NO CHANGE
   B. figures in early Greek myths were
   C. figure in early Greek myths was
   D. figure in early Greek myths were

4. A. NO CHANGE
   B. Greek gods were Zeus, who threw
   C. Greek gods was Zeus, who throws
   D. Greek gods was Zeus who threw

5. A. NO CHANGE
   B. also lived on Mount Olympus; they
   C. also lived on Mount Olympus—they
   D. also lived on Mount Olympus, they

6. The last sentence in this passage is:
   A. a simple sentence.
   B. a compound sentence.
   C. a complex sentence.
   D. a compound-complex sentence.

Revising and Editing Skills

1. A	**4.** A
2. B	**5.** D
3. B	**6.** C

TEACHING NOTE

Activate Prior Knowledge
Tell students that when they take a revising and editing test, it is a good idea to refresh their memories about the skills they will have to use. One way is to study the passage before they preview the questions about it. Use this test as an example. Ask students to read the paragraph, and then decide whether they think the sentences are clear. Give students time to edit the sentences to improve word order and punctuation. Then have students answer the test questions. Afterward, ask them whether activating prior knowledge helped them feel more confident when they took the test.

> For more information, see the Language Arts Handbook Section 8, Test-Taking Skills.

Program Resources

For more study and practice with test-taking skills, see the *Exceeding the Standards: Test Practice* resource:
• SAT Practice Test, pp. 20–23

Words in Use

Teaching Words
authority, 831
counterparts, 831
guile, 831
deceit, 831
paraphrase, 832
generous, 833
mischievous, 833
arrogant, 833

KEY TERMS

Remind students that reading comprehension tests give a short piece of writing and then ask several questions about it. The questions often ask students to interpret the passage. Urge students to keep the following tips in mind:

- Begin by skimming all the questions.
- Read the passage with the questions in mind. If time permits, read the passage twice before answering any questions.
- Reread the first question carefully.
- Locate the portion of the passage to which the question refers. Read it slowly and carefully.
- Answer the first question.
- Repeat this process to answer all the rest of the questions.

Reading Skills

Carefully read the following passage. Then, on a separate piece of paper, answer each question.

from "Why the Owl Has Big Eyes"

Raweno, the Everything-Maker, was busy creating various animals. He was working on Rabbit, and Rabbit was saying: "I want nice long legs and long ears like a deer, and sharp fangs and claws like a panther."

"I do them up the way they want to be; I give them what they ask for," said
5   Raweno. He was working on Rabbit's hind legs, making them long, the way Rabbit had ordered.

Owl, still unformed, was sitting on a tree nearby and waiting his turn. He was saying: "Whoo, whoo, I want a nice long neck like Swan's, and beautiful red feathers like Cardinal's, and a nice long beak like Egret's, and a nice crown of plumes like
10   Heron's. I want you to make me into the most beautiful, the fastest, the most wonderful of all birds."

Raweno said: "Be quiet. Turn around and look in another direction. Even better, close your eyes. Don't you know that no one is allowed to watch me work?" Raweno was just then making Rabbit's ears very long, the way Rabbit wanted them.

15   Owl refused to do what Raweno said. "Whoo, whoo," he replied, "Nobody can forbid me to watch. Nobody can order me to close my eyes. I like watching you, and watch I will."

Then Raweno became angry. He grabbed Owl, pulling him down from his branch, stuffing his head deep into his body, shaking him until his eyes grew big with fright,
20   pulling at his ears until they were sticking up at both sides of his head.

"There," said Raweno, "that'll teach you. Now you won't be able to crane your neck to watch things you shouldn't watch. Now you have big ears to listen when someone tells you what not to do. Now you have big eyes—but not so big that you can watch me, because you'll be awake only at night, and I work by day. And your
25   feathers won't be red like cardinal's but gray like this"—and Raweno rubbed Owl all over with mud—"as punishment for your disobedience." So Owl flew off, pouting: "Whoo, whoo, whoo."

Then Raweno turned back to finish Rabbit, but Rabbit had been so terrified by Raweno's anger, even though it was not directed at him, that he ran off half done. As a
30   consequence, only Rabbit's hind legs are long, and he has to hop about instead of walking and running. Also, because he took fright then, Rabbit has remained afraid of most everything....

Differentiated Instruction

Enrichment

Tell students who like this story that it comes from a Native American culture, that of the Iroquois. Encourage them to use library and Internet resources to find out more about Raweno and the culture Raweno represents.

English Language Learning

Pair English learners with native speakers to read this story together. Ask native speakers to help their partners get the point of the story and identify the main character traits of Raweno, Rabbit, and Owl. Ask English learners to write down words they would like to look up in a dictionary.

1. In line 3, what is the rabbit's most likely motivation for asking for sharp fangs and claws like a panther?
   A. It wanted to be able to defend itself.
   B. It wanted to attack humans.
   C. It wanted to attack the owl.
   D. It wanted to fight a panther.

2. What does the quotation that begins in line 4 suggest about Raweno's character?
   A. He is cruel.
   B. He is unpredictable.
   C. He is generous.
   D. He is mischievous.

3. Lines 12–17 contribute mainly to which literary element?
   A. setting
   B. conflict
   C. simile
   D. theme

4. Based on the context, the word *crane* in line 21 is used as a:
   A. noun.
   B. adjective.
   C. verb.
   D. adverb.

5. Which word *best* describes Owl's character?
   A. curious
   B. wise
   C. arrogant
   D. grateful

6. Which of the following *best* describes the theme of this story?
   A. It is best to avoid discussion.
   B. Do not be arrogant.
   C. Owls are curious animals.
   D. Rabbits are afraid of everything.

7. This story is told from which of the following points of view?
   A. first-person
   B. second-person
   C. third-person limited
   D. third-person omniscient

8. Based on the story, why is Rabbit frightened of everything?
   A. He is ashamed of the way he looks.
   B. He is smaller than all the other animals.
   C. He thinks Owl might still be around.
   D. He does not have claws and fangs.

9. Which of the following *best* describes the genre of this story?
   A. drama
   B. myth
   C. fable
   D. epic poem

10. Which of the following *best* describes the character Raweno?
    A. He is a god.
    B. He is a trickster.
    C. He is a symbol.
    D. He is an allegory.

Teach the Workshop

Reading Skills
1. A
2. C
3. B
4. C
5. C
6. B
7. D
8. C
9. B
10. A

Students may offer different answers for Question 9. Make sure their responses agree with the definitions you have taught for myth, fable, and allegory.

Test-Taking Skills

Choose the Best Answer
Tell students that a key skill in answering multiple-choice questions is deciding which is the *best* answer available. Note that many times, they will be able to think of good answers to a question. However, not all of those answers will be offered as choices. Model this skill using a question from the sample.

Question 8. The question asks for the reason Rabbit is frightened of everything. The last paragraph suggests that Rabbit stayed frightened because he never went back to get fangs and claws from Raweno. Based on this, either answer C or answer D could be correct. I'm going to pick C, because Rabbit was terrified by Raweno's anger. I think that's the best answer.

Language Arts Handbook

1 Reading Strategies & Skills

1.1 The Reading Process

The reading process begins before you actually start to read. All readers use a reading process, even if they don't think about it. By becoming aware of this process, you can become a more effective reader. The reading process can be broken down into three stages: before reading, during reading, and after reading.

> Refer to the following pages for unit Reading Models:
> Fiction Reading Model, p. 8
> Nonfiction Reading Model, p. 256
> Poetry Reading Model, p. 465
> Drama Reading Model, p. 610
> Folk Literature Reading Model, p. 726

BEFORE READING

BUILD BACKGROUND

- Think about the **context** you as a reader bring to the selection based on your knowledge and experiences. What do you know about the topic? What do you want to know?

SET PURPOSE

- **Preview** the text to set a purpose for reading. Skim the first few paragraphs and glance through the selection to figure out what it's about and who the main characters are. What can you learn from the art or photos?

USE READING SKILLS

- Apply **reading skills** such as determining the author's purpose, analyzing text structure, and previewing new vocabulary.

DURING READING

USE READING STRATEGIES

- **Ask questions** about things that seem unusual or interesting, like why a character might have behaved in an unexpected way.
- **Visualize** by forming pictures in your mind to help you see the characters or actions.
- **Make predictions** about what's going to happen next. As you read, gather more clues that will either confirm or change your predictions.
- **Make inferences,** or educated guesses, about what is not stated directly. Things may be implied or hinted at, or they may be left out altogether.

- **Clarify** your understanding of what you read by rereading any difficult parts.

ANALYZE LITERATURE

- Determine what **literary elements** stand out as you read the selection. Ask whether the characters are engaging and lifelike. Determine if there is a strong central conflict or theme.

MAKE CONNECTIONS

- Notice where there are **connections** between the story and your life or the world beyond the story. Be aware of feelings or thoughts you have while reading the story.

AFTER READING

REFER TO TEXT

- Think about the facts. **Remember details** like characters' names, locations or settings, and any other things that you can recall.
- Determine the **sequence of events** or the order in which things happened.
- **Reread** the story to pick up any details you may have missed the first time around.
- Try to **summarize** the story in a sentence or two based on the events.

REASON WITH TEXT

- **Analyze** the text by breaking down information into smaller pieces and figuring out how those pieces fit into the story as a whole. Your knowledge of literary tools can help you analyze the author's technique.
- **Evaluate** the text. **Synthesize** and **draw conclusions** by bringing together what you have read and using it to make a decision or form an opinion. Decide if you agree with the author's views.

Framework for Reading

BEFORE READING

ASK YOURSELF

- ❏ What's my purpose for reading this?
- ❏ What is this going to be about?
- ❏ How is this information organized?
- ❏ What do I already know about the topic?
- ❏ How can I apply this information to my life?

DURING READING

ASK YOURSELF

- ❏ What is the best way to accomplish my purpose for reading?
- ❏ What do I want or need to find out while I'm reading?
- ❏ What is the essential information presented here?
- ❏ What is the importance of what I am reading?
- ❏ Do I understand what I just read?
- ❏ What can I do to make the meaning more clear?

AFTER READING

ASK YOURSELF

- ❏ What did I learn from what I have read?
- ❏ What is still confusing?
- ❏ What do I need to remember from my reading?
- ❏ What effect did this text have on me?
- ❏ What else do I want to know about this topic?

1.2 Using Reading Strategies

Reading actively means thinking about what you are reading as you read it. A **reading strategy,** or plan, helps you read actively and get more from your reading. The following strategies can be applied at each stage of the reading process: before, during, and after reading.

Reading Strategies
- Build Background
- Set Purpose
- Ask Questions
- Visualize
- Make Predictions
- Make Inferences
- Clarify
- Make Connections

BUILD BACKGROUND

Each reader brings his or her own context to a selection based on prior knowledge and experiences. What do you know about the topic? What do you want to know? Before and during reading, think about what you already know about the topic or subject matter. By connecting to your prior knowledge, you will increase your interest in and understanding of what you read. Fill in the first two columns of a K-W-L Chart before you read. Fill in the last column after you finish reading.

K-W-L Chart

What I _Know_	What I _Want_ to Learn	What I Have _Learned_
Queen Elizabeth I was the queen of England a long time ago and never married.	Why didn't she marry?	Elizabeth I was the daughter of King Henry VIII who had six wives. Her father had her mother beheaded.

SET PURPOSE

Before you begin reading, think about your reason for reading the material. You might be reading from a textbook to complete a homework assignment, skimming a magazine for information about one of your hobbies, or reading a novel for your own enjoyment. Know why you are reading and what information you seek. Decide on your purpose for reading as clearly as you can. Be aware that the purpose of your reading may change as you read.

Preview the text to set a purpose for reading. Skim the first few paragraphs and glance through the selection to figure out what it's about and who the main characters are. What can you learn from the art or photos? Fill in a Reader's Purpose Chart at each stage of reading to set a purpose for reading and to help you attain it.

Reader's Purpose Chart

Before Reading
Set a purpose for reading
I want to read "Seventh Grade" because it could be a story about people my age and I could see if they are like me.

During Reading
Take notes on what you learn

After Reading
Reflect on your purpose and what you learned

ASK QUESTIONS

Think and reflect by asking questions to further your understanding of what you are reading. Asking questions helps you to pinpoint parts of the text that are confusing. You can ask questions in your head, or you may write them down. Ask questions about things that seem unusual or interesting, like why a character might have behaved in an unexpected way. What do you wonder about as you read the text? Use a Generate Questions Bookmark like the following to record your questions as you read.

Generate Questions Bookmark

Page #	What I Wonder About
214	How does Victor think he's going to make Teresa be his girl?

VISUALIZE

Reading is more than simply sounding out words. It is an active process that requires you to use your imagination. When you visualize, you form a picture or an image in your mind of the action and descriptions in a text. Each reader's images will be different based on his or her prior knowledge and experiences. Keep in mind that there are no "right" or "wrong" visualizations. Visualize by forming pictures in your mind to help you see the characters or actions. Use a Visualization Map to draw pictures that represent key events in a selection. Write a caption under each box that explains each event. Draw the events in the order they occur.

Visualization Map

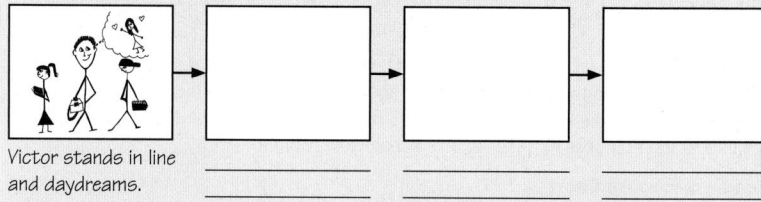

Victor stands in line and daydreams.

MAKE PREDICTIONS

When you **make predictions** during reading, you are making guesses about what the reading is going to be about or what might happen next. Before you read, make predictions based on clues from the page and from what you already know about the topic. As you read, gather more clues that will either confirm or change your predictions.

Prediction Chart

Guesses	Reasons	Evidence
The portrait salesman is going to steal Don Mateo's money.	The picture Don Mateo gives him is his only picture of his son, so I'm guessing something will go wrong with it.	The salesman keeps talking about how his new manager wants payment in cash. The salesman also seems frightened and timid and says it will take a month to deliver the picture.

MAKE INFERENCES

Making an inference means putting together the clues given in the text with your own prior knowledge. Make inferences, or educated guesses, about what is not stated directly. Things may be implied or hinted at, or they may be left out altogether. By paying close attention to what you read, you will be able to make inferences about what the writer is trying to communicate. Use an Inference Chart to document your conclusions.

Inference Chart

Text	What I Infer
In "Papa's Parrot," the parrot says, "Where's Harry?"	Harry's father has been lonely, saying "Where's Harry?" so many times that the parrot learned how to say it.
Detail from Text	Conclusions

CLARIFY

Check that you understand what you read and identify text that is confusing or unclear. If you encounter problems or lose focus, it may be helpful to use **Fix-Up Ideas,** such as rereading difficult parts, reading in shorter chunks, going back and reading aloud, or changing your reading rate. (See Monitor Comprehension on page 834 for more information.)

MAKE CONNECTIONS

Notice where there are **connections** between the story and your life or the world beyond the story. Be aware of feelings or thoughts you have while reading the story.

Connections Chart

Page #	Event	Reminds Me of
392	The Sibley Guide to Birds describes wild turkeys.	I've eaten turkey at Thanksgiving dinner.

1.3 Using Reading Skills

Using the following skills as you read helps you to become an independent, thoughtful, and active reader who can accomplish tasks evaluated on tests, particularly standardized tests.

Reading Skills

- Identify Author's Purpose and Approach
- Skim and Scan
- Find the Main Idea
- Determine Importance of Details
- Understand Literary Elements
- Meaning of Words
- Use Context Clues
- Take Notes
- Analyze Text Organization

- Identify Sequence of Events
- Compare and Contrast
- Evaluate Cause and Effect
- Classify and Reorganize Information
- Distinguish Fact from Opinion
- Identify Multiple Levels of Meaning
- Interpret Visual Aids
- Monitor Comprehension
- Summarize
- Draw Conclusions

IDENTIFY AUTHOR'S PURPOSE AND APPROACH

Author's Purpose

A writer's **purpose** is his or her aim or goal. Being able to figure out an author's purpose, or purposes, is an important reading skill. An author may write with one or more of the purposes listed in the following chart. A writer's purpose corresponds to a specific mode, or type, of writing. A writer can choose from a variety of forms while working within a mode.

Purposes of Writing

Mode of Writing	Purpose	Examples
expository	to inform	news article, research report
narrative	to express thoughts or ideas, or to tell a story	personal account, memoir
descriptive	to portray a person, place, object, or event	travel brochure, personal profile
persuasive	to convince people to accept a position and respond in some way	editorial, petition

Once you identify what the author is trying to do, you can evaluate, or judge, how well the author achieved that purpose. For example, you may judge that the author of a persuasive essay made a good and convincing argument. Or, you may decide that the novel you are reading has a boring plot.

Before Reading
Identify the author's purpose, the type of writing he or she uses, and the ideas he or she wants to communicate.

During Reading
Gather ideas that the author communicates to the readers.

After Reading
Summarize the ideas the author communicates. Explain how these ideas help fulfill the author's purpose.

Author's Approach

The literary elements, the terms and techniques used in literature, make up the **author's approach** to conveying his or her main idea or theme. Understanding the author's approach in fiction involves recognizing literary elements such as *point of view, tone,* and *mood.* What perspective, or way of looking at things, does the author have? What is his or her attitude toward the subject? Is the writing serious or playful in nature? What emotions is the writer trying to evoke in the reader? (See Understand Literary Elements on page 828.)

SKIM AND SCAN

When you **skim,** you glance through material quickly to get a general idea of what it is about. Skimming is an excellent way to get a quick overview of material. It is useful for previewing a chapter in a textbook, for surveying material to see if it contains information that will be useful to you, and for reviewing material for a test or an essay.

When you **scan,** you look through written material quickly to locate particular information. Scanning is useful when, for example, you want to find an entry in an index or a definition in a textbook chapter. To scan, simply run your eye down the page, looking for a key word. When you find the key word, slow down and read carefully.

To **skim** a text, preview the following:	When you **scan** a text, you may be looking for the following:
• titles • headings • bold or colored type • topic sentences • first/last paragraphs of sections • summaries • graphics	• specific information • key words • main ideas • answers to questions

FIND THE MAIN IDEA

The **main idea** is a brief statement of what you think the author wants you to know, think, or feel after reading the text. In some cases, the main idea will actually be stated. Check the first and last paragraphs for a sentence that sums up the entire passage. The author may not tell you what the main idea is, and you will have to infer it.

In general, nonfiction texts have main ideas; literary texts (poems, short stories, novels, plays, and personal essays) have themes. Sometimes, however, the term *main idea* is used to refer to the theme of a literary work, especially an essay or a poem. Both deal with the central idea in a written work.

A good way to find the main or overall idea of a whole selection (or part of a selection) is to gather important details into a Main Idea Map like the one below. Use the details to determine the main or overall thought or message.

Main Idea Map

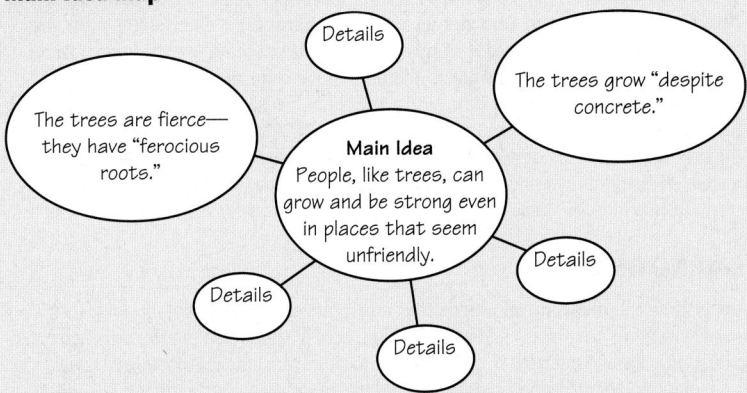

DETERMINE IMPORTANCE OF DETAILS

The main ideas are what the selection is about; the minor ideas and details provide support for the main ones. To identify supporting details, you need to do the following:
• **Locate basic facts,** such as names, dates, and events.
• **Determine the importance** of those facts to the understanding of the piece. Some facts or details will be more important than others.

1 READING STRATEGIES & SKILLS **841**

- **Interpret** subtly stated details. These details can help clarify the author's stance or purpose, or they may give fuller meaning to the basic facts.
- **Understand the function** of a part of a passage. Is the author providing information, supporting a previously made point, presenting a conflicting argument, building suspense? Pay attention to how your understanding of a topic or your feelings toward it change as you read.
- **Make inferences,** or educated guesses, about how the author uses the supporting details to achieve his or her desired result. Put together clues from the text with your known prior knowledge to make inferences. A Main Idea Map or an Inference Chart can help you keep track of your ideas.

UNDERSTAND LITERARY ELEMENTS

Literary elements are the terms and techniques that are used in literature. When you read literature, you need to be familiar with the literary terms and reading skills listed below. These literary elements are explained in more detail in the Introduction to Fiction on page 4.

- **Recognize Mood and Tone** The atmosphere or emotion conveyed by a literary work is called **mood.** A writer creates mood by using concrete details to describe the setting, characters, or events. **Tone** is the writer's attitude toward the subject or toward the reader of a work. Examples of different tones that a work may have include familiar, ironic, playful, sarcastic, serious, and sincere.
- **Understand Point of View** The vantage point, or perspective, from which a story or narrative is told is referred to as **point of view.** Stories are typically written from the following points of view:

  first-person point of view: narrator uses words such as *I* and *we*
  second-person point of view: narrator uses *you*
  third-person point of view: narrator uses words such as *he, she, it,* and *they*
- **Analyze Character and Characterization** A **character** is a person (or sometimes an animal) who takes part in the action of a story. Characterization is the literary techniques writers use to create characters and make them come alive.
- **Examine Plot Development** The plot is basically what happens in a story. A **plot** is a series of events related to a central conflict, or struggle. A typical plot involves the introduction of a conflict, its development, and its eventual resolution. The elements of plot include the exposition, rising action, climax, falling action, and resolution. A graphic organizer called a Plot Diagram (page 6) can be used to chart the plot of a literature selection.

MEANING OF WORDS

To understand the **meaning of words** that are unfamiliar, use vocabulary skills, such as prior knowledge of word parts and word families, context clues (see the following section), and denotation and connotation. Other helpful resources include footnotes, glossaries, and dictionaries. For more information, refer to the Language Arts Handbook, section 2, Vocabulary & Spelling, page 836.

USE CONTEXT CLUES

You can often figure out the meaning of an unfamiliar word by using context clues. **Context clues** are words and phrases near a difficult word that provide hints about its meaning. The context in which a word is used may help you guess what it means without having to look it up in the dictionary.

Different types of context clues include the following:
- **comparison clue:** shows a comparison, or how the unfamiliar word is like something that might be familiar to you
- **contrast clue:** shows that something contrasts, or differs in meaning, from something else
- **restatement clue:** uses different words to express the same idea
- **examples clue:** gives examples of other items to illustrate the meaning of something
- **cause-and-effect clue:** tells you that something happened as a result of something else

TAKE NOTES

Taking or making notes helps you pay attention to the words on a page and remember important ideas. *Paraphrase,* or write in your own words, what you have read and put it into notes you can read later. Taking or making notes is also a quick way for you to retell what you have just read. Since you cannot write in, mark up, or highlight information in a textbook or library book, make a response bookmark like the one that follows and use it to record your thoughts and reactions. As you read, ask yourself questions, make predictions, react to ideas, identify key points, and/or write down unfamiliar words.

Response Bookmark

Page #	Questions, Predictions, Reactions, Key Points, and Unfamiliar Words
319	Will Robert be as horrified by the Chinese dinner as the narrator thinks he will?

Making notes in **graphic organizers** helps you organize ideas as you read. For instance, if you are reading an essay that compares two authors, you might use a Venn Diagram to collect information about each author. If you are reading about an author's life, you may construct a Time Line. As you read a selection, create your own method for gathering and organizing information. You might use your own version of a common graphic organizer or invent a new way to show what the selection describes.

Common Graphic Organizers

Cause-and-Effect Chart, page 831
Classification Chart, page 832
Connections Chart, page 825
Drawing Conclusions Log, page 835
Fact from Opinion Chart, page 832
Generate Questions Bookmark, page 824
Inference Chart, page 825
K-W-L Chart, page 823
Levels of Meaning Chart, page 833
Main Idea Map, page 827

Prediction Chart, page 824
Pro and Con Chart, page 831
Reader's Purpose Chart, page 823
Response Bookmark, above
Sequence Map, page 830
Summary Chart, page 835
Time Line, page 830
Venn Diagram, page 831
Visualization Map, page 824

ANALYZE TEXT ORGANIZATION

Text organization refers to the different ways a text may be presented or organized. If you are aware of the ways different texts are organized, you will find it easier to understand what you read. For example, familiarity with typical plot elements—the exposition, rising action, climax, falling action, and resolution—is important for understanding the events in a short story or novel. Focusing on signal words and text patterns is important for understanding nonfiction and informational text. For instance, transition words, such as *first*, *second*, *next*, *then*, and *finally*, might indicate that an essay is written in chronological, or time, order. Common methods of organization are shown in the following chart.

Methods of Organization

Chronological Order	Events are given in the order they occur.
Order of Importance	Details are given in order of importance or familiarity.
Comparison and Contrast Order	Similarities and differences of two things are listed.
Cause and Effect Order	One or more causes are presented followed by one or more effects.

IDENTIFY SEQUENCE OF EVENTS

Sequence refers to the order in which things happen. When you read certain types of writing, such as a short story, a novel, a biography of a person's life, or a history book, keep track of the sequence of events. You might do this by making a Time Line or a Sequence Map.

Time Line

To make a Time Line, draw a line and divide it into equal parts like the one below. Label each part with a date or a time. Then add key events at the right places along the Time Line.

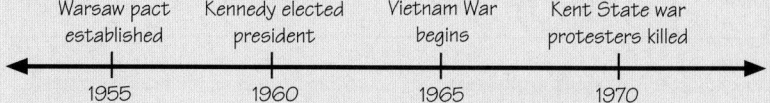

Sequence Map

In each box, draw pictures that represent key events in a selection. Then write a caption under each box that explains each event. Draw the events in the order in which they occur.

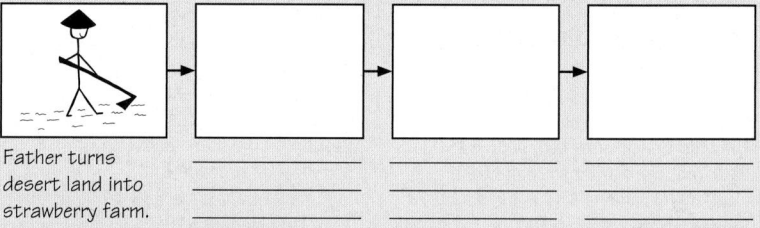

COMPARE AND CONTRAST

Comparing and contrasting are closely related processes. When you **compare** one thing to another, you describe similarities between the two things; when you **contrast** two things, you describe their differences. To compare and contrast, begin by listing the features of each subject. Then go down both lists and check whether each feature is shared or not. You can also show similarities and differences in a *Venn Diagram*. A Venn Diagram uses two slightly overlapping circles. The outer part of each circle shows what aspects of two things are different from each other. The inner, or shared, part of each circle shows what aspects the two things have in common.

Venn Diagram

Another method for comparison and contrast is to use a Pro and Con Chart like the one below to take notes on both sides of an argument.

Pro and Con Chart

Arguments in Favor of Exploring Outer Space (PRO)	Arguments Against Exploring Outer Space (CON)
Argument 1: We must continue to explore outer space. **Support:** The space effort has a history of creating scientific discoveries such as Teflon and transistors.	**Argument 1:** **Support:**

EVALUATE CAUSE AND EFFECT

When you evaluate **cause and effect,** you are looking for a logical relationship between a cause or causes and one or more effects. A writer may present one or more causes followed by one or more effects, or one or more effects followed by one or more causes. Transitional, or signal, words and phrases that indicate cause and effect include *one cause, another effect, as a result, consequently,* and *therefore.* As a reader, you determine whether the causes and effects in a text are reasonable. A graphic organizer like the one below will help you to recognize relationships between causes and effects. Keep track of what happens in a story and why in a chart like the one below. Use cause-and-effect signal words to help you identify causes and their effects.

Cause-and-Effect Chart

CLASSIFY AND REORGANIZE INFORMATION

To **classify** is to put into classes or categories. Items in the same category should share one or more characteristics. A writer may group things to show similarities and name the categories to clarify how one group is similar or different from another. For example, whales can be classified by their method of eating as *baleen* or *toothed*. Classifying or reorganizing the information into categories as you read increases your understanding.

The key step in classifying is choosing categories that fit your purpose. Take classification notes in a chart like the one that follows to help you organize separate types or groups and sort their characteristics.

Classification Chart

Category 1 Electron	Category 2 Nucleus	Category 3 Atom
Items in Category	Items in Category	Items in Category
Details and Characteristics	Details and Characteristics	Details and Characteristics

DISTINGUISH FACT FROM OPINION

A **fact** is a statement that can be proven by direct observation. Every statement of fact is either true or false. The following statement is an example of fact:

Many Greek myths deal with human emotion. (This statement is a fact that can be proven by examining the content of Greek myths.)

An **opinion** is a statement that expresses an attitude or a desire, not a fact about the world. One common type of opinion statement is a *value statement*. A value statement expresses an attitude toward something.

Ancient Greece produced some **beautiful** and **inspiring** myths. (The adjectives used to describe myths express an attitude or opinion toward something that cannot be proven.)

Fact from Opinion Chart

Fact: The Endurance was shipwrecked, but the crew survived on the ice of the Antarctic. Proof: Historical records, Shackleton's diary	Opinion: Support:

IDENTIFY MULTIPLE LEVELS OF MEANING

There is often more than one purpose to a story or nonfiction work. Though there is always a main idea or theme, other levels of meaning are nonetheless important in understanding the overall meaning of the selection. As you read, take note of the multiple levels of meaning, and record them in a Levels of Meaning Chart like the one on the following page.

Levels of Meaning Chart

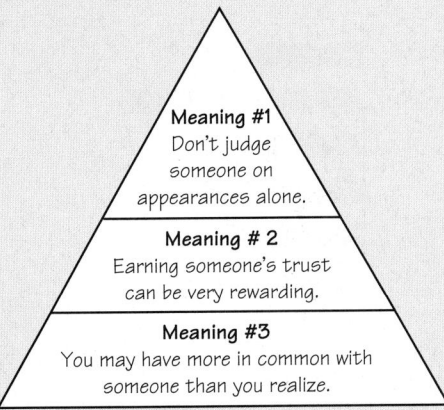

INTERPRET VISUAL AIDS

Visual aids are charts, graphs, pictures, illustrations, photos, maps, diagrams, spread-sheets, and other materials that present information. Many writers use visual aids to present data in understandable ways. Information visually presented in tables, charts, and graphs can help you find data, see trends, discover facts, and uncover patterns.

Pie Chart

A **pie chart** is a circle that stands for a whole group or set. The circle is divided into parts to show the divisions of the whole. When you look at a pie chart, you can see the relationships of the parts to one another and to the whole.

362 Sometimes like, sometimes dislike poetry

136 Strongly like poetry

68 Strongly dislike poetry

Total: 566 students

Bar Graph

A **bar graph** compares amounts of something by representing the amounts as bars of different lengths. In the bar graph shown on the next page, each bar represents the value in dollars of canned goods donated by several communities to a food drive. To read the graph, simply imagine a line drawn from the edge of the bar to the bottom of the graph. Then read the number. For example, the bar graph on the next page shows that the community of Russell Springs donated $600 worth of goods during the food drive.

DOLLAR VALUE OF DONATED GOODS TO CANNED FOOD DRIVE

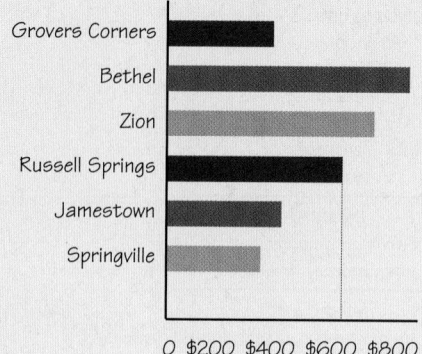

Map

A **map** is a representation, usually on a surface such as paper or a sheet of plastic, of a geographic area showing various significant features of that area.

MONITOR COMPREHENSION

All readers occasionally have difficulty as they read. As you read, you should always **monitor,** or pay attention to, your progress, stopping frequently to check how well you are understanding what you are reading. If you encounter problems or lose focus, use a **fix-up idea** to get back on track. The following **fix-up ideas** can help you "fix up" any confusion or lack of attention you experience as you read. You probably use many of these already.

- **Reread** If you don't understand a sentence, paragraph, or section the first time through, go back and reread it. Each time you reread a text, you understand and remember more.
- **Read in shorter chunks** Break a long text into shorter chunks. Read through each "chunk." Then go back and make sure you understand that section before moving on.

- **Read aloud** If you are having trouble keeping your focus, try reading aloud to yourself. Go somewhere private and read aloud, putting emphasis and expression in your voice. Reading aloud also allows you to untangle difficult text by talking your way through it.
- **Ask questions** As you read, stop and ask yourself questions about the text. These questions may help you pinpoint things that are confusing you or things that you want to come back to later. You can ask questions in your head, or jot them down in the margins or on a piece of paper.
- **Change your reading rate** Your reading rate is how fast or slow you read. Good readers adjust their rate to fit the situation. In some cases, when you just need to get the general idea or main points of a reading, or if the reading is simple, you will want to read through it quickly and not get bogged down. Other times, such as when a text is difficult or contains a lot of description, you will need to slow down and read carefully.

SUMMARIZE

Summarizing is giving a shortened version of something that has been said or written, stating its main points. When you summarize a selection, you are **paraphrasing,** or restating something using other words in order to make it simpler or shorter. Summarizing what you have read will help you identify, understand, and remember the main and supporting points in the text. Read and summarize short sections of a selection at a time. Then write a summary of the entire work. Use a Summary Chart like the one below.

Summary Chart

Summary of Section 1: The village blacksmith is a mighty, strong man.
Summary of Section 2: He makes an honest living and doesn't owe any man.
Summary of Section 3: He works long hard days every day of the week.
Summary of Section 4: The children love to watch him work at the forge and bellows.
Summary of the Selection: The village blacksmith is a valuable member of the community.

DRAW CONCLUSIONS

When you **draw conclusions,** you are gathering pieces of information and then deciding what that information means. Drawing conclusions is an essential part of reading. It may be helpful to use a graphic organizer such as a chart or log to keep track of the information you find while you are reading and the conclusions you draw.

Drawing Conclusions Log

Key Idea Eshu was trying to trick the farmers to ruin their friendship. **Supporting Points** Eshu wore a cap that was black on one side and red on the other.	Key Idea **Supporting Points**	Key Idea **Supporting Points**
Overall Conclusion Eshu wore his cap that way so that the friends would have seen different things.		

For additional instruction and practice refer to the Vocabulary & Spelling Workshop, Use Context Clues, on page 423.

2 Vocabulary & Spelling

2.1 Using Context Clues

You can often figure out the meaning of an unfamiliar word by using context clues. Context clues, or hints you gather from the words and sentences around the unfamiliar word, prevent you from having to look up every unknown word in the dictionary. The chart below defines the types of context clues and gives you an example of each. It also lists words that signal each type of clue.

Context Clues	
comparison clue	shows a comparison, or how the unfamiliar word is like something that might be familiar to you
signal words	*and, like, as, just as, as if, as though*
EXAMPLE Joan was as nimble as a mountain goat as she hiked along the steep, rocky trail. (A mountain goat is extremely agile and sure on its feet. Nimble must mean "agile.")	
contrast clue	shows that something contrasts, or differs in meaning, from something else
signal words	*but, nevertheless, on the other hand, however, although, though, in spite of*
EXAMPLE Hsuan is very reflective, but his friend Ku Min is known for jumping into things without thinking about them. (The word *but* signals a contrast between Hsuan's and Ku Min's ways of doing things. If Ku Min jumps in without thinking, Hsuan must think things through more thoroughly. *Reflective* must mean "thoughtful, meditative.")	
restatement clue	uses different words to express the same idea
signal words	*that is, in other words, or*
EXAMPLE I know Kayesha will prevail in the student council election; I have no doubt that she's going to win! (As the information after the semicolon indicates, *prevail* means "win.")	
examples clue	gives examples of other items to illustrate the meaning of something
signal words	*including, such as, for example, for instance, especially, particularly*
EXAMPLE Trevor has always been interested in celestial bodies such as planets, stars, and moons. (If you know enough about the examples listed, you can tell that celestial bodies are visible bodies in the sky.)	
cause-and-effect clue	tells you that something happened as a result of something else
signal words	*if/then, when/then, thus, therefore, because, so, as a result of, consequently*
EXAMPLE I hadn't planned on going to the party, but the host invited me in such a cordial way that I felt welcome. (If the host's cordial invitation helped the speaker feel welcome, you can guess that *cordial* means "friendly.")	

Program Resources

For more study and practice with vocabulary and spelling, see the *Exceeding the Standards: Vocabulary & Spelling* resource.

2.2 Breaking Words Into Base Words, Word Roots, Prefixes, and Suffixes

Many words are formed by adding prefixes and suffixes to main word parts called base words (if they can stand alone) or word roots (if they can't). A prefix is a letter or group of letters added to the beginning of a word to change its meaning. A suffix is a letter or group of letters added to the end of a word to change its meaning.

➤ For additional instruction and practice refer to the Vocabulary & Spelling Workshop, Prefixes, Roots, and Suffixes, on page 176.

Word Part	Definition	Example
base word	main word part that can stand alone	form
word root	main word part that can't stand alone	struc
prefix	letter or group of letters added to the beginning of the word	pre–
suffix	letter or group of letters added to the end of the word	–tion

Common Prefixes		
Prefix	**Meaning**	**Examples**
anti–/ant–	against; opposite	antibody, antacid
bi–	two	bicycle, biped
circum–	around; about	circumnavigate, circumstance
co–/col–/com–/con–/cor–	together	cooperate, collaborate, commingle, concentrate, correlate
counter–	contrary; complementary; opposite	counteract, counterpart
de–	opposite; remove; reduce	decipher, defrost, devalue
dia–	through; apart	dialogue, diaphanous
dis–	not; opposite of	dislike, disguise
dys–	abnormal; difficult; bad	dysfunctional, dystopia
ex–	out of; from; away	explode, export, extend
extra–/extro–	outward; outside; beyond	extraordinary, extrovert
hyper–	too much, too many, extreme; above	hyperbole, hyperactive
hypo–	under	hypodermic, hypothermic
il–, im–, in–, ir–	not	illogical, impossible, inoperable, irrational
	in; within; toward; on	illuminate, imperil, infiltrate, irrigate
inter–	among; between	international, intersect
intra–/intro–	into; within; inward	introvert, intramural
mis–	wrongly	mistake, misfire
non–	not	nonsense, nonsmoker

Common Prefixes

Prefix	Meaning	Examples
out–	in a manner that goes beyond	outrun, outmuscle
over–	excessive	overdone, overkill
post–	after; later	postgame, postpone
pre–	before	prefix, premature
pro–	before; forward	proceed, prologue
re–	again; back	redo, recall
retro–	back	retrospect, retroactive
semi–	half; partly	semicircle, semidry
sub–/sup–	under	substandard, subfloor, support
super–	above; over; exceeding	superstar, superfluous
trans–	across; beyond	transatlantic, transfer, transcend
ultra–	too much; too many; extreme	ultraviolet, ultrasound
un–	not	unethical, unhappy
under–	below; short of a quantity or limit	underestimate, understaffed
uni–	one	unicorn, universe

Common Suffixes

Noun Suffixes	Meaning	Examples
–ance/–ancy/–ence/–ency	quality; state	defiance, independence, emergency
–age	action; process	marriage, voyage
–ant/–ent	one who	defendant, assistant, resident
–ar/–er/–or	one who	lawyer, survivor, liar
–dom	state; quality of	freedom, boredom
–ion/–tion	action; process	revolution, occasion
–ism	act; state; system of belief	plagiarism, barbarism, Buddhism
–ist	one who does or believes something	ventriloquist, idealist
–itude, –tude	quality of; state of	multitude, magnitude
–ity/–ty	state of	longevity, piety
–ment	action or process; state or quality; product or thing	development, government, amusement, amazement, ointment, fragment
–ness	state of	kindness, happiness

Common Suffixes

Adjective Suffixes	Meaning	Examples
–able/–ible	capable of	attainable, possible
–al	having characteristics of	personal, governmental
–er	more	higher, calmer, shorter
–est	most	lowest, craziest, tallest
–ful	full of	helpful, gleeful, woeful
–ic	having characteristics of	scientific, chronic
–ish	like	childish, reddish
–ive	performs; tends toward	creative, pensive
–less	without	hapless, careless
–ous	possessing the qualities of	generous, joyous
–y	indicates description	happy, dirty, flowery
Adverb Suffixes	**Meaning**	**Examples**
–ly	in such a way	quickly, studiously, invisibly
–ward, –ways, –wise	in such a direction	toward, sideways, crosswise
Verb Suffixes	**Meaning**	**Examples**
–ate	make or cause to be	fixate, activate
–ed	past tense of verb	walked, acted, fixed
–ify/–fy	make or cause to be	magnify, glorify
–ing	indicates action in progress (present participle); can also be a noun (gerund)	running, thinking, being
–ize	bring about; cause to be	colonize, legalize

Common Word Roots

Word Root	Meaning	Examples
act	do	actor, reaction
ann/annu/enni	year	annual, bicentennial
aqu	water	aquarium, aquatic
aster, astr	star	asteroid, astronomy
aud	hear	audition, auditorium
bene	good	beneficial, benefactor
bibl, bibli	book	Bible, bibliography
chron	time	chronic, chronological
cred	believe; trust	credit, credible
cycl	circle	bicycle, cyclone

Common Word Roots		
Word Root	**Meaning**	**Examples**
dem/demo	people	democracy, demagogue
derm	skin	dermatologist, hypodermic
dic/dict	say	dictate, dictionary
fer	carry	transfer, refer
fin	end	finish, infinite
flect/flex	bend	deflect, reflex, flexible
hydra, hydro	water	hydrate, hydrogen
ign	fire	ignite, ignition, igneous
ject	throw	projector, eject
lect/leg	read; choose	lecture, election, legible
liber	free	liberate, liberal
log/logue	word; speech; discourse	logic, monologue
luc/lumin	shine; light	lucid, luminous
mal	bad	malevolent, malodorous
man/manu	hand	manufacture, manual
metr	measure	metric, metronome
ped	foot; child	pedal, pediatrics
phon/phony	sound; voice; speech	symphony, microphone
phot	light	photography, photon
physi	nature	physical, physics
pop	people	popular, populate
port	carry	transport, portable
psych	mind; soul	psychology, psychic
reg	rule	register, regulate
rupt	break	disrupt, interruption, rupture
scrib/script	write	describe, prescription
spec/spect/spic	look	speculate, inspect, specimen
ter/terr	earth	inter, terrestrial, terrain
therm	heat	thermal, hypothermia
vid/vis	see	video, visual
vol/volv	turn	evolution, revolve

2.3 Using a Dictionary

When you can't figure out a word using the strategies already described, or when the word is important to the meaning of the text and you want to make sure you have it right, use a dictionary. There are many parts to a dictionary entry.

pole¹ (pōl) *n.* [ME, from OE *pal,* from L *palus,* stake.] 1. a long, slender, generally rounded piece of wood 2. [Sports] the inside position on the starting line of a race-track: *qualified in the time trials to start on the pole*

pole² (pōl) *n.* [ME, from L *polus,* from Gr *polos,* axis of the sphere.] 1. the extreme part of an axis through a sphere 2. either of two related opposites

The **pronunciation** is given immediately after the entry word. The dictionary's table of contents will tell you where you can find a complete key to pronunciation symbols. In some dictionaries, a simplified pronunciation key is provided at the bottom of each page.

An abbreviation of the **part of speech** usually follows the pronunciation. This label tells how the word can be used. If a word can be used as more than one part of speech, a separate entry is provided for each part of speech.

An **etymology** is the history of the word. In the first entry, the word *pole* can be traced back through Middle English (ME) and Old English (OE) to the Latin (L) word *palus,* which means "stake." In the second entry, the word *pole* can be traced back through Middle English to the Latin word *polus,* which comes from the Greek (Gr) word *polos,* meaning "axis of the sphere."

Sometimes the entry will include a list of **synonyms,** or words that have the same or very similar meanings. The entry may also include a **usage illustration,** which is an example of how the word is used in context.

2.4 Exploring Word Origins and Word Families

The English language expands constantly and gathers new words from many different sources. Understanding the source of a word can help you unlock its meaning.

One source of new words is the names of people and places associated with the thing being named. Words named for people and places are called **eponyms.**

EXAMPLES

hamburger Originally known as "Hamburg steak," the hamburger takes its name from the German city Hamburg.

spoonerism The slip of the tongue whereby the beginning sounds of words are switched is named after the Rev. William A. Spooner, who was known for such slips. For example, after a wedding, he told the groom, "It is kisstomary to cuss the bride."

> For additional instruction and practice refer to the Vocabulary & Spelling Workshop, Using Dictionaries and Thesauruses, on page 668.

VOCABULARY & SPELLING

Another source for new words is **acronyms.** Acronyms are words formed from the first letter or letters of the major parts of terms.

EXAMPLES

sonar, from sound navigation ranging

NATO, from North American Treaty Organization

Some words in the English language are borrowed from other languages.

EXAMPLES

deluxe (French), **Gesundheit** (German), **kayak** (Inuit)

Many words are formed by shortening longer words.

EXAMPLES

ad, from advertisement

lab, from laboratory

stereo, from stereophonic

Brand names are often taken into the English language. People begin to use these words as common nouns, even though most of them are still brand names.

EXAMPLES

Scotch tape   Xerox   Rollerblade

2.5 Understanding Multiple Meanings

Each definition in the entry gives a different meaning of the word. When a word has more than one meaning, the different definitions are numbered. The first definition in an entry is the most common meaning of the word, but you will have to choose the meaning that fits the context in which you have found the word. Try substituting each definition for the word until you find the one that makes the most sense. If you come across a word that doesn't seem to make sense in context, consider whether that word might have another, lesser known meaning. Can the word be used as more than one part of speech, for example, as either a noun or a verb? Does it have a broader meaning than the one that comes to your mind?

Keep in mind that some words not only have multiple meanings but also different pronunciations. Words that are spelled the same but are pronounced differently are called **homographs.**

2.6 Understanding Denotation and Connotation

The **denotation** of a word is its dictionary definition. Sometimes, in order to understand a passage fully, it is helpful to know the connotations of the words as well. A **connotation** of a word is an emotional association the word has in addition to its literal meaning. For example, the words *cheap* and *thrifty* both denote "tending to spend less money," but *cheap* has a negative connotation similar to "stingy," whereas *thrifty* has a positive connotation involving being responsible with money. The best way to learn the connotation of a word is to pay attention to the context in which the word appears or to ask someone more familiar with the word.

For additional instruction and practice refer to the Vocabulary & Spelling Workshop, Denotation and Connotation, on page 16.

Connotation Chart

Negative	Neutral	Positive
weird	unusual	unique
freakish	different	remarkable
bizarre	uncommon	extraordinary
abnormal	rare	unequaled
mob	group	congregation

2.7 Spelling

SPELLING RULES

Always check your writing for spelling errors, and try to recognize the words that give you more trouble than others. Use a dictionary when you find you have misspelled a word. Keep a list in a notebook of words that are difficult for you to spell. Write the words several times until you have memorized the correct spelling. Break down the word into syllables and carefully pronounce each individual syllable.

Some spelling problems occur when adding prefixes or suffixes to words or when making nouns plural. Other spelling problems occur when words follow certain patterns, such as those containing *ie/ei*. The following spelling rules can help you spell many words correctly.

PREFIXES AND SUFFIXES

Prefixes

A **prefix** is a letter or a group of letters added to the beginning of a word to change its meaning. When adding a prefix, do not change the spelling of the word itself.

EXAMPLES

mis– + perception = misperception   anti– + social = antisocial
im– + possible = impossible   al– + mighty = almighty
in– + conceivable = inconceivable

Suffixes

A **suffix** is a letter or a group of letters added to the end of a word to change its meaning.

The spelling of most words is not changed when the suffix *–ness* or *–ly* is added.

EXAMPLES

shy + –ness = shyness   strange + –ly = strangely
forgive + –ness = forgiveness   bad + –ly = badly
eager + –ness = eagerness   splendid + –ly = splendidly

If you are adding a suffix to a word that ends with *y* following a vowel, usually leave the *y* in place.

EXAMPLES

employ   employs   employing   employed
defray   defrays   defraying   defrayment
buoy   buoys   buoying   buoyancy

For additional instruction and practice refer to the Vocabulary & Spelling Workshop, Spelling with Prefixes and Suffixes, on page 464.

VOCABULARY & SPELLING

2 VOCABULARY & SPELLING **857**

If you are adding a suffix to a word that ends with *y* following a consonant, change the *y* to *i* before adding any ending except *–ing*.

EXAMPLES

bury	buried	burying
copy	copied	copying
supply	supplied	supplying
magnify	magnified	magnifying

Double the final consonant before adding a suffix beginning with a vowel (such as *–ed*, *–en*, *–er*, *–ing*, *–ence*, *–ance*, or *–y*) in words ending in a single consonant preceded by a single vowel if the word is either a single syllable or ends in a stressed syllable.

EXAMPLES

regret	regrettable	regretting
quit	quitter	quitting
fan	fanned	fanning
refer	referred	referring
plot	plotted	plotting
deter	deterrence	deterring
rot	rotten	rotting

If you are adding a suffix that begins with a vowel to a word that ends with a silent *e*, usually drop the *e*.

EXAMPLES

tune	tuning
oblige	obligation
pursue	pursuable
grieve	grievous

If you are adding a suffix that begins with a consonant to a word that ends with a silent *e*, usually leave the *e* in place.

EXAMPLES

spite	spiteful
achieve	achievement
state	stately
lame	lameness

EXCEPTIONS

awe	awful
wise	wisdom
nine	ninth
due	duly

If the word ends in a soft *c* sound (spelled *ce*) or a soft *g* sound (spelled *ge*), keep the *e* when adding the suffixes *–able* or *–ous*.

EXAMPLES

acknowledge	acknowledgeable
enforce	enforceable
outrage	outrageous

PLURAL NOUNS

Plural Nouns

Most noun plurals are formed by simply adding –s to the end of the word.

EXAMPLES

surface + –s = surfaces   platelet + –s = platelets
mouthful + –s = mouthfuls   refrigerator + –s = refrigerators

The plural of nouns that end in *o, s, x, z, ch,* or *sh* should be formed by adding *–es.*

EXAMPLES

tomato + –es = tomatoes   buzz + –es = buzzes
loss + –es = losses   inch + –es = inches
fox + –es = foxes   flash + –es = flashes

The exception to the rule above is that musical terms and certain other words that end in *o* are usually made plural by adding *–s.* Check a dictionary if you aren't sure whether to add *–s* or *–es.*

EXAMPLES

piano + –s = pianos   soprano + –s = sopranos
solo + –s = solos   vibrato + –s = vibratos

Form the plural of nouns that end in *y* following a consonant by changing the *y* to an *i* and adding *–es.*

EXAMPLES

democracy	democracies
fairy	fairies
fallacy	fallacies
fifty	fifties
filly	fillies

Nouns that end in *f* or *fe* must be modified, changing the *f* or *fe* to *v,* before adding *–es* to the plural form.

EXAMPLES

shelf	shelves
knife	knives
scarf	scarves
leaf	leaves
calf	calves

SPELLING PATTERNS

The ie/ei Spelling Pattern

A word spelled with the letters *i* and *e* and has a long *e* sound is usually spelled *ie* except after the letter *c.*

EXAMPLES

belief	conceive
piece	receive
field	deceit

EXCEPTIONS

leisure	either

Use *ei* when the sound is not long *e.*

EXAMPLES

forfeit   surfeit   foreign   height

EXCEPTIONS

science   mischief   sieve

If the vowel combination has a long *a* sound (as in *eight*), always spell it with *ei.*

EXAMPLES

weight   reign   vein

When two vowels are pronounced separately in a word, spell them in the order of their pronunciation.

EXAMPLES

siesta   patio   diode   transient

The "Seed" Sound Pattern

The "seed" ending sound has three spellings: *–sede, –ceed,* and *–cede.*

EXAMPLES

Only one word ends in *–sede: supersede*

Three words end in *–ceed: proceed, succeed, exceed*

All other words end in *–cede: accede, concede, recede, precede, secede*

Silent Letters

Some spelling problems result from letters written but not heard when a word is spoken. Becoming familiar with the patterns in letter combinations containing silent letters will help you identify other words that fit the patterns.

- Silent *b* usually occurs with *m.*

EXAMPLES

dumb   bomb   climb   lamb

- Silent *b* also appears in *debt* and *doubt.*

- Silent *c* often appears with *s.*

EXAMPLES

scissors   scent   scenic   science

- Silent *g* often appears with *n.*

EXAMPLES

design   resign   gnome   foreign

- Silent *gh* often appears at the end of a word, either alone or in combination with *t* (*–ght*).

EXAMPLES

fright   freight   sought   wrought

- Silent *h* appears at the beginning of some words.

EXAMPLES

hourly   heir   honestly   honor

- Silent *h* also appears in a few other words, as in *rhythm* and *ghost.*

- Silent *k* occurs with *n.*

EXAMPLES

knack   knight   knot   kneecap   knapsack

- Silent *n* occurs with *m* at the end of some words.

EXAMPLES

condemn   solemn   column   autumn

- Silent *p* occurs with *s* at the beginning of some words.

EXAMPLES

psyche   psychosis   psoriasis

- Silent *s* occurs with *l* in some words.

EXAMPLES

island   islet   aisle

- Silent *t* occurs with *s* in a few words.

EXAMPLES

listen   hasten   nestle

- Silent *w* occurs at the beginnings of some words.

EXAMPLES

wreak   wrong   wraith   wrapper

- Silent *w* also occurs with *s* in a few words, such as *sword* and *answer.*

Letter Combinations

Some letter combinations have a different pronunciation when combined and can cause spelling problems.

- The letters *ph* produce the *f* sound.

EXAMPLES

sphinx   photograph   alphanumeric   phosphate

- The letters *gh* produce the *f* sound usually at the end of a word. (Otherwise, they are silent.)

EXAMPLES

cough   enough   neigh   weigh

- The letter combination *tch* sounds the same as *ch.*

EXAMPLES

sketch   pitch   snitch   hatch
such   hunch   grouch   torch

If the letters *c* and *g* have soft sounds (of *s* and *j*), they will usually be followed by *e, i,* or *y.*

EXAMPLES

cyclone   circle   regent
giant   cent   gyroscope
outrageous   region

If the letters *c* and *g* have hard sounds (of *k* and *g*), they will usually be followed by *a, o,* or *u.*

EXAMPLES

candid	gasket	conjugate
congeal	garland	gun
convey	argument	cunning

Spelling Patterns of Borrowed Words

Many words borrowed from other languages follow the spelling patterns of the original language. For example, some English words borrowed from French, Spanish, and Italian follow letter patterns of the language of origin.

• The final *t* is silent in many words borrowed from French.

EXAMPLES

croquet	ballet

• The letter combinations *eur* and *eau* appear at the end of many words with French origin.

EXAMPLES

amateur	bureau	grandeur
chauffeur	plateau	tableau

• The letter combination *oo* appears in many words borrowed from the Dutch language.

EXAMPLES

roost	cooper	toot

Many plural Italian words end in *i.*

EXAMPLES

ravioli	manicotti	linguini

Many words of Spanish origin end in *o.*

EXAMPLES

machismo	tomato	patio

Compound Nouns

A **compound noun** consists of two or more nouns used together to form a single noun. Sometimes they are written as one word *(football, uptown)*; other times they are written separately *(picnic table, tennis shoes)*. Some compound nouns are connected with hyphens *(great-grandfather, fly-by-night)*. Consult a good dictionary when you are not sure of the form of compounds.

Numerals

Spell out numbers of *one hundred* or less and all numbers rounded to hundreds. Larger round numbers such as *seven thousand* or *three million* should also be spelled out.

EXAMPLES

Joe Morgan hit more than **twenty** home runs and stole at least **thirty** bases in the same season **four** times in his career.

Joe DiMaggio was the first baseball player to receive an annual salary of more than **a hundred thousand** dollars.

Use a hyphen to separate compound numbers from twenty-one through ninety-nine.

EXAMPLES

forty-two birds   one hundred soldiers
seventy-four candles   sixty thousand dollars

Use a hyphen in a fraction used as a modifier, but not in a fraction used as a noun.

EXAMPLES

The glass is **two-fifths full** of water.

After an hour, I had mowed **three fourths** of the backyard.

Use Arabic numerals for numbers greater than one hundred that are not rounded numbers.

EXAMPLES

Our company sent out **493,745** mailings in just **145** days this year.

My uncle boasted that he has read **1,323** books thus far in his life.

If a number appears at the beginning of a sentence, spell it out or rewrite the sentence.

EXAMPLES

incorrect
356 years ago, my ancestors moved to North America.
correct
Three hundred fifty-six years ago, my ancestors moved to North America.
correct
My ancestors moved to North America **356** years ago.

Use words to write the time unless you are writing the exact time (including the abbreviation AM or PM). When the word *o'clock* is used for time of day, express the number in words.

EXAMPLES

Our meeting will start at **a quarter after ten.**

At **eight-thirty,** the show will begin.

I was born at **5:22 PM** on a Monday.

You have until **three o'clock** to finish the proposal.

Use numerals to express dates, street numbers, room numbers, apartment numbers, telephone numbers, page numbers, exact amounts of money, scores, and percentages. Spell out the word *percent.* Round dollar or cent amounts of only a few words may be expressed in words.

EXAMPLES

May 27, 1962   three hundred dollars
(402) 555-1725   Apartment 655
5219 Perret Street   38 percent
pages 49–73 $1.6 billion (or $1,600,000,000)
seventy cents $2,634

When you write a date, do not add *–st, –nd,* or *–th.*

EXAMPLES

incorrect
August 17th, 1968   November 5th
correct
August 17, 1968   November 5 or the fifth of November

COMMON SPELLING ERRORS

Pronunciation is not always a reliable guide for spelling because words are not always spelled the way they are pronounced. However, by paying attention to both letters that spell sounds and letters that are silent, you can improve some aspects of your spelling. Always check a dictionary for the correct pronunciations and spellings of words that are new to your experience.

Extra Syllables

Sometimes people misspell a word because they include an extra syllable. For example, *arthritis* is easily misspelled if it is pronounced *artheritis,* with four syllables instead of three. Pay close attention to the number of syllables in these words.

EXAMPLES

two syllables

foundry   carriage   lonely

three syllables

privilege   boundary   separate

Omitted Sounds

Sometimes people misspell a word because they do not sound one or more letters when pronouncing the word. Be sure to include the underlined letters of these words even if you don't pronounce them.

EXAMPLES

barbarous	candidate	drowned	mischievous	sophomore
gratitude	governor	grocery	quantity	literature

Homophones

Words that have the same pronunciation but different spellings and meanings are called **homophones.** An incorrect choice can be confusing to your readers. Knowing the spelling and meaning of these groups of words will improve your spelling.

EXAMPLES

allowed/aloud	coarse/course	compliment/complement
sole/soul	alter/altar	site/sight/cite
hear/here	some/sum	plain/plane
ascent/assent	lead/led	capital/capitol
threw/through	bear/bare	who's/whose
night/knight	wait/weight	peace/piece
brake/break	pair/pear	buy/bye/by
weak/week		

Commonly Confused Words

Some other groups of words are not homophones, but they are similar enough in sound and spelling to create confusion. Knowing the spelling and meaning of these groups of words will also improve your spelling.

EXAMPLES

access/excess	farther/further	nauseous/nauseated
accept/except	principle/principal	stationary/stationery
formally/formerly	passed/past	alternate/alternative
literal/literally	desert/dessert	loose/lose

COMMONLY MISSPELLED WORDS

Some words are often misspelled. Here is a list of 150 commonly misspelled words. If you master this list, you will avoid many errors in your spelling.

absence	enormous	parallel
abundant	enthusiastically	pastime
academically	environment	peasant
accessible	exhaust	permanent
accidentally	existence	persistent
accommodate	fascinating	phenomenon
accurate	finally	physician
acknowledgment	forfeit	pneumonia
acquaintance	fulfill	prestige
adequately	guerrilla	privilege
adolescent	guidance	procedure
advantageous	hindrance	prophesy
advisable	hypocrite	prove
ancient	independent	receipt
annihilate	influential	referred
anonymous	ingenious	rehearsal
answer	institution	relieve
apparent	interference	resistance
article	irrelevant	resources
attendance	irresistible	responsibility
bankruptcy	judgment	rhythm
beautiful	league	schedule
beggar	leisure	seize
beginning	license	separate
behavior	lightning	sergeant
biscuit	liquefy	siege
breathe	magnificent	significance
business	manageable	souvenir
calendar	maneuver	sponsor
camouflage	meadow	succeed
catastrophe	mediocre	surprise
cellar	miniature	symbol
cemetery	mischievous	synonymous
changeable	misspell	temperature
clothes	mortgage	tomorrow
colossal	mysterious	transparent
column	naïve	twelfth
committee	necessity	undoubtedly
conceivable	nickel	unmistakable
conscientious	niece	unnecessary
conscious	noticeable	vacuum
consistency	nucleus	vehicle
deceitful	nuisance	vengeance
descendant	nutritious	villain
desirable	obedience	vinegar
disastrous	occasionally	weird
discipline	occurrence	whistle
efficiency	orchestra	withhold
eighth	outrageous	yacht
embarrass	pageant	yield

> For additional instruction and practice refer to the Grammar & Style Workshop, Sentence Types, on page 296.

3 Grammar & Style

3.1 The Sentence

THE SENTENCE

In the English language, the sentence is the basic unit of meaning. A **sentence** is a group of words that expresses a complete thought. Every sentence has two basic parts: a subject and a predicate. The **subject** tells whom or what the sentence is about. The **predicate** tells information about the subject.

EXAMPLE

sentence
The old professor | read the dusty manuscript.
   (subject)   **(predicate)**

A group of words that does not have both a subject and a predicate is called a **sentence fragment.** A sentence fragment does not express a complete thought.

EXAMPLES

sentence fragment The baker.
(The fragment does not have a predicate. The group of words does not answer the question *What did the baker do?*)
sentence fragment Frosted the chocolate cake.
(The fragment does not have a subject. The group of words does not answer the question *Who frosted the chocolate cake?*)
sentence fragment In his kitchen.
(The fragment does not have a subject or predicate. The group of words does not tell what the sentence is about or tell what the subject does.)
complete sentence The baker frosted the chocolate cake in his kitchen.

FUNCTIONS OF SENTENCES

There are four different kinds of sentences: *declarative, interrogative, imperative,* and *exclamatory.* Each kind of sentence has a different purpose. You can vary the tone and mood of your writing by using the four different sentence types.

- A **declarative sentence** makes a statement. It ends with a period.

EXAMPLE
Your cat would like to eat her supper now.

- An **interrogative sentence** asks a question. It ends with a question mark.

EXAMPLE
When will your cat eat her supper?

- An **imperative sentence** gives an order or makes a request. It ends with a period or an exclamation point. An imperative sentence has an understood subject, most often *you*.

EXAMPLES
(You) Please feed your cat.
(You) Look in the cupboard for the cat food.

Program Resources

You will find additional lessons on grammar and style in the *Exceeding the Standards: Grammar & Style* resource.

- An **exclamatory sentence** expresses strong feeling. It ends with an exclamation point.

EXAMPLE

Your cat is really hungry!

SIMPLE AND COMPLETE SUBJECTS AND PREDICATES

In a sentence, the **simple subject** is the key word or words in the subject. The simple subject is usually a noun or a pronoun and does not include any modifiers. The **complete subject** includes the simple subject and all the words that modify it.

The **simple predicate** is the key verb or verb phrase that tells what the subject does, has, or is. The **complete predicate** includes the verb and all the words that modify it.

In the following sentence, a vertical line separates the complete subject and complete predicate. The simple subject is underlined once. The simple predicate is underlined twice.

EXAMPLE

 (complete subject)   (complete predicate)

The large black <u>umbrella</u> | <u>shielded</u> my brother and sister from the rain.

Sometimes, the simple subject is also the complete subject, and the simple predicate or verb is also the complete predicate.

EXAMPLE

<u>Jesse Owens</u> | <u>ran</u>.

To find the simple subject and simple predicate in a sentence, first break the sentence into its two basic parts: complete subject and complete predicate. Then, identify the simple predicate by asking yourself, "What is the action of this sentence?" Finally, identify the simple subject by asking yourself, "Who or what is performing the action?" In the following sentences, the complete predicate is in parentheses. The simple predicate, or verb, appears in boldface.

EXAMPLES

one-word verb   Three energetic monkeys (**climbed** up the tree.)
two-word verb   Three energetic monkeys (**are climbing** up the tree.)
three-word verb   Three energetic monkeys (**have been climbing** up the tree.)
four-word verb   Three energetic monkeys (**might have been climbing** up the tree.)

COMPOUND SUBJECTS AND PREDICATES

A sentence may have more than one subject or predicate. A **compound subject** has two or more simple subjects that have the same predicate. The subjects are joined by the conjunction *and, or,* or *but.*

A **compound predicate** has two or more simple predicates, or verbs, that share the same subject. The verbs are connected by the conjunction *and, or,* or *but.*

EXAMPLES

compound subject
<u>Ice</u> and <u>snow</u> | <u>make</u> travel difficult in the winter.
compound predicate
Some <u>teachers</u> | <u>show</u> videos and <u>play</u> CDs during their classes.

> For additional instruction and practice refer to the Grammar & Style Workshop, Simple and Compound Subjects, on page 407.

> For additional instruction and practice refer to the Grammar & Style Workshop, Simple, Complete, and Compound Predicates, on page 571.

➤ For additional instruction and practice refer to the Grammar & Style Workshop, Simple, Compound, Complex, and Compound-Complex Sentences, on page 543.

The conjunctions *either* and *or* and *neither* and *nor* can also join compound subjects or predicates.

EXAMPLES

compound subject

Either <u>Peter</u> *or* <u>Paul</u> | <u>sings</u> the national anthem before each game.
Neither <u>yesterday</u> *nor* <u>today</u> | <u>seemed</u> like a good time to start the project.

compound predicate

Her <u>dogs</u> | *either* <u>heard</u> *or* <u>smelled</u> the intruder in the basement.
The police <u>inspector</u> | *neither* <u>visited</u> *nor* <u>called</u> last night.

A sentence may also have a compound subject and a compound predicate.

EXAMPLE

compound subject and compound predicate

John and Diane | drove to the lake and fished all afternoon.

SENTENCE STRUCTURES

A **simple sentence** consists of one independent clause and no subordinate clauses. It may have a compound subject and a compound predicate. It may also have any number of phrases. A simple sentence is sometimes called an independent clause because it can stand by itself.

EXAMPLES

Three bears emerged from the forest.

They spotted the campers and the hikers and decided to pay a visit.

The three bears enjoyed eating the campers' fish, sandwiches, and candy bars.

A **compound sentence** consists of two sentences joined by a semicolon or by a coordinating conjunction and a comma. Each part of the compound sentence has its own subject and verb. The most common coordinating conjunctions are *and, or, nor, for, but, so,* and *yet.*

EXAMPLES

compound sentence

Grover Cleveland served as president from 1885 to 1889**;** he served a second term in the White House from 1893 to 1897.

compound sentence

An economic downturn gripped the nation during Cleveland's second term**, and** his popularity with Americans dwindled.

A **complex sentence** consists of one independent clause and one or more subordinate clauses. The subordinate clauses in the examples below are underlined.

EXAMPLES

<u>When you finish your report</u>, remember to print it out on paper <u>that contains 25 percent cotton fiber</u>.

Jim will water the lawn <u>after he returns home from the baseball game</u>.

3.2 The Parts of Speech

IDENTIFYING THE PARTS OF SPEECH

Each word in a sentence performs a basic function or task. Words perform four basic tasks; they name, modify, express action or state of being, or link.

There are eight different parts of speech. Each part of speech is defined in the following chart.

> For additional instruction and practice refer to the Grammar & Style Workshop, Nouns: Proper, Plural, Possessive, and Collective, on page 490.

Part of Speech	Definition	Example
noun	A **noun** names a person, place, thing, or idea.	**Apples, oranges,** and **potato chips** were the only **items** on the **list.**
pronoun	A **pronoun** is used in place of a noun.	Fanny whispered to **her** friend as **they** waited for **their** new teacher.
verb	A **verb** expresses action or a state of being.	Playful fox cubs **tumbled** out of the den and **chased** one another across the field.
adjective	An **adjective** modifies a noun or pronoun. The most common adjectives are the articles *a, an,* and *the.*	**Tattered** curtains hung in the **dark** windows of the **gray, sagging** house.
adverb	An **adverb** modifies a verb, an adjective, or another adverb.	**Sharply** turning to the left, the bicyclist **nearly** caused an accident.
preposition	A **preposition** shows the relationship between its object—a noun or a pronoun—and another word in a sentence. Common prepositions include *after, around, at, behind, beside, off, through, until, upon,* and *with.*	**During** winter, we often sit **by** the fireplace **in** the evening.
conjunction	A **conjunction** joins words or groups of words. Common conjunctions are *and, but, for, nor, or, so,* and *yet.*	**Neither** Grant **nor** Felix felt tired after two miles, **so** they ran another mile.
interjection	An **interjection** is a word used to express emotion. Common interjections are *oh, ah, well, hey,* and *wow.*	**Wow!** Did you see the dive he took from the high jump?

3.3 Nouns

NOUNS

A **noun** is a part of speech that names a person, place, idea, or thing. In this unit, you'll learn about the different kinds of nouns and what they name.

EXAMPLES

people Sidney, teacher, mother, photographer

places city, Wrigley Field, Kentucky

ideas admiration, addition, relief, plan

things checkerboard, butterfly, flight, ring

Types of Nouns	Definition	Examples
common noun	names a person, place, idea, or thing	mother, garage, plan, flower
proper noun	names a specific person, place, or thing; begins with capital letter	John Adams, New York City, Monroe Doctrine
concrete noun	names a thing that can be touched, seen, heard, smelled, or tasted	ruler, mirror, giggle, garbage, banana
abstract noun	names an idea, a theory, a concept, or a feeling	approval, philosophy, faith, communism
singular noun	names one person, place, idea, or thing	governor, tree, thought, shoe
plural noun	names more than one thing	governors, trees, thoughts, shoes
possessive noun	shows ownership or possession of things or qualities	Jan's, Mrs. Wilson's, women's, intern's
compound noun	made up of two or more words	staircase, picnic table, brother-in-law
collective noun	names groups	organization, platoon, team

3.4 Pronouns

PRONOUNS

A **pronoun** is used in place of a noun. Sometimes a pronoun refers to a specific person or thing.

Pronouns can help your writing flow more smoothly. Without pronouns, your writing can sound awkward and repetitive.

The most commonly used pronouns are *personal pronouns, reflexive and intensive pronouns, demonstrative pronouns, indefinite pronouns, interrogative pronouns,* and *relative pronouns.*

Types of Pronouns	Definition	Examples
personal pronoun	used in place of the name of a person or thing	I, me, we, us, he, she, it, him, her, you, they, them
indefinite pronoun	points out a person, place, or thing, but not a specific or definite one	one, someone, anything, other, all, few, nobody
reflexive pronoun	refers back to a noun previously used; adds –self and –selves to other pronoun forms	myself, herself, yourself, themselves, ourselves
intensive pronoun	emphasizes a noun or a pronoun	me myself, he himself, you yourself, they themselves, we ourselves
interrogative pronoun	asks a question	who, whose, whom, what, which
demonstrative pronoun	points out a specific person, place, idea, or thing	this, these, that, those
relative pronoun	introduces an adjective clause	that, which, who, whose, whom
singular pronoun	used in place of the name of one person or thing	I, me, you, he, she, it, him, her
plural pronoun	used in place of more than one person or thing	we, us, you, they, them
possessive pronoun	shows ownership or possession	mine, yours, his, hers, ours, theirs

➤ For additional instruction and practice refer to the Grammar & Style Workshop, Personal and Possessive Pronouns, on page 480.

➤ For additional instruction and practice refer to the Grammar & Style Workshop, Reflexive and Intensive Pronouns, on page 501.

PRONOUNS AND ANTECEDENTS

The word that a pronoun stands for is called its **antecedent.** The antecedent clarifies the meaning of the pronoun. The pronoun may appear in the same sentence as its antecedent or in a following sentence.

EXAMPLES

Where is **Michael? He** is at the library.
(*Michael* is the antecedent of *He*.)

Amy's black **dog** barks loudly because **he** is hungry.
(*Dog* is the antecedent of *he*.)

A pronoun should agree in both number (singular or plural) and gender (masculine, feminine, or neutral) with its antecedent.

EXAMPLES

number

singular	**Robert Frost** wrote many poems. "Stopping by Woods on a Snowy Evening" is perhaps **his** most well-known poem.
plural	The visiting **poets** were asked if **they** would give a reading on Saturday night.

gender

masculine	**Robert Frost** was born in California, but **he** was raised in Massachusetts and New Hampshire.
feminine	**Toni Morrison** begins **her** writing day before dawn.
neutral	The **poem** is titled "Birches," and **it** is one of my favorites.

Singular pronouns are used with some nouns that are plural in form but singular in meaning, such as *economics, electronics, gymnastics, linguistics, mathematics, measles, news,* and *physics*.

EXAMPLES

My younger brother has the **measles.** I hope I don't catch **it.**
Would you like to try **gymnastics? It** is excellent exercise.

Plural pronouns are used with some nouns that are plural in form but refer to single items, such as *pliers, eyeglasses, pants, scissors,* and *shorts*.

EXAMPLES

I can't find my **eyeglasses.** Have you seen **them?**
The **pants** fit you well, but **they** need hemming.

Agreement between a relative pronoun—*who, whom, whose, which,* and *that*—and its antecedent is determined by the number of the antecedent.

EXAMPLES

Marie, who has always enjoyed **her** rural life, has surprisingly decided to move to the city. (*Who* is singular because it refers to the singular noun *Marie. Her* is used to agree with *who*.)

All who wish to vote by absentee ballot should complete **their** ballots and mail **them** to the county clerk's office. (*Who* is plural because it refers to the plural pronoun *All. Their* is used to agree with *who. Them* is used to agree with *ballots.*)

> For additional instruction and practice refer to the Grammar & Style Workshop, Pronoun-Antecedent Agreement, on page 56.

GRAMMAR & STYLE

For additional instruction and practice refer to the Grammar & Style Workshop, Nominative and Objective Pronouns, on page 72.

PRONOUN CASES

Personal pronouns take on different forms—called *cases*—depending on how they are used in sentences. Personal pronouns can be used as subjects, direct objects, indirect objects, and objects of prepositions. In the English language, there are three case forms for personal pronouns: *nominative, objective,* and *possessive.* The following chart organizes personal pronouns by case, number, and person.

Personal Pronouns

	Nominative Case	Objective Case	Possessive Case
Singular			
first person	I	me	my, mine
second person	you	you	your, yours
third person	he, she, it	him, her, it	his, her, hers, its
Plural			
first person	we	us	our, ours
second person	you	you	your, yours
third person	they	them	their, theirs

Indefinite Pronouns

An **indefinite pronoun** points out a person, place, or thing, but not a particular or definite one. The indefinite pronouns are listed below.

Singular	Plural	Singular or Plural
another	both	all
anybody	few	any
anyone	many	more
anything	others	most
each	several	none
each other		some
either		
everybody		
everyone		
everything		
much		
neither		
nobody		
no one		
nothing		
one		
one another		
somebody		
someone		
something		

EXAMPLES

singular

Something makes a ticking noise in the night.

Everyone is welcome to join us at the picnic.

plural

Many are eager to participate in the summer festival.

Several were missing the necessary information.

Verbs

VERBS — PREDICATES

Every sentence can be divided into two parts: the **subject** and the **predicate.** The following sentence is divided between the complete subject and the complete predicate.

EXAMPLE

The barn **owl** | **glided** slowly over the cornfield.

The subject of a sentence names whom or what the sentence is about. The predicate tells what the subject does, is, or has. A **verb** is the predicate without any complements, linkers, or modifiers. In other words, the verb is the simple predicate.

Verbs are the **expressers** of the English language. Verbs are used to express action or a state of being. They tell whether the action is completed, continuing, or will happen in the future. Verbs also express all kinds of conditions for the action. Verbs in the English language can be from one to four words long. When a main verb is preceded by one or more helping verbs, it is called a **verb phrase.**

EXAMPLES

Dale **mows** his neighbors' lawns.

Dale **is mowing** his neighbors' lawns.

Dale **has been mowing** his neighbors' lawns.

Dale **might have been mowing** his neighbors' lawns.

The following chart lists the different types of verbs and their functions, along with examples of how they are used.

Type of Verb	Definition	Examples
action verb	names an action	howl, wobble, skitter, flutter, fly
helping verb	helps a main verb express action or a state of being	My dogs will howl when a siren sounds. A butterfly has been fluttering above the daisies.
linking verb	connects a noun with another noun, pronoun, or adjective that describes or identifies it; the most common linking verbs are formed from the verb *to be*	The butterfly is a monarch. It seems to float in the breeze.
transitive verb	has a direct object	The scientist remembered the secret code.
intransitive verb	does not have a direct object	My brother snores.
irregular verb	has a different past tense form and spelling	forget/forgot think/thought write/wrote

VERB TENSES

The Simple Tenses

Verbs have different forms, called **tenses,** which are used to tell the time in which an action takes place. The **simple tenses** of the verb are **present, past,** and **future.**

For additional instruction and practice refer to the Grammar & Style Workshop, Consistent Verb Tense, on page 219.

The **present tense** tells that an action happens now—in present time.

EXAMPLES

present tense singular	The green frog **jumps** into the pond.
present tense plural	The green frogs **jump** into the pond.
present tense singular	The teacher **walks** down the hall.
present tense plural	The teachers **walk** down the hall.

The **past tense** tells that an action happened in the past—prior to the present time. The past tense of a regular verb is formed by adding *–d* or *–ed* to the present verb form.

EXAMPLES

past tense singular	The green frog **jumped** into the pond.
past tense plural	The green frogs **jumped** into the pond.
past tense singular	The teacher **walked** down the hall.
past tense plural	The teachers **walked** down the hall.

The **future tense** tells that an action will happen in the future. The future tense is formed by adding the word *will* or *shall* before the present verb form.

EXAMPLES

future tense singular	The green frog **will jump** into the pond.
future tense plural	The green frogs **will jump** into the pond.
future tense singular	The teacher **shall walk** down the hall.
future tense plural	The teachers **shall walk** down the hall.

The Perfect Tenses

The **perfect tenses** of verbs also express present, past, and future time, but they show that the action continued and was completed over a period of time or that the action will be completed in the present or future. The perfect tense is formed by using *has, have,* or *had* with the past participle.

EXAMPLES

present perfect singular	Vera **has baked** the birthday cake. The birthday cake **has been baked** by Vera.
present perfect plural	Vera and Hans **have baked** the birthday cake. (have or has + past participle)
past perfect singular	Vera **had baked** the birthday cake. The birthday cake **had been baked** by Vera.
past perfect plural	Vera and Hans **had baked** the birthday cake. (had + past participle)
future perfect singular	Vera **will have baked** the birthday cake. The birthday cake **will have been baked** by Vera.
future perfect plural	Vera and Hans **will have baked** the birthday cake. (will have or shall have + past participle)

Complements

COMPLEMENTS FOR ACTION VERBS

A sentence must have a subject and a verb to communicate its basic meaning. In the following sentences, the subject and verb express the total concept. There is no receiver of the verb's action.

EXAMPLES

We talked.

I never lose.

The tree fell.

Many sentences that include action verbs, however, need an additional word or group of words to complete the meaning.

EXAMPLES

The soldiers climbed.

The soldiers climbed the wall.

The group of words *The musicians tuned* contains a subject *(musicians)* and a verb *(tuned)*. Although the group of words may be considered a sentence, it does not express a complete thought. The word *instruments* completes the meaning expressed by the verb *tuned*. Therefore, *instruments* is called a **complement** or a completing word. The *completers* for action verbs are **direct objects** and **indirect objects.**

Direct Objects

A **direct object** receives the action in the sentence. It usually answers the question *what?* or *whom?* To find the direct object, find the action verb in the sentence. Then ask *what?* or *whom?* about the verb.

EXAMPLES

I **found** a **coin** in the pond. (*Found* is the action verb. What did I find? *Coin* is the direct object.)

The dog **jumped** the **fence.** (*Jumped* is the action verb. What did the dog jump? *Fence* is the direct object.)

Remember to use object pronouns for a direct object.

singular me, you, him, her, it
plural us, you, them

EXAMPLES

Betty told **us** to drive west.

Evan questioned **him** about the wallet.

Indirect Objects

Sometimes the direct object is received by someone or something. This receiver is called the **indirect object.** It comes before the direct object and tells *to whom* the action is directed or *for whom* the action is performed. Only verbs that have direct objects can have indirect objects.

EXAMPLE

Seth **sold** Karl a **car.** (*Sold* is the action verb. *Car* is the direct object because it tells what Seth sold. *Karl* is an indirect object. It tells to whom Seth sold a car.)

To identify the indirect object: (1) Look for a noun or a pronoun that precedes the direct object. (2) Determine whether the word you think is a direct object seems to be the understood object of the preposition *to* or *for*.

COMPLEMENTS FOR LINKING VERBS

A **linking verb** connects a subject with a noun, a pronoun, or an adjective that describes it or identifies it. Linking verbs do not express action. Instead, they express state of being and need a noun, a pronoun or an adjective to complete the sentence meaning.

In each of the following sentences, the subject and verb would not be complete without the words that follow them.

EXAMPLES

The chocolate cake **was** rich.
(The verb *was* connects the subject *cake* with a word that describes it—*rich*.)

The wind and rain **are** cold.
(The verb *are* connects the compound subject *wind and rain* with a word that describes it—*cold*.)

Most linking verbs are forms of the verb *to be*, including *am, are, is, was,* and *been*. Other words that can be used as linking verbs include *appear, feel, grow, smell, taste, seem, sound, look, stay, feel, remain,* and *become*. When *to be* verbs are part of an action verb, they are helpers.

3.7 Agreement

SUBJECT AND VERB AGREEMENT

A **singular** noun describes or stands for *one* person, place, thing, or idea. A **plural noun** describes or stands for *more than one* person, place, thing, or idea.

EXAMPLES

singular nouns	book	apple	rose	mouse	child
plural nouns	books	apples	roses	mice	children

In a sentence, a verb must be singular if its subject is singular and plural if its subject is plural. In other words, a verb must agree in number with its subject.

EXAMPLES

singular subject and verb	The apple seems ripe.
plural subject and verb	The apples seem ripe.
singular subject and verb	A rose smells lovely in the evening.
plural subject and verb	The roses smell lovely in the evening.
singular subject and verb	A mouse runs across the room.
plural subject and verb	The mice run across the room.

> For additional instruction and practice refer to the Grammar & Style Workshop, Subject-Verb Agreement, on page 48.

COMPOUND SUBJECT AND VERB AGREEMENT

A **compound subject** consists of two or more subjects that share the same verb.

EXAMPLE

> Frank and Wyatt ride horses in the corral. (The compound
> subject—*Frank and Wyatt*—shares the verb *ride*.)

A compound subject must have either a singular or a plural verb, depending on how the parts of the subject are connected.

Use a singular verb:
- when the compound subject is made up of singular nouns or pronouns connected by *either/or* or *neither/nor.*

EXAMPLES

> **singular verb**
>
> Either Tom or Jesse **looks** like a good choice to start the game.
>
> Neither sword nor axe **prevents** me from finishing this quest.

Use a plural verb:
- when the compound subject is connected by the coordinating conjunction *and.*
- when the compound subject is formed from plural nouns or pronouns.

EXAMPLES

> **plural**
>
> Cars and trucks **park** in the field.
>
> Either cats or dogs **provide** good companionship.

When a compound subject consists of a singular subject and a plural subject connected by *or* or *nor,* use a verb that agrees in number with the subject that is closer to it in the sentence.

EXAMPLES

> Either Kevin or his sisters **watch** the children in the park. (*sisters watch*—plural)
>
> Neither the players nor their coach **endorses** the statement of the owner. (*coach endorses*—singular)

INDEFINITE PRONOUN AND VERB AGREEMENT

An **indefinite pronoun** does not refer to a specific person, place, or thing. Some indefinite pronouns are always singular and take singular verbs: *anybody, anyone, anything, each, either, everybody, everyone, everything, much, neither, nobody, no one, nothing, one, somebody, someone, something.*

EXAMPLES

> **singular**
> **Nobody** knows the size of the universe.
>
> **Something** occurs at noon every day.

Some indefinite pronouns are always plural and take plural verbs: *both, few, many, others, several.*

EXAMPLES

> **plural**
> **Many** of our presidents **were** military officers.
>
> **Both understand** that this must never happen again.

Modifiers

ADJECTIVES

Adjectives modify nouns by telling specific details about them.

EXAMPLES

noun	a car
a little more specific	an orange car
more specific yet	the fast orange car
even more specific	a sporty, fast orange car

Some adjectives tell *how many* or *what kind* about the nouns or pronouns they modify.

EXAMPLES

There were **several** cars in the lot.

They chose the car with the **tinted** windows.

Other adjectives tell *which one* or *which ones*.

EXAMPLES

Our car has rust spots.

Those cars in the junkyard were once very expensive.

The **articles** *a, an,* and *the* are the most commonly occurring adjectives. *A* and *an* refer to any person, place, or thing in general. *The* refers to a specific person, place, or thing.

EXAMPLES

A fence can be made of wood or metal. (*A* refers to a fence in general.)

The gate on **the** fence is open. (*The* refers to a specific gate on a specific fence.)

A **proper adjective** is formed from a proper noun. Proper adjectives are capitalized and often end in *–n, –an, –ian, –ese,* or *–ish.*

EXAMPLES

African mahogany trees are valued for their hard, reddish brown wood.

Furniture and ships are often built with durable **Asian** teakwood.

Type of Adjective	Definition	Examples
adjective	modifies nouns and pronouns; answers the questions *what kind? which one? how many?* and *how much?*	**shiny** pennies **hieroglyphic** inscription **dozen** roses **one** mistake
article	*a* and *an* refer to an unspecified person, place, thing, or idea; *the* refers to a specific person, place, thing, or idea	**A** problem has developed. I peeled **an** orange. **The** tomatoes are ripe.
proper adjective	is formed from proper nouns; is capitalized; often ends in *–n, –an, –ian, –ese,* or *–ish*	**Serbian** restaurant **Victorian** England **Chinese** calendar **Jewish** tradition

ADVERBS

Adverbs modify verbs, adjectives, or other adverbs. Many times adverbs will tell us *how, when, where, why* or *to what extent.*

EXAMPLES

adverbs modify verbs

The children sing **cheerfully.** (*Cheerfully* tells how they sing.)

Eagles **usually** fly **high** in the summer sky. (*Usually* tells when they fly in the sky; high tells where they fly.)

adverbs modify adjectives

These noble birds are **especially** graceful. (*Especially* tells to what extent they are graceful.)

Some rare birds are **nearly** extinct. (*Nearly* tells to what extent the birds are extinct.)

adverbs modify adverbs

The eagles swoop down on their prey **very** quickly. (*Very* tells to what extent they swoop down on their prey quickly.)

The birds grip **so** strongly, few animals can escape their clutches. (*So* tells how strongly they grip.)

POSITION OF ADVERBS

An adverb can be placed before or after a verb it modifies. Sometimes an adverb can be separated from a verb by another word or words.

EXAMPLES

The coin collector **carefully examined** the rare silver coin.

Eager to find out when it was minted, he **looked carefully** through the magnifying glass.

He **polished** the coin **carefully** to reveal the embossed date.

Note, however, in the following examples, how changing the position of an adverb changes the meaning of the sentence.

EXAMPLES

He **only** worried about money. (He did nothing else but worry about money.)

He worried **only** about money. (He worried about nothing else but money.)

3.9 Prepositions and Conjunctions

PREPOSITIONS AND CONJUNCTIONS

Prepositions and conjunctions are the linkers of the English language. They are used to join words and phrases to the rest of a sentence. They also show the relationships between ideas. Prepositions and conjunctions help writers vary their sentences by connecting sentence parts in different ways.

A **preposition** is used to show how its object, a noun or a pronoun, is related to other words in the sentence. Some commonly used prepositions include *above, after, against, among, around, at, behind, beneath, beside, between, down, for, from, in, on, off, toward, through, to, until, upon,* and *with.*

EXAMPLES

A whale swam **under** our boat.

We had to crawl **through** the tunnel **between** the two buildings.

A **conjunction** is a word used to link related words, groups of words, or sentences. Like a preposition, a conjunction shows the relationship between the words it links. Some of the most commonly used conjunctions are *and, but, for, nor, or, yet, so, if, after, because, before, although, unless, while,* and *when.* Some conjunctions are used in pairs, such as *both/and, neither/nor,* and *not only/but also.*

EXAMPLES

I found leaves **and** twigs in the yard.

He stopped running **after** he twisted his ankle.

Neither the plaintiffs **nor** the defendants understand the ruling.

3.10 Interjections

An **interjection** is a part of speech that expresses feeling, such as surprise, joy, relief, urgency, pain, or anger. Common interjections include *ah, aha, alas, bravo, dear me, goodness, great, ha, help, hey, hooray, hush, indeed, mercy, of course, oh, oops, ouch, phooey, really, say, see, ugh,* and *whew.*

EXAMPLES

Hey, that's not fair!

Goodness, you don't need to get so upset.

Hush! You'll wake the baby.

Why, of course! Please do join us for dinner.

3.11 Phrases

A **phrase** is a group of words used as a single part of speech. A phrase lacks a subject, a verb, or both; therefore, it cannot be a sentence. There are three common kinds of phrases: prepositional phrases, verbal phrases, and appositive phrases.

PREPOSITIONAL PHRASES

A **prepositional phrase** consists of a preposition, its object, and any modifiers of that object. A prepositional phrase adds information to a sentence by relating its object to another word in the sentence. It may function as an adjective or an adverb.

EXAMPLES

adjectives
Ted bought a car **with a sunroof.** (The prepositional phrase *with a sunroof* tells what kind of car Ted bought. The phrase is an adjective, modifying the noun *car.*)

adverbs
The fog drifted **over the hill.** (The prepositional phrase *over the hill* tells where the fog drifted. The phrase is an adverb, modifying the verb *drifted.*)

> For additional instruction and practice refer to the Grammar & Style Workshop, Phrases, on page 264.

VERBAL PHRASES

Verbals are verb forms that act as namers or modifiers.

A **participle** is a verb form ending in *–ing, –d,* or *–ed* that acts as an adjective, modifying a noun or a pronoun. A **participial phrase** is made up of a participle and all of the words related to the participle, which may include objects, modifiers, and prepositional phrases. The entire phrase acts as an adjective.

EXAMPLES

Climbing carefully up the tree, Elijah was able to reach the cat. (The participle *climbing,* the adverb *carefully,* and the prepositional phrase *up the tree* make up the participial phrase that modifies *Elijah.*)

Jim came up with the idea for the mural **painted on the building.** (The participle *painted* and the prepositional phrase *on the building* make up the participial phrase that modifies *mural.*)

A **gerund phrase** is a phrase made up of a gerund (a verb form ending in *–ing*) and all of its modifiers and complements. The entire phrase functions as a noun.

EXAMPLES

Waiting for the bus is boring for Tracy. (The gerund phrase functions as the subject of the sentence.)

Tracy hates **waiting for the bus** at the corner. (The gerund phrase functions as the direct object of the sentence.)

Sometimes the *to* of an infinitive phrase is left out; it is understood.

EXAMPLES

Jerry helped **[to]** paint the house.

I'll go **[to]** feed the cat.

APPOSITIVE PHRASES

An **appositive phrase** is a group of words made up of an appositive and all its modifiers. The phrase renames or identifies a noun or a pronoun.

EXAMPLES

Dr. George, **the former football coach,** is our new professor. (The appositive phrase renames the noun *Dr. George.*)

The television show ***Let's Make a Deal*** used to be very popular. (The appositive phrase identifies which show used to be very popular.)

The first example above, *the former football coach,* is a **nonessential,** or **nonrestrictive, appositive phrase.** It is not necessary to the meaning of the sentence; it is not needed to identify Dr. George, since we already know that he is our new professor. Therefore, it is set off with commas.

The second example, *Let's Make a Deal,* is an **essential,** or **restrictive, appositive phrase.** It is necessary for understanding the sentence because it identifies which particular television show, since we do not already know which one. This appositive phrase is not set off with commas.

For additional instruction and practice refer to the Grammar & Style Workshop, Verbals: Participles, Gerunds, and Infinitives, on page 622.

For additional instruction and practice refer to the Grammar & Style Workshop, Independent and Dependent Clauses, on page 190.

For additional instruction and practice refer to the Grammar & Style Workshop, Adjective and Adverb Clauses, on page 389.

GRAMMAR & STYLE

3.12 Clauses

A **clause** is a group of words that contains a subject and a verb and that functions as one part of speech. There are two types of clauses—independent and subordinate.

An **independent clause,** sometimes called a *main clause,* has a subject and a verb and expresses a complete thought. Since it can stand alone as a sentence, it is called *independent.*

EXAMPLE

   Abraham Lincoln is often called the "Great Emancipator."

A **subordinate clause** or *dependent clause* has a subject and a verb, but it doesn't express a complete thought. It can't stand alone. It must be attached to or inserted into an independent clause. When you combine subordinate clauses with independent clauses, you form complete sentences.

EXAMPLES

   When the bell rang, the students ran out of the room. (The subordinate clause *when the bell rang* is attached to an independent clause.)

   The dog **that barked all night** slept throughout the day. (The subordinate clause *that barked all night* is inserted into the independent clause *The dog slept throughout the day.*)

3.13 Common Usage Problems

INCORRECT SUBJECT-VERB AGREEMENT

A subject and its verb must agree in number. Use singular verb forms with singular subjects and plural verb forms with plural subjects.

Intervening Words

A prepositional phrase that comes between a subject and a verb does not determine whether the subject is singular or plural.

EXAMPLES

   The **captain** on the bridge **gazes** across the sea. (*captain gazes,* singular)

   The **detective,** in addition to the police, **looks** for clues at the house. (*detective looks,* singular)

   The **players** on the team **practice** diligently. (*players practice,* plural)

   The **books** in the back of the store **are** only half price. (*books are,* plural)

In some cases, the *object* of the preposition controls the verb.

EXAMPLES

   Jim and his brother **plan** strategy before each game.

   Cars, trucks, and motorcycles **roar** past our house.

Compound Subjects

Use a plural verb with most compound subjects connected by *and.*

EXAMPLES

Charlotte and her boss **review** the budget once a month.

Otters, beavers, and alligators **live** near bodies of water.

INCORRECT USE OF APOSTROPHES

Use an apostrophe to replace letters that have been left out in a contraction.

EXAMPLES

it's = it is   don't = do not   I'll = I will

Use an apostrophe to show possession.

Singular Nouns

Use an apostrophe and an *s* ('s) to form the possessive of a singular noun, even if it ends in *s*, *x*, or *z*.

EXAMPLES

Rachel's notebook   Frank's lizard   Conan's ring
lynx's paw   jazz's history   boss's desk

Plural Nouns

Use an apostrophe and an *s* ('s) to form the possessive of a plural noun that does not end in *s*.

EXAMPLES

women's shirts   children's books   people's candidate

Use an apostrophe alone to form the possessive of a plural noun that ends in *s*.

EXAMPLES

rodents' food   the boys' locker room   the ships' sails

Do not add an apostrophe or 's to possessive personal pronouns: *mine, yours, his, hers, its, ours,* or *theirs.* They already show ownership.

EXAMPLES

Our cars are painted; **theirs** are still rusty.

The shark opened **its** mouth.

DOUBLE NEGATIVES

Make sure that you use only one of the following negatives in each sentence: *not, nobody, none, nothing, hardly, can't, doesn't, won't, isn't, aren't.* A **double negative** is the use of two negative words together when only one is needed. Correct double negatives by removing one of the negative words or by replacing one of the negative words with a positive word.

EXAMPLES

double negative
We won't hardly make it in time.

corrected sentence
We will hardly make it in time. We won't make it in time.

double negative

Nell wasn't never able to win the big prize.

corrected sentence

Nell was never able to win the big prize. Nell wasn't ever able to win the big prize.

DANGLING AND MISPLACED MODIFIERS

A **dangling modifier** has nothing to modify because the word it would logically modify is not present in the sentence. In the following sentence, the modifying phrase has no logical object. The sentence says that a whale was flying.

EXAMPLE

Flying above the ocean, a whale was spotted.

You can eliminate dangling modifiers by rewriting the sentence so that an appropriate word is provided for the modifier to modify. You can also expand a dangling phrase into a full subordinate clause.

EXAMPLES

Flying above the ocean, we saw a whale.

As we flew above the ocean, we spotted a whale.

A **misplaced modifier** is located too far from the word it should modify.

EXAMPLE

I found a penny during my morning jog on a park bench.

You can revise a misplaced modifier by moving it closer to the word it modifies.

EXAMPLES

I found a penny on a park bench during my morning jog.

On a park bench I found a penny during my morning jog.

During my morning jog, I found a penny on a park bench.

FORMS OF *WHO* AND *WHOM*

Who and *whom* can be used to ask questions and to introduce subordinate clauses. Knowing what form of *who* to use can sometimes be confusing. The case of the pronoun *who* is determined by the pronoun's function in a sentence.

nominative case   who, whoever

objective case   whom, whomever

EXAMPLES

Who wrote the novel *One Hundred Years of Solitude?* (Because *who* is the subject in the sentence, the pronoun is in the nominative case.)

Did you say **who** called? (Because *who* is the subject of the subordinate clause, the pronoun is in the nominative case.)

Whoever returns my wallet will receive a reward. (Because *whoever* is the subject in the sentence, the pronoun is in the nominative case.)

Whom did you visit? (Because *whom* is the direct object in the sentence, the pronoun is in the objective case.)

> For additional instruction and practice refer to the Grammar & Style Workshop, Dangling Modifiers, on page 776.

> For additional instruction and practice refer to the Grammar & Style Workshop, Misplaced Modifiers, on page 764.

3.14 Commonly Misused Words

The following chart contains an alphabetic list of words and phrases that often cause usage problems.

Word/Phrases	Correct Use	Examples
a, an	Use *a* before words beginning with a consonant sound. Use *an* before words beginning with a vowel sound, including a silent *h*.	While walking in the woods, Jonah saw **a** coyote. **An** orangutan has a shaggy, reddish brown coat and very long arms. It is hard to find **an** honest politician in this town.
accept, except	*Accept* is a verb meaning "to receive willingly" or "to agree." *Except* is a preposition that means "leaving out" or "but."	I wish you would **accept** this token of my appreciation. Everyone has apologized for the misunderstanding **except** the mayor.
affect, effect	*Affect* is a verb that means "to influence." The noun *effect* means "the result of an action." The verb *effect* means "to cause" or "to bring about."	You can't let the audience **affect** your concentration. We saw the **effect** of last night's storm throughout the town. Peter will **effect** the proposed reorganization when he takes office.
ain't	This word is nonstandard English. Avoid using it in speaking and writing.	**nonstandard:** I ain't going to study English this semester. **standard:** I **am not** going to study English this semester.
all ready, already	*All ready* means "entirely ready or prepared." *Already* means "previously."	Speaking with each team member, I determined that they were **all ready** to play. Sandy **already** finished her homework before soccer practice.
all right	*All right* means "satisfactory," "unhurt," "correct," or "yes, very well." The word *alright* is not acceptable in formal written English.	**All right,** let's begin the meeting. Is your ill father going to be **all right?**
a lot	*A lot* means "a great number or amount" and is always two words. Because it is imprecise, you should avoid it except in informal usage. *Alot* is not a word.	We found **a lot** of seashells on the beach. Your brother had **a lot** of help planning the surprise party.
altogether, all together	*Altogether* is an adverb meaning "thoroughly." Something done *all together* is done as a group or mass.	He was **altogether** embarrassed after tripping on the sidewalk. The family members were **all together** when they heard the good news.
anywheres, everywheres, somewheres, nowheres	Use these words and others like them without the *s: anywhere, everywhere, somewhere, nowhere.*	The little gray dog was **nowhere** to be found. Yolanda never goes **anywhere** without her cell phone.
at	Don't use this word after *where.*	Where are your brothers hiding?
bad, badly	*Bad* is always an adjective, and *badly* is always an adverb. Use *bad* after linking verbs.	I developed a **bad** cold after shoveling the heavy, wet snow. Tom feels **bad** about losing your favorite CD. We **badly** need to find another relief pitcher.

Word/Phrases	Correct Use	Examples
beside, besides	*Beside* means "next to." *Besides* means "in addition to." *Besides* can also be an adverb meaning "moreover."	The yellow plant is sitting **beside** the purple vase. I bought socks and shoes **besides** a new shirt and jacket. There is nothing worth watching on TV tonight; **besides,** I have to study for a test.
between, among	Use *between* when referring to two people or things. Use *among* when you are discussing three or more people or things.	While on vacation, I divided my time **between** Paris and Brussels. The thoughtful pirate divided the loot **among** his shipmates.
bring, take	Use *bring* when you mean "to carry to." It refers to movement toward the speaker. Use *take* when you mean "to carry away." It refers to movement away from the speaker.	You need to **bring** your backpack home. Don't forget to **take** the garbage out to the curb tonight.
bust, busted	Do not use these nonstandard words as verbs to substitute for *break* or *burst*.	**nonstandard:** I busted my leg sliding into third base. The barrel busted after the extra batch was added. **standard:** I **broke** my leg sliding into third base. The barrel **burst** after the extra batch was added.
can, may	The word *can* means "able to do something." The word *may* is used to ask or give permission.	**Can** you speak a foreign language? You **may** borrow my red sweater.
choose, chose	*Choose* is the present tense, and *chose* is the past tense.	I **choose** to start work at 6:00 AM each day. Randy **chose** to quit his job after working only three days.
could of	Use the helping verb *have* (which may sound like *could of*) with *could, might, must, should, ought,* and *would*.	**nonstandard:** We could of won the game in overtime. **standard:** We **could have** won the game in overtime.
doesn't, don't	*Doesn't* is the contraction of *does not*. It is used with singular nouns and the pronouns *he, she, it, this,* and *that*. *Don't* is the contraction of *do not*. Use it with plural nouns and the pronouns *I, we, they, you, these,* and *those*.	Jason **doesn't** know what to make for lunch. We **don't** answer the phone during dinner.
farther, further	Use *farther* to refer to physical distance. Use *further* to refer to greater extent in time or degree or to mean "additional."	I walked **farther** today than I did yesterday. The board members will discuss this issue **further** at the meeting. The essay requires **further** revision before it can be published.
fewer, less	Use *fewer*, which tells "how many," to refer to things that you can count individually. *Fewer* is used with plural words. Use *less* to refer to quantities that you cannot count. It is used with singular words and tells "how much."	I see **fewer** fans coming out to the ballpark each year. Jasmine has more experience and thus needs **less** training than Phil.
good, well	*Good* is always an adjective. *Well* is an adverb meaning "ably" or "capably." *Well* is also a predicate adjective meaning "satisfactory" or "in good health." Don't confuse *feel good*, which means "to feel happy or pleased," with *feel well*, which means "to feel healthy."	Charles was a **good** pilot during the war. Leslie felt **good** [pleased] after bowling three strikes in a row. Shirley paints **well** for someone with no formal training. Not feeling **well,** Samuel stayed home from school today.

Word/Phrases	Correct Use	Examples
had ought, hadn't ought	The verb *ought* should never be used with the helping verb *had*.	**nonstandard:** Ted had ought to find another route into town. **standard:** Ted **ought** to find another route into town. **nonstandard:** She hadn't ought climb that tree. **standard:** She **ought** not climb that tree.
hardly, scarcely	Since both of these words have negative meanings, do not use them with other negative words such as *not*, *no*, *nothing*, and *none*.	**nonstandard:** That music is so loud I can't hardly hear myself think. **standard:** That music is so loud I can **hardly** hear myself think. **nonstandard:** Shane hadn't scarcely enough gas to make it back home. **standard:** Shane had **scarcely** enough gas to make it back home.
he, she, they	Do not use these pronouns after a noun. This error is called a double subject.	**nonstandard:** Jed's brother he is a famous actor. **standard:** Jed's brother is a famous actor.
hisself, their-selves	These are incorrect forms. Use *himself* and *themselves*.	**nonstandard:** Paul talks to hisself when mowing the lawn. **standard:** Paul talks to **himself** when mowing the lawn. **nonstandard:** The panel talked among theirselves about the Holy Roman Empire. **standard:** The panel talked among **themselves** about the Holy Roman Empire.
how come	Do not use in place of *why*.	**nonstandard: How come** you didn't call me last night? **standard: Why** didn't you call me last night?
in, into	Use *in* to mean "within" or "inside." Use *into* to suggest movement toward the inside from the outside.	The children were **in** the kitchen. The children raced **into** the kitchen.
its, it's	*Its* is a possessive pronoun. *It's* is the contraction for *it is*.	The radio station held **its** annual fundraiser. **It's** too late tonight to start another game.
kind, sort, type	Use *this* or *that* to modify the singular nouns *kind*, *sort*, and *type*. Use *these* and *those* to modify the plural nouns *kinds*, *sorts*, and *types*. *Kind* should be singular when the object of the preposition following it is singular. It should be plural when the object of the preposition is plural.	This **kind** of ice cream is my favorite. These **types** of problems are difficult to solve.
kind of, sort of	Do not use these terms to mean "somewhat" or "rather."	**nonstandard:** He feels kind of sluggish today. **standard:** He feels rather sluggish today.
lay, lie	*Lay* means "to put" or "to place." *Lay* usually takes a direct object. *Lie* means "to rest" or "to be in a lying position." *Lie* never takes a direct object. (Note that the past tense of *lie* is *lay*.)	Please **lay** the blanket on the bed. I **laid** the blanket on the bed. **Lie** down on the bed and take a nap. Mary **lay** down on the bed and took a nap.
learn, teach	*Learn* means "to gain knowledge." *Teach* means "to give knowledge." Do not use them interchangeably.	Betty took lessons to **learn** how to fly a small airplane. I would like to find someone to **teach** me how to sew.

Word/Phrases	Correct Use	Examples
like, as	*Like* is usually a preposition followed by an object. It generally means "similar to." *As, as if,* and *as though* are conjunctions used to introduce subordinate clauses. *As* is occasionally a preposition: *He worked as a farmer.*	The alligator was motionless **like** a rock on the riverbank. The spider spun its web **as** the unsuspecting fly flew into the silky trap. Roger looks **as though** he's not feeling well.
of	This word is unnecessary after the prepositions *inside, outside,* and *off.*	The feather pillow slid **off** the bed. People gathered **outside** the stadium before the game. Please put the chattering parrot **inside** its cage.
precede, proceed	*Precede* means "to go or come before." *Proceed* means "to go forward."	The calf-roping competition will **precede** the bull-riding event. If you hear the alarm, **proceed** down the stairs and out the exit.
quiet, quite	Although these words sound alike, they have different meanings. *Quiet* is an adjective that means "making little or no noise"; *quite* is an adverb meaning "positively" or "completely."	The house became **quiet** after the baby finally fell asleep. Unfortunately, our bill for the car repairs was **quite** large.
real, really	*Real* is an adjective meaning "actual." *Really* is an adverb meaning "actually" or "genuinely." Do not use *real* to mean "very" or "extremely."	The table is very sturdy because it is made of **real** oak. Heather was **really** (not *real*) excited about trying out for the play.
reason...because	*Reason is because* is both wordy and redundant. Use *reason is that* or simply *because.*	**nonstandard:** The reason I am in a good mood is because today is Friday. **standard:** The reason for my good mood is that it is Friday. **standard:** The reason for my good mood is that today is Friday. **standard:** I am in a good mood because today is Friday.
regardless, irre-gardless	Use *regardless, unmindful, heedless,* or *anyway.* *Irregardless* is a double negative and should never be used.	**nonstandard:** Irregardless of the rain, the concert will still be held as scheduled. **standard: Regardless** of the rain, the concert will still be held as scheduled.
rise, raise	*Rise* is an intransitive verb that means "to move upward." It is an irregular verb that does not take a direct object. *Raise* is a transitive verb that means "to lift or make something go upward." It is a regular verb that takes a direct object.	The sun **rises** and sets every day. Perry **raised** his hand to ask a question.
scratch, itch	*Scratch* means "to scrape lightly to relieve itching." *Itch* means "to feel a tingling of the skin, with the desire to scratch."	Please do not **scratch** the mosquito bites. The mosquito bites on my leg still **itch.**
set, sit	*Set* is a transitive verb meaning "to place something." It always takes a direct object. *Sit* is an intransitive verb meaning "to rest in an upright position." It does not take a direct object.	Please **set** the pitcher of milk on the table. Let's **sit** outside on the back deck.
some, somewhat	*Some* is an adjective meaning "a certain unspecified quantity." *Somewhat* is an adverb meaning "slightly." Do not use *some* as an adverb.	**nonstandard:** The pressure on her schedule has eased some. **standard:** The pressure on her schedule has eased **somewhat.** **standard:** I need to find **some** index cards before starting my report.

Word/Phrases	Correct Use	Examples
than, then	*Than* is a conjunction used in comparisons. *Then* is an adverb that shows a sequence of events.	Hank's lawn is greener **than** Dale's lawn is. We went to the post office and **then** drove to the mall.
that	*That* is used to refer either to people or things. Use it to introduce essential, or restrictive, clauses that refer to things or groups of people. Do not use a comma before *that* when it introduces an essential clause.	The tree **that** fell in the storm was more than one hundred years old. An automobile **that** never needs repairs is rare.
their, there, they're	*Their* is the possessive form of *they*. *There* points out a place or introduces an independent clause. *They're* is the contracted form of *they are*.	Our neighbors inspected **their** roof after the hailstorm. When you arrive at the airport, I will be **there** waiting. I don't think **they're** going to be visiting us this summer.
them	*Them* is a pronoun. It should never be used as an adjective. Use *those*.	**nonstandard:** Remember to return them books to the library. **standard:** Remember to return **those** books to the library.
this here, that there	Do not use. Simply say *this* or *that*.	**nonstandard:** This here is the best coffee shop in town. **standard: This** is the best coffee shop in town. **nonstandard:** That there is an antique rocking chair. **standard: That** is an antique rocking chair.
to, too, two	*To* is a preposition that can mean "in the direction of." *Too* is an adverb that means both "extremely, overly" and "also." *Two* is the spelling for the number 2.	Please carry the luggage **to** the car. Leah has **too** many boxes in the attic. Tony and Liz are excellent students, **too.** I bought **two** pairs of blue jeans.
try and	Use *try to* instead.	**nonstandard:** Try and find the umbrella before you leave. **standard: Try to** find the umbrella before you leave.
use to, used to	Be sure to add the *-d* to *use* to form the past participle.	**nonstandard:** Rory use to enjoy singing in the choir. **standard:** Rory **used to** enjoy singing in the choir.
way, ways	Do not use *ways* for *way* when referring to distance.	**nonstandard:** We traveled a long ways from home. **standard:** We traveled a long **way** from home.
when, where	When you define a word, don't use *when* or *where*.	**nonstandard:** A *perfect game* is when a bowler throws twelve strikes resulting in a score of 300. **standard:** A *perfect game* is twelve strikes resulting in a score of 300.
where, that	Do not use *where* to mean "that."	**nonstandard:** I read where school will start a week earlier in August. **standard:** I read **that** school will start a week earlier in August.

Word/Phrases	Correct Use	Examples
which, that, who, whom	*Which* is used to refer only to things. Use it to introduce nonessential, or nonrestrictive, clauses that refer to things or to groups of people. Always use a comma before *which* when it introduces a nonessential clause.	Our garage, **which** was built last year, is already showing signs of wear. The panel, **which** was assembled to discuss the election, will publish its conclusions.
who, whom	*Who* or *whom* is used to refer only to people. Use *who* or *whom* to introduce essential and nonessential clauses. Use a comma only when the pronoun introduces a nonessential clause.	Lyle is the man **who** rescued us from the fire. Abraham Lincoln, **whom** many admired, issued the Emancipation Proclamation.
who's, whose	*Who's* is a contraction for *who is* or *who has*. *Whose* is the possessive form of *who*.	**Who's** going to make dinner tonight? **Whose** pig is running loose in my garden?
without, unless	Do not use the preposition *without* in place of the conjunction *unless*.	**nonstandard:** I am not leaving without I have your endorsement. **standard:** I am not leaving **without** your endorsement. **standard:** I am not leaving **unless** I have your endorsement.
your, you're	*Your* is a possessive pronoun. *You're* is a contraction for the words *you are*.	Ron repaired **your** leaky kitchen faucet. **You're** very skilled at repairing things!

3.15 Punctuation

EDITING FOR PUNCTUATION ERRORS

When editing your work, correct all punctuation errors. Several common punctuation errors to avoid are the incorrect use of end marks, commas, semicolons, and colons.

Punctuation Reference Chart

Punctuation	Function	Examples
End Marks	tell the reader where a sentence ends and show the purpose of the sentence; periods are also used for abbreviations.	Our next-door neighbor is Mrs**.** Ryan**.**
Periods	with **declarative** sentences	The weather forecast predicts rain tonight**.**
	with **abbreviations**	
	personal names	**N.** Scott Momaday, **W. W.** Jacobs, Ursula **K.** Le Guin
	titles	**Mr.** Bruce Webber, **Mrs.** Harriet Cline, **Ms.** Steinem, **Dr.** Duvall, **Sen.** Hillary Clinton, **Gov.** George Pataki, **Capt.** Horatio Hornblower, **Prof.** Klaus
	business names	Tip Top Roofing **Co.**, Green **Bros.** Landscaping, Gigantic **Corp.**
	addresses	Oak **Dr.**, Grand **Blvd.**, Main **St.**, Kennedy **Pkwy.**, Prudential **Bldg.**
	geographical terms	Kensington, **Conn.**, San Francisco, **Calif.**, Canberra, **Aus.**
	time	2 **hrs.** 15 **min.**, **Thurs.** morning, **Jan.** 20, 21st **cent.**

> For additional instruction and practice refer to the Grammar & Style Workshop, Punctuation: Dashes, Semicolons, and Colons, on page 693.

Punctuation	Function	Examples
	units of measurement	3 **tbsp.** olive oil 1/2 **c.** peanut butter 8 **oz.** milk 5 **ft.** 4 **in.** 20 **lbs.**
	exceptions: metric measurements, state names in postal addresses, or directional elements	**metric measurements** cc, ml, km, g, L **state postal codes** MN, WI, IA, NE, CA, NY **compass points** N, NW, S, SE
Question Marks	with **interrogative** sentences	May I have another serving of spaghetti**?**
Exclamation Points	with **exclamatory** sentences	Hey, be careful**!**
Commas	to separate words or groups of words within a sentence; to tell the reader to pause at certain spots in the sentence	Casey was confident he could hit a home run**,** but he struck out.
	to separate items in a series	The magician's costume included a **silk scarf, black satin hat,** and **magic wand.**
	to combine sentences using *and, but, or, nor, yet, so,* or *for*	An infestation of beetles threatened the summer squash and zucchini crops**, yet** the sturdy plants thrived. I'll apply an organic insecticide**, or** I'll ignore the garden pest problem.
	after an introductory word, phrase, or clause	**Surprisingly,** fashions from the 1970s are making a come-back. **Frayed and tight-fitting,** denim bellbottoms remain a fashion hit.
	to set off words or phrases that interrupt sentences	Harpers Ferry**, a town in northeastern West Virginia,** was the site of John Brown's raid in 1859. The violent raid**, however,** frightened people in the North and South. **An abolitionist leader,** Brown was captured during the raid and later executed.
	between two or more adjectives that modify the same noun and that could be joined by *and*	A **warm,** [and] **spicy** aroma enticed us to enter the kitchen. Steaming bowls of chili satisfied the **tired,** [and] **hungry** travelers.
	to set off names used in direct address	**Olivia,** the zinnias and daisies need to be watered. Please remember to turn off the back porch light**, John.**
	to separate parts of a date	The United States Stock Exchange collapsed on October **28, 1929.** The stock market crash in October 1929 precipitated a severe economic crisis.
	to separate items in addresses	Gabriel García Márquez was born in **Aracataca, Colombia.** My brother will be moving to **1960 Jasmine Avenue, Liberty, Missouri 64068.**
Semicolons	to join two closely related sentences	It was a beautiful summer morning**;** we took advantage of it by going on a picnic.
	to join the independent clauses of a compound sentence if no coordinating conjunction is used	Marjory Stoneman Douglas was a pioneer conservationist. She formed a vigorous grassroots campaign to protect and restore the Everglades. Marjory Stoneman Douglas was a pioneer conservationist**;** she formed a vigorous grassroots campaign to protect and restore the Everglades.

> For additional instruction and practice refer to the Grammar & Style Workshop, Comma Use, on page 162.

Punctuation	Function	Examples
	between independent clauses joined by a conjunction if either clause contains commas	Douglas was a writer, editor, publisher, and tireless advocate for the protection of the Everglades**;** and President Clinton awarded her the Medal of Freedom in 1993 for her work.
	between items in a series if the items contain commas	Members of Friends of the Everglades **wrote petitions; contacted local groups, political organizations, and governmental agencies; and gathered public support** for the restoration of the Everglades.
	between independent clauses joined by a conjunctive adverb or a transitional phrase	**conjunctive adverb** Starting in 1948, the Central and Southern Florida Project ditched and drained the Everglades**; consequently,** the four million acre wetland was reduced by half. **transitional phrase** Douglas knew that restoration of the Everglades would be a daunting task**; in other words,** she knew that it would take the combined efforts of local, state, and federal groups working in unison.
Colons	to mean "note what follows"	Make sure you have all your paperwork in order**:** passport, visa, and tickets.
	to introduce a list of items	*The Tragedy of Romeo and Juliet* explores **these dominant themes:** civil strife, revenge, love, and fate. The main characters in the play are **as follows:** Romeo, Juliet, Paris, Mercutio, Tybalt, and Friar Lawrence. The role of Juliet has been played by **the following actresses:** Norma Shearer, Susan Shentall, and Olivia Hussey.
	to introduce a long or formal statement or a quotation	Shakespeare's prologue to *Romeo and Juliet* begins with **these memorable lines:** Two households, both alike in dignity, In fair Verona, where we lay our scene, From ancient grudge break to new mutiny, Where civil blood makes civil hands unclean. John Dryden made **the following remark about Shakespeare:** "He was the man who of all modern, and perhaps ancient poets, had the largest and most comprehensive soul." Nearly everyone recognizes **this line by Shakespeare:** "All the world's a stage."
	between two independent clauses when the second clause explains or summarizes the first clause	Shakespeare deserves the greatest of praise**:** his work has influenced and inspired millions of people over the centuries. For Romeo and Juliet, their love is star-crossed**:** If they tell their feuding parents of their love, they will be forbidden from seeing each other. On the other hand, by keeping their love secret, they follow a path that leads, tragically, to their deaths.
	between numbers that tell hours and minutes, after the greeting in a business letter, and between chapter and verse of religious works	Our English class meets Tuesdays and Thursdays from **9:00** AM to **10:00** AM Dear Juliet**:** Please meet me on the balcony at midnight. Ecclesiastes **3:1–8**

Punctuation	Function	Examples
	not after a verb, between a preposition and its object(s), or after *because* or *as*	**after a verb** **incorrect** Three of Shakespeare's most famous plays are: *Romeo and Juliet, Macbeth,* and *Hamlet.* **correct** These are three of Shakespeare's most famous plays: *Romeo and Juliet, Macbeth,* and *Hamlet.* **between a preposition and its object(s)** **incorrect** I have seen performances of Shakespeare's plays in: London, New York, and Chicago. **correct** I have seen performances of Shakespeare's plays in the following cities: London, New York, and Chicago. **after *because* or *as*** **incorrect** Shakespeare was a great playwright because: he had an extraordinary skill in depicting human nature and the universal struggles all people experience. **correct** Shakespeare was a great playwright because he had an extraordinary skill in depicting human nature and the universal struggles all people experience.
Ellipsis Points	to show that material from a quotation or a quoted passage has been left out	"Doing something does not require discipline...it creates its own discipline."
	if material is left out at the beginning of a sentence or passage	...The very thought of hard work makes me queasy.
	if material is left out in the middle of a sentence	The very thought...makes me queasy.
	if material is left out at the end of a sentence	It's hard work, doing something with your life....I'd rather die in peace. Here we are, all equal and alike and none of us much to write home about....
Apostrophes	to form the possessive case of a singular or plural noun	the **window's** ledge, **Carlos's** father, **jazz's** beginnings, **wolves'** howls, twenty-five **cents'** worth, **countries'** treaties, **students'** textbooks
	to show joint or separate ownership	**Zack and Josh's** experiment, **Lisa and Randall's** cabin, **Sarah's** and **Jason's** schedules, **Steve's** and **John's** trumpets
	to form the possessive of an indefinite pronoun	**anyone's** guess, **each other's** notes, **everybody's** dream
	to form a contraction to show where letters, words, or numerals have been omitted	**I'm** = I am **you're** = you are **she's** = she is **o'clock** = of the clock **they're** = they are
	to form the possessive of only the last word in a compound noun, such as the name of an organization or a business	brother-in-**law's** sense of humor; Teller, Teller, and **Teller's** law firm; Volunteer Nursing **Association's** office
	to form the possessive of an acronym	**NASA's** flight plan, **NATO's** alliances, **UNICEF's** contributions
	to form the plural of letters, numerals, and words referred to as words	two **A's**, **ABC's**, three **7's**, twelve **yes's**
	to show the missing numbers in a date	drought of **'02**, class of **'06**

Punctuation	Function	Examples
Underlining and Italics	with titles of books, plays, long poems, periodicals, works of art, movies, radio and television series, videos, computer games, comic strips, and long musical works and recordings	**books:** *To Kill a Mockingbird, Silent Spring, Black Elk Speaks* **plays:** *The Tragedy of Romeo and Juliet, The Monsters Are Due on Maple Street* **long poems:** *Metamorphoses, The Odyssey* **periodicals:** *Sports Illustrated, Wall Street Journal, The Old Farmer's Almanac* **works of art:** *The Acrobat, In the Sky, The Teacup* **movies:** *Il Postino, North by Northwest, Cast Away* **radio/television series:** *Fresh Air, West Wing, Friends, Animal Planet* **videos:** *Yoga for Strength, Cooking with Julia, Wizard of Oz* **computer games:** *Empire Earth, Age of Wonders II* **comic strips:** *Zits, Foxtrot, Overboard* **long musical works/recordings:** *Requiem, Death and the Maiden, La Traviata*
	with the names of trains, ships, aircraft, and spacecraft	**trains:** *Sunset Limited* **ships:** *Titanic* **aircraft:** *Air Force One* **spacecraft:** *Apollo 13*
	with words, letters, symbols, and numerals referred to as such	The word **filigree** has a Latin root. People in western New York pronounce the letter **a** with a harsh, flat sound. The children learned that the symbol **+** is used in addition. Your phone number ends with four **7**'s.
	to set off foreign words or phrases that are not common in English	Did you know the word **amor** means "love"? The first Italian words I learned were **ciao** and **pronto**.
	to place emphasis on a word	Why is the soup **blue**? You're not going to borrow **my** car.
Quotation Marks	at the beginning and end of a direct quotation	"Do you want to ride together to the concert?" asked Margaret. "Don't wait for me," sighed Lillian. "I'm running late as usual."
	to enclose the titles of short works such as short stories, poems, articles, essays, parts of books and periodicals, songs, and episodes of TV series	**short stories:** "Gwilan's Harp," "Everyday Use" **poems:** "Hanging Fire," "Mirror" **articles:** "Where Stars Are Born," "Ghost of Everest" **essays:** "Thinking Like a Mountain," "It's Not Talent; It's Just Work" **parts of books:** "The Obligation to Endure," "Best Sky Sights of the Next Century" **songs:** "At the Fair," "Johnny's Garden" **episodes of TV series:** "The Black Vera Wang," "Isaac and Ishmael"
	to set off slang, technical terms, unusual expressions, invented words, and dictionary definitions	We nicknamed our dog **"Monkey"** because he moves quickly and loves to play tricks. My mother says that **"groovy"** and **"cool"** were the slang words of her generation. Did you know that the word *incident* means **"a definite, distinct occurrence"**?

Punctuation	Function	Examples
Hyphens	to make a compound word or compound expression	**compound nouns:** great-grandfather Schaefer, great-uncle Tom **compound adjectives used before a noun:** best-known novel, down-to-earth actor, real-life adventure **compound numbers:** ninety-nine years, twenty-five cents **spelled-out fractions:** one-half inch, three-fourths cup
	to divide an already hyphenated word at the hyphen	Finally, after much coaxing, our **great-grandfather** told his stories.
	to divide a word only between syllables	**incorrect:** After hiking in the woods, the novice ca-mpers became tired and hungry. **correct:** After hiking in the woods, the novice **camp-ers** became tired and hungry.
	with the prefixes *all-*, *ex-*, *great-*, *half-* and *self-*, and with all prefixes before a proper noun or proper adjective	**all**-purpose, **ex**-husband, **pre**-Industrial age, **great**-grandparent, **half**-baked, **self**-expression
	with the suffixes *-free*, *-elect*, and *-style*	fragrance-**free** detergent, mayor-**elect** Kingston, Southern-**style** hospitality
Dashes	to show a sudden break or change in thought	"I say it did," replied the other. "There was no thought about it; I had just—What's the matter?"
	to mean *namely*, *that is*, or *in other words*	Our puppy knows only two commands—*sit* and *stay*. The hotel rates were surprisingly reasonable—less than a hundred dollars—for a double room.
Parentheses and Brackets	around material added to a sentence but not considered of major importance	Toni Cade Bambara (1939–1995) grew up in Harlem and Brooklyn, New York. The Taj Mahal (a majestic site!) is one man's tribute of love to his departed, beloved wife. More grocery stores are stocking natural food ingredients (for example, whole grains, soy products, and dried fruits).
	to punctuate a parenthetical sentence contained within another sentence.	When the quilt is dry (it shouldn't take long), please fold it and put it in the linen closet. The piping-hot funnel cakes (they were covered with powdered sugar!) just melted in our mouths. The vitamin tablets (aren't you supposed to take one every morning?) provide high doses of vitamins A and E.
	to enclose words or phrases that interrupt the sentence and are not considered essential to meaning.	They took pasta salad and fruit (how could we have forgotten dessert?) to the summer concert.
	to enclose information that ex-plains or clarifies a detail in quoted material	A literary critic praised the author's new book, "She [Martha Grimes] never fails to delight her devoted fans with witty dialogue, elegant prose, and a cast of characters we'd like to consider our friends." Another literary critic wrote, "[Martha] Grimes is the queen of the mystery genre."

3.16 Capitalization

EDITING FOR CAPITALIZATION ERRORS

To avoid capitalization errors, check your draft for proper nouns and proper adjectives; geographical names, directions, and historical names; and titles of artworks and literary works.

Capitalization Reference Chart

Category/Rule	Examples
Proper Nouns and Proper Adjectives	
Proper Nouns	
Names of people	Sojourner Truth, Franklin D. Roosevelt, Martin Luther King Jr.
Months, days, and holidays	October, Wednesday, Memorial Day
Names of religions, languages, races, and nationalities	Baptist, Catholicism, Chilean, Buddhism, French, Hispanic, Greek, African American
Names of clubs, organization, businesses, and institutions	Little League, American Heart Association, Pratt-Read Company, Webster Bank
Names of awards, prizes, and medals	Emmy Award, Nobel Peace Prize, Purple Heart, Pulitzer Prize
Proper Adjectives	
Proper adjectives formed from proper nouns	Japanese gardening, English class, Caribbean music, Alaskan oil drilling
Proper nouns used as adjectives	Senate bill, Agatha Christie masterpiece, California coast, Franklin stove
I and First Words	
The pronoun *I*.	Next week I will leave on my trip to Yellowstone National Park.
First word of each sentence.	The oldest of the U.S. national parks is noted for its beauty, wildlife, and geysers.
First word of a direct quotation.	"That mountain stands taller than any other in the state," the guide reported with pride to his group of tourists.
First lines of most poetry. (Follow the capitalization of the original poem.)	And far as the eye of God could see Darkness covered everything, Blacker than a hundred midnights Down in a cypress swamp.
First word in a letter salutation and the name or title of the person addressed.	Dear Dad, My dear Aunt Nola, Dear Madam
First word in letter closings.	Sincerely yours, Yours truly, Fondly, Warm wishes
Family Relationships and Titles of Persons	
Capitalize the titles or abbreviations that come before the names of people.	Admiral Michael Chase, Ms. Gloria Steinem, Senator Dodd, Mr. and Mrs. Douglas, Dr. Watson, Chief Justice Oliver Wendell Holmes
Person's title as a proper noun.	Can you meet us on Tuesday, Rabbi? It's time to start rounds, Doctor.
Words showing family relationships when used as titles or as substitutes for a name.	Uncle Fred, Grandmother Parker, Father, Cousin Sam
Abbreviations	
Social titles after a name.	My teacher is named **Mr.** Franks. Can't you ask **Prof.** Pardoe to help us in the soup kitchen?
Abbreviate the titles of organizations.	Northeastern **Mfg.** Connecticut Yard Workers **Assoc.**

Category/Rule	Examples
Parts of government, and business, with the initials of each word in the title.	**NATO** (North Atlantic Treaty Organization) **USMC** (United States Marine Corps) **IBM** (International Business Machines) **SNET** (Southern New England Telephone)
Abbreviate address titles.	Stoughton **St.**, Fort **Rd.**, Park **Ave.**
Time Designations	
Time abbreviations BCE (BC), CE (AD), AM, and PM	Hatshepsut, who lived from 1503 to 1482 **BCE**, was one of five women to reign as Queen of Egypt. The cruel Caligula ruled Rome until **CE** 41. My appointment was for 9:30 **AM**, and I'm not happy about waiting. We have a 7:00 **PM** dinner reservation at my favorite restaurant.
Geographical Names, Directions, and Historical Names	
Names of cities, states, countries, islands, and continents	**cities:** Honolulu, Moscow, Guatemala City **states:** Georgia, Iowa, New Mexico **countries:** Zimbabwe, Belgium, Ecuador **islands:** Tahiti, Cayman Islands, Cyprus **continents:** North America, Europe, Africa
Names of bodies of water and geographical features	Black Sea, Snake River, Sahara Desert, Mount McKinley
Names of buildings, monuments, and bridges	Woolsey Hall, Empire State Building, Vietnam Veterans Memorial, Golden Gate Bridge
Names of streets and highways	Railroad Avenue, New England Turnpike, Palm Drive, Route 153
Sections of the country	the Sunbelt, the Pacific Coast, the Southeast, the Midwest
Names of historical events, special events, documents, and historical periods	**historical events:** Battle of the Bulge, World War I **special events:** Summerfest, Boston Marathon **documents:** Magna Carta, Declaration of Independence **historical periods:** Reconstruction, Industrial Age
Titles of Artworks and Literary Works	
First and last words and all important words in the titles of artworks and literary works, including books, magazines, short stories, poems, songs, movies, plays, paintings, and sculpture	*Transworld Skateboarding* (magazine), *Too Close to the Falls* (book), "The Cask of Amontillado" (short story), *Birches at Sunrise* (painting), "Polka Dots and Moonbeams" (song), *The Lion in Winter* (movie)
Titles of religious works	Hebrew Bible, Koran, Old Testament

> For additional instruction and practice refer to the Grammar & Style Workshop, Fragments and Run-on Sentences, on page 321.

3.17 Writing Effective Sentences

SENTENCE FRAGMENTS

A sentence contains a subject and a verb and should express a complete thought. A **sentence fragment** is a phrase or clause that does not express a complete thought but that has been punctuated as though it did.

EXAMPLES

complete sentence   The gray fox ran across the field.

sentence fragment   Ran across the field. (The subject is missing.)

sentence fragment   The gray fox. (The verb is missing.)

sentence fragment   Across the field. (The subject and verb are missing.)

RUN-ON SENTENCES

Take a look at the following examples of run-on sentences. In the first run-on, no punctuation mark is used between the run-on sentences. In the second run-on, a comma is used incorrectly.

EXAMPLES

The umpire watched the two teams warm up before the game his headache had gone away.

At the start of the American Revolution, about three million people lived in the thirteen colonies, about one third of them supported the British government.

You can correct a run-on by dividing it into two separate sentences. Mark the end of each idea with a period, question mark, or exclamation point. Capitalize the first word of each new sentence.

EXAMPLE

The umpire watched the two teams warm up before the game. His headache had gone away.

You can also correct a run-on by using a semicolon. The second part of the sentence is not capitalized. Use a semicolon to join two sentences only if the thoughts are closely related.

EXAMPLE

At the start of the American Revolution, about three million people lived in the thirteen colonies; about one third of them supported the British government.

SENTENCE COMBINING AND EXPANDING

A series of short sentences in a paragraph can make your writing sound choppy and uninteresting. The reader might also have trouble understanding how your ideas are connected. By **combining and expanding sentences,** you can connect related ideas, make sentences longer and smoother, and make a paragraph more interesting to read.

One way to combine sentences is to take a key word or phrase from one sentence and insert it into another sentence.

EXAMPLES

short, choppy sentences
The girl rode a bicycle. It was pink.

combined sentence (with key word)
The girl rode a pink bicycle.

short, choppy sentences
We took a trip in the summer. We went to the Texas coast.

combined sentence (with key phrase)
We took a summer trip to the Texas coast.

Another way of combining sentences is to take two related sentences and combine them by using a coordinating conjunction—*and, but, or, so, for, yet,* or *nor.* By using a coordinating conjunction, you can form a compound subject, a compound verb, or a compound sentence. Be sure to use a comma before the coordinating conjunction that links two sentences.

EXAMPLES

two related sentences
Stephen lived close to the ocean. He often sailed on his boat in the summer.

combined sentence
Stephen lived close to the ocean, **and** he often sailed on his boat in the summer. (compound sentence)

two related sentences
Dandelions sprang up in the backyard. There were also broadleaf weeds.

combined sentence
Dandelions **and** broadleaf weeds sprang up in the backyard. (compound subject)

two related sentences
Rain beat down upon the trail. It drenched the weary travelers.

combined sentence
Rain beat down upon the trail **and** drenched the weary travelers. (compound verb)

VARYING SENTENCE STRUCTURE

Just as you probably wouldn't like to eat the same thing for breakfast every morning, your readers don't enjoy reading the same sentence pattern in every paragraph. By **varying sentence beginnings** you can give your sentences rhythm, create variety, and keep your readers engaged. Sentences often begin with a subject. To vary sentence beginnings, start some sentences with a one-word modifier, a prepositional phrase, a participial phrase, or a subordinate clause.

EXAMPLES

subject
She usually finishes her test before the rest of the class.

one-word modifier
Usually, she finishes her test before the rest of the class.

prepositional phrase
Before lunch he plans the following day's activities.

participial phrase
Humming a lively tune, the warden reviewed the parole cases.

subordinate clause
Since it rarely rains where he lives, Jeff leaves the top down on his convertible.

WORDY SENTENCES

A **wordy sentence** includes extra words and phrases that can be difficult, confusing, or repetitive to read. When you write, use only words necessary to make your meaning clear. Revise and edit your sentences so that they are not unnecessarily wordy or complicated.

Replace a group of words with one word.

EXAMPLES

wordy
I quit my job **because of the fact that** the company wanted me to work overtime each week.

revised
I quit my job **because** the company wanted me to work overtime each week.

Replace a clause with a phrase.

EXAMPLES

wordy
When the batter hit the ball over the fence into the stands, the crowd cheered wildly.

revised
When the batter hit the ball over the fence, the crowd cheered wildly.

Delete a group of unnecessary or repetitive words.

EXAMPLES

wordy
What I think is your book will appeal to children in grade school.

revised
I think your book will appeal to grade school children.

wordy
Joe suffers from insomnia, **and he doesn't sleep well at night.**

revised
Joe suffers from insomnia.

USING PARALLELISM

A sentence has **parallelism** when the same forms are used to express ideas of equal—or parallel—importance. Parallelism can add emphasis, balance, and rhythm to a sentence. Words, phrases, and clauses that have the same form and function in a sentence are called **parallel.**

EXAMPLES

not parallel
The singers **took** the stage, **dazzled** the crowd, and then **had returned** to their dressing rooms. (The highlighted verbs are not in the same tense.)

parallel

The singers **took** the stage, **dazzled** the crowd, and **returned** to their dressing rooms.

not parallel

The performers are **talented, lively,** and **dance.** (The three highlighted words include two adjectives and one verb.)

parallel

The performers are **talented, lively,** and **energetic** dancers.

MAKING PASSIVE SENTENCES ACTIVE

A verb is **active** when the subject of the verb performs the action. It is **passive** when the subject of the verb receives the action.

EXAMPLES

active

Lenny bought Rachel a scarf.

passive

A scarf was bought for Rachel by Lenny.

USING COLORFUL LANGUAGE

When you write, use words that tell your readers exactly what you mean. **Colorful language**—such as precise and lively nouns, verbs, and modifiers—tells your readers exactly what you mean and makes your writing more interesting.

Precise nouns give your reader a clear picture of who or what is involved in the sentence.

EXAMPLES

original sentence

The cat walked into the building.

revised sentence

The Siamese cat walked into the grocery **store.**

Colorful, vivid verbs describe the specific action in the sentence.

EXAMPLES

original sentence

Her brother ran across the yard.

revised sentence

Her brother darted across the yard.

Modifiers—adjectives and adverbs—describe the meanings of other words and make them more precise. Colorful or surprising modifiers can make your writing come alive for your readers.

EXAMPLES

original sentence

The tired farmer planted the last row of corn.

revised sentence

The exhausted farmer wearily planted the last row of corn.

▶ Refer to the following pages for the unit Writing Workshops:

Expository Writing (Responding to a Short Story), pp. 126–131

Narrative Writing (Writing a Short Story), pp. 238–245

Expository Writing (Cause-and-Effect Essay), pp. 362–367

Expository Writing (Compare-and-Contrast Essay), pp. 524–529

Narrative Writing (Personal Narrative), pp. 594–599

Persuasive Writing (Persuasive Essay), pp. 710–715

Expository Writing (Research Report), pp. 820–827

WRITING

4 Writing

4.1 The Writing Process

All writers—whether they are beginning writers, famous published writers, or somewhere in between—go through a process that leads to a complete piece of writing. The specifics of each writer's process may be unique, but for every writer, writing is a series of steps or stages.

The Writing Process

Stage	Tasks
1. Prewriting	Plan your writing: choose a topic, audience, purpose, and form; gather ideas; arrange them logically.
2. Drafting	Get your ideas down on paper.
3. Revising	Evaluate, or judge, the writing piece and suggest ways to improve it. Judging your own writing is called self-evaluation. Judging a classmate's writing is called peer evaluation.
	Work to improve the content, organization, and expression of your ideas.
	Proofread your writing for errors in spelling, grammar, capitalization, and punctuation. Correct these errors, make a final copy of your paper, and proofread it again.
Writing Follow-Up: Publish and Present	Share your work with an audience.
Reflect	Think through the writing process to determine what you learned as a writer, what you accomplished, and what you would like to strengthen the next time you write.

While writing moves through these stages, it is also a continuing cycle. You might need to go back to a previous stage before going on to the next step. Returning to a previous stage will strengthen your final work. Note also that you can take time to reflect on your writing between any of the other stages. The more you reflect on your writing, the better your writing will become.

1 PREWRITE

In the prewriting stage of the writing process, you decide on a purpose, audience, topic, and form. You also begin to discover your voice and gather and organize ideas.

Prewriting Plan

Set Your Purpose	A **purpose,** or aim, is the goal that you want your writing to accomplish.
Identify Your Audience	An **audience** is the person or group of people intended to read what you write.
Find Your Voice	**Voice** is the quality of a work that tells you that one person wrote it.
Select Your Topic	A **topic** is simply something to write about. For example, you might write about a sports hero or about a cultural event in your community.
Select a Writing Form	A **form** is a kind of writing. For example, you might write a paragraph, an essay, a short story, a poem, or a news article.

Program Resources

Additional writing workshops are available in the *Exceeding the Standards: Writing* resource.

Set Your Purpose

When you choose your mode and form of writing, think about what purpose or aim you are trying to accomplish. Your purpose for writing might be to inform, to tell a story, to describe something, or to convince others to see your viewpoint. Your writing might have more than one purpose. For example, a piece of writing might inform your readers about an important event while persuading them to respond in a specific way.

Mode of Writing	Purpose	Form
expository	to inform	news article, research report
narrative	to express thoughts or ideas, or to tell a story	personal account, memoir, short story
descriptive	to portray a person, place, object, or event	travel brochure, personal profile, poem
persuasive	to convince people to accept a position and respond in some way	editorial, petition, political speech

Identify Your Audience

An **audience** is the person or group of people intended to read what you write. For example, you might write for yourself, a friend, a relative, or your classmates. The best writing usually is intended for a specific audience. Choosing a specific audience before writing will help you make important decisions about your work. For an audience of young children, for example, you would use simple words and ideas. For an audience of your peers in an athletic group, you would use jargon and other specialized words that your peers already know. For an adult audience, you would use more formal language.

Use the following questions to help identify your audience.

- Who will be most interested in my topic?
- What are their interests and values?
- How much do they already know about the topic?
- What background information do they need in order to understand my ideas and point of view?
- What words, phrases, or concepts will I need to define for my audience?
- How can I capture my audience's interest from the very start?

Use Appropriate Language

Formal Versus Informal English To write effectively, you must choose your language according to your audience, purpose, and the occasion or situation. **Formal English** contains carefully constructed, complete sentences; avoids contractions; follows standard English usage and grammar; uses a serious tone; and uses sophisticated vocabulary. **Informal English** contains everyday speech and popular expressions, uses contractions, and may include sentence fragments.

Formal English is appropriate for school essays, oral or written reports, interviews, and debates. Informal English is appropriate for communication with friends, personal letters or notes, and journal entries.

EXAMPLES

formal English
I am very pleased that I received a perfect score on the math exam.

informal English
I'm so pumped that I aced that math exam!

Find Your Voice

Voice is the quality of a work that tells you that one person wrote it. Voice makes a person's writing unique. In your writing, you should strive to develop your own voice, not to imitate the voices of others. Be true to your own voice, and your experience will speak directly to the experience of others.

Select Your Topic

A **topic** is simply something to write about. For example, you might write about a sports hero or about a cultural event in your community. Here are some ideas that may help you find interesting writing topics:

Ways to Find a Writing Topic	
Check your journal	Search through your journal for ideas that you jotted down in the past. Many professional writers get their ideas from their journals.
Think about your experiences	Think about people, places, or events that affected you strongly. Recall experiences that taught you important lessons or that you felt strongly about.
Look at reference works	Reference works include printed or computerized dictionaries, atlases, almanacs, and encyclopedias.
Browse in a library	Libraries are treasure houses of information and ideas. Simply looking around in the stacks of a library can suggest good ideas for writing.
Use mass media	Newspapers, magazines, radio, television, and films can suggest good topics for writing. For example, a glance at listings for public television programs might suggest topics related to the arts, to history, or to nature.
Search the Internet	Search key words in a search engine or web browser to expand on your ideas. Make sure to keep your work original and avoid plagiarizing from websites.

Select a Writing Form

Another important decision that a writer needs to make is what form his or her writing will take. A form is a kind of writing. Once you've identified your topic, your purpose for writing, and your audience, a particular form of writing may become immediately obvious as the perfect one to convey your ideas. But, sometimes, an unexpected choice of form may be even more effective in presenting your topic. The following chart lists some of the many different forms of writing.

Forms of Writing

adventure	brochure	directions	fantasy
advertisement	character sketch	editorial	history
advice column	children's story	epitaph	human interest story
agenda	comedy	essay	instructions
apology	consumer report	eulogy	interview questions
autobiography	debate	experiment	itinerary
biography	detective story	fable	journal entry
book review	dialogue	family history	letter

magazine article	obituary	proposal	speech
memorandum	parable	radio or tv spot	sports story
minutes	paraphrase	recommendation	statement of belief
movie review	petition	research report	summary
mystery	play	résumé	tall tale
myth	police/accident	science fiction	tour guide
narrative	report	short story	want ad
newspaper article	poster	song lyrics	

Gather Ideas

After you have identified your purpose, audience, topic, and form, the next step in the prewriting stage is to gather ideas. There are many ways to gather ideas for writing.

- **Brainstorm** When you **brainstorm,** you think of as many ideas as you can, as quickly as you can, without stopping to evaluate or criticize them. Anything goes—no idea should be rejected in the brainstorming stage.
- **Freewrite Freewriting** is simply taking a pencil and paper and writing whatever comes into your mind. Try to write for several minutes without stopping and without worrying about spelling, grammar, usage, or mechanics.
- **Question** Ask the **reporting questions** *who, what, where, when, why,* and *how* about your topic. This questioning strategy is especially useful for gathering information about an event or for planning a story.
- **Create a Graphic Organizer** A good way to gather information is to create a **graphic organizer,** such as a Venn Diagram, Sensory Details Chart, Time Line, Story Map, or Pro-and-Con Chart. For examples, see the Language Arts Handbook, section 1, Reading Strategies and Skills, page 821.

Organize Your Ideas

Writing Paragraphs After you have gathered ideas for a piece of writing, the next step is to organize these ideas in a useful and reader-friendly way. The most basic organization of ideas occurs in forming paragraphs. A good paragraph is a carefully organized unit of writing. It develops a sequence in narrative writing or develops a particular topic in informational or persuasive writing.

Paragraphs with Topic Sentences Many paragraphs include a topic sentence that presents a main idea. The topic sentence can be placed at the beginning, middle, or end of the paragraph. Topic sentences usually appear early on in the paragraph and are commonly followed by one or more supporting sentences. Often these supporting sentences begin with transitions that relate them to the other sentences or to the topic sentence. This type of paragraph may end with a clincher sentence, which sums up what has been said in the paragraph.

EXAMPLE

<u>Whether it's rock or Bach, music that's played too loud can put more than a temporary damper on your hearing</u>. At most rock concerts and many night clubs, the sound intensity is high enough to cause irreversible damage to the delicate sensor cells lining the inner ear. Car and home stereo equipment and headphones can also harm your hearing when the volume is cranked up too high.

from "Hearing Under Seige"
by Bob Ludlow

Paragraphs Without Topic Sentences Most paragraphs do not have topic sentences. In a narrative piece of writing, many paragraphs state a series of events, and no sentence in the paragraph sums up the events. In good narrative writing, the sequence of events appears in chronological order. Descriptive writing may contain paragraphs organized spatially—in the order in which the speaker or narrator sees, hears, feels, smells, and tastes things in a given situation.

Write Your Thesis Statement

One way to start organizing your writing, especially if you are writing an informative or persuasive essay, is to identify the main idea of what you want to say. Present this idea in the form of a sentence or two called a thesis statement. A **thesis statement** is simply a sentence that presents the main idea or the position you will take in your essay.

Example thesis for a persuasive essay

The development at Rice Creek Farm should be stopped because it will destroy one of the best natural areas near the city.

Example thesis for an informative essay

Wilma Rudolph was an athlete who succeeded in the elite sport of tennis before the world was willing to recognize her.

Methods of Organization

The ideas in your writing should be ordered and linked in a logical and easily understandable way. You can organize your writing in the following ways:

Methods of Organization	
Chronological Order	Events are given in the order they occur.
Order of Importance	Details are given in order of importance or familiarity.
Comparison-and-Contrast Order	Similarities and differences of two things are listed.
Cause-and-Effect Order	One or more causes are presented followed by one or more effects.

To link your ideas, use connective words and phrases. In informational or persuasive writing, *for example, as a result, finally, therefore,* and *in fact* are common connectives. In narrative and descriptive writing, words like *first, then, suddenly, above, beyond, in the distance,* and *there* are common connectives. In comparison-contrast organization, common phrases include *similarly, on the other hand,* and *in contrast.* In cause-and-effect organization, linkers include *one cause, another effect, as a result, consequently, finally,* and *therefore.*

Create an Outline An **outline** is an excellent framework for highlighting main ideas and supporting details. To create a rough outline, simply list your main ideas in some logical order. Under each main idea, list the supporting details set off by dashes.

EXAMPLE

What Is Drama?
Definition of Drama
—Tells a story
—Uses actors to play characters
—Uses a stage, properties, lights, costumes, makeup, and special effects
Types of Drama
—Tragedy
　　—Definition: A play in which the main character meets a negative fate

—Examples: *Antigone, Romeo and Juliet, Death of a Salesman*
—Comedy
   —Definition: A play in which the main character meets a positive fate
   —Examples: *A Midsummer Night's Dream, Cyrano de Bergerac, The Odd Couple*

2 DRAFT

After you have gathered your information and organized it, the next step in writing is to produce a draft. A **draft** is simply an early attempt at writing a paper. Different writers approach drafting in different ways. Some prefer to work slowly and carefully, perfecting each part as they go. Others prefer to write a discovery draft, getting all their ideas down on paper in rough form and then going back over those ideas to shape and focus them. When writing a discovery draft, you do not focus on spelling, grammar, usage, and mechanics. You can take care of those details during revision.

Draft Your Introduction

The purpose of an introduction is to capture your reader's attention and establish what you want to say. An effective introduction can start with a quotation, a question, an anecdote, an intriguing fact, or a description that hooks the reader to keep reading. An effective introduction can open with a quotation, question, anecdote, fact, or description.

EXAMPLES

"That's one small step for man, one giant leap for mankind." With these words, Neil Armstrong signaled his success as the first man to set foot on the moon...

What would it be like if all the birds in the world suddenly stopped their singing?

When my brother was nineteen, he volunteered in a homeless shelter making sure people had a safe place to spend the night. He told me once that he would never forget the time he met...

Draft Your Body

When writing the body of an essay, refer to your outline. Each heading in your outline will become the main idea of one of your paragraphs. To move smoothly from one idea to another, use transitional words or phrases. As you draft, include evidence from documented sources to support the ideas that you present. This evidence can be paraphrased, summarized, or quoted directly. For information on proper documentation, see the Language Arts Handbook 5.5, Documenting Sources, page 904.

Draft Your Conclusion

In the conclusion, bring together the main ideas you included in the body of your essay and create a sense of closure to the issue you raised in your thesis. There is no single right way to conclude a piece of writing. Possibilities include:

- Making a generalization
- Restating the thesis and major supporting ideas in different words
- Summarizing the points made in the rest of the essay
- Drawing a lesson or moral
- Calling on the reader to adopt a view or take an action
- Expanding on your thesis or main idea by connecting it to the reader's own interests
- Linking your thesis to a larger issue or concern

3 REVISE

Evaluate Your Draft

Self- and Peer Evaluation When you evaluate something, you examine it carefully to find its strengths and weaknesses. Evaluating your own writing is called **self-evaluation.** A **peer evaluation** is an evaluation of a piece of writing done by classmates, or peers. The following tips can help you to become a helpful peer reader, to learn to give and receive criticism, and to improve your writing.

Tips for evaluating writing
- **Check for content** Is the content, including the main idea, clear? Have any important details been left out? Do unimportant or unrelated details confuse the main point? Are the main idea and supporting details clearly connected to one another?
- **Check for organization** Are the ideas in the written work presented in a logical order?
- **Check the style and language** Is the language appropriately formal or informal? Is the tone appropriate for the audience and purpose? Have any key or unfamiliar terms been defined?

Tips for delivering helpful criticism
- **Be focused** Concentrate on content, organization, and style. At this point, do not focus on proofreading matters such as spelling and punctuation; they can be corrected during the proofreading stage.
- **Be positive** Respect the writer's feelings and genuine writing efforts. Tell the writer what you like about his or her work. Answer the writer's questions in a positive manner, tactfully presenting any changes you are suggesting.
- **Be specific** Give the writer concrete ideas for improving his or her work.

Tips for benefiting from helpful criticism
- **Tell your peer evaluator your specific concerns and questions.** If you are unsure whether you've clearly presented an idea, ask the evaluator how he or she might restate the idea.
- **Ask questions to clarify comments that your evaluator makes.** When you ask for clarification, you make sure you understand your evaluator's comments.
- **Accept your evaluator's comments graciously.** Criticism can be helpful, but you don't have to use any or all of the suggestions.

Revise for Content, Organization, and Style

After identifying weaknesses in a draft through self-evaluation and peer evaluation, the next step is to revise the draft. Here are four basic ways to improve meaning and content:
- **Adding or Expanding** Sometimes writing can be improved by adding details, examples, or transitions to connect ideas. Often a single added adjective, for example, can make a piece of writing clearer or more vivid.

EXAMPLE

draft   Wind whistled through the park.

revised   The **bone-chilling** wind whistled through the park.

- **Cutting or Condensing** Often writing can be improved by cutting unnecessary or unrelated material.

EXAMPLE
draft   Will was firmly determined to find the structure of the DNA molecule.

revised   Will was determined to find the structure of the DNA molecule.

EXAMPLE
draft   Several things had been bothering Tanya.

revised   Several personal problems had been bothering Tanya.

- **Moving** Often you can improve the organization of your writing by moving part of it so that related ideas appear near one another.

After you've revised the draft, ask yourself a series of questions. Think of these questions as your "revision checklist."

REVISION CHECKLIST

Content
- ❑ Does the writing achieve its purpose?
- ❑ Are the main ideas clearly stated and supported by details?

Organization
- ❑ Are the ideas arranged in a sensible order?
- ❑ Are the ideas connected to one another within paragraphs and between paragraphs?

Style
- ❑ Is the language appropriate to the audience and purpose?
- ❑ Is the mood appropriate to the purpose of the writing?

Proofread for Errors

When you proofread your writing, you read it through to look for errors and to mark corrections. When you mark corrections, use the standard proofreading symbols as shown in the following chart.

Proofreader's Symbols

Symbol and Example	Meaning of Symbol	Symbol and Example	Meaning of Symbol
The very first time	Delete (cut) this material.	gebril	Change the order of these letters.
dog life	Insert (add) something that is missing.	end. "Watch out," she yelled.	Begin a new paragraph.
George	Replace this letter or word.	Love conquers all.	Put a period here.
All the horses (king's)	Move this word to where the arrow points.	Welcome friends.	Put a comma here.
french toast	Capitalize this letter.	Get the stopwatch	Put a space here.
the vice-President	Lowercase this letter.	Dear Madam	Put a colon here.
housse	Take out this letter and close up space.	She walked he rode.	Put a semicolon here.
book keeper	Close up space.	name-brand products	Put a hyphen here.
		cats meow	Put an apostrophe here.
		cat's cradle stet	Let it stand. (Leave as it is.)

After you have revised your draft, make a clean copy of it and proofread it for errors in spelling, grammar, and punctuation. Use the following proofreading checklist.

Proofreading Checklist

Spelling
- [ ] Are all words, including names, spelled correctly?

Grammar
- [ ] Does each verb agree with its subject?
- [ ] Are verb tenses consistent and correct?
- [ ] Are irregular verbs formed correctly?
- [ ] Are there any sentence fragments or run-ons?
- [ ] Have double negatives been avoided?
- [ ] Have frequently confused words, such as *affect* and *effect*, been used correctly?

Punctuation
- [ ] Does every sentence end with an end mark?
- [ ] Are commas used correctly?
- [ ] Do all proper nouns and proper adjectives begin with capital letters?

WRITING FOLLOW-UP

Publish and Present

Some writing is done just for oneself—journal writing, for example. Most writing, however, is meant to be shared with others. Here are several ways in which you can publish your writing or present it to others:

- Submit your work to a local publication, such as a school literary magazine, school newspaper, or community newspaper.
- Submit your work to a regional or national publication.
- Enter your work in a contest.
- Read your work aloud to classmates, friends, or family members.
- Collaborate with other students to prepare a publication—a brochure, online literary magazine, anthology, or newspaper.
- Prepare a poster or bulletin board, perhaps in collaboration with other students, to display your writing.
- Make your own book by typing or word processing the pages and binding them together.
- Hold an oral reading of student writing as a class or school-wide project.
- Share your writing with other students in a small writers' group.

Reflect

After you've completed your writing, think through the writing process to determine what you learned as a writer, what you learned about your topic, how the writing process worked or didn't work for you, and what skills you would like to strengthen.

Reflection can be done on a self-evaluation form, in small-group discussion, or simply in silent reflection. By keeping a journal, however, you'll be able to keep track of your writing experience and pinpoint ways to make the writing process work better for you. Here are some questions to ask as you reflect on the writing process and yourself as a writer:

- Which part of the writing process did I enjoy most and least? Why? Which part of the writing process was most difficult? least difficult? Why?
- What would I change about my approach to the writing process next time?
- What have I learned in writing about this topic?
- What have I learned by using this form?
- How have I developed as a writer while writing this piece?
- What strengths have I discovered in my work?
- What aspects of my writing do I want to strengthen? How can I strengthen them?

4.2 Modes and Purposes of Writing

Types of writing generally fall within four main classifications or modes: expository, narrative, descriptive, and persuasive. Each of these modes has a specific purpose. See the Mode of Writing Chart on page 826.

Expository Writing

The purpose of **expository writing** is to inform, to present or explain an idea or a process. News articles and research reports are examples of informative expository writing. One function of expository writing is to define, since a definition explains what something is. Another function of expository writing is to analyze and interpret. For example, a book review is writing that analyzes and interprets a piece of literature to inform an audience about its worth. Similarly, a movie review evaluates and judges for its viewing audience how well a movie accomplishes its purpose.

Narrative Writing

Narrative writing tells a story or relates a series of events. It can be used to entertain, to make a point, or to introduce a topic. Narrating an event involves the dimension of action over time.

Narratives are often used in essays, reports, and other nonfiction forms because stories are entertaining and fun to read. Just as important, they are a good way to make a point. Biographies, autobiographies, and family histories are also forms of narrative writing.

Descriptive Writing

The purpose of **descriptive writing** is to entertain, enrich, and enlighten by using a form such as fiction or poetry to share a perspective. Descriptive writing is used to describe something, to set a scene, to create a mood, to appeal to the reader's senses. Descriptive writing is often creative and uses visual and other sensual details, emotional responses, and imagery. Poems, short stories, and plays are examples of descriptive writing.

Persuasive Writing

The purpose of **persuasive writing** is to persuade readers or listeners to respond in some way, such as to agree with a position, change a view on an issue, reach an agreement, or perform an action. Examples of persuasive writing are editorials, petitions, political speeches, and essays.

5.1 Research Skills

Learning is a lifelong process, one that extends far beyond school. Both in school and on your own, it is important to remember that your learning and growth are up to you. One good way to become an independent lifelong learner is to master research skills. Research is the process of gathering ideas and information. One of the best resources for research is the library.

How Library Materials Are Organized

Each book in a library is assigned a unique number, called a call number. The call number is printed on the spine (edge) of each book. The numbers serve to classify books as well as to help the library keep track of them. Libraries commonly use one of two systems for classifying books. Most school and public libraries use the Dewey Decimal System.

Dewey Decimal System	
Call Numbers	Subjects
000–099	Reference and General Works
100–199	Philosophy, Psychology
200–299	Religion
300–399	Social Studies
400–499	Language
500–599	Science, Mathematics
600–699	Technology
700–799	Arts
800–899	Literature
900–999	History, Geography, Biography[1]

1. Biographies (920s) are arranged alphabetically by the name of the person whose life is treated in each biography.

How to Locate Library Materials

If you know the call number of a book or the subject classification number you want, you can usually go to the bookshelves, or stacks, to obtain the book. Use the signs at the ends of the rows to locate the section you need. Then find the particular shelf that contains call numbers close to yours.

Library collections include many other types of publications besides books, such as magazines, newspapers, audio and video recordings, and government documents. Ask a librarian to tell you where to find the materials you need. To find the call numbers of books that will help you with your research, use the library's catalog. The catalog lists all the books in the library (or a group of libraries if it is part of a larger system).

Internet Libraries It is also possible to visit the Internet Public library online at **http://www.ipl.org/.** The Internet Public Library is the first public library of the Internet. This site provides library services to the Internet community by finding, evaluating, selecting, organizing, describing, and creating quality information resources; teaches what librarians have to contribute in a digital environment; and promotes the importance of libraries.

Computerized Catalogs Many libraries today use computerized catalogs. Systems differ from library to library, but most involve using a computer terminal to search through the library's collection. You can usually search by author, title, subject, or key word.

EXAMPLE COMPUTERIZED CATALOG SEARCHES

Search By	Example	Hints
Author	gould, stephen j	Type last name first. Type as much of the name as you know.
Title	mismeasure of man	Omit articles such as *a, an,* or *the* at the beginning of titles.
Subject	intelligence tests; ability-testing	Use the list of subjects provided by the library.
Key words	darwin; intelligence; craniology	Use related topics if you can't find anything in your subject.

If your library has a computerized catalog, you will need to learn how to use your library's particular system. A librarian can help you to master the system. The following is a sample book entry screen from a computerized catalog.

Author	Wallace, David Rains, 1945—
Title	The Quetzal and the Macaw: The Story of Costa Rica's National Parks
Publication info.	Sierra Club Books, 1992
No. of pages/size	xvi, 222 p. : maps : 24 cm.
ISBN	ISBN 0-87156-585-4
Subjects	National parks and reserves—Costa Rica—History
	Costa Rica. Servicio de Parques
	Nacionales—History
	Nature conservation—Costa Rica—History
Dewey call number	333.78

Interlibrary Loans Many libraries are part of larger library networks. In these libraries, the computerized catalog covers the collections of several libraries. If you want a book from a different library, you will need to request the book at the library's request desk or by using its computer. Ask your librarian to help you if you have questions. He or she will be able to tell you when the book will be shipped to your library.

Using Reference Works

Most libraries have an assortment of reference works in which knowledge is collected and organized so that you can find it easily. Usually, reference works cannot be checked out of the library.

Types of Dictionaries You will find many types of dictionaries in the library reference section. The most common is a dictionary of the English language. Examples include *Merriam Webster's Collegiate Dictionary,* the *American Heritage Dictionary,* and the multi-volume *Oxford English Dictionary*. Other word dictionaries focus on slang, abbreviations and acronyms, English/foreign language translation, and spelling. Biographical, historical, scientific, and world language dictionaries are also some of the works you will find in the reference section.

Using a Thesaurus A thesaurus is a reference book that groups synonyms, or words with similar meanings. Suppose that you are writing an essay and have a word that means almost but not quite what you want, or perhaps you find yourself using the same word over and over. A thesaurus can give you fresh and precise words to use. For example, if you look up the word *sing* in a thesaurus, you might find the following synonyms listed:

sing (v.) carol, chant, croon, hum, vocalize, warble, yodel

Using Almanacs, Yearbooks, and Atlases **Almanacs** and **yearbooks** are published each year. An almanac provides statistics and lists, often related to recent events. In an almanac you can find facts about current events, countries of the world, famous people, sports, entertainment, and many other subjects. An overview of the events of the year can be found in a yearbook. Some of the more widely used almanacs and yearbooks are *The Guinness Book of World Records;* the *Information Please, Almanac, Atlas, and Yearbook;* the *World Almanac and Book of Facts;* and the *World Book Yearbook of Events.*

An **atlas** is a collection of maps and other geographical information. Some atlases show natural features such as mountains and rivers; others show political features such as countries and cities. If you need to locate a particular feature on a map in an atlas, refer to the gazetteer, an index that lists every item shown on the map.

Using Biographical References and Encyclopedias A **biographical reference** contains information on the lives of famous people. Examples include *Who's Who,* the *Dictionary of American Biography,* and *Contemporary Authors.*

Encyclopedias provide a survey of knowledge. General encyclopedias, such as *World Book,* contain information on many different subjects. Specialized encyclopedias, such as the *LaRousse Encyclopedia of Mythology,* contain information on one particular area of knowledge. The topics in an encyclopedia are treated in articles, which are usually arranged in alphabetical order. If you look up a topic and do not find it, check the index (usually in the last volume). The index will tell you where in the encyclopedia your topic is covered.

Using Indexes, Appendices, and Glossaries An **index** lists in alphabetical order the subjects mentioned in a book or collection of periodicals and pages where these subjects are treated. Indexes help you locate possible sources of information about your topic. An index can be at the back of a book of nonfiction, or it can be a published book itself. Indexes are available as bound books, on microfilm, and online on the Internet.

An **appendix** provides additional material, often in chart or table form, at the end of a book or other writing.

A **glossary** lists key words in a book and their definitions.

Primary and Secondary Sources

Primary sources are the original unedited materials created by someone directly involved in an event or speaking directly for a group. They may include firsthand documents such as diaries, interviews, works of fiction, artwork, court records, research reports, speeches, letters, surveys, and so on.

Secondary sources offer commentary or analysis of events, ideas, or primary sources. They are often written significantly later and may provide historical context or attempt to describe or explain primary sources. Examples of secondary sources include dictionaries, encyclopedias, textbooks, and books and articles that interpret or review original works.

	Primary Source	Secondary Source
Art	Painting	Article critiquing the artist's technique
History	Prisoner's diary	Book about World War II internment camps
Literature	Poem	Literary criticism on a particular form of poetry
Science	Research report	Analysis of results

See the Language Arts Handbook 5.3, Media Literacy, page 902, for information on using newspapers, periodicals, and other forms of media to document your research.

5.2 Internet Research

The Internet is an enormous collection of computer networks that can open a whole new world of information. With just a couple of keystrokes, you can access libraries, government agencies, high schools and universities, nonprofit and educational organizations, museums, user groups, and individuals around the world.

Keep in mind that the Internet is not regulated and everything you read online may not be verified or accurate. Confirm facts from the Internet against another source. In addition, to become a good judge of Internet materials, do the following:

- **Consider the domain name of the resource.** Be sure to check out the sites you use to see if they are commercial (.com or .firm), educational (.edu), governmental (.gov), or organizational (.org or .net). Ask yourself questions like these: What bias might a commercial site have that would influence its presentation of information? Is the site sponsored by a special-interest group that slants or spins information to its advantage?

Key to Internet Domains

.com	commercial entity
.edu	educational institution
.firm	business entity
.gov	government agency or department
.org or .net	organization

- **Consider the author's qualifications.** Regardless of the source, ask these questions: Is the author named? What expertise does he or she have? Can I locate other online information about this person? Evaluate the quality of information.
- **How accurate is the information?** Does it appear to be reliable and without errors? Is the information given without bias?
- **Check the date posted.** Is the information timely? When was the site last updated?

Keep Track of Your Search Process

- ❏ Write a brief statement of the topic of your research.
- ❏ Write key words or phrases that will help you search for this information.
- ❏ Note the search engines that you will use.
- ❏ As you conduct a search, note how many "hits" or Internet sites the search engine has accessed. Determine whether you need to narrow or expand your search. Write down new key words and the results of each new search.
- ❏ Write down all promising sites. As you access them, evaluate the source and nature of the information and jot down your assessment.
- ❏ As you find the information you need, document it carefully according to the directions in Citing Internet Sources, page 906.
- ❏ Keep a list of favorite websites, either in your research journal or in your browser software. This feature may be called bookmark or favorites. You can click on the name of the site in your list and return to that page without having to retype the URL (Uniform Resource Locator).

Search Tools

A number of popular and free search engines allow you to find topics of interest. Keep in mind that each service uses slightly different methods of searching, so you may get different results using the same key words.

All the Web	http://www.alltheweb.com
AltaVista	http://www.altavista.com
Go	http://www.go.com
Yahoo	http://www.yahoo.com
Excite	http://www.excite.com
HotBot	http://www.hotbot.com
WebCrawler	http://www.webcrawler.com
Google	http://www.google.com

Search Tips

- To make searching easier, less time consuming, and more directed, narrow your subject to a key word or a group of key words. These key words are your search terms. Key search connectors, or Boolean commands, can help you limit or expand the scope of your topic.

  AND (or +) narrows a search by retrieving documents that include both terms—for example: Ulysses Grant AND Vicksburg.

  OR broadens a search by retrieving documents that include any of the terms—for example: Ulysses Grant OR Vicksburg OR Civil War.

  NOT narrows a search by excluding documents containing certain words—for example: Ulysses Grant NOT Civil War.

- If applicable, limit your search by specifying a geographical area by using the word *near*—for example, golf courses near Boulder, Colorado.
- When entering a group of key words, present them in order, from the most important to the least important key word.
- If the terms of your search are not leading you to the information you need, try using synonyms. For example, if you were looking for information about how to care for your garden, you might use these terms: *compost, pest control,* and *watering*.
- Avoid opening the link to every page in your results list. Search engines typically present pages in descending order of relevancy or importance. The most useful pages will be located at the top of the list. However, skimming the text of lower order sites may give you ideas for other key words.
- If you're not getting the desired results, check your input. Common search mistakes include misspelling search terms and mistyping URLs. Remember that URLs must be typed exactly as they appear, using the exact capital or lowercase letters, spacing, and punctuation.

For information on citing Internet sources, see the Language Arts Handbook 5.6, Documenting Sources.

5.3 Media Literacy

The term **media,** in most applications, is used as a plural of *medium,* which means a channel or system of communication, information, or entertainment. *Mass media* refers specifically to means of communication, such as newspapers, radio, or television, which are designed to reach the mass of the people. *Journalism* is the gathering, evaluating, and disseminating, through various media, of news and facts of current interest. Originally, journalism encompassed only such printed matter as newspapers and periodicals. Today, however, it includes other media used to distribute news, such as radio, television, documentary or newsreel films, the Internet, and computer news services.

Newspapers are publications usually issued on a daily or weekly basis, the main function of which is to report the news. Newspapers also provide commentary on the news, advocate various public policies, furnish special information and advice to readers, and sometimes include features such as comic strips, cartoons, and serialized books.

Periodicals are publications released at regular intervals, such as journals, magazines, or newsletters. Periodicals feature material of special interest to particular audiences. The contents of periodicals can be unrelated to current news stories—however, when dealing with the news, periodicals tend to do so in the form of commentaries or summaries.

Technical writing refers to scientific or process-oriented instructional writing that is of a technical or mechanical nature. Technical writing includes instruction manuals, such as computer software manuals, how-to instructional guides, and procedural memos.

Electronic media include online magazines and journals, known as webzines or e-zines; computer news services; and many web-based newspapers that are available on the Internet. The web is by far the most widely used part of the Internet.

Multimedia is the presentation of information using the combination of text, sound, pictures, animation, and video. Common multimedia computer applications include games, learning software, presentation software, reference materials, and web pages. Most multimedia applications include links that enable users to switch between media elements and topics. The connectivity provided by these links transforms multimedia from static presentations with pictures and sound into a varied and informative interactive experience.

Visual media, such as fine art, illustrations, and photographs, are used extensively in today's visually stimulating world to enhance the written word. Visual arts offer insights into our world in a different way than print does. Critical viewing or careful examination of a painting or photograph can help you to comprehend its meaning and be able to compare and contrast the visual image with a literary work or other piece of writing.

5.4 Evaluating Sources

To conduct your research efficiently, you need to evaluate your sources and set priorities among them. Ideally, a source will be:

- **Unbiased** When an author has a personal stake in what people think about a subject, he or she may withhold or distort information. Investigate the author's background to see if she or he is liable to be biased. Using loaded language and overlooking obvious counterarguments are signs of author bias.
- **Authoritative** An authoritative source is reliable and trustworthy. An author's reputation, especially among others who conduct research in the same field, is a sign of authority. Likewise, periodicals and publishers acquire reputations for responsible or poor editing and research.
- **Timely** Information about many subjects changes rapidly. An astronomy text published last year may already be out of date. In other fields—for instance, algebra—older texts may be perfectly adequate. Consult with your teacher and your librarian to decide how current your sources must be.
- **Available** Borrowing through interlibrary loan, tracing a book that is missing, or recalling a book that has been checked out to another person takes time. Make sure to allow enough time for these materials.

- **Appropriate for your level** Find sources that present useful information that you can understand. Materials written for "young people" may be too simple to be helpful. Books written for experts may presume knowledge that you do not have. Struggling with a difficult text is often worth the effort, but if you do so, monitor your time and stay on schedule.

5.5 Documenting Sources

As you use your research in your writing, you must document your sources of information.
- Credit the sources of all ideas and facts that you use.
- Credit original ideas or facts that are expressed in text, tables, charts, and other graphic information.
- Credit all artistic property, including works of literature, song lyrics, and ideas.

Keeping a Research Journal A research journal is a notebook, electronic file, or other means to track the information you find as you conduct research. A research journal can include the following:
- A list of questions you want to research. (Such questions can be an excellent source of writing topics.)

EXAMPLES

How did the Vietnam Veterans Memorial come to be? Why is it one of the most visited memorials in America?

Where can I find more artwork by Faith Ringgold?

Why was Transcendentalism such an important literary movement in America but not in Europe?

Avoiding Plagiarizing Plagiarism is taking someone else's words or thoughts and presenting them as your own. Plagiarism is a very serious problem and has been the downfall of many students and professionals. Whenever you use someone else's writing to help you with a paper or a speech, you must be careful either to **paraphrase,** put the ideas in your own words; **summarize** the main ideas; or to use **quotation marks.** In any case, you must document your sources and give credit to the person whose ideas you are using. As you do research, make sure to include paraphrases, summaries, and direct quotations in your notes.

Informal and Formal Note-Taking

Informal Note-Taking Take informal notes when you want information for your own use only, and when you will not need to quote or document your sources. You would take informal notes when preparing materials to use in studying, for instance, as you watch a film or listen to a lecture.

Informal note-taking is similar to outlining. Use important ideas as headings, and write relevant details below. You will not be able to copy every word, nor is there any need to. Write phrases instead of sentences. You will also want to record information about the event or performance, including the date, time, place, speaker, and title, as applicable.

EXAMPLE

quotation
"Jerzy Kosinski came to the United States in 1957, and in 1958 he was awarded a Ford Foundation fellowship."

notes

Jerzy Kosinski
—came to US 1957
—Ford Foundation fellowship 1958

Formal Note-Taking Take formal notes when you may need to quote or document your sources. When you are keeping formal notes for a project—for instance, for a debate or a research paper—you should use 4″ x 6″ index cards.

Preparing Note Cards

1. Identify the source at the top right corner of the card. (Use the source numbers from your bibliography cards.)
2. Identify the subject or topic of the note on the top line of the card. (This will make it easier to organize the cards later.)
3. Use a separate card for each fact or quotation. (This will make it easier to organize the cards later.)
4. Write the pertinent source page number or numbers after the note.

EXAMPLE

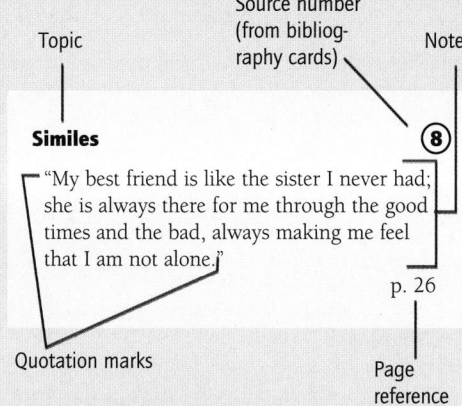

Topic

Source number (from bibliography cards)

Note

Similes

⑧

"My best friend is like the sister I never had; she is always there for me through the good times and the bad, always making me feel that I am not alone."

p. 26

Quotation marks

Page reference

Bibliographies and Bibliography Cards

If you are writing a research paper, your teacher will ask you to include a bibliography to tell where you got your information. A bibliography is a list of sources that you used for your writing. A source is a book, a magazine, a film, or any other written or audiovisual material that you use to get information. As you work on your paper, you should be writing down on note cards the information for each source that you use.

EXAMPLE

2

Van Lawick-Goodall, Jane.

In the Shadow of Man

Boston: Houghton, 1971.

Peabody Institute Library

599.8

For each source used, prepare an index card with complete bibliographical information. Include all of the information in the following chart when preparing your cards.

Information to Include on a Bibliography Card	
Author(s)	Write the complete name(s) of all author(s), editor(s), and translator(s).
Title	Write the complete title. If the piece is contained in a larger work, include the title of the larger work. (For example, write the name of the encyclopedia as well as the name of the article you used.)
Publisher	Write exactly as it appears on the title page.
Place and date of publication	Copy this information from the title page or copyright page of a book. For a magazine, write the date of the issue that you used.
Location and call number	Note where you found the book. If it is in a library collection, write the call number.
Card number	Give each bibliography card that you prepare a number. Write that number in the top right-hand corner of the card and circle it. When you take notes from the source, include this number on each note card so that you will be able to identify the source of the note later on.

The following chart shows the correct form for citing different types of bibliography entries, following the *Modern Language Association (MLA) Style Manual.* Note that all citations should include the medium of the publication, such as *print*, *film*, or *Web*.

MLA Forms for Works Cited

Book	Douglass, Frederick. *Escape from Slavery: The Boyhood of Frederick Douglass in His Own Words.* New York: Alfred A. Knopf, 1994. Print.
Magazine article	Reston, James, Jr. "Orion: Where Stars Are Born." *National Geographic.* December 1995: 90–101. Print.
Encyclopedia entry	"Lewis and Clark Expedition." *Encyclopedia Americana.* Jackson, Donald. 1995 ed. Print.
Interview	Campbell, Silas. Personal interview. 6 February 2007.
Film	*The Big Heat.* Dir. Fritz Lang. With Glenn Ford and Gloria Grahame. Writ. Sidney Boehm. Based on the novel of the same title by William P. McGiven. 90 min. Columbia, 1953. Film.

Citing Internet Sources

To document your Internet sources, use your research journal to record each site you visit (See the Language Arts Handbook, 5.2 Internet Research, page 879) or make bibliography cards as you search. An Internet source entry should include the following general pieces of information:

- Name of the author, if available, last name first, followed by a period.
- Title of the source, document, file, or page in quotation marks, followed by a period.
- Date of the material if available, followed by a period.
- Name of the database or online source, underlined or italicized, and followed by a period.
- Medium of publication (Web).
- Date the source was accessed (day, month, year).

- Provide an electronic address, URL, only when needed to locate the source or if required by your instructor. Enclose the URL in angle brackets (< >), followed by a period. Avoid showing network and e-mail addresses as underlined hyperlinks. Note that when line length forces you to break a Web address, always break it after a slash mark.

The *Modern Language Association Style Manual* acknowledges that all source tracking information on the Internet may not be obtainable. Therefore, the manual recommends that if you cannot find some of this information, cite what is available.

EXAMPLES
Armstrong, Mark. "That's 'Sir' Mick Jagger to You." 17 June 2002. E! Online, Inc. Web. 17 June 2009 <http://www.eonline.com/News/Items/0,1,10110,00.html>.

For sites with no name of the database or online source:
Chachich, Mike. "Letters from Japan Vol 1" 30 March 1994. Web. 17 June 2009 <http://www.chachich.com/cgi-bin/catlfj?1>.

For sites with no author:
"The Science Behind the Sod." 13 June 2002. *MSU News Bulletin*. Web. 17 June 2009 <http://www.newsbulletin.msu.edu/june13/sod.html>.

For e-mail messages:
Daniel Akaka (senator@akaka.senate.gov). "Oceanic Exploration Grant." E-mail to Al Franken (senator@franken.senate.gov). 17 June 2009.

Parenthetical Documentation Parenthetical documentation is currently the most widely used form of documentation. To use this method to document the source of a quotation or an idea, you place a brief note identifying the source in parentheses immediately after the borrowed material. This type of note is called a parenthetical citation, and the act of placing such a note is called citing a source.

The first part of a parenthetical citation refers the reader to a source in your List of Works Cited or Works Consulted. For the reader's ease in finding the source in your bibliography, you must cite the work according to how it is listed in the bibliography.

EXAMPLES

For works listed by title, use an abbreviated title.

Sample bibliographic entry
"History." *Encyclopedia Britannica: Macropædia*. 1992 ed. Print.

Sample citation
Historians go through three stages in textual criticism ("History" 615).

For works listed by author or editor, use the author's or editor's last name.

Sample bibliographic entry
Brown, Dee. *Bury My Heart at Wounded Knee: An Indian History of the American West*. New York: Holt, 1970. Print.

Sample citation
"Big Eyes Schurz agreed to the arrest" (Brown 364).

When the listed name or title is stated in the text, cite only the page number.

Brown states that Big Eyes Schurz agreed to it (364).

For works of multiple volumes, use a colon after the volume number.

Sample bibliographic entry

Pepys, Samuel. *The Diary of Samuel Pepys.* Eds. Robert Latham and William Matthews. 10 vols. Berkeley: University of California Press, 1972. Print.

Sample citation

On the last day of 1665, Pepys took the occasion of the new year to reflect, but not to celebrate (6: 341–2).

For works quoted in secondary sources, use the abbreviation "qtd. in."

Sample citation

According to R. Bentley, "reason and the facts outweigh a hundred manuscripts" (qtd. in "History" 615).

For classic works that are available in various editions, give the page number from the edition you are using, followed by a semicolon; then identify the section of the work to help people with other editions find the reference.

Footnotes and Endnotes

In addition to parenthetical documentation, footnoting and endnoting are two other accepted methods.

Footnotes Instead of putting citations in parentheses within the text, you can place them at the bottom or foot of the page; hence the term *footnote.* In this system, a number or symbol is placed in the text where the parenthetical citation would otherwise be, and a matching number or symbol at the bottom of the page identifies the citation. This textbook, for example, uses numbered footnotes in its literature selections to define obscure words and to provide background information.

Endnotes Many books use endnotes instead of footnotes. Endnotes are like footnotes in that a number or symbol is placed within the text, but the matching citations are compiled at the end of the book, chapter, or article rather than at the foot of the page. Footnote and endnote entries begin with the author's (or editor's) name in its usual order (first name, then last) and include publication information and a page reference.

EXAMPLES

Book with one author

[1]Jean Paul-Sartre, *Being and Nothingness* (New York: The Citadel Press, 1966) 149–151. Print.

Book with one editor and no single author

[2]Shannon Ravenel, ed., *New Stories from the South: The Year's Best, 1992* (Chapel Hill, NC: Algonquin Books, 1992) 305. Print.

Magazine article

[3]Andrew Gore, "Road Test: The Apple Powerbook," *MacUser,* December 1996: 72. Print.

6.1 Workplace and Consumer Documents

Applied English is English in the world of work or business, or *practical* English. Entering a new school, writing a professional letter, applying for a job, reading an instructional manual—these are but a few of the many situations you may encounter that involve **workplace and consumer documents.** You can apply English skills to many real-world situations, using your reading, writing, speaking, and listening abilities to help you be successful in any field or occupation you choose to pursue.

6.2 Writing a Step-by-Step Procedure

A **step-by-step procedure** is a how-to or process piece that uses directions to teach someone something new. Written procedures include textual information and sometimes graphics. Spoken procedures can be given as oral demonstrations. They can include textual and graphic information and other props. Examples of step-by-step procedures include an oral demonstration of how to saddle a horse; instructions on how to treat a sprained ankle; a video showing how to do the perfect lay-up in basketball; and an interactive Internet site allowing the user to design and send a bouquet of flowers.

Guidelines for Writing a Step-by-Step Procedure

- Demonstrate the steps. If you are showing how to make something, create several different samples to show each step of the procedure. For example, if you are showing how to make a wooden basket, you might want to display the raw materials, the started basket, the basket halfway finished, and then the finished product.
- Be prepared. The best way to prevent problems is to anticipate and plan for them. Rehearse an oral demonstration several times. If you are preparing the procedure in written form, go through your directions as if you knew nothing about the process. Anticipate what it would be like to learn this procedure for the first time. See if you can follow your own directions, or have a friend work through the procedure and offer suggestions for improvement.
- Acknowledge mistakes. If you are sharing a procedure "live" as an oral demonstration and you can't talk around or correct a mistake, tell your audience what has gone wrong, and why. If you handle the situation in a calm, direct way, the audience may also learn from your mistake.
- Know your topic. The better you know it, the better you will be able to teach others.

6.3 Writing a Business Letter

A **business letter** is usually addressed to someone you do not know personally. Therefore, a formal tone is appropriate for such a letter. Following appropriate form is especially important when writing business letters. If you follow the correct form and avoid errors in spelling, grammar, usage, and mechanics, your letter will sound professional and make a good impression. Above the salutation, a business letter should contain the name and title of the person to whom you are writing and the name and address of that person's company or organization (see the model on the following page).

One common form for a business letter is the block form. In the **block form,** each part of the letter begins at the left margin. The parts are separated by line spaces.

Begin the salutation with the word *Dear,* followed by the courtesy or professional title used in the inside address, such as Ms., Mr., or Dr., and a colon. If you are not writing to a specific person, you may use a general salutation such as *Dear Sir or Madam.*

In the body of your letter, use a polite, formal tone and standard English. Make your points clearly, in as few words as possible.

End with a standard closing such as *Sincerely, Yours truly,* or *Respectfully yours.* Capitalize only the first word of the closing. Type your full name below the closing, leaving three or four blank lines for your signature. Sign your name below the closing in blue or black ink (never in red or green). Proofread your letter before you send it. Poor spelling, grammar, or punctuation can ruin an otherwise well-written business letter.

One of the most frequently used types of business letters is an **application letter,** which you would write to apply to a school or for a job. In an application letter, it is important to emphasize your knowledge about the business and the skills that you can bring to the position.

Guidelines for Writing a Business Letter

- Outline your main points before you begin.
- Word process your letter, if at all possible. Type or print it on clean 8 1/2" x 11" white or off-white paper. Use only one side of the paper.
- Use the block form or another standard business letter form.
- Single space, leaving a blank line between each part, including paragraphs.
- Use a standard salutation and a standard closing.
- Stick to the subject. State your main idea clearly at the beginning of the letter. Keep the letter brief and informative.
- Check your spelling, grammar, usage, and punctuation carefully.

6.4 Writing a Proposal

A **proposal** outlines a project that a person wants to complete. It presents a summary of an idea, the reasons why the idea is important, and an outline of how the project would be carried out. Because the proposal audience is people who can help carry out the proposal, a proposal is both informative and persuasive.

EXAMPLES

- You want funding for an art project that would benefit your community.

- Your student council proposes a clothing drive for disaster relief.

- You and a group of your friends want to help organize a summer program for teens your age.

Guidelines for Writing a Proposal

- Keep the tone positive, courteous, and respectful.
- State your proposal and rationale briefly and clearly.
- Give your audience all necessary information. A proposal with specific details makes it clear what you want approved, and why your audience—often a committee or someone in authority—should approve it.
- Use standard, formal English.
- Format your proposal with headings, lists, and schedules to make your proposed project easy to understand and approve.

6.5 Writing a Public Service Announcement

A **public service announcement,** or **PSA,** is a brief, informative article intended to be helpful to the community. PSAs are written by nonprofit organizations and concerned citizens for print in local newspapers, for broadcast by television and radio stations, and for publication on the Internet.

EXAMPLES

- an article by the American Cancer Society outlining early warning signs of cancer

- an announcement promoting Safety Week

- an informative piece telling coastal residents what to do during a hurricane

Guidelines for Writing a Public Service Announcement

- Know your purpose. What do you want your audience to know from reading or hearing your piece?
- State your information as objectively as possible.
- As with most informative writing, use the 5 *Ws* and an *H*—*who, what, where, why, when,* and *how*—questioning strategy to get your important information at the beginning of your story.
- Keep your announcement brief. Local media are more likely to publish or broadcast your piece if it is short and to the point.
- Include contact information in case the media representative has any questions. You might also include contact information in the PSA itself.
- Key or type your PSA in conventional manuscript form. Make sure the text is double-spaced and that you leave margins of at least an inch on all sides of the page.
- At the end of the PSA, key "END" to designate the end of the announcement.
- Be aware of print and broadcast deadlines and make sure your material is sent on time.

> Refer to the following pages for the unit Speaking and Listening Workshops:

Giving and Actively Listening to Oral Summaries, pp. 132–133

Giving and Actively Listening to Literary Presentations, pp. 246–245

Giving and Actively Listening to Informative Presentations, pp. 368–369

Giving and Actively Listening to Expository Presentations, pp. 530–531

Giving and Actively Listening to Narrative Presentations, pp. 600–601

Giving and Actively Listening to Persuasive Presentations, pp. 716–717

Giving and Actively Listening to Research Presentations, pp. 828–829

> Refer to the following pages for the unit Viewing Workshop: Critical Viewing, pp. 454–455.

SPEAKING & LISTENING

7 Speaking & Listening

7.1 Verbal and Nonverbal Communication

When a person expresses meaning through words, he or she is using verbal communication. When a person expresses meaning without using words, for example by standing up straight or shaking his or her head, he or she is using nonverbal communication. When we speak to another person, we usually think that the meaning of what we say comes chiefly from the words we use. However, as much as sixty percent of the meaning of a message may be communicated nonverbally.

Elements of Verbal Communication

Element	Description	Guidelines for Speakers
Volume	Loudness or softness	Vary your volume, but make sure that you can be heard.
Melody, Pitch	Highness or lowness	Vary your pitch. Avoid speaking in a monotone (at a single pitch).
Pace	Speed	Vary the speed of your delivery to suit what you are saying.
Tone	Emotional quality	Suit your tone to your message, and vary it appropriately as you speak.
Enunciation	Clearness with which words are spoken	When speaking before a group, pronounce your words more precisely than you would in ordinary conversation.

Elements of Nonverbal Communication

Element	Description	Guidelines for Speakers
Eye contact	Looking audience members in the eye	Make eye contact regularly with people in your audience. Try to include all audience members.
Facial expression	Using your face to show your emotions	Use expressions to emphasize your message— raised eyebrows for a question, pursed lips for concentration, eyebrows lowered for anger, and so on.
Gesture	Meaningful motions of the arms and hands	Use gestures to emphasize points. Be careful, however, not to overuse gestures. Too many can be distracting.
Posture	Position of the body	Keep your spine straight and head high, but avoid appearing stiff. Stand with your arms and legs slightly open, except when adopting other postures to express particular emotions.
Proximity	Distance from audience	Keep the right amount of distance between yourself and the audience. You should be a comfortable distance away, but not so far away that the audience cannot hear you.

Program Resources

To expand upon speaking and listening skills, see the *Exceeding the Standards: Speaking & Listening* resource.

7.2 Listening Skills

Active Versus Passive Listening

Active listening requires skill and concentration. The mind of a good listener is focused on what a speaker is trying to communicate. In other words, an effective listener is an active listener. Ineffective listeners view listening as a passive activity, something that simply "happens" without any effort on their part. **Passive listening** is nothing more than hearing sounds. This type of listening can cause misunderstanding and miscommunication.

ADAPTING LISTENING SKILLS

Just as different situations require different types of listening, different tasks or goals may also require different listening strategies and skills.

Listening for Comprehension

Listening for comprehension means listening for information or ideas communicated by other people. For example, you are listening for comprehension when you try to understand directions to a friend's house or your teacher's explanation of how to conduct a classroom debate.

When listening for comprehension, your goal is to reach understanding, so it is important to recognize and remember the key information or ideas presented. Concentrate on getting the **main points or major ideas** of a message rather than all the supporting details. This can prevent you from becoming overwhelmed by the amount of information presented.

You might also use a technique called **clarifying and confirming** to help you better remember and understand information. This technique involves paraphrasing or repeating back to the speaker in your own words the key information presented to make sure that you have understood correctly. If the situation prevents you from using the technique—for instance, if there is no opportunity for you to respond directly to the speaker—it can still be helpful to rephrase the information in your own words in your head to help you remember and understand it.

Listening Critically

Listening critically means listening to a message in order to comprehend and evaluate it. When listening for comprehension, you usually assume that the information presented is true. Critical listening, on the other hand, includes **comprehending and judging** the arguments and appeals in a message in order to decide whether to accept or reject them. Critical listening is most useful when you encounter a persuasive message such as a sales pitch, advertisement, campaign speech, or news editorial.

When evaluating a persuasive message, you might consider the following:
- Is the speaker trustworthy and qualified to speak about this subject?
- Does the speaker present logical arguments supported by solid facts?
- Does the speaker use unproven assumptions to make a case?
- Does the speaker use questionable motivational appeals, such as appeals to fear or to prejudice?

These questions can help you decide whether or not to be convinced by a persuasive message.

Listening to Learn Vocabulary

Listening to learn vocabulary involves a very different kind of listening because the focus is on learning new words and how to use them properly. For instance, you have a conversation with someone who has a more advanced vocabulary and use this as an opportunity to learn new words. The key to listening in order to learn vocabulary is to **pay attention to how words are used in context.** Sometimes it is possible to figure out what an unfamiliar word means based simply on how the word is used in a sentence.

Once you learn a new word, try to use it several times so it becomes more familiar and you become comfortable using it. Also be sure to look up the word in a dictionary to find out whether it has other meanings or connotations of which you are not aware.

Listening for Appreciation

Listening for appreciation means listening purely for enjoyment or entertainment. You might listen appreciatively to a singer, a comedian, a storyteller, an acting company, or a humorous speaker. Appreciation is a very individual matter and there are no rules about how to appreciate something. However, as with all forms of listening, listening for appreciation requires attention and concentration.

7.3 Collaborative Learning and Communication

Collaboration is the act of working with one or more other people to achieve a goal. Many common learning situations involve collaboration.
- Participating in a small-group discussion
- Doing a small-group project
- Tutoring another student or being tutored
- Doing peer evaluation

Guidelines for Group Discussion

- **Listen actively.** Maintain eye contact with the speakers. Make notes on what they say. Mentally translate what they say into your own words. Think critically about whether you agree or disagree with each speaker, and why.
- **Be polite.** Wait for your turn to speak. Do not interrupt others. If your discussion has a group leader, ask to be recognized before speaking by raising your hand.
- **Participate in the discussion.** At appropriate times, make your own comments or ask questions of other speakers.
- **Stick to the discussion topic.** Do not introduce unrelated or irrelevant ideas.
- **Assign roles.** For a formal dicussion, choose a group leader to guide the discussion and a secretary to record the minutes (the main ideas and proposals made by group members). Also draw up an agenda before the discussion, listing items to be discussed.

Guidelines for Projects

- **Choose a group leader** to conduct the meetings of your project group.
- **Set a goal** for the group. This goal should be some specific outcome or set of outcomes that you want to bring about.
- **Make a list of tasks** that need to be performed.
- **Make a schedule** for completing the tasks, including dates and times for completion of each task.
- **Make an assignment sheet.** Assign certain tasks to particular group members. Be fair in distributing the work to be done.

- **Set times for future meetings** You might want to schedule meetings to evaluate your progress toward your goal as well as meetings to actually carry out specific tasks.
- **Meet to evaluate** your overall success when the project is completed. Also look at the individual contributions of each group member.

7.4 Asking and Answering Questions

There are many situations in which you will find it useful to ask questions of a speaker, or in which you will be asked questions about a presentation. Often a formal speech or presentation will be followed by a question-and-answer period. Keep the following guidelines in mind when asking or answering questions.

Guidelines for Asking and Answering Questions

- **Wait to be recognized.** In most cases, it is appropriate to raise your hand if you have a question and to wait for the speaker or moderator to call on you.
- **Make questions clear and direct.** The longer your question, the less chance a speaker will understand it. Make your questions short and to the point.
- **Do not debate or argue.** If you disagree with a speaker, the question-and-answer period is not the time to hash out an argument. Ask to speak with the speaker privately after the presentation is over, or agree on a later time and place to meet.
- **Do not take others' time.** Be courteous to other audience members and allow them time to ask questions. If you have a follow-up question, ask the speaker if you may proceed with your follow up.
- **Do not give a speech.** Sometimes audience members are more interested in expressing their own opinion than in asking the speaker a question. Do not give in to the temptation to present a speech of your own.
- **Come prepared for a question-and-answer period.** Although you can never predict the exact questions that people will ask you, you can anticipate many questions that are likely to be asked. Rehearse aloud your answers to the most difficult questions.
- **Be patient.** It may take some time for audience members to formulate questions in response to your speech. Give the audience a moment to do so. Don't run back to your seat the minute your speech is over, or if there is an awkward pause after you invite questions.
- **Be direct and succinct.** Be sure to answer the question directly as it has been asked, and to provide a short but clear answer.

7.5 Conducting an Interview

In an interview, you meet with someone and ask him or her questions. Interviewing experts is an excellent way to gain information about a particular topic. For example, if you are interested in writing about the art of making pottery, you might interview an art teacher, a professional potter, or the owner of a ceramics shop.

When planning an interview, you should do some background research on your subject and think carefully about questions you would like to ask. Write out a list of questions, including some about the person's background as well as about your topic. Other questions might occur to you as the interview proceeds, but it is best to be prepared. For guidelines on being a good listener, see Language Arts Handbook 7.2, Listening Skills, page 913. Guidelines for interviewing appear on the following page:

Guidelines for Conducting an Interview

- **Set up a time in advance.** Don't just try to work questions into a regular conversation. Set aside time to meet in a quiet place where both you and the person you are interviewing can focus on the interview.
- **Explain the purpose** of the interview. Be sure the person you are interviewing knows what you want to find out and why you need to know it. This will help him or her to answer your questions in a way that is more useful and helpful to you.
- **Ask mostly open-ended questions.** These are questions that allow the person you are interviewing to express a personal point of view. They cannot be answered with a simple "yes" or "no" nor a brief statement of fact. The following are all examples of open-ended questions:

    "Why did you become a professional potter?"
    "What is the most challenging thing about owning your own ceramics shop?"
    "What advice would you give to a beginning potter?"

    One of the most valuable questions to ask at the end of the interview is, "What would you like to add that I haven't asked about?" This can provide some of the most interesting or vital information of all.
- **Tape-record the interview** (if possible). Then you can review the interview at your leisure. Be sure to ask the person you are interviewing whether or not you can tape-record the session. If the person refuses, accept his or her decision.
- **Take notes** during the interview, whether or not you are also tape-recording it. Write down the main points and some key words to help you remember details. Record the person's most important statements word for word.
- **Clarify spelling and get permission** for quotations. Be sure to get the correct spelling of the person's name and to ask permission to quote his or her statements.
- **End the interview on time.** Do not extend the interview beyond the time limits of your appointment. The person you are interviewing has been courteous enough to give you his or her time. Return this courtesy by ending the interview on time, thanking the person for his or her help, and leaving.
- **Write up the results** of the interview as soon as possible after you conduct it. Over time, what seemed like a very clear note may become unclear or confusing. If you are unclear of something important that the person said, contact him or her and ask for clarification.
- **Send a thank-you note** to the person you interviewed as a follow-up.

7.6 Public Speaking

The nature of a speech, whether formal or informal, is usually determined by the situation or context in which it is presented. **Formal speeches** usually call for a greater degree of preparation, might require special attire such as a suit or dress, and are often presented to larger groups who attend specifically to hear the presentation. A formal speech situation might exist when presenting an assigned speech to classmates, giving a presentation to a community group or organization, or presenting a speech at an awards ceremony. **Informal speeches** are more casual and might include telling a story among friends, giving a pep talk to your team at halftime, or presenting a toast at the dinner table.

Types of Speeches

The following are four common types of speeches:
- **Extemporaneous:** a speech in which the speaker refers to notes occasionally and that has a specific purpose and message. An example would be a speech given at a city council meeting.

- **Informative:** a speech used to share new and useful information with the audience. Informative speeches are based on fact, not opinion. Examples would include a speech on how to do something or a speech about an event.
- **Persuasive:** a speech used to convince the audience to side with an opinion and adopt a plan. The speaker tries to persuade the audience to believe something, do something, or change their behavior. Persuasive speeches use facts and research to support, analyze, and sell an opinion and plan. Martin Luther King's famous "I Have a Dream" speech and Nelson Mandela's "Glory and Hope" speech are examples of persuasive speeches.
- **Commemorative:** a speech that honors an individual for outstanding accomplishments and exemplary character. Examples would be a speech honoring a historical figure, leader, teacher, athlete, relative, or celebrity.

Guidelines for Giving a Speech

A speech should always include a beginning, a middle, and an end. The **beginning,** or introduction, of your speech should spark the audience's interest, present your central idea, and briefly preview your main points. The **middle,** or body, of your speech should expand upon each of your main points in order to support the central idea. The **end,** or conclusion, of your speech should be memorable and should give your audience a sense of completion.

- **Be sincere and enthusiastic.** Feel what you are speaking about. Apathy is infectious and will quickly spread to your audience.
- **Maintain good but relaxed posture.** Don't slouch or lean. It's fine to move around a bit; it releases normal nervous tension. Keep your hands free to gesture naturally instead of holding on to note cards, props, or the podium so much that you will "tie up" your hands.
- **Speak slowly.** Oral communication is more difficult than written language and visual images for audiences to process and understand. Practice pausing. Don't be afraid of silence. Focus on communicating with the audience. By looking for feedback from the audience, you will be able to pace yourself appropriately.
- **Maintain genuine eye contact.** Treat the audience as individuals, not as a mass of people. Look at individual faces.
- **Speak in a genuine, relaxed, conversational tone.** Don't act or stiffen up. Just be yourself.
- **Communicate.** Focus on conveying your message, not "getting through" the speech. Focus on communicating with the audience, not speaking at or to it.
- **Use strategic pauses.** Pause briefly before proceeding to the next major point, before direct quotations, and to allow important or more complex bits of information to sink in.
- **Remain confident and composed.** Remember that listeners are generally "for you" while you are speaking, and signs of nervousness are usually undetectable. To overcome initial nervousness, take two or three deep breaths as you are stepping up to speak.

7.7 Oral Interpretation

Oral interpretation is the process of presenting a dramatic reading of a literary work or group of works. The presentation should be sufficiently dramatic to convey to the audience a sense of the particular qualities of the work. Here are the steps you need to follow to prepare and present an oral interpretation:

Guidelines for Oral Interpretation

1. **Choose a cutting,** which may be a single piece; a selection from a single piece; or several short, related pieces on a single topic or theme.
2. **Write** the introduction and any necessary transitions. The introduction should mention the name of each piece, the author, and, if appropriate, the translator. It should also present the overall topic or theme of the interpretation. Transitions should introduce and connect the parts of the interpretation.
3. **Rehearse,** using appropriate variations in volume, pitch, pace, stress, tone, gestures, facial expressions, and body language. If your cutting contains different voices (a narrator's voice and characters' voices, for example), distinguish them. Try to make your verbal and nonverbal expression mirror what the piece is saying. However, avoid movement—that's for drama. Practice in front of an audience or mirror, or use a video camera or tape recorder.
4. **Present** your oral interpretation. Before actually presenting your interpretation, relax and adopt a confident attitude. If you begin to feel stage fright, try to concentrate on the work you are presenting and the audience, not on yourself.

Interpreting Poetry

Here are some additional considerations as you prepare to interpret a poem. The way you prepare your interpretation of a poem will depend on whether the poem you have chosen is a lyric poem, a narrative poem, or a dramatic poem.

- A **lyric poem** has a single speaker who reports his or her own emotions.
- A **narrative poem** tells a story. Usually a narrative poem has lines belonging to the narrator, or person who is telling the story. The narrator may or may not take part in the action.
- A **dramatic poem** contains characters who speak. A dramatic poem may be lyrical, in which characters simply report emotions, or narrative, which tells a story. A dramatic monologue presents a single speaker at a moment of crisis or self-revelation and may be either lyrical or narrative.

Before attempting to dramatize any poem, read through the poem carefully several times. Make sure that you understand it well. To check your understanding, try to paraphrase the poem, or restate its ideas, line by line, in your own words.

7.8 Telling a Story

A story or narrative is a series of events linked together in some meaningful fashion. We use narratives constantly in our daily lives: to make a journal entry, to tell a joke, to report a news story, to recount a historical event, to record a laboratory experiment, and so on. When creating a narrative, consider all of the following elements:

Guidelines for Storytelling

- **Decide on your purpose.** Every story has a point or purpose. It may be simply to entertain or to share a personal experience, but it may have a moral or lesson.
- **Select a focus.** The focus for your narrative will depend largely on your purpose in telling it.
- **Choose your point of view.** The storyteller or narrator determines the point of view from which the story will be told. You can choose to speak in the *first person,* either as a direct participant in the events or as an observer (real or imagined) who witnessed the events firsthand, or in the *third person* voice to achieve greater objectivity.

- **Determine sequence of events.** The sequence of events refers to the order in which they are presented. Although it might seem obvious that stories should "begin at the beginning," this is not always the best approach. Some narratives begin with the turning point of the story to create a sense of drama and to capture the listeners' interest. Others begin at the end of the story and present the events leading up to this point in hindsight. Wherever you choose to begin the story, your narrative should present events in a logical fashion and establish a clear sense of direction for your listeners.
- **Determine duration of events.** Duration refers to how long something lasts. Everyone has experienced an event that seemed to last for hours, when in reality it only took minutes to occur. A good storyteller can likewise manipulate the duration of events in order to affect the way listeners experience them.
- **Select details carefully.** Make them consistent with your focus and make sure they are necessary to your purpose. A well-constructed story should flow smoothly, and should not get bogged down by irrelevant or unnecessary detail. Details can also establish the tone and style of the story and affect how listeners react to the events being described.
- **Choose characters.** All stories include characters who need to be developed so that they become real for listeners. Try to provide your listeners with vivid, concrete descriptions of the mental and physical qualities of important characters in the story. Remember that listeners need to understand and relate to the characters in order to appreciate their behavior.
- **Create dialogue.** Although it is possible to tell a story in which the characters do not speak directly, conversation and dialogue help to add life to a story. As with detail, dialogue should be used carefully. It is important that dialogue sound authentic, relate to the main action of the story, and advance the narrative.

7.9 Participating in a Debate

A debate is a contest in which two people or groups of people defend opposite sides of a proposition in an attempt to convince a judge or an audience to agree with their views. Propositions are statements of fact, value, or policy that usually begin with the word "resolved." The following are examples of typical propositions for debate:

RESOLVED   That lie detector tests are inaccurate. (proposition of fact)

RESOLVED   That imagination is more important than knowledge. (proposition of value)

RESOLVED   That Congress should prohibit the sale of handguns to private citizens. (proposition of policy)

The two sides in a debate are usually called the affirmative and the negative. The affirmative takes the "pro" side of the debate and argues in favor of the proposition, whereas the negative takes the "con" side and argues against the proposition. Using a single proposition to focus the debate ensures that the two sides argue or clash over a common topic. This allows the participants in the debate to develop their logic and ability to argue their positions persuasively.

Guidelines for Participating in a Debate

- **Be prepared.** In a debate, it will never be possible to anticipate all the arguments your opponent might make. However, by conducting careful and thorough research on both sides of the issue, you should be able to prepare for the most likely arguments you will encounter. You can prepare briefs or notes on particular issues in advance of the debate to save yourself preparation time during the debate.

- **Be organized.** Because a debate involves several speeches that concern the same basic arguments or issues, it is important that you remain organized during the debate. When attacking or refuting an opponent's argument, or when advancing or defending your own argument, be sure to follow a logical organizational pattern to avoid confusing the audience or the other team.
- **Take notes** by turning a long sheet of paper sideways. Draw one column for each speaker, taking notes on each speech going down one column, and recording notes about a particular argument or issue across the page as it is discussed in each successive speech.
- **Be audience-centered.** In arguing with your opponent, it is easy to forget the goal of the debate: to persuade your audience that your side of the issue is correct.
- **Prepare in advance** for the most likely arguments your opponents, will raise. Use time sparingly to organize your materials and think of responses to unanticipated arguments. Save time for the end of the debate, during rebuttal speeches, when it will be more valuable.

7.10 Preparing a Multimedia Presentation

Whether you use a simple overhead projector and transparencies or a PowerPoint presentation that involves graphics, video, and sound, multimedia technology can add an important visual element to a presentation. Consider the following guidelines to create a multimedia presentation:

Guidelines for a Multimedia Presentation

- **Use effective audiovisuals** that enhance understanding. The multimedia elements should add to the verbal elements, not distract from them. Be sure the content of the presentation is understandable, and that the amount of information—both verbal and visual—will not overwhelm audience members.
- **Make sure the presentation is clearly audible and visible.** Video clips or graphics may appear blurry on a projection screen or may not be visible to audience members in the back or on the sides of the room. Audio clips may sound muffled or may echo in a larger room or a room with different acoustics. When creating a multimedia presentation, be sure the presentation can be easily seen and heard from all parts of the room.
- **Become familiar with the equipment.** Well before the presentation, be sure you know how to operate the equipment you will need, that you know how to troubleshoot if the equipment malfunctions, and that the equipment you will use during the presentation is the same as that which you practiced with.
- **Check the room** to be sure it can accommodate your needs. Once you know where you will make your presentation, be sure the necessary electrical outlets and extension cords are available, that lights can be dimmed or turned off as needed, that the room can accommodate the equipment you will use, and so on.
- **Rehearse with the equipment.** Make sure that you can operate the equipment while speaking at the same time. Be sure that the multimedia elements are coordinated with other parts of your presentation. If you will need to turn the lights off in the room, make sure you can operate the equipment in the dark and can still see your note cards.

8.1 Preparing for Tests

Tests are a common part of school life. You take tests in your classes to show what you have learned in each class. In addition, you might have to take one or more standardized tests each year. Standardized tests measure your skills against local, state, or national standards and may determine whether you graduate, what kind of job you can get, or which college you can attend. Learning test-taking strategies will help you succeed on the tests you are required to take.

The following guidelines will help you to prepare for and take tests on the material you have covered in class.

Preparing for a Test

- **Know what will be covered on the test.** If you have questions about what will be covered, ask your teacher.
- **Make a study plan** to allow yourself time to go over the material. Avoid last-minute cramming.
- **Review the subject matter.** Use the graphic organizers and notes you made as you read as well as notes you took in class. Review any study questions given by your teacher.
- **Make lists** of important names, dates, definitions, or events. Ask a friend or family member to quiz you on them.
- **Try to predict questions** that may be on the test. Make sure you can answer them.
- **Get plenty of sleep** the night before the test. Eat a nutritious breakfast on the morning of the test.

Taking a Test

- **Survey the test** to see how long it is and what types of questions are included.
- **Read all directions and questions carefully.** Make sure you know exactly what to do.
- **Plan your time.** Answer easy questions first. Allow extra time for complicated questions. If a question seems too difficult, skip it and go back to it later. Work quickly, but do not rush.
- **Save time for review.** Once you have finished, look back over the test. Double-check your answers, but do not change answers too readily. Your first responses are often correct.

8.2 Strategies for Taking Standardized Tests

Standardized tests are given to large groups of students in a school district, a state, or a country. Statewide tests measure how well students are meeting the learning standards the state has set. Other tests, such as the SAT (Scholastic Aptitude Test) or ACT (American College Test), are used to help determine admission to colleges and universities. Others must be taken to enter certain careers. These tests are designed to measure overall ability or skills acquired so far. Learning how to take standardized tests will help you to achieve your goals.

You can get better at answering standardized test questions by practicing the types of questions that will be on the test. Use the Test Practice Workshop questions in this book and other sample questions your teacher gives you to practice. Think aloud with a partner or small group about how you would answer each question. Notice how other students tackle the questions and learn from what they do.

TEST-TAKING SKILLS

> Refer to the following pages for the unit Test Practice Workshops:

Writing Skills:
Literary Response, p. 134
Literary Response, p. 248
Expository Essay, p. 370
Descriptive Essay, p. 456
Expository Essay, p. 532
Personal Essay, p. 602
Persuasive Essay, p. 718
Research Report, p. 816

Revising and Editing Skills:
135, 249, 371, 457, 533, 603, 719, 817

Reading Skills:
136–137, 250–251, 372–373, 458–459, 534–535, 604–605, 720–721, 832–833

Program Resources

For more study and practice with test-taking skills, see the *Exceeding the Standards: Test Practice* resource.

In addition, remember these points:

- **Rule out some choices** when you are not sure of the answer. Then guess from the remaining possibilities.
- **Skip questions that seem too difficult** and go back to them later. Be aware, however, that most tests allow you to go back only within a section.
- **Follow instructions exactly.** The test monitor will read instructions to you, and instructions may also be printed in your test booklet. Make sure you know what to do.

8.3 Answering Objective Questions

An **objective question** has a single correct answer. The following chart describes the kinds of questions you may see on objective tests. It also gives you strategies for tackling each kind of question.

Description	Guidelines
True/False You are given a statement and asked to tell whether the statement is true or false.	• If any part of a statement is false, then the statement is false. • Words like *all*, *always*, *never*, and *every* often appear in false statements. • Words like *some*, *usually*, *often*, and *most* often appear in true statements. • If you do not know the answer, guess. You have a 50/50 chance of being right.
Matching You are asked to match items in one column with items in another column.	• Check the directions. See if each item is used only once. Also check to see if some are not used at all. • Read all items before starting. • Match those items you know first. • Cross out items as you match them.
Short Answer You are asked to answer the question with a word, phrase, or sentence.	• Read the directions to find out if you are required to answer in complete sentences. • Use correct spelling, grammar, punctuation, and capitalization. • If you cannot think of the answer, move on. Something in another question might remind you of the answer.

8.4 Answering Multiple-Choice Questions

On many standardized tests, questions are multiple choice and have a single correct answer. The guidelines below will help you answer these kinds of questions effectively.

- **Read each question carefully.** Pay special attention to any words that are bolded, italicized, written in all capital letters, or otherwise emphasized.
- **Read all choices** before selecting an answer.
- **Eliminate** any answers that do not make sense, that disagree with what you remember from reading a passage, or that seem too extreme. Also, if two answers have exactly the same meaning, you can eliminate both.
- **Beware of distractors.** These are incorrect answers that look attractive because they are partially correct. They might contain a common misunderstanding, or they might apply the right information in the wrong way. Distractors are based on common mistakes students make.
- **Fill in circles completely** on your answer sheet when you have selected your answer.

8.5 Answering Reading Comprehension Questions

Reading comprehension questions ask you to read a passage and answer questions about it. These questions measure how well you perform the essential reading skills. Many of the Reading Assessment questions that follow each literature selection in this book are reading comprehension questions. Use them to help you learn how to answer these types of questions correctly. Work through each question with a partner using a "think aloud." Say out loud how you are figuring out the answer. Talk about how you can eliminate incorrect answers and determine the correct choice. You may want to make notes as you eliminate answers. By practicing this thinking process with a partner, you will be more prepared to use it silently when you have to take a standardized test.

The following steps will help you answer the reading comprehension questions on standardized tests.

- **Preview the passage and questions** and predict what the text will be about.
- **Use the reading strategies** you have learned to read the passage. Mark the text and make notes in the margins.
- **Reread the first question carefully.** Make sure you know exactly what it is asking.
- **Read the answers.** If you are sure of the answer, select it and move on. If not, go on to the next step.
- **Scan the passage** to look for key words related to the question. When you find a key word, slow down and read carefully.
- **Answer the question** and go on to the next one. Answer each question in this way.

8.6 Answering Synonym and Antonym Questions

Synonym or antonym questions give you a word and ask you to select the word that has the same meaning (for a synonym) or the opposite meaning (for an antonym). You must select the best answer even if none is exactly correct. For this type of question, you should consider all the choices to see which is best. Always notice whether you are looking for a synonym or an antonym. You will usually find both among the answers.

8.7 Answering Sentence Completion Questions

Sentence completion questions present you with a sentence that has one or two words missing. You must select the word or pair of words that best completes the sentence. The key to questions with two words missing is to make sure that both parts of the answer you have selected work well in the sentence.

8.8 Answering Constructed-Response Questions

In addition to multiple-choice questions, many standardized tests include **constructed-response questions** that require you to write essay answers in the test booklet. Constructed-response questions might ask you to identify key ideas or examples from the text by writing a sentence about each. In other cases, you will be asked to write a paragraph in response to a question about the selection and to use specific details from the passage to support your answer.

Other constructed-response questions ask you to apply information or ideas from a text in a new way. Another question might ask you to use information from the text in a particular imaginary situation. As you answer these questions, remember that you are being evaluated based on your understanding of the text. Although these questions may offer opportunities to be creative, you should still include ideas, details, and examples from the passage you have just read.

The following tips will help you answer constructed-response questions effectively:

- **Skim the questions first.** Predict what the passage will be about.
- **Use reading strategies** as you read. Underline information that relates to the questions and make notes. After you have finished reading, you can decide which of the details you have gathered to use in your answers.
- **List the most important points** to include in each answer. Use the margins of your test booklet or a piece of scrap paper.
- **Number the points** you have listed to show the order in which they should be included.
- **Draft your answer to fit** in the space provided. Include as much detail as possible in the space you have.
- **Revise and proofread** your answers as you have time.

8.9 Answering Essay Questions

An essay question asks you to write an answer that shows what you know about a particular subject. A simplified writing process like the one below will help you tackle questions like this.

1. Analyze the Question

Essay questions contain clues about what is expected of you. Sometimes you will find key words that will help you determine exactly what is being asked. See the chart below for some typical key words and their meanings.

Key Words for Essay Questions	
analyze; identify	break into parts, and describe the parts and how they are related
compare	tell how two or more subjects are similar; in some cases, also mention how they are different
contrast	tell how two or more subjects are different from each other
describe	give enough facts about or qualities of a subject to make it clear to someone who is unfamiliar with it
discuss	provide an overview and analysis; use details for support
evaluate; argue	judge an idea or concept, telling whether you think it is good or bad, or whether you agree or disagree with it
explain	make a subject clearer, providing supporting details and examples
interpret	tell the meaning and importance of an event or concept
justify	explain or give reasons for decisions; be persuasive
prove	provide factual evidence or reasons for a statement
summarize	state only the main points of an event, concept, or debate

2. Plan Your Answer

As soon as the essay prompt is clear to you, collect and organize your thoughts about it. First, gather ideas using whatever method is most comfortable for you. If you don't immediately have ideas, try freewriting for five minutes. When you **freewrite,** you write whatever comes into your head without letting your hand stop moving. You might also gather ideas in a cluster chart like the one below. Then, organize the ideas you came up with. A simple outline or chart can help.

3. Write Your Answer

Start with a clear thesis statement in your opening paragraph. Your **thesis statement** is a single sentence that sums up your answer to the essay question. Then follow your organizational plan to provide support for your thesis. Devote one paragraph to each major point of support for your thesis. Use plenty of details as evidence for each point. Write quickly and keep moving. Don't spend too much time on any single paragraph, but try to make your answer as complete as possible. End your essay with a concluding sentence that sums up your major points.

4. Revise Your Answer

Make sure you have answered all parts of the question and included everything you were asked to include. Check to see that you have supplied enough details to support your thesis. Check for errors in grammar, spelling, punctuation, and paragraph breaks. Make corrections to your answer.

ACT. An **act** is a major division of a play. There are two acts in Israel Horowitz's *A Christmas Carol* (Unit 7).

ALLEGORY. An **allegory** is a work in which characters, events, or settings symbolize, or represent, something else. Olivia E. Coolidge's retelling of the Greek myth "Phaëthon, Son of Apollo" (Unit 8) is an allegory.

ALLITERATION. Alliteration is the repetition of initial consonant sounds. Though alliteration usually refers to sounds at the beginnings of words, it can also be used to refer to sounds within words. In Galway Kinnell's poem "Blackberry Eating" (Unit 5), for example, the s sound is repeated several times:

> I squeeze, squinch open, and splurge.
> in the silent, startled, icy, black language
> of blackberry-eating in late September.

ALLUSION. An **allusion** is a reference to a well-known person, event, object, or work from history or literature. For example, the title of Borden Deal's story "Antaeus" (Unit 2) is a literary allusion to the Greek myth of Antaeus, a giant who was extremely powerful as long as his feet touched the earth, but became weak once he was lifted off the ground.

ANALOGY. An **analogy** is a comparison of two things that are alike in some ways but otherwise quite different. Often an analogy explains or describes something unfamiliar by comparing it to something more familiar.

ANECDOTE. An **anecdote** is usually a short account of an interesting, amusing, or biographical incident. Anecdotes are sometimes used in nonfiction writing as examples to help support an idea or opinion. In "Names/Nobres" (Unit 3), Julia Alveraz tells several anecdotes to underscore the idea that a person's name can be important to his or her identity.

ANTAGONIST. An **antagonist** is a character or force in a literary work that is in conflict with a main character, or protagonist. The antagonist of Tomás Rivera's story "The Portrait" (Unit 1), is the portrait salesman who has cheated everyone out of their money. *See* Character.

ARTICLE. An **article** is an informational piece of writing about a particular topic, issue, events, or series of events. Articles usually appear in newspapers, professional journals, or magazines, or on websites. An

editorial is an article meant to give an opinion. A *review* is an article that is a critical evaluation of a work, such as a book, play, movie, or musical performance. "The Size of Things" by Robert Jastrow (Unit 4) is an example of a familiar type of news—a science article.

ASSONANCE. Assonance is the repetition of vowel sounds in stressed syllables. An example is the repetition of the long *i* sound and the short *a* sound in the following line from Galway Kinnell's poem "Blackberry Eating" (Unit 5):

> the fat, overripe, icy, black blackberries.

ATMOSPHERE. *See* Mood.

AUTOBIOGRAPHY. An **autobiography** is the story of a person's life, written by that person. *Off the Court* by Arthur Ashe (Unit 3) is an example of an autobiography. *See* Biography *and* Memoir.

BALLAD. A **ballad** is a poem that tells a story and is written in four- to six-line stanzas, usually meant to be sung. Most ballads have regular rhythms and rhyme schemes and feature a refrain, or repetition of lines.

BIAS. Bias is a personal judgment about something, or a mental leaning in one direction or another.

BIOGRAPHY. A **biography** is the story of a person's life, told by someone other than that person. Milton Meltzer's "Elizabeth I" (Unit 3) is a biography. *See* Autobiography.

CHARACTER. A **character** is an individual that takes part in the action of a literary work. A character is usually a person but may also be a personified plant, animal, object, or imaginary creature. The main character, or protagonist, has the central role in a work and is in conflict with the antagonist.

Characters can also be classified in other ways. *Major characters* play significant roles in a work, and *minor characters* play lesser roles. A *flat character* shows only one quality, or character trait. Tokubei, the wealthy merchant, in *The Inn of Lost Time* by Lensey Namioka (Unit 1) is a flat character. A *round character* shows the multiple character traits of a real person. A *static character* does not change during the course of the action. A *dynamic character* does change.

CHARACTERIZATION. Characterization is the act of creating or describing a character. Writers create characters using three major techniques: showing what characters say, do, or think; showing what other characters say or think about them; and describing what physical features, dress, and personalities the characters display. The first two methods may be considered examples of *indirect characterization,* in which the writer *shows* what a character is like and allows the reader to judge the character. The third technique is considered *direct characterization,* in which the writer *tells* what the character is like. *See* Character.

CHORUS. In drama, a **chorus** is a group of actors who speak directly to the audience between scenes, commenting on the action of the play. In classical Greek drama, the chorus conveyed its message through a series of *odes,* or serious poems, which it sang throughout the play.

CHRONOLOGICAL ORDER. When telling a story in **chronological order,** the writer unfolds events in the order in which they occurred.

CLIMAX. The **climax** is the high point of interest and suspense in a literary work. The term also is sometimes used to describe the turning point of the action in a story or play, the point at which the rising action ends and the falling action begins. The climax in Ernest Hemingway's "A Day's Wait" (Unit 1) occurs when the narrator comes home to find Schatz causing a commotion. He refuses to let anyone into his room and asks his father how long he has to live. *See* Plot.

COMEDY. A **comedy** is any lighthearted or humorous literary work with a happy ending, especially one prepared for the stage or the screen. Comedy is often contrasted with tragedy, in which the hero meets an unhappy fate. Comedies typically show characters with human limitations, faults, and misunderstandings. The action in a comedy usually progresses from initial order to a humorous misunderstanding or confusion and back to order again. Standard elements of comedy include mistaken identities, word play, satire, and exaggerated characters and events. "A Defenseless Creature" by Neil Simon (Unit 7) is a comedy. *See* Tragedy.

CONFLICT. A **conflict** is a struggle between two forces in a literary work. A plot introduces a conflict, develops it, and eventually resolves it. There are two types of conflict: external and internal. In an *external conflict,* the main character struggles against another character, against the forces of nature, against society or social norms, or against fate. In an *internal conflict,*

the main character struggles against some element within himself or herself. In Ray Bradbury's "The Foghorn" (Unit 1), the conflict is external, between the main characters and a force of nature, a strange sea creature attracted by the sound of the foghorn. *See* Plot.

CONNOTATION. The **connotation** of a word is the set of ideas or emotional associations it suggests, in addition to its actual meaning. For example, the word *inexpensive* has a positive connotation, whereas the word *cheap* has a negative connotation, even though both words refer to "low cost." *See* Denotation.

CONSONANCE. **Consonance** is a kind of rhyme in which the consonant sounds of two words match, but the preceding vowel sounds do not, as in the words *wind* and *sound.* In Diana Rivera's poem "Under the Apple Tree" (Unit 5) the author repeats the "ks" sound in the words "trunks," "necks," "strokes," and "specks."

CONTEXT. The conditions under which a literary work occurs make up its **context.** Context is closely related to setting, but focuses more on the environment of the time and place. Two common types of context include historical and cultural.

COUPLET. A **couplet** is two lines of verse that rhyme. These lines from Robert Frost's "Once by the Pacific" (Unit 6) provide an example:

> There would be more than ocean-water broken
> Before God's last *Put out the Light* was spoken.

A *closed couplet* is a pair of rhyming lines that present a complete statement. A pair of rhyming iambic pentameter lines is also known as a *heroic couplet.*

DENOTATION. The **denotation** of a word is its dictionary meaning without any emotional associations. For example, the words *dirt* and *soil* share a common denotation. However, dirt has a negative connotation of uncleanliness, whereas soil does not. *See* Connotation.

DÉNOUEMENT. *See* Plot.

DESCRIPTION. A **description** is a picture in words. *Descriptive writing* is used to portray a character, an object, or a scene. Descriptions include *sensory details* — words and phrases that describe how things look, sound, smell, taste, or feel. In her poem "How to Eat a Poem" (Unit 5), Eve Merriam appeals to the sense of touch when she compares reading a poem to eating something juicy:

> Pick it up with your fingers and
>   lick the juice
> that may run down your chin.

DIALECT. A **dialect** is a version of a language spoken by the people of a particular place, time, or social group. A *regional dialect* is one spoken in a particular place. A *social dialect* is one spoken by members of a particular social group or class. The following is an example of dialect from Toni Cade Bambara's story "The War of the Wall" (Unit 1):

> "Watcha got there, sweetheart?" he asked the
>   twin with the plate.
> "Suppah," she said all soft and countrylike.

DIALOGUE. **Dialogue** is conversation between two or more people or characters. Plays are made up of dialogue and stage directions. Fictional works are made up of dialogue, narration, and description. When dialogue is included in fiction or nonfiction, the speaker's words are enclosed in quotation marks.

DICTION. **Diction,** when applied to writing, refers to the author's choice of words. Much of a writer's style is determined by his or her diction, the types of words that he or she chooses. *See* Style.

DRAMA. A **drama** is a story told through characters played by actors. Dramas are divided into segments called *acts.* The script of a drama is made up of dialogue spoken by the characters and stage directions. Because it is meant to be performed before an audience, drama features elements such as lighting, costumes, makeup, properties, set pieces, music, sound effects, and the movements and expressions of actors. Two major types of drama are comedy and tragedy. *See* Comedy, Dialogue, Stage Directions, *and* Tragedy.

DRAMATIC IRONY. *See* Irony.

DRAMATIC MONOLOGUE. A **dramatic monologue** is a poem written in the form of a speech of a single character to an imaginary audience.

DRAMATIC POEM. A **dramatic poem** relies heavily on literary devices such as *monologue* (speech by a single character) or *dialogue* (conversation involving two or more characters). Often dramatic poems tell stories. Types of dramatic poetry include the dramatic monologue and the soliloquy. *See* Dramatic Monologue *and* Soliloquy.

EPIC. An **epic** is a long story, often told in verse, involving heroes and gods. Grand in length and scope, an epic provides a portrait of an entire culture, of the legends, beliefs, values, laws, arts, and ways of life of a people. *The Odyssey* and *Beowulf* are examples of epics.

EPIPHANY. An **epiphany** is a moment of sudden insight in which the nature of a person, thing, or situation is revealed.

ESSAY. An **essay** is a short nonfiction work that presents a single main idea, or *thesis,* about a particular topic.

- An *expository,* or *informative, essay* explores a topic with the goal of informing or enlightening the reader.
- A *persuasive essay* aims to persuade the reader to accept a certain point of view. Louis L'Amour's "The Eternal Frontier" (Unit 3) is an example of a persuasive essay.
- A *personal essay* explores a topic related to the life or interests of the writer. Personal essays are characterized by an intimate and informal style or tone. "Fish Cheeks" (Unit 3) is a personal essay by Amy Tan.

EXPOSITION. In a plot, the **exposition** provides background information, often about the characters, setting, or conflict. Exposition is also another word for *expository writing,* the type of writing that aims to inform or explain. *See* Plot.

EXTENDED METAPHOR. An **extended metaphor** is a point-by-point presentation of one thing as though it were another. The description is meant as an implied comparison, inviting the reader to associate the thing being described with something that is quite different from it.

FABLE. **Fables** are brief stories, often with animal characters, told to express morals. Famous fables include those of Aesop retold by James Reeves and Joseph Jacobs in Unit 8.

FALLING ACTION. *See* Plot.

FANTASY. A fantasy is a literary work that contains highly unrealistic elements. Included as fantasy are stories that resemble fairy tales, involve the supernatural, or have imaginary characters and settings. Joan Aiken's "The Serial Garden" (Unit 1) contains elements of fantasy. *See* Magical Realism *and* Science Fiction.

FAIRY TALES. Fairy tales are stories that deal with mischievous spirits and other supernatural occurrences, often in medieval settings.

FICTION. Fiction is any work of prose that tells an invented or imaginary story. The primary forms of fiction are the novel and the short story. *See* Novel *and* Short Story.

FIGURATIVE LANGUAGE. Figurative language is writing or speech meant to be understood imaginatively instead of literally. Many writers, especially poets, use figurative language to help readers to see things in new ways. Types of figurative language, or **figures of speech,** include *hyperbole, metaphor, personification, simile,* and *understatement.*

FIGURES OF SPEECH. *See* Figurative Language.

FLASHBACK. A **flashback** interrupts the chronological sequence of a literary work and presents an event that occurred earlier. Writers use flashbacks most often to provide background information about characters or situations. In the short story "The Inn of Lost Time" by Lensey Namioka (Unit 1), Zenta remembers the time when he and the wealthy merchant Tokubei stopped their journey at an inn where the innkeeper tried to swindle the merchant. This flashback helps explain Zenta's wariness toward his current hosts.

FOLK LITERATURE. Folk literature, or *folklore,* refers to a body of cultural knowledge and beliefs passed from one generation to the next, both orally and in writing. Much of folk literature originated as part of the *oral tradition,* or the passing of a work, an idea, or a custom by word of mouth from generation to generation.

FOLK TALE. A **folk tale** is a brief story passed by word of mouth from generation to generation. Types of folk tales include fairy tales, tall tales, parables, and fables. Zora Neale Hurston's retelling of the African-American folk tale "How the Snake Got Poison" (Unit 8) is an example of a folk tale that offers an explaination for a feature in the natural world.

FOOT. *See* Meter.

FORESHADOWING. Foreshadowing is the act of presenting hints to events that will occur later in a story. In Joseph Bruchac's "Jed's Grandfather" (Unit 2), the main character's dreams suggest coming difficulties.

FREE VERSE. Free verse is poetry that does not use regular rhyme, meter, or stanza division. Free verse may contain irregular line breaks and sentence fragments and tends to mimic the rhythm of ordinary speech. Most contemporary poetry is written in free verse. "Unfolding Bud" by Naoshi Koriyama (Unit 5) is an example of poem written in free verse.

GENRE. A **genre** (zhän′ rə) is a type or category of literary composition. Major genres of literature include fiction, nonfiction, poetry, and drama. *See* Drama, Fiction, Poetry, *and* Prose.

HAIKU. A **haiku** is a traditional Japanese three-line poem containing five syllables in the first line, seven in the second, and five again in the third. The syllable pattern is often lost when a haiku is translated into English. A haiku presents a single vivid image, often of nature or the seasons, intended to evoke in the reader a specific emotional or spiritual response.

HERO. A **hero** is a character whose actions are inspiring and courageous. In early literature, a hero was often part divine and had remarkable abilities, such as magical power, superhuman strength, or great courage. Phaëthon in Olivia Coolidge's "Phaëthon, Son of Apollo" (Unit 8) is one such hero. In contemporary literature, the term *hero* often refers to any main character. The mongoose Rikki-Tikki-Tavi is the hero of Rudyard Kipling's story "Rikki-Tikki-Tavi" (Unit 1).

HYPERBOLE. A **hyperbole** (hī pür′ bə lē′) is an overstatement, or exaggeration, used for dramatic effect.

IAMB. *See* Meter.

IAMBIC PENTAMETER. *See* Meter.

IDIOM. An **idiom** is an expression that cannot be understood from the meanings of its separate words but must be learned as whole.

IMAGE. An **image** is a picture formed in the mind of a reader.

IMAGERY. Imagery is language that creates pictures by appealing to the senses of sight, sound, touch, taste, and smell. *See* Description *and* Figurative Language.

INFORMATIONAL TEXT. An **informational text** is a form of nonfiction that aims to convey or explain information. Examples of informational texts include reference materials, articles, editorials, and how-to writing.

IRONY. Irony is the difference between appearance and reality—in other words, what seems to be and what really is. Types of irony include the following:

dramatic irony, in which something is known by the reader or audience but unknown to the characters; *verbal irony,* in which a character says one thing but means another; and *irony of situation,* in which an event occurs that violates the expectations of the characters, the reader, or the audience. In Elizabeth Bishop's "The Filling Station" (Unit 6), the station and its workers are dirty and greasy, but we learn by the poet's descriptions of details of extraneous items of decoration that the station is quite cared for and loved.

LEGEND. A **legend** is a story that is passed down through generations and is often based on real events or characters from the past. Unlike myths, legends are usually considered to be historical; however, they may contain elements that are fantastic or unverifiable.

LYRIC POEM. A **lyric poem** is a highly musical type of poetry that expresses the emotions of a speaker. Lyric poems are often contrasted with narrative poems, which have storytelling as their main purpose. "Gold" by Pat Mora (Unit 5) is a lyric poem. *See* Poetry.

MEMOIR. A **memoir** is a type of autobiography that focuses on one incident or period in a person's life. Annie Dillard's *An American Childhood* (Unit 3) is a memoir about her childhood. *See* Autobiography.

METAPHOR. A **metaphor** is a comparison in which one thing is spoken or written about as if it were another. This figure of speech invites the reader to make a comparison between the writer's actual subject, the *tenor* of the metaphor, and another thing to which the subject is likened, the *vehicle* of the metaphor. In "Feel Like a Bird" (Unit 5), May Swenson uses the following metaphors to describe a bird by comparing it to a person:

> lands on star-toes
> finger-beak in
> feather-pocket
> finds no Coin

See Extended Metaphor *and* Figurative Language.

METER. **Meter** is a regular rhythmic pattern in poetry. This pattern is determined by the number of beats, or stresses, in each line. Stressed and unstressed syllables are divided into rhythmical units called *feet.* Feet commonly used in poetry are as follows:

Type of Foot	Stress Pattern	Example
iamb (iambic)	an unstressed syllable followed by a stressed syllable	in**sist**
trochee (trochaic)	a stressed syllable followed by an unstressed syllable	**free**dom
anapest (anapestic)	two unstressed syllables followed by one stressed syllable	unim-**pressed**
dactyl (dactylic)	one stressed syllable followed by two unstressed syllables	**fe**verish
spondee (spondaic)	two stressed syllables	**baseball**

Terms used to describe the number of feet in a line include the following:

> *monometer* for a one-foot line
> *dimeter* for a two-foot line
> *trimeter* for a three-foot line
> *tetrameter* for a four-foot line
> *pentameter* for a five-foot line
> *hexameter,* or Alexandrine, for a six-foot line
> *heptameter* for a seven-foot line
> *octameter* for an eight-foot line

A complete description of the meter of a line includes both the term for the type of foot used most often in the line and the term for the number of feet in the line. The most common meters are iambic tetrameter and iambic pentameter. The following are examples of each:

iambic tetrameter

⏑ / | ⏑ / | ⏑ / | ⏑ /
O slow | ly, slow | ly rose | she up

iambic pentameter

⏑ / | ⏑ / | ⏑ / | ⏑ / | ⏑ /
The cur | few tolls | the knell | of part | ing day

MOOD. **Mood,** or atmosphere, is the emotion created in the reader by part or all of a literary work. The writer can evoke in the reader an emotional response—such as fear, discomfort, longing, or anticipation—by working carefully with descriptive language and sensory details. "The Foghorn" by Ray Bradbury (Unit 1) has a lonely, mysterious mood.

944 LITERARY TERMS HANDBOOK

MORAL. A **moral** is a lesson that relates to the principles of right and wrong and is intended to be drawn from a story or other work of literature.

MOTIF. A **motif** is any element that appears in one or more works of literature or art. Examples of common folk tale motifs found in oral traditions throughout the world include granting of three wishes, the trial or quest, and the magical metamorphosis, or transformation of one thing into another. "Cinderella," "The Ugly Duckling," and the Arthurian "Sword in the Stone" are examples of the transformation motif, in which persons or creatures of humble station are revealed to be exceptional. Much can be revealed about a literary work by studying the motifs within it.

MOTIVATION. A **motivation** is a force that moves a character to think, feel, or behave in a certain way. Lester Simons, in "The 11:59" by Patricia McKissack (Unit 1), is motivated by fear of death to try to escape the 11:59.

MYTH. A **myth** is a traditional story, rooted in a particular culture, that deals with gods, goddesses, and other supernatural beings, as well as human heroes. Myths often embody religious beliefs and values and explain natural phenomena. Every early culture around the globe has produced its own myths. Ingri and Edgar Parin d'Aulaire's "Persephone and Demeter" (Unit 8) is a Greek origin myth.

NARRATION. **Narration** is a type of writing that tells a story, or describes events.

NARRATIVE POEM. A **narrative poem** is one that tells a story. Edgar Allan Poe's "Annabel Lee" (Unit 6) is an example of a narrative poem. *See* Poetry.

NARRATOR. A **narrator** is a character or speaker who tells a story. The writer's choice of narrator is important to the story and determines how much and what kind of information readers will be given about events and other characters. The narrator in a work of fiction may be a major or minor character or simply someone who witnessed or heard about the events being related. A *reliable narrator* gives a trustworthy account of events. An *unreliable narrator* cannot be trusted because he or she comments on and offers opinions about events. *See* Point of View *and* Speaker.

NONFICTION. **Nonfiction** writing explores real people's lives, places, things, events, and ideas. Essays, autobiographies, biographies, and news articles are all types of nonfiction. *See* Prose.

NOVEL. A **novel** is a long work of fiction. Often novels have involved plots, many characters, and numerous settings.

ODE. An **ode** is a poem to honor or praise someone or something.

ONOMATOPOEIA. **Onomatopoeia** is the use of words or phrases that sound like the things to which they refer. Examples of onomatopoeia include words such as buzz, click, and pop. In "The Highwayman" by Alfred Noyes (Unit 6), *tlot-tlot, tlot-tlot* is an example of onomatopoeia.

ORAL TRADITION. The **oral tradition** is the passing of a work, an idea, or a custom by word of mouth from generation to generation. Common works found in the oral traditions of peoples around the world include folk tales, fables, fairy tales, tall tales, nursery rhymes, proverbs, legends, myths, parables, riddles, charms, spells, and ballads. *See* Folk Tale, Legend, Myth, *and* Parable.

PARALLELISM. **Parallelism** is a rhetorical device in which a writer emphasizes the equal value or weight of two or more ideas by expressing them in the same grammatical form. *See* Rhetorical Device.

PERSONIFICATION. **Personification** is a figure of speech in which an animal, a thing, a force of nature, or an idea is described as if it were human or is given human characteristics. For example, in the poem "Under the Apple Tree" (Unit 5) Diana Rivera uses personification to describe apple blossoms:

> here, under the apple tree,
> where a crowd of petals close their
>   eyes...."

PERSUASION. **Persuasion,** or *persuasive writing,* is intended to change or influence the way a reader thinks or feels about a particular issue or idea.

PLOT. A **plot** is the series of events related to a central conflict, or struggle. A plot typically introduces a conflict, develops it, and eventually resolves it. A plot often contains the following elements, although it may not include all of them and they may not appear in precisely this order:

- The **exposition,** or introduction, sets the tone or mood, introduces the characters and setting, and provides necessary background information.
- The **rising action** is where the conflict is developed and intensified.

- The **climax** is the high point of interest or suspense.
- The **falling action** consists of all the events that follow the climax.
- The **resolution,** or dénouement (dā' nü män´), is the point at which the central conflict is ended, or resolved.

POETRY. Poetry is a major type of literature. It features imaginative and musical language carefully chosen and arranged to communicate experiences, thoughts, or emotions. It differs from prose in that it compresses meaning into fewer words and often uses meter, rhyme, and imagery. Poetry is usually arranged in lines and stanzas as opposed to sentences and paragraphs, and it can be more free in the ordering of words and the use of punctuation. Types of poetry include narrative, dramatic, and lyric. *See* Dramatic Poem, Lyric Poem, Meter, Narrative Poem, *and* Rhyme.

POINT OF VIEW. Point of view is the vantage point, or perspective, from which the story is told—in other words, who is telling the story. In **first-person** point of view, the story is told by someone who participates in or witnesses the action; this person, called the narrator, uses words such as *I* and *we* in telling the story. **Second-person** point of view uses the word *you* and addresses the reader directly, positioning the reader in the story. In **third-person** point of view, the narrator usually stands outside the action and observes; the narrator uses words such as *he, she, it,* and *they*. There are two types of third-person point of view: limited and omniscient. In *limited point of view,* the thoughts of only the narrator or a single character are revealed. In *omniscient point of view,* the thoughts of all the characters are revealed. Piri Thomas's "Amigo Brothers" (Unit 2) is told from a third-person omniscient point of view. *See* Narrator.

PRIMARY SOURCE. *See* Source.

PROSE. Prose is the broad term used to describe all writing that is not drama or poetry, including fiction and nonfiction. Types of prose writing include novels, short stories, essays, and news stories. Most biographies, autobiographies, and letters are written in prose.

PROSE POEM. A **prose poem** is a passage of prose that makes such extensive use of poetic language that the line between prose and poetry becomes blurred.

PROTAGONIST. A **protagonist** has the central role in a literary work. In Tomás Rivera's "The Portrait" (Unit 1), Don Mateo is the protagonist. *See* Antagonist.

PROVERBS. Proverbs, or *adages,* are traditional sayings, such as "You can lead a horse to water, but you can't make it drink."

PURPOSE. A writer's **purpose** is his or her aim, or goal. People usually write with one or more of the following purposes: to inform or explain *(expository writing);* to portray a person, place, object, or event *(descriptive writing);* to convince people to accept a position and respond in some way *(persuasive writing);* and to express thoughts or ideas, or to tell a story *(narrative writing).*

QUATRAIN. A **quatrain** is a stanza of poetry containing four lines. *See* Stanza.

REFRAIN. A **refrain** is a line or group of lines repeated in a poem or song. Many ballads contain refrains.

REPETITION. Repetition is a writer's intentional reuse of a sound, word, phrase, or sentence. Writers often use repetition to emphasize ideas or, especially in poetry, to create a musical effect. *See* Rhetorical Device.

RESOLUTION. *See* Plot.

RHETORICAL DEVICE. A **rhetorical device** is a technique used by a speaker or writer to achieve a particular effect, especially to persuade or influence. Common rhetorical devices include parallelism, repetition, and rhetorical questions. *See* Parallelism, Repetition, *and* Rhetorical Question.

RHETORICAL QUESTION. A **rhetorical question** is a question asked for effect but not meant to be answered. In the essay "Ships in the Desert" (Unit 4), Al Gore asks the rhetorical question: "What does it mean . . . that children playing in the morning surf must now dodge not only the occasional jellyfish but the occasional hypodermic needle washing in with the waves?"

RHYME. Rhyme is the repetition of sounds in words. Types of rhyme include the following:

- *end rhyme* (the use of rhyming words at the ends of lines)
- *internal rhyme* (the use of rhyming words within lines)
- *exact rhyme* (in which the rhyming words end with the same sound or sounds, as in *moon* and *June*)
- *slant rhyme* (in which the rhyming sounds are similar but not identical, as in *rave* and *rove*)

- *sight rhyme* (in which the words are spelled similarly but pronounced differently, as in *lost* and *ghost* or *give* and *thrive*)

RHYME SCHEME. A **rhyme scheme** is the pattern of end rhymes designated by assigning a different letter of the alphabet to each rhyme. In the following verse from "The Village Blacksmith" by Henry Wadsworth Longfellow (Unit 5), the rhyme scheme is *abcb*.

> His hair is crisp, and black, and long,
> His face is like the tan;
> His brow is wet with honest sweat,
> He earns whate'er he can,

RHYTHM. **Rhythm** is the pattern of beats, or stresses, in a line poetry. Rhythm can be regular or irregular. A regular rhythmic pattern in a poem is called a *meter*. *See* Meter.

RISING ACTION. *See* Plot.

ROMANCE. **Romance** is a term used to refer to the following four types of literature:
- medieval stories about the adventures and loves of knights
- novels and other fiction involving exotic locations and extraordinary or mysterious events and characters
- nonrealistic fiction in general
- in popular, modern usage, love stories of all kinds

SATIRE. **Satire** is humorous writing or speech intended to point out errors, falsehoods, foibles, or failings. It is written for the purpose of reforming human behavior or human institutions.

SCENE. A **scene** is a short section of a play that usually marks changes of time and place.

SCIENCE FICTION. **Science fiction** is highly imaginative fiction containing fantastic elements based on scientific principles, discoveries, or laws. Rod Serling's drama "The Monsters Are Due on Maple Street" (Unit 7) is an example of science fiction.

SENSORY DETAILS. *See* Description.

SETTING. The **setting** of a literary work is the time and place in which it occurs, together with all the details used to create a sense of a particular time and place. Writers create setting by various means. In drama, the setting is often revealed by the stage set and the costumes, though it may be revealed through what the characters say about their environs. In fiction, setting is most often revealed by means of description of such elements as landscape, scenery, buildings, furniture, clothing, the weather, and the season. It can also be revealed by how characters talk and behave. The setting of Lensey Namioka's "The Inn of Lost Time" (Unit 1) includes both the geographic location of Japan and the eighteenth century—the time period in which the story takes place.

SHORT STORY. A **short story** is a brief work of fiction. Short stories are typically crafted carefully to develop a plot, a conflict, characters, a setting, a mood, and a theme, all within relatively few pages. *See* Fiction *and* Genre.

SIMILE. A **simile** is a comparison of two seemingly unlike things using the word "like" or "as." Alfred Noyes uses this figure of speech in "The Highwayman" (Unit 6):

> His eyes were hollows of madness, his hair like mouldy hay,

SONNET. A **sonnet** is a fourteen-line poem, usually in iambic pentameter, that follows one of a number of different rhyme schemes. The *English, Elizabethan,* or *Shakespearean* sonnet is divided into four parts: three quatrains and a final couplet. The rhyme scheme of such a sonnet is *abab cdcd efef gg.* The *Italian* or *Petrarchan* sonnet is divided into two parts: an octave and a sestet. The rhyme scheme of the octave is *abbaabba.* The rhyme scheme of the sestet can be *cdecde, cdcdcd,* or *cdedce.* Robert Frosts's "Once by the Pacific" (Unit 6) is a sonnet. *See* Stanza *and* Rhyme Scheme.

SOURCE. A **source** is evidence of an event, an idea, or a development. A *primary source* is direct evidence, or proof that comes straight from those involved. Primary sources include official documents as well as firsthand accounts, such as diaries, letters, photographs, and paintings done by witnesses or participants.

SPEAKER. The **speaker** is the character who speaks in, or narrates, a poem—the voice assumed by the writer. The speaker and the writer of a poem are not necessarily the same person. The speaker in Edna St. Vincent Millay's poem "The Courage That My Mother Had" (Unit 2) wishes she had inherited her mother's courage. *See* Narrator.

SPEECH. A **speech** is a public address that was original delivered orally. "Queen Elizabeth's Speech to Her Last Parliament" (Unit 3) is an example of a speech.

SPIRITUALS. Spirituals are religious songs from the African-American folk tradition.

STAGE DIRECTIONS. Stage directions are notes included in a play, in addition to the dialogue, for the purpose of describing how something should be performed on stage. Stage directions describe setting, lighting, music, sound effects, entrances and exits, properties, and the movements of characters. They are usually printed in italics and enclosed in brackets or parentheses.

STANZA. A **stanza** is a group of lines in a poem. The following are some types of stanza:

two-line stanza	couplet
three-line stanza	triplet or tercet
four-line stanza	quatrain
five-line stanza	quintain or quintet
six-line stanza	sestet
seven-line stanza	septet
eight-line stanza	octave

STEREOTYPE. A **stereotype** is an overgeneralization about a group of people based on a lack of knowledge and experience.

STYLE. Style is the manner in which something is said or written. A writer's style is characterized by such elements as word choice (or *diction*), sentence structure and length, and other recurring features that distinguish his or her work from that of another. One way to think of a writer's style is as his or her written personality.

SUSPENSE. Suspense is a feeling of expectation, anxiousness, or curiosity created by questions raised in the mind of a reader or viewer.

SYMBOL. A **symbol** is anything that stands for or represents both itself and something else. Writers use two types of symbols—conventional, and personal or idiosyncratic. A *conventional symbol* is one with traditional, widely recognized associations. Such symbols include doves for peace; the color green for jealousy; winter, evening, or night for old age; wind for change or inspiration. A *personal* or *idiosyncratic symbol* is one that assumes its secondary meaning because of the special use to which it is put by a writer. In Sandra Cisneros's "Four Skinny Trees" (Unit 2), the trees are symbols of the narrator's experience growing up in the city.

TALL TALE. A **tall tale** is a story, often lighthearted or humorous, that contains highly exaggerated, unrealistic elements. Stories about Paul Bunyan are tall tales.

TANKA. A **tanka** is a traditional Japanese poem consisting of five lines, with five syllables in the first and third lines and seven syllables in the other lines (5-7-5-7-7). The syllable pattern is often lost when a tanka is translated into English. Tanka uses imagery to evoke emotions in the reader, but its images are often more philosophical and less immediate than those in a haiku. See Haiku.

THEME. A **theme** is a central message or perception about life that is revealed through a literary work. Themes may be stated or implied. A *stated theme* is presented directly, whereas an *implied theme* must be inferred. Most works of fiction do not have a stated theme but rather several implied themes. A *universal theme* is a message about life that can be understood by people of most cultures. A stated theme of Marta Salinas's "The Scholarship Jacket" (Unit 2) is that earning something is different from buying something. An implied theme is that it is important to stand up for what you believe.

THESIS. A **thesis** is a main idea that is supported in a work of nonfiction. The thesis of "The Eternal Frontier" by Louis L'Amour (Unit 3) is that it is humankind's destiny to explore outer space.

TONE. Tone is the emotional attitude toward the reader or toward the subject implied by a literary work. Examples of the different tones that a work may have include familiar, ironic, playful, sarcastic, serious, and sincere. In the short story "The War of the Wall" (Unit 1), Toni Cade Bambara employs a combative tone.

TRAGEDY. A **tragedy** is a work of literature, particularly a drama, that tells the story of the fall of a person of high status. It celebrates the courage and dignity of a tragic hero in the face of inevitable doom. Sometimes that doom is made inevitable by a tragic flaw. Today, the term *tragedy* is used more loosely to mean any work that has an unhappy ending. *See* Comedy, Tragic Hero, *and* Tragic Flaw.

TRAGIC FLAW. A **tragic flaw** is a weakness of personality that causes the tragic hero to make unfortunate choices.

TRAGIC HERO. A **tragic hero** is the main character in a tragedy.

TRICKSTER. The **trickster,** who is either an animal or a shape-shifter, is more than an annoyance to the mythical gods: He or she is often responsible for bringing important gifts to humanity, such as fire. Judith Gleason's "Eshu" (Unit 8), a Yoruban folk tale, is an example of a trickster tale.

VOICE. **Voice** is the way a writer uses language to reflect his or her unique personality and attitude toward topic, form, and audience. A writer expresses voice through tone, word choice, or diction, and sentence structure. *See* Diction *and* Tone.

Glossary of Vocabulary Words

Pronunciation Key

Vowel Sounds

a	hat	i	sit	ü	blue, stew	ə	extra
ā	play	ī	my	oi	boy		under
ä	star	ō	go	ou	wow		civil
e	then	ô	paw, born	u	up		honor
ē	me	ù	book, put	ʉ	burn		bogus

Consonant Sounds

b	but	j	jump	p	pop	th	the
ch	watch	k	brick	r	rod	v	valley
d	do	l	lip	s	see	w	work
f	fudge	m	money	sh	she	y	yell
g	go	n	on	t	sit	z	pleasure
h	hot	ŋ	song, sink	th	with		

A

ab·sent·mind·ed·ly (ab' sənt mīn´ dəd lē) *adv.*, lost in thought; unaware

a·bund·ance (ə bʉn´ dən[t]s) *n.*, wealth; riches; surplus of money and possessions

a·byss (ə bis´) *n.*, bottomless pit; something too deep to measure

am·ber (am´ bər) *adj.*, yellowish red; *n.*, hardened sap

am·bi·tion (am bi´ shən) *n.*, drive to succeed

a·nal·y·sis (ə na´ lə səs) *n.*, act of separating something into its parts to examine them

an·ti·dote (an´ ti dōt') *n.*, remedy

ap·pall·ing (ə pôl´ iŋ) *adj.*, inspiring disgust

ap·pre·hen·sive·ly (a' pri hen[t]´ siv lē) *adv.*, in a way that shows fear or caution

ar·dent (är´ dənt) *adj.*, warmth of feeling characterized by eager support

ar·is·toc·ra·cy (a' rə stä´ krə sē) *n.*, noble or privileged class; government by people who belong to the noble class

as·cend (ə send´) *v.*, move upward; rise

a·skew (ə skyü´) *adj.*, out of line; crooked

as·ton·ish·ing (ə stä´ ni shiŋ) *adj.*, amazing; very surprising

as·tute (ə stüt´) *adj.*, possessing practical intelligence and the ability to make good decisions

a·veng·ing (ə venj´ iŋ) *adj.*, taking revenge or punishing someone for something

B

bar·rage (bə räzh´) *n.*, outpouring of many things at once

bar·ren (ber´ ən) *adj.*, unable to reproduce or bear fruit; desolate

bear (ber) *v.*, carry; bore (past tense)

bel·lows (be´ lōz') *n.*, device that expands and contracts to draw in and force out air, used to increase the intensity of a fire

ben·e·dic·tion (be' nə dik´ shən) *n.*, blessing

be·nign (bi nīn´) *adj.*, posing no threat

bleak (blēk) *adj.*, windy; cold; raw

blun·der (blʉn´ dər) *v.*, make a serious error in judgment; make a thoughtless mistake

brace (brās) *n.*, grove that provides shelter from wind

bran·dish (bran´ dish) *v.*, wave threateningly

brawn·y (brô´ nē) *adj.*, muscular, strongly built

brood (brüd) *v.*, dwell on a gloomy subject; worry

by·gone (bī´ gôn') *adj.*, long ago; in the distant past

C

cache (kash) *n.*, stored supply, often hidden

cha·ot·ic (kā ät´ ik) *adj.*, in a state of disorder or confusion

chide (chīd) *v.*, express mild disapproval

cleft (kleft) *n.*, space made when something breaks open

co·los·sal (kə lä´ səl) *adj.*, of a very large degree or amount

co·in·ci·dence (kō in[t]´ sə den[t]s) *n.*, chance occurrence

com·mence·ment (kəm men[t]s´ mənt) *adj.*, graduation

com·pen·sate (käm´ pən sāt') *v.*, balance, offset, repay

com·po·sure (kəm pō´ zhər) *n.*, calmness of mind or appearance

com·pul·sion (kəm pəl´ shən) *n.*, irresistible impulse to perform an act

com·pul·so·ry (kəm pʉl´ sə rē) *adj.*, required by a law or rule

con·clu·sive·ly (kən klü´ siv lē) *adv.*, in a way that ends debate or discussion

con·geal (kən jēl´) *v.*, change from liquid to solid due to cold temperature

con·jec·ture (kən jek´ chər) *v.*, predict; guess

con·sol·i·dat·ed (kən sä´ lə dā təd) *adj.*, joined together; compacted

con·vic·tion (kən vik´ shən) *n.*, belief; self-confidence; boldness

cos·mic (käz´ mik) *adj.*, relating to the universe as a whole

cour·te·ous (kʉr´ tē əs) *adj.*, polite; well mannered

cow·er (kaʉ´ [ə]r) *v.*, shrink and tremble as from anger, threats, or blows

cred·i·bil·i·ty (kre' də bi´ lə tē) *n.*, believability; ability to inspire belief

crev·ice (kre´ vəs) *n.*, narrow opening resulting from a split or crack

cro·chet (krō´shā´) *n.*, needlework made by interlocking loops of thread using a hooked needle

cul·ti·va·ted (kʉl´ tə vāt' əd) *adj.*, prepared for growing plants

cun·ning (kʉ´ niŋ) *adj.*, clever or tricky

D

de·duce (di düs´) *v.*, infer

def·er·ence (de´ fə rən[t]s) *n.*, respectful yielding

de·i·ty (dē´ə tē) *n.*, god or goddess

de·jec·ted·ly (di jek´ təd lē) *adv.*, sadly; showing lack of confidence

del·i·cate·ly (del´ i kət lē) *adv.*, carefully; cautiously

de·lin·e·ate (di li´ nē āt') *v.*, describe

des·e·crate (des´ i krāt') *v.*, treat with disrespect

des·o·late (de´ sə lət) *adj.*, lonely, sad

des·ti·tute (des´ tə tüt') *adj.*, without money or other basic necessities for survival; extremely poor

dev·a·stat·ing (de´ və stā' tiŋ) *adj.*, overwhelming

dif·fuse (di fyüs´) *adj.*, spread out loosely and widely

din (din) *n.*, loud noise

dire (dī´ [ə]r) *adj.*, desperate; horrifying

di·rec·tive (də rek´ tiv) *n.*, order or form of guidance

dis·il·lu·sioned (dis' ə lü´ zhənd) *adj.*, disappointed; dissatisfied

dis·may (dis mā´) *n.*, sudden loss of courage; shock

dis·pel (di spel´) *v.*, break up; make vanish

dis·solve (di zälv´) *v.*, melt; reduce to liquid form

dis·suade (di swād´) *v.*, deter a person from a course of action by persuasion

do·main (dō mān´) *n.*, land that a person owns; rightful territory

dom·i·nant (dä´ mə nənt) *adj.*, having the most control or influence

driv·el (dri´ vəl) *v.*, drool

drought (draʉt) *n.*, period of dry weather; lack of rain

dub (dʉb) *v.*, give a nickname

dusk (dʉsk) *n.*, darker stage of twilight

E

e·go·tism (ē´ gə' ti zəm) *n.*, large sense of self-importance; conceit

em·er·ald (em´ rəld) *adj.*, bright green

em·u·late (em´ yə lāt') *v.*, imitate

en·croach·ing (in krōch´ iŋ) *adj.*, trespassing; creeping slowly into a territory with the object of stealing it

ep·i·dem·ic (e' pə de´ mik) *n.*, outbreak of contagious disease that spreads rapidly

e·rode (i rōd´) *v.*, wear away, usually through natural forces such as weather

eth·ni·ci·ty (eth ni´ sə tē) *n.*, belonging to a racial, cultural, or national group

ex·alt·ed (ig zōlt´ ed) *adj.*, held in high regard

ex·as·per·at·ed (ig zas´ pə rāt' ed) *adj.*, irritated

ex·tra·ne·ous (ek strä´ nē əs) *adj.*, not essential; not a part of the main idea

F

fe·roc·i·ty (fə räs´ ət ē) *n.*, fierceness or intensity

flail (flāl) *v.*, swing

flour·ish (flʉr´ ish) *v.*, grow luxuriously

flush (flʉsh) *adj.*, having a red color to the skin

fond·ness (fän[d]´ nəs) *n.*, affection; having a liking

for·feit (for´ fət) *v.*, lose or fail to win the right to something by some error, offense, or crime

for·lorn (fər lôrn´) *adj.*, sad; lonely; hopeless

G

gid·dy (gi´ dē) *adj.*, feeling dizzy or unsteady

gnarled (när[ə]ld) *adj.*, misshapen

gran·di·ose (gran´ dē ōs') *adj.*, magnificent; grand

grum·ble (grʉm´ bəl) *v.*, mumble unhappily

H

ha·bit·u·al (hə´ bi ch [ə] wel) *adj.*, behaving in a certain manner by habit

hack (hak) *v.*, chop or cut forcefully

high-strung (hī´ strʌŋ´) *adj.*, nervous; extra sensitive

I

im·passe (im´ pas') *n.*, situation with no escape

im·plore (im plōr´) *v.*, beg

in·ca·pac·i·tat·ed (in' kə pa´ sə tāt' ed) *adj.*, unable to engage in normal activities; disabled

in·ces·sant·ly (in' se´ sənt lē) *adv.*, constantly

in·cor·po·rate (in kôr´ pə rāt') *v.*, combine into one body

in·ert (i nʉrt´) *adj.*, still; unmoving

in·ev·i·ta·ble (i ne´ və tə bəl) *n.*, unavoidable situation

in·flu·en·za (in' flu['] en´ zə) *n.*, viral disease characterized by fever, muscular aches, and respiratory distress

in·tent (in tent´) *n.*, purpose

in·ter·cede (in' tər sēd´) *v.*, come between to cause a change

in·tri·cate (in´ tri kət) *adj.*, elaborate

ir·i·des·cence (ir' ə de´ sən[t]s) *n.*, show of rainbow colors that seem to shimmer and change when viewed from different angles

K

kind·ling (kin´ [d] liŋ) *n.*, material used to start a fire, often dry sticks

L

la·bor·i·ous (lə bôr´ ē əs) *adj.*, produced by hard work

la·den (lād´ən) *adj.*, weighed down

lam·en·ta·tion (la' mən tā´ shən) *n.*, expression of sorrow or regret

lar·va (lär´ və) *n.*, early wingless form of a newly hatched insect; larvae (lär´ vī) *n. pl.*

lav·ish (la´ vish) *adj.*, abundant; rich

lib·er·a·tion (li' bə rā´ shən) *n.*, state of being free or of achieving civil rights

lithe·ly (līth´ lē) *adv.*, bending easily

lo·co·mo·tion (lō' kə mō´ shən) *n.*, power or act of moving from one place to another

lu·mi·nous (lü´ mə nəs) *adj.*, emitting or reflecting steady, glowing light

M

man·i·fes·ta·tion (ma' nə fə stā´ shən) *n.*, example; instance

ma·nip·u·late (mə nip´ yə lāt') *v.*, treat or operate with the hands in a skillful manner

mas·ter·piece (mas´ tər pēs') *n.*, artist's greatest work

mea·ger (mē´ gər) *adj.*, lacking in quantity or quality

mes·mer·ize (mez´ mə rīz') *v.*, fascinate, spellbind

mi·li·tia (mə li´ shə) *n.*, citizens' army

mis·sion·ar·y (mi´ shə ner' ē) *n.*, person sent to other countries or remote areas to spread a religion and, sometimes, to care for people

mys·ti·cal (mis´ ti kəl) *adj.*, having a spiritual quality; mysterious

N

noi·some (nôi´ səm) *adj.*, offensive smell; objectionable

O

ob·sessed (əb sest´) *adj.*, preoccupied

o·di·ous (ō´ dē əs) *adj.*, hateful or disgusting

o·men (ō´ mən) *n.*, prophetic sign

om·i·nous (äm´ ə nəs) *adj.*, foreboding or foreshadowing evil

P

peak·ed (pē´ kid) *adj.*, thin and drawn, as from sickness

per·il (per´ əl) *n.*, danger; exposure to harm

per·pet·u·al (pər pe´ chə wəl) *adj.*, going on forever

pe·ti·tion (pə ti´ shən) *n.*, formal request

phe·nom·e·non (fi nä´ mə nän') *n.*, extremely unusual or extraordinary thing or occurrence

phys·i·o·log·i·cal·ly (fi' zē ə lä´ ji k[ə] lē) *adv.*, relating to bodily function

pluck (plʌk) *v.*, pull off or out

poi·gnant (poi´ nyənt) *adj.*, deeply affecting or touching; somber

pre·cip·i·tous (pri si´ pə təs) *adj.*, very steep

pred·a·tor (pred´ at ər) *n.*, animal that gets food by capturing and eating other animals

pre·lim·i·nar·y (pri li´ mə ner' ē) *adj.*, preparing for the main action or event

pre·rog·a·tive (pri räg´ ət iv) *n.*, special power or privilege

pres·tige (pre stēzh´) *n.*, status; standing in general opinion

pri·me·val (prī mē´ vəl) *adj.*, from the earliest ages

pros·per·i·ty (prä spər´ ə tē) *n.*, condition of being successful or thriving, especially economic well-being

prov·i·dence (präv´ əd əns) *n.*, valuable gift; godsend

pro·vi·sion (prə vi´ zhən) *n.*, arrangement made beforehand to deal with a certain need

prov·o·ca·tion (präv' ə kā´ shən) *n.*, something that calls forth an action or emotion

R

ra·di·ant (rā´ dē ənt) *adj.*, shining bright

rapt (rapt) *adj.,* mentally engrossed or absorbed

rav·en·ous (raʹ və nəs) *adj.,* very eager for food

re·buff (ri bəfʹ) *n.,* refusal to meet an advance or offer

re·cruit (ri krütʹ) *v.,* hire or engage the services

reel (rēl) *v.,* stumble as the result of a hard hit

re·frain (ri frānʹ) *n.,* phrase or verse in a song or poem that is repeated throughout

re·gret·ful·ly (ri gretʹ fə lē) *adv.,* with a sense of loss or sorrow

re·press (ri presʹ) *v,.* hold in by self-control

re·tal·i·ate (ri taʹ lē ātʹ) *v.,* respond to an action by doing a similar thing back, usually in a negative sense, such as repaying one injury by inflicting another

rev·e·la·tion (reʹ və lāʹ shən) *n.,* act of revealing or showing, usually something astonishing or enlightening

root (rüt) *v.,* dig in the ground

rum·pled (rʉmʹ pəld) *adj.,* wrinkled

S

sage (sāj) *n.,* wise man

sau·cy (sô sē) *adj.,* bold

scav·en·ger (scavʹ ən jər) *n.,* animal that gets food by eating the dead bodies of other animals

scep·ter (sepʹ tər) *n.,* tall staff or baton that a ruler carries as a symbol of authority

scowl (skau̇[ə]l) *v.,* lower the eyebrows, as if squinting or frowning

scrag·gly (skraʹ g[ə]lē) *adj.,* uneven or ragged in growth or form

seg·re·gate (segʹ ri gāt') *v.,* separate a race, class, or ethnic group from the rest of the population; set apart

shield (shēld) *v.,* protect, guard, or defend against

sin·ew·y (sinʹ yü' ē) *adj.,* powerful; strong, lean, and clearly displaying muscles and tendons

snipe (snīp) *v.,* shoot from a hidden position; direct an attack

sole (sōl) *adj.,* only

spec·i·fy (speʹ sə fī') *v.,* state explicitly

spec·ter (spekʹ tər)

splurge (splʉrj) *v.,* indulge oneself extravagantly or spend a lot of money

spry (sprī) *adj.,* energetic; lively

staunch·est (stônchʹ est) *adj.,* most loyal or committed

stu·pen·dous (stu̇ penʹ dəs) *adj.,* marvelous; awe-inspiring

sub·se·quent (sʉbʹ si kwənt) *adj.,* following in time, order, or place

sulk·i·ly (sʉlʹ kə lē) *adv.,* moodily silent

sup·ple (sʉʹ pəl) *adj.,* flexible

surge (sʉrj) *v.,* rise and move forward

swag·ger (swaʹ gər) *n.,* walk with an insolent air; strut

T

taunt (tänt) *v.,* mock; jeer at

taw·ny (täʹ nē) *adj.,* warm sandy color

te·di·um (tēʹ dē əm) *n.,* boredom

ter·mi·nate (tʉrʹ mə nāt') *v.,* end

tes·ti·fy (tesʹ tə fī') *v.,* make a statement based on personal knowledge or belief; give evidence

teth·er (teʹ t͟hər) *n.,* rope or chain that allows an animal to move in a limited area

trance (tran[t]s) *n.,* state of detachment from one's physical surroundings; stunned or dazed state

trans·for·ma·tion (tran[t]s fər māʹ shən) *n.,* change in composition, structure, or outward form and appearance

trans·lu·cen·cy (tran[t]s lüʹ sənt sē) *n.,* quality of being transparent or allowing some light to pass through

tread (tred) *v.,* walk on, along, or across; trod (past tense)

trough (trôf) *n.,* long, shallow container

trudge (trʉjʹ) *v.,* walk heavily; plod

U

un·bid·den (ʉn' biʹ dən) *adj.,* not asked or invited

un·com·mon·ly (ən' käʹ mən lē) *adv.,* amazingly

un·pre·ce·dent·ed (ʉn' preʹ sə den' təd) *adj.,* unheard of; new

V

ven·ture (ven[t]ʹ shər) *v.,* undertake the risks and dangers of an action

ver·i·fy (verʹ ə fī') *v.,* test or check for correctness

void (vôid) *n.,* emptiness

W

wane (wān) *v.,* approach an end

war·y (werʹ ē) *adj.,* cautious

wea·ri·ly (wirʹ ə lē) *adv.,* tiredly

with·drawn (wit͟h drônʹ) *adj.,* introverted; unresponsive

world·ly (wʉr[ə]ldʹ lē) *adj.,* of or related to this world

wor·ri·some (wʉrʹ ē səm) *adj.,* causing worry

writhe (rīt͟h) *v.,* twist and turn

wrought (rôt) *v.,* (archaic) past tense of *work;* created, shaped, or formed through hard work; formed by hammering, as on metal

Y

yawn·ing (yôʹ niŋ) *adj.,* wide open

Holy Cow! Press. "Jed's Grandfather" from *Turtle Meat and Other Stories* by Joseph Bruchac. Reprinted by permission of Holy Cow! Press.

Houghton Mifflin Company. "The Aqualung" from *The New Way Things Work* by David Macaulay. Compilation copyright © 1988, 1998 Dorling Kindersley Ltd., London. Text copyright © 1988, 1998 David Macaulay, Neil Ardley. Illustrations copyright © 1988, 1998 David Macaulay. Reprinted by permission of Houghton Mifflin Co. All rights reserved. "Blackberry Eating" from *Mortal Acts, Mortal Words* by Galway Kinnell, copyright © 1980 by Galway Kinnell. Reprinted by permission of Houghton Mifflin Company. All rights reserved. "Phaethon, Son of Apollo" from *Greek Myths* by Olivia E. Coolidge. Copyright © 1949 by Olivia E. Coolidge; copyright renewed © 1977 by Olivia E. Coolidge. Adapted by permission of Houghton Mifflin Company. All rights reserved. "Ships in the Desert" from *Earth in the Balance* by Al Gore. Copyright © 1992 by Senator Al Gore. Reprinted by permission of Houghton Mifflin Company. All rights reserved. "St. Crispian's Day Speech" from *Henry V* by William Shakespeare, edited by G. Blakemore Evans, The Riverside Shakespeare. Copyright © 1974 by Houghton Mifflin Co.

Jerry Izenberg. "Roberto Clemente: A Bittersweet Memoir" from *Great Latin Sport Figures* by Jerry Izenberg. Reprinted by permission of the author.

Coleman A. Jennings. Excerpt from "Braille: The Early Life of Louis Braille" from *Theater for Children*, edited by Coleman A. Jennings. Copyright © 2005 by Coleman A. Jennings. Reprinted by permission of Coleman A. Jennings.

Liveright Publishing Corporation. "the/ sky/ was," copyright © 1925, 1953, E.E. Cummings, copyright © 1991 by the Trustees for the E.E. Cummings Trust. Copyright © 1976 by George James Firmage, from *Complete Poems: 1904–1962* by E.E. Cummings, edited by George J. Firmage. Reprinted by permission of Liveright Publishing Corporation.

Carol Mann Agency. "The Size of Things" by Robert Jastrow, copyright © 1990 by Robert Jastrow, published by W. W. Norton. Reprinted with permission from Carol Mann Agency.

MBA Literary Agency. "The Smallest Dragonboy" by Anne McCaffrey from *A Gift of Dragons* is reprinted by kind permission of the author.

Milkweed Editions. "Achieving Perspective" from *Firekeeper: Selected Poems* by Pattiann Rogers, Minneapolis: Milkweed Editions, 2005. Copyright © 2005 by Pattiann Rogers. Reprinted with permission from Milkweed Editions.

William Morris Agency, LLC. "A Christmas Carol: Scrooge and Marley" by Israel Horowitz. Copyright © 1994 by Fountain Pen, LLC. All rights reserved. Reprinted by permission of William Morris Agency, LLC on behalf of the author. *Let me Hear You Whisper* by Paul Zindel. Copyright © 1974 by Paul Zindel. Used in electronic form by permission of William Morris Agency, LLC on behalf of the author.

Ashley Matin Moss. "Antaeus" by Borden Deal. Reprinted by permission of Ashley Matin Moss.

Museum of New Mexico Press. "The Force of Luck" by Rudolfo A. Anaya from *Cuentos*. Reprinted by permission of Museum of New Mexico Press.

The Nation. "Dust Changes America" by Margaret Bourke-White. From *The Nation*, May 22, 1935. Reprinted with permission of *The Nation*.

National Audubon Society. "Wild Turkey" from *The Bird Biographies of John James Audubon* selected and edited by Alice Ford. Copyright © 1957 by Alice Ford. Reprinted by permission of National Audubon Society.

The New York Times. "A Black Athlete Looks At Education" by Arthur Ashe from *The New York Times*, February 5, © 1977 The New York Times. All rights reserved. Used by permission and protected by the copyright laws of the United States. The printing, copying, redistribution, or retransmission of the material without express written permission is prohibited.

Naomi Shihab Nye. "The Lost Parrot" from *Hugging the Jukebox* by Naomi Shihab Nye. Reprinted by permission of the author.

Fifi Oscard Agency. Excerpt from *Off the Court* by Arthur Ashe. Reprinted by permission of Fifi Oscard Agency.

Penguin Books Ltd. From *The Narrow Road to the Deep North and Other Travel Sketches* by Matsuo Basho, translated with an introduction by Nobuyuki Yuasa (Penguin Classics, 1966). Copyright © Nobuyuki Yuasa, 1966. Reprinted by permission of Penguin Books Ltd.

Penguin Group (USA) Inc. "Death in the Open," from *The Lives of a Cell* by Lewis Thomas. Copyright © 1973 by The Massachusetts Medical Society. Used by permission of Viking Penguin, a division

LITERARY ACKNOWLEDGMENTS

Cover (top left) © The Gallery Collection/Corbis; (top right) Medioimages/Photodisc; (bottom left) Stock Xpert; (bottom right) © Brand X/SuperStock; **i** Medioimages/Photodisc; **iii** © The Gallery Collection/Corbis; (top right) Medioimages/Photodisc; (bottom left) Stock Xpert; (bottom right) © Brand X/SuperStock; **viii** (top and bottom) PhotoDisc; (middle) © SHAMIL ZHUMATOV/Reuters/Corbis; **ix** (top) © Raymond Gehman/CORBIS; (middle) Media Bakery; (bottom left) © age fotostock/SuperStock; (bottom right) PhotoDisc; **x** (top) © Getty Images; (middle) Jupiter Images; (bottom left) iStock photo; **xi** (top) © Austin J. Stevens/Animals Animals–Earth Scenes—All rights reserved; (middle) Jupiter Images; **xii** (top and bottom right) iStockphoto; (left) PhotoDisc; **xiii** (top) © Raymond Gehman/CORBIS; (middle) PhotoDisc; (bottom) Jupiter Images; **xiv** (top and middle) PhotoDisc; (bottom) Jupiter Images; **xv** (top) Royalty-Free/Corbis; (middle) PhotoDisc; (bottom) iStockphoto; **xvi** (middle) Jupiter Images; (bottom) © SHAMIL ZHUMATOV/Reuters/Corbis; **xvii** © CORBIS; **xviii** Shutterstock; **xix** (top) Shutterstock; (middle) PhotoDisc; (bottom) © age fotostock/SuperStock; **xx** Jupiter Images; **xxi** (top) Media Bakery; (bottom) PhotoDisc; **xxii** Macduff Everton/Getty Images; **xxiii** (top) Jupiter Unlimited; (middle) Media Bakery; (bottom) Shutterstock; **xxiv** Yoruba Eshu Elegba Figure, Abeokuta, Southwest Nigeria, mid 19th century (carved wood)/© Royal Albert Memorial Museum, Exeter, Devon, UK/The Bridgeman Art Library; **xxv** (top) Shutterstock; (middle) *The Rattle Snake* (w/c on paper), Bartram, William (1739–1823)/© The Right Hon. Earl of Derby/The Bridgeman Art Library; (bottom) © Bettmann/CORBIS.

Unit 1

2 (top) Jupiter Images; (bottom left) Courtesy of JFK Presidential Library and Museum; (bottom middle) © Bettmann/CORBIS; (bottom right) Courtesy of Lensey Namioka; **3** (top) © Ralph A. Clevenger/CORBIS; (bottom left) Courtesy of Library of Congress; (bottom middle) Courtesy of Leslie Marmon Silko; (bottom right) Courtesy of Library of Congress; **4** © Bettmann/CORBIS; **5** Courtesy of Library of Congress; **6** © 2007 PunchStock; **9** Courtesy of Library of Congress; **10** © Geoffrey Clements/CORBIS; **12** Jupiter Images; **13** © Getty Images; **17** (all) Jupiter Images; **18** Courtesy of JFK Presidential Library and Museum; **19** Jupiter Images; **21** Courtesy of Library of Congress; **26** Courtesy of Library of Congress; **27** The Granger Collection, New York; **29** Jupiter Images; **30** Courtesy of Lensey Namioka; **31** Jupiter Images; **33** © Christie's Images/CORBIS; **37** iStock photo; **39** © Condé Nast Archive/CORBIS; **40** © Asian Art & Archaeology, Inc./CORBIS; **49** Courtesy of Tomás Rivera; **50** Courtesy of the United States Marine Corps; **52** © Bettmann/CORBIS; **57** Courtesy of Library of Congress; **58** © Wolfgang Flamisch/zefa/Corbis; **59** Jupiter Images; **61** Courtesy of NASA; **63** © William J. Weber; **63–71** (border) © IBID photo; **64** © David Butow/CORBIS SABA; **67** Jupiter Images; **68** Photodisc; **69** © Flip Schulke/CORBIS; **73** © Bettmann/CORBIS; **74** © Ralph A. Clevenger/CORBIS; **78** *The Loch Ness Monster*, illustration, c. 1935 (litho), D'Achille, Gino (20th century)/Private Collection/The Bridgeman Art Library; **79** AP Images; **85** (all) Courtesy of Library of Congress; **86** *Rikki-Tikki-Tavi*, illustration from *The Jungle Book* by Rudyard Kipling (1865–1936) published in Paris, 1937 (colour litho), Collot, Andre (d. 1976)/Bibliotheque Nationale, Paris, France, Archives Charmet/The Bridgeman Art Library; **89** Jupiter Images; **93** *Rikki-Tikki-Tavi*, illustration from *The Jungle Book* by Rudyard Kipling (1865–1936) published in Paris, 1930 (colour litho), Soulas, Louis Joseph (1905–1954)/Bibliotheque Nationale, Paris, France, Archives Charmet/The Bridgeman Art Library; **98** © Austin J. Stevens/Animals Animals–Earth Scenes—All rights reserved; **101** © age footstock/SuperStock; **103** Copyright © AUSTIN J. STEVENS/Animals Animals–Earth Scenes—All rights reserved; **105** (top) © Jason Hosking/zefa/Corbis; (bottom) Courtesy of Leslie Marmon Silko; **108** © Kevin Fleming/CORBIS; **109** © C3066 Hinrich Baesemann/dpa/Corbis; **110** © Peter Turnley/CORBIS; **111** (top) Jupiter Images; (bottom) Courtesy of Joan Aiken; **113** Courtesy of Dover Flowers; **114** Jupiter Images; **116** Courtesy of Dover Flowers; **117** Jupiter Images; **118** Royalty-Free/Corbis; **122** Jupiter Images; **125** Jacket cover from *Tuck Everlasting* by Natalie Babbitt. Jacket design copyright © 1975 by Natalie Babbitt. Reprinted by permission of Farrar, Straus and Giroux, LLC; Jacket cover *Eragon* by Christopher Raolini. Copyright © 2003 by John Jude Palencar, from Eragon (Book Inheritance) by Christopher Paolini. Used by permission of Alfred A. Knopf, an imprint of Random House Children's Books, a division of Random House, Inc.; Cover from *Zazoo* by Richard Mosher (Boston:

Graphia, 2004.); **126** (left) Jupiter Images; (right) © Bettmann/CORBIS; **127** Jupiter Images; **132** Eileen Ryan Photography.

Unit 2

138 (top) © Ashley Cooper/Corbis; (bottom left) © Ulf Andersen/Getty Images; (bottom middle) Courtesy of Gary Soto; (bottom right) Courtesy of Cherylene Lee; **139** (top) Smithsonian American Art Museum, Washington, DC/Art Resource, NY; (bottom left) Time & Life Pictures/Getty Images; (bottom middle) Courtesy of Piri Thomas; (bottom right) © Time & Life Pictures/Getty Images; **140** (top) © Benelux/ zefa/Corbis; (bottom) © Patrick Bennett/CORBIS; **141** (top) © Getty Images/Marvin E. Newman; (bottom) Courtesy of Cherylene Lee; **142** © Getty Images/Marvin E. Newman; **145** © Cherylene Lee; **147** © SOQUI TED/CORBIS SYGMA; **148** © Louie Psihoyos/CORBIS; **150** © Vince Streano/CORBIS; **152** Shutterstock; **153** (left) iStockphoto; (right) © Blue Lantern Studio/CORBIS; **155** iStockphoto; **158** © Michael S. Lewis/CORBIS; **161** Royalty-Free/Corbis; **163** Courtesy of Piri Thomas; **164** *The Big Fight* (oil on canvas on wood), Crook, P. J. (b. 1945)/Private Collection/The Bridgeman Art Library; **166–167** Image Source; **169** PhotoDisc; **170** *Boxer Right* (acrylic on canvas), Tatham, Carol (Contemporary Artist)/Private Collection/The Bridgeman Art Library; **173** AP Images; **174** AP Images; **177** © Ulf Andersen/Getty Images; **178** Royalty-Free/Corbis; **179** iStockphoto; **181** Time & Life Pictures/Getty Images; **182** Jupiter Images; **184** Royalty-Free/Corbis; **185–189** PhotoDisc; **191** (top) © Martin Benjamin 2007; (bottom) Time & Life Pictures/Getty Images; **192** © Raymond Gehman/CORBIS; **195** © Michael & Patricia Fogden/ CORBIS; **196** PhotoDisc; **197** PhotoDisc; **199** (top) Smithsonian American Art Museum, Washington, DC/Art Resource, NY; (bottom) Photo by Marcia Corbino; (background) Jupiter Images; **200** Jupiter Images; **201** Smithsonian American Art Museum, Washington, DC/Art Resource, NY; **203** Courtesy of Library of Congress; **204** iStockphoto; **207** Courtesy of Library of Congress; **209** iStockphoto; **210** (top) © Patrick Bennett/Corbis; (bottom) © Ashley Cooper/ CORBIS; **212** Courtesy of Gary Soto; **213** © Tim Pannell/CORBIS; **215** Jupiter Images; **220** (top) Jupiter Images; (bottom) Courtesy of Cynthia Rylant; **221** PhotoDisc; **222** Jupiter Unlimited; **224** (top) iStockphoto; (bottom) Creative Commons Attribution Sharealike 2.0 License; **227** iStockphoto; **230** *Ms*

Fr *2810 f.55v Dragons and other beasts* (vellum), Boucicaut Master, (fl.1390–1430) (and workshop)/ Bibliotheque Nationale, Paris, France/The Bridgeman Art Library; **233** © Gary Bell/zefa/Corbis; **237** *The Outcasts of 19 Schuyler Place* by E.L. Konigsburg. Jacket illustration © 2004 E.L. Konigsburg. Reprinted with the permission of Atheneum Books for Young Readers, an imprint of Simon & Schuster Children's Publishing Division from *The Outcasts of 19 Schuyler Place* by E.L. Konigsburg; *Al Capone Does My Shirts* by Gennifer Choldenko. Copyright © 2004 by Gennifer Choldenko. Reprinted by permission of Penguin Group (USA), Inc.; Jacket design by Philomena Tuosto from *Holes* by Louis Sachar. Jacket design copyright © 1998 by Pilomena Tuosto. Reprinted by permission of Farrar, Straus and Giroux, LLC; *Romiette and Julio* by Sharon Draper. Copyright © 1999 by Sharon Draper. Reprinted by permission of FPG/Getty Image; Jacket Cover from *Pictures of Hollis Woods* by Patricia Reilly Giff. Used by permission of Random House Children's Books, a division of Random House, Inc.; Book cover *The Chosen,* copyright © 1967, from *The Chosen* by Chaim Potok. Used by permission of Ballantine Books, a division of Random House, Inc.; **238** (left) Jupiter Images; (right) Courtesy of The Anacostia Museum Archives, Smithsonian Institution; **240** Jupiter Images; **246** Eileen Ryan Photography.

Unit 3

252 (top) The Jacob and Gwendolyn Lawrence Foundation/Art Resource, NY; (bottom left) © Bettmann/CORBIS; (bottom middle) AP Images; (bottom right) © Getty Images; **253** (top) © Bridgeman Art Library/National Portrait Gallery, London, UK; (bottom left) AP Images; (bottom middle) AP Images; (bottom right) © Lynn Goldsmith/CORBIS; **254** (left) PhotoDisc; (right) © Bettmann/CORBIS; **255** PhotoDisc; **257** G. Richard Howard/Time & Life Pictures/Getty Images; **258** The Jacob and Gwendolyn Lawrence Foundation/Art Resource, NY; **260** PhotoDisc; **262** PhotoDisc; **265** Courtesy of Milton Meltzer; **266** © Bridgeman Art Library/ National Portrait Gallery, London, UK; **269** *Queen Elizabeth I in procession with her Courtiers* (c. 1600– 1603) from *Memoirs of the Court of Queen Elizabeth* after an oil attributed to Robert Peake (c. 1592– 1667) at Sherborne Castle, published in 1825 (w/c and gouache on paper), Essex, Sarah Countess of (d. 1838)/Private Collection, The Stapleton Collection/ The Bridgeman Art Library; **272** G.11631.B.L. Title

Page with a Portrait of Shakespeare, from *Mr. William Shakespeare's Comedies, Histories and Tragedies*, edited by J. Heminge and H. Condell, engraving by Droeshout, 1623/British Library, London, UK, © British Library Board. All Rights Reserved/The Bridgeman Art Library; **277** © Roy Rainford/Robert Harding World Imagery/Corbis; **278** Shutterstock; **281** Royalty-Free/Corbis; **282** AP Images; **283** Media Bakery; **285** © Robert Harding Picture Library Ltd/Alamy; **287** Jupiter Images; **289** © IBID Photo; **291** AP Images; **292** Royalty-Free/Corbis; **294** PhotoDisc; **297** © Getty Images; **298** © Jerry Cooke/CORBIS; **304** © Bettmann/CORBIS; **307** Associated Press; **310** Jupiter Images; **312** © Lynn Goldsmith/CORBIS; **313** © Bettmann/CORBIS; **314** © Getty Images; **315** AP Images; **317** AP Images; **318** © Phil Schermeister/CORBIS; **319** PhotoDisc; **322** (top) © Star Ledger; (bottom) AP Images; **323** © Bettmann/CORBIS; **324** iStockphoto; **329** © Bettmann/CORBIS; **331** © Bettmann/CORBIS; **333–336** Jupiter Images; **337** Shutterstock; **340** Bloomsbury USA/Walker & Co.; **341** The Granger Collection, New York; **343** The Newark Museum/Art Resource, NY; **344** Courtesy of Library of Congress; **348** iStockphoto; **349** © Faith Ringgold; **352** Courtesy of Library of Congress; **354** Sharrer, Honore D. (1920–) © Smithsonian American Art Museum, Washington, DC/Art Resource, NY; **356** (top) PhotoDisc; (bottom) © Bettmann/CORBIS; **357–359** PhotoDisc; **361** Cover from *The Forbidden Schoolhouse* by Suzanne Jurmain. Copyright © 2005 by Suzanne Jurmain. Jacket cover photo © Doug Mindell. Reprinted by permission of Houghton Mifflin Company. All rights reserved; Cover from *George Washington, Spymaster; How the Americans Outspied the British and Won the Revolutionary War* by Thomas B. Allen. Reprinted by permission of National Geographic Society; Cover from *5,000 Miles to Freedom: Ellen and William Craft's Flight from Slavery* by Dennis and Judith Fradin. Reprinted by permission of National Geographic Society; Jacket cover from *Big Annie of Calumet* by Jerry Stanley. Used by permission of Crown Publishers, a division of Random House, Inc.; From *The Kidnapped Prince: The Life of Olaudah Equiano* adapted by Ann Cameron, copyright © 1995 by Ann Cameron. Jacket illustration copyright © 1995 by Dan Andreasen. Used by permission of Alfred A. Knopf, an imprint of Random House Children's Books, a division of Random House, Inc.; *Bad Boy: A Memoir* by Walter Dean Myers. Reprinted by permission of HarperCollins Publishers; **362** (left) Jupiter Images; (right) AP Images; **363** Jupiter Images; **368** Eileen Ryan Photography.

374 (top) © Corbis; (bottom left) Courtesy of Jennifer Armstrong; (bottom middle) Time & Life Pictures/Getty Images; (bottom right) AP Images; **375** (top) *Drought Stricken Area*, 1934 (oil on canvas), Hogue, Alexandre (1898–1994)/Dallas Museum of Art, Texas, USA/The Bridgeman Art Library; (bottom left) © Robert Maass/CORBIS; (bottom middle) © Carolynne Bailey (bottom right) Time & Life Pictures/Getty Images; **376** Jupiter Images; **377** PhotoDisc; **378** Time & Life Pictures/Getty Images; **379** © CORBIS; **382** © Roger Ressmeyer/CORBIS; **386** © STScl/NASA/Corbis; **387** © Aaron Horowitz/CORBIS; **390** © Carolynne Bailey; **394** Jupiter Images; **396** © Robert Maass/CORBIS; **396–397** © SHAMIL ZHUMATOV/Reuters/Corbis; **398** iStockphoto; **400** Royalty-Free/Corbis; **403** © Canadian Museum of Civilization/CORBIS; **404–405** Shutterstock; **408** (top) Time & Life Pictures/Getty Images; (bottom) AP Images; **409** *Quetzalcoatl, the plumed serpent, god of the wind, learning and the priesthood, master of life, creator and civiliser, patron of every art and inventor of metallurgy* (manuscript)/Biblioteca Nazionale Centrale, Florence, Italy/The Bridgeman Art Library; **412** Jupiter Images; **415** Courtesy of Jennifer Armstrong; **416** © Hulton-Deutsch Collection/CORBIS; **421** (all) PhotoDisc; **425** Storycloth, Mee Vang; Private collection; **426** © Dave Bartruff/CORBIS; **428** AP Images; **430** © Reuters/Corbis; **432** Courtesy of Library of Congress; **433–436** © 1936 Arthur Rothstein; **438** *Drought Stricken Area*, 1934 (oil on canvas), Hogue, Alexandre (1898–1994)/Dallas Museum of Art, Texas, USA/The Bridgeman Art Library; **440** (top) *Dead fox lying in the Undergrowth*, 1865 (oil on canvas), Degas, Edgar (1834–1917)/Musée des Beaux-Arts, Rouen, France, Peter Willi/The Bridgeman Art Library; (bottom) © Bettmann/CORBIS; **446** AFP/Getty Images; **447** Cover from *The New Way Things Work* by David Macaulay. Compilation copyright © 1988, 1998 Dorling Kindersley Ltd., London. Illustrations copyright © 1988, 1998 David Macaulay. Reprinted by permission of Houghton Mifflin Company. All rights reserved; *A Drop of Water* by Walter Wick. Text and photographs copyright © 1997 by Walter Wick. Reprinted by permission of Scholastic Inc.; *Pick Me Up* by David Roberts and Jeremy Leslie. Reprinted by permission of John Brown Publishing Ltd.; *Raptor! A Kid's Guide to Birds of Prey* by Chirstyna and René Lauback, and Charles W. G. Smith. Copyright © 2002 by Christyna Lauback, René Lauback, and Charles W. G. Smith. Reprinted by permission of Storey Publishing; *Photography: An*

Illustrated History by Martin W. Sandler. Copyright © 2002 by Martin W. Sandler. Reprinted by permission of Oxford University Press; *Universe* edited by Martin Rees. Copyright © 2005 Dorling Kindersley Limited. Reprinted by permission of DK Publishing; **448** (left) Shutterstock; (right) AP Images; **449** Jupiter Unlimited; **454** Eileen Ryan Photography.

Unit 5

460 (top) © Shutterstock; (bottom left) © Oscar White/CORBIS; (bottom middle) © Corbis; (bottom right) © Oscar White/CORBIS; **461** (top) *Mother Courage II*, 1974 (oil on canvas), White, Charles Wilbert (1918–1979)/National Academy Museum, New York, USA/The Bridgeman Art Library; (bottom left) Courtesy of Library of Congress; (bottom middle) © Bettmann/CORBIS; (bottom right) Courtesy of Library of Congress; **462** © Edmond Van Hoorick/SuperStock; **463** Superstock; **464** Shutterstock; **466** Courtesy of Pat Mora; **467** Shutterstock; **469** © Oscar White/CORBIS; **470** Shutterstock; **473** © age fotostock/SuperStock; **474** © age fotostock/SuperStock; **475** Courtesy of Library of Congress; **478** The Pierpont Morgan Library/Art Resource, NY; **481** © Oscar White/CORBIS; **482** Fine Art Photographic Library, London/Art Resource, NY; **485** Courtesy of Library of Congress; **486** © David David Gallery/SuperStock; **488** Shutterstock; **491** Courtesy of Library of Congress; **492** *Mother Courage II*, 1974 (oil on canvas), White, Charles Wilbert (1918–1979)/National Academy Museum, New York, USA/The Bridgeman Art Library; **496** *The Apple Tree II*, 1916 (oil on canvas), Klimt, Gustav (1862–1918)/Private Collection/The Bridgeman Art Library; **498** *Johnny Appleseed* (1774–1847) (colored engraving), American School, (19th century)/Private Collection, Peter Newark American Pictures/The Bridgeman Art Library; **502** © CORBIS; **503** © Edmond Van Hoorick/SuperStock; **505** Eve Merriam: Photo by Bachrach; **506–508** Shutterstock; **511** © Christie's Images/CORBIS; **513** iStockphoto; **515** © Bettmann/CORBIS; **516** © Eddi Böhnke/zefa/Corbis; **518** (top) Jupiter Images; (bottom) Eve Merriam: Photo by Bachrach; **519** PhotoDisc; **520** Courtesy of Library of Congress; **521** iStockphoto; **522** *The Navajo* (oil on canvas), Dixon, Maynard (1875–1946)/Private Collection, Photo © Christie's Images/The Bridgeman Art Library; **523** *The Invisible Ladder: An Anthology of Contemporary American Poems for Young Readers* edited by Liz Rosenberg. Compilation copyright © 1996 by Liz Rosenberg. Reprinted by permission of

Henry Holt & Company; Cover from *War and the Pity of War*, edited by Neil Philip. Jacket illustrations copyright © 1998 by Michael McCurdy. Reprinted by permission of Clarion Books, an imprint of Houghton Mifflin Company. All rights reserved; *Becoming Joe DiMaggio* by Maria Testa. Text copyright © 2002 by Maria Testa, illustration copyright © 2002 by Scott Hunt. Reprinted by permission of Candlewick Press, Inc.; *Ancient Voices* by Kate Hovey. Jacket illustration © 2004 Murray Kimber. Reprinted with the permission of Margaret K. McElderry Books, an imprint of Simon & Schuster Children's Publishing Division from *Ancient Voices* by Kate Hovey, illustrated by Murray Kimber; *I Am the Darker Brother: An Anthology of Modern Poems by African Americans* edited by Arnold Adoff. Reprinted by permission of James Ransome; *The The Dream on Blanca's Wall: Poems in English and Spanish* by Jane Medina, illustration by Robert Casilla. (Wordsong, an imprint of Boyds Mills Press, 2004.) Reprinted by permission of Boyds Mills Press, Inc.; **524** (left) PhotoDisc; (right) © Bettmann/CORBIS; **525** (all) Jupiter Images; **528** Time & Life Pictures/Getty Images; **530** InspireStock Images.

Unit 6

536 (top) Media Bakery; (bottom left and middle) Courtesy of Library of Congress; (bottom right) Time & Life Pictures/Getty Images; **537** (top) Art Resource, NY; (bottom left) © Bettmann/CORBIS; (bottom middle) Courtesy of Library of Congress; (bottom right) © Bettmann/CORBIS; **538** Jupiter Images; **539** (bottom) Courtesy of Library of Congress; (background) Media Bakery; **540–541** Media Bakery; **544** Courtesy of Library of Congress; **545** *Downpour at Etretat* (oil on canvas), Courbet, Gustave (1819–1877)/Musée des Beaux-Arts, Dijon, France, Giraudon/The Bridgeman Art Library; **547** (top) Courtesy of Library of Congress; (bottom) Time & Life Pictures/Getty Images; **548** *Found Drowned*, 1848–1850 (oil on canvas), Watts, George Frederick (1817–1904)/© Trustees of the Watts Gallery, Compton, Surrey, UK/The Bridgeman Art Library; **550** Erich Lessing/Art Resource, NY; **551** *The Highwaymen* (oil on canvas), Rowlandson, George Derville (1861–1930)/Private Collection, Haynes Fine Art at the Bindery Galleries, Broadway/The Bridgeman Art Library; **553** Jupiter Images; **557** © Bettmann/CORBIS; **558** Courtesy of Library of Congress; **563** Courtesy of Library of Congress; **564** © University of Virginia; **568** Courtesy of the African American Registry; **569** Courtesy of

Library of Congress; **572** Courtesy of Naomi Shihab Nye; **573** iStockphoto; **576** Getty Images; **577** (foreground) © SuperStock, Inc./SuperStock; (background) Courtesy of Library of Congress; **578** Courtesy of Library of Congress; **580** ANNELINDSAY Photography; **581** © Thomas Holton/Getty; **582** Shutterstock; **584** (top) Art Resource, NY; (bottom) © Bettmann/CORBIS; **585** PhotoDisc; **586** (top) © Josephine Trotter/SuperStock; (bottom) © Bryce Milligan; **587** PhotoDisc; **588** © CORBIS; **590** iStockphoto; **591** (top) *Canterbury Meadows,* 1862 (oil on panel), Cooper, Thomas Sidney (1803–1902)/Art Gallery of New South Wales, Sydney, Australia, Gift of W. A. Little 1928/The Bridgeman Art Library; (bottom) Courtesy of Library of Congress; **592** PhotoDisc; **593** *Poetry for Young People* by William Carlos Williams edited by Christopher McGowan. Text copyright © 2004 by Chistopher McGowan, Illustration copyright © by Robert Crockett. Reprinted by permission of Sterling Publishing Co., Inc.; *Remember the Bridge: Poems of a People* by Carole Boston Weatherford. Text copyright © 2002 by Carole Boston Weatherford; Book cover *Laughing Out Loud, I Fly: Poems in English and Spanish* by Juan Felipe Herrera. Used by permission of HarperCollins Publishers; *Poetry for Young People* by Walt Whitman, edited by Jonathan Levin. Text © 1997 by Jonathan Levin. Illustration © 1997 by Jim Burke. Reprinted by permission of Sterling Publishing Co.; *I am Wings: Poems About Love* by Ralph Fletcher. Text copyright © 1994 by Ralph Fletcher. Photographs copyright © 1994 by Joe Baker. Reprinted by permission of Joe Baker; Cover from *A Wreath for Emmett Till* by Marilyn Nelson, illustrated by Philippe Lardy. Jacket painting © 2005 by Philippe Lardy. Reprinted by permission of Houghton Mifflin Company. All rights reserved; **594** Courtesy of Library of Congress; **595** Jupiter Images; **600** Jupiter Images.

Unit 7

606 (top) Macduff Everton/Getty Images; (bottom left) AFP/Getty Images; (bottom middle) Courtesy of the Library of Congress; (bottom right) AP Images; **607** (top) © Michael Brosilow; (bottom left) Courtesy of Library of Congress; (bottom middle) © Roger Ressmeyer/CORBIS; (bottom right) © Bettmann/CORBIS; **608** Media Bakery; **611** AP Images; **612** *An Old Woman and her Dog Startled by Male Company* (pen & ink and w/c on paper), Rowlandson, Thomas (1756–1827)/Private Collection, © Chris Beetles, London, U.K./The Bridgeman Art Library;

620 Shutterstock; **623** AFP/Getty Images; **624** © Michael Brosilow; **628** © Michael Brosilow; **634** *The Crawlers* (Woodbury type), Thomson, John (1837–1921)/Victoria & Albert Museum, London, UK/The Bridgeman Art Library; **636** © Michael Brosilow; **638** © Michael Brosilow; **640** © Michael Brosilow; **642** Shutterstock; **643** *Tower Bridge from Cherry Garden Pier,* c. 1900 (w/c on paper), Dixon, Charles Edward (1872–1934)/Private Collection, Bourne Gallery, Reigate, Surrey/The Bridgeman Art Library; **646** © Michael Brosilow; **650** © Michael Brosilow; **654** © Michael Brosilow; **657** *Silent Night,* 1891 (oil on canvas) by Viggo Johansen (1851–1935), © Hirschsprungske Samling, Copenhagen, Denmark/The Bridgeman Art Library, Nationality/copyright status: Danish/out of copyright; **661** © Michael Brosilow; **663** © Michael Brosilow; **665** (top) Jupiter Images; (bottom) *Marley's Ghost,* 1843. John Leech. Dickens House Museum, London; **666** (left) *Scrooge's Third Visitor,* 1843. John Leech. Dickens House Museum, London; (right) *The Last of the Visitors,* 1843. John Leech. Dickens House Museum, London; **669** © Roger Ressmeyer/CORBIS; **670** Jupiter Unlimited; **673** *Faraday's Magnetic Laboratory,* 1852 (w/c on paper), Moore, Harriet Jane (1801–1884)/The Royal Institution, London, UK/The Bridgeman Art Library; **681** Jupiter Unlimited; **683** Shutterstock; **684** ISSOUF SANOGO/AFP/Getty Images; **687** (all) Courtesy of Library of Congress; **688** Courtesy of Photofest, Sir Lawrence Olivier as Henry V in a 1944 film version of Shakespeare's play; **690** *Balaclava,* 1889 (oil on canvas), Charlton, John (1849–1917)/© Blackburn Museum and Art Gallery, Lancashire, UK/The Bridgeman Art Library; **691** Helmet, c. 1855 (gilt metal), English School, (19th century)/Courtesy of the Council, National Army Museum, London, UK/The Bridgeman Art Library; **694** (top) © Macduff Everton/Getty Images; (bottom) © Bettmann/CORBIS; **698** © H. Armstrong Roberts/CORBIS; **704–705** © Digital Art/CORBIS; **709** Cover from *The Jumbo Book of Drama* written by Deborah Dunleavy and illustrated by Jane Kurisu, is used by permission of Kids Can Press Ltd., Toronto. Text © 2004 Deborah Dunleavy. Illustrations © 2004 Jane Kurisu; *Plays of Black Americans: the Black Experience in America, Dramatized for Young People* edited by Sylvia E. Kamerman. Copyright © 1987, 1994 by Sylvia K. Burrack. Reprinted by permission of Plays, Inc.; *Plays from Hispanic Tales* by Barbara Winther. Copyright © 1998 by Barbara Winther. Reprinted by permission of Plays, Inc.; *Greek Theatre* by Stewart Ross. Copyright © 1996 by Wayland Publishers Limited. Reprinted by permission of Contemporary Publishing Group, Inc.; *Shakespeare's Theater* by Jacqueline Morley and John James. Reprinted by permission of Simon & Schuster; *Seattle Children's Theatre: Six Plays for Young Readers* by Marisa Smith. Reprinted by permission of Smith and Kraus Publishers, Inc.; **710** Courtesy of Library of Congress; **711** © Royalty-Free/Corbis; **716** Radius Images.

Unit 8

722 (top) Detail depicting the deceased led by Horus before Osiris, c. 1250 BC (painted papyrus), Egyptian, 19th Dynasty (c. 1297–1185 BC)/British Museum, London, UK/The Bridgeman Art Library; (bottom left) Courtesy of Judith Ortiz Cofer; (bottom middle) © Joanne Ryder/Writer Pictures; (bottom right) Courtesy of Judith Gleason; **723** (top) Jupiter Images; (bottom left) Writers Pictures/@Joseph Campbell Foundation; (bottom middle) Courtesy of Library of Congress; (bottom right) AFP/Getty Images; **724** © Dennis Degnan/CORBIS; **725** (all) © Blue Lantern Studio/CORBIS; **727** Courtesy of D'Aulaire; **728** *The Rape of Persephone by Hades* (colour litho), English School, (19th century)/Bibliotheque des Arts Decoratifs, Paris, France, Archives Charmet/The Bridgeman Art Library; **730** © Sal Maimone/SuperStock; **733** Courtesy of Judith Gleason; **734** Yoruba Eshu Elegba Figure, Abeokuta, Southwest Nigeria, mid 19th century (carved wood)/© Royal Albert Memorial Museum, Exeter, Devon, UK/The Bridgeman Art Library; **738** Courtesy of Geraldine Harris; **739** (background) © Rosemary Calvert/SuperStock; **739** (foreground) Detail depicting the deceased led by Horus before Osiris, c. 1250 BC (painted papyrus), Egyptian, 19th Dynasty (c. 1297–1185 BC)/British Museum, London, UK/The Bridgeman Art Library; **741** SuperStock; **743** © Christine Osborne/CORBIS; **744** Shutterstock; **748** Time & Life Pictures/Getty Images; **753** © Bettmann/CORBIS; **754** PhotoDisc; **755** *The Trail of Tears*, 1942. Robert Lindneux. The Granger Collection, New York; **757** (bottom) © Joanne Ryder/Writer Pictures; (background) Jupiter Images; **758** Jupiter Images; **761** iStockphoto; **765** *Aesop*, 1640 (oil on canvas), Velasquez, Diego Rodriguez de Silva y (1599–1660)/Prado, Madrid, Spain, Giraudon/The Bridgeman Art Library; **766** *The Ant and the Grasshopper* from 'Aesop's Fables' series (offset from linocut), Bawden, Edward (1903–1989)/© Chelmsford Museums, Essex, UK/The Bridgeman Art Library; **767** The Art Archive/Bibliothèque Nationale Paris/Marc Charmet; **768** © Araldo de Luca/CORBIS; **771** *The Chariot of Apollo*, 1907–1910 (oil on canvas), Redon, Odilon (1840–1916)/Fitzwilliam Museum, University of Cambridge, UK/The Bridgeman Art Library; **773** © Bettmann/CORBIS; **777** (top) Writers Pictures/© Joseph Campbell Foundation; (bottom) AFP/Getty Images; **778** Jupiter Images; **779** Jupiter Unlimited Images; **780** © Art Archive; **782** iStockphoto; **786** Kunak McGann, The O'Brien Press; **787** © Asian Art & Archaeology, Inc./CORBIS; **789** Roof of the Naiku, Shinto shrine, dedicated to Amaterasu, the sun goddess, Ise. Ise, Japan, Photo Credit: Werner Forman/Art Resource, NY; **790** Shutterstock; **792** Courtesy of Judith Ortiz Cofer; **793** © Leslie Hinrichs/SuperStock; **796** (top) © Patti Mollica/SuperStock; **796** (bottom) AP Images; **799** © The Grand Design/SuperStock; **803** (top) *The Rattle Snake* (w/c on paper), Bartram, William (1739–1823)/© The Right Hon. Earl of Derby/The Bridgeman Art Library; (bottom) Courtesy of Library of Congress; **805** Cover from *Horse Hooves and Chicken Feet: Mexican Folktales,* edited by Neil Philip. Jacket illustrations copyright © 2003 by Jaqueline Mair. Reprinted by permission of Clarion Books, an imprint of Houghton Mifflin Company. All rights reserved; *Peace Walker: The Legend of Hiawatha and Takenawita* by Carrie J. Taylor. Reprinted by permission of Tundra Books of Northern New York; *Beowulf* by Michael Morpurgo ISBN: 978-1-58049-348-2. Copyright © 2005 Prestwick House. Reprinted by permission of Prestwick House Inc.; *The Legend of Lord Eight Deer: An Epic of Mexico* retold and illustrated by John M.D. Pohl. Copyright © 2002 by John M.D. Pohl. Reprinted by permission of Oxford University Press; *The Four Corners of the Sky* by Steve Zeitlin. Text copyright © 2000 by Steve Zeitlin and illustration copyright © 2000 by Chris Raschka. Reprinted by permission of Henry Holt & Company; From *The Story of King Arthur and His Knights* by Howard Pyle, copyright © 1986 by New American Library. Used by permission of Signet, an imprint of Penguin Group (USA) Inc.; **807** Image courtesy of Michael Thompson **809** Jupiter Images; **815** (Top) © Carrie Wendel/iStockphoto LP; (bottom) Image by Larry D. Moore, used under a Creative Commons License. **817** © powerlines/iStockphoto LP; **828** Eileen Ryan Photography.

834 (top left) Shutterstock; (top right) iStockphoto; (bottom left) © Bettmann/CORBIS; (bottom right) Royalty-Free/Corbis.

Index of Skills

Reading Strategies & Skills/Literary Elements

act, 609
adaptions, 316, 414
allegory, 770, 775
alliteration, 463, 474, 481, 482, 483
allusion, 211
analogy, 396, 406
analyze, 8, 256, 316, 414, 431, 465, 610, 644, 726, 835
antagonist, 5, 7, 17, 609
ask questions, 8, 256, 351, 465, 610, 726, 835, 838, 849
assonance, 474
author's approach, 840
author's perspective, 560
author's purpose, 152, 282, 286, 481, 568, 570, 747, 765, 840
autobiography, 255, 257, 259, 261, 262, 263
bar chart, 847–848
biography, 255, 265, 268, 269, 270, 274, 275
build background, 8, 256, 465, 610, 726, 835, 837
cast, 609
cause and effect, 9, 12, 49, 63, 141, 144, 147, 149, 151, 502, 580, 611, 613, 614, 738, 792, 845
cause-and-effect chart, 845
cause-and-effect clue, 843
cause-and-effect order, 844
character, 5, 17, 18, 19, 20, 22, 23, 25, 28, 212, 218, 609, 621, 842
characterization, 17, 322, 339, 786, 791
chart, 377
chronological order, 7, 844
clarify, 8, 256, 271, 385, 465, 610, 726, 835, 839
classification chart, 846
classify, 846
climax, 6, 9, 49
comedy, 608

compare and contrast, 181, 386, 510, 572, 775, 844–845
compare translations, 514
compare versions, 644
comparison clue, 843
comparison-and-contrast order, 844
comprehension, 378, 380, 381, 383, 384, 469, 471, 727, 728, 730
conclusions, 340, 351
concrete poem, 462, 515, 517
conflict, 7, 9, 49, 57, 62, 199, 211, 757, 763
connections, 8, 276, 619, 729
connections chart, 839
consonance, 474
context, 835
context clues, 73, 154, 160, 199, 257, 259, 312, 340, 415, 485, 842–843
contrast appearance and reality, 583
contrast clue, 843
creation myths, 724
description, 297, 311, 386, 408, 414, 415, 422, 426
descriptive writing, 840
determine importance, 841–842
diagram, 377
dialect, 63, 71
dialogue, 609, 669, 686
diction, 687, 692
distinguish fact from opinion, 265, 273, 295
drama, 606, 610, 613, 616, 617, 621
draw conclusions, 57, 163, 390, 392, 393, 623, 770, 786, 835, 849
drawing conclusions log, 849
dynamic characters, 17
effects of form on meaning, 475, 477
end rhyme, 473
essay, 255, 281
evaluate, 8, 256, 465, 610, 726, 791, 835
examples clue, 843
exposition, 6

expository essay, 281
expository writing, 840
external conflict, 7
fable, 725, 765, 769
fact, 846
fact from opinion chart, 295, 846
fact vs. opinion, 846
facts and opinions, 2
falling action, 6
fantasy, 4
fiction, 4, 5
figurative language, 415, 463, 464
film, 575
first-person point of view, 842
fix-up ideas, 839, 848–849
flashback, 7
flat character, 17
folk literature, 722, 724, 757
folk tale, 725, 733, 735
foot, 474
foreshadowing, 7
framework for reading, 836
free verse, 462, 495, 500
generate questions bookmark, 838
graphic organizers, 843
Greek myth, 732
haiku, 462, 510, 514
half rhyme, 473
hero myth, 724
horror, 4
hyperbole, 463, 464, 576, 579
ideas, 355
illustration, 377
image, 463, 464, 560
imagery, 415, 421, 463, 464, 466, 467, 468
implied theme, 153
inference chart, 839
inferences, 8, 11, 150, 256, 267, 268, 465, 610, 726, 736
informational text, 376, 378, 379, 383, 384, 388
internal conflict, 7
internal rhyme, 473
interpret, 8, 256, 465, 609, 610, 726, 842
introductions, 340, 351
irony, 580, 583
judgments, 8, 256, 465, 610, 726

Vocabulary Skills

Grammar & Style

Writing

formal English, 903–904
freewrite, 905
gather ideas, 905
graphic organizer, 905
historical essay, 431
humorous poem, 479
informal English, 903–904
interview questions, 439
introduction, 907
invitation, 290
jingle, 351
journal entry, 152, 223, 422, 446, 686
letter, 15, 62, 104, 406, 566
list, 388
literary analysis, 47, 585, 590, 592, 621, 708, 756, 775
literary critique, 556
literary response, 134, 152, 180, 211, 248, 295, 422, 442, 472, 521, 542, 579, 763
lyric poem, 500
monologue, 494
myth, 745
narrative essay, 483
narrative poem, 556, 692
narrative writing, 238, 903, 911
neatness, 528
newspaper editorial, 355, 500
order of importance, 712
order of importance organization, 906
organization, 128, 450, 526, 906–907
outline, 439, 906–907
paragraph, 28, 84
parallel structure, 714
paraphrasing, 810
passive voice, 452
peer evaluation, 908
personal essay, 360, 566, 602
personal letter, 295, 316, 504, 579
personal narrative, 494, 594
persuasive essay, 509, 710, 718
persuasive paragraph, 316, 575
persuasive speech, 732
persuasive techniques, 718
persuasive writing, 62, 84, 903, 911
plot diagram, 439

poem, 198, 468, 483, 509, 542, 795
point-by-point organization, 526
point of view, 242
positive form, 714
prewrite, 902–907
problem-and-solution essay, 406
problem-and-solution order, 596
proofread, 909–910
publish and present, 910
punctuating dialogue, 242
propose, 902, 903
questions, 47, 218, 360, 566
quotations, 242
reflect, 910–911
reporting question, 905
research essay, 71
research report, 686, 806, 830
response to piece of literature, 126
response to short story, 126
retelling of myth, 732
review, 263
review of play, 644
review of poem, 517
revise, 908–910
rhetorical devices, 718
scene, 621
screenplay, 263
script, 175
self-evaluation, 908
sentence variety, 130
short story, 218, 238, 489, 560
spatial order, 450
speech, 161, 351
story summary, 55
subject-by-subject organization, 526
summary, 745, 824
superlative form, 714
taking notes, 785
thesis, 718
thesis statement, 525, 906
tone, 128, 240
topic, 902, 904
topic sentence, 128, 905–906
transitions, 526, 528
travel brochure, 583
voice, 902, 904
wordiness, 366
writing process, 902–911

Research & Documentation

advertisements, 351
African-American athletes, 316
African-American sports heroes, 310
ancestry, 570
Ancient Egypt, 741
animal languages, 683
animals, 446
aqualung, 83
archaeological site details, 152
attitudes toward nature, 403
biography, 279
birds, 394, 395, 472
blacksmith's bellows, 489
changing names, 564
chart, 28
chart of Fahrenheit and Celsius equivalents, 62
city living, 210
civil rights, 69
Crimean War, 691
cultural identity, 289
description, 177, 180
desert life, 468
divine order in kingdom, 741
documenting sources
 bibliographies and bibliography cards, 919–920
 citing Internet sources, 920–921
 formal note-taking, 919
 informal note-taking, 918–919
 note cards, 919
 parenthetical documentation, 921–922
 plagiarism, 918
 quotation marks, 918
 research journal, 918
 summarize, 918
Dominican Republic, 285
dragons, 236
dreams, 198
Egyptian sun god, 743
England, industry and reform in, 634
environment, 406, 498
fables, 769
famous awards, 161

Applied English

Speaking & Listening

Test-Taking Skills

INDEX OF SKILLS

INDEX OF TITLES AND AUTHORS